The Papers of
HENRY CLAY

The Papers of
HENRY CLAY

Melba Porter Hay
Editor

Carol Reardon
Associate Editor

Volume 10
CANDIDATE, COMPROMISER,
ELDER STATESMAN
January 1, 1844-
June 29, 1852

THE UNIVERSITY PRESS OF KENTUCKY

"My ambition is that we may enter a new and larger era of service to humanity."

Dedicated to the memory of
JOSIAH KIRBY LILLY
1861-1948
President of Eli Lilly and Company
Founder of Lilly Endowment, Inc.

Whose wisdom and foresight were devoted to the service of education, religion, and public welfare

ISBN: 978-0-8131-0060-9
Library of Congress Catalog Card Number: 59-13605

Scholarly publisher for the Commonwealth, serving Bellarmine College, Berea College, Centre College of Kentucky, Eastern Kentucky University, The Filson Club, Georgetown College, Kentucky Historical Society, Kentucky State University, Morehead State University, Murray State University, Northern Kentucky University, Transylvania University, University of Kentucky, University of Louisville, and Western Kentucky University.

Editorial and Sales Offices: Lexington, Kentucky 40508-4008

CONTENTS

PREFACE

As senior editor and director of *The Papers of Henry Clay* since July, 1987, I am greatly indebted to those who have assisted the project. Chief among these is Robert Seager, II, senior editor 1979-1987, who not only trained me in the craft of editing but also selected me as his successor. Dr. Seager, now retired and living in Washington, D.C., remains a consultant for the project and continues to provide unfailing moral support and professional advice. Carol Reardon, associate editor 1987-1989, has cheerfully proofread galleys of this volume from her new post at the University of Georgia. Mackelene G. Smith and Anna B. Perry have continued their superb work as editorial assistants. They were joined in August, 1989, by Kenneth H. Williams, who ably assisted in completing the latter stages of this volume. Also contributing to the project were student typists Kimberly Montgomery, Stacy Greene, Shannon O'Neill, and Angelia Wilson.

The editorial policies that guided volumes 7 through 9 are continued in volume 10, except that very brief remarks made on the Senate floor have been placed in the calendar of unpublished documents. As before, a majority of the letters written by Clay, as well as the most important of his incoming mail have been printed in full. A few of the less important letters written by Clay, along with most of the incoming mail and his more extensive remarks in Senate, have been summarized. To help the reader distinguish between the casual and the formal in Clay's Senate statements, his observations have been divided into three categories—remark, comment, or speech—as their length and importance warrant. The *Remark in Senate* is a brief, offhand, unprepared statement; the *Comment in Senate* is a more sustained, though extemporaneous, response; the *Speech in Senate* is an extensive, carefully prepared declaration of his position on an important national issue. Marginal and peripheral Clay materials have been placed in the calendar of unpublished documents, which contains the name of the correspondent, location, and general subject of each item. Every known Clay document for 1844-52 have been printed in full, summarized, or calendared herein.

In keeping with the editorial practices established with volume 7, letter headings have been standardized and salutations, closings, and subscriptions have been omitted. Volume and page numbers are omitted in citations of encyclopedias and dictionaries that are arranged alphabetically. Abbreviations used in the footnotes are explained in the table below. All documents, except those calendared, have been extensively cross-referenced and subject indexed. In documents printed in full, cross-references to relevant materials in this and earlier volumes appear in footnotes. In summarized documents cross-references are enclosed in brackets and inserted in the text. Documents printed in full and direct quotations in summaries have been transcribed literally, as far as possible, with no silent emendations. Letters, words, and punctuation marks supplied by the editors for clarifications are inserted in the text within brackets, as are identifying materials such as first names.

The use of *sic* to denote errors in spelling is limited to proper names and to those rare instances in which a misspelling might cause confusion. Interlineations and raised letters have been lowered to the line and substantive decipherable cancellations have been placed in footnotes. Ellipsis marks at the end of a letter printed in full indicate that a brief social pleasantry, not a part of the closing, has been omitted. Readers should be aware that letters not in Clay's hand often contain errors originating in the work of an amanuensis or copyist.

Two more points concerning editorial methodology need to be made. When a letter referred to in the text has not been found, a footnote designating it as "not found" appears only if no date is given for the letter; when a specific date is mentioned, enabling the reader to determine whether the letter referred to actually appears, no footnote is used. Second, when a Clay correspondent or person mentioned in the letters cannot be identified, the notation "not identified" has been inserted after the name in the index. Otherwise, an identification of the person will be found in this or an earlier volume. Cross-references have been supplied to the identifications of many of the less noted persons. A serious effort has been made to identify all Clay correspondents.

The editors had hoped to be able to include in this volume the approximately one thousand Clay documents received too late for inclusion in proper chronological sequence in earlier volumes. It became apparent, however, that one volume would not be enough to encompass those letters along with the mass of documents from 1844-52. A supplementary volume will therefore be published. In addition to the recently discovered letters, it will include an errata, a comprehensive bibliography of works cited in the series, and a calendar of Clay artwork, including busts, statues, paintings, and engravings.

Finally, the editors and staff sincerely thank the Lilly Endowment, Inc., for its generous support of the early volumes. In addition, we thank the National Historical Publications and Records Commission, the University of Kentucky Research Foundation, the University Press of Kentucky, and Dr. Wimberly C. Royster, vice president for Research and Graduate Studies at the University of Kentucky, for the funds that have made possible the editing and publishing of this volume.

Melba Porter Hay
May, 1990

SYMBOLS & ABBREVIATIONS

The following symbols are used to describe the nature of the originals of documents copied from manuscript sources.

AD	Autograph Document
AD draft	Autograph Document, draft
ADI	Autograph Document Initialed
ADS	Autograph Document Signed
AE	Autograph Endorsement
AEI	Autograph Endorsement Initialed
AES	Autograph Endorsement Signed
AL	Autograph Letter
AL draft	Autograph Letter, draft
ALI	Autograph Letter Initialed
ALI copy	Autograph Letter Initialed, copy
ALI draft	Autograph Letter Initialed, draft
ALS	Autograph Letter Signed
ALS draft	Autograph Letter Signed, draft
AN	Autograph Note
AN draft	Autograph Note, draft
ANI draft	Autograph Note Initialed, draft
ANS	Autograph Note Signed
Copy	Copy not by writer (indicated "true" is so certified)
D	Document
DS	Document Signed
L	Letter
L draft	Letter, draft
LI draft	Letter Initialed, draft
LS	Letter Signed
N	Note
N draft	Note, draft
NS	Note signed

The following, from the *Symbols Used in the National Union Catalog of the Library of Congress* (9th ed., rev.; Washington, 1965), indicate the location of the original documents in institutional libraries of the United States.

CBPac	Pacific School of Religion, Berkeley, California
CHi	California Historical Society, San Francisco, California
CSmH	Henry E. Huntington Library and Museum, San Marino, California
Ct	Connecticut State Library, Hartford, Connecticut
CtHi	Connecticut Historical Society, Hartford, Connecticut

CtHT	Trinity College, Hartford, Connecticut
CtY	Yale University, New Haven, Connecticut
CU	University of California, Berkeley, California
CU-B	University of California, Bancroft Library, Berkeley, California
DCU	Catholic University of America Library, Washington, D.C.
DeHi	Historical Society of Delaware, Wilmington, Delaware
DGU	Georgetown University Library, District of Columbia
DGW	George Washington University Library, District of Columbia
DLC	Library of Congress, Washington, D.C.
DLC-HC	Library of Congress, Henry Clay Collection
DLC-TJC	Library of Congress, Thomas J. Clay Collection
DNA	United States National Archives Library, Washington, D.C. Following the symbol for this depository, the letters A and R mean Applications and Recommendations; M, Microcopy; P and D of L, Publication and Distribution of the Laws; R, Reel; and RG, Record Group.
GU	University of Georgia, Athens, Georgia
I	Illinois State Library, Springfield, Illinois
ICHi	Chicago Historical Society, Chicago, Illinois
ICN	Newberry Library, Chicago, Illinois
ICU	University of Chicago, Chicago, Illinois
IEN	Northwestern University, Evanston, Illinois
IGK	Knox College, Galesburg, Illinois
In	Indiana State Library, Indianapolis, Indiana
InHi	Indiana Historical Society, Indianapolis, Indiana
InNd	University of Notre Dame, Notre Dame, Indiana
InU	Indiana University, Bloomington, Indiana
KHi	Kansas State Historical Society, Topeka, Kansas
Ky	Kentucky State Library & Archives, Frankfort, Kentucky
KyBB	Berea College, Berea, Kentucky
KyHi	Kentucky Historical Society, Frankfort, Kentucky
KyLo	Louisville Free Public Library, Louisville, Kentucky
KyLoF	The Filson Club, Louisville, Kentucky
KyLxT	Transylvania University, Lexington, Kentucky
KyU	University of Kentucky, Lexington, Kentucky
L-M	Louisiana State Museum Library, New Orleans, Louisiana
LNHT	Tulane University Library, New Orleans, Louisiana
LU-Ar	Louisiana State University, Department of Archives and Manuscripts, Baton Rouge, Louisiana
MB	Boston Public Library, Boston, Massachusetts
MBAt	Boston Athenaeum, Boston, Massachusetts
MCM	Massachusetts Institute of Technology, Cambridge, Massachusetts
MdAA	Hall of Records. Archives, Annapolis, Maryland
MdBJ	Johns Hopkins University, Baltimore, Maryland
MdBP	Peabody Institute, Baltimore, Maryland
MdHi	Maryland Historical Society, Baltimore, Maryland
MeB	Bowdoin College, Brunswick, Maine
MeWC	Colby College, Waterville, Maine
MH	Harvard University, Cambridge, Massachusetts

MH-BA	Harvard University, Graduate School of Business Administration Library
MHi	Massachusetts Historical Society, Boston, Massachusetts
MiD	Detroit Public Library, Detroit, Michigan
MiU	University of Michigan, Ann Arbor, Michigan
MiU-C	University of Michigan, William L. Clements Library, Ann Arbor, Michigan
MnHi	Minnesota Historical Society, St. Paul, Minnesota
Mo	Missouri State Library, Jefferson City, Missouri
MoSHi	Missouri Historical Society, St. Louis, Missouri
MoSW	Washington University, St. Louis, Missouri
MoU	University of Missouri, Columbia, Missouri
MWA	American Antiquarian Society, Worcester, Massachusetts
MWiW	Williams College, Williamstown, Massachusetts
NBuHi	Buffalo Historical Society, Buffalo, New York
Nc-Ar	North Carolina State Department of Archives and History, Raleigh, North Carolina
NcU	University of North Carolina, Chapel Hill, North Carolina
NGos	Goshen Library and Historical Society, Goshen, New York
NhD	Dartmouth College, Hanover, New Hampshire
NhHi	New Hampshire Historical Society, Concord, New Hampshire
NHi	New-York Historical Society, New York City
NIC	Cornell University, Ithaca, New York
NjHi	New Jersey Historical Society, Newark, New Jersey
NjMoHP	Morristown Edison National Historical Park, Morristown, New Jersey
NjP	Princeton University, Princeton, New Jersey
NjR	Rutgers–The State University, New Brunswick, New Jersey
NN	New York Public Library, New York City
NNC	Columbia University, New York City
NRHi	Rochester Historical Society, Rochester, New York
NRU	University of Rochester, Rochester, New York
NUtM	Munson-Williams-Procter Institute, Utica, New York
O	Ohio State Library, Columbus, Ohio
OC	Public Library of Cincinnati and Hamilton County, Cincinnati, Ohio
OCHP	Historical and Philosophical Society of Ohio, Cincinnati, Ohio
OClWHi	Western Reserve Historical Society, Cleveland, Ohio
OFH	Rutherford B. Hayes Library, Fremont, Ohio
OHi	Ohio State Historical Society, Columbus, Ohio
OTU	University of Toledo, Toledo, Ohio
PHarH	Pennsylvania Historical and Museum Commission, Harrisburg, Pennsylvania
PHC	Haverford College, Haverford, Pennsylvania
PHi	Historical Society of Pennsylvania, Philadelphia, Pennsylvania
PP	Free Library of Philadelphia, Philadelphia, Pennsylvania
PPiU	University of Pittsburgh, Pittsburgh, Pennsylvania
PPL	Library Company of Philadelphia, Philadelphia, Pennsylvania
PPPrHi	Presbyterian Historical Society, Philadelphia, Pennsylvania
PPRF	Rosenbach Foundation, Philadelphia, Pennsylvania

PSC	Swarthmore College, Swarthmore, Pennsylvania
PSC-Hi	Swarthmore College, Friends Historical Library, Swarthmore, Pennsylvania
PU	University of Pennsylvania, Philadelphia, Pennsylvania
PWbH	Wyoming Historical and Geological Society, Wilkes-Barre, Pennsylvania
RPB	Brown University, Providence, Rhode Island
Sc	South Carolina State Library, Columbia, South Carolina
ScU	University of South Carolina, Columbia, South Carolina
THaroL	Lincoln Memorial University, Harrogate, Tennessee
THi	Tennessee Historical Society, Nashville, Tennessee
TxDaHi	Dallas Historical Society, Dallas, Texas
Vi	Virginia State Library, Richmond, Virginia
ViHi	Virginia Historical Society, Richmond, Virginia
ViU	University of Virginia, Charlottesville, Virginia
ViW	College of William and Mary, Williamsburg, Virginia
VtHi	Vermont Hstorical Society, Montpelier, Vermont
WHi	State Historical Society of Wisconsin, Madison, Wisconsin
Wv-Ar	West Virginia Department of Archives and History Library, Charleston, West Virginia

The following abbreviations are used in the footnotes of this volume:

AHA	*Alabama Historical Quarterly*
BDAC	*Biographical Directory of the American Congress 1774-1961*
BDGUS	*Biographical Directory of the Governors of the United States 1789-1978.* Robert Sobel & John Raimo, eds. Westport, Ct.: Meckler Books, 1978
CAB	*Cyclopedia of American Biography.* James G. Wilson & John Fiske, eds. New York: D. Appleton & Company, 1888
DAB	*Dictionary of American Biography.* Allen Johnson, ed. New York: Charles Scribner's Sons, 1927, 1964
DNB	*Dictionary of National Biography.* Sir Leslie Stephen & Sir Sidney Lee, eds. London: Oxford University Press, 1917
FCHQ	*Filson Club History Quarterly*
GHQ	*Georgia Historical Quarterly*
HRDUSA	*Historical Register and Dictionary of the United States Army 1789-1903.* Reprint ed. Urbana: University of Illinois Press, 1965
IHQ	*Illinois Historical Quarterly*
JAH	*Journal of American History*
JER	*Journal of the Early Republic*
JNH	*Journal of Negro History*
JSAH	*Journal of the Society of Architectural Historians*
JSH	*Journal of Southern History*
LHQ	*Louisiana Historical Quarterly*
MHM	*Maryland Historical Magazine*
MPP	*A Compilation of the Messages and Papers of the Presidents 1789-1902.* James D. Richardson, comp. 10 vols. Washington: Bureau of National Literature and Art, 1904

NCAB	*National Cyclopedia of American Biography*. New York: James T. White & Company, 1898
NCHR	*North Carolina Historical Register*
NEGHR	*New England Historical and Genealogical Register*
OH	*Ohio History*
PMHB	*Pennsylvania Magazine of History and Biography*
RKHS	*Register of the Kentucky Historical Society*
SCHM	*South Carolina Historical Magazine*
THQ	*Tennessee Historical Quarterly*
VMHB	*Virginia Magazine of History and Biography*
WMH	*Wisconsin Magazine of History*
WMQ	*William and Mary Quarterly*
WPHM	*Western Pennsylvania Historical Magazine*

The Papers of HENRY CLAY

To UNKNOWN RECIPIENT [1844]

I am not a professor of religion; and, as I have remarked on all occasions, I regret that I am not; I hope that I s[h]all be. The longer I live the more sensible I become of its utility; the more profoundly penetrated with its truth; the more entirely convinced that the religion of Christ, is of all religions, best; and it alone can af[f]ord us an adequate solace in the hour of affliction[.]

Copy. NjHi.

To Octavia Walton LeVert, Mobile, January 1, 1844. Thanks her for her letter introducing and recommending the artist [James H.] Wise. Regrets that he must postpone sitting for Wise "until a future period." Looks forward to seeing her and her husband, Dr. [Henry] LeVert, again in Mobile about February 20. ALS. KyU. Written from New Orleans. Clay arrived in Mobile on February 26, 1844, remaining there until March 5. For the LeVerts, see her entry in *NCAB*, 6:440-41 and Edward T. James *et al.* (eds.), *Notable American Women, 1607-1950, A Biographical Dictionary*, 4 vols. (Cambridge, Mass., vols. 1-3, 1971; vol. 4, 1980), 2:394-95.

Wise's full-length portrait of Clay, best known through John Sartain's engraving, was executed some time before March 15, 1844, when it was announced in the newspaper. See Washington *Daily National Intelligencer*, March 15, 1844; and Clifford Amyx, "The Portraits of Henry Clay." 2 vols. Typed. Profusely Illustrated. Special Collections, University of Kentucky Library, 1980, vol. A:1.86.

On January 6, 1844, Clay again wrote Mrs. LeVert from New Orleans, thanking her for her letter of January 4, giving his proposed travel schedule in January (to and from Lafourche Parish, January 8-15; to and from Natchez, January 22-29) and accepting her kind invitation to stay at the LeVerts' home when he reaches Mobile. Hopes he can see her if she visits New Orleans prior to his going to Mobile. Notes that he is staying at the house of Dr. William N. Mercer in Carondelet Street, near the St. Charles Hotel. ALS. KyU.

From William Browne, Fredericksburg, Va., January 5, 1844. Encloses an invitation from the local Clay Club to stop and visit Fredericksburg on his journey from Raleigh to Washington. Assures him that the club, "certainly the first in Virginia," has a large and enthusiastic membership. Agrees with Clay that the club members "regret that a 'necessity should exist for appealing to the feelings & passions of our fellow citizens, rather than to their reasons & their judgments,' to secure the triumph of our Friend & our principles—But we must plead full justification in seizing on and using the most effective weapons in our reach, without a too strict enquiry into their legitimacy, when our principles & our best interests are threatened with ruin & destruction—" Copy. KyU. Addressed to Clay in New Orleans. For Browne, see 4:109.

On February 6, 1844, Clay replied to Dr. Browne with thanks, refusing the invitation because he "may not pass that way" and because "The continued excitement, incident to my meeting, successively, large concourses of my fellow Citizens is prejudicial to my strength and health." Notes that the trip "has drawn me much more before the public than I wished to have been." ALS. KyU.

From Francis Y. Porcher, Charleston, S.C., January 6, 1844. On behalf of the Clay Club of Charleston, invites him to visit their city "and give us as much of your time as you may have at your disposal." Comments on Clay's long service to his country, and says that "we believe that you are especially calculated at the present juncture of our political affairs to preside over our wide extended country, to harmonize conflicting interests, to reconcile sectional prejudices and jealousies, and to draw still closer those ties which alone constitute us a great, a happy and a powerful nation." Adds that the Clay Club of Charleston anticipates "all these national benefits from your administration" and desires "to give you in advance . . . their confidence and profound respect." Copy. Printed in Charleston *The Courier*, March 9, 1844.

Clay replied from New Orleans on February 5, 1844, accepting the invitation and saying he hoped his reception would be "private and unceremonious." Plans to stay there two or three days but cannot yet designate the day of his arrival. *Ibid.* See Speech in Charleston, April 6, 1844.

Porcher was a physician in Charleston and a leading Unionist during the nullification crisis of 1832-33, although by 1860 he had become a secessionist. James Petigru Carson, *Life, Letters, and Speeches of James Louis Petigru* (Washington, D.C., 1929), 60, 72, 320, 363.

From Jared S. Dawson, Bellefontaine, Ohio, January 17, 1844. Responds to Clay's inquiry about the value of his lands in Logan County, Ohio [9:368-69]. Reports that he has examined the tract, in company with the tenant who lives thereon, and opines that it would bring four to five dollars per acre if sold now, although its true value is nearly twice that. Advises Clay not to sell. Points out, however, that the tenant has cleared and/or inclosed about 48 acres and that he should be charged $40 rent in cash and kind for 1844. He should be asked to pay the taxes on the property and work out the balance of the rent due by cutting rails to sell or to repair the fencing. The tenant, who has had "peac[e]able possession of the premises for 20 years," has countered with an offer of $30 annual rent. "I gave him 20 days to think on the subject." ALS. DLC-TJC (DNA, M212, R14). For Dawson, a land agent and prominent resident of Bellefontaine, see *History of Logan County and Ohio* (Chicago, 1880), 345, 510.

To WILLIAM C. PRESTON New Orleans, January 19, 1844

[Outlines his proposed journey from New Orleans through Alabama, Georgia, South Carolina, North Carolina (Raleigh), Virginia, to Washington. Continues:][1]

This tour[2] has been undertaken with great reluctance, on account of causes exclusively personal to myself. Among them is, my distrust of my physical strength to bear the excitements incident to the journey. I must therefore entreat my friends to spare me as much as possible, which I hope they will not hesitate to do in So. Carolina, as I do not expect it entertains any design to vote for or kill me, altho' I have great fears of the generous hospitality which, notwithstanding, I am sure it will be disposed to extend to me.

Our friend [Alexander] Porter is gone—a great loss public & private, and one of my best and truest friends. With a majority of one or two on joint ballot in the Louisiana Legislature, I nevertheless entertain some fears that we may not get a Whig Successor. . . .[3]

ALS. NcD. 1. On Jan. 6, 1844, writing from New Orleans Clay informed the Clay Club of Montgomery, Ala., that he plans to leave for Mobile on Feb. 25 and would depart from there on March 1, 2, or 3, "according to circumstances." Adds: "You can judge better than I the requisite time to make the voyage to Montgomery." Copy. Printed in Washington *Daily National Intelligencer*, Feb. 5, 1844. On March 10, 1844, from Shade Grove near Columbus, Ga., Clay wrote to Dr. F.M. Robertson, outlining the proposed itinerary for his travel through Georgia. Copy. Printed in Jonesborough (Tenn.) *Whig, and Independent Journal*, March 27, 1844. On April 10, 1844, Clay wrote Samuel Mordecai in Petersburg, Va., saying that he plans to leave Raleigh for Petersburg on the 18th and arrive there that night. Copy. Printed in Richmond *Enquirer*, April 16, 1844. 2. Clay left New Orleans for Mobile, Ala., on Feb. 24, 1844. He arrived in Mobile the following day and remained there until March 5 when he left for Montgomery. From there he traveled to Columbus, Ga., where he arrived on March 11 and remained until March 14. He made a speech in Macon on March 18 and one in Milledgeville on March 19. He arrived in Savannah on March 21, leaving there for Augusta on March 25. On April 1 he arrived in Columbia, S.C., and moved on to Charleston on April 6. He traveled to Wilmington, N.C., on April 9 or 10 and left there for Raleigh on April 10 or 11, arriving in Raleigh on April 12. He left there for Petersburg, Va., on April 18 which he reached the same day. He left Petersburg for Norfolk on April 20, was detained by fog, and got to Norfolk on the 21st. On April 23 he made a speech in Portsmouth, Va. He reached Washington, D.C., on April 26. 3. Alexander Porter had died on Jan. 13, 1844. The Louisiana legislature met on Jan. 29 and elected Whig Henry Johnson to replace him in the U.S. Senate. Johnson took the seat on Feb. 12, 1844. *BDAC*; Washington *Daily National Intelligencer*, Feb. 1, 8, 1844.

To JAMES BROWN CLAY

New Orleans, January 22, 1844

I received your two letters of the 4h. and 9h. instant. but I have received none from Thomas [Hart Clay]. Henry [Clay, Jr.] will write you about his horse. I should be glad if you would make some equitable arrangement with Bradley[1] to take the Woodpecker filly.

I send you enclosed a power of Atto. from Henry to sign one and endorse another note for $5000 which I left with you to be discounted at the N[orthern]. Bank [of Kentucky] along with two others that I also left. I wish you to attend to that business particularly, I think the 20h. Feb. is the time. I also enclose the first number of a draft for the sum of $ [2] to pay the discount on the four notes.[3] The second I will send via Washn. City.

It will be time, on my return home, to decide on your proposal about Water retting hemp. In the mean time, I expect Mr. [Albert] Florea to put in Hemp all the hemp ground I have, including the new ground & piece at Mansfield.

Tell Thomas that I think he had better make a contract with Mr_____ (I forget his name) of Clarke [*sic*, Clark County] for his Crop of hemp offered us, at the market price between the time of the delivery and the first of Sept. paying interest upon every ten tons from time to time as delivered. I think the probability is that hemp will fall below rather than rise above the price of four dollars at which you state it now to be.

My health has been generally good but I am suffering just now with cold & its effects. I shall leave here about the 20h. next month. Any letters for me after the 10h. had better be addressed to me at Augusta Georgia via Washn. until the 10h. March, after that to Charleston until the 25h. March, after that to Raleigh until the 10th Apl. & after that to Washn.

Poor Judge [Alexander] Porter is dead, and I regret that uncertainty should exist about his successor.[4] A rumor has got into circulation, I believe without foundation, that he has left me a legacy. . . . [P.S.] Since writing the above, I have received a letter from Thomas.[5] And I wish you would say to him to try and engage both [James] Shelby and [Philip B.] Hockadays hemp on the terms I have proposed above.

ALS. DLC-TJC (DNA, M212, R10). Printed in Calvin Colton, *The Life, Correspondence, and Speeches of Henry Clay*, 6 vols. (New York, 1864), 4:483-84. 1. Possibly James L. Bradley who owned a stable on the Maysville Turnpike, six miles from Lexington. Lexington *Observer & Kentucky Reporter*, May 4, 1844. 2. Figure omitted in text. 3. See 9:789-90, 806-7. 4. Clay to Preston, Jan. 19, 1844. 5. Not found.

From James Morrison Harris, Baltimore, January 22, 1844. Thanks him for his letter of December 1, 1843, in which Clay had stated that the remission of the legacy from the estate of "Aunt Morrison" [Esther Montgomery (Mrs. James) Morrison] would occur in about March or April, 1844. Points out that he has two outstanding $600 notes, both held by George Baughman, a personal friend, that will be coming due at about that same time. Adds that both are secured by the expected legacy. Asks Clay to hold the legacy subject to Baughman's order. Copy. DLC-TJC (DNA, M212, R14). Addressed to Clay in New Orleans. Endorsed by Clay: "Sent a check for $1500 on the Bank of Philada. 30h. March 1844 payable to both. H.C."

For Harris, see 3:740. Baughman, who dealt in commercial transactions, lived in the 9th ward of Baltimore. Population Schedules of the Sixth Census of the United States (M704, R160), vol. 3.

To Clement Carrington *et al.*, New Orleans, January 23, 1844. Regrets that he will not be able to accept their invitation to greet the members of the Clay Club of Charlotte County, Virginia, after his visit in Raleigh, N.C., in April. Is pleased to learn from them, however, that the people of Charlotte are now "candidly reviewing their former opinions adverse to a protective tariff; and that many of them are disposed now to believe that reasonable and moderate protection, short of prohibition, is beneficial to the Consumer by augmenting the supply. The nonexistence of Manufactures in the U. States would leave to Foreign Countries a monopoly, in the supply of American consumption. The prohibition of the fabrics of Foreign Countries would transfer that monopoly to the Home manufactures in the United States; but the monopoly would be modified and moderated, progressively, by competition arising at home. The true interests of the Consumer are best promoted by a compet[it]ion between the Foreign and the National supply. The inevitable tendency of that competition is to reduce prices, as all experience has demonstrated. A duty never augments the price, to the extent of its amount, but in the case of an inadequate supply of the article, on which it is imposed, to the demand for that article. But the reduction of prices is not the only, nor the greatest, advantage of the establishment of Manufactures in our Country. They create an ability to purchase those cheaper articles, by the Home market which arises for the products of Agriculture and of labor." ALS. InU.

To JAMES B. CLAY New Orleans, January 24, 1844

I sent the other day a power of Atto: from Henry [Clay, Jr.] to you to execute on his part the notes for $5000. which I left with you for renewal with the N[orthern]. Bank of K[entucky]. and also the first number of a draft of which I now enclose the second for the sum of $511:50 to pay the discount on the four notes.[1] I hope that business will have your particular attention.

ALS. DLC-TJC (DNA, M212, R10). 1. Clay to James B. Clay, Jan. 22, 1844.

To JOHN J. CRITTENDEN New Orleans, January 24, 1844

I received your favor of the 2d. and 8h. inst. The object of the latter is attained by the death of our excellent friend Judge [Alexander] Porter, so far as respects a vacancy. I wish I could add that it would be certainly filled by a Whig.[1] That is very uncertain, altho' my hopes preponderate a little over my fears. A few days will supersede all speculation.

I thank you for the information contained in your's of the 2d. If Mr. [John] Tyler's present dispositions do not lead you to attach an undue importance to them, nor induce the Senate to confirm nominations which they ought to reject, they are not to be regretted. Among those nominations are [Caleb] Cushings,[2] Profits [*sic*, George Proffit][3] and [John C.] Spencer's,[4] the latter decidedly the most important of them all. Does any man believe these men true or faithful or honest? If Spencer be confirmed, he will have run a short career of more profligate conduct and good luck than any man I recollect.

My departure from this City I have fixed between the 20h. and 25h. Feb. and my arrival at Raleigh the 12th April. I shall leave Mobile the first of March. I have therefore appropriated about one month and a half for the tour of Alabama Georgia and So. Carolina.[5]

Generally my health has been good, altho' just now I am a little out of sorts.

ALS. DLC-John J. Crittenden Papers (DNA, M212, R20). 1. Clay to Preston, Jan. 19, 1844. 2. See 9:803-4. 3. Tyler nominated Proffit as envoy extraordinary and minister plenipotentiary to Brazil on Dec. 18, 1843. The nomination was rejected on Jan. 11, 1844, by 33 to 8 votes. U.S. Sen., *Executive Journal*, 6:209-10. 4. Tyler nominated Spencer on Jan. 9, 1844, to be associate justice of the Supreme Court. It was rejected on Jan. 31 by a vote of 26 to 21, resubmitted on June 17, 1844, but withdrawn that same day. *Ibid.*, 207-8, 227, 229, 353-54. See also 9:804. 5. Clay to Preston, Jan. 19, 1844.

Speech on the *Wabash*, New Orleans, *ca.*, Late January, 1844. After being welcomed on board the new packet *Wabash*, Clay replies thanking them for their tribute to him and saying: "You have rightly conceived the motives, if you have exaggerated the value, of my public services. With a truly American heart, every beat of which has been for my country, I have sought by my humble exertions to establish its character, advance its fame, and strengthen and secure all its interests, at home and abroad. . . . I thought it requisite that we should sustain and encourage the exertions of our Domestic Industry. I know that some good men have supposed my zeal transported me too far." Notes that he has learned from experience that "while the policy is to be maintained with firmness, it should be exercised with wisdom, moderation and stability." Emphasizes that "Above all, our Government and all our systems of policy should be ever administered in reference to the preservation of our glorious Union—that permanent and transcendent object which is the sole guarantee of our liberty." Warns, however, that "without harmony between the parts, union may exist in form, but its spirit and its vigor will have fled." Copy. Printed in New-York *Daily Tribune*, February 15, 1844.

To Benjamin W. Leigh *et al.*, February 5, 1844. Replies to an invitation of the Whigs of Richmond, Va., to visit that city on his return home from Portsmouth. Says it would be a "very great pleasure" to meet his numerous friends "in the Capitol of our native State, where I passed so many of my youthful days," but he cannot extend the journey beyond its present route or give "it the character of a political tour." Copy. Printed in New-York *Daily Tribune*, February 26, 1844. For Clay's itinerary, see Clay to Preston, January 19, 1844.

To WILLIAM A. GRAHAM[1] New Orleans, February 6, 1844

I received your friendly letter, an acknowledgment of which has been delayed by my absence from this City. I should be most happy in meeting Mrs. Graham and yourself, and accepting the hospitalities of your house. I am sure that I should be no where more tranquil or happy; but I am afraid that it will not be in my power. We will see when I get to Raleigh. I have announced the 12h. of April for my arrival there, where I purpose remaining a few days.[2]

I anticipate the necessity of stopping a day or two at Wilmington, and a short time at the other places indicated by you on the route from that place to Raleigh. But I must trust to my friends to spare me as much fatigue as possible. I am particularly desirous to avoid public entertainments with their train of excitements. Some recent experience of them admonishes me of the absolute necessity of my avoiding them.

I saw, with very great pleasure, your nomination as Govr. of the old North State, and I cherish the confident hope of your easy election.[3] Still I should have preferred that you were in another situation,[4] where the whole Union would have been benefited by your services.

I congratulate you on the bright and cheering prospect of the Whig Cause. There is scarcely a speck in the whole political horizon. . . .

ALS. Nc-Ar. 1. For Graham, see *BDAC.* 2. For his itinerary, see Clay to Preston, Jan. 19, 1844. While in Raleigh Clay stayed with Gov. John M. Morehead. Raleigh *Register and North Carolina Gazette,* April 16, 1844. For Morehead, see *DAB* and *BDAC.* 3. Graham defeated Democratic candidate Michael Hoke in the 1844 North Carolina gubernatorial race by a vote of 42,586 to 39,433. He was inaugurated on Jan. 1, 1845. *BDGUS,* 3:1131. In the North Carolina state legislative elections, 26 Whigs and 24 Democrats were chosen for the state senate while 71 Whigs and 49 Democrats were selected for the state house. Raleigh *Register and North Carolina Gazette,* August 16, 1844. In the U.S. House race, 3 Whigs and 2 Democrats were elected. *Congressional Quarterly's Guide to U.S. Elections* (Washington, 1975), 582. 4. Probably the U.S. Senate.

To Committee of Whigs of Pennsylvania, February 10, 1844. Declines their invitation to attend the meeting in Philadelphia to celebrate Washington's birthday. Notes, however, that "the birth of no man that ever lived is so well entitled to perpetual commemoration, as a rare blessing, bestowed on mankind by the goodness of Providence. . . . Most justly has he acquired the title of the father of his country. . . . The task of recalling the purer days of the Republic, during which he lived and figured, and of renewing the unadultered republican principles which he so fondly cherished and successfully enforced, by distinguished celebration of the anniversary of his birth, and by other appropriate means, is eminently worthy the Whig citizens of . . . Philadelphia." Copy. Printed in Washington *Daily National Intelligencer,* February 27, 1844. Written from New Orleans and addressed to John Lindsey *et al.*

The Whigs of Philadelphia, meeting in Musical Fund Hall on February 22, 1844, honored Washington by reading his Farewell Address. Clay's reply to their invitation was also read to the assembly. Washington *Daily National Intelligencer,* February 26 and 27, 1844.

To Leonard Marbury, February 12, 1844. Hopes to visit "the Ship Genl Washington" before leaving New Orleans but cannot fix a date. Adds: "I shall endeavor to seize some unoccupied moment to surprize you with an unceremonious visit." ALS. MdAA. Written in New Orleans. Marbury was captain of the ship *General Washington.*

To JOHN J. CRITTENDEN New Orleans, February 15, 1844

Genl. [Charles] F. Mercer has just arrived here from Texas and brings intelligence which has greatly surprized me, but which in part I cannot believe to be true. It is in substance, that it has been ascertained by a vote in Secret Session, or in some other way, that 42 American Senators are in favor of the annexation of Texas,[1] and have advised the President [John Tyler] that they will confirm a treaty to that effect; that a negotiation has been opened accordingly in Texas, and that a treaty will be speedily concluded &c.[2]

Is this true? Especially that 42 Senators have concurred in the project?

Do address me instantly both at Montgomery, in Alabama, and Columbus in Georgia, and give me such information as you feel at liberty to communicate.

If it be true, I shall regret extremely that I have had no hint of it.

ALS. DLC-John J. Crittenden Papers (DNA, M212, R20). 1. On Jan. 16, 1844, Sec. of State Abel P. Upshur informed the U.S. chargé in Texas William S. Murphy that a two-thirds majority in the Senate favored annexation of Texas. Claude Hall, *Abel Parker Upshur* (Madison, Wisc., 1963), 204, 206-12; William R. Manning (ed.), *Diplomatic Correspondence of the United States . . .*, 12 vols. (Washington, 1932-39), 12:59-65. 2. The Tyler administration had begun negotiating in the fall of 1843 for a treaty of annexation with Texas. Such a treaty was signed on April 12, 1844, and submitted to the Senate on April 22, with both the treaty and Tyler's message concerning it to remain secret. The information, however, was leaked to the press, and when the treaty came to a vote on June 8, 1844, it was defeated by a vote of 35 to 16. Tyler then attempted to annex Texas by a joint resolution of Congress, thereby avoiding the two-thirds majority necessary for Senate ratification, but adjournment occurred before it came to a vote. When the 28th Congress, 2nd Session convened in Dec., 1844, Tyler again recommended annexation by joint resolution. It passed the House by a vote of 120 to 98 but stalled in the Senate. Finally, the annexation resolution passed the Senate on Feb. 27, 1845, by 27 to 25 votes and the House the following day by 132 votes to 76. The resolution admitting Texas to the Union was passed by the House on Dec. 16, 1845, by 141 to 56 votes; it passed the Senate on Dec. 22 by 31 to 14, and was signed by President James K. Polk on Dec. 24, 1845. U.S. Sen., *Executive Journal*, 6:126-27, 146, 157, 162, 188-89, 257, 262, 271, 277-79, 311-12; Justin H. Smith, *The Annexation of Texas* (corrected ed., New York, 1941); Frederick Merk, *Fruits of Propaganda in the Tyler Administration* (Cambridge, Mass., 1971), 95-128, 221-52; Charles M. Wiltse, *John C. Calhoun: Sectionalist* (New York, 1951), 199-216. For the treaty of annexation, see Clive Parry (ed.), *The Consolidated Treaty Series*, 231 vols. (Dobbs Ferry, N.Y., 1969), 99:261-69. See also 9:35-36.

To Richard Henry Bayard, Washington, D.C., February 27, 1844. Has received Bayard's letter of February 16 inviting him to visit Mrs. [Mary S.] Bayard and daughters in Wilmington, Delaware, while on his present trip. Notes that he has long wanted to tour the Eastern shore of Virginia but now feels that after passing through North Carolina, "I shall be in no condition to meet anywhere large concourse[s] of my fellow citizens." Promises, however, that should he travel up the peninsula and reach Delaware, "I will avail myself of your friendly invitation and stop at your house." LS. DLC-James Asheton and Richard Henry Bayard Papers (DNA, M212, R20). Letter written from Mobile, Ala. See Clay to Preston, January 19, 1844, for his itinerary.

To JAMES WATSON WEBB Mobile, Ala., February 29, 1844

Your favour of 20th of December, addressed to me at Lexington, followed me to this place; The Post Master of that City [Joseph Ficklin] misunderstood me. I was about to leave home for a period of at least five months, and as some forty or fifty newspapers daily came to me, I stated to him that I did not wish that they should come in my absence. I have always taken a deep interest in the perusal of the Inquirer [*sic*, New York *Courier & Enquirer*]; At the same time, I felt myself under great obligations to yourself and other friends for transmitting your Papers, altho' I was no Subscriber, & if you think proper to continue to send it [to] me, after my return in May, I shall feel greatly obliged.

I offer you congratulations, on the bright and cheering prospects of the success of our cause; but I agree with you, that there should be no relaxation in our exertions. . . .[1]

LS. KyLoF. 1. James K. Polk won the 1844 presidential election with 170 electoral votes and 1,337,243 popular votes, carrying the states of Alabama, Arkansas, Georgia, Illinois, Indiana, Louisiana, Maine, Michigan, Mississippi, Missouri, New Hampshire, New York, Pennsylvania, South Carolina, and Virginia. Clay garnered 1,299,068 popular and 105 electoral votes, carrying Connecticut, Delaware, Kentucky, Maryland, Massachusetts, New Jersey, North Carolina, Ohio, Rhode Island, Tennessee, and Vermont. Liberty party candidate James G. Birney received 65,608 popular but no electoral votes. Thomas H. McKee, *The National Conventions and Platforms of All Political Parties, 1789 to 1905; Convention, Popular and Electoral Vote* (New York, 1906; reprint, 1971), 56-57.

Speech to Committee of Tuscaloosa, Alabama, Whigs, late February or early March, 1844. Speaking in Mobile in a response to an invitation to visit Tuscaloosa, explains his position on the tariff. Says he looks back "with conscientious satisfaction in my agency in the passage of the Compromise [Tariff] Law [8:604, 621-22, 626-27]. The motives which governed me on that occasion, have been so often publicly avowed, that it is not necessary now to repeat them. A leading one, was the preservation of that Union, which is at once the basis and guarantee of all our rights, privileges and liberties, as a nation of freemen. It was then, as it had been long manifest to me, that the spirit of mutual concession and compromise which presided at the birth of our Constitution, should be borne in mind during the administration of the Government. With that spirit, extremes are wholly incompatible. Ultraism would have prevented the formation of the Constitution, as it may in process of time, endanger its existence." Notes that there are so many different interests in the country that each one ought to know that it cannot have all it wants. Uses the tariff to illustrate this point, noting that the extremes of opinion on this issue favor either free trade or prohibitory duties. Asks: "What then ought to be done?" Advocates a middle course with a tariff for revenue, adjusted to provide "reasonable protection to American interests." Copy, extract. Printed in Raleigh *Register and North Carolina Gazette*, March 15, 1844.

Clay was in Mobile from February 25 to March 5 and this speech was delivered sometime during that period. Raleigh *Register*, March 8, 1844; Washington *Daily National Intelligencer*, March 12, 1844.

To LUCRETIA HART CLAY Mobile, Ala., March 2, 1844

I arrived here a few days ago, and during my sojourn I stay at the house of Dr. [Henry] Levert. It is impossible that I could be treated with more kindness than I am by them. They have made a deep and grateful impression on my feelings. The people of the City all manifest towards me the most friendly feelings. The other night they gave me a splendid ball.[1]

John [Morrison Clay] arrived the day before I left N. Orleans, and as I intended to stop a week here, I advised him to remain there and join me at the end of the week. I shall leave this place to proceed on my journey tuesday next, and he will arrive the day before.

I ought to have mentioned to you before that I have remitted to Mr. [John J.] Astor $5000. & if I should be taken off you will find deposited with the Bank of Philada six or seven thousand dollars and a small balance with the Bank of Commerce at N. York.

I wish you would say to Thomas [Hart Clay] and James [Brown Clay] that I think they had better close with [2] of Clarke [*sic*, Clark County] for his hemp at four dollars and the rise. His hemp being of the previous years growth (at least much of it) is worth more than that of last year. There seems to be a general belief that the price of Bag. & Rope will advance some thing, but I apprehend not a great deal. I shall endeavor to dispose of what Thomas is making at Savannah or Charleston.

I shall not write to you again until I reach Augusta. I have a most arduous journey before me. My greatest difficulty is to restrain the enthusiasm of my friends and to avoid the entertainments which they are pressing me to accept. A part of the road, I understand, is very bad. I hope to be able to get through the journey, but I approach it with fear and trembling. I have appointed the 12h. of April to reach Raleigh, and I suppose it will be the last of the month before I get to Washington.

Give my love to James & Susan,[3] and Henry Duralde.

ALS. DLC-TJC (DNA, M212, R10). 1. Clay arrived in Mobile on Feb. 25 and left for Montgomery on March 5. The ball was held on Feb. 28, 1844. Mobile *Register and Journal*, Feb. 26, 29, March 6, 1844. 2. Name omitted. See Clay to James B. Clay, Jan. 22, 1844. 3. James Brown Clay had married Susan Maria Jacob, the daughter of John J. Jacob of Louisville on Oct. 12, 1843. Louisville *Daily Journal*, Oct. 14, 1843.

To Mrs. Foster, Columbus, Georgia, March 13, 1844. Thanks her for the "tranquil and pleasant" night he spent "under your hospitable roof." ALS. KyU. Mrs. Foster was probably the wife of Congressman Thomas F. Foster of Columbus. See *BDAC*.

From Citizens of Berkeley County, Martinsburg, Va. (W. Va.), March 14, 1844. Mention "some historical recollections connected with your fame," viz: "It was here, in this very county . . . on the 14th of June, 1824, that your name was first presented to the people of Virginia, as a candidate for that exalted station, for which you now stand nominated in the hearts of near two millions of your admiring countrymen"; "It was here . . . that the electoral ticket was framed and announced, which presents your claim to the suffrages of your native State." Also, Berkeley County "gave you her confidence without reserve in 1824, and she has continued that confidence without change or shadow to the present hour." Copy. Printed in F. Vernon Aler, *Aler's History of Martinsburg and Berkeley County, West Virginia* (Hagerstown, Md., 1888), 109-10.

The freeholders of Berkeley County had met in the courthouse in Martinsburg on June 14, 1824, nominated Clay for president, and appointed a committee of correspondence to promote his election. Frankfort (Ky.) *Argus of Western America*, July 28, 1824.

To The National Clay Club, Philadelphia, March 17, 1844. Reports receiving their letter of February 24 and reading it with "concern and regret." Says that it was his intention to answer their letter of the previous autumn, and "I have a strong conviction, although I would not assert positively, that I replied to it, prior to my departure from home." Adds that his correspondence "occupies, when I am at home, my time constantly." Hopes "your failure to receive my reply . . . was unattended with any disadvantage."

States that it "is to be inferred from your letter" that "there are . . . differences among my Philadelphia friends," and notes that "I deeply regret the existence of the jealousies and misconceptions among those between whom nothing but harmony and cordial cooperation should prevail." Expresses his "very high opinion of the motives, objects, and services of the National Clay Club," because many of them "are my personal, and all of them my political, friends." Adds that "Most happily concord, harmony, and union characterize the votaries of our cause generally throughout the Union, and I should be greatly disappointed and mortified if Philadelphia formed an exception." LS. ViU. Written from Macon, Ga.; addressed to Henry White, David S. Brown, John B. Myers, Francis N. Buck, and William Reynolds.

Henry White (1793-1860) was a prominent wholesale grocer in Philadelphia for more than forty years. His business, located at 23 S. Water Street, was named White, Stevens & Co. until about 1859 when it was changed to White, Hart & Co. For many years White lived on Walnut Street, but his residence at the time of his death was 1703 Locust Street. Information supplied by Joel T. Loeb, The Historical Society of Pennsylvania.

David S. Brown was a commission merchant in Philadelphia, John B. Myers an auctioneer, and both Francis N. Buck and William Reynolds were merchants. *M'Elroy's Philadelphia Directory for 1844*, 7th ed. (Philadelphia, 1844).

On the same day, March 17, Clay wrote Henry White, enclosing the above letter and saying that it could be read to the National Clay Club but should not be published. Copy. Printed in Colton, *Clay Correspondence*, 4:484.

Speech in Milledgeville, Ga., March 19, 1844. Although suffering from a cold, Clay acknowledges "the very eloquent" introductory speech of Gov. George Walker Crawford and expresses his pleasure at being able to visit Georgia "as a private citizen, seeking no honor." Notes a desire for "his reception to be freed from every party bias, and to meet every Georgian with the toleration and kindness, he really felt for all parties. . . . The contest was not with enemies of the country, but between two great parties aiming at the good of the country but differing in the means of accomplishing so great an object. . . . With regard to the great questions of public interest, which were now before the people, why should he speak? Was there a doubt of his opinions in regard to one of them? His spoken, recorded, and printed opinions were before the world; and they remained unaltered. He would therefore, limit his remarks to a few topics, which had . . . acquired a peculiar importance to himself."

In reference to the honor Gov. Crawford has done him in comparing his trip through Georgia to that of Gen. Lafayette in 1825, he recalls his own role in the House of Representatives in 1825 in the election of John Q. Adams as president. Mentions that William H. Crawford had been his first choice among the three candidates, but that Crawford's paralysis had rendered him "out of the question." Thus, he had supported Adams over Andrew Jackson who was "too rash, impetuous, and inexperienced." Notes that he had shown a manuscript version of his defense to his constituents [4:143-66] to General Lafayette who had suggested deleting the "full and strong account of the personal afflictions of Mr. Crawford," because "a thing so painful ought not to be brought to Mr. Crawford's eyes." "By all means," Clay had replied, "they shall be left out, and they were left out."

In reference to Gov. Crawford's allusion to Clay's role in the Missouri Compromise [2:669-70, 740-48, 775-77, 785-86; 3:15-22, 26-29, 32-33, 46-47, 49-50] and the Compromise Tariff of 1833 [8:604, 621-22, 626-27], gives a brief "account of his agency in these transactions." Remembers how he "had the happiness to wring . . . the positive promise" from the House Committee to vote for the admission of Missouri to the Union. Notes that he "has been charged with arrogance and dictation, to the measures of the late senate; but he repudiated *not debts*, but dictation to the senate." Recalls that "if he had ever acted dictator," it was on the occasion of a near breakup of the conference committee which was attempting to work out the Compromise tariff. On that occasion he had thrown "himself into the door and said, 'gentlemen you shall not go out of this door, till you have acted on this question—the senate and house of representatives have referred it to us, and it must be reported back to them; this is your duty, and you have to do it.' " When the measure was prepared for final action by Congress, the opposition it still encountered caused him to "despair of carrying it through; but, at the crisis . . . Mr. [John C.] Calhoun came forward and gave it his support. Thus it was saved and thus perhaps, the evils which then menaced the country averted." As for President Jackson, the compromise tariff "was urged on him by his most influential friends" who "used arguments and even threats before they were successful." Adds that his views of the tariff have remained unchanged. Avers that "Experience had taught us a great lesson . . . that a tariff laid on an article, did not increase its price, and often reduced it." Also, "Mr. Clay repeated his aversion to all extremes; he was a compromise man, and on the tariff question he was for a judicious use of the protective power, for the purpose of fostering *American industry*."

Reiterates his support for the distribution of the proceeds of the sales of the public lands to the states, pointing out that "Two states were distinguished for their contributions to this great fund, Virginia and Georgia." Asks: "Ought not these states to derive some benefit, from the sales of this vast property? . . . this fund in the hands of the states, would. . . . be a permanent common fund, and a great bond to the union." Emphasizes that he "was, and always had been, the friend of Georgia—he wished to see her covering all her territory and enjoying all the blessings which Providence had alloted to her." Is "particularly gratified *that her last legislature had remedied the defects in her currency and provided for the re-establishment of her credit*." Adds, however, that as a U.S. senator, he "had voted against the ratification of the treaty, by which she had acquired her Cherokee land. Treaties, like other contracts, must have two parties, and both must be willing. In this case, the senate had before them proof—irresistible proofs, that the treaty was induced by *corruption*, made without authority and against the wishes of almost the whole Cherokee nation. He could not consider this the act of one nation treating with another, and therefore *voted against it*."

Apologizes "for the lengthy and desultory remarks into which he had been drawn. They were demanded by feelings which it would have been wrong for him to suppress." Copy. Printed in *Niles' Register* (April 20, 1844), 66:119-20; reprinted from the Milledgeville *Union* and described as a "brief and imperfect, but interesting outline of an extended speech made by Mr. CLAY."

For George Walker Crawford, see *DAB* and *BDAC*; the latter erroneously gives his middle name as "Washington." When Crawford began his first administration in 1843, he urged the legislature to conclude rapidly the affairs of the Central Bank of Georgia, a state-owned bank which had been forced to end active operation in 1841 because it could not redeem its large number of paper notes. Believing that as long as its depreciated bills were in circulation the state's credit was in question, he proposed that certificates of deposit bearing 8% interest be issued to redeem the notes still in circulation. By January, 1844, a large quantity of the notes had been burned, thus retiring more of the bank's circulation. With this and also with the resumption of specie payments by the state treasury, Georgia's economic condition markedly improved during 1844. See Len G. Cleveland, "George W. Crawford of Georgia, 1798-1872," Ph.D. dissertation, University of Georgia, 1974, pp. 108-112, 135-36, espec. 109-10.

For the New Echota Treaty, signed on December 29, 1835, and proclaimed on May 23, 1836, by which Georgia acquired the Cherokee lands, see Parry, *Treaty Series*, 85:409-20. Clay voted against ratification when it was approved by the Senate on May 16, 1836. U.S. Sen., *Executive Journal*, 4:545-46.

To WILLIAM C. PRESTON

Milledgeville, Ga.,
March 20, 1844

I received at this place your favor of the 15th inst. I have made such arrangements, in reference to my journey, that I hope to leave Augusta for Columbia in the cars on Tuesday the 2d of April, and to arrive that night at Columbia.[1] I am accompanied by my youngest son [John Morrison Clay] only and one servant.[2] I can remain in Columbia only on Wednesday and Thursday, which days you and my friend Col. [Wade] Hampton must divide between you as you please. I wish to leave Columbia on Friday the 5th of April for Charleston, where I can only remain two or three days, as I am bound to reach Raleigh on the night of the 11th of April. I should have been glad to have given you more of my time at Columbia, which I should have been able to have done but for an excursion to Madison and Greensborough [*sic*] which I have not been able to resist Dawson[3] in making.

With respect to the mode of my passing my time at Columbia, in regard to which you have kindly enquired, I desire it to be as quiet as possible. I wish no parade, no public meetings on my account, and no public speeches. In spite of myself I have been drawn out at Macon, Columbus,[4] and this place[5] to make speeches of more than an hour's duration at each, in the open air, and I find unless I stop that I shall get the Bronchitis. I am now as hoarse as a circuit rider; otherwise my health and strength are very good. . . .

LS. Vi. 1. For Clay's itinerary, see Clay to Preston, Jan. 19, 1844. 2. Probably Clay's body slave, Charles Dupuy. 3. Probably William C. Dawson of Greensboro, Ga. See *BDAC*. 4. Speeches at Columbus and Macon, given on March 12 or 13 and 18, respectively, have not been found. 5. Speech in Milledgeville, March 19, 1844.

Speech in Savannah, Ga., March 22, 1844. Expresses his appreciation for the warmth of their greeting, and adverts "to the attempt through the medium of anonymous communications to influence the public mind against him here, and censured the 'few leading Democrats' who had attempted to array against him an unfriendly feeling, foreign to the dictates of a liberal Southern hospitality. He was always pleased . . . to exchange civilities with his democratic brethren wherever he might be, and . . . prior to leaving his lodgings, several citizens of that party had called to pay their respects to him. He defended himself from the charge of making an electioneering tour. . . . He was anxious to see the state of Georgia." Inquires "several times why 'the few democrats' should seek to poison the public mind against him. He brought with him neither 'war, pestilence nor famine.' He did not mean to bear away, even if he could do so, any of the fair daughters of Georgia, whom he saw before him; he had an estimable wife at home, with whom he was sufficiently blest already. Mr. [Martin] Van Buren and himself had long been accustomed to the interchange of civilities; he had had the pleasure of dispensing the hospitalities of Ashland to the ex-president [9:680-81], and he should be happy to extend a similar reception to that gentleman's friends here."

Briefly refers to the Missouri Compromise [2:742-48, 775-78, 785-88] and the Compromise Tariff of 1833 [8:604, 621-22, 626-27], as well as to "the last war [of 1812]." Says "that war was necessary not only to the vindication of the national honor, but to the . . . integrity of our rights. He was however a *peace* man emphatically. Peace was what he wanted.—*Time and patience* were the elements which this country wanted to place her in a condition of prosperity and happiness in comparison with which ancient republics would sink into insignificance." Regarding the tariff, "He rejected either extreme of a high tariff and of free trade." Asserts that "the proceeds of the sales of public lands . . . belonged to the states, to the thirteen [old states] that had acquired them by their blood and treasure, as well as to the new states in which they lie."

Details his reasons for believing in the necessity of a national bank, saying: "If exchanges were now in a good condition, experience has shown that they would not continue so. If the state banks now paid specie, facts had shown that with a revival of prosperity the inflation of paper currency would re-commence, because there was no national regulator to check these spurious issues. The state banks as we all know, are also powerless to furnish a national currency with which a citizen of this great country can travel from one end of it to the other. The practice of the most enlightened European governments has shown that a national currency was necessary; the national government could alone ordain it, and it was just as important to the national interest to have it, as it was to regulate commerce, or to provide a navy or an army." Notes that he "*has* changed his mind" about the national bank "as all honest men ought to change their minds, when they find that more mature experience in public affairs, and more enlarged observation have convinced them of their error." Recalls how President [George] Washington had been "slow to be convinced of the propriety of signing the first bank charter, but he . . . *did* sign it. Mr. [James] Madison refused to sign the re-charter and he, too, became convinced after viewing the disastrous condition of the currency during the eventful period of 1811-1816. . . . At this time we can appreciate both the intelligence and patriotism of those who thus modified their views." Points to the problems resulting from President [Andrew] Jackson's veto of the recharter of the second national bank [8:434, 552-53].

Remarks that the Whigs are often accused "of avowing no distinct principles." Denies that this is true, asking: "But what were the democratic principles? He did not know, unless it was *opposition to every thing whig*." Criticizes the Democrats for opposing the one term principle for the president, for opposing the law providing for the election of members of Congress by district [9:724-25], and for their support of the presidential veto power—"a power so dangerous to those liberties when carelessly exercised." Copy. Printed in *Niles' Register* (April 13, 1844), 66:106-7.

For Clay's reversal on the national bank in 1816, see 2:200-205, 342-44, 413-14, 552-53, 697, 723; for his proposal of constitutional amendments to limit the president to one term and to abolish the veto power, see 9:312-13, 608-9, 775-76. For definition of the "old states," the seven "new states," and the "nine land states" relative to the distribution of public land sales receipts, see 8:540 and 9:489.

To JOHN M. BERRIEN Savannah, Ga., March 23, 1844

I write under your hospitable roof, where the kindness of Mrs. [Eliza] Berrien supplies me with every thing to render my sojourn here highly comfortable and agreeable. I arrived on Thursday night, and shall remain here until Monday morning. I expect to reach Washington in one of the last days of April. I hope you and my other friends in the Senate from the South will not allow yourselves, before my arrival, to decide in favor of lending yourselves to the fraudulent purpose of changing the Tariff of 1842.[1] I find every where at the South and South West the support of the combined principle of Revenue and Protection far stronger than I had anticipated. Indeed the Whigs appear to be nearly, if not quite, unanimous. But that I remember you predicted to me, near two years ago, would probably be the case.

My reception here and everywhere that I have been, during my journey, has been most enthusiastic. Nothing could exceed the fervor of the demonstrations which have been made in this ancient city.

Mrs Berrien will no doubt inform you that, with the exception of some slight indisposition on her part, your family are all well. . . .

LS. NcU. 1. For the Tariff of 1842, see 9:628, 646-47. For proposals in 1844 to change the tariff, see Clay to Clayton, *ca.* Late August, 1844.

To JOHN J. CRITTENDEN Savannah, Ga., March 24, 1844

I arrived here on the 21st inst. and shall leave it to-morrow morning. My reception every where from Mobile to this place has been marked by extraordinary enthusiam.[1] I have borne the fatigues of the journey better than I feared, indeed I have nothing to complain of but a hoarseness produced by public speaking, into which I have been reluctantly drawn.

I received at Montgomery, and Columbus both your letters relating to Texas,[2] and I find that subject is producing great excitement at Washington. I have forborne hitherto to express any opinion with regard to it. I reserve for my arrival at Washington the consideration of the question whether it is not necessary to announce my opinions. I think I can treat the question in a manner very differently from any treatment which I have yet seen of it, and so as to reconcile all our friends, and many others, to the views which I entertain. Of one thing you may be certain, that there is no such anxiety for the annexation here at the South as you might have been disposed to imagine. I take pleasure in also informing you that I have not seen one Whig during my journey who is not satisfied with the ground on which I place the principle of protection in connection with a tariff for revenue. And you may say to the Southern Senators who belong to our party that they may with perfect safety and confidence vote against the fraudulent tariff which is cooking up in the House.

I adhere to my purpose of reaching Raleigh by the 12th of next month, and of getting to Washington towards the end of April. I expect to pass by Columbia and Charleston. My son John [Morrison Clay] alone accompanies me, and acts on this occasion as my Amanuensis.

LS. DLC-John J. Crittenden Papers (DNA, M212, R20). 1. For his itinerary, see Clay to Preston, Jan. 19, 1844. 2. Crittenden's letters have not been found; however, for the Texas question, see Clay to Crittenden, Feb. 15, 1844.

To Samuel Weir, Columbia, S.C., March 27, 1844. Acknowledges receipt of the resolutions in his honor passed by the Richland Clay Club of Columbia. Says he plans to reach that city on April 2 and that he desires it to be "wholly of a private nature" without parades, public meetings, or a barbecue. Adds, however, that he will take pleasure in meeting the citizens of Richland County and Columbia in "any unceremonious manner." Copy. Printed in Charleston *Courier*, April 4, 1844. Written from Augusta, Ga.

Weir was editor of the Columbia (S.C.) *Southern Chronicle* and an active Whig partisan. Information supplied by Wylma Wates, South Carolina Department of Archives and History.

To WILLIAM C. PRESTON Augusta, Ga., March 28, 1844

I recd. your favor addressed to me at this place. I have been compelled to abandon my trip to Madison and Greensboro', in consequence of fatigue[.][1] The result is to throw a little more time on my hands. I shall leave Augusta on monday the first of Apl. instead of tuesday the 2d. for Columbia, where I hope to arrive on that same (monday) evening. I *must* leave Columbia on thursday (this day week) for Charleston,[2] to a Comee. from which, which has met me here, I have made that engagement. This variation in my movements does not lessen the time I had appropriated to you.

Would it not be best to keep undivulged my arrival on monday instead of tuesday? and thus spare me all parade.

I find I must restrain the excitement to which I am constantly exposed. Quiet, quiet, quiet, is my greatest want.

ALS. MB. 1. Clay to Preston, Jan. 19, 1844. 2. See Speech in Charleston, S.C., April 6, 1844.

To JOHN PENDLETON KENNEDY Augusta, Ga., March 29, 1844

I received since my arrival at this place your favor of the 22d of February, transmitting me an invitation to visit Baltimore, and to attend the Young Men's Convention of Ratification.[1] Enclosed[2] I send an answer to it, which after perusing I will thank you to forward to its destination.

I congratulate you most heartily upon the issue of your own election[3] and that of the Maryland elections generally.[4] It was a glorious commencement of the campaign of this year. I shall seize the first leisure which I can command to peruse your publications which so greatly contributed to bring it about.[5] I anticipate also much satisfaction from the perusal of your defence of the Whig Congress,[6] all of which I have not yet read.

We shall run our adversaries hard if not beat them in Illinois,[7] Missouri,[8] Arkansas,[9] and Alabama.[10] We shall beat them in Louisiana[11] and Mississipi [*sic*],[12] and our friends in this State[13] count upon its giving us a majority of not less that [*sic*, than] ten and probably fifteen thousand.

LS. MdBP. 1. See 9:887. 2. Enclosure not found. 3. Kennedy had been reelected to the U.S. House in the Maryland congressional election which had been postponed from the fall of 1843 until early 1844 in order for the legislature to pass a new districting bill. Charles H. Bohner, *John Pendleton Kennedy, Gentleman from Baltimore* (Baltimore, 1961), 163-64. The date of the congressional election is erroneously given as 1843 in *Guide to U.S. Elections*, 578 and in 9:870. 4. For the Maryland elections held in Oct., 1843, see 9:870. In the 1844 state elections in Maryland, Whig Thomas G. Pratt defeated Democrat James Carroll for the governorship by 35,040 votes to 34,495. *BDGUS*, 2:664. Whigs also carried both houses of the state legislature, winning the senate by 15 seats to 6 for the Democrats and the house by 61 seats to 21. *Niles' Register* (Oct. 5, 1844), 67:67. In addition, Clay carried Maryland's 8 electoral votes with 35,984 popular votes to 32,676 for James K. Polk, and 3,308 for James G. Birney. McKee, *National . . . Popular and Electoral Vote*, 56-57. 5. Probably a reference to a series of letters, defending the protective system, which he had written to the "Mechanics and Workingmen" of Baltimore which had been published in the newspapers as a part of his bid for reelection. Georgia P. Spelman, "The Whig Rhetoric of John Pendleton Kennedy, Spokesman for Industry," Ph.D. dissertation, Indiana University, 1974, pp. 138-42. 6. See 9:894 and Clay to Kennedy, June 10, 1844. 7. In the 1844 Illinois elections Democrats carried the state senate by 12 seats to 8 for the Whigs and the state house by 76 to 36 seats. Theodore C. Pease, *Illinois Election Returns 1818-1848* (Springfield, Ill., 1923), 380-406. In the congressional races, Democrats won 6 seats and the Whigs 1. *Guide to U.S. Elections*, 580. Also, Polk won Illinois's 9 electoral votes, winning 57,920 popular votes to 45,528 votes for Clay, and 3,570 for Birney. McKee, *National . . . Popular and Electoral Vote*, 56-57. 8. In the 1844 Missouri elections, Democrats carried the state senate 25 seats to 8 for the Whigs and the house by 55 to 45. *Niles' Register* (August 31, 1844), 66:444. Democrats also won 4 seats in the U.S. House to 1 for the Whigs. *Guide to U.S. Elections*, 580. John C. Edwards, a Democrat, was elected governor over Whig Charles H. Allen by 36,978 votes to 31,357. *BDGUS*, 2:843. Polk carried Missouri's 7 electoral votes, winning 41,369 popular votes to Clay's 31,251. McKee, *National . . . Popular and Electoral Vote*, 56-57. 9. In the 1844 elections in Arkansas, Democrat Thomas S. Drew defeated Whig Lawrence Gibson by 8,859 to 7,244 votes, with Independent Richard C. Byrd garnering 2,507. *BDGUS*, 1:65. Democrat Archibald Yell won the U.S. House seat. *Guide to U.S. Elections*, 580. In the state senate Democrats won 21 seats to 4 for the Whigs and 64 house seats to 11 for the Whigs. *Niles' Register* (Dec. 14, 1844), 67:226. Polk defeated Clay with 9,546 to 5,504 popular votes, winning all 3 of Arkansas's electoral votes. McKee, *National . . . Popular and Electoral Vote*, 56-57. 10. In the 1844 elections in Alabama, Democrats won the state senate by 20 seats to 13 for the Whigs and the state house by 68 to 32. In a special election for the U.S. House, Democrat William Yancey defeated Whig Daniel Watraus. *Guide to U.S. Elections*, 580. Polk carried Alabama over Clay by 37,740 popular votes to 26,084, receiving all 9 electoral votes. McKee, *National . . . Popular and Electoral Vote*, 56-57. 11. In Louisiana's 1844 elections, Democrats carried the state senate 9 seats to 8 for the Whigs, while Whigs won the house 34 to 26. *Niles' Register* (July 20, 1844), 66:336. In the congressional elections, Whigs won 1 seat, Democrats 2, and the States' Rights Democrats 1. *Guide to U.S. Elections*, 580. Polk carried Louisiana and its 6 electoral votes with 13,782 popular votes to 13,083 for Clay. McKee, *National . . . Popular and Electoral Vote*, 56-57. 12. Polk carried Mississippi by 25,126 to 19,206 for Clay, winning its 5 electoral votes. McKee, *National . . . Popular and Electoral Vote*, 56-57. There was no other major election in Mississippi in 1844. 13. In Georgia's 1844 congressional elections, Whigs and Democrats each won 4 seats. *Guide to U.S. Elections*, 580. Polk carried Georgia 44,177 to 42,106 for Clay, winning all 10 electoral votes. McKee, *National . . . Popular and Electoral Vote*, 56-57.

To JOHN BROWN FRANCIS[1] Augusta, Ga., March 31, 1844

I duly received, in this city, your favor[2] transmitting certain resolutions adopted at a meeting of the Law and Order members of the General Assembly held in Providence in February last;[3] and I request you to convey to them my profound acknowledgments for the friendly and flattering allusion to my name in some of the resolutions.

I congratulate your State upon its successful vindication of social order and the authority of the law.[4]

The principles avowed and attempted to be enforced, by subverting the existing Government in Rhode Island, struck at the foundations of all safety and security in civilized society. They were revolutionary, without being characterized by a manly spirit of open and fearless resistance. In rebuking and repudiating them, Rhode Island has rendered an important service to the cause of order, stability, and free institutions; and having achieved a decisive triumph over disorder and anarchy, I have no doubt that she will not tarnish the lustre of it by any act of useless and uncalled for severity. . . .

Copy. Printed in Washington *Daily National Intelligencer*, April 16, 1844. 1. For Francis (1791-1864), former Rhode Island governor who entered the U.S. Senate in 1844, see *DAB*; *BDAC*. 2. Francis had written Clay on Feb. 19, 1844, transmitting the resolutions of the convention and saying, "Your generous support, at a time when few politicans dared to evince any sympathy for us, cannot but increase the attachment to you already so strong in our State." Copy. Printed in Washington *Daily National Intelligencer*, April 16, 1844. 3. The Law and Order members of the Rhode Island general assembly had met on Feb. 14, 1844, and strongly criticized the Dorr party [9:714-16], while endorsing Clay for president. *Manufacturers and Farmers Journal and Providence and Pawtucket Advertiser*, Feb. 15, 1844. 4. See 9:714-16.

Speech to Mr. Shepherd and the Cabinet Makers of Columbia, S.C., *ca*. April 2, 1844. Thanks them for their address, saying: "You are not, probably, aware of the connection existing between me and the mechanical class to which you belong. . . . my only surviving full brother [Porter Clay] was once a very excellent Cabinet Maker." Adds that he has "ever thought it desirable to see our country enjoying a real and practical independence of the rest of the world. . . . I have believed that our artizans ought to be protected, and still think they should be protected, against the rival productions of foreign artizans." Copy, summary. Printed in Knoxville *Register*, May 1, 1844.

Shepherd, heading the deputation of Columbia cabinet makers, had greeted Clay, promising him "our undivided support," and adding: "As *Cabinet Makers* we know you to be a *master workman*, and in electing you *chief Boss*, we confidently expect to see the best *Cabinet work since* the days of Washington; and the people will not be obliged to pay or be under the least necessity to send to France or England, as Mr. [Van] Buren did for furniture to furnish the White House." *Ibid.*

To Francis Y. Porcher, Charleston, S.C., April 3, 1844. Reports that he had intended to leave Columbia for Charleston on April 4, but a cold and his fear that "a portion of the religious community of Charleston might feel wounded by public manifestations to which the occasion of my first visit to that city may possibly give rise, during a week [Easter] which recal[l]s a recollection of memorable and solemn events connected with our religion." Thus, "I have determined to postpone my departure . . . to Saturday morning [April 6], which will enable me to arrive there that evening." Plans to stay until Tuesday afternoon. Copy. Printed in Charleston *Courier*, April 4, 1844. Written from Columbia, S.C.

From "Many of Your Fellow Citizens," Charleston, S.C., *ca.* April 4, 1844. Noting that the "Texas and Oregon questions having assumed a position of paramount importance" in public affairs, they ask: "1. Are you for or against the annexation of Texas [9:35; Clay to Crittenden, February 15, 1844] to the United States? 2. Are you for or against giving the notice required by the Treaty with Great Britain [9:828-29] before either Government can occupy the Oregon Territory, and proceeding at the expiration of the notice to take posession of that country?" Copy. Printed in Charleston (S.C.) *Mercury*, April 4, 1844.

Speech in Charleston, S.C., April 6, 1844. In "a speech of thrilling eloquence and great ability, occupying near two hours," Clay expresses his thanks to the "various committees, to the throng of citizens, and especially to the assemblage of fair ladies, who had united to greet him." Mentions that he had been "greatly assisted" in the settlement of the Missouri question [2:669-70, 740-48, 775-78, 785-88; 3:15-22, 26-29, 32-33, 46-47, 49-50; 8:786-88] by "his personal friend the lamented William Lowndes," who "of all the statesmen with whom he had mingled in the counsels of the country, he had found . . . to be 'the wisest, the purest, the best.' " Adds that "there were others largely entitled to share in whatever credit" the Compromise Tariff of 1833 [8:604, 621-22, 626-27] "conferred on its authors." Asserts that in both cases "he was actuated only by the desire to harmonize and perpetuate our political union, without which our liberties, our prosperity, and our greatness would be inevitably destroyed." Alluding "to the motives of his present tour," denies the charge, made by "the selfish and ungenerous," that he is making "an electioneering tour." Maintains that his visit to New Orleans was "purely on a matter of business; and his return home furnished him . . . a favorable opportunity to visit . . . Alabama, Georgia, South Carolina, and North Carolina. . . . It was said he was a candidate for the presidency. He could not deny that from the St. John's to the banks of the Sabine, spontaneous demonstrations, unsought and unprompted by him, had been made in his favor; but he had never yet consented or declared to anyone that he was a candidate for the presidency—at present he was a plain farmer, earning his labor by the sweat of his brow, or rather by the joint sweat of himself and those who labored with him—and however near the period of final decision might be, he had reserved the right of such decision for the proper moment and the proper occasion."

Enters, then, "into a frank and fearless exposition of his views on the great questions of the tariff and currency." States that he has always "been in favor of the protective policy to a certain extent," and that he had "been active in effecting the compromise [tariff] of 1833" in an effort to preserve "the peace and the great interests of the country." Does not maintain that the doctrine of "any congress could bind its successors," but the "state of the country which led to the passage of that compromise made him feel it an obligation of honor to adhere to it in good faith." Denies that he has "ever countenanced its violation in the slightest particular." Avers that "the principle of home valuation was an essential and indispensable feature of that concession," but denies "that the principle of the compromise required a maximum rate of duty to be fixed at 20 per cent." Continues with a "brief vindication of a moderate protective policy," and concludes "this branch of his subject by declaring himself in favor of a system of protection, moderate, reasonable, certain and durable—yielding no more revenue than is necessary for an honest and economical administration of the government, and within that limit, discriminating in the imposition of duties, between those articles which do and those which do not enter into competition with domestic industry—throwing the heavier duty on the former and the lighter duty on the latter. . . . on this basis this great question must be settled—*that we must live together*, we cannot do otherwise—and there must be some common ground on which we should meet. . . . safety and peace could only be found by taking the middle path. That neither interest or section could expect to have it all their own way. . . . Each interest must concede something, and thus a system of equivalents must give satisfaction to all."

Believes in regard to the currency that "the idea of an exclusively metallic circulation" is a "mere delusion," and that banks will continue to exist under the auspices of the states. Thus, a national bank is necessary "to regulate and control the system and keep it from explosion and mischief"; also insists that it is "necessary to secure a national currency" and "to prevent the monied and commercial interests of the country from being placed at the mercy of the monied power of foreign states." Argues that "it was in Wall street among foreign capitalists, that the northern opposition to a national bank was most vigorous, and this spoke volumes of its connexion with the true interests and welfare of the country."

Says, in conclusion, that "he had set out on his present tour, with the intention to keep his lips sealed, but he had been compelled to speak. That he was no preacher and could not give a sermon—no doctor and could not deliver a lecture on medicine—no poet and could not sing soft strains for the amusement of the audience. . . . he trusted he would be pardoned, for being silent on subjects of which he knew nothing, and for speaking out freely on subjects with which he professed to be familiar." Copy. Printed in *Niles' Register* (April 13, 1844), 66:105-6.

For William Lowndes, see *DAB* and *BDAC*.

Speech in Wilmington, N.C., April 9 or 10, 1844. Expresses his pleasure at being in North Carolina for the first time. Recalls that two years ago he was invited to attend a convention in Raleigh but declined, when he learned that he was being considered as a presidential candidate. Notes that he had promised to come at some future date and that a large number of the members of the last session of the North Carolina legislature wrote him "calling on me for a fulfillment of that promise. I have felt that I must come now or never, and as I am a man of my word, I come now. I come for no political end, to effect no object of personal aggrandizement."

Continues, saying: "I am a Whig! I am so because I believe the principles of the Whig party are best adapted to promote the prosperity of the country. I seek to change no man's allegiance to his party, be it what it may. A life of great length and experience, has satisfied me, that ALL PARTIES AIM AT THE COMMON GOOD OF THE COUNTRY." Adds that members of both the Whig and Democratic parties believe "that their policy is patriotic. I take the hand of one as cordially as of another—for all are Americans. I place *country* far above all parties. Look aside from that and parties are no longer worthy of being cherished. As to the Democratic party, I think much better of it than some of them think of themselves. *I* never said of them that they entertained the doctrine, that 'to the victors belong the spoils,' as an eminent member of the party did." States that in exercising suffrage himself, he always chooses a man "whose general course gave a guaranty of uprightness and honesty. That he never expected a man's opinions to conform altogether to his own, any more than in selecting a wife (and here he turned playfully to the ladies,) a man can expect his lady love to be free from all possible defects."

Thanks them for their many kindnesses, saying his physical ability cannot sustain any more strain. Copy, summary. Printed in Raleigh *Register and North Carolina Gazette*, April 19, 1844. The Raleigh *Register* article states that the speech was given on "Tuesday last," in other words, on April 9; however, the Washington *Daily National Intelligencer* of April 15, 1844, states that he did not arrive at Wilmington until April 10.

SPEECH IN RALEIGH, N.C.[1] April 13, 1844

Friends and Fellow citizens, Ladies and Gentlemen of North Carolina.

A long cherished object of my heart is accomplished. I am at your Capital and in the midst of you. I have looked forward to this my first visit to North

Carolina, with anxious wishes, and with high expectations of great gratification; and I am happy to say that my fondest anticipations have been more than realized. Wherever I have passed on my way to your city, wherever I have stopped, at the depots of railroads, in country town or village, it has been my good fortune to receive the warmest demonstrations of respect and kindness, from all parties, from both sexes, and from every age; but no where have I met, no where had I expected such a distinguished reception, and such enthusiastic greetings as those with which my arrival here has been attended. I am rejoiced to be with you this day, to stand surrounded by you in the shade of this magnificent Capitol, a noble monument of your public liberality and taste; and while my grateful heart has been warmed, by the thrilling grasp of each outstretched hand, and my eye cheered by the smiles and beauty of the fair daughters of North Carolina, who have honored this occasion by their presence, I cannot but rejoice, and I do rejoice, that I am an American citizen, and feel that, though far removed from my immediate home and friends, yet I tread here the soil of my own country, am in the midst of my friends and countrymen and can exclaim in the language of the Scottish bard "that this, this is indeed, my own my Native land." I own that I have been truly and greatly but agreeably surprized. I had expected to find some hundreds, perhaps a few thousands assembled here to meet and greet me. I did not expect to witness such an outpouring. I did not expect to see the whole State congregated together, but here it is! From the mountains and from the sea board, from the extremities, and from the centre, I see around me the sons and the daughters of the good old North State! A State, which has earned this estimable title by the purity, simplicity, and efficiency of its institutions; by its uniform patriotism and inflexible virtue, by its quiet, unobtrusive, and unambitious demeanor, and by its steady and firm attachment to the union; of which it is one of the surest props and pillars—A noble title, of which although it is not proud, because it is not in its nature to be proud, its sister States may well envy and emulate her. For these hearty manifestations of your respect and esteem I thank you all. I thank my fair countrywomen for gracing this meeting by their countenance and presence. I thank your worthy Chief Magistrate [John M. Morehead] for the generous manner in which he has represented your hospitality. I thank the various committees for the kindness and attentions which I have received at their hands, and, particularly, the committee who did me the honor to meet me on the borders of your State, and escort me to this city.

I am here, fellow citizens, in compliance with your own summons. Warm and repeated invitations to visit this State and my own ardent desire to see it, to form the acquaintance and to share the hospitalities of its citizens, have brought me in your presence. I have come with objects, exclusively social and friendly. I have come upon no political errand. I have not come as a propagandist. I seek to change no man's opinion, to shake no man's allegiance to his party. Satisfied and contented with the opinions which I have formed upon public a[f]fairs, after thorough investigation and full deliberation, I am willing to leave every other man in the undisturbed possession of his opinions. It is one of our great privileges, in a free country, to form our own opinions upon all matters of public concern. Claiming the exercise of it for myself I am ever ready to accord to others equal freedom in exercising it for themselves. But, inasmuch as the manner in which we may exercise the rights, appertaining to us, may exert, reciprocally, an influence upon each other, for good or for evil, we owe the mutual duty of considering fairly, fully, and disinterestedly, all measures of public policy which may be proposed for adoption.

Although, fellow citizens, I have truly said that I have not come to your State with any political aims or purposes, I am aware of the general expectation, entertained here, that I should embrace the occasion to make some exposition of my sentiments and views in respect to public affairs. I do not feel at liberty to disappoint this expectation. And yet I must declare, with perfect truth, that I have not and never had any taste for these public addresses. I have always found them irksome and unpleasant. I have not disliked public speaking, but it has been public speaking, in legislative Halls, on public measures affecting the welfare of my country, or before the tribunals of justice. It has been public speaking, in which there was a precise and well defined object to be pursued, by a train of thought and argument, adapted to its attainment.

Without presuming to prescribe to any body else the course which he ought to pursue in forming his judgment upon political parties, public measures, and the principles which ought to guide us, I will state my own. In respect to political parties, of which I have seen many, in this country, during a life which is now considerably protracted, I believe in the main, most of them think, or have persuaded themselves to believe, that they are aiming at the happiness of their country. Their duties and their interests, well understood, must necessarily urge them to promote its welfare. They are, it is true, often deceived, deceived by their own passions and prejudices, and still more by interested demagogues, who cloak and conceal their sinister designs. Political parties, according to my humble opinion of their legitimate sphere of action, ought, to be regarded as nothing more than instruments, or means, subordinate, but important instruments or means, in effecting the great purposes of a wise administration of government; highly useful when not factious and controlled by public[2] virtue and patriotism; but, when country is lost sight of, and the interests of the party become paramount to the interests of the country, when the government is seized by a party and is not administered for the benefit of the people, and the whole people, but to advance the purposes and selfish aims of itself, or rather of its leaders, then is such a party, whatever may be the popular name it may assume, highly detrimental and dangerous. I am a Whig, warmly attached to the party, which bears that respected name, from a thorough persuasion that its principles and policy are best calculated to secure the happiness and prosperity of our common country; but, if I believed otherwise, if I were convinced that it sought party or individual aggrandizement, and not the public good, I would instantly and forever abandon it, whatever might be the consequences to myself, or whatever the regrets which I might feel in separating from veteran friends. My opinions upon great and leading measures of public policy have become settled convictions, and I am a Whig because that party seeks the establishment of those measures. In determining with which of the two great parties of the country, I ought to be connected, I have been governed by a full consideration and fair comparison of the tendency of their respective principles, measures, conduct and views. There is one prominent and characteristic difference between the two parties, which eminently distinguishes them, and which, if there were no other, would be sufficient to decide my judgment. And that is, the respect and deference uniformly displayed by the one, and the disregard and the contempt exhibited by the other to the constitution, to the laws and to public authority. In a country, where a free and self-government is established, it should be the pleasure, and it is the bounden duty, of every citizen to stand by and uphold the constitution and laws, and support the public authority; because they are *his* constitution—*his* laws, and the public authority emanates from *his* will. Having concurred, by the exercise of his privileges, in the adoption of the constitution, and in the passage of the laws, any outrage or violation attempted of either ought to be regarded as an offence against himself, an offence against the majesty of the people. In an arbitrary and absolute government, the subject may have some excuse for evading the edicts and ukases of the monarch, because they are not only promulgated, without consulting his will, but sometimes against the wishes and the interests of the people. In that species of government, the power of the bayonet enforces a reluctant obedience to the law. With a free people, the fact that the laws are their laws, ought to supply, in a prompt and voluntary rally to the support of the public authority, a force more peaceful, more powerful, and more reasonable than any derivable from a mercenary soldiery.

It is far from my intention or desire to do the least injustice to the party to which I am opposed; but I think that in asserting the characteristic difference between the two parties which I have done, I am fully borne out by facts, to some of which, only, on this occasion, can I refer, and these shall all be of a recent nature.[3]

The first, to which I shall call your attention, has occurred during the present session of Congress. The variety in the mode of electing members to the House of Representatives of the United States, some being chosen by whole states, and others by separate districts, was long a subject of deep and general complaint.[4] It gave to the States unequal power in the councils of the nation. Mississippi or New-Hampshire, for example, by a general ticket, securing the election of its members to the House of Representatives, all of one political party, might acquire more power, in that House, than the State of New-York, which, electing its members by districts, might return an equal or nearly an equal number of members of both the parties. According to the general ticket system, it is impossible that the elective franchise can be exercised with the same discretion and judgment as under the district system. The elector cannot possess the same opportunity, under the one system as under the other, of becoming acquainted with and ascertaining the capacity and fidelity of the candidate for his suffrage. An elector, residing in one extreme of the State, cannot be presumed to know a candidate living at a distance from him, perhaps at the other extreme. By the general ticket, the minority in a State is completely smothered. From these, and other views of the subject, it has been long a patriotic wish entertained that there should be some uniform mode, both of electing members to the House of Representatives and cho[o]sing electors of President and Vice President. I recollect well, some twenty years ago, when public opinion appeared to be almost unanimous upon this subject. Well, the last Whig Congress, in order to prevent the abuses, and to correct the inequality, arising out of the diverse modes of electing members of the House of Representatives, passed an act requiring that it should be uniform and by districts.[5] This act was in conformity with an express grant of power contained in the constitution of the United States, which declares that "the times, places, and manner of holding elections for senators, and representatives shall be prescribed in each state by the legislature thereof; *but the congress may, at any time, by law, make or alter such regulations, except as to the places of choosing senators.*" With that reasonable, equal, and just act of Congress every Whig state, whose legislature assembled in time after its passage, strictly complied, and laid off their respective States into districts accordingly. But the four States, with Democratic legislatures, of Georgia, Mississippi, Missouri, and New Hampshire refused to conform to the law, treated it with contemptuous neglect, and suffered the elections for members of the House of Representatives to proceed, in total disregard of its provisions. This was a new species of nullification, not less reprehensible than that which was attempted formerly in another state, though admitting of a more easy and peaceful remedy. That remedy was to refuse to allow the members, returned from the four States, to take their seats in the House of Representatives, which they had no constitutional or legal right to occupy. That question the present House of Representatives had to decide. But it was predicted, long before they assembled, confidently predicted, that the members from the four refractory States, would be allowed to take their seats, the constitution and the law notwithstanding. Why was it so predicted? Was it not because it was known, from the general character and conduct of the dominant party, in the House, that it would not hesitate to trample under foot both law and constitution, if necessary to the accomplishment of a party object? Accordingly, the question recently came up in the House, and the members from the four states were admitted to their seats. And what, fellow citizens, do you suppose was the process of reasoning by which this most extraordinary result was brought about? Congress you have seen is invested with unlimited power to make regulations as to the times, places, and manner of holding elections for representatives, or to *alter* those which might have been previously made by the state legislatures. There is nothing in the grant of the power, which enjoins upon Congress to exercise the whole of it, or none. Considerations of obvious convenience concur in leaving to the several States themselves, the fixation of the times and places of holding those elections. In that, each State may be governed by its sense of its own convenience, without injuriously affecting other states. But it is different with the *manner* of holding elections, that is whether it be by general ticket or by the district system. If some states elect by a general ticket, it gives to them an undue advantage over those states which elect by the district system. The manner, therefore, of holding elections was a fit subject, and the only fit subject, contained in the grant of power, for congressional legislation. If congress had legislated beyond that, it would have overreached the convenience and necessity of the case. But the dominant party, in the present House of Representatives, have strangely assumed, that congress could not execute a part of the granted power, without the whole. According to their logic the major does not include the minor. In their view government cannot execute a part of a power with which it is entrusted without it executes the whole of a power vested in it. If this principle be true, when applied to a part of the constitution, it would be equally true in its application to the whole constitution; but there are many parts of the constitution that never have been and probably never will be executed. And, if the doctrine of the dominant party, in the House of Representatives, be sound all the laws enacted by congress since the commencement of the government are null and void, because Congress has not executed all the powers of government with which it is entrusted. The doctrine applied to the enjoyment of private property would restrain a man from using any part of his property, unless he used the whole of it.

The case of the New Jersey election[6] is familiar with every body. There the Whig members who presented themselves at Washington, to take their seats, bore with them the highest credentials, under the great seal of their state, demonstrating their right to occupy them. They had been regularly declared and returned elected members of the House of Representatives, by the regular authorities, and according to the law of the state of New Jersey. Agreeably to the uniform usage, which had prevailed in that House from the commencement of the government, and according to the usage which prevails in every representative body, they had a right to demand to be admitted to their seats, and to hold and occupy them, until any objections which might exist against them should be subsequently investigated. In the case of the four states already noticed, it was important to the interests of the dominant party, in order to swell their majority, that the members returned should be allowed to take their seats, although elected contrary to law. In the New Jersey case, it was important to the dominant party to enable it to retain its majority, to exclude the Whig members, although returned according to law. The decision in both cases was adapted to the exigency of party interest, in utter contempt, both of constitution and law. And it is worthy of observation that, in the decision against the Whig members of New Jersey, members, who boast of being emphatically the patrons and defenders of State rights, concurred in trampling under foot the laws and authorities of that state.

In connection with the subject on which I am now addressing you, the manner of admission of Michigan into the union is worthy of notice. According to the usage which had uniformly prevailed, prior to the admission of the states of Michigan and Arkansas, a previous act of Congress was passed, authorizing the sense of the people of the territory to be taken, in convention, and regulating the election of members to that body, limiting their choice to citizens of the United States residing in the territory. Michigan, without the sanction of a previous act of Congress, undertook, upon her sole authority, to form a constitution, and demanded admission into the Union.[7] In appointing members to that convention, a great number of aliens, as well as citizens of the United States, were allowed to vote, against the earnest remonstrances of many resident citizens. Under these circumstances she applied to Congress to be admitted into the Union. No one questioned or doubted that she was entitled to be received whenever she presented herself, regularly and according to law. But it was objected against her admission, that she had assumed to act against all usage, without the authority of congress, and that contrary to the constitution and laws of the United States she had permitted aliens to partake of the elective franchize. The danger was pointed out, of allowing aliens unnaturalized, and without renouncing their allegiance to foreign sovereigns and potentates, to share in that great and inestimable privilege. But all objections were unavailing, the dominant party under the hope of strengthening their interests, in spite of all irregularity and in contravention of law admitted Michigan as a State into the Union.

In intimate connection with this case the subject of Dorrism[8] may be noticed. Rhode Island had an existing government of long duration, under which her population had lived happily and prosperously. It had carried her triumphantly through the war of the revolution, and borne her into the union, as one of the original thirteen independent sovereign states. Under the operation of it, the people of no state in the union, in proportion to her population, had displayed more valor patriotism and enterprize. Dorr did not find his ambitious aspirations sufficiently gratified under this venerable government, and he undertook to subvert it. Asserting the principle that every people have a right to alter, modify and change their government whenever they think proper—an abstract principle which, with cautious limitations, may be true without consulting the established government and the public authorities, he undertook to beat up for recruits, to hold irregular elections, at which persons qualified and unqualified, dead and living, were pretended to have voted, and thus securing a heterogeneous majority, he proceeded to form a new constitution and to set a new government. In the mean time, the legitimate and regular government proceeded in operation and prepared to sustain itself and put down the insurrectionary proceeding. Dorr flew to arms and collected a military force, as irregular and heterogeneous as his civil majority had been. But on the first approach of military force, on the part of the legitimate and regular government, Dorr took to his heels and ignominiously fled leaving his motley confederates to fare as they might. Now fellow citizens what had been the conduct of the two parties in respect to this insurrection which, at one time, seemed to be so threatening? The Whigs, every where, I believe to a man, have disapproved and condemned the movement of Dorr. It has been far otherwise with our opponents. Without meaning to assert that the whole of them countenanced and supported Dorr, every body knows that all the sympathy and encouragement, which he has received, have been among them. And they have introduced the subject into the present House of Representatives. We shall see what they will do with it. You can readily comprehend and feel what would be the effects and consequences of Dorrism here at the South, if Dorrism were predominant. Any unprincipled adventurer would have nothing to do but to collect around him a mosaic majority black and white aliens and citizens, young and old, male and female, overturn existing governments and set up new ones, at his pleasure or caprice! What earthly security, for life liberty or property, would remain, if a proceeding so fraught with confusion disorder and insubordination, were tolerated and sanctioned!

Then there is Repudiation—that dark and foul spot upon the American name and character—how came it there? The stain has been put there by the Democratic majority of the Legislature of Mississippi.[9] Under special pleas, and colorable pretexts, which any private man of honor and probity would scorn to employ, they have refused to pay the debts of that State—debts contracted by the receipt of an equivalent expended within the State! The Whigs of that State, who are the principle Tax-paying portion of the population, with remarkable unanimity, are in favor of preserving its honor and good faith, by a reimbursement of the debt; but the Democratic majority persists in refusing to provide for it. I am far from charging the whole of the Democratic party with this shameful public fraud, perpetrated by their brethern in the State of Mississippi. Without the State, to their honor be it said, most of them disapproved; and within the State there are many honorable exceptions, among the Democrats.

Other examples might be cited to prove the destructive and disorganizing tendency of the character tendency and principles of the Democratic party, but these will suffice for this occasion. If, the systems and measures of public policy of the two parties are contrasted and compared, the result will be not less favorable to the Whig party. With the Whig party there prevails entire concurrence as to the principles and measures of public policy which it espouses. In the other party we behold nothing but division and distraction. Their principles, varying at different times and in different latitudes. In respect to the tariff, whilst in some places, they are proclaiming that free trade is the true Democratic doctrine, and the encouragement of domestic industry federal heresy, in other parts of the Union, they insist that the Democrats are alone to be relied upon to protect the industry of the country, and that the Whigs are opposed to it.

That is a great practical and administrative question, in respect to which there is happily now prevailing among the Whigs, throughout the whole Union, a degree of unanimity as unprecedented as it is gratifying. From New Orleans to this place, I have conversed with hundreds of them, and I have not met with a solitary one, who does not assent to the justice and expediency of the principle of a tariff for revenue, with discriminations for protection. On this interesting question, fellow citizens it is my purpose to address you, with the utmost freedom and sincerity, and with as little reserve as if I were before an audience in the State of Kentucky. I have long given to this subject the most impartial and deliberate consideration, of which my mind is capable. I believe that no great Nation ever has existed, or can exist, which does not derive within itself, essential supplies of food and raiment and the means of defence. I recollect no example to the contrary in ancient or modern times. Although Italy did not itself afford all those supplies, to Ancient Rome the deficiency was drawn from her subjugated provinces. Great Britain, although her commerce encompasses the world supplies herself mainly from the little island under her immediate dominion. Limited and contracted as it is, it furnishes her with bread and other provisions for the whole year, with the exception only of a few days; and her manufactures, not only supply an abundance of raiment and means of defence, but afford a vast surplus for exportation to foreign countries.

In considering the policy of introducing and establishing manufactures in our Country, it has always appeared to me that we should take a broad and extensive view, looking to seasons of war, as well as peace, and regarding the future, as well as the past and the present. National existence is not to be measured by the standard of individual life. But it is equally true, both of nations and of individuals, that, when it is necessary, we must submit to temporary and present privations, for the sake of future and permanent benefits. Even if it were true, as I think I shall be able to show it is not, that the encouragement of domestic manufactures would produce some sacrifices, they would be compensated, and more than counterbalanced, by ultimate advantages secured, combining together seasons of peace and of war. If it were true that the policy of protection enhanced the price of commodities, it would be found that their cheapness, prevailing in a time of peace, when the foreign supply might be open to us, would be no equivalent for the dearness in a period of war, when that supply would be cut off from us. I am not old enough to recollect the sufferings of the soldiery and population of the United States, during the war of Independence; but history and tradition tell us what they were; they inform us what lives were sacrificed, what discomforts existed, what hardships our unclad and unshod soldiers bore, what enterprizes were retarded or paralyzed. Even, during the last war, all of us, who are old enough to remember it, know what difficulties, and, at what great cost, the necessary clothing and means of defence were obtained. And who does not feel conscious pride and patriotic satisfaction that these sufferings, in any future war, will be prevented, or greatly alleviated, by the progress which our infant manufactures have already made. If the policy of encouraging them wisely, moderately, and certainly, be persevered in, the day is not distant when, resting upon our own internal resources, we may be perfectly sure of an abundant supply of all our necessary wants and, in this respect, put Foreign Powers and Foreign wars at defiance. I know that, from extreme suffering and the necessity of the case, manufactures, in the long run, would arise and sustain themselves, without any encouragement from Government, just as an unaided infant child would learn to rise, to stand, and to walk; but, in both instances, great distress may be avoided, and essential assistance, derived from the kindness of the parental hand.

The advantages arising from the division of the labor of the population of a country are too manifest to need being much dwelt upon. I think the advantage of a home, as well as foreign markets, is equally manifest; but the home market can only be produced by diversified pursuits, creating subjects of exchange, at home as well as abroad. If one portion of the population of a country be engaged in the business of manufacturing, it must derive its means of subsistence, from the agricultural products of the country in exchange for their fabrics. The effect of these mutual exchanges is beneficial to both parties and the whole Country.

The great law, which regulates the prices of commodities, is that of supply and demand. If the supply exceed the demand, the price falls; if the demand exceed the supply the price rises. This law will be found to be invariably true. Any augmentation of supply is beneficial to the consumer; but, by establishing manufactures, in the United States, an additional supply is created. Again, another principle, universally admitted to be beneficial to consumption, is, the principle of competition. If Europe alone supply the American consumption of manufactures, Europe will enjoy a monopoly in that supply. That monopoly, it is true, will be subject to the competition which may exist in Europe; but it would be still restricted to that competition. By the existence of manufactures, in the United States, an additional competition is created, and this new competitor enters the American market, contending for it with the previous European competitors. The result is, an increase in the aggregate of supply and a consequent reduction in price. But it has been argued, that the fabrics manufactured in America take the place only of so many which had been before manufactured in Europe; that there is no greater consumption in consequence of the home manufacture than would exist without it; and that it is immaterial to the consumer whether the theatre of manufacture be Europe or the United States. But I think this is an extremely contracted and fallacious view of the subject. Consumption is greater in consequence of the existence of manufactures at home. They create a demand for labor, which would not exist without them, and the employment of labor creates an ability to consume, which would not exist without it. How could the American labor, employed in manufactures, at home, supply its consumption of European commodities, if it were deprived of that employment? What means of purchase would it possess? It is in vain to point to Agriculture; for every department of that is already producing superabundantly. It cannot be questioned that the chief cause of the reduced price of Cotton is the excess of production. The price of it would rise, if less were produced, by diverting a portion of the Labor employed in its cultivation to some other branch of industry. This new pursuit would furnish new subjects of exchange and those who might embark in it, as well as those who would continue in the growth of cotton, would be both benefited by mutual exchanges. The day will come, and is not distant, when the South will feel an imperative necessity voluntarily to make such a diversion of a portion of its labor. Considering the vast water power, and other facilities of manufacturing, now wasting and unemployed, at the South, and its possession, at home, of the choice of the raw material, I believe the day will come when the Cotton Region will be the greatest manufacturing region of Cotton in the world.

The power of consuming manufactured articles, being increased, in consequence of the domestic establishment of manufactures, by the wages of labor which they employ, and by the wealth which they create, there is an increase also in the use and consumption of Cotton and other raw materials. To the extent of that increase, the Cotton grower is directly and positively benefited, by the location of manufactures at home instead of abroad.

But suppose it were true that the shifting to a certain extent of the theatre of manufactures, from Foreign Countries to our own, did not increase consumption at all, and did not augment the demand for Cotton, there would be no just ground of complaint with the Cotton planter, and the most that he could say is, that it would be a matter of indifference to him. All that would happen to him would be, a substitution of a certain number of American customers, for an equal number of European customers. But ought it to be, can it be, a matter of indifference to him, whether any portion of his fellow Citizens in the U.S. are in a state of prosperity or adversity? If, without prejudice to him, his own Countrymen can acquire a part of the wealth which arises out of the prosecution of manufacturing industry, instead of the foreigner, ought he not to rejoice at it? Is it to him a matter of no consequence that a certain amount of wealth created by manufactures, shall be in his own Country, instead of being in foreign Countries? If here, its influence and effects will be felt, directly or indirectly, in all the departments of human business, and in a greater or less degree in all parts of the Country. It becomes a clear addition to the aggregate wealth of the nation, increasing its resources, and forming a basis of taxation and revenue in seasons of War or peace, if necessary.

But the advantage, resulting from domestic manufactures, in producing an American competition with the European competition, augmenting the supply of manufactured articles, and tending consequently to a reduction of prices, is not the sole advantage great as that is. A double market is produced both in the *purchase* of fabrics for consumption, and in the *sale* of productions of Agriculture. And how superior is the home to any other market, in the conditions of its proximity, its being under our own control, and its exemption from the contigency of War! It has been argued, however, that we sell no more than we should do if we were deprived of the home market. I have shown that to be otherwise. The importance of opening new markets is universally admitted. It is an object of the policy of all nations. If we could open a new market for 400.000 bales of Cotton with any Foreign power should we not gladly embrace it? Every one owns the benefit which arises out of various markets. All who reside in the neighbourhood of large Cities or market towns, are sensible of the advantage. It is said that our Manufactures absorb only about 400.000 bales of Cotton, which is a very small part of the total crop. But suppose that were thrown upon the market of Liverpool, already overstocked & glutted? It would sink the price far below what it now is. France consumes also about 400.000 bales. If the market of Havre were closed, and that quantity were crowded into the market of Liverpool would not the effect be ruinous to the cotton grower? Our American market is growing, annually increasing, and, if the policy of the country can only become firmly fixed, the time will come, I have no doubt when the manufacture of cotton in the United States will exceed that of England. I do not desire to see any market closed, domestic or foreign. I think it our true interest to cherish and cultivate all. But I believe it to be our indispensable duty to afford proper and reasonable encouragement to our own.

But it must be borne in mind that, although cotton is by far the most important of our agricultural products, it is not the only one. Where should we find a market for our Indian corn, if it were not for the existence of our manufactures? We should absolutely have none. My friend Mr. Pettigru [*sic*, Ebenezer Pettigrew], who sits before me, can find no market for his Corn in North Carolina; because his neighbours, like himself, are occupied in producing it. Nor can he find any in foreign Countries. But he meets with a good sure and convenient market in Boston and Providence, and other Northern Capitals. Where should we seek a market for the flour, provisions, and other raw agricultural produce now consumed by our manufacturers? If their present business were destroyed, they would be employed themselves in producing cotton, corn, provisions, and other agricultural produce, thus augmenting the quantity and inevitably leading to a further decline of prices.

It has been contended that the effect of affording legal encouragement to domestic manufactures is, to enhance the price of commodities, and to impose a tax upon the consumer. This argument has been a thousand times refuted. It has been shown again and again that the price of almost every article, on which the system of encouragement has effectually operated, has been reduced to the consumer. And this was the necessary consequence of that law of supply and demand and that principle of competition to which I have before adverted. It was foretold long ago by myself and other friends of the policy. But it is in vain that we appeal to facts. It is in vain that we take up article by article, and comparing present, with former prices, show the actual and gradual reduction. The free trader has mounted his hobby, and he has determined to spur and whip him on, rough shod, over all facts obstacles and impediments that be in his way. It was but the other day, I heard of one of these free trade orators, addressing an audience, and depicting, in the most plaintive and doleful terms, the extreme burdens and oppressive exactions, arising out of the abominable tariff. Why, says he, fellow citizens every one of you that wears a shirt, is compelled to pay six cents a yard more for it than you otherwise would do, in order to increase the enormous wealth of Northern capitalists. An old man in the crowd, shabbily dressed, and with scarcely any thing but a shirt on, stopped the eloquent orator and asked him how that could be? for says he "I have a good shirt on that cost me only 5 1/2 cents per yard and, I should like to know how I paid a duty of 6 cents."

These ingenious and indefatigable theorists, not only hold all facts and experience, in contempt, but they are utterly inconsistent with themselves. At one time, they endeavour to raise the alarm, that the tariff would put an end to all foreign commerce, and thus drying up our principal source of revenue, in imports, it would become necessary to resort to direct taxes and internal taxation. In process of time, however, their predictions were falsified, and the system was found to produce an abundant revenue. Then, they shifted their ground, the treasury, said they, is overflowing, the tariff is the cause and the system must be abandoned! If they had have taken the trouble to enquire, they might have ascertained that, although England is the greatest manufacturing Nation in the world, in amount, extent, and variety, she nevertheless draws a vast revenue from customs.

Allow me to present you, fellow-citizens, with another view of this interesting subject. The government wishes to derive a certain amount of revenue from foreign imports. Let us suppose the total annual amount of imports to be $100.000000. and the total annual amount of revenue, to be raised from it, to be $20.000000. Is it at all material, whether that $20.000000 be spread, in the form of duties, equally over the whole 100.000.000 or that it be drawn from some 50000000 or more of the imports, leaving the rest free of duty? In point of fact, such has been the case for several years. Is not a compensation found, for the duty paid upon one article, by the exemption from duty of another article? Take the wearing apparel of a single individual, and suppose you have a duty of $2. to raise upon it, is it of any consequence to him whether you levy the whole $2. upon all parts of his wearing apparel equally, or levy it exclusively upon his coat and his shirt, leaving the other articles free? And if, by such discriminations as I have described, without prejudice to the consumer, you can raise up, cherish, and sustain domestic manufactures, increasing the wealth and prosperity, and encouraging the labor, of the nation ought it not to be done?

We are invited, by the partizans of the doctrine of Free trade to imitate the liberal example of some of the great European powers. England, we are told, is abandoning her restrictive policy, and adopting that of free trade. England adopting the principles of free trade! Why, where are her Corn laws? Those laws which exclude an article of prime necessity—the very bread which sustains human life—in order to afford protection to English agriculture. And, on the single article of American tobacco, England levies annually an amount of Revenue equal to the whole amount of duties, levied annually, by the U. States upon all the articles of import, from all the foreign nations of the world, including England. That is her free trade! And as for France, we have lately seen a State paper, from one of her high functionaries, complaining in bitter terms of the American tariff of 1842,[10] and ending with formally announcing to the world that France steadily adhered to the system of protecting French industry!

But, fellow Citizens, I have already detained you too long on this interesting topic, and yet I have scarcely touched it. For near thirty years it has agitated the Nation. The subject has been argued and debated a thousand times, in every conceivable form. It is time that the policy of the Country should become settled and fixed. Any stable adjustment of it, whatever it may be, will be far preferable to perpetual vascillation. When once determined, labor, enterprize and commerce can accommodate themselves accordingly. But in finally settling it, the interests of the whole Union, as well as all its parts, should be duly weighed and considered, in a paternal and fraternal spirit. The Confederacy consists of 26 States, besides territories, embracing every variety of pursuit, every branch of human industry. There may be an apparent, there is no real, conflict between these diversified interests. No one State, no one section, can reasonably expect or desire that the common Government of the whole should be administered, exclusively according to its own peculiar opinion, or so as to advance only its particular interest, without regard to the opinion or the interests of all other parts. In respect to the Tariff, there are two schools holding opposite and extreme doctrines. According to one, perfect freedom in our foreign trade, with no or very low duties, ought to prevail. According to the other the restrictive policy ought, on many articles, to be pushed, by a high and exorbitant tariff, to the point of absolute prohibition. Neither party can hold itself up as an unerring standard of right and wisdom. Fallibility is the lot of all men, and the wisest know how little they do know. The doctrine of free trade is a concession to Foreign powers, without an equivalent, to the prejudice of native industry. Not only without equivalent, but in the face of their high duties, restrictions and prohibitions applied to American products. To foreign Powers, our rivals, jealous of our growth and anxious to impede our onward progress. Encouragement of domestic industry is a concession to our own fellow-citizens, to those, whose ancestors shared in common, with our ancestors, in the toils of the revolution; to those who have shared with us in the toils and sufferings of our day; to those whose posterity are destined to share with our posterity in the trials in the triumphs and the glories that await them. It is a concession to those who are bone of our bone and flesh of our flesh, and who in some other beneficial form do make and are ready to make equivalent concessions to us. It is still more; it is a concession by the whole to the whole; for every part of the country possesses a capacity to manufacture and every part of the country more or less does manufacture. Some parts have advanced farther than others, but the progress of all is forward and onward.

Again, I ask what is to be done in this conflict of opinion between the two extremes which I have stated? Each believes, with quite as much confidence as the other, that the policy which he espouses is the best for the country. Neither has a right to demand that his judgment shall exclusively prevail. What, again, I ask is to be done? Is compromise or reconciliation impossible? Is this glorious union to be broken up and dissolved and the hopes of the world, which are concentrated in its fate to be blasted and destroyed forever? No, fellow citizens, no the Union must be preserved. In the name of the people of this noble old state, the first to announce the independence of the United States by the memorable declaration of Mecklenburg,[11] and which has ever since been among the most devoted and faithful to the preservation of this union; in the name of the people of my own gallant state; and, in the name of the whole people of the United States, I feel authorized to say, that this union will not, must not, shall not be dissolved. How then can this unhappy conflict of opinion be amicably adjusted and accommodated? Extremes, fellow citizens, are ever wrong. Truth, and justice, sound policy, and wisdom always abide in the middle ground, always are to be found in the juste milieu. Ultraism is ever baneful, and if followed, never fails to lead to fatal consequences. We must reject both the doctrines of free trade and of a high and exorbitant tariff. The partizans of each must make some sacrifices of their peculiar opinions. They must find some common ground, on which both can stand, and reflect that, if neither has obtained all that it desires, it has secured something and what it does not retain has been gotten by its friends and countrymen. There are very few who dissent from the opinion that, in time of peace, the federal revenue ought to be drawn from foreign imports, without resorting to internal taxation. Here is a basis for accommodation, and mutual satisfaction. Let the amount, which is requisite for an economical administration of the government, when we are not engaged in war, be raised exclusively on foreign imports, and in adjusting a tariff, for that purpose, let such discriminations be made as will foster and encourage our own domestic industry. All parties ought to be satisfied with a tariff for revenue and discriminations for protection. In thus settling this great and disturbing question, in a spirit of mutual concession and of amicable compromise, we do but follow the noble example of our illustrious ancestors, in the formation and adoption of our present happy constitution. It was that benign spirit that presided over all their deliberations, and it has been in the same spirit that all the threatening crises, that have arisen during the progress of the administration of the constitution, have been happily quieted and accommodated.

Next, if not superior in importance to the question of encouraging the National industry is that of the National currency. I do not purpose to discuss the point, whether a paper representative of the precious metals, in the form of bank notes, or in other forms, convertible into those metals, on demand, at the will of the holder be, or be not desirable and expedient. I believe it could be easily shown, that, in the actual state of the commercial world, and considering the amount and distribution of the precious metals throughout the world such a convertible paper is indispensably necessary. But that is not an open question. If it were desirable that no such paper should exist, it is not in the power of the general government, under it[s] present constitution, to put it down or prevent its creation and circulation. Such a convertible paper has existed, does exist, and probably will always exist, in spite of the general government. The twenty six states, which compose the union, claim the right and exercize the right, now not to be controverted, to authorize and put forth such a convertible paper, according to their own sense of their respective interests. If even a large majority of the States were to resolve to discontinue the use of a paper representative of specie, the paper would nevertheless be created and circulated, unless every state in the Union abandoned its use, which nobody believes is ever likely to happen. If some of the states should continue to employ and circulate such a paper, it would flow into and be current in other States, that might have refused to establish banks. And, in the end, the States which had them not would find themselves, in self defense, compelled to charter them. I recollect, perhaps my friend near me (Mr. B.W. Leigh) if he be old enough, may also recollect, the introduction of Banks in our native State. Virginia adopted slowly and reluctantly the Banking system. I recollect, when a boy, to have been present in 1792 or 1793 when a debate occurred in the Virginia legislature on a proposition, I think it was, to renew the charter of a bank in Alexandria, the first that ever was established in that state, and it was warmly opposed and carried with some difficulty. Afterwards Virginia, finding herself surrounded by states that had banks, and that she was subject to all their inconveniences, whatever they might be, resolved to establish banks upon a more extensive scale, and accordingly did establish two principle banks with branching powers, to secure to herself whatever benefits might arise from such institutions. The same necessity that prompted, at that period, the legislation of Virginia would hereafter influence states having no banks, but adjactent to those which had. It follows, therefore, that there are and probably always will be local banks. These local banks are often rivals, not only acting without concert but in collision with each other, and having very imperfect knowledge of the general condition of the whole circulation of the United States, or the state of our monetary relations with foreign Powers. The inevitable consequence must be, irregularity in their movements, disorder and unsoundness in the currency, and frequent explosions. The existence of local banks, under the authority and control of the respective states, begets a necessity for a United States Bank, under the authority and control of the general government. The whole power of government is distributed in the United States between the states and the federal government. All that is general and national appertains to the federal government, all that is limited and local to the state governments. The states cannot perform the duties of the general government, nor ought that [*sic*, they] to attempt to perform, nor can it so well execute, the trusts confided to the state governments. We want a National army, a National navy, a National post office establishment, National laws regulating our foreign commerce and our coasting trade, above all, perhaps, we want a National currency. The duty of supplying these national means of safety, convenience and prosperity must be executed by the general government, or it will remain neglected and unfulfilled. The several states can no more supply a national currency than they can provide armies, and navies for the National defence. The necessity for a National institution does not result merely from the existence of local institutions, but it arises also out of the fact that all the great commercial nations of the world have their banks. England, France, Austria & Russia, Holland, and all the great Powers of Europe have their national banks. It is said that money is power, and that to embody and concentrate it in a bank is to create a great and dangerous power. But we may search the records of history, and we shall find no instance, since the first introduction of banking institutions, of any one of them having sought to subvert the liberties of a country or to create confusion and disorder. Their well being depends upon the stability of laws and a legitimate and regular administration of government. If it were true that the creation of a bank is to embody a monied power, is not such a power in the hands of the general government necessary to protect the people against the monied power in the form of banking institutions in the several states, and in the hands of Foreign Governments? Without it, how can the commerce of the United States cope and compete with the commerce of foreign Powers having national banks? In the commercial struggles, which are constantly in operation between nations, should we not labor under great and decided disadvantage, if we had no bank and they had their banks? We all recollect, a few years ago, when it was alleged to be the policy of the bank of England to reduce the price of our great Southern staple. In order to accomplish that object, the policy was adopted of refusing to discount the notes and bills of any English houses engaged in the American trade. If a bank of the United States had been in existence at that time, it could have adopted some measure of counteraction; but there was none and the bank of England effected its purpose.

It has been asked, what will you have banks merely because the monarchies of Europe have them? Why not also introduce their King Lords and Commons, and their aristocracy? This is a very shallow mode of reasoning. I might ask, in turn, why have armies, navies, laws regulating trade or any other national institutions or laws, because the monarchies of the old world have them? Why eat, or drink, cloathe or house ourselves, because Monarchs perform these operations? I suppose myself the course of true wisdom, and of common sense, to be to draw from their arts, and sciences and civilization, and political institutions, whatever is good, and avoid whatever is bad.

Where, exclusive of those who oppose the establishment of a bank of the United States upon constitutional ground, do we find the greatest opposition to it? You are, fellow citizens, perhaps not possessed of information, which I happen to have acquired. The greatest opposition to a bank of the United States will be found to arise out of a foreign influence, and may be traced to the bankers and brokers of Wall street in New York, who are wielding a foreign capital. Foreign Powers and foreign capital see, with satisfaction, whatever retards the growth, checks the prosperity; or arrests the progress of this country. Those, who wield that foreign capital, find, from experience, that they can employ it to the best advantage, in a disordered state of the currency, and when exchanges are fluctuating and irregular. There are no sections of the Union which need a uniform currency, sound and every where convertible into specie, on demand, so much as you at the South and we in the West. It is indispensable to our prosperity. And, if our brethern at the North and the East, did not feel the want of it themselves, since it will do them no prejudice they ought, upon principles of sympathy and mutual accommodation, to concur in supplying what is so essential to the business and industry of other sections of the Union. It is said that the currency and exchanges have improved and are improving, and so they have & are. This improvement is mainly attributable to the salutary operation of the tariff of 1842, which turned the balance of foreign trade in our favor. But such is the enterprize and buoyancy of our population that we have n[o] security for the continuation of this state of things. The balance of trade may take another direction, new revulsions in trade may take place, seasons of distress and embarrassment we must expect. Does any body believe the local banking system of the United States is competent to meet and provide for these exigencies? It is the part of a wise government to anticipate and provide, as far as possible, for all these contingencies. It is urged against banks that they are often badly and dishonestly administered, and frequently break, to the injury and prejudice of the community. I am far from denying that banks are attended with mischief and some inconvenience; but that is the lot of all human institutions. The employment of steam is often attended with most disastrous consequences, of which we have had recent melancholy examples. But does any body, on that account, think of proposing to discontinue the agency of steam power either on the Land or the Water? The most that is thought of is, that it becomes our duty to increase vigilance and multiply precautions; against the recurrence of accidents. As to banks, the true question is, whether the sum of the inconvenience of dispensing with them would not be greater than any amount of which they are productive? And, in any new charters that may be granted, we should anxiously endeavor to provide all possible restrictions, securities, and guaranties against their mismanagement, which reason or experience may suggest.

Such are my views of the question of establishing a bank of the United States. They have been long, and honestly, and sincerely entertained by me, but I do not seek to enforce them upon any others. Above all, I do not desire any bank of the United States, attempted or established, unless, and until, it is imperatively demanded, as I believe demanded it will be, by the opinion of the people.

I should have been glad, fellow Citizens, if I had time and strength to make a full exposition of my views and opinions upon all the great measures and questions that divide us and agitate our Country. I should have been happy to have been able to make a full examination of the principles and measures of our opponents, if we could find out what they are, and contrast them with our own. I mean them no disrespect; I would not use one word to wound the feelings of any one of them; but I am really and unaffectedly ignorant of the measures of public policy which they are desirous to promote and establish. I know what they oppose. I know that they stand in direct opposition to every measure which the Whigs espouse; but what are their substitutes? The Whigs believe that the Executive power has, during the two last and the present administrations, been intolerably abused; that it has disturbed the balances of the Constitution; and that, by its encroachments upon the co-ordinate branches of the Government, it has become alarming and dangerous. The Whigs are therefore desirous to restrain it within Constitutional and proper limits. But our opponents, who assume to be emphatically the friends of the people, sustain the Executive in all its wildest and most extravagant excesses. They go for Vetos in all their variety, for Sub treasuries, standing armies, treasury circulars! Occupying a similar ground with the Tories of England, they stand up for power and prerogative against privilege and popular rights. The Democrats or Republicans of 1798-9, taught by the fatal examples of all history, were jealous and distrustful of Executive power. It was of that department that their fears were excited, and against that their vigilance was directed. The Federalists of that day, imbibing the opinion from the founders of the Constitution, honestly believed that the Executive was the weakest branch of the Government, and hence they were disposed to support & strengthen it. But experience has demonstrated their error, and the best part of them have united with the Whigs. And the Whigs are now in the exact position of the Republicans of 1798-9. The residue and probably the larger part of the Federalists joined our opponents, and they are now in the exact position of the Federalists of 1798-9, with this difference, that they have shut their eyes against all the lights of experience, and pushed the Federal doctrines of that day far beyond the point to which they were ever carried by their predecessors.

But I am trespassing too long on your patience, and must hasten to a close. I regret that I am too much exhausted, and have not time to discuss other interesting subjects that engage the public attention. I should be very glad to express to you my views on the Public domain; but I have often, on the floor of the Senate and on other public occasions, fully exposed them.[12] I consider it the common property of the nation and the whole nation. I believe it to be essential to its preservation and the preservation of the fund, which may accrue from its Sales, that it should be withdrawn from the theatre of party politics, and from the temptations and abuse, incident to it, whilst it remains there. I think that fund ought to be distributed, upon just and liberal principles, among all the States, old as well as new. If that be not done there is much ground to apprehend, at no very distant period, a total loss of the entire domain. Considering the other abundant and exhaustless resources of the General Government, I think that the proceeds of the Sales of the public lands may be well spared to the several States to be applied by them to beneficent local objects. In their hands, judiciously managed, they will lighten the burden of Internal taxation, the only form of raising Revenue to which they can resort, and assist in the payment of their debts or hasten the completion of important objects, in which the whole Union, as well as themselves, are interested & will be benefited.

On the subject of Abolition, I am persuaded it is not necessary to say one word to this enlightened assemblage. My opinion was fully expressed in the Senate of the U. States a few years ago,[13] and the expression of it was one of the assigned causes of my not receiving the nomination as a Candidate for the Presidency in December 1839.[14] But, if there be any one who doubts or desires to obtain further information about my views, in respect to that unfortunate question, I refer him to Mr. [Hiram] Mendenhall of Richmond in Indiana.[15]

I hope and believe fellow-citizens that brighter days and better times are approaching. All the exhibitions of popular feeling, all the manifestations of the public wishes, this spontaneous and vast assemblage, deceive us if the scenes and the memorable event of 1840 are not going to be renewed and reenacted. Our opponents complain of the means which were employed to bring about that event. They attribute their loss of the public confidence to the popular meetings, and processions, to the display of banners, the use of log cabins, the Whig songs, and the exhibition of coons; which preceded the event of .40. How greatly do they deceive themselves! What little knowledge do they display of human nature! All these were the mere jokes of the campaign. The event itself was produced, by a strong, deep, and general conviction pervading all classes, and impressed by a dear bought experience, that a change of both measures and men was indispensable to the welfare of the country. It was a great and irresistible movement of the people. Our opponents were unable to withstand and were borne down by a popular current, far more powerful than that of the mighty father of waters. The symbols and insignia, of which they complain, no more created or impelled that current than the objects which float upon the bosom of the Mississippi give impetus to the stream. Our opponents profess to be great friends of the poor, and to take a great interest in their welfare, but they do not like the log cabins in which the poor dwell! They dislike their beverage of hard cider[.] They prefer sparkling champaign, and perhaps their taste is correct, but they ought to reflect that it is not within the poor man's reach. They have a mortal hatred to our unoffending coons, and would prefer any other quadruped. And, as for our Whig songs, to their ears they appear grating and full of discord, although chanted by the loveliest daughters, and most melodious voices of the land! We are very sorry to disoblige our Democratic friends, but I am afraid they will have to reconcile themselves, as well as they can, to our log cabins, hard cider, and Whig songs. Popular excitement, demonstrating a lively interest in the administration of public affairs is far preferable to a state of stillness, of sullen gloom and silent acquiescence, which denotes the existence of despotism, or a state of preparation for its introduction. And we need not be disturbed, if that excitement should sometimes manifest itself, in ludicrous, but innocent, forms. But our opponents seem to have short memories. Who commenced that species of display and exhibition of which they now so bitterly complain? Have they already forgotten the circumstances attendant on the campaigns of 1828 and 1832? Have they forgotten the use which they made of the hog—the whole hog, bristles and all? Has the scene escaped their recollection, of bursting the heads out of barrels, not of hard cider, but of beer, pouring their contents into ditches, and then drinking the dirty liquid? Do they cease to remember the use which they made of the hickory, of hickory poles, and hickory boughs. On more occasions than one, when it was previously known that I was to pass on a particular road, have I found the way obstructed by hickory boughs, strewed along it. And I will not take up your time by narrating the numerous instances of mean low and vulgar indignity to which I have been personally exposed. Our opponents had better exercise a little philosophy on the occasion. They have been our masters, in employing symbols and devices to operate upon the passions of the people. And, if they would reflect and philosophize a little, they would arrive at the conclusion, that, whenever an army or a political party achieves a victory over an adversary, by means of any new instrument or stratagem, that adversary will be sure, sooner or later, to employ the same means.

I am truly glad to see our opponents returning to a sense of order and decency. I should be still happier if I did not fear that it was produced by the mortification of a past defeat, and the apprehension of one that awaits them ahead, rather than any thorough reformation of manners. Most certainly, I do not approve of appeals to the passions of the people, or of the use of disgusting or unworthy means to operate on their senses or their understanding. Although I can look and laugh, at the employment of hogs and coons, to influence the exercise of the elective franchize, I should be glad to see them entirely dispensed with. I should greatly prefer to see every free citizen of the United States deliberately considering and determining how he can best promote the honor and prosperity of his country, by the exercise of his inestimable privileges, and coming to the polls unaffected by all sinister exertions, and there independently depositing his suffrage. I should infinitely prefer to see calumny, falsehood and detraction totally abandoned, and truth sincerity, honor and good faith alone practiced in all our discussions. And I think I may venture to assure our opponents that, whenever they are prepared to conduct our public discussions and popular elections, in the manner and upon the principles which I have indicated, the Whig Party will be as prompt in following their good example, as they were slow and reluctant to imitate their bad one. The man does not breathe who would be more happy than I should be, to see all parties united, as a band of brothers, to restore our beloved country to what it has been, to what it is so capable of being, to what it ever should be, the great model of self government, the boast of enlightened and liberal men throughout the world, and, by the justice, wisdom, and beneficence of its operation, the terror and the dread of all tyrants. I know and deplore, deeply deplore, the demoralization which has so extensively prevailed in our country, during a few past years. It should be to every man, who has an American heart, a source of the deepest mortification, and most painful regret. Falsehood and treachery, in high places, peculation and fraud among public servants, distress embarrassment and ruin, among the people, distracted and disheartened at home, and treated with contempt and obloquy abroad, compose the sad features, during the period to which I have adverted of our unfortunate national picture. I should rejoice to see this great country once more itself again, and the history of the past fifteen years shrouded, in a dark and impenetrable veil. And why shall we not see it? We have only to will it, to revive and cultivate the spirit which won for us, and bequeathed to us, the noble heritage which we enjoy; we have only to rally around the institutions and interests of our beloved country, regardless of every other consideration, to break, if necessary, the[16] chains of party, and rise in the majesty of freemen, and stand out and stand up, firmly resolved to dare all and do all, to preserve, in unsullied purity, and perpetuate unimpaired the noble inheritance, which is our birth-right, and sealed to us with the blood of our fathers[.]

One word more, fellow-citizens, and I am done. I repeat that I had anticipated much gratification from my visit to your State. I had long anxiously wished to visit it, to tread the soil on which American Independence was first proclaimed; to mingle with the descendants of those who were the first to question the divine right of Kings, and who, themselves, are surpassed by none in devotion to the cause of human liberty, and to the Constitution and the Union, its best securities. Only one circumstance has happened to diminish the satisfaction of my journey. When I left my residence in December, I anticipated the happiness of meeting, among others, your GASTON,[17] then living. I had known him long and well, having served with him more than a quarter of a century ago in the House of Representatives[.] He united all the qualities which command esteem and admiration—bland, pure, patriotic, eloquent, learned and pious, and was beloved by all who knew him. Whilst we bow in dutiful submission to the will of Divine Providence, who, during the progress of my journey, has called him from his family and from his country, we cannot but feel and deplore the great loss which we have all sustained. I share it largely with you, fellow-citizens, and it is shared by the whole Union. To his bereaved family and to you, I offer assurances of my sincere sympathy and condolence.

We are about, Fellow-citizens, finally to separate. Never again shall I behold this assembled multitude. No more shall I probably ever see the beautiful City of the Oaks. Never more shall I mingle in the delightful circles of its hospitable and accomplished inhabitants. But you will never be forgotten in this heart of mine. My visit to your State is an epoch in my life. I shall carry with me every where, and carry back to my own patriotic State a grateful recollection of the kindness, friendship and hospitality which I have experienced so generously at your hands. And whatever may be my future lot or destiny, in retirement or public station, in health or sickness, in adversity or prosperity, you may count upon me, as an humble but zealous co-operator with you, in all honorable struggles to replace the Government of our Country, once more, upon a solid, pure and patriotic basis. I leave with you, all that it is in my power to offer, my fervent prayers that one and all of you may be crowned with the choicest blessings of Heaven, that your days may be lengthened out to the utmost period of human existence, that they may be unclouded, happy and prosperous, and that, when this mortal career shall terminate, you may be translated to a better and brighter world.

Farewell, Fellow-Citizens, ladies and gentlemen—an affectionate farewell to all of you!

AD, partially in Clay's hand, some pages missing from manuscript. Henry Clay Memorial Foundation, Lexington, Ky. Also printed in Raleigh *Register and North Carolina Gazette*, June 28, 1844. It was published in pamphlet form under the title, *Mr. Clay's Speech, Delivered in the City of Raleigh, April 13, 1844* (N.p., 1844). 1. Reporters from the Raleigh *Register* took notes on the speech as it was given and then transmitted their version to Clay who revised and returned it to them for publication. The manuscript and Raleigh *Register* versions are virtually identical except for some changes in punctuation and capitalization. Considered to be a major statement of Whig principles and platform, the speech was subsequently carried by other newspapers as well, but often with considerable variation in wording. 2. Pages of manuscript missing; the following is from the Raleigh *Register and North Carolina Gazette*, June 28, 1844. 3. Manuscript follows from this point. 4. See 9:707, 742-43. 5. *Ibid.* 6. See 9:248. 7. After Michigan voters on Oct. 2, 1832, approved a proposal to form a state government, the legislative council on Jan. 7, 1833, sent a memorial to that effect to Congress requesting authorization to proceed. Although Congress had not acted on the memorial, an election was held on April 4, 1835, to select delegates to a constitutional convention. These delegates were required to be U.S. citizens, but voters choosing them only had to be free, male, white, 21 years of age, and residents of Michigan for 3 months. This became a major political issue, as did the fact that Michigan held the convention, drafted a constitution, and conducted elections without congressional authorization. The Michigan state government operated in fact, but without the approval of Congress, from Nov., 1835 until Jan. 26, 1837, when it was finally admitted to the Union. Alec R. Gilpin, *The Territory of Michigan 1805-1837* (East Lansing, 1970), 148-91. See also 8:808. 8. See 9:714-16. 9. *Ibid.* 10. See 9:628. 11. See 8:774-75. 12. See, for example, 9:486-93, 682-83, 686. 13. See 9:278-83. 14. See 9:91-92, 115-17. 15. See 9:777-82. 16. Manuscript ends here; remainder is from Raleigh *Register.* 17. For William Gaston, who had died in Raleigh on Jan. 23, 1844, see *BDAC.*

To JAMES B. CLAY Raleigh, N.C., April 14, 1844

I arrived here on the 12th, very much fatigued, but my general health is pretty good. I have a note in the Branch Bank for fifteen hundred dollars due about the 1st of next month. Enclosed I send you a check for eighteen hundred dollars, fifteen hundred of which I wish applied to the payment of that note, and the balance to the payment of my interest due to the [Transylvania] University. I expect to reach Washington towards the last of this month and to remain there until the 4th or 5th. of May, and shall be glad to hear from you at that place.

Tell Thomas [Hart Clay] that there is a fair prospect of selling the bagging & rope at Savannah and Charleston, and that I adhere to the opinion that it is best to send them there after I get home.

Give my love to your Mamma [Lucretia Hart Clay] and tell her I will write her before I leave this place. Remember me also to Susan [Jacob Clay].

LS. DLC-TJC (DNA, M212, R10). Printed in Colton, *Clay Correspondence*, 4:486.

To OCTAVIA WALTON LEVERT Raleigh, N.C., April 14, 1844

I have only time to drop you a line to say that I arrived here on the evening of the 12h. a good deal fatigued but with better general health than I expected. My reception has been cordial & enthusiastic beyond all description. I consider the fatigues of my journey as now substantially terminated, and that henceforward I shall have comparative ease and quiet.

I have been much disappointed in not finding here any letter from Mobile. How has this happened? I have written twice to you, since we parted at Montgomery.

My warm regards to the Dr. [Henry LeVert] and Kisses to the Graces.[1]

P.S. A letter will find me at Washn. until the 5h. May, enveloped to Willis Green Esq. of the H[ouse]. of R[epresentatives].

ALS. KyU. Printed in Colton, *Clay Correspondence*, 4:486. 1. Madam LeVert's daughters were Octavia Walton, Claudia Eugenia, and Sally Walker. She later had Henrietta Caroline who was named for Henry Clay and known as Cara Netta. Her only son apparently died without being named. Information supplied by Caldwell Delaney, Director, City of Mobile Museum Department.

To WILLIE P. MANGUM Raleigh, N.C., April 14, 1844

I received here your favor of the 9th. inst. and I am greatly obliged by the views opinions and information which it contains. It relieved me from some solicitude which I had felt. I think you need entertain no fears that your own opinions will not be fully sustained and supported by your constituents.[1] Indeed throughout the whole of that portion of the South, which I have traversed, I have found a degree of indifference or opposition to the measure of annexation which quite surprized me. I have forborne to make any exposition of the sentiments which I entertain upon the subject; but it is my intention after my arrival at Washington to make such an exposition if I deem it necessary.[2] I can easily avail myself for that purpose of any one of several letters of enquiry which have been addressed to me. I do not entertain the slightest apprehension of any injury to our cause from the publication of my opinions. On the contrary I believe it would be benefitted and strengthened.

My reception at the Capital of your State has been cordial and enthusiastic,[3] and attended by numbers, far surpassing my most sanguine anticipations.

LS. NcD. 1. For the Texas annexation issue, see Clay to Crittenden, Feb. 15, 1844. Mangum shared Clay's opposition to annexation. Shanks, *Papers of Willie P. Mangum*, 4:76, 92-94, 127-28. 2. Clay to Editors of Washington *Daily National Intelligencer*, April 17, 1844. 3. Speech in Raleigh, N.C., April 13, 1844.

To WILLIAM A. GRAHAM Raleigh, N.C., April 15, 1844

I received at this place your favor of the 11th. inst., and I regret extremely to hear of your continued indisposition, not only on account of itself, but because it deprives me of the satisfaction of having the gratification of seeing you in your own State, as I always hoped to do. For that purpose, I should be delighted to visit you at your own residence, but it is one of the privations incident to my journey that the public takes complete possession of me, leaving me no leisure for individual intercourse. Were I a freeman, at liberty to do as I please, I should accept the tender of your hospitality with great avidity, but my engagements to the public deny me that happiness. . . .

LS. NcU.

From "Fellow Citizen," Charleston, S.C., *ca.* April 16, 1844. States that circumstances prevented his having "addressed to you this communication whilst you were in our midst." Presents now "as candidly and as clearly . . . as I understand them, the chief propositions which were urged by you in your late address [Speech in Charleston, April 6, 1844]. . . . by reducing them to a logical form, I have endeavored to bring more pointedly to your own view and to the view of all, what I conceive to be the false principles upon which they proceed, and the sophistry, (if you will excuse a term which is used in no odious but in its logical sense) which they seem to embody." Avers that he does so "in no spirit of hostile controversy or fancied triumph."

Attacks, at great length in a series of so-called syllogisms, Clay's arguments in favor of protection and a national bank. Concludes that Clay's contentions "present themselves to my own mind in a light which exhibits them as wholly at variance with truth." Adds that "I trust that this may convince you that our opposition to the party to which you belong, to the principles you profess, and to your own elevation to the Executive Office, is not founded merely in a personal hostility to yourself, or a bigotted devotion to the person of another, but in an intelligent and settled objection to the wisdom of the measures you propose."

Declaring that he "is no 'preacher' by profession," calls, nevertheless, "for the blessing of God upon your steps—that He may bless you in your home, in your person and in your deliberations, and above all, with the fear of God in your heart." Copy. Printed in Charleston (S.C.) *Mercury*, April 16, 1844.

To JOHN J. CRITTENDEN Raleigh, N.C., April 17, 1844

I transmit herewith a letter intended to be published in the [Washington *Daily National*] Intellr.[1] on the Texas question.[2] In my opinion, it is my duty to present it to the public. And in that [George] Badger, the Governor [John M. Morehead] & [Edward] Stanly (to whom I have confidentially read it) concur. I wish you to confer with [Willie P.] Mangum, [John M.] Berrien, [James T.] Morehead, Stevens [*sic*, Alexander Stephens] of Georgia & any other friends you please about it. I leave to you & them to determine *the time* of the publication, whether before or after my arrival at Washington.[3] To slight modifications of its phraeseology I should have no objections.

I leave here tomorrow for Petersburg, and leave that for Portsmouth on saturday afternoon. I shall leave Norfolk if I can wednesday the 24h.

Do me the favor to forward the inclosed letter to my wife [Lucretia Hart Clay].

ALS. DLC-John J. Crittenden Papers (DNA, M212, R20). 1. Clay to Editors of Washington *Daily National Intelligencer*, April 17, 1844. 2. See 9:35-36; Clay to Crittenden, Feb. 15, 1844. 3. It was published in the *Intelligencer* on April 27, 1844.

To THE EDITORS OF THE Raleigh, April 17, 1844
WASHINGTON *DAILY NATIONAL INTELLIGENCER*
[JOSEPH GALES & WILLIAM W. SEATON]

Subsequent to my departure from Ashland, in December last, I received various communications from popular assemblages and private individuals, requesting an expression of my opinion upon the question of the Annexation of Texas to the United States. I have forborne to reply to them, because it was not very convenient, during the progress of my journey, to do so, and for other reasons. I did not think it proper, unnecessarily, to introduce at present a new element among the other exciting subjects which agitate and engross the public mind. The rejection of the overture of Texas, some years ago, to become annexed to the United States, had met with general acquiescence.[1] Nothing had since occurred materially to vary the question. I had seen no evidence of a desire being entertained, on the part of any considerable portion of the American people, that Texas should become an integral part of the United States. During my sojourn in New Orleans, I had, indeed, been greatly surprised, by information which I received from Texas, that, in the course of last fall, a voluntary overture had proceeded from the Executive of the United States to the Authorities of Texas to conclude a treaty of Annexation;[2] and that, in order to overcome the repugnance felt by any of them to a negotiation upon the subject, strong and, as I believed, erroneous representations had been made to them of a state of opinion in the Senate of the United States favorable to the ratification of such a treaty. According to these representations, it had been ascertained that a number of Senators, varying from thirty-five to forty-two, were ready to sanction such a treaty. I was aware, too, that holders of Texas lands and Texas scrip, and speculators in them, were actively engaged in promoting the object of annexation. Still, I did not believe that any Executive of the United States would venture upon so grave and momentous a proceeding, not only without any general manifestation of public opinion in favor of it, but in direct opposition to strong and decided expressions of public disapprobation. But it appears that I was mistaken. To the astonishment of the whole nation, we are now informed that a treaty of annexation has been actually concluded, and is to be submitted to the Senate for its consideration. The motives for my silence, therefore, no longer remain, and I feel it to be my duty to present an exposition of my views and opinions upon the question, for what they may be worth, to the public consideration. I adopt this method as being more convenient than several replies to the respective communications which I have received.

I regret that I have not the advantage of a view of the treaty itself, so as to enable me to adapt an expression of my opinion to the actual conditions and stipulations which it contains. Not possessing that opportunity, I am constrained to treat the question according to what I presume to be the terms of the treaty. If, without the loss of national character, without the hazard of foreign war, with the general concurrence of the nation, without any danger to the integrity of the Union, and without giving an unreasonable price for Texas, the question of annexation were presented, it would appear in quite a different light from that in which, I apprehend, it is now to be regarded.

The United States acquired a title to Texas, extending, as I believe, to the Rio del Norte, by the treaty of Louisiana.[3] They ceded and relinquished that title to Spain by the treaty of 1819,[4] by which the Sabine was substituted for the Rio del Norte as our western boundary. This treaty was negotiated under the Administration of Mr. [James] Monroe, and with the concurrence of his Cabinet, of which Messrs. [William H.] Crawford, [John C.] Calhoun, and [William] Wirt, being a majority, all Southern gentlemen, composed a part. When the treaty was laid before the House of Representatives, being a member of that body, I expressed the opinion, which I then entertained, and still hold, that Texas was sacrificed to the acquisition of Florida.[5] We wanted Florida; but I thought it must, from its position, inevitably fall into our possession; that the point of a few years, sooner or later, was of no sort of consequence, and that in giving five millions of dollars and Texas for it, we gave more than a just equivalent. But, if we made a great sacrifice in the surrender of Texas, we ought to take care not to make too great a sacrifice in the attempt to re-acquire it.

My opinions of the inexpediency of the treaty of 1819 did not prevail. The country and Congress were satisfied with it, appropriations were made to carry it into effect, the line of the Sabine was recognised by us as our boundary, in negotiations both with Spain and Mexico, after Mexico became independent, and measures have been in actual progress to mark the line, from the Sabine to Red river, and thence to the Pacific ocean. We have thus fairly alienated our title to Texas, by solemn national compacts, to the fulfilment of which we stand bound by good faith and national honor. It is, therefore, perfectly idle and ridiculous, if not dishonorable, to talk of resuming our title to Texas, as if we had never parted with it. We can no more do that than Spain can resume Florida, France Louisiana, or Great Britain the thirteen colonies, now composing a part of the United States.

During the administration of Mr. [John Q.] Adams, Mr. [Joel R.] Poinsett, Minister of the United States at Mexico, was instructed by me, with the President's authority, to propose a re-purchase of Texas;[6] but he forbore even to make an overture for that purpose. Upon his return to the United States, he informed me, at New Orleans, that his reason for not making it was, that he knew the purchase was wholly impracticable, and that he was persuaded that, if he made the overture, it would have no other effect than to aggravate irritations, already existing, upon matters of difference between the two countries.

The events which have since transpired in Texas are well known. She revolted against the Government of Mexico, flew to arms, and finally fought and won the memorable battle of San Jacinto, annihilating a Mexican army and making a captive of the Mexican President.[7] The signal success of that Revolution was greatly aided, if not wholly achieved, by citizens of the United States who had migrated to Texas. These succors, if they could not always be prevented by the Government of the United States, were furnished in a manner and to an extent which brought upon us some national reproach in the eyes of an impartial world. And, in my opinion, they impose on us the obligation of scrupulously avoiding the imputation of having instigated and aided the Revolution with the ultimate view of territorial aggrandizement. After the battle of San Jacinto, the United States recognised the independence of Texas, in conformity with the principle and practice which have always prevailed in their councils of recognising the Government "*de facto*," without regarding the question *de jure*.[8] That recognition did not affect or impair the rights of Mexico, or change the relations which existed between her and

Texas. She, on the contrary, has preserved all her rights, and has continued to assert, and so far as I know yet asserts, her right to reduce Texas to obedience, as a part of the Republic of Mexico. According to late intelligence, it is probable that she has agreed upon a temporary suspension of hostilities; but, if that has been done, I presume it is with the purpose, upon the termination of the armistice, of renewing the war and enforcing her rights, as she considers them.

This narrative shows the present actual condition of Texas, so far as I have information about it. If it be correct, Mexico has not abandoned, but perseveres in the assertion of her rights by actual force of arms, which, if suspended, are intended to be renewed. Under these circumstances, if the Government of the United States were to acquire Texas, it would acquire along with it all the incumbrances which Texas is under, and among them the actual or suspended war between Mexico and Texas. Of that consequence there cannot be a doubt. Annexation and war with Mexico are identical. Now, for one, I certainly am not willing to involve this country in a foreign war for the object of acquiring Texas. I know there are those who regard such a war with indifference and as a trifling affair, on account of the weakness of Mexico, and her inability to inflict serious injury upon this country. But I do not look upon it thus lightly. I regard all wars as great calamities, to be avoided, if possible, and honorable peace as the wisest and truest policy of this country. What the United States most need are union, peace, and patience. Nor do I think that the weakness of a Power should form a motive, in any case, for inducing us to engage in or to depreciate the evils of war. Honor and good faith and justice are equally due from this country towards the weak as towards the strong. And, if an act of injustice were to be perpetrated towards any Power, it would be more compatible with the dignity of the nation, and, in my judgment, less dishonorable, to inflict it upon a powerful instead of a weak foreign nation. But are we perfectly sure that we should be free from injury in a state of war with Mexico? Have we any security that countless numbers of foreign vessels, under the authority and flag of Mexico, would not prey upon our defenceless commerce in the Mexican gulf, on the Pacific ocean, and on every other sea and ocean? What commerce, on the other hand, does Mexico offer, as an indemnity for our losses, to the gallantry and enterprise of our countrymen? This view of the subject supposes that the war would be confined to the United States and Mexico as the only belligerents. But have we any certain guaranty that Mexico would obtain no allies among the great European Powers? Suppose any such Powers, jealous of our increasing greatness, and disposed to check our growth and cripple us, were to take part in behalf of Mexico in the war, how would the different belligerents present themselves to Christendom and the enlightened world? We have been seriously charged with an inordinate spirit of territorial aggrandizement; and, without admitting the justice of the charge, it must be owned that we have made vast acquisitions of territory within the last forty years. Suppose Great Britain and France, or one of them, were to take part with Mexico, and, by a manifesto, were to proclaim that their objects were to assist a weak and helpless ally to check the spirit of encroachment and ambition of an already overgrown Republic, seeking still further acquisitions of territory, to maintain the independence of Texas, disconnected with the United States, and to prevent the further propagation of slavery from the United States, what would be the effect of such allegations upon the judgment of an impartial and enlightened world?

Assuming that the annexation of Texas is war with Mexico, is it competent to the treaty-making power to plunge this country into war, not only without the concurrence of, but without deigning to consult Congress, to which, by the Constitution, belongs exclusively the power of declaring war?

I have hitherto considered the question upon the supposition that the annexation is attempted without the assent of Mexico. If she yields her consent, that would materially affect the foreign aspect of the question, if it did not remove all foreign difficulties. On the assumption of that assent, the question would be confined to the domestic considerations which belong to it, embracing the terms and conditions upon which annexation is proposed. I do not think that Texas ought to be received into the Union, as an integral part of it, in decided opposition to the wishes of a considerable and respectable portion of the Confederacy. I think it far more wise and important to compose and harmonize the present Confederacy, as it now exists, than to introduce a new element of discord and distraction into it. In my humble opinion, it should be the constant and earnest endeavor of American statesmen to eradicate prejudices, to cultivate and foster concord, and to produce general contentment among all parts of our Confederacy. And true wisdom, it seems to me, points to the duty of rendering its present members happy, prosperous, and satisfied with each other, rather than to attempt to introduce alien members, against the common consent and with the certainty of deep dissatisfaction. Mr. [Thomas] Jefferson expressed the opinion, and others believed, that it was never in the contemplation of the framers of the Constitution to add foreign territory to the confederacy, out of which new States were to be formed. The acquisitions of Louisiana and Florida may be defended upon the peculiar ground of the relation in which they stood to the States of the Union. After they were admitted, we might well pause awhile, people our vast wastes, develop our resources, prepare the means of defending what we possess, and augment our strength, power, and greatness. If hereafter further territory should be wanted for an increased population, we need entertain no apprehensions but that it will be acquired by means, it is to be hoped, fair, honorable, and constitutional.

It is useless to disguise that there are those who espouse and those who oppose the annexation of Texas upon the ground of the influence which it would exert, in the balance of political power, between two great sections of the Union. I conceive that no motive for the acquisition of foreign territory would be more unfortunate, or pregnant with more fatal consequences, than that of obtaining it for the purpose of strengthening one part against another part of the common Confederacy. Such a principle, put into practical operation, would menace the existence, if it did not certainly sow the seeds of a dissolution of the Union. It would be to proclaim to the world an insatiable and unquenchable thirst for foreign conquest or acquisition of territory. For if to-day Texas be acquired to strengthen one part of the Confederacy, tomorrow Canada may be required to add strength to another. And, after that might have been obtained, still other and further acquisitions would become necessary to equalize and adjust the balance of political power. Finally, in the progress of this spirit of universal dominion, the part of the Confederacy which is now weakest, would find itself still weaker from the impossibility of securing new theatres for those peculiar institutions which it is charged with being desirous to extend.

But would Texas, ultimately, really add strength to that which is now considered the weakest part of the Confederacy? If my information be correct, it would not. According to that, the territory of Texas is susceptible of a division into five States of convenient size and form. Of these, two only would be adapted to those peculiar institutions to which I have referred, and the other three, lying west and north of San Antonio, being only adapted to farming and grazing purposes, from the nature of their soil, climate, and productions, would not admit of those institutions. In the end, therefore, there would be two slave and three free States probably added to the Union. If this view of the soil and geography of Texas be correct, it might serve to diminish the zeal both of those who oppose and those who are urging annexation.

Should Texas be annexed to the Union, the United States will assume and become responsible for the debt of Texas, be its amount what it may. What it is, I do not know certainly; but the least I have seen it stated at is thirteen millions of dollars. And this responsibility will exist, whether there be a stipulation in the treaty or not expressly assuming the payment of the debt of Texas.[9] For I suppose it to be undeniable that, if one nation becomes incorporated in another, all the debts, and obligations, and incumbrances, and wars of the incorporated nation, become the debts, and obligations, and incumbrances, and wars of the common nation created by the incorporation.

If any European nation entertains any ambitious designs upon Texas, such as that of colonizing her, or in any way subjugating her, I should regard it as the imperative duty of the Government of the United States to oppose to such designs the most firm and determined resistance, to the extent, if necessary, of appealing to arms to prevent the accomplishment of any such designs. The Executive of the United States ought to be informed as to the aims and views of foreign Powers with regard to Texas, and I presume that, if there be any of the exceptionable character which I have indicated, the Executive will disclose to the co-ordinate departments of the government, if not the public, the evidence of them. From what I have seen and heard, I believe that Great Britain has recently formally and solemnly disavowed any such aims or purposes—has declared that she is desirous only of the independence of Texas, and that she has no intention to interfere in her domestic institutions.[10] If she has made such disavowal and declaration, I presume they are in the possession of the Executive.

In the future progress of events, it is probable that there will be a voluntary or forcible separation of the British North American possessions from the parent country. I am strongly inclined to think that it will be best for the happiness of all parties that, in that event, they should be erected into a separate and independent Republic. With the Canadian Republic on one side, that of Texas on the other, and the United States, the friend of both, between them, each could advance its own happiness by such constitutions, laws, and measures, as were best adapted to its peculiar condition. They would be natural allies, ready, by co-operation, to repel any European or foreign attack upon either. Each would afford a secure refuge to the persecuted and oppressed driven into exile by either of the others. They would emulate each other in improvements, in free institutions, and in the science of self-government. Whilst Texas has adopted our Constitution as the model of hers, she has, in several important particulars, greatly improved upon it.

Although I have felt compelled, from the nature of the inquiries addressed to me, to extend this communication to a much greater length than I could have wished, I could not do justice to the subject, and fairly and fully expose my own opinions in a shorter space. In conclusion, they may be stated in a few words to be, that I consider the annexation of Texas, at this time, without the assent of Mexico, as a measure compromising the national character, involving us certainly in war with Mexico, probably with other foreign Powers, dangerous to the integrity of the Union, inexpedient in the present financial condition of the country, and not called for by any general expression of public opinion.

Copy. Printed in Washington *Daily National Intelligencer*, April 27, 1844; also in Colton, *Clay Correspondence*, 3:25-31. 1. See 9:226-27. 2. Clay to Crittenden, Feb. 15, 1844. 3. Parry, *Treaty Series*, 57:27-48. 4. *Ibid.*, 70:1-30, espec. 4. 5. See 2:810-16. 6. See 6:308-9, 540. 7. See 9:20. 8. See 9:35-36. 9. The first treaty of annexation, which was signed on April 12, 1844, but never ratified, provided that Texas would cede its public lands to the U.S. and that the U.S. would assume the public debt of Texas up to $10,000,000. The joint resolution which admitted Texas into the Union, however, allowed the new state to retain its public lands and apply the income to its debts. Stanley Siegel, *A Political History of the Texas Republic, 1836-1845* (Austin, Texas, 1956), 244; Parry, *Treaty Series*, 99:261-69. 10. Clay was probably referring to a letter of Dec. 26, 1843, from Lord Aberdeen to Richard Pakenham, Great Britain's minister to the U.S., restating the British position favoring the independence of Texas, opposing slavery there, but disavowing any intention of acting "directly or indirectly, in a political sense, on the United States through Texas." Aberdeen instructed Pakenham to show the dispatch to the U.S. secretary of state, and John C. Calhoun found it unanswered when he assumed that office on April 1, 1844, after A.P. Upshur's death. Manning, *Diplomatic Correspondence*, 7:246-50; Wiltse, *John C. Calhoun: Sectionalist*, 3:168-69.

To JOHN J. CRITTENDEN Petersburg, Va., April 19, 1844

I transmitted to you from Raleigh a letter[1] on the subject of the Annexation of Texas for publication. I observe, with the greatest attention, all that is passing in regard to it, as far as it is visible to my eye. I feel perfectly confident in the ground which I have taken, and feel moreover that it is proper and politic to present to the public that ground. I leave to you and other friends merely the question of deciding when my exposition shall appear. I cannot consent to suppress or unreasonably delay the publication of it. I think it ought to appear not later than this day or tomorrow week.[2] I entertain no fears from the promulgation of my opinion. Public sentiment is every where sounder than at Washington.

I should be glad to receive at Norfolk, if you feel authorized to send me confidentially, a copy of the Treaty.[3] I leave here tomorrow evening for Norfolk, from which I shall take my departure on wednesday or thursday next.

ALS. DLC-John J. Crittenden Papers (DNA, M212, R20). 1. Clay to Editors of Washington *Daily National Intelligencer*, April 17, 1844. 2. It appeared on April 27. 3. Of the annexation of Texas. Clay to Crittenden, Feb. 15, 1844.

Speech in Petersburg, Va., April 19, 1844. In a speech of two hours' length, "delivered in the finest style imaginable," Clay discusses "the great questions of a Bank, Abolition, the Tariff, and Distribution." Devotes, however, the first half hour to an editorial by Thomas Ritchie in the Richmond *Enquirer*. Notes that the editorial warned Democrats in Petersburg "to be on their guard. . . . Mr. Clay comes among us, in the character of a political intriguer—not as a native of the State, nor as a stranger, entitled to our general hospitality—but as an Electioneerer to woo our suffrages, and to promote his own ambition. . . . As such, it becomes every Democrat to receive him—not to be caught by any affection of manner—by any idle appeal to the generous, old-fashioned hospitality of the State." Clay then asks the Democrats of Petersburg "if Mr. Ritchie had not shown a reckless partizan spirit? . . . Did his friend of the Enquirer hold the intelligence of the 'Democrats' of Petersburg, in such low esteem that he must needs step in like an anxious guardian, and say to his simple, obedient, but unsuspecting Wards, *be on your* guard? Guard against what and whom? What was the approaching danger that extorted this shriek of alarm from head quarters in Richmond? Did Mr. R. suppose he were the devil, and had come to torment a portion of the 'Democracy' before their time? Did he think he had brought with him a loathsome disease, that would destroy this beautiful city? . . . Ah! his old friend feared the effect of his 'affectation of manner'—his *winning ways* to catch 'Democrats.' He was sorry that Mr. R. had so little confidence in the truth of the cause he was trying to uphold, and so poor an opinion of the intellects of the members of his party here. He had a better opinion of them by far, than Mr. R. had—he believed them to be honest in their opinions, and . . . he further believed that they were freemen, and independent citizens, incapable of being dictated to, or turned about, either by himself or the venerable old gentleman of the Enquirer. But . . . the veritable Editor of the Enquirer, has not only attempted to deprive me of the hospitalities, extended to a stranger, even by a Hottentot, or the savages of our Western wilderness—but he has denied me the cherished honor of having been born in this Ancient and renowned Commonwealth! I swear . . . that I was born in the Slashes of Old Hanover! [Tremendous applause!] I am, said he, a native of Virginia, and I will continue to be a native born citizen of this proud Commonwealth, the avowals of *Tom Ritchie* to the contrary notwithstanding! [Loud and long continued cheering!]" Continues, saying that he has "been denied the character of a candid and honest man, a character he had labored to establish for himself, for the last forty years of his life. He had avowed every sentiment he held, over and over again, & he held none that he had not published, and that was not known and read of all men. . . . The truth was, the old gentleman of the Enquirer, had so long ago bid adieu to these virtues, to-wit, candor and honesty, that he was unwilling to recognize them, even as *old acquaintances* when he met with them in others! [Loud cheering!]"

Comments also that while his traveling through several states is viewed by Ritchie as electioneering, "it was patriotic in Mr. [Martin] Van Buren, about three years ago, to travel through the same States, and to continue on through various other States, through which Mr. C. never expected to pass! He was a free man, an American citizen, and would go wherever it suited him. If others crossed his way, he would meet them kindly if they desired; otherwise if they would have it so[.] And once for all, he would meet any prominent man of the Democratic party, before the free people of this country and discuss his principles, and the principles and acts of the Whig party. [Loud cheering!] He did not intend to be understood as giving a *challenge*, but to signify his willingness to meet any man of their party in discussion, and the more so, since he was charged with coming before them with a mask over his face." Copy, extract. Printed in Jonesborough (Tenn.) *Whig, and Independent Journal*, May 1, 1844.

Ritchie's editorial warning Virginians against Clay had appeared in the Richmond *Enquirer* on April 16, 1844.

To JOHN J. CRITTENDEN Norfolk, Va., April 21, 1844

I arrived here this morning from Petersburg, and found your letter of the 18h. You must have recd. that evening or next day my communication on the Texas question.[1] I stated at Petersburg to several friends that it would appear on saturday next, or at farthest on monday the 29h. and I *wish* it to appear accordingly.[2]

I do not entertain the smallest apprehension from the publication of my opinions. If the importance of the subject may be underrated, it may be overrated too. Caution may degenerate into timidity. And I cannot help thinking that there is at Washington a state of intense feeling which creates nervous sensibility, and a local atmosphere which prevents the easy penetration of truth. I am perfectly sure that the degree of favor which prevails at the South towards annexation is far less than is believed at Washington. If the Senate will fulfill its duty to the Country, and realize the expectations which are entertained of it, I feel certain that no mischief will ensue. I hope the rejection will be prompt, firm and dignified, and by a majority.[3]

Mr. [Martin] V[an]. B[uren]. if he does not alter his position, stands opposed.[4] We shall therefore occupy common ground. And his present attitude, renders it necessary that I should break silence. If he change his position, and come out for annexation, it will be so much worse for him. The public mind is too fixed on the Presidential question, the current is running too strong and impetuous to be now affected by Texas.

I hope to arrive at Washn. the last of this week, perhaps thursday next. I requested [Willis] Green to procure me two or three rooms, if possible, on the hill, for a week or ten days. I wish you would aid him in getting them for me.

ALS. DLC-John J. Crittenden Papers (DNA, M212, R20). 1. Clay to Editors of Washington *Daily National Intelligencer*, April 17, 1844; Clay to Crittenden, April 17, 1844. 2. Clay to Crittenden, April 19, 1844. 3. Clay to Crittenden, Feb. 15, 1844. 4. Van Buren's letter of April 20, 1844, to William H. Hammet opposing Texas annexation was published in the Washington *Globe* the same day (April 27) that Clay's Raleigh letter of April 17 to the editors of the Washington *Daily National Intelligencer* appeared in that paper. Van Buren's statement has been widely viewed as the reason he lost the Democratic presidential nomination. Donald B. Cole, *Martin Van Buren and the American Political System* (Princeton, N.J., 1984), 393-97; John Niven, *Martin Van Buren, The Romantic Age of American Politics* (New York, 1983), 516-36. See also 9:704.

From James Jarvis, Portsmouth, Va., April 22, 1844. Describes himself as "an humble Induvidual," and recalls first seeing Clay "in the Speakers Chair of the House of Representatives." Praises him for his "Great attachment to the *Union*," noting that "When I first heard your voice I was what was then called a democrat as you were, You have not changed. I have not changed. Yet there are some amongst us who say we are not of the old and pure school. I maintain that the Whig party are the *real* democratic party." Asks for "a letter in answer to this" for the purpose of passing "it down to my Children and Grand Children &c to show to them what were my political feelings in the life time of Henry Clay!" Encloses a letter from George Washington to Henry Knox [not found], saying "were it the Presidency it should be Yours. I beg you to accept it from a true Whig after Your own order." ALS. DLC-TJC (DNA, M212, R10).

Jarvis is probably the James Jarvis who served as a captain in the Navy in the War of 1812. William Maxwell (ed.), *Virginia Historical Register and Literary Advertiser*, 6 vols. (Richmond, Va., 1848), 1:137-41.

SPEECH IN NORFOLK April 22, 1844

Mr. Clay deferred his remarks on the tariff until he should address the people of Portsmouth.[1] He gave a beautiful and powerful argument in support of an institution for the establishment of a national currency: *A Bank*—which carried conviction to many who had doubted on that subject; that a national currency, through the agency of a United States Bank, was not only necessary to the wholesome operations of business throughout the country, but in harmony with the Constitution and our federal system in all its parts. Mr. Clay said that in 1811 he made a speech against a United States Bank.[2] With that speech the Democrats now were desperately enamored. Oh, it was a lovely speech! the most beautiful and conclusive speech he had ever delivered. He also made a speech in 1816 in favor of a Bank.[3] If the party would place the two side by side, then he would be satisfied with whatever verdict his country might render! In 1811 the country was at peace; but so soon as war was declared the want of a Bank was immediately felt; disorder, chaos, and confusion reigned throughout the land; the paper in every State was depreciated; the public finances got into disorder; the credit was gone; its paper every where was greatly below par. In 1816 a proposition for a Bank was made; his experience from 1811 to that time proved to him that he was mistaken; he changed his opinion with the Republicans of that day, [James] Madison and others.[4] The Bank was then a Republican measure. It was opposed by Federalists alone. A Bank was necessary for the interest of the whole country. Private Banks were established in different States to counteract those of other States. Suppose 20 States should say we will have banks, and the other States should refuse to charter any: then these six States will be flooded with the paper of the twenty, at various scales of depreciation, to the great injury of the community, and for the benefit of swarms of Brokers. Was it not necessary then to have a National Bank to control and regulate the currency? In private Banks there was no security. Do we not frequently hear of their bursting in various sections of this extensive country; the currency is getting better, it is true, and we are indebted for it to the Whig Tariff of 1842; but when the balance of trade shall be against us, we shall have the same distress we had before. No one State can perform the duties of the General Government.

We want, then, a National Currency as well as national laws; England has her National Bank; France has her National Bank; we have a National Army, a National Navy, for the protection of the country; and if we want these National Armies and National Navies, so we want a National Currency. We have been told that a National Bank is dangerous to liberty; all history disproves the assertion; the liberty of the country has never been endangered by a National Bank. Banks only prosper when the country prospers. Some say, why should we imitate the monarchies of Europe and have our Banks like England and France, for example? He might retort the argument and say, why have an Army and a Navy, because countries governed by monarchies have them? The most powerful opposition to a National Bank is in Wall street, where reside English bankers with English capital; should we have a sound currency, these English capitalists would be shorn of their enormous profits which they derive from a disordered currency.—Virginia may not desire a National Bank, because she does not need it; but will the people of one State refuse to promote an institution which will benefit all the others? Will you be so selfish as to refuse to do good to others because you do not want the benefit yourselves? It has been my invariable rule to do all for the Union. If any man wants the key of my heart, let him take the key of the Union, and that is the key to my heart. Without Union we shall be liable to all the evils of Tyranny, subject to be trodden under foot by some military chieftain. Every man who reflects upon the prospects of our country, the next twelve years, may see what will be our destiny, provided we remain UNITED.

I am . . . a Whig, as you all know, and have Whig principles. What the Democratic principles are I know not. They assail our principles without letting us know what they themselves maintain. Mr. Clay then proceeded to lay open the great and distinctive principles avowed by the Whig party: A national currency, which could only be secured by the establishment of an institution which should give it the same value in every part of the country; a tariff for revenue, adequate to the wants of an economical administration of the Government, and giving incidental protection to American industry; distribution of the proceeds of the public lands, (the revenue which a leader of the Democratic party had long since admitted was not required for the General Government.) To these Mr. Clay added the firm ground which the Whigs had taken against the Executive assumption of powers not conferred by the Constitution. Within the last fifteen years it had shot madly from its legitimate sphere of action: the vetoes and dismissals from office without cause were in rapid progress to realize the portentous remark of Patrick Henry on the Federal Government at its birth, that it had "an awful squinting at monarchy." Indeed, the power of the Executive had already been upheld, while the Representative power had been humbled in the dust. Executive power must be confined to its constitutional limits; and this was what the Whig party was struggling for while the Democratic party are striving to extend it by upholding its assumptions.[5] Which, said he, is the most democratic of the two parties? Mr. Clay said he should be delighted to hear what the champions of the other party had to advance in opposition to these Whig principles. They are opposed to protection and in some parts of the Union they are for free trade. For himself, he was in the veritable sense of the word a *democrat*, and he should live and die a republican. The democratic party of the present day profess to be of the Jefferson School, and yet they are carrying out the principles against which he warned them many years ago:—They are upholding the extension of Executive power: they go with the Executive against their own representatives; they go for its power and praise it for all its extravagance.

Mr. C. felt grateful for the attendance of the Democrats, and if he had mistaken their views he would be glad if any one of their leaders would correct him.

Copy, summary. Printed in Hodges, Todd, & Pruett (pub.), *The Campaign of 1844* (Frankfort, Ky., 1844), 77-78. 1. His speech at Portsmouth, Va., on April 23 has not been found. 2. See 1:527-39, 542-44. 3. See 2:138, 178-80, 182-85. 4. For previous explanations of his switch on the national bank issue, see 2:200-205, 210, 216-19. 5. For his constitutional amendment proposals, see 9:636-40.

From Isaac T. Preston, New Orleans, April 26, 1844. Reports that the case of John B. Humphreys's heirs [9:303, 796, 800] "against you has been decided in your favor." Says the "half belonging to you as Executor of Mrs [Ann Hart "Nancy"] Brown is deposited in Bank subject to your draft upon me or other disposition that may be agreeable to you[.] I am under obligations to your son [Henry Clay, Jr.]. Who argued the case before the Supreme Court with great credit to himself and advantage to the cause." Mentions that he still must settle with the estate some rent and other charges which he owes and that a house and some land must be sold and the proceeds divided among the heirs. Lists the "Debt from Humphreys Heirs To the estate of James

Brown" as $9,000 plus interest of $4,643 accrued since January 1, 1834, for a total of $13,643 of which half, or $6,821.50, is due Clay as executor for Mrs. Brown. ALS. DLC-TJC (DNA, M212, R14).

Writing from Washington, Clay replied to Preston on May 4, 1844, saying that he had written to his son "conveying an authority to receive the part belonging to Mrs. Brown's Estate [9:82-84], and transmitting a receipt for $500 to you for my fee for arguing the cause at the former term &c." Asks Preston "to deduct your own fee, my fee, & $250 as a fee to my son, and divide the nett balance equally between the two Estates, paying over to my son the portion coming from Mrs. Browns Estate." Adds that "Mason Brown expresses his satisfaction with my charge, and I am persuaded will be satisfied with the above arrangement." ALS. Henry Clay Memorial Foundation, Lexington, Ky.

Clay wrote Mason Brown from Lexington on May 25, 1844, saying that "the last suit brought by the Heirs of Mr. Humphreys has been decided by the Supreme Court of Louisiana in our favor." Mentions that his son, Henry Clay, Jr., and Isaac T. Preston argued the case and that Preston has collected the amount of the Judgment. Requests "that, before you pay the money over, you will retain $250, your half of my fee, and $125, your half of the fee I engaged to pay Henry." Copy. KyU.

Isaac T. Preston sent Clay a check on June 4, 1844, for the fees of Clay and Henry Clay, Jr., for arguing the case. Adds that he is also sending a draft "for the net half of the amount received belonging to the Heirs of Mrs. Brown." LS. DLC-TJC (DNA, M212, R14). In another letter written from New Orleans the same day, Preston informed Clay of additional charges deducted from the settlement. *Ibid.*

On September 10, 1844, George Washington Anderson wrote Clay that he (Anderson) had just been appointed guardian of Sarah Hart. Also sends receipts showing that his wife, Eleanor Hart Anderson, daughter of Thomas Hart, Jr., has received $350 and Sarah Hart $116 from Clay as "Executor of Mrs Nancy Brown . . . from J.B. Humphreys' Estate." ALS. *Ibid.* Sarah Hart was the infant daughter of Thomas P. Hart, eldest son of Thomas Hart, Jr.

Clay wrote Mason Brown from New Orleans on December 29, 1846, to inform him that a "judicial sale is to be made of the House and lot in this City belonging to the Estates of Mr. & Mrs. Brown." This will be done "in consequence of the difficulty of getting all the persons, interested in the property, to unite in conveying the requisite authority to make the sale." Adds that "I have no intention of purchasing; but I thought you might like to know of the intended sale." Notes that the sale will be on January 22, 23, or 24. ALS. KyHi.

A document, dated April, 1847, and signed by Henry Clay as executor for Nancy Brown, indicates that Mrs. Brown's house sold for $5,025. After expenses the net sum to be distributed was $2,455.26 in six equal parts of $409.21. The document notes that "Mrs Brown died intestate, and her interest in it passed to her heirs, of whom her mother [Susannah Gray Hart] having survived her, became one. Mrs Hart, by her will, left her interest to her daughter Lucretia [Hart Clay], in consequence of the great losses sustained through her son John [Hart] by H[enry] Clay [2:718, 795, 898-99]. Hence Mrs Hart being entitled to an equal portion with the brothers and sisters of Mrs Brown, Mrs Clay as her representative is entitled to one sixth, and in her own right to another one sixth." ADS. KyU.

Clay received a receipt from James Shelby, dated June 16, 1847, indicating that $136.40 had been paid to his children as heirs of their mother, Mary Shelby, from the sale of the Brown house in New Orleans. AD, in Clay's hand, signed by James Shelby. DLC-TJC (DNA, M212, R19). See also 8:739-40.

To REVERDY JOHNSON

Washington, April 29, 1844

I cannot reconcile it to my sense of delicacy and propriety to attend either of the Whig Conventions this week in Baltimore.[1] Such is my deliberate judgment. I hope my friends will acquiesce in my determination, and not urge me to revoke it, which I cannot do.

Copy. Printed in Hodges, Todd, & Pruett, *The Campaign of 1844*, 51. Addressed to Johnson in Baltimore. 1. For the National Whig convention, see 9:753-54; for the Whig Young Men's Ratification convention, see 9:887.

From Beverley C. Sanders, Baltimore, April 29, 1844. Asks "whether you entertain the same high opinion now which you expressed last summer in relation to the College at Lexington [Transylvania]." Is considering sending his son there, and wonders if it is "an institution suitable to place a Boy 13 years of age, who has no friends residing there."

Notes that "Baltimore is all life & animation all the world seems to be wending hither—The weather is propitious and all things promise a glorious day on 2d." Adds that the "whigs hope to see you here after the Convention of ratification [9:887]," and invites him to "visit us at our house." Also includes a receipt for a check Clay has sent "which closes the account." ALS. DLC-HC (DNA, M212, R5).

For Sanders, a businessman who later moved to San Francisco and lived for a time in Russia, see *MHM*, 67:156-70 and New York *Times*, December 27, 1883.

To George W. Blunt, New York, N.Y., April 30, 1844. Thanks him for the offer of a female "Setter" which he accepts, commenting: "I have no great attachment for dogs because they kill sheep, but some of my family like them better, and I sometimes overcome my repugnance to them, and get attracted by their fidelity." Instructs him to send the dog to William A. Bradley "of this city [Washington, D.C.]," and "I will carry her with pleasure to Ashland." Copy. Printed in Frederick Van Wyck, *Recollections of an Old New Yorker* . . . (New York, *ca.* 1932), 27.

Blunt was a hydrographer who established a publishing house which specialized in nautical works. He also served as first assistant of the U.S. Coastal Survey and on the Board of Pilot Commissioners. See *DAB*.

To JOHN M. BERRIEN *et al.*[1] Washington, May 2, 1844

I have the honor to acknowledge the receipt of your letter, dated yesterday at Baltimore, communicating my nomination, by the National Whig Convention there assembled[2] to the people of the U. States as a Candidate for the office of President of the U. States. Confidently believing that this nomination is in conformity with the desire of a majority of the people of the U. States, I accept it, from a high sense of duty, and with feelings of profound gratitude. I request you, Gentlemen, in announcing to the Convention my acceptance of the nomination, to express the very great satisfaction I derive from the unanimity with which it has been made. . . .

ALS. MdBJ. 1. On May 1, 1844, John M. Berrien, Jacob Burnet, Erastus Root, Abbott Lawrence, and William S. Archer had informed Clay of his nomination for the presidency by the Whig National convention meeting that day in Baltimore. Express "our earnest hope, that the wish of your assembled fellow citizens in which 'all with one voice' have united, and in which their personal feelings, and . . . the best interests of this great people are involved, may meet your prompt and cheerful acquiescence." Copy. Printed in *Niles' Register* (May 18, 1844), 66:186. 2. See 9:753-54.

To Editors of the Washington *Daily National Intelligencer*, May 3, 1844. Explains that during his current trip he has received "numerous invitations to visit my fellow citizens at various points of the Union." Has transmitted answers declining most of these invitations, "but, as I may have omitted to reply to some of them and as others addressed to me may not have reached me . . . I request to be allowed through the National Intelligencer to communicate a general and respectful answer, and to state the ground on which I shall feel constrained to place any similar invitations with which I may be in future honored." Writes that "If it were suitable and proper," he would like to accept such invitations; but, does not believe he should do so, because of his nomination for the presidency [Clay to Berrien *et al.*, May 2, 1844]. Continues: "The election of a Chief Magistrate . . . is one of the gravest and most momentous functions which the People can exercise. It is emphatically, and ought to be exclusively, their own business.—Upon the wisdom of their choice depend the preservation and soundness of free institutions, and the welfare and prosperity of themselves. In making it, they should be free, impartial, and wholly unbiased by the conduct of a candidate himself. Not only, in my opinion, is it his duty to abstain from all solicitation, direct or indirect, of their suffrages, but he should avoid being voluntarily placed in situations to seek, or in which he might be supposed to seek, to influence their judgment. Entertaining these views of what becomes a candidate for the exalted office of President of the United States, I shall act in strict conformity with them." Concludes that he cannot accept any more invitations to public meetings until the election is over and that he wants to return home "as quietly and quickly as possible." Copy. Printed in Washington *Daily National Intelligencer*, May 4, 1844. Written in Washington.

From Charles F. Mercer, Tallahassee, Fla., May 6, 1844. States that "I have risen, with unqualified approbation, from the perusal of your letter [Clay to Editors of the Washington *Daily National Intelligencer*, April 17, 1844], on the subject, which so deeply interests our whole country, the annexation of Texas." Notes that "Perhaps, no man, in our union, would more largely profit, than I should, by the immediate annexation of that country, to ours." Discusses his large landholdings in Texas, adding: "yet, I have never wavered, in opinion, on this subject, in that war with Mexico for the acquisition of Texas, would be, as dishonorable, as it would be unjust." Writes that he "was fearful, that the expression of any hostility, on your part, to the contemplated treaty of annexation [Clay to Crittenden, February 15, 1844] . . . would be used, to your prejudice, in the ensuing contest for the presidency." Thinks, however, that "the public annunciation that the treaty had been submitted to the Senate" and the meeting of the National Whig convention in Baltimore [Clay to Berrien *et al.*, May 2, 1844] "left you no longer at liberty to withhold your opinion." Adds: "I hope no unjust, or improper use will be made of an act, which comports, in my opinion, with the best trait of your public character; and I shall, within my limited sphere of action, employ all the means, which my Texian [*sic*] interests can supply, to defeat any such purpose, wherever I go." ALS. NHi.

To THURLOW WEED Washington, May 6, 1844

Your letter of the 8th. of January has been only received by me since my arrival at this place, and hence the delay in my transmission of an answer. I do not now recollect the purport of the letter from Mr Dickinson to which you refer.[1] but you may be assured that it made no unfavorable impression on my mind towards any body, much less [2] [William H.] Seward whose determination to give [3] efficient support to the Whig cause I have never doubted.

The nomination of Mr [Theodore] Frelinghuysen was no doubt unexpected by you as it certainly was by me.[4] I think nevertheless it is a most judicious selection, and if he does not add any strength which however I think he will do he will take away none from the ticket. The only regret about it is that the friends of so many able and good men should have been disappointed in regard to the selection of their favorites.

I do not think I ever witnessed such a state of utter disorder, confusion and decomposition as that which the Democratic Party now presents. Many believe that their Convention will now abandon Mr [Martin] Vanburen [*sic*] and take up some one else.[5] That is not my opinion, unless he chooses voluntarily to withdraw. For I think he is really the strongest man of their Party.

I am sure you will be pleased to hear from me that I am firmly convinced that my opinion on the Texas question will do me no prejudice at the South.[6]

Copy. NcD. 1. Andrew B. Dickinson, a Whig senator in the New York legislature and a friend of Weed and Seward. Harriet A. Weed (ed.), *Autobiography of Thurlow Weed*, 2 vols. (Boston, 1883), 1:440-42. See Seward to Clay, Oct. 25, 1844. 2. Name covered at this point. 3. Word covered at this point. 4. See 9:733. 5. See 9:752. 6. Clay to Editors of Washington *Daily National Intelligencer*, April 17, 1844.

To JOHN WHITE Washington, May 6, 1844

I have received your note, bringing to my notice a certificate[1] subscribed by five gentlemen,[2] members of the present House of Representatives, all of them my political opponents, which you inform me is going the rounds of the Locofoco papers. The object of that certificate seems to be to verify the correctness of an extract taken from the National Intelligencer of the 1st of July 1820. In that extract I am stated by a former member of the House of Representatives (I believe not living) to have remarked, in a debate which occurred a year before, to the following effect: "If gentlemen will not allow us to have black slaves they must let us have *white ones*, for we cannot cut our firewood, and black our shoes, and have our wives and daughters work in the kitchen."[3]

I think you attach an importance to this miserable attempt to prejudice me which it does not merit. Here is an extract from the files of the Intelligencer, under date near twenty four years ago, not from any speech of mine, but from a speech of a another member of Congress. He does not undertake to give my *words*, but merely states his impression of the *effect* of certain words used by me a year before.[4]

During the long and arduous discussions of what was called the Missouri question,[5] I was so engrossed with the importance of the subject, and so deeply apprehensive of the awful consequences which it involved, that I never wrote out or corrected any speech of mine made during the progress of the debate. On the last and most important occasion of the agitation of that question, I made an elaborate speech of several hours duration,[6] no part of which, I believe, was ever reported by any of the stenographers, as it certainly never was by me.

I certainly will not undertake to recite what were the precise words used by me on the occasion of any of the numerous speeches, short or long, which I made in Congress on the Missouri question; but this I undertake to assert, with the most perfect confidence, that I never used the words, or any words which would bear the import of the extract to which I have alluded. I am confident of it because I never entertained such a sentiment in my life. I never conceived a contingency in which I would favor or countenance reducing white men to slavery. To such an imputation I may oppose the tenor of a whole life, during which my humble exertions have been constantly directed to the preservation of liberty at home and the encouragement of its establishment in foreign countries. If I have not been able to extend these exertions to the black race held in bondage in this country, it has been because of considerations and convictions, sincerely and honestly entertained, embracing the peace and happiness of both the white and black races, which have been often presented to the public.

It is quite possible that, in arguing upon the existence of the institution of slavery in this country, I may have contended that the black race supplied those domestic offices which, under the names of "help," "menial servants," and "domestics," are to be found in every state of civilized society, and consequently relieved the white race from the performance of those offices. If I have ever employed such an argument, (of which I have no recollection) it is apparent how erroneous inferences may have been drawn from it which it did not authorize.

I have no desire to disparage the industry of the wives of any of the certifiers to the extract, nor to boast of that in my own family; but I venture to say that no one of them performs more domestic industry with her own hands than my wife [Lucretia H. Clay] does at Ashland. . . .

Copy. Printed in Hodges, Todd, & Pruett, *The Campaign of 1844*, 92. 1. The certificate is printed in the Cincinnati *Enquirer and Message*, April 23, 1844. 2. The five congressman signing the certificate were: Samuel Simons (Conn.), Andrew Kennedy (Ind.), John P. Hale (N.H.), Moses G. Leonard (N.Y.), Thomas J. Henley (Ind.). 3. This appeared in the Washington *Daily National Intelligencer* on July 1, 1820. 4. The speech was given by Charles Rich of Vermont on Feb. 17, 1820, and was reported in *ibid.* 5. For the Missouri Compromise, see espec. 2:669-70, 742-45, 775-78, 785-86; 3:15-16, 18-22, 26-33, 46-47, 49-50; 8:786-88. 6. Probably his speech of Jan. 29, 1821. See 3:18-20.

From William Henry Russell, St. Louis, Mo., May 7, 1844. Reports that Dr. Frederick Gilmer has paid "the amount of your Exr against him [9:611-12, 731, 748]." Writes that he (Russell) has already sent a check for $300 to James Brown Clay and is now sending to Clay $135 plus "Mr [William] Porters statement." Notes that Porter, though "putatively a good whig," has violated "an understanding between us" by charging Clay "a fee."

States that "I am here & have been for the last week in attendance upon a great mass [Democratic] convention that come off on the 3rd Inst, and I really think that it was the most splendid affair that I ever witnessed *any where.*" Adds that "strangers who were here . . . thought that there were no Locos in the State; = That they had either been killed off by pestilence or had gone to Nauvoo with Jos[eph] Smith [9:384] or were now wending their way to Oregon—"

Mentions that in the last six weeks he has visited "many portions of our State and assisted in forming Clay clubs, making speeches . . . and no where did I meet with a sensible man who doubted our ability to carry Mo triumphantly [Clay to Kennedy, March 29, 1844] . . . and it matters not whether we run against their best and selected candidate or against one started in every State in the Union. . . . In the remotest counties in the Platte purchase the confidence of the Whigs is equally strong, where formerly they were incensed against you by the circulation of the vile slander that you considered them land pirates [squatters; 9:134-35]."

States that since he has been in St. Louis, "I have received very great and unwanted attention from a Colo [Joshua] Brant late of the army, a man of great wealth and influence; whose wife [Sarah] is a neice of Colo [Thomas Hart] Benton, and who has always been Bentons private organ here, and doubtless shares his unlimited confidence; = He actually imposed upon me the task of furnishing him a list of 15 of my best Whig friends that he might invite them to dine with me at his house which was done—Is it an overture of Bentons to join the Whig ranks, and if so must we take him and his friends, not as leaders, but as common soldiers, or is it best to continue with the Penn party to wage a war against him, which will so effectually use him up, that his hides will not hold shuks; = A hint communicated to me through my brother Tom [Russell] will determine my course—" ALS. DLC-HC (DNA, M212, R5).

The Mr. Porter whom Russell mentions is probably William Porter of Troy, Mo., named in a promissory note from Gilmer to Clay, dated November 9, 1841, which appears as a calendar item in volume 9. Porter has not been further identified.

The St. Louis County Democratic "mass convention" to which Russell refers was attended by only 48 Democrats who nominated candidates for the state house and senate. St. Louis *Morning Missouri Republican*, May 6, 1844.

For Benton's niece and her husband, see William N. Chambers, *Old Bullion Benton, Senator From the New West* (Boston, 1956), 228.

Shadrack Penn, editor of the St. Louis *Missouri Reporter*, was leader of the soft money faction of the Democrat party and a leading opponent of Thomas Hart Benton. The Whigs were allied with the Penn party against Benton and remained so in the 1844 election. Missouri Whigs fielded candidates only for the general assembly and local offices and supported the independent ticket of the soft money Democrats for other offices. If Benton did, indeed, seek an alliance with the Whigs, he was unable to effect it. John V. Mering, *The Whig Party in Missouri* (Columbia, Mo., 1967), 112-17.

To Unknown Recipient, May 7, 1844. Reports that "I am better to day, and free from pain, altho' the swelling in my face is not entirely gone down. I should have gone to see you and our other friends in your Mess but for the blustering character of the day." Adds that he hopes to have that pleasure tomorrow. Concludes: "You are an excellent physician, and I shall follow your prescription." ALS. DeHi.

From Robert Garrett & Sons, Baltimore, May 9, 1844. Report that Clay's 23 bales of hemp sold on April 17 for the net sum of $338.11 which, with interest to date of $1.24, totals $339.35. Note that the "rate was the highest procured for unhackled, during this Season." ALS. DLC-TJC (DNA, M212, R19). For Garrett, a well-known Baltimore shipper, banker, importer, and hotel owner, see George W. Howard, *The Monumental City, its Past History and Present Resources* (Baltimore, 1873), 124-29.

On May 10, 1844, Clay acknowledged receipt of their letter reporting the sale of his hemp, adding that "I hope to find on reaching home a quantity on hand if it has not been already forwarded which I will consign to your House." L, signature removed. DLC-Garrett Family Papers (DNA, M212, R21).

From JOHN SLOANE Columbus, Ohio, May 9, 1844

Permit me to congratulate you on the happy termination of the meeting at Baltimore;[1] as well [as] the wholesome condition of our affairs in all parts of the union. I have for some time been looking for our opponents to fall back on the slander of bargain and sale &c.[2] Foiled as they are, in every thing in the way of principles and measures, it was natural that they should place their reliance on that which required nothing but assertion.

Stale and discredited as that story is, I had rather hoped that our friends would have let them have the entire field to themselves, and in no case agree to assume the defensive. But the course of some of the whigs in Congress, has perhaps made it necessary to meet the enemy again on the same old field—[3]

In Ohio, I think this will be their only reliance: but I can see nothing indicating the least success from its use. I send you two papers[4] from which you will see how the matter is treated here. We have no whig paper of standing here; and hence, I chose to sign my name to the article I prepared in the case.[5]

The address of the Locofocos has nothing in the way of character to sustain it. Such of the signers as are not decidedly infamous on the score of veracity; are extremely insignificant: too much so to warrant any one in reviewing their production. Whether it will eventually require any notice, I am not yet decided.[6]

Were I refered to, by some one else, I could give information on the case perhaps more direct than any other person. It is this: about the time mentioned by [James] Buchanan; or perhaps some earlier, I met with Genl. [Sam] Houston at Mr Fletchers Boarding-house, and was accosted by him on the subject of the vote of Ohio. I told him there had been no general consultation among the members. He then observed, by g—d, what a most splendid administration it would make with "Old Hickory [Andrew Jackson] for President and Mr Clay Secretary of State." To this I assented. He then went on to address himself more earnestly to me, and said, "I feel a strong hope you will all vote for Hickory, and in that event, you know your man can get any thing he may want. To all this I replied in substance, that the vote [of] the Ohio delegation when given, I had no doubt would be satisfactory to the citizens of the State.[7]

This conversation was in my full recollection at the time I made my statement which was appended to your address;[8] and an allusion of a general nature was made to it. Why I did not specify the facts as they took place was, my knowledge of the relation which existed between Jackson, and Houston, and the great probability that the latter would not dare to do—other than deny the whole. This in the then temper of the public mind, I thought might do more harm than good. What I may ultimately do in that behalf, will depend on after developments[.]

Our friends in Ohio are in high spirits and our enemies depressed in a corresponding degree. Although their gazettes are as boastful as ever, in private conversation they hardly speak of a hope.[9]

ALS. DLC-HC (DNA, M212, R5). Printed in Colton, *Clay Correspondence*, 4:486-87. 1. See 9:754. 2. For the corrupt bargain charge relating to the presidential election of 1824-25, see indexes in 7:660, 719; 8:911; 9:934; see also 9:648-49, 659, 696-97, 709-10. 3. Democrat Linn Boyd had brought up the charge again in the House on April 30, 1844, and John White of Ky. had replied in Clay's defense. For the running debate, see *Cong. Globe*, 28 Cong., 1 Sess., 550-51, 566-68. During this encounter, Boyd proposed finding and publishing the Jan., 1825 correspondence between Clay and Francis P. Blair [4:9-11, 46-48], which allegedly proved that a bargain had been made. These letters were published during the 1844 campaign. See Clay to Leigh, July 3, 1844. 4. Not found, but see below. 5. On May 8, 1844, Sloane's signed letter, dated April 26, 1844, had been published in the Columbus *Weekly Ohio State Journal.* Sloane asserted that there was no proof that a bargain had been made between Clay and John Quincy Adams, but maintained that Andrew Jackson had attempted to make a deal with Clay, citing comments in the 1827 published addresses of James Buchanan [6:888] and Jackson [6:949] as evidence. 6. The Address of the Young Men's Democratic State Central Committee of Ohio, reasserting the corrupt bargain charge, was reprinted in the Cincinnati *Gazette* on May 10, 1844. It was signed by Charles B. Flood, Thomas J. Morgan, Jacob Medary, S.D. Preston, and Charles A. Loomis. 7. See 6:573 and George T. Curtis, *Life of James Buchanan*, 2 vols. (New York, 1883), 2:514. 8. See 6:573, 1394-96. 9. For the 1844 vote in Ohio, see Clay to Berrien, July 16, 1844.

To S.W. WHITING[1] Washington, May 9, 1844

I received the notes which you sent me through Mr. [Willie P.] Mangum, of my Speech at Raleigh,[2] which, with those previously given me there by Col. Gales,[3] were thought to furnish a full outline of the Speech. I desired very much to have been able to return from this City the Speech with such corrections as struck me to be necessary; but such have been the crowds of people constantly pouring in upon me, ever since I have been here, that I have found it to be utterly impossible to command the time requisite to that labor. The Conventions at Balto[4] gave rise to a large portion of the Company which has called on me; & as I declined going there, I did not think it right to lock myself up and refuse to receive them.

Today, for the first time, I looked into the notes, and to my great surprize and regret I found that some of the sheets are mis-paged; and this has created a confusion, and a necessity for greater care and labor on my part. I am now brought to the painful conclusion that I cannot, during the few days I shall remain here, complete the revisal in a manner satisfactory to myself or worthy of my North Carolina friends. I must take the notes home with me, & make the corrections there, where alone I shall be able to secure the requisite leisure, and transmit the Speech to Raleigh.

Personally I have no particular desire for the publication of the Speech, because there is nothing of great consequence in it that I had not before said, in some form or other or upon some occasion. But if my friends are at all anxious about its publication, I will certainly gratify their wishes.

Should it become necessary to account for the delay in its appearance, Col Gales (to whom I request you to present my respects) can say in his paper that it has been owing to Mr. Clays utter inability, from constant company and incessant engagements, to revise the notes. He may add that as soon as that can be done, and the Speech shall be received it will appear, unless you can dispense with the publication of it altogether.[5]

ALS. NcU. 1. Whiting is probably Seymour Webster Whiting (1816-55), a banker, writer, and treasurer of the Raleigh and Gaston Railroad. Grady L.E. Carroll, Sr., *They Lived in Raleigh* (Raleigh, 1977), 1:126. 2. Speech in Raleigh, April 13, 1844. 3. Weston R. Gales, owner of the Raleigh *Register and North Carolina Gazette*, was the brother of Joseph Gales, Jr., owner with William W. Seaton of the Washington *Daily National Intelligencer*. Joseph Gales, Sr., had founded both papers. Robert N. Elliott, *The Raleigh Register, 1799-1863* (Chapel Hill, 1955), 37, 57, 72, 74, 87-88. 4. For the Whig National convention, see 9:754 and Clay to Berrien, May 2, 1844. 5. The speech was printed in the Raleigh *Register* of June 28, 1844.

To John Thornly, Philadelphia, May 10, 1844. Thanks him for "the two pair of Indian rubber over shoes, one intended for my wife, and the other for myself." Adds: "You justly appreciate my feeling in supposing that I take a lively concern in the success of every branch of our American manufactures." LS. NjR.

To CLAY CLUB OF DAUPHIN COUNTY, PA. Washington, May 11, 1844

I received the letter which you did me the honor to address to me,[1] inviting me, prior to my return home, to visit the capitol of Pennsylvania. Subsequent to its date, I thought it right to announce to the public my determination to make no visits, nor attend any public meetings which might be deemed political, until the presidential election was decided. To that determination I shall adhere. It deprives me of the pleasure of accepting your friendly invitation.[2]

Gentlemen, I agree with you—"No state in this Union would be benefitted more by the permanent establishment of a sound whig policy than Pennsylvania." I have had the great satisfaction, always, to agree with Pennsylvania in regard to public measures, whenever the genuine feelings of Pennsylvania have been fairly expressed. There was not merely a cordial concurrence, but an intimate friendship, between her Findlay [*sic*], Smilie, Lacock, Roberts, Brown, and other distinguished sons, and me, in the congress which declared the last war.[3] I united also with the survivors of them, or other eminent citizens of that state, in laying the foundation of the national prosperity, after a return of peace. I have no recollection of any important public measure respecting what I have differed from Pennsylvania. I was perfectly aware that "the time was when the people of Pennsylvania were made to believe that you were not their friend." Acting under the maxim that honesty was the best policy, and upon the conviction that truth is omnipotent, and public justice certain, I bore the unmerited reproaches cast upon me, as became me. I have not been disappointed. I stand vindicated, in the hearts, and by the spontaneous acclamations of my fellow citizens. The industry and malignity of my enemies will no doubt prompt perseverance in these attacks. Perversions of my language, misrepresentations of my course, old scraps from tattered and obsolete newspapers—even fabrication and forgery are and will continue to be employed to vituperate and vilify me. But like all preceding assaults, they will be unavailable, and I shall remain invulnerable to them all.

In the meantime, I congratulate you on the bright and cheering prospects of the establishment of that whig policy so essential, I believe, not only to the prosperity of Pennsylvania, but to that of the whole union. I happened to be in the house of representatives when an important part of that policy signally triumphed. The tariff of 1842[4] has been bitterly denounced, and gross epithets applied to it. Its repeal was pronounced to be a favorite object of our political opponents. They have a majority of some fifty or sixty in the house. A bill to repeal that tariff has been pending a great part of the present session of congress.[5] And yet, yesterday, on a test vote, a majority of the house decided against the repealing bill, *leaving the tariff of* 1842 in FULL and SALUTARY OPERATION![6] This decision was an involuntary concession of our political oponents to the *wisdom and beneficence of whig policy*, produced by the returning prosperity of the country, and the enlightened opinion of the people.

But, gentlemen, I have a much higher gratification than any which could be derived from that decision of the house of representatives. It is that the people of the United States, from the St. Johns to the Sabine, who have been so long divided and agitated on the question of the *encouragement of domestic industry*, are about to settle down in *union* and *harmony*, upon the equitable basis of raising, in time of peace, the amount of revenue requisite to an economical administration of the government, *exclusively* from foreign imports, by a tariff so adjusted as that, by proper *discriminations*, just and reasonable *encourgement shall be extended to American industry.* May this happy union and harmony pervade all other great measures of public policy, and nothing occur to disturb the peace, to sully the character, or check the onward and glorious march of our country.

Copy. Printed in *Niles' Register* (June 8, 1844), 66:235. 1. The invitation, dated April 25, 1844, has not been found; however, in printing Clay's reply *Niles' Register* states that the letter mentioned Clay's strong support for the tariff and Pennsylvania's obligation to him for that position. 2. Clay to Editors of Washington *Daily National Intelligencer*, May 3, 1844. 3. For William Findley, John Smilie, Abner Lacock, Jonathan Roberts, and Robert Brown, see *BDAC*. 4. See 9:628. 5. Clay to Clayton, *ca.* Late August, 1844. 6. By a vote of 105 to 99, the House had voted to table the bill to modify and amend the Tariff Act of 1842. A motion to reconsider that action was defeated 103 to 99. U.S. H. of Reps., *Journal*, 28 Cong., 1 Sess., 900.

From THEODORE FRELINGHUYSEN New York, May 11, 1844

I have been rather, impatiently waiting for my lame arm,[1] to write a few lines to my honored friend,—that I might express to you the heartfelt gratification, that I feel at the recent association of my humble name with yours—a distinction as honorable as it has been to me surprising.[2] And should the results of the fall elections confirm the nomination, of which there now seems very strong indications, it will I assure you be among my richest political privileges, to contribute any mite of influence in my power, to render prosperous & lasting in benefits, the administration of a patriot, whose elevation I have long desired. Our names, have been brought together, here, by the voice of our fellow men. My prayer for you & my own soul, shall be fervent, that thro' the rich grace of our Savior, they may be found written in the Book of Life, of the Lamb, that was slain for our sins. My good wife [Charlotte Mercer Frelinghuysen], who has never ceased to cherish the hope of your eventual elevation to the chief magistracy, unites with me in kindest respects to Mrs. [Lucretia Hart] Clay & yourself.

P.S.—My hand is still lame & can write only, in irregular characters.

LS. DLC-HC (DNA, M212, R5). Printed in Colton, *Clay Correspondence*, 4:487-88. 1. Words "to enable me" have been stricken. 2. See 9:733, 753-54.

To Octavia Walton LeVert, Mobile, Ala., May 13, 1844. States that he is "greatly grieved by the illness of your dear little Claudia, and fervently hope that this letter will find her fully restored to health. Your fatigue in nursing her must have been very severe."

Adds that he is leaving Washington today and that he writes "amidst perpetual interruptions of friends calling to bid me farewell. Indeed, my dear friend, no language can adequately describe the scenes of excitement, of exertion, and of crowds through which I have passed since I left you. A thousand times have I wished & sighed for the quiet of my room at your house. Address me hereafter at Ashland, under cover to Garret[t] Davis at Paris (K). Adieu my ever dear friend. My best wishes to the Dr. [Henry LeVert] and to your mother [Sally M. Walker Walton], and affectionate kisses for me to your sweet girls." Copy. Printed in *Uncle Remus's The Home Magazine* (June, 1907), 18-19.

From Joseph Smith, Nauvoo, Ill., May 13, 1844. States that "Your answer to my inquiry, 'What would be your rule of action towards the Latter-Day Saints, should you be elected President of the United States?' has been under consideration since last November [9:881]." Believes that "So far as you have made public declarations, they have been made, like your answer to the above [9:890-91], soft to flatter, rather than solid to feed the people." Says Clay's answer of the previous fall "resembles a lottery vendor's sign with the goddess of Good-luck sitting on the car of fortune, astraddle of the horn of plenty, and driving the merry steeds of beatitude, without reins or bridle, that I cannot help exclaiming, O frail man! what have you done that will exalt you? Can anything be drawn from your *life, character*, or *conduct*, that is worthy of being held up to the gaze of this nation as a model of *virtue, charity, and wisdom*?"

Asks why as a U.S. senator Clay had not used all honorable means to restore the rights and property taken from the Mormons when they were exiled from Missouri. Asserts that "when the Missouri compromise was entered into by you [2:669-70, 740-48, 775-78, 785-86; 3:15-22, 26-29, 32-33, 46-47, 49-50], for the benefit of *slavery*, there was a mighty shrinkage of *western honour*; and from that day" Clay has been marked "as a *blackleg* in politics, begging for a chance to *shuffle* yourself into the presidential chair." Believes that in his attempt "to shoot at that chalk line of a [John] Randolph [5:208-9, 211-12]," Clay "disgraced his own fame, family, and friends." Attacks at great length Clay's stance on political issues such as the national bank, the tariff, and Texas annexation. In regard to the latter, states that "the 'annexation of Texas' has touched your pathetic sensibilities of national pride so acutely, that the poor Texians [*sic*], your own *brethren*, may fall back into the ferocity of Mexico, or be sold at auction to British stock-jobbers; and all is well, for 'I,' the old senator from Kentucky, am fearful it would militate against my interest in the north, to enlarge the borders of the Union in the south."

Contends that "when fifteen thousand free citizens . . . are robbed and driven from one State to another without redress or redemption, it is not only time for a candidate for the presidency to *pledge* himself to execute judgment and justice in righteousness . . . but it is his bounden duty . . . to call for a union of all honest men, and appease the wrath of God." Adds that "If words were not wind, and imagination not a vapour," Clay's expressed sympathy for their sufferings "might coax out a few Mormon votes; such 'sympathy' for their suffering under injustice, might heal some of the sick yet lingering amongst them; raise some of the dead, and recover some of their property, from Missouri; and finally, if thought was not a phantom, we might, in common with other religious communities, *'you think,' enjoy the security* and protection of the constitution and laws. But during ten years, while the Latter-Day Saints have bled, been robbed, driven from their own lands, paid oceans of money into the treasury to pay your renowned self and others for legislating and *dealing* out equal rights and privileges to those *in common with all other religious communities*, they have waited and expected in vain! . . . It is currently rumored that your dernier resort for the Latter-Day Saints is to emigrate to Oregon or California. Such cruel humanity, such noble injustice, such honourable cowardice, such foolish wisdom, and such vicious virtue, could only emanate from Clay." Copy. Printed in Henry Mayhew, *The Mormons: Or Latter-Day Saints* . . . , 3rd ed. (London, 1852), 138-43.

A Mormon state convention in Illinois met on May 17, 1844, and nominated Joseph Smith for president. This candidacy apparently was intended to influence the policies of the Liberty party. Smith, however, was shot and killed on June 27, 1844. Earlier in the year Smith himself had proposed moving the Mormons to the Oregon Territory or California. These plans were later enlarged to include Texas and most of the West. Fawn M. Brodie, *No man knows my history, The Life of Joseph Smith* (New York, 1971), 356-66; Joseph Smith, *History of the Church of Jesus Christ of Latter Day Saints*, 6 vols., (2nd rev. ed., Salt Lake City, 1948-51), 6:187-89, 214-17, 226-27, 255-61, 268-70, 275-77, 281-83, 367-76.

Speech in Washington, Pa., May 16, 1844. States, in part: "I rejoice . . . to find that the Old Keystone State is about to resume her proper place in the Federal Arch. I trust she will soon be where I found her during the last War [of 1812]. Her Delegation in Congress, every man, was compelled to vote to sustain the present Tariff. The voice of public opinion is omnipotent." Copy, excerpt. Printed in *Manufacturers and Farmers Journal and Providence and Pawtucket Advertiser*, May 23, 1844. For contemporary efforts to repeal or modify the Tariff of 1842, see Clay to Clayton, *ca.* Late August, 1844.

To JOHN SLOANE Lexington, May 21, 1844

I have duly received your friendly letter of the 9th. inst and share with you in gratification at the bright prospects of success, which our political cause presents. Indeed there can Scarcely be I think now a doubt that we shall truimph with more eclat than we did in 1840. I am very happy to inform you that from all the information which I derived during my late Southern tour and from what I have since received I am perfectly convinced that my opinion upon the Texas question[1] will do us no prejudice.

It is now quite manifest that our opponents intend to place their main reliance, in their attack upon me, on the revival of the old story of bargain &c.[2] With you I am inclined to think that it would have been better to take no notice of it, and I do not believe they will be able to make much out of it. I have been thinking of assuming the offensive instead of the defensive position and carrying the war into Africa. In other words, I have under consideration whether I will not charge upon [Andrew] Jackson and his friends the attempt to bargain and intrigue to secure his election in 1825. [James] Buchanan said in my own presence and in that of Gov. [Robert P.] Letcher the same thing in substance that [Sam] Houston said to you[.] With two such witnesses as you and Letcher I think the charge would be pretty well established.[3] I told Buchanan many years ago that I would prove what he had said but he begged hard, and I have hitherto forborne to do it. I do not know, until I see Letcher, whether he would be willing now to come out with a statement of what he knows. I will consider well the propriety of taking this step, before I make any publication, and should be glad if you would do so likewise. Perhaps it might not be amiss for you to consult with some of our discreet friends in Ohio, as to the expediency of the course and its probable effect in your State.[4] I shall be glad to hear from you after you and those whom you may consult shall have given to the subject such consideration as it may deserve.

LS. MH. 1. Clay to Editors of Washington *Daily National Intelligencer*, April 17, 1844. 2. For the corrupt bargain charge, see the following index references—7:660; 8:911; 9:934. 3. Sloane to Clay, May 9, 1844. 4. No such publication was made by Clay or Letcher, because Letcher opposed making a public statement on the matter. See correspondence between Letcher and Buchanan in John Bassett Moore, *The Works of James Buchanan*, 12 vols. (reprint ed., New York, 1960), 6:59, 63-64; Curtis, *Life of James Buchanan*, 2:512-13; Letcher to Clay, July 6, 1844.

From V.G. Audubon, New York, May 22, 1844. Sends nos. 95 to 100 "of the Birds of America" and asks for payment of $27 in full for the work. Adds: "I take the liberty of congratulating You on your Prospects for the Presidency, which all our family sincerely support & hope to see realized." ALS. DLC-TJC (DNA, M212, R10).

For Victor Gifford Audubon (1809-60), son of John James Audubon, see Alice

Ford, *John James Audubon* (Norman, Okla., 1964), 74, 135-39, 297-99, 404-5, 412, *passim*. See also 8:554.

To THEODORE FRELINGHUYSEN Lexington, May 22, 1844

I received, with very great pleasure, your friendly letter of the 11h. instant. I reciprocate most cordially all the kind feelings which it expresses. From considerations of delicacy and propriety, which *you* can well appreciate, I scrupulously forbore to intimate any preference which I might have, if I had any, among our friends, of a Whig Candidate for the V. Presidency. If the decision had depended on me, it would have been a painful office to discriminate between several gentlemen, of great merit and high abilities. Altho' I remained passive, I did not fail to remark the public manifestations, in various quarters, respecting different gentlemen held up to public view. Your nomination took me by surprize, but it was an agreeable surprize.[1] It has taken uncommonly well. No other nomination, I am sure, would have given more, if so much, general satisfaction. And I think that the ticket has derived strength from it. I feel honored by the association between us. And having co-operated with you, in the Legislative department, during a period of great excitement and trial,[2] it will afford me high satisfaction, if, by the blessing of providence, we shall be spared, and by the People shall be called upon, to unite our counsels together, in other spheres of the public service, to promote the happiness and prosperity of our Country.

I have received many letters requesting my opinion in regard to Foreigners and the Naturalization laws, to which I have as yet returned no answers. My silence has been mainly produced by a reluctance to throw new issues into the existing contest. Foreigners may be divided into three classes. 1st. Those who are already naturalized. 2. Those who are now in the U.S. but not yet naturalized and 3dly. Those who may hereafter arrive in the U.S. or may arrive after the passage of a new law of naturalization. My opinion is, that naturalized Citizens should enjoy all the privileges and protection, at home and abroad, of native Citizens, subject only to Constitutional exceptions; and that foreigners, now resident in the U. States, should be allowed to be naturalized as the laws now stand, without any change in their enactments. But that with respect to the class who may arrive subsequent to the passage of a new law, further restrictions upon naturalization ought to be imposed. What should be their precise character is matter of detail, on which I have not formed a definitive opinion.

I limit myself simply to the exposition of my views, without now offering the reasons which induce me to entertain them. If I express any opinion to the public it must be the above. But my object is to ask you, if you think it would be expedient to promulgate this opinion?[3] What effect would it have in N. York, N. Jersey or elsewhere? And if you think it proper I should be glad if you would confer with some other discreet friends, and let me know the result of your joint consideration of the matter. It is right to apprize you that I have this day addressed a similar request to Mr. [Millard] Fillmore now in N. York. I am happy to tell you that he acquiesces with entire cheerfulness in your nomination. . . .

ALS. NN. 1. See 9:733. 2. Probably a reference to the nullification controversy and cooperation on the Compromise Tariff of 1833. 3. Clay ultimately decided not to make a public statement on the naturalization law. See Clay to Davis, August 31, 1844; Clay to Webb, Oct. 25, 1844.

From William Fielding, Sidney, Shelby County, Ohio, May 29, 1844. Recalls sending a letter, dated January 17, 1829 [7:600-601], "In which I feebly attempted to portray the feelings of disappointment I felt at the political misfortune that befel[l] our Common Country, the Novr. previous." Rejoices that now everything has changed and "you . . . have been declared to be, the man, whom a grateful people, are determined *NOW* to honor." Exclaims: "Henry Clay!!! A name beyond the reach of eulogy: A name that calumny, detraction, and base ingratitude; have only served to brighten."

Writes to obtain permission "to read in our Clay Club, the confidential reply [not found] you made to my letter." Calls for God's blessing and direction "in all the high responsibilities that are to rest upon you." ALS. O.

Fielding is probably Dr. William Fielding of Sidney. See F.E. Scoby & B.L. McElroy, *Historical Collections of Ohio* . . . , 2 vols. (Cincinnati, 1907), 2:594.

To R.E. CONSTABLE Lexington, June 1, 1844

I received your favor and thank you for the friendly motives which prompted it.

I must refer you for my opinion on the question of completing the Cumberland road, through the states of Ohio, Indiana, and Illinois, to a speech I made at Indianapolis in the autumn of 1842.[1] It was published in the papers of that place and other papers; but I regret that I have no copy to send you.

The substance of what I said was, that an estimate ought to be made of the expense of finishing the road in the three states, to be stoned or gravelled where stone or gravel could conveniently be obtained at a reasonable expense; and where they could not be so procured, to be cleared, graded and bridged; and that appropriations from time to time should be made by the general government as the state of its finances would admit to complete the road; the money to be expended in each of the three states under the direction of the respective states.

Copy. Printed in *Niles' Register* (July 6, 1844), 66:291. 1. See 9:782-85.

To JOHN P. JACKSON[1] Lexington, June 4, 1844

I received your letter of the 28th ultimo and am very happy to learn that the Whig nominations at Baltimore[2] have been received with so much enthusiasm in New Jersey. Whilst I share in the common regret, amongst the Whigs, that so many good and true men, who had high and just pretensions for the office of Vice President, were necessarily put aside, nothing could be more agreeable and gratifying to me than the association of Mr [Theodore] Frelinghuysen's name with my own.[3] I have long and intimately known that gentleman; and no man stands higher in my estimation, as a pure, upright and patriotic citizen. I served with him, with great pleasure, in the Senate of the United States, and shall never forget the memorable session of 1833-34. He always seemed self poised and bore himself uniformly with great ability and dignity. There was a vein of benignity and piety, running through all his conduct and speeches, which it was refreshing and delightful to contemplate.

Such, my dear sir, is briefly, my opinion of this most worthy, and excellent man. But I cannot forbear expressing to you that I doubt the propriety of any publication of it. Considering the present attitude, in which we both stand, before the American People, my motives in speaking as I have done of my associate might be misconceived or misrepresented.

LS. NjR. Addressed to Jackson in Newark, N.J. 1. Jackson (1805-61) was a lawyer who had served as speaker of the New Jersey general assembly and was in 1844 clerk of Essex County. William H. Shaw, *History of Essex and Hudson Counties, New Jersey,* 2 vols. (Philadelphia, 1884), 1:261-62. 2. See 9:753-54; Clay to Berrien *et al.*, May 2, 1844. 3. See 9:733.

To WILLIAM FIELDING Lexington, June 5, 1844

I have received your favor,[1] and offer you my thanks for the warm and friendly feelings of attachment and confidence towards me which it expresses.

Referring to any answer from me, in reply to a letter I received from you in January 1829,[2] you request permission to read it before a Club of which you are a member. I have preserved no copy of it, and retain no recollection of its contents, but if it relate altogether to public affairs, I can have no objection to the use you desire to make of it.

Reciprocating all your friendly wishes, and especially that you may be under the constant protection of Divine Providence, . . .

ALS. O. 1. Fielding to Clay, May 29, 1844. 2. See 7:600-601.

To Donald MacLeod, Nashville, Tenn., June 5, 1844. Thanks him for sending a copy of the proceedings of the Whig meeting of ratification held in Nashville on May 11 and "communicating the congratulations of the Clay club of Davidson county upon my unanimous nomination, as the Whig candidate for President, by the Baltimore Convention."

Notes that "You also kindly convey to me assurances of the determination of the Whigs of Davidson county and the State of Tennessee to use their most zealous and devoted exertions to give effect to the Whig nominations at Baltimore [Clay to Berrien, July 16, 1844]. I regard these assurances as equivalent to success in Tennessee, where the political campaign of 1843 was conducted, by the Press, in public discussions before assemblies of the people, and in every other suitable form with a degree of zeal, energy, and ability, which, if ever equaled, have never been surpassed in the United States [9:817-18]. In the campaign of this year, besides their own firm resolves and patriotic determinations, the Whigs of Tennessee will have the satisfaction to know that every where, throughout the Union, there will be a hearty cooperation in their efforts." Copy. Printed in Jonesborough (Tenn.) *Whig, and Independent Journal,* June 26, 1844.

Donald MacLeod was editor of the Nashville *Republican Banner* from the summer of 1843 until March 24, 1845. Will T. Hale, *A History of Tennessee and Tennesseans*, 7 vols. (New York, 1913), 2:512.

The Whigs of Nashville and Davidson County had met on May 11, 1844, to ratify the nominations of the National Whig convention. MacLeod played a major role, praising the selection of Clay and Frelinghuysen and introducing resolutions supporting a tariff for revenue and protection, a sound currency, distribution of the proceeds from the sale of public lands, and restriction of the president's veto power. Nashville *Republican Banner*, May 13, 1844.

From Unknown Woman, Philadelphia, June 6, 1844. Sends from the ladies of Philadelphia a quilt, "Fashioned by their heads and wrought by their hands." Notes that it "has not been spoiled by a multiplicity of counsellors for although nearly one hundred ladies have participated in it, it has come out fair and square, showing once more what may be accomplished when there is an unanimity of feeling." States that they tender this gift "not to propitiate your favor in any way, but to intimate to you that we have appreciated your conduct in the many harassing affairs in which you have taken an active part—that your judgment we respect, and thinking that one who has so striven for the good of his country deserves our love, has led us to take this silent way of showing our affection." Says they believe "that when elected to that office which the voice of the people destines for you . . . our government may regain that high tone of honor which was infused into it by those who first filled the presidential chair." Adds that "we have endeavored, in making this quilt, to have it so soft and light that you should not know it rested upon you save by the comfort it gave, and a wish that through many a long cold night, when testing the advantage of it, it may bring to your kindly remembrance your well wishers, those ladies of Philadelphia, whose representative I have the honor to be." Copy. Printed in Philadelphia *United States Gazette*, July 13, 1844.

Clay replied to the representative of the Philadelphia ladies on June 20, 1844, thanking the ladies for the quilt which "is remarkably light and soft, and exquisitely beautiful." Adds: "But, my dear Miss, much as I prize this elegant and tasteful production, I appreciate infinitely higher the sentiments of confidence, attachment, and affection with which I am honored by the ladies who offered it to my acceptance." Notes also that "I owe it to your whole sex to acknowledge, that their approval of the Whig cause has strengthened my confidence in its goodness, and cheered and encouraged me in exertions to establish its principles."

Referring to their belief that he is destined to become president, states: "I should be most happy, in the event which you have supposed, if I could be an humble instrument in the hands of Providence to accomplish the patriotic objects which you have specified. All that I dare promise is, that if my life should be spared, and I should be placed in the high and responsible station to which you allude, my constant and earnest endeavors shall be employed to attain those objects." *Ibid.*

This quilt, made of satin and velvet with embroidered flowers, was displayed for a time in the store of Cochran, Christy & Co. in Philadelphia. Lexington *Observer & Kentucky Reporter*, June 19, 1844.

To WILLIE P. MANGUM Lexington, June 7, 1844

I take the liberty of troubling you herewith, with a package containing my speech, delivered at Raleigh in April last.[1] You will oblige me very much if you will have it put under another cover if necessary, give it your frank and transmit it to its address without delay.

Are our Democratic friends serious in the nominations which they have made at Baltimore of candidates for President and Vice President?[2] I have supposed that their object was to get rid of the Conventions, and ultimately to get rid of Mr [James K.] Polk, and bring out Mr [Martin] Van Buren; or retaining Mr Polk, as the candidate for the South West, to bring Mr Van Buren out, in some form, as the candidate for the North. In that way they might calculate to be able to throw upon Mr Polk all the Democratic votes for Texas, and upon Mr Van Buren all the Democratic votes against Texas. But nous verrons. It is of very little consequence to us what their real designs may be; for no matter how many candidates or who they bring out, we must beat them with ease if we do one half of our duty.

LS. NcU. 1. Speech in Raleigh, April 13, 1844. 2. See 9:752.

To JOHN P. KENNEDY Lexington, June 10, 1844

I received your Defense of the Whigs[1] and thank you for it. I have read it with uncommon satisfaction. I regret that the pleasure of perusing it had been so long delayed. It is composed with great ability, and if extensively circulated, as it ought to be and I hope will be, it is destined to have powerful effect. A cheap edition ought to be struck off, and it should be in the hands of and studied by all the Clubs.[2] I hope this will be done. I remember an anecdote, which you might introduce into a new edition, as illustrative of the spirit by which that portion of the Federalists, who left us and joined the Jackson party, were actuated. Stopping at Washington in Penna. on my way to or from Congress, some years ago, I asked the late Thomas McGiffin Esq. of that place what had made James Ross of Pittsburg[h] a Jackson man?[3] Why, said he, Ross was here (Washn. Pa.) a few nights ago, and I asked him that very question. He was some what excited by liquor, and replied: that if [John Q.] Adams, [Henry] Clay or [William H.] Crawford were elected, the Republican Admons of [Thomas] Jefferson, [James] Madison and [James] Monroe would be continued, and there would be no chance for the Federalists; but that [Andrew] Jackson was a rash intemperate and violent man, and, if elected, would throw every thing into confusion, and the Federalists might again get into power! There was patriotism for you!

I am awaiting anxiously for an account of the closing scenes of the Session. The Democratic nominations could not have been better for our cause.[4] The only regret attending them is that persons more worthy of a contest with us had not been selected. Still it is a wise maxim, in politics as well as War, never to despise an enemy, and to prepare for battle as if he were the most formidable foe. . . .

ALS. MdBP. 1. See 9:894. 2. Kennedy's *Defense of the Whigs* came out in Feb., 1844 and was later published in an inexpensive bound pamphlet edition by Horace Greeley. Bohner, *John Pendleton Kennedy*, 152-53. See also 9:894. 3. For McGiffin, see 4:382; for Ross, see 3:757. 4. See 9:752.

From W.M. Kidd, June 13, 1844. Sends a memorandum of Mrs. Sarah Thompson, narrated by her on May 1, 1813, at age 64, giving the genealogy of Clay's mother, Elizabeth Hudson. The memorandum, witnessed by Charles Tait, reads: "My Paternal Grand Father was named John Hudson. He was an Englishman and lived and died in the County of Hanover State of Virginia. He married Elizabeth Harris and had the following children Viz: George, Christopher, John, William, Charles, David, Cuthbert and Thomas. There were also, I think, three daughters. My Father's name was Charles who settled in the County of Prince Edward. In the year 1776 being dissatisfied with the times, on account of the dispute then existing between the Mother Country and her colonies, he left home for the more Southern States, and never returned. It was said he died in the lower part of Georgia on his way to St. Augustine. About the year 1770, I visited my Grand Mother who lived about 7 miles from Hanover Town or Page's Ware House, as it was more commonly called. My Uncle George was then an Inspector of Tobacco at that Ware House. He had no Son, and only two daughters, viz: Elizabeth and Polly. The latter married a Mr. Watkins and the former a Mr. Clay. My Grand Father had only one brother, named Charles, of whose family I know nothing, except that a daughter of his named Sarah married Col. Richard Holland, of Prince Edward. My Great Uncle Charles was a merchant and said to be wealthy. My Grand Father died suddenly and intestate, by which means my uncle George being the oldest son, heired all the Land, and thereby became much wealthier than the rest of the family."

Kidd concludes: "Charles Hudson, the brother of your Grand Father is my Mother's Grand Father, making you and her Second Cousins." Copy. InHi.

To JOHN W. CLARK[1] Lexington, June 14, 1844

I received your favor with the number of the Southerner, containing the article addressed "Truth."[2] It is an able vindication of me from the charge of which it treats,[3] and I thank you for it. If you had chosen to pursue this subject further, you might have adverted to Gen. [Andrew] Jackson's endorsement of the charge of 1827, and his offer to name his witness to prove it; my demand of this witness; his bringing forward the honorable James Buchanan; Mr. Buchanan's total denial of what Gen. Jackson professed to believe he would prove;[4] and finally Carter Beverly [*sic*, Beverley] (of whom Gen. Jackson had made use as an organ to bring out the charge from him) having, not a great while before his death, addressed me a letter[5] expressing his disbelief of the charge, owned that he had wronged me, and stating his wish to repair the injury, &c.

It ought to be gratifying to my friends that my enemies are driven to this stale charge, disproved and refuted near twenty years ago, as their only attack on my public character. . . .

Copy. Printed in Louisville *Courier Journal*, August 11, 1884. 1. Clark (1797-1849) was proprietor of a literary and periodical agency in Jackson, Mississippi. William D. McCain, *The Story of Jackson, A History of the Capital of Mississippi*, 2 vols. (Jackson, Miss., 1953), 1:78. 2. Not found. 3. See corrupt bargain charge in indexes of 7:660; 8:911; 9:934. 4. For Buchanan's statement, see 6:887; see also Sloane to Clay, May 9 and June 20, 1844; Clay to Sloane, May 21, June 14, and June 28, 1844; Letcher to Clay, July 6, 1844. 5. See 9:648-49.

To JOHN SLOANE Lexington, June 14, 1844

I wrote you some days ago,[1] in answer to your favor,[2] respecting the conversation between you and President [Sam] Houston, in[3] relation to the Presidential election in 1825, but have not since heard from you. I have it still under advisement whether I shall not exhibit to the world the proofs of the intrigues of [Andrew] Jackson and his friends. In that case, I should rely mainly on your testimony & that of Govr. [Robert P.] Letcher. The latter has some scruples about testifying in consequence of his friendly relations with [James] Buchanan; but I believe that he may be finally prevailed on to testify.[4]

If I determine to take this course, would you prefer simply a reference to your name, or previously to furnish your testimony? If it be indifferent to you, I should prefer the latter.

ALS. MH. 1. Clay to Sloane, May 21, 1844. 2. Sloane to Clay, May 9, 1844. 3. The word "respect" is stricken. 4. Clay to Sloane, May 21, 1844.

To JOSEPH GALES & WILLIAM W. SEATON Lexington, June 15, 1844

I will thank you to publish the enclosed article "Mr. Clay and his revilers"[1] in the [Washington *Daily*] Nat. Intellr., with the two corrections of typographical errors which I have pointed out. Perhaps you may choose to add some thing of your own testimony. It might be expedient to draw public attention conspicuously to the fact that Mr. [James K.] Polk lent himself to the propogation of the old calumny last year.[2] Was that the cause of his selection? Or [Andrew] Jackson's motive for desiring it?

I congratulate you on the rejection of the Texas treaty.[3]

ALS. InU. Letter marked "(Confidential)." 1. The article from the Lexington *Observer & Kentucky Reporter* of June 15 was published in the Washington *Daily National Intelligencer* on June 22, 1844. It strongly defended Clay against both the corrupt bargain and gambling charges. 2. See 9:818-20. 3. Clay to Crittenden, Feb. 15, 1844.

To HENRY WHITE Lexington, June 15, 1844

I received and thank you for your friendly letter of the 5h. inst. I am rejoiced to hear that the merchants of Phila. are animated by such liberal and patriotic zeal. The honble G[arrett]. Davis may be relied on as a gentleman of perfect honor and probity.[1]

Whatever we may think of the nominations of our opponents,[2] it is always wisest, in politics as well as War, Never to despise an enemy but to go to work as if Napoleon or Wellington were in the field. If we act in that way, and according to that maxim, we shall drive our opponent out of the Union to find refuge in Texas.

I thank you for the list of the Mercantile houses which have manifested so much liberality; and shall be gratified to receive the further one you promise. I hope their patriotic endeavors will be rewarded by good, stable and honest administration of the Government.

I shall be most happy to serve you with the Planters of Louisiana, if I can. Should I meet any of them this summer, as is probable, I will mention your House in terms corresponding with my high opinion of it.

ALS. ViU. 1. Garrett Davis and Willis Green of Kentucky were actively involved in promoting Clay's candidacy at this time, especially through the distribution of campaign literature. See Clay to Green, *ca.* June 25, 1844, and August 24, 1844; also Clay to White, Sept. 19, 1844. 2. See 9:752.

To Octavia Walton LeVert, Mobile, Ala., n.d. [probably early summer, 1844]. Reports that he has received her last two letters, the first describing her illness and that of her daughters and the second telling of their restoration to health. Feels, nevertheless, "the deepest concern on account of the gloom and desolation which exist in Mobile, and especially in your quarter of it, by the departure of so many of the inhabitants. And then that dreadful scourge of the yellow fever! of which you tell me so many serious apprehensions are entertained. Ah! my dear friend, I pray you to take all possible care of yourself, and fly the moment the Destroyer appears. Tell the Doctor [Henry LeVert] that I hold him responsible for your life and safety. I am continually shocked and grieved by the death of friends, one after another, in constant succession. But the loss of such a friend as you are would be a blow from which I should hardly be able to recover. You tell me, indeed, that you scarcely expect ever to see me again. In that I trust you are mistaken. The kindness of Providence would not have permitted the formation of a friendship so pure and so ardent as ours, if we were never to meet again." Wonders if she will visit Dr. William N. Mercer next December at Laurel Hill, because "I cherish a faint hope that I may be able to go there and escape our rigorous winter one or two months."

Mentions that since his return from the South, he has "been unwell but not seriously." Also, "I find very little repose. Letters without end, and Company without cessation, and without any respect even to the Sabbath, keep me constantly occupied."

Continues: "You ask where my defense against the charge of Genl. [Andrew]

Jackson, growing out of Mr. [John Q.] Adams's election is to be obtained. It consisted 1st of my Address to my Constituents in March 1825 [4:143-66], which is contained in any of the collections of my Speeches. And 2dly of a pamphlet issued by me in 1827 [6:1394-96] with a large mass of documentary proof, and a Supplement published in 1828 [7:339], with additional proof. These are both in Niles's Register of those years; but a copy of the whole is about to be republished, and I will send you one." Believes the Whig cause is gaining strength and "that the victory will be more signal that it was in 1840."

In conclusion, implores her to take care of her health, because "Your loss would occasion me a similar affliction—the greatest that ever befel[l] me—which I experienced when my lamented daughter Anne [Brown Clay Erwin] was taken from me [8:808-9]." ALS. KyLoF.

In 1843 an outbreak of yellow fever in Mobile took 750 lives and apparently caused much anxiety about the possibility of a recurrence in 1844. Madame LeVert also suffered from fits of despondency, which may have contributed to her sense of "gloom and desolation." Information supplied by Caldwell Delaney, City of Mobile Museum Department.

To ANSON G. HENRY Lexington, June 17, 1844

I recd. your friendly letter. Subsequent to its date, you will probably have seen a letter from me to the Honble John White,[1] contradicting the story of my being willing to make slaves of white men. If it has not reached you, I have no doubt it will, as it has been extensively published at the Eastward. It was a poor tale, and demonstrates the desperate means to which our opponents resort. It ought to be gratifying to my friends that my enemies are put to such shifts in their assaults upon me.

I am rejoiced to hear of your flattering prospects in Illinois.[2] You will have heard that they have given you [James K.] Polk to combat, who is opposed to every interest and stands counter to every prejudice of Illinois. You certainly will not allow the State to go for him.[3]

ALS. I. Letter marked "(Private)." 1. Clay to White, May 6, 1844. 2. Clay to Kennedy, March 29, 1844. 3. *Ibid.*

To PETER SKEN SMITH Lexington, June 17, 1844

I received your favor, transmitting news papers containing an account of the great meeting of the American Republican party in Philada.[1] It was a powerful demonstration[.] At the bottom it has a right spirit; and, if conducted with discretion and prudence, it cannot fail ultimately to do good. But it is worthy of serious consideration whether it be expedient to throw any new issues into the Presidential canvass.

I have no recollection of having ever proposed in the H. of Representatives any amendment to the Naturalization laws. The case of Elliott [*sic*, Benjamin C. Elliot] at N[ew].O[rleans]. proves that there is something in the administration of the Law or in the Law itself or in both.[2]

ALS. DLC-HC (DNA, M212, R5). Letter marked "(Confidential)." 1. At the American Republican (or Native American) party meeting in Philadelphia on June 7, Smith had attacked the House Judiciary Committee for tabling the party's petition calling for a change in the naturalization laws. Michael Feldberg, *The Philadelphia Riots of 1844* (Westport, Conn., 1975), 135; Henry R. Mueller, *The Whig Party in Pennsylvania* (New York, 1922), 104-12. See also Ewing to Clay, June 23, 1844. 2. Judge Elliot of the city court of Lafayette, La., had been impeached and convicted of issuing illegal naturalization certificates. *Manufacturers and Farmer's Journal and Providence and Pawtucket Advertiser*, April 18, 22, 1844.

To HENRY M. BRACKENRIDGE Lexington, June 18, 1844

I recd. your friendly letter, and thank you for the information which it communicates. I shall read your revised Speech,[1] with pleasure, when it arrives.

My Southern Tour,[2] although some times very fatiguing, was full of gratification. It enabled me to perceive, in the Southern Atlantic States, the true cause of those complaints which have been directed against the Tariff. It is the inferiority of these exhausted Lands to those of the valley of the Mississippi.

Mrs. Levert, the Lady of Dr. [Henry] Levert at whose house I tarried in Mobile, is your old friend Octavia [Walton], and a most fascinating and talented lady she is. She is now the mother of three little daughters, and she continues to cultivate the Spanish and French which you taught her, to which she has added Italian.

I hope you will find it convenient to execute your desire to visit Kentucky this summer. I shall be most happy to see your here under my roof[.]

ALS. PPiU. 1. Probably Brackenridge's *Speech Delivered in Broadhurst's Grove on the Evening of the 6th October, 1843* (Pittsburgh, 1843), 17 pp. This speech concerned the tariff, public lands, and national bank. 2. Clay to Preston, Jan. 19, 1844.

To THOMAS EWING Lexington, June 19, 1844

I have received several letters from individuals, requesting my opinion as to the expediency of a modification of the naturalization laws. I have hitherto forborne to answer these letters from a reluctance unnecessarily to introduce any new issues into the presidential canvass: but I do not know but that a necessity will arise for giving publicity to my opinions.

Foreigners may be divided into three classes. First, those who have been naturalized; Secondly those who are residing in the United States, but not yet naturalized; and Thirdly those who might arrive in the United States after the passage of a new na[t]uralization law. My opinions are with respect to the first class, that they ought to be allowed to enjoy all the rights and privileges, secured to them by the constitution and laws of the country, including the elective franchize and eligibility to office. As to the second class, good faith requires that they should be allowed to be naturalized according to the provisions of the existing laws without any further restrictions. But as to the third class, I think, considerable additional restrictions ought to be imposed upon the process of naturalization. These may consist of a limitation of the power to naturalize, to particular tribunals, or the further extension of the probationary period or both together. The precise extent and nature of these restrictions is matter for legislative detail, and need not be more particularly specified. These are the opinions which I deliberately entertain, and which I must publicly express, if I publicly express any opinion. My object in writing to you is to request you to inform me, as early as may be convenient, whether the promulgation of these opinions will have any and what effect in the State of Ohio.[1] I learn that representations are industriously made in certain quarters that I am opposed to all foreigners, and that I am in favor of depriving those who have been naturalized of all their rights and privileges.

ALS. KyLoF. 1. Ewing to Clay, June 23, 1844.

From Archibald Hawkins, Baltimore, June 20, 1844. Reports that Mr. J.H. Green, "the reformed gambler," has given him a letter [not found] from Amos Kendall which he sends on to the "malignant author's generous Benefactor [Clay]" as "additional proof of the serpentine gratitude of the *magnanimous* Amos Kendall!" Adds that this is not the only letter which Green has received from Kendall, and that "At my request he has treated them with silent contempt." Continues: "During the last two weeks, the Locofoco *clique* of this city, at the instigation of Kendall, have sought in vain, to have an interview with Mr. G. at the office of a Notary who is one of the *clique*! They have approached him in various ways, but these good honest patriots . . . find that they cannot for their honest souls; nay, for the very life's blood of their ragged Democracy, make any other out of that reformed gambler but a gentleman and a *solid* Whig!"

Notes that "I need scarcely add that I am a whig when I inform you that I have named a son for HENRY CLAY, the honored living Orator, statesman & Patriot." ALS. DLC-HC (DNA, M212, R5). A postscript, dated October 22, 1844, states that by an oversight "this letter was not posted till today having remained in my desk undiscovered up to this morning."

Archibald Hawkins is listed in the 1842 and 1845 *Baltimore City Directories* as a teacher who lived at 58 E. Pratt Street. Information supplied by Donna Ellis, Maryland Historical Society.

Jonathan H. Green (1813-87), a Mississippi riverboat gambler, reformed in 1842 and began a lecture tour. See *CAB*.

From Stephen F. Miller, Tuscaloosa, Ala., June 20, 1844. Sends an editorial he has written in the Tuscaloosa *Monitor* of June 19, 1844, concerning "your Texas letter [Clay to Editors of Washington *Daily National Intelligencer*, April 17, 1844]." The editorial "intended to repel the construction given by Southern Democrats to a particular passage" in which Clay had used the term "Confederacy." Contends in the editorial that the term was used "in a special sense, and qualified by the 'integrity of the Union,' which did not apply to the people, as a mass. The Union can never be in danger except from disaffection or violence of some one or more of its members." Adds that "You readily understand the object of your opponents in impressing the people of the South with the belief that you were propitiating a certain influence at the North, by the terms 'a considerable and respectable portion of the Confederacy,' in reference to the annexation of Texas." Believes the charge is unjust, but warns that the annexation question [Clay to Crittenden, February 15, 1844] "is pushed here with great assiduity by the Democrats," because their nomination of a Tennessean for president [9:752] "and the circumstances under which it was made, afford them no other ground to rally upon." Comments that the tariff is now better understood in the South and "has lost its terrors with the people." Believes, however, that "Some very sound Whigs regret that in your Texas letter you did not leave a door open for annexation at a future time," but emphasizes that he has "maintained that you say not a word to preclude your support . . . when it can or shall be properly introduced."

Reports that many Democrats admit "that the Whigs would probably have obtained the vote of Alabama in a contest with Mr. [Martin] Van Buren, obnoxious as he was to them on account of his Texas letter [Clay to Crittenden, April 21, 1844]," but they now boast that "Polk and Texas will sweep the State [Clay to Kennedy, March 29, 1844]." Promises, nevertheless, that the "Whigs will use all fair and manly exertions to prevent it." Copy. Printed in Stephen F. Miller, *The Bench and Bar of Georgia* . . . , 2 vols. (Philadelphia, 1858), 2:386-87.

Stephen F. Miller (1805-67) was a lawyer who edited the Tuscaloosa *Monitor* from 1840 to 1847 and then helped edit *DeBow's Review*. *NCAB*, 9:263.

From John Sloane, Wooster, Ohio, June 20, 1844. Has received Clay's letter of June 14. Notes that he has decided to make his statement tomorrow on the subject of the presidential election by the House of Representatives in 1825. Continues: "I see by the newspapers from various parts that the subject is being agitated and, in Ohio, the Locofoco candidate for governor is hurling from the stump. Why Gov [Robert P.] Letcher should feel any delicacy about making a statement, out of any relation of amity between him and [James] Buchanan, I am at a loss to imagine. Mr B, by his equivocation, & want of directness in his answer to [Andrew] Jacksons appeal, put himself beyond all claim upon the forbearance of any one. . . . the cautious manner in which he spoke of Jackson, left it beyond dispute, that it was his object that his statement should not be so understood, as to do justice between the parties." Adds that "When my statement reaches you, and you have that of Gov Letcher, you can determine how you will dispose of them. I always intended to make the facts known to you, if for no other purpose, that it might go into the history of the case after we have gone hence." ALS. DLC-HC (DNA, M212, R5). Printed in Colton, *Clay Correspondence*, 4:488-90. See also Sloane to Clay, May 9, 1844, and Clay to Sloane, May 21 and June 14, 1844.

To Philip B. Hockaday *et al.*, June 21, 1844. Declines an invitation to attend a mass meeting of the Whigs of Missouri, to be held in Lexington, Mo., in July. Does not feel he can attend with propriety any political meetings during the presidential canvass. Acknowledges the strong inducements for visiting which they list: "old friends and neighbors, the largest body of good land in all the Mississippi valley, producing 1,000 lbs. of hemp to the acre, a rapid growth in population, wealth, and improvements, and, although last, not least a radical and extensive revolution, going on in politics." Adds: "I would know that you are Kentuckians from the complacency with which you speak of all these fine things." Rejoices "in the prospects of the deliverance of the state of Missouri from the yoke of locofocoism of which I receive a flattering account from all quarters. Next to Virginia, which gave me birth, and to Kentucky, which adopted and cherished me, there is no state in the Union which I would feel more gratified with the support of than Missouri. I have ever entertained a kind of parental feeling towards that state. Among the arduous struggles which I have had in public life, that was incomparably the greatest in which I ever participated, for the admission of Missouri into the Union [2:669-70, 740-48, 775-77, 785-86; 3:15-22, 26-33, 46-47, 49-50; 8:786-88].—I claim nothing, I am entitled to nothing, on that account. I merely did my duty. Missouri honored me with her first love. In reviewing the past, I am unconscious of ever having done any thing justly to forfeit her esteem and confidence. Being now in the evening of a long life, it would be a great satisfaction to me, before I terminate my mortal career once more to meet Missouri on terms of friendship and affection [Clay to Kennedy, March 29, 1844]."

Expounds "on the bright and cheering prospects of the whig cause throughout the whole Union," adding that "The whigs know that the maxim 'never despise an enemy' is as wise and sound in politics as it is in war and they mean to combat as if Napoleon or Wellington, instead of Col. [James K.] Polk, were in the field." Copy. Printed in *Niles' Register* (August 17, 1844), 66:402.

Hockaday, an attorney, lived in Boone County, Mo., then moved to Montgomery County, Mo., where he died. William Bryan, *A History of the Pioneer Families of Missouri* (St. Louis, 1876), 340. Hockaday had also lived in Kentucky. See 8:607.

Missouri honored Clay "with her first love" by casting its 3 electoral votes for him in 1824, the first presidential election after its admission to statehood. McKee, *National . . . Popular and Electoral Vote*, 21-22.

From Thomas Ewing, Lancaster, Ohio, June 23, 1844. Agrees with the views on naturalization expressed in Clay's letter of June 19, but "would regret extremely the necessity" of injecting it into the presidential campaign. Believes if no new issue is brought up, the Whigs are "certain of success," but that a new issue could cause defeat. Says for this reason he was "troubled at the nomination of Mr [Theodore] Frelinghuysen—It brought into the canvass a new element." Notes that the question of modifying the naturalization laws has been raised by the native American organizations in New York and Philadelphia and is due "especially to the riots, burning, & Massacre in the latter City—You conscientiously think the law ought to [be] *changed*, to the disadvantage of Foreigners, seeking naturalization—and I entirely concur with you—but the expression of this opinion if made now, is brought out by reason of those burnings & massacres & will be seized upon by our adversaries . . . as an approval of, or a concession to the savage & intolerant spirit by which they were dictated." Believes that the charge that Clay is hostile to naturalized citizens can be countered with opinions he has already expressed, but fears an additional statement will cost him the support of Catholic friends "who are goaded almost to madness by what they consider a concerted attack upon their religious liberty & their political rights—" Furthermore, thinks that friends will agree to the propriety of saying nothing at the moment, while "*enemies* . . . are entitled to no answer." Adds, however, "whatever you find necessary to do in the matter, we will make the best we can of it—" ALS. KyLoF.

In the spring of 1844 the American Republican (nativist) party in New York organized its forces against voting and office-holding by foreigners. In New York City their candidate, James Harper, won the mayoral election in April, and the party also won a majority of the seats for alderman and assistant alderman. Hoping to obtain additional votes for Clay in the November election, the Whigs agreed to a fusion ticket with the American Republicans. The Whigs were to support American Republican candidates for Congress and the state legislature, while the American Republicans were to vote for the Whig presidential and gubernatorial candidates. This coalition helped elect four American Republican congressmen, two state senators and thirteen assemblymen, but it could not carry the city for Clay. William Henry Seward and other upstate Whigs had correctly feared that the alliance with the American Republicans would weaken the Whigs in the state as well as in the nation [Seward to Clay, November 7, 1844]. Jabez D. Hammond, *The History of Political Parties in the State of New York* . . . , 3 vols. (Syracuse, 1842-53), 3:477-78, 481-82; Ira M. Leonard, "The Rise and Fall of the American Republican Party in New York City, 1843-1845," *New-York Historical Society Quarterly* (April, 1966), 50:151-92. See also Ray Allen Billington, *The Origins of Nativism in the United States, 1800-1844* (reprint ed., New York, 1974), 522-612.

Much the same opposition to political activity by aliens and recently naturalized citizens existed in Pennsylvania. Rioting between Protestants and Irish Catholics broke out in May of 1844 in the Philadelphia suburb of Kensington and at Southwark in July. Similar riots in New York City were narrowly averted. Nativists from both New York and Pennsylvania flooded Congress with petitions for a new naturalization law that would lengthen the time required for aliens to become citizens. Feldberg, *The Philadelphia Riots*.

Following the 1844 election, charges of voting fraud by illegally naturalized foreigners resulted in further demands for reform of the naturalization laws as well as immigration restriction. Ray Allen Billington, *The Protestant Crusade, 1800-1860* (New York, 1938), 193-211. John M. Berrien attempted to get a bill passed in the 28th Congress, 2nd Session to tighten up naturalization procedures. He collected evidence from all over the country to prove there had been fraud in the 1844 elections. Although he contended that he sought only safeguards in the naturalization process rather than substantial changes, his proposals failed. Royce C. McCrary, Jr., "John MacPherson Berrien of Georgia (1781-1856): A Political Biography," Ph.D. dissertation, University of Georgia, 1971, pp. 294-95. The Senate's investigation of the frauds were published in *Sen. Docs.*, 28 Cong., 2 Sess., no. 173, pp. 1-197. This report documented frauds in several states, including the crucial ones of New York, Pennsylvania, and Louisiana.

Frelinghuysen's nomination had injected a "new element" into the election, because he had been connected with evangelical organizations for so long that he was considered anti-Catholic. Billington, *Origins of Nativism*, 541.

To NICHOLAS DAVIS Lexington, June 24, 1844

I received your letter of the 15th inst., requesting my interposition in behalf of Mr Thos. D. Tatum, to obtain his discharge from confinement in the castle of Perote in Mexico.[1] It would afford me great satisfaction to be able to accomplish that object, but I am not sure that I can be of any service to him. I knew Gen. Santa Anna when he was in this country, and he paid me some very high compliments for the interest which I had taken in the independence of the Spanish American colonies. Subsequently, I animadverted, with a good deal of severity, in the Senate of the U. States,[2] on some expressions which Santa Anna had made use of, in a public document, reflecting indiscriminately upon the conduct of the people in the Valley of the Mississip[p]i. He felt a good deal hurt with my remarks, as our late Minister to Mexico[3] informed me by letter. I do not know whether he continues to entertain any feelings of resentment towards me. But, at all events, prompted by humanity, and your friendly application, I have addressed to him the enclosed letter, which Capt. Tatum had better forward either directly to its address or through some public organ of the U States in Mexico. My political relations with the gentleman lately appointed minister to Mexico[4] are not very friendly and I do not therefore feel at liberty to address him directly; but if my interposition is likely to be of any avail, I think the enclosed letter will be more probably successful than if the application were made through the minister.

I am much gratified with the political information communicated in your letter, and I congratulate you upon the bright prospects which surround our cause in every quarter. Of the triumphant success of the Whig cause by even a larger majority than was given in 1840, there cannot now be a doubt.

LS. DLC-HC (DNA, M212, R5). 1. Tatum had been a member of a Texas expedition led by Captain William S. Fisher when they were captured at Mier on Dec. 26, 1842. Tatum and four others were released from prison on August 25, 1844; all other prisoners on Sept. 16, 1844. Joseph M. Nance (ed.), *Mier Expedition Diary, A Texan Prisoner's Account* (Austin, Tex., 1978), 33-34, 143-44, 147-48, 194. 2. See 9:684. 3. Waddy Thompson. 4. Wilson Shannon. See Clay to Santa Anna, June 24, 1844; Santa Anna to Clay, August 23, 1844.

From W. Ogden Niles, Washington, D.C., June 24, 1844. Assures Clay that "The motive which induced the revival of the loathsome and infamous calumny about 'Bribery and Corruption' was perfectly understood here." Notes that "even the endorsement of *certain honorable members of the house*! failed to excite any other sensations than those of scorn at their baseness and laughter at their folly [Clay to White, May 6, 1844]." Feels "pained and mortified at the averments of your chief accuser's [Andrew Jackson] recent letter," because he always "felt satisfied that even he, when the softening influences of time, and charity which pleads most for justice to our fellow men . . . would have . . . induced him openly and frankly to have retracted the charge, at least to have confessed that he might have misunderstood the alleged negociator [Robert P. Letcher], and that there was nothing in your past life which afforded any ground for the impression that you were a party to the supposed overture; for, in preferring the charge against you, he admits that in supposing *you were privy to the* *proposition he may have done you injustice.* Animated by the spirit which I had hoped your accuser would have invoked in your behalf, I will not further comment upon that letter, than to say, that, in the face of the prompt denial of the party adduced as the principal witness, the recent disclaimer [9:648-49] of the propagator [Carter Beverley] of the story of the slightest belief in its truth and the common opinion of all honorable minds, it is one of the most extraordinary papers ever penned, and exhibits an intensity of hatred and adherence to exploded falsehood utterly revolting to all my opinions of common justice and common honesty; and will do more to lessen his fame than all the efforts of his friends to enhance it; for it will confirm the impression that he is not only distitute of an enlightened mind, but wants a magnanimous heart."

Has concluded that "it would not be displeasing to you, even at this late day, to have another witness of the baseness of the charge in the person of my late father [Hezekiah Niles]." Continues: "A short time after the election my father was in Washington, and attended the first levee, or party, given by the president elect [John Q. Adams] (and I believe he held levees every fortnight whilst Secretary of State) and there met General Jackson, who, after greeting him with much cordiality, took him by the arm, and, forcing his way thro' the crowd, led him to the passage, or hall, where he entered into a free discussion of all the matters connected with the election; and again and again expressed himself satisfied with the result; saying, among other things, that he was not fit for the presidential chair—that he could not get on—that his proper place was at the head of an army, &c, &c,. During that conversation not one word escaped him which betrayed the slightest suspicion that he had been unfairly dealt with, or that any improper influences had been exerted in the election. About the interview I cannot be mistaken, (and my father may have mentioned it to you) for I have heard him frequently describe it, and well remember his indignant manner and language in spurning the charge and all who are [*sic*, have] affected a belief in it. Indeed, the mode in which he repelled it converted General Jackson into his most relentless enemy."

Says he has provided "This incident in the chain of testimony," because "it is monstrous to suppose that, if General Jackson believed in the overture, he would have sanctioned the bargain by presenting himself at Mr. Adams' levee; and above all, have acknowledged to my father, your avowed partisan, that he was satisfied with the result, &c." Copy, typescript. InHi. For the corrupt bargain charge in previous volumes see the indexes in 7:660, 8:911, 9:934.

Jackson had written a letter on May 3, 1844, to the editors of the Nashville *Union*, denying that he had ever recanted on his charge of a corrupt bargain between Clay and Adams and strongly reasserting his belief in it. This letter was published in the Nashville *Union* on May 4 and in the Washington *Globe* on May 18.

To SANTA ANNA Lexington, June 24, 1844

An application has been made to me, in behalf of Mr Thomas D. Tatum, a prisoner now in the Castle of Perote, formerly under the command of Col. [William S.] Fisher, and captured at Mier, to intercede with your Excellency for his discharge.[1] I am not acquainted personly with the young man, but I have received favorable accounts of him; and [ve]ry strong and interesting [reco]mmendations have been made to me of the high respectability and great worth of his father, Capt Tatum of the state of Alabama[.]

I am sensible of the informality of this appeal to your Excellency, which regularly ought to pass through the Minister of the U States at Mexico;[2] but in cases which affect our humane feelings, I am sure your Excellency will readily excuse any departure from established forms. I might, by way of apology, also add that I believe the newly appointed American Minister has not repaired yet to his official post.

I am wholy unacquainted with the particular circumstances attending the case of young Tatum, I suppose, like many other young men, impelled by a romantic passion for adventure and War, he indiscreetly engaged in an expedition, in which there was judgement displayed neither in the plan nor the execution.

Should your Excellency be able to reconcile the exercise of clemency with those considerations of policy which, as the head of the republic, you may feel bound to respect, and liberate this unfortunate young man, you will gladden the heart of his venerable and excellent father, and greatly oblige one who, with high considerations, subscribes himself resp[e]ctfully . . . [3]

Copy, manuscript torn. DLC-HC (DNA, M212, R5). 1. Clay to Davis, June 24, 1844. 2. Waddy Thompson had resigned as U.S. minister to Mexico and Tyler had appointed former Ohio governor Wilson Shannon, a Democrat, to that post. Shannon did not arrive in Mexico City until August 26, 1844. Nance, *Mier Expedition Diary*, 144. 3. Santa Anna to Clay, August 23, 1844.

To WILLIS GREEN *ca.* June 25, 1844[1]

. . . I should think that the circulation of documents proving the beneficial operation of the Tariff, and the opposition to it of Col. [James K.] Polk and our opponents, would be beneficial.[2] And also documents relating to the Texas Treaty,[3] especially at the North. I h[ave no]t seen Mr. [James T.] Morehead's retrenchment Tariff,[4] but I have heard it well spoken of.

I wish you would request, *on your own account*, the publication of the enclosed article[5] in the Richmond Whig, and have it extensively republished in other papers. You[6] comprehend the draft of it. The facts and[7] which it contains may be relied on. I suppose the [Washington *Daily National*] Intellr. will publish it.

[John J.] Crittenden passed through Lexn. friday night but I have not yet seen him.

I have been unwell, since my return home, but feel now much better.

I should be glad to be advised of the movements of the Executive. Will [John] Tyler retire?[8] Send me occasionally the Madisonian. How long will you remain in the City?

ALS. KyLoF. 1. Date and half of first page is missing; however, the letter is postmarked June 25. 2. On July 13, 1844, the Lexington *Observer & Kentucky Reporter* printed an article dealing with Polk's opposition to the Tariff of 1842. The article also contained statistics showing that custom house receipts for 1844 were triple those of the same period of 1843. 3. For Texas annexation, see Clay to Crittenden, Feb. 15, 1844. The documents referred to may be those which accompanied the treaty. See *Sen. Docs.*, 28 Cong., 1 Sess., no. 341. 4. James T. Morehead had made a report in the Senate on June 15 in regard to retrenchment and reform of the tariff, but he did not yet have a bill prepared. He did not report such a bill in either the 28th Congress, 2nd Session or the 29th Congress. *Cong. Globe*, 28 Cong., 1 Sess., 688. 5. Enclosure not found. 6. Manuscript torn; several words missing. 7. *Ibid.* 8. Clay to Green, August 24, 1844.

To UNKNOWN RECIPIENT Frankfort, Ky., June 26, 1844

No public event, which has happened for a long time, has given me such deep concern as the recent division, and the cause of the division of the Methodist Episcopal Church of the U. States, both on account of the welfare and prosperity of the Church itself, and the danger with which the example is fraught.[1]

ANS. Courtesy of Mrs. W.A. Hifner, Lexington, Ky. 1. Northern and Southern factions of the Methodist Episcopal Church split, primarily over the issue of slavery, during the 1844 General Conference which met in New York City from May 1 to June 11. Emory S. Bucke (ed.), *The History of American Methodism*, 3 vols. (New York, 1964), 2:11-85.

To JOHN SLOANE Lexington, June 28, 1844

I recd. your favors, including the Statement,[1] and thank you for them. I shall be glad to receive also your opinion promised from Cincinnati as to the expediency of the publication. My own inclines to it. [Robert P.] Letcher & [John J.] Crittenden I believe doubt. I shall at all events prepare a publication whether it be made or not. My principal objection to it is the abuse which I apprehend you might be exposed to. [Sam] Houston may deny your statement. Why was it not before made? &c. will be urged. Is it not probable that Judge [John C.] Wright[2] had a similar conversation with Houston?

I should be very glad if you could come over and see me. Why can't you? There is to be a great Convention at Lexn. on the 3d[3] & one day from Cincinnati would put you down at Lexn.

ALS. MH. 1. Statement not found, but see Sloane to Clay, May 9 and June 20, 1844, and Clay to Sloane, May 21 and June 14, 1844. 2. For Wright, see 2:874. 3. A mass meeting of the Whigs of Kentucky was called in compliance with a recommendation by the National Whig convention held in Baltimore. Thomas Metcalfe was elected president of the meeting. Those attending adopted nine resolutions, including one which approved of the nomination of Clay and Theodore Frelinghuysen, one which criticized President Tyler's Texas annexation treaty, and one which rejected a proposition for a convention of "*the Slave States*" to secure Texas. Lexington *Observer & Kentucky Reporter*, July 6, 1844.

To FRED J. COPE Lexington, Ky. June 29, 1844

I have received your favor, stating that our political opponents represent me as being a friend to protection at the North, and for free trade in the South; and you desire an expression of my opinion under my own hand, for the purpose of correcting this misrepresentation. I am afraid that you will find the effort vain to correct misrepresentations of me. Those who choose to understand my opinions can have no difficulty in clearly comprehending them. I have repeatedly expressed them as late as this spring, and several times in answer to letters from Pennsylvania.[1] My opinions, such as they are, have been recently quite as freely expressed at the South as I ever uttered them at the North. I have everywhere maintained that in adjusting a Tariff for revenue, discrimination ought to be made for protection; that the Tariff of 1842[2] has operated most beneficially, and that I AM UTTERLY OPPOSED TO ITS REPEAL. These opinions were announced by me at public meetings in Alabama, Georgia, Charleston in South Carolina, and in Virginia.[3]

Copy. Printed in Hodges, Todd, & Pruett, *The Campaign of 1844*, 196. Addressed to Cope in Pittsburgh, Pa. 1. For example Clay to Committee of the Whigs of Pennsylvania, Feb. 10, 1844; Clay to National Clay Club, Philadelphia, March 17, 1844; Clay to Clay Club of Dauphin County, Pa., May 11, 1844. 2. See 9:628, 646. 3. Speech to Committee of Tuscaloosa Whigs, late Feb. or early March, 1844; Speech in Milledgeville, Ga., March 19, 1844; Speech in Savannah, Ga., March 22, 1844; Speech in Charleston, S.C., April 6, 1844; Speech in Petersburg, Va., April 19, 1844.

To STEPHEN MILLER Lexington, July 1, 1844

I received and thank you for your friendly letter,[1] and the copy of the [Tuscaloosa] Monitor. You have justly conceived my meaning, when I referred in my 'Texas letter'[2] to a considerable and respectable portion of the *Confederacy.* And you might have strengthened your construction of the paragraph, by reference to the fact that, at the date of my letter, the States of Ohio, Vermont and Massachusetts had, almost unanimously, declared against annexation;[3] the Legislature of Georgia had declined to recommend it, and other States were believed to be adverse to the measure. As to the idea of my courting the Abolitionists it is perfectly absurd. No man in the United States has been half as much abused by them as I have been.

I consider the Union a great political partnership; and that new members ought not to be admitted into the concern at the imminent hazard of its dissolution. Personally, I could have no objection to the annexation of Texas; but I certainly would be unwilling to see the existing Union dissolved or seriously jeoparded for the sake of acquiring Texas. If any one desires to know the leading and paramount object of my public life, the preservation of this Union will furnish him the key.

From developments now being made in South Carolina, it is perfectly manifest that a party exists in that State seeking a dissolution of the Union[4] and for that purpose employing the pretext of the rejection of Mr. [John] Tyler's abominable treaty.[5] South Carolina, being surrounded by slave States, would, in the event of a dissolution of the Union, suffer only comparative evils; but it is otherwise with Kentucky. She has the boundary of the Ohio extending five hundred miles on three free States.—What would her condition be in the event of the greatest calamity that could befal this Nation?

In Kentucky, the Texas question will do the Whig cause no prejudice. I am glad to perceive, in the proceedings of the Clay Club of Tuscaloosa, a similar belief expressed as to Alabama.[6] It was a bubble, blown up by Mr. Tyler in the most exceptionable manner, for sinister purposes, and its bursting has injured no body but Mr. [Martin] Van Buren.

Retaining an agreeable recollection of the pleasure which I derived from forming your acquaintance last spring. . . .

Copy. Printed in Hodges, Todd, & Pruett, *The Campaign of 1844*, 165, and Colton, *Clay Correspondence*, 4:490-91. This document is referred to as Clay's "first Alabama letter." 1. Miller to Clay, June 20, 1844. 2. Clay to Editors of Washington *Daily National Intelligencer*, April 17, 1844. 3. In 1838 both houses of the Ohio legislature adopted resolutions against the annexation of Texas. Also resolutions from citizens of Ohio opposing annexation were presented to the U.S. House and Senate in 1843 and 1844. Francis P. Weisenburger, *The Passing of the Frontier, 1825-1850*, in Carl Wittke (ed.), *The History of the State of Ohio*, 6 vols. (Columbus, Ohio, 1941-44), 3:433; U.S.H. of Reps., *Journal*, 28 Cong., 1 Sess., 87-88, 104, 240, 274, 276, 426, 879, 1096, 1164; U.S. Sen., *Journal*, 28 Cong., 1 Sess., 193, 206, 210-11, 220, 224, 233, 241, 245, 252, 255, 275, 280, 289, 337. In Dec., 1843 the Massachusetts legislature passed a joint resolution asking its senators and representatives to vote against Texas annexation. This resolution was introduced in the U.S. Senate on March 6, 1844, and tabled; it was brought up again on March 25 and referred to the Committee on Foreign Relations. Samuel F. Bemis, *John Quincy Adams and the Union* (New York, 1956), 463; *Cong. Globe*, 28 Cong., 1 Sess., 346, 428. A similar resolution from the Vermont legislature was introduced in the Senate on March 6, 1844. *Cong. Globe*, 28 Cong., 1 Sess., 346. 4. As early as March, 1844, Robert Barnwell Rhett of South Carolina had called for "Texas or disunion." Although Calhoun tried to modify this position somewhat, it built into the so-called "Bluffton Movement," a radical cry for annexation of Texas and repeal of the Tariff of 1842. Wiltse, *John C. Calhoun: Sectionalist*, 187-98; Laura A. White, *Robert Barnwell Rhett: Father of Secession* (New York, 1931), 68-84. 5. Clay to Crittenden. Feb. 15, 1844. 6. The Clay Club of Tuscaloosa met on June 13, 1844. The members approved resolutions to ask other Clay Clubs of the South if they had abandoned Clay because of his April 17 letter on Texas annexation; to assert that, although they favored annexation, "we are not Texas mad"; to oppose the free trade doctrine of Polk; and to declare that Clay would be elected president. Lexington *Observer & Kentucky Reporter*, July 17, 1844.

To BENJAMIN W. LEIGH Lexington, July 3, 1844

I have thought you might desire to see my famous letters to Mr. [Francis P.] Blair, and therefore send Copies.[1] The originals have not the blanks which these copies contain, and I really do not recollect the names that were in them. These copies are from copies certified by Blair. I have no objection to your shewing them to any person you please; but I do not wish them published without my previous consent. I gave permission, when the investigation was proceeding in the Legislature of K[entucky]. some seventeen or eighteen years ago,[2] to any gentleman to inspect them that pleased, and hundreds then or since have accordingly perused them. Is there any necessity for their publication? Ought I to yield to the call for them? Ought I to consent to the exhibition to the public of letters which are private and playful and[3] in terms of familiarity that render them unfit for the public eye?[4] I confess too that I am a little ashamed of ever having been on terms of such intimacy with so great a scoundrel as I now believe Blair to be.

I am now *considering* whether I shall not attack the Jackson party.[5] I have strong proof in my power or possession to prove that, at the epoch of 1824-5, they were the guilty party in tampering to secure [Andrew] Jackson's election. I have a strong inclination to carry the War into Africa. If I do not finally do so, it will be not from the want of proof but from considerations of policy. P S. Should I determine on offensive operations, I shall publish these letters, which, it is not true, that I ever *refused* to allow to be published. No such application was ever made to me[.]

ALS. ViU. Letter marked "(Private)." 1. Of Jan. 8 and Jan. 29, 1825. See 4:9-10, 46-48. 2. See 7:54, 74-76, 118, 121. 3. The word "which" has been stricken. 4. For the publication history of these letters, see 4:10. 5. Sloane to Clay, May 9, 1844.

To H. PETWAY[1] Lexington, July 3, 1844

I received your friendly letter, and thank you for the information which it contains, and for the sentiments of attachment and confidence which you have so long entertained for me, and to which you still kindly adhere. I hope your fears as to the influence which the Texas question[2] may exercise in Tennessee[3] will not be realized. It was a trap set by Mr. [John] Tyler but it has caught no body but Mr. [Martin] V[an]. Buren. Some of the Democrats have seized hold of it as a plank to save themselves upon, but it will not avail them. You will find, in the sequel, that an immense majority of the people of the U.S. are opposed to the Treaty.[4] And now that a party has sprung up in So. Carolina which announces the alternative Texas or a dissolution of the Union,[5] the eyes of every friend of the Union must be opened.

Whatever may be the result in a few States of the present contest, I do not entertain a doubt that in Novr. the Whigs will achieve a more signal and decisive victory than was won in 1840.[6]

ALS. THi. Addressed to Petway in Nashville, Tenn. 1. Petway is probably Hinchey Petways, a farmer from Davidson County, Tenn. Murpha T. Rudd, *1850 Census Tennessee* (Evanston, Ill., 1975), 112. 2. Clay to Crittenden, Feb. 15, 1844. 3. For the 1844 presidential election in Tennessee, see Clay to Berrien, July 16, 1844. 4. Clay to Crittenden, Feb. 15, 1844. 5. Clay to Miller, July 1, 1844. 6. Clay to Webb, Feb. 29, 1844.

From Joshua R. Giddings, Jefferson, Ohio, July 6, 1844. In regard to the upcoming presidential election, reports that "Our people of all political parties regard the great question to be whether the nation shall assume upon itself the support of Slavery in the States? Whether the people of the free States shall be involved in the expense of its maintainance?" Says these questions "are pressed upon our attention in the official Correspondence accompanying the Texas treaty [Clay to Crittenden, February 15, 1844], and we regard them as importan[t] and even vital to our institutions." Notes that "From your Texas letter [Clay to Editors of Washington *Daily National Intelligencer*, April 17, 1844] and the analysis of whig doctrines given in your Speech at Raleigh [April 13, 1844] we regarded you as opposed to these propositions." Continues: "In the 9th article of the whig faith as given in your published remarks you state 'The maintainance *exclusively* by the several States of their own local and peculiar institutions.' to be a fundamental doctrine of the whig party. On the 4th Inst the [Washington *Daily*] National Intelligencer arrived with your Raleigh Speech as written out by yourself. In it we find no allusion to the above doctrine. This has led many to apprehend that we have mistaken your views on this all important point. Indeed the absence of all allusion to it in your Speech as written by yourself has created great apprehensions in the minds of many of your friends. I regard it as important that we should be informed on the subject [Clay to Giddings, July 19, 1844]. Indeed our people feel that they have the right to understand your sentiments in respect to this important question now pressed upon us by the opposite party." Asks that "you cause your views on this point to be made public in Such way as your judgement may dictate." Emphasizes the importance of this issue which "Can only be appreciated by those who understand the deep feeling which now pervades the minds of a portion of the people of all the free States against all participation in the support of the institution of slavery—If I have myself mistaken your views on this point I beg you will inform me at your earliest leisure." AL, draft. OHi. Letter marked "Confidential."

From WILLIAM LAWRENCE & J.E. WHARTON[1] Washington, Ohio, July 6, 1844

This day, in a political discussion in this place, upon the subject of the election of John Q. Adams President of the United States by the House of Representatives, in Congress, in February, 1825, and the appointment of yourself by Mr. Adams as Secretary of State immediately thereafter, the undersigned mutually agreed to address this note to you, and respectfully request of you a letter, authorizing the publication of a certain letter, claimed by your opponents to be in the possession of Francis P. Blair,[2] and which they also claim fully establishes, from your own hand, the validity of the charge of corruption, bargain, &c.,[3] which they have brought against you. We hope you will immediately authorize Mr. Blair to make public that or any other evidence in his possession relating to the matter.

You will please direct an answer to J.E. Wharton, of Wheeling, Virginia [West Virginia], and a copy of the same to William Lawrence, Washington, Guernsey county, Ohio.

Copy. Printed in *Kendall's Expositor* (August 14, 1844), 4:303. 1. At various times Lawrence was a judge and member of the Ohio house of representatives. F.E. Scobey & E.W. Doty, *The Biographical Annals of Ohio*, 3 vols. (Springfield, Ohio, 1902), 1:283; Emilius O. Randall, *History of Ohio . . .*, 5 vols. (New York, 1912), 5:144, 156-57. James E. Wharton was the Whig editor of the Wheeling *Times & Advertiser* in the 1840s and he later edited the Wheeling *Daily Gazette*. Charles A. Wingerter, *History of Greater Wheeling and Vicinity*, 2 vols. (Chicago, 1912), 1:473. 2. See 4:9-11, 46-48. 3. For the corrupt bargain charge, see index references 7:660; 8:911; 9:934.

From ROBERT P. LETCHER Frankfort, July 6, 1844

I send you, enclosed, a short *Love-letter*, which I reced. a day or two ago, from my old friend *Buch* [James Buchanan].[1] He writes like a man, as you will see, who feels the *force of his subject*. You can retain it, until I see you.

The more I have thought about your making a publication in regard to that miserable old calumny, the less inclined I am to think favorably of it.[2] Every thing appears to be progressing so smo[o]thly for the Whig cause, "better let it be."

Owing to the illness of my wife, I regret very much I could not witness the proceedings of the great Whig meeting in Lexington the 3d. Inst. I am very glad to hear it went off beautifully. Mrs L. is now much better. she requests me to say, she was entirely too ill to think of the Tomattoes. should she not be well enough to meet Mrs Tubman at Ashland Thu[r]sday next I will write you in due time to supply her place.[3]

I made a calculation last night very carefully, of the Govrs election. I took up each county in the state, and the result was nine thousand three Hundred of a majority for [William] Owsley. It can not be less than that, and may be 1500 more. I am perfectly satisfied, if there is an error in the calculation its on the safe side.[4]

P.S. Col. [Richard M.] Johnson was here a day or two since—I had a short interview with him—He is not the happiest man in the world, nor is he the most amiable. He has taken to hard swearing. I have not heard as many oaths uttered by any gentleman within the same space of time the last 10-years of my life.

ALS. DLC-HC (DNA, M212, R5). Printed in Colton, *Clay Correspondence*, 4:491. Endorsed by Clay on verso: "Mr. Letcher [With Buchanan letter]." 1. In this letter Buchanan wrote that he did not know what good it would do to publish his conversation with Clay about the possibility of Clay's becoming Jackson's secretary of state. Also, he did not want his conversation with Jackson concerning the "corrupt bargain," which had been published in August, 1827, to be reprinted now. Moore, *Works of James Buchanan*, 6:59. See also Sloane to Clay, May 9 and June 20, 1844; Clay to Sloane, May 21, June 14, June 28, 1844. 2. Clay to Sloane, May 21, 1844. 3. Emily Thomas Tubman, who owned a large plantation in Georgia, visited family and friends in Lexington and Frankfort each summer. She was a strong supporter of the American Colonization Society, having offered to send all 144 of her own slaves to Liberia (69 accepted). Clay had been appointed her legal guardian in 1803 upon the death of her father. James M. Gifford, "Emily Tubman and the African Colonization Movement in Georgia," *GHQ* (Spring, 1975), 59:10-11. 4. In the 1844 elections in Kentucky, Whig gubernatorial candidate William Owsley defeated Democrat William O. Butler by a vote of 59,680 to 55,040. *BDGUS*, 2:519. In the elections for the state legislature, Whigs won 64 seats in the lower house to 35 for the Democrats, with 1 neutral, while in the state senate Whigs won 26 seats to 12 for the Democrats. Frankfort *Commonwealth*, August 27, 1844. In the presidential election Clay carried Kentucky over Polk by a vote of 61,255 to 51,988. McKee, *National . . . Popular and Electoral Vote*, 56.

To Robert Garrett & Sons, Baltimore, July 8, 1844. Asks that they deposit $300 of the money from "the sales of my water rotted hemp" to his account at the Merchant's Bank of Baltimore to the credit of Rezin D. Shepherd of New Orleans. Says that some days ago he forwarded about two tons of cleaned hemp "by the way of Pittsburgh, and the [Pennsylvania Portage] canal," but is not pleased with either "the quantity of hemp gotten out" or the degree to which it was cleaned. L, signature removed. DLC-Garrett Family Papers (DNA, M212, R21).

The Pennsylvania Portage and Canal System went from Pittsburgh to Philadelphia with eastern and western sections connected by the Allegheny Portage Railway. Richard Morris (ed.), *Encyclopedia of American History* (New York, 1953), 424-25.

On July 15, 1844, Robert Garrett & Sons wrote Clay acknowledging his letter and sending the cashier's acknowledgment for the deposit made to Shepherd. Hope the next shipment will arrive in good condition. ALS. DLC-TJC (DNA, M212, R14).

R.D. Shepherd wrote Clay on July 29, 1844, acknowledging receipt of the $300, "being for the Amount of Interest due on your note on the 7 proximo." Notes that

"I am well Satisfied with the Mules and Horses purchased for me by Mr Hunt but I don't think I will again undertake with my People to break a young Kentucky Mule and have however got through with them without accident." *Ibid.* Mr. Hunt is probably John M. Hunt. See 8:495.

To WILLIAM P. THOMASSON Lexington, July 8, 1844

I received your friendly letter of the 5th. inst. I have had many letters from individuals, some requesting that I would, and some that I would not, express an opinion on the naturalization laws. How am I to comply with the wishes of both parties? I think it inexpedient to gratify our opponents with new issues. Besides, I entertain strong doubts as to the propriety of my expressing any opinion on public questions, since I became formally a candidate for the Presidency. You cannot conceive what a multitude of questions are constantly put to me, assuming every var[i]ety of form, and often making suppositious cases which may be never realized. What right have my opponents to attribute to me a wish to alter the naturalization laws? Without meaning to commi[t] myself one way or the other, in this letter, on the question, it seems to me that my published speeche[s] (that of 1832 particularly on the tariff)[1] afford ampl[e] materials to my friends for defending me against any charge of illiberality towards foreigners. Wheth[er] there ought to be any modification of the naturalizat[ion] laws or not is a question depending upon public opinion, of which I ought not to deprive myself of the benefit, but, if placed at the head of public affairs, ought to be left to be guided by it, and by the counsel of my constitutional advisers as well as my own judgment. I think the decision which you say the committee of the House of Representatives made in the case of Botts and Jones by which they assumed that the States had a right to admit aliens to exercise the elective franchize was manifestly erroneous. . . . [2]

LS. KyLoF. Letter marked "(Private and confidential)." 1. Speech in Senate, Feb. 2, 3, 6, 1832, in 8:455-56 where reference to naturalization has been omitted by editors. For the speech in its entirety, see Colton, *Clay Correspondence*, 5:437-86, espec. 5:451. 2. On Dec. 7, 1843, John Q. Adams had presented in the House a memorial of John M. Botts of Virginia contesting the seat of John W. Jones. This memorial was referred to the Committee on Elections which reported in favor of Jones on May 21, 1844. On June 6 the House unanimously resolved that Jones was entitled to the seat. U.S.H. of Reps., *Journal*, 28 Cong., 1 Sess., 30, 948, 1014.

To WILLIAM G. BROWNLOW[1] Lexington, July 15, 1844

I have just received your favor, and it does not surprise me to learn that opponents are seeking to make the impression that I was instructed to go against the bankrupt law. Our legislature gave no instructions to me on the subject of the bankrupt law.[2] Resolutions of instruction were pending before the legislature, but they were lost by a disagreement between the two houses.[3] You may boldly assert this, and proof, if necessary, can be furnished from Frankfort.

Copy. Printed in *Niles' Register* (August 17, 1844), 66:402. 1. Brownlow was editor of the Jonesborough (Tenn.) *Whig, and Independent Journal* at this time and later served in the U.S. Senate. *BDAC*. 2. See 9:408-9, 784-85. 3. See 9:784-85.

From Alexander Plumer *et al.*, West Newton, Pa., July 15, 1844. Write as members of the Whig and Anti-Masonic parties of Fayette and Westmoreland counties in Pennsylvania and as "your political admirers and friends." In order to be able conscientiously "to swell your electoral vote at the approaching Presidential election," ask whether or not Clay, if challenged to fight a duel, would reject the invitation. After giving many Biblical allusions and quotations, continue: "But what, it may be asked, has all this to do with Mr. Clay, who has so decidedly revealed himself as hostile to duelling in the recent occurrence between Messrs. [Jonathan] Cilley and [William] Graves [9:153, 157, 164-65, 334, 643-45, 656-58, 661-65]? Well, now, that, fortunately, is the very point of time and fact of which we designed to avail ourselves, for proof of Mr. Clay's prevailing affinity with duelling. Then he shall be his own witness. His exculpatory letter to Mr. [Henry A.] Wise, of that period [9:662-65], set forth that while the affair between Cilley and Graves was yet in embryo, his colleague and friend, Graves & Co., called upon him at his room, in Washington, for advice in the matter. Desirous, as he alleges, of putting an end to the difficulty between the belligerents, he obtained from Mr. Graves a sight of the challenge, read it, and suggested amendment, with the friendly design just noticed. Whereupon it was agreed that Mr. Clay should himself embody his amendment in a new draft. This was submitted, adopted, forwarded, and accepted, and the murder ensued. Now can any one doubt who was principal and accessory in this matter? Mr. Clay pleads that he wished to effect peace. We don't doubt it. So does every duellist profess a purpose of peace, in his preliminary correspondence, if he can effect it agreeably to his spurious code of honor. But, then, this is the very thing which we entirely and most cordially eschew and abhor, and which we invite Mr. Clay to go and do likewise; and then he can have no difficulty how to act when a friend again calls upon him in a similar emergency." Aver that Clay's "Christian friendship for Mr. Graves" should have caused him to admonish Graves, and if that failed, he should "have taken upon him forthwith to inform the proper authorities of the meditated defilement. Thus the whole affair would have been quashed. Divine and human law would have been honored, instead of being infringed." Noting, however, that "that occasion has passed," if Clay, "now, in the winter of life," will repudiate dueling. Copy. Printed in *Kendall's Expositor* (September 3, 1844), 4:331-33.

For Alexander Plumer (1786-1875)—a merchant, trader, and builder who had been a Jackson Democrat, then an Anti-Masonic leader and later was involved with the Whig and Republican parties—see George D. Albert (ed.), *History of the County of Westmoreland, Pennsylvania* . . . (Philadelphia, 1882), 661-62. See Clay to Plumer *et al.*, August 1, 1844.

From WILLIAM C. RIVES "Castle Hill" [near Charlottesville, Va.]
July 15, 1844

[Sends a letter he had received the previous autumn from Count Louis B.C. Serurier,[1] the former minister of France to the U.S., in which the Count asked to be remembered to John C. Calhoun, Daniel Webster, "& above all Mr. Clay, one of the greatest of your citizens." Also forwards a letter just received from his son in London.[2] Continues:]

I take the liberty of adding to these, copies of a speech made by me on the Tariff,[3] & of another on the Texas question.[4] You will perceive from the latter that I am decidedly in favour of the restoration of our ancient limits in that quarter, whenever it can be accomplished honorably & peaceably; & I will say to you frankly that the motive of the particular proposition I submitted was to pass the question over into your hands, beleiving sincerely that you are the only man in the Union whose practised ability & weight of character & influence, both at home & abroad, are competent to effect the object in a way to satisfy these essential conditions. From all I have seen & heard, since my return from Washington, I have been led to the conclusion that a large majority of your friends in Virginia are in favour of the acquisition of Texas, but they are, like myself, anxious to commit so great a question to an able & patriotic guardianship, which would, of itself, be a pledge to the country, that every thing that can & ought to be done, will be done.—

May I venture to ask, my dear sir, that the length of my speech on the Tariff will not deter you from looking over it, at some moment of leisure. There are some views in the latter half of it, connected with our early constitutional history, & the natural clamps & holdings of our Union, which I trust may be seasonable, at the present moment; & I have been so much flattered by a general conformity in the opinions I have expressed, upon this leading question of national policy to the views so lucidly & impressively delivered by you in your able speech at Raleigh,[5] (which I have just read with very great pleasure), that I am encouraged to hope the whole speech will meet your approbation.—

We have seen, with concern, that your health had been somewhat deranged since your return home from your long & fatiguing excursion, but we trust it is now entirely re-established. . . .

ALS, draft. DLC-William C. Rives Papers (DNA, M212, R22). 1. See 6:1044. 2. Neither enclosure has been found. Rives's son, Francis Robert Rives, served as secretary of legation in London from 1842-45. Alexander Brown, *The Cabells and their Kin* (Boston, 1895), 414-15. 3. Rives had addressed the Senate for three hours on May 27, 1844, in support of retaining the Tariff of 1842, which he had originally voted against. *Cong. Globe*, 28 Cong., 1 Sess., 626. 4. Rives had spoken in secret session on June 6, 1844, on the Texas annexation treaty. Washington *Daily National Intelligencer*, June 13, 1844. 5. Speech in Raleigh, April 13, 1844.

To JOHN M. BERRIEN Lexington, July 16, 1844

I received your friendly letter under date the 8h. at N. York, sketching your future plan of campaign,[1] as well as your previous operations. The papers had apprized me of some of the latter, and had demonstrated that you were working hard and working well. You should take care and not overtask yourself. I hope that you will find plain and easy sailing in Georgia.[2] Such all my accounts assure me will be the case. Still it is wisest always to combat, without regard to the weakness of the foe, as if Napoleon or Wellington were in the field.

You ask me to explain the cause of the defeat which you anticipated for the Whigs in Louisiana.[3] That State has answered for herself, in the most satisfactory manner.[4] I regard it as certain for us in Novr.[5] as any State in the Union. In this State the candidate of our opponents has the advantage of personal popularity, and that fact will probably diminish our majority. But we entertain no fears of the result.[6] Nor of that in Indiana.[7] Our majority in Ohio[8] will be immense. A fierce struggle is in progress in Tennessee.[9] Our friends are nevertheless very confident of success.

My health is now excellent. . . .

ALS. NcU. 1. Berrien conducted a campaign tour in the North for Clay, starting at Carlisle, Pa., on June 29. In his speeches Berrien praised the protective tariff and said the South did not want to annex Texas. McCrary, "John MacPherson Berrien," Ph.D. dissertation, University of Georgia, 1971, p. 288. 2. Clay to Kennedy, March 29, 1844. 3. *Ibid.* 4. Whigs had won control of the Louisiana house of representatives. See *ibid.* 5. *Ibid.* 6. Letcher to Clay, July 6, 1844. 7. Polk carried Indiana over Clay by a vote of 70,181 to 67,867, with Liberty party candidate James G. Birney receiving 2,106. McKee, *National . . . Popular and Electoral Vote*, 56. In the 1844 elections to the Indiana state legislature, with 1/3 of each body up for selection, Whigs concluded with a majority of 55 to 45 seats in the house, while seats were evenly distributed 25 to 25 in the senate. *Niles' Register* (August 31, 1844), 66:444. 8. Clay carried Ohio over Polk by a vote of 155,057 to 149,117 with Birney receiving 8,050. In the state elections in Ohio in 1844, Whigs won 20 seats in the state senate to 16 for the Democrats and won 40 seats in the state house to 32 for the Democrats. Lexington *Observer & Kentucky Reporter*, Oct. 16, 1844. Whig Mordecai Bartley defeated Democrat David Todd for the governorship by a vote of 146,333 to 145,062. *BDGUS*, 3:1203. In the congressional race Democrats won 13 seats to 5 for the Whigs. *Guide to U.S. Elections*, 580. 9. Clay carried Tennessee over Polk by a vote of 60,030 to 59,917. McKee, *National . . . Popular and Electoral Vote*, 56.

To WILLIAM A. MOORE & M.W. BOYD[1] Lexington, July 16, 1844

I have received your letter, stating that you had not seen any opinion of mine expressed on the question of the assumption, by the General Government, of the State debts. If you had perused my speeches, and attended to my votes in Congress, you would not have wanted any information in respect to my opinions. At both the Sessions of Congress of 1839-40 and 1840-41 I expressed myself in the Senate against the assumption of the State debts.[2] Nor have I since expressed or entertained any contrary opinion. In putting, as you do, the suppositious case of the passage of a bill by Congress, assuming the State debts, and enquiring what in that contingency, I would do, if I were elected President, and whether I would exercise the Veto, you assume the existence of an event highly improbable. Should it be the pleasure of the People to place me at the head of their public affairs, I hope there will be no difference in opinion, as to the proper course of conducting them, between the legislative and executive departments. And I deem it improper to anticipate any such difference, and disrespectful towards Congress, to announce, in advance, if it were to occur what I would do with any bill which its sense of duty might prompt it to pass. Should a conflict of opinion exist, I should avail myself of all the lights within my reach furnished by the constitution by Congress, by my constitutional advisers, and by public opinion and decide according to my conscientious convictions of duty.

I have been and yet am most anxious for the distribution of the proceeds of the sales of the public lands, among the several States.[3] If that measure were adopted, it would afford all the assistance to the indebted States which could be properly rendered by the General Government.

ALS. KyU. 1. No such names in Bourbon County appear in the 1840 or 1850 Kentucky censuses. 2. See 9:376, 390-92, 396, 492. 3. See 9:486-94, 686.

To Alexander Williams *et al.*, Greeneville, Tenn., July 17, 1844. Declines their invitation to attend a mass meeting in Greenville, because, as the Whig candidate for president, "I have felt constrained, by considerations of delicacy and propriety, from attending political meetings of the people." Adds, however, that "if I occupied a different position from that which has been assigned me, the gallant and patriotic State of Tennessee would stand in no need of any aid which I could render." ALS. NcD.

To THOMAS B. STEVENSON Lexington, July 18, 1844

I received your favor of the 13th. inst. with its enclosure. I have sent a slip from the Bay State Democrat to Mr [William G.] Brownlow, the source of the information respecting Mr [Daniel] Webster, published in that paper, and requested him to correct the error.[1] It will be better that the correction and the error should have a common origin. If he fail or decline to do it, I will adopt some other suitable mode to have it rectified. I am inclined to think that you gentlemen of the press do not lash [William O.] Butler sufficiently for his silence for near 30 years, in regard to the slander of the Kentucky troops.[2] During all that time he has been zealously supporting the slanderer [Andrew Jackson], supporting all his violent measures, supporting his lieutenant, Martin Van Buren, and is now supporting his other lieutenant James K. Polk. During all that time also he has been opposing the measures of public policy, which a majority of the people of Kentucky desired, and opposing me. Now, after the lapse of near 30 years of silence on his part, he comes out and says, for the first time, that he did not approve of the slander upon the Kentucky troops.[3] He says this when for the first time he is appealing to the people of Kentucky for their suffrages. Why has he been so long silent? Why has he always supported the slanderer of every thing that is Kentuckian? And what is the difference between concurring in the slander and endorsing the slanderer? We should have a pretty time of it with one of Jackson's lieutenants at Washington and another at Frankfort, and the old man in his dotage at the Hermitage dictating to both.

LS. Courtesy of Dr. Thomas D. Clark, Lexington, Ky. Printed in Colton, *Clay Correspondence*, 3:458. Copy in OCHP. 1. The Boston *Bay State Democrat* had printed an article called "CLAY'S OPINIONS OF WEBSTER," which quoted William G. Brownlow as asserting that Clay looked upon Webster with "utter contempt and detestation." Brownlow stated in the Jonesborough (Tenn.) *Whig, and Independent Journal* of August 14, 1844, that he himself had made the statement about Webster in a speech in Baltimore in May, and he had not attributed it to Clay; the sentiment was his own. He denied that he had ever heard Clay say anything at all derogatory about Webster. 2. For Jackson's "slander" of Kentucky troops at the Battle of New Orleans, see 2:11-12. 3. On July 2, 1844, Thomas B. Stevenson reported in the Frankfort *Commonwealth* that he had seen a letter from C.S. Morehead claiming that Butler had called on him to help make it known that the gubernatorial candidate had never written anything to support Jackson's accusation that the Kentuckians "ingloriously fled" at the Battle of New Orleans. Stevenson noted, however, that while Butler might not have *written* anything to support that contention, he reportedly had *said* that "the Kentuckians *did* run and it was useless to deny it." Stevenson's editorial contended that Butler had been presumed to agree with Jackson because of their long and close association.

To JOSHUA R. GIDDINGS Lexington, July 19, 1844

I received, and thank you for, your friendly letter of the 6th instant, and I am extremely happy to receive the encouraging accounts which it communicates of the progress of the Whig cause. I had before received, from other sources, highly gratifying information of the zeal and ability with which you were sustaining it. The omission in my Raleigh speech, as published,[1] of the principle of "the maintenance exclusively by the several States of their own local and peculiar institutions," was altogether accidental and without any design. I adhere faithfully to that principle, which I have on various occasions announced. The declaration of that principle by me once is as good as a thousand times; for I hope all men will do me the justice to suppose that I intend faithfully to execute, as far as I can, every public pledge or promise or assurance I may make. The Raleigh speech, as corrected by me, was written out by the aid of notes taken by a stenographer at the time it was delivered, and there are other omissions of what I said in the delivery of it unintentionally made. Your own experience in the preparation for the Press of speeches previously delivered, will have suggested to you how impracticable it is to write them out exactly as they were delivered. I have great repugnance to appearing before the public without an urgent necessity. You will understand and appreciate my motives. But if a suitable occasion shall occur I will take pleasure in complying with your request again to announce the principle, the omission of which in the Raleigh speech has occasioned your regret.

I offer you cordial congratulations upon our success in Louisiana.[2] I consider that State as certain for us in November as any State in the Union;[3] and I am happy to be able to add that the Whig cause will sustain no prejudice from the Texas question[4] anywhere at the South or Southwest.

Copy. OHi. Printed in George W. Julian, *The Life of Joshua R. Giddings* (Chicago, 1892), 162-63. 1. Speech in Raleigh, April 13, 1844. 2. Whigs had won control of the Louisiana house. Clay to Kennedy, March 29, 1844. 3. *Ibid.* 4. Clay to Crittenden, Feb. 15, 1844.

From O.H. Berg, Baltimore, July 20, 1844. Sends pages he has translated from his father's two brochures bearing "upon the Quintuple Treaty and the Institution of Slavery." Says he has "extracted, strictly compiled, and as faithfully translated" from German "all that relates to the above two questions." Also encloses a copy of the Quintuple Treaty in his father's handwriting. Notes that he is dedicating the pages to Clay, and adds: "Perhaps you may not have as yet read the two above questions treated in their mutual bearing upon each other . . . and if, in the perusal of these pages, you should find only half as much satisfaction as I take delight in dedicating them to you, my labours, insignificant though they be, will be most happily rewarded." ALS. DLC-HC (DNA, M212, R6).

For the Quintuple Treaty of December 20, 1841, between Austria, Great Britain, Prussia, and Russia (signed but not ratified by France) for the suppression of the African slave trade, see Parry, *Treaty Series*, 92:437-69. Olof Berg, father of O.H. Berg, had written two pamphlets in German dealing with the treaty. See *The National Union Catalog. Pre-1956 Imprints* . . . (Chicago, 1979), 48:112. See also Berg to Clay, January 29, 1845.

To BENJAMIN W. LEIGH Lexington, July 20, 1844

I recd. your favor of the 10h. inst. I am vexed with applications, chiefly from Virginia, to allow the publication of my [Francis P.] Blair letters.[1] Such an one has come to me from a Comee. at Lynchburg.[2] I have written to them declining the publication, for the present, but authorizing any of them to peruse the letters in your hands. Should they therefore make the application to you, I will thank you to shew them. Indeed, I have no objection to any *gentleman* of either party reading the letters. There is an entire congruity between the letters, and what is contained in my address to my Constituents of March 1825, and in my letters to Judge [Francis T.] Brooke and Walthal Watkins of the same period.[3] I have but two objections to their publication, one of which is the violation of the confidence due to private correspondence, and the other is the allusion to an infirmity of Mr. [John Q.] Adams,[4] whose feelings I am unwilling to wound.

I have not yet received all the proof I expect to establish "bargain intrigue & corruption," upon [Andrew] Jackson and his friends.[5] My judgment favors the publication. That of those friends whom I have consulted is adverse to it. I think I owe it to the truth of history, to the Country and to my self. But I shall be guided, at least as to the time of the publication, by the views & wishes of my Tennessee friends. In that State there will be a most animated and fierce contest. The excitement now exceeds that of 1840. We shall succeed in the State.[6]

I have seen Orator Shinn's letter.[7] Whatever may be his motives, or his view of the coincidence between Jackson and my self, as to public measures, his support is very acceptable and it is from an excellent locality.

As our opponents in Virginia chiefly rely upon the Texas question,[8] our friends cannot press with too much vigor and constancy, the design of the Nullifiers in So. Carolina to dissolve the Union, if they can.

Our majority in K[entucky]. will not be as great for our Govr. in Augt. as it ought to be, owing to the want of tact in canvassing, and a want of personal popularity.[9] In Novr. I think we shall have as large a majority as we had in 1840.[10]

ALS. ViU. 1. For the letters to Blair and their publication, see 4:9-10, 46-48. For the corrupt bargain, see index references in 7:660; 8:911; 9:934. 2. No such letter has been found. 3. For the letter to Brooke, see 4:45-46; no letter to Watkins has been found. 4. Clay's joking reference [4:9] to a friend of Adams coming "with tears in his eyes" was an allusion to Adams's "infirmity of a watery eye [3:187]." 5. Sloane to Clay, May 9 and June 20, 1844; Clay to Sloane, May 21, June 14, and June 28, 1844. 6. Clay to Berrien, July 16, 1844. 7. Wilson K. Shinn, a Virginia state senator from the Harrison County district (now West Virginia) and a leading Democrat, had made an address to the public opposing the election of James K. Polk and George M. Dallas and announcing his support for Clay. Franklin (Tenn.) *The Western Weekly Review*, July 26, 1844. 8. Clay to Crittenden, Feb. 15, 1844. 9. Letcher to Clay, July 6, 1844. 10. In 1840 William Henry Harrison had carried Kentucky over Martin Van Buren by 58,489 votes to 32,616, while Clay carried the state in 1844 over James K. Polk by only 61,255 to 51,988. McKee, *National . . . Popular and Electoral Vote*, 44, 56.

From James C. Johnston, Edenton, N.C., July 24, 1844. Sends a painting of the George Washington family which he has had Henry Inman execute. Asks that it be presented "with my best respects to Mrs [Lucretia Hart] Clay as a mark of the high esteem I have for her character." Continues: "I present this Painting to her because I think there is a great similarity in her Character to that of Mrs. [Martha] Washington who remained at Mount Vernon and attend[ed] to Genl. Washingtons domestic affairs while he was fighting to establish the Independence of our Country. So Mrs Clay has directed herself to your concerns at Ashland while you have been fighting with the greatest mental enemy to preserve that independence. But for Washington we might still have been colonies of Great Britain & but for *you* we should certainly have been her tributaries." Adds that if Mrs. Clay will think the painting worthy of a place at Ashland, "I shall be truly gratified and highly honored." ALS. DLC-TJC (DNA, M212, R10).

James Cathcart Johnston (1782-1865) of Hayes Plantation held one of the largest estates in North Carolina and was the son of U.S. senator and Revolutionary War patriot Samuel Johnston. *NCHR* (July, 1983), 60:357 and (October, 1984), 61:431.

For Henry Inman, who had painted a Clay portrait in 1840, see Amyx, "Portraits of Henry Clay," Special Collections, University of Kentucky, vol. A:1.52.

To THOMAS M. PETERS & JOHN M. JACKSON[1] Lexington, July 27, 1844

I have received your favor informing me that my views, as disclosed in my letter from Raleigh,[2] on the question of the Annexation of Texas,[3] are misconceived, if not misrepresented in your quarter; and that it is supposed that I have changed my opinion from what it was in 1819.[4] I endeavored to express myself in that letter as explicitly as I could, and I do not think now that it can be fairly misinterpreted.

In 1819, when I addressed the House of Representatives, the Executive had negotiated the treaty with Spain, by which Texas was ceded to that power, but Congress had not then given any sanction to the cession.—I believe now, as I thought then, that the Treaty-making power is not competent, without the concurrence of Congress, to cede away any Territory belonging to the United States.[5] But Congress, by repeated acts, subsequently manifested its approbation of the treaty; and these acts rendered it as valid and obligatory upon the U. States, as if Congress had given its assent, prior to the conclusion of the treaty. At that period of 1819, Texas as claimed by us, was unpeopled. No hostile incursions had been made into it by citizens of the United States. In 1825 and 1827, there were but few inhabitants of Texas, consisting of some colonists, planted there under the authority of Mexico. At neither of the three periods above mentioned had any State or section, in this Union, manifested any opposition to Texas composing a part of it. It has been said that Mr. [John Quincy] Adams' administration offered to negotiate with Mexico for Texas, notwithstanding the existence of a war between Spain and Mexico, and that it could not therefore have believed that the acquisition of Texas, at that time, would have involved the U. States in war with Spain.—Hence it is argued that the ratification of the late treaty could not have compromitted our peace.

Mr. Adams thought it desirable to obtain Texas. Two foreign powers claimed it.—Mexico was in possession, and Spain was doing nothing to assert and enforce her claim. Her representative had even gone so far as to stipulate, in a convention, to acknowledge the Independence of Mexico, although that convention was not ratified by Spain.[6]

Mr. Adams had a right to authorize the negotiation of a treaty for the acquisition of Texas with both or either of the powers claiming it. It was natural that he should begin with that power which had the possession of Texas.[7] Spain had interposed no obstacle. She had made no declaration that she would regard the acquisition of Texas as an act of war. In point of fact, no overture was formally made to Mexico to purchase Texas, no negotiation was opened, no treaty was concluded. If a negotiation had commenced, or if a treaty had been signed, and Spain had protested, the prudent and cautious policy which characterized Mr. Adams' administration, would undoubtedly have prompted him to quiet Spain, and accommodate the matter, previous to the annexation of Texas to the U. States, and without plunging them in war with Spain. How totally different are all the circumstances, under which, with Mr. Adams' authority, I authorized the overture to Mexico, from those which attended the recent treaty of Mr. [John] Tyler![8] So far from Mexico being silent, she repeatedly and solemnly declared that she would consider annexation as war with her. Texas was no longer an uninhabited country. It had been wrested from the dominion of Mexico by citizens, many of whom went armed from the U. States. The war between Mexico and Texas had not been terminated by any treaty of Peace. Mr. Tyler not only did not consult Mexico, but he announced that her assent to the annexation was altogether unnecessary. And he proceeded to conclude a treaty, embracing a large extent of Territory, and a numerous population, not comprehended in the Texas which the U. States ceded to Spain in 1819.

In the mean time too, a powerful opposition had arisen in the U. States against the annexation of Texas to them. Several States had declared, through their Legislatures, against it, and others, if not whole sections of the Union, were believed to be adverse to it.[9] This was the opposition to the measure, to which, in my Raleigh letter, I alluded, when I spoke of a 'considerable and respectable portion of the *confederacy*.' I did not refer to persons but to States or sections.

Under such circumstances, I could not but regard the annexation of Texas, at this time, as compromitting the honor of my country, involving it in a war, in which the sympathies of all christendom would be against us, and endangering the integrity of the Union. I thought then, and still believe, that national dishonor, foreign war, and distraction and division at home were too great sacrifices to make for the acquisition of Texas.

But, gentlemen, you are desirous of knowing by what policy I would be guided, in the event of my election as Chief Magistrate of the United States in reference to the question of the annexation of Texas. I do not think it right to announce in advance, what will be the course of a future administration in respect to a question with a Foreign power. I have, however, no hesitation in saying that, far from having any personal objection to the annexation of Texas, I should be glad to see it, without dishonor—without war, with the common consent of the Union, and upon just and fair terms. I do not think that the subject of slavery ought to affect the question, one way or the other. Whether Texas be Independent, or incorporated in the United States, I do not believe it will prolong or shorten the duration of that institution. It is destined to become extinct, at some distant day, in my opinion, by the operation of the inevitable laws of population. It would be unwise to refuse a permanent acquisition, which will exist as long as the globe remains, on account of a temporary institution.

In the contingency of my election, to which you have adverted, if the affair of acquiring Texas should become a subject of consideration, I should be governed by the state of fact, and the state of public opinion existing at the time I might be called upon to act. Above all, I should be governed by the paramount duty of preserving this Union entire, and in harmony, regarding it as I do as the great guaranty of every political and public blessing, under Providence, which, as a free people, we are permitted to enjoy.

Copy. Printed in Tuscumbia *North Alabamian*, August 16, 1844. This letter is referred to as Clay's "Second Alabama letter." 1. Thomas M. Peters of Lawrence, Ala., an 1834 graduate of the University of Alabama, was elected to the state house of representatives in 1845 and to the state senate in 1847. He also served as a judge on the state supreme court. William Garrett, *Reminiscences of Public Men in Alabama* (Atlanta, Ga., 1872), 440. John M. Jackson was a resident of Moulton, Lawrence County, Ala. Information supplied by the Alabama Department of Archives and History. 2. Clay to Editors of Washington *Daily National Intelligencer*, April 17, 1844. 3. Clay to Crittenden, Feb. 15, 1844. 4. For Clay's statements in favor of annexing Texas in the period 1819-21, see 2:769, 771, 803-16. 5. For the Adams-Onis Treaty, signed on Feb. 22, 1819, first ratified on Feb. 24, 1819, and, due to delays by Spain, brought up and again approved on Feb. 19, 1821, see Parry, *Treaty Series*, 70:1-30. The treaty went into effect on Feb. 22, 1821. See also Clay's speech of April 3, 1820, on the Adams-Onis Treaty [2:803-16]; and Bemis, *John Quincy Adams and the Foundations of American Foreign Policy*, 338-40, 350-51. 6. A Mexican uprising against Spain had begun by 1808. On August 24, 1821, the Spanish viceroy signed the so-called Treaty of Cordova, which granted Mexico its independence. This act was repudiated by the Spanish Cortes by decree in 1822, the same year the U.S. recognized the independence of the former colonies of Spain. In 1825 the Mexican government formally received a U.S. minister; Spain, however, did not officially recognize Mexico's independence until 1836. George L. Rives, *The United States and Mexico 1821-1848*, 2 vols. (New York, 1913), 1:27-50. 7. See 6:308-10, 540. 8. Clay to Crittenden, Feb. 15, 1844. 9. Clay to Miller, July 1, 1844.

From Oran Follett *et al.*, Columbus, Ohio, August, 1844. Reporting on Clay's letter of July 27 to Thomas M. Peters and John M. Jackson [see above], state that its "effect in this quarter is not happy." Note that "You of course know enough of the public feeling both in this State and New-York, to be satisfied, that the only hope of the Whigs in carrying them, is, in largely neutralizing the vote that ordinarily would be given for the 3rd [Liberty] party candidates. The impressions created by the reading of that letter, materially affect the efforts of our friends in that direction." Add that they, themselves, have no difficulty in reconciling the letter to his previous statements concerning Texas, but "all are not able to do so." Therefore, suggest that Clay write someone in New York, "(Mr. [Millard] Fillmore, for instance,) . . . and express yourself on Annexation [Clay to Crittenden, February 15, 1844; Clay to Editors of Washington *Daily National Intelligencer*, April 17, 1844], without particular allusion to any moving cause for such renewed expression, so as to leave the impression distinctly upon the public mind, unmixed with individual preferences or opinion, of what would be your course in case of your Election." Believe that such an action may be "highly useful, and may become necessary." Assure him, however, that they have "full conviction of being able to carry this State [Clay to Berrien, July 16, 1844] for the Whig Ticket throughout." Copy. OCHP. Signed by most of the Ohio Whig Central Committee.

For Oran Follett, prominent Ohio Whig and editor of the *Ohio State Journal*, see Edgar Allen Holt, *Party Politics in Ohio, 1840-1850* (Columbus, Ohio, 1931), 15.

To ALEXANDER PLUMER *et al.* Lexington, August 1, 1844

I duly received your letter of the 15th ultimo, on the subject of duelling, and I appreciate fully the friendly, pious and patriotic motives which prompted you to address it to me. Pernicious as the practice undoubtedly is, I hope you will excuse me when I say that there are other questions, in our public affairs, of much higher and more general importance. The victims or votaries of that practice are but few in number, and bear no comparison with the immense number of sufferers from the rejection of wise measures of national policy, or the adoption of those of an opposite character.

I expressed in strong terms of condemnation my opinions against duelling, in a letter which I addressed to my constituents, in March, 1824,[1] which is to be found in the published collection of my speeches. Again, within a few years past, I gave evidence of my strong disapprobation of it, by voting, in the United States Senate, for the bill for suppressing duelling in the District of Columbia.[2]

With these proofs of my sentiments, I think, gentlemen, you ought to be satisfied. But you ask me whether, if I were challenged to fight a duel, I would reject the invitation. Considering my age, which is now past 67, I feel that I should expose myself to ridicule if I were to proclaim whether I would or would not fight a duel. It is certainly one of the most unlikely events that can possibly be imagined, and I cannot conceive a case in which I should be provoked or tempted to go to the field of combat. But, as I cannot foresee all the contingencies which may possibly arise, in the short remnant of my life, and for the reason which I have already stated, of avoiding any exposure of myself to ridicule, *I cannot reconcile it to my sense of propriety to make a declaration one way or the other.*

You have, gentlemen, done me some, but not full justice, in respect to the affair of the lamented [Jonathan] Cilley.[3] When I first obtained any knowledge of his difficulty with Mr. [William J.] Graves, I did not think that there was the smallest occasion for a combat between them. I believed, from the first, that the matter would be amicably accommodated: to that end all my exertions were directed. I did not know that it was not accommodated until the day when, and after the parties went out to fight. On that day I was confined to my room by illness, and it was altogether accidental that I obtained information that the parties had gone out. But I was neither informed as to the place nor the hour of their meeting. Contrary to the impression which you entertain, I did advise the employment of the police to arrest the parties and prevent the duel. The constables accordingly went out in search of them, but like myself, being ignorant of the time and place of their meeting, they mistook their route, and failed in the accomplishment of the object. If you would read attentively the whole of my correspondence with Mr. [Henry A.] Wise, to which you have referred, you will find that it sustains the preceding statement.[4]

Copy. Printed in Lexington *Observer & Kentucky Reporter*, Sept. 4, 1844; also Colton, *Clay Correspondence*, 3:451-52. 1. It was March 26, 1825. See 4:146-49. 2. See 9:153. 3. See 9:153, 157, 164-65, 334, 643-45, 656-58, 661-65. 4. See 9:661-65.

To EPES SARGENT Lexington, August 7, 1844

I received your favor of the 29th ultimo with the copy of the [New York] Republic which accompanied it.[1] It had been before pretty regularly sent to me, by whom I know not. But its columns then did not appear to me to possess much interest. Mr Wykoff [*sic*, Henry Wikoff][2] has wisely determined to give it a more decided character, and I am glad that it comes out in support of our cause. I perused the two articles in the number you sent me to which you called my attention. They are both well written. Mr. Wykoff, if he had health, has sufficient talent to conduct a paper with ability. Under your management I hope the Republic will avoid collisions with other Whig papers in the city of New York. Such collisions injure a good cause, and injure the parties to them. I regret the eccentricities of the [New York] Tribune to which you refer.[3] They detract from the merit of the paper which otherwise is very great. On statistics and the state of elections and public opinion throughout the Union I regard Mr [Horace] Greeley as surpassed by no other Editor in the Union. This day terminates our election in Kentucky, and if results in other parts of the State shall equal those in my neighborhood, our success will come up to that of 1840.[4]

You probably saw an article which about a month ago went the rounds of the News papers, headed "Mr Clay and his revilers":[5] The accuracy of the statements in that article may be entirely relied upon and if you should have occasion to prepare another edition of my biography I would be glad if you would incorporate them in it.[6]

All the information that reaches me in respect to the influence upon our cause of the Texas question[7] satisfies me that it will do it no prejudice, and I do not entertain a doubt that we shall get a majority of 2/3 of the slave states.[8]

I find the extent of my correspondence and the number of strangers that are constantly calling upon me are very oppressive. To lighten my burden as to the first, I have to engage the services of my son John [Morrison Clay], as an Amanuensis, and he has written this letter upon my dictation. . . .

LS. MCM. 1. The New York *Republic* was issued early in 1844 by Henry Wikoff and lasted only about one year. Originally, it was edited as a free trade journal by Duff Green. Then it was taken over by Clay Whigs and edited by John O. and Epes Sargent. Frederick Hudson, *Journalism in the United States, 1690-1872* (New York, 1873; reprint ed., Ann Arbor, Mich., 1964),

577. 2. For Henry Wikoff, better known as Chevalier Wikoff, see *CAB*. 3. Probably a reference to Greeley's support for a variety of reforms, including Association, an Americanized version of Fourierism. Glyndon G. Van Deusen, *Horace Greeley, Nineteenth Century Crusader* (New York, 1953), 64-96. 4. For the 1844 state and presidential elections in Kentucky, see Letcher to Clay, July 6, 1844. 5. Clay to Gales & Seaton, June 15, 1844. 6. See 9:536. Another revised edition of Sargent's *The Life and Public Services of Henry Clay* was published by Greeley & McElrath in 1848. "Mr. Clay and His Revilers" was not included in it. 7. Clay to Crittenden, Feb. 15, 1844. 8. For states carried by Clay, see Clay to Webb, Feb. 29, 1844.

To A.G. SECKEL Lexington, August 8, 1844

I received your letter containing a hand bill published by the liberty party in your town, in which they attribute to me the expression, "if we cannot have black slaves we must have white ones," &c. I never used such expressions in my life; and in a letter addressed by me to the Hon. John White last spring, I positively contradicted them.[1] That letter was extensively published in the newspapers.

Copy. Printed in Pittsburgh *Daily Gazette and Advertiser*, Sept. 20, 1844. 1. Clay to White, May 6, 1844.

From Robert L. Caruthers, Lebanon, Tenn., August 12, 1844. Reports that the Democratic newspapers in the state are charging "that you do not embrace in your system of protection of American industry by a discriminating tariff, the agricultural interest." Also, "It is . . . insisted that you regard a bankrupt law as one of the Whig measures to be carried out in the event of their success." Notes that "your position on both these subjects are well understood by all candid men, yet as you have manifested a disposition to affirm and re-affirm your opinions on all and every subject to the full satisfaction of friends and foes, I will ask of you an answer to the following questions." Inquires, therefore, if "in making discriminations in a revenue Tariff with a view to protection of American industry would you include the agricultural as well as manufacturing and other interests?" Secondly, asks if he is in favor of reviving the Bankrupt law, "and when you voted against the repeal of that law in 1842 before it went into force, did you consider yourself instructed by the Legislature of Kentucky to vote differently?" Copy. Printed in Jonesborough (Tenn.) *Whig, and Independent Journal*, September 11, 1844. For Clay's role in the earlier Bankrupt law, see 9:408-9, 784-85, and Clay to Brownlow, July 15, 1844.

From William Driver *et al.*, Nashville, August 12, 1844. Send Clay a set of horseshoes "made by us at the head of the Liberty Pole in Nashville, 62 feet from the ground." Ask him to put the shoes on his saddle horse. Copy. Printed in Nashville *Republican Banner*, September 6, 1844.

Clay replied from Lexington on August 31, 1844, thanking them for the present. States: "The associations with which the manufacture of these Shoes is connected—between Heaven and Earth, on a Liberty Pole, 62 feet from the ground, in Nashville—give to your present an extraordinary interest." Promises to use it as they have requested. Closes: "May all your strokes, in Politics and on the Anvil, ever be as well directed as those which were employed in making these Shoes!" *Ibid.*

From Amos Kendall, [Washington, D.C.], *ca.* August 14, 1844. Addresses Clay "not as a friend or as an enemy, but as '*the embodiment of Whig principles.*' " Denies that a personal attack is part of his object, but adds that he will not "hesitate to speak . . . of those traits of character which render you unfit for the Chief Magistracy of a Christian people."

Argues that in all civilized nations that do not have despotic governments, "there are always two parties which may be called the *Democracy* and the *Aristocracy*. The principles of Democracy are those of the Moral Code . . . so beautifully illustrated. . . . in the single command—'*Do unto others as you would have them do unto you.*' " Explains that "Equality of rights is a precept of the Moral Code, and is asserted in the Declaration of Independence, as the only just basis of political institutions." Advocates, however, an "*Aristocracy of Nature*," such as Clay possessed "when his youthful eloquence filled the bosoms of the ardent Kentuckians with patriotic devotion, and rallied them almost as one man against the usurpations of the elder [John] Adams and his political counsellors. But at this point men diverge in their political opinions and actions, and here an *artificial* Aristocracy commences. Democrats are content with the advantages which God, nature, and their own industry and good conduct give them; Aristocrats seek to increase and enlarge those advantages by the laws and institutions of society." Charges that the Federalist party was the aristocratic party and that it now goes by the name of Whig. States: "And you, sir, are proclaimed by that Party to be '*the embodiment of Whig principles.*' You are 'the embodiment' of the principles of that Party, which, not content with the advantages which God and nature have given them over their fellow men, seek to make the great mass of their countrymen work for their emolument and live for their aggrandizement. . . . Their plan of government is based on a direct violation of moral principle, on depriving the mass of rightful power, and taking from them without an equivalent, the fruits of their industry. A *moral* man could not be a *true* 'embodiment' of such principles. . . . The *true* 'embodiment' of their principles must be a man who thinks so lightly of the lives of others that he is ready to kill them for a hasty word or a trespass against the arbitrary rules of a lawless etiquette." Continues at length, castigating Clay for his dueling, swearing, card playing, and his position on the Dorr Rebellion [9:714-15].

Also accuses Clay and the Whig party of planning to increase taxes and the power of the national government to the detriment of the states and the liberty of the people. Claims that the result would be "*to make our Government an Aristocracy of wealth, as that of Great Britain now is.*" Says the chief means of accomplishing this objective is a national bank. Expounds at length on the unconstitutionality of such an institution, recalling "your speech in 1811 [1:527-40]" to that effect. Attacks him also for changing his stand on the bank in 1816 [2:199-205]. Charges that "Henry Clay has adopted the Federal principle of *stretching* the Constitution rather than ask the States for amendments." Notes that in arguing against the bank in 1811, Clay had said the bank was "*one of the* CAUSES *out of which the Republican and Federal Parties originally sprang.*" Adds that "You have adopted the Federal principles and measures which were '*the causes of the political divisions in this country.*' You have gone over to '*the camp of the enemy.*' " Copy. Printed in *Kendall's Expositor* (August 14, 1844), 4:291-98. Designated as Tract No. 19. Clay's speeches attacking the Alien and Sedition Acts have not survived, but see 8:243, 269; 9:161-62, 249.

In Tract No. 20, addressed to Clay, Kendall continues his attack on the national bank. Asserts that so great was the "mischief exhibited by the late Bank in its attempt to extort a new charter from an unwilling people, that many of its original advocates are now among its strongest opponents [8:432-33]. Among these is "*George M. Dallas*, the Democratic candidate for the Vice Presidency." Outlines in detail reasons why he believes the power of a national bank is inevitably so great that it threatens popular government. Contends: "That power pervades the Union, and may, at any moment, be put forth to check, regulate or destroy; to make a good speculation or maintain a safe currency; to distress trade or promote it; to save the National Bank at the expense of the State Banks; to facilitate the action of the government or to thwart it; to put down one President and make another; to sustain the government or overthrow it." As evidence, charges that the branches of the Second B.U.S. drove the Bank of Kentucky out of business. Adds that "such effects a Bank of the United States can produce upon the interior Banks whenever it chooses, simply by curtailing its own business in particular Branches, receiving the Notes of the doomed State Banks, and presenting them for payment. . . . No man who traces effects back to their causes can now doubt, that the course pursued by the Bank of the United States operated largely in filling Kentucky with the cry of Relief, and led to a train of palliative measures which protracted for many years the sufferings which that institution was instrumental in producing." Cites as further evidence of the dangerous power of the B.U.S. the fact that it was entirely independent of state authority following the Supreme Court ruling in *McCulloch* v. *Maryland* which declared that "the States have no constitutional power to tax the Bank of the United States." Asks: "Who was in the West the great Bank leader in this war upon the reserved rights and powers of the States? . . . It was HENRY CLAY."

Maintains that "After its successful conflict with the States, the Bank exercised undisputed dominion over the trade and currency of the country until 1829." Asserts that although Nicholas Biddle made every effort "to ingratiate himself into the favor not only of the President, but of all his leading friends, in the Cabinet and out," General [Andrew] Jackson considered the bank "so dangerous to Liberty . . . that he said, 'I cannot sleep upon my pillow if I fail to call the attention of the People to the subject on the first opportunity.' " Says the bank's officials became alarmed at the president's pronouncements and "entered into an alliance with the leaders of a political party, to acquire the mastery of the Government. The Bank wanted a new charter, and *Henry Clay* wanted to be President. It was as well understood between the parties as if they had signed a bond, that the Bank was to make Clay President, and that in consideration thereof, Clay and his friends should give a new charter to the Bank." When Congress passed a recharter bill, "Gen. Jackson met it with a direct veto [8:552]. . . . *Bank or no Bank* was thus made the issue at the Presidential election in 1832, and the People decided against a Bank by an overwhelming majority [8:367-68]." Still, the bank hoped "to throw itself into the Presidential election of 1836, decide the contest, and obtain a new charter from the Administration it should bring into power. The expiration of its charter in 1836, the year of the election, would afford it plausible reasons for curtailing its loans and distressing the country." Details Jackson's efforts to forestall such an event by early removal of the government's deposits [8:583-84] from the B.U.S. Charges that "a perfect concert of action was established between *you*, as the leader in Congress, and *Mr. Biddle*, as Manager of the Bank. *His* province was to distress the country by extraordinary and needless retrenchments. . . . *Your* province was to denounce the President in the Senate as a tyrant and usurper, instigate your political partizans to the same course, charge on him all the public distresses you knew the Bank was wantonly producing, and, echoing the Bank press throughout the land, add alarm and panic to actual suffering." Adds that "Firm as the Pillars of Hercules stood the President and the House of Representatives. The waves of the bank-troubled ocean dashed themselves into foam at their feet, and retired, exhausted and conquered by their own violence. . . . the record of *your* glory in that infamous war, is the resolution of the Senate condemnatory of General Jackson's greatest act, *surrounded by blank lines, there inscribed by the order of a just and indignant people* [8:735; 9:12-14]." Asserts that "With any other leader than Gen. Jackson to marshal the Democracy, the Bank would have succeeded." Contends that "To establish another Bank, therefore, is *to establish a new Government*. It is to create a power which *the People's* Government is not strong enough to resist. . . . That *Henry Clay* and *Theodore Frelinghuysen* should be the advocates of such a Government, does not surprise us. . . . They have no faith in the capacity of the People to govern themselves. They are willing to obey the public will when it accords with their views; and they want a machine to control and nullify it when it does not." Copy. Printed in *Kendall's Expositor* (August 27, 1844), 4:313-19. The charter of the Bank of Kentucky was repealed in 1822 and the bank was given seven years to conclude its business.

For the chaotic Old Court-New Court struggle in Kentucky during that period, see Samuel M. Wilson, *History of Kentucky*, 2 vols. (Louisville, 1928), 2:124-28.

In Tract No. 22, also addressed to Clay, Kendall blames the Bank of the United States for the Panic of 1837 and the depression which followed, stating that "to the expansions of loans and circulation by the Bank of the United States, after the close of the deposite war in 1834, is mainly to be ascribed that general expansion of bank loans and credit which plunged the country into embarrassments and distresses . . . from which it has not yet entirely recovered." The "evils which the Bank caused" were then blamed on the [Van Buren] administration, causing it to be overthrown in 1840. Believes that if the bank had not stopped payment by that time and its "frauds and corruptions" been exposed, "you, *Henry Clay*," would have demanded at the Extra Session of Congress in 1841 that its charter be restored. Instead, because its corruption was so notorious, "you . . . proclaimed yourself in favor of a new Bank . . . established on the same principles—'an old fashioned Bank'—clothed . . . with superior powers. To this day, you persist in this Bank project, dangerous as you once proclaimed it, and as it has since proved itself to be, to the power of the people over their Government." Denies that Jackson's policies were responsible for the financial panic and depression, and predicts that "a hundred years hence . . . Andrew Jackson will as far outshine Henry Clay . . . as the bright sun . . . outshines the pale moon." Copy. Printed in *Kendall's Expositor* (September 10, 1844), 4:344-47.

To CAROLINE L. BROWN Lexington, August 16, 1844

Altho' I am, as you anticipated, almost insupportably burthened with an extensive correspondence, I can not deny myself the pleasure of acknowledging the receipt of your friendly letter, and tendering my acknowledgments for the opinions with which you honor me. These opinions have descended to you from your lamented father,[1] who always distinguished me by his attachment and confidence.

I look forward, my dear Madam, to the event which you so kindly and so fervently desire, I will not say with indifference, but with far less solicitude than that which is entertained by many of my friends. Should it happen, it will bring after it for me constant care and anxiety, and the greatest responsibility; and I know enough of the vanity of all earthly things to feel that I shall experience no corresponding equivalents for the sacrifices and vexations I shall encounter. All that I dare hope is that, by the aid and blessing of Providence, I may not entirely disappoint the expectations of my friends. . . . [2]

ALS. KyU. 1. Neither Mrs. Brown nor her father has been identified. 2. Caroline L. Brown again wrote Clay from Cincinnati on Nov. 22, 1844, informing him that when she had corresponded during the summer she had not doubted that "the more intelligent & moral portion of the people of Ohio" would achieve their "long cherished wish" to see Clay become president. Asserts, however, "Do not suppose, my dear *sir*, because the event has proved that I was mistaken in my anticipations, that I am going to write you a letter of condolence!" Thinks that to have won by such means "as have been resorted to, & to have proved successful, in the case of J.K. Polk—then indeed, there would have been cause for grief & sorrow; for a victory achieved by such means would have brought disgrace & dishonor with it." Feels the American people "have made a man their Representative, about whom they thought nothing and whom they care less." Adds that "I am beginning to think that he may very well represent those who placed him there,—& from my heart I wish the Nullifiers, the Tylerites, the Dorrites, the Mormons, the New York Abolitionists & the ignorant & deluded foreign population, which rests a dead weight upon us—'Much joy' of their President." Says that Clay's loss "came upon me like a 'thunderbolt from a clear sky,' & even yet,—it is only at intervals that I am able to realise the full extent of the misfortune that has befallen our Country." ALS. DLC-HC (DNA, M212, R6).

To J.G. GOBLE[1] Lexington, August 16, 1844

I received your friendly letter, with the enclosed slip,[2] cut from a newspaper, and I appreciate, and am thankful for the motives which prompted you to address me. I wish you would obtain and peruse the correspondence which passed between Messrs. [Henry A.] Wise, [William J.] Graves and me, respecting the lamentable affair between Messrs. Graves and [Jonathan] Cilley, published about three years ago.[3] I have not a copy of it; but you can obtain it in New-York.

It establishes 1st, That the draft which I suggested of the challenge was made expressly with the view of leading to an adjustment of the dispute amicably, and not, as alleged in the slip you forwarded, to close the door.

2d. That I never believed that the controversy would occasion a hostile meeting, but continually thought that it ought to be, and would be, amicably settled.

3d. That I was ignorant that the parties were to meet in combat, and at what hour they were to meet.

And 4th. That when I accidentally heard that they had gone out to fight, although I did not know the hour, nor the place, I advised the police to be called out; but they missed the parties, in consequence of their having taken an unexpected route.

I was not upon the ground, and had nothing whatever to do with the conduct of the combat. My agency as far as I had any in the whole transaction, was directed to the object of an amicable settlement of the difficulty.

Copy. Printed in Hodges, Todd, & Pruett, *The Campaign of 1844*, 198. 1. For Goble (1799-1859), a Newark, N.J., physician, see Shaw, *History of Essex and Hudson Counties*, 1:309-10. 2. Not found. 3. See 9:643-45, 648, 656-58, 661-65.

To WILLIAM E. ROBINSON Lexington, August 16, 1844

I am mortified and concerned that you should deem it necessary to address the enquiries to me contained in your letter of the 6h. inst. My opinions, on the topics to which you refer, have been again and again expressed, in Speeches letters &c. long since published. I cannot allow myself, upon the eve, as it were, of a great election, to renew the expression of them. I will not subject my motives to the imputation to which they might be exposed, by such a renewal of the expression of them.

The experiment is now in progress, whether partizans of the Locofocos' can, by falsehood calumny and detraction, break down the Whig cause, which they have despaired of affecting by reason argument and truth.

I am mortified that you should, for a moment, have been influenced by the operations of that system.

Whenever I change my opinions (which I have done but once in my life, on any great national question)[1] I shall announce the change myself, and not leave it to my enemies to do it for me.

ALS. NjMoHP. Letter marked "(Private)." Addressed to Robinson in New Haven, Connecticut. 1. On the national bank. See 2:200-205, 342-44, 413-14, 552-53, 697, 723.

To WILLIAM C. RIVES Lexington, August 19, 1844

Absence from home has delayed my acknowledgment of your obliging letter of the 15h. Ulto. I return the letter of Mr. Serrurier [*sic*, Louis B.C. Serurier] with many thanks for the opportunity of perusing it. He is a most worthy person, towards whom I have ever cherished feelings of the highest respect. Should you write to him, I pray you to present to him my constant and cordial regard. As for myself, my correspondence is already too oppressive to think of adding to it. Mr. [James] Madison once told me that the correspondents of Mr. [Thomas] Jefferson were killing him. My own experience assures me of the possibility of such a homicide.

I perused your Speech on the Tariff[1] with great and unaffected satisfaction. Its historical allusions and reminiscences were extremely apposite and finely illustrative. It will do great good. Nothing, in the aspect of public affairs, affords me more gratification than the perfect unanimity which prevails among our party, in all quarters of the Union, on this long agitated question. If our people engaged in importations would only be prudent, we should soon regain our lost prosperity. This year they have been too adventurous. Two more years of such excessive importations would bring about another commercial revulsion.

If Texas can be received into the Union, it must be after the revival of harmony among the various sections of the Confederacy.[2] The course recently taken by yourself, and Whig members of the Senate and H. of R. from the South, in respect to the principle of protection,[3] will have a most salutary tendency, in reviving a better state of feeling. I have always believed that the steady and united opposition of the South, in former times, to that principle, was the principle cause of abolition and of engendering other bad feelings at the North. They traced that opposition to Slavery, which they believed was consolodated and combined against all measures tending to Northern prosperity. Hence they attacked Slavery, sought its abolition, and sought to deprive it of all representation. The present liberality of the South, in regard to protection, will undeceive them, and I hope will lead to more concord and contentment among the members of our Union. To this desirable object, I trust, the new Whig administration will direct its exertions. And it is possible that a condition of the public mind may ensu[e], which would reconcile all parts of our Country to the annexation of Texas.

The result of the August elections is quite satisfactory. The battle of November has been fought this month, and with more advantages on the side of our opponents than they will enjoy in the Autumn. We have much reason to hope for Missouri.[4] If I am to credit numerous accounts which come to me from our parent State [Virginia], strong hopes may be indulged of her support.[5]

I have been two or three times indisposed, since my return home, the effects of the exertion and excitement incident to my Southern tour, I suppose; but I have at no time been seriously ill or confined to my bed. I am now very well. . . .

ALS. DLC-William C. Rives Papers (DNA, M212, R22). 1. Rives to Clay, July 15, 1844. 2. Clay to Crittenden, Feb. 15, 1844. 3. During the 28th Congress, 1st Session, Rives, John M. Berrien, and other southerners in the House and Senate had spoken and voted against repeal of the Tariff of 1842. Several also had campaigned for Clay and had endorsed a tariff for revenue with some protection. U.S.H. of Reps., *Journal*, 28 Cong., 1 Sess., 102, 160-61; McCrary, "John MacPherson Berrien," Ph.D. dissertation, University of Georgia, 1971, pp. 279, 288-89; Clay to Clayton, *ca.* Late August, 1844. 4. Clay to Kennedy, March 29, 1844. 5. James K. Polk won Virginia's 17 electoral votes with 49,570 popular votes to Clay's 43,677. McKee, *National . . . Popular and Electoral Vote*, 56-57.

To ROBERT L. CARUTHERS Lexington, August 20, 1844

I received your letter of the 12th instant. You surprise me by the statement of some opinions which are attributed to me. Nothing can be more unfounded than the assertion that I am unfriendly to the protection of agriculture. I consider that interest in all its departments as the predominant interest in the United States. Cotton Hemp, Wool, manufactures of Tobacco, and other articles of agricultural product[ion] are now protected, and if the measure of protection be inadequate no man in the United States would be willing to go further than I would in extending sufficient protection. I have never held or expressed any other sentiments. The substance of what I have said and which is to be found in my published speeches, is that agriculture in the United States, owing to our distance from European countries, needs but little *direct* protection. But the principal aim in introducing and protecting manufactures is to benefit agriculture by opening a home market for its surplus productions. Expressions disparaging to agriculture or rather to the habits of those who pursued it have been put into my mouth, and paraded at the head even of newspapers. I never used these expressions. They have been forged or fabricated by political enemies. Of all the pursuits of man, I consider the cultivation of the earth as the most honorable. It is my own pursuit, and any reflecting man must at once perceive that I could say nothing derogatory from it.

I have already stated in a letter which has been published that the General Assembly of Ky. gave me no instructions to vote for the repeal of the Bankrupt Law.[1] Instructions were pending before the Legislature but they fell by a disagreement between the two Houses.[2]

I consider that the American people have expressed a decided disapprobation of the late Bankrupt Law, and for one, in deference to that opinion, I do not desire to see that law revived or any other Bankrupt Law passed.

I congratulate you on the satisfactory result of the August elections. . . .[3]

Copy. Printed in Jonesborough (Tenn.) *Whig, and Independent Journal*, Sept. 11, 1844. 1. For the Bankrupt law, see 9:408-9. The published letter was Clay to Brownlow, July 15, 1844. 2. See 9:784-85. 3. In Tennessee. See Clay to Berrien, July 16, 1844.

To UNKNOWN RECIPIENT Lexington, August 20, 1844

I received your favor of the 8th instant. If you will be so good as to turn to my speech on the preemption bill,[1] pages 182 and 183, Greeley & McElrath's edition,[2] you will find a strong and decisive expression of my opinion against the assumption of the State debts.[3] I have never expressed or entertained any other opinion. The only relief which I have thought ought to be afforded to the States, in the payment of their debts, was that which would incidentally arise out of a distribution of proceeds of the sales of the public lands among all the States. But that distribution has no necessary connexion with the existence of State debts. It was proposed by me prior to the contraction of most of them. It is proper to add, that, for the sake of the credit of our common country, I fervertly desire to see every State honorably fulfilling all of its obligations. . . .

Copy. Printed in Washington *Daily National Intelligencer*, Oct. 8, 1844. 1. Of Dec. 19, 1836. See 8:873. 2. See 9:871. 3. For other statements on the issue of state debts, see 9:376, 390-92, 396, 492.

To JOHN M. CLAYTON Blue Licks [Nicholas County, Ky.], August 22, 1844

I have to thank you for several obliging letters. Your supposition is right as to the oppressive extent of my Correspondence. It is utterly impossible to answer all the letters which I receive. I am afraid that I cannot reply to many that deserve it. Mr. [James] Madison once remarked to me that Mr. [Thomas] Jefferson's correspondents were killing him; but they were furnished by a population of about ten millions. Mine are supplied by a population of near twenty millions. I can feel and conceive the possibility of a homicide, committed in the mode which Mr. Madison suggested.

I request you to attribute to the above cause my omission to express to you before the satisfaction I derived from the perusal of your admirable Speech on the Compromise law.[1] No man knew better the motives and considerations which prompted its passage than you did, and you have ably and truly exposed them. We were upon terms of the most confidential intimacy and friendship. You daily, in the Senate, sat near me. You knew of my consultations with the practical manufacturers, and their coincidence in opinion with us. I believe it was upon your invitation that the lamented [E.I.] Dupont came from Delaware and conferred with us.[2] Upon more occasions than one, whilst gazing upon the care-worn countenances and haggard looks of some of the delegation in Congress from South Carolina,[3] you said to me, "Clay these are fine fellows. It won't do to let old [Andrew] Jackson hang them. We must save them." You lived in a mess of some seven or eight Senators, and it was your mess[4] that insisted upon the Home valuation,[5] as a sine qua non. Mr [John C.] Calhoun opposed it. Your mess persevered. The fate of the bill was threatened, but he, at the last moment, withdrew his opposition, and the bill finally passed[.]

I have again and again asserted, on the floor of the Senate, that two principal objects were aimed to be accomplished. One was to avert a Civil War. The other was to preserve the policy of protection. It was threatened, by Mr. Verplank's [*sic*, Gulian C. Verplanck][6] bill, with total subversion; and I believed then and believe now, that, if the Compromise had not passed,[7] at the next Session of Congress, all traces of that policy would have been effaced from the Statute book.

You and I both maintained that the measure of protection preserved by the Compromise would be sufficient until about 1842. But we were haunted by our opponents to know what would be its conditions when that period arrived. We replied there were the home valuation, cash duties, a long list of free articles &c. But I said also, let us take care of ourselves now; the people of 1842 may be trusted to take care of themselves. Public opinion, in the meantime, may become more enlightened, & the wisdom of the protective policy may be demonstrated. I have not been disappointed. My predictions have been fulfilled. The people of 1842, the Whigs at least every where, and many of the Democrats, are now fully persuaded that the industry of this great Country ought not to be prostrated at the feet of Foreign powers. Every where the cry is for a Tariff for Revenue, with discriminations for protection. Every where the preservation of the Tariff of 1842,[8] which has worked so well, and is delivering us from embarrassments, is loudly demanded.

The circumstance which led to, or attended, the enactment of the Compromise may be curious and interesting, as matters of history; but, in respect to the policy of protection, the great, practical, absorbing question is shall the Tariff of 1842 be preserved or repealed? That question is to be solved in November next. I have repeatedly expressed my opinion, unequivocally, in favor of it.

I thought we achieved a great triumph in placing the Protective policy, by the Compromise act, without the reach and beyond the term of Genl. Jackson's administration. And we availed ourselves of the fact that the South Carolina delegation were much more anxious that the difficulty should be settled by us than by Genl. Jackson.

You tell me that I am accused of having abandoned the Protective policy. That would distress me exceedingly, if I were not accused of all sorts of crimes and misdemeanors. I believe I have been charged with every crime enumerated in the Decalogue. I laugh at the streights to which our opponents are driven. They are to be pitied. Shrinking from all the issues, arising out of the great questions of National policy, which have hitherto divided the Country, they have no other refuge left but in personal abuse, detraction and defamation. I have lived down their attacks heretofore, and with the blessing of Providence, I hope to survive those which they are now directing against me. Most certainly my surprize at the attempt to make me out a friend of free trade with Foreign Countries, and an opponent of the Protective policy, ought not to be greater than that of my Competitor [James K. Polk] at the effort to establish his friendship to the Protective policy.[9]

AL, signature removed. DLC-John M. Clayton Papers (DNA, M212, R20). Also printed in *Kendall's Expositor* (Sept. 10, 1844), 4:340-41; and Colton, *Clay Correspondence*, 1:259-61 with minor omissions. 1. Clayton had spoken at a Whig mass meeting in Wilmington, Delaware, on June 15, 1844. He had endorsed the protective tariff and defended Clay against the charge of having abandoned protection in his Compromise Tariff of 1833. Washington *Daily National Intelligencer*, July 4, 1844. See also Clay to Clayton, *ca.* Late August, 1844 and August 29, 1844. 2. E.I. Dupont, as well as other prominent manufacturers, had consulted with Clay while he was working on his plan for the Compromise Tariff of 1833. Merrill D. Peterson, *Olive Branch and Sword—The Compromise of 1833* (Baton Rouge, 1982), 67. 3. John C. Calhoun. 4. Clayton's mess in the winter of 1832-33 had consisted of himself, Samuel Bell (Sen., N.H.), John Holmes (Sen., Me.), Samuel A. Foote (Sen., Conn.), Arnold Naudain (Sen., Del.), Asher Robbins (Sen., R.I.), Elisha Whittlesey (Rep., Ohio). Perry M. Goldman & James S. Young, *The United States Congressional Directories 1789-1840* (New York, 1973), 257. In his speech in Wilmington (see note 1 above) Clayton specifically had mentioned Bell, Naudain, Foote, and Holmes as having helped devise the 1833 tariff. 5. The protectionist group comprising Clayton's mess had reportedly insisted on certain crucial amendments, including a provision for home valuation, as the price for their support of the compromise bill. Clay then also endorsed the principle of home valuation, and it was incorporated in the bill. See Peterson, *Olive Branch and Sword*, 74-77. 6. See 8:608. 7. See 8:604, 619-22, 626-27. 8. See 9:628. 9. On June 19, 1844, Polk had written a letter to J.K. Kane of Philadelphia, announcing his support of a tariff for revenue with incidental protection to home industry. This was widely viewed as an attempt to present himself as a protectionist in the North, although he had been a life-long foe of the protective tariff. To an emissary from Calhoun, however, he gave assurance that he was still opposed to protection. Merrill D. Peterson, *The Great Triumvirate: Webster, Clay, and Calhoun* (New York, 1987), 363; Eugene I. McCormac, *James K. Polk, A Political Biography* (Berkeley, 1922), 260-61.

From Santa Anna, Tacubaya, Mexico, August 23, 1844. States that he has received Clay's letter of June 24 and has followed its recommendation to free Thomas D. Tatum, a prisoner at the fort of Perote. Has ordered Tatum to be turned over to the American consul in Vera Cruz. Copy, in Spanish. InHi. See also Clay to Davis, June 24, 1844. Translated by Professors Kathleen Kulp-Hill and Norris MacKinnon, Eastern Kentucky University.

To WILLIS GREEN Blue Licks [Nicholas County, Ky.], August 24, 1844

Being here to drink the water for a few days, I recd. at this place your favor of the 19h. from which I perceive you continue to have your hands full. Don't you apprehend that Mrs. [Ann A.] Green will apply for a Divorce? I like the Catholic Layman[1] very much. In certain Localities, it is calculated to have good effect. I wrote to [Garrett] Davis for half a dozen copies. I enclosed to him yesterday a letter for J[ohn]. M. Clayton, supposing that you had left the City. Be pleased to forward it.

We have done as well as I feared in K[entucky]. not as well as I hoped; but in Novr. all will be right.[2]

You will see next week in the Reporter an article about the slander of my gambling here.[3]

So [John] Tyler has withdrawn! And that upon the promise of a Mission, made by our opponents![4] There were suitable equivalents in that bargain; for nothing was given and nothing will be received.

A condensed form of the proofs, arguments &c concerning the old bargain Story[5] will be useful at certain points.

My respects to Davis.

ALS. KyLoF. 1. Samuel M. Semmes, a lawyer and judge of Cumberland, Md., had made an address to the Clay Club of Cumberland on June 28, 1844, in which he cited examples from Clay's career that demonstrated his friendliness to foreigners and Catholics. This address was published in *Extracts from a Pamphlet Entitled: "Religious Liberty in Danger"; A Vindication of the Whig party from the Charge of Hostility to Catholics and Foreigners, By a Catholic Layman* (n.p., 1844) and in the Lexington *Observer & Kentucky Reporter*, August 17, 1844. For Semmes, see Harry W. Newman, *The Maryland Semmes and Kindred Families* (Baltimore, 1956), 65, 80-81. 2. Letcher to Clay, July 6, 1844. 3. John M. McCalla spread stories stating that Clay had recently won several hundred dollars while at Blue Licks and had gambled on board the boat from Wheeling to Maysville on his recent return from Washington. The paper later published letters from the proprietors of Blue Licks and other witnesses denying these charges. Lexington *Observer & Kentucky Reporter*, August 31, 1844. 4. Through intermediaries, Tyler agreed to withdraw from the presidential contest and support Polk; in exchange, Tyler and his supporters would be welcomed into the Democratic party. A rumor also circulated that Tyler was to be appointed as American minister to the Court of St. James's. Tyler made his formal withdrawal on August 20. Oliver P. Chitwood, *John Tyler, Champion of the Old South* (New York, 1939), 379-83, and Robert Seager II, *And Tyler Too, A Biography of John and Julia Gardiner Tyler* (New York, 1967), 231-37. 5. See 7:660; 8:911; 9:648-49, 659-60, 696-700, 934.

From MAJOR A. WILLCOX & W.H. HARDEE[1] Halifax, N.C., August 27, 1844

As much has been said in relation to your letter addressed to Mr. [Francis P.] Blair many years ago,[2] in regard to the election of the Hon: J.Q. Adams to the Presidency, when & where you were accused of bargain & corruption in that election;[3] We have thought proper to ask of you, if you ever in a solitary instance refused directly or indirectly to permit the letter to be published, if not, we respectfully ask will you now give your consent to publish it?[4]

Since the Hon: L[inn]. Boyds' expose of the matter in Congress,[5] the Whigs have been losing ground in this State, and we have no doubt unless the letter is published [James K.] Polk & [George M.] Dallas will carry it in Novr. next.[6]

An answer at your earliest convenience is requested—

Copy. Printed in Shanks, *Papers of Willie Person Mangum*, 4:192. Enclosed in Clay to Mangum, Sept. 11, 1844. 1. Willcox was a member of the North Carolina legislature from 1825-38.

Shanks, *Papers of Willie Person Mangum*, 4:192. Hardee has not been identified. 2. See 4:9-11, 46-48. 3. See subject index 7:660; 8:911; 9:934; also 9:659-60, 696-97. 4. For the publication history of the letters, see 4:10, 48. 5. Sloane to Clay, May 9, 1844. 6. Clay to Graham, Feb. 6, 1844.

To JOHN M. CLAYTON N.p., n.d., *ca.* Late August, 1844

I send you the enclosed[1] to dispose of as you please. [Robert P.] Letcher, if necessary, will come out on the Compromise [Tariff of 1833];[2] but is it necessary? Is it not somewhat of a collateral if not obsolete issue? Had we not better pin them on the Repeal or Preservation of the Tariff of 1842?[3] That is a plain practical question, within the comprehension of the dullest capacity.

AN. DLC-John M. Clayton Papers (DNA, M212, R20). Addressed to Clayton in New Castle, Delaware. Editors have concluded from the content of this undated document, as well as statements made by Clay in his letters to Clayton of August 22 and 29, that this note probably was written between the dates of those letters. 1. Not found. 2. For Letcher's role in the Compromise Tariff of 1833, see 8:608; 9:329-30 and Peterson, *Olive Branch and Sword*, 54, 68-69, 81, 83; Maurice G. Baxter, *One and Inseparable, Daniel Webster and the Union* (Cambridge, Mass., 1984), 219, 555. 3. Throughout the 28th Congress, 2nd Session, free trade supporters in the House and Senate attempted to modify or repeal the Tariff of 1842. All these efforts failed. Clay's allies generally opposed any change in the tariff. For the various proposals, see U.S. Sen., *Journal*, 28 Cong., 1 Sess., 39, 313-15, *passim*; U.S.H. of Reps., *Journal*, 28 Cong., 1 Sess., 151, 160; Harold Von Holst, *The Constitutional and Political History of the United States*, 8 vols. (Chicago, 1881-92), 2:528-31; and Charles F. Adams (ed.), *Memoirs of John Quincy Adams*, 12 vols. (Philadelphia, 1876), 11:471, 473, 530, 543-44; 12:6, 14-17, 19-21, 25.

From Charles Burchard & John J. Foote, Hamilton, Madison County, N.Y., August 28, 1844. Write as "political friends" who desire not only "the maintainance of Whig measures & principles, but that some measure be devised for the peaceable & gradual abolition of slavery in our country." Ask, therefore, for "an expression of your views in reference to the emancipation of slaves throughout the United States & Whether in your opinion any means can be devised consistent with our obligations to the southern states, that would tend to ultimate emancipation without injury to the interests & rights of our southern bretherin & without endangering the union[.] And also whether you can as Presedent should you be elected to that office, consistently cooperate with any proper efforts for such a purpose—" Add that from his early espousal of emancipation in Kentucky [1:10-14], as well as his "impartial course . . . towards the north & south & from the fact that the annexation of Texas was sought for the purpose of checking all efforts for universal liberty & for political power & that you without consulting any personal interests raised you[r] voice . . . against the attempt [Clay to Editors Washington *Daily National Intelligencer*, April 17, 1844], we have been lead to believe that you were at heart opposed to slavery & . . . that . . . at a proper time . . . you would use your influence for its removal." They promise that his reply will be confidential, unless he gives permission "to express the sentiment to a few who feel & act with us." Mention also that "one of us" writing is "the 'Charles Burchard' about whom so much ado is made in consequence of his letter in the Hamilton Palladium & extensively republished in other papers by the Loco Focos & Abolitionists." Copy, draft. Courtesy of Prof. Alfred G. Engstrom, University of North Carolina.

On June 25, 1844, Burchard had addressed the abolitionists of Madison County, explaining that he was abandoning the Liberty party and endorsing Henry Clay. He believed James G. Birney could not carry a single state, and a vote for him would aid in Polk's election. He did not want to be instrumental in any way in helping the cause of Polk and Texas annexation. His entire speech was republished in the Rochester *Daily Democrat* on July 8, 1844. He was strongly attacked by some abolitionists for taking this position. See *ibid.*, July 22, 1844.

John J. Foote, who owned hardware and drug stores in Hamilton, was later a state senator and in 1860 a presidential elector for Abraham Lincoln. John E. Smith, *Our County and Its People: A Descriptive and Biographical Record of Madison County, New York* (Boston, 1899), 194-95, 248, 250, 252, 301; Mrs. L.M. Hammond, *History of Madison County, State of New York* (Syracuse, N.Y., 1872), 441, 454.

To JOHN M. CLAYTON Lexington, August 29, 1844

I wrote you a few days ago and have now to acknowledge the receipt of your favor of the 21st instant. I have read with very great satisfaction your piece in reply to the Ex member of Congress—[1] It is a triumphant vindication of your previous speech.[2] Both taken together appear to me to have exhausted the whole subject of the Compromise Act.[3]

I had seen the piece in the Madisonian charging Mr. [Daniel] Webster with having furnished that paper with an article containing an alleged paragraph in the original draught of the Compromise Act abandoning the Protective policy.[4] I am quite sure that there was no such paragraph in that draught, which however can be ascertained by resort to the files of the Senate. I have written to Mr [Garrett] Davis requesting him to procure a Copy for me from the files. But even if there were such a paragraph it was like any other first thought which unless it was persisted in amounts to nothing— The true question is, what was the shape in which I presented the bill to the Senate, and not what were any previous immature speculations[.] There seems to be a direct issue between Mr Webster and the Editor of the Madisonian,[5] and it strikes me to be best to let them settle it between themselves[.]

I repeat[6] that I think you have said and written all that is requisite about the Compromise Act, and I submit to you, whether a further protraction of that subject might not withdraw the public attention too much from the real issues in the present contest, to a collateral and subordinate one.

It seems to me that in Pennsylvania the points to be pressed are the Tariff, and Col [James K.] Polks hostility to it, and the Distribution of the proceeds of the Public lands. The strongest proofs should be laid before the Public of that hostility. On the other hand my known attachment to both those measures of policy should be urged on all suitable occasions. If by such an exhibition of our respective views Pennsylvania remains unmoved, I know not what would operate upon her. I sent you my last letter through Willis Green at Washington City.

LS. DLC-John M. Clayton Papers (DNA, M212, R20). 1. Clayton had written a letter on August 13, 1844, in reply to an unnamed Philadelphia man who asked him whether or not he had read Pennsylvania Congressman Charles Brown's attack on the speech Clayton had delivered at Wilmington on June 15. Clayton emphasized that "The Journals of Congress and Registers of Debates . . . will support every statement I have made, and will fix the charge of misrepresentation upon any ignorant demagogue, who, for his own poor purposes, may have sought to contradict me." Furthermore, "the business of detecting and exposing errors and falsehoods, when uttered by such a man as your Charles Brown, would be like fishing with a pin hook." This letter was printed in the Philadelphia *United States Gazette* on August 14, 1844. 2. Clay to Clayton, August 22, 1844. 3. See 8:604, 619-22, 626-27. 4. The article, which appeared in *The Madisonian* on August 14, 1844, claimed Webster had verified that Clay's original draft of the Compromise Tariff of 1833 had included the words that after June 30, 1842, "such duties shall be laid without reference to the protection of any domestic articles whatever." 5. John B. Jones. 6. See Clay to Clayton, *ca.* Late August, 1844.

To JOSEPH R. INGERSOLL Lexington, August 29, 1844

I thank you for your friendly letter transmitting [to] me [one] from [Christopher] Hughes,[1] and I am happy to perceive that he appears to be in good spirits. Besides the assurances which you give me of the exertions which our friends are making in Pennsylvania I receive concurring intelligence to the same effect from various other parts of the Keystone state. Nothing has surprised me so much as the attempt now making in Pennsylvania to represent Mr [James K.] Polk as the friend and myself as the foe of Protection.[2] If it should succeed I shall distrust the power of the press and of truth.

I am happy to inform you that although I have been several times indisposed since my return home, my health is now very good.

LS. NcD. 1. Not found. 2. For charges that Clay had abandoned the protective system, see Clay to Clayton, August 29, 1844. For Polk's attitude toward the tariff, see Clay to Clayton, August 22, 1844.

To David P. Hart, Lexington, Ky., August 30, 1844. For the payment of $3,500 conveys to Hart "the factory at present occupied by Thomas H. Clay and about Thirteen acres of land attached thereto. Said Clay reserves to himself the Machinery &c &c or such portions of it as has been agreed upon between his son Thomas H. Clay and the said David Hart." ADS. DLC-TJC (DNA, M212, R19).

From John Bayless, August 31, 1844. Gives bill of sale for a thirteen-year-old slave named Allen, sold to Clay for $525. DS. DLC-TJC (DNA, M212, R19).

See Deed of Emancipation for Charles Dupuy, December 9, 1844.

On January 1, 1845, Garrett Watts sold a Negro man named Thornton, "aged about twenty Eight Years," to Clay for $600. Warrants that Thornton "is sound in body & mind and a slave for life." ALS. DLC-TJC (DNA, M212, R19).

On February 23, 1845, Chilton Allen wrote Clay attesting to the character of Allen Armstrong and saying that he "will be good for any Warrantee he may make you in the sale of his slaves. They are free from any incumbrance." *Ibid.* Another letter of the same date from H. Frazer [?] attested to the excellent qualities of the slave Jim which he had bought from Armstrong. *Ibid.* The following day, February 24, Allen Armstrong, Winchester, Ky., sold to Clay the slaves James (or Jim), 24 years old, and his wife Sidney, 19 years old, for a total of $1,100. He warranted that the title to them was free from any encumbrance or defect. Contract witnessed by H.I. Bodley. ADS. *Ibid.*

On April 4, 1846, Clay, along with Wallace Kirkwood of Washington, D.C., Benjamin Merrill of Salem, Mass., and Elijah Porter of New York City, for the sum of $505 deeded to Arsenious Harvey and James S. Harvey a parcel of land in the District of Columbia from the estate of Henry Ault. The Ault estate had been willed to Kirkwood, in trust, "to Sell and dispose of . . . with the approbation of the President for the American Colonization Society for the time being," all proceeds to go to the Colonization Society. Kirkwood, with the approbation of Clay as president, had deeded this land to Merrill and Porter on February 6, 1844, but the deed was faulty, thus requiring Kirkwood and Clay, as well as Merrill and Porter, to sign the new deed conveying the parcel of land to the Harveys. DS, signed by Kirkwood, Clay, Merrill, and Porter. KyU.

Clay purchased "a negro boy of light complexion named Lewis about twenty three years of age" from A. Warner on May 21, 1846. Bill of Sale; price not given. AD, by Clay, signed by Warner. DLC-TJC (DNA, M212, R19). Warner was probably Alfred Warner, a Lexington manufacturer. Julius P.B. MacCabe, *Directory of the City of Lexington . . . 1838 & '39* (Lexington, 1838).

On December 25, 1847, Clay purchased from Edwin Poage "a negro man named

Charles Lilly, and Emilly his wife" for the sum of $1,000. Under the agreement Poage could repurchase the two slaves for $1,000 "any time within four years," but this right could not be assigned to another party. Agreement between Poage and Clay. ADS, by Clay, signed also by Poage. DLC-HC (DNA, M212, R6). A receipt to Clay, signed by Poage and dated December 29, 1847, is written on the bottom of the agreement.

On July 7, 1848, Clay sold a mulatto boy named Henry, age 15 years, to John Raine for the sum of $500. The boy, who was the son of Mary Anne Dupuy, was to be freed by Raine when he reached the age of 28. Copy. KyLxT. Attached is a receipt, dated July 10, 1848, by D.P. Faulds, indicating that he had received the boy for Raine, and he "is now at the Galt House [in Louisville] in my possession for said Raine." ADS. *Ibid.* Witnessed by Thomas Smith. Endorsed by Clay on verso: "Mulatto Henry. Proof of his right to his freedom at the age of 28." Raine is probably John A. Raine of Hardin County, Ky., who had previously served as coroner and deputy sheriff of the county and in 1848 was farming and selling goods. William H. Perrin *et al.*, *Kentucky, A History of the State* . . . , 8 vols. (reprint ed., Louisville, 1979), 3:980.

On August 31, 1848, John Raney [*sic*, Raine] acknowledged receipt of Henry, "a son of Mary Anne and grand son of Aaron and Lotty [Dupuy] . . . and . . . I have bought the said boy upon the condition that he is to be free when he completes his twenty-Eighth year. . . . or at my death if I should die sooner." DS. DLC-HC (DNA, M212, R6).

Also on August 31, Thomas Smith wrote Clay from Louisville enclosing Raine's receipt. Notes that the "probability is so strong that Henry will be free . . . too soon for his own good" under the stipulation regarding Raine's death that "I felt inclined to take the responsibility of suggesting 21 years of age, as the earliest period of his liberation from service." ALS. DLC-TJC (DNA, M212, R11).

On November 20, 1848, Clay transferred to his grandson James, son of James B. Clay, ownership of "the negro boy Solomon aged from Eight to Ten years old, the son of my slaves." ADS. *Ibid.*

Clay transferred to his son John M. Clay on November 27, 1848, ownership of slaves Harvey, John, and Bob. ADS. Henry Clay Memorial Foundation, Lexington, Ky.

On July 17, 1849, James B. Clay sold to his father "my negro man Lewis for the Sum of Seven hundred Dollars." DS. DLC-TJC (DNA, M212, R19).

See also Last Will and Testament of Henry Clay, July 10, 1851.

To GEORGE M. DAVIS Lexington, August 31, 1844

I received your favor. I had previously seen the result of the Election in your State [Illinois],[1] which I confess some what disappointed me. With respect to your suggestion that I should make some public declaration of my opinions on the subjects of the Naturalization Laws and the Native American party, I must say, that, after much consideration, I have thought it best to leave the existing contest to be decided on the issues now before the public, without adding any new one. Those subjects only affect particular localities, in some of which, it is true, that public opinion is much divided. Some of my most discreet friends coincide with me in this course.[2]

Mean time, I transmit herewith, a Lexn. Reporter, containing a Speech of a Mr. [Samuel M.] Semmes, which comprehends abundant matter for defending me against the charge of illiberality towards foreigners.[3]

The August elections have fulfilled all our expectations, in the results in Kentucky,[4] Indiana[5] & No. Carolina.[6] I never counted upon Illinois, altho' I cherished some hope of it. I believe that we shall give our opponents a complete drubbing in November.[7]

ALS. ViU. Letter marked "(Private)." 1. Clay to Kennedy, March 29, 1844. 2. Clay to Ewing, June 19, 1844; Ewing to Clay, June 23, 1844. 3. Clay to Green, August 24, 1844. 4. Letcher to Clay, July 6, 1844. 5. Clay to Berrien, July 16, 1844. 6. Clay to Graham, Feb. 6, 1844. 7. Clay to Webb, Feb. 29, 1844.

To DANIEL C. WICKLIFFE Lexington, September 2, 1844

The editor[1] of a neighboring print, (the Kentucky Gazette, of Lexington) calling my attention to a letter of C[assius]. M. Clay, Esq., under date the 10th July 1844, and addressed to Col. J.J. Speed[2] of Ithaca, has appealed to me, with so much earnestness and with a purpose of such unaffected sincerity, to say whether I approve or disapprove of that letter, that I have not the heart to deny to that Editor the very great gratification which he will derive from the perusal of this note, especially when it gives me so little trouble to write it.

Mr. C.M. Clay's letter was written without my knowledge, without any consultation with me, and without any authority from me. I never saw it until I read it in the public prints. That gentleman is an independent citizen, having a perfect right to entertain and avow his own opinions. I am not responsible for them, as he is not for mine. So far as he ventures to interpret my feelings, he has entirely misconceived them. I believe him to be equally mistaken as to those in the circle of my personal friends and neighbors, generally.

In my speech, addressed to the Senate of the U.S.,[3] and in resolutions which I offered to that body,[4] in my address to Mr. [Hiram] Mendenhall,[5] about two years ago, and on various other public occasions, I have fully, freely, and explicitly, avowed my sentiments and opinions, on the subject of the Institution of Slavery and Abolition. I adhere to them, without any reservation. I have neither entertained, nor expressed publicly or privately, any others. And my friends and neighbors generally, so far as I have interchanged sentiments with them, coincide entirely with me.

The sentiments and opinions, so expressed by me, may be briefly stated to be: 1st. That Congress has no power or authority over the institution of Slavery. 2d. That the existence, maintenance and continuance of that Institution depend, exclusively, upon the power and authority of the respective States, within which it is situated. And 3d. That Congress cannot interfere with slavery in the District of Columbia, without a violation of good faith to the States of Maryland and Virginia, implied, if not expressed, in the terms, objects, and purposes of the grant of ten miles square to the General Government.

So far from the success of the Whig cause having any injurious tendency, as has been alleged, I believe it will have a powerful effect in tranquilizing and harmonizing all parts of the Union, and in giving confidence, strength and security to all the great interests of our country.

I hope that your editorial neighbor will be now satisfied. And as I trust that I do not exaggerate the pleasure which this renewed expression of my views and opinions will give him, is it too much to anticipate that he will forthwith renounce the error of his ways and come straight out a staunch and sterling Whig?

Copy. Printed in Lexington *Observer & Kentucky Reporter*, Sept. 4, 1844; and Lexington *Kentucky Gazette*, Sept. 7, 1844. 1. J. Cunningham was editor of the *Gazette*, Wickliffe of the *Observer & Reporter*. Extant copies of the *Gazette* do not contain the editor's call for Clay's response.

2. Col. John James Speed, Jr. (1803-67), was a prominent merchant of Ithaca, N.Y., who had been a presidential elector and an unsuccessful candidate for Congress. There is also a possibility C.M. Clay's letter was written to John James, Sr. (1777-1859), who was also known as Col. Speed. W.T. Hewitt, *Landmarks of Tompkins County New York*. John H. Selkrey, ed. (Syracuse, N.Y., 1894), 24, 278-79; Thomas Speed, *Records and Memorials of the Speed Family* (Louisville, Ky., 1892), 47-52. C.M. Clay's letter to Speed appeared in the New-York *Daily Tribune*, August 13, 1844. In it he wrote that "If Whiggery means anything it means opposition to tyranny—all tyranny. . . . I regard no aristocracy in Europe so coercive and anti-republican as the Southern states." He also predicted that Henry Clay would lose 3 or 4 slave states because of his opposition to the annexation of Texas. He said he did not mean to say that Henry Clay was an emancipationist "but I believe his feelings are with the cause." 3. See 9:278-83. 4. See 9:123-26. 5. See 9:777-82.

From JOHN C. WRIGHT Cincinnati, September 5, 1844

On the other leaf you will find the statement of my conversation with Louis McLane, which I promised you.[1] My apology for not preparing it sooner is, that my engagements scarcely leave me a moment of leisure[.]

I have your letter on the subject of the Blue Lick lie, and you will have seen in the [Cincinnati *Daily*] gazette the use made of it.[2] I should certainly with you [have] felt no little mortification, had I thought it *necessary* to call upon *you* to refute so improbably [*sic*, improbable] a calumny. But the charge was reiterated upon the face of *my denial*, and the proof in writing said to exist under these circumstances I thought it proper that you see the charge and have an opportunity to say if *any* circumstance had taken place out of which to fabricate the story. I know well, Sir, that even the Father of lies himself could hardly keep pace with the supporters of [James K.] Polk, in inventing and giving circulation to lies, and I do not often heed them.

Upon the whole our prospects are as favorable as when I had the pleasure of meeting you. Our opponents are very active and unscrupulous in the use of the means they employ. The small majority in Ky has been wary in all its charges & has passed away. Your late letter on [the] Texas question[3] has given the rascals a new impulse. Liberty men, Locofocos and timid Whigs use the letter as bug-a-boo to the anti-annexation. We defend it, as in accordance with [what] you before said, and I think it will leave little injurious impression upon the minds of our friends. But the public mind is excited—men are confederated together in appeals to the very worst passions of our nature, and the public mind is feverish, and unstable. This will not be more than a nine day's topic of vituperation. With the old issues we are safe, depend upon it. All we want is to bring the voters out.

ALS. DLC-HC (DNA, M212, R5). Printed in Colton, *Clay Correspondence*, 4:492-93. Endorsed by Clay on verso: "Statem[en]t concerning the P. Election of 1825 McLean [*sic*] &c." 1. Wright's statement, addressed to Clay and dated Sept. 5, 1844, reported that both he and Louis McLane had been members of the U.S. House in 1825 and on the committee "to report rules for the government of the House in conducting the [presidential] election. He was known to be in favor of Mr. [William H.] Crawford, and I was in favor of Mr [John Q.] Adams." Asserts that on the morning of the election he had walked with McLane "from the Committee room to the House" and that McLane asked "if we could elect Mr. Adams? I answered that we could elect him, as I thought on the first ballot. I trust in God you will succeed, said he, and on the first ballot, and save the country from the curse of Jacksonism. You know I must vote for Crawford on the first ballot as my State [Delaware] voted for him; but we all know he cannot be elected, and I sincerely hope you will elect Mr. Adams. We separated and took our seats. In a short time the vote was taken and Mr. Adams got the votes of thirteen states and was declared duly elected. This is the substance of the conversation, if not the very words. Mr. McLane spoke openly, with energy, and I thought sincerely[.]" ALS. DLC-HC (DNA, M212, R5). Printed in Colton, *Clay Correspondence*, 4:493-94. 2. Clay's letter to Wright has not been found. Wright, the editor of the Cincinnati *Daily Gazette*, had written an editorial on August 20, 1844, calling John M. McCalla's allegations about Clay's gambling [Clay to Green,

August 24, 1844] "An Unmitigated Lie." In a Sept. 2 editorial Wright noted that he had "addressed a note to Mr. Clay" on the subject, and that Clay "authorizes us to say that the whole Tale in all its particulars is a base, and infamous calumny, utterly destitute of all Foundation." 3. Clay to Peters & Jackson, July 27, 1844; see also Clay to Editors of Washington *Daily National Intelligencer*, April 17, 1844, and Clay to Miller, July 1, 1844.

To ANDREW G. BURT[1] Lexington, September 6, 1844

I have no hesitation in saying, in reply to your favor, that in my opinion all our rights in the Oregon Territory[2] ought to be firmly and inviolably maintained. I did all that I could at Ghent[3] to accomplish that object, and should continue to exert myself to the same end, in whatever situation I might be placed. P.S. I have a great repugnance, without a strong necessity, to be published; altho' of course I desire no concealment of the above opinion.

ALS. OCHP. Addressed to Burt in Cincinnati, Ohio. 1. For Burt, a Cincinnati banker, see Merrill J. Mattes, *Indians, Infants and Infantry, Andrew and Elizabeth Burt on the Frontier* (Denver, Colo., 1960), 10. 2. See 9:828-29. 3. The Treaty of Ghent contained a formula for reciprocal restitution of territory captured by each side in the war. Although the peace commissioners had been instructed that Astoria, a post at the mouth of the Columbia River in the Oregon Territory that had been in U.S. hands before the war, should be included in any reciprocal restoration, this was not specifically mentioned in the treaty nor was the related boundary issue settled. Frederick Merk, *The Oregon Question, Essays in Anglo-American Diplomacy and Politics* (Cambridge, Mass., 1967), 6-10. For the Treaty of Ghent, see Parry, *Treaty Series*, 63:421-30.

To CHARLES BURCHARD & JOHN J. FOOTE Lexington, September 9, 1844

On the subjects of which your friendly letter to me treats,[1] I have so often, during a long life, expressed myself, that in the present nervous and sensitive state of the public mind, I think it best to write nothing for publication. There is a propensity to perve[r]sion of every thing proceeding from me, among our political opponents, that I think that silence generally is the course of duty with me. We must beat our opponents, on the present issues before the public; especially on those in which we are for the Tariff,[2] and against Annexation,[3] whilst they are the reverse. Why multiply these issues? Or distract the public mind with others?

Nevertheless I thank you for your friendly letter, to which I could not forbear transmitting this brief reply, altho' my correspondence is oppressive, almost beyond endurance.

ALS. Courtesy of Prof. Alfred G. Engstrom, University of North Carolina. Letter marked "(Private)." 1. Burchard & Foote to Clay, August 28, 1844. 2. Clay to Clayton, *ca.* Late August, 1844. 3. Of Texas. Clay to Crittenden, Feb. 15, 1844.

To THOMAS C. MILLER[1] ***et al.*** Lexington, September 9, 1844

I this day received your letter addressing two inquiries to me—"first. Are you in favor of the tariff act of 1842:["][2] And, second. "Would you, if elected, support that act as it is, without modification, or would you be in favor of modifying it?"

I have so often, gentlemen, expressed my opinion in favor of the tariff of 1842, that the only regret I feel is that you should deem it at all necessary to request any renewed expression of it. Nevertheless, I take pleasure in complying with your request in saying that I am of opinion that the operation of the tariff of 1842 has been eminently salutary; that *I am decidedly opposed to its repeal*; that I should regard its repeal as a great National calamity; and that I am unaware of the necessity of any modification of it. I am, therefore, opposed alike to its repeal or modification. A fixed and stable policy is what the country now most needs, and I sincerely hope that the Tariff of 1842 may be maintained, and thus afford a security for that desideratum.

Copy. Printed in *Niles' Register* (Oct. 5, 1844), 67:75. 1. For Miller, a former Democratic member of the Pennsylvania house from Cumberland County and a prominent figure in the Buckshot War, see Charles M. Snyder, *The Jacksonian Heritage, Pennsylvania Politics 1833-1848* (Harrisburg, Pa., 1958), 135. 2. See 9:646-47.

To THOMAS M. BOND Lexington, September 10, 1844

I duly received your favor of the 29th ultimo. You will have seen an editorial article in the [Washington *Daily*] National Intelligencer of the 5th inst.[1] which I presume will afford you satisfaction in respect to the enquiry contained in your letter. I confess I feel surprize and mortification that it should be deemed necessary to ascertain whether, now near thirty eight years ago, I was, when I first took my seat in the Senate of the U States, a few months under or over thirty years of age. No man knows his own age, except by information from others; and I was less likely to obtain correct information of mine than most men, my father having died when I was a mere infant and my mother having moved to Kentucky in the year '92 when I was a boy scarcely 15 years of age. But I repel with scorn and indignation the charge of perjury. I neither took, nor was required to take, any oath with respect to my age. I did not elect myself to the Senate of the U States, but I was chosen by the Legislature. Kentucky three times elected me afterwards to the Senate of the U. States and twice give me her vote for the President of the U. States. The Senate did not controvert my right to a seat. And I ask, in all candor and liberality, if both the Legislature of Kentucky and the Senate of the U. States were content, whether any body else after the lapse of near thirty years can now justly impeach my conduct? This far fetched objection shows the desperation of our opponents and how little they can really find to upbraid me with. I think it ought to be treated by our friends with contempt.

I offer you, my dear sir, my thanks for the friendly motives which have prompted your letter. Mine is not intended for publication, but for your own satisfaction.

ALS. PSC-Hi. Letter marked "(Private)" and addressed to Bond in Wheatland, Loudon County, Virginia. 1. The editorial defended Clay for having taken his seat in the U.S. Senate when he was only 29 years and 7 months old, rather than the constitutionally required age of 30. It also pointed out that there had been other cases of a similar nature.

To ENOS COOPER[1] Lexington, September 10, 1844

[Thanks him for the "half a dozen pair of ladies and gentlemen's white and black kid gloves" just received and comments on their superiority. Adds that "if we can obtain a sufficient supply of such American gloves, we need no longer be dependent, for that article, upon Europe." Continues:]

I have attentively perused your observations, in regard to the manufacture of kid gloves, and the inadequacy of the protection at present afforded by our laws. They seem to me to possess great weight; and I cannot doubt that the views you present, upon being properly laid before Congress, will command attention and exert influence. What strongly recommends the encouragement of this branch of manufacture is, that it would bring into active employment a great amount of female labor, which is now idle or unprofitably occupied.

But, my dear sir, it is useless now to speculate upon the advantages of cherishing this or any other branch of American manufactures. The question is now depending before the American people, whether the doctrines of free trade or fair protection to American industry, shall prevail. In a period of less than sixty days, that question will be settled. Perhaps no State in the Union will exercise more influence in settling it than the State of Pennsylvania.[2] If it should be determined, in conformity with the policy of the whigs, we may confidently anticipate just protection to every branch of manufactures for which the country is ripe. Should the opposite party prevail, we may bid adieu to national prosperity, so far as it depends upon the encouragement of domestic manufactures, and resume our dependence upon foreign countries. In any and every event, I tender you my cordial wishes for your success, happiness and prosperity.

Copy. Printed in *Kendall's Expositor* (Oct. 1, 1844), 4:394. 1. Cooper's glove manufactory was located at N.E. St. John and Willow in Philadelphia. *McElroy's Philadelphia Directory for 1844.* 2. Polk carried Pennsylvania in 1844, receiving 167,533 votes to 161,203 for Clay, and 3,138 for Birney. McKee, *National . . . Popular and Electoral Vote*, 56.

From Samuel S. Seward, Florida, Orange County, N.Y., September 10, 1844. Although not a personal acquaintance, writes because "I read your letter at Raleigh [Clay to Editors of Washington *Daily National Intelligencer*, April 17, 1844] with extacy of Joy I conceived it precisely what the people wanted my blood run warm through my Veins. . . . Then Clay and [Theodore] Frelinghuysen triumphantly waived on every Banner Then the Opposition seemed conscious all was gone. Then every vile Slander passed by you as A shaddow—And in your answer to Messrs [Thomas M.] Peters and [John M.] Jackson [Clay to Peters & Jackson, July 27, 1844] you say you do not think it right to announce in advance what will be the course of A future administration in respect to A question with A foreign power, Had your letter ended here no exceptions could have been taken. But your after Ideas relative to the annexation of Texas however guarded they may be have been so garbled misconstrued & abused by The Locos as to completely resussitate revive and put new annimation into their followers[.] Their theme now is [James K.] Polk & Clay hold the same doctrines as to Texas and as we have a pure unexceptionable nominee we will elect Mr Polk."

Adds that "my heart & Soule is made up in Henry Clay not so much of his spended [*sic*, splendid] talents but because I thought under providence he was destined to be the salvation of our beloved Country—And I humbly implore that if any thing can be done to arrest the ardour & violance of those lying distructives with their tory Polk that it may be spedily attended to." Notes also that "The citisens of this portion of the Union are extreamly hostile to Slavery and nothing in the most remote shape can be favourably received." ALS. NGos.

For Samuel S. Seward, father of William Henry Seward, see Glyndon G. Van Deusen, *William Henry Seward* (New York, 1967), 3-6, 11, 22-23, 36, 90-91, 116.

From HENRY CLAY, JR. Louisville, September 11, 1844

I have just been reading the letter of Mr C[assius]. M. Clay and your note relating to it in the Lexington paper.[1] I have but little doubt that in Mr C's remark that those most under your influence approximate him in sentiment he means me among others. Now I have great reluctance and unfeigned diffidence in expressing any opinion of news on a political subject at this crisis. But I entertain other feelings much stronger and more decided such as the most profound regret that any opinion of mine should be used in any the remotest degree to your injury or annoyance and an entire disapprobation of such use but above all when such an opinion seems to have been misunderstood by the gentleman who has thus used it.

These remarks I hope will excuse me to you in adverting at all to opinions so unimportant in their influence as mine. In a conversation which I had with Mr C.M. Clay at Maysville I felt a desire to know if he was really an Abolitionist. If I understood him he declared that he was only in favour of legal and constitutional means of effecting a gradual emancipation of the slaves of Ky. I agreed with him expressing a desire that this might at some time or other be brought about and further in considering slavery a great curse to Ky. I think our conversation extended no further than as to these two points. I listened rather than lead in conversation for I believed Cassius to be in a false position on the subject of slavery and I desired to understand him. As to my own opinion which was not then in question and which I did not give in detail I may remark that I would consider it worse, than idle at a moment like the present—the most unpropitious in my judgment—to urge the subject of gradual emancipation. It can only be effected with the consent of the people of Ky and ought only to be carried with a full regard to vested rights of property and the legal and constitutional obligations belonging to the subject. My views principally regard the welfare of the white race, that of the black I consider secondary. Indeed I have serious doubts if the emancipation of the blacks would not ultimately lead to their extermination and disappearance from among us as we have seen that other inferior race the Indian gradually disappear although free.

I learn that Mr Clay entertains the opinion that no slave holder after you, if you should be elected, will ever be President of the United States. This indicates an entire division of opinion between him and me. Looking as I do principally at the good of the White race and embracing the black only in that great sphere of duties in which I include foreigners and all mankind other than the White citizens of the U. States upon whom alone I lavish my hearts best affections, two great paramount ideas rise in my mind two fixed principles about which revolve all minor considerations namely the liberty of the people and the Union of the States. These principles too I consider almost inseparable. It will be enough then to prove the entire discordance of Mr C.M. Clay's opinion and mine to remark that I consider his sentiment just referred to as a direct and fearful attack upon the Union of the States. The establishment of such a rule in the selection of the President would be the beginning of the end of this Government. The expression of such an opinion opens the way and points out the plainest and shortest road to the consummation of our national ruin. I dissent from it therefore and deplore its expression[.]

I am sure that Mr Clay would not purposely misrepresent me—I regret if his allusion meant me that he did not more thoroughly understand my views—It is however possible that he referred to other persons. I take it there is nothing new or strange in my opinions. I think I stand upon the ground occupied by Washington Jefferson Madison and all the fathers of the country. Besides as the period for action has not arrived and as I am not called upon now to decide I desire the benefit of mature consideration of all future events and circumstances as affecting the great question of emancipation. Fearing innovation I shall much rejoice if you are right in your opinion that a law of population will relieve us from the difficulties and embarassments of this subject. In any event I consider the liberty and Union of the Whites as subjects infinitely superior in importance to the gradual emancipation of the blacks. What we now want is repose. The public mind is now too excited and sensitive to arrive at just conclusions about our own interest and welfare as involved in the question. I therefore consider him as an enemy though perhaps an unwitting one both to the interests and happiness of the Whites and the Blacks who at a season so inopportune as the present rashly and improperly stirs the question of emancipation. With the abolitionists I need hardly say I can hold no communion of any sort. I believe them wrong in their principles wrong in their action wrong in every thing.

AL, incomplete. Henry Clay Memorial Foundation, Lexington, Ky. 1. Clay to Wickliffe, Sept. 2, 1844.

To JOSHUA R. GIDDINGS Lexington, September 11, 1844

Your friendly letter of the 4th inst. which I have just received, affords me a good opportunity of writing to you, which I very much desired. I am extremely sorry that my letters to Alabama[1] should have produced any unfavorable impressions in your portion of Ohio. It was not my intention, in those letters, to vary the ground in the smallest degree which I had assumed in my Raleigh letter.[2] It had been represented to me that in that letter I had displayed a determined opposition to the annexation of Texas to the United States, although the whole Union might be in favor of it, and it could be peacefully and honorably effected upon fair and just terms. It was my purpose, in those Alabama letters, to say that no personal or private motives prompted me to oppose annexation; but that my opinion in opposition to it was founded solely upon public and general considerations. I therefore said that if by common consent of the Union, without national dishonor, without war, and upon just conditions, the object of annexation could be accomplished, I did not wish to be considered as standing in opposition to the wishes of the whole confederacy, but on the supposition stated would be glad to see those wishes gratified.

Could I say less? Can it be expected that I should put myself in opposition to the concurrent will of the whole nation, if such should be its will? You appear to have rightly conceived me; and I think any one who will take a fair and candid view of all my letters together, must be satisfied with their import, and perfectly convinced of my entire consistency. But, my dear sir, as I had learned from Pittsburg[h] that my last Alabama letter was operating mischievously there, I have addressed a letter to James Dunlop, Esq.,[3] and others, in which I reaffirmed all the sentiments and opinions which I expressed in my Raleigh letter, and go the length of saying that if three such States as Ohio, Massachusetts, and Vermont were to manifest a decided opposition to the annexation of Texas, it ought not to be annexed to the United States. That letter will be published, will probably reach you by the time that this does, and I confidently anticipate will be satisfactory.

My position is very singular. Whilst at the South I am represented as a Liberty man, at the North I am decried as an ultra supporter of slavery; when in fact I am neither one nor the other. This peculiarity of position exposes me to a cross-fire from opposite directions, and rendered it indispensably necessary that I should come out a few days ago with a note in relation to a letter of Cassius M. Clay, Esq., first published in the "Tribune."[4] That letter, although I have no doubt it was written with the best intentions, was doing great mischief to the Whig cause even here in Kentucky, and there was much reason to apprehend that it would be much more extensively prejudicial in the States of Tennessee, Georgia, North Carolina, and Louisiana, upon whose vote we have strong reason for counting. You, I trust, will be satisfied with the position taken in my note,—that the existence, maintenance, and continuance of the institution of slavery depend exclusively upon State power and authority. As you had expressed regret that my Raleigh speech should have omitted that principle, I thought the occasion a suitable one for reasserting it. I shall be very sorry if Mr. Clay should be at all wounded by my note. Such was not my intention, and if he had been here, he would have felt the imperative necessity for it.

Copy. OHi. Printed in Julian, *The Life of Joshua R. Giddings*, 164-65. Letter marked "(Confidential)." 1. Clay to Miller, July 1, 1844; Clay to Peters & Jackson, July 27, 1844. 2. Clay to Editors of Washington *Daily National Intelligencer*, April 17, 1844. 3. Letter not found. James Dunlop was a prominent attorney and president of the Central Clay Club in Pittsburgh, Pa. *The Twentieth Century Bench and Bar of Pennsylvania* (Chicago, 1903), 2:840; *WPHM* (Winter, 1957), 40:243. 4. Clay to Wickliffe, Sept. 2, 1844.

To WILLIE P. MANGUM Lexington, September 11, 1844

I was very happy to receive your favor of the 23d of July. Your election did not turn out quite [as] well as you anticipated,[1] and its result was the reverse of what was anticipated when I was at Raleigh, at which time no fears were entertained for the election of the Governor, but great apprehensions were entertained about the Legislature. What is the present state of your prospects?[2] Our opponents are manifestly making great exertions every where, and affect if they do not feel great confidence in the issue of the contest.[3] Their whole system now seems to be directed to the propagation of the most detestable libels and lies. Is it producing any effect in North Carolina? If I am to credit the enclosed letter[4] it is doing us mischief there. Do you know the writers of it? The old story to which they allude I thought had been buried so low that it could never rise to the surface again. Our friends at Washington have been getting up an abridged history of all the facts, documents, and proofs respecting that old story, and if you think it worth while I wish you would write to [Willis] Green and have some of them distributed in your State. The [Francis P.] Blair letters[5] to which the enclosed refers, or rather copies of them are in the possession of Benj. Watkins Leigh of Richmond with authority to show them to any gentleman that may be desirous of perusing them. The truth is that so far as relates to the charge against me, they contain str[ong] corroborative proof of its falsity: but they are sportive, playful, and written in all the familiarity of private correspondence to the violation of which in any case I do not wish to give my sanction.

I am greatly obliged to you for the friendly solicitude you entertain about my health, and I am happy to inform you that it is now very good. I hope this letter will find yours equally so. Owing to the great extent of my correspondence, I am obliged to obtain the assistance of one of my sons who writes this letter as my amanuensis upon my dictation.

LS. DLC-Willie P. Mangum Papers (DNA, M212, R22). Addressed to Mangum at Red Mountain, Orange County, N.C. 1. Clay to Graham, Feb. 6, 1844. 2. *Ibid.* 3. Clay to Webb, Feb. 29, 1844. 4. Enclosure not found. 5. For the Blair letters, see 4:9-11, 46-48; also Clay to Leigh, July 3, 1844. For the corrupt bargain issue, see 7:660; 8:911; 9:934.

From Thomas C. Reyburn *et al.*, Baltimore, *ca.* September 11, 1844. Write to inquire if there was any truth to the report that when Clay heard of the nomination of James K. Polk by the Democrats, he had exclaimed, " 'beat again by hell[']; I desire to know the truth of this . . . because it is in the mouths of many of the opposite party who are continually trying to exercise their miserable wit by its repetition, and it has been flatly pronounced by me and others a miserable contemptible and absurd lie . . . we should like to have from you at an early period a positive Contradiction or the contrary." ALS. DLC-John Pendleton Kennedy Papers (DNA, M212, R21). Undated, but postmarked September 11. Clay enclosed this letter in Clay to Kennedy, September 16, 1844.

To RICHARD HENRY BAYARD Lexington, September 14, 1844

I was extremely sorry to learn the indisposition of Mrs. [Mary S.] Bayard, with her old complaint, by your favor received to day.[1] I am afraid that the climate of little Willie [Wilmington], with all her partiality for it, is unsuited to her constitution.

I thank you for the interesting information which you communicate. I am afraid that you and other friends are most too sanguine. The Loco's, beyond all question, are every where making the most desperate efforts by the most devilish means. They have so metamorphised me that you will not be able to recognize me when I next meet you.

I received a letter from Professor [Nathaniel Beverley] Tucker, written by your advice. I was not surprized by what he said respecting Mr. [Daniel] Webster.[2] [Louis] McLane's course is in perfect character.[3] He has a hereditary title to insincerity. He once said to Dr. [Henry] Huntt at West point that great wrong had been done to me, and that he meant to contribute all in his power to rendering me justice.

My affectionate regards to Mrs. Bayard and the young ladies. Tell her that I received her friendly letter giving me an enthusiastic account of the Mass Meeting at Wilmington.[4]

ALS. DLC-Richard Henry Bayard Papers (DNA, M212, R20). 1. Letter not found. 2. Not found, but see Tucker to Clay, Dec. 25, 1844. 3. Reference obscure, but see Wright to Clay, Sept. 5, 1844. 4. Probably the convention at Wilmington on June 15 at which John M. Clayton presided. See Clay to Clayton, August 22, 1844, and Washington *Daily National Intelligencer*, June 19, 1844.

To JOHN PENDLETON KENNEDY Lexington, September 16, 1844

I have received the enclosed letter signed by persons whom I do not know about which I take the liberty to trouble you. They make, you will perceive, an enquiry of me whether I ever used certain silly expressions which they quote in reference to Mr [James K.] Polk's nomination.[1] I need hardly say to you that I never uttered the foolish expressions in my life, and I should write to that effect to them, but for my apprehension that they would publish my letter, which would make me appear supremely ridiculous. Will you do me the favor to show them this denial on my part of the expressions attributed to me?

Is it not wonderful that our friends will give credit to, or allow themselves to be affected by the lies of our opponents, when they will not believe or listen to our incontestable truths?

What are your prospects in Maryland?[2] Is there any effort making to unite the Catholics against us?[3] And if so, with what success is it attended. . . .

LS. DLC-John Pendleton Kennedy Papers (DNA, M212, R21). 1. Reyburn *et al.* to Clay, Sept. 11, 1844. 2. Clay to Kennedy, March 29, 1844. 3. There apparently was no such organized effort.

To EDMUND H. TAYLOR Lexington, September 17, 1844

I recd. today your favor of the 14h. I should have no objection to your furnishing copies of my [Francis P.] Blair letters[1] to Mr. [Benjamin] Hardin, *upon your own authority*, and under the restriction that they should not be published. It is now too late for their publication, if it were ever expedient.[2] And I do not wish to give my countenance to the violation of private correspondence, under any circumstances.

ALS. KyHi. Letter marked "(Confidential)." 1. See 4:9-11, 46-48. 2. Clay to Leigh, July 3, 1844.

To EDGAR ATWATER Lexington, September 18, 1844

I have received your favor of the 9th instant,[1] and appreciate and thank you for the friendly motives which prompted it. I take pleasure, in compliance with your request, in saying that I adhere to every feeling, sentiment, and opinion expressed in my Raleigh letter[2] upon the subject of the annexation of Texas, and that it was far from my intention to vary in the smallest degree from them by either of my two letters addressed to Alabama.[3] It is only by a gross perversion of their contents that any discrepancy with the Raleigh letter is made out. It was my purpose, among other things, to say in my Alabama letters that I had no private or individual motives to object to annexation; that my objections were founded altogether upon public and political consideration, and that if the United States, by common consent, desired annexation, and it could be affected without national dishonor, without war, and upon just terms, I should be glad to see the people of the United States gratified. These letters were written in consequence of statements at the South being boldly put forth that I stand out in oppositon to annexation, although the whole people of the United States might desire it. Parts of paragraphs and expressions in my Alabama letter have been torn from the context, and a color attempted to be given to my meaning, which I never attempted. Some of my opponents are constantly treating me with the greatest unfairness. They have gone the length even of forging for me language which I never used, and of garbling and shamefully perverting that which I did employ.

Copy. Printed in *Kendall's Expositor* (Oct. 22, 1844), 4:437. 1. Atwater, writing from Portage County, Ohio, on Sept. 9, 1844, asked Clay "to state, over your signature, whether the letter written by you upon the annexation of Texas, a short time previous to your nomination, is a just exposition of the sentiments you now entertain upon that subject." Copy, excerpt. Printed in *Kendall's Expositor* (Oct. 22, 1844), 4:437. 2. Clay to Editors of Washington *Daily National*

Intelligencer, April 17, 1844. 3. Clay to Miller, July 1, 1844; Clay to Peters & Jackson, July 27, 1844.

To CASSIUS M. CLAY Lexington, September 18, 1844

I received your favor of the 10th instant, in which you state that you will be in Boston on the 19th, where it is impossible this letter can reach you; and I therefore send it to the Hon. Willis Green, to be forwarded to you. I am perfectly persuaded of your friendly intentions, and feel grateful for them. But you can have no conception, unless you had been here, of the injury which your letter to the *Tribune*[1] was doing; and that was nothing in comparison to that which it was likely to inflict on the Whig cause in the States of Tennessee, North Carolina, and Georgia. Our friend, John Speed Smith, as well as others, thought it even endangered the State of Kentucky. This effect resulted from your undertaking to speak of my private feelings and those of my near and particular friends, and your statement that you had been ten years operating in the Abolition cause.

Under these circumstances, there was an absolute necessity for the note which I published,[2] although I regretted it extremely. I endeavored so to shape it as not to wound your feelings, and I hope I did not.

Had you been here, you would have concurred with myself and other friends in thinking it indispensable.

You must be well aware of the very great delicacy of my position.

At the North I am represented as an ultra supporter of the institution of slavery, whilst at the South I am described as an Abolitionist; when I am neither the one nor the other. As we have the same sirname, and are, moreover, related, great use is made at the South against me, of whatever falls from you. There, you are even represented as being my son; hence the necessity of the greatest circumspection, and especially that you should avoid committing me.

You are watched wherever you go; and every word you publicly express will be tortured and perverted as my own are.

After all, I am afraid you are too sanguine in supposing that any considerable number of the Liberty men can be induced to support me. How can that be expected after they have voted against Mr. [William] Slade [Jr.]?[3]

With sentiments of my thankfulness for your friendly purposes, and with my best respects for Mrs. [Mary Warfield] Clay, I am truly and faithfully your friend,

Copy. Printed in Cassius M. Clay, *The Life of Cassius Marcellus Clay. Memoirs, Writings, and Speeches*. . . . (Cincinnati, 1886), 101-2. 1. Clay to Wickliffe, Sept. 2, 1844. 2. *Ibid.* 3. In 1844 abolitionists fielded a candidate in the Vermont gubernatorial election against Slade, the anti-slavery Whig candidate. Nevertheless, Slade, with 26,265 votes, defeated Democrat Daniel Kellogg who received 21,187 votes, and abolitionist candidate William Shafter who had 3,618 votes. *BDGUS*, 4:1573 and *Niles' Register* (Oct. 26, 1844), 67:115.

To JOSEPH PAXTON[1] Lexington, September 19, 1844

I received your favor of the 5h. inst. and perused with much interest the encouraging accounts you give of the Whig prospects in Pennsylvania.[2] I sincerely hope that they may be realized. Being myself an ardent friend of the Tariff of 1842, I should lament if Pennsa should bring it into jeopardy, by supporting the other party. Upon her course greatly depends the fate of the Tariff. If the Key stone of the Federal Arch should give way, the whole policy of protection might be prostrated.

I do not write for publication, being almost ashamed of having so often appeared in the public prints.

ALS. Courtesy of Dr. Thomas D. Clark, Lexington, Ky. 1. Joseph Paxton (1786-1861) was one of the first to manufacture iron on a large scale in Pennsylvania. See *CAB*. 2. Clay to Cooper, Sept. 10, 1844; Clay to White, Sept. 19, 1844.

To JOHN PURDUE & GODLOVE S. ORTH Lexington, September 19, 1844

I have received your favor,[1] and am obliged to you for the friendly motive which induced you to address me. I think a deliberate and candid view of my two Alabama letters[2] would lead to the conclusion, that there was no departure in them from the grounds taken in my Raleigh letter.[3] Most certainly none was intended. When I spoke of having no personal objections to annexation, I meant that my opinion was formed altogether upon public and general grounds, and did not proceed from any private or individual motives. So in the other letter to Alabama, when I said that if the annexation of Texas could be effected with the common consent of the Union, without national dishonor, without war, and upon fair and just terms, I meant that I did not wish to be considered as standing in opposition to the general will. I am opposed to immediate annexation. I am opposed to it whilst a war is raging between Texas and Mexico. And I should be opposed to it, at all times, and under all circumstances, unless there was a degree of concurrence among the states composing our Union, amounting to or approximating towards unanimity.

Heretofore there has been considerable opposition to the Protective Policy in the Slave States; but at this time I regret to be obliged to say, that I think that Policy is more in danger in the Free States than in the Slave States. And this favorable result in the Slave States has been brought about by the whigs. It is for example much more secure in Kentucky, Tennessee, Georgia, North Carolina, and Virginia, than it is in Indiana, or I fear even in Pennsylvania.

Copy. Printed in *Kendall's Expositor* (Oct. 22, 1844), 4:437-38. 1. Letter not found. For Purdue, a leading businessman from Lafayette, Ind., see *DAB*. For Orth, a Lafayette lawyer and later a congressman, see *DAB* and *BDAC*. 2. Clay to Miller, July 1, 1844; Clay to Peters & Jackson, July 27, 1844. 3. Clay to Editors of Washington *Daily National Intelligencer*, April 17, 1844.

To WILLIAM B. TAYLOR[1] Lexington, September 19, 1844

I received your favor of the 4th inst. and I have very regularly received the newspapers which you have kindly transmitted to me. Until the receipt of your letter I was not aware to whom I was indebted for them.[2] I agree with you that the prospects of the Whig cause are very encouraging; but our opponents are every where making the most strenuous exertions and they ought to be met by countervailing efforts. P.S. Many thanks for your friendly feelings towards me.

LS. NHi. 1. *The New-York City Directory for 1844 and 1845* (New York, 1845), 341, lists Taylor's address as Post Office, 179 Grand. Taylor has not been otherwise identified. 2. On Dec. 24, 1844, Clay again wrote Taylor, thanking him for the copies of the New York *Herald* which Taylor had sent him. Explains that "in my retirement . . . I have occasion for not more papers than the few that I subscribe for." Requests that Taylor no longer "incur the trouble and expense of transmitting any other papers to me." ALS. NHi.

To HENRY WHITE Lexington, September 19, 1844

Many thanks for your obliging letter of the 11th instant and for its interesting contents. It demonstrates very great and patriotic activity on the part of the Commercial Committee[1] and I hope that the success of its labors may correspond with its good intentions. We feel the greatest anxiety about the issue of your Governor's election[2] and our intelligence concerning it is somewhat conflicting.

You are aware that there is a Whig Committee at Washington consisting of the Hon. Messrs Garrett Davis and Willis Green,[3] the object of which is to distribute documents, of which a great many have been sent to Pennsylvania. I understand the funds of the Committee are getting low and if you should have any surplus in your Exchequer they will be very glad to receive some assistance.

I should be very happy should it be in my power to serve your house with the sugar planters of Louisiana and I authorise you at any time to refer them to my name.

LS. ViU. Printed in Colton, *Clay Correspondence*, 4:494. 1. The "Commercial Committee" evidently consisted of a group of merchants in Philadelphia who actively supported the Whig cause. For example, in Sept. White chaired a meeting of merchants in Philadelphia to consider the propriety of closing their businesses on Oct. 1 to attend the mass convention of Whigs scheduled to meet in the city that day. Philadelphia *United States Gazette*, Sept. 27, 1844. 2. In the 1844 gubernatorial election in Pennsylvania, Whig Joseph Markle who received 156,040 votes, lost to Democrat Francis R. Shunk, who had 160,322. *BDGUS*, 3:1305. Twelve Democrats, 10 Whigs, and 2 Native Americans were elected to Congress from Pennsylvania in 1844. *Guide to U.S. Elections*, 581. In the state senate elections Democrats won 21 seats to 11 for the Whigs and 1 for the Native Americans. In the state house, Democrats won 51 seats to 41 for the Whigs, and 8 for the Native Americans. *Niles' Register* (Oct. 9, 1844), 67:112. 3. Clay to White, June 15, 1844.

To MARY S. BAYARD Lexington, September 21, 1844

I duly received your friendly letter of the 9h. inst as I had that which you kindly previously addressed to me, communicating an account of your great & enthusiastic Convention at Wilmington.[1] I omitted to acknowledge that last, as I should have done, and, in a late letter to Mr. [Richard H.] Bayard, I requested him to apologize to you for me, which I hope he did. I am greatly obliged by the friendly interest which you continue to take in me, and I assure you that it is all most cordially reciprocated. And I am thankful for the communication of the observations made by you, during your late journey and at Saratoga. In the circle in which [words missing] have no doubt that the prospects of the Whigs [words missing] bright and cheering, but their opponents are [words missing] when, making the most strenuous exertions and resorting to the most unscrupulous means. My hopes are strong that we shall defeat them, but I am prepared for any event. I care less for myself, than I do of those great interests of our Country, which are at hazard in the contest.

In answer to your friendly enquiries about my health, I am happy to tell you that it was never better than at this time. After my return in the Spring, I had two or three slight, [words illeg.] indispositions, the probable consequences of my arduous and exciting Southern journey;[2] but they have passed away, and I am now perfectly well.

I regreted extremely to learn f[rom Mr.] Bayard that you had been revisited by your old complaint[3] immediately on your return to your favorite little Willie [Wilmington]. Why will it treat you so ill? Positively you must quit such an ungrateful place. I was very sorry also to hear of the ill health of your daughter,[4] and sincerely hope that this letter will find you both, and all the rest of your family, in good health. Do me the favor to present my affectionate regards to all of them, and to my good friend Miss Milligan,[5] and all the other friends who think of me in Wilmington. And do not forget that other letter promised me.

ALS. DeHi. 1. Clay to Clayton, August 22, 1844; Clay to Bayard, Sept. 14, 1844. 2. Clay to Preston, Jan. 19, 1844. 3. Reference obscure, but see Clay to Bayard, Sept. 14, 1844. 4. Reference obscure. 5. Possibly a daughter of John J. Milligan, a Delaware congressman and judge. See *BDAC*.

To JOSHUA R. GIDDINGS Lexington, September 21, 1844

Before I received your favor of the 16th instant, I had addressed a letter to you[1] which I presume you have since received, but which had not reached you at the date of yours.

In that letter I expressed my great reluctance on account of the necessity, arising out of the letter of C[assius] M. Clay Esq,[2] of my publishing my note to the Lexington Observer.[3] I stated what I still believe, that there was great danger of the loss of 4 slave states if I left Mr Clay's letter unnoticed. I stated to you also, that I expected a letter which I addressed to Pittsburg[h] would be published,[4] but it has not been and why I do not know.

I regret extremely the state of things which you describe in Ohio; the loss of its Electoral vote will I fear lead to the inevitable defeat of the Whig party.[5] Always prepared myself, for any event, and ready to acquiesce in any decision of the People of the U States, I should deplore that defeat less on my own account than that of our common country.

I transmit enclosed a letter in reply to one which you forwarded from Mr Hendry;[6] but I sincerely hope it may not be published, because the public mind is in such a state of excitement, that any thing from me at this time is liable to the greatest perversion.

In certain States, which you can well imagine, it might occasion us a much greater loss than any gain in your quarter; and I must add that I am afraid all your Patriotic efforts to conciliate the support of the Liberty party are vain and fruitless. Their course in Vermont, although our friend Mr [William] Slade [Jr.][7] was the Candidate there for Governor, and their more recent course in Maine,[8] cannot have escaped your observation. Another reason for not publishing my letter to Mr Hendry is, that I have had many letters from New York Pennsylvania and Ohio requesting me to forbear writing letters for publication Notwithstanding which I am almost daily importuned to write others.

I thought you would have been pleased with that part of my note, drawn from me by Mr Clay's letter, in which I state that the power over the Institution of Slavery in the Slave States is vested exclusively in them.

I will transmit to you in a few days an Editorial article[9] on the subject of my three letters,[10] in regard to Texas, with which I hope you will be well pleased[.]

LS. DLC-Giddings/Julian Papers (DNA, M212, R21). Letter marked "(Private & Confidential)." 1. Clay to Giddings, Sept. 11, 1844. 2. Clay to Wickliffe, Sept. 2, 1844. 3. *Ibid.* 4. The letter to James Dunlop mentioned in Clay to Giddings, Sept. 11, 1844. 5. Clay to Berrien, July 16, 1844. 6. Letter not found. Mr. Hendry is probably Samuel Hendry, a lawyer who with Giddings had been a founder of the Ashtabula County Historical and Philosophical Society. William W. Williams, *History of Ashtabula County, Ohio* . . . (Philadelphia, 1878), 30-31, 40, 43, 114, 151. 7. Clay to C.M. Clay, Sept. 18, 1844. 8. In the 1844 gubernatorial race in Maine, Democrat Hugh Johnson Anderson won with a vote of 48,942 to 38,501 for his Whig rival, Edward Robinson, and 6,410 votes for minor candidates. *BDGUS*, 2:605. In the congressional elections Democrats won 10 seats and Whigs 1. *Guide to U.S. Elections*, 580. Of those seats up for election in the state legislature, Democrats won 65 in the house while Whigs won 30 and the Liberty party 1. In the state senate Democrats won 20 seats to 3 for the Whigs. Portland (Me.) *Daily Argus*, Sept. 18, 1844. Polk carried Maine with 45,719 votes to 34,378 for Clay, and 4,836 for Liberty party candidate Birney. McKee, *National . . . Popular & Electoral Vote*, 56. It was generally believed that, but for the abolitionist vote, the Whigs would have carried Maine. The abolitionists drew almost all their 5,000 votes from the Whigs, while many other Whigs stayed away form the polls because of the abolitionists. New-York *Daily Tribune*, Sept. 2, 12, 1844. 9. Probably Clay to Gales & Seaton, Sept. 23, 1844. 10. Clay to Editors of Washington *Daily National Intelligencer*, April 17, 1844; Clay to Miller, July 1, 1844; Clay to Peters & Jackson, July 27, 1844.

From Robert Walsh, Jr., Paris, France, September 22, 1844. States that President John Tyler and Secretary of State John C. Calhoun have nominated him as U.S. consul in Paris. Reports that he had not sought the post and hesitated accepting it, because "the emoluments were reduced below my gains from literary efforts: the offic[e], moreover, having become a mere mercantile speculation in the hands of Mr. [Daniel] Brent's successor, was brought, altogether to a sorry plight." Has decided to accept the post, however, since it is "capable of being rendered particularly useful & creditable to the country as an entrepot of information for both th[e] American & French governments in the trade, statistics, commercial legislation & diplomacy of Europe & th[e] United States," and because of the favorable response the nomination has received from the Paris generals, the press, and many of his friends. Hopes "to reorganize and replenish the Consulate in a way to raise it to its proper estimation here and at home." Adds that "I doubt I should have overcome my general reluctance, if I had not counted on your kindness and protection in the event of your election to the Presidentship. It would be . . . too severe a mortification to be encountered that you should remove me." Notes that since he left the U.S. eight years ago, "I have taken no share in party politics; I can have no claims as a mere partisan. . . . On the Tariff question, I am with the Whigs; on the Abolition & the Texas points, more with their adversaries: You yourself, I perceive, differ, on these, materially from a considerable portion of the Whig denomination." ALS. DLC-HC (DNA, M212, R5). For Walsh, see 2:325.

Lorenzo Draper was confirmed as Daniel Brent's replacement on March 15, 1841. Draper was recalled and Walsh nominated on December 17, 1844. His appointment was confirmed on December 23, 1844. U.S. Sen., *Executive Journal*, 5:377, 379; 6:361, 370.

To THE EDITORS OF THE WASHINGTON *DAILY NATIONAL INTELLIGENCER* [JOSEPH GALES, JR. & WILLIAM W. SEATON] Lexington, September 23, 1844

Since my nomination at Baltimore in May last, by the Whig Convention,[1] as a candidate for the office of President of the United States, I have received many letters propounding to me questions on public affairs, and others may have been addressed to me which I never received. To most of those which have reached me, I have replied; but to some I have not, because either the subjects of which they treated were such as that, in respect of them, my opinions, I thought, had been sufficiently promulgated, or that they did not possess, in my judgment sufficient importance to require an answer from me. I desire now to say to the public, through you, that considering the near approach of the Presidential election, I shall henceforward respectfully decline to transmit for publication any letters from me in answer to inquiries upon public matters.

After my nomination, I doubted the propriety, as I still do, of answering any letters upon new questions of public policy. One who may be a candidate for the Chief Magistracy of the nation, if elected, ought to enter upon the discharge of the high duties connected with that office, with his mind open and uncommitted upon all new questions which may arise in the course of its administration, and ready to avail himself of all the lights which he may derive from his Cabinet, from Congress, and, above all, from the public opinions.

If, in advance, he should commit himself to individuals who may think proper to address him, he may deprive the public and himself of the benefit of those great guides. Entertaining this view, it was my intention, after my nomination, to decline answering for publication all questions that might be propounded to me. But, on further reflection, it appeared to me that if I imposed this silence upon myself, I might, contrary to the uniform tenor of my life, seem to be unwilling frankly and fearlessly to submit my opinions to the public judgment. I therefore so far deviated from my first purpose as to respond to letters addressed to me, making inquiries in regard to subjects which had been much agitated. Of the answers which I so transmitted, some were intended exclusively for the satisfaction of my correspondents, without any expectation on my part of their being deemed worthy of publication. In regard of those which have been presented to the public, misconceptions and erroneous constructions have been given to some of them which I think they did not authorize, or which, at all events, were contrary to my intentions.

In announcing my determination to permit no other letters to be drawn from me on public affairs, I think it right to avail myself of the occasion to correct the erroneous interpretation of one or two of those which I had previously written. In April last, I addressed to you, from Raleigh,[2] a letter in respect to the proposed treaty, annexing Texas to the United States, and I have since addressed two letters to Alabama upon the same subject.[3] Most unwarranted allegations have been made that those letters were inconsistent, with each other, and, to make it out, particular phrases or expressions have been torn from their context, and a meaning attributed to me which I never entertained.

I wish now distinctly to say that there is not a feeling, a sentiment, or an opinion expressed in my Raleigh letter, to which I do not adhere. I am decidedly opposed to the immediate annexation of Texas to the United States. I think it would be dishonorable, might involve them in war, would be dangerous to the integrity and harmony of the Union, and, if all these objections were removed, would not be effected, according to any information I possess, upon just and admissible conditions.

It was not my intention, in either of the two letters which I addressed to Alabama, to express any contrary opinion. Representations had been made to me that I was considered as inflexibly opposed to the annexation of Texas under any circumstances; and that my opposition was so extreme that I would not waive it, even if there were a general consent to the measure by all the States of the Union. I replied, in my first letter to Alabama, that personally I had no objection to annexation. I thought that my meaning was sufficiently obvious, that I had no personal, private, or individual motives for opposing, as I have none for espousing the measure, my judgment being altogether influenced by general and political considerations, which have ever been the guide of my public conduct.

In my second letter to Alabama, assuming that the annexation of Texas might be accomplished without national dishonor, without war, with the general consent of the States of the Union, and upon fair and reasonable terms, I stated that I should be glad to see it. I did not suppose that it was possible I could be misunderstood. I imagined every body would comprehend me as intending that, whatever might be my particular views and opinions, I should be happy to see what the whole nation might concur in desiring under the conditions stated. Nothing was further from my purpose than to intimate any change of opinion as long as any considerable and respectable portion of the Confederacy should continue to stand out, in opposition to the annexation of Texas.

In all three of my letters upon the subject of Texas, I stated that annexation was inadmissible, except upon fair and reasonable terms, if every other objection were removed. In a speech which I addressed to the Senate of the United States more than three years ago, I avowed my opposition, for the reasons there stated, to the assumption, by the General Government, of the debts of the several States.[4] It was hardly, therefore, to be presumed that I could be in favor of assuming the unascertained debt of a foreign State, with which we had no fraternal ties, and whose bad faith or violation of its engagements can bring no reproaches upon us.

Having thus, gentlemen, made the apology which I intended, for my omission to answer any letters of inquiry upon public affairs which I may have received; announced my purpose to decline henceforward transmitting answers for publication to any such letters that I may hereafter receive; and vindicated some of those which I have forwarded against the erroneous constructions to which they have been exposed, I have accomplished the purpose of this note.

Copy. Printed in Washington *Daily National Intelligencer*, Oct. 1, 1844. 1. See 9:753-54. 2. Clay to Editors of Washington *Daily National Intelligencer*, April 17, 1844. 3. Clay to Miller, July 1, 1844; Clay to Peters & Jackson, July 27, 1844. 4. See 9:390-92.

To WILLIS GREEN & GARRETT DAVIS Lexington, September 23, 1844

Enclosed I transmit a letter for publication in the [Washington *Daily National*] Intellr.[1] One of its objects is to correct the perversions made of previous letters from me. If I am to credit numerous letters which I have recd. my two Alabama letters[2] have created some unfavorable impressions in particular localities.

I submit it to you to publish the enclo[sure] or not, as you have perhaps a better view of the whole ground than I have. Perhaps it will be well to take [Joseph] Gales [Jr.] into your counsel, as he is a very discreet Counseller. You are at liberty also to make [word missing] [rea]sonable alterations in the letter.

How are your pulses? High or low[?] The result in Maine[3] has affected the nerves of some of our friends.

AL, manuscript torn and signature removed. KyLoF. Letter marked "(Confidential)." 1. Clay to Gales & Seaton, Sept. 23, 1844. 2. Clay to Miller, July 1, 1844; Clay to Peters & Jackson, July 27, 1844. 3. Clay to Giddings, Sept. 21, 1844.

From "Montgomery," *ca.* September 23, 1844. Writes a pamphlet addressed "To Henry Clay," which was enclosed in a letter of September 23, 1844, from Levi S. D'Lyon to James K. Polk, and which attacks Clay at length for his position on the national bank and Texas. Charges that a Bank of the United States is "pernicious" to the interests of the people, and, "if not subversive to their sovereignty, certainly fatal to its proper and independent exercise." Adds that when previously a presidential candidate, "You set yourself up, like Nebuchadnezer [*sic,* Nebuchadnezzar] of old, for an image of Idolatry, and the type of your worship was a Golden Calf. You thought to ride into office on the back of the Bank of the United States. You had the enchanted key. At the sound of your voice, 'open sesame', and millions upon millions flooded the western states, in the shape of discounts to favored individuals who bore the mark of the beast."

Claims that "Again, after being once more five times too often announced by political devotees for the same exhalted station," Clay has used "disgusting, bullying" language to denounce "the present President of the United States [John Tyler]" for his veto of "the Bill of Abominations, the Bill for forging golden fetters for the liberties of the people, the new Bank Bill the child of your begetting [9:528-29]." Asks how long "since the ablest of your field marshals [Daniel Webster], the great constitutional lawyer declared in his speech to a Whig assemblage at Faneuil Hall .... that a United States Bank was an exploded idea [9:787-88]?"

Continues: "The Texan question found you asleep, and dreaming, in your Ashland shades. . . . The sagacious mind of the President had conceived and accomplished the measure. . . . Your manifests appeared, and *Texas was voted down* [Clay to Crittenden, February 15, 1844]. And do you think your late confessed penitence, your eating your own words [Clay to Miller, July 1, 1844; Clay to Peters & Jackson, July 27, 1844], will serve to blot out your offence to your injured country. . . . Your country is confessedly a fond mother, but she is jealously tenacious of her rights; and inflexibly severe in her demands on the devotion of her children, upon magnanimous and disinterested motives upon pure and patriotic principles. Her *soaring Eagle perches on her loftiest cliffs,* where the hawk would strive in vain to make his eyry." AD. DLC-James K. Polk Papers, series 2, reel 28.

To JAMES WATSON WEBB Lexington, September 23, 1844

I congratulate you on your safe return to the U. States of which I had heard prior to the receipt of your friendly letter of the 16th instant.[1] I hope you have come back in good health and spirits. Your retort of cui bono in regard to my Alabama letters[2] is perhaps just. I am glad however that you concur in the sentiments which they express. The principal object of the last was to discriminate clearly between the case of Mr [John] Tylers Treaty[3] and that of the overture during Mr [John Q.] Adams' administration[4] which was authorised to be made for the purchase of Texas. But, from this day forward, I shall cease to write any letters for publication. I am gratified to find you speaking with so much confidence as to the result of the election in New York.[5] From the tone of some of your papers and from the small Whig majority which Mr [John C.] Hamilton informed me had been estimated by the Syracuse Convention,[6] I was led to entertain some apprehensions about it. I think the success of the Whigs is sure with the vote either of New York Pennsylvania[7] or Virginia[8] but they cannot afford to lose all three of those States. My information from Virginia is very encouraging as it is from Pennsylvania in regard to the Presidential Election, but not in respect to that of Governor.[9]

I concur with you entirely in the mode of conducting the canvass, recommended in the slip that you sent me from the Courier.[10]

I will thank you to present my respects to John C. Hamilton Esq, and tell him that I received his last letter. Mr [John J.] Crittenden has gone to Ohio and Indiana. But Mr [James T.] Morehead wrote to me that he intended to go to Rochester.

P.S. This letter is written by an Amanuensis, upon my dictation.

LS, postscript in Clay's hand. KyU. Endorsed: "Explaining his Alabama letter; which, I fear will lose him this State & the *Presidency*." 1. Webb had just returned from Europe. See Washington *Daily National Intelligencer*, Sept. 6, 1844. 2. Clay to Miller, July 1, 1844; Clay to Peters & Jackson, July 27, 1844. 3. Clay to Crittenden, Feb. 15, 1844. 4. Clay to Peters & Jackson, July 27, 1844. 5. Polk carried New York State in 1844 by a vote of 237,588 to Clay's 232,482 and Birney's 15,812. McKee, *National . . . Popular and Electoral Vote*, 56. 6. Hamilton (1792-1882) was a New York City lawyer and at this time president of the 5th Ward Clay Club. *CAB*; New-York *Daily Tribune*, August 29, 1844. The Whig convention to nominate candidates for state office had assembled at Syracuse on Sept. 11. It nominated Millard Fillmore for governor, Samuel J. Wilkin for lieutenant governor, and John A. Collier and Willis Hall for presidential electors. Francis Granger served as president of the convention. Philadelphia *North American*, Sept. 14, 1844; Washington *Daily National Intelligencer*, Sept. 16, 1844. 7. Clay to Cooper, Sept. 10, 1844. 8. Clay to Rives, August 19, 1844. 9. For Pennsylvania, see Clay to White, Sept. 19, 1844. Virginia had no gubernatorial election in 1844. 10. The New York *Courier & Enquirer* of Sept. 7, 1844, had urged strong organization for the campaign and the spread of documents, speeches, and arguments for the Whig cause. It asserted: "No effort should be relaxed."

To IGNATIUS MATTINGLY Lexington, September 26, 1844

In reply to your friendly letter,[1] I have to say that, on the subject of the post office rule, according to which, as you state, that Department forbears appointing Editors as deputy post masters, I have formed no opinion one way or the other.[2] I do not deem it right, in advance of an event, which may or may not happen, to consider or decide, much less to announce by what rule I should be governed in the administration of any branch of the patronage of the Government. Should it be the pleasure of the people of the U.S. to call me to the Chief Magistracy I shall endeavor to discharge all the duties of the office faithfully and honestly, and with whatever ability I may possess. But to no mortal man can I, prior to the termination of the Election, hold out any assurance or promise of any office whatever.

I am sure you must approve of the delicacy and propriety of this reserve.

Certainly, I do not desire the publication of this note.

Copy. Printed in Louisville *Courier-Journal Magazine*, Sept. 21, 1952, p. 28. Letter marked "(Private)." 1. Not found. 2. In 1841 President Tyler had ordered the acting postmaster general not to appoint editors of political newspapers as postmasters. This order irritated the press, because the custom of editors acting as postmasters extended back to colonial times. James E. Pollard, *The Presidents and the Press* (New York, 1973), 219, 228.

To JOB W. RAY[1] Lexington, September 26, 1844

Having expressed my opinion on numerous occasions, in public speeches, in letters which have been published, and in other forms within the last six months, in favor of a Tariff for Revenue, with discrimination for *Protection*, and against the repeal of the Tariff of 1842, you will excuse me for expressing my surprise that you should deem it necessary to call on me for a reiteration of it. My respect alone for you prompts the present reply, which, for the reason above stated, surely does not need publication.

No man in the nation is more deeply penetrated with the wisdom of the Protective policy than I am; and not one would more sincerely deplore its overthrow than I should.

Copy. Printed in Lexington *Observer & Kentucky Reporter*, Nov. 9, 1844. 1. Ray had written Clay on Sept. 12, 1844, from Allegany, Md., asking him to state his views "unreservedly" on the subject of the tariff, noting that it is "the article of political faith which chiefly interests and most widely divides the people in the manufacturing districts." Adds that although Clay's views on the tariff have been widely reported in the newspapers, "such channels, cannot be indubitably relied on." Copy. Printed in *ibid.* Also printed in *Niles' Register* (Nov. 16, 1844), 67:170 which states that Ray was writing for himself and his fellow iron workers and that an identical letter addressed to James K. Polk had not been answered. Ray probably worked at Mt. Savage Iron Works in Allegany County. See James W. Thomas & T.J.C. Williams, *History of Allegany County, Maryland*, 2 vols. (n.p., 1923), 1:489-90.

To CHARLES LANMAN Lexington, September 28, 1844

I have only time, through an amanuensis who writes upon my dictation, to make a brief acknowledgment of the receipt of your friendly letter,[1] and to thank you for the kind sentiments towards me which it expresses. I most sincerely hope that the prospect which you present of the enthusiasm which prevails in the Whig cause may terminate in its successful issue, less on my own account than that of our common country. I believe that such will be the result, if the Whigs put forth their earnest exertions, undismayed by the boasting and bragging of their opponents.[2]

I am greatly obliged by the offer, which you kindly make, of the two volumes which you have composed,[3] and I should be most happy to receive them. At present, I know of no opportunity by which they can be conveyed. Perhaps some one may shortly present itself.

Copy. Printed in Charles Lanman, *Haphazard Personalities; Chiefly of Noted Americans* (Boston, 1886), 124-25. 1. Not found. 2. Clay to Webb, Feb. 29, 1844. 3. Lanman (1819-95), who at various times worked in a mercantile house, edited newspapers, and served as librarian of the War Department and the U.S. House, wrote several books; it has not been determined which ones he proposed sending Clay. *DAB*.

To WILLIAM McCONKEY, JR. Lexington, September 28, 1844

I received a day or two ago your friendly letter under date of the 4th of July last, transmitting a note from our good friend Mr [Christopher] Hughes. I perused your letter with very great satisfaction and sincerely wish that the same pure sentiments of patriotism & disinterestedness which animate you, were more prevalent in the country. For your friendly and favorable feelings & opinions, in respect to myself, I request your acceptance of my acknowledgements. Hitherto throughout life I have been anxious to deserve the esteem of good men and such will continue to be my desire through the remnant of my days. Sometimes misunderstood, oftener misrepresented, I have nevertheless persevered, & shall continue to persevere, in the even tenor of my way. . . . P.S. To save myself from the labor of my extensive correspondence, I write by an Amanuensis, upon my dictation.

LS, postscript in Clay's hand. KyLoF. Addressed to McConkey in Baltimore, Md. 1. For McConkey, see *MHM*, 73:387 and the Christopher Hughes Papers at MiU-C.

To BENJAMIN W. LEIGH Lexington, September 30, 1844

I am very much urged by Mr [John H.] Pleasants and other friends in Virginia, to allow the publication of my [Francis P.] Blair letters,[1] of which copies are in your possession[.] My own opinion from the first has been, that their publication, so far from injury would benefit me in respect to the charge of bargain &c. You know the motives which have restrained me from allowing them to be published[.][2] The question now is, whether it is not too late? Whether there is time to prevent the false interpretations, and misrepresentations to which their publication would now give rise. I have never been asked to consent to their publication by Blair, by [Thomas] Ritchie, by [Linn] Boyd or by any of the leaders of that party. If you and other friends think for the sake of Virginia or the cause, that their publication is desirable I will not object to it. If it be done, it would perhaps be best to say, that it was done by friends of Mr Clay upon their own responsibility; or to say that yielding to the strong entreaties of friends he has overcome his repugnance to the publication of a correspondence which was private playful and sportive, and reluctantly consented to a violation of the sanctity which belongs to private correspondence, and permitted the publication of private letters, which were written under its sanctity. If the publication should be made, it should be brought forward in a very striking and imposing manner. Credit should be claimed for me, which I think I deserve for abstaining from the publication on account of the private playful and familiar character of the letters, although the evidence which they contain in regard to the public charge, is really beneficial to me. It should be asserted, that the publication is now made to put down efectually and forever, a vile charge which has been revived after having been most fully and completely refuted. It should be further stated that copies of these letters with the consent of Mr Clay, given in a letter which he addressed to the late John Harvey [*sic*, Harvie] in the year 1827,[3] were placed in the hands of Col. Richard H Taylor of Frankfort for public inspection; that they have been examined by hundreds of persons of both parties, and perfectly accessible to any person who was desirous of perusing them. It should be further stated, that no person who has examined them has ventured to state or assert, that they contained anything prejudicial to Mr Clay. It should be added that there is really nothing in them, which he does not substantially state in his letter to his constituents in March 1824[4] to be found in the public collection of his speeches, and in Niles Register, and extracts from that letter should be made, to shew its conformity with the Blair letters. The latter part of the second letter, in which I avow, as the fact was, that in my vote for Mr [John Q.] Adams in 1825, I discarded all personal or private motives, and looked exclusively to the public good of my country, should be emphatically and strikingly set forth.

It is proper that I should state how the copys of the letters in your possession, had been procured. Col Taylor before mentioned, has in his custody copies of the letters certified by Blair. Those which you have, are copies from those certified copies. Blair may be challenged to produce the originals, to be submitted to any person acquainted with my hand writing (Willis Green Jr [Joseph] Gales [Jr.] or Mr [Philip R.] Fendal[l] for example) and they will be found to conform, I presume to the copies which you have.

To relieve myself from the very great burthen, under which I am, of correspondence this letter has been written by an amanuensis upon my dictation, although I am happy to tell you, that my health is now excellent and never was better[.]

LS. ViU. 1. See 4:9-11, 46-48. 2. Clay to Leigh, July 20, 1844. 3. See 6:226-27, 327. 4. See 4:143-66.

To LEMUEL MOFFITT & JAMES M. BLOSS Lexington, September 30, 1844

I received your friendly & respectful letter[1] to which I hope you will excuse me for returning only a brief reply. Nothing was further from my intention than to express, in either of my Alabama letters,[2] on the subject of Texas any feeling sentiment or opinion contrary to those which I had expressed in my Raleigh letter.[3] And I respectfully conceive that no person, who will make a candid & careful examination of all three of my letters, will discern any conflict between them. I adhere to every part from beginning to end, of my Raleigh letter. It has only been by the grossest perversion and misrepresentation of my letters, that any attempt has been made to establish a conflict between them.

I was very sorry for the necessity which I sincerely believed existed for the publication of my note in reference to the letter of Col. C.M. Clay.[4] That gentleman was actuated I have no doubt by the most friendly and patriotic purposes. But, without his intention, his letter, if it remained unnoticed by me, was calculated to do very great prejudice to the Whig cause. Insomuch that I verily believe it hazarded the loss of four or five States before which they had every reason to count.

In that note of mine I expressed no new opinion; it, on the contrary, merely reaffirmed opinions which I had several times expressed on the floor of the Senate. I have intimated in that note no purpose of exercising the veto in the event of my election as President. I have in no case whatever in the remotest degree, ever signified any purpose of using the veto in any case whatever. Should I be elected I hope that during my Administration no contingency will arise in which I may be called upon to exercise it. Most certainly, I should never employ it as it has been.

After all, Gentlemen, do you not attach an undue importance to the Slavery question in the District of Columbia? Ask our friend Mr. [Joshua R.] Giddings if he thinks there is any possibility for the passage of a bill to abolish Slavery in that District during the period of the next four years.

This letter is written for your own satisfaction and not for publication; for it seems that every new letter from me becomes the parent of misconception if not perversion, I have therefore determined to write no other letters for publication between now and the election.

LS. ICHi. Letter marked "(Private)." Addressed to them in Kelloggsville, Ashtabula County, Ohio. 1. Not found. For Moffitt & Bloss, both judges in Ashtabula County, see Williams, *History of Ashtabula County, Ohio*, 30, 118, 141, 202. 2. Clay to Miller, July 1, 1844; Clay to

Peters & Jackson, July 27, 1844. 3. Clay to Editors of Washington *Daily National Intelligencer*, April 17, 1844. 4. Clay to Wickliffe, Sept. 2, 1844.

From Alexander Campbell, Albany, N.Y., October 1, 1844. Introduces Joseph Gist of Brooke County, Va. (West Virginia), who is visiting "Kentucky to encrease his Knowledg[e]" of agriculture and "desires to see your splendid farm and fine stock and to have before him the best models of agriculture and the management of stock."

Adds that "I am glad to hear of the improvement of your health and vigor under all the excitement and party violence which you have to encounter." Looks forward to a great victory for the country. AL, manuscript torn. DLC-HC (DNA, M212, R5).

For Alexander Campbell, minister and founder of Buffalo Seminary in Bethany, Va. (W. Va.), see *DAB*. Joseph Gist later served as a delegate to the second convention called for the secession of Western Virginia from Virginia. Virgil A. Lewis, *How West Virginia Was Made* . . . (Charleston, W. Va., 1909), 79.

From Charles A. Davis, New York, October 4, 1844. Reports that "I liked your letter of 23 Ulto. to [Joseph] Gales [Jr.] & [William W.] Seaton remarkably well and think you have put the whole matter of 'questions and answers' on an exactly right footing—giving alike good reasons why you deviated from your original plan and why you now return to it—"

Does not believe that losing some local elections foreshadows defeat in the presidential election. Believes that "7/10 of the young Voters . . . And the Women" are Whigs, and "in addition to this the native Am: party almost to a man can't fail to Vote the full Whig Electoral ticket . . . and as this party drew into its ranks a great many former Loco focos—that latter will 'suffer some' by the operation or I am mistaken[.] I feel just as sure that this state will vote right as I am of any thing not yet positively proven [Clay to Webb, September 23, 1844]."

Predicts that Silas "Wright will run several hundred some (of their own side) say 1500 above the Polk Electoral ticket. . . . the party will no doubt make the difference as palpable as possible—their desire wd. be to Elect Wright & defeat Polk [Clay to Sargent, October 29, 1844]." Notes also that "Our Stock Market in Wall Street vibrates just as reports are pro or con—but opinions there are not worth a Cent." Believes "the largest party by odds in the Country is the party I belong to which sees greater benefit in general prosperity than in precarious emoluments of office—& that party will tell its story next Nov."

Concludes: "The returns from Balto. are not as good as desired but the reason is just here—the *Catholic* question there is strong and the *natives* have not attempted a real rally there as they did here last Spring—but our boys are at it in Phila.—and you will see a Vote in that City that will astonish you—they are as Excited there as we were here last spring [Ewing to Clay, June 23, 1844]—and just so it wd. be in all our atlantic Cities—where that feeling is Excited *and acts*—All goes right our Cause is just & our votes will tell it." ALS. DLC-HC (DNA, M212, R5).

In the 1844 elections in Baltimore, Democrats won 5 seats in the state house of delegates to represent Baltimore City and 5 more for Baltimore County. New-York *Daily Tribune*, October 4, 1844. In Baltimore City, Democrat James Carroll won 9,190 votes for governor to 7,995 for Whig Thomas G. Pratt. Philadelphia *North American and Daily Advertiser*, October 4, 1844. In the presidential election in November, Polk carried Baltimore City over Clay by a vote of 8,887 to 8,414 and won Baltimore County 2,716 to 2,301. New-York *Daily Tribune*, November 16, 1844. For the Maryland State elections, see Clay to Kennedy, March 29, 1844.

In the Philadelphia city mayoral election, Whig Peter McCall won with 5,534 votes to 4,889 for the American Republican candidate and 4,093 for the Democratic candidate. For both the common council and the select council, 13 Whigs, 1 American Republican, and 1 Democrat were elected. One Whig, 1 Democrat, and 2 Nativists were elected to Congress from the 3 congressional districts in Philadelphia City and County. Whig Joseph Markle also carried Philadelphia City and County in the gubernatorial election over Democrat Francis R. Shunk 9,262 to 5,257. Native Americans carried Philadelphia County in the legislative elections, sending 8 men to the lower house and 1 to the state senate. Philadelphia *North American and Daily Advertiser*, October 9, 10, 11, 14, 1844; Snyder, *The Jacksonian Heritage*, 186. In the presidential election Clay carried Philadelphia City and County, winning 22,403 votes to Polk's 17,591, and Birney's 161. Philadelphia *North American and Daily Advertiser*, November 2, 1844. For the Pennsylvania state elections, see Clay to White, September 19, 1844; for the Pennsylvania presidential vote, see Clay to Cooper, September 10, 1844.

To BRANTZ MAYER Lexington, October 4, 1844

I received your obliging letter of the 7th ulto. with a copy of the Baltimore American, containing the Article to which you refer, shewing the practicability of opening a market for our great Southern staple in Mexico.[1] I perused it with satisfaction. Our commerce with Mexico has greatly declined within a few years past, from causes sufficiently obvious. I hope that a better state of things may arise. Whilst we have been neglecting our interests with that great country, Great Britain has been assiduously taking care of hers and has drawn to her shores a great portion of the precious metals, which ought to have come to us.

I should be glad to receive your work on Mexico,[2] as well on account of the recollection which I retain of our former acquaintance, as because of the personal opportunities which your residence at Mexico gave you of acquiring valuable information.

LS. MH. 1. The article appeared in the Sept. 6, 1844, issue of the Baltimore *American & Commercial Advertiser* as an open letter to Henry Clay. Signed by "M." and dated Sept. 2, 1844, it argued that the annexation of Texas would neither be just to Mexico nor beneficial to the Union. It also detailed the growing antagonism between the U.S. and Mexico that followed the Texas uprising. The author asserted that commerce between the two countries had declined as a result but suggested remedies that would promote better relations and increase trade. "M." further recalled how in 1818 Clay had argued that the U.S. had a deep interest in South American independence and contended that "What was true of these countries in 1818 is true still." 2. In 1844 Mayer, who had gone to Mexico in 1841 as secretary of the U.S. legation, published *Mexico as It Was and as It Is*, a controversial work because of his comments about the Catholic Church. See *DAB*.

To ANDREW G. BURT Lexington, October 9, 1844

I only recd. to day your favor of the 5h. You will have seen that I have announced my resolution to answer no letters for publication, between now and the Presidential election.[1]

For your own private satisfaction, I will say that I do not belong to the Native American party, nor have I ever expressed any opinion in favor of their particular creed. At the same time, I desire to be understood as open to any conviction, which future reflection, information, and public sentiment may prompt, in regard to the Naturalization laws, especially to prevent such abuses as occurred at N. Orleans.[2]

ALS. OCHP. Letter marked "(Private)." Addressed to Burt in Cincinnati, Ohio. 1. Clay to Gales & Seaton, Sept. 23, 1844. 2. Clay to Smith, June 17, 1844.

To Fernando C. Putnam, Freehold, Monmouth County, N.J., October 9, 1844. Thanks him "for the interest which you kindly take in my present and future welfare." States: "Although I am not a member of any Christian Church, I have a profound sense of the inappreciable value of our Religion, which has increased and strengthened as I have advanced in years; and I sincerely hope that I may yet be inspired with that confidence in the enjoyment of the blessings, in another state of existence, which it promises, that disarms death of all its terrors." ALS. DLC-HC (DNA, M212, R6).

Putnam was the rector (1843-50) of St. Peter's Episcopal Church in Freehold, N.J. Franklin Ellis, *History of Monmouth County, New Jersey* (Philadelphia, 1885), 417.

From Joseph Knore, Pittsburgh, Pa., October 11, 1844. Writes "to put you in possession of the first *good* news from a state, which has a larger debt of gratitude to pay to you, sir than to any other of our distinguished men." Gives a tally comparing the Whig and Democratic votes of 1840 with those of the recent election, and concludes that "Unless in the 24 Counties to be heard from the Loco's gain 2581 over their majority of 1840—the state is ours—" Adds: "I say they cant gain 2581 because—In the East they are not gaining in the ratio. . . . I beleive the state is ours—I have taken great pains to arrive at the truth—The state at all events is safe in November—I have stumped our county [Allegheny] and it has done better than I expected."

Adds that "In the course of my duty in Court as a member of the Committee on Naturalization—I discovered facts which made me dread that vote—1200 were admitted citizens within 3 months—about 3/4 Locos [Ewing to Clay, June 23, 1844].—That and the 300 abolition vote [Clay to Clayton, December 2, 1844] reduced our 3047 = I am determined to raise the 3047 on the 1st November." ALS. KyLxT.

For the 1844 Pennsylvania state elections, see Clay to White, September 19, 1844; for the 1844 presidential election in Pennsylvania, see Clay to Cooper, September 10, 1844.

In Allegheny County, Pa., Whig Joseph Markle won 8,105 votes in the gubernatorial election, while Democrat Francis R. Shunk received 5,863. *Niles' Register* (November 2, 1844), 67:131. In the presidential election Clay carried Allegheny County with 8,083 votes to 5,743 for Polk and 435 for Birney. *The Tribune Almanac for the Year 1836 to 1868* . . . , 2 vols. (New York, 1868), 1:45.

From George Washington Anderson, Louisville, October 14, 1844. Reports having paid Clay's account of $10.25 for fish and packing to the Exchange Hotel. Adds that "Our news from Pensylva [Clay to White, September 19, 1844] is very cheering, we believe the Locos will elect their Governor—Ohio, has done well [Clay to Berrien, July 16, 1844]—very well—Our items as to New Jersey, are propitious." ALS. DLC-TJC (DNA, M212, R14). Endorsed by Clay: "G.W. Anderson [Rect for fish]." For Pennsylvania's vote in the 1844 presidential election, see Clay to Cooper, September 10, 1844.

The Exchange Hotel, P.W. Bibb proprietor, was located at the corner of Main and 6th streets in Louisville. John B. Jegli, *Louisville, New-Albany, Jeffersonville, Shippingport and Portland Directory, For 1845-1846* . . . (Louisville, 1845), 79.

In the 1844 New Jersey gubernatorial election, which was the first by popular vote in that state, Whig Charles C. Stratton defeated Democrat William Thompson by a vote of 37,949 to 36,591. *BDGUS,* 3:1018-19. Four Whigs and 1 Democrat were elected to Congress from New Jersey. *Guide to U.S. Elections,* 580. In the state legislative elections Whigs carried the senate by a majority of 7 seats and the assembly by 22 seats. New-York *Daily Tribune,* October 11, 1844. Clay carried New Jersey over Polk by a popular vote of 38,318 to 34,495, winning all 7 electoral votes. McKee, *National . . . Popular and Electoral Vote,* 56-57.

To JOSHUA R. GIDDINGS Lexington, October 14, 1844

I was glad to learn that you were gratified by the perusal of my letter to the Edit. of the Intellr.[1] My only regret in writing it was that there should have existed any occasion for it, which there would not have been if my previous letters had not been greatly perverted.

The information conveyed in your letter of the 9h that noble Ashtabula has given a majority of 2400 for the Whigs relieves me from all fears about the Ohio election.[2]

As my letter to Mr. H. has not been *I hope it may not be published.*[3] Not that I have the smallest doubt of the opinion I expressed, but that it may give rise to fresh perversions.

ALS. Courtesy of James de T. Abajian, San Francisco, Calif. Addressed to Giddings at Jefferson, Ashtabula County, Ohio. 1. Clay to Gales & Seaton, Sept. 23, 1844. 2. Clay to Berrien, July 16, 1844. 3. Probably Mr. Hendry. See Clay to Giddings, Sept. 21, 1844.

From Samuel S. Seward, Florida, Orange County, N.Y., October 14, 1844. Reports that "Saturday the 12 was A proud day for the Empire State Old Orange & the neighboring State and Countys turned out truly in Masss." Writes that "Thousands on Thousand of all classes of Citizens" turned out "in conveyances of every description," while "highminded farmers . . . became so interested. In behalf of their bleeding Country that it loosened their Tongues [and] Men who had never addresed an Audiance mounted a stage on their Waggon publiclify proclaimed the Whig principles—and the . . . support of Clay & [Theodore] Frelin[g]huysen, [Millard] Fillmore and [Samuel Jones] Wilkins [*sic*, Wilkin] as the only Safeguards of our Country [Clay to Sargent, October 29, 1844]." Adds that speakers "addressed the people for about three hours showing forth in glowing coullers the train of misrule & destruction that was heaped on the deluded Country by unworthy dishonest locofoco self stiled Democrat[s]." Copy. NGos.

The Orange County Whig meeting at Goshen, N.Y., was estimated to number between 10,000-12,000. New-York *Daily Tribune*, October 14, 16, 1844.

From John R. Wilson, Alton, Ill., October 15, 1844. Warns that "the man who pretends to be your Agent is Cutting Selling and Makeing [a]way with" the timber "on your land in the Bottom." Recommends that Clay "Make an Agent of John Smettsen that lives in the Bottom Just Above me" in order to "prevent any tresspassing what Ever." Adds that "if they are Allowed to Go on they will Ruining [*sic*, ruin] all the Best timber you have." ALS. DLC-TJC (DNA, M212, R14).

To PETER SKEN SMITH Lexington, October 16, 1844

Many thanks for the agreeable information communicated in your favor of the 9h. The Natives [Native Americans], in supporting [Joseph] Markle so nobly, in the two Philadas., have demonstrated their patriotism and their fidelity to principle.[1] Perseverance in a similar course will secure for them the warm sympathy and the good wishes of hundreds of thousands, who are not now formally united with them.

From the information which has reached me, I suppose that Markle is defeated but by a majority so lean as to ensure the success of the Whigs next month.[2]

ALS. DLC-TJC (DNA, M212, R10). Letter marked "(Confidential)." Addressed to Smith in Philadelphia. 1. Davis to Clay, Oct. 4, 1844. 2. *Ibid.* For the Pennsylvania presidential election, see Clay to Cooper, Sept. 10, 1844; for the state elections, see Clay to White, Sept. 19, 1844.

To JOHN P. FOOTE[1] *et al.* Lexington, October 17, 1844

Mr. [Thomas D.] Jones[2] has made a capital likeness of me—credible to him as an artist, and to the arts themselves. I think it must prove to be perfected satisfactory to yourselves, and my Cincinnati friends. I take pleasure in adding that I found in Mr Jones, a modest, sensibly, and agreeable gentleman, and that he was in ever ready to consult my convenience.

Copy. Printed in Lexington *Observer & Kentucky Reporter*, Nov. 9, 1844. 1. For Foote, see 3:868. 2. For Jones, a Cincinnati stone mason who began to produce busts about 1842, see George C. Groce & David H. Wallace, *The New-York Historical Society's Dictionary of Artists in America 1564-1860* (New Haven, 1957), 358 and Amyx, "Portraits of Henry Clay," Special Collections, University of Kentucky Library, vol. A:1.55.

From Thomas C. Patrick, Clay's Prairie, Ill., October 17, 1844. Has received a letter from Thomas Hart Clay asking "how the crops of corn is this year upon Clays Prairie or its neighborhood." Reports that "thire scarsley any corn on the Prairie and crops are lite in its neighborhood." Adds: "I hoap you will succeed in your Election." ALS. DLC-TJC (DNA, M212, R10).

To DANIEL ULLMANN Lexington, October 18, 1844

I received your friendly letter of the 7th inst. from which I am happy to perceive that, notwithstanding your removal to the interior of Pennsylvania, you continue to take a lively interest in the Whig cause, and your long cherished friendship for me remains undiminished. We are just now receiving the returns of the Pennsylvania election, and most of them have reached me.[1] I infer from them that our candidate for Governor [Joseph Markle] is defeated by a majority of some four or five thousand; but if I am to credit the confident assurances of my numerous correspondents we shall experience a better result next month.[2] The interior of the State does not appear to have done as well as we could have wished; and I am apprehensive, notwithstanding your hopes and those of other friends, that the Northern part of the State has fallen short. I am very glad to assure you that I feel perfectly confident that the Whig cause will triumph next month. Should Pennsylvania share in that triumph, I believe that the electoral vote will be greater than it was in .40.[3] I am glad to be able to inform you that my health is perfectly good.

P.S. This letter is written by an Amanuensis on my dictation.

LS. NHi. Addressed to Ullmann in Philipsburg, Centre County, Pa. 1. Clay to White, Sept. 19, 1844. 2. Clay to Cooper, Sept. 10, 1844. 3. In 1840 William Henry Harrison carried Pennsylvania's 30 electoral votes, winning a total of 234 to 60 for Martin Van Buren. In 1844 Polk carried Pennsylvania and received a total of 170 electoral votes to 105 for Clay. McKee, *National . . . Popular and Electoral Vote*, 45, 57.

To F.M. WRIGHT Lexington, October 21, 1844

I duly received your letter of the 12th inst., and I regret that you should deem it necessary to address me on the subject of the vile slander to which you call my attention. Two or three other letters of the same import, have reached my neighborhood and it is remarkable that, in no instance, has the name of the slanderer been given. The charge as you state it, is, that I was seen attending a horse race in the District of Columbia, on the Sabbath, and that I bet and won a thousand dollars on the issue of the race. It is an infamous falsehood, from beginning to end, without the smallest color of foundation for it. I never attended a horse race on the Sabbath in my life, in the District of Columbia, or any where else upon earth, and I believe there never was a horse race run upon that day in the District of Columbia. The charge is a vile and atrocious fabrication.

Copy. Printed in Lexington *Observer & Kentucky Reporter*, Nov. 27, 1844.

From WILLIAM H. SEWARD Auburn, N.Y., October 25, 1844

Your friend Mr. [John] Lee[1] has just delivered to me your letter of the 13th. of October. I have adopted your suggestion and hope that beneficial results may follow, though the mischief to which you refer has gone almost too far and too long unchecked.

I will not undertake to give you an opinion of the probable result of the election in this state, upon which perhaps is suspended the whole question and of course the fate of the Country.[2] Candidates receive favorable reports enough, and speculations adverse are unwise. I think however that the election will not prove as close a one as many suppose and the present setting of the current is clearly and strongly in our favor—I believe not without fear that this current is flowing rapidly enough to give us success. It has been proved that letters *from* you can be stolen.[3] It may therefore be assumed that letters *to* you might suffer the same fate. I will not indulge in speculations on the tendency of the different masses. The result is so near at hand as about to supersede prophecy.

I am very happy that it has fallen in your way to write to me, because it gives me an opportunity without apparent intrusion to say something which has been too long unsaid. During the course of the past year I have learned that different persons, politically and presently friends of my own have addressed you with good motives sometimes refering to me in terms of indiscreet friendship, under circumstances which might lead you to suppose that I was privy to the communications. I will not specify any of them: But I desire to say in regard to them all that I knew nothing of any letters that have been addressed to you by any body until after they were sent and when I was subsequently informed of their contents by their writers, except a letter written by our mutual friend Mr [Thurlow] Weed disclosing from a very strange letter which our friend A[ndrew]. B. Dickinson wrote to you as he stated to us last winter—[4]

Again, people have speculated as usual in the newspapers adopting sometimes the opinion that I supported you with some object of personal advantage, and at other times that since I disclaimed such objects I could not be sincere in my support. Now my private feelings and views are those so often publicly expressed. I not only do not look for consideration from your administration but I am so situated and entertain such notions that I should not under any circumstances accept any from any Administration.

With an abiding and profound respect and reverence for your character and public services which heartily engages me in your support, since you are the representative of the Whig party. I have nevertheless greater devotion to the party and have never been your partisan nor that of any other leader—My views and my actions are on public grounds alone[.] Allow me I pray you to say so much and perhaps so widely from a desire to be understood by one to whom I know I have been much misrepresented and who has had little opportunity to know the truth or falsehood of such representations.

Sincerely trusting that your Election may crown the wishes of the great mass of enlightened and generous citizens by whom you are supported and may redound to the welfare of the Country and your own lasting power[.]

ALS. DLC-HC (DNA, M212, R6). 1. See Lee to Clay, Nov. 2, 1844. 2. Clay to Webb, Sept. 23, 1844. 3. Clay to C.M. Clay, Sept. 18, 1844, had been stolen and published. 4. Reference obscure, but see Clay to Weed, May 6, 1844.

To JAMES WATSON WEBB Lexington, October 25, 1844

I received to day your letter of the 18th. inst. I stand pledged to the Public to write no more letters for publication, on public affairs, prior to the presidential election, and nothing, not even the presidency, would induce me to violate my pledge.[1] Several months ago I addressed three or four letters to different friends, and amongst others to Messrs. [Theodore] Frelinghuysen and [Millard] Fillmore communicating my opinions in regard to foreigners and the naturalization laws.[2] These opinions coincide substantially with yours, as disclosed in the editorial article which you have transmitted to me. Whilst every one of my correspondents concurred with me, most of them deemed it inexpedient to introduce a new issue into the present contest, and, in deference to their judgments, I forbore to publish my opinions.

I received the other day a similar letter to yours from Hiram Ketchum Esq and I referred him to my letter to Mr Frelinghuysen wh[ich] I presume that gentleman has preserved. I refe[r] you also to it, with authority, with their concu[rrence] to make any proper use of it, short of its p[ublication.]

I think without any fresh e[vidence] of opinion from me my sentiments might [word missing] inferred from the whole of my public career. Every pulsation of my heart is American and nothing but American. I am utterly opposed to all foreign influence in every form and shape. I objected in the Senate to Aliens being allowed any privileges under our preemption laws.[3] I have forborne to interfere in behalf of the Irish repeal movement.[4] I am in favor of American industry, American institutions, American order, American liberty. Whilst I entertain all these feelings and sentiments, I wish our Country, forever, to remain a sacred asylum for all unfortunate and oppressed men whether from religious or political causes.

I am cheered by the intelligence which you give me as to the prospects of the Whig cause in New York.[5] I am more deceived than I ever was in my life, if our cause should not carry seventy two electoral votes, from the Western side of the Alleghany Mountains, given by the States of Ohio, Kentucky, Tennessee Indiana, Louisiana, and Mississip[p]i.[6] God grant us a safe deliverance in this the greatest crisis in which our Country has ever been.

LS, manuscript torn. CtY. Letter marked "(Confidential)." 1. Clay to Gales & Seaton, Sept. 23, 1844. 2. Clay to Frelinghuysen, May 22, 1844. The letter to Fillmore has not been found, but on naturalization, see Clay to Ewing, June 19, 1844. 3. For example, see 9:136. 4. See 9:883-84. 5. Clay to Webb, Sept. 23, 1844. 6. Clay to Webb, Feb. 29, 1844.

To JOHN Q. ADAMS Lexington, October 26, 1844

I received under your frank a Copy of your recent discourse pronounced in Boston,[1] and thank you for it. I had previously read it with the highest satisfaction. It appears to me that you have annihilated Jackson and [Aaron

V.] Brown and G[eorge]. W. Irving [*sic*, Erving], or, as Genl [Andrew] Jackson has him, *Erwin*.[2]

In the last of the two letters which I addressed to Alabama, on the subject of Texas,[3] and which have been so greatly perverted by Locofoco's, my main object was to discriminate between the case of the overture authorized by you for the purchase of Texas[4] and Mr. [John] Tylers treaty.[5] I did not enlarge upon nor state all the points of difference, but intended to present a clear distinction briefly between the two transactions.

You will have seen that I have finally yielded to the publication of my letters to [Francis P.] Blair.[6] There is an expression in one of them, which I hope you will excuse, and for which I owe you an apology.[7] The truth is that it constituted my chief objection to the publication of the letters. But I thought I might rely upon your indulgence and liberality, especially as such an improper use was made of the nonpublication of them.

The great contest, fraught with such important consequences to our Country, will now soon be decided. The elections of the current year have been remarkable for the closeness of the majorities which determined them. Still, if I am to judge of the final result by the information which I have received, the Whigs will succeed by a large Electoral majority. I think they will pass the Mountains from the West with seventy two Electoral votes, given by Ohio, Tennessee, Kentucky, Indiana, Louisiana and Mississippi.[8]

I request you to present my respectful Compliments to Mrs. [Louisa Johnson] Adams, in which Mrs. [Lucretia Hart] Clay joins me.

ALS. MHi. 1. Adams spoke to the Young Men's Whig Club of Boston on Oct. 7, 1844, and defended his actions in the Adams-Onis Treaty of 1819. In their correspondence to each other, Andrew Jackson and Tennessee Congressman Aaron V. Brown had attacked the treaty for giving up the U.S. claim to Texas. Adams denounced this as a conspiracy by Jackson, Brown, George W. Erving, and Charles J. Ingersoll "to justify the robbery of Texas from Mexico, by the pretence that Texas had been . . . treacherously surrendered to Spain." Adams, *Memoirs of John Quincy Adams*, 12:78, 84; Washington *Daily National Intelligencer*, Oct. 12, 1844. 2. Jackson wrote in his letter to Brown that Erving (or Erwin as he called him) had claimed that while serving as minister in Madrid during the Monroe administration he had laid the foundation for a treaty with Spain that would cede the Floridas to the U.S. and settle the U.S.-Mexican boundary at the Rio Grande. He was never given the power to sign the treaty, however. Instead, negotiations were transferred to Washington, and there the Adams-Onis Treaty established the boundary at the mouth of the Sabine River zigzaging to the 42nd parallel west to the Pacific Ocean, and the U.S. gave up its claim to Texas. Among other things, Adams argued in his address that no official correspondence existed between Erving and the Monroe administration to verify Erving's claims. The Jackson-Brown correspondence, as well as Adams's address, are printed in the Washington *Daily National Intelligencer*, Oct. 12, 1844. See also Rives, *The United States and Mexico*, 1:620-21. 3. Clay to Peters & Jackson, July 27, 1844. 4. See 6:308-10, 540. 5. Clay to Crittenden, Feb. 15, 1844. 6. See 4:9-11, 46-48. 7. Clay to Leigh, July 20, 1844. 8. Clay to Webb, Feb. 29, 1844.

To WILLIAM B. CAMPBELL Lexington, October 26, 1844

I have received and cordially thank you for your letter of the 18th instant. I am highly gratified with the cheering prospects of the Whig cause in Tennessee,[1] which it communicates. I receive concuring accounts from other friends; but there is no one upon whose judgement & information I place greater reliance than yours.

I am happy to inform you that my advices from all quarters of the Union are encouraging in the highest degree. Judging from the strong assurances which are given me, I believe that the Whigs will carry all the four great States of New York[2] Pennsylvania[3] Virginia[4] and Ohio,[5] and I think there is a fair prospect of a larger Electoral vote than was given to Gen [William Henry] Harrison in 1840.[6] But a few weeks will now decide the contest, and it is happy that the Nation will soon be relieved from the extraordinary state of excitement which exists.

I am glad to inform you that I enjoy excellent health[.]

LS. NcD. 1. Clay to Berrien, July 16, 1844. 2. Clay to Webb, Sept. 23, 1844. 3. Clay to Cooper, Sept. 10, 1844. 4. Clay to Rives, August 19, 1844. 5. Clay to Berrien, July 16, 1844. 6. Clay to Ullmann, Oct. 18, 1844.

To CALVIN COLTON Lexington, October 26, 1844

I duly received your favor of the 18th instant, communicating your desire to prepare and compose a work, to be entitled, "The Life and Times of Henry Clay," and you invite an expression of my opinion of such an undertaking, and the contribution of any materials toward it in my possession. Such a work, truly and faithfully written, might be made very interesting. But every thing will depend upon its execution. I believe you possess sufficient ability to perform the task, if you have sufficient time and sufficient materials. However, this is a moment of too great interest and excitement either to decide definitely upon the propriety of such a work, or for me to make now any contributions toward its composition. I hope we shall both live some years yet, and have many opportunities of seeing and conferring with each other upon the subject, after which we can come to a satisfactory conclusion.[1]

A few weeks more will decide the arduous contest in which we have been engaged, and if I am to credit the confident assurances which I receive from all quarters, there is no doubt of a triumphant result.[2]

My health is excellent, although I write by the hand of an amanuensis.

Copy. Printed in Colton, *Clay Correspondence*, 4:494-95. 1. Colton published *The Life and Times of Henry Clay*, 2 vols. (New York, 1846); *The Private Correspondence of Henry Clay* (New York, 1855); *The Works of Henry Clay*, 6 vols. (New York, 1855). They were republished in 7 vols. in 1897. 2. Clay to Webb, Feb. 29, 1844.

From JOHN M. MOREHEAD Raleigh, October 29, 1844

Before this will probably reach you the die will be cast for the weal or woe of the Republic.[1]

The Elections which will come off within one week will determine the succesion to the Presidency—My hopes are sanguine—But the Democracy are moving heaven & earth—aye & Things under the earth to triumph in the contest—[2]

My confidence is still unshaken in the good sense of the American people.

It is impossible that James K. Polk can succeed—I will not believe it.

I am just from the North—I was in Baltimore on the day of their Election—was in Phil & New Jersey on the eve of theirs: & in New York as the news of our successes would arrive. I was much among the politicians; witnessed the excitement, & was glad to fan the whig flame whenever & wherever I could do so, with propriety.

I have very *great confidence* that we shall carry Pennsylvania[3] & New York[4] & our friends say—that Senator [Silas] Wright will add but little weight to the Democratic Ticket[5]—I met a sqad of Ohio & Pennsylvania politicians in Phila & gave them a challenge in behalf of the "Old North" to give the largest majority, in proportion to the vote which they readily accepted.[6]

I only wish they may *beat us*—for I think we are safe here[7]—although the foulest slanders & basest rumors are resorted to—to affect our Elections—

Our whigs are holding mass meetings all over the State, to try to rouse our people—that is all we have to fear—& it is difficult to induce them to believe that J.K. Polk is serious opposition.

They promise well & I think will certainly give you a much better vote than they gave [William A.] Graham[8]—which I promised to send you—& should have done—had not Mr Hines[9] done so—

On my return I saw Seymme [*sic*] of the Petersburg Intelligencer—and he spoke most confidently of the success of the Whigs in Va[.][10]

Our enemies here have been proclaiming the victory in Arkansas[11]—a small matter to make such a noise about—but it seems to *wake up* Old Rip.[12]

Madam [Ann Eliza Lindsay Morehead] accompanied me to the north & on our return we spent a day in Washington—she thought it probable she would not attend yr inauguration on the 4t March—but postpone her visit until she could have the pleasure of paying her respects to Mrs [Lucretia Hart] Clay—In the meantime she wished to pay a visit to the White House—but would not go a foot if I went—she had no idea of letting the Govr of N.C. call upon Captain [John] Tyler.—I yielded of course & she & some other ladies accompanied by Gov. [Edward B.] Dudley made the [ca]ll—If our men were such whigs as our ladies we have nothing to fear—

The Democratic papers will have you dead—withdrawn &c &c—but our whigs here will vote for you dead or alive—They are prepared for all manner of democratic Trickery—

I have written to day an epistle to our southern friends at New Sweden who hold their soci[e]ty meeting next monday, the day of our Election—to bring them to the polls—

Genl W. Greene [*sic*, Willis Green] was gone to Yorktown & I did not have the pleasure of seeing him—I was at the Whig Head Quarters—. The Ladies join me in wishes for yr success—

ALS. DLC-HC (DNA, M212, R6). 1. Clay to Webb, Feb. 29, 1844. 2. *Ibid.* 3. Clay to Cooper, Sept. 10, 1844. 4. Clay to Webb, Sept. 23, 1844. 5. Clay to Sargent, Oct. 29, 1844. 6. For Pennsylvania's vote, see Clay to Cooper, Sept. 10, 1844; for Ohio's, see Clay to Berrien, July 16, 1844. 7. Clay to Graham, Feb. 6, 1844. 8. Graham had won the North Carolina gubernatorial race in 1844. See *ibid.* 9. Probably Richard Hines. 10. John W. Syme, an ardent Whig, who was editor of the Petersburg *Intelligencer* from 1838-58. He served in the Virginia General Assembly from 1845-50. Lester J. Cappon, *Virginia Newspapers 1821-1935* (New York, 1936), 150-51. For Virginia's vote, see Clay to Rives, August 19, 1844. 11. Clay to Kennedy, March 29, 1844. 12. Edward B. Dudley. See *DAB*.

To EPES SARGENT Lexington, October 29, 1844

My frequent absence from home during the last few weeks have delayed my acknowledgement of the receipt of your several favors transmitting the memoranda with which I had supplied you for the biography.[1] I have received them all in safety and thank you for the punctuality with which you have returned them.

We are all looking with anxiety to New York to compensate at her approaching election for disappointments which have existed elsewhere—[2]

LS. MCM. 1. See 9:536. 2. In the New York state elections on Nov. 4, 39 Whigs, 69 Democrats, and 18 Native Americans were chosen for the assembly. New-York *Daily Tribune*, Nov. 9, 1844. In the gubernatorial race Democrat Silas Wright defeated Whig Millard Fillmore by a vote of 241,087 to 231,060 while Democrat Addison Gardiner defeated Whig Samuel J. Wilkin for lieutenant governor. *BDGUS*, 3:1079. In the congressional elections 21 Democrats, 9 Whigs, and 4 Native Americans were chosen. *Guide to U.S. Elections*, 580. For the New York presidential vote, see Clay to Webb, Sept. 23, 1844.

From J. Lee, Baltimore, November 2, 1844. Reports that he left for New York on October 21 and "delivered your letter [not found]" to Gov. William Henry Seward at Auburn. States that Seward "entered warmly into the subject,—but regretted that his political engagements to address the people would prevent him from accompanying me to the City;—& as a substitute proposed Mr Thurlow Weed, whom he recommended as being very intimate with the Bishop [John Hughes], & a man of great tact." Notes, however, that Weed was "in the West on a political mission from the Whig State Committee at Albany, distributing funds & documents," and that they were unable to reach him. Explains he then returned to New York City "with Gov. Seward's letter to the Bishop,—& he requested me to shew him a copy of your letter."

Reports that the "Bishop was very kind & cordial. . . . He desired me to assure you that he entertained the highest respect for you . . . that he was deeply impressed with the marked difference between your sentiments & political career, & the sentiments & conduct of the intolerant Whigs who were made prominent by the party in the City of New York;—& while he hoped for their defeat on the Legislative ticket, he wished sincerely for the success of your Electoral ticket . . . & that he beleived his brethern would be divided on the Presidential vote." Believes the Bishop "will interpose the influence of his opinion, whenever it can be made to bear with effect." Points out that there are separate and distinct boxes in which to vote for state officers and for presidential electors.

Adds that Seward thinks the abolitionists "have the power to decide the vote of New York, being 16,000 strong,—and his efforts are chiefly directed to induce them to abandon [James G.] Birney & vote for you, as the only means of preventing the annexation of Texas." Thinks Birney's "late conduct" will help produce this result. Mentions that "accounts from Pennsa are contradictory, & rather unfavorable [Clay to Cooper, September 10, 1844]—We shall maintain our position in Maryland [Clay to Kennedy, March 29, 1844] on the 4*th*." Draft, signed. DLC-HC (DNA, M212, R9).

Lee was probably John Lee, former Maryland congressman and friend of Clay. See *BDAC*. Seward wrote Catholic Bishop John Hughes, urging his support for Clay. This was an apparent attempt to appeal to Catholic voters in New York, who had been driven away from the Whig party because of its alliance with the Nativists. Van Deusen, *William Henry Seward*, 102. See also Ewing to Clay, June 23, 1844. For John Hughes, archbishop of the archdiocese of New York, see *NCAB*, 1:193-95.

James G. Birney had been nominated for the Michigan legislature by the Democrats in the late summer of 1844. Whigs then accused him of allying with Polk in order to defeat Clay. Betty Fladeland, *James Gillespie Birney: Slaveholder to Abolitionist* (Ithaca, N.Y., 1955), 241-46.

To HENRY JOHN SHARPE Lexington, November 3, 1844

I duly received your favor of the 15th ultimo, transmitting a copy of some verses which you have done me the honor to compose;[1] and I offer you my thanks and acknowledgements for the friendly and flattering allusions which you have made to my name—Your composition breathes a poetic spirit, far superior to that which is to be found generally in the songs and verses of which the present excited Presidential contest has been the occasion. By the time this letter reaches you, that contest will be decided,[2] and I hope its result may be such as to render your lyric more appropriate than it would be, before the election, or if the Whigs should be defeated.

LS. NcD. 1. Sharpe was a commission merchant whose business was located at 46 Pine, New York City. Doggett, *New York City Directory 1844-45*. The poem—"Hurrah! 'The Work is Done!' "—was published as *Poems by the Late Henry John Sharpe, Esq.* (London, 1859) and can be found in the microfilm series "American Poetry 1609-1900": Segment III, 1851-1870. Reel 156, New Haven, Ct. 2. Clay to Webb, Feb. 29, 1844.

To ORAZIO DE ATTELLIS SANT'ANGELO[1] Lexington, November 5, 1844

I received your friendly letter of the 24th ultimo,[2] with the pamphlet[3] which accompanied it, for which please to accept my thanks. The good intentions which animate you, and the able and enlightened views which you present, in regard to our foreign population, ought to be attended with the best and happiest effects. I am afraid that all foreigners who come to this country do not sufficiently appreciate the blessings which it offers, and that they sometimes act with indiscretion. For one, I must say, that whilst I hope the United States may always remain an asylum to the unfortunate, the oppressed, and the persecuted of other climes, I hope that it will be ever governed by true and genuine American feelings, sentiments and interests.

I pray you to accept, sir, my grateful acknowledgements for the kind interest you take in the vindication of my name and character from the foul and unexampled aspersions with which I have been assailed.

Copy. Printed in New York *Daily Herald*, Nov. 17, 1844. 1. Sant'Angelo is identified in his pamphlet as the former editor of the *Correo Atlantico* and one deeply versed in Mexican politics. He had been a U.S. resident for 21 years and a citizen for 16. 2. Sant'Angelo had written Clay from New York on Oct. 24 enclosing a pamphlet, and expressing his support of Clay's candidacy. Notes that the press is saying that the outcome of the election "depends entirely upon this State, and consequently, upon the result in the city of New York." Says he has written and distributed this pamphlet because there are thousands of adopted citizens in New York City "whose suffrages may cause the balance to turn in favor of your holy cause, and whose credulity has heretofore been successfully practised upon by your unconscientious adversaries." Hundreds of copies of the pamphlet have been distributed to "those, whose cry was 'Polk and [George M.] Dallas,' and I have learned from many sources . . . that very many of them have changed their watchword to 'Clay and Frelinghuysen!' " Asserts that after twenty-one years in the U.S., "I could not refrain from allowing myself the pleasure . . . of telling some bitter but wholesome truths to the people; and thus taking the noblest revenge on that proverbial republican ingratitude, which is the distinguishing trait of those who have basely attempted to blacken the character of the only American, in whom I have found all the qualities necessary to make the Great Chief of a Great Nation." Copy. Printed in New York *Daily Herald*, Nov. 17, 1844. Sant'Angelo sent copies of these two letters to the *Herald* with the comment: "Thinking that the true sentiments about 'naturalization' candidly expressed by Mr. Clay . . . may serve to show the injustice done to him at the polls both by a large part of the 'natives,' and a still larger portion of the 'adopted citizens,['] I take the liberty of respectfully requesting the publication of the . . . correspondence." 3. The pamphlet was titled *The Texas Question Reviewed by an Adopted Citizen* . . . (New York, 1844). It presented an argument against Texas annexation and was distributed to other adopted citizens.

From WILLIAM HENRY SEWARD Auburn, N.Y., November 7, 1844

Bad news needs no herald. The Election in this state[1] leaves us to rest a last hope upon Virginia,[2] and this is hoping against all previous expectation.

There would be great hazard of error in conjectures concerning the cause of our defeat here and propably no benefit could result from the wisest retrospect. Yet I have found it impossible to avoid recurring to political campaigns with a curiosity to ascertain what agencies produced the results.

The Whig party in the State of New York gave 13,000 majority for General [William Henry] Harrison in 1840, and 2700 Abolition votes. During the three years thereafter the Abolition Party gained 13,000 chiefly from the Whig Party. I was never able to see how we could safely expect to get in 1844 a return of this loss from our Adversary upon the issues we presented until the annexation of Texas[3] was made a political question, and then I allowed myself to hope that Whig Abolitionists would return in part, and that we should either obtain some aid from the Loco Foco Party or that many would pass from them to the Abolition Party. The election in Vermont[4] and Maine[5] in September shewed that this was our only ground of hope and gave us assurance that much could be effected in that way. What has been done has equalled my expectations, and I think that we should have saved the State of New York in that manner, but for the entrance of another and very ruinous element into the canvass. The jealousy of the Whig party or of a portion of it, against foreigners and Catholics[6] has been a serious evil which I have endeavored to correct and was quite successful though the effort exhausted much of my personal popularity which was cheerfully sacrificed. In the Spring the class in question were somewhat divided and were greatly mollified. The unhappy tragedy at Philadelphia[7] awakened religious prejudices and animosities and the Whigs in that city and New York thought they could strengthen themselves by coalition with the Native Americans. A change of the Naturalization laws to affect future immigrants was proposed and too readily approved by the Whig Press of the cities. It seemed to me to require no sagacity to discern that this would be regarded as preliminary to a general attempt to disfranchise the citizens already naturalized, and so would rouse the entire voluntary population against you. Hating pres-cription [*sic*, proscription] for its own sake and sincerely believing in the wisdom and safety and justice of universal suffrage, I endeavored to check the tendency to Native Americanism. But the aid it promised was too seductive to our friends already imbued with its spirit, and in an evil hour they adopted it. Our tickets were not framed to guard against the danger Native Americanism produced. Your own known magnanimity was not sufficient to satisfy a mass alarmed by the general action of the Party and especially of its Press. The Native Americans gave us one vote only for two of which they deprived us, and the result is our defeat in the state.

Our friend Mr Willis Hall will tell you I think that foreseeing the danger from this cause and the Slavery question in 1842 I counselled against your being brought forward as a candidate until the latest hour—declaring what was true that you had not and could not have any competition. But advice so unpalatable to ardent friends coupled with remembrances of supposed injustice to you in 1840,[8] only brought suspicion on myself without obtaining the delay or rather the moderation which seemed so necessary. There remained for me only to prove by greater efforts, dis-claiming and rejecting all personal benefits that I was as truly a Whig and as truly a friend of Henry Clay as those who converted the Whig party into a merly personal one and thereby released from your support all who from any cause might be or become prejudiced against you[.]

Frankly my dear Sir, this letter is written under a belief that all is lost. But with a hope as fondly cherished as any I ever indulged that Providence may have decided that you shall enjoy the reward of a life of chivalrous and devoted patriotism. Should that be the case I shall be found among the most faithful of your supporters and defenders, and the last one of them all who comes to seek your favor even for the dearest friend I have. It was so that I supported Harrison and so that I wished to be supported when I held a station of scarcely less difficulty though of humbler dignity . . .

ALS. NRU. 1. Clay to Webb, Sept. 23, 1844. 2. Clay to Rives, August 19, 1844. 3. Clay to Crittenden, Feb. 15, 1844. 4. For the state elections in Vermont, see Clay to C.M. Clay, Sept. 18, 1844. In the presidential election Clay won Vermont's 6 electoral votes, carrying the state with 26,770 popular votes to 18,041 for Polk and 3,954 for Birney. McKee, *National . . . Popular and Electoral Vote*, 56-57. 5. Clay to Giddings, Sept. 21, 1844. 6. Ewing to Clay, June 23, 1844. 7. *Ibid.* 8. See 9:91-92, 115-17, 288.

From James Watson Webb, New York City, *ca.* November 7, 1844. Writes that "My predictions in yesterdays letter are more than verified—The City is safe—the State is safe [Clay to Webb, September 23, 1844]—the Country is safe [Clay to Webb, February 29, 1844]—& you are to be, God willing, the next Presidt of the U.S." ALS. DLC-HC (DNA, M212, R6). Endorsed on cover: "Nothing but *Abolition* can injure us.—We have already gained 2.000 on our estimates, which elected [William Henry] Seward by 7.500—" with only the "by 7.500" in Clay's hand. Letter is postmarked November 8. Endorsed by Clay: "Col. J.W. Webb."

The New-York *Daily Tribune*, November 18, 1844, gives the "official" election returns for New York City as Clay, 26,385; Polk, 28,302; and Birney, 7,600. For the state elections in New York, see Clay to Sargent, October 29, 1844.

From THEODORE FRELINGHUYSEN New York City, November 9, 1844

I address you this morning with very different feelings, from my expectations, a week ago.[1] The alliance of the foreign vote,[2] & that most impracticable of all organizations, the abolitionists,[3] has defeated the strongest national vote, ever given, to a Presidential candidate—The Whigs in this City & State,[4] have struggled most nobly. all classes of American citizens—have ardently cordially & with the freest sacrifices, contended for your just claims to patriotic confidence—& could you this morning, behold, the depression of spirit, & sinking of heart, that pervade the community, I am sure, that you would feel 'well, in very truth, my defeat, has been the occasion of a more precious tribute & vindication, than even the majority of members—[']

The abolitionists were invincibly obstinate—& seemed resolved, to distinguish their importance right or wrong. The combination of adverse circumstances has often struck me in the progress of the canvass. At the south I was denounced as an abolitionist—rank & uncomprising—Here, the abolit[ionist]s have been rancorous in their hostility a short time since Wm Jay (of illustrious name) assailed me in his Anti Slavy. prints by a harsh, unchristian & intolerant article,[5] in the form of a letter addressed to me, but sent to the winds. Its object was no doubt to drive the party together & it had, I suppose, some influence, that way—Altho', it was too bitter & irrational to accomplish much. And then the foreign vote was tremendous—More than 3000, it is confidently said, have been naturalized in this city alone, since the 1st Octr.[6] It is an alarming fact, that this foreign vote has decided the great questions of American policy—& counteracted a nation's gratitude.

But my dear Sir, leaving this painful subject, let us look away to brighter

& better prospects; and surer hopes—in the promises & consolations of the Gospel of our Saviour—As sinners, who have rebelled against our Maker we need a Saviour or we must perish—And this Redeemer has been provided for us—Prophecy declared him from the earliest period of our fall, in Paradise—& the Gospel makes known the faithful fulfil[l]ment—"Come unto me, cries this exalted Saviour, come unto me all ye that are weary & heavy laden & I will give you rest." Let us then repair to Him. He, will never fail us, in the hour of peril & trial. Vain is the help of man—& frail & false, all trust in an arm of flesh:—but he that trusteth in the Lord, shall be as Mount Zion itself that can never be removed—I pray my honored friend, that your heart may seek this blessed refuge—stable as the everlasting hills—& let this be the occasion to prompt an earnest, prayerful & [blank space] the Lord grant, it may be a joyful search after the truth as it is in Jesus Christ—With affectionate regards to Mrs. [Lucretia Hart] Clay, in which my good wife [Charlotte M. Frelinghuysen], sorely tried, heartily unites . . .

ALS. DLC-HC (DNA, M212, R6). Endorsed by Clay on verso: "Answd Theo. Frelinghuysen." Printed in Colton, *Clay Correspondence*, 4:495-96. 1. Clay to Webb, Feb. 29, 1844. 2. Ewing to Clay, June 23, 1844. 3. Clay to Clayton, Dec. 2, 1844. 4. Clay to Webb, Sept. 23, 1844; Webb to Clay, *ca.* Nov. 7, 1844. 5. The letter, dated Oct. 1, 1844, and published as a pamphlet titled *Letter of the Honorable William Jay, to Hon. Theo. Frelinghuysen* (New York, 1844), 8pp., attacked Frelinghuysen for saying he was not an abolitionist but rather a member of the American Colonization Society and that he believed Congress could not legislate against slavery in the states. It also attacked the strength of his religious and moral beliefs because he refused to endorse the cause of abolition. 6. According to *Niles' Register* (Nov. 2, 1844), 67:144, the number of persons naturalized in New York City in the previous three months was said to be more than 5,000.

From MILLARD FILLMORE Buffalo, N.Y., November 11, 1844

I have thought for three or four days that I would write you. But really I am unmanned. I have no courage or resolution. All is gone. The last hope which hung first upon the city of New York[1] and then upon Virginia[2] is finally dissipated, and I see nothing but despair depicted in every countenance.

For myself I have no regrets. I was nominated much against my will, and though not insensible to the pride of success, yet I feel a kind of relief at being defeated.[3] But not so for you or for the nation. Every consideration of justice—every feeling of gratitude—conspired in the minds of honest men to insure your election; and though always doubtful of my own success, I could never doubt yours till the painful conviction was forced upon me.

The abolitionists and foreign Catholics have defeated us in this state. I will not trust myself [to] speak of the vile hypocrisy of the leading abolitionists now. Doubtless many acted honestly but ignorantly in what they did. But it is clear that [James G.] Birney and his associates sold themselves to Locofocoism; and they will doubtless receive their rewards.

Our opponents by pointing to the native Americans and to Mr. Frelinghysen [*sic*, Theodore Frelinghuysen], drove the foreign catholics from us, and defeated us in this state.[4] But it is vain to look at the causes by which this infamous result has been produced. It is enough to say that all is gone—And I must confess that nothing has happened to shake my confidence in our ability to sustain a free government so much as this. If with such *issues* and such *candidates* as the *national* contest presented we can be beaten, what may we not expect? A cloud of gloom hangs over the futu[re.] May God save the country, for it is evident the people will not.

ALS. DLC-HC (DNA, M212, R6). Endorsed by Clay on verso: "Answd Millard Fillmore." Printed in Colton, *Clay Correspondence*, 4:497. 1. For New York City, see Webb to Clay, *ca.* Nov. 7, 1844; for New York State, see Clay to Webb, Sept. 23, 1844. 2. Clay to Rives, August 19, 1844. 3. Defeated for governor. See Clay to Sargent, Oct. 2, 1844. 4. Ewing to Clay, June 23, 1844.

From J.W. Mighels, Portland, Me., November 11, 1844. Says he is unknown to Clay, but identifies himself as "a *native born* Whig" and a "part of that majority of *native born* citizens of the United States which has cast its electoral vote for HENRY CLAY." Charges that the Locofocos have smuggled in "*British paupers* . . . to vote us down, (two or three hundred of whom will cast their votes against us in this city, this day, and who hold the ballance of power in this state & in this country.)" Adds: "I have this moment returned from the polls, but alas! with what an overwhelming sense of shame and indignation! Knowing that we are to be prostrated in the dust by an army of *Irish* paupers, set on and marsheled by their *infernal* priest!!! God Almighty save us!!!" Predicts that "Twenty thousand *Irish paupers* will come into the field this day in Maine, and every one of them will vote against us. Throw one half of them out of the ballot box and we should carry the state, over Locofocoism, *Irish pauperism*, & *Abolissionism*." States that "altho. our hearts are broken and bleeding . . . we feel proud of our *candidate*." Reports that when news of New York's election results [Clay to Webb, September 23, 1844] arrived, "all our friends turned pale, and the little children, even, burst into tears! My own little boy of 14. was so much affected that he came near fainting in the Clay club room, and passed a sleepless night."

Believes "that the time has come . . . to adopt some measures to 'protect' ourselves against the poluted streams that are even now flowing in upon us from the *alms houses* of Europe." Recommends modification of the naturalization law, but "As to the expediency of forming a '*Native American* party,' I am in doubt about it. I fear it would not avail. . . . Can you advise us?" ALS. DLC-HC (DNA, M212, R6). Endorsed by Clay on verso: "J.W. Mighels." For the Native American movement, see Ewing to Clay, June 23, 1844. For the presidential vote in Maine, see Clay to Giddings, September 21, 1844.

From Unknown Correspondent, Maysville, Ky., November 12, 1844. Notifies Clay that "All, sir, is lost [Clay to Webb, February 29, 1844]." Writes that a steamer just arrived from Wheeling, Va. (W. Va.), and "her passengers and officers report that New York has gone for [James K.] Polk by 6 or 8000 majori[t]y [Clay to Webb, September 23, 1844]. . . . They had on board Baltimore papers of Saturday, and there is no mistake, I presume about the matter[.] **HENRY CLAY,** the orator, statesman and patriot, is beaten, and by such a man! Great God to what degradation has our country brought herself?" Copy. Printed in *Manufacturers and Farmers Journal and Providence and Pawtucket Advertiser*, November 21, 1844.

Clay said in a speech, *ca.* mid-November, 1844, to a group of friends who came to inform him of the election results: "My friends, it would be ridiculous for me to say I do not feel disappointed—but I feel so chiefly for you and for our country; as regards myself, I am relieved from a load of anxiety. I have ever been ready and willing to serve my country, even with my life. I allowed my name to be used in the late contest, because it was unanimously called for, for the sake of the Union; and I am consoled by the fact that I have been supported by the intelligence and patriotism of the nation. Now, I hope to spend the remainder of my days in peace and quiet." Copy. Printed in the Milledgeville (Ga.) *Southern Recorder*, November 26, 1844.

From Stephen M. Chester, New York, November 13, 1844. Writes, "Though personally unknown to you," to "unbosom sympathies, which I am sure I share with all the good & virtuous around me." Adds: "I have not a doubt that a *majority of* the *constitutional freemen* of the Union have deposited their votes for your election. We have been defeated by the organized minions of a treacherous Administration, & the anti american machinations of foreign capitalists & the Hierarchy of Rome [Ewing to Clay, June 23, 1844]; to say nothing of the *asinine falsity* of the *Abolition party* [Clay to Clayton, December 2, 1844], which *itself alone* & *inevitably sacrificed* the *Empire State.*" Believes that "we have many consoling considerations to restore our equanimity." For instance, thinks if the Catholics can be convinced "that the Government is *their own* . . . they will be obedient as the serfs of [Daniel] OConnell to him; but if the Government were Whig, they would be as tumultuous in their gatherings, & as loud in their murmurs, as those very serfs toward the throne of Britain.—The Whigs on the contrary, virtuous & intelligent, always submit gracefully to any Dynasty *constitutionally* placed over them." Asks: "Is it not best then in a Republic, that the turbulent elements of the body politic should *conceive* themselves *identified* with the *Laws*, and that the Government itself should find its constitutional checks, in the wisdom & the patriotism of a powerful minority." Thinks "As a 'Looker on in Venice' you can exert perhaps an almost equal influence on the councils of the nation, without a personal exposure to the rude collisions of the Forum."

Refers to James K. Polk as "a man of straw," as "nothing in himself, but *all the world*, as an *embodiment* of *party.* The party had therefore, in his nomination, nothing to do but organize & gather numbers. . . . He was presented as the native Deity of Free trade to the South,—the Tutelar of the Manufacturing interests to Pennsylvania [Clay to Clayton, August 22, 1844]:—Like the cameleon he was made to change his hue to that of the nearest object, & to glow through all the colors of the prism, as he made the grand tour of the Union:—How could a *consistent character* contend with such a *political Harlequin* of *contradictions*?" Continues: "The organiza[tion of] our opponents, was as systematic, as its policy was jesuitical . . . th[e] merits of citisenship, & the portions of the ballot box almost every [where] at their control, whence was political honesty to find an Aegis [ag]ainst the shafts of ambuscade? . . . Ours was an open, frank, sincere avowal of our principles, & we have the proud consciousness that the aristocracy of intelligence & wealth, & highsouled patriotism of the country, was *all with us.*"

In conclusion states that after "reading over this hasty letter I am prompted by my prudence to [sup]press it but my feelings endorse it so fully as one most expressive of the Whigs feeling every where that I must risk your displeasure at my uncourteous tirade against a 'hapless' fellow being [Polk]." Identifies himself as "a cypher in the political world—a mere business man—formerly a partner of John Devereux in N Carolina—now a carpet dealer in N.Y. My maternal Grandfather was Chief Justice [Stephen Mix] Mitchell of Conn[ecticu]t." ALS. DLC-HC (DNA, M212, R6). Endorsed by Clay on verso: "Mr. Chester [Presidl Election]."

Chester's carpet business was located at 191 Broadway in New York City. Doggett, *New-York City Directory for 1844 & 1845.* Chester's mother, Elizabeth Mitchell, had married Stephen Chester, sometime sheriff of Hartford, Conn. Edward Salisbury, *Family-Histories and Genealogies*, 3 vols. (n.p., 1892), 1:179.

From JOHN J. CRITTENDEN Frankfort, Ky., November 13, 1844

The intelligence brought to us this morning has terminated all our hopes, our suspense & our anxieties in respect to the Presidential election—We now know the worst—[James K.] Polk is elected, & your friends have sustained the heaviest blow that could have befallen them.[1] You will feel, I trust, no other concern about—it than that which naturally arises from your sympathy with those friends. You are perhaps the only man in the Nation that can lose nothing by the result—Success could have added nothing to your name, and nothing I beleive to your happiness—You occupy now, but too truly, the position described as presenting the noblest of human spectacles,

"A great man struggling with the storms of fate and nobly falling with a falling State."

Some little business in the Federal court, which now meets on the first monday of December, hastens my departure for Washington, and I intend to set out for that place, by the river route, on monday next—I shall endeavour to carry with me a heart as light as possible, but deeply impressed with the difficulties and troubles that overhang the country. To prevent them from becoming fatal, will, it seems to me, require great care and prudence. It seems that we can only [*sic*, gain] wisdom by suffering ruin, and I am strongly tempted to leave the Polkites to dispose of the Tariff among themselves, & as they please—The people have preferred Mr Polk, and are they not entitled to the benefit of his measures?

I shall hope occasionally to be favoured with your views on public affairs, & the oftner you may please to give them, the more acceptable will it be.

ALS. NcD. Printed in Colton, *Clay Correspondence*, 4:498 with last two paragraphs deleted; these paragraphs also have been crossed out on the ALS version. 1. Clay to Webb, Feb. 29, 1844.

From Cornelius L.L. Leary, Baltimore, November 14, 1844. Identifies himself as a mechanic who has "used my effort, aye, my *honest* effort to acquit myself of the pressing debt of gratitude which I felt I owed you." Writes that the result of the presidential election has left him with "inexpressible agony," adding: "I am too well acquainted with your character to suppose that this result will affect you as it has affected your friends: that consciousness of purity of motive and of unbending rectitude . . . will still support you in the trying crisis." Is glad that his family, "native born American citizens and competent voters," as well as the state of Maryland [Clay to Kennedy, March 29, 1844] have supported Clay. Asserts that "You are the *only* choice of the great American party, standing upon a broad American platform supported and dependent upon an American Constitution as framed, understood and construed by the Patriot Fathers of the Republic." Fears for the country, because "The very fountain of our political system from whence all authority and power flow is revoltingly corrupt. The ballot box is poisoned by gross ignorance and wanton perjury. The ermine of justice is spotted and the judicial Bench disgraced by undisguised partisan conduct that in the better days of the Republic would have condemned the actors to merit infamy."

Admits that some members "of the class to which I belong have oppo[sed] your elevation and it is because I keenly feel the reproach which this fact awakens, that I have thus ventured to address you." Wishes Clay contentment in retirement, and hopes he "will recognise Maryland, Kentucky [Letcher to Clay, July 6, 1844] and their sister Whig States as having heartily accorded to you that tribute of Justice and Gratitude which an ungrateful country has failed to bestow." ALS. DLC-HC (DNA, M212, R6). Endorsed by Clay on verso: "C. L L Leary [Condolence]." Printed in Colton, *Clay Correspondence*, 4:498-500. For Leary, a Baltimore lawyer and congressman, see *BDAC*.

From Philip S. Galpin *et al.*, New Haven, Conn., November 16, 1844. Transmit proceedings of a Whig meeting, held in New Haven on November 14. Express "pain & mortification" at the "deplorable result of the late Election [Clay to Webb, February 29, 1844]." Assert that "you are President in the hearts of a vast majority of the intelligent & patriotic Citizens of the Country, where you can never be defeated, &

where the poisoned shafts of calumny can never reach you." State that "We are proud, Sir, of our City, for the vote she gave you, which was larger than ever given before to any candidate in a contested election, & we are proud of our State, that amid all the deceptions & slanders . . . she has given you a majority worthy of her character & of the intelligence of her citizens." Conclude by saying Clay is "in our affections second only to the Father of his Country." ALS. DLC-HC (DNA, M212, R6). Endorsed by Clay on verso: "New Haven [Resolutions &c. P. Election]." Printed in Colton, *Clay Correspondence*, 4:500-501.

Galpin was mayor of New Haven from 1842-46 and 1856-60. He was a carpet manufacturer and was also in the insurance business. Robert A. Dahl, *Who Governs? Democracy and Power in an American City* (New Haven, 1961), 13, 25; Edward E. Atwater, *History of the City of New Haven* (New York, 1887), 458. Galpin chaired the meeting of November 14 which praised Clay and the Whig party. A copy of the resolutions passed at the meeting is in DLC-HC (DNA, M212, R6).

Clay carried the city of New Haven by 1,735 votes to 1,267 for Polk. New-York *Daily Tribune*, November 6, 1844. He carried Connecticut with 32,832 votes to Polk's 29,841 and Birney's 1,943. McKee, *National . . . Popular and Electoral Vote*, 56-57.

On December 17, 1844, Clay wrote Galpin *et al.* acknowledging receipt of a copy of the proceedings of the New Haven meeting which manifested a "patriotic spirit . . . worthy of Connecticut, worthy of its renowned seat of learning, and worthy of the Whig cause." Pledges that his "obligations to Connecticut . . . will be faithfully remembered whilst I continue to live."

Sets forth his views on "the policy of the Country in regard to the protection of industry," which, until "a few months ago, seemed to be rapidly acquiring a permanent and fixed character." The North had reproached the South and Southwest "for want of sufficient interest and sympathy in its welfare." When "the Slave States were fast subscribing to the justice and expediency of a Tariff, for Revenue, with discriminations for protection," a "sufficient number" of the Northern states "abandoned what was believed to be their own cherished policy and have aided, if not in its total subversion in exposing it to imminent hazard." As a result, "Discouragement has taken the place of confidence . . . enterprize is checked, and no one knows to what employment he can now safely direct his exertions." Fears a decline in the "Home market . . . at a time when the Foreign market is absolutely glutted with American productions, Cotton especially." Sees the "final and not distant result" to be "a drain of the Specie of the Country, with all its train of terrible consequences."

Believes that a Whig victory would have secured the distribution of the proceeds of the sales of the public lands, "and that great national inheritance would have been preserved for the benefit of the present and future generations." Shall be "agreeably disappointed if it not be wasted in a few years by graduation and other projects of alienation."

Touches briefly on other key elements of Whig policy "aimed at the purity of the Government, the greater prosperity of the People, and additional security to their liberties and to the Union." Views his party as "most anxious to avoid a Foreign War, for the sake of acquiring a Foreign territory, which . . . could not fail to produce domestic discord, and expose the character of the Country, in the eyes of an impartial World to severe animadversions."

Urges "a fair trial" for the newly elected administration, with the "anxious desire that the evils we have apprehended may not be realized." Hopes "to visit once more New England, and especially New Haven," which gave him "the largest majority ever given by that City in a contested election." Copy. DLC-HC (DNA, M212, R6). Printed in Colton, *Clay Correspondence*, 4:514-16.

From I.C. Ray, New Bedford, Mass., November 16, 1844. Rejoices with Clay, not at his defeat in the presidential election, but because "now thee is forced from political turmoil" and will now be able to enjoy "the luxuries of domestic comfort." Reports that in New England "the late contest . . . has been against the annexation of Texas; and boldly have the sons of the Puritans spoken against that wicked scheme, gotten up by Tyler & Co. to extend the withering curse of slavery, and to put the day farther distant . . . when religious and political freedom would be extended to all." Says that the Quakers have believed that Clay would free his slaves if elected president, and urges that the election loss "not interfer with thy carrying out that great act of justice, if thee has given anyone to understand thee should." Believes Clay can "shine brightly on the page of moral history" if he should take up the cause of freeing the slaves. Regrets "for any moral subject to be mixed with politics," and would like to separate the anti-slavery movement from politics and "bring the moral and religious influence of the land to bear upon slavery. In that event, the system would not live one year—I mean, if our religion was according to the morality of Jesus Christ. But our religion is our politics, and our code of morals our Constitution, and it will take a long time to change them." Adds that he has "looked forward . . . for thee to do something that would set the wheels going towards emancipation." Remains certain that thousands would follow suit if they only had a leader. Copy. Printed in Boston *The Liberator*, April 11, 1845.

To MARY S. BAYARD Lexington, November 18, 1844

I received your letter of the 4h. The forebodings of the defeat of the Whig party, which you appear to have entertained even at its date, are realized.[1] Your kind and soothing letter reached me most opportunely, for it came to me in the same mail that bore intelligence which satisfied me that our cause was lost. The spirit of religion, of philosophy and of friendship which it embodied served to weaken the blow which fell upon me. I will not disguise, my dear friend, that I felt the severity of that blow, more perhaps because two weeks ago it was altogether unexpected by me here. Then, indeed, the fulfillment of the wild prophecy of [William] Miller[2] would have hardly excited more astonishment than what has just happened. But, much as this sad event effects me personally, I feel much more for my Country and my friends. I am but a poor mortal, whose life has nearly reached the ordinary limit of human existence. But the Country comprehends many millions, and the Nation, it is to be hoped, will remain for ages to come. And my friends, by this event, are cut out of that share in the conduct of public affairs to which, from their virtues, their talents and their cruel proscriptions, they were justly entitled.

This painful event is another striking example of the uncertainty of all human concerns; and should lead us to cherish other and higher hopes in another and better world.

I cannot tell you how much I was gratified by the re-assurance of your friendship, come what might. You have proved yourself to me the best of friends, the cordial and sympathising friend in need. I never can forget how in 1840 you manifested your friendship. I shall ever remember the scene in the Eastern portico of the Capitol, when a sense of the injustice which you supposed had been done me,[3] overcame your feelings and you gave vent to your tears. But I turn from the contemplation of public affairs.

I was happy to learn from your letter that your health was re-established. But these frequent attacks should urge you to more care, and should induce Mr. [Richard Henry] Bayard to take you from Wilmington, attached as you may be to it, if its climate, as you apprehend, be the cause of your illness.

I know not my dear friend when, if ever, I shall again have the satisfaction of seeing you, and of drawing comfort and consolation from your conversation and society. Be that as it may, I shall ever bear in memory and cherish an affectionate remembrance of our friendship, and of the many happy hours I have passed in your company.

I pray you to present to Mr. Bayard, the young ladies[4] and to his sister[5] the warm regards of . . .

ALS. Anonymous Owner. Copy in KyU. 1. Clay to Webb, Feb. 29, 1844. 2. Miller, the leader of a millennialist religious group, had predicted that the second coming of Christ would occur in 1843 or 1844. After the event did not occur on several of the dates he had foretold, he refused to name a specific time but still insisted that the second coming would happen in the immediate future. See Miller's article in *DAB* and Dick Everett, "The Adventist Crisis, 1831-1844," Ph.D. dissertation, University of Wisconsin, 1930. 3. Probably a reference to Clay's 1839 loss of the Whig presidential nomination. See 9:361-65, 368, 384, 462-63. 4. The Bayards had 5 daughters—Mary, Caroline, Elizabeth, Harriet, and Louisa. Thomas A. Glenn (ed.), *Some Colonial Mansions and Those Who Lived in Them* . . . , 2 vols. (Philadelphia, 1897), 1:362. 5. For Bayard's sister Ann Caroline Bayard, see Clay to Bayard, Sept. 22, 1847.

From WILLIAM C. RIVES Castle Hill,[1] November 18, 1844

It seems now certain that every calculation, founded on the natural relation of cause & effect & derived from the usual evidences of public opinion, has been reversed & set at naught in the recent Presidential election.[2] The result is most deeply to be deplored for the country; but you, my dear sir, have but little cause to regret it personally. While it has saved you from the cares of a most thankless & harrassing office, it has secured to you a still higher place in the hearts of your countrymen & upon the imperishable records of History.—And when the vote which has been cast in the election comes to be analysed it will be seen that, throwing out one or two petty factions whose narrow-minded hostility a peculiar combination of circumstances had armed with the power of mischief, the voice of a large majority of the *american* people has decreed to you the pre-eminence due to your patriotism, your principles & your services. It is, indeed, a melancholy reflection that the odds & ends of faction should ever have it in their power thus to disappoint a nation's award. But history is full of such examples, ennobled by their very sacrifice. Cato was disappointed of the Consulate; but this only evoked the more, the notice of history & even of his own countrymen to assign him the first place among the patriots & benefactors of his age—

It has been some consolation to us, amid our disappointment in this state, as I hope it will be a gratifying circumstance to yourself that your native county of Hanover (nearly balanced by her party divisions as she has been for many years) gave you a much larger majority than she has given for any party or cause, within the present generation.[3] I am happy to add that this county also[4] upon which extraordinary efforts were directed by the holding of the State Convention of our adversaries in it,[5] nobly seconded the lead of Hanover by increasing her majority for you considerably beyond that given for Genl [William Henry] Harrison in 1840. And, indeed, your acquaintance with our political geography will enable you at once to see that but for three or four irreclaimable counties of large extent, which light has as yet very imperfectly penetrated, Virginia & Kentuckey [*sic*] would have stood side by side in this great struggle.—[6]

I pray you, my dear sir, to accept the cordial assurances of the great & distinguished respect . . .

ALI, draft. DLC-William C. Rives Papers (DNA, M212, R22). 1. His estate near Charlottesville, Va. 2. Clay to Webb, Feb. 29, 1844. 3. Clay won 558 votes in Hanover County, Va., to Polk's 482. *Niles' Register* (Jan. 4, 1845), 67:276. 4. Clay carried Albemarle County, Va., over Polk by a vote of 912 to 702. *Ibid.* 5. The Virginia Democratic State convention, with over 600 delegates, had met in Charlottesville on Sept. 10, 1844. *Ibid.* (Sept. 21, 1844), 67:42. 6. For Virginia's presidential vote, see Clay to Rives, August 19, 1844; for Kentucky's, see Letcher to Clay, July 6, 1844.

From Samuel Boyd Tobey, Providence, R.I., November 18, 1844. Although unknown to Clay, writes that "I cannot well refrain from writing thee on the close of the present election—I do not condole with thee on the inauspicious result on thy own account—for surely to be placed in the Presidential chair would bring many onerous duties and add nothing to the honored name of Henry Clay—but my condolence is for my country in consequence of the *radical* and *downward* tendency manifested by the votes of the people, many of whom, being aliens in our land, have little interest in our Institutions." Predicts that if "this course of things be not arrested, the experiment of self-government will prove a failure here as it has heretofore done in other Republics." Hopes Clay will retain "the elasticity which thou hast always displayed when pressed most heavily," and that he may again come forth as the "champion and deliverer" of his country.

Asserts that he knows "of no member of the Society of Friends in our little State that did not give his vote for thee for President." Says his "wife and four boys are out and out *whigs* and of course thorough friends of Henry Clay." Asks for "a single line from thee, that my children . . . may look upon thy autograph." ALS. DLC-HC (DNA, M212, R6). Endorsed by Clay on verso: "Ansd Dr Saml Boyd Tobey."

Tobey was a leading Providence physician. Welcome Arnold Greene, *The Providence Plantations* (Providence, R.I., 1886), 208.

From George T.M. Davis *et al.*, Alton, Ill., November 19, 1844. As "Whigs of the City of Alton," write to express their "deep mortification and disappointment" at Clay's recent defeat [Clay to Webb, February 29, 1844] and "to assure you of our continued and undiminished confidence in you as an American, a Philanthropist and a Statesman." Assert: "*To us*, defeat in sustaining you and those American principles for which you have so assiduously and fearlessly battled for the last thirty years and upwards, is infinitely more honor in our estimation, than to have had our exertions crowned with success under such a leader and with such AntiAmerican principles as James K Polk and those he and his friends advocated. *To us*, it is a proud, and will ever remain an enduring reflection that in this contest you have received the support, and the suffrages of a large majority of *the free born citisens* of this vast nation." Believe that Clay's defeat while "contending for American Industry, and American Manufacturers, while our opponents have succeeded with the banner of a foreign land as their Emblem, and by the aid and influence of British interests, and British Capital, is indeed a source of never failing consolation."

Refer to Clay as "Father of the great American System . . . the product of your mighty mind and gigantic intellect." Are afraid that the nation will now be humbled "under the dominion of a 'Free Trade' Administration . . . to the humiliating condition of being dependent to a great extent, upon the pauper labor & Capital of England for our necessary supplies." Predict, however, that the country will eventually "be rescued from the fangs of the corrupt and dishonest, now elevated to power, not by the voice of American freemen! but by the purchased suffrages of a Foreign legion, unacquainted with the principles or the policy of our Government, and brought here to subdue and overpower the honest industry and labor of our own citizens." Add that "we now turn to you for Council and advice as to the best course to be pursued, to save our country from disunion, and our people from being reduced to a condition worse than the vassals of Europe." LS, by 15 people. DLC-HC (DNA, M212, R6). Endorsed by Clay on verso: "Ansd. Alton address."

For the impact of nativism and frauds in the 1844 presidential election, see espec. Ewing to Clay, June 23, 1844, and Seward to Clay, November 7, 1844. For George T.M. Davis (1810-88)—a lawyer at this time in Alton, Ill., and later editor of the Louisville *Courier*—see Rossiter Johnson (ed.), *The Twentieth Century Biographical Dictionary of Notable Americans* . . . (Boston, 1904).

The New-York *Morning Courier and Enquirer* had reported on September 24, 1844, that "British Gold is being spent freely throughout the country to promote Mr. Polk," apparently because of his free trade stance. North Carolina Congressman Thomas Clingman made a similar reference to British gold in the House on January 6, 1845. *Cong. Globe*, 28 Cong., 2 Sess., 97. Thomas L. Clingman, *Selections from the Speeches and Writings of Thomas L. Clingman, of North Carolina* (Raleigh, N.C., 1878), 185-86. The Lexington *Observer & Kentucky Reporter* of September 25, 1844, charged that British agents even then were in Kentucky and throughout the United States distributing free trade tracts and money to secure the election of Polk and the demise of the Tariff of 1842.

From Francis S. Bronson, LaGrange, Ga., November 20, 1844. Deplores Clay's loss of the presidential election [Clay to Webb, February 9, 1844], saying "the *majority* have been triumphed over by the triumvirate, [Andrew] Jackson, [John C.] Calhoun, and [Martin] Van Buren—by these combined influences have we been beaten, with the assistance of a large Foreign vote [Ewing to Clay, June 23, 1844; Roman to Clay, December 2, 1844], thrust upon us, against the very letter and spirit of our Constitution—and this, too, done in our very midst, by the Locofoco officers of State. I write no idle tale—no dream—no imagination—'tis true." Asserts: "We want a leader, *we must have one—that task* devolves upon you, though heavy it may be." Believes that unless the "spirit of foreign interference" is checked, "we are ruined and undone forever: The Constitution and Laws of this Union will become a by-word & a reproach to us." Thinks that "To avoid the threatening dissolution . . . we have but one alternative—resort to it immediately, & we are saved—procrastinate, and we are politically damned & dead, as a people & as a nation." Contends that "The evil can be remedied—it must be done by the amalgamation of the Whig Party with the Native Americans [Clay to Clayton, December 2, 1844]—for, indeed, I regard the two parties synonymous: the issue has been made, & the result has proven to be, *American vs. Foreign*." Proclaims that "The whole State of Georgia is ready for the question—Alabama and Louisiana are ready. . . . I beg you, Sir, in behalf of our country, and in the name of God, whom I revere, come forward once more to the rescue."

States that in Georgia "thousands of votes . . . have been cast against us by foreigners, who have not been in our country for a greater period than one & two years—yet, these men, (beasts, I should have said,) have sworn to their nativism, & declared their residence to entitle them to the elective franchise. They *have* been naturalized! Were they entitled, is a question that can never be tried in this Locofoco, foreign, antiparty, State." Begs Clay "to answer this letter in detail." In a postscript marked private adds: "Never was there a time when the hearts of freemen have been so sorely tried. The whole exertions of the more discreet in our party have, for weeks tended to prevent bloodshed—so much & so great was the feeling among our disappointed friends. As for myself, I have wondered that I have not been murdered a dozen times over. Fraud of every conceivable character has been practiced bribery & corruption resorted to—and even by men who claimed to be the followers of Jesus Christ—forgot the *sanctum sanctorum* and sought aid from both Beelzebub, & from the blinded zealots, who thought their ministers to be saints—this is the game—& by this and the foreigners were we beaten in Georgia." ALS. DLC-HC (DNA, M212, R6). Endorsed by Clay on verso: "Dr Bronson La Grange."

For the Georgia election, see Clay to Kennedy, March 29, 1844. For the nativist movement, see Ewing to Clay, June 23, 1844.

Although Georgia did not have a large foreign population, the state did seem to experience a significant degree of voting fraud in the 1844 election. According to the Macon *Georgia Messenger* of December 12, 1844, an estimated 9,502 more votes were cast than there were legal voters in the state. See also Washington *Daily National Intelligencer*, December 10, 1844; Colton, *Clay Correspondence*, 2:430-43; McCrary, "John MacPherson Berrien," Ph.D. dissertation, University of Georgia, 1971, pp. 294-95.

From John P.B. Maxwell *et al.*, Belvedere, N.J., November 20, 1844. Report their disappointment at Clay's loss [Clay to Webb, February 29, 1844]. Believe, however, that his election to the presidency could not "add one ray to the brilliancy of such a life as yours. . . . your name belongs to history and to posterity." State that "Upon us falls the loss of national honor and the blight of that prosperity which was just beginning to rise under the influence of the only Whig measure [Tariff of 1842] which treason and folly permitted us to realize [9:528-29, 543-44, 553, 556-57]." Note that "a great majority of those who are American in feeling and American by birth have been true to their country and to you; and that when fanaticism calumny and falsehood have done their worst in the contest they must yet have failed but for the aid of the refuse of other lands who have basely repaid the protection our country has afforded them by sacrificing her interests and her honor." Point out that "our State [New Jersey] . . . has again proved herself true Whig [Anderson to Clay, October 14, 1844] and worthy of her [Theodore] Frelinghuysen." Praise Clay further and ask him to visit. LS, by 100 people. DLC-HC (DNA, M212, R6). Endorsed by Clay on verso: "Ansd. Address [Belvedere N. Jersey]."

Clay writing on December 18, 1844, thanked them for their "friendly address, on the subject of the late Presid[entia]l election." Attributes defeat to "an extraordinary combination, embracing some very conflicting elements."

Believes the Whigs should be consoled by their "principles and measures" which "stand free from reproach." Expresses his gratification "that, in conjunction with my excellent friend, Mr. [Theodore] Frelinghuysen, I was honored by the suffrage of his native State," and appreciates their "kind invitation to visit your part of New Jersey." ALS. KyLoF.

For John P.B. Maxwell—lawyer, editor, and twice congressman from New Jersey—see *BDAC*.

To WILLIAM HENRY SEWARD Lexington, November 20, 1844

I duly received the two letters[1] which you did me the favor to address to me, one written immediately after the interview of Mr. [John] Lee, of Maryland,[2] with you, and the other on the 7th instant, after the termination of the presidential election in New York.[3] I feel greatly obliged by your prompt attention to my request communicated through Mr. Lee.

Throughout this whole political campaign I have never doubted your good intentions, and have been constantly persuaded of your having employed your best exertions. The sad result of the contest is now known;[4] it is also irreversible, and we are only left to deplore that so good a cause, sustained by so many good men, has been defeated—defeated, too, by a combination of the most extraordinary adverse circumstances that perhaps ever before occurred. But it is now useless and unavailing to speculate upon the causes of the unfortunate issue of the contest. We are also too much under the excitement which it produced, and under depression created by that issue, calmly and deliberately to look through the gloom which hangs over the future. It will be time enough to do that after the public has recovered from the disappointment which it has just experienced.

As for myself, it would be folly to deny that I feel the severity of the blow most intensely. I feel it for myself, but, unless my heart deceives me, I feel it still more for my country and my friends. I had hoped to have been an humble instrument in the hands of Providence to arrest the downward tendency of our Government. I had hoped to have it in my power to do justice to those able, valuable, and virtuous friends, who have been so long and cruelly proscribed and persecuted. But it has been otherwise decreed, and my duty now is that of resignation and submission, cherishing the hope that some others more fortunate than myself may yet arise to accomplish that which I have not been allowed to effect.

You are in the prime of life, endowed with great ability, and I trust that you will long be spared in health and prosperity to render great and good service to our common country.

Such will continue to be the prayer of your friend . . .

Copy. Printed in Frederick W. Seward, *Autobiography of William H. Seward From 1801 to 1834 with a Memoir of His Life, and Selections From His Letters From 1831 to 1846* (New York, 1877), 733-34. 1. Seward to Clay, Oct. 25 and Nov. 7, 1844. 2. Lee to Clay, Nov. 2, 1844. 3. Clay to Webb, Sept. 23, 1844. 4. Clay to Webb, Feb. 29, 1844.

To WILLIAM H. WEED Lexington, November 20, 1844

I received your letter[1] and thank you for the friendly sentiments towards me which it conveys. I share with you in deep regret on account of the unexpected issue of the Presidential Election.[2] It is however now past and irrevocable. It would be useless and unavailing to bewail the event. To me personally it is of little importance, for I cannot expect much more to prolong my life. It is far otherwise with the country, and I confess, when I look at the causes and the consequences of the event, I cannot but indulge the most fearful forebodings. Let us however cherish the hope that they may not be realised, and that Providence has yet in store for us some blessings which, in his infinite wisdom and goodness, he has not yet thought proper to disclose. Reciprocating your kind personal wishes towards me . . .

LS. NjP. Addressed to Weed in New York City. 1. Letter not found. This correspondent is probably William Henry Weed (1782-1845), a New York City merchant, who is referred to in William R. Cutter, *New England Families Genealogical and Memorial*, 4 vols. (New York, 1914), 1:408. 2. Clay to Webb, Feb. 29, 1844.

To OCTAVIA WALTON LEVERT Lexington, November 21, 1844

I cannot, my ever dear friend, sufficiently apologise to you for my delay in acknowledging the receipt of your two last very agreeable letters.[1] I was delighted to learn, by that of October, that you and your's had all passed through the perils of a Mobile summer, without injury or serious danger. May you all long survive to enjoy health, happiness and every other blessing!

To tell the truth I postponed writing to you 'till after the Presidential election, under the hope that I might be able to communicate to you what I know would have been agreeable intelligence. That hope has not been realized; and, as you will have heard 'ere this letter reaches you, the election has terminated adversely to the Whigs.[2] This has been a most unlooked for & astounding event, causing many hearts to bleed freely. I did not dream of such an issue of the contest three short weeks ago. I will not deny that it has created with me the profoundest regret, not on my own account only nor principally but on account of my Country and my friends. I had hoped to be an humble instrument, in the hands of Providence, to arrest the downward tendency of the Government. And I had ardently hoped also to have it in my power to contribute towards doing justice to that large body of enlightened virtuous and patriotic political friends, who have been so long and so cruelly proscribed. But it has been otherwise decreed, and to the irreversible decree it is my duty to submit in a spirit of Christian resignation. I will not trouble you, my dear Octavia, with speculations on the causes or the consequences of this sad event. I sincerely wish that the fearful forebodings, which fill my mind may, in the sequel, be found to be groundless.

I believe that I shall have to remain at home this winter. My private affairs render this necessary, and altho' I should be most happy to be with such friends as yourself and your good husband [Henry LeVert] and your charming little girls,[3] I have no great inclination for mixing in the gay or busy world. Dr. [William N.] Mercer has, by this time, left Laurel Hill and entered his winter quarters in Carondelet Street.[4] Such at least he wrote me was his intention.

I will not write more at present. Let me have the satisfaction of an occasional line from you; for I shall ever cherish the deepest interest in the welfare of yourself and your family. Present my warm regards to Dr. Levert, your father and mother [George & Sally Walton], and embrace the girls . . .

P.S. Do me the favor to present my respectful compliments to Madame Hubbell.

ALS. CSmH. 1. Letters not found. 2. Clay to Webb, Feb. 29, 1944. 3. Clay to LeVert, April 14, 1844. 4. In New Orleans.

From Allan B. Magruder, Charlottesville, Va., November 21, 1844. Though unknown to Clay, expresses his "unaffected mortification at the result of the late Presidential election [Clay to Webb, February 29, 1844]." Notes that "As the former editor of the Virginia Advocate—a Whig Journal—published in this place, I derive no little gratification from the reflection that long before the public wish for your election to the Presidency of the United States, had found expression in a formal nomination [9:753-54], it was my fortune to rank among the earliest of the public Journalists of the Country who unfurled the banner inscribed with those great Whig principles which, under your auspices, we desired to see reduced to practice in the administration of the National government." Contends that "If the Whigs have failed in the late contest, it has not been because they lacked the energy, the will or the lawful power to achieve success. We have seen the will of a large majority of the qualified voters of the Country—if the native sons of the soil (as I sincerely believe) contemned & set aside by a combination of foreign force & domestic fraud & ignorance against which the intelligence and virtue of the Country have, alas! been arrayed in vain [Ewing to Clay, June 23, 1844]."

Testifies at length to his respect for Clay, noting that "Your career as the great Statesman of the age has happily illustrated those virtues & abilities which office cannot enhance & which the retirement of private life will tend still further to dignify

& adorn." ALS. DLC-HC (DNA, M212, R6). Endorsed by Clay on verso: "Answd A B. Magruder."

For Allan B. Magruder, a lawyer and father of writer Julia Magruder, see the daughter's entry in James, *Notable American Women*, 2:485; also *The Magazine of Albemarle County History*, 6:64; 21:37.

From Ambrose Spencer, Albany, N.Y., November 21, 1844. Referring to "the disastrous result, of the efforts of the whig party to do justice to you," states: "It is pretty well ascertained that had New York given you her vote, you would have been elected [Clay to Webb, February 29, 1844]. This consideration is very mortifying to us—and yet, I venture to affirm, that in no state of the Union had you warmer or more vigilant & vigorous supporters. Every thing that could be effected by human means, was done—I knew many, very many men, who laid aside all other business & directed themselves night & day in the good cause. The result of our canvass shows what mighty efforts have been made—You received 232,411 votes—[James K.] Polk recd. 237,432—[James G.] Birney 15,875—what a monstrous poll—You received 6594 more votes than [William Henry] Harrison did in 1840, when his majority exceeded 12,000—You will perceive that the abolition vote lost you the election, as 3/4ths of these were from whigs converted into abolitionists—The foreign vote also destroyed your election—& there was yet another distinct cause, the utter mendacity frauds & villainies of Locofocoism—This untoward event, has produced universal gloom, & has shaken public confidence to an unexpected extent—Even many of those who voted for Polk, now that he is elected, deeply regret this result[.] God only knows to what we are destined—One sentiment seems to obtain universally, that the naturalization laws must be altered—That they must be repealed & the door forever shut on the admission of foreigners to citizenship, or that they undergo a long probation—I am for the former—" Believes the Germans and Irish "can never understandingly exercise the franchise" and because of "their ignorance are naturally inclined to go with the loafers of our own population—"

Does not offer Clay condolence, because "the country not you are to be sufferers. . . . You have been spared the toils of four years hard service, which could not have raised you higher in the affections & confidence of your friends & admirers." Concludes: "Your administration would have put at rest all contention on the duty & necessity of protecting American industry—on the distribution of the proceeds of the public lands & on many other vexed questions; which are now set afloat & put in jeopardy—In yielding my hearty support to the whig cause, you are aware, that I had no earthly motives but the public good—I confess that in doing all I could to promote your election, there was an additional motive, the deep respect, & affection I felt for you individually, founded on your public services & on those personal qualities, which on our first acquaintance took a lodgment in my heart, never to be effaced—" ALS. DLC-HC (DNA, M212, R6). Endorsed by Clay on verso: "Ansd. Ambrose Spencer." Printed in Colton, *Clay Correspondence*, 4:501-2. For the nativist movement which opposed allowing recent immigrants to vote, see Ewing to Clay, June 23, 1844.

Spencer's numbers for the New York presidential vote in 1844 are slightly smaller than the official tally. See Clay to Webb, September 23, 1844. In 1840 Harrison had received 225,817 votes to 212,519 for Martin Van Buren, and 2,798 for Birney. McKee, *National . . . Popular and Electoral Vote*, 44.

From Thomas Nevitt, Fairfax County, Va., November 23, 1844. Writes that the election result [Clay to Webb, February 29, 1844] "has produced a sensation in my breast, I can not describe, a dark gloom I can not penetrate, has cast a shadow over my brightest prospects, and enveloped in doubt & uncertainty all my future hopes." Asserts that "The landing of the British armies in the late war, the takin[g] of

Washington, the burning of the Capitol & other public buildings, are but trifiling events when compared with the present: then we had an honorable enemy to fight against; now we have had an unprincipaled party aided by foreign votes & foreign influence to contend with, a party who taxed their ingenuity to invent the most unblushing falsehoods and heaping upon you the vilest, abuse, but all this would have availed naught, had they not caped the climax of their infamy by adding the spurious and illegal foreign vote." Adds: "You are defeated in part by the very cause which in the early and virtuous days of our Republic would have secured your election, the open, frank, manly and undisguised manner you have always expressed your political views & opinions." Assures Clay that he occupies "a deep seated and abide-ing place in the hearts and affections of every true Whig." Concludes with a request for "your *likeness*, with your name written by yourself attached to it; I wish to place it by the side of [George] Washington's that my children may be taught to venerate them alike." ALS. DLC-HC (DNA, M212, R6). Endorsed by Clay: "Thomas Nevitt."

From William C. Preston, Columbia, S.C., November 23, 1844. Writes that he is "astounded with the result of the elections [Clay to Webb, February 29, 1844]" and has been "solely occupied with these gloomy and fortuitous occurrences." Believes that for Clay "they effect you in no more but as depriving you of the means of further patriotic usefulness. You have long since passed that point where office could confer additional celebrity—or add an inch to the noble preeminence which history will assign you—Tho' your name will not appear in the dull chronology of official succes-sion—the times will be known as those in which the wisdom courage & eloquence of Clay were displayed for the glory of his country." Believes "It would be vain and painful to speculate on the causes which have led to this result. . . . For the present the Whig party of the South is dispersed—and we cannot know our position until the heat & smoke of the conflict have passed away." ALS. DLC-HC (DNA, M212, R6). Endorsed by Clay: "Wm. C. Preston Answd. Presl. Election." Printed in Colton, *Clay Correspondence*, 4:503.

From John L. Lawrence, New York City, November 25, 1844. States that the "mor-tification felt at the result of the late Presidential election [Clay to Webb, February 29, 1844], which has cast an unprecedented gloom over the enlightened & patriotic portion of the Nation & particularly of this City, has been too deeply participated by myself to leave me in spirits to write to you sooner on that subject. . . . There is no consolation in the reflection, that the defeat has been produced by fraud and deception—by lying practices and unprincipled combinations—since that very fact but strengthens a gloomy anticipation of the coming fate of our Government." Be-lieves, however, that "apart from the ability which the possession of the Executive chair would have afforded you of . . . advancing the national welfare—it cannot be lamented by you personally. In your public career, you have sowed broadcast through-out the land, seeds which, if permitted to vegetate, will yield abundant prosperity and blessings, with whose enjoyment your name must be inseparably connected by your fellow citizens. At the recent contest you have been sustained, by almost the entire mass of the intelligent and worthy among them; forming a support both in reference to the men and the motives, such as no other person in this Country could have called forth. The bauble of the Presidency, seeing into what hands it has some-times fallen, and is about to be placed, could add nothing to the reputation which the wise and just award to you, and which the Historian will record."

Asks Clay not to make a "premature decision in the negative" about returning to the public councils, adding that "I feel confident . . . that if it be necessary that your exertions be again interposed to save the Country, they will not be withheld." ALS. DLC-HC (DNA, M212, R6). Endorsed by Clay: "Answd. Jno. L–Lawrence Esq."

From Joseph Hoxie, New York, November 26, 1844. Acknowledges receipt of Clay's letter of October 29, "enclosing a note for my daughter for which she desires me to thank you." Feels he is not yet "in a frame of mind to speak of recent events in the political affairs of the Country." Adds that " 'My sleep has departed from me', & my appetite fails. . . . of all the troubles & afflictions I have been called to struggle with, none has troubled me like the present. . . . nothing has so crushed me to the earth, and depressed my spirits as the result of our late political contest [Clay to Webb, February 29, 1844]." ALS. DLC-HC (DNA, M212, R6). Endorsed by Clay: "Answd. Joseph Hoxie."

Hoxie's three daughters were Maria, Josephine, and Elsie. It is not known to which one of these Clay had written, since neither that note nor the letter with which it was enclosed have been found. For the daughters, see Leslie R. Hoxie, *The Hoxie Family, Three Centuries in America* (Ukiah, Ore., 1950), 65.

From J. Phillips Phoenix, New York City, November 26, 1844. Reports that "I see by the papers that you have determined to retire from public life—Would it not be well to wait the movement of your friends on this important subject? Although politically defeated, you enjoy the confidence of the Country to a greater extent than you ever have done—no person has a stronger hold upon the feelings of the american people—" Adds that "On saturday evening, we met (about 50) to close up the expenses of the late campaign, and during the supper 'Henry Clay for 1848' was received, with the most enthusiastic applause." ALS. DLC-HC (DNA, M212, R6). Endorsed by Clay: "J.P. Phenix [*sic*]."

For Phoenix, who later served in the U.S. House, see *BDAC*.

From Neilson Poe, Baltimore, November 26, 1844. Recalls that when writing Clay "on the morning after the Presidential Election in Maryland [Clay to Kennedy, March 29, 1844]," he promised to report to "you early intelligence from other quarters." Says, however, that he did not do so after he realized it would not be "a task which I should find pleasure in discharging." Recalls that it has been "nearly ten years since, as the Editor of a public journal, I took the initiative in presenting your name as a candidate for the Presidency—The advice of men more influential than myself, at that time, and at a subsequent period led to the designation of another individual." Was happy when Clay received the nomination in 1844, and "felt that my long delayed but never abandoned expectations were to be gratified." Does not offer condolence for the loss, however, because "I feel the triumph of envy hatred, malice & all uncharitableness in the recent contest more severely than you can, and it is I & such men as I am, who most need to be consoled." Urges Clay to "address . . . the Whigs of the Union" and "admonish them to stand by the principles they have professed." ALS. DLC-HC (DNA, M212, R6). Endorsed by Clay: "Nelson [*sic*] Poe."

Neilson Poe (1809-84), second cousin of Edgar Allan Poe, was a lawyer and journalist. In 1839 he was editor of the Baltimore *Commercial Chronicle and Daily Marylander*. George E. Woodberry, *The Life of Edgar Allan Poe, Personal and Literary*, 2 vols. (New York, 1909), 1:379; *MHM*, 37:421-22.

From Epes Sargent, New York City, November 26, 1844. Asserts that "We have been robbed of our lawful President by the seven thousand fraudulent votes cast for Mr. [James K.] Polk in this city [Webb to Clay, *ca.* November 7, 1844]. No man, who has had opportunities of investigating the subject, entertains a doubt of this fact. Our opponents have had in their pay a gang, who have voted twenty times severally at the late election with impunity. What resistance can we offer to such a terrible system so long as the party in power reject a registry law and every other measure calculated to preserve the ballot box from corruption?" Asks: "What high-souled man will hereafter be ambitious to fill the highest office in the gift of our people—when he sees it the reward of partizan servility and not of magnanimous public services? I have heard of old men, who came home, sickened and died on being assured of the result of the election." Expresses the sense of gratitude the public feels toward Clay, and hopes "that your friends will long be privileged to look to you for counsel and encouragement in their efforts for the public good." ALS. DLC-HC (DNA, M212, R6). Endorsed by Clay: "Answd. Epes Sargent."

According to *Niles' Register* (November 2, 1844), 67:144, over 5,000 immigrants had been naturalized in New York City in the three months prior to the election. For views similar to Sargent's, see Horace Greeley, *Recollections Of A Busy Life* . . . (New York, 1868), 165-66; also see Ewing to Clay, June 23, 1844.

From Ruth L. Farnurre, Newburgh, N.Y., November 27, 1844. Assures Clay that the Whigs of Newburgh "have indeed strove manfully to resist the principles of Locofocoism," and that their village "has merrily resounded with the cheering songs of Clay and Frelinghuysen Union and Protection . . . and our bright hopes blasted yet that love for *Harry of the West* which has so strongly manifested itself far from being abated is doubly increased." Writes that she is fifteen years old and that her father is a great Clay supporter. Asks for an answer to her letter "as a New Years gift." ALS. DLC-HC (DNA, M212, R6). Endorsed by Clay: "Nov. 1844 Ruth L. Farnurre."

From Christopher Hughes, London, England, November 27, 1844. Addresses Clay as "my chief—my old Master—my venerated & beloved Friend!" As he prepares to leave by steamer for Rotterdam and The Hague, "I will not lose a moment in conveying to you—the heart felt emotion—amazement—& grief—with which I have received the news—just arrived—of the result of the Presidential Election [Clay to Webb, February 29, 1844]. Great God! is it possible! . . . England is astounded . . . for in you and on your election depends, in the minds of this people and Government, the maintenance of harmony and peaceful relations between the two nations." Asserts that "Since our first acquaintance in 1814, when we left our country to send home peace to our people, I have never—no, never—deserted you, in thought, in heart, or in deed! Never have I disguised my preference, my respect, my love and admiration for you; and I have prized, as the greatest success and honor of my life, your friendship for me, and the cheerful, amiable, playful, affectionate familiarity that you have always permitted and tolerated in me, your pupil and your friend. I know you have always loved me and trusted me. My eyes now run over—before God they do!"

Recalls that they wept together "on the 2d December, 1814, the day we signed the peace of Ghent—when you threw your arms around my neck in bidding me adieu, seeing how sad I was; and exclaimed—'Hughes! my friend, what is the matter with you? I see that you are unhappy.' I told that I was mortified at finding—that—in the last '*despatches*' to the Government at home—(which I myself had copied & was to bear home—with the Treaty)—there was *no mention* of my name—by my Ministers—whom I had served with so much zeal—fidelity & honour—& that this—mortified & pained me. You told me—there had been such a sentence—at the close of the last Despatch: that it had been erased—as not properly belonging to a *public* Document—& was repeated in all your *private* Letters—to Secy. of State [James Monroe] & to Mr. [James] Madison—that admirable & incomparable man—whom I knew & loved. This did not appease me—& I said—Good God! are not the character & conduct of public 'servants—when they are honourable—proper in the public & *published* archives of the Country?' But I loved you—my excellent & kind-hearted Friend—for the kindness & tenderness of your conduct! You embraced me—you wept like a child—Your heart was full of the pride & pleasure & comfort of having achieved peace for Your Country."

Informs Clay that after signing the Treaty of Ghent "ye—my—chief—had signed yr last *despatch—at* Made. Van C–s [Van Canighams or Van Caneghems; see 5:1043-44]—which I was to bear! & the good lady thought it was '*The Treaty*' & the Pen you used—is in a Glass Case—in her House—sacredly preserved—to this day—for Made. Van C. continued to believe that the Peace had been made under her Roof—& boasted of it till her death—25 years after! & showed me—proudly—'The Precious Pen!' " Contends that "*No man* knows you—*as well*—as *I do*! No! Not one!—& I ever have loved & esteemed you; & it is my pride to feel—*so have you me*! Why I could see comfort in your heart and manner—whenever I have been with you! You seemed to feel—as if there was a safety—an ease—a pleasing security—when I was with you! Again & again May God bless & preserve! I write incoherently! You would not believe my emotion. My head is confused!" ALS. DLC-HC (DNA, M212, R6), first page only. Printed in full, with minor variations, in Colton, *Clay Correspondence*, 4:503-6.

From Peter H. Silvester, Coxsackie, Greene County, N.Y., November 27, 1844. Writes in behalf of the Coxsackie Clay Club to say "that you have been our political idol & that we esteem you as highly & love you as dearly as we ever have done—In defeat, more than in victory—" Adds that "There is one consolation to us . . . that is, that your name will live—, yes, it must, it shall live forever, in undying, honorable fame." States that "Your nomination was but the spontaneous & unanimous outbreaking of the feelings of a great majority of the intelligent & patriotic freeman of the land—By them, you have been supported, with the whole heart & soul & strength: with an intensity of feeling & exertion almost unparalleled & every whig heart is stricken down & mourns that this republic has exhibited such an instance of ingratitude. . . . We point with unutterable pride to the fact that we cast our votes for the man 'who would rather be right, than be President—' " ALS. DLC-HC (DNA, M212, R6). Endorsed by Clay on verso: "Answd. Cocksachie Clay Club." Printed in Colton, *Clay Correspondence*, 4:506-7.

For Silvester, a lawyer and later a congressman from New York, see *BDAC*.

To JOHN J. CRITTENDEN Lexington, November 28, 1844

I received your very kind letter written just before your departure for Washington. It is hardly necessary to say that I deeply sympathize with you, in consequence of the most unexpected and disastrous result of the presidential election.[1] As to myself, it is of but little importance. But I deplore it on account of the country and of our friends. I had cherished the fond hope of being an humble instrument, in the hands of Providence, to check the downward tendency of our Government, and to contribute to restore it to its former purity. I had also hoped to be able to render some justice to our enlightened and patriotic friends, who have been so long and so cruelly persecuted and proscribed. But these hopes have vanished, and it is useless and unavailing to lament the irrevocable event.

It will be more profitable to seek to discern the means by which the Country may be saved from the impending dangers. I regret that they are not visible to me. Still it is our duty, to the last, to struggle for its interests, its honor, and its glory. And it is in that spirit that I venture to offer a few suggestions. It seems to me that the Whigs, or some of them, in Congress would do well to have an early consultation and to adopt some system of future action. We, I think, should adhere to our principles; for believing in their wisdom and rectitude it is impossible that we can abandon them. The recent election demonstrates that, although the Whigs are in the minority, it is a large minority, embracing a large portion of the virtue, wealth, intelligence, and patriotism of the Country. That minority constitutes a vast power which, acting in concert, and with prudence and wisdom, may yet save the country. Then, there are the errors which we confidently fear and believe our opponents will commit, in the course of their administration, an exposure of which must open the eyes of the people and add to the Whig strength. In your letter you intimated an inclination to leave the dominant party free, to carry out their principles, undisturbed by the Whigs. I confess I am inclined to agree with you in that opinion. For, unless there is a practical operation and experience of the opposite systems of the two parties, I do not see how the Country will ever settle down in a stable and permanent policy. As a general rule, I think that the dominant party ought to be allowed to carry out their measures, without any other opposition than that of fully exposing their evil tendency to the people, if they have such a tendency. Of course, I do not mean that members should vote contrary to their conscientious convictions or to the will of their Constituents. But I suppose that there are members, in both branches of Congress, who can vote in conformity with the will of their Constituents without violating their own Convictions, and thus leave the other party at liberty to establish its own policy. If that party should attempt to embody in a tariff just enough of protection, on the one hand, and of free trade, on the other, to secure its ascendancy and further to deceive and mislead the people, such partial legislation ought to encounter the most determined opposition. That is the course, I confess, which I most apprehend they will pursue. They will give protection where it is necessary to the preservation of their power, and they will deny it to States, with whose support they can dispense.

There is a great tendency amongst the Whigs to unfurl the banner of the *Native* American party.[2] Whilst I own I have great sympathy with that party I do not perceive the wisdom, at present, either of the Whigs absorbing it, or being absorbed by it. If either of those contingencies were to happen, our adversaries would charge that it was the same old party, with a new name or with a new article added to its creed. In the mean time, they would retain all the foreign vote, which they have consolidated, make constant further accessions, and perhaps regain their members who have joined the Native American party. I am disposed to think that it is best for each party, the Whigs and the Natives, to retain their respective organizations distinct from each other, and to cultivate friendly relations together. If petitions be presented, to alter the naturalization laws, they ought to be received and respectfully dealt with. There can be no doubt of the greatness of the evil of this constant manufacture of American Citizens out of foreign emigrants, many of whom are incapable of justly appreciating the duties incident to the new character which they assume. Some day or other this evil will doubtless be corrected. But is this country ripe for the correction? And will not a premature effort instead of weakening add strength to the evil?

I perceive, in several quarters, a wish expressed that I should return to the Senate. I desire to say to you, that I have not the remotest thought of doing so, even if a vacancy existed. I can hardly conceive of a state of things in which I should be tempted to return to Congress. My anxious desire is to remain, during the remnant of my days, in peace and retirement.

Do me the favor to present me affectionately to all our friends, in the Senate, and particularly to Messrs. [John M.] Berrien, [Richard H.] Bayard, and [William C.] Rives, from whom I have received very friendly letters. I may write to them perhaps on some other occasion.

LS. DLC-John J. Crittenden Papers (DNA, M212, R20). 1. Clay to Webb, Feb. 29, 1844. 2. Ewing to Clay, June 23, 1844.

From PHILIP HONE New York, November 28, 1844

I hesitate and doubt whether I ought to add to the annoyance which I know you experience at this time, but I cannot deny myself the privilege of writing to you, not to condole with you on your recent defeat.[1] I know you feel little regret on your own account, but to give vent to my own sorrow, to deplore the infatuation of my Countrymen, and to mingle my prayers with yours, that the evils we anticipate from the unexpected result of the late Election may be averted and the people made happy against their own wayward wills.

You, and the holy cause of which you were the honored representative, have been sacrificed to fraud, corruption and misrepresentation, and the Instruments used to effect the object, were foreign voters made to order, and mischeivous sectarians, who prefer to trust the success of their theory to the uncertain measures of an untried Administration than to one pledged to support the glorious Constitution and to maintain its guaranties.

The result of this election has satisfied me that no such man as Henry Clay can ever be President of the United States. The party leaders, the men who make Presidents, will never consent to elevate one greatly their superior—they suffer too much by the Contrast, their aspirations are checked, their power is circumscribed, the clay cannot be moulded into an Idol suited to their worship. Moreover a Statesman, prominent as you have been for so long a time, must have been identified with all the leading measures affecting the interests of the people, and those interests are frequently different in the several parts of our widely extended Country. What is meat in one section is poison in another. Give me therefore a Candidate of an inferior grade, one whose talents, patriotism and public services have never been so conspicuous as to force him into the first ranks. He will get all the votes which the best and wisest man could secure, and some which for the reasons I have stated, he could not.

But the especial object of my writing is to remove any unfavorable impressions (if such there be) from your mind as to the miserable result here.[2] The loss of New York was fatal to the cause of the Whigs, but I pray your [*sic*, you] dear Sir to attribute no part of this misfortune to a want of exertion on the part of your friends in the City of New York. Never before did they work so faithfully, and never, I fear, will they again. the Man, and the cause were equally dear to the noble Whigs, and every honorable exertion was made, every personal sacrifice submitted to, every liberal oblation poured upon the Altar of patriotic devotion—Nine tenths of our respectable Citizens voted for Clay and [Theodore] Frelinghuysen, the merchants, the professional men, the mechanics an[d] working men, all such as [live] by their skill, and the labour of their honest hands, who have wives whom they cherish and children whom they strive to Educate and make good citizens. Men who go to church on Sundays, respect the laws and love their Country. Such Men to the number of 26385 redeemed their pledge to God and the Country; but alas! the numerical strength lies not in those classes, foreigners who have "no lot or inheritance" in the matter, have robbed us of our birth-right, the "Sceptre has departed from Israel." Ireland has re-conquered the Country which England lost, but never suffer yourself to believe that a single trace of of [*sic*] the name of Henry Clay is obliterated from the swelling hearts of the whigs of New York[.]

ALS. DLC-HC (DNA, M212, R6). Endorsed by Clay on verso: "Philip Hone." Printed in Colton, *Clay Correspondence*, 4:507-9. 1. Clay to Webb, Feb. 29, 1844. 2. For New York State, see Clay to Webb, Sept. 23, 1844; for New York City, see Webb to Clay, *ca.* Nov. 7, 1844.

To ISAAC A. PENNYPACKER[1] Lexington, November 28, 1844

I received and thank you for your friendly letter communicating some of the causes which occasioned the recent most unexpected defeat of the Whigs in Pennsylvania.[2] They are curious as matters of history; but I apprehend there is no present remedy.

I am grateful for the good opinion of me which prompts you to desire my return to the National Councils; but I have no intention of doing so. My desire is to pass the remnant of my days in private life. Grateful to my ardent and faithful friends, I shall never cease to cherish the warmest affection for them, and, in my private station, to co-operate with them in advancing the happiness and prosperity of our country.

Copy. Printed in Samuel W. Pennypacker, *The Autobiography of a Pennsylvanian* (Philadelphia, 1918), 48. 1. Pennypacker (1812-56) was a physician who practiced in Phoenixville and Philadelphia. See *ibid.* 2. Clay to Cooper, Sept. 10, 1844.

From M. & R.H. Sweeney, Wheeling, Va. (W. Va.), November 28, 1844. State that they have sent Clay "a large Glass Vase, which was made at our Glass Manufactory in this city, and which was thought worthy of a medal by the Franklin Institute of Philadelphia, when exhibited at the recent Fair in competition with similar manufactures from other parts of the United States." Ask him to accept the vase as a token of their gratitude for his support of American manufactures which has allowed them to reach their "present degree of perfection." Copy. Printed in Wheeling *Times and Advertiser*, December 27, 1844. Also printed in Gary E. Baker, "The Flint Glass Industry in Wheeling, West Virginia: 1829-1865," M.A. thesis, University of Delaware, 1986, pp. 180-81.

Clay replied on December 14, 1844, thanking them for the vase, which arrived "in perfect condition." Notes that it surpasses "in magnitude and splendor any production of Cut-glass which I have ever seen. . . . The Vase is a triumphant vindication of the wisdom of that policy, to the establishment of which I have devoted my utmost endeavors, respecting which, however, others should share largely in the merit which you are pleased to assign me." Regrets the vase "has not some more conspicuous place than in my humble dwelling." Copy. Printed in Wheeling *Times and Advertiser*, December 27, 1844. Also printed in Baker, "The Flint Glass Industry," 181-82.

Robert H. (1814-45) and Michael Sweeney (1809-75) bought shares in the glassworks in 1843, and Robert became general business manager. Baker, "The Flint Glass Industry," 60-63.

The Franklin Institute of the State of Pennsylvania, for the Promotion of the Mechanic Arts was established in Philadelphia in 1824 for the purpose of diffusing knowledge, educating artisans, and awarding prizes for useful improvements in the arts. Bruce Sinclair, *Philadelphia's Philosopher Mechanics, A History of the Franklin Institute 1824-1865* (Baltimore, 1974), 3-4, 20, 32.

From John H. Westwood, Baltimore, November 28, 1844. States that now that the election is over, "I can address you without the fear of selfishness, or a desire of ingratiating myself to your notice for personal motives." Describes himself as "one of your early and fast friends," who believes that "when the name of [Andrew] Jackson and others of your vile traducers shall be forgotten, yours shall be remembered and live in the affections of all lovers of liberty."

Asserts that "It was foreign influence aided by the Irish and Dutch vote that caused our defeat. As a proof, in my native City alone, in the short space of two months there were over 1000 naturalized[.] Out of this number 9/10 voted the loco foco ticket. Thus men who could not speak our language were made citizens and became politicians too, who at the poles were the noisy revilers of your fair fame—"

Adds that "Notwithstanding the ingratitude of the Irish and German voters if the Abolitionist[s] of New York had done their duty, all would have been well [Clay to Webb, September 23, 1844]." Notes that "I am proud of Old Maryland she never voted for a Loco Foco President and I trust never will." Writes that he has a fourteen-year-old son named Henry whom he believes "will not disgrace his name." ALS. DLC-HC (DNA, M212, R6). Endorsed by Clay: "Jno. H. Westwood." Printed in Colton, *Clay Correspondence*, 4:509-10.

John H. Westwood is listed as a bacon dealer at 46 Pitt Street in the 1842 *Baltimore City Directory* and at 138 N. Exeter in the 1845 directory. Information supplied by Donna Ellis, Maryland Historical Society.

From George A. Coffey, Danville, Columbia Co., Pa., November 29, 1844. Identifies himself as "a Pennsylvanian, and a Methodist preacher," who has "from my earliest boyhood . . . been your admirer, your friend, your supporter." Expresses his disappointment over Clay's loss of the presidential election [Clay to Webb, February 29, 1844], writing that "you are defeated only by foul fraud." Asserts that "I admire you, and *love* you more than ever." ALS. DLC-HC (DNA, M212, R6). Endorsed by Clay: "Answd. Revd. Geo. A. Coffey."

To L.J. Moses, Charleston, S.C., November 29, 1844. Acknowledges receipt of a letter of October 22 "informing me of the birth of your son . . . and of your having bestowed my name upon him." Thanks Moses for this compliment and "For the sentiments of confidence and attachment which you kindly entertain towards me." ALS. Courtesy of Mrs. Henry Clay Moses, New Rochelle, N.Y.

Moses was a clerk in the Southwestern Bank from 1840-48. See Barnett A. Elzas, *The Jews of South Carolina* . . . (Philadelphia, 1905; reprint ed., Spartanburg, S.C., 1972), 170, 205.

From Charles Olivier, Parish of St. Mary, La., November 29, 1844. Writes of "the disgrace which weighs upon the Louisianians" as a result of the recent presidential election [Clay to Webb, February 29, 1844; Clay to Kennedy, March 29, 1844]. Asserts that "ambitious intriguers have employed all the means which have been put in operation from time to time to act upon the masses; appeals to every bad passion, the hostile instinct of the poor against the rich, lies and calumnies &c &c. and at last the lever, already too powerful of that surplus population of Europe which is yearly vomited upon our shores." Adds that "your enemies themselves pay the tribute of admiration to your high capacities, truly American, and under whatever color it is done, are surprised that Henry Clay has not received the palm due to his eminent services! they recall to mind Aristides Banished, Socrates poisoned."

Writes that he is sixty-six years old, is sick, and "I expect nothing nor could I expect any favor, I am a Louisianian. I have been bound by friendship to Judge [Alexander] Porter 30 years. You know how much he was attached, to you, and he often spoke to me of you. Permit me then to join to the expression of my respect, the sincere devotion that I profess to you." ALS, in French, with contemporary translation by unknown person. InU.

Olivier had been a delegate to the Louisiana constitutional convention of 1811-12. He owned an interest in the Metairie Race Course and was a horseracing enthusiast. Wendell Holmes Stephenson, *Alexander Porter, Whig Planter of Old Louisiana* (Baton Rouge, 1934), 13, 124, 127-28.

To JAMES MADISON PENDLETON[1] Lexington, November 29, 1844

My feelings prompt me to offer you my cordial acknowledgments for your friendly letter of the 21st. inst. I entertain sentiments of the liveliest gratitude for the kind interest you have taken and continue to cherish in me. And I am greatly obliged by the desire you manifest that I should seek, in the resources of Religion, consolation for all the vexations and disappointments of life. I hope you will continue your prayers for me, since I trust that I am not altogether unworthy of them. I have long been fully convinced of the paramount importance of the Christian Religion. I have for many years fervently Sought its blessings. I shall persevere, in seeking them, and I hope ultimately to attain a firm faith and confidence in its promises. There is nothing for which I feel so anxious. May God, in his infinite mercy, grant what I so ardently desire!

Should you pass this way at any time, I shall be most happy to see you. Mean while accept my thanks and my wishes for your happiness here & hereafter.

ALS. TxDaHi. Printed in Colton, *Clay Correspondence*, 4:509. 1. For Pendleton, a Baptist minister and educator in Kentucky, see *DAB*.

From Thomas H. Baird, Pittsburgh, Pa., November 30, 1844. In regard to "The result of the late elections [Clay to Webb, February 29, 1844]," asserts that "No man ever before received so glorious a testimonial. I believe in fact you had a majority of the *legal* votes throughout the Union. One thing however is certain. You had nine tenths of the virtue, intelligence & respectability of the Nation on your side.—We failed on obtaining your election through the fraud & falsehood of our opponents, who will soon feel the effects of their folly & crime.—The defeat is nothing to you: it is the people who are to be the sufferers—until delusion is dispelled & they rise in their strength to cast off the oppressors."

Believes that Clay will "be vindicated . . . by your election to the Presidency four years hence." States that "In a letter, which I see published in the New York Tribune, it is intimated that you are determined to withdraw from public life.—I hope you have formed no such purpose. The Whig party regard you as the only man upon whom we can rally with one heart and one mind. If you leave us we shall fall into divisions which will impair our union & prevent our success. . . . Our opponents are astonished at their unexpected conquest. Thousands of them in this State, are alarmed—and would gladly retract if they could, their ill advised action. The Liberty [party] men are ashamed of their course—and wish it was undone." Therefore, contends that "There is no reason why you should retire." ALS. DLC-HC (DNA,

M212, R6). Endorsed by Clay: "Tho. H. Baird Nov. 30. 1844 P. Election." Printed in Colton, *Clay Correspondence*, 4:497.

A letter in the New-York *Daily Tribune* of November 26, 1844, dated November 19 and reported to be from a friend of Clay, had stated that "*Mr. Clay will never again return to public life.*"

From William D. Lewis, Philadelphia, November 30, 1844. Believes that only "a very small number . . . can realize as much sorrow . . . as myself" as a result of Clay's loss of the presidential election [Clay to Webb, February 29, 1844]. Says he had "looked to your elevation to the Presidency as a great personal delight to myself, and the harbinger of long continued prosperity to the nation." Asserts that "This glorious and beneficial result has been prevented, through wicked and unprincipled men, by frauds upon the elective franchise as monstrous as they are unprecedented; by fanaticism both religious & political without a paralell in our history." Adds that "the bitterest reflection was that you had been defrauded out of the honor designed for you by a majority of your own countrymen, through the instrumentality of foreigners whose illegal votes had been bought up for the purpose by unprincipled demagogues."

Asserts that "the gallant party which sustained you fought a noble battle, and it fought that battle under its own banners on which your name and principles were boldly emblazoned, the same in the South & in the North, in the East and in the West. And it is a party numbering in its ranks a large majority of the most intelligent and patriotic of our citizens. To have been nominated with perfect unanimity by such a class, to have been supported by it with so much devotion, and to know how their hearts were riven by their failure of success, each one feeling almost that your case was his own, should give you no inconsiderable grounds of consolation." Adds that Clay has lost nothing in the election and still retains "the admiration of the world." Hopes Clay will not again enter public life. Notes also that "whatever this stupid & degraded State [Pennsylvania] may have done [Clay to Cooper, September 10, 1844], Philadelphia performed her part in a manner which must forever redound to her favor [Davis to Clay, October 4, 1844]." ALS. DLC-HC (DNA, M212, R6). Endorsed by Clay on verso: "Wm. D. Lewis." Printed in Colton, *Clay Correspondence*, 4:510-11.

From Lorenzo D. McCabe, Athens, Ohio, November 30, 1844. Writes that as an orphan he "sought sanctuary in the house of a Lady who taught me to love thy character and honor thy name." Identifies himself as a Methodist minister of the Ohio Conference, and asks for "a word with the signature of Henry Clay." Consoles Clay, noting "That your support was from the wise, the good, and the truly patriotic." Writes he has shed bitter tears over Clay's loss [Clay to Webb, February 29, 1844] and "the degradation of my Nation in being led by so vile a party, headed by so meagre so imbecile a leader [James K. Polk]." Believes that "Unlike other public men your friends are disinterested and their friendship deep and fervent, Your enemies may be bitter but by so much are your admirers stronger and holier." ALS. DLC-HC (DNA, M212, R6). Endorsed by Clay on verso: "Answd The Revd. L.D. McCabe."

McCabe (1817-97), who had graduated from Ohio University in 1843, joined the faculty of Ohio Wesleyan in 1845 as professor of mathematics. He later became professor of philosophy and twice served as acting president. William Coyle, *Ohio Authors and their Books . . . 1796-1950* (Cleveland, 1962), 404.

From George H. Chrisman, Harrisonburg, Va., December 1, 1844. Reports that as a result of the election "the right judging and right thinking part of our Citizens" acted "as if overwhelmed with some private calamity" at the news of Clay's defeat in New York [Unknown Correspondent to Clay, November 12, 1844]. Is astonished that on a trip through the countryside, he discovered "among the democracy" after "talking with some twenty or thirty persons . . . but one man [who] made any inquiry about the result of the Election." Could not account for this attitude because "they had all been marshaled but a few days before at the polls, and cast their votes against you [Clay to Rives, August 19, 1844], not indeed with the same unconcern they now manifested, for they were anxious to vote, but with the same indifference for the Interest and honour of the Country." Believes, however, that "these men are worthy and good citizens, compared with the foreign and fraudulent Voters, that decided the vote of New York, against you [Ewing to Clay, June 23, 1844]."

Writes that he spent "all night with a Democrat, of some intelligence" who believed Clay "would rank among the wise statesmen and patriots of the Country" and who agreed "it was hard that such a Man, should be set aside by his Country men for Col. [James K.] Polk." Continues: "When your character extorts such praises as these from your enemies, May not your friends be excused, for mixing up with an enlightened and patriotic solicitude for the true Interests of the Country, a warm and ardent personal devotion to your Character as a States man & a man?"

Assures Clay, despite his defeat, that so many of "the good the wise and the true, of your Country men, shall have pronounced their verdict of condemnation, upon the foul Calumnies of Genl. [Andrew] Jackson, who was one omnipotent for mischief," that he should have "unerring evidence of what the decision of posterity must be." Views "this evidence of the returning justice" as "a consolation," and hopes Clay "may live to witness that full and overwhelming condemnation, which your Country must pronounce upon your defamers." ALS. DLC-HC (DNA, M212, R6). Endorsed by Clay on verso: "Decr. 1844 Geo–H. Christman [*sic*]."

George H. Chrisman (1799-1870) was a substantial planter and slaveowner in Rockingham County. John H. Harrison, *Settlers by the Long Grey Trail* (Dayton, Va., 1935), 464.

To JOHN M. CLAYTON Lexington, December 2, 1844

I duly received your friendly letter of the 16h. Ulto. In the general wreck of our Cause, I was delighted that little Delaware stood up firm and faithful[.][1] She is a noble and patriotic State, and I am not surprized at your great attachment to her. Whilst all my friends there are entitled to my warmest acknowledgments, I must request you to be my organ in expressing them particularly to the du Ponts—Alfred and all of them—for their friendly and powerful aid, without which we should not have triumphed.[2] I hope that you will not fail to execute this commission.

We have been defeated by a most extraordinary combination of adverse circumstances[.] If there had been no Native party, or if all its members had been truer to its own principles; or if the recent foreigners had not been all united against us; or if the foreign Catholics had not been arrayed on the other side;[3] or if the Abolitionists had been true to their avowed principles;[4] or if there had been no frauds,[5] we should have triumphed. It required the union of all these elements, conflicting as some of them are, to defeat us, and unfortunately the union existed[.]

But regrets are now useless and unavailing[.] You ask what is now to be done? I wish I could clearly see a satisfactory answer. I can only make suggestions. I think we should stand by our principles and by our arms and continue to endeavor to enlighten the public. We cannot if we would abandon our principles, which are founded in truth[.] Then, our opponents, unless we are greatly deceived, in their character and designs will, by the course of their administration, furnish abundant cause of public dissatisfaction. I freely confess that I see in the future only dim glimpses of light. Discouraged we cannot but be. Still we should not yield to ignoble feelings of despair. We have a Country to save, and, by doing our whole duty towards accomplishing that object, we may have the smiles of Providence, but, should we fail, we will have the conscious satisfaction of feeling that we have made our utmost exertions[.]

I do not see the wisdom of assuming a new name, and giving up our separate organization. With the Natives, we have strong sympathies, and ought to cultivate amicable relations; but if the two parties were to unite, our foes would charge that it was the same Whig party, with a new name, or a new article added to its creed. Whilst they would be constantly making accessions of strength from the foreign source, and perhaps might draw from the Native party the democrats who have joined it[.][6]

In an aggregate vote of upwards of 2 1/2 millions we are only beaten some thirty or forty thousand, and that by means already adverted to.[7] The Whig minority, minority though it be, is a great power, which judiciously wielded may yet save the Republic[.] And when we contemplate the intelligence, virtue, wealth & patriotism combined in that minority, our hopes and confidence are strengthened[.]

I wish you had removed to Philada some years ago, or could now remove. Altho' your residence in Delaware ought to have been a recommendation, it prevented you from receiving from the Balto. Convention last May the nomination for V.P.[8] Had you been nominated, the Catholics would not have been so united against us, and I am not sure that a different issue of the election might not have taken place. In saying this, I desire not to be understood as justifying in the slightest degree their unfounded prejudices against Mr. [Theodore] Frelinghuysen, or uttering one word against him, whom I regard as one of the best of men.[9] You will be prominent among those towards whom the Whig party will hereafter naturally look for a Candidate for the Chief Magistracy, and your position in Philada. would favor the selection.

As for myself, I have not the remotest purpose of returning to the Senate, as some seem to desire, even if a vacancy existed. It is my wish to pass the remainder of my life in peaceful retirement.

ALS. DLC-John M. Clayton Papers (DNA, M212, R20). 1. Clay won Delaware's 3 electoral votes with a popular vote of 6,278 over Polk's 5,996. McKee, *National . . . Popular and Electoral Vote*, 56-57. 2. For Alfred V. DuPont, eldest son of E.I. DuPont and a presidential elector in 1844, see *NCAB*, 6:456-57. 3. Ewing to Clay, June 23, 1844. 4. For the Liberty party vote in 1844, see Clay to Webb, Feb. 29, 1844. Since the Democratic party in 1844 was committed to the annexation of Texas, which would increase slave territory, the Whig and Liberty parties vied for the anti-slave vote. Whig leaders appealed to abolitionists to vote for Whig candidates who might stop Texas annexation rather than throw away their votes on the Liberty party slate. Following the election, many observers felt the Liberty party had taken away enough votes from Clay, especially in New York, to give Polk the victory. See Fladeland, *James Gillespie Birney*, 227-51. 5. Ewing to Clay, June 23, 1844; Roman to Clay, Dec. 2, 1844. 6. Although nativists and Whigs had attempted an alliance in certain areas of the country for the election of 1844, nativists in 1845 attempted to form a national party of their own by calling for a convention to meet in Philadelphia on July 4. They failed in this effort, since both Whigs and Democrats stressed to their supporters the importance of party loyalty. Also, many Whigs blamed the nativists for Clay's defeat; thus, without Whig support, the nativists lost much of their political clout in the mid-1840s. Ira M. Leonard & Robert D. Parmet, *American Nativism, 1830-1860* (New York, 1971), 76-79. 7. Clay to Webb, Feb. 29, 1844. 8. See 9:733, 754. 9. Ewing to Clay, June 23, 1844.

From John C. Hamilton, New York, December 2, 1844. Has waited to write until "the first moments of our National reverse [Clay to Webb, February, 29, 1844]" was past in order to give "precedence . . . to those who have had . . . nearer relations with you than has been my privilege." Does not want to "dwell on the circumstances of our defeat," but wonders if "the result of this election is indicative of our destinies." Continues: "Democracy, if it has shewn great levity, is not the less stern in its decrees. In your person it has assailed the most powerful opponent of its excesses, & may now trample & riot in its usurpations—*where* this will end may be foreseen—*when* is less obvious." Fears that "the general standard of our National morals will sink more & more—year after year amid frequent & sudden changes which prevent the formation of established character." Copy. InHi.

To OBADIAH MEAD[1] Lexington, December 2, 1844

I received[2] . . . letter [and thank] you for the sentiments of confidence and friendship towards me which it conveys. The issue of the P. election,[3] of which it treats is less important to me than to our Country an[d to my frie]nds, altho' I do not pretend to feel indifferent to it [on my] own account. It is how ever passed and irrevocable [and a]ll regrets about it are vain and unavailing. Let [us] hope that the fearful apprehensions which are entertained of its consequences may not be realized.

I shall ever feel the liveliest gratitu[de] for the support with which I have been honored in Connecticut.[4]

ALS. Ct. Addressed to Mead in Fairfield Co., Conn. 1. For Mead (1785-1878), a deacon in the Congregational Church of North Greenwich, see D. Hamilton Hurd, *History of Fairfield County, Connecticut* . . . (Philadelphia, 1881), 384. 2. Manuscript mutilated. 3. Clay to Webb, Feb. 29, 1844. 4. Galpin to Clay, Nov. 16, 1844.

From Andre B. Roman, St. James Parish, La., December 2, 1844. Assures Clay that "When posterity shall wonder that you did not obtain the first office in the gift of your country-men," their answer will "raise you higher than the office could ever have done: it is because 'he had rather be right than president'!" Believes that citizens' inability to open their eyes to "the distressful experience of fifteen years of demagogism and bareface corruption" might well offer "splendid proof of the incapacity of men for self government. . . . unless we find the means of restoring the lost sanctity of the ballot-box."

Argues that "our naturalization laws must be reformed [Ewing to Clay, June 23, 1844]." In addition, "most of the states have extended too far the elective franchise," resulting in "a system of deception, bribery and perjury" in which "almost every foreigner who lands on our shores is manufactured into an american elector, before he can form an opinion of the rights he has to execute."

Informs Clay that Louisiana's "meager majority" for James K. Polk [Clay to Kennedy, March 29, 1844] "was obtained through the grossest, the most infamous frauds." Plaquemine Parish "which had never at any previous election polled more than 340 votes, gave a locofoco majority of 970!" Believes Clay "undoubtedly received the majority of, the legal votes of Louisiana, although she is numbered against you as well as Pen[n]sylvania & N–York, where locofocoism has triumphed by falsehoods, misrepresentations & the help of foreign influence." ALS. DLC-HC (DNA, M212, R6). Printed in Colton, *Clay Correspondence*, 4:512. Endorsed by Clay on verso: "Answd A.B. Roman [Presidt. Election]."

According to an anonymous article titled "The Election Frauds in Plaquemine Parish, Louisiana in 1844," written soon after the 1844 election and originally published in the New York *Nation*, February 27, 1879, pp. 146-47, a Democratic judge from Plaquemine Parish had chartered two steamboats, put on board some 350 people to whom he supplied liquor, and took them to three polling places in the parish to vote for Polk. Most of these people were Irish and German immigrants. The article charged that the Plaquemine sheriff prevented Whigs from New Orleans from interferring with this action and also cooperated with Loco Focos to prevent Whigs from voting. See *LHQ* (July, 1927), 10:402-6. See also Ewing to Clay, June 23, 1844.

To ALEXANDER WILLIAMS Lexington, December 2, 1844

I duly recd. and thank you for your friendly letter.[1] The conduct of young Howard,[2] as represented in it, surprizes me. Neither myself nor my family recollect of his ever having dined but once in my house. He has not been here since his return to the University. I do not remember having ever met him any where in company, and I am not sure that I should recognize him if I were to see him. If he stated that he had seen me intoxicated, and gambling, his statements were absolutely untrue, and destitute of all foundation whatever.

I share with you, my dear Sir, in deep regrets on account of the most unexpected issue of the Presidential election.[3] It has been brought about by the most extraordinary combination of circumstances. There is no alternative but submission to the event, with a determination to adhere to our principles and to persevere in our endeavors to save the Country. Amidst the greatest discouragements, it some times happens, in the dispensations of an all wise Providence, that unexpected deliverance is sent us. Such must be our hope.

I owe to you and to my numerous warm hearted friends a debt of gratitude which I can never pay.

ALS. NcD. Addressed to Williams at Greeneville, Tenn. 1. Letter not found. For Williams, see Goldene F. Burgner, *Greene County, Tennessee Wills, 1783-1890* (Easley, S.C., 1981), 75, 109; Byron & Barbara Sistler (transcribers), *1850 Census Tennessee* (Evanston, Ill., 1976), 7:69. 2. John K. Howard of Greeneville, Tenn., was a junior at Transylvania University. *Annual Announcement of Transylvania University for 1843-44* (Lexington, 1844), 7. 3. Clay to Webb, Feb. 29, 1844.

From Thomas L. McKenney, near Portland, Me., December 3, 1844. Had hoped to congratulate Clay on his victory, but instead "I write amidst 'muffled drums.' " Describes the campaign as one "when the flag of your principles was flung to the breeze from every hill top, and spire, and when the valleys, every where rang with the enthusiastic shouts of the 'Intelligent and Patriotic'; and when woman—lovely woman, alive as in Roman times, and as in American Revolutionary times . . . mingled with the masses of the Sons of Liberty, wreathing with her smiles their efforts, and their hopes." Mourns that Clay's opponents "have succeeded by fraud . . . making of American Liberty, and American rights, a *farce*. . . . Never before were such base shifts made to defeat the will of the people. . . . Earth itself, and Hell would seem to have been ransacked by the most active and worst of spirits to find elements for your destruction!!" Adds that "you are, at this moment the choice of an immense majority of the legal, Intelligent & Patriotic voters," and if there had been no fraud, Clay "would be in *fact*, as you are of *right*, President of the U. States." Calls "Prophetic" Clay's announcement that " '*War Pestilence* & *Famine*' were preferable, to the elevation of Andrew Jackson to the Presidency." Is consoled only by "the thought that we are in the hand of God!" ALS. DLC-HC (DNA, M212, R6). Endorsed by Clay on verso: "Thos. L. McKenney Esq. Prest. Election."

For Maine's vote in the 1844 elections, see Clay to Giddings, September 21, 1844.

To JOSEPH HOXIE Lexington, December 4, 1844

I will not delay a moment acknowledging the receipt this morning of your truly feeling and friendly letter of the 26t. ultimo.[1] I am perfectly sure of the sincerity and truth of every sentiment expressed by you. The sad result of the presidential election has filled the nation with grief.[2] My own heart has bled and still bleeds for my Country, for my friends, and for myself, although it is perhaps to me of no great importance. That event is now irrevocable, and, however much we may deplore the means by which it was brought about, submission to it is the only alternative. I regret it because I had indulged the fond hope of being an humble instrument, in the hands of Providence, of bringing back the Government to its former purity, and doing some justice to able, enlightened, and patriotic friends. That hope is now forever fled. My dear sir, The subject of this letter is not one for many words, reciprocating all your kind and friendly wishes . . . P.S. I dictate to one of my sons who writes this.

LS, with postscript in Clay's hand. KyBB. Letter marked "(Private)." 1. Hoxie to Clay, Nov. 26, 1844. 2. Clay to Webb, Feb. 29, 1844.

Speech of Judge Joseph R. Underwood to Clay on behalf of Kentucky Presidential Electors, Lexington, Ky., December 4, 1844. Announces that "yesterday, at Frankfort, we performed our official duty in obedience to the will of the people of Kentucky," by casting their unanimous vote for Clay and Theodore Frelinghuysen. Believes that "The machinations of your enemies, their frauds upon the elective franchise [Ewing to Clay, June 23, 1844], and their duplicity with the people in promulgating opposite principles in different sections [Clay to Clayton, August 22, 1844]" led to Clay's defeat. Views as "incalculable" the impact of Clay's defeat on the future of the nation: "God grant that the confederacy may not hereafter mourn over the result in dismembered fragments!" Criticizes the "verbal slanders and printed libels" as stains upon "the character of our country and its institutions," not as injuries to Clay's "moral reputation." Is disappointed that "protection of American labor, a national currency connected with a fiscal agent for the government, the distribution among the States of the proceeds of the public lands, further constitutional restriction upon executive power and patronage, and a limitation upon the eligibility of the president for a second term" cannot be advanced by a Clay administration. Hopes to "find consolation in the general prosperity," but if the "apprehended evils come, we shall enjoy the happy reflection of having done our duty." Copy. Printed in Colton, *Clay Correspondence*, 3:16-17.

Speech to Kentucky Presidential Electors, Lexington, December 4, 1844. Expresses his gratitude for the kindness "which has prompted this visit from the Governor [William Owsley], the Presidential Electors of Kentucky and some of my fellow citizens in private life." States that "I am under the greatest obligations to the people of Kentucky. During more than forty years of my life, they have demonstrated their confidence and affection towards me, in every variety of form." Is filled with "overflowing gratitude" for the vote they "gave yesterday . . . as the Electoral College of Kentucky." Also expresses gratitude to the other states that have voted for him, as well as "the million and a quarter of freemen, embracing so much virtue, intelligence and patriotism, who, wherever residing, have directed strenuous and enthusiastic exertions to the same object. Their effort has been unavailing, and the issue of the election has not corresponded with their anxious hopes and confident expectations." Notes that "I will not affect indifference to the personal concern which I had in the political contest, just terminated; but, unless I am greatly self-deceived, the principal attraction to me of the office of President of the United States, arose out of the cherished hope that I might be an humble instrument, in the hands of Providence, to accomplish public good. I desired to see the former purity of the general Government restored, and to see dangers and evils, which I sincerely believed encompassed it, averted and remedied. I was anxious that the policy of the country, especially in the great department of its domestic labor and industry should be fixed and stable, that all might know how to regulate and accommodate their conduct. . . . The future course of the Government is altogether unknown, and wrapt in painful uncertainty. I shall not do the new Administration the injustice of condemning it in advance. On the contrary, I earnestly desire that, enlightened by its own reflections, and by a deliberate review of all the great interests of the country, or prompted by public opinion, the benefit may be yet secured of the practical execution of those principles and measures, for which we have honestly contended, that peace and honor may be preserved, and this young, but great nation may be rendered harmonious[,] prosperous, and powerful."

Believes the "Whig party has fully and fairly exhibited to the country the principles and measures . . . best adapted to secure our liberties." Adds that "For myself, I have the high satisfaction to know that I have escaped a great and fearful responsibility; and that, during the whole canvass, I have done nothing inconsistant with the dictates of the purest honor. No mortal man is authorised to say that I held to him the promise of any office or appointment whatever."

Asks: "What now is the duty of the Whig party? I venture to express any opinion with the greatest diffidence. The future is enveloped in a veil impenetrable by human eyes. I cannot contemplate it without feelings of great discouragement. But I know of only one safe rule, in all the vicissitudes of human life, public and private, and that is conscientiously to satisfy ourselves of what is right, and firmly and undeviatingly to pursue it under all trials and circumstances, confiding in the great Ruler of the Universe for ultimate success. The Whigs are deliberately convinced of the truth and wisdom of the principles and measures which they have espoused. It seems, therefore, to me that they should persevere in contending for them; and that, adhering to their separate and distinct organization, they should treat all who have the good of their country in view with respect and sympathy, and invite their co-operation in securing the patriotic objects which it has been their aim and purpose to accomplish."

Plans in retirement to enjoy "peace and tranquility," but "I shall never cease, whilst life remains, to look, with lively interest and deep solicitude, upon the movement and operations of our free system of Government, and to hope that, under the smiles of an all-wise Providence the Repub[lic] may be ever just, honorable, prosperous and great." Copy. Printed in Philadelphia *United States Gazette*, December 17, 1844, from the Lexington *Observer & Kentucky Reporter*, December 10, 1844.

The electors to whom this speech was made were: Benjamin Hardin, Joseph R. Underwood, R.A. Patterson, Philip Triplett, W.W. Southgate, W.R. Grigsby, John Kincaid, L.W. Andrews, Green Adams, B. Mills Crenshaw, Leslie Combs, and William J. Graves.

To ALFRED BRUNSON Lexington, December 5, 1844

I have this moment recd. your letter,[1] and lose no time in saying that the threatened division of the Methodist Church gave me the deepest distress.[2] I know of but one other event of the year, and that is the issue of the late election, that gave me so much pain.[3] Entertaining the profoundest respect for that Church, I deplored the division, both on account of the Church, and its political consequences. I yet hope that a merciful Providence may avert that sad and great evil.

I would willingly do any proper thing in my power to restore union and harmony in the Church; but I fear that I can do nothing. Alarmed by the menaced rupture, I have conversed fully with my friend Dr. [Henry B.] Bascom about it, and I know that he is equally penetrated with a sense of the danger.

I tender you my thanks for the good opinion you entertain of me.

ALS. WHi. Addressed to Brunson in Prairie du Chien, Wisconsin Territory. 1. Letter not found. For Brunson (1793-1882), who long served as a missionary of the Methodist Episcopal Church in the Wisconsin area, see *WMH* (Dec., 1918), 2:129-48. 2. Clay to Unknown Recipient, June 26, 1844. 3. Clay to Webb, Feb. 29, 1844.

From Ursin Bouligny, Jr., New Orleans, December 6, 1844. Remits to Clay a total of $950, including $875 for the sale of "Ten Mules & the Bull" to Mr. [Samuel] Packwood and "$75 for the Bull I bought of you for Mr. Valcour[?] Horne." Reports that two more of Clay's bulls were sold but then returned, because "the color is strongly objected to and they are found to be not old enough."

Complains about the "frauds & rascality" that cost Clay the support of Louisiana [Clay to Kennedy, March 29, 1844], including "Parishes giving more votes or as many as there are white inhabitants of all sexes & ages living in them. Steam Boats chartered to convey voters in the same day at different Polls, and every other species of fraud." Believes that Clay's loss in Louisiana was due to the "foreign vote, which went nearly *en masse* against you." ALS. DLC-TJC (DNA, M212, R14). Endorsed by Clay: "Answd. U. Bouligny, Jr [Mules & Calves]." See also Ewing to Clay, June 23, 1844; and Roman to Clay, December 2, 1844.

For Samuel Packwood, a sugar planter of Plaquemine Parish, La., see Herbert A. Kellar (ed.), *Solon Robinson, Pioneer and Agriculturist*, 2 vols. (Chicago, 1936), 2:180-81.

From OCTAVIA WALTON LEVERT Mobile, Ala., December 6, 1844

Your letter of Novr 21st[1] my ever dearest friend reached me yesterday, I hasten to tell you what true happiness it imparted to me. I can sincerely say with the Poet,

"It came when my bosom was lonely & dark"
"Like the Beacon's glad blaze to the Mariners bark."

Your letters are always welcome, but this last one, was especially dear, for it brought me the tidings of your good health, and kindly remembrance of those who love you so dearly, and whose thoughts are ever with you in the sunshine or in darkness.

My Mind is a perfect chaos when I dwell upon the Events that have occured within the last few weeks. It seems to me I wander in a world of frightful Dreams, from which I must awake. My heart refuses to credit the sad reality. Ah! had I the eloquence of all living languages melted into one, I could not shadow forth the deep deep sorrow that has thrilled my inmost soul in the defeat of our Party and Principles.[2] When the Democratic Cannon reached my ears, it sounded like the Requiem for the Dead, and the bitterest tears flowed like the raindrops from my eyes. Never until that moment could I believe, Truth and Justice would not prevail.

Among the indications of 'decadence' of the Republics of Olden Times, was ingratitude to the Great & Wise, *then* as thier [*sic*, their] punishment from an avenging God came the avalanche of Northern Barbarians which swept away all but thier memory. In the dim mists of the Future, I trace the downfall of this Republic to similar causes.[3] Ingratitude to you, my noble friend, who for so many years have been the sentinel on the Watch-Tower, gaurding her Liberties, and pouring out the treasures of your great and mighty Mind in her service. Yes, I feel the patriotic blood of my brave Grand-Sire[4] rush in indignant torrents to my heart, when I see the Country for which he fought and bled swayed and governed by Foreign Babarians, for the President, is thier President. You are the chosen of the American People, honor to them, but scorn, and "war to the knife" to those Traitors who joined *that Rabble*, and placed a Pigmy, where the Giant should rule. The vengeance of heaven will surely fall upon them. Gloom and sadness have folded themselves like a dark Mantle around every true hearted Whig. I cannot be reconciled to the decree. But, I will cease, let me only say dear, dearest friend, nought that Time can bear on its tide, can ever change, the deep and true affection I feel for you.

Ah! why will you not come South this winter? I am so grieved to learn you are not coming. In my "Fancy's wanderings," I had pictured to myself our meeting again this winter; then I had built some "airy fabrics" that you might go this Winter to Havana, and take me with you, but alas! they have all vanished! Dr [Henry] L[eVert]. begs me to present him to you in the most affectionate manner, and says he trusts you will alter your determination, and come to the Sunny South where warm and devoted friends will greet you. I shall not leave home this season; If you had visited N.O. I should have flown thither to welcome you, and have endeavoured to induce you to sojourn with us a few weeks, but as you will not be there, I shall remain here, and spend a dull dull winter. We are all quite well, but we are sad in spirit, we clung to the hope of seeing you this winter, but in that also, we are disappointed. Mamma[5] was so grieved when the news from New York[6] arrived, she was taken really ill; both Papa[7] & herself desire thier kindest regards to you. The children grow finely[.] [The]y speak of you every day, and send you thier sweetest kisses. Our friend Gen [Charles F.] Mercer passed thro' here two days since, he spent an hour with me, and we spoke of you the whole time; he is going to Tallahassee, will return and pass the winter in N.O. where he thought to meet you. The Gen is overwhelmed with grief at the result, says he considers it the greatest misfortune of his life. I had a letter recently from my Aunt in Augusta, she had heard, from you, thro' Mrs [Emily Thomas] Tubman she mentioned the marriage of your Grand-Daughter.[8] Whom did she marry?—Let me have the happiness of hearing from you very soon, I do hope in your answer to this letter you will say your [*sic*, you are] coming to us. Farewell, my dearest, dear friend, croyes moi, toujours deoniee a vous.

My friend Madame H[ubbell]. sends her love to you, she was so distressed about about [*sic*] the election, that she said thank God, she was born under the Spanish Flag, for she con[si]dered the name of American disgraced by thier [in]gratitude to you.

AL. DLC-HC (DNA, M212, R6). Endorsed by Clay on verso: "Mrs. LeVert." 1. Clay to LeVert, Nov. 21, 1844. 2. Clay to Webb, Feb. 29, 1844. 3. Apparently a reference to election frauds. See Ewing to Clay, June 23, 1844; Roman to Clay, Dec. 2, 1844. 4. George Walton, Signer of the Declaration of Independence. 5. Sally Walker Walton. 6. Clay to Webb, Sept. 23, 1844. 7. George Walton (Jr.). 8. No granddaughter had gotten married. See Clay to LeVert, Jan. 21, 1845.

To The Reverend Lorenzo D. McCabe, Athens, Ohio, December 6, 1844. Thanks McCabe for his recent letter [McCabe to Clay, November 30, 1844] and "the kindness towards me which it evinces." Claims his defeat saved him "a heavy responsibility." Is consoled by the feeling "that I stand free from any self reproach," and is gratified by the support of "the intelligent, the virtuous and the patriotic members of the community." Appreciates McCabe's interest in "my happiness in another and better world. I have ever felt a deep sense of the unappreciable value of religion. I shall seek to entitle myself to the benefit of its promises." Copy, extract. Printed in The Rendell's Inc., *The American Frontier . . . Explorations and Settlements to the Mississippi River: Autograph Letters, Etc.*, 1: 287.

To AMBROSE SPENCER Lexington, December 6, 1844

I share in all the feelings of regret and mortification, expressed in your friendly letter,[1] about the sad issue of the Presidential election.[2] It is a great blow which has fallen unexpectedly. May it not prove calamitous to our Country! I will not disguise that I felt it on my own account; but whatever wishes I entertained about the office, if I know my own heart, proceeded from a desire to do public good, and to render justice to able, virtuous and patriotic friends, who have been long cruelly persecuted. On account of our Country and of them, no previous event has ever inflicted on me so deep a wound.

I have no doubt that our friends in your State [New York][3] did all that men could do to avert this painful catastrophe.

It is a great consolation to me, my dear friend, to know that I enjoyed your confidence, and received your support and that of so many other able and enlightened men. It is a further consolation to me to feel that I am not justly liable to any self reproach. I have moreover escaped a heavy responsibility. . . .

ALS. PHi. 1. Spencer to Clay, Nov. 21, 1844. 2. Clay to Webb, Feb. 29, 1844. 3. Clay to Webb, Sept. 23, 1844.

From William McLain, Washington, December 7, 1844. Informs Clay of the annual meeting of the American Colonization Society, to be held at Washington on January 21, 1845. Asks him to "attend and preside on that occasion, and then visit Richmond, Norfolk, Baltimore, Phila. New York, Providence, New Haven, Boston, Lowell, Salem &c. and address public assemblies in all those cities." Assures Clay that "most of these places" had requested his visit and "our great cause would receive a powerful impulse from Your advocacy."

Among the "subjects of vital importance" to be taken up at the annual meeting that require Clay's attention is "the ground taken by the British Government in relation to our Colony." Encloses an extract [not found] of "the dispatch of Capt. W. Jones, Senior Officer, Commanding the British Squadron on the West coast of Africa, addressed to our Governor [Joseph J. Roberts] . . . from which you will learn the nature of the trouble."

Requests "an early reply" so he can "make the ne[c]essa[r]y arrangements" with those "[wh]o are solicitous to know if they may hope to be honored with a visit" from Clay. If he cannot attend, asks "the ai[d] of You[r] opinion as t[o] the cou[rse] best t[o] b[e] persued with reference t[o] the stand taken by the British Goverment." Copy, nearly illegible. DLC-American Colonization Society Papers, Letters Sent, vol. 8, p. 434.

For William McLain, who in 1844 had succeeded Ralph R. Gurley as secretary of the American Colonization Society, see P.J. Staudenraus, *The African Colonization Movement, 1816-1865* (New York, 1961), 239-40.

Joseph J. Roberts, governor of the colony of Liberia, received Jones's dispatch, dated September 9, 1844, which stated that Liberia was not a sovereign country and could not impose duties or regulate the trade of British subjects who had settled in the area and acquired property. When the U.S. government refused to accept sovereignty, the colonization society in 1846 ordered Liberia to declare its independence. Jones's dispatch is printed in the *African Repository & Colonial Journal* (July, 1845), 21:225. See also Staudenraus, *African Colonization Movement*, 241.

From William Newton Mercer, New Orleans, La., December 7, 1844. Assures Clay that even in defeat he remains "the first man in our Country." Reports that disappointment "seemed to pervade all classes," and even "men of the opposite faction express their regret at the success of their party." Believes Clay prefers "reputation to power, and the approbation of the victorious & intelligent to the dignity of office," and, therefore, "you have rather gained than lost by the defeat of your party."

Invites Clay to visit him in Mississippi or in New Orleans. Offers to accompany him "wheresoever you may wish to go.—even to Cuba."

Concludes: "I have it from the best authority that in the event of your election, there would have been no difficulty in the arrangement of the Texas question [Clay to Crittenden, February 15, 1844],—which, from the confidence reposed in you by the Governments of France & England, would have been referred mainly to your own attainment," a possibility dashed by "a few thousand voters, alien in feeling as in blood, & without legal qualifications [Ewing to Clay, June 23, 1844]," who "nullified the suffrages & frustrated the wishes of a decided majority of our countrymen." ALS. DLC-HC (DNA, M212, R6). Printed in Colton, *Clay Correspondence*, 4:513. Endorsed by Clay on verso: "Ansd. Dr. Mercer."

From J. Young *et al.*, Burdette, Tompkins Co., N.Y., December 7, 1844. As representatives of the "Burdette Clay Club," express regret at Clay's defeat, but "would not consent to exchange the approbation of our own consciences, for all the glory which will follow the giddy applause, & loud exultation of the successful party." Regret that Clay, "who has so long & so steadily stood forth, the able, the independent, & the unconquered champion of the people's rights, & the people's interests . . . should feel the cold ingratitude" of the American citizens.

Describe the "self-styled & self-constituted" Democratic party, "aided by a powerful foreign & irresponsible influence [Ewing to Clay, June 23, 1844]," as an "array of political interests of the most discordant character imaginable, & a combination as unholy in its conception, as it is destructive in its operations." Wonder "whether the American people will sustain them" in their attempts to "squander the public lands for party purposes," to "abrogate the present Tariff [Clay to Clayton, *ca.* Late August, 1844], & thereby paralyze one of the most vital interests of our country," or wrest "from a neighboring Republic a part of her possessions, in gross violation of all national law."

Leave to future historians to do Clay "that justice which has [been] denied by your cotemporaries" for his "successful efforts to silence scivil commotion" during the nullification crisis [8:604, 619-22, 626-27] and his "able advocacy of our common country, while engaged in the second War of Independence." LS, probably by Young. DLC-HC (DNA, M212, R6). Endorsed by Clay on verso: "Ansd. Burdette C. Club N.Y. [Address—election]."

Deed of Emancipation for Charles Dupuy, Lexington, Ky., December 9, 1844. Clay, "in consideration of the fidelity, attachment and services of Charles Dupey [*sic*,

Dupuy], the son of Aaron and Charlotte . . . do liberate and emancipate the said Charles Dupey, from this day, from all obligations of service to me or my representatives, investing him, as far as any act of mine can invest him, with all the rights and privileges of a freeman." ADS. KyU. Recorded in Fayette County Deed Book 22, p. 299.

To SHEPPARD C. LEAKIN[1] *et al.* Lexington, December 9, 1844

I received your circular letter written in behalf of the election of Reverdy Johnson Esq to the Senate of the U. States, by the State of Maryland. Coinciding entirely with you in opinion as to the great merit and ability of that gentleman, I should be most happy to see him in a station in which I am confident he would render highly beneficial service to his own State and to the Union.[2] But, residing as I do in another and a distant State, you wil[l] appreciate the feelings and principles which appear to me to render any interference, in the election, on my part indelicate and improper.

LS. Courtesy of St. George L. Sioussat, Washington, D.C. Letter marked "(Confidential)."
1. For Leakin, see 5:993-94. 2. Reverdy Johnson was elected to the U.S. Senate and served from 1845 until he resigned March 7, 1849. See *BDAC* and *NCAB*, 4:371-72.

From Leverett Saltonstall, Salem, Mass., December 10, 1844. Blames Clay's defeat on "the falsehoods & deceptions resorted to, by the friends of Mr [James K.] Polk, and the obstinate & mad course of the *Liberty party* [Clay to Clayton, December 2, 1844], so called." Recalls Clay frequently saying "that we mistook, in treating the abolition party, too mildly—that we ought to come out at once & decidedly against them or they would make trouble for us." Considers such "political abolitionists" to be "so perverse—so unprincipled" that "There is no excuse for them. Their conduct has been utterly inconsistent with their professed principles." Claims that they became "utterly indifferent" to the issue of Texas annexation [Clay to Crittenden, February 15, 1844] "when the danger of what they professed to abhor and dread was imminent." Believes their strongest desire was "the election of Mr P[olk]. & the success of his party," while maintaining "a deadly spite against the Whig party, from which 99/100's of them seceded." Remains convinced that "the bulk of them will sink into the loco-foco party" where they will "receive the reward of their profligacy." Believes Liberty party leaders such as James G. Birney were correct when they asserted that the "aboli[tionis]ts had more to hope from the election of Mr Polk than yourself." Blames defeat on "fraudulent conspiracies & representations & gross & most atrocious calumnies," with New York deciding the election "by a plurality vote of about 5000, & of there having been 15000 abolition votes & what is worse, no doubt from 5 to 10000 illegal votes [Ewing to Clay, June 23, 1844; Clay to Webb, September 23, 1844]!"

Comments extensively on the state of major political parties in the United States. Views the Whig party as embracing a large "proportion of the virtue—honor & intelligence of the Country, & of those who hold any stake in the community." Sees "Demagogueism" as "the greatest vice of our Country." Fears for America's future "when men holding the most eminent station will (to speak plainly) lie—& wilfully deceive the people—state what they know to be false, and address themselves to the lowest passions & prejudices, of the lowest & most ignorant classes." Believes that the Democrats carried Pennsylvania [Clay to Cooper, September 10, 1844] and New York in this way and claims that irrelevant issues, such as the injection of "*Dorrism.* . . . the question of the imprisonment of a fellow who had stirred up civil war in a State" into Rhode Island's election [9:714-16], deflected attention away from Clay's campaign. Remains indignant about "the vile attacks on your private character—for the mere purpose of the election," especially those delivered by "migratory orators who roamed over the country." Publicly defended Clay from the "vile slanders" but considers "this mode of electioneering" to be "barbarous—murderous." Rejoices that "Old Mass[achusett]s has done nobly" in supporting Clay, but finds "danger in the moment of victory. . . . a new party—*Native American*—has sprung up in Boston" and defeated the Whig candidates for city offices. Concludes that the "Whig party, as pure & honorable & patriotic a party as ever existed in any Country, seems to be doomed to misfortune—if not to dissolution." ALS. DLC-HC (DNA, M212, R6). Endorsed by Clay on verso: "Answd. L. Saltonstall [P. election]."

In the 1844 elections in Massachusetts Whig incumbent Governor George Nixon Briggs defeated Democrat George Bancroft by a vote of 69,570 to 54,714, with Liberty party candidate Samuel Sewell receiving 9,635. *BDGUS*, 2:702. Ten Whigs were elected to Congress. *Guide to U.S. Elections*, 380. In the presidential race Clay carried Massachusetts's 8 electoral votes, winning 67,418 popular votes to Polk's 52,846, with Liberty party candidate Birney receiving 10,860. McKee, *National . . . Popular and Electoral Vote*, 56-57.

The Boston municipal elections in 1844-45 were complicated by the appearance of the Native American party which split off from the Whigs. At the December 9, 1844, election for city officials, no mayoral candidate received a majority and only 3 of 8 aldermen were elected; those 3 had the support of both the Whig and Native American parties. After several more inconclusive elections, Thomas A. Davis, the Native American candidate, was finally chosen mayor on February 21, 1845. Melvin G. Holli & Peter d'A. Jones (eds.), *Biographical Dictionary of American Mayors, 1820-1980* (Westport, Conn., 1981), 98; Charles M. Wiltse *et al.* (eds.), *The Papers of Daniel Webster, Correspondence*, 7 vols. (Hanover, N.H., 1974-86), 6:62-63, 66-67.

From Samuel G. Arnold, Harvard University, Cambridge, Mass., December 15, 1844. Recalls how he once met Clay in Providence, R.I.: "It is among the most pleasant recollections of my childhood." States that Rhode Island "feels her debt" to Clay " 'the Father of the American system' " who "raised a warning voice and called on the patriots of the land to sustain the cause of Liberty and Law [9:714-16]." Although "she never can repay" this debt, she has given Clay "a majority of more than twenty one per cent." of her vote. Notes that "your name has become identified among us" with " 'Law and Order.' "

States that he is related to Tristam Burges "whom you long knew in Congress." Sends Clay a whalebone stick and a copy of the " 'Address to the people of the U. States' by the Law & Order party of R.I., setting forth . . . the actual facts involved in the late controversy." ALS. DLC-HC (DNA, M212, R6). Excerpt printed in Colton, *Clay Correspondence*, 1:58. Endorsed by Clay on verso: "Saml. G. Arnold [Presidl Election &c] Decr. 15, 1844."

For Arnold (1821-80), a lawyer and later lieutenant governor of Rhode Island and U.S. senator, see *BDAC* and *DAB*. Arnold probably met Clay in Providence in October, 1833. See 8:664.

Clay carried Rhode Island in 1844 by 7,322 votes to 4,867 for Polk and 107 for Birney. McKee, *National . . . Popular and Electoral Vote*, 56-57.

The *Address to the People of the United States in Relation to the People and Government of Rhode Island* was published in Providence in 1844. It attacked the Dorr Rebellion and Dorr's so-called "People's Constitution."

To JOHN J. CRITTENDEN Lexington, December 16, 1844

Will you do me the favor to have some such article as the enclosed published in the [Washington *Daily*] N[*ational*]. Intell[*igence*]r.?[1] My postage is greivous, amounting to between three and four hundred dollars per annum at the least. The recent election has not yet diminished it. And then the insulting and exulting letters which are addressed to me!

I see Mr. [George] McDuffie has presented a resolution for annexing Texas. What will be its fate in the Senate?[2] Will not amendments be offered to it—refusing to admit without the consent of Mexico, refusing to assume the debts of Texas &c? And will not the Northern Senators propose that, if admitted, that shall be done, on the exclusion of slavery &c[.]

I am curious to witness the progress of this measure.

ALS. DLC-John J. Crittenden Papers (DNA, M212, R20). 1. On Dec. 24, 1844, editors of the Washington *Daily National Intelligencer* announced that they had been asked to express Clay's thanks for the newspapers sent him and to say that he wished only to receive those to which he subscribed. They noted that his postage was enormous and that he no longer had the franking privilege. 2. McDuffie had presented a joint resolution for annexing Texas. It was referred to the committee on foreign relations on Dec. 10 and was not acted upon again during the session. U.S. Sen., *Journal*, 28 Cong., 2 Sess., 28-29. For the resolution that finally passed, approving the annexation of Texas, see Clay to Crittenden, Feb. 15, 1844.

To WILLIAM McLAIN Lexington, December 16, 1844

I recd. your favor of the 7h. inst. with its enclosure. It would afford me very great satisfaction to be able to attend the meeting of the [American] C[olonization]. Society at its approaching Session, if I could; but indispensable engagements at home, to say nothing of the season of the year, prevent me. I cannot pass the mountains this winter. In view of this state of things, while I am as solicitous as ever for the success of the great and humane cause of Colonization, I am thinking of resigning the office of President of the association, the duties of which I cannot personally discharge in a manner satisfactory to myself.[1]

The extract from the despatch of Captn. [W.] Jones, a British officer, which you have sent me,[2] excites regret & surprize. It is a new proof that the British spirit of trade prompts the Government of the British isles, if Captn. Jones truly represents it, to disregard all considerations of humanity & benevolence which stand in the way of its commercial pursuits[.] You ask my advice as to the treatment of that despatch. I know of nothing that can be done but to combat its reasoning, and to appeal for protection to our own Government.[3] If the British power is directed against the Colony, resistance would be unavailing without the support of our Government.

ALS. DLC-American Colonization Society Records (DNA, M212, R20). 1. Clay remained president of the colonization society until his death. 2. McLain to Clay, Dec. 7, 1844. 3. *Ibid.*

To JOHN WATKINS[1] Lexington, December 16, 1844

I received and thank you for your friendly letter, communicating the causes of the Whig defeat in La.[2] Of these I had been advised through other channels.[3]

The general issue of the election is greatly to be deplored on account of the Country, and the patriotic party which has been defeated. My personal concern in the event is not entitled to much consideration.

The future, in respect to public affairs, is very discouraging. Still, confiding in the principles for which we have contended, we ought not to relax in the discharge of our public duty.

Present my warm regard to Mrs. Watkins.

P.S. Mrs. [Lucretia Hart] Clay has sent a lot of fine hams to N. Orleans recently, to be disposed of [by] Mr. [Thomas S.] Kennedy of the firm of [Worsley,] Kennedy & Foreman.

ALS. NjP. 1. There were a number of men named John Watkins living in New Orleans at this time; this is probably the one listed as a "gentleman," residing at 195 Esplanade in the 1846 *New Orleans City Directory*. He is not to be confused with Dr. John Watkins, a mayor of New Orleans, who had died in 1812. Information supplied by the City of New Orleans Public Library. Nor, apparently was he Clay's half-brother by that name who had lived in Woodford County, Ky., and died in Missouri. He may, however, have been the son of Clay's aunt Mary Hudson Watkins, who married John Watkins, brother of Clay's stepfather Henry Watkins. Zachary F. Smith & Mary Clay Rogers, *The Clay Family*. Filson Club Publications, No. 14 (Louisville, 1899), 7, 19, 26. 2. Clay to Kennedy, March 29, 1844. 3. Roman to Clay, Dec. 2, 1844.

From William T. Gould, Augusta, Ga., December 18, 1844. Claims the Whigs were defeated in Georgia "by a most 'unholy alliance' of the most discordant materials—and worse than that, by fraud the most unparralelled, and falsehood the most bare-faced [Clay to Kennedy, March 29, 1844]." Views "The preposterous hum bug of Texas" as the key to the party's loss in that state, "fooled and bamboozled as our Cherokee people were, by the mode in which democracy availed itself of that hobby." Cares little "for the mere defeat of my *party*, as such; for I have a[l]ways been an old fashioned federalist, & [am] accustomed to being in the minority." Assures Clay that "the office of President could add nothing to your fame, nor brighten one line of your history" and is glad he has "been saved from the toils, vexations, & annoyances of office." Believes Clay has "greater cause for congratulation, than the gentleman [Polk], who has been forced into the place you ought to occupy, by party discipline & double dealing."

Regrets greatly "the degraded position of my country." For the last twenty years "the tendency of our institutions was downwards." Sees the United States as "Controlled by demagogues—ruled by faction—her affairs regulated by vagabonds—her rulers chosen by men who have no interest but in plundering her!" Wonders "what, but a blind resolve to do so, can lead men of standing & influence [to] put themselves under the control of the worthless & the ignorant?" Asks "After the complimentary Ball, given by the great men of New York to the leader of the 'Empire Club,' is there a 'lower depth,' for the ruling party to sink to?" Believes "the wise & the good" must "quit electioneering, & take to their prayers, for verily, an overruling Providence only can save us."

Reports that Georgia Whigs "shall continue to show an unbroken front." They "are buckling on our armor for the contest next fall," and intend "to make [George W.] Crawford stand another poll, for Governor, whether he will or not" and hope to "keep him in the traces," although he is "a restive nag, & somewhat given to 'take the studs.' " If he can be defeated, however, "the game is up." ALS. DLC-HC (DNA, M212, R6). Endorsed by Clay on verso: "[Decr. 18. 1844 P. Election] Wm. T Gould Augusta Ga."

For William T. Gould (1799-1882), a lawyer and proprietor of a law school in Augusta, see William Northern, *Men of Mark in Georgia*, 4 vols. (Atlanta, Ga., 1910), 2:85-88.

The term "our Cherokee people" evidently refers to the district once occupied by the Cherokee Indians or to Cherokee County, both of which were carried by Polk in the presidential election. *The Whig Almanac 1845* (New York, 1845), 48.

The Empire Club, founded by Captain Isaiah Rynders a short time before the election of 1844, was a Democratic Club located at No. 28 Park Row, New York City. It was an auxiliary of Tammany Hall, whose members frequently broke up Whig meetings and often ran afoul of the law. Clingman, *Selections from the Speeches and Writings of Hon. Thomas L. Clingman*, 187-88; Gustavus Myers, *The History of Tammany Hall* (New York, 1917), 136-38; M.R. Werner, *Tammany Hall* (New York, 1928), 68.

George W. Crawford, a Whig, was elected in 1845 to a second term as Georgia's governor. He won 41,514 votes, while his Democratic opponent, Matthew H. McAllister, won 39,763. *BDGUS*, 1:294.

From Eliza S. Turner, Athens, Tenn., December 18, 1844. Although "entirely unknown to you, either personally or by character," hopes nonetheless to "extort an answer" about the recent election. Recalls that "Never . . . was there such a damp, a general damp thrown over the minds of a people" who had tried to elect "one who is deservedly viewed as the preserver of the union." Sees Clay as "the ever firm supporter of republican principles which are invincible." Describes Theodore Frelinghuysen as "the ever ardent and sincere christian, exerting his every energy in sending abroad the word of life." Criticizes the "expressions of hatred towards the supporters of truth from a certain class of bigots (I mean the Roman Catholics) who would rather burn that Holy Book, and let their deluded followers perish for want of it." Claims their "malignant slanders" against Clay and Frelinghuysen to be like "a straw . . . thrown against the wind [Ewing to Clay, June 23, 1844]." Desires Clay's views on "what you believe will be the final results of the interference of foreign emigrants in the elections of this union, so as to elect James K. Polk, who, by his policy has pretended to favour both the north and the South [Clay to Clayton, August 22, 1844]" and whether or not this might lead "to a disolution of the Union."

Concludes: "If I ever travel for the benefit of my health, I believe my feelings will lead me Ashlandward." ALS. DLC-HC (DNA, M212, R6). Endorsed by Clay on verso: "Mrs Turner [P. election] Decr. 18. 1844." Mrs. Turner was probably Ann Eliza Turner, wife of William A. Turner. They were heirs to the Ames Manor House in LaGrange, Tenn. See *THQ* (Summer, 1979), 38:271.

From Benjamin J. Leedom, New York City, N.Y., December 20, 1844. As a "member of a peaceable Society who do not profess to take much interest in the political contests of the day," mourns over "the prostration of those high and glorious principles of which thou hast been so long the great and unwearied champion, that prostration brought about by fraud and calumny [Ewing to Clay, June 23, 1844]." Had hoped that "like Cincinnatus thou too wouldst have left the scenes of domestic life and once more been heard in our Legislative halls." Felt so strongly about the late election that just as "My venerated Grandsire left the peaceful society . . . to stand by the Father of his country in the dark hour which tried the Souls of men . . . his decendant in [18]44" cast his vote for Clay "as an heirloom to my children." ALS. DLC-HC (DNA, M212, R6). Printed in Colton, *Clay Correspondence*, 4:516-17. Endorsed by Clay on verso: "Answd Benjn. J. Leedom. Decr. 20. 1844 Presl. Election."

Leedom ran a hardware business at 23 Liberty in New York City. John Doggett, Jr., *New-York City Directory for 1844 & 1845* (New York, 1845).

From Gilbert H. Sayres, Jamaica, Long Island, N.Y., December 21, 1844. Thanks Clay for "a beautiful copy of your farewell in the Senate [9:691-96]" and hopes that "the young Gentleman your grandson" has already conveyed this acknowledgment. Hoped to address Clay "as President Elect of the U.S–," but suggests that "perhaps a merciful God . . . has turned away the load that might have shortened your useful life." Notes that he has witnessed every presidential election since Thomas Jefferson's administration "with more or less anxiety but never have I seen my country so disappointed and Cast down as at present." Cannot recall "a case before where the good and intelligent ranged themselves on one side and the worthless on the other so completely as in the late contest," and hopes that God "can restrain the 'madness of the people'—"

Informs Clay of the exertions of John A. King and James D.P. Ogden on his behalf during the campaign. Asserts that the "Roman Catholic vote of our State was Cast not indeed so much against the venerable name of Clay but because that name was associated with [Theodore] Frelinghuysen [Ewing to Clay, June 23, 1844]. It was with them a question of the *Bible*." Had not counted on "the abolition vote . . . tho' stra[n]gely enough it was the most direct vote on their part for Slavery [Clay to Clayton, December 2, 1844]." Urges Clay to "reconsider take a second sober thought & return to the Senate," but prays, in any event, "that the close of a life so closely identified with our countrys history may be cheered and comforted by the precious hopes and promises of the Gospel." Praises "your answer to the Electors of Kentucky—it was as eve[r]ybody thinks—just as it should be eve[r]y way proper, and becoming the Statesman that uttered it [Clay to Kentucky Presidential Electors, December 4, 1844]." ALS. DLC-HC (DNA, M212, R6). Endorsed by Clay on verso: "Answd. The Revd G.H. Sayres Dcr. 1844 Presidential Election."

From William Tuttle, Newark, N.J., *ca.* December 23, 1844. Although "personally a stranger to you," praises Clay's "undaunted zeal" in "the cause of civil and religious freedom," and expresses disappointment at Clay's defeat and "the stigma this national *blot* has cast on our common country."

Warns that "when that venerated patriot and enlightened statesman, the Junior [John Quincy] Adams, was forced into exile, to make place for Gen [Andrew] Jackson, whose chief stepping stone was his military fame . . . not a few esteemed it a judgment from Heaven in wrath sent upon the people." Believes "the degradation of national character, national morals, and the unparalle[le]d sufferings" of the nation may lead to the destruction of the "civil and religious liberty bequeathed us by the blood, the treasure, and the toils of our fathers."

Suggests that Clay's defeat reflects the truth of the charge "*Republics are ungrateful*!" Voters in New Jersey, however, "proved themselves worthy the Whigs of former days [Anderson to Clay, October 14, 1844]." The Democrats not only lost the presidential contest in that state, but also were defeated in the state elections held under the new constitution, which was "shaped much to their liking" and supported by "the monied influence of [Robert F.] Stockton and [William] Thompson." ALS. DLC-HC (DNA, M212, R6). Endorsed by Clay on verso: "Ansd. Wm. Tuttle."

William Tuttle, a Newark bookseller, had been instrumental in raising funds for the Newark Library Society. *Proceedings of the New Jersey Historical Society* (October, 1953), 71:269-70, 275.

The second constitution of New Jersey had been adopted by popular referendum in the summer of 1844. It removed property qualifications for voting, divided the government into three distinct branches, and provided for an amendment process. The governor was to be elected by popular vote for a 3-year term and could not succeed himself. Robert B. Harmon, "Government and Politics in New Jersey: An Information Source Survey," in *Public Administration Series: Bibliography* (Monticello, Ill., March, 1979), No. 197. Charles C. Stratton, the Whig candidate, had beaten Democrat William Thompson in the first gubernatorial election held under the new constitution. For the 1844 elections in New Jersey, see Anderson to Clay, October 14, 1844.

From Adam Beatty, "Prospect Hill," near Washington, Mason County, Ky., December 24, 1844. Views Clay's defeat as a "wound . . . inflicted on the honor and best interests of our country," but one which may "redound to your temporal and eternal good." Believes James K. Polk won "by the most shameful and abominable frauds, practiced to an extent, which . . . must create the most awful apprehensions as to the future destinies of our free institutions, and the perpetuity of the Union." Criticizes the "foulest and most unprincipled means" used by Clay's opponents "to excite the bitter hatred of our recently naturalized citizens, Roman Catholics, and abolitionists against whig principles [Ewing to Clay, June 23, 1844; Clay to Clayton, December 2, 1844]." Recalls the words of "an eminent modern historian" who wrote " 'that the great body of man kind are incapable of judging correctly on public affairs.' " Fears that the United States will struggle until " 'the decay of interests, *the experience of suffering, or the extinction of passions*,' " but hopes that "truth may in the end prevail, and . . . our republican institutions may yet be saved." ALS. DLC-HC (DNA, M212, R6). Printed in Colton, *Clay Correspondence*, 4:517-18; copy in NN. Endorsed by Clay on verso: "Adam Beatty Esq [Presidt. Election] 24 Decr. 1844."

From NATHANIEL BEVERLEY TUCKER Williamsburg, Va., December 25, 1844

I beg you to pardon me, for not having, long since, acknowledged the very kind message[1] you were so good as to send through General Coombs [*sic*, Leslie Combs]. Domestic affliction at the time, the pressure of business then and since, and bad health of late excuse me to myself for seeming indifference to a compliment of which any man might be proud, and kindness for which any man ought to be grateful.[2] When I recollected the prompt and candid attention which you had uniformly paid to every unauthorized communication I have heretofore intruded on you, I felt as if I had reason to reproach myself that our correspondence should have ceased on my part. But if you remember the general character of my last letter, and your reply, in connexion with the exciting controversy which immediately followed, you must be sensible, that, so far as I took any part in that, it must necessarily be antagonist to your own.[3] Under such circumstances, to have pretended to commune with you, on the politics of the day, would have been disingenuous or foolish, if indeed the latter is not always and necessarily implied in the former.

I did take some part in the business of the day; tho' it was no more than to endeavour to stimulate J[ohn]. T[yler]. to "assume a virtue which I knew he had not."[4] I succeeded, in part, tho' I cared little for such success, when I saw, that he would continue to disable himself to effect any good purpose, by making it manifest to all, that in whatever he did, or refused to do, he acted solely with a view to the gratification of his own sordid ambition. As soon as he made that clear, I ceased to hold any communication with him. The death [of] my most intimate friend [Abel P.] Upshur has put an end to my connexion with public men and public affairs.[5]

I have never ceased to regret that your opinions did not permit you to take the position which I indicated in my last letter to you. I am not more sure now than I was then, that you never could succeed as the candidate of a party of which Mr. [Daniel] Webster was a member. He is certainly a man of transcendent abilities, but infinitely more formidable as a friend than as an enemy. That he defeated your nomination by the Harrisburg Convention, I never doubted;[6] and when he drew out from the Cabinet, and took his place under your banner,[7] I was quite sure that he would manage to place you in some false position, and thus effect your defeat. What would have been the vote of Virginia but for his machinations and some other kindred causes, I am not prepared to say, as I never canvassed those details, which enable men to form opinions on such matters. But I can speak confidently, when I say, that the difference between [James K.] Polk's majority[8] and [Martin] Van Burens in 1840.[9] was mainly owing to him, and to the conduct of those here, who, following his lead, *unwhigged* (to use their own word) every man who did not agree to disclaim, renounce, and deride opinions and principles, which so many deem, not only sound, but essential to the preservation of the country from disunion, on the one hand, and from, that worst of all despotisms, a vast consolidated democracy on the other. All such were put to the ban.

It is not easy, I find, for men to resist the contagion of other men's excitement; and I have often had occasion to remark, that, sooner than not be a-doing, many will do what they really disapprove. Thus it was, that, while some few of those who thought as I did, continued to support you with considerable ardor, the great body became the equally ardent supporters of Mr. Polk. For my part, I thought I had lived long enough, to be excused from taking any part in the controversy, and claimed leave, as I could not do what I wished, to do nothing. But I will frankly say, that, looking to the temper and views avowed by your supporters in this part of the world, I had begun to look to their success with serious apprehension. When I saw men, who had never held up their heads since 1801., rejoicing in the hope of an earthly resurrection, and heard the doctrines then exploded proclaimed as the true reading of the constitution, I could not help dreading the consequences. What is to come now? I can not anticipate. Anarchy and misrule, I fear, as the consequence of a weak government. How the government is to be otherwise than weak, in the hands of one put up by contending factions, each of which will claim him for a tool, and endeavour to counteract what may not favour its own views, it is hard to see. That the most desperate and wicked of these factions will strive hardest for the mastery, [an]d, acting out its nature, be most eager in its opposition to whatever [manuscript torn; words missing] m[ay] be most nearly right, is to be expected. With such factions [words missing] too much the nature of opposition to combine on such [words missing] ions. If this be so; then it is still in your power, my dear Sir, [words missing] at privacy to which you are unworthily condemned, to serve your country as efficiently, and more nobly, than in the high station to which your friends have wished to raise you. Of your fair claims to the first place in the union (apart from differences of opinion, which do not affect your merit) I always speak as frankly, as if I had not been made to dread your triumph. In what will seem to you the choice of evils to be presented by Mr. P's administration, it will be for your master mind to decide for your friends. The spirit of party might dictate to them to force their adversaries upon the greater. You, I am persuaded, would choose differently, and your magnanimity will prefer to aid your enemy to make the best & not the worst, *for the country*, of the difficulties of his situation. Believing this, I say no more than the truth, when I add the assurance of my very high respect & sincere good wishes.

ALS. NjR. 1. Not found, but see Clay to Tucker, Jan. 11, 1845. 2. Tucker's daughter Lucy had died in the fall of 1844. For his writing, teaching, and illness during this time, see Robert J. Brugger, *Beverley Tucker, Heart over Head in the Old South* (Baltimore, 1978), 154-55, 166. 3. Possibly a reference to the differences between Tucker and Clay on the national bank issue in 1841. See *ibid.*, 140-43. 4. Tucker attempted to advise John Tyler on the bank issue and urged him to stand apart from both political parties. See *ibid.* 5. Secretary of State

Upshur was killed in the explosion of a cannon during the firing of a ceremonial salute aboard the *Princeton* on Feb. 28, 1844. Hall, *Abel Parker Upshur*, 211-12. 6. See 9:251-52, 875. 7. See 9:722-23, 882-83. 8. Clay to Rives, August 19, 1844. 9. See 9:452.

To ADAM BEATTY Lexington, December 26, 1844

I received to day your friendly letter,[1] for which and the kind motives which prompted it accept my thanks. The late blow that has fallen upon our Country is very heavy. I hope that she may recover from it; but I confess that the prospect ahead is dark and discouraging. But, perhaps, my personal concern in the election, small as it ought to be regarded, may be sufficient to obscure my vision.

I am afraid that it will be yet a long time, if ever, that the People will recover from the corrupting influences and effects of Jacksonism. I pray God to send them a happy deliverance. . . .

ALS. NN. 1. Beatty to Clay, Dec. 23, 1844.

From Orlando Fish, New York City, *ca.* January, 1845. "Deprived as we are doomed to be, of the pleasure of having you at our *head*," hopes Clay will "allow us the minor pleasure of having ourselves at *yours*, for a brief period by accepting this Hat, and may it afford you, sir, what you have so zealously labored to secure to us—*Protection.*" Copy. Printed in Edna T. Whitley, *Kentucky Ante-Bellum Portraiture* (Paris, Ky., 1956), 120.

Clay replied on January 29, 1845, extending "many and cordial thanks." Adds: "The Hat might have 'protected' a better and wiser head than mine, but no head was ever covered by a better or more elegant hat." Copy. *Ibid.*

Fish was a hatter whose shop was located at 137 Broadway, New York City. Doggett, *New-York City Directory for 1844 & 1845.*

To Mary Cosby Shelby, "Grassland," Fayette County, Ky., January, 1845. Thanks her for "the pair of socks, knit by your own hands," which are "very soft and neat, and highly creditable to your taste & industry." Concludes: "Mrs. Clay, who usually knits my Socks, yields the palm of beauty to yours!" Copy. KyU.

Mary C. Shelby (1826-56), daughter of Thomas Hart Shelby and granddaughter of Gov. Isaac Shelby, lived at "Grassland," her father's estate. Shortly before her death she married George S. Shanklin. Lucy G. Shelby, *Grassland Days and Grassland Ways* (Lexington, 1957), 4, 9, 21, 27-28.

From Ebenezer Pettigrew, Magnolia, Tyrrell Co., N.C., January 1, 1845. Mourns Clay's defeat: "The storm is over, and we the people of the United States are shipwrecked, & I fear too much damaged ever to be repaired." Predicted the results "for weeks before it . . . as it is natural for me to look on the dark side of every subject." Attempted to prepare himself for "the evil day" that marked "the beginning of the end of the peace, prosperity & happiness of this rising country, if it did not begin in the year 1829, with the reign of Hickory the 1st [Andrew Jackson]." Had hoped that Clay's election would "stay the downward tendency of this government." Remains proud, however, that "North Carolina is numbered among the Law & Order party, though differing with so many of its neighboring states [Clay to Graham, February 6, 1844]."

Blames "malcontents" for allowing "demagogues . . . without principle & without honesty" to "rake the pit for voters" and elect James K. Polk, "a third rate man. Yea, a no-rate man." Under "the dictation of artfule, designing, dishonest, & irresponsable men," believes "the government must necessarily run into anarchy &

confusion." On naturalization states that "My opinion has been for forty years that there should be no citizens of the United States except those born within its limits." Believes that "Had that been the law, we should not now be like men in a thunder squall waiting with trembling anxiety for the next clap." Feels for Clay's "disappointment in being prevented by *corruption*, after more than forty years of devotion to your countrys good, from doing to it the greatest service that could fall to the lot of any man," but asserts that he can "now rest in repose under a perfect knowledge that you retire into private life, with the highest honours that can fall to any man now living."

Concludes: "I omited to mention that in 1829, I was unreserved in saying that I gave this U.S. goverment thirty years to continue; which has been my unwavering opinion & declaration up to this time, & I fear my time will be found too long, & I farther fear that God has given us up as unworthy of his love & protection, & to a hard heart & reprobate mind, at all events politically." ALS. DLC-HC (DNA, M212, R6). Printed in Colton, *Clay Correspondence*, 4:518-20.

From John Quincy Adams, Washington, D.C., January 4, 1845. Transmits to Clay from Commodore Jesse D. Elliott "a bronze medal which he has caused to be struck in honour of Mr. J[ames]. Fenimore Cooper, as a tribute of gratitude for Mr Cooper's defence and vindication of the Commodores character" from "certain charges" made by "the public against him." Is pleased to forward the medal that Elliott proposes to distribute to "a limited number of . . . certain distinguished persons . . . and then to have the die broken."

Acknowledges Clay's letter "written shortly before the unexpected and inauspicious issue of the recent Presidential election [Clay to Adams, October 26, 1844]." Had hoped that "under your guidance the Country would have recovered from the downward tendency into which it has been sinking—but the glaring frauds by which the election was consummated [Ewing to Clay, June 23, 1844] afford a sad presentiment of what must be expected hereafter." ALS. DLC-HC (DNA, M212, R6). Copy in MHi-Adams Papers, Letterbook, Private, no. 15 (MR154); also printed in Colton, *Clay Correspondence*, 4:520-21.

The charges against Elliott involved his actions in commanding the *Niagara* in the Battle of Lake Erie on September 10, 1813. Elliott was under the command of Oliver Hazard Perry who later sought to have him court-martialed for failing to come to Perry's support during the battle. James F. Cooper's *History of the Navy*, published in 1839, gave an account of the battle which was favorable to Elliott. For Elliott, see *DAB*.

From Lewis Jacob Cist, Cincinnati, Ohio, January 4, 1845. Sends a copy of a four-stanza poem he wrote as "a feeble tribute to the talents, worth, and long tried public Services, which have made your honoured name a household word." Relates to Clay as an "illustration of the feelings still thus entertained for you by even the humblest of your friends," an exchange between "an honest Sailor, whose Motto has ever been 'Clay and Protection,' " and an exultant "Loco friend." Continues: "I had rather now (said the worthy Tar) walk from here to Ashland, and to take Henry Clay by the hand, than accept the best Office in James K. Polk's gift!" Is proud to offer his literary efforts to "the private Citizen, who has no honours at his Command with which to reward the Sycophantic herd which ever flocks around the Successful aspirant for Office." ALS. DLC-HC (DNA, M212, R6). A copy of Cist's poem "To Henry Clay" was enclosed with this letter.

Clay replied to Cist on January 8, 1845, and thanked him for "the verses which you have done me the honor to address to me." Adds: "I am so much praised in them that it does not become me to express any opinion of their merit, as a poetic composition. If I could divest myself of the bias, which they naturally create, I should say that it was of a very high order." Explains that he would "have much less felt" his defeat "if it were not for the deep affliction which it has produced with a large portion of the intelligence and worth of the Country, and of which, from all quarters, from both sexes, and in every form, I daily receive some touching evidence." Concludes: "Indeed I almost tremble to receive my mail." ALS. NHi.

For Cist (1818-85), a banker, writer, and secretary of the zoological society in Cincinnati, see Johnson, *Twentieth Century Biographical Dictionary.*

To DAVID FRANCIS BACON Lexington, January 6, 1845

I received to day and thank you for your friendly letter. Of your constant, arduous and efficient services in the Whig cause, I was fully aware, and often saw satisfactory evidence.[1] You will render a great additional service to the whole Country, if you succeed in developing & exposing the frauds, perpetrated, as you believe, in the late election in N. York.[2] Assuming their existence, I hope some remedy will be found for them, other than that which proved so fatal to antient Republics[.]

You are yet young; I am otherwise. May you live to see all the dangers which overhang our Country dispelled!

ALS. CtY. 1. For example, see 9:868. 2. Ewing to Clay, June 23, 1844; Clay to Webb, Sept. 23, 1844; Webb to Clay, *ca.* Nov. 7, 1844; Frelinghuysen to Clay, Nov. 9, 1844.

To JOHN J. CRITTENDEN Lexington, January 9, 1845

I recd. your favor of the 3d. and transmit enclosed a letter to Judge [Joseph] Story. I am not surprized at his disgust with his service on the bench of the S[upreme]. Court. Among the causes of regret on account of our recent defeat, scarcely any is greater than that which arises out of the consequence that the Whigs cannot fill the two vacancies in the S. Court.[1]

I see that they have got up Texas in the House,[2] and I anticipate that some scheme of annexation will be cooked up there, whatever fate may attend it in the Senate. I think that the resolution of our friends in this body is wise to leave it to Mr. [James K.] Polk.[3] Among my fears, one is that it will, if annexed, disturb the Territorial balance of the Union and lead to its dissolution.

[Robert P.] Letcher, of whose silence you complain, bears badly our recent defeat. Time, the great physician, may heal his wounds.

I sometimes have occasion to use another's Supers[c]ription and wish you would send me some half a dozen of franked envelopes.

ALS. DLC-John J. Crittenden Papers (DNA, M212, R20). 1. Justice Smith Thompson had died on Dec. 19, 1843, and Justice Henry Baldwin in April, 1844. For a time Senate Whigs defeated the nominations of replacements because they hoped a Whig president would be chosen in the 1844 election. Thompson's seat was eventually filled by Samuel Nelson, who was confirmed on Feb. 14, 1845; Baldwin was replaced by Robert C. Grier on August 4, 1846. Before Baldwin's confirmation, Story had died and been replaced by Levi Woodbury. U.S. Sen., *Executive Journal*, 6:395-96 and 7:135; Carl B. Swisher, *Roger B. Taney* (New York, 1935), 431-44. 2. Clay to Crittenden, Feb. 15, 1844. 3. *Ibid.*

To JOSEPH STORY Lexington, January 9, 1845

Our mutual friend Mr. [John J.] Crittenden, communicated to me many friendly messages and kind expressions from you, which I was very happy to receive, and the spirit of all of which I cordially reciprocate. I was truly distressed to learn from him, confidentially, that you entertain serious thought of finally retiring from the Bench.[1] I sincerely hope that you will reconsider the matter, and come to a different conclusion. You are the only remaining member, of what the Supreme Court of the U. States, in its bright and better days, once was. And your retirement from it, as it now is, would be a very great National misfortune. In anticipation of an event, which has not happened, scarcely anything gave me more satisfaction, than that I might have the power of placing on the Bench, with the concurrence of the Senate, two new members, worthy of the ancient renown of the court, and worthy of an association with you.[2] It has not been allowed me to enjoy that gratification, and I can well conceive the discomfort of your official situation, present, and prospective. But this is a world of trial and suffering, and ought you not to bear your full share for the sake of our common Country? Everything, it is true, has a downward look and tendency, but who knows what a good Providence may yet bring forth for us all! In his will we are bound to submit; in his mercy, we may hope. The result of the Presidential election surprised everybody but those who knew of the fraudulent means employed to produce it.[3] I shared the common surprise; but the event affects me less by its direct influence upon me, than by the sympathy excited for our Country, and our friends, of which evidence, almost daily reaches me in the most touching forms, in prose and poetry from both sexes. Never was so fine an opportunity wantonly lost of uniting the various sections of our Country upon leading measures of National policy, that of protection especially. You, in the free States, are chiefly to be reproached. Henceforward you ought to cease to upbraid us with slavery. The leaders of the Abolitionists—what do they deserve to have said of them![4] In early and middle life I desired to be preserved from the grumbling and murmuring incident to old age. I wish now to avoid taking too desponding a view of our public affairs; but, in spite of all my efforts, very few glimpses of light and hope, break through the darkness of the gloomy future. I pray God that my fears may not be realized. But I ought to annoy no one, nor you particularly, with my fearful forebodings.

Copy. MH. Letter marked "(Confidential)." 1. Editors have determined from its content and from Clay to Crittenden, Jan. 9, 1845, that this letter was written to Joseph Story. He had been appointed to the Supreme Court in 1811 and served until his death on Sept. 10, 1845. Intending to retire in March, 1845, he postponed that action in order to write opinions for a backlog of cases already argued in his circuit. Gerald T. Dunne, *Justice Joseph Story and the Rise of the Supreme Court* (New York, 1970), 423-30; William W. Story, *Life and Letters of Joseph Story . . .*, 2 vols. (Boston, 1851), 2:523-29, 544-48. 2. Clay to Crittenden, Jan. 9, 1845. 3. Ewing to Clay, June 23, 1844. 4. Clay to Clayton, Dec. 2, 1844.

To JOHN CARR Lexington, January 11, 1845

I received your friendly letter, and thank you for the kind feelings toward me which it expresses. Your suggestion that I would prepare a journal of my public life, embracing a narrative of all the slanders which have been so profusely propagated against me, is received in the same friendly spirit in which it was made. As to the calumnies circulated against me, many of them, I dare say, never reached me, and I wish to forget them and their vile authors as soon as I can. I hope God will forgive them. I do not desire to soil myself by any contact with them. The best demonstration of their falsehood is the testimony in my favor, borne by my neighbors, and by the people of Kentucky, uniformly, during a period of upward of forty years. . . .

Copy. Printed in Colton, *Clay Correspondence*, 4:521.

To EPES SARGENT Lexington, January 11, 1845

I am in arrear in our correspondence but not in friendly feelings towards you. I have been unwilling to think or to say much about the late Presidential election.[1] It was the result of such an extraordinary combination of heterogeneous and conflicting elements! The event is not the less important, for good or evil, to our Country, its character, its institutions and its harmony. I fear the worst, but try to hope for the best.

So far as I am personally concerned, I am not sure that I ought to regret it. I should have ceased, long since, to feel any disappointment about it, if it were not for the sympathy for friends, who pour forth their griefs to me in the most touching and affecting language. Nor are these expressions confined to any section of the Union, or to either sex.

In one aspect of the event, its tendency has been to make me think rather more of myself than I had been accustomed to do; for it has manifested the existence of a confidence in, and an affectionate attachment towards, me, of which I had previously no adequate conception. This feeling, on the part of my numerous friends, excites a degree of distress which no personal interest or concern that I had in the election could have produced.

For what you have done, so well done, for you[r] friendly feelings towards me, and for your kind assurance, in your letter of the 26h. of November, that your affectionate regard for me will ever continue unabated, I offer you, all that I have to tender, my grateful acknowledgments, and a reciprocal assurance of lasting respect and esteem.

I am endeavoring to separate myself as much as I can from this world; but, in spite of all my wishes for seclusion, great numbers call to see me at this place, and as I know that their purpose is friendly and respectful, I have not the heart to receive or treat them unkindly. I have been constrained to diminish the news papers kindly sent me, and now I see only the [Washington *Daily National*] Intell[*igence*]r. and one or two others from beyond the mountains. In the former, I have the satisfaction to peruse your letters, from the great American focus of intelligence &c—

ALS. MCM. Addressed to Sargent in New York City. Endorsed in strange hand: "Willis Green M C Free." 1. Clay to Webb, Feb. 29, 1844.

To NATHANIEL BEVERLEY TUCKER Lexington, January 11, 1845

I duly received your favor of the 25h. Ulto. Genl [Leslie] Combs had previously informed me of your having received my friendly message through him in the spirit in which it was sent[.][1]

The Presidential election is past and I say and think about it as little as possible. The result was the consequence of a most extraordinary combination of causes, some of them conflicting, which has ever occurred. You think that Mr. [Daniel] Webster's support was one of them.[2] Perhaps so. But I have had no correspondence with him, direct or indirect, since 1841. It is strange that he should have injured the Whigs, when we look at some of the elements employed on the other side.[3] What is to be thought of those, who profess to support a strict construction of the Constitution, and are contending for the annexation of Texas by Congressional action?[4] They forfeit all consideration of respect to principle, without any compensation, if there could be any compensation in the violation of principle, by the acquisition. For Texas will leave the political balance between the South & North undisturbed.

I see great difficulties ahead. I should despair of the Republic, if my temperament admitted of despair. Entertaining a very bad opinion of all the sections of the party which has brought Mr. [James K.] Polk into power, I can scarsely conceive of any state of things which would induce me to give my humble countenance to any of them. But for our common Country, there are no sacrifices which a private man, and one that desires always to be private, could make, that I am not ever ready to make.

ALS. ViW. Addressed to Tucker at Williamsburg, Va. 1. Tucker to Clay, Dec. 25, 1844. 2. *Ibid.* 3. For example, see Ewing to Clay, June 23, 1844; Clay to Clayton, August 22, 1844 and Dec. 2, 1844. 4. Clay to Crittenden, Feb. 15, 1844.

To GARRETT DAVIS Lexington, January 13, 1845

I take the enclosed letter[1] to be from fictitious persons, addressed to me by some wag. Will you do me the favor to inquire of the member from Pennsa. representing Chambersburg[2] whether my conjecture be correct? If it be a genuine letter from ladies, I should be sorry to treat it with any neglect.

I see that you are in the midst of Texas. There is ample choice in the variety of the propositions to annex it to the U.S. Will either of them succeed?[3]

ALS. KyLoF. 1. Not found. 2. Moses McClean. See *BDAC*. 3. Clay to Crittenden, Feb. 15, 1844.

To EBENEZER PETTIGREW Lexington, January 13, 1845

I have received and perused your kind letter in the same friendly spirit in which it was written.[1] I must own that the result of the Presidential election took me by surprize.[2] I did not expect it. It was brought about by an extraordinary combination of causes, and some of them very conflicting. All the cliques, and particular parties went against us; but with you it is unnecessary to dwell on them. I can hardly say whether I have been more affected by the event, from any personal or direct interest which I had in it, or by the sympathy for friends who have, in great numbers, addressed me in the most pathetic and touching terms. I had no previous conception of the extent of the affectionate attachment to me which has been demonstrated since the election. This is a source both of consolation and grief—grief that *such* friends should be so sadly disappointed in their patriotic wishes to arrest the downward tendency of our Government.

But it is the future that fills me, as it does you, with alarm. I can discern in it, I confess, but few glimpses of light and hope. My greatest trust is in the mercy and goodness of Providence, who may have provided some mode of deliverance which he has not yet deigned to disclose. You speak of the law of naturalization, but what expectation can be indulged of any modification of that, by a party which has so greatly profited by it?[3]

I am truly rejoiced that your good State [North Carolina] and your County [Tyrrell] realized our hopes.[4] I shall never forget my visit to Raleigh, nor the friendly feelings, greetings and hospitality which, from the time I had the pleasure of meeting you at Wilmington until I left the confines of your State, every where welcomed me.[5] I too regretted not seeing more of you at your Capital [Raleigh]; but I conjectured and appreciated the kind forbearance which kept you from me[.]

I have other reasons gratefully to remember N. Carolina—the most beautiful ornamental article in my house, a magnificent picture of the Washington family, by [Henry] Inman, admired by all who visit me, was recently presented to Mrs. [Lucretia Hart] Clay by our good friend Mr. [James C.] Johnston, to whom, when you see him, I request you to offer the affectionate regards of . . . [6]

ALS. Nc-Ar. 1. Pettigrew to Clay, Jan. 1, 1845. 2. Clay to Webb, Feb. 29, 1844. 3. Ewing to Clay, June 23, 1844. 4. For North Carolina, see Clay to Graham, Feb. 6, 1844. In Tyrrell County Clay won 283 votes to 92 for Polk. *Niles' Register* (Dec. 7, 1844), 67:211. 5. Clay to Preston, Jan. 19, 1844. 6. Johnston to Clay, July 24, 1844.

To JOHN M. BERRIEN Lexington, January 14, 1845

I have felt the same sort of reluctance to write to you, as you did to me, prior to your departure from home,[1] after the Presidential election. Its result was so unexpected, to say nothing of the means by which it was brought about. In Georgia, as elsewhere, I observe that you were defrauded.[2] What are we to come to, if there can be no preventive or corrective of these alarming frauds?

I hardly know whether I have not been more grieved by the event, from sympathy excited by the wailing and pathetic letters which I have received from affectionate friends than from any personal interest I had in it. It appears to me that they will never cease pouring out their afflictions on me in the most heartrending terms.

But my chief object now, in writing to you, is to express my warm regard, to assure you that I believe you did all that could be prompted by the most ardent patriotism, and to request that you will do me the favor to present to Mrs. [Eliza Hunter] Berrien, the the young ladies of your family, and to Captain [James] Hunter my grateful and friendly respect and esteem.

I will not say one word on passing public affairs, which I observe is in a state to give all of you much vexation & concern.

ALS. NcU. 1. For the Senate. 2. For the Georgia vote, see Clay to Kennedy, March 29, 1844. For the Georgia frauds, see Bronson to Clay, Nov. 20, 1844.

To JOHN QUINCY ADAMS Lexington, January 15, 1845

I duly received your favor with the bronze medal which, at the instance of Commodore [Jesse D.] Elliott, you were kind enough to forward to me. Should an occasion occur, without inconvenience to you, I will thank you to make to him such acknowledgments as may be due from me for this testimonial of his gratitude to Mr. J[ames]. F[enimore]. Cooper.[1]

I concur with you in thinking that the issue of the recent Presidential election opens, in the future, prospects far more discouraging than any of its immediate results, bad as they may be. It has saved me from a heavy burthen, and I should cease to think much of it, but that I am daily reminded of the event by the most pathetic letters, bewailing it in terms which excite great sympathy. My chief trust is in the agency of a merciful Providence, which I hope may be directed to the preservation of our free institutions from the abuses and corruption, with which they are imminently threatened to be destroyed. That neither you nor I may ever witness this fatal end of them, and that, during life, you may enjoy all earthly happiness and prosperity is the fervent prayer of . . .

ALS. MHi. 1. Adams to Clay, Jan. 4, 1845.

To CAROLINE L. BROWN Lexington, January 15, 1845

I hope that you will not conclude, from the delay which has intervened in my transmitting an answer to your kind letter,[1] respecting the late Presidential election, that I was insensible to the friendly feelings towards me, which prompted it. It was far otherwise with me, and altho' late, I request you to accept my grateful thanks.

Like you, the event took me by surprize; but, so far as I had any personal concern in it, I should long since have ceased to be much affected by it but for the pathetic letters addressed to me, by both sexes, bewailing what has occurred, and which come to me daily. These excite lively sympathy, and, on account of Country and friends, I can not but feel profound regrets. These regrets are much heightened by the few glimpses of light and hope which are discernable in the future. I should utterly despair, if it were not for the trust that I repose in the goodness of Providence, who may, in his wise dispensations, have provided some security for us not visible to mortal eyes. . . .

ALS. KyU. On attached sheet: "Mrs. Caroline L. Brown. Cincinnati Ohio." 1. Brown to Clay, Nov. 22, 1844.

To JOHN A. ROCKWELL[1] Lexington, January 18, 1845

I have received your kind letter informing me that yourself and other friends, with the view of manifesting their esteem and regard for me, have contributed the requisite sum to constitute me a Director of the "American Seamens' friend Society,"[2] and that the proper testimonial of my appointment will be transmitted to me. That has not yet arrived, but, when received, I will forward my formal acceptance of the appointment.[3] In the mean time I hasten to express my acknowledgments to you, and the other friends associated with you, for the distinguished compliment thus paid me. Entertaining with you and them a lively and grateful sense of the great value of the services of Seamen, both as agents of Commerce, and as defenders of our Flag, I am gratified always with the adoption of any measure tending to their comfort and that of their families. They take care of our interests on the water, and it is but a reciprocal duty that we should attend to their's on the land. I regret that my distance from the theatre of the operations of the Society will not allow me to bestow that personal attention upon them, which, differently situated, I should be happy to render.

I will thank you to be my organ in communicating to the gentlemen mentioned in your letter my great obligations for the honor done me.

ALS. Ct. 1. For Rockwell (1803-61)—a Connecticut lawyer, judge, and congressman—see *BDAC* and *Who Was Who in America; Historical Volume 1607-1896* (Chicago, 1963). 2. This organization was established for the purpose of founding chaplaincies, building seamen's churches, and promoting mental and moral culture among seamen. *The Acts of the Apostles of the*

Sea, An Eighty Years Record of the Works of the American Seamen's Friend Society (New York, 1909), 6, 42, 46. 3. Clay's acceptance has not been found.

To Octavia Walton LeVert, Mobile, Ala., January 21, 1845. Apologizes for waiting so long to answer her letter [LeVert to Clay, December 6, 1844]. Thanks her for confirming "that our friendship was, on your part, as on mine, sincere and independent of adverse or prosperous fortunes, which might befal either of us." Is grateful for all the "demonstrations of affectionate attachment to me," some of which "have been made in the most enthusiastic form, and by both sexes (I pray you not to be jealous) in the most touching manner." Thinks so highly of her "eloquent indignation, on account of the issue of the contest" that he "read a part of your letter to an *author* . . . and he insisted upon taking an extract. You must not therefore be surprized if some day or other you see what you have so well said in print."

Remains undecided about visiting the South during the winter because "so far as climate is concerned . . . our autumn and winter hitherto have been as mild and genial as Mobile itself." Relates the invitation of "our good friend Dr. [William N.] Mercer" to visit Louisiana and his offer "to accompany me to Cuba, or any where else I might choose to go." Writes that if he could have been sure that "you, and Dr. [Henry] LeVert and Dr. Mercer" would visit Cuba with him, he would have found "the jaunt altogether irresistible."

Expresses his regret that "your good Mama [Sally M. Walker Walton]" took his defeat badly but remains satisfied that he claimed "a warm and generous support from a large portion of the virtue, intelligence and religion of our Country."

Explains that "It is not correct . . . that I have had a granddaughter married. Altho' I am not very young, I have no granddaughter yet old enough to be married." ALS. KyU.

The author to whom Clay was referring was Calvin Colton who spent the winter of 1844-45 at Ashland preparing to write his *Life, Correspondence, and Speeches of Henry Clay.* He included in 2:451 an excerpt of Mrs. LeVert's letter to Clay of December 6, 1844.

To WILLIAM P. THOMASSON Lexington, January 25, 1845

I should have embraced, with pleasure, the kind offer of correspondence which you made, just before your departure from K[entucky]. if I had any thing to communicate from my quiet abode. I have written to and received from Washington very few letters during the present Session. Congress appears to be full of embarrassment with the variety of Texas propositions,[1] a defaulting Clerk &c.[2] And I suppose the issue of the former is as uncertain there as to one at a distance it seems to be.

I visited Frankfort this week and remained there three days. They have passed in the lower house a stringent and very good Election Law and most likely will do nothing else of much importance.[3] The disposition prevails to have a short Session, and the Legislature will probably adjourn about the 10h. prox:[4]

ALS. KyLoF. 1. Clay to Crittenden, Feb. 15, 1844. 2. Caleb J. McNulty, clerk of the House of Representatives, had just been dismissed from the position for embezzlement of $219,149.49 of public money. U.S.H. of Reps., *Journal*, 28 Cong., 2 Sess., 223-24, 230; *House Docs.*, 28 Cong., 2 Sess., no. 121, p. 3. 3. "A bill the better to protect the purity of elections" passed the lower house on Jan. 20, 1845, and the senate on Feb. 8. Among other things, it set penalties for voting more than once, for voting by non-residents, for using some one else's naturalization papers, and for punishing judges who received illegal votes. It also set rules for determining residency and required taking an oath and the presentation of naturalization papers before voting. Ky. H. of Reps., *Journal* . . . 1844-1845, pp. 158-59; Ky. Sen., *Journal* . . . 1844-

1845, p. 276; Ky. Gen. Assy., *Acts* . . . 1844-1845, pp. 39-43. 4. The legislature adjourned on Feb. 10, 1845.

From O.H. Berg, Baltimore, Md., January 29, 1845. Apologizes to Clay for the lateness of the delivery of the translations of his father's pamphlets, which he originally intended to dispatch the previous July [Berg to Clay, July 20, 1844]. Explains that the man to whom the packet of documents had been entrusted found them "too heavy to allow its being franked by him, and to my great mortification it was not returned to me until yesterday." Hopes Clay will excuse his packing the items "into three parts in order to save the heavy postage." Also forwards a copy of "Wilmer & Smith's newsletter dated Liverpool Jany 4. 1845" which contains an article on Ireland that "strange to say, agrees for several lines nearly word for word with what my father wrote three years ago." Retains his copy of the Quintuple Treaty "because I hardly doubt but what you have a copy," but will send it on if needed "at a moments warning." ALS. DLC-HC (DNA, M212, R6).

Wilmer and Smith published the Liverpool *European Times* from 1843-68. *Tercentenary Handlist of English and Welsh Newspapers, Magazines and Reviews* (London, 1966).

To JOHN PENDLETON KENNEDY Lexington, January 31, 1845

Not being sure whether the enclosed letter from Balto. be genuine or not, I will thank you to satisfy yourself on that point, and if it be genuine, to transmit my answer,[1] and if not to suppress it.

Notwithstanding the weighty considerations against the Annexation of Texas by any act of Congress, so powerfully urged by yourself and others, a report reached us to day that the measure had been carried in the House by a majority of 22![2] God save the Commonwealth!

ALS. MdBP. 1. The enclosed letter has not been found; Clay's answer may be Clay to Stewart *et al.*, Jan. 31, 1845. 2. Clay to Crittenden, Feb. 15, 1844.

To John M. Stewart *et al.*, Baltimore, January 31, 1845. Reports receiving their letter informing him of the organization in Baltimore of the Henry Clay Institute, designed to give "strength and dissemination to the principles of the Whig party." Thanks them and agrees to be made an honorary member. Copy. Printed in Lexington *Observer & Kentucky Reporter*, March 8, 1845.

A number of John Stewarts appear in John Murphy (pub.), *The Baltimore Directory for 1845*, but none have the middle initial "M."

To Miss Estramadura Acee, Talbot County, Ga., February 1, 1845. Thanks her for her letter [not found], and states that the "Javelin, which you did me the favor to present to me, constantly remains in our parlor, and always reminds me of the occasion, when you did me the honor to express towards me feelings of attachment & confidence." Notes that the presidential election "Cannot now be reversed, and it is best to submit to it as one, of the dispensation[s] of providence." In regard to giving her advice, suggests she consult her father and her own reflection, because "From these sources, you have already learnt that Modesty, Virtue, an amiable temper intelligence and religion are the jewells which best adorn the female Character." Copy, by A.S. Barnes. DLC-HC (DNA, M212, R6).

Miss Acee, the daughter of Dr. A.L. Acee, married Gustavus A. Miller, a lawyer from Mocksville, N.C., in 1849. Buster W. Wright (comp.), *Abstracts of Marriages Reported in the Columbus (Georgia) Enquirer 1832-1852* (Columbus, 1980), 48.

To BRANTZ MAYER & J. MORRISON HARRIS Lexington, February 1, 1845

I have received your letter,[1] communicating your purpose to establish a new journal in Balto. to sustain the principles of the Whig party, and stating your opinion that a change ought to be effected in the existing Naturalization laws. In respect to the latter object you ask my advice in the conduct of your paper.

In a reply I made to an address from the Kentucky P[residential] electors in Dec.[2] I briefly stated what I thought ought to be the course of the Whig party, which was to maintain its own principles and denomination, but to treat all other parties and persons, seeking the good of the Country, with sympathy and respect. I adhere to that opinion.

It is easier to perceive the evil of the great facility with which vast numbers of foreigners are annually naturalized, and the influence with which they, strangers to our institutions, act upon our Government, than it is to discover an adequate remedy.[3] I have long thought that all abuses under the laws ought to be provided against, and that some further restrictions upon the process of naturalization itself should be imposed. But how is this to be accomplished? The party, profiting by the Foreign vote, is in possession of power. If the Whigs were to announce such a purpose, as amongset [*sic*, amongst] their aims, the other party, already opposed to it, would draw back from the Native American party all its members, who have joined this party, and would, by that means, and by annual accessions from the Foreign source, augment still more the Democratic strength, and totally defeat all modification of the Naturalization laws.

Believing that an avowal by the Whigs of the doctrines of the Native American party, or an incorporation of the two parties together would lead to that result, I have supposed it best that the two parties should remain separate & distinct, each struggling, in its own sphere, to uphold and carry out its own principles.[4] Perhaps, in process of time, the N. American party may draw off from the Locofoco's a sufficient number to throw them into the minority, *if they can be permanently detached from the Locofoco party.*

The evil of the Foreign element in our population is most felt in the large Cities, where the aliens first collect; and the formation of Native American parties hitherto has been principally limited to those Cities. In the Country, not much sympathy has been manifested with the N.A. party. You must have observed that recently, in the Ohio Legislature, altho' a majority of it be Whig, a resolution passed, I believe unanimously, against the principles of the N.A. party.[5]

I confess to you that I am always some what apprehensive of men and of parties who have but a single idea. It has so happened that they have, in the end, been generally turned against the Whigs. Witness the course both of the Abolition and Native American parties in N. York during the late Presidential election.[6] I am aware that some of them voted with us; but a sufficient number, in direct opposition to their avowed principles, voted against us, to defeat our cause.

Perhaps Locofoco's, who join the N.A party, may, after acting a long time with it, become so estranged from their original party as never, on any occasion, to return to it. That is the only hope from it, the only chance.

You are apprized that the State of Illinois, and I believe Michigan, admits aliens to vote, although not naturalized.[7] But the object of the N.A. party is to prevent exercise of the elective franchise on the part of foreigners here after, by closing the door or prolonging the period of naturalization. It is obvious that no modification, not even a repeal, of the Naturalization laws would reach the mischief of which they complain, in those two States. My opinion is, that they have no authority to allow aliens to vote; but an opposite opinion is maintained, which is quite as likely to prevail as mine. Supposing the N. laws totally repealed, if, notwithstanding, unnaturalized foreigners should be permitted to enjoy the elective franchise, what object will have been accomplished by the N. American party?

I have thus, gentlemen, in compliance with your wish expressed the views I entertain. You perceive that they all terminate in the conclusion which I expressed to the Kentucky Presidential electors.

ALS. MHi. Letter marked "(confidential)." 1. Not found. 2. Clay to Kentucky Presidential Electors, Dec. 4, 1844. 3. Ewing to Clay, June 23, 1844. 4. Clay to Clayton, Dec. 2, 1844. 5. The Ohio legislature had passed a resolution in Dec., 1844, urging its senators and representatives in Congress to oppose any change in the naturalization laws, especially any alteration that would extend the required waiting period before naturalization. *Journal of the House of Representatives of the State of Ohio*, 43 Gen. Assembly, 1 Sess. (Columbus, Ohio, 1844), 30, 59, 79. 6. Ewing to Clay, June 23, 1844; Seward to Clay, Nov. 7, 1844; Clay to Clayton, Dec. 2, 1844. 7. The Illinois constitution permitted any adult male alien to vote if he had resided in the state for 6 months. In 1839, in an attempt to overrule this provision, the Whigs attempted a test case in the state court of appeals, but Democrats countered by legislating the court of appeals out of existence and adding five new members to the state supreme court, thus enabling the provision to endure. Thomas J. Curran, *Xenophobia and Immigration, 1820-1930* (Boston, Mass., 1975), 31. The Michigan constitution provided that any free white male at least 21 years old, who had lived in the state 6 months, could vote in all general elections in the county or district where he had resided for at least 30 days before the election. No person who was not a citizen could vote, however, "until he shall have declared his intention of becoming a citizen . . . according to the law." Harold M. Dorr (ed.), *The Michigan Constitutional Convention of 1835-36* (University of Michigan Publications, History and Political Science, 1940), 13:468.

To CALVIN COLTON

Lexington, February 3, 1845

I am sorry that after having remained in Lexington, I hope agreeably, for two months, you should be about to leave us in not as good health as you have enjoyed during your sojourn.

With respect to the composition of the work which you have so much at heart,[1] and which brought you to this city, I think now, as I stated to you at first, that every thing depends upon the execution, that most important word in language. You have shown me most, if not all you have written, and, as I formed the subject of it, perhaps I am not a competent, as I certainly am not an impartial, judge. But, unless I am already biased, I do think that, so far, you have made good progress, and may ask leave to sit again. What you have written may require an attentive revisal, and some new arrangement of its parts, before it is finally sent to the press, that bourne from which a traveler does not always safely return.

I need not say that by far the most important, the historical, part of your work remains to be entered upon. I hope you will get successfully through it, to accomplish which, I hardly need say, will require great patience, much research and study, and a large measure of candor and impartiality.

I can not part from you without the expression of fervent wishes for your success and fame, and for your health and prosperity.

Copy. Printed in Colton, *Clay Correspondence*, 4:521-22. 1. Clay to Colton, Oct. 26, 1844.

To MARY S. BAYARD Lexington, February 4, 1845

Before the receipt of your letter of the 18th Ulto., my dear and estimable friend, I had seen in the newspapers the result of the Senatorial election in Delaware. It took me by great surprize; for I had understood previously, I thought from a reliable source, that Mr. [John M.] Clayton had abandoned all thought of being a Candidate, and I anticipated your husband's [Richard H. Bayard] re-election with entire confidence.[1] I believe I mentioned to you, in a former letter, that my interposition in behalf of Mr. Clayton's election had been requested, and that I had positively declined all interference.[2] I regret Mr. Bayard's disappointment very much, as I know he took pleasure in the station, and discharged its duties with great diligence and ability. I should deeply regret if Mr. Clayton, for whom as well as for Mr. B. I have always entertained sentiments of sincere friendship, has resorted to any unworthy acts to secure his election. I hope on that subject there is some mistake or misconception.

I should also regret your being deprived of your annual visit to the City, if you did not assure me that it is totally changed, and has lost all its attractions. Your testimony is corroborated by that of another friend, who writes me from Washington, "Times are changed, and men are changed and things are changed." I own, with you, that I can discern scarcely a faint glimpse of light breaking through the dark gloom of the future. My only trust is in Providence, who may, in his inscrutable dispensations, have provided some means of safety and deliverance for our Country, which he chooses to conceal from our vision.

Among my occupations here, during the winter, I have been reading and studying some interesting theological works, and I hope and believe that I have been benefited by them and by my reflections on them.

You ask me if I am happy? Ah! my dear friend, who on earth is happy? Very few, I apprehend, if any. Public affairs, and our recent defeat, give me now no great concern, except when I peruse a bewailing and deploring letter from some distressed friend. Then indeed my heart bleeds, for the moment, for my Country and my friends. As for myself, I *know* that I have done my duty, and that I have honestly and zealously strove for the honor, for the prosperity, and for the true glory of the nation.

It would be an inexpressible satisfaction to me if I were near you, and we could occasionally meet and mutually console each other, and breathe that pure air which I have ever found in the atmosphere around you. I hope some day or other to enjoy that satisfaction, altho' I am unable now to foresee when or where. And I assure you that it is a high hope that I indulge, if circumstances should never allow us to meet again below, that we *shall* meet in a far better, brighter and happier world.

You conveyed to me the kind regards of your daughters,[3] but you mentioned nothing about their settlement and establishment in life. Present my warm respects to Mr. B. and to them . . .

ALS. Anonymous Owner. Copy in KyU. 1. The Wilmington *Delaware Gazette* reported on Oct. 8, 1844, that Clayton's friends had promised him Bayard's Senate seat, despite the "arduous labors" of Bayard to retain it. On Nov. 19 the paper stated that it was generally believed Clayton would be elected because of his influence over the Whigs of Delaware and because circumstances had prevented him from becoming a member of the president's cabinet. Clayton was elected by the Delaware legislature in Jan., 1845. Washington *Daily National Intelligencer*, Jan. 18, 1845. See also Richard A. Wire, "John M. Clayton and the Search for Order: A Study in Whig Politics and Diplomacy," Ph.D. dissertation, University of Maryland, 1971, pp. 147, 189. 2. Not found. 3. Mary, Caroline, Elizabeth, Harriet, and Louisa.

To James Alfred Pearce, Washington, D.C., February 4, 1845. Reports that "We are looking with anxiety to the issue of the Texas resolution in the Senate [Clay to Crittenden, February 15, 1844]. The papers speak with doubt of its fate there, which excites my surprize." Copy. Printed in *MHM* (1922), 17:178. For Pearce, see *BDAC*.

To Robert Garrett & Sons, Baltimore, Md., February 9, 1845. Acknowledges receipt of a certificate of deposit to the credit of Rezin D. Shepherd made by the Garretts at his request. Informs them that "as I did not sooner hearer [*sic*, hear] from you, I forwarded to the Cashr. of the Bank a check for the amount, and directed that, if you had previously made the deposite, to place it to my credit."

Plans to send them his hemp in the spring. "I expect to forward a much larger quantity than I ever did, and it shall be in much better order than the last parcel. I purpose sending it by N. Orleans, as the charges are less by that route." AL, signature removed. DLC-HC (DNA, M212, R21). See Clay to Garrett & Sons, July 8, 1844.

To JOSEPH STORY — Lexington, February 9, 1845

I am not surprized that the weighty, some of them painful motives, enumerated in your friendly letter of the 22d. Ulto, should prompt you to desire to retire from the bench of the S. Court, deeply as I, in common with many others, will lament that event.[1] We shall regard the last remaining light of the truly august old Court as extinguished. Your friends would rejoice if you could reconcile it to your feelings to continue; but most certainly, after what you have said to me, the question should be left to your exclusive judgment.

I lament that there is nothing in the political prospects before us to encourage you to abide in your station. If indeed this Nation be resolved to cast away the blessings which encompass it, and to add another sad example to those which History records, of the corruption & downfall of Republics, no organization of the Supreme Court, however enlightened virtuous & patriotic its members might be, can avert the calamity.

I should be very reluctant to assert that such will be our fate; but passed and passing events fill me with awful apprehensions . . .

ALS. ViU. 1. Clay to Story, Jan. 9, 1845.

From Sarah F. & Jared Coffin, Brighton, Mass., February 11, 1845. Miss Coffin hopes Clay will accept "this purse," which she describes as "a trifling token of my regard."

Her father, Jared Coffin, adds as a postscript that he has put into "the purse she has Sent you . . . $500.00 as A Present you will Pl[e]as[e] accept." Informs Clay that he has "left the purse and money with Abbott Lawrence to be sent directly to Kentucky or to Garrett Davis in Washington." Adds that he has "written the Particklars to Mr Davise [*sic*] what is Doing for you in the City of Boston." ALS, by both Sarah F. Coffin and Jared Coffin. DLC-HC (DNA, M212, R6).

Coffin was a whaling captain, who sailed out of Nantucket and who served in the Massachusetts general court in 1829 and 1833. Alexander Starbuck, *The History of Nantucket* (Rutland, Vt., 1969), 637, 728.

To Henry Clay, Jr., Louisville, Ky., February 12, 1845. Writes from the Northern Bank of Kentucky "to say that they have agreed to discount your note; but it is done upon the usual condition that the amount or any part of it must be subject to calls, if the interest of the Bank makes it necessary. What produced some hesitation yesterday, about the discount of the note, arose out of an understanding that you wanted the loan positively a year." ALS. Henry Clay Memorial Foundation, Lexington, Ky.

From B. Johnson Barbour, Barboursville, Va., February 16, 1845. Proclaims his affection for Clay as "based upon a love of all that is bright and noble in human nature" and "not the growth of a day." Continues: "I claim the privilege of speaking as an original Whig—as one baptized in the faith at the fountain—as one who was taught to love the Whig Cause when he knew no better, and who now Knows nothing better than to love it." Assures Clay that his "love for its great Representative was coeval." Was taught in his earliest years "by him who was your constant friend [James Barbour] to honor the pure statesman and patriot pursued by calumny but still laboring with undiminished ardor for an ungrateful Country—I felt then that when the vile passions and prejudices of the day had passed away that you would have your merited reward from an approving posterity . . . that you would be hailed as the wondrous Architect that had strengthened and adorned the noble edifice whose foundation was won by the Valor of [George] Washington and whose cornerstone was laid by the wisdom of [James] Madison."

Views Clay's defeat as a dashed hope for "the firm reestablishment of our great Conservative Cause." Believes the loss resulted from "Double dealing defamation and Slander" wrought by "A motley party without principle or principles, with fraud for the means and the election of a Demagogue for the end." Complains that "Domestic corruption and foreign putrescence wakened to overwhelm the Virtue and Honesty of the Country—Plaquemine [Roman to Clay, December 2, 1844] and Tammany [Frelinghuysen to Clay, November 9, 1844] have stifled the voice of the American People, and the late contest has only established the melancholy facts—that frauds upon the ballot box have perfect impunity—that Mediocrity is Merit—and that every excess may be committed in the name of a spurious Democracy."

Suggests to Clay that, considering the corruption pervading the country, his defeat "is perhaps better for your fame. . . . But little pleasure could be felt by the President of a Nation where [Thomas] Dorr found mourners [9:714-16]—Disunion advocates—Where a Lust of Territory overrules every principle of law, all fear of consequence, and all sense of Justice—Where Rebellion puts the power of the state at defiance. . . . Such are the terrible symptoms by which we are surrounded, telling of the decay of Virtue and Honor, the only safeguard of a Republick."

Hopes that "the time may return when Patriotism will be no Crime, nor long services a subject of reproach." ALS. DLC-HC (DNA, M212, R6). Postmarked from Gordonsville, Va. Printed in Colton, *Clay Correspondence*, 4:522-23.

Benjamin Johnson Barbour (1821-94) was the son of James Barbour and a graduate of the University of Virginia. He later served as a member of the Virginia house of delegates. Information supplied by Ann L.S. Southwell, Alderman Library, University of Virginia.

To PETER CROMWELL Lexington, February 17, 1845

I received your letter[1] and thank you for the friendly sentiments towards me which it conveys. The regret and disappointment which you express, on account of the issue of the late Presidential election, are shared by a vast number of our fellow Citizens; and I do not know whether I have not been more affected on their account than my own.

You ask my opinion of the future. I wish that I was able to form and communicate one that was satisfactory. I entertain many serious apprehensions. There is a tendency to disorder, to unsettle every thing, to violence and to war, that is truly alarming. My hope is that the People, 'ere it be too late, will perceive impending dangers and guard against them. My fear is that every thing will be sacrificed to the absorbing spirit of party. My chief trust is in Providence, who may have reserved, for the preservation of our Country, some means which he has not yet deigned to disclose to us.

ALS. ViU. Letter marked "(Private)." Addressed to Cromwell at Fishkill Landing, N.Y.
1. Not found.

From JOHN TILFORD Lexington, February 17, 1845

I received a communication some days ago covering the sum of *$5000*, which I was directed to apply to the payment of a note[1] of yours due to the Northern Bank Kentucky for that amount which I have accordingly done, and now enclose it[.]

I am not informed by the Communication from whom this money comes, other than that they are *your friends* and of their desire to render your remaining years free from pecuniary cares, and with the avowel that it is only part of a debt they owe you for your long and valued Services in the cause of our country and its institutions[.][2]

ALS. DLC-HC (DNA, M212, R6). 1. See 9:789-90. 2. On Feb. 21, 1845, Tilford wrote Clay again, informing him of the receipt of an additional $5000 "to apply to the payment of another of your notes due the Northern Bank Kentucky," contributed by "friends of yours . . . to relieve your declining years from all apprehension of pecuniary embarrassments." ALS. DLC-HC (DNA, M212, R6). See also Lawrence to Clay, March 13, 1845; Clay to Lawrence, March 20, 1845.

From Ursin Bouligny, Jr., New Orleans, La., February 18, 1845. Encloses a copy of his current account with Clay for recent livestock transactions, especially the sale of a "small white bull." Announces his intention to visit Clay "this summer," and assures him that if he can get "a good lot of mules [I] think it likely that I can trade with you for it." Is interested in purchasing them, because "I can I think without any difficulty place" 50 to 70 mules "amongst my Planters at fair prices." Informs Clay that "none will do but first rate mules the height is not of as much consequence as some suppose—what our Planters want are mules about 15 Hands thick well set-and not long legged." ALS. DLC-TJC (DNA, M212, R19).

The account of Bouligny's transactions for Clay, also dated February 18, 1845, accompanied this letter. ADS. *Ibid.*

From Thomas Smith, Louisville, Ky., February 19, 1845. Informs Clay that the "late Sales of B[agging]. & R[ope]. at New Orleans are not encouraging to Man[ufacture]rs." Complains that the "prices obtained will barely pay cost—and the vacuum will be filled at once by shipments from this place—so that the stock will continue excessive . . . while the production remains undiminished." Reports only a "slight curtailment in one of the factories here" and has "advised all our manufacturing Constituents not to *engage* hemp, but to buy from day to day" to "keep it upon the market in the producer's hands. . . . the way Cotton is now bought, and Bag. & Rope, and every thing else, of which there is a full supply." Expects, however, "a demand for the article . . . to spring up in the Eastern markets."

Foresees little market for "Thomas's article" in Mississippi, as it is best "adapted to Georgia & Carolina," but asks if he should contract at 12¢, if he can get that price. Adds: "Good hemp rope will be in brisk demand, but ordinary tow rope will be heavy & low all the year." ALS. DLC-TJC (DNA, M212, R14).

The account accompanied this letter, showing that Clay owed $46. ADS. *Ibid.*

On February 25, 1845, Kennedy, Smith & Co. wrote Clay from Louisville acknowledging receipt of his check for $46. State that "the late movement in New Orleans in Bagging and Rope has had the effect to bring some purchasers to this market." Advise Clay to send them his rope: "we promise our best exertions—Mr. Smith, will Send us up orders from below, and we have no doubt but we can put your Rope in Some of them. First Rate Rope is Scarce, and will soon sell readily." Opine that "the Spring prices this year will be as good, if not better than any during the course of it." LS. *Ibid.*

Kennedy, Smith & Co., of which Thomas Smith was a partner, were commission merchants who dealt in bagging and rope from their offices at 568 Main Street in Louisville. Jegli, *Louisville . . . Directory, For 1845-1846.*

From A.C. Bayard, New York City, February 20, 1845. Derives comfort from Clay's "letters to my Sister [Mary S. Bayard] and your public addresses" because in them, despite his defeat, he reveals that he is "sustained by the magnanimity of your own mind. . . . a spirit which can rise above disappointment." Is thankful that Clay "could refer every thing, and trust every thing, to a Wisdom which is unerring.—That in your own impressive language to my sister you considered 'this painful event as a striking example of the uncertainty of all human concerns, & should lead us to cherish other and higher hopes for another & better world [Clay to Bayard, November 18, 1844].' "

Believes the election "was treacherously dealt with." Assures Clay: "From the North and the South the East & the West, indeed from every part of the land, there came up such a simultaneous burst of feeling, such an expression of love and gratitude towards you, such a just appreciation of your services, that it afforded abundant evidence that you are *first* in the hearts of the American people." Fears that "in not permitting us to be guided by your councils the Righteous Governor of the Universe intended our punishment." Describes Clay's "elevated and enduring fame. . . . so appreciated, so loved and so remembered" as "perhaps the highest earthly reward that can be enjoyed by the Benefactor of his country." Adds, however, that such fame "is all of this world" and "the 'honor which comes from men' and as such does not satisfy me." Believes "indeed it is a much 'higher attainment to be able to *look down* upon any thing humanly great than to *look up* to it.' " Hopes Clay will not remain "content with any thing less enduring than truth, virtue and holiness" and will rely "on the Omnipotent arm which can alone impart strength" to all those who "have been 'wrecked by the same storm & must be rescued by the same Saviour.' " Insists that "your Eagle flight must not stop short of Heaven." ALS. DLC-HC (DNA, M212, R5).

Despite Clay's endorsement naming "Catharine Bayard" as the author, this letter probably was written by Ann Caroline Bayard, sister of Richard H. Bayard. No "Catharine" appears in the family genealogy as a sister of Richard H. Bayard. Joseph G.B. Bulloch, *A History and Genealogy of the Families of Bayard . . .* (Washington, D.C., 1919), 67; and information supplied by the Historical Society of Delaware.

To JOHN TILFORD — Lexington, February 22, 1845

I received your favor dated yesterday enclosing a cancelled note of mine for five thousand dollars, which had been held by the Northern Bank of Kentucky, over which you preside.[1] The payment of this note, you inform me, has been made by a remittance confidentially forwarded to you, by some friends of mine for the kind purpose of relieving my declining years from all apprehension of pecuniary embarrassment.

As I am not informed of the names of my friends, who have performed the signal act of liberality and kindness, I cannot address myself directly to them. I must therefore request the goodness of you (presuming that you are aware of some channel through which they may be approached) to convey to them my deep and grateful sense of this distinguished testimony of their friendship, and of the delicate manner in which it has been rendered.[2] I should hesitate to acquiesce in what has been so kindly done but, from the hope that their benevolent design, of relieving me from pecuniary embarrassment, has not been attended with any embarrassment to themselves. I trust that they will do my heart the justice to believe that, in a reversal of our respective conditions, it would irresistably prompt me to hasten to their relief.[3]

ALS. DLC-HC (DNA, M212, R6). 1. Tilford to Clay, Feb. 17, 1845. 2. Lawrence to Clay, March 13, 1845. 3. For Clay's debts see Lawrence to Clay, March 13, 1845, and Clay to Lawrence, March 20, 1845.

From S.C. Salisbury, Cincinnati, Ohio, February 24, 1845. Acknowledges receipt of "Duplicate Contracts." Subscribes to all of Clay's alterations "but one & that is the guarranty required." Explains that he just bought his partner's interest in their business, and "in doing so I was determined Never to place my self or business in Jeop[ard]y. by a reciprocal or Mutual Indorsements that if under any circumstances My Business ever required additional Credit, that Credit I would pay a price for." Points out that "under my present agreement, I make Nothing Nor ask Nothing for my Services & it could not be Expected of me to pay for a guaranty under such Circumstances." Adds: "If I ask a friend to Indorse, I lay my self under alike obligation, which I would Not do for My Father, prefering to pay Cash rather than" acquire "an obligation." ALS. DLC-TJC (DNA, M212, R14).

According to their agreement of February 22, 1845, Clay was to sell Salisbury one thousand yards of cotton bagging during the year. This bagging would be manufactured by Thomas Hart Clay and would be delivered free of charge. Salisbury was to pay 12 1/2 cents per yard, and, "if upon the sale thereof, it nets more than twelve and a half cents per yard, the excess of that price is to be paid by the said Salisbury to the said Clay." A note in Clay's hand added: "I do hereby guaranty the punctual payment by S.C. Salisbury of the bills which may, from time to time, be drawn upon him by Henry Clay of Ashland." DS, by Salisbury, signed also by Clay. DLC-TJC (DNA, M212, R19). Endorsed by Clay on verso: "S.C. Salisbury with H. Clay Agreemt. [Answd. his letter on 4h. Mar. 1845, declining the contract]."

For S.C. Salisbury & Co., a cordage manufacturer located at Warehouse No. 4, Broadway, in Cincinnati, see Kimball & James, *Business Directory for the Mississippi Valley: 1844 Including . . . Cincinnati* (Cincinnati, 1844), 96.

To WILLIAM O. NILES Lexington, February 25, 1845

I received your letter[1] communicating your desire and purpose to revive the Register,[2] formerly edited with so much ability by your lamented father [Hezekiah Niles], and make it what it was, under his auspices, the successful expounder and defender of the System of protection of American industry[.] That system, from causes on which I will not dwell, is destined to encounter, during the approaching administration, a fierce and formidable attack. It will need all the exertions of its friends to sustain it. I should be very glad to see the Register once more engage in supporting so good a cause, and I most heartily wish you success if you should engage in conducting it. You have enjoyed great advantages in having the benefit of your fathers instructions and example, besides other opportunities which you have possessed; and as you will commence the work at about the same age at which he first undertook it, I do not see why you may not give to it its former renown. I cannot doubt but that you will receive a liberal patronage. If we could see the pens of two such men as Hez[ekiah]. Niles & Mat[hew]. Carey employed, as their pens were, in upholding the American System, firmly, perseveringly but moderately, I should have great hopes that it would survive the blow meditated against it. And why should not the sons supply the place of the sires?

ALS. DLC-Charles H. Hart Autograph Collection (DNA, M212, R21). Addressed to Niles in Washington, D.C. 1. Not found. 2. The Niles family sold *Niles' Weekly Register* in 1839 after Hezekiah died; it continued as *Niles' National Register*, edited by Jeremiah Hughes, until 1849. Apparently William O. Niles was not affiliated with it after 1839. Hudson, *Journalism in the United States*, 307. See also 9:75.

From Sarah L.B. French, Warrenton, Va., February 27, 1845. Encloses "a circular of the Henry Clay statue Society of Virginia," explaining that "the Whig ladies have proposed erecting your Statue at the Capitol of Virginia your native state." Explains that his cause is especially dear to them because "the foulest slanders ever envented for party purposes" were used against him during the recent presidential election. They desire to "teach our Sons to honor your name—and imitate your noble deeds." ALS. DLC-HC (DNA, M212, R6).

The Ladies Clay Association, with Lucy (Mrs. James) Barbour as president and Julia (Mrs. Benjamin W.) Leigh as one of the vice presidents, commissioned Joel T. Hart to sculpt the statue. It was completed in 1859 and unveiled and dedicated in Richmond on April 12, 1860. Mary W. Scott & Louise F. Catterall, *Virginia's Capitol Square, Its Buildings & Its Monuments* (Richmond, Va., 1957), 29-30; Washington *Daily National Intelligencer*, November 18, 1845. See also Amyx, "Portraits of Henry Clay," Special Collections, University of Kentucky Library, A:146j.

From Central Clay Committee of the City of New York, David Francis Bacon, secretary, New York City, March 4, 1845. Review for Clay "their original purpose and their labors" in support of his presidential campaign in 1844. Although "they might have done much more, they are content to point to the fact that the city of New York gave for Henry Clay in 1844 six thousand more votes than it gave for William Henry Harrison in 1840, as an evidence that something has been done here for the redemption of their original pledges." Point out that "This is the whole net gain of the Whig vote in the *state* of New York since 1841, and is a sufficient testimonial of the appreciation of the merits of Henry Clay by the freemen of the greatest city of America."

To combat the "agencies of fraud and crime" that, unfortunately had resulted in the "depositing in the ballot-boxes of this city and State at least 15,000 illegal votes,—most of them being introduced under deliberate perjury [Ewing to Clay, June 23, 1844]," had endeavored "to inform the people of the character and measures and principles involved in the contest." Report that "In these efforts, we have circulated at our expense more than a quarter of a million of documents, have given our time and means, have employed agents here and throughout the State, have conducted a correspondence with many hundred individuals in the same connexion, have convoked numerous great meetings, which we have caused to be effectively addressed by devoted and capable speakers; and we concluded these labors by the display, in grand procession, through the streets of our city, of the largest assemblage and most splendid demonstration of the mechanic arts and of their operations and political associations that was ever witnessed in this country." Although the "laboring classes have been, in vast numbers, instructed in the history of National legislation" and "will remain Whig through years to come," regret that the committee's labors, "so beneficial in immediate effect, have been rendered vain as to the actual result of the election, by fraudulent votes."

Blame Clay's defeat largely on recent immigrants, such as the "5,500 foreigners" who were "naturalized, during the year 1844 in this city alone, and about twice as many in other parts of the State, ninety nine-hundredths of whom of course voted against us [Frelinghuysen to Clay, November 9, 1844]." Are discouraged that "the great result was produced by the votes of more than 100,000 men who a few years before were the subjects of European monarchs and aliens from our Republican Institutions."

Nonetheless, "at this particular point of time, in the void present," the day on which a victorious Clay would have taken the oath of office as president, "we for a moment forget our dark forebodings. . . . For in looking among the wrecks of that vain hope, we find that all which embodied and personified our principles, which gave life and reality to our purpose, is left to us unchanged in HENRY CLAY." Praising "the defender of the Union and its Republican Constitution, the chief advocate of every measure of beneficial and protective legislation, the unchanging and dauntless opposer of tyranny and corruption," salute Clay as "great, honorable, just, pure, patriotic and wise—still first of living men, and 'first in our hearts'—still 'right,' and willing to 'be right rather than be President'."

Remember Clay's defeat as "a 'child's first grief:' fathers and their children wept together the death of patriotic hopes." Contend, however, that "our glowing spirits and burning words shall bear you better witness. The granite shall sooner moulder than these living memorials shall fail." Vow to "remember you, HENRY CLAY, while the memory of the glorious or the sense of good remains in us. . . . we will never know a triumph which you do not share in life, whose glory does not accrue to you in death. We will remember you while the national peace and prosperity continues; and when the war-clouds now darkening and muttering over the horizon have risen to overcast the clear and placid sky yet above us, and have burst over the whole land, the people will remember you too; and all will remember you when the bloodhounds so long baying on our track, and the wolves now howling around the fold, shall have rent the prey, where the vultures are already screaming for the offal." Copy. Printed in Lexington *Observer & Kentucky Reporter*, March 22, 1845; printed in part in Colton, *Clay Correspondence*, 2:454-56. A copy of this address was "enclosed in a silver case of elegant workmanship, and forwarded to Ashland" to commemorate the day on which Clay would have been sworn in as president. See Clay to Bacon, April 28, 1845.

From Charles Martin, Martinsburg, Va. (W. Va.), March 4, 1845. Although a stranger to Clay, assures him that "your name has been familiar to me since my father first taught me to pronounce it in connection with the name of John Quincy Adams, in 1824." Rejoiced after Clay's nomination in 1844 "that the time had come to show that 'Republics are *not* ungrateful.' " Had hoped to look upon Clay's victory as "a proud personal victory for yourself over your malignant foes: but above all, as a noble triumph of correct principles." Continues: "Sir, had you been my father, your defeat could have occasioned me but little more grief. Everything calculated to destroy faith in the Republic, was connected with that unlooked for event."

Remains appalled by the "unfounded, unscrupulous, and malignant attacks . . . upon both your public and private character." Wonders: "Could the judgment of my country men be so perverted, or their minds so shackled, as to sacrifice the nation's highest interest and honor, to secure the triumph of *party*, and *party* only? Was it possible that the most unblushing attempts to deceive the people could succeed, even for a moment?" Fears that American voters "offered a large reward to the selfish and unscrupulous partizan" while destroying "every incentive to noble, generous, and patriotic efforts in the country's service." Hopes Clay will take consolation in knowing that he was "nobly supported by the noblest hearts and purest hands of this great nation, while your defeat was effected by a combination of means which your opponents must ever contemplate with burning shame." ALS. DLC-HC (DNA, M212, R6).

From Stephen Russell, Lyme, Huron Co., Ohio, March 4, 1845. Expresses the disappointment and grief of Ohio Whigs at Clay's defeat, and admits they have seen much "that militates against the adage that 'truth is mighty and must prevail.' " Intends, nonetheless, "to keep good our organization labor hope—and struggle on."

Reviews Whig victories in Ohio during the late election: "On the Western Reserve (containing 11 Counties) there was not a single Loco Foco elected to Co. or state office. . . . The Whigs made a clean sweep." Mentions "an incident which I think a pretty little commontary on the relative merits of the parties." Continues: "Richland Co. in this state was one of the counties according to the census of–40 that contained the greatest No. in proportion to the population unable to read and write. The Co. gave about 2600 majority for [James K.] Polk. Ashtabula where it would appear from s[ai]d census the inhabitants were best informed—descendents of the Pilgrim Fathers—with a village school house at every cross roads a church spire to every 800 souls—gave almost as great a majority for the other ticket." Consoles Clay: "Let the excelling chuckle of the victorious demagogue the conte[m]ptuous sneer of the envious—and the sardonic grin of the revengeful pass alike for what they are worth."

Looks upon Clay's "situation as ten thousand times more to be coveted than the situation of J.K. Polk—From what I have seen and heard I can form some conception of the load of responsibilities &c of which he is and is a while to be the center. It will be enough to make a well man sick and a sick man crazy." ALS. DLC-TJC (DNA, M212, R10).

Stephen Russell had settled in Lyme, Ohio, in 1814 and was for many years an active businessman and stock dealer there. William W. Williams, *History of the Fire Lands, Comprising Huron and Erie Counties, Ohio* (Cleveland, Ohio, 1979), 378-79, 387.

From John S. Williams, Cincinnati, Ohio, March 4, 1845. Reminds Clay that he owes $2.00 for "the 2d Vol of the 'American Pioneer.' " Admits "the Amt is small but being in need it will serve as a great Auxilliary." ALS, copy. DLC-TJC (DNA, M212, R14).

The *American Pioneer* was the organ of the Logan County (Ohio) Historical Society, and Williams was the editor and publisher. The various numbers of the *American Pioneer* were published either in Chillicothe or Cincinnati. Frank L. Mott, *A History of American Magazines 1741-1850* (New York, 1930), 422; Peter G. Thomson, *A Bibliography of the State of Ohio* (Cincinnati, Ohio, 1880), 11-12.

To CALVIN COLTON Lexington, March 5, 1845

I received your favors from Washington and from Philadelphia,[1] the latter making inquiries concerning my paternal ancestors. I am sorry that I am unable to communicate to you any minute information about them. All that I know, in the general, is that they came from England to the colony of Virginia, some time after its establishment, and settled, I believe, on the south side of James River. The descendants of the original stock are very numerous, and much dispersed, many of them residing in Virginia and Kentucky. A branch, or branches of the family remained in England, and among their descendants was Mr. J. Clay, recently quite a distinguished member of the British House of Commons.[2]

My maternal ancestors also came from England, and settled in Hanover county, Virginia, about the beginning of the last century. George Hudson, my maternal grandfather, died about the year 1770, in that county.[3]

This is about as much as I can inform you in regard to my ancestors, and from this statement, you will, I hope, be able to incorporate all that is material in your narrative.

My family is well, and unite with me in assurances of our warm regard.

Copy. Printed in Colton, *Clay Correspondence*, 4:524. 1. Not found. 2. Printed in Colton, 4:524 is an undated note from Clay to Colton, saying that "I am sorry that you should have any trouble about my English namesakes. I am not sure that two of them have been members of the House of Commons. One, I know, has been, because I have read a speech of his, and have corresponded with him, although I can not now lay my hands upon any letter of his. . . . Most probably it was William. When I wrote you last, I thought his name was J. Clay, being uncertain whether it was John or Joseph. It was probably William. It is not a matter of much consequence, and perhaps you had better confine what you say to the one of whom you know something." For William Clay, see 9:6. 3. For George Hudson, who died in 1770, see Smith & Rogers, *The Clay Family*, 37-38, 53-55.

To Charles Hall, New Haven, Conn., March 7, 1845. Acknowledges a "testimonial of my being made a member for life of the American Home Missionary Society, in virtue of a contribution made for that object by the ladies of the Durand Society of New Haven." Asks Hall to thank them "for this distinguished proof of their highly—appreciated esteem and regard, and to assure them that I share with them a profound sense of the surpassing importance of the Christian religion." Hopes that "the labors of the society would fully correspond with the pious and religious motives which prompted its establishment." Copy. Printed in Colton, *Clay Correspondence*, 1:57.

According to the 1845 *New Haven City Directory*, the Durand Society was a benevolent organization, led by Mrs. C.W. Jarman as president. Mrs. Jarman was a member of Center Church (First Congregational), and it is possible the Durand Society was affiliated with that church. Information supplied by Diane E. Kaplan, archivist, Yale University Library.

The American Home Missionary Society had been formed in New York in 1826. See Colin B. Goodykoontz, *Home Missions on the American Frontier* (Caldwell, Idaho, 1939), 173-79.

To Charles W. Ridgely, Baltimore, March 7, 1845. Acknowledges receipt of Ridgely's letter informing him that, "by the contribution of two ladies of Baltimore," Clay had "been made a member for life of the Baltimore Sabbath Association." Asks Ridgely to extend his gratitude "for this proof of their valued regard and esteem, and to assure them that I share with them in sentiments of profound reverence for the Sabbath, as a religious institution." Thanks Ridgely for "the copy of the pamphlet containing the proceedings of the Association." Copy. Printed in Frankfort *Commonwealth*, August 15, 1845.

Ridgely was secretary of the Baltimore Sabbath Association, formed in 1844 to promote "the better observance of the Lord's day." *First Anniversary Meeting of the Baltimore Sabbath Association Held on the 13th January, 1845* (Baltimore, 1845), 18 pp.

To Mrs. Mary S. Gove, Cincinnati, Ohio, March 8, 1845. Offers to receive Mrs. Gove, who is "travelling in the West for health and literary improvement," at Ashland "if you think proper to come so far to visit an old and retired person." Adds as a postscript: "I am at a loss, as not unfrequently happens, to address you whether as a single or married lady. I adopt the latter mode, because if you are not married you *ought* to be, of course, when it pleases you." ALS. KyU. Addressed on attached sheet in Clay's hand: "Mrs. Mary S. Gove Cincinnati Ohio."

From Abbott Lawrence, Boston, Mass., March 13, 1845. Informs Clay that he had "determined quietly to raise from your friends and mine, a few thousand dollars" to help reduce the "pecuniary obligations which might press upon you." Discovered, however, "a general movement among our people to raise a large sum for *an individual*, for whom I have more than once in by gone years *successfully* exerted my self, to clear him of debt.—I could not under *past and present circumstances* unite in *this* movement, and maintain my own self respect." Hesitated, then, to proceed with "*my plan* to raise a small sum for the relief of a friend for whom I entertain the truest friendship." Raised "the sum of $4750—$500 of which was placed in my hands as a voluntary tribute . . . by Mr. Jared Coffin [Coffin & Coffin to Clay, February 11, 1845]." Intends to send the remaining $4250 "to John Tilford Esq President of the Northern Bank of Kentucky to be applied to the payment of your debt to that Bank." Adds that he "*could* raise a larger sum of money—from the persons who have contributed on this occasion, and *much more* if I were to make a general appeal to your friends." ALS. DLC-HC (DNA, M212, R6). Letter marked "Private & Confidential." See also Tilford to Clay, February 17, 1845; Clay to Tilford, February 22, 1845.

Among those who agreed to contribute $500, in addition to Lawrence and Coffin, were: Thomas H. Perkins, Nathan Appleton, Peter C. Brooks, William Appleton, Edmond Dwight, Theodore Lyman, and William Lawrence. In addition, Martin Brimmer contributed $250.

On March 13 John Tilford wrote Henry White in Philadelphia reporting that Clay owes $7,000 to the Northern Bank of Kentucky which is secured by a mortgage on Ashland; that he owes $8,500 to John J. Astor (the remainder of the $15,000 being for his son Henry, Jr.); and $10,000 to some individual in New Orleans. He reports that this comprises the bulk of Clay's indebtedness as far as he knows, and that he expects $3,500 to arrive shortly from New Orleans and about $5,000 from Boston to help defray Clay's debts. ALS. DLC-HC (DNA, M212, R6).

Tilford wrote Clay on March 20, 1845, that he had received $4,250 "from friends who are desireous of contributing to free you from pecuniary cares" to be applied to "the payment of that much of your indebtedness" to the Northern Bank of Kentucky. *Ibid.*

On April 2, 1845, Tilford again wrote Clay to inform him of the receipt of an additional "five Thousand Dollars which I am directed to apply to the payment of debts due this Institution." Pays off Clay's remaining debt to the bank of $2,728.75 and "the residue of the money $2271.25 I applied in part payment of a note of yours due to Miss [Sidney] Edmiston." *Ibid.* Endorsed on verso by Clay: "John Tilford—[The last of my notes to the N. Bank paid and a part of my debt to Miss Edmiston, the residue of it I paid the same day]."

Also on April 2, 1845, Miss Edmiston signed a receipt for $2,271.25 to be credited to "a note held by me on the Hon: Henry Clay." DS. *Ibid.* See also Clay to Lawrence, March 20, 1845.

To HENRY CLAY, JR. Lexington, March 17, 1845

I received your letter by Mr. Bryant.[1] Your children are very well and were here yesterday. I do not believe that you could have made a better provision for them than that which you have done. Should you go to N[ew]. O[rleans]., besides the immediate object of your journey, the case of Dubreuils heirs may be worthy of your attention. I learn that the Court has decided the exception against us on the ground that the U. States cannot be sued. I have great confidence, in previous decisions of the S. Court of the U.S., that the ground can not be maintained. An appeal has been taken to the Supreme Court of Louisiana, which I understand will be probably tried this Spring.[2] I wish that you could attend to it. I have communicated to Mr. [Gustavus] Schmidt[3] my views of that question of jurisdiction. It is doubtful whether [Samuel] Judah[4] can assist in the argument. I have not yet heard from France as to the order of Rochemore.[5]

It would afford me very great pleasure if you could be elected to Congress from the Louisville District. I know nothing or next to nothing of the probability of the success of a Whig Candidate. [William O.] Butler, I think it probable, will be the Candidate on the other side. I hope that your connection with me, if it do not benefit, may not injure you, should you determine to be a Candidate.[6]

My friends are kindly doing something towards my pecuniary relief. They have addressed themselves directly to the N[orthern]. Bank of K[entucky]. & paid off the two notes of $5000. each given respectively by you and me, and I have reason to believe that they will do at least as much more for me.[7] This will relieve me from all solicitude on a pecuniary score.

Mr. Bryant brought me a purse from a Nantucket whaler, a good friend of mine, containing $500. which he kindly contributed to my relief.[8]

I have felt some hesitation, and experienced some mortification, in yielding to these friendly efforts to assist me.

I should be glad to learn if you finally resolve, to go to N. Orleans. I do not wish to go myself, unless there should be an imperative necessity for the voyage.

Dubreuils case is far from being certain. On the points now in issue, if the decision of the S. Court of Louisiana be against us, a writ of error will be to the S. Court of the U. States; but my confidence in this tribunal is much diminished, and even if it should decide that point for us, it is not certain that we should finally succeed.

P.S. Martin Duralde [III] has been very ill, with a hemorrage, which we feared was from the lungs. He is now better, but not well.

John [Morrison Clay] too has exhibited decided symptoms of mental aberration. Altho' now better, we have the greatest fears about him.[9]

ALS. Henry Clay Memorial Foundation, Lexington, Ky. 1. Not found. 2. Dubreuil Villars had been employed to help construct fortifications around French New Orleans and was authorized to use lands not needed for the fortifications and not already occupied. He could make improvements on this land and use it until the Crown needed it. Later the fortifications were abandoned and rebuilt, and the lands Villars had used changed hands. After Louisiana was purchased by the U.S., the state claimed title to the lands and turned them over to the U.S. to construct a federal mint. In 1850 in its final decision, the Louisiana Court ruled against the heirs of Dubreuil Villars. For a discussion of this case, see Charles J. Bayard (ed.), "Documents, The Clay-Judah Correspondence," *RKHS* (Jan., 1969), 67:80-85. 3. Schmidt (b. Sweden 1795–d. 1877) was a leader of the New Orleans bar. *Ibid.*, 81. 4. Judah (b. New York 1798–d. Indiana 1869) was a leading Indiana lawyer. *Ibid.*, 81. 5. Vincent Gaspard Pierre de Rochemore had been the intendant of Louisiana 1758 to *ca.* 1762. *Ibid.*, 83. 6. Henry Clay, Jr., announced that he would not run for Congress from the Louisville district but would support the Whig cause. Louisville *Daily Journal*, April 22, 1845. In the congressional race Whig William P. Thomasson defeated Democrat Elijah Nuttall. *Guide to U.S. Elections*, 582. 7. Tilford to Clay, Feb. 17, 1845; Clay to Tilford, Feb. 22, 1845. 8. Coffin & Coffin to Clay, Feb. 11, 1845. 9. For John Morrison Clay's mental problems, see Clay to Henry Clay, Jr., April 5, 1845.

To JOHN M. BERRIEN Lexington, March 19, 1845

I cannot allow your friendly letter of the 13h. inst to remain unacknowledged, if for no other reason than that of communicating to Mrs. [James] Hunter[1] my grateful obligations for her very friendly message. Tell her, I pray you, that it does not become me to attribute ingratitude to the Nation, on my account, but my heart prompts me to own the gratitude which it feels to individual kindness, to her sex, and to herself particularly. My hopes, as to our Country, dark and dismal as prospects seem, are that we may be yet taken care of by a wise and merciful Providence. Tell Mrs. [Eliza Hunter] Berrien too that I am thankful to her for the proofs of friendship[2] which she has given to me, and for the feelings of sympathy excited in her breast by our recent defeat[.]

I shall read with attentive interest your Speech on the Texas question,[3] when I get it. I am happy to bear my humble testimony to your manly bearing and your fidelity to peace honor and the Constitution of our Country. I am not surprized at your desire to retire from the scenes of a public life which offers so little to cheer the patriot and to animate to honorable exertion. And yet I should be extremely sorry to hear of your quitting the Senate.[4]

The arrangement of the Committees (and what an arrangement it is!)[5] attracted & fixed my attention. Great God, what have we come to! . . .

ALS. NcU. 1. Berrien's mother-in-law. 2. As one indication of her support, Mrs. Berrien had written a song to Clay. See 9:854. 3. A summary of Berrien's speech against Texas annexation appears in *Cong. Globe*, 28 Cong., 2 Sess., 343-44; for the complete text, see Washington *Daily National Intelligencer*, March 16, 1845. 4. Berrien resigned from the Senate on Nov. 7, 1845, and was subsequently reelected on Nov. 14, 1845, to fill his own unexpired term. McCrary, "John MacPherson Berrien," Ph.D. dissertation, University of Georgia, 1971, pp. 303-5. See also Clay to Berrien, Dec. 12, 1845. 5. Traditionally no standing committees were appointed during an executive session of Congress, but in March, 1845, during the executive session of the 29th Congress, the Democratic majority appointed committees after arranging to keep Vice President George M. Dallas always in the chair so that no president pro tempore could be chosen. Dallas then appointed extreme expansionist William Allen of Ohio as chairman of the Foreign Relations Committee along with two other men who advocated an Oregon boundary of 54 degrees 40′. In general, these committee appointments gave expansionist Democrats power that was out of proportion to their strength in the Senate and enabled chairmen to claim seniority when the regular session of Congress began in Dec., 1845. This whole procedure, especially Allen's appointment as chairman in both March and Dec., was decried by the Whig press. Merk, *The Oregon Question*, 374-80.

To ABBOTT LAWRENCE Lexington, March 20, 1845

I hasten to acknowledge the receipt this morning of your obliging letter,[1] with its highly interesting enclosures. I know not how adequately to express the deep and grateful sense which I feel for the very great obligations under which you and my other friends in Massachusetts have placed me.

But I owe it to you and them to explain the cause of any pecuniary embarrassment which has befallen me. Never, never for a moment, in my whole life, have I been subjected to any on my own proper account. Twice have I been seriously embarrassed for others, towards whom, however, I must say that I have no just reproaches to make. Once, about twenty years ago, by a brother of Mrs. [Lucretia Hart] Clay, a most honorable and estimable person now no more. I quitted Congress, in consequence of it, and in a few years of successful and laborious practice of my profession relieved myself.[2] Again, about three years ago, a son of mine [Thomas Hart Clay], engaged in the manufacture of hemp, proved unfortunate, more by the times than from his fault.[3] He made an assignment, providing equally for all his creditors, of whom I was the largest, his debt to me of about $25.000 being equal to the aggregate amount of theirs. I attended the sale of his property, and authorized the Auctioneer to proclaim that all his creditors should be first paid, and that if any thing were left I would take it.[4] This liberal course did not prevent sacrifices of his property; and, in the sequel, they were all paid to the last cent, and I received nothing.

I had means nevertheless to meet all my engagements; but it would have been necessary to sell Ashland, the best property I have, endeared to me by time and many other precious associations. My own judgment prompted me to sell it, and to live afterwards, in an humbler way, upon the residue of my means. My friends remonstrated, and insisted upon an endeavor to sell my outlands, and to collect my other scattered resources, and preserve this property to my family. Hence the proposal which, I understand, some of them made to you and other friends, of my outlands, with which they were acquainted.

It would have been more compatible with my feelings, if a sale could have been effected of them; but a generous and noble response has been made to the proposal from Boston, Philadelphia, N. York and from N. Orleans.[5] Not without some feelings of repugnance, I yield to the kind wishes of my friends, and retain my out lands.

The assistance which has been thus liberally afforded me, relieves me from all solicitude, and leaves only a small remnant of debt; which I can meet without any sacrifice or difficulty.

I observe what is so kindly intimated in some of the notes, which you have forwarded, of a readiness to contribute further to my aid. I am infinitely obliged by those good friends, but I cannot consent to any further contributions from them.

I pray you to excuse this long letter. I thought it due to the friendship, so highly appreciated by me, which you honor me by entertaining, and due to my self.

But the main object of my addressing you was to express to you, and to request you to convey to the kind friends who have so generously associated with you, in coming to my relief, my profound and grateful obligations for their signal & distinguished generosity. I trust that, in the resolutions of the capricious wheel of fortune, your and their condition and mine will never be reversed; but if that should unhappily, as to you and them, be the case, God knows with what pleasure my heart would prompt me to fly to your and their assistance.

I have never been desirous of inordinate wealth. I have been only anxious to live in a manner corresponding with the circle in which I move, and to possess the means of doing so. This desire I shall now be able to gratify, without the indulgence of any habits of extravagance or ostentatious display, to which neither Mrs. Clay or myself has ever been prone. . . . P.S. The acceptable present of my estimable friend Mr. J[ared]. Coffin came to me in perfect safety. I have already written to him, in anticipation of its arrival.[6]

ALS. MH. Letter marked "(Confidential)." 1. Lawrence to Clay, March 13, 1845. 2. For Clay's involvement in the financial problems of his wife's brother John Hart and nephew Thomas P. Hart, see 2:396-98, 794-95. 3. See 9:791-93, 806-7. 4. *Ibid.* 5. Tilford to Clay,

Feb. 17, 1845; Clay to Tilford, Feb. 22, 1845; Lawrence to Clay, March 13, 1845. 6. Coffin & Coffin to Clay, Feb. 11, 1845.

To JOHN BRAND Lexington, March 24, 1845

I send enclosed the last of the series of notes[1] which you, kindly lending me your credit when it was of great benefit to me,[2] executed, paid off and cancelled.

Next to the pleasure, which the performance of a friendly office excites, is that of knowing that the object of it has received it with thanks and gratitude. Your own heart assures you of the first, and mine prompts me now to convey a sincere assurance of the last.

ALS. KyLoF. 1. Not found. 2. Probably a reference to the Deed of Trust for "Ashland" for which Brand held a promissory note or notes. See 9:789-90.

To Henry L. Ellsworth, Washington, D.C., March 24, 1845. Provides a cover letter for "two of the most enterprizing and reputable citizens of Louisville." Suggests only that if their "experiment be successful, by *which an efficient Hempbrake* has been invented, as they seem to suppose, it would be difficult to magnify too much its importance." ALS. ViU.

Ellsworth was commissioner of the U.S. Patent Office from 1835-45. *DAB*. No patent for a hemp-brake was issued to anyone from Louisville until 1853 when one was issued to L.W. Colver; however, a patent was issued to R. Deering, Sr., of Louisville on June 25, 1845, for "Hemp, Preparation of." *Subject Matter Index of Patents for Inventions Issued by the U.S. Patent Office, 1790-1873 inclusive* (Washington, D.C., 1874), 717-18.

To MARTHA K. BUCKINGHAM Lexington, March 31, 1845

I received your letter[1] informing me that your mother had bequeathed to yourself and your two sisters $1000, to be appropriated by you and them, as you might deem best, for the promotion of the immediate emancipation of the slaves in the United States; and that it has occurred to you that the benevolent design of your mother might be well executed by applying that sum in aiding the circulation of a paper which Mr. Cassius M. Clay purposes publishing in support of the cause of emancipation of the slaves in Kentucky.[2] You do me the honor to ask my advice as to the direction of the bequest to that object.

I am much more sensible of the compliment you have paid me than I am able to offer you any very satisfactory advice.

At all times there have been in Kentucky many individuals in favor of a *gradual* emancipation of slaves, similar to that which was adopted by Pennsylvania, during the Revolutionary war.[3] At no time has any body, or at least any considerable number of persons, been in favor of *immediate* emancipation. I sincerely believe that the number, in favor of gradual emancipation, would now be much greater than it is but for the unhappy agitation of the question of abolition in the free States. What proportion of the population of K. is in favor of gradual emancipation, at present, I have no means of judging, and can only be matter of conjecture. I am inclined to believe that it is not greater, relatively to those who are opposed to it, than it was in the years 1798-9.[4]

My belief is that Mr. Clay's effort is made at an inauspicious period, and that it will be unsuccessful. Time would do a great deal, if its operations, and the calm reflection of the public mind were left undisturbed by the excitement of passions. It has been by such excitement that abolitionists, contrary no doubt to the intention of the honest portion of them, have done much prejudice to the cause which they espoused. The annexation of Texas,[5] should it be consummated, will prolong the duration of Slavery, by opening to it a new theatre.

I am not in consultation with Mr. Clay about the project of his paper, of which I know nothing except what I derive from the public prints and general rumor. If he should go for immediate emancipation, he will find no partizians in this State. And, if he should even confine his exertions to the object of a gradual emancipation, I doubt whether he will add many to the number of those among us who are in favor of that plan. But if he limit himself to a *gradual* emancipation, it is worthy of your consideration whether such a purpose falls within the scope of your mother's bequest, which is directed to *immediate* emancipation.

If I were to offer any advice to you, it would be to withhold the application of the money, for the present, and until Mr. Clay's plan is further developed, and the reception of it by the public is seen.

ALS. Courtesy of Elsie O. and Philip D. Sang, River Forest, Illinois. Letter marked "Private." Addressed to Mrs. Buckingham at Putnam, Ohio. 1. Not found. 2. A prospectus for the *True American*, an emancipationist newspaper published by Cassius M. Clay, had appeared in the Lexington *Observer & Kentucky Reporter* on Feb. 19, 1845. The first issue appeared on June 3, 1845, but publication was suppressed by mob action on August 18. Clay revived it in Cincinnati on Oct. 8, 1845, and it survived there for about a year. John C. Vaughan took charge of the paper after Cassius Clay went to fight in the Mexican War. David L. Smiley, *Lion of White Hall* (Madison, Wisc., 1962), 80-82, 90-102, 115, 265; *History and Record of the Proceedings of the People of Lexington . . . in the Suppression of the "TRUE AMERICAN"* . . . (n.p., n.d.). 3. Pennsylvania had passed an act in 1780 providing that all current slaves would remain in servitude for the remainder of their lives, but all Negroes born after the passage of the act would become free at age 28. Robert L. Brunhouse, *The Counter-Revolution in Pennsylvania 1776-1790* (Harrisburg, Pa., 1942), 81. 4. At that time Clay had advocated gradual emancipation. See 1:5-7, 12-14. 5. Clay to Crittenden, Feb. 15, 1844.

From Emiline Rockwell, Norwich, Conn., March 31, 1845. On behalf of the "Whig Ladies of Norwich . . . more than three hundred of their number," presents Clay with "a pair of silver Pitchers as a memorial of the value which they attach to the distinguished public services which you have rendered your country through a long and eventful public life." Promises Clay that "whenever you may favor Conn with a visit, her Whig daughters will vie with the sons of her soil in tendering you a hearty welcome." ALS. DLC-TJC (DNA, M212, R10).

To HENRY CLAY, JR. Lexington, April 2, 1845

Enclosed is a letter which came to me for you. I am happy to inform you that my good friends have contributed $24.750 towards my relief, which has been applied to the payment of my debt.[1] The whole of that to the N[orthern]. Bank is paid, and $5000 have been directed to the payment of so much of the [John J.] Astor debt.[2] I learn indirectly that a further sum is coming to my assistance;[3] but if no more come, the remnant of my debt will occasion me no solicitude.

I regret to inform you that John [Morrison Clay] is becoming more and more deranged, and, painful as it will be, I fear there will be no alternative but the hospital.[4] Thus providence mixes afflictions and blessings! Our duty is that of perfect submission to his will.

We are all well, except Martin Duralde [III], who continues in a situation creating apprehension. Your children[5] are quite well and appear contented and happy.

ALS. Henry Clay Memorial Foundation, Lexington, Ky. Addressed to Henry Clay, Jr., in Louisville, Ky. 1. Tilford to Clay, Feb. 17, 1845; Clay to Tilford, Feb. 22, 1845; Lawrence to Clay, March 13, 1845; Clay to Lawrence, March 20, 1845. 2. For Clay's debts to Astor, see 2:686; 3:857; 8:763; 9:846. 3. Astor to Clay, April 28, 1845. 4. See Clay to Henry Clay, Jr., April 5, 1845. 5. Anne (1832-1918) and Thomas Julian (1840-63) were staying in Lexington. Henry Clay III was in Louisville, possibly with his mother's family. See Clay to Henry Clay, Jr., April 8, 1845.

To HENRY CLAY, JR. Lexington, April 5, 1845

I lament to inform you that we have been compelled to place John [Morrison Clay] in the Hospital.[1] He had been getting worse for some days past. The night before last he was roaming about in the woods until two o'clock in the morning. Altho' he offered violence to no one, he was wild and boisterous in his language; and it was often incoherent. The painful conviction was at length forced upon me that it was necessary, and a duty on my part, to have him confined. It has greatly afflicted me. He threatened his own life, and declared to more than one that he intended to terminate it last night. His passion for Miss J——[2] revived, and yesterday he attempted to see her, but she, being advised of his situation, properly declined to receive him. He went in a carriage quietly to the Hospital, without any resistance. I was afraid of the effect of this last stroke upon your poor mother; but she was satisfied of the propriety of the measure, and her resignation to the will of God enables her to bear what has happened better even than I do.

Mr. Milton[3] handed me yesterday $15 received upon your fellowship in the University. What shall I do with it? Are you not owing about that sum to Mrs. Tibbatts?[4]

Your children continue well; and, except Martin [Duralde III] we are all well here. His situation is very critical.[5]

ALS. Henry Clay Memorial Foundation, Lexington, Ky. Addressed to Henry Clay, Jr., in Louisville, Ky. 1. Lunatic Asylum of Kentucky, located in Lexington. 2. Reference obscure. 3. William E. Milton, secretary and treasurer of the Board of Trustees of Transylvania University. 4. Possibly the wife of Thomas Tibbatts who appears as a resident in Lexington in the 1840 census. 5. Clay to Henry Clay, Jr., March 17, 1845.

From Robert Garrett & Sons, Baltimore, Md., April 5, 1845. Send Clay a copy of their current account with him, "Having recently closed your lot of Hemp." Express regret for "the delay in closing Sales of this parcel—the bad cleaning being in frequent instances the only impediment to Sales at better rates." Inform Clay that the supply of "Prime Clean W[ater]. R[etted]. . . . is small & as the importations of Russia [hemp], have been unusually light . . . we trust Hemp [prices] will be favorably Affected." ALS. DLC-TJC (DNA, M212, R14). Enclosed is an account sheet that indicates Clay's hemp was sold on August 24 and December 14, 1844, and January 20 and March 28, 1845, netting a total price of $285.36. Charges against the account for freight, drayage, storage, fire insurance, labor, advertising, and commission amounted to $211.54.

Clay responded on April 12, 1845, questioning "one charge of yours that I am inclined to think you ought not to make, and that is for storage. . . . It has always seemed to me that it ought to be considered as included in commissions; that every Commission merchant ought to be prepared to receive the articles consigned to him." Admits that if the charge is "right in principle, your's is moderate enough." Warns, however, "that the charges on hemp sent to the Eastern Cities are so great that, unless they can be reduced, I am afraid that the producer will have to stop the business. They amount to about $40 per ton!" Informs them that he has sent via New Orleans "3908 lb. of Water retted hemp, which you will find much better cleaned than the last parcel I forwarded." Intends also to send "several tons of very superior water retted hemp . . . through the interior route by Pittsburg[h]." Wishes to "try both routes, and ascertain which is the best and least expensive." ALS. DLC-Garrett Family Papers (DNA, M212, R21).

On May 21, 1845, Clay wrote again, wondering if the "15 bales of Water retted hemp" which he "shipt to you from N.O. early in April" arrived safely in Baltimore. Hopes, as well, that the "16 bales of the same description of hemp" which he shipped "through the route of the Interior, by the way of Cincinnati" arrived in good condition. Suggests he may forward to them "several tons in course of preparation" unless "I should be tempted to direct it to Boston, in consequence of the very favorable state of the market there." AL, signature removed. *Ibid.*

To Dr. W.A. Booth, Sommerville, Tenn., April 7, 1845. Responds to questions about his views on "the unfortunate controversy which has arisen in the Methodist Episcopal Church of the United States [Clay to Unknown Recipient, June 26, 1844]." Asserts: "I have long entertained, for that church, sentiments of profound esteem and regard, and I have the happiness of numbering among its members some of the best friends I have in the world. I will add, with great truth, that I have witnessed, with much satisfaction, the flourishing condition of the church, and the good sense and wisdom which have generally characterized the administration of its affairs." Regrets to learn of "the danger of a division of the church, in consequence of a difference of opinion existing on the delicate and unhappy subject of slavery. A division, for such a cause, would be an event greatly to be deplored, both on account of the church itself, and its political tendency. Indeed, scarcely any public occurrence has happened, for a long time, that gave so much real concern and pain, as the menaced separation of the church, by a line, throwing all the free States on one side, and all the slave States on the other." Doubts that "such separation would necessarily produce a dis[s]olution of the political Union of these States; but the example would be fraught with imminent danger." Hopes "to hear of an adjustment of the controversy, a reconciliation between the opposing parties in the church, and the preservation of its unity," but refuses to offer an "opinion on either of the plans of compromise and settlement." Copy. Printed in the Portsmouth (N.H.) *Journal of Literature & Politics*, May 17, 1845. Printed in Colton, *Clay Correspondence*, 4:525-26.

This letter was a response to a query advanced both to Clay and to James K. Polk: "Will the division of the Methodist Episcopal Church, into two separate organizations, (slavery being the cause of the division, and the dividing line,) be likely to affect the civil connexion between the slave and the non-slaveholding states? If so, will it strengthen or weaken the bonds of the Union?" Unlike Clay, Polk did not offer an answer to this question. Portsmouth *Journal of Literature & Politics*, May 17, 1845.

William A. Booth of Sommerville, Tenn., had proposed a compromise to prevent a North-South split in the Methodist Episcopal Church. In 1845 he published in Sommerville a pamphlet, *The Writings of William A. Booth, M.D. During the Controversy Upon Slavery, Which Ended in the Division of the Methodist Episcopal Church*, which detailed his role in the affair.

To HENRY CLAY, JR. Lexington, April 8, 1845

Since I wrote you the other day about the unhappy condition of John [Morrison Clay],[1] I received your letter of the 5h. Out of the money which has been contributed by my good friends to my relief, five thousand dollars have been divided to be paid to Mr. [John J.] Astor. That, with the $5000 which I paid the winter the last will reduce the original debt from $20.000 to $10.000.[2] I mean to write in a week or two and propose a further indulgence of two years for this latter sum, and to state positively that it is the last indulgence that will be asked. I entertain all confidence that it will be granted, and consequently that you need not allow this subject to distress you.

I am afraid that John's case is hopeless. He exhibited strong and unequivocal demonstration of derangement, and I understand manifested it more decisively than his unfortunate brother [Theodore W. Clay] did when he was first put in the Hospital. We shall make the best arrangements we can for the comfort of them, and among others I have sent a servant to the Hospital to attend on them.[3]

I find it extremely hard to bear this last sad affliction. It has put in requisition the utmost fortitude I can command.

I am not surprized that you should be dissatisfied with boarding in a Tavern, and leading a life of inactivity. I fervantly wish that you were engaged in some useful and agreeable employment. Thomas [Hart Clay] & James [Brown Clay] are both building dwelling houses,[4] and both will leave here when they are finished, some time next fall. If you do not go to Congress, suppose you come and live with us? You would save expence, be near your two children,[5] and might bring Henry [Clay III] with you. To us it would be no additional expense, and if it were as I can do but little for you during my life, I should be happy to assist you in that way. Perhaps we might be able to mark out some business in which we might be both beneficially engaged. Thomas's factory has capacity to work double the number of the looms now in operation. I own one third of the hands, the other two thirds being hirelings. I am satisfied that, if we owned all the hands, with attention and economy, the business might be made profitable. I believe too that by judicious purchases of hemp, and baleing and exporting it money may be made, and I am now prepared for baling and packing it at Mansfield.

These are matters which I submit to your consideration. I think you ought to resolve upon some steady pursuit.

Your children are both well. They were with us, as usual, last Sabbath.

ALS. Henry Clay Memorial Foundation, Lexington, Ky. Addressed to Henry Clay, Jr., in Louisville, Ky. 1. Clay to Henry Clay, Jr., April 5, 1845. 2. See 8:763 and Clay to Henry Clay, Jr., April 2, 1845. 3. The Fayette County property tax roll for 1846 lists Theodore W. Clay, still in the asylum, as owning property consisting of one slave. Ky. State Archives microfilm of property tax roll. 4. In 1837 Clay had bought at auction a portion of the "Mansfield" property which adjoined "Ashland" and which had originally belonged to Col. John Todd. Clay had a house, also called "Mansfield," built on the site in 1845-46 for his son Thomas Hart Clay. The house was designed by Thomas Lewinski, a Lexington architect. Also in 1845-46, Clay assisted James B. Clay in building a house called "Clay Villa," which was also designed by Lewinski. Clay Lancaster, "Major Thomas Lewinski: Emigre Architect in Kentucky," *JSAH*, no. 4, 11:14; Elizabeth M. Simpson, *Bluegrass Houses and Their Traditions* (Lexington, 1932), 375-82. 5. Anne and Thomas Julian.

From Rezin D. Shepherd, New Orleans, La., April 8, 1845. Thanks Clay for the "receipt for the deposit made to my Credit" in the Merchants Bank, Baltimore; but, assures him that in the future he need not go to the expence of sending the receipt, because "all that is necessary . . . is a mere notification from yourself . . . giving me the date of the Deposit in order that I may debit the Bank with the amount & endorse the same on the Bond."

Informs Clay that "Our friend Touro . . . has this day put on board the steam Boat Sultana . . . Two half pipes of Medeira Wine, of which he begs your acceptance." Describes one pipe as "orderd by our late Senator Nichols [*sic*, Robert C. Nicholas], in 1840 from the House of Marsh & co of Madeira, a high priced wine," while the other "is from a Cargo of a direct Importation into this port [marked with asterisk and noted at bottom of page: "from the House of Blackburn"] . . . and is a more Common wine, at all times, usful in House Keeping." ALS. DLC-HC (DNA, M212, R6).

Judah Touro (1775-1854) was a wealthy New Orleans merchant. See *LHQ* (January, 1928), 11:67-86. For Clay's business with Shepard, see 9:1, 174.

From John R. Thompson, Charlottesville, Va., April 8, 1845. Although "a very young man, whose only claim upon your notice is a passionate admiration for your exalted character," reminds Clay that "I had once or twice, indeed, the honor of being presented to you," most recently "in the month of may last," when "my friend the Hon'ble W.C. Rives, our great Senator, accompanied me to see you at Col. Bradley's in Washington."

Offers his condolences on the outcome of the recent presidential election "as an original Whig, as a native of that [']Gibraltar of Whig principles', *the city* of Richmond, which has always stood up nobly for you, thro' good & evil report, and, where, forty five years ago in the Office of Chancellor [George] Wythe, you laid the imperishable foundations of that greatness, which has since overshadowed the world." Adds: "Your own generous Kentucky has not been more faithful to your fortunes." Had looked forward to the day of Clay's victory "as the day when the people of our beloved country would assert their long violated rights, when the malevolence of a vile herd of defamatory enemies would be silenced forever." Condemns the frauds which "stifled the voice of the people" and were "effected by a motley party of Dorrites [9:715-16] & Agrarians, Mormons [9:881], & Repudiators [9:714, 813-14], the voters of Plaquemine [Roman to Clay, December 2, 1844] & the Outlaws of the Empire Club [Gould to Clay, December 18, 1844]." Blames the opposition party for setting "the plainest provisions of our blessed Constitution . . . at naught, in the passage of the Texas Bill [Clay to Crittenden, February 15, 1844]," and foresees "a dark pall" over the future if "that sacred instrument can be trampled upon by peculation & Cupidity."

Calls to Clay's attention the "patriotic exertions of the women of Virginia, to erect a statue in commemoration of your virtues [French to Clay, February 27, 1845]." Continues: "I was yesterday informed by Mrs. Lucy Barbour, the venerable & distinguished Lady, who gave to the work its first impulse, that success is certain and that next summer the corner stone will be laid. We will erect it upon our Capitol Square in Richmond." ALS. DLC-HC (DNA, M212, R6). Printed in Colton, *Clay Correspondence*, 4:526-27.

The Col. Bradley referred to was possibly William A. Bradley, former mayor of Washington, D.C. James T. White & Co. (eds.), *Notable Names in American History* (Clifton, N.J., 1973).

From Catherine Thorn *et al.*, Troy, N.Y., April 18, 1845. On behalf of "the Whig Ladies of Troy," present Clay with a "testimonial of respect, but we hope you will not measure that respect by the smallness of our gift." Point out "with much pride and pleasure," that "our little City fought nobly for Henry Clay and his principles." Assure him that "to none are your name and fame dearer than to the Whig Women of Troy." LS. DLC-HC (DNA, M212, R6).

Clay replied on May 5, 1845, thanking them for the "neat and chastely tasteful Silver Waiter." Adds that coincidentally another box arrived along with it "containing a pair of beautiful Pitchers presented to us by the Ladies of Norwich, in Connecticut, members of Whig families." Recalls with pleasure the trips he previously made to Troy and appreciates the "confidence manifested in me by the city of Troy, at the Presidential election in November last." Adds that nothing in retirement cheers him more "than the approbation with which I am honored, by so large a portion of your sex." Copy. Printed in Lexington *Observer & Kentucky Reporter*, May 31, 1845.

Clay carried Rensselaer County, N.Y., which includes the city of Troy, by 6,359 votes to Polk's 5,616 and Birney's 191. New York *Daily Herald*, November 22, 1844.

Catherine Thorn was possibly the wife of James Thorn, Troy's mayor in 1862-63. Arthur J. Weise, *Troy's One Hundred Years* (Troy, N.Y., 1891), 326.

From William Newton Mercer, New Orleans, La., April 22, 1845. Expresses with "not the slightest hesitation" his opinion on "a late movement on the part of your friends [Tilford to Clay, February 17, 1845; Clay to Tilford, February 22, 1845; Lawrence to Clay, March 13, 1845]" to pay Clay's debts. Understands that Clay is "somewhat doubtful, whether it would not be more consistent with the independence of your previous life" to "reject the kindly office thus proferred." Believes that "in all ages signal, publick services, have been rewarded by National benefactions." Continues, however, that "if Republicks are ungrateful, it is the more necessary that private individuals should perform the duty neglected by the publick authorities." Asks, moreover, "Would it not be ungracious to repel the friendly hand that is tendered; to mortify those who are warmly attached to you, and to consult—shall I venture on the word?—your *pride*, at the expense of their feelings?" Concludes: "My dear Friend, you must submit, there is no remedy; for, if your suspicions are correct, you cannot overcome the precautions which may have been adopted to guard against this very contingency."

Had hoped to visit the North and "to see some of my ancient friends in the middle states" and "to pass on to Kentucky" to visit Clay, but now offers "to attach myself to you, and to conform to your route and your wishes. An excursion during the summer unattended by care or anxiety, a winter spent in New Orleans, which is a *sine qua non*, and occasional excursions to Cuba and elsewhere, will reinvigorate your health and add years to your life." Asks only "for permission to visit some land which I have in Illinois."

Writes that Gen. [Charles Fenton] Mercer has suggested that "the assent of Texas to an union with us is by no means certain," because some of her principal men, "are opposed to it and that Huston [*sic*, Sam Houston], who is also considered hostile, has the decision in his own hands."

Sends the regards of his daughter Anna ("as is the case with most of her sex, your warm and staunch friend"), as well as some of her friends. ALS. DLC-HC (DNA, M212, R6). Printed in Colton, *Clay Correspondence*, 4:527-28.

On his trip South in the winter of 1845-46, Clay left Ashland on December 18 for Louisville where he embarked on a steamboat for Natchez, arriving there about January 12, 1846, after many delays due to ice on the river. He reached New Orleans on January 19 and remained there until March 22. Traveling to St. Louis by way of Natchez, he left Missouri on April 17 and reached Ashland on April 22. He visited neither Cuba nor Mobile on this trip. See Clay to Lucretia Hart Clay, January 12, 19, 24, 1846, and March 16, 1846; also Clay to LeVert, March 17, 1846; Clay to Mercer, March 23, 1846.

To DUDLEY SELDEN Lexington, April 23, 1845

I received your favor of the 15h. instant. On the subject of the Chesapeak[e] and Ohio Canal, of which it treats, I have always felt a lively interest, and regretted extremely the impediments which have hitherto prevented its completion. I rejoice that the Legislature of Maryland has made provision for the accomplishment of that desirable object, and sincerely hope that it may be attended with full success.[1]

I am not particularly acquainted with the skill which has been exhibited in the management of the Canal, nor with the competency of its present President.[2] Without reference to his qualifications, I should think that, if the Company are determined to make a change of that officer, and could engage the services of the honble R[ichard]. H. Bayard,[3] they would make a great acquisition. I have known this gentleman long and intimately. He may be perfectly relied on for probity, fidelity, and great industry, as well as good judgment and discretion. I have no knowledge whatever of what may be his disposition to embark on such an undertaking. I suppose that he has not much experience in works of this kind, but a man of his ability and indefatigability would soon acquire the requisite practical knowledge.

I observed, with much interest, the Canvass in which you engaged for the Mayoralty of N. York, and the issue of the election.[4] Altho there is some evil in the facility with which foreigners are let in to the enjoyment of our political privileges, indiscriminately, it is local & limited in its operation. Most certainly the naturalized Citizens can accomplish nothing of themselves, and can only exert an influence on our institutions by the co-operation of a very large portion of our Native born Citizens. The formation of a National party, upon the sole ground of an amendment of the law of naturalization,[5] appears to me to be too narrow a basis to uphold any National party. Surely there are other desirable objects of good Government, besides any change that might be made in that law. The Whigs have always suffered from parties having but one object, or a single idea. I do not know how it happens, but such parties in the end, directly or indirectly, have almost always tended to the benefit of our opponents.

Many causes, no doubt, concurred to defeat the Whigs last fall, and the concurrence of all of them was necessary to that result.[6] Among those causes, was the existence of the Native American party.[7] If it had never existed, I believe that the Whigs would have been successful. They were charged by their opponents with being natives, and, crediting this charge, vast numbers of naturalized Citizens, in the interior of the States, who otherwise would have voted with us, cast their votes against us. Whilst in the Cities, many of the Natives voted with the very party which most bitterly denounced them. I know that there were numerous exceptions, many of the Natives who honorably and zealously supported our cause, but they could not control others of their party. The Whigs were placed between two fires; and they lost a great deal more by the imputation of Nativism than they gained from the ranks of the natives.

But I will not dwell longer on this painful subject, which I should not have touched but for your allusion to it.

ALS. KyU. Addressed to Selden at New York City. 1. The legislature of Maryland had passed a bill in March, 1845 providing that the Chesapeake and Ohio Canal Co. could issue $1,700,000 in construction bonds on the mortgage of its revenues when it received guaranties from interested parties for 195,000 tons of trade annually for five years. Walter S. Sanderlin, *The Great National Project, A History of the Chesapeake and Ohio Canal. Johns Hopkins University Studies in Historical and Political Science* (Baltimore, 1946), 64:152. 2. John M. Coale, president 1843-51. *Ibid.*, 304. See also 8:734, 742, 828; 9:497. 3. Bayard did not become president of the canal company. 4. In the New York City mayoral election on April 8, 1845, Democrat William Havemeyer had defeated Whig Dudley Selden as well as Native American, Working Man, and Abolition party candidates. *Niles' Register* (April 12, 1845), 68:96; Holli & Jones, *Biographical Dictionary of American Mayors.* 5. Clay to Ewing, June 19, 1844; Ewing to Clay, June 23, 1844. 6. Clay to Webb, Feb. 29, 1844. 7. Ewing to Clay, June 23, 1844.

To JOHN R. THOMPSON Lexington, April 23, 1845

I duly received your friendly letter[1] and thank you for it. The sentiments which it conveys, your nativity in a City so endeared to me as that of Richmond, and your sterling Whig principles rendered unnecessary any apology for addressing me. Indeed, my dear Sir, in spite of any unfavorable opinion entertained of me in our native State [Virginia], I can never cease to venerate our common mother, and to cherish the most friendly recollection of the many excellent friends, of both sexes, who there honor me with their esteem and confidence.

The result of the Presidential election, so unexpected to us all, would have affected me personally but for a short time, if it had not been for the numerous letters which I received from all quarters, couched in the most touching terms, bewailing the event as a great National calamity. I have in this way been more afflicted, I believe, on account of my friends than by any personal disappointment of my own. I sincerely hope that the consequences of the event may not be as injurious as was anticipated, although I confess I have seen enough, since the 4h. of March, to keep alive my worst apprehensions, to say nothing of the fatal measure of Annexation[2] which preceded it, and which is fairly attributable to the election[.] Without adverting to the character of some of the individuals composing the new Cabinet,[3] or that of many persons recently appointed to public office, the single fact of the recent arrangement of the Senate's Committees[4] proclaims the Nation's degradation.

The unconstitutional manner,[5] more than the simple act, of Annexation ought to fill every enlightened patriot with alarm and apprehension. It will, I fear, totally change the peaceful character of the Republic, converting us in the end into a warlike, conquering Nation, until we raise up some Military Chieftain who will conquer us all. I should not be surprized, even during the short remnant of my days, to witness an insurrection in Canada—a declaration of Independence—Recognition by the U. States—and finally a resolution of Annexation passed by a majority of the two houses of Congress! After what has passed, what opposition could be made to such a resolution? And the annexation of Canada may be followed by that of California—Mexico—Cuba &c &c until the identity of the Nation is lost in dilution.

But I will not dwell on these painful reflection[s].

I have seen, with feelings of lively gratitude, the movement of the Ladies of Va.[6] to which you allude. As it is their own kind affair, I have supposed it my duty to remain a passive spectator. To day I had the pleasure of a short visit from Miss Taliaferro,[7] the grand daughter of my good friend Mrs. [Lucy] Barbour, who gave the first impulse to that movement.

I have read, with much satisfaction, the copy of the verses[8] which you sent me, and which possess a merit far beyond the ordinary compositions for such occasions as called them forth. Accept my thanks for the flattering reference to my name.

ALS. NN. Addressed to Thompson at the University of Virginia. 1. Thompson to Clay, April 8, 1845. 2. Clay to Crittenden, Feb. 15, 1844. 3. Polk's cabinet consisted of James Buchanan (State); Robert J. Walker (Treasury); William L. Marcy (War); John Y. Mason (Attorney General); Cave Johnson (Postmaster General); George Bancroft (Navy). Joseph N. Kane, *Facts About the Presidents* (New York, 1974), 76. 4. Clay to Berrien, March 19, 1845. 5. Reference is to use of a joint resolution passed by a simple majority in both houses of Congress rather than Senate ratification of the treaty which requires a 2/3 majority. 6. French to Clay, Feb. 27, 1845. 7. Lucy, daughter of James and Lucy Barbour, married John S. Taliaferro and had four daughters—Lucy, Elizabeth, Lindsey, and Cornelia—and two sons. It has not been determined which of these daughters visited Clay. Neil W. Sherman, *Taliaferro-Toliver Family Records* (Peoria, Ill., 1960), 29; Raleigh Green, *Genealogical and Historical Notes on Culpeper County, Virginia* (Culpeper, Va., 1900), 53. 8. Not found, but enclosed with letter of Thompson to Clay, April 8, 1845.

To Central Clay Committee of the City of New York, April 25, 1845. Reports that Willis Green has delivered to him "the address which you did me the honor to make on the 4th March last, enrolled on parchment, and enclosed in a silver case." Notes that "I received it with emotions of grateful sensibility," and continues: "Waiving all considerations of the causes and consequences of the recent presidential election, of which it treats, as a past and irrevocable event, on which I have neither inclination, nor would it perhaps be fitting for me to expiate, I take pleasure in expressing my profound and grateful sense of the great, persevering and efficient labors of the Central Clay committee of the city of New York during the canvass which preceded the election." Feels "high and lasting obligations" to those who displayed such "ardent attachment and generous confidence towards me" during the campaign.

States: "My situation is peculiar. I have been in spite of unexpected discomfiture, the object of honors and of compliments usually rendered only to those who are successful and victorious in the great enterprises of mankind;—to say nothing of other demonstrations, the letters, the addresses . . . which I have received since the election from every quarter. . . . I have been quite as much if not more affected by them than I was by any disappointment or personal interest of my own in the event of the contest." Copy. Printed in *Niles' Register* (May 17, 1845), 68:162. Addressed to James K. Wood, Benjamin Drake *et al.* Benjamin Drake was a physician at 35 Bowery, New York City. Wood has not been identified. Doggett, *New-York City Directory for 1844 & 1845.* See also Central Clay Committee of the City of New York to Clay, March 4, 1845.

To HENRY CLAY, JR. Lexington, April 27, 1845

I received your letter, transmitting a check for your part of the interest on the [John J.] Astor debt.[1] I had previously sent the interest, and written to Mr. A. requesting a further indulgence of two years, with an assurance that it was the last positively that I would ask. There has not yet been time enough to receive an answer.

I saw your letter in the Journal about the representative in Congress from your district, and think that it was very properly and happily composed.[2] From what I have seen I suppose Mr. [James M.] Bullock of Shelby will be the Candidate.[3]

Poor John [Morrison Clay] continues to be a source of great affliction to us.[4] The most distressing circumstance in his case is that his reason is sufficient to enable him to comprehend his situation, and to feel his confinement with the keenest pain, and yet is not enough to make it, perhaps, prudent or safe to liberate him. If he were unconscious, we should be less afflicted. That is the condition of his unfortunate brother [Theodore W. Clay], and I fear will ultimately become his own.[5]

I am inclined to make one more experiment with John here; and if he exhibit again such wildness of conduct as he did, when we were compelled to send him to the Hospital, to return him to it finally, or at least until he is unquestionably restored to his mind, if it should please God ever to restore him.

Your children[6] are doing very well, and I should reject almost any arrangement by which they should be taken away from their present eligible situation. But if carried to Louisville they would no where there be under better care than that of Mrs. [Nannette Price] Smith and yourself.

I wish you would say to Martin Duralde [III] that I received his letter, and hope that his opinion of his condition is worse than the actual state of his health authorizes. We shall be glad to see him here whenever he can come.

ALS. Henry Clay Memorial Foundation, Lexington, Ky. Addressed to Henry Clay, Jr., in Louisville, Ky. 1. Clay to Henry Clay, Jr., April 2, 1845; Astor to Clay, April 28, 1845. 2. Clay to Henry Clay, Jr., March 17, 1845. 3. James M. Bullock of Shelby County, who had served in the lower house of the state legislature and as Kentucky's secretary of state, announced his candidacy for election to Congress. The Whig party, however, nominated William P. Thomasson for the seat. See Clay to Henry Clay, Jr., March 17, 1845. For Bullock, see Lewis & Richard H. Collins, *History of Kentucky*, 2 vols. (Cynthiana, Ky., 1874; reprint, 1966), 2:709. 4. Clay to Henry Clay, Jr., April 2, 1845; Clay to Henry Clay, Jr., April 5, 1845. 5. See 8:442-43. 6. Anne and Thomas J. were in Lexington; Henry III in Louisville.

From William B. Astor, New York City, N.Y., April 28, 1845. Informs Clay that "Messrs. Tucker Cooper & Co have already paid the amt: of interest due 1st May on your bond." Adds that his father, John Jacob Astor, "assents to your request to extend the payment of your bond for two years; unless you should find convenient to reduce the amount of it by the payment of $5000 which he would prefer." ALS. DLC-TJC (DNA, M212, R10).

A receipt from John Jacob Astor for $450 "by the Hands of Messrs. Tucker Cooper & Co" was sent to Clay on April 28, 1845. DS. DLC-TJC (DNA, M212, R19).

A second receipt notes that on May 2, 1845, Astor received from "John Tilford Esqr. two drafts amounting to $1500 say Fifteen Hundred dollars" to be applied to Clay's "debtors bond to me." DS. DLC-HC (DNA, M212, R6).

On May 9, 1845, John Tilford of the Northern Bank of Kentucky informed Clay that he had received "Some days ago . . . from friends of yours" the $1500, which he had then forwarded to Astor. Encloses Astor's receipt, most likely that noted immediately above, to Clay. ALS. *Ibid.*

A personal note from John Jacob Astor followed, dated May 9, 1845, acknowledging receipt "on the 26th ulto: from Mr. John Tilford of the Northern Bank of Kentucky dfts for $1500." LS, signed by William B. Astor for John Jacob Astor. *Ibid.* Letter is postmarked from New York City.

On October 30, 1845, William B. Astor acknowledged receipt of $364.18 "which pays the interest say $359 58/100 due on your bond the 1st proxo & leaves a balance of $4 60/100 to your credit." ALS. *Ibid.* See also Clay to Henry Clay, Jr., April 2, 1845.

Clay received a note from William B. Astor, dated February 25, 1846, acknowledging a payment of $700 "to be applied toward payment of your bond to my father." ANS. MH.

Clay received another note from W.B. Astor, dated February 27, 1846, acknowledging receipt of another payment of $1,000. ANS. DLC-TJC (DNA, M212, R10).

To DAVID FRANCIS BACON Lexington, April 28, 1845

Genl. Willis Green delivered to me the address of the 4h. March last from the Central Comee. of N.Y. a few days ago.[1] I doubted whether an answer was expected from me or not; but I concluded to send a brief acknowledgment of its receipt,[2] which accompanies this letter.

To you, my dear Sir, who I conjecture to be the Author of the Address, I always intended to express my very great obligations for the ability, eloquence, and ardent attachment to me, which it manifests. Indeed, I should not half express my feelings, if I did not convey to you my cordial thanks for the many and signal proofs you have constantly given of your friendship to me.[3] I regret that you have not been engaged in a better, or at least more successful, cause. That it was not successful was not owing to any want of powerful, persevering and well-directed exertion on your part.

May you long live to enjoy health happiness & prosperity; and live too to see ultimately triumphant those principles which you have labored, with such patriotic zeal, and such ardent devotion, to establish for the benefit of our Country.

ALS. CtY. Addressed to Bacon at New York City. Letter marked "(Private)." 1. Central Clay Committee of the City of New York, March 4, 1845. 2. Clay to Central Clay Committee of the City of New York, April 25, 1845. 3. Bacon was secretary of the committee. See above; see also 9:866-68, 872; Clay to Bacon, Jan. 6, 1845.

To CALVIN COLTON Lexington, April 28, 1845

I duly received your letter of the 17th instant. Compression is your forte in composition; but is there not danger of your elaborating too much the old calumny of bargain, etc.?[1] The division you propose of the subject appears to me to be natural and suitable[.]

When I meet Governor [Robert P.] Letcher I will endeavor to prevail on him to give the certificate you desire.[2] He may perhaps consent to furnish it to be used only in the contingency of his death. If living, and the statement of Mr. B.'s[3] agency should be denied, appealed to as he is as a witness, I am sure he would be willing to testify. You will find Mr. [James] Buchanan's speech, what you want, in Gales and Seaton's Congressional Debates, although I can not refer you to the page.[4] Governor Letcher could refer to it.

It would be well not to publish Colonel Sloan's [*sic*, John Sloane] statement until I hear from Mr. [James] Reilly, the Texan Chargé des Affaires. I endeavored, through him, to procure from General [Sam] Houston a confirmation of Colonel Sloan's testimony, and have not yet learned what success attended the effort.[5]

Mr. [John Q.] Adams' appeal to heaven was at Maysville,[6] I think in November 1843, on the occasion of his visit to Cincinnati. He made a very strong defense of me in 1829[7] in answer to some address from New Jersey,[8] which you will no doubt be able to find in Niles' Register.

Copy. Printed in Colton, *Clay Correspondence*, 4:528-29. 1. For the corrupt bargain, see index entries 7:660; 8:911; 9:934. 2. Clay to Sloane, May 21, 1844. 3. James Buchanan. See Letcher to Clay, July 6, 1844. 4. When Buchanan spoke on Thomas Chilton's retrenchment resolution on Feb. 4, 1828, he alluded to the corrupt bargain. His speech is in *Register of Debates*, 20 Cong., 1 Sess., 1360-78 and Moore, *Works of James Buchanan*, 1:286-312, espec. 289-91. Writing to Letcher on June 27, 1844, Buchanan asserted that in this speech he had done Clay "ample justice but no more than justice." Moore, *Works of James Buchanan*, 6:59. 5. Sloane to Clay, May 9, 1844; Clay to Sloane, May 21, 1844; Letcher to Clay, July 6, 1844. 6. See

9:891. 7. See 8:24-25. 8. Adams's defense of Clay was published in *Niles' Register* (April 11, 1829), 8:1-2. It was given in response to a letter from Robert Lee *et al.*, a committee in Rahway, N.J., which represented Essex and Middlesex counties. The committee had also written Clay. For that letter and Clay's response see 8:1-2.

To JOHN L. LAWRENCE Lexington, April 30, 1845

I received your letter of the 21st. inst,[1] without the newspapers to which it refers. But I received a newspaper from Baltimore containing what occurred in the British House of Commons on the Oregon subject.[2] It excites no surprize with me. I have all along apprehended that serious difficulty would arise out of the headlong course of our Government in respect to Oregon, at the very moment when a negotiation is in progress with Great Britain for the settlement of the dispute about that Territory.[3] It has ever appeared to me, that it was altogether premature to attempt a settlement on the Pacific Ocean, and assume the consequent duty of its defence, by the requisite military and naval means, at a time when we have quite enough to defend the coasts of the Atlantic Ocean and the Gulph of Mexico. True wisdom seemed to me to point out, that, whilst we sustained and upheld all our territorial rights, beyond the Rocky Mountains, we should direct our present exertions to the increase of population and strength, and the improvement and development of our resources, on this side of those mountains.

But, if it were deemed expedient, at this time, to settle Oregon, it was highly indiscreet to attempt it, without regard to the feelings or rights of Great Britain, at the very moment of the pendency of a negotiation.

I am very apprehensive, my dear sir, that we are shortly to have war with both England and Mexico. The party in power has not the moral courage to do right. [James K.] Polk and [James] Buchanan would never dare settle the question of Oregon without a total surrender on the part of Great Britain of all her pretensions and she is not going to yield them.[4] Besides, she sees in that most fatal and unconstitutional precedent, of the annexation of Texas,[5] dangers to all her American possessions ahead, which she may perhaps think it is best at once to meet. She may also deem it expedient to secure the alliance of Mexico. Should this latter power take the prudent course, which has been intimated, of excluding from her ports our commerce and navigation and of terminating all diplomatic intercourse with us, she will be in a position prepared to take advantage of any circumstances when the measure of annexation shall be consummated. That may take place at the next session of Congress and at the same time the crisis of our difficulties with England will arise.

Mexico, single handed, could not affect us much by any belligerent operations. Alone and unaided she will probably not attempt, if she acts wisely, any active hostile operations.[6] But the non intercourse, to which she has a right to resort, without its being any just cause of war to us, will affect most injuriously our commerce and manufactures, to say nothing of the diversion which it will occasion of the precious metals from this Country. But Mexico, acting as an ally of Great Britain, is capable of inflicting upon us much mischief, especially on the Pacific. Together they would speedily achieve the conquest of the whole of Oregon. We should have, in the event of war, to seek indemnity in Canada and what that would cost us, in blood and treasure, we may calculate from our experience during the last war and from the present ample state of defence which exists in Canada.

Upon the whole, my dear sir, whilst I sincerely hope for the preservation of peace, I confess that, looking at the temper which prevails in England, alike in the ministry and the opposition, and the temper and the men in power in this country, I am forced to believe that there is strong probability of war.

Lord Russell[7] appears to have went somewhat at large into the British title to Oregon, and if his speech should be reported in full I should be very glad, if you get hold of it, if you would send it to me.

P.S. I have dictated the above to an Amanuensis.

LS, postscript in Clay's hand. ViU. Letter marked "(Private)." Addressed to Lawrence at New York City. 1. Letter not found, but see below. 2. On April 4, 1845, both houses of parliament debated the Oregon question in response to Polk's inaugural message. *Niles' Register* (April 26, 1845), 68:113. For Polk's message in which he declared that the U.S. title to Oregon was "clear and unquestionable," see James D. Richardson (comp.), *A Compilation of the Messages and Papers of the Presidents 1789-1902*, 10 vols. plus supplements (Washington, D.C., 1904), 4:373-82, espec. 381. 3. See 9:829. 4. *Ibid.* 5. Clay to Crittenden, Feb. 15, 1844. 6. In fact, the U.S. went to war with Mexico on May 13, 1846, and the treaty ending the war was ratified by the U.S. on March 13, 1848, with official exchange of ratifications taking place on May 30, 1848. For more on the Mexican War, see K. Jack Bauer, *The Mexican War, 1846-1848* (New York, 1974); Otis A. Singletary, *The Mexican War* (Chicago, 1960); Justin H. Smith, *The Annexation of Texas* (New York, 1941); Rives, *The United States and Mexico.* 7. Lord John Russell, first Earl Russell (see *DNB*), had strongly disputed the American claim to the Oregon Territory and had asserted that England's stronger claim would be upheld. See *Niles' Register* (April 26, 1845), 68:114.

To HENRY CLAY, JR. Lexington, May 6, 1845

Mr. [John J.] Astor accedes to the postponement of the residue of our debt to him for another period of two years, under the assurance which I have given him that it is the last that will be asked.[1]

Since I last wrote to you, I have again taken John [Morrison Clay] out of the Hospital, and he has been calm and rational.[2] I pray to God that he may so continue.

I have begun today an improvement in my house by pulling down the Eastern projection in the dining room, with the view of rebuilding & carrying it up to the roof. I think it will add to our comfort.

I have received a letter from the French Minister.[3] The order could not be found at Paris for the occupation of a part of the plantation of Claude Villars,[4] but they found an order, dated in Jany 1760, for the fortification of N. Orleans, of which however they omitted to send me a Copy, which I have now requested.

Your children are well.[5]

ALS. Henry Clay Memorial Foundation, Lexington, Ky. 1. Astor to Clay, April 28, 1845. 2. Clay to Henry Clay, Jr., April 5, 1845. 3. Alphonse J.Y. Pageot. 4. Clay to Henry Clay, Jr., March 17, 1845. See also Clay to Wilde, May 10, 1845. 5. Thomas Julian and Anne.

To JOHN JAY[1] Lexington, May 7, 1845

I received your letter,[2] transmitting a Copy of a Report of a Committee of the New York Historical Society,[3] upon the subject of the expediency of adopting a National name for the Country and the People of the United States; and I have attentively perused it. In compliance with your request, I have now the pleasure briefly to express the views of the question which strike me.

There is undoubtedly some inconvenience in the want of a more specific and exclusive name, descriptive of the Country and the inhabitants of this portion of the new world; but I respectfully think the inconvenience is exaggerated. If happily our present Union should continue unbroken, I believe that, in process of time, in consequence of the greater power, population & influence of the U. States than any other Nation, either in North or South America, the United States, will be empatically called and known as "The United States," and the inhabitants as "Americans". Whilst the other Confederacies of States will be called and described as the United States *of Mexico* &c, and their inhabitants, Mexicans, Peruvians &c.

If the great calamity of a dissolution of the Union should befal us, no common name that we might adopt would, in that direful contingency, be applicable to any of its dissevered parts.

There would be much if not insuperable difficulty in the adoption of any new name. Besides others, I am not sure that it would not excite with some frightful apprehension of a consolodation.

Between the proposed names of "Alleghania" and "Washington," I should think the latter decidedly preferable. And I should be glad, that it might be adopted by universal consent, that our Country should ever remain one and indivisible, that its inhabitants, to the latest posterity, should be called Washingtonians, and that they should ever fondly cherish both the name and the virtues of the Father of his Country.

ALS. NHi. Addressed to Jay at "Historical Rooms City of New York." 1. For John Jay (1817-94), grandson of Chief Justice John Jay and a New York City lawyer, see *DAB*. 2. Not found. 3. Washington Irving had first proposed changing the name of the United States to "Allegania." This was adopted by the New-York Historical Society and promoted in its report in the spring of 1845. *Niles' Register* (April 12, 1845), 68:88. This proposal was ultimately dropped. Louisville *Daily Journal*, May 21, 1845.

To Richard Henry Wilde, New Orleans, La., May 10, 1845. Informs him that "I have entered into an agreement with the Heirs of Dubreuil [Clay to Henry Clay, Jr., March 17, 1845] for the recovery of a property of large value in the lowest Faubourg of N. Orleans," although he admits that "My confidence on the merits of the claim is not absolute." Since "the claim includes the Mint. . . . The inferior Court has decided against the jurisdiction upon the ground, I understand, that the U.S. are not suable." Hopes that the Louisiana Supreme Court will hear the case, but has not been advised "whether it will be tried at the present term of that Court."

Desires "to obtain a copy of a document which *may* be very important" and has "engaged the French minister [Alphonse J.Y. Pageot] to write to France" for it. Has heard, however, that, while "the particular document desired would not be found . . . another was found for the erection of a fosse around the City of N. Orleans for its defense, dated in 1760."

Informs Wilde that "in the conduct of the case my son Henry [Clay, Jr.], Mr. [Samuel] Judah of Vincennes and Mr. [Gustavus] Schmidt of the N. Orleans bar. . . . were to share equally in expence & in profits." Invites Wilde "to look carefully into the case, and if you think well of it I would propose to divide equally with you my share in expense & profit. I think my son, and, perhaps, the other gentlemen, would agree, if it be your pleasure, to make you equally interested with us all." ALS. CSmH.

To LORD ASHBURTON [ALEXANDER BARING] Lexington, May 14, 1845

[Introduces some citizens from Lexington who are visiting London. Continues:]

Your Lordship happily contributed to the preservation of the peace between our respective Countries by a treaty,[1] the best eulogy of which is that it was heartily approved by vast majorities in both Nations, and only condemned by a few in each, for directly opposite reasons. If the tone of the organs of the two Governments, in regard to Oregon, be not deceptive, another occasion is nigh at hand for the pacific interposition of your Lordship.[2] I am sure that I shall have your concurrence, in the wish, that some means may be devised for averting the calamity of a War between the U. States and G. Britain, respecting a territory so distant from them both, and at present so unimportant to either. . . .

ALS. KyLoF. Addressed to Ashburton in London. 1. See 9:405. 2. Ashburton was not one of the negotiators of the Oregon settlement. See 9:828-29.

To Octavia Walton LeVert, Mobile, Ala., May 20, 1845. Expresses his disappointment "in being unable to go to N. Orleans during the last winter" and hopes she appreciates "what a sacrifice I made in being deprived of the pleasure of meeting you." Intends to pass "next winter, if God spare me . . . with my good friend Dr. [William N.] Mercer [Mercer to Clay, April 22, 1845], and we purpose going to Cuba, Texas &c, one or all of them." Would be "delighted" if "we could have the happiness of the company of Dr. [Henry] Levert and yourself!" Fears, however, that the doctor's "slavish profession will not allow him to go."

Refuses to discuss recent events "of a public nature. . . . But there is one of a private character, respecting which your friendship for me entitles you to a fuller explanation than you can derive from the papers." Explains: "It is true that I became involved to the amount of about $25.000 in consequence of responsibility for one of my sons. But my outlands alone, without touching this valuable estate, (which with its slaves &c is worth about $70.000) or other property, were sufficient to pay the debt, if a sale of them could be effected at a fair price. A schedule of them was made and transmitted to some of the Cities, and they were offered for sale. But the moment that my friends were aware of this embarrassment, they proceeded in a quiet manner, without any parade, to raise the requisite sum for my relief. Having ascertained my creditors, they addressed themselves directly to them, took up my notes and caused them to be sent to me cancelled. Nothing could exceed the delicacy and respect to my feelings with which the whole business was conducted. The names even of my generous benefactors have not been communicated to me, and I am left only to conjecture. The first information which I generally got of the movement was to receive one of my cancelled notes [Tilford to Clay, February 17, 1845]." Adds: "I am thus left, my dear friend, in possession of this estate unencumbered . . . and free from all pecuniary care."

Regrets that she is "confined to Mobile—a delightful City in the winter, but I apprehend quite unhealthy in the summer and autumn." Had hoped "to meet you somewhere this summer," but "Except for a short excursion of business to St. Louis and Alton [Illinois], which I am about to make, I shall not be much absent from home until the winter, unless possibly I may make a flying trip to some of the Springs." ALS. KyU.

To DANIEL M. BARRINGER[1] Lexington, May 23, 1845

I received your letter respecting the claim of the Heirs of Col. R[ichard]. Henderson[2] to lands in K[entucky]. and take pleasure in answering it; but I possess only very general information on the subject. What I know is, that the State of Virginia, in consideration of the purchase from the Indians of a large part of the present State of Kentucky by Richard Henderson & Co. granted to them 200.000 acres of land lying at the mouth of Green river, in the County of Henderson. The land is now held by persons, deriving title from the different members of the Company. It was divided between them, and the part of each member assigned to him by miles & bound[ary]. My wifes father [Thomas Hart] was interested in the Company and received and sold his share. I am not able to say what was done with that of Richard Henderson; but, if it were never sold by himself or his heirs, (which however I apprehend was done) I presume that it might be now recovered. Their best course to pursue would be for one of them to proceed to the town of Henderson, situated on the Ohio river 150 miles below Louisville, and there investigate the state of the title. I imagine that the records in Henderson (the seat of justice of Henderson County) will exhibit the true condition of the title.

A similar grant of 200.000 acres of land, lying in Powells Valley, was made by the State of No. Carolina to R. Henderson &Co for their purchase of a large part of the present State of Tennessee. This land was also divided between the members of the Company, and has been sold out by some if not all of them.

The Company was not very fortunate in the selection of land which it made; but it is worth looking after.

As you wrote at the instance of the Grandchildren of Col. R. Henderson, I would suggest the propriety of their ascertaining whether their grandfather or his heirs did not sell their interests in the above grants.

The land lies 200 miles distant from me.

There were various persons in N. Carolina interested in the grants besides Col. H. Among them, I think were a Mr. Alvin [*sic*][3] and a Mr. Bullock.[4] [P.S.] 24 May. Since I wrote the foregoing I have seen Col Alvis,[5] who lives on the grant of R.H. & Co. He tells me that Col. H. or his heirs long ago sold his interest in the grant.

ALS. NcU. 1. For Barringer, a congressman from North Carolina, see *BDAC* and *DAB*. 2. For Richard Henderson and his land speculations, see *DAB* and Thomas D. Clark, *A History of Kentucky* (Lexington, 1954), 41-45. 3. Walter Alves (or Alvis) was one of the signers of the 1797 ordinance of Richard Henderson & Co. which established the town of Henderson, Ky. Edmund L. Starling, *History of Henderson County, Kentucky* . . . (Henderson, Ky., 1887), 801-2. 4. Probably Leonard H. Bullock who helped negotiate the treaty by which Richard Henderson & Co. acquired the land from the Cherokees. See *NCAB*, 2:496. 5. One of Walter Alves's sons—William J., James, Robert, Haywood, or Walter. *Ibid.*, 266.

From M[ary] MacGregor, New York City, May 29, 1845. Extends belated thanks for Clay's autograph: "*Ordinarily*, I consider a favor of that sort, as balanced, by the solicitation which procures it: but in the present instance, I am happy and proud to acknowledge the weight of an obligation."

Compares her feelings about Clay's defeat, "the great shock that so unexpectedly struck our beloved Country in November last," to "the first paroxisms of private grief" when "tears cannot flow, and scarcely sighs escape." Adds: "Expectations of national prosperity were crushed; and Hope, veiled in grief, became the companion of Despair."

Hopes that with the passage of "time, which usually blunts the edge of every misfortune," he can "contemplate the National calamity with more composure than at first." Was permitted by "My friend and neighbor, Mr. [Theodore] Frelinghuysen" to read "an interesting letter which he had recieved from you" just after the election. Relates that Frelinghuysen's "chief regret, was not on his own account, but on that of the Country, which would thereby be deprived of the wisdom & policy of an administration which would have been second only, to that of Washington's." Adds: "Could but the pen of any one of your many friends have been transformed into the wand of Aladdin, how quickly had every ill judged, fraudelent vote, been converted into a righteous and legal one, thereby securing to our noble Republic, that blessing which her pride had coveted—her exigencies demanded—and which Justice would have sanctioned with a loud Amen." ALS. DLC-HC (DNA, M212, R6).

M. MacGregor was Mary MacGregor, widow of John MacGregor of 8 Washington Square, New York City. Information supplied by New York Public Library.

From Wade Hampton, Columbia, S.C., June 3, 1845. Presents Clay with "Margaret Woods, the Bay Filly you saw in my stables, by Priam out of Maria West." Assures Clay that "To me she is of but little value, having her dam still breeding, her half sister Fanny, besides others of the same family." Adds: "She was foaled in 1840; at 3 yrs old she won the Trial stakes at Nashville . . . a very promising filly, but . . . she was utterly ruined by the Trip. She has been put to Herald, & I hope may prove in foal." ALS. Josephine Simpson Collection, Lexington, Ky.

When Clay obtained Margaret Woods, she was in foal to Herald and subsequently produced Heraldry at Ashland. John Hervey, *Racing in America*, 3 vols. (New York, 1844), 2:45.

To John F.H. Claiborne, New Orleans, La., June 9, 1845. States that "about the period when I last heard from you, and before the letter which I addressed to Mr. [George] P[rentice]. had reached him, the [Louisville *Daily*] Journal contained some paragraphs attacking you with great personality. After Mr. P. received my letter, he informed me that he would conform to the request which I had addressed to him, and I have not since observed that you have been the object of any animadversions in the Journal." ALS. DLC-HC (DNA, M212, R6). Addressed to Claiborne at New Orleans.

For John F.H. Claiborne, former Mississippi congressman and at this time a newspaper editor in New Orleans, see *DAB*. The Louisville *Daily Journal* had assailed him as a man guilty "of seduction, forgery, and larceny." See Louisville *Daily Journal*, April 1, 17, 18, 1845.

To JOSEPH MERREFIELD[1] Lexington, June 14, 1845

Absence from home has delayed my acknoweldging the Receipt of your letter, and tendering my thanks for the friendly Sentiments towards me, which it contains.—Acquiescing as I have done, with the Result of the late Presidential Election,[2] I am entirely reconciled to the retirement from the Cares and responsibility of public life, which was its Consequence to me. I Sincerely hope that the honor and the welfare of the Country may be Secure under the direction of those, who have been appointed to take care of them. And whether I ever emerge from this retirement or not (I think it improbable that I ever shall) I Shall never cease to cherish fervent hopes and wishes for the glory and prosperity of our Confederacy.

Copy, enclosed in a letter from Joseph Merrefield to Carl Schurz, August 29, 1885. DLC-Carl Schurz Papers (DNA, M212, R22). Letter marked "(Private)." 1. Merrefield, a wealthy Quaker merchant, moved from Philadelphia to Baltimore in 1870 when he was elected to the board of Johns Hopkins Hospital. Related by marriage to Johns Hopkins, he subsequently became treasurer of the hospital. He continued his mercantile endeavors in Baltimore and became a noted philanthropist, especially for his support of Boy's Home and the Association for the Improvement of the Condition of the Poor. Alan M. Chesney, *The Johns Hopkins Hospital and The Johns Hopkins University School of Medicine*, 3 vols. (Baltimore, 1943, 1958, 1963), 1:10, 143; 2:331. Information courtesy of James K. Stimpert, Eisenhower Library, Johns Hopkins University. 2. Clay to Webb, Feb. 29, 1844.

To HENRY CLAY, JR. Lexington, June 21, 1845

I recd your letter transmitting the discount I paid on the discount of your notes at the Banks,[1] which was all right.

My health is not entirely restored, and that of your mother [Lucretia Hart Clay] has not been good, but she is better.

The rest of the families here are well.

I am daily occupied in sitting for my portrait to Mr. [George] Healy—a most unpleasant occupation, altho' he seems to be an artiste of real talent.[2]

Our love to your children.

ALS. Henry Clay Memorial Foundation, Lexington, Ky. Letter addressed to Henry Clay, Jr., at Louisville, Ky. 1. On June 11, 1845, Clay had written to Henry Clay, Jr., acknowledging receipt of "two of your notes, both of which have been discounted." Suggests he make "a partial paymt. to the N[orthern]. Bank [of Kentucky], when your note becomes mature there," in hopes that "it will continue the rest of it." Reports he has paid "$11 toward the discount of the Branch, the residue of $1:40 stood there to your credit," and "shall advance the discount at the other Bank, when due." *Ibid.* 2. This Healy portrait of Clay is in the National Portrait Gallery, Washington, D.C. For Healy, see *DAB*.

To [ROBERT C.] WINTHROP[1] Lexington, June 26, 1845

I recd. your friendly letter transmitting an invitation from the Boston Lyceum[2] to deliver next autumn its annual lecture, and return an answer enclosed. I am sorry that I could not accept it. I purpose next winter, with the double view of business and to enjoy a Southern winter, to go to N. Orleans. If I were to go to Boston, it would have the effect either of preventing my going to N.O. or of obliging me to be much longer absent from home than I ought or wish to be. Frankly too, I must say to you, that I have no taste, perhaps no qualification, for these public literary discourses. I have declined hundreds of applications, and if I were to engage in this new and untried career, I do not know how I should discriminate or where stop.

Do me the favor to present my affectionate regards to our good friend Mr. Abbott Lawrence,[3] and say to him that he and other friends would form a much [more] powerful motive to me to visit Boston than the eclat of a public discourse.

ALS. MHi. Letter marked "(Private)." 1. Addressed only to "The Honorable Mr Winthrop"; it is probably Robert C. Winthrop, a Whig friend of Clay's. 2. Letter not found. The Boston Lyceum was founded in 1829 to provide lectures, dramatic performances, debates, etc. to the community. Carl Bode, *The American Lyceum, Town Meeting of the Mind* (New York, 1956), 50. 3. Lawrence to Clay, March 13, 1845; Clay to Lawrence, March 20, 1845.

To COURTLANDT S. PALMER[1] Lexington, June 27, 1845

I am greatly obliged by the friendly expressions towards me contained in your letter,[2] and should be glad to deliver a walking cane, produced on this farm [Ashland], according to your request, to any person who would call and receive it for you. I am not sufficiently acquainted with any safe mode by which I could send it. If it were forwarded by any of the ordinary channels of commerce, I should think that there would be ten chances to one against its safely reaching its destination.

If you persist therefore in desiring such an article, I must request you to designate some person to receive it here.

ALS. Courtesy of J. Winston Coleman, Lexington, Ky. Letter addressed to Palmer in care of N.W. Easton, New York City. 1. For Palmer, one of the wealthiest businessmen in New York City, see *CAB*. 2. Not found.

To Henry Clay, Jr., Louisville, Ky., July 2, 1845. Reminds him that "I had engaged Mr [Richard H.] Wilde . . . in the case of Dubreuils heirs [Clay to Henry Clay, Jr., March 17, 1845]." Has learned that the Louisiana "Supreme Court had decided the question in our favor" concerning "the exception to the jurisdiction." Asks him to "write to Judge [Thomas] Bishop at Vincennes" in preparation for the trial. Needs to prove especially "the heirship, and the locality of the ground." Stresses the importance of acquiring "the right of [Gilbert de] St Maxent's heirs . . . for 3 or four thousand dollars." Adds: "Perhaps we may be able to get the Heirs of Dubreuil to give the heirs of St Maxent some 10.15 or 20 thousand dollars, in the contingency of success." Comments that Samuel Judah, another attorney on the case, "has done nothing," and wishes "we could, get rid of him." Hopes to obtain a "Copy of the order about the Fortifications" from "the French Minister at Washn. [Alphonse J.Y. Pageot]" to help their case. ALS. Henry Clay Memorial Foundation, Lexington, Ky.

Gilbert Antoine de St. Maxent, a wealthy Louisiana merchant, had been involved in the 1768 revolt against Spain. Charles Gayarré, *History of Louisiana*, 4 vols. (New York, 1854), 3:98; *Louisiana Studies* (Fall, 1986), 27:407-37.

Thomas Bishop was also a lumber dealer and a member of the board of trustees of Vincennes University. *RKHS*, 67:83.

To HENRY CLAY ________[1] Lexington, July 7, 1845

Your parents have done me the honor to give my name to you. On that account, and at the request of your good mother, I address this note, which she wishes to preserve for your perusal, when, by the lapse of time, you shall have attained an age that will enable you to comprehend and appreciate its friendly purport.

Your parents entertain fond hopes of you, and you ought to strive not to disappoint them. They wish you to be good, respected, eminent. You can realize all their most sanguine hopes, if you firmly resolve to do so, by judicious employment of your time and your faculties. Shun bad company, and all dissipation, its inevitable consequence. Study diligently and perseveringly. You will be surprised at the ease with which you will master branches of knowledge, which on a first view, will frighten you. Make honor, probity, truth, and principle your invariable guide. Be obedient, and always affectionately respectful to your parents. Assiduously cultivate virtue and religion, the surest guarantee of happiness both here and hereafter. In your intercourse with your fellow beings, be firm, but at the same time, bland, courteous, and obliging. Recognize at all times the paramount right of your

Country to your most devoted services, whether she treats you ill or well, and never let selfish views or interests predominate over the duties of patriotism.

By regulating yourself according to these rules, you may become respected and great, be an ornament to your Country, and a blessing to your parents. That such may be your destiny is the sincere wish of their and your friend.

Copy. Printed in Morton and Griswold's *Western Farmer's Almanac*, Louisville, Ky., 1859, p.5. 1. Addressed to "My dear little Namesake."

To F.S. Pecantet [?], Nashville, Tenn., July 9, 1845. Thanks him for his "generous sentiments of respect and admiration" but refuses "to make any reproaches on account of the issue of a popular election with which my name was associated." Remains grateful "for the many proofs which my Country has given me of its esteem . . . and to be satisfied with the consciousness of having, in all situations, faithfully sought to perform my public duty." Adds: "Should History deign to notice me, I have no fears that it will pronounce a different judgment." ALS. THi.

To HENRY CLAY, JR. Lexington, July 10, 1845

I received your letter of the 6h. and was happy to observe that your spirits were better. The contract you have made with Mr. Sutton may turn out well, if you can realize the price you have stipulated to give him, or thereabouts. I have *hopes* that prices of those articles may rise in the fall.[1] I think you would do well to ship to Payne & Harrison. You run a risk of low water for the last of your receipts of those articles.

I shall be happy to continue to endorse for you, and reassure you that you labored altogether under a misconception as to my disposition on that subject.

We should be glad to see you and your children here. If you cannot all come, had you not better let Henry [Clay III] come?

We have now fine prospects of good crops.

ALS. Henry Clay Memorial Foundation, Lexington, Ky. 1. Reference obscure, but see Clay to Henry Clay, Jr., Oct. 14, 1845.

To JOHN J. CRITTENDEN Lexington, July 11, 1845

I am very sorry that the illness of yourself and son has prevented your coming up to sit to Mr. Healey [*sic*, George P.A. Healy].[1] I hope that both of you have now recovered.

Mr. Healey, being anxious to take another portrait of me, I have reluctantly consented to sit to him again upon this condition, that you will come here and remain at Ashland, whilst your picture is in progress, and that we shall sit to him alternately. He will come out early every morning (for I can not accommodate him in lodging here) and continue throughout the day, and in that way he will sooner get through his work, and I trust with less fatigue to us.

I hope that you will accede to this arrangement & come here as soon as you can.

ALS. DLC-Crittenden Papers (DNA, M212, R20). 1. Clay had written Crittenden, *ca.* July 7, 1845 (dated only "Monday morning"), inviting him to come on Wednesday to start sitting for his portrait. Reports that Healy is "flattered by the honor of taking your portrait," that he charges $150, and that "You must make up your mind to rather unusually long sittings." ALS. Danville Public Library, Danville, Ky. The Danville Public Library owns the Healy portrait of Crittenden.

To Worsley, Foreman & Kennedy, New Orleans, La., July 11, 1845. Expresses his thanks for the "information . . . as to the state of the Bagg[in]g and rope market, and the statistics which it furnishes as to those articles." Regrets "the dullness of your market" and their inability "to sell my articles." Warns: "By the first of Sept. I shall need funds very much, and should be very glad to receive a remittance by that time."

While filling "some contracts with planters in Mississippi," has sent "a small lot of bagging to Payne & Harrison" to "assist the sale of some rope of mine." Asks the difference "between time & cash sales," and desires if they can't sell for cash, to "sell to undoubted purchasers on time, if you can effect a sale that will pay interest." ALS. KyU.

From "A GOLD PEN"[1] New York City, July 12, 1845

Designed by my Maker for actual service, and ambitious to hold a situation where I can gain the highest honor, and confer the greatest benefit on Mankind, I am emboldened, at the suggestion of a friend, to present myself before you, to solicit your patronage and favor. Truth, compels me to admit, that I have but little to recommend me to your notice. Although I derive my origin from a rich and powerful family, to whom, even Princes pay court, and whose influence is felt throughout the World, I am myself without influence—without the attraction of peculiar beauty—am worth but little money, and wholly destitute of intellectual endowments. Yet, kind Sir, if *you* will take me *by the hand*, and admit me to your intimate companionship—to your treasury of thoughts—I shall soon become familliar with all that is noble in sentiment, lofty in conception, wise in judgement, beautiful in imagery, honest in purpose, and truthful in expression.

Thus *guided*, I cannot fail to impart pleasure and instruction to the world; and to gain in return, the world's admiration and applause.

Insignificant as I may appear in comparison with such of my elegant relations as have lately been presented to you, I yet hope you will deign to listen to my application—will give me a place near your person . . .

LS. DLC-HC (DNA, M212, R6). Printed in Colton, *Clay Correspondence*, 4:529-30. 1. Although this letter was addressed to Henry Clay, it was transmitted with a note written on a separate sheet: "Mrs. [Mary] MacGregor, being a stranger to Mrs. [Lucretia Hart] Clay—though not so to her amiable character—begs her to pardon the liberty she takes, in requesting her acceptance of the accompanying trifle." Thus, it appears that Mrs. MacGregor is the author of the letter.

From Ursin Bouligny, Jr., New Orleans, La., July 17, 1845. Regrets that his letter of March 25, 1845, "has by some accident miscarried," because "all the instructions were contained in it, for the forwarding of the Mules." Urges Clay to send the mules "at once or as soon as possible," since "they are wanted now and if here I could dispose of them at once and at handsome profits." Fears that if Clay does not act quickly, "those who want them in our neighbourhood . . . should buy out of the first droves that will make their appearance in the market." Hopes to "prevent that if I can, by writing to those planters that I expect some down and inviting them to wait until our lot reaches here." Suggests that Clay ship the mules at once if "the River should still be in good Boating order . . . with instructions to land them at *Gov. A B Roman's Plantation*—40 Miles from New Orleans on the right Bank of the river and *immediately opposite the Jefferson College.*" Asks Clay to "advise me of the probable time" of the boat's arrival so "I can then have a watch placed on the Bank . . . if it should pass in the night." Advises Clay that he intends to send any mules "that are too fine for Planters use . . . to the city where better prices can be had for them." If the mules cannot be sent by boat, requests Clay to "start them from Kentucky, by land, at the very earliest period," because "Our Planters will have a very heavy crop to take in, and I think will have to purchase a great many mules for this and a number of years to come." Describes the increase in the culture of sugar cane as "extraordinary." Reminds Clay "that I am doing a general Commission business and that I should be pleased to receive consignments of produce from your part of the country." ALS. DLC-TJC (DNA, M212, R14).

For more on the growth of the sugar cane industry, see United States Beet Sugar Association, *The Beet Sugar Story* (Washington, D.C., 1959).

To Robert Triplett, Owensboro, Ky., July 19, 1845. Thanks Triplett for the "three sheets of your essay on a system of National education." Believes it "would do well, if it had money to start it, and was afterwards well executed. There lies the whole difficulty. The word 'execution' is the most important in language." Doubts the success of Triplett's proposition "to raise the requisite funds by an appeal to Mr [John J.] Astor. . . . He is a german by birth of strong and vigorous mind, and who, I have no doubt, has fully deliberated and firmly resolved on the disposition . . . of his vast estate." Fears that Astor "would be found immovable" in light of "the example of [Stephen] Girards immense Estate wasted before him, after having been dedicated to Education [7:848]." Decides he cannot approach Astor with the plan, even though he views education "as the best, if not the only, means of saving our sinking Country. I am sick, sick, whenever I think of its sad condition." ALS. KyU.

To HENRY CLAY, JR. Lexington, July 22, 1845

Henry [Clay III] has been with us a week, behaving very well. He intended to return tomorrow, in conformity with your orders; but, as he and we should be happy for him to remain another week, I told him that I would assume the authority of detaining him, and that I was sure you would consent to the extension of his furlough, which I hope you will do:

We are all well. Wm. [C.C.] Claiborne [Jr.] and his family are with us, and we should be glad to have you occupying the only spare room we have remaining.

ALS. Henry Clay Memorial Foundation, Lexington, Ky.

To J.G. Vandervolgen *et al.*, Albany, N.Y., July 31, 1845. Thanks "the Watchmen of the city of Albany," for their gift of a saddle and its "appendages." Promises "always to put the saddle upon the right horse" and to "cherish a proud recollection of the friendly source whence it came." Also thanks them for their compliments regarding "my origin, my career, and my retirement from public life." Affirms "the purity and disinterestedness of the motives" which have prompted his public service. Copy. Printed in Lexington *Observer & Kentucky Reporter*, August 30, 1845.

John Vandervolgen is listed as a fur cutter at 76 Second, Arbor Hill, Albany in L.G. Hoffman's *Albany Directory and City Register, 1846-7* (Albany, 1846). He is given as a "Captain of the Watch" in S. Wilson's *1844 Albany City Guide* (Albany, 1844).

To JOHN TILFORD Lexington, August 4, 1845

It is proper that I should say that you handed to me to day a Certificate of deposite with the Phenix [*sic*] Bank of N. York for five thousand dollars,[1] made by some liberal and kind friends of mine, with the view of relieving me from pecuniary embarrassment; that I endorsed and returned the certificate to you; and that you appropriated the whole of the amount to the payment of my debts in a manner perfectly satisfactory to me.

Unable to address myself directly to the good friends from whom this act of generosity has proceeded, because they have, with the greatest delicacy, kept me uninformed as to their names, I must request you to express to your correspondent the sentiments of profound gratitude and thankfulness with which they have filled me.

You inform me that it was their friendly purpose to have discharged the whole of the debt which, in my own right, I owe Mr. [John J.] Astor;[2] but that they were prevented from accomplishing it by some difficulty in arranging the form of the acquittance. I request you also to express my great obligations for that kind intention. It will be, I am sure, agreeable to my friends to know that the extent of the assistance which they have, with so much kindness, and so much delicacy, rendered to me is such as to place me perfectly at ease in my circumstances. Never ambitious of great wealth, thanks to their goodness and generosity I am now allowed to retain ample means to live in comfort, and to continue to dispense the accustomed hospitalities at Ashland, where I shall always be delighted to see any of them.

I beg therefore that they will no longer cherish any feelings of solicitude in respect to my pecuniary affairs.

I cannot conclude without expressing to you, my dear Sir, my thanks and obligations for the fidelity and friendly consideration, with which you have executed this and other similar trusts confided by my friends to your hands.

ALS. NN. 1. See also Tilford to Clay, Feb. 17, 1845; Lawrence to Clay, March 13, 1845. 2. Astor to Clay, April 28, 1845.

From Thomas Hinde, Mount Carmel, Ill., August 7, 1845. Writes Clay a series of six letters "embracing *Rem[in]iscences* of Kentucky."

In #1, recalls his arrival in Kentucky from " 'Old Hanover' County Virginia, a memorable region [that] gave us birth." Remembers Clay as "the first lawyer I ever heard address a Court." Describes in detail his first visit to "the metropolis Frankfort," when he found the parlor of his boarding house "crowded with Great men . . . perhaps yourself and many others" and was pleased to be "introduced into the Circle of the greatest Constellation of talent . . . unsurpassed by any in this Union."

In #2, reminisces about Kentucky political and judicial leaders of the early nineteenth century, especially Isaac Shelby, James Garrard, George Nicholas, Alexander Scott Bullitt, and John Adair. After a visit to Richmond, Va., realized that he "could not find at the bar with the Randolfs [*sic*], Wickhams, Wirts, Calls, Hay's, Botts' & others, the learned in the law, the glow and shining genius of . . . yourself and others" in Kentucky.

In #3, reviews "the Old Appellate Court of Kentucky—& its Judges." Describes Judges George Muter [1:272], Benjamin Sebastian [1:271], Caleb Wallace [1:222], and Thomas Todd [1:27].

In #4, turns his attention to "the primitive characters and persons of Kentucky," especially Daniel Boone and Simon Kenton and their families and personality traits.

In letter #5, wishes to "review the Condition of old Kentucky as to Society . . . from our first knowledge of it up to the period of the last war [of 1812]."

Discusses the establishment of newspapers in Kentucky, Ohio, and Tennessee. Also considers the monthly literary magazines and musical compositions. Recalls the "immoralities of these early days" when "drinking and frolicking was in a great degree counter balanced, by the hilarity and good humor and kind feelings which pervaded all classes of people." Comments as well on the scarcity of currency on the frontier and the driving of Western livestock to markets in Baltimore.

Continues in letter #6 to discuss Kentucky's "cabin schools" which "turned out more talent than Transylvania University or any university of the nation within the same space of time." Attributes the success of these schools either to "the flow of genius or talent of that period, or from the talent and capacity of the Teachers of that early day." Comments also on the "scanty collection—of various descriptions" of school texts used during the period. Hopes that the efforts of early Kentucky schools would "Stimulate our Country Schools in the wish to secure good Teachers and procure good books—and they then can Secure all the advantages, which might be obtained in Academies Primaries or Universities."

A final letter, dated August 8, 1845, considers "the first settlers of Kentucky" and the "difficulties they had to encounter." While the "Indian wars, the building of forts—the deaths by fire arms, tomahawk and scalping knives are written down," wonders about "the other deprivations of the early inhabitants." Examines briefly a number of subjects: clothing, wolves, the water supply, problems with overgrazing, the scarcity of fruit, the amusements of the young people, and the emergence of a stratified society. Praises early Kentuckians: "Both men and women of the early day had muscle and mighty bone." ALS. WHi.

To J. MUIR[1] Lexington, August 7, 1845

I received your kind letter and thank you for the friendly sentiments which it conveys. I have ceased to have any, I never had many, personal regrets on account of the issue of the Presidential election. Those which I most felt were excited for my country and for my friends. They remain undiminished. And for no portion of them were my sympathies more strongly awakened than for our country women. Their hearts, every where, assured them of the deep and durable interests involved in the contest, and intuitively prompted them to avert all calamity from our land, if they could. Mine gratefully owns the kind partiality which they manifested toward me. The ladies of Alexandria [Va.] are entitled to a large share of the great obligation which I owe to their whole sex.

I return the blank notes which you transmitted, with my name affixed to each as you desired. I add a similar one for Mrs. Mandell.

I will thank you to make my respects and my acknowledgments to the poet mechanic, of whose versification you have sent a specimen so creditable to his talent.[2]

Copy. Printed in Colton, *Clay Correspondence*, 4:530. 1. Muir is possibly John Muir, a hardware dealer, who appears in the Alexandria city census for 1860. Information supplied by Ann L.S. Southwell, Alderman Library, University of Virginia. 2. Reference obscure; poem not found.

To Octavia Walton LeVert, Mobile, Ala., August 8, 1845. Expresses his thanks for her "kind tender . . . of the hospitality of your house, of the use of the same chamber, of the services of the same Amanuensis &c." Wishes to visit Mobile "Should I not have the gratification of seeing you elsewhere." Hopes that "the contemplated trip to Cuba will be executed, and that we shall have the pleasure of your Company in the party [Mercer to Clay, April 22, 1845]." Expects "to concert the arrangements for the voyage to Cuba" with Dr. William Newton Mercer. Adds: "Independent of the pleasure which we should derive from your Society, your tact and talent, and your knowledge of the Spanish language would be of infinite advantage to us." Anticipates "no obstacle to your going, if Dr. [Henry] LeVert will accompany you, or . . . if he will confide you to our care." Intends "to descend the [Mississippi] river early in December" and wishes to voyage to Cuba "early in January."

Reports meeting "a number of persons from Mobile here this summer," and writes that they "were able to give me some agreeable tidings of you."

Sends his best wishes for her entire family. "I sincerely hope that the mineral waters of Arkansas will restore your broken health." Requests her to kiss "the graces . . . for me—God bless them" and expects to find the oldest "almost as tall as her mother, so much do two years in the female life affect the growth of a young lady [Clay to LeVert, April 14, 1844]." Presents his "respectful and affectionate regards to Dr. LeVert."

Concludes: "The desolate state of Mobile . . . will continue to awaken great solicitude for your health and that of your family. . . . I hope that you will omit no precaution to preserve a life and health so dear to your friends, and to none more so than to me." ALS. Courtesy of Caldwell Delaney, Mobile, Ala.

To THOMAS B. STEVENSON Lexington, August 12, 1845

I received your letter informing me that a new and revised edition is about to be published of Dr. [Henry B.] Bascom's pamphlet,[1] in respect to the divisions which have unhappily arisen in the Methodist Church.[2] I perused a copy of the first edition with very great satisfaction, and consider it as distinguished by uncommon ability. Besides the particular questions involved in the controversy, between the Southern and Northern sections of the Methodist church, it treats of other subjects (slavery and abolition) in a masterly manner, and well adapted to make a deep and lasting impression upon all patriotic and religious minds open to the reception of great and important truths. The intention of Dr. Bascom to divide the principal topics of the work into suitable chapters will be an agreeable facility to the reader of it.

An unwarrantable interpretation has been given to a letter which I addressed several months ago to Dr. Boothe [*sic*, William A. Booth], in regard to the menaced separation of the Methodist church.[3] It was my purpose, in that letter, to confine myself strictly to an expression of my great regret of the consequences to the Church and to the Union, which I apprehended from the separation, without intimating any opinion whatever as to which of the two parties to the controversy was in the wrong. I understand that my letter has been construed to imply that I thought the Southern division of the Church in error, which is certainly not the opinion that I do really entertain.

My profound regrets on account of the division of the Church, *for the cause which brought it about*, remain undiminished. I know that there are very high authorities for cherishing the belief that the event will add strength instead of creating danger to our political union. I anxiously hope that experience may demonstrate the correctness of that and the fallacy of my opinion.

ALS. Courtesy of Mrs. Kenneth W. Warren, Wellerby Hills, Mass. Letter is addressed to Stevenson at Frankfort, Ky. Printed in Colton, *Clay Correspondence*, 3:458. 1. Letter not found. Bascom's pamphlet, *Methodism and Slavery: With Other Matters in the Controversy Between the North and the South* . . . , was published in Frankfort, Ky., in 1845. 2. Clay to Unknown Recipient, June 26, 1844. 3. Possibly Clay to Booth, April 7, 1845.

To Calvin H. Wiley, Oxford, S.C., August 12, 1845. Regrets that he "cannot advise your establishment in Lexington to pursue the profession of law." Describes the Lexington bar as "excessively crowded. . . . there are not more than two or three of them who make annually as much as $3000." Explains: "The age of Lexington, the density of our population, and the existence of Transylvania University in the City all contribute to bring to the Bar a greater number of members than find profitable employment." Recommends that he consider going "to one of the new States or Territories," and that he visit "the place to which he proposes to go. . . . Such a tour of observation is worth all that it could cost, and would lead to much more satisfactory results than any which can be obtained from the representations of others." ALS. Courtesy of Mr. R.D. Hay, Winston-Salem, N.C.

Wiley (1819-87), an attorney, had settled in Oxford, S.C., in 1841 and remained there, editing the Oxford *Mercury* for a time. He later served in the state legislature before turning to the ministry in 1855. *DAB*.

To UNKNOWN RECIPIENT[1] Lexington, August 14, 1845

I have received your letter. It is not correct as you supposed, that the culture of hemp and flax was introduced into Kentucky by me, although for many years I have cultivated hemp, and sometimes flax. There is a very great amount of hemp produced in Kentucky, more than in any other state; but flax is not cultivated more extensively than it is perhaps in New Jersey. Nor have our people made greater progress in the manufacture of Linen. There is a great deal of course tow cloth made, but very little fine linen. Now and then a piece is made in some private family. There is no manufacture of linen either for wearing or bleaching in this State.

I agree with you that linen is one of the objects of manufacture, to which the industry of our country ought to be in due time applied.

Copy. Printed in Lexington *Observer & Kentucky Reporter*, Sept. 13, 1845. 1. Identified only as a citizen of Baskinridge, N.J.

From Robert Garrett & Sons, Baltimore, Md., August 15, 1845. Send to Clay an account of the "Sales of your two lots of Hemp (via N. Orleans & the interior route, which were received in equally good order)," and include a "statement of a/c Showing balance Subject to yr. order at Sight $344.49."

In answer to Clay's queries [Garrett & Sons to Clay, April 5, 1845] in his letter of April 12, admit that they are "desirous that our charges in Western produce should be as low as practicable & altho' it is the usage in this market, to charge Storage on Hemp, we never do, unless the period we are forced to hold be unusually long." Add that hemp violates "our general Insurance Policies which compels us to keep a separate Ware house for its exclusive Storage."

Report that they "have given the Sales of your Water R[etted]. Hemp our best attention & have had to encounter the prejudices of our manufacturers, who still most decidedly prefer Russia." Apologize for delaying the sale of Clay's hemp, but could not sell earlier "Unless we would have yielded to lower prices." Note that dew rotted hemp brings a better price and that they sold "this day . . . 200 Bales good Ky [hemp] at $96.00 per ton," but find "we cannot always promise speedy Sales of W. R." unless "the order & quality, will gradually improve . . . so that less delay & difficulty, will be experienced in selling."

Enclose "a sample of Italian Hemp, which commands $200 @ $220 per tons. . . . on account of its peculiar strength & softness for the manufactures of packing yarn." Concludes: "The nearer the Kentucky articles can be brought to this quality, & order, the higher prices it will command." ALS. DLC-TJC (DNA, M212, R14).

A copy of Clay's account for the sale of 31 bales of hemp showing a balance of $344.49 in his favor is also included. DS. *Ibid.*

Clay responded on September 12, 1845, reporting that he had "this day drawn" his $344.49. Is satisfied "that you have done the best you could with the hemp," but complains of "one small charge that I do not think right. It is for Fare. The rope &c with which the hemp is baled ought to be worth at least the price per pound of the hemp, if not more. That charge is not made at Boston. Your own charges are reasonable. And I think nothing ought to be paid for storage, or rather that is covered by commissions." Thanks them "for the specimen of Italian hemp, which I hope we may be able to imitate."

Intends to "consign to you as soon as the rivers get up a large quantity of hemp." Asks "the best time of the year for you to receive it" and whether or not it is "sufficient to bale it and bind it with rope, without any covering." AL, signature removed. DLC-Garrett Family Papers (DNA, M212, R21).

To MRS. FOSTER[1]

White Sulphur Springs, Va. (W. Va.), August 26, 1845

I must express to you, my dear Mrs. Foster, my regrets that I did not see you at the moment of your departure from this place yesterday. Painful as the ceremony *some times* is of taking leave of one's friends, it was my intention to have performed it towards you, and for that purpose I started to go to your lodgings, but being stopt on my way once or twice (you know I am scarcely a free agent) when I reached the neighbourhood of your Cottage, I saw the Stage which bore you away rapidly moving towards the gate.

But, my dear friend, I should not have troubled you with this long apology if it did not afford me the occasion of expressing my thanks and obligations for the books which you kindly sent me by Genl. [Leslie] Combs. They are all highly interesting and display the good taste and judgment with which they were selected. One of them (Eothen)[2] I have been particularly anxious to peruse.

I hope soon to have the pleasure of seeing you in K[entucky]. when we will talk of these and *other* matters. . . .

ALS. THaroL. 1. Possibly Jane Mebane Lytle Foster, wife of Ephraim Foster. See Ephraim Foster's entry in *DAB*. 2. Alexander W. Kinglake (1809-91) made an eastern tour which he described in *Eothen, or Traces of Travel Brought Home from the East* (1844). He later wrote an 8-volume history of the Crimean War. See *DNB*.

To CALVIN COLTON

Blue Sulphur, Va. (W. Va.), September 5, 1845

I received your favor, proposing to send the proofs to me of your first volume.[1] I am now *en route* to Ashland, where I shall be glad to receive them, hoping to find in the introduction, as intimated in your previous letter, an exoneration of me from any responsibility for the composition of the work. It is the best if not only mode of correcting the error committed in the prospectus.

I saw Judge [Francis T.] Brooke at the White Sulphur Springs. He tells me that he has packed up a large bundle of my letters, and placed them in the care of a friend, to be delivered to you. He thinks that you may derive useful matter from them. He has returned to St. Julien, his residence near Fredericksburg.

I have also received a package of some forty of my letters addressed to the late J[osiah]. S. Johnston, Senator from Louisiana, sent me by the widow of his only son.[2] I will try to find some person to forward them by to you from Lexington.

I have not yet heard from General [Sam] Houston;[3] but Mr. Reiley [*sic*, James Reily], the husband of my wife's niece,[4] still believes I shall receive a communication from him.

Copy. Printed in Colton, *Clay Correspondence*, 4:530-31. 1. Not found, but see Clay to Colton, Feb. 3, 1845. 2. Maria Williams Johnston was the widow of William Stoddard Johnston who had died in 1839. William Preston Johnston (comp.), *The Johnstons of Salisbury, With a Brief Supplement Concerning the Hancock, Strother and Preston Families* (New Orleans, 1897), 72-74. 3. Sloane to Clay, May 9, 1844; Clay to Sloane, May 21, 1844, June 14, and June 28, 1844. 4. Ellen Ross Reily, daughter of Eliza Pindell and George Ross, was the granddaughter of Lucretia Hart Clay's sister Eliza Hart Pindell. Sarah S. Young, *Genealogical Narrative of the Hart Family* (Memphis, 1882), 10-11.

To Aaron Barton, Livermore Falls, Me., September 11, 1845. Thanks him for communicating his friendly sentiments. Notes that "You express regret as to the issue of the [presidential] contest [Clay to Webb, February 29, 1844]: If you could see me in this quiet, and agreeable abode, I am persuaded you would think that I ought to be thankful for it. Certainly, I have escaped a high responsibility, and been able to avoid any disappointment which my administration of the Executive department might have created." LS. MeWC.

Barton is listed as one of the "Selectmen, assessors, overseers of the poor" in Livermore in the period 1839-43. Ira T. Munroe, *History of the Town of Livermore . . .* (Lewiston, Me., 1928), 251.

To WILLIAM PAINE *et al.*[1] Lexington, September 12, 1845

I have the honor to acknowledge the receipt of your official letter, transmitting to me a Copy of a resolution adopted by the Whig Convention, assembled in Portland [Maine] on the 7h. Ulto., in which it has been pleased to express its continued confidence in me,[2] and to declare its conviction that a majority of the American people is in favor of the principles of the Whig party, and that the issue of the last Presidential election ought not to be regarded as a proof to the contrary.

This testimonial, emanating from a body so patriotic and distinguished as was that Convention, is received and will be cherished by me, with feelings and sentiments of profound gratitude, and I request your acceptance, in behalf of the Convention, of my respectful acknowledgments.

Believing, as I sincerely do, that the policy & principles of the Whig party, are best adapted to the welfare of our Country, and that its present prosperity is attributable to them, I hope that the Whig Convention of Maine may have correctly interpreted the opinion of a majority of the American people. So far as legislation is concerned, whether there will be a conformity or not to those principles and that policy, by the dominant party, will be probably demonstrated during the approaching Session of Congress. In any event, let us all unite in prayers for the happiness and glory of our common Country.

ALS. CtY. 1. William Paine (1806-61), a graduate of Bowdoin College and a lawyer, represented Bangor in the state legislature for 7 consecutive terms. In 1848 he returned to Portland, his birthplace, where he remained until his death. Information courtesy of Elizabeth S. Maule, Maine Historical Society. 2. The Maine Whig convention had met in Portland and adopted 8 resolutions, 7 of which pertained to Henry Clay and their continued support for him. Kennebec *Journal*, August 15, 1845.

To Paul Henry Langdon, Wilmington, N.C., September 13, 1845. Encloses the "trifling object which you requested," possibly Clay's autograph, with regrets "that it is not some thing more worthy of your acceptance." Views his defeat in the 1844 presidential election "with resignation and philosophy." Adds: "It has long ceased to give me any personal concern. Perhaps I ought to felicitate myself on my escape from great responsibilities, in meeting which I might have failed to accomplish all that my ardent friends anticipated." Recalls "my agreeable visit last year to North Carolina [Clay to Porter, January 19, 1844]," but doubts if he can ever return. ALS. NcD.

Langdon (b. 1826) was the son of Samuel Langdon and Mary Jane Halsey of Wilmington, N.C., and grandson of Samuel Langdon, president of Harvard University during the American Revolution. He served as a captain in the Confederate Army during the Civil War. Information supplied by Patricia Gantt, Wilson Library, University of North Carolina at Chapel Hill.

To Lewis Shanks, Memphis, Tenn., September 13, 1845. Acknowledges an invitation to attend "the Western and South Western Convention" scheduled "to meet at Memphis the 12h. of November." Sympathizes "with all who have at heart the welfare of our whole Country, and every part of it." Is pleased to learn that while the convention "has more particularly in view the advancement of the interests of the sections of the Union in which we reside," it "contemplates nothing adverse to other sections, or to the common tye which happily binds all together." Regrets that "indespensible engagements" prevent his attending, but hopes "the Convention may be characterized by harmony, moderation and wisdom" and add "fresh strength and stability to the Union itself." ALS. MH.

Lewis Shanks (1801-61)—a general practitioner in Memphis—was one of the founders of the Memphis Medical College, where he served as dean and as professor of obstetrics and diseases of women and children. He was also a Memphis city alderman for seven years. O.F. Vedder, *History of the City of Memphis and Shelby County, Tennessee* . . . , 2 vols. (Syracuse, N.Y., 1888), 2:99.

The Western and Southwestern convention met in Memphis, attended by approximately 564 delegates from twenty states. They adopted twenty resolutions calling for federal, state, and private support for internal improvements, especially roads and railroads, that would more closely unite the region. Memphis *Weekly Appeal*, November 14, 21, 1845; Washington *Daily National Intelligencer*, November 15, 24, 29, 1845.

To WILLIAM A. BOOTH Lexington, September 15, 1845

A temporary absence from home has delayed my acknowledgment of the receipt of your favor of the 7th ultimo. I have not received the pamphlet to which it refers.[1] But any expression of my opinion, as to your plan of compromise between the two divisions of the Methodist Church, would be now wholly unimportant, if at any time it would have been worth any thing, since a separation seems to be inevitable.[2] When such is the case, in human affairs, I think the best way is to seek to avoid any mischievous consequences.

I must continue to regret the separation, because I believe it to have an evil tendency. Others think differently; and my hope is that they may, in the end, prove to be right, and I wrong.

It was not my intention, in my former letter, to impute any error to the Southern portion of the Church, on the unhappy subject of Slavery, the immediate cause of division.

My opinion is, that the existence of Slavery, or the fact of owning slaves, in States which authorize the institution of Slavery, does not rightfully fall within the jurisdiction of Ecclesiastical bodies. The law of the land is paramount, and ought not to be contravened by any spiritual tribunal.

Copy. Printed in Colton, *Clay Correspondence*, 4:531. 1. Probably Booth's pamphlet on the Methodist split. See Clay to Booth, April 7, 1845. 2. Clay to Unknown Recipient, June 26, 1844.

To CALVIN COLTON Lexington, September 16, 1845

I received your favor of the 2d instant. I have really no coat of arms, and if I had, I should doubt the propriety of the use of it suggested by you. In lieu of it, would it not be better to employ some object drawn from those interests which I have sought to promote in the National Councils? A loom, shuttle, anvil, plow, or any other article connected with manufactures, agriculture, or commerce. I wrote you from the Blue Sulphur.[1]

Copy. Printed in Colton, *Clay Correspondence*, 4:532. 1. Clay to Colton, Sept. 5, 1845.

To Harmon C. Westervelt, New York City, September 20, 1845. Acknowledges his letter "communicating the desire of Mr [William] Fischerman to make and present me a pair of boots, and . . . to obtain from me an old boot or some other adequate measure of the leg and foot which he kindly desires to cover."

Fears that "the old boot . . . might never reach its destination. It would be an inconvenient customer to the P[ost]. Office department . . . and, if sent through any other, it might, by mistake, get upon some other leg & foot, and lead its strange companion a dance." Transmits instead "a paper measure of my leg and foot, taken by a plain but worthy boot and shoe maker in Lexn." who "Like Mr. Fischerman . . . is a foreigner and like him also a good whig." ALS. ViU. Addressed to Westervelt at 47 Nassau St., New York City. Letter endorsed in strange hand: "The boots were made in an elegent & comfortable manner under my superintendance, with the hair (undressed inside) and were as beautiful a specimen of the Mechanic art as I remember to have seen—Mr Clay recd them & expressed his kind acknowledgements to Mr Fisherman [*sic*] personnally—"

Westervelt was a lawyer at 47 Nassau h. 31 Greenwich, while William Fischerman was a boot and shoemaker at 7 Nassau, New York City. Doggett, *New York City Directory for 1844-45.*

From CASSIUS M. CLAY Lexington, September 25, 1845

In the late outrage against my person, my constitutional rights as a loyal citizen of a free commonwealth and against the liberty of the press, your name was currently used as having given sanction and approval to the lawless action of the Rebels of the 18th of august.[1]

It is further stated that you were waited upon by some lovers of "Law-and order" between the first actual movement and its consummation on Monday, and persuaded to remain in Kentucky, in order to save if things were pushed to extremity my life—and that you refused and departed on saturday the 14th to the Virginia springs, thus leaving me here to perish under that tide which you had assisted in raising.[2]

When I remember that I have devoted all the days of my manhood—my purse—my person and my honor to the success of the whig cause, which would result very certainly in your personal elevation,[3] I cannot in justice to myself or to you allow these reports though vague and indirect in authority to pass without hearing from yourself the whole truth. M[adison]. C. Johnson Esq will hand you this and receive your answer.

ALS. DLC-TJC (DNA, M212, R10). 1. Clay to Buckingham, March 31, 1845. 2. It is not known what role, if any, Henry Clay played in planning the dismantling of the office of the *True American*, but he was at the Blue Sulphur spa when it occurred. His son James B. Clay served as secretary of the Committee of Sixty which was responsible for the action. In the spring of 1848 C.M. Clay repeated the charges made in this letter, declared his personal enmity for H. Clay, and announced his opposition to him as the Whig candidate for president. Smiley, *Lion of Whitehall*, 99, 130-31. See also *History and Record of the Proceedings of the People of Lexington . . . in the Suppression of the "TRUE AMERICAN"* . . . (n.p., n.d.). 3. For C.M. Clay's role in the 1844 presidential election, see Clay to Wickliffe, Sept. 2, 1844; Clay to C.M. Clay, Sept. 18, 1844.

From Joel Tanner Hart, Baltimore, Md., September 26, 1845. Informs Clay that "Mr Christopher Hughes, who was with you when Minister to Ghent . . . desires that I shall be introduced to him by a letter from yourself, and to be handed, or sent to him by me." Suspects that Hughes "wishes me to execute your Bust for him in marble; and would like to have a word from you about the artist." Reports that Hughes "has a number of very fine specimens of art, yet seems to hold your Bust in the highest veneration of them all." ALS. ICU.

On October 4, 1845, Clay provided the requested letter to Hughes, introducing Hart as "a native & self taught, artist of very great merit" who "has made a Bust of me, which has commanded, I believe, the unanimous approbation of all who have seen it." Copy, in Hart's hand. *Ibid.*

Clay had already provided Hart with several other letters of introduction. On September 2, 1845, he introduced Hart to Mrs. Lucy Barbour as "a most worthy and respectable citizen, and . . . an artist of uncommon merit" who "desires to consult you on a subject on which, from considerations of delicacy, which you will justly appreciate, I cannot say one word, except to express my obligations of profound grattitude [French to Clay, February 27, 1845]." *Ibid.*

Also on September 2, 1845, he introduced Hart to Benjamin W. Leigh as "an Artist of uncommon merit, in whose welfare I share, with the whole community, of which he is a member, a lively interest." *Ibid.*

Another letter of introduction dated September 2, 1845, to Abbott Lawrence describes Hart as "a self-made artist of great merit and promise, which he has evinced in the modelling and execution of several works of art, and among these the best bust of me, in the unanimous opinion of my friends and neighbors, which has been hitherto produced." *Ibid.*

Joel T. Hart executed his first bust of Clay in 1842 and exhibited it at the Philadelphia Artists' Fund Show in 1845. There were many duplicates of this bust made by Hart and (without his permission) by his former employer Mahlon Pruden of Lexington. He also did several full-length statues of Clay, including the one commissioned by Mrs. Barbour and the Whig ladies of Richmond, Va., which was completed in 1859. For Hart, see *NCAB*, 6:514; *DAB*; and Amyx, "Portraits of Henry Clay," Special Collections, University of Kentucky, vol. A.

To Charles Edwards Lester, Genoa, September 26, 1845. Belatedly thanks Lester for the gift of a snuffbox: "From the devices on the box, and its Moscow manufacture, it is highly probable that the tradition which accompanies it is well founded. It is, at all events, an excellent box and such as even an Emperor might have used. And I assure you that my obligations to you are just as great whether the box was ever worn by Peter the Great or not."

Discusses the work and "Autobiography of Mr. [Hiram] Powers," and recalls when Powers "was engaged, in the Capitol at Washington, in taking the Busts of Col. [William C.] Preston and some other gentlemen." Remembers visiting Powers at his studio and his "wish to take my head." Had replied then "that I would consider of it . . . if I could command the time." Adds: "You can imagine what repugnance one has to sit to an artist, who has submitted to that operation more than one hundred times. I was aware of the great merit of Mr. Powers, and my not sitting to him did not proceed from any insensibility to it."

Contends: "It is a mistake that, after Mr. Powers' application, I agreed to sit *during that winter* to another artiste." Had sat "at intervals" for a portrait painter "at the urgent insistance of Col. Preston." Believes "about that time, perhaps the same winter, a foreign artiste made a marble bust of me" but the sitting "did not exceed ten minutes, and that was given at the earnest entreaty of a Lady-friend."

Attributes his "repugnance to sitting" to "the repeated failures, both of painters and sculptors, to exhibit a correct likeness of me. Mr. [Horatio] Greenough utterly failed." ALS. MHi.

Charles E. Lester (1815-90)—a lawyer, Presbyterian minister, and writer—was at this time consul at Genoa. *DAB*. Hiram Powers (1805-73), residing at this time in present-day Italy, produced about 150 busts during his lifetime, including those of Chief Justice John Marshall, Andrew Jackson, John C. Calhoun, and Daniel Webster. *DAB*. Lester wrote Powers's "autobiography"—*The Artist, the Merchant, and the Statesman, of the Age of the Medici and of Our Own Times* (New York, 1845)—from information provided by Powers.

Clay may have sat in 1838 for Frederick August Ferdinand Pettrich at the request of Margaret Bayard Smith. See 9:196-97. The portrait for which Clay sat "at intervals" in 1837 may have been the one executed by George Cook. See 9:371.

To HENRY GRINNELL & EZRA NYE Lexington, September 27, 1845

I duly received your friendly letter, informing me of the building of a packet ship, to fly between the ports of New York and Liverpool, by Messrs. Grinnell, Minturn & Co.[1] to which I have had the honor of having my name applied; and that a portrait of the Ship,[2] in full sail, had been taken, representing her as having just passed Sandy Hook [N.J.], and exhibiting interesting objects on the adjacent land. This picture you have done me the favor to send to me, free of all expense, by the way of Cincinnati.

I postponed, Gentlemen, answering your kind letter, until the arrival of the painting here; and I now have the pleasure of informing you that I this day safely received it. I tender you my cordial thanks and my grateful acknowledgments for it. It is a beautiful and splendid object of art, presenting a magnificant Ship, highly creditable to the enterprize of the owners, and the skill and taste of its construction, as well as the pencil of the artiste who painted it.[3] I had frequently before heard of this fine ship, and I am highly gratified to find that she merits the renown which she has acquired. We will preserve the picture, as one of the most cherished ornaments of our house, and exhibit it to our friends, who may visit us, with the highest satisfaction, and with feelings of never ceasing gratitude to the friendly source whence it comes.

I thank you also, Gentlemen, for your obliging offer of a free passage to Europe in this noble vessel. It is not probable that I shall ever again make a voyage to Europe; but if I should have occasion ever hereafter to visit it, there is no Ship in which I would take a passage with so much pleasure as in yours'. P.S. During the transportation of the picture from N.Y. to Cincinnati, I was informed that it had been slightly defaced, in a storm, in the Northern part of Ohio; but it was carefully retouched at the latter City, and no vestige of any injury is now visible.

ALS. KyLoF. Addressed to Grinnell & Nye at New York City. 1. Henry Grinnell, with his brother Moses and brother-in-law Robert B. Minturn, were shipping merchants who owned a line of Liverpool packets. Moses Y. Beach (ed.), *The Wealth and Biography of the Wealthy Citizens of the City of New York* (New York, 1846), 13, 21. 2. The painting "Henry Clay, Packet Ship E. Nye, Commander," was drawn by William Marsh in 1845 and lithographed and published by S. Palmer in New York City the same year. G.K. Hall & Co., *The Mariners Museum, Newport News, Virginia, Catalog of Marine Prints and Paintings*, 3 vols. (Boston, Mass., 1964), 1:180; 3:118, 332. 3. *Ibid.*

To Robb, Winebrener & Co., Philadelphia, Pa., October, 1845. Requests them to "make and send me . . . a Surtout; a pair of pantaloons of black color, and two waistcoats." Notes that they "have my measure, but will make a small allowance for my good health & undiminished size." Leaves to them "the selection of colors &c. I do not wish to be too much in nor too much out of the prevailing fashion." ALS. ICHi. Letter addressed to James B. Clay in Philadelphia, who delivered it to Robb and Winebrener, "Merchant Tailors," at 102 Chestnut Street. *M'Elroy's Philadelphia Directory for 1845*, 8th ed.

On November 3, 1845, John H. McCalla sent Clay a bill, dated October 22, 1845, for $70.00: $42.00 for a "Surtout Coat Super Brown Cloth," $13.00 for "Pantaloons" of "Blk French doe skin," $7.00 for one satin vest, $7.50 for one "fancy Cashmere" vest, and a 50 cent fee for the box in which the items were shipped to Lexington. ALS. DLC-TJC (DNA, M212, R14).

McCalla was a tailor at 12 N. 8th Street, Philadelphia. *M'Elroy's Philadelphia Directory for 1845.*

To HENRY CLAY, JR. Frankfort, Ky., October 14, 1845

I came down here yesterday, and shall not return until the day after to-morrow. Before I left Lexn. I ascertained that your note at the N[orthern]. Bank [of Kentucky] was not due until the 17h. and I deposited your note for its partial renewal, which I have no doubt will be done. At the Branch B[ank]. [of Kentucky] I requested Mr [Thomas Hart] Pindell to pay your note out of my funds, or let it lie over until my return, which he said he would do. Your business therefore will not suffer until I get back, when I suppose I shall receive from you your bill on P[ayne]. & H[arrison]. which I had returned for your signature.[1]

I wish you would say to Mr. [Thomas] Smith that I sent a Barrel of old Bourbon to his house, thro' the Rail Road, which I wish carefully forwarded to Dr. H[enry]. S. Levert of Mobile free from expense to him. I wrote to him (Mr. Smith) about it by Dr. [Lewis or Louis] Marshall.[2]

ALS. Henry Clay Memorial Foundation, Lexington, Ky. Letter addressed to Henry Clay, Jr., at Louisville, Ky. 1. Clay to Henry Clay, Jr., July 10, 1845. 2. On Oct. 17, 1845, now in Lexington, Clay again wrote Henry Clay, Jr., that he had "to day transacted your business in the Banks." Reports "that I paid for you 1st. Discount on the new & payment on the old note," amounting to $1043.40, "2 Amt. of your note at the B[ranch]. Bank [of Kentucky]," amounting to $600. Also received "for you proceeds of bill on P[ayne]. & Harrison," a sum of $1449, leaving a balance "overpaid by me" of $194.40. Invites Henry Clay, Jr., and his children to visit Ashland as "Our house is now less crowded." Announces his intention "to pass the winter at the South, and . . . to go to N.O. in December." Does not think Henry Clay, Jr., also needs to go if "no other object but that of the Dubreuil case [Clay to Henry Clay, Jr., March 17, 1845] would carry you to N.O." ALS. Henry Clay Memorial Foundation, Lexington, Ky. Letter addressed to Henry Clay, Jr., at Louisville, Ky.

To RICHARD H. BAYARD Lexington, October 21, 1845

A friend of mine is largely interested in a debt due from the Pennsa. Bank of the U. States, and has requested me to obtain any information I can as to the present or ultimate prospects of the payment of the debt.[1] Knowing that you are one of the Trustees of that unfortunate institution may I ask the favor of you to communicate to me the desired information, confidentially or otherwise, as you may think proper? I believe the Courts have sustained the validity of the several deeds of trust made by the Bank; but I have heard of no dividends being declared, nor of what progress the Trustees have made.

I was much gratified to hear from Dr. [William N.] Mercer and Miss [Eliza] Young[2] (who were here a short time ago) that the Sea Bath at New Port [*sic*, Newport, R.I.] had restored the health of Mrs. [Mary S.] Bayard. But I am afraid the climate of Wilmington, so injurious to her, will bring back her complaint.

Your sister writes me that your brother James [A. Bayard, Jr.] is about to remove to N. Orleans. As he had established himself in N. York, I regret the necessity of a second removal.[3] But as I learn that he will, en route, call on me, I shall be happy to see him and to render him any service in my power.

Present me affectionately to Mrs. Bayard and your daughters.

ALS. KyLxT. Addressed to Bayard at Wilmington, Del. 1. The friend was Isaac Shelby, Jr. See Clay to Bayard, May 7, 1846. Many lawsuits resulted from the insolvency of the U.S. Bank of Pennsylvania. While the stockholders recovered nothing, "the result for the creditors appears indeterminable." The final settlement did not occur until 1866 or 1867. Bray Hammond, *Banks and Politics in America From the Revolution to the Civil War* (Princeton, N.J., 1957), 517, *passim.* For the problems of the U.S. Bank of Pennsylvania, see also 9:446, 500. 2. Eliza Young was a wealthy cousin of Mercer's late wife, Anna Butler Mercer. Pierce Butler, *The Unhurried Years* . . . (New Orleans, 1948), 20, 26, 28, 35-37, 41, 44, 46. 3. Apparently James decided against moving to New Orleans. He practiced law in New York City from 1843 to 1846, then moved back to Delaware. *DAB.*

To H. Hays & Co., Louisville, Ky., October 21, 1845. Acknowledges their "having deposited at the Agricultural Store of Messrs. [C.J.] Sanders and [J.T.] Davidson in Lexington a plough, manufactured at your establishment in Louisville, expressly for me . . . as a token of your regard for me, as the friend of the laboring man, in the various departments of industry."

Reports that the plough "has not yet reached its destination, in consequence of the unexampled curiosity of the public to see it." Compliments "the beauty and taste displayed in its construction, both in the wood and metallic parts of it," so elegant that "many ladies have regretted that they could not adorn their parlours with such a splendid article." Intends "to give it a fair trial myself, when the public will allow me to bring it to Ashland." Copy. KyLo.

Sanders and Davidson's Grocery and Agricultural Store was located at the corner of Main and Limestone streets. Lexington *Observer & Kentucky Reporter*, October 18, 1845.

To WILLIAM L. HODGE Lexington, October 24, 1845

I have recd. and thank you for your friendly letter dated in this month, and chiefly relating to the case and the calumny against me of the Revd. Mr. [William A.] Scott.[1] I regret, on his account, that it has taken such a serious turn, as I should have been satisfied that his tale should have passed, as the thousand and one calumnies against me have, for what they are worth. But your friendly enquiries are entitled to an answer.

I have been five times to N. Orleans. The first in the Spring of 1819, then in the winter 1829-30, then in that of 1830-31. again in that of 1842-43 and lastly in the winter of 1843-44.

I understand that the specifications of the Revd. Mr. Scott fix the time of the misconduct which he imputes to me to the occasion of my ascent of the Mississippi river in the Spring (March or Feby) 1830,[2] on board the Steamboat Philada. commanded by Anderson Miller Esqr. On that occasion, besides others, I was accompanied by Thomas Smith Esq and his lady [Nannette Price Smith], Miss Crittenden[3] (now the lady of Chapman Coleman Esq) and Miss Sidney Edmiston of Lexington, a most excellent & exemplary lady, of the Presbyterian Society. Without having consulted any of these persons, I confidently appeal to each and all of them for the refutation of the accusations of Mr. Scott.

On board of Steamboats every body knows that one gets fatigued and resorts to books, to music, to the company of ladies, and sometimes to cards pour passer le tems. I do not deny that I have resorted occasionally to all these resources, during long and exhausting voyages.

But the point of the Revd. Mr. Scotts charge is, that I continued to play at Cards to a late hour on Saturday night, trenching upon the Sabbath, and that when the morning arrived and it was announced that there was to be Divine Service, I scornfully refused to attend it, and shut myself up in my State room.

Now, this charge in all its parts & aspects I positively and utterly deny.

I never trespassed on the Sabbath, in my whole life, on board of any Steam boat, at Cards or any other game.

I never in my whole life treated with disrespect the performance of Divine Service.

It is quite possible that I may have met, on some occasion, upon Steam boats or elsewhere, a ranting, canting, presumptuous person, assuming to be a Clergyman, whom I thought it would be misspending my time to listen to. I do not say that the Revd. Mr. Scott is or ever was such a person. I have no recollection of ever making any voyage, up or down the Mississippi or any other river with him. I have no recollection of ever having seen him, prior to the winter before the last when, one Sabbath day, I went to hear him preach, and I add, with pleasure, that I was edified by his Sermon.

But according to my recollection (of course on such a subject, and at a time so distant I do not mean to be absolutely positive) no whist, the only game at Cards which I have played for many years, was played by me on board the Philadelphia during the voyage before mentioned.

Altho' the two Reverend Gentlemen (Mess. Scott & [James A.] Lyon) have conjured up quite an imposing tale against me, they do not appear to concur very exactly in their respective statements. That is the common fate of fabrication. Still I had no desire that either of them should have been subjected to the ordeal of a formal investigation of his conduct. I should have been content to have left both to the operations of their consciences, and especially to the self-examination whether, whilst so shocked with imaginary irregularities, falsely imputed to me, neither of them ever supported any man for high office, to whom far greater irregularities were truly and justly ascribable.

As I hope, in a few weeks, to have the pleasure of seeing you at N.O. I forbear now touching on the other topics of your letter. . . .

ALS. Courtesy of Charles P. Whittemore, New Canaan, Conn. 1. Letter not found. The Rev. William A. Scott, pastor of the First Presbyterian Church of New Orleans (1843-54), was reputed to have told the Rev. James A. Lyon, pastor of a church in Columbia, Mississippi, that he had witnessed Clay's playing cards on Sunday. These rumors surfaced in the summer of 1844. Lyon affirmed that he had heard Scott so state, but Scott denied it. A complaint was then made to Presbyterian authorities about the veracity of Scott's denial. The case was carried through ecclesiastical courts to the Louisiana General Assembly and was finally decided in Scott's favor in 1847. Whether or not Clay had played cards on the Sabbath was not the issue in Scott's case. James Smylie, *Brief History of the Trial of the Rev. William A. Scott . . .* (New York, 1847). For Lyon, see *ibid.*, 12 and New Orleans *Daily Picayune*, Feb. 8, 1845. 2. See 8:66, 289, 309, 322. 3. Ann Mary, daughter of John J. Crittenden.

To Charles J. Hadermann, Louisville, Ky., November 1, 1845. Acknowledges his expressions of regret "on account of the issue of the late Presidential election," which are "shared by a large portion of the good and intelligent of the population of the U. States, native and foreign." Although "surprized and sorry to see how many of your Countrymen, and others of foreign birth were deluded by misrepresentation and the acts of demagogues," believes that as "they become more versed in our institutions and their operation, they will themselves regret that delusion." Praises Hadermann's "desire to spread light and truth before them."

Asserts that he has "no control" over "Mr. [Calvin] Coltons' Biography of me, which is shortly to appear [Clay to Colton, February 3, 1845]." Adds: "It was undertaken indeed against my opinion of its expediency; but I have no doubt that it will contain a considerable addition to facts and circumstances already before the public." Presumes Hadermann "can obtain permission by or through the Revd. C. Colton, whose address is Carlton House, City of N. York," if he "wishes to make any such use of it as is mentioned in your letter." ALS. KyLoF.

Hadermann was a teacher living at 98 Second Street. Jegli, *Louisville . . . Directory, For 1845-1846.*

To Thomas Lewinsky [*sic*, Lewinski], Lexington, Ky., November 1, 1845. Clay sends "his mare for a week or two" for Lewinski's personal use. Adds: "She is pretty well broke, but H.C. hopes will improve in her gaits under the Major." AN, in third person. Courtesy of Russell des Cognets, Florida.

For Lewinski—soldier, architect, and military engineer—see Clay Lancaster, "Major Thomas Lewinski: Emigre Architect in Kentucky," *JSAH*, no. 4, vol. 11.

To SUSAN JACOB [Mrs. James B.] CLAY Lexington, November 3, 1845

I was glad to hear by your letter and from Thomas [Hart Clay] that dear little Lucy[1] had recovered. I am sorry that you did not come up with him, as the weather was then finer than, I fear, we shall have again this fall.

Tell James [Brown Clay], who I hope will return this week, that I have a very satisfactory letter from Mr. [Ursin] Bouligny [Jr.]. He had sold 52 of the Mules for $6185, and he hoped to get for the remaining ten one hundred dollars a piece. He also sent me a Check for the buggy horse, which I shall retain until his arrival.[2]

I wish you would also say to James that I should be glad if he would make some final arrangement with Mr. Churchill about the partnership Monarch[3] filly, which we jointly own. He may name a price, or I will, to give or take.

We are all well, and all unite in love to you, and do not omit to kiss precious Lucy . . .

ALS. DLC-TJC (DNA, M212, R10). Addressed to Susan Clay in care of J.J. Jacob, Esq., Louisville, Ky. 1. Letter not found. James and Susan's daughter Lucy Jacob Clay was born in 1844 or 1845 and died at age 19. Charles Kerr (ed.), *History of Kentucky*, 5 vols. (Chicago,

1922), 3:7. Lucy suffered from some unspecified spinal affliction. Glyndon G. Van Deusen, *The Life of Henry Clay* (Boston, 1937), 382. 2. Letter and check not found. 3. For Monarch, see 9:480-81.

To THOMAS W.H. MOSELEY Lexington, November 4, 1845

I request you to attribute the delay in answering your favor[1] to no want of respect to you, and to no want of interest on the subject of it.

I feel very greatly for the free portion, as well as that in slavery, of the African Race. I fear that the project of colonizing the province, on one of the Islands of the Pacific Ocean, as suggested by you, will not be practicable. I do not think in the first place, that any aid in planting such a Colony, will be derived from the Federal Government. 2dly That none will be obtained from the Brittish Government, as supposed by you. 3dly That it will be greatly more expensive to colonize on the Shores of the Pacific, than in Liberia. With respect to the repugnance of the Free blacks to going to Africa, it ari[s]es out of their disinclination to leaving the place of their nativity. They would, in the sequel, be equally opposed to going to the Pacific, or anywhere else beyond the United States. I adhere to all my opinions, often and sincerely expressed, that Africa, from whence their Ancesters were drawn, is the best quarter of the Globe in which they can be beneficially colonized. In expressing this opinion, I mean to offer no opposition to any other, which may be proposed and be attempted to be executed, In, whatever mode the U.S. may get rid of the Free Blacks, I believe it will be better for them and for the whites.

I am happy to see you located, I hope, happily in Ohio. It is a fine State, and has a fine population.

I offer you also congratulations on the result of the rece[nt] elections in Ohio[.][2]

Copy. DLC-TJC (DNA, M212, R10). Letter addressed to Moseley at Covington, Ky. 1. Letter not found. 2. In the recent state elections in Ohio, Whigs had won 21 seats in the senate to 15 for the Democrats, as well as carrying the house by 44 to 28 seats. *Niles' Register* (Nov. 15, 1845), 69:162. There were no gubernatorial or congressional elections in Ohio in 1845.

To SAMUEL JUDAH Lexington, November 14, 1845

I recd. today your favor. I have not heard from Mr. [Gustavus] Schmidt since the decision of the S[upreme]. C[our]t. of Louisiana,[1] but I recd. a very satisfactory letter from Mr. [Richard H.] Wilde,[2] who assisted in the argument before that Ct. and has taken a lively interest in the case. I think we ought to interest him in it. Both he and Mr. Schmidt think it all important to unite by purchase the title of the heirs of [Gilbert de] St. Maxent to ours. Without that they have not as much confidence as I could wish.

I have recd. through the French Minister at Washn. [Alphonse J.Y. Pageot] the only document which I could procure from the archives of France. It is a general order for the fortification of N[ew]. O[rleans]. dated in 1760 and made in Council. [Vincent Gaspard Pierre de] Rochemore was present, but the order attributed to him could not be found.

We may anticipate that the defense will be of a nature requiring us to prove every thing. I presume it will be put in during this month.

I expect to reach N.O. by Xmas. I think it desirable that a meeting should take place there about that time of yourself and Mr. [Thomas] Bishop, in order that we may determine upon future proceedings, & particularly whether an attempt shall be made to purchase out the heirs of St. Maxent. Shall I expect you & him?

ALS. Courtesy of Charles J. Bayard, Fort Collins, Colo. Letter addressed to "Saml. Judah Esq. Counsellor at Law Vincennes Inda." 1. Clay to Henry Clay, Jr., March 17, 1845. 2. Not found.

To Mrs. Ann Warner, Baltimore, Maryland, November 17, 1845. Extends thanks for "the very tasteful and comfortable Counterpane, wrought by your own venerable hands." Since he "was at a loss to know to what post office to address you. . . . I have to request your Senator, the honorable R[everdy]. Johnson, to give this letter its proper direction." Expresses his gratitude for the sentiments "which prompted the tender of a present," and hopes "we both meet hereafter in that world of eternal bliss, which is promised by our holy religion." Copy. Printed in Baltimore *American & Commercial Advertiser*, January 3, 1846.

Mrs. Warner had died on November 16 at age 94. Her obituary appeared in the Baltimore *American & Commercial Advertiser* on November 18, 1845.

To Benjamin Balch, Newburyport, Mass., November 20, 1845. Acknowledges receipt of "a plan of the 'National Life Insurance Company of Massachusetts.' " Although "proposed as President of the Company," cannot "reconcile it to my sense of propriety to accept the appointment." Offers nonetheless his "best wishes for the success of the contemplated Company." ALS. ViU.

Balch is probably the Benjamin Balch (1774-1860) who learned the watchmaking trade with his cousin Daniel in Newburyport. Galusha B. Balch, *Genealogy of the Balch Family in America* (Salem, Mass., 1897), 91. No reference to the proposed life insurance company has been found in the histories of Newburyport.

From William Adams *et al.*, New York City, November 22, 1845. Present to Clay "in the name of the Gold and Silver artizans of the City of New York the accompanying Silver Vase as a small tribute of the deep respect entertained by them for your many valuable services . . . in elevating the working men of this country." Believe that "*protection* to *American Industry* so long and zealously advocated by you will entitle you more than any other American statesman to the thanks and gratitude of the mechanical portion of your fellow citizens." Praise his "exertions in the promotion of the Tariff Bill of 1842 [9:628]: and especially in procuring for us at that time *after all other means had failed an Adequate* and just protection against foreign importation." State that "for several years previous to its passage the business of the Gold and Silver artizans had been gradually declining until we found ourselves upon the very brink of ruin in competeing with foreign manufacturers, the Anvil no longer rang with the gladsome notes of well paid industry." Since the tariff of 1842, however, "the business of the Gold and Silver Artizans . . . enjoys as great a state of prosperity as the most sanguine could desire." ALS. DLC-TJC (DNA, M212, R10). Letter signed by 173 others. Adams was a silversmith whose business was located at 185 Church, New York City. Doggett, *New-York City Directory for 1844-45.*

From New Orleans in February, Clay wrote Adams *et al.*, acknowledging their gift. Expresses his regret that "I was not at home when Mr [William] Adams did me the honor" of presenting the silver vase. Insists that he would have been "most happy" to have received Adams and "treated him, under my own roof, with . . . high respect and hospitality." Explains his absence: "When I took my departure for New Orleans, from Ashland in December last, near a month had elapsed after I had been advised of the Vase having left N. York, and, as the Winter commenced very early, with uncommon rigor, I concluded that it might not reach its destination, until the Winter broke up."

Thanks the artisans for "this splendid article," presented "as a testimonial of their sense of my public services." Retains "a lively recollection of an interview I had with a Committee of the Gold & Silver Artisans of N. York in the year 1841 when the Tariff, at the Extra Session, was in progress through the Senate. They fully satisfied me that the measure of protection to their interests, as the bill had passed the house, was inadequate, and I took pleasure in prevailing on the Senate to render it more effectual. . . . without the remotest expectation of its entitling me to any such generous manifestation of feelings as that with which I am now honored." Although he has not yet seen the vase, eagerly awaits "an opportunity of examining this distinguished testimonial; but Mrs. [Lucretia Hart] Clay and other members of my family represent it as exquisitely beautiful & elegant." Hopes that the "Gold & Silver Artisans of the City of New York may long continue, under the influence of wise and protective laws, to enjoy the measure of prosperity which, I am happy to learn from you, now rewards their industry." Copy. Printed, in facsimile, in *The Jewelers' Circular-Weekly*, March 22, 1916; copy in DLC-TJC (DNA, M212, R10).

To JOHN J.H. STRAITH[1] Lexington, November 24, 1845

I received your letter, communicating your wish to be appointed to the Medical Professorship in Transylvania University, vacated by the death of Dr. [William H.] Richardson,[2] and transmitting some very strong testimonials, in support of your application, from gentlemen of high standing well known to me.

I am not officially connected with Transylvania University in any manner; but I will nevertheless place your application with the testimonials received by me in the proper hands, to receive full and deliberate consideration. I must however add that, prior to the accept [*sic*, receipt] of your letter, I had recommended another gentleman for the vacant chair.[3]

The appointment, I learn, will not be made until sometime in January next. And it is my intention to leave home next week for the South, and as I shall be absent several months, I would suggest the expediency of your transmitting any other recommendations if you should think proper to send any other, to the address of Madison C. Johnson Esq President of the Board of Trustees of the University.[4] Nor do I think that you should be discouraged in making any honorable exertions to secure the appointment by the fact of my having recommended another.

ALS. KyLxT. Addressed to Straith at Charles Town, Jefferson Co., Va. (W. Va.) 1. Straith (1812-78) was a physician who specialized in obstetrics and gynecology and served as a professor at Winchester Medical College. Information supplied by Prof. John E. Stealey, III, Dept. of History, Shepherd College, Shepherdstown, W. Va. 2. Letter not found. For Richardson, see 3:137. 3. Reference obscure. 4. Samuel Annan, a graduate of Edinburgh and founder of Washington University in Baltimore, replaced Richardson. *Catalog of the Medical Department of Transylvania University for the Session 1845-46* (Lexington, 1846).

From Charles Augustus Davis, New York City, November 25, 1845. Expresses his views on the development of railroads, hoping that the government will recognize such endeavors as "worthy of private enterprise" and do as much as it can "Constitutionally in granting Public lands or *the rent* of any good enterprise to do so." Believes railroads or "*internal Communications* . . . appear by experience thus far to be one of the most if not the most efficient *means*" of protection. Adds that "Roads can protect where a Tariff could not & protect without doing injury to any interest but good to all."

Relates a trick he had played on some fellow Clay supporters when he described a man "so old and decripet he can scarcely write his name . . . yet just so sure as any new invention in agricultural implements appears at our institute here or some singular kind of Cattle or Hogs are Exhibited I am sure to get some enquiry from him about them[.] he never feels easy unless *Ashland* has the best and latest breed or invention." Then showed them Clay's previous letter with its "two pages of neat penmanship," noting "that is pretty well done for *a very old and infirm gentleman*." When he exhibited Clay's signature, "up went a unanimous burst of joy.—among the number were two who had of late been hinting at *new candidates*." Adds: "The fact is my good Sir—we have no other *man*—the 'Expediency men' might as well try to convince a good old Lady that a cup of brown stock was better than *Cat nip* Tea for a child squalling with a stomach ache as to convince the mass there is *any other man* or *name* but yourself & yr. own—if you are willing." ALS. DLC-HC (DNA, M212, R6). Letter marked "Private chat."

The American Institute of New York City had been formed in 1828 to exhibit and promote agricultural, commercial, manufacturing, and artistic interests throughout the U.S. Kellar, *Solon Robinson*, 1:525-26.

From William Newton Mercer, Laurel Hill, Adams County, Mississippi, November 25, 1845. Apologizes for his recent hasty departure from Lexington, but "Miss [Eliza] Young, to whom I referred the decision, determined to proceed immediately, lest we might be delayed indefinitely, as the waters had already began to fall at Maysville." Assures Clay that "my family as well as myself look forward with great pleasure, to a renewal of the times so gratifying to us all, in former winters." Expects to be able to "spare you a little while with [William St. John] Elliot & other friends near Natchez, but rely confidently on seeing you during the second week of December in Canal Street, where *mutato nomine*, every thing will be as formerly in Carondelet Street."

In a postscript mentions he has sent Clay on the *Uncle Sam* a filly named Magnolia who was foaled on March 4, 1841, "by Imp. Glencoe, d. Imp. Myrtle by Manchester, G.d. Bobodilla, by Bobadil, Pythoness by Sorcerer, Princess by Sir Peter, Dungannon, Turf, Herod &c &c." ALS. Josephine Simpson Collection, Lexington, Ky. Letter marked "*P.T.O.*"

Clay often stayed with William St. John Elliot at his plantation "D'Evereux" near Natchez. Harnett T. Kane, *Natchez on the Mississippi* (New York, 1947), 198-201.

For Magnolia, who foaled 13 stakes winners, see Amelia Clay Van Meter Rogers, "Ashland, Home of Henry Clay," M.A. thesis, University of Kentucky, 1934, pp. 22-23.

From Samuel Judah, Vincennes, Ind., December 2, 1845. Informs Clay that "after the opinion of the Sup. court [of Louisiana] was given—the Defts. asked a rehearing," and expects "that only little progress can be made this winter." To prepare for court, "the order of [Vincent Gaspard Pierre de] Rochemore 'or some thing equivalent' is essential [Clay to Judah, November 14, 1845]." Hopes that "If the original cannot be found in France. . . . a copy may exist in New Orleans. . . . amongst the papers of the city council." Wonders if Louisiana law would "compel the production of Such a paper for one benefit." Suggests that "the 'Something equivalent' . . . must be found in the History of Louisiana—in the records of the Land Office and in the dicisions of the courts and recitals in co[n]temporaneous conveyances." Believes the greatest need is "patient investigation and certain legal knowledge." Summarizes the case: "Either Debuil [*sic*, Dubreuil] Villars was or was not the Granter—and either the Government did or did not reclaim the possession for fortifications.—If Villars was not the Granter—neither our clients nor [Gilbert Antoine de] St. Maxent have title.—If Villars was the granter then the land belongs to our clients unless it has been sold. That the 2 a. 12 t. was not sold is shewn by the reservation in the act of sale. . . . The St. Maxent title cannot be good—unless ours is good.—" Adds that "The Rochemore order is material as a confirmation of the possession of Villars, and as an explanation of the exception in the act of Sale and of the possession of the government." Will try to be in New Orleans for a few weeks in January "if assured that the time can be spent by some of us in the investigation of the course." ALS. DLC-HC (DNA, M212, R6).

On December 16, 1845, Clay wrote Judah that he "was not aware of . . . a petition for a re hearing, in the Villars case." Doubts there is any need to make preparations until "the disposition of that petition" is determined, and Judah "need not go down [to New Orleans] until you hear." Informs Judah that "I have paid $58:13 and my son Henry about $30. I will thank you to make provision for meeting your portion of the Costs." ALS. InU. See Clay to Henry Clay, Jr., March 17, 1845.

To William B. Craig, Mercersburg, Pa., December 3, 1845. Transmits the autograph that Craig requested and thanks him for his "friendly sentiments." Appreciates his efforts to "lessen regrets on account of the issue of the last Presidential election." Assures him that "My personal interest in the event was not worthy of much consideration; and I shall soon pass away." Hopes that "the fears, which, in common with so many others, I have felt, should not be realized." ALS. KyU.

Craig is probably William Boyd Craig (b. 1827) who graduated from Jefferson College in 1853 and the Western Theological Seminary in 1856. He was pastor of several different churches following his ordination in 1856. *Biographical Annals of Franklin County, Pennsylvania . . .* (Chicago, 1905), 683.

To JOHN M. BERRIEN Lexington, December 12, 1845

I attentively observed, with friendly interest, the proceedings of the Georgia Legislature recently, in respect to yourself and the appointment of a Senator.[1] I think you ultimately gained a signal triumph, of which you may be pround, and which entitles you to the congratulations of your friends, and I now come to offer mine. I was glad to see you consent to return to the Senate, although I fear you will have but little personal satisfaction in that body, with such majorities as are against the Whigs in both houses.[2] Unless, indeed, as some times happens, when there seems to be no hope, cheering light suddenly & unexpectedly breaks upon us. I went, I remember, to the Senate this time thirteen years ago, with feelings of discouragement almost bordering on despair, immediately after Genl [Andrew] Jackson's second election.[3] I never at one Session accomplished more than I did during that Session.[4]

I expected 'ere this to have been at Natchez or N. Orleans, but a most rigorous and premature spell of winter has embargo'd me. I hope a thaw in a few days will let me off, and that I shall be able to reach one of those Cities before the close of the year.

I will thank you to present my affectionate regards to Mrs. [Eliza Hunter] Berrien . . .

ALS. NcU. 1. Clay to Berrien, March 19, 1845. 2. McKee, *National . . . Popular and Electoral Vote*, 57, gives the party affiliations of the members of the 29th Congress as: Senate—30 Democrats, 25 Whigs, 1 vacancy; House—141 Democrats, 78 Whigs, and 6 American party members. Morris, *Encyclopedia of American History*, 406, describes its membership as: Senate—31 Democrats, 25 Whigs; House—143 Democrats, 77 Whigs, 6 others. 3. See 8:599-603. 4. Especially the Compromise Tariff of 1833. See 8:604, 619-22, 626-27.

To HENRY WHITE *et al.* Lexington, December 16, 1845

I received today at this place the letter which, on the first instant, you did me the honor to address to me, from the hands of Henry White Esq. one of the subscribers to it.[1] He at the same time delivered to me the book, beautifully printed and bound, entitled, "A testimonial of gratitude and affection to Henry Clay," containing the proceedings of a meeting of my friends in the City of Philadelphia, publicly held at the County Court house, on wednesday evening December 19h. 1844, in pursuance of a call of the National Clay Club;[2] and containing also several thousand names of both sexes, young, and old, of those who have done me the great honor of contributing a testimonial to my public services, to the principles and measures which I have endeavored, to establish, and to my exertions in the common cause which we have espoused.

It is utterly impossible, Gentlemen, for me to find language of sufficient force and strength, to express to you the emotions of gratitude and thankfulness excited in my breast by this precious and affecting testimonial. It will be ever warmly cherished by me throughout my life, and be preserved and transmitted to my descendants as the most honorable legacy which I could bequeath to them. And I request you to say, to one and all of the Contributors, that their respective names are not more indelibly recorded in the splendid book, which they have sent me, than in grateful impressions on my heart.

I am also charged by Mrs. [Lucretia Hart] Clay to present her cordial and respectful thanks (to which I beg leave to add my own) to the Ladies and Gentlemen who have had the goodness to send her a Casket of rich jewels, which Mr. White kindly delivered into her own hands, for their highly valuable present. Her grateful obligations for it, she enjoins me to say, are not at all diminished by the reflection that considerations apart from any merits of her own, have prompted the generous offer of it to her acceptance.

I embrace the occasion to bear my testimony, and to tender my thanks to you, Gentlemen, the Trustees appointed under the authority of the public meeting in Philadelphia before mentioned, for the delicacy, the fidelity and the honor with which you have executed the Trust confided to you. And I have great pleasure in expressing my thanks and gratitude to Mr. White, in particular, for the great trouble and inconvenience which he has encountered, by preforming a long journey, at a most inclement season, to fulfill the commission entrusted to him.

ALS. ViU. Printed in Colton, *Clay Correspondence*, 4:532-33. 1. Henry White *et al.*, representing the Whigs of Philadelphia, had written Clay on Dec. 1, 1845, asking him to accept "the Book which accompanies this letter," which "contains an expression of gratitude from your Whig brethren here." The Philadelphia Whigs also sent "a Casket of Jewells, manufactured in this city, for Mrs. [Lucretia Hart] Clay. . . . as a mark of their high consideration and respect for the worth and virtues of the lady of one to whom the country owes a debt of gratitude that can never be repaid." Copy. Printed in Colton, *Clay Correspondence*, 4:532 where it is misdated as Dec. 21, 1845. The "Casket of Jewells" included a "Brilliant bracelet, studded with diamonds . . . with appropriate accompanyings completing a set, all placed in a rich casket. . . . This work is from the establishment of Bailey & Kitchen." The memorial given to Clay was bound in red velvet with a gold clasp and binding and inscribed with the name Henry Clay. It was prepared by Messrs. Carey & Hart. Baltimore *American & Commercial Advertiser*, Dec. 6, 1845. 2. The National Clay Club had held a meeting at the county courthouse of Philadelphia on Dec. 19, 1844, to decide how most appropriately to express with a "proper testimonial" the feelings of Whigs toward Clay. John Sargeant presided over the meeting. Washington *Daily National Intelligencer*, Dec. 21, 1844.

From William McLain, Washington, D.C., January 2, 1846. Encloses a letter from J.M. Witherspoon of Greensboro, Ala., and asks "if you will authorise the Exrs. to hire out the negroes as they suggest." Informs Clay that "Our Annual Meeting [of the American Colonization Society] takes place the 20 of this Month" and hopes that he will attend. ALS. DLC-American Colonization Society Papers (DNA, M212, R20). Addressed to Clay at New Orleans.

On January 19, 1846, Clay acknowledged McLain's letter with "its enclosures from Mr. J.M. Witherspoon; and I have just written to him, giving the authority, as suggested in your letter, to hire out, the slaves devised to me as President of the A.C.S. at a private instead of a public hiring." Adds: "And when hired I have requested him to inform me the amount, and to whom hired. I have desired him also to keep me informed if there should be any contest about the will of the late Revd. Thomas S. Witherspoon, by which the above slaves were devised to me." ALS. *Ibid.*

Also on January 19, 1846, Robert H. McFadden wrote from Greensboro, Greene Co., Ala., to inform Clay of the contents of the last will and testament of "Thomas Sydenham Witherspoon a distinguished minister of the Presbyterian Denomination" who "departed this life on the 19th day of October 1845." Witherspoon had willed "to the President of the American Colonization Society, who shall be in office at my death" a total of 26 slaves "with the increase of the females" in that group. As executor of the will, McFadden wishes to carry out its provisions and "would transport the slaves immediately but for the difficulty which our laws interpose." Continues: "The Statute laws of Alabama, prescribe the mode in which emancipation shall be effected, which will be found in Clay, 'Digest of the laws of Alabama['] *545.* a reference to which will show that there is no provision for emancipation by will—Our Supreme Court have determined that emancipation by will is contrary to the policy of our laws." Since "the fact is obvious that emancipation was *intended.* . . . I propose that you as President of the American Colonization Society should institute suit against me for the Slaves—that I may be deprived of the property by judgement of the Courts." Suggests that "the Hon H.I. Thornton of Eutaw, who is engaged in the practice of law in this County . . . would no doubt cheerfully raise the question for the benefit of these Slaves." ALS. *Ibid.* Addressed to Clay at New Orleans.

On January 26, 1846, Clay informed McLain that he would send McFadden's proposal to the A.C.S. board "& advise that it be acceded to, with the qualification that the agreed case be tried in the Federal instead of a State Court. If the Board coincide with me, a letter had better be addressed to Mr. Thornton to prepare & try the case. He is worthy of all confidence. He is the brother in law of Mr. [John J.] Crittenden of the Senate." ALS. *Ibid.* Sent from New Orleans to McLain in Washington.

Thomas S. Witherspoon, a South Carolina native and a graduate of Union College, New York, was a popular minister of the Presbyterian church in Greensboro, Ala., until declining health caused his resignation in 1843. At that time he was elected by the Synod to the Alabama Professorship at Oglethorpe University in Georgia. James Williams Marshall, *The Presbyterian Church in Alabama* (Montgomery, Ala., 1977), 60, 68, 71-72, 85-86.

For Robert McFadden, a planter and large landowner, see William E. Wadsworth Yerby, *History of Greensboro, Alabama* (Northport, Ala., 1963), 194.

Section 37 of the Alabama law provided that the judge of a county court could emancipate slaves upon petition of the owner, while section 38 provided that if, after emancipation and removal, a slave returned to the state, he could be sold again as a slave for life. There was no provision for emancipation by will. Clement C. Clay, *A Digest of the Laws of the State of Alabama: Containing all the Statues of a Public and General Nature . . .* (Tuscaloosa, 1843), 539-46, espec. 545.

To W.L. WOODWARD Lexington, January 3, 1846

I duly received your favor,[1] and take pleasure in answering it. The desire to trace out your ancestry is very natural. I have often felt it in respect to mine, but I have no written, and very imperfect traditional accounts of them. I am apprehensive, however, that my parental stock is different from the family of Clays described by you, as having been established in Middletown, Connecticut. My ancestors emigrated from England, and settled in the colony of Virginia, early, I believe, in the 17th century. My father was born there, not far from Richmond, on the south side of James River. He removed to Hanover county, shortly before my birth in that county. His name was John, and he was sometimes called Sir John Clay (as I have seen in the record of judicial proceedings), but he had no legitimate right to that title. It was a soubriquet which he somehow acquired. He had but one brother, Edward Clay, who removed at an early period into North Carolina, where he lived and died, leaving a large family.

I never knew my father, who died in my infancy, nor my grandfather. Left an orphan, struggling for subsistence and education, and removing, before I reached my majority, to this State, where I plunged first into an active professional business, and then into political affairs, I have had but little leisure to prosecute inquiries concerning my ancestors. And now, I shall so soon meet them in another, and I hope a better state, that I have thought it hardly necessary to institute any. I think it is quite probable that the Clays, from whom we both descended, were originally of the same family, although it may not be practicable now to trace the exact degree of connection. When I was in England, I met with some persons bearing the name of Clay, and from conversation with them, I had reason to suppose that we all sprung from the same stock.

I am very thankful for the assurance contained in your letter, that your family have all done me the honor to entertain confidence in me, and that those of them who are entitled to the exercise of the elective franchise, have voted with the Whigs. I shall be most happy, if, during the remnant of my life, I shall continue to merit their good opinion.

I pray you to communicate my respectful regards to your venerable grandfather, and accept for yourself assurances of the respect and esteem, and the wishes for your welfare and happiness of your friend and obedient servant.

P.S. My father was a Baptist preacher. Mr. Eleazer Clay[2] near Richmond, Va., was also a Baptist preacher for more than sixty years, and my only surviving full brother[3] is a preacher of the same denomination.

Copy. Printed in Colton, *Clay Correspondence*, 4:533-35. 1. Not found. 2. For Eleazer Clay (1744-1836), see Smith & Rogers, *The Clay Family*, 83. 3. Porter Clay.

To LUCRETIA HART CLAY Natchez, Miss., January 12, 1846

I arrived here this morning. Thursday next, it will be four weeks since we left Louisville. During our voyage in the Ohio the Boat was repeatedly stopt for days together by the floating ice and by the low water on the Bars. On one occasion only I believe were we in danger, being enclosed in the Ice without being able to move the wheels or to steer the boat. When she did move she was carried off helplessly by the mass of floating ice, and we were thrown against a ledge of rock, but no injury was done her[.]

When we entered the Mississippi I hoped that our misfortunes had terminated, but here too they followed us[.] We stuck on several Bars, and were detained several days by them. During the whole voyage we had a great many passengers, and, except for its extraordinary length, we should have passed our time agreeably enough. With the exception of bad colds, my health has been pretty good.

We met the Uncle Sam, which brought down my Stock, on her return to Louisville from N. Orleans. I presume that she delivered it all safely. Henry's [Clay, Jr.] Jack was received by Mr. [William St. John] Elliot, and I am glad to find that he is pleased with him.

I shall remain a few days with Mr. Elliot, and then proceed to N. Orleans, where I hope to arrive on the 18h. or 19h. instant.

Hitherto I have been at a very trifling expence, since I left home, and I shall incur very little during my absence, unless I go to Cuba, which is rendered some what doubtful, in consequence of my great detention on my voyage.

I am most anxious to hear from home, and hope that I shall find at N.O. some letters from there. I fear that you have suffered much with the Cold from its great severity here, where they complain much of it.

Give my love to all, and tell them not to omit to write to me.

ALS. DLC-TJC (DNA, M212, R10).

From [James H.] Muse & [Edwin T.] Merrick, Clinton, La., January 15, 1846. Nothing Clay's trip to New Orleans, address him on "the subject of your claim against the estate of the late Robert Slaughter [9:52, 475-76]." Although they had informed Clay "that there were funds still to be distributed (about $1200)," have learned "the attorney who represented the executor (a nonresident) remitted the funds to him." Report: "There is therefore nothing available at present within our reach out of which we could enforce the payment of your claim." Suggest Clay contact Judge Thomas Gibbes Morgan regarding a judgment "to the amount of, say, five or six thousand dollars out of which your claim may be realized." ALS. DLC-TJC (DNA, M212, R10).

For Merrick (1808-97), a New Orleans lawyer and subsequently chief justice of Louisiana, see *DAB*. He and Muse had opened a partnership under the name Muse & Merrick in Clinton, La., in 1838. For Muse, see Merrick article in *DAB*.

Thomas Gibbes Morgan, at one time collector of the Port of New Orleans and later judge of the district court of Baton Rouge, was the father of Sarah Morgan Dawson and Judge Philip Hickey Morgan of the Second District Court, Parish of Orleans and later of the Louisiana Supreme Court. Sarah Morgan Dawson, *A Confederate Girl's Diary*, ed. by James I. Robertson, Jr. (Bloomington, Ind., 1960), xxxiii-xxxv. In 1846 his law office was located at 15 St. Charles Street, New Orleans. *Michel & Company's New Orleans Annual and Commercial Register for 1846* (New Orleans, 1846).

On January 30, 1846, Clay responded to Judge Morgan's "obliging note of yesterday [not found], in respect to the debt due me from the Estate of R. Slaughter." Although he intends to make inquiries and perhaps might contest "the Judgment agt. In Williams Dix &c," fears "that the prospect of success in securing my debt may not be sufficiently encouraging to hazard expences about my small demand." ALS. LU-Ar.

On March 2, 1846, L.D. Brewer of St. Francisville, La., sent Clay "the Bond of Robt. Slaughter and R.C. Ballard, in your favor for the sum of $5000, which was placed in the hands of Muse, Merrick, & Brewer, for collection." Had intended to forward the bond to Clay "before you left the residence of Mr Taylor in Pointe Coupee but I failed to see Dr [William N.] Mercer. (the gentleman to whom you requested me to deliver it.)" Asks Clay to "excuse my non compliance with your wishes." ALS. DLC-TJC (DNA, M212, R14).

From Nicholas Carroll, New York City, January 16, 1846. Informs Clay that "a 'parcel of us' who have some regard for you were asking each other tonight why it wouldn't be better for you to pull up stakes out West & come to this City." As an inducement, "an honorable, popular & responsible Institution would make you President with a salary of $4,000 or $4,500." Wishes "to know *without delay* whether you could & would accept" and must have his "decision on or before the 10th. of Feby." Offers "no vouchers other than the true heart [that] is devoted to Henry Clay & all that belong to him." ALS. DLC-HC (DNA, M212, R6). Letter marked "*Private*."

Carroll was a member of the Democratic Whig Young Men of New York City and an "agent" at 180 Prince. Doggett, *New-York City Directory for 1844-45*. The "Institution" to which he refers is unknown.

To LUCRETIA HART CLAY New Orleans, La., January 19, 1846

I arrived here from Natchez this morning and am now comfortably lodged in Dr. [William N.] Mercer's new house. North East Storm is now raging here, as bad as any you have in K[entucky]. and I have seen no one but the Dr's family. I received today a letter of the 2d. inst from James [Brown Clay], the only one I have yet recd. since I left home. There is a good deal in his letter which I was glad to be informed of. Tell him that I shall endeavor to see Mr. [Ursin] Bouligny [Jr.] tomorrow, and that I will lose no time in making a remittance to him to meet our note in the N[orthern]. Bank.

I have not yet heard of the arrival of the Stock I sent down; but as Mr. [William St. John] Elliot received Henrys [Clay, Jr.] Jack safely, I presume the others got safely to their destinations.

The winter here, as with you, has been extremely bad. I have not found many letters here from any quarter. As James writes me that he has sold one of my working mules, I think Mr. [Ambrose] Barnett[1] had better break one of the others. I hope he will take good care of all my stock, including the three young Jacks which ought to be weaned & put under the care of Abraham.[2]

I suppose you will have sent off your hams. I will speak to W[orsley], Forman [*sic*, Foreman] & Kennedy about selling them.

I will write to James after setling with Bouligny. Tell John [Morrison Clay] that I had expected to hear from him 'ere now.

My love to all at Ashland & to James's family including little Lucy [Jacob Clay].

ALS. DLC-TJC (DNA, M212, R10). 1. For Barnett, Clay's overseer, see Peterson, *The Great Triumvirate*, 377. 2. A slave.

To THOMAS HART CLAY New Orleans, La., January 24, 1846

I arrived here a few days ago, after a very long and fatiguing Voyage, in better health than could have been expected. I stopt a few days at Natchez & am now comfortably lodged at Dr. [William N.] Mercer's. The Steam boat which run between this & Havana is discontinued. There is some prospect of its resuming its voyages, in which case I may go to Cuba, but otherwise it is not so certain[.]

I have received your letter of the 10h. inst. and was very sorry to hear of the killing of my Calves, which appears very strange. I do hope that you and John [Morrison Clay] will see that Mr. [Ambrose] Barnett pays attention to my Stock. The brood mares and the young Jacks I am very anxious about.

Magnolia (the name of the mare presented to me by Dr. Mercer) is by Glencoe out of the imported mare Myrtle.[1]

Our bagging here is not sold. The market is low & dull. I have not heard from Savannah one word.

I am very glad to hear that the heckler & scutcher[2] are doing better, and promise to fulfill your expectations. As to the hemp you may send here, I will see W[orsley]. F[oreman]. & Kennedy about it, and direct them to sell it, if it can be done at a fair price. You do not inform me how the machine has succeeded in breaking hemp. I hope that the hands you hired will turn out well and that you will keep them constantly employed.

Your letter & the one I recd. from James [Brown Clay] are the only letters I have recd. since I left home.

My love to Mary [Mentelle Clay] & your children.[3]

ALS. MH. 1. Mercer to Clay, Nov. 25, 1846. 2. A heckler was an implement for cleaning flax or hemp. A scutcher was an implement used to separate the wood from the valuable fiber of flax and hemp. For the processing of hemp, see James F. Hopkins, *A History of the Hemp Industry in Kentucky* (Lexington, 1951), 58-64. 3. Thomas's children at this time were Lucretia Hart, Henry Boyle, and Thomas Hart.

To JAMES BROWN CLAY New Orleans, February 2, 1846

I recd. your letter of the 15h. Ulto. and I am glad to hear that you & Susan [Jacob Clay] are happy to be in your new house,[1] and I hope your bad colds did not prove serious.

On the 21st Ulto. I sent in duplicate by the way of the river and by Mobile & Balto. a check on N. York for $5646:67 at forty days after date. I hope one or both of them reached you in safety, to enable you to meet our note in the N[orthern]. Bank.[2]

I am greatly distressed by the unhappy occurrence to Fayette Shelby.[3] Would not the sad event enable you to make up your difficulty with his father [James Shelby] by expressing your sympathy with him, and tendering any professional advice you can give him?

In consequence of the Steam boat having discontinued her voyages to the Havana, I believe that I shall relinquish my intention of going there.

I have not yet finally settled with [Ursin] Bouligny [Jr.], but expect to do so in a few days, after, which I will remit whatever may be coming to you.[4]

I am a little afraid of some neglect on the part of [Ambrose] Barnett & wish you would look occasionally into his movements at Ashland.[5]

Give my love to Susan and kisses to Lucy [Jacob Clay].

ALS. DLC-TJC (DNA, M212, R10). Addressed to J.B. Clay at Lexington. Noted under postmark: "Henry [Clay, Jr.] arrived in N.O. 2 Feb." 1. Clay to Henry Clay, Jr., April 8, 1845. 2. On Jan. 21, 1846, from New Orleans Clay sent a draft on William N. Mercer for $5,646.67 to Messrs. A. & J. Dennistoun, New York with the endorsement "Pay to James B. Clay on order H. Clay." DS, partially printed. DLC-TJC (DNA, M212, R10). Clay also wrote James B. Clay on Jan. 21, 1846, informing him that "I transmit enclosed the second number of a draft, the first of which I have sent by Louisville for $5646:67 to be applied to the paymt of our note at the N. Bank & the bal. to be accounted for by you." ALS. *Ibid.* 3. On Jan. 10, 1846, an intoxicated Lafayette Shelby left a party at the Phoenix Hotel, got into a fight with Henry M. Horine, pulled a gun, and killed Horine. Shelby was arrested for murder and denied bail. He swore in an affidavit that he fired only when he believed Horine was about to draw a knife. Clay defended Shelby at his trial, which started July 1, 1846. The jury failed to reach a verdict, and Shelby was released on bail. The case was continued several times, and when Shelby failed to appear for trial in Sept., 1848, the bail bond was forfeited, and he fled to Texas. He did not return to Lexington until 1862, by which time the case virtually had been forgotten.

Horine, a native of Jessamine County, was employed at a Lexington grocery at the time he was killed. J. Winston Coleman, Jr., *Henry Clay's Last Criminal Case* (Lexington, 1950), 1-20. 4. Bouligny to Clay, July 17, 1845. 5. Clay to Thomas Hart Clay, Jan. 24, 1846.

To THOMAS HART CLAY New Orleans, February 2, 1846

I have just returned from examining your first shipment of hemp, which has safely arrived. It looks very rough and unsightly, but appears clean. It is not even well corded, one or two bales having come loose at the ends. I am now satisfied that it ought to be covered, that is the sides not the ends, with bagging. I am sure that the additional price will more than compensate the additional expence.

There is no market for hackled or scutched hemp[1] here at present. W[orsley]. F[oreman] and Kennedy shewed me a very portly looking article, admirably put up of Missouri hemp, which they had unsuccessfully offered at $105. I have consequently diverted the shipment of it to N York to Charles P. Leverick,[2] who is here, and who has a very high reputation. Mr. [Thomas S.] Kennedy has, he tells me, engaged the freight at six dollars per ton, and I shall, have it insured[.]

I am very apprehensive that the price of all descriptions of dew retted hemp in the Eastern markets will be low, and you had better feel your way slow & cautiously, not contracting for too much, nor at two high prices. Can you make any sales in Louisville? What have you done with the Water retted hemp? [James] Morrison Pindell,[3] who is here, told me that he had instructed Mr Minton, if he did not buy it, to let us put it in with some of his in a contract at $154, delivered at Louisville. You had better see Mr. M about it. I received your letter of the 14h. as I had that of the 10h. I am truly unfortunate with my Stock, and regret the losses very much, especially of the hogs.[4]

The price you had to give for your hands was higher than I hoped you would have been able to get them at. But I hope that the two branches of business in which you have engaged may turn out well. Economy & industry ought to be your watchwords, without which you cannot succeed.

H[enry]. C[lay]. Duralde is here, and Martin [Duralde III] at Cuba. Poor boys, I do not see how they are to get along. Neither Henry nor his father [Martin Duralde, Jr.] has engaged in any business yet, and seem entirely at a loss what to do. Nor have either of them any means except what they are to get from Mr. Erwin,[5] who has paid them in bonds.

I have at last heard from Mr. Holt,[6] who has remitted me $700 only, that being the amt of all the sales he had made. He says that some of the bagg marked with the Arrow brand was brought to Savannah & sold at 12 Cents, a price at which he would not sell ours; but he hoped to make some further sales before the last year's crop was closed.

In consequence of the Steam boat not running between here and Cuba, I think I shall give up going to that island. I shall probably make one or two excursions from N. Orleans.

Give my love to your Mama [Lucretia Hart Clay], to Mary [Mentelle Clay] and to all the children.[7]

P.S. Captain Shalerofa informs me that a barrel has been put on board the Peytona addressed to Ashland for me. It had better be sent for to the Depot[.]

I sent up by Pat. (Johns boy)[8] a whole parcel of seed of the Arbor Vita & Laura Mundi[9] & directed him to deliver them at Louisville to Henry [Clay, Jr.] As he is coming away, Mr [Thomas] Smith had better be written to about them[.][10]

ALS. DLC-HC (DNA, M212, R6). 1. See Clay to Thomas H. Clay, Jan. 24, 1846. 2. For Leverick, New York City businessman and banker, see William T. Bonner, *New York, The World's Metropolis 1623-4—1923-4* . . . (New York, 1924), 492. 3. Son of Thomas H. Pindell and great-nephew of Lucretia Hart Clay. 4. Ashland's proximity to Lexington made it easy for dogs to kill livestock. Clement Eaton, *Henry Clay and the Art of American Politics* (Boston, 1957), 75; see also Clay to Beatty, April 29, 1847. 5. Probably James Erwin. 6. Of Holt & Atchison in Savannah. See Clay to Berrien, Sept. 26, 1846. 7. Lucretia Hart, Henry Boyle, and Thomas Hart Clay. 8. Reference obscure. 9. Shrubs. 10. On Feb. 7, 1846, Clay again wrote Thomas to inform him of the arrival of "45 bales of your hemp. . . . Like the former parcel it shows the want of covering & I repeat that I think you had better incur that expence." Has sent the "former parcel of 29 bales" to Leverick in New York. Adds: "I saw some of Richardsons today, which was covered all round, and six times corded. It looked very well." Notes that charges total about $30 per ton, so that "I fear . . . that the profit if any, will be very small." Advises his son: "Your success depends 1st. upon the quality of the hemp, 2dly. on the price, and 3dly. on the neatness with which it may be handled. I repeat that I would not engage with a rush in the business, until you felt the market." Points out that "There was a considerable sale of hemp the other day but at low prices." ALS. DLC-HC (DNA, M212, R6). Addressed to Thomas Hart Clay at Lexington.

To Samuel Judah, Vincennes, Ind., February 6, 1846. Informs Judah that "The Supreme Court of La. has overruled the petition for a rehearing in the case of Dubreuils heirs [Clay to Henry Clay, Jr., March 17, 1845], and I understand that the U.S. have no intention, in the present state of the cause to take it up to their Supreme Court." Adds that "In consequence of the adoption of a new Constitution. . . . much progress cannot be made in the cause, beyond preparing what will require some time & be attended with more expence than I anticipated." Considers it "important to unite [Gilbert Antoine de St.] Maxents title if it can be procured, to that of Dubreuils heirs." Doubts that "the sale of 1758 did not pass their right to the land occupied by the fortifications, subject to the Kings right to use it for that purpose." Has learned that "the State of La. has obtained from the Archives of France Copies of all documents & papers . . . relating to the Colony of La. and that they have arrived." Intends to ask Gustavus Schmidt and Richard H. Wilde to search through the papers again "to ascertain if those, made at . . . my request, overlooked [Gaspard Pierre de] Rochemores order." ALS. Courtesy of Professor Charles J. Bayard, Fort Collins, Colo. Letter is postmarked from New Orleans.

The 1845 Louisiana constitution lifted property qualifications for voting and holding office and granted suffrage to white males twenty-one years of age or over who had been U.S. citizens for 2 years and had resided in the state for 2 consecutive years prior to the election. It also reorganized the judicial system, creating a supreme court with appellate jurisdiction only and judges appointed for 8 years, as well as district courts with judges appointed for 6 years. Melvin Evans, "A Study in the State Government of Louisiana," in *Louisiana State University Studies*, no. 4 (Baton Rouge, 1931), 28-33; Perry H. Howard, *Political Tendencies in Louisiana* (Baton Rouge, 1957), 47-51.

To LUCRETIA HART CLAY New Orleans, February 17, 1846

I have remitted to Mr. [John Jacob] Astor since I have been here $700 on a/c of my debt to him. I have also sent him the first number of a Check for $1000. I send you enclosed the second number of the same check, which you will keep until my return home.

I am without any late letters from Ashland, and am very anxious about things there. I hope that you have got through the winter without much trouble. Thomas [Hart Clay] wrote me a terrible account about losses of my stock, and I trust that they have ceased.[1]

If Mr. [Ambrose] Barnett is in want of work beasts, I wish that you would tell him to break some of my Mules.

I owe John [Morrison Clay] $25 on a/c of his part of one of the bull calves which has been sold, the other is not yet sold. If he wants that sum I should be glad that it should be paid to him, if you have it to spare[.]

I go to day up the Coast for a few days.

My love to all at home.

ALS. DLC-TJC (DNA, M212, R10). 1. Thomas's letter not found, but see Clay to Thomas H. Clay, Feb. 2, 1846.

From Eustis & Chaplin, Natchez, Miss., March 5, 1846. Inform Clay that "Mr [William St. John] Elliot has stated to us that you hold a certificate of deposit of the Agt [Agricultural] Bank for some 3000 dollars—which you desire to collect or secure by proceeding." Gave Elliot copies, for Clay's information, of "the late acts of the Mississippi Legislature upon the subject of the Bank." State that a "Judgt of ouster was entered against the Agt Bank at the May term 1845—upon demurrer to the Court charging mere insolvency, neglect to redeem their notes.—(without fraud or wilful neglect)—" Note that the courts ascertained "that it was best to surrender to the Trustee. The trustee is therefore now in possession of the assets of the Bank." Believe that "the Bank notes, in existence do not amount to 500,000 Dollars" and that "the amt of good debts due to the Bank largely exceeds that sum—300000 at least." Since the "effect of this legislation, here has been to depreciate the paper to a lower point, than it had ever reached before," suspect that Clay will recover his funds only if "a purchaser (residing in another state) of a bill . . . can sue in the Federal court" and force the paper to "rise rapidly." ALS. DLC-HC (DNA, M212, R6).

Horatio Eustis and E.K. Chaplain were law partners, neighbors, and brothers-in-law. Their wives, Catherine and Amenaide, respectively, were the daughters of Henry Chotard, a wealthy planter and businessman who owned a huge plantation near Natchez called "Somerset." *Biographical and Historical Memoirs of Mississippi . . .*, 2 vols. (Chicago, 1891), 1:542; and information supplied by the Mississippi Department of Archives and History.

The act passed by the recent legislative session, entitled "An Act to amend an act entitled an act to prescribe the mode of proceeding against incorporated banks for a violation of their corporate franchises . . . approved July 26, 1843," gave persons holding certificates of deposit, bills, bonds, etc. of insolvent banks up to 12 months to present their claims to commissioners appointed by the courts. It also established the order of distribution of funds to be made by trustees. Those whose claims had been proven to the commissioners were fourth on the list of those to be paid. The trustees had been appointed under the 1843 act. *Laws of the State of Mississippi, Passed . . . in January, February And March, A.D. 1846* (Jackson, Miss., 1846), 118-23.

To THOMAS HART CLAY New Orleans, March 9, 1846

I received your letter of the 20h. Ulto. and I was glad to learn from you that you had purchased no hemp since I left home; for according to existing prospects, I am really afraid that it will prove a losing business. There is little or no demand for the article here. Heckled hemp has been sold as low as 92$ per ton, and I do not observe from the price currents of Eastern markets that it is doing much better there. The greater part of what you have sent here has been shipt to New York.[1] Freights are now however high, being 10 to 11 dollars per ton. Mr. [Thomas S.] Kennedy thinks that they will fall when the market is relieved from the Cotton now pressing on it. Bagging and rope continue dull and low.

I hope that you will purchase little or none until my return. If you buy any it should be only that of the best quality, and at the lowest price. If the business is to occasion loss it had better not be prosecuted. Could not Henry Watkins[2] employ his hands in some profitable way, breaking hemp, or even breaking stone?

I have been quite unwell for some days with a bad cold, and I am still confined to the house; but I hope that it is passing off.

My intention is to return by St. Louis, with the hope of being able to sell the land there belonging to James [Brown Clay][3] and me. And it will be about the 10h. April before I expect to reach home.

We have had much cold weather here for this climate. Henry [Clay] Duralde's mare sold for $115 but the expences on her will reduce very much the net price.

Give my love to your mother [Lucretia Hart Clay], and to Mary [Mentelle Clay] and her children [Lucretia Hart, Thomas Hart, & Henry Boyle Clay] and to John [Morrison Clay].

ALS. DLC-HC (DNA, M212, R6). 1. Clay to Thomas H. Clay, Feb. 2, 1846. 2. Clay to Thomas H. Clay, Dec. 25, 1849. 3. See 8:801; 9:40, 45-46, 48-49, 87-88, 90, 818.

To LUCRETIA HART CLAY New Orleans, March 16, 1846

I send by the Peytona to day a hogshead of brown sugar, two barrels of White, one in loaf and the other crushed, a box of black tea (presented by Dr. [William N.] Mercer) two boxes, one containing my embroidered portrait, and the other a lamp stand worked, and some Orange trees for James [Brown Clay]. I hope they will all arrive safe. I intend some of the brown sugar for Thomas [Hart Clay]. I cannot get all the seed here, of which Mr. George[1] made a memo: but I shall send some others. I have sent two parcels of Arbo Vita Seed and plenty of the Laura Mundi.

I shall leave here on saturday next for Natchez, where I shall remain three or four days and then proceed to St. Louis, which I hope to reach by the first or second of April. I may remain there about a week, and then return home.

I have had a very bad cold which confined me nearly a week. I am now however recovered from it.

The residue of the bagging at this place has been sold at 11′ pr. There now only remains that at Savannah.

I have written to James to supply you with money, if you want any, out of funds of mine in his hands.

I am endeavoring to secure something out of the deposite I have with the Agricultural Bank at Natchez which is put in jeopardy by a late act of the Legislature.[2]

Tell John [Morrison Clay] that I would be glad if he would write to me at Natchez.

My love to all at home.

P.S. I have another parcel of trees—just arrived—five Japan plumbs or Quince trees, which go by the Peytona[.]

ALS. DLC-TJC (DNA, M212, R10). 1. Possibly Joseph George, a Lexington grocer. MacCabe, *Directory of the City of Lexington . . . 1838 & '39.* 2. Eustis & Chaplain, March 5, 1846.

From Horace Greeley, New York City, March 17, 1846. Although he has not written much to Clay since "the Country's great disaster," presents a copy of a work by an "author . . . who, though born beneath another sky, has devoted many years of his life to the pursuits of a practical Artisan and Inventor among us, and especially to the improvement and perfection of the Machinery employed in our Manufactures." Describes this unknown work as "the only labor of his life which has not been of a thoroughly practical character."

Hopes Clay will welcome the writing "as one more evidence that the Arts of Peace are attaining their proper place in the estimation of mankind; and that War, with its desolating atrocities and horrors, is destined no longer to be the *only* subject of Historical blazonry and commemmoration." Trusts that this token "from a member of that great body of American Manufacturers and Artisans who naturally regard you, the most eminent champion and constant guardian of their interests . . . will not be regarded by you otherwise than with kindly allowance if not with positive favor." ALS. DLC-HC (DNA, M212, R6).

To Octavia Walton LeVert, Mobile, Ala., March 17, 1846. Is sorry to learn "you have been affected by the prevailing Influenza." Adds: "For ten days I have been quite ill with it, in so much that Dr. Luzenburg daily attended me four of five days. Nearly all last week I was confined to my room." Regrets that his illness "has deprived me of the pleasure of visiting Mobile, enjoying the hospitality of your house and seeing my good friends in your City." Leaves New Orleans "sadly mortified and chagrined that I could not go to Mobile."

Notes that "I sit today to Mr. Parker, and shall give him some other sittings prior to my departure, chiefly because you desired it, and because I have an opportunity there of seeing some beautiful portraits, *one* of which especially interests me."

Writes of "a great Fancy ball & masked, at the St Charles [Hotel]" but "did not attend, owing to my indisposition. It is spoken of as a very splendid affair." Suspects, however, that "you are as well informed as to what occurs here, as if you were with us."

Encourages her to visit "our watering places in Kentucky this summer" since "such a jaunt would greatly benefit you." Concludes: "I shall be soon, my dear friend, far, far from you, but I shall never cease to feel the constant solicitude of your happiness, and that of all those connected with you," and regrets his inability to visit her family. ALS. Courtesy of Caldwell Delaney, Mobile, Ala. Written from New Orleans.

For Dr. Charles A. Luzenberg, founder of the New Orleans Medical School, see *CAB*. For C.R. Parker, a portrait and historical painter who visited New Orleans in 1826, 1832, 1838, and 1845-46, see Groce, *Dictionary of Artists in America.* No Parker portrait of Clay has been located; however, Clay did sit for Dennis Malone Carter about this time and it is possible he confused the two names. Amyx, "Portraits of Henry Clay," 2 vols., Special Collections, University of Kentucky, vol. A; New Orleans *Daily Picayune*, March 22, 1846.

To WILLIAM NEWTON MERCER Natchez, Miss., March 23, 1846

I arrived here a little before midnight, amidst darkness, mud and rain, after a most disagreeable to day, and we lodged the residue of the night in the stationary boat.

Finding it very uncertain when the Maria will return, I have determined to take a passage to St. Louis in the Harry of the West,[1] if I can get one; and I have therefore to request the favor of you to engage a State room for me, and to desire the Captn. to take me up here. I should be glad, if it be practicable, to know what day and at what time, night or day, she will arrive here.[2]

I forgot to mention to you that the 2 Vols of [Adolphe] Thiers[3] were sent for from the St Charles, as having been left by mistake at your house, and were accordingly returned. . . .

ALS. LU-Ar. Addressed to Mercer at Canal Street in New Orleans. 1. "Harry of the West" was a steamboat built in 1843 which measured 490 in tonnage and had a cargo capacity of 750 tons. Louis C. Hunter, *Steamboats on the Western Rivers* (Cambridge, Mass., 1949), 652. 2. On March 24, 1846, Clay again wrote Mercer, this time from "D'Evereux," William St. John Elliot's plantation near Natchez. Explains: "When I wrote to you yesterday, I was not aware that the Princess was so soon to return to N. Orleans. If therefore she goes back to St. Louis, *and you have not engaged for me a passage in the Harry,* I will thank you to take one in the Princess. The accounts I have received of the other Boat are less favorable." Still wishes to meet the boat at Natchez, but "since I may possibly go to Vicksburg . . . I will leave a message" if plans change. ALS. LU-Ar. Addressed to Mercer at Canal Street in New Orleans. 3. For Thiers—French statesman, journalist, and historian—see *Encyclopedia Britannica,* 11th ed. The two volumes were probably part of Thiers' 10-vol. *Histoire de la Revolution Francaise.*

To Elizabeth A. Linn, St. Louis, Mo., April 17, 1846. Regrets "not finding you at home" before he left to return to Kentucky. "I desired to again express to you my high satisfaction in meeting you here, and renewing the agreeable intercourse which I enjoyed in your society in Washington city." Wishes also "once more, to assure you of my deep sympathy and condolence on account of your great bereavement." Hopes her "promising children," especially her son, "will maintain and add to the reputation of his father [Lewis F. Linn], who was a bright ornament to the highest council in our country." Copy. Printed in E.A. Linn and N. Sargent, *The Life and Public Services of Dr. Lewis F. Linn* (New York, 1857), 391-92. Written from St. Louis on the day of his departure.

Lewis F. Linn had died on October 3, 1843. His children were Augustus and Mary Linn. *Ibid.*, 62, 418.

From Lord Morpeth [George Howard], Castle Howard, near Molton, England, April 17, 1846. Apologizes for "breaking in at all upon the repose of Ashland (a repose however against the cause of which I protest in common with the sound sense of mankind at large)" but asks on a friend's behalf "whether you happen to know any thing of a Mr William Cavendish" who may have accompanied Clay "upon your return to America in 1815-16 (?), and if so, what befell him."

Comments on current diplomatic and political affairs: "I think upon our side there would be a sincere adverse to any conflict between us [over Oregon]." On another topic, adds: "I am afraid I must not bespeak *your* sympathy for our Free Trade movement. It rather hangs fire during its progress through the Legislature, but I am inclined to believe that the House of Lords will pass the bill."

Enquires "after your stock of cattle; we are rather proud of our breed in this place, and sold two short horned cows last autumn for . . . 300 (Pounds) . . . a good price." Wonders if "your servant Charles [Dupuy] is still with you." ALS. DLC-HC (DNA, M212, R6). Printed in Colton, *Clay Correspondence*, 4:535-36. Sent to Clay by way of Liverpool and postmarked in Boston, Mass., on May 5, 1846.

The Free Trade movement in Britain culminated in a new customs law and repeal of the corn laws on June 6, 1846. The latter set the duty on corn at a shilling a quarter beginning in 1849 and allowed a small protective duty in the interim. The new customs law abolished duties on live animals and most kinds of meat and reduced the duty on butter, cheese, and other foods. Duties on many manufactured items were either reduced or abolished. William L. Langer (ed.), *An Encyclopedia of World History*, 4th ed. (Boston, 1968), 661; Wilbur D. Jones & Arvel B. Erickson, *The Peelites, 1846-1857* (Columbus, Ohio, 1972), *passim.*

To THOMAS B. STEVENSON Lexington, April 27, 1846

My son Henry [Clay, Jr.] will have informed you that owing to the bad weather, he did not carry with him to Frankfort, [George P.A.] Healys portrait of me.[1] The truth is, it is in a frame, and cannot be conveniently carried, at least, without being box up, and I must also add that it is Mrs [Lucretia Hart] Clays, it having been presented to her by the Artist; she prises it highly, and is not willing to part from it unless you are more desirous than you ought to be to have a portrait of me. Would not one of [John] Dodges fine engravings[2] satisfy the friendly feelings which prompt you.

Copy. OCHP. 1. Clay to Henry Clay, Jr., June 21, 1845. 2. See 9:880.

To NATHAN SARGENT Lexington, April 28, 1846

I reached home in good health a few days ago, after an absence of four months, and found here your favor of the 13h. March, which had followed me from N[ew]. O[rleans]. and for which I thank you.

I perceive that, after great divisions in each of the two houses of Congress among members even of the same party, the two houses themselves have disagreed. Should they finally disagree, and leave the Oregon question where it has been so many years, I for one shall not regard it as National misfortune.[1] Then, negotiation may be again tried, with a better prospect of success than if the proposed notice, in any form, be given.[2] For if it be given, England cannot fail to discern the quo animo, and she will be less likely to negotiate, in an amicable spirit, with a threat of total expulsion from Oregon suspended over her head, than if no such menace is thrown out. Putting herself on her dignity and pride, she may say that she will make no proposal whatever towards an accommondation of the difficulty, but will receive any that we may choose to offer.

I have never been, during the last year, and am not now, without fears for the peace of the Country. I am far from believing that England is quite as averse from War with this Country as she is believed to be at Washington.[3] These fears are not allayed by the more moderate form of notice adopted in the Senate. The President [James K. Polk] *at his discretion* is to give the notice. But will he not feel bound to give it?

After having formally and publicly announced to Congress and to the world his opinion that the notice ought to be given, can it be expected that, when fully authorized, he will forbear to give it? Will he not be urged by those whom he deems his best friends, the Ultra's of the party, to give the notice?[4] And may he not have deluded himself into the honest belief that the giving of the notice will facilitate our acquisition of the whole Territory? But I stop. I have not written so much on public affairs to Washington, since the commencement of the present Session of Congress.

I concur with you entirely in believing that it would be altogether premature, and highly indiscreet and impolitic for the Whig party to make any movement whatever, in favor of any body, in respect to the next Presidential election.

I request you to communicate my warm regards to Mr. [Joseph] Chandler.

ALS. ViU. Letter marked "(Confidential)." Addressed to Sargent at Washington. 1. See 9:828-29. 2. After months of debate and several versions, a "joint resolution of notice to Great Britain to annul and abrogate the convention [of 1827] betweeen Great Britain and the United States" which had provided for joint occupation of Oregon passed the House 142 to 46 and the Senate 42 to 10 on April 23, 1846. It was signed by Polk on April 29. *Cong. Globe*, 29 Cong., 1 Sess., 716, 720; Washington *Daily National Intelligencer*, April 30, 1846. For the debate, see Merk, *The Oregon Question*, 368-88. 3. For British sentiments on Oregon, see Norman A. Graebner, *Empire on the Pacific* (New York, 1955), 140-43; and McCormac, *James K. Polk*, 583. 4. One version of the joint resolution, proposed by John J. Crittenden, had earlier passed the Senate. It would have placed on the president full responsibility for serving the notice. Merk, *The Oregon Question*, 387.

From William B. Astor, New York City, April 30, 1846. Acknowledges receipt of "a draft for $250 . . . payable by White, Stevens & Co Philadelphia &, a check for $95 . . . $300 [of] which shall be applied to your bond, held by my father [John Jacob Astor]." Has already applied to the bond "the $1000 draft [Clay to Lucretia Hart Clay, February 17, 1846] sent me sometime as well as the $700 previously sent." Encloses a statement of Clay's current account with Astor. ALS. MH-BA. The attached statement indicates that as of May 1, 1846, Clay had paid off $1700 of the principle on a $10,000 bond and had overpaid by $13.10 the amount of interest due on the bond.

To MARY S. BAYARD Lexington, May 7, 1846

Upon my return home my dear friend, some days ago, among the many letters which had reached here, during my absence, I was delighted to recognize your well known hand.[1] But, upon eagerly opening and perusing it, I was truly grieved with the sad misfortune which had befallen your poor dear Lizzie [Elizabeth Bayard]! Hard has been her fate! And then that she should have lost her love by that once so terrible disease of the small pox, which has now so long been, almost, banished from the world! Give my love to poor Lizzie, and assure her of my cordial sympathy. Tell her that distressing as the event has been necessarily to her it has not been quite as bad as that of a young lady, whom I saw a few weeks ago at Port Gibson. She was married in the morning, and her husband was a corpse before night! Your daughter is young, and will feel with painful sensibility her severe loss. But I hope that she will survive it, and live a long and happy life.

I returned home, after four months absence, in good health. I had a most disagreeable voyage down the river, owing to ice and low water. I passed my time chiefly in N. Orleans, with my good friend Dr. [William N.] Mercer. I did not go to Cuba, as I had intended, in consequence of there being no Steam boat plying between N.O. and Havanna [*sic*], and I was unwilling to encounter the discomforts of a small confined Sail-vessel.

No! my dear friend, I had not forgotten, and can never forget you and your family. I often talked of you with Dr. Mercer, Miss [Eliza] Young, Mrs. [Catherine Bingaman, (Mrs. Stephen)] Duncan &c &c but much oftener thought of you. You inquire what disposition I shall make of myself this summer. I have formed no plan, come to no resolution. I have some reluctance to leave home, after such a long absence recently from it. If I could get to you and other friends at the Eastward through the air, or by a simple act of volition, I should surprize you, on some early summer day, in little Willie

[Wilmington, Del.]. But the crowds I should have to encounter, the exciting scenes through which I might be obliged to pass, dissuade me from undertaking the journey. And yet I am not much better situated at home. Not a day passes that some stranger does not come here; nor am I sure in any one of the twenty four hours that I shall be free from Company. Yesterday afternoon, amidst rain, I had four distinct visits from six strangers, and two of them ladies. Your friendship for me prompts you to regard all these things as *triumphs* and with satisfaction. But to me they are excessively (what shall I say?) oppressive. I am obliged to supply, when these strangers come, all the capital of conversation, and you know I never liked much talking. They come to look and to listen, and a monysyllable is all that I can sometimes get from them. I am occasionally tempted to wish that I could find some obscure and inaccessible hole, in which I could put myself, and enjoy quiet and solitude during the remnant of my days.

But you did not inform me where you purpose passing the ensuing summer. I should have been glad to know, because if I could not join you which I should be most happy to do I could at least hear of and perhaps some times from you.

I saw a good deal of my fair Secretary (how come you to make her a brunnette?) in N. Orleans.[2] She was as gay as ever, and attended more balls, parties, operas, theatres in the same time than I ever saw any person before. Of course I was not with her on many of these occasions; nor did I put in requisition her excellent talents as a Secretary.

I am aware, my dear friend, that some of my partial & enthusiastic friends still cherish hopes about me, as you inform me. But I do not cherish any desire, nor entertain any serious expectation, of ever having my name again presented to the public as a Candidate. I have had my turn and my troubles and why should I wish to renew them? I am now free from responsibility of public affairs, and I have profited, in every way, by my retirement. I think I ought to be let alone.

Do me the favor to offer my warm regards to Mr. [Richard Henry] Bayard and to all your family. And rest assured of the unalterable esteem and regard . . .

ALS. DeHi. 1. Not found. 2. Reference obscure.

To Richard H. Bayard, Wilmington, Del., May 7, 1846. Inquires for further information "about a debt due to a friend of mine [Clay to Bayard, October 21, 1845] from the late Bank of the U.S. of Penna." Recalls Bayard's answer that "a large sum was tyed up by the U.S. and that if it were released, a dividend would be made among Creditors." Adds: "I have seen a statement in the papers that the matter has been compromised between the Government and the Bank, and if so, I suppose that some dividend has been, or will be declared." Admits that the "friend above alluded to is Isaac Shelby Esqr, a son of the late Govr [Isaac] Shelby, who holds by assignment a Judgment against the Bank for upwards of $50.000 with several years interest." Believes that the "Judgment was obtained by Bache, and I understand that the Trustees or Agents of the Bank are dissatisfied with him, and perhaps with James Erwin, who held some control over the judgment, on account of the use which one or both of them attempted to make of the Judgment." Assures Bayard, however, that Shelby, "the present assignee," is "an innocent and bona fide holder" of the judgment. Hopes Bayard will, therefore, "throw light on the prospects of my friend's now or hereafter realizing the debt due him." ALS. KyLxT. Endorsed on cover: "Henry Clay May 7h. 1846 Ansd. May 24h. and sent him Copy of Report of Stockholders of Bk. U S. Made on 4h. May inst and published on 5h May inst in United States Gazette. And a Copy of letter from Herman Cope Esq to Joshua Levis Esq agent of Mr. Isaac Shelby Dated. Apl. 26h. 1845, the two furnished all the information I could give."

The article in the Philadelphia *United States Gazette* of May 5, 1846, stated that the trustees of the U.S. Bank of Pennsylvania had used assets of the bank assigned them by the courts to discharge judgments to the amount of $291,649.76. They hoped next to settle claims arising under the 4th preference in the assignment—indemnity of all other sureties for any loss sustained by responsibility of the bank. The 5th assignment would then be made to all creditors of the bank except holders of post notes secured by the assignment of May 1. It further stated that many claims against the bank were being contested by the trustees through litigation, and, until these were settled, it would be impractical to pay a dividend to other creditors. In addition, many claims by the bank were being resisted by the debtors, and much time would be needed for legal proceedings to settle them.

To EUGENE ROUSSEL[1] Lexington, May 18, 1846

. . . The progress of American manufactures, during the last quarter of a century, ought to excite in the heart of every American citizen feelings of patriotic satisfaction. Every hope which I entertained at the commencement of the policy which fostered them,[2] has been realized and more than realized, and every prediction of the friends of that policy, as to quality, abundance, and cheapness, the effects of competition, and the operation upon the revenue of the General Government, has been fulfilled, and every counter prediction of the foes of the policy has completely failed.

I should, therefore, regard with deep regret the abandonment of a system from which such manifold benefits have sprung. Nor ought we, I think, to be seduced into a change of policy by the delusive example of any foreign power.[3]

The question of Protection, its degree, and its duration, is a question depending upon the state of circumstances in each particular nation.—Some nations, owing to the great perfection their manufactures have attained, may need no protection for them, and others may require more or less, or for a longer or a shorter time. If I were an English subject, I would be in favor of free trade for Great Britain, because the great variety and perfection of her manufactures, and her great advantages in the distribution of them, would enable her to maintain a successful competition in most of the markets in the world. When we have acquired more skill, accumulated more capital, and had more time to bring our manufactures to maturity and perfection, we shall be better prepared to consider whether we ought to adopt practically the doctrine of Free Trade. In the meantime, it is my firm belief that the destruction of our American Manufactures would ultimately be injurious to Great Britain in the commerce between the two countries, as it would most certainly be highly prejudicial to the United States.

Hoping that we may be preserved from such a calamity, and that you and all others engaged in Domestic Industry, in all its branches, may continue to enjoy the protecting care of our common Government[.]

Copy, extract. Printed in Lexington *Observer & Kentucky Reporter*, July 11, 1846. Letter addressed to Roussel at Philadelphia, Pa. 1. Roussel was a manufacturer and importer of perfumes, soaps, shaving creams, etc., located at 114 Chestnut and 44 Prune streets. John G. O'Brien, *Philadelphia Wholesale Business Directory and United States, South America and West Indian Circular for the Year 1845* (Philadelphia, 1845). 2. For examples of Clay's views on the tariff, see 8:604, 619-22, 626-27; 9:628, 646-47. 3. For Britain's recent move toward free trade, see Morpeth to Clay, April 17, 1846.

To MRS. F. EUSTIS[1] Lexington, May 19, 1846

Mrs. [Lucretia Hart] Clay, since my return home, has desired me to acknowledge for her the rect. of your friendly letter, with the several articles referred to in it, all of which came safe to hand. Those intended for Mrs. [Charlotte] Mentelle were delivered to her. Mrs. Clay is greatly obliged for your kind presents, which she found excellent, and requests me to tender her thanks, to what I beg leave to add my own. We are both gratified to hear of your daughter's continued good health, and Mrs. Clay thanks her for her present of a bag. We have had so little warm weather, that there has not been much occasion yet for employing the machine you kindly sent to make Ice cream. It seems well adapted to its object.

Poor Mr. [Augustus Waldemarde] Mentelle is in the hands of the Doctors for a serious operation.[2] He is not thought at present to be in great danger, but until he gets out of their hands, I shall not regard him safe.

The several branches of my family are well, and desire to be particularly remembered to you. James [Brown Clay] & Susan [Jacob Clay] are in their new house,[3] & Thomas [Hart Clay] & Mary [Mentelle Clay] hope soon to go into theirs.[4]

We shall all be happy again to see you here, & hope that we shall some day or other enjoy that satisfaction.

Do us the favor to present our warm regards to Mrs. [Julie Duralde] Clay, Mr. Eustis,[5] Mr. & Mrs. [William C.C.] Claiborne [Jr.] and to Maltida.[6]

ALS. DLC-George Eustis Papers (DNA, M212, R21). 1. It is not clear to whom Clay was writing; it would seem likely to be Mrs. George Eustis; however, her name was Clarisse Allain Eustis. 2. Mentelle died on June 26, 1846. George W. Ranck, *History of Lexington Kentucky* (Cincinnati, 1872), 354. 3. Clay Villa. 4. Mansfield. 5. Possibly George Eustis. 6. Possibly Marie Mathilde Eustis (b. July 3, 1831), daughter of George Eustis. *NEHGR* (April, 1878), 32:217.

To Farnham Plummer, Boston, Mass., May 26, 1846. Advises him that "My son [Thomas Hart Clay] had intended to ship a considerable quantity of Dew retted hemp this year; but the low price of the article in the Eastern markets has discouraged him and for the present he has ceased shipping." Adds that he himself has already "sold most of my water retted hemp in Louisville at $150 per ton." Expresses a willingness "here after to consign some of my hemp to you," but concludes that "I have found your old partners quite attentive & regular in their correspondence, and I should not regard it as right to quit them." ALS. KyLoF.

Farnham Plummer, commission merchant, operated his business from "19 and 20 Commercial wf. house 18 Franklin place." Charles Stimpson, *Boston Directory for 1847-48* (Boston, 1848).

From "B," Nashville, Tenn., June 1, 1846. Although "unknown to you—feels much gratified—that through a course of a well ordered Providence you have again returned after an absence of four months to your own 'Beautiful ashland' in perfect health." Prays that it may "be the pleasure of Heavan to . . . make you a Great & special blessing—to this perturbed and distracted Nation."

Desires to "take the liberty of discourseing a litle to you" in a "very strange and unexpected manner" which "may surprise you—but suffer no surprise—Simple truth has no cause to blush—though clad in a homely garb and comeing from the humblest of mortals."

Admits that "Since the last presidential Ellection" he had feared the "great Evils—that seemed comeing on our goverment & nation—but recently those sad feelings have left me." Adds: "what may surprise you—those hopes have grown from . . . a strange & singular dream—with its interpretation as presented to my mind when I awoke." Intends to narrate it even if "you are one of that class who discard all such things" because "the great God is witness that—what that I shall speak is true."

Recounts the dream: "I was in the midst of a large assembly of all ranks of persons—in which there was a most beautifull little girl—about Eight or ten years old—clad in tattered garments" who appeared "destitute of Parents or affectionate guardians." When the crowd attempted to decide who should "rear—cloth[e], & protect her . . . all by consent—agreed that you was the most proper person though advanced in life, to take charge of the damsel." You "accepted the little girl—with great cordiality—promiseing to do all things required."

Continues: "now—as God lives—this Earth stands . . . the following interpretation presented itself to my mind—the little damsel . . . was our goverment & nation—in a neglected and tattered condition—Beautifull in itself—but in bad keeping—the assembly—was the people of this nation—assigneing the care of the little girl—or goverment to you."

Believes that James K. Polk's "distructive policy, and arrant folly—more fully manifested—among which that of geting this nation—in to a foolish war with Mexico already—and perhaps with England soon" will cause "our goverment & nation" to "present quite a tattered garb—and barefooted but doubtless—it will prove an Excellent Eye salv[e]—to 'open the Eyes of the blind' and let them see—the necesaty of giveing the goverment—in charge of hands more capable—of takeing care of it." Quotes John J. Crittenden's "late speach" in which he had said that " 'it was by a strange and mysterious providence that the preasant Executive, came in to office,' " but adds that "I am persuaided God is about to let the Errors of this nation—correct them."

Recalls "two other dreams of singular charector. . . . that Genl. [William Henry] Harrison would tryumph" and "the dolefull tale of Polks tryumph." Wishes he could speak to Clay in person but "not knowing wheather you may spurn the writer and what he has spoken—or not—therefore think it most prudent—not to tell now my true name." Asks Clay to acknowledge receipt of the letter "by a small note—to B— 'Montgomerys P.O. Sumner Cty Ten—' " ALI. DLC-HC (DNA, M212, R6). Letter marked "(private)." Endorsed by Clay: "Anonymous—[A dream]."

To JOHN J. CRITTENDEN Lexington, June 1, 1846

Having recd. under your frank a letter from Mr. Fry,[1] I transmit the enclosed answer, which I will thank you to deliver.

From this unfortunate Mexican War,[2] I turn with much more anxiety to the Oregon question. Altho' I share in the hopes which appear to be entertained by the public, both in G. Britain & the U. States, that it will be amicably settled, I have seen nothing, in an authentic shape, to dispel my fears of a rupture, increased by the giving of the notice,[3] and by hostilities with Mexico.

ALS. NcD. 1. Probably Cary Harrison Fry, a graduate of West Point in the Class of 1834 and major of the 2nd Kentucky Volunteers, Henry Clay, Jr.'s regiment in the Mexican War. He was the senior surviving officer of the regiment after the Battle of Buena Vista. USMA,

Register, 186. See also Fry to Clay, March 22, 1847. 2. Clay to Lawrence, April 30, 1845. 3. See 9:829 and Clay to Sargent, April 28, 1846.

To DUDLEY SELDEN Lexington, June 4, 1846

I received your obliging letter, transmitting a Copy of one which you had addressed to Mr. [Richard Henry] Wilde, in respect to researches which he and I had requested you to make in the public archives at Havana. Be pleased to accept my thanks for your kind attention to our request. Genl. [Robert Blair] Campbell will no doubt complete the researches.[1]

The object of my trips to the South has been rather to preserve than to acquire health, by escaping our more rigorous winters. I have much reason to be thankful for what I enjoy. It is now so long before the next winter that I cannot undertake to say whether I shall be able or not then to visit Cuba. The pleasure of such a visit, which I have long desired to make, would be greatly augmented, if I can accomplish it, by finding you there. It is quite uncertain whether we may not both be prevented from going by a state of War with G. Britain, the danger of which I consider as much encreased by the fact of giving notice to terminate the treaty of joint occupation of Oregon,[2] and by the breaking out of hostilities with Mexico.[3]

ALS. KyLoF. Addressed to Selden at New York City. 1. General Campbell was consul at Havana. This research related to the case of the heirs of Dubreuil Villars. See Clay to Henry Clay, Jr., March 17, 1845. 2. See 9:829 and Clay to Sargent, April 28, 1846. 3. Clay to Lawrence, April 30, 1845.

To "A MERCANTILE HOUSE OF HIGH STANDING" IN NEW YORK CITY Lexington, June 5, 1846

I postponed answering your favor[1] until the arrival of the articles to which it refers, which you have been kind enough to present to me. They reached here yesterday in safety, and I request your acceptance of my thanks for them. The pleasure which we shall derive from using them, will be much increased by the fact, that both the raw material and the fabric are American. Their excellence attests the perfection which this important branch of woollen manufactures has attained in the United States, and it is the more gratifying because of the great difficulties with which they have constantly had to contend[.]

On both sides of the Atlantic, the policy of affording protection to domestic manufactures appears to be under consideration in the national legislatures. The British Minister has brought forward a measure embracing the doctrines of free trade,[2] not however without exceptions of several, and some very important articles.—The manufactures of Great Britain have reached a very high degree of perfection, by means of her great capital, her improved skill and machinery, her cheap labor, and under a system of protection long, perseveringly, and rigorously enforced. She moreover possesses immense advantages for the sale and distribution of her numerous manufactures, in her vast colonial possessions, from which those of foreign powers are either entirely excluded, or admitted on terms very unequal with her own.

I am not therefore surprised that under these favorable circumstances, Great Britain should herself be desirous to adopt, and to prevail on other nations to adopt the principles of Free Trade. I shall be surprised if any of the great nations of the continent should follow an example, the practical effects of which will be so beneficial to her and so injurious to them.

The propriety of affording protection to Domestic manufactures, its degree, and its duration, depend upon the national condition and the actual progress which they have made.—Each nation, of right, ought to judge for itself. I believe that history records no instance of any great and prosperous nation, which did not draw its essential supplies of food and raiment from within its own limits. If all nations were just commencing their career, or if their manufactures had all made equal progress, it might perhaps be wise to throw open the markets of the world to the freest and most unrestricted competition. But it is manifest, that while the manufactures of some have acquired all the maturity and perfection of which they are susceptible, and those of others are yet in their infancy, struggling hard for existence, a free competition between them must redound to the advantage of the experienced and skilful, and to the injury of those who are just beginning to naturalize and establish the arts.

No earthly gratification to the heart of a Statesman can be greater than that of having contributed to the adoption of a great system of National Policy, and of afterwards witnessing its complete success in its practical operation.—That gratification can be enjoyed by those who were instrumental in establishing the policy of protecting our Domestic Manufactures—Every promise which they made has been fulfilled—Every prediction which they hazarded as to the quality and quantity of the Domestic supply, as to the reduction of prices, as to the effect of competition at home, and as to the abundance of the public revenue, has been fully realized. And it is no less remarkable that every counter prediction without exception, of the opponents of the policy, has, in the sequel, been entirely falsified.

Without tracing particularly the operation of our earlier Tariffs, adjusted to both the objects of Revenue and Protection, and coming down to the last, it seems to me that if there ever were a beneficial effect from any public measure fully demonstrated, it is, that the Tariff of 1842,[3] beyond all controversy, relieved both the Government and the people of the United States, from a state of pecuniary embarrassment bordering on bankruptcy.

Entertaining these views and opinions, I should deeply regret any abandonment of the policy of protection, or any material alteration of the Tariff of 1842, which has worked so well.[4] If its operation had been even doubtful, would it not be wiser to wait further developments from experience, before we plunge into a new and unexplored theory? Scarcely any misfortune is so great to the business and pursuits of a people as that of perpetual change. . . .

Copy. Printed in the Lexington *Observer & Kentucky Reporter*, July 11, 1846. 1. Letter not found. 2. For the British Free Trade movement, see Lord Morpeth to Clay, April 17, 1846. At this time Sir Robert Peel was prime minister, but a struggle was going on between Conservatives of the Peel government and Whigs led by Lord John Russell who succeeded Peel as prime minister in July, 1846. Langer, *Encyclopedia of World History*, 661. 3. See 9:628. 4. For the Tariff of 1846 which lowered duties, see Clay to Greeley, June 23, 1846.

From Harry I. Thornton, Eutaw, Ala., June 8, 1846. Acknowledges "a communication from W[illiam]. McLane [*sic*, McLain] Esqr. the agent of the American Colonization society, on the subject of the bequest of his slaves, by the late Revd. Thos Sydenham Witherspoon [McLain to Clay, January 2, 1846]." Submits "a few suggestions for your better consideration" in the handling of this case. Notes: "The

Constitution of Ala. refers the subject of emancipation of slaves, to the Legislature," which has "prescribed the mode *of procedure* in the matter, *which is*, by *Deed* of the master &c. The Supreme Court of the State has adjudicated upon the subject, & have holden, that . . . emancipation cannot be effected by *Will*; neither by a direct bequest of freedom to the slave, nor by a direction to the Extr. as trustee, to carry out such intention." Believes Witherspoon understood the law and "framed his will, so as to accomplish his object, in the only way that it could be done; which was to bequeathe his slaves *as property*, to such legatee, as he believed, would do, what he clearly desired to be done," and that "you are the legatee of the slaves, and intended to be so by Mr W., from, a well grounded confidence, that you would effectuate his desire." Foresees potential legal problems from the wording of Witherspoon's will which may raise qûestions about " 'who is the legatee.' " Suggests that "you transfer to the Society by deed of release, or quitclaim, all interest vested in you" by the will "so that by inhibiting the transfer, I can maintain the right of the Society to recover, no matter which is the legatee." Such a move "would only be to protect *your* interest, & your answer would be only an acknowledgment of the transfer of any interest derived to you under, or through the will."

Intends to "observe your wishes . . . & file the Bill in the Federal Court." Warns, however, that "if the bequest should be considered as a violation of the settled policy of the State, I should fear that the Federal Court would, (it being a matter of State concern) adopt the State decision." ALS. DLC-HC (DNA, M212, R6).

On June 22, 1846, Clay responded to Thornton that "I concur with you in opinion that the bequest is to me of the slaves mentioned, in my own right and as property, altho' if I have any control in the matter, I shall certainly carry out the intentions of the devisor, by having the slaves sent to Liberia." Adds that "My impression was, and is, that the best course to pursue is to bring a suit in my name, as a Citizen of the State of K[entucky]. and as being the P[resident]. of the C[olonization]. S[ociety]. at the time of the death of Mr. W. and now, in the Circuit Court of the U.S. for the District of Alabama against his Exors. They, I understand, will not do more than make a formal defence." Believes that "this course is, probably, preferable to that of my making a transfer of the slaves to the American Colonization Society," because "It will keep more out of view the emancipation of the Slaves, about which a difficulty may arise under the laws of Alabama." Notes that the "Court will not know, and will have no right to know, whether I may hold the Slaves as my own property, or what disposition I may choose to make of them." Adds, however, that "if it be deemed best that I should transfer the Slaves to the Society, I have no sort of objection to doing so." Expects "the Society . . . to defray the expense of any litigation, to which the bequest may give rise." ALS. CU. Addressed to Thornton at Eutaw, Ala.

To WILLIAM OWSLEY Lexington, June 20, 1846

I have not felt at liberty to withhold from your Excellency a view of the enclosed strong letter[1] in behalf of Mr. [Calvin] Fairbanks [*sic*].[2] I am not acquainted with the writer of it, but I have informed him that I would transmit his letter to you, beyond which I should not interfere in the case.

ALS. Ky. 1. Not found. 2. Calvin Fairbank, a Methodist minister, and Delia Webster, a teacher, had been arrested on Sept. 30, 1844, for spiriting three slaves out of Lexington to Ohio. In Dec., 1844 Webster was sentenced to two years in prison and Fairbank to fifteen years. Gov. Owsley pardoned Webster on Feb. 24, 1845, and more than four years later Gov. John J. Crittenden pardoned Fairbank. J. Winston Coleman, Jr., "Delia Webster and Calvin Fairbank—Underground Railroad Agents," *FCHQ* (July, 1943), 17:129-42.

To Horace Greeley, New York City, June 23, 1846. Notes that of the many important events that have recently occurred, "not the least, is the unfortunate War with Mexico

[Clay to Lawrence, April 30, 1845]. Altho' I foretold, I lament its existence. A war between two neighboring Republics! Between them because the stronger one has possessed itself of Territory claimed by the weaker! Produced immediately by the transfer of the Army from Corpus Christi to the Rio Bravo [Rio Grande], a transfer which the president [James K. Polk] had the indiscretion to direct at *the very moment* when he was making professions of a desire to settle by amicable negotiation, the question of whether Mexico or the U.S. should have the ground which our Army was then directed forceably to occupy! This unhappy War never would have occurred if there had been a different issue of the Presidential contest of 1844 [Clay to Webb, February 29, 1844]; for in that case the annexation of Texas [Clay to Crittenden, February 15, 1844] would not have happened." Continues: "I wonder what the violent portion of the Abolitionists now think . . . having contributed to produce the present state of things [Clay to Clayton, December 2, 1844]? Their calumnies on me I observe are continued, with the view of lessening just indignation against their conduct, by making me out as wholly unworthy of support."

Predicts that the "Tariff of 1842 [9:6] . . . is doomed . . . a law will be passed protecting favored interests (Iron, Coal, Sugar, for example) and leaving all others to the mercy of Free trade." Asks also "to place my name on the list of subscribers to the [New York] *Tribune*," because he receives no other New York paper, "and there is none in which I expect to find more intelligence." Copy, extract. Printed in "List 65," *Catalog of Joseph Rubinfine* (February, 1981), Pleasantville, N.J.

In late 1845 Polk had sent John Slidell on a mission to Mexico to try to negotiate the boundary of Texas at the Rio Grande. When Slidell was not immediately successful, Gen. Zachary Taylor received orders on February 3, 1846, to advance into the disputed territory. In late April, Mexican troops crossed in force north of the river into the disputed territory. On May 11, Polk sent his war message to Congress, which approved a declaration of war two days later. Bauer, *The Mexican War*, 48-49, 68-69.

The Tariff of 1846, often called the Walker Tariff for its chief author Secretary of the Treasury Robert Walker, moderated protection rather than applying free trade principles. Signed into law on July 30, 1846, it remained in effect until 1857 [9 *U.S. Stat.*, 79-86]. Frank W. Taussig, *The Tariff History of the United States* (New York, 1888), 114-15; MacCormac, *James K. Polk*, 672-78; James P. Shenton, *Robert John Walker: A Politician from Jackson to Lincoln* (New York, 1961), 79-86.

To Octavia Walton LeVert, Mobile, Ala., June 25, 1846. Regrets "that your duties to one of the best of mothers [Sally Walker Walton], and to your husband [Dr. Henry LeVert] and children confine you this summer to Mobile. You should really pay us a visit. You will find the Kentucky of the present day widely different from the Kentucky you formerly saw. Great improvements have been made, especially about our numerous watering places."

Assures her "My disappointment in not going to Mobile, after your departure from N[ew]. O[rleans]. was even greater than yours. It had constituted a principal object of my visit to the South."

Reflects upon "The same trumpet of War, which you so well describe as sounding in Mobile" that already "has summoned several thousand Kentuckians to repair to the field of battle [Clay to Lawrence, April 30, 1845]. Of the volunteers from this State, a vast proportion of them are Whigs, who disapproved of the measures which have led to this unfortunate War. Among them is my son Henry [Clay, Jr.], who goes as Lt. Col. in one of our Regiments [2nd Kentucky Volunteers]. We cannot but admire and approve the patriotic and gallant spirit which animates our Country men, altho' we might wish that the cause in which they have stept forth was more reconcilable with the dictates of conscience."

Informs her that "G. Britain has tendered her mediation to the belligerents. Our

Oregon controversy [9:829] being now amicably settled, I hope . . . some other means will be found to terminate a War so afflicting to humanity and to the friends of Free Government."

Since his return from the South, "altho' I have, daily almost, crowds of visitors I find myself comparatively so quiet here" that "I do not seek professional employment; but now and then some is forced upon me. . . . I have to appear in defence of Lafayette Shelby to be tried next week for killing a young man last winter [Clay to James B. Clay, February 2, 1846]. It is a very hard case, but for the sake of his numerous and highly respectable connections, I hope to be able to secure his acquittal." ALS. KyLoF.

Three regiments of Kentucky Volunteers, totaling 2,604 men, were mustered into service in May and June of 1846. *House Exec. Doc.* 48, 29 Cong., 2 Sess., p. 7.

From Lewis J. Cist, Cincinnati, Ohio, July 4, 1846. At the request of "my learned friend Dr. [Hermann E.] Ludewig, (whose visit to you, at Ashland, in Janny 1845, you probably remember)," presents a "Copy of a work, recently published by him, on the 'literature of American Local History.' " Asks Clay to accept as well "the accompanying Copy of a little Volume of Poems published by me during the past winter." Offers the gift "from my desire to omit no opportunity . . . to testify the warm and *unabated* admiration, and attachment with which, *as an American*, and *a Whig*, I am proud to regard your longtried public worth and Services to your Country." ALS. NHi.

On August 5, 1846, Clay wrote Cist that he had received Ludewig's work "for which I have addressed a letter, making my acknowledgments, directly to him." Believes that the "Dr. has rendered a good service . . . to his adopted Country. Judging . . . by those states with which I am most familiar, I think it remarkably correct and complete." Thanks Cist "for the interesting volume of your own poems" which he has read "with very great satisfaction." Adds that "many of your 'Trifles' appear to me to display a genuine spirit of poetic inspiration. And the purity of their morals and patriotism cannot be contested." Hopes Cist "will continue to employ your leisure hours in contributing, in this way, to the amusement and instruction of the Community." ALS. MWiW.

For Ludewig (1808-56), a lawyer and writer who settled in New York City after immigrating to the U.S. in 1844, see *CAB*. Ludewig privately published *Literature of American Local History* in New York in 1846.

Cist's volume of poetry was called *Trifles in Verse*.

To William B. Wedgwood, New York, July 30, 1846. Acknowledges Wedgwood's plan for presenting him "with some large and liberal testimonial of a pecuniary nature, by the Whigs of the U. States" but feels "constrained to express my disapprobation of it." Remains impressed by the "numerous testimonies of the attachment and esteem of my Whig brethren" which "have poured in on me" since the presidential election. Adds: "Many of my friends too, in the most delicate & unostentatious manner imaginable, have contributed to my relief from pecuniary embarrassment. . . . by applying directly to my creditors and cancelling my obligations held by them. And I remain even to this day ignorant of the names of most of these generous contributors [Tilford to Clay, February 17, 1845; Lawrence to Clay, March 13, 1845]." Refuses to "think of giving my consent to any further appeal to the purses of my friends" to avoid the "possibility of my being a burden to any part of the community." Although grateful for Wedgwood's interest, responds that his efforts are not necessary: "It is true that I am not rich; but I am now nearly free from debt, and I possess a competency to enable me, to live in comfort during the remnant of my days, and to fulfill some of the duties of hospitality." ALS. KyU.

Wedgwood, a Maine native and New York City attorney, was a close friend of

Horace Greeley and an active Whig. He authored several works, including one on the constitution and laws of New York, and in 1857 he established a law school. William B. Wedgwood, *Civil Service Reform* (Portland, Me., 1883), 89-107.

To John W. Graves *et al.*, July 31, 1846. Acknowledges an invitation to "a general meeting of our fellow-citizens from Georgia and other adjacent States, at the base of Stone Mountain in DeKalb County, for the purpose of promoting the important inter[e]sts of scientific Agriculture and Internal Improvements generally." Realizes that "many of the most distinguished sons of Georgia, and some whom I have the honor to number among my personal friends" will be in attendance, and he would enjoy the opportunity "to consult with them on the highly interesting subjects which bring them together." Adds: "From what I saw and heard, when I was in Georgia, two years ago, I was satisfied that that State, in a quiet and unostentatious but effective way, had accomplished more, in the great improvement by Railroads, which distinguishes the present age, than any state in the Union." Regrets that he "did not receive your obliging invitation in time to make the neccessary arrangements for so long a journey," and "must content myself with the . . . fervent hope" that the meeting's "deliberations may contribute to the promotion of the laudable objects in view." Copy. Printed in the Lexington *Observer & Kentucky Reporter*, September 9, 1846.

John W. Graves was the owner of the site on which the hotel at Stone Mountain Depot was built. Graves called for a meeting there in 1846 to discuss non-political issues. Out of this meeting, held on August 17, 1846, grew the Southern Agricultural Society. James C. Bonner, *A History of Georgia Agriculture 1732-1860* (Athens, Ga., 1964), 116; David W. Lewis, *Transactions of the Southern Central Agricultural Society from its Organization in 1846 to 1851* (Macon, Ga., 1852), iii-viii.

From James Hamilton, Savannah, Ga., August 12, 1846. Regrets missing Clay in New Orleans "when you did me the honor to call at my Lodgings and that I should have been so unfortunate, as to have found on my calling at Dr [William Newton] Mercers, that you had left the City." Had hoped for "an opportunity of reiterating to you, the assurances of my high personal esteem, which a mere temporary difference of opinion on a Question of national policy [Texas annexation], would have no power to impair." Wonders if "your successful Rival for the Presidency [James K. Polk], will have occasion to envy you, in your retirement, or you him in his distinction," but concludes that "defeat can be turned into triumph . . . emphatically your case." Assures Clay that if he had won, "you would have been surrounded by ten thousand false friends & scycophants soliciting your patronage. Your defeat revealed to you your true ones with testimonies of devoted & enthustic attachment. . . . *Such reveries* are reserved in this World for few Men."

If they had met in New Orleans, he had intended to ask Clay "if you had seen my reply to a Mr. [John Randolph] Bryan of this state, (who was a sort of *protege* of the late Mr [John] Randolph) *in* relation to your duel with the latter." Explains that Bryan "took me to task for some inaccuracies in my narrative of the Duel, (the joint result of a lapse of Memory & time on my part) & next for not *doing justice* to Mr R." Promises to send a copy of his reply, "which was published some six weeks after you left the South," if Clay has not seen it.

Proceeds "to the business part of this letter" which has "rather the attraction of usefulness, than sentiment." At his home "on the Chattahoochee about 18 Miles below Columbus [Georgia] . . . on the Alabama side. . . . there is a large demand for Mules for the Plough." Because it is "a great corn growing Country not deficient in pasturage," believes many people would be induced to raise Mules, extensively, if we had stationed at some suitable stand a first *Rate Jack*." Adds that "Mr. Troy [*sic*, Edward Troye] the Portrait Painter . . . was so struck with the probable advantages of this locality that he proposed selling me half on a fine young Jack . . . which came originally out of your Stock, I believe and that he should stand at my place for our joint account." Although the mule was too young "to let to Mares the first year," it became "one of the most magnificent Animals of his kind I ever saw." When his "first Season was about to commence, in March last," however, he was "seized with a disease, called the Big head, of which he died," leaving "15 Mares . . . waiting for him on the public Road." Asks Clay if "you have a spare Jack & whether you would be willing to enter with me into any copartnership like that, I formed with Mr Troy." Assures Clay that, if he "should desire to make such an arrangement, there are several horse and Mule Dealers, who come every Oct to Columbus Geo from Lexington & its vicinity, who would gladly to oblige us both bring out the Jack." ALS. DLC-HC (DNA, M212, R6).

John Randolph Bryan was John Randolph's godson and was married to Randolph's niece. He also served as his godfather's second in the duel with Henry Clay [5:211-12]. Bryan's and Hamilton's writings on the duel have not been found. William C. Bruce, *John Randolph of Roanoke*, 2 vols. (New York, 1922), 1:33; 2:54, 538-40.

For Edward Troye, painter of blood horses, see *DAB*. For Hamilton's involvement in the Texas issue, see *DAB*.

From Charles D. Drake, St. Louis, Mo., August 13, 1846. Sends a check to pay $150 on Dr. Frederick G. Gilmer's [9:612] note to Clay. Reports that Gilmer intends to "send me the receipts for the payment of the two preceding notes," apparently for sums of $200 and $300. Adds that Gilmer "has had the land surveyed, & will immediately send me the Surveyor's description of it, to be sent to you to make out the deed by; & that as soon as the deed is forwarded, or soon after, he will pay the balance, with 10% interest as he agreed." ALS. DLC-TJC (DNA, M212, R14). For Drake, see 6:1089-90.

Clay's deed transferring ownership of a tract of 234 97/100 acres to Dr. Gilmer at a price of $1150 was "made and entered into" on September 14, 1846. DS. Mo. Lincoln Co. (Mo.) Deedbook, vol. G, pp. 588-89.

To Oliver Brooks & Co., Philadelphia, Pa., August 17, 1846. Offers thanks for "the beautiful Hat, and Box which contains it, which you have done me the favor to present to me." Notes that the "fine Hat *fits* my *head* as exactly as if it had been used, instead of the customary block." Adds that "it will ever be my pride" to wear "hats of American manufacture." Copy. Printed in the Lexington *Observer & Kentucky Reporter*, September 9, 1846. Addressed to Oliver Brooks & Co. at "S.W. corner Third and Walnut streets Philadelphia."

Oliver Brooks & Co. had written Clay on June 26, 1846, tendering the "Hat and Box made by us expressly for you to guard that head which has so long and so nobly advocated the protection of American manufactures." Copy. Printed in Lexington *Observer & Kentucky Reporter*, September 5, 1846.

To CHRISTOPHER HUGHES Lexington, August 17, 1846

I recd. your kind letter from the Falls of Niagara,[1] and hope this may reach you, on your return home, with my congratulations. Your contemplation of that wonderful natural curiosity has excited feelings not always produced by a first view of it. Mine coincided with yours, but the interest of the spectacle was increased the more I examined and dwelt upon it. When you reach Quebec, you will behold the next finest, grandest, natural object which I have seen on this Continent[.][2]

Your letters are always highly acceptable, but the last was not less so because it was totally silent on politics. I am not surprized that your visit to Washington inspired nothing but disgust. It is there, and in the measures which have arisen and issued from there, that we see the degredation, and, I fear, the decline of our Country.

And you went to Boston to conduct Mr. [John Quincy] Adams in safety to Washington! Would your visit not have had a better object if it had been to *prevent* his leaving home?[3]

Why have you not been to see me this summer? Last year, I wrote you that we had in my house four families; but now we have only my own, and should have received, and entertained you, in our plain way, with the greatest pleasure. I hope that you may still find some opportunity to visit us. If the American, whose curiosity never prompted him to visit the Falls of Niagara, deserved Lord Byron's reproach;[4] how much more does the American merit it who has never seen the vast Western valley?

I do not know when I can occupy the rooms which you have kindly provided for me in Balto. I sincerely hope to take possession of them, some day or other. I have appropriated my winters to the South, and desire to pass the next there. I think that a gentleman of your size and age would find the sun of N. Orleans warmer and more genial, in the winter, and more conducive to his health, than that of the Monumental City [Baltimore]. Suppose you come out in December and go with me? You may do all the talking, and I the thinking. Each of us would then have what is most agreeable to him.

My respects to your daughter [Margaret Smith Hughes] . . .

ALS. MiU-C. 1. Not found. 2. Probably Montmorency Falls, which rises more than 100 feet higher than Niagara Falls. W.P. Percival, *The Lure of Quebec* (Toronto, 1941), 188-90. 3. Clay did not approve of Adams's frequent introduction of anti-slavery petitions in the House. Also, he may have felt that Adams's health was too precarious for him to return to the House. Adams, *Memoirs of John Quincy Adams*, 12:215, 218. 4. Possibly a reference to the comment on Americans in Canto I, verse 131 of Byron's *Don Juan*. Truman G. Steffan (ed.), *Byron's Don Juan*, 4 vols. (Austin, 1957), 2:92.

To Francis Lieber, August 20, 1846. Acknowledges his query to learn "whether I was, or when I would be at home," and writes that he would regret it extremely if Lieber should have to "return from the West without my having the pleasure of seeing you." Explains that "My family has been laboring under a severe domestic affliction, and in the hope of deriving some relief from it, I intend to go to the Blue Licks on saturday" for five or six days. Hopes that Lieber will find it "agreeable and convenient" to exchange "friendly salutations . . . there or at Lexington."

Expresses his obligations to "our friend Col. [William C.] Preston for the kind messages" he sent through Lieber. Regrets that Preston "has recently sustained a great loss in the death of his mother [Sarah Campbell Preston]," but "was glad to see him appointed one of the Regents in the Smithsonian institute [9:387]." ALS. ScU.

Preston was named to the first Board of Regents of the Smithsonian Institution, which held its initial meeting on September 7, 1846. Polk had signed the act creating the Smithsonian on August 10, 1846. Paul H. Oehser, *Sons of Science, The Story of the Smithsonian* . . . (New York, 1949), 25.

Clay's domestic affliction may have been the mental illness of his son John Morrison Clay or the death of his grandson Martin Duralde III, or both. See McClellan to Clay, September 17, 1846, and Clay to Mercer, November 14, 1846.

To Albro, Hoyt & Co., Elizabethtown, N.J., September 10, 1846. Acknowledges receipt of an oil cloth, designed by this company to meet the precise dimensions of the hall at Ashland. In looking back on his career, contemplates "no part of my public exertions . . . with more satisfaction than the support which . . . I constantly, zealously and faithfully gave to the industry of my own country. Its prosperity or adversity has been [as] infallibly marked, by the adequacy or inadequacy of protection, as the thermometer indicates heat or cold." Believes that "the system of protection . . . has pushed the nation forward half a century in advance of where it would have been, if the doctrines of free trade had always prevailed in our public councils." Fears that "the tariff recently established [Clay to Greeley, June 23, 1846], which has sought to subvert the previous system" will cause "great injury to the general business of the country, and ultimately to the revenue of the government." If foreign importations do not increase, "the treasury must experience a large *deficit*" unless there is "an equivalent increase in the value of our exports, or the balance must be adjusted in specie." Doubts "we shall be able to effect payment, by additional exportation. . . . We in the West, do not believe that the relaxation in the British system of restriction [Morpeth to Clay, April 17, 1846] is going to create any considerable demand for the surplus of our agricultural produce." Feels that the United States will, "in the event of an excess of importations," be required to "pay for them in the precious metals," a move that would cause "commercial disorder" and "embarrassment in every department of business." Admits it "may turn out that our importations may continue to flourish and increase; that the country will continue to prosper; and that the revenue of the government will be ample." If so, concludes that "I shall be most happy to find these results realized, and that I have erroneously entertained the opinions to which I have so long sincerely adhered." Copy. Printed in *Niles' Register* (September 26, 1846), 71:52-53.

Albro, Hoyt & Co. were the manufacturers of floor oil clothes. *Ibid.*

From Dr. George McClellan, Philadelphia, Pa., September 17, [1846]. Reports: "I have just got [out] of my bed under a sudden paroxysm of chill & fever to pay my last visit to poor Martin Duralde [III]." Had attended him "the past three days . . . during Dr [Nathaniel] Chapman's absence on a visit to Baltimore." Informs Clay that Duralde fell "very ill at the American Hotel about ten days ago" and was moved to "the Columbia Hotel (formerly the Marshall House)," where "every comfort & attend[ance] for him" was provided. Although Chapman held "very faint hopes of him when he left," McClellan "began to be flattered that he might get on during Monday & Tuesday. His delirium & loss of appetite dissappeared & he took a fair quantity of light nourishment—But Yesterday morning I was called out early (at sun rise) to see him under a new aspect. He was labourin[g] under frightful convulsions from a congestion of the brain. Since that attack he sunk into total insensibility & prostration[.] He has just expired." Advises Clay that there will be "a private funeral day after tomorrow" and the body will be placed "in a Vault in Ronaldson's ground on South 9th St."

Explains the disposition of Duralde's effects: "We have counted the money in his Wallet & find $143 dolls in southern notes—and a certificate of a number of Lottery purchased by him in Baltimore. . . . also a memorandum of a deposit of $1300 dolls May 5. 1846 in the City Bank of New Orleans. Mr [Peter L.] Ferguson the chief proprietor of the Hotel will take charge of his watch, trunk, & effects to transmit to his family whenever you notify me of the course you wish to have pursued. I need not say to you that such a claim upon our regards will always be responded to by every Whig heart here."

Because he is "very ill & tremulous to night—& have to write this letter almost in the dark at a crowded bar," concludes that he cannot express "half the regards I feel for you & every member of your family." Adds in a postscript: "I ought to say in justice to Mr Ferguson . . . that he has been exceedingly kind & assiduous in his attentions to poor Martin ever since Chapman left town." ALS. DLC-TJC (DNA, M212, R10). See Ferguson to Clay, November 17, 1846.

For the Columbia House on the northside of Chestnut Street, adjoining the Arcade on the west, see J. Thomas Scharf, *History of Philadelphia 1609-1884*, 3 vols. (Philadelphia, 1884), 2:994.

To George L. Taylor, New York City, September 23, 1846. Sends through "J. Hoxy [*sic*, Joseph Hoxie]" the autograph Taylor requested "but must beg you to excuse my not transmitting the extract from one of my Speeches which you desired." Receives "with pleasure your avowal of being a Whig. But whatever party predominates in our public Councils, patriotism enjoins us to wish for the happiness and welfare of our country." ALS. Ct.

To Dr. GEORGE McCLELLAN Lexington, September 24, [1846]

I received your friendly letter, communicating the death of my Grandson Martin Duralde.[1] Distressing as the event is, it did not take us by surprize. We had long looked for and feared it. About 18 months ago he was attacked with an hoemorrage of the lungs, which subsequently often was renewed.[2] He passed last winter in the island of Cuba, with the view to benefit his health, but did not realize our hopes. He joined us in the Spring, and left us to try the virtues of the Red Sulphur Spring in Virginia. But there too he failed in accomplishing his object, and went thence to old Point Comfort,[3] where his last letters received here bear date. From that place, I presume, he proceeded to Philadelphia, where the career of the poor fellow was terminated.

It is a great consolation to us to know that, in his last days, he suffered for nothing, and had the kind attention and care of yourself, Dr. [Nathaniel] Chapman and Mr. [Peter L.] Ferguson. I pray you to accept yourself, and to present to them, my grateful acknowledgments for the kindness shewn to him.

He carried with him & received after he left me altogether the sum of about $1500, of which the sum mentioned by you is all that remains.

With respect to his body, I will thank you to have it buried in a private and decent manner, marking the spot of his interment, so that it may be known, to allow of some stone or monument being placed over it, if, after consulting with his father [Martin Duralde, Jr.] in N. Orleans, it shall be deemed necessary:

The money he left may be applied to the payment of expences incident to his illness and funeral,[4] and I will thank you to advise me, if it be insufficient for those objects, what further sum may be requisite.

In regard to his cloathes, watch, papers and other effects, I will be obliged to you to get Mr. Ferguson to have them securely put up in his trunk, and have that passed over to Mr. Rockhill,[5] with a request from me that he will have the goodness to have it directed to me, and forwarded via Pittsburg[h] to the care of Messrs. January & Son, Maysville, Kentucky.

Ah! my dear friend, I hope you have had a less measure of affliction than has fallen to my lot. Death, ruthless death, has deprived me of Six affectionate daughters,[6] all that I ever had, and has now commenced his work of destruction, with my descendents, in the second generation[.] I bow submissively to the despensations of an All-wise and merciful Providence, thankful that I have been myself so long spared, altho' spared to witness and to feel these great domestic misfortunes, not to speak of others which I have painfully experienced.

ALS. ViU. 1. McClellan to Clay, Sept. 17, 1846. 2. Clay to Henry Clay, Jr., March 17, 1845. 3. A sea resort with post office at Fortress Monroe, near Norfolk, Va. Leon E. Seltzer (ed.), *The Columbia Lippincott Gazetteer of the World* (New York, 1952). 4. The bill of D.P. Moore & W.H. Moore, undertakers, for $54.32, dated Sept. 17, 1846, included $8.00 for interment in the Philadelphia Cemetery and $3.00 for digging the grave. The bill from Columbia House, dated Sept. 21, 1846, was for $47.63, and a bill from J.P. Wilson Neill's Drug and Medicine Store, dated Oct. 5, 1846, for medicine totaled $4.50. All in DLC-TJC (DNA, M212, R10). 5. Possibly T.C. Rockhill, Jr., an attorney at 152 Walnut in Philadelphia. *M'Elroy's Philadelphia Directory for the Year 1845.* 6. Henrietta (1800-1801); Susan Hart Clay Duralde (1805-25); Anne Brown Clay Erwin (1807-35); Lucretia (1809-23); Eliza (1813-25); Laura (1816-16).

To JOHN M. BERRIEN Lexington, September 26, 1846

You were kind enough to recommend to me the House of Messrs. Holt and Atchison of Savannah, as factors of probity, and worthy of confidence, and I found them to merit your opinion. After the dissolution of the firm I continued to transact business with Mr. [Asa] Holt,[1] from whom I recd. a letter in April last informing me of the sale of a quantity of Cotton bagging, and promising to transmit me the a/c of Sales. Since then I have not heard from him, although I have twice written to him requesting the promised account. I have feared that he may be dead, or that some accident may have befallen him.[2] And my present object is to request the favor of any information you can give me about him.

The Sale was made upon a credit of six months, and as the time has not expired that may be the cause of his omission to forward me the a/c; but I do not think it a sufficient reason for the omission.

I request you to present my affectionate regards to Mrs. [Eliza Hunter] Berrien and your family, and to Captain [James] Hunter.

ALS. NcU. 1. In addition to being a shipping merchant, Holt represented Chatham County in the Georgia state house in 1843. Ben W. Fortson, Jr., *Georgia Official and Statistical Register 1977-1978* (Atlanta, 1978), 1419. 2. The April letter has not been found; however, on Feb. 22, 1847, William B. Astor wrote Clay that he had received a draft from Asa Holt for $1669.38, plus another check for $167.00 from an unspecified source, "which have been credited you on your bond." Copy. MH.

To THOMAS L. FORTUNE[1] Lexington, October 12, 1846

I have recd. your letter on the subject of the Hemp brake which you have invented, and sincerely hope that it may realize all your wishes and expectations.[2] But I have seen so many hemp brakes tried & failed that I cannot make a positive engagement to take one of your's until I see it tested by actual experiment. Several within my knowledge have been constructed on the principle of the common hand brake and have failed.[3]

If you will erect one on my farm, and I find it answering your description, or even if it will break out and clean one half of what you state it can do to the hand, that is 250 lb per day to the hand, I would gladly pay you the price you ask for it, that is one hundred dollars.

I have the horse power; and my situation on the Turnpike road is well adapted to the exhibition of your Machine to Hemp raisers. And I will afford you any facilities of timber &c in my power.

ALS. KHi. Addressed to Fortune at Frankfort, Ky. 1. Thomas L. Fortune of Liberty, Mo., patented a hemp brake on Sept. 3, 1846. He patented another one on July 26, 1864, at which time he listed his residence as Weston, Mo. *Subject Matter Index of Patents for Inventions*, 717. 2. Letter not found. On Oct. 16, 1846, Clay again wrote Fortune to extend thanks "for your generous offer of your patent right to your Machine for breaking hemp." Hopes to meet Fortune "in Frankfort on monday" or "tuesday next . . . when we will converse further on the subject." ALS. KHi. Addressed to Fortune at Frankfort, Ky. 3. For a description of hemp brakes and the way they worked, see Hopkins, *Hemp Industry in Kentucky*, 58-59.

To DANIEL MALLORY Lexington, October 12, 1846

I recd. your favor of the 5h. inst. and in answer to the only topic in it requiring a reply, I have to state that I have never said to any one that I would or would not be a Candidate for the Presidency at the next election. I have remained perfectly passive. Altho' I have been interrogated on that point, at various times, and on some occasions by collective bodies, I have observed entire silence.

My friends would do well to credit no reports of my intention, but such as may be announced under my own signature, if such an annunciation should ever be necessary.

ALS. MH. Letter marked "(Confidential)."

To EPES SARGENT Lexington, October 17, 1846

I recd. today your friendly letter of the 12h. inst. I regret extremely, and sympathise, most cordially, with you, on account of the domestic afflictions, to which you have been exposed. We too have had great and severe ones, in the past summer; but being accustomed to such visitations we are, perhaps, able to bear them better than you can.[1]

I did not forget the expression of your wish, some months ago, to make an addition to the Life of me which you had previously prepared, and my promise to supply some memoranda for that purpose.[2] But I supposed that your wish was dependent upon conditions, not likely to be realized, and therefore I have not prepared the memo: promised. But as you persevere in it, I will, in the course of the ensuing winter, or earlier, if it be requisite, communicate such facts and matter as may enable you to execute your contemplated purpose. I can easily do so from here, if I remain here, or from N. Orleans, if as is probable I shall go there. In either case, transmitting what I may have occasion to note through some Congressional friend.

On the subject of the next Presidency, I have been, and shall continue, a passive looker on. I am not unaware of, and am profoundly grateful for, the confidence and attachment which continue to impel many of my warm and ardent friends to turn their attention towards me. But whether it will be expedient to use again my name; and whether the circumstances of the Country, and those which are personal to me, may be such as to allow or authorize it, are grave questions, which should not be hastily or prematurely decided. Without any consideration of me, I do think it the true interest of the Whig party to move slowly and cautiously on the subject of their Candidate for the next Presidency. The public mind should be left, undisturbed and undiverted, to consider and to feel the disastrous effects of this most calamitous administration. Nothing could be more desirable to it, or perhaps more conducive to its future success, than to withdraw public attention from the ruin with which its measures, foreign & domestic, are fraught, and to engage in a hot struggle, prematurely began, for the Presidential office.

I deplore the divisions in the Whig party, and those especially which prevail in N. York.[3] Our friends there, it has always appeared to me, do not sufficiently estimate the injurious effects without the State of a defeat within it. Beyond its limits, people can not comprehend how we may lose, for example, the Governor, and yet carry an Electoral ticket for President; nor how an election is suffered to go by default, when there existed a power to prevent it.

If there be a desire to ensure the election, two years hence, of a Whig President for the U.S. you may be sure that it is of the first importance to secure the election of a Whig Governor at your approaching election.[4] How extremely desirable, then, is it that all divisions should be merged in one united and patriotic exertion to elect Mr. [John] Young! I knew him well in Congress, and from the sentiments of respect and esteem, with which he inspired me, for his patriotism his ability and his industry, I should not hesitate, were I a Citizen of your State, to throw into his support the utmost zeal and exertion which I could employ, even if I felt a preference for any other eminent Citizen of your State.

I am very thankful to your brother [John O. Sargent] for his unabated attachment to me, and I request you to assure him of my undiminished esteem and friendship for him. Such an assurance to you would be entirely unnecessary. . . .

ALS. MCM. Letter marked "(Confidential)." 1. Sargent's sister Arria (b.1827) had died of tuberculosis in Roxbury, Mass., on June 23, 1846. Emma W. Sargent & Charles Sprague Sargent (eds.), *Epes Sargent of Gloucester and His Descendants* (Boston, 1923), 30. See also Sargent to Clay, Feb. 27, 1847. For Clay's afflictions, see Clay to Lieber, August 20, 1846. 2. For Sargent's previous edition, see 9:536. See also Clay to Sargent, August 7, 1844. 3. Divisions existed in New York concerning John Young's nomination as the Whig candidate for governor. Young endorsed the war with Mexico, sympathized with the Anti-Rent party, and let it be known that, if elected, he would pardon the Anti-Rent rioters. For a discussion of Whig divisions, see John A. Garraty, *Silas Wright* (New York, 1949), 377-87; DeAlva Stanwood Alexander, *A Political History of the State of New York*, 3 vols. (New York, 1906), 2:114-23; Hammond, *History of Political Parties . . . in New York*, 3:673-98. See also Greeley to Clay, Nov. 15, 1846. 4. In the gubernatorial election in New York in Nov., 1846, Whig John Young defeated Democrat Silas Wright by a vote of 197,627 to 192,361. *BDGUS*, 3:1080. In the congressional race Whigs won 21 seats to 12 for the Democrats and one Anti-Rent Whig. *Guide to U.S. Elections*, 583. Whigs won 5 of 8 seats up for election in the state senate and 68 seats in the assembly, with Democrats winning 50 and Anti-Renters 10 assembly seats. Thus, Whigs controlled the assembly, but Democrats still controlled the state senate. Alexander, *Political History of New York*, 2:120.

To JOSEPH HOXIE Lexington, November 2, 1846

I was very glad to learn, by your letter of the 26th. ultimo, that you had arrived safely at home after a delightful journey through the State of Ohio and by Lake Erie. And that you found family and friends all well. My letter addressed to George L Taylor,[1] to your care, was in answer to one from a young man, which you yourself brought and delivered to me. I know nothing of him beyond the information which I derived from that letter. Enclosed I transmit a brief note to Mr Meade,[2] on the subject of Indian Corn ground with the cob as suitable food for cattle and horses. Nothing can be finer for that purpose.

I shall look with trembling and anxiety to the result of your election in New York.[3] Should it be favourable, I shall begin again to entertain hopes for our Country which were almost previously extinguished. For you, for your health, and for your prosperity they will ever be fondly cherished. . . . P.S. The above has been written by my son John [Morrison Clay] upon my dictation.

LS. Henry Clay Memorial Foundation, Lexington, Ky. 1. Clay to Taylor, Sept. 23, 1846. 2. Note not found. On Nov. 4, 1846, Clay again wrote Hoxie to inform him that "the brief note which I hastily wrote to your friend the other day, expressing my opinion of the value of Indian corn ground in the Cob, as food for horses and cattle, contains an inaccuracy." Qualifies his earlier note: "I ought to have said, 'that the Cob when thus ground forms a substitu[t]e for, and *in a great measure* supersedes the necessity for hay or other rough food.' " Comments again on the New York state elections: "I hope that, before I hear of the result, I may venture to tender you congratulations on it." ALS. KyU. 3. Clay to Sargent, Oct. 17, 1846.

From Charles A. Davis, New York City, November 5, 1846. Reports that "the aspect of things in all this quarter has an awful squinting ag[ains]t the present party in power." Cites the tariff, the administration's Sub-Treasury policy, and the Mexican War as being issues New Yorkers regard with distrust. Discusses at length his own views on the tariff. Writes that he looked into the subject closely last summer while in England and has decided that tariff protection can be replaced by a policy of " '*reducing to its lowest cost the Expense of transit*—between points of production and points of consumption.'—in other words when we can, (as we surely can) lay down on our sea board the productions of our interior—as cheap as like things can be brought to us from abroad—our protection is complete—when we can do this cheaper (as we can by a good system of Roads & Canals) we are not only fully protected but become the Exporter to those we now receive from.—and in addition to this have entire national protection in War as in peace now my notion is that you take up this question and if found in your judgment to be worthy of a higher position *as a means of protection* . . . so to place it before the people." Assures Clay that he still has an enthusiastic following in New York City and hopes that he "will not for a moment listen to any suggestion that any body else of the Whig party can carry any thing like your general influence over the whole Country." Comments on the health and vitality of the British economy and gives the reasons why it thrives. Concludes with the observation that "Our present [New York] Election I regard as a spontaneous Erupting of good principles and indebted to no particular set of men [Clay to Sargent, October 17, 1846]." ALS. DLC-HC (DNA, M212, R5).

The bill to establish a Sub-Treasury (or Independent Treasury) was introduced in the House on December 19, 1845. It passed the House 123 to 67 on April 2, 1846, and the Senate 28 to 25 on August 1. The House agreed to the Senate's amendments on August 5 and the bill was finally approved on August 6. U.S. H. of Reps., *Journal*, 29 Cong., 1 Sess., 621; *Cong. Globe*, 29 Cong., 1 Sess., 596, 1176; U.S. Sen., *Journal*, 29 Cong., 1 Sess., 482, 529.

To OCTAVIA WALTON LEVERT Lexington, November 6, 1846

It has been a long, long time, my ever dear friend, since I had the pleasure of addressing you; and I frankly acknowledge that I stand in arrear to you, not in affectionate remembrance, but in our correspondence. The past summer has been however one of great affliction to us. We lost our eldest grandson (Martin Duralde) who died in the City of Philadelphia;[1] our son Col H[enry]. Clay [Jr.] met with a serious accident in Mexico,[2] and our youngest son John [Morrison Clay], whom you may recollect, has been painfully affected.[3] Both of these have now got better, and I feel in better spirits once more to address you, my excellent friend.

I have been constantly looking to Mobile, with great anxiety for its health, and for the safety and welfare of the good friends whom it contains. Several of its inhabitants, and among others Mrs. Smith and her sister Miss Deshea, have visited Lexington during the summer, but they were there whilst we were in the midst of our troubles, and I therefore saw less of them than I could have wished, under more favorable circumstances.

In your last, you informed me that you had sent your dear little Octavia to her aunt, at Augusta, to divert her from intense study and re-establish her strength and health.[4] I hope that, in that object, you have been completely successful.

You speak of the War with Mexico. It is one in which the hearts of our people are not engaged, and of which unhappily we can discern no prospect of a speedy termination. What a waste of precious human life it occasions, more by the climate than by the sword! And what a waste of treasure too! It was begun without any necessity, and in folly, and is conducted without wisdom. Aiming for the conquest of Mexico, the Executive at Washn. [James K. Polk] appears to have thought that it was best to overlook and neglect the most direct and shortest road to that [Mexico] City, and to pursue that which is most hazardous & circuitous. And how Genl [Zachary] Taylor is to keep up his long line of communication and receive indispensable supplies of provisions, munitions of War, and re-enforcements, God only knows, for I am sure neither the President nor Secretary of War [William L. Marcy] does. I tremble for the fate of the gallant General and his gallant army.[5]

Except our domestic distresses, we have had a most pleasant year, and nothing can surpass the beauty of the weather at this time. I have made but one or two short excursions from home, during the Summer, to neighbouring water places, where I found some agreeable company. If this fine weather were to continue, I should, so far as climate is concerned, be without apology for leaving home, during the ensuing winter; but it will not continue, and I have besides other motives for going South. I expect to go hence for Mississippi and Louisiana in three or four weeks, but may not reach N. Orleans until towards the last of December. It is my wish and present purpose to visit Mobile, but you know that one cannot always do what one desires. What is your plan of winter campaign? Do you operate at Mobile or on the larger theatre of the Crescent City? If I had the choice, I must confess that I should prefer seeing you at Mobile, where one may be able to *see you*. At N. Orleans, your meteor like movements allow only a glimpse to be caught of you.

I pray you to present me, most affectionately, to Dr [Henry] LeVert, to your good mother [Sally Walker Walton], and Mrs. Hubble & Mrs. Stewart. And embrace all the graces most tenderly for their and your Faithful friend. P.S. Should you write to me, be pleased to address me at N. Orleans.

ALS. KyLoF. 1. McClellan to Clay, Sept. 17, 1846. 2. Henry Clay, Jr., to Clay, Feb. 12, 1847. 3. Clay to Henry Clay, Jr., March 17, 1845. 4. Reference obscure. 5. The Polk administration was slow to develop a comprehensive military strategy. Initially, at least, the president was preoccupied chiefly with the acquisition of California. Polk also hoped that the Mexican government could be forced to negotiate by applying gradually increasing pressure without mounting a major offensive; American victories at Palo Alto and Resaca de la Palma in May, 1846, and the occupation of Monterey in September were directed toward this end. Polk also ordered Gen. Stephen W. Kearney to capture and occupy Santa Fe, the capital of New Mexico, with his "Army of the West." Polk and Secretary of War William L. Marcy also ordered Taylor's advance into Northern Mexico to secure the Rio Grande boundary, as well as a naval blockade of Mexico's Pacific ports, including the seizure of San Francisco. After these initial objectives were achieved, Gen. Winfield Scott launched a final major offensive against Mexico City, which was captured after a joint army-navy expedition against Vera Cruz, a long march inland over mountainous terrain, and the storming of the capital city's defenses. For a complete discussion of American military strategy and its execution, see K. Jack Bauer, *Zachary Taylor: Soldier, Planter, Statesman of the Old Southwest* (Baton Rouge, 1985), 167-87, *passim*; Singletary, *The Mexican War*, 25, *passim*; Rives, *The United States and Mexico*, 2:195-96, 202-3, 207-12. For Taylor's many problems concerning troops, transportation, and supplies, see Bauer, *The Mexican War*, 36, 84-89, 130-36, 145-57, *passim*.

To BENJAMIN B. SMITH Lexington, November 7, 1846

I recd. your favor, transmitting a biographical sketch of Judge [Benjamin] Sebastian. Whilst I greatly loved & admired him, I must frankly say that, considering both his virtues and his errors (such at least as the world attributed to him) I doubt the expediency of publishing any memoir of him. You have not praised too highly his social qualities, his dignity of deportment, nor his general attractions. Perhaps, you have, his influence in Kentucky,[1] of which I however do not pretend to be a competent judge, as, when in 1797 I arrived in the State it was in the wane.

If I had written the article which you have prepared, I should have made some alteration in its structure. I would have introduced the last paragraphs, which I have enclosed in brackets, in the earlier part of the article, where I have marked brackets.

I think you have made an error in dates, which I have indicated. I am not sure either that you have not expressed too strongly the sanction supposed to have been given by Col. [George] Nicholas, Judge [Harry] Innis &c to Judge Sebastians Spanish connections.[2] You wd. do well, on this subject, to confer with Judge [Samuel Smith] Nicholas of Louisville, the son of Col. Nicholas.

I was not aware that at a public meeting of the People of K[entucky]. persons had been deputed to repair to Madrid or N. Orleans to negotiate about the navigation of the Mississippi, nor that any persons actually went on that mission. But it may have escaped my knowledge. On my arrival in this State, all was quiet on that subject, in consequence of the Spanish treaty of 1795.[3] When, afterwards, about 1800, the interruption occurred in the right of depôt at N. Orleans, the flame again burst out, but it was extinguished by the subsequent treaty of Louisiana.[4]

ALS. NN. 1. See 1:270-71. 2. *Ibid.*; 1:319-20. 3. Pinckney's Treaty. See Parry, *Treaty Series*, 53:11-31. 4. The Louisiana Purchase. See Parry, *Treaty Series*, 57:27-48.

Speech to Dr. Boyd McNairy, Lexington, Ky., November 12, 1846. Acknowledges the gift of a silver vase delivered by McNairy for "a large circle of Tennessee ladies," and views the "precious testimonial of their inestimable respect and regard" as "a proud incident in my life, ever to be remembered with feelings of profound gratitude and delight." Believes that "If, indeed, their kind wishes in relation to the issue of the last Presidential election had been gratified. . . . We should have preserved, undisturbed, and without hazard, peace with all the world, have had no unhappy war with a neighboring sister-republic, and, consequently, no deplorable waste of human life." In addition, "We should have saved the millions of treasure which that unnecessary war has and will cost" and used it "to improve every useful harbor" in the nation. States that "We should not have subverted a patriotic system of domestic protection . . . for the visionary promises of an alien policy of free trade, fostering the industry of foreign people and the interests of foreign countries." Adds: "The beneficial Tariff of 1842 [9:628], which raised both the people and the government of the

United States out of a condition of distress and embarrassment, bordering on bankruptcy, to a state of high financial and general prosperity, would now be standing unimpaired, in the statute-book, instead of the fatal Tariff of 1846 [Clay to Greeley, June 23, 1846], whose calamitous effects will, I apprehend, sooner or later, be certainly realized."

Notes that all these problems had been "foretold prior to that [Presidential] election," but they had been "denied, disbelieved, or unheeded." Nonetheless, warns "that we should not indulge in unavailing regrets as to the incurable past," and instead "derive from it instructive lessons for our future guidance."

Accepts "with greatest pleasure, the splendid and magnificent vase of silver." Since it was "Wrought by American artists, tendered by my fair countrywomen, and brought to me by an ever-faithful, ardent, and distinguished friend, it comes with a triple title to my grateful acceptance."

Expresses to McNairy "my great obligations for the faithful and uninterrupted friendship which, in prosperous and adverse fortune, and amid all the vicissitudes of my checkered life, you have constantly, zealously, and fearlessly displayed." Copy. Printed in Colton, *Clay Correspondence*, 3:44-45. Dated from report in Lexington *Observer & Kentucky Reporter*, November 14, 1846.

From John Davis, Worcester, Mass., November 13, 1846. Comments extensively on the chief political issues of the day: "the policy of the [James K. Polk] administration is enough to excite public alarm without Coon skins, hard cider, log cabins, or even a song or a hurrah—As far as my observation has extended the revolution has been accomplished almost without argument or effort. The sense of the public is manifestly opposed to the doings of Congress. The [Mexican] war [Clay to Lawrence, April 30, 1845] is daily becoming unpopular and the revenue act [Clay to Greeley, June 23, 1846] meets with condemnation every where. The opinion too is gaining ground that the administration is weak and insincere."

Wonders "whether the whigs can learn wisdom from the past and understand the necesity of a hearty and cordial cooperation." Agrees with Clay's "suggestion that the act of 42 [9:628] is a popular act having brought with it not only relief but prosperity." Believes the act's opponents "were warned of the hazard which they would incur by its repeal—but they believed that the Shiboleth, democracy, would carry them safe through any absurdity." Expounds further on protectionism: "We of the old school of whigs desire to have a law that shall give ample protection to all branches of industry which require it and we are not for measuring the degree by the wants of those who have the greatest skill and the most ample means but by the strength of the more feeble, We wish to see industry advance into new employments and to witness the spread of the mechanic and manufacturing arts into all parts of the country. Nothing else I am confident can give to the Union so sure a guarantee of future prosperity." Explains his views on "the proposition called the compromise" that some believed "the whigs had hastily and inconsiderately rejected . . . upon political considerations"; "To this I have answered . . . that it proposed a surrender which could never be reclaimed. . . . many were of opinion that it would not be suited to the condition of the weak. Moreover it proposed to reduce the revenue when it was agreed on all hands that we needed more than all we could raise and the worst feature in it was the supplying the deficiency created by the reduction—by a duty upon tea & Coffee greater than the duty upon the articles needing protection. . . . This seemed to me to be a violation of fundamental principles." Adds that the Whigs "must now be convinced of the great attachment to the law of 1842 & of the powerful hold which it has upon public opinion—The democrats made their own issue—they demanded its repeal and a disclaimer of the fundamental doctrines which it sustained—They have carried their point and the people the great court for the correction of errors are now revising their doings and pronouncing judgment upon them." When "additional revenue will be required," asks "shall we in raising such revenue disclaim the doctrine of protection and for one I am prepared if forced upon the alternative to be a party to the disclaimer or to vote against the proposed measure, to vote against." Concludes: "In good time the question of [the] presidency will arise & must be decided in a manner which will unite our whole strength—There will [be] cliques but they must be discountenanced & all must be defered to the judgment of a convention of wise men." ALS. DLC-HC (DNA, M212, R6).

Daniel Webster had considered proposing a compromise on the tariff bill that would have reduced all duties, whether specific or ad valorem, by 25%, with an 8 1/2% reduction 5 years later. This was finally proposed by Sen. Simon Cameron of Pa. and rejected. This was similar to a compromise proposed to Polk by certain Pennsylvanians. Isaac Holmes in the House presented an amendment to set the duties on tea and coffee at 20% ad valorem, which was defeated. Wiltse, *Papers of Daniel Webster: Correspondence*, 6:183-84; *Cong. Globe*, 29 Cong., 1 Sess., 1178; Milo Milton Quaife (ed.), *The Diary of James K. Polk*, 4 vols. (Chicago, 1910), 2:42, 45-47.

To Thomas Washington, Nashville, Tenn., November 13, 1846. Acknowledges "your friendly communication, addressed to me at the instance of Ladies in Tennessee," and confirms that "the splendid vase which they have done me the honor to present to me" was "safely delivered to me" by "our mutual friend Dr. [Boyd] McNairy." Adds: "Nothing could surpass the considerate delicacy with which the Whig Ladies of Tennessee have arranged the manufacture, and the presentation of this rich testimonial of their friendly confidence and esteem." Reflects that "In our passage through public life, and amidst the vicissitudes to which it is incident, it is cause of the highest consolation and satisfaction to be assured of the countenance and approbation of any respectable portion of our fellow-beings. But I confess that my gratification is much greater, in receiving such testimony, from the other sex than from my own. Their virtues and attractions, and the impartiality and disinterestedness of their position, impress a more sterling value upon their award." ALS. THi.

To WILLIAM N. MERCER Lexington, November 14, 1846

I duly recd., my dear friend, your letter from Laurel Hill of the 26h. Ulto. and was happy to learn that you had passed in that delightful abode, an agreeable summer, in quiet and good health with all your family.[1] I should indeed have been better pleased if you had come hither, as more conducive to your strength and health.

We have had a full measure of affliction, but thank God, with the exception of the death of my oldest Grandson, Martin Duralde,[2] an event which we had long apprehended, it is now all removed. My son Henry [Clay, Jr.] has recovered from an accidental injury which he had recd. and which occasioned us much uneasiness,[3] and my son John [Morrison Clay] is again restored to the use of his mind.[4] We indulge the hope that it may be now preserved to him.

I regret that it will not be in my power to join you at Laurel Hill. My present intention is to leave Louisville about the first of next month, perhaps in the next trip of the Peytona, for N. Orleans; but, as I purpose stopping a short time in Mississippi, it may be the 20h. of Decr. before I reach the Crescent City.

I must reserve for the occasion of our meeting an interchange of views on the present state of public affairs. The plan of the Campaign for conducting the Mexican War has been most unwise and unskilful, I think, in making the Rio Bravo [Rio Grande] and Camargo the base of military operations.[5] It should have been (if any invasion of Mexico were decided on) to have taken La Vera Cruz, or to have blockaded it by land and water, and marched the Army from that point, or its neighbourhood, to the attack of the City of Mexico, if it were to be attacked.[6] By pursuing this latter route, besides other advantages which it afforded, a distance of some 7 or 8 hundred miles would have been saved. As it is, I do not discern how Genl. [Zachary] Taylor can possibly maintain, unbroken, his long line of operations, through which his supplies and reinforcements must pass. I confess that I have the greatest apprehensions for him.

Victories have been achieved recently in the U.S, much more important and consequential, than those in Mexico, brilliant as these have been. The results of late elections have, I hope and believe, sealed the fate of the present most disastrous Administration.[7]

I enclose an account of an occurrence at Ashland, which may reach you earlier than through the papers, the perusal of which may be interesting, for a moment, to my young friend Anna [Mercer].[8] Do me the favor, along with it, to present to her my affectionate regards, and also to Miss [Eliza] Young and Miss [Mary D.] Kemble.[9]

ALS. LU-Ar. 1. Laurel Hill was Mercer's plantation near Natchez, Miss. 2. McClellan to Clay, Sept. 17, 1846. 3. Henry Clay, Jr., to Clay, Feb. 12, 1847. 4. Clay to Henry Clay, Jr., March 17 and April 5, 1845. 5. Clay to LeVert, Nov. 6, 1846. 6. *Ibid.* See also Clay to Greeley, June 23, 1846. 7. For example, New York and Pennsylvania. See Clay to Sargent, Oct. 17, 1846, and Clay to Littell, Nov. 17, 1846, respectively. 8. Reference obscure. Mercer's daughter Anna died in 1851 at the age of 19. Butler, *The Unhurried Years*, 20; William Mercer Green, *Memoir of Rt. Rev. James Hervey Otey* . . . (New York, 1885), 47-48. 9. Mary D. Kemble married Gen. William H. Sumner of Jamaica Plain, Mass., on April 18, 1848. New Orleans *Daily Picayune*, April 19, 1848.

From HORACE GREELEY New York City, November 15, 1846

I have delayed for months to answer your kind letter of August last,[1] because we were in such a state of confusion here that I could say nothing of interest that the next week might not contradict. I thought I would wait till after Election,[2] and then explain to you our troubles here; but now it seems to me that the result explains itself well enough, and I shall say very little about it. It is very unpleasant that there should be such bickerings among Whigs as are manifested here, but I cannot see how they can be helped without giving up the State to the common adversary.[3] It was hard for me this Fall to be placed in a position of seeming hostility to Mr. [Millard] Fillmore, who has ever been my warm friend, and whom I love and esteem; but it was just as certain as sunrise to-morrow that we could carry the State with Mr. [John] Young and would probably lose it with Mr. Fillmore; and how could we hesitate? Our noble friend Hamilton Fish[4] has got exactly the vote Mr. Fillmore would have received had he been put up, as was contemplated, and commended as the enemy of the Anti-Renters,[5] &c. Those who were influential in making the nomination of Mr. Young were not Mr. Young's personal friends so much as Mr. Fillmore's—I surely was not—but only asked what name would best subserve the Whig cause. We knew that the other party would be disorganized by Young's nomination, while it would be united and incited to exertion by Fillmore's. So we chose, and our Congressional triumph is among the fruits of that choice. For all practical purposes, our delegation in the next Congress stands 25 with us to 9 against us, and one other ([Ausburn] Birdsall)[6] was elected by one vote, but is not very reliable. Our friends abroad begged us to do every thing with reference to Congress, and we have done our very best for that. Six Members are chosen wholly or in part by the Counties comprised within the 'Anti-Rent' or Manorial region; of these, five were against and one for us last Congress; now five for us and one against, who is elected by less than 300 votes in a district which gave nearly 2,000 for [James K.] Polk. And every one of these five is an old-fashioned Whig, who did all he knew how for the cause in 1844.[7] So of all our 25 admitted Whigs. They comprise a delegation superior in talent and capacity to any we have sent from this State for many years.

One unwelcome but inevitable result of the Whig triumphs this Fall is the springing up of a large growth of Presidential aspirants.[8] Happily we are just now in a minority in both branches of congress, and this can do little harm; but Washington will be overrun with cabals and intrigues for the succession; and when we come to have a majority in the House, as I trust we shall a year hence, it will prove a serious impediment to any proper conduct of the public business. It seems to me, if we are to have a National Convention at all, it should meet about the last week in November of next year, settle the candidates, and have the matter over.[9]

At present, there is a considerable and increasing band of drummers and canvassers for this or that aspirant perambulating the Country. In this City, and vicinity they make no impression. The wiser politicians, in their own esteem, refuse to be committed; the great mass, who act from the heart rather than the head, protest that they won't hear of any other candidate than the old one [Clay], at least until he publicly and peremptorily refuses to run. I think Judge [John] McLean has been injured here by industrious but injudicious canvassers in his behalf.[10]

Perhaps it may be well to await the developments on the other side before nominating. It now appears here that the friends of Mr. [John C.] Calhoun are resolved that he shall run any how.[11] On the other hand, Silas Wright's friends are organizing to bring him into the field.[12] The Calhoun leaders here gave us some help in the late contest—quietly, of course. Of course, Messrs. [John J.] Crittenden and [Garrett] Davis will be prepared to give wise counsel to our small but inspirited band in the present Congress, from where the call of a Convention will probably emanate.

ALS. DLC-HC (DNA, M212, R6). 1. Not found. 2. Clay to Sargent, Oct. 17, 1846. 3. *Ibid.* 4. Hamilton Fish, the Whig candidate for lieutenant governor, had been defeated by Democrat Addison Gardiner despite the victory of the Whigs in the governor's race and other state contests. Garraty, *Silas Wright*, 379. For Fish, see *BDAC*; *DAB*. 5. The Anti-Rent party in New York arose from discontent over the survival of manorial rights in the patroonships along the Hudson River. The Anti-Renters briefly controlled the votes of about ten counties, generally located south and west of Albany. In the summer of 1845, Anti-Rent disturbances in Columbia, Delaware, and Schoharie counties resulted in at least one death. Herbert D.A. Donovan, *The Barnburners, A Study of the Internal Movements in the Political History of New York State and of the Resulting Changes in Political Affiliation 1830-1852* (Philadelphia, 1974), 12, 76, 78, 115; Hammond, *History of Political Parties in New York*, 3:579-84, 600-601, 661-65, 683-85, 691-92; Garraty, *Silas Wright*, 356-61, 376-81. 6. For Birdsall, see *BDAC*. 7. Clay to Sargent, Oct. 17, 1846. 8. Many Whigs still hoped Clay would accept the party's nomination in 1848, despite his age and his apparent unwillingness to run again after his 1844 defeat. In the event Clay decided not to run, John J. Crittenden emerged as a likely candidate, but he refused to be considered and began in 1846 to tout Zachary Taylor for the office. Others with presidential ambitions and at least some supporters were Daniel Webster, Winfield Scott, John McLean, and Thomas Corwin. Albert D. Kirwan, *John J. Crittenden: The Struggle for the Union* (Lexington, Ky., 1962), 200-223; George R. Poage, *Henry Clay and the Whig Party* (1936; reprint ed., Gloucester, Mass.,

1965), 153-80; Norman A. Graebner, "Thomas Corwin and the Election of 1848," *JSH* (Feb., 1951), 17:162-79; Betty C. Congleton, "Contenders for the Whig Nomination in 1848 and the Editorial Policy of George D. Prentice," *RKHS* (April, 1969), 67:119-33. 9. The Whig National convention took place in Philadelphia on June 7-9, 1848, with John M. Morehead of N.C. as chairman. On the 4th ballot Taylor was nominated over Clay, Scott, Webster, McLean, and John M. Clayton. Millard Fillmore was nominated vice president on the 2nd ballot. McKee, *National . . . Popular and Electoral Vote*, 62-65. 10. For McLean's candidacy, see Francis P. Weisenburger, *The Life of John McLean, A Politician on the United States Supreme Court* (Columbus, Ohio, 1937), 105-28. 11. For Calhoun's attempt to win the Democratic nomination, see Wiltse, *John C. Calhoun: Sectionalist*, 225-27, 261, 289-90, 297-98, 318-20. 12. For the possibility of Wright's candidacy, see Garraty, *Silas Wright*, 337-38, 392-94, 403-6. Wright, however, died on August 27, 1847.

To ADONIRAM CHANDLER Lexington, November 16, 1846

I recd. your favor of the 8h. inst. but have not yet recd. the Addresses to the late Fair of the American Institute, to which you refer.[1] They will doubtless hereafter come to hand, and, whether they do or not, I thank you for your kind intention to put me in possession of such interesting documents.

I unite with you in congratulations on the late signal triumphs of the Whigs,[2] holding out, as they do, better and brighter prospects for our common Country.

I regret the existence of divisions among our political friends in your City.[3] I can make myself no party to them, and I would adjure all, who are, to seek to unite in one common band of patriotic brothers and friends. Those divisions cannot possibly benefit our cause but most certainly will tend to its prejudice.

I am not unaware that some, who now co-operate heartily with the Whigs, formerly thought it best not to promote the wishes of my friends.[4] But does not policy, as well as justice, prompt that, believing in their sincerity as I am inclined to do, they should be now treated with kindness and confidence? . . .

ALS. NcD. 1. For the American Institute, see Davis to Clay, Nov. 25, 1845. 2. Clay to Sargent, Oct. 17, 1846. 3. *Ibid.* 4. More naturalized citizens and Anti-Renters were supporting the Whigs by 1846. Van Deusen, *Horace Greeley*, 104-5.

From William McLain, Washington, D.C., November 16, 1846. Encloses a letter [not found] "from a colored man, who has very lately become much excited about Liberia. If it is like some he has written it may afford you a *smile*." Notes that "We launched on last Saturday the Liberia Packet of which I enclose you a print. She is a beautiful vessel, possessing every accommodation—" ALS. DLC-Records of the American Colonization Society (DNA, M212, R20).

From Peter L. Ferguson, Philadelphia, Pa., November 17, 1846. Sends Clay a check for $71.55, "being bal: of money left by your grandson M[artin Duralde, III]: a[ft]er paying sundr[y] exps:" Assures Clay that the "money was counted . . . after Mr Ds death by Doct: [George] McClellan and myself, & amtd: as we then thought, to $143.—b[ut] afterwards I found in another pocket of the book $50. = N: York note rolled up in the smallest po[ssible] space." Informs Clay that all bills were "approved by Dr McC. who directed me about 2 weeks since to remit you the bal:" Adds that "Mr Josiah Randa[ll] called two days since with your letter" that enquired "about a Diamond finger ring & breast pin. Mr D. did n[ot] wear either at the time of his death, nor do I recollect seeing them during his stay at our house. I am positive that when Dr McC. & myself collected his effects, neither was among them. His pocket book I will forward with Hat & Cane. . . . so soon as an opportunity offers."

Ferguson's account of medical and funeral expenses includes the following charges: $4.50 for medicines; $56.32 for "Undertakers bill"; $47.63 to cover "Bagley Mackenzie [*sic*] & Co; board bill"; $11.00 to pay Drs. Nathaniel Chapman and McClellan; and $2.00 for other services. ALS. DLC-TJC (DNA, M212, R11).

Bagley McKenslie was a partner with Ferguson in the Columbia House where Duralde died. Scharf, *History of Philadelphia*, 2:994.

To JOHN S. LITTELL Lexington, November 17, 1846

I received your friendly letter of the 9th. inst and am greatly obliged by your kind intention to send me a copy of Graydon's Memoirs.[1] I should receive it with pleasure, & no doubt would peruse it with profit. I saw that you were a candidate for Congress on the Native American ticket.[2] I did not, for a moment, suppose that in assuming that position you had abandoned any of your long cherished Whig principles.

There is much in the principles of the Native American party to commend it to deliberate consideration; but as a separate and distinct party I have not imagined that it could succeed in the United States.[3] Its tendency is to distract and divide the Whigs, for it is not to be believed that the other party, to any considerable extent, will unite with the Native American. The other party [Democrat] has profited too largely by the Foreign vote to authorise us to expect that, as a party, it will give any considerable support, or countenance, to the Native Americans.[4] If any modification of the Naturalization laws shall ever be effected, it will not be at the instance, only the cooperation of the Democratic party.[5]

The political evils which flow from the foreign population are confined to localities, and do not pervade the interior of the Union. Hence I suppose that the principles of the Native American party alone can never form a basis of a party commensurate with the whole union. I unite with you in congratulations on the recent signal triumphs of the Whigs.[6] They encourage us to hope for a better administration of the General government. Such a desirable result I think inevitable if the Whigs should be wise, and not allow themselves to be intoxicated by their present successes. I look on passing scenes with calmness though not with indifference. I am often addressed to know if I would consent to the use of my name again as a candidate for the Presidency. Although full of gratitude to my friends for their past confidence and support, I have deemed it most befitting to remain silent on these appeals, answering neither yea nor nay. In my opinion it is too soon now to agitate the question of the next Presidency. The public mind, I think, had better be left to the full, undisturbed, and undivided consideration of the disastrous measures of the last session of Congress. It will be time enough, hereafter, from amongst the living and the worthy, to select a suitable person to accomplish the changes so desirable in the General Administration. . . . P.S. Graydon's Memoirs might be sent to Mr. Marshall, bookseller &c. Lexington.

Copy. DLC-HC (DNA, M212, R6). Printed in Colton, *Clay Correspondence*, 4:536-37. Letter marked "*Copy.*" 1. Alexander Graydon (1752-1818), a Revolutionary War officer and member of the Pennsylvania convention that ratified the U.S. Constitution, had published his *Memoirs of a Life* . . . in Harrisburg, Pa., in 1811. Littell republished it in Philadelphia in 1846. For Graydon, see *DAB*. 2. In the 1846 congressional election Littell was defeated by Democrat Charles J. Ingersoll by a vote of 3,786 to 3,519, with the Whig candidate running third. Philadelphia *U.S. Gazette*, Oct. 16, 1846. In all, 16 Whigs, 7 Democrats, and 1 Native American were elected to Congress from Pennsylvania. *Guide to U.S. Elections*, 584. In the elections for the state house of representatives, 45 Whigs and 29 Democrats were chosen. Eleven state senators were selected in 1846, leaving the Whigs with a total of 18 seats in the senate to 14 for the Democrats and 1 for the Native Americans. Philadelphia *U.S. Gazette*, Oct. 16, 17, 1846. 3. Clay to Ewing, June 19, 1844; Clay to Clayton, Dec. 2, 1844. 4. Clay to Smith, June 17, 1844; Ewing to Clay, June 23, 1844; Frelinghuysen to Clay, Nov. 9, 1844; Roman to Clay, Dec. 2, 1844. 5. Ewing to Clay, June 23, 1844. 6. Clay to Sargent, Oct. 17, 1846.

To Arthur Wells, November 17, 1846. Concurs "in congratulations on the recent triumphs of the Whigs [Clay to Sargent, October 17, 1846; Clay to Littell, November 17, 1846] and it adds to my pleasure that their success has been achieved on great and vital principles of policy." Suggests that "If the Whigs are hereafter wise, and do not prematurely agitate distant questions, there is much reason to hope that the administration of our General Government may be again brought back to a just comprehension and a faithful support of sound principles of National policy." LS. ViU.

To EPES SARGENT Lexington, November 18, 1846

I duly received your favor of the 27th. ultimo and, although I had no expectation of the publication of any part of my last letter,[1] addressed to you, I am entirely satisfied with the use you made of an extract from it.[2] I shall be very happy if it contributed, in the smallest degree, to the election of Mr [John] Young.[3] On that and other recent gratifying events I tender you cordial congratulations. This being a dark and unpleasant November day, I determined to remain at home and employ it in the preparation of some additional matter for your contemplated new edition of my life. I accordingly prevailed upon my son John [Morrison Clay] to act as my Amanuensis, and to write out the four sheets which I now send you. They are transmitted, just in the form which I dictated to him, without copying or revisal. I request you to treat them with the utmost freedom and to incorporate them, or any part of them, or not, in your work, as you please. Of course, you will have to interweave them with the text in the manner which you may deem most proper, if you think them worthy of any place in your book. I request you also not to consider yourself bound by the language which I have employed, as I have no doubt you will be able to improve it, as, perhaps, I could myself if I had time to revise and review it. I think you can have no difficulty in making the addition which the publishers desire to your pamphlet.[4] You might draw many facts perhaps from the work of Mr [Calvin] Colton, and dress them up to your own taste. He, I think, has erred in too copiously publishing from my speeches and writings.[5] Possibly you have gone a little too much upon the opposite extreme. Circumstances, which have occurred, in connexion with me, since the period at which your work terminates, may furnish you with some additional matter. Such, for example, as the manner in which I bore the defeat in 1844, my speech addressed to the Electors of Kentucky who came here from Frankfort to visit me,[6] after having deposited their suffrages, my late address in answer to Dr [Boyd] McNairy,[7] which will reach you about the time this letter does &c &c.

In dictating the matter, on the enclosed sheets,[8] I had no memorandum to guide me, but was governed by a memory, in whose fidelity I have entire confidence. P.S. I have not employed the services of my son, in consequence of ill health. It was never better, and I go in a few days to N. Orleans not [to] regain but to retain it.

Possibly from that City, I may transmit to you more matter, if any thing material shall occer. Would not your last chapters bear greater amplification?

LS, postscript in Clay's hand. MCM. 1. Clay to Sargent, Oct. 17, 1846. 2. Reference obscure; Sargent's letter of Oct. 27 has not been found. 3. Clay to Sargent, Oct. 17, 1846. 4. Clay to Sargent, August 7, 1844. 5. Clay to Colton, Sept. 5, 1845. 6. Speech to Ky. Presidential Electors, Dec. 4, 1844. 7. Speech to McNairy, Nov. 12, 1846. 8. Not found.

To HORACE GREELEY Lexington, November 21, 1846

I recd. today your favor of the 15h. inst. and feel greatly obliged by the explanations and information which it communicates. I was previously at a loss to comprehend why Mr. [Millard] Fillmore was not taken up, as the Whig Candidate in your State.[1] The reasons you assign would seem to be sufficient; but I hope that Mr. F. of whom I entertain a very high opinion, as indeed I do of Mr. [John] Young, will be made to understand them. Should the Whig party hereafter succeed, as there appears now great reason to hope, Mr. Fillmore, ought not to be; and I hope will not be, forgotten.

For almost the first time, the Whigs have, in your State, been benefited by the accession of a local or peculiar party, that is the Anti renters.[2] Will you be able in your Legislature, without the sacrifice of principle, to satisfy them? I hope so, but there lies the danger in future.

New York has nobly acquitted herself of her duty to herself and to the Union; and the gratifying result of recent elections there and elsewhere[3] revives hopes for our Country which were before almost extinct.

You tell me that one consequence of these events is to bring forward a large number of Presidential aspirants.[4] That is not at all surprising. But I do most heartily concur with you in thinking that at present, and for some time to come, it would be unwise in the Whig party and the Whig press to agitate the question of the succession. It is better to leave the Public to consider & feel yet longer the effects of the disastrous measures of the last Session of Congress, and to let it be undisturbed and undiverted by any new question. It would be highly gratifying, and probably conducive to the interests of the other party, to divert public attention from its misdeeds to what is always an exciting and engrossing subject.

If the eagerness of some gentlemen or their friends will not allow them to wait patiently, it will be well for the Whig Press to leave them to the consequences of their own indiscreet and premature movements.

Messrs. [John J.] Crittenden and [Garrett] Davis, both of whom I expect to see in the course of the next week, (I do not suppose that I shall see any other members of our delegation) will carry to Washington my views as to the future. As to myself, whilst I have deliberately foreborne to say yes or no to any one, on the question of the use of my name, as a Candidate for the next President, I will say to you that it depends on conditions as to my life, health, vigor of mind and body, and general manifestations of a desire to place me at the helm, of the existence of which I must be allowed to judge, at the proper time.

I expect to leave home in about a week for N. Orleans, where I go to pass the winter, not on account of ill health, for my health was never better, but to retain what I have. I shall be happy to hear from you there, if you should have occasion to address me.

ALS. NUtM. 1. Clay to Sargent, Oct. 17, 1846; Greeley to Clay, Nov. 15, 1846. 2. Greeley to Clay, Nov. 15, 1846. 3. Clay to Sargent, Oct. 17, 1846. 4. *Ibid.*

From John Bailhache, Alton, Ill., November 23, 1846. Acknowledges receipt of "a Copy of the Patent for your Land, which will probably enable me to find the lines and corners with sufficient certainty [9:108]." Reports that "I have had several applications for the purchase of the Timber on portions of your Land, and also for very small Tracts of the Land itself." Has "just received an offer for the whole, which I will submit at once in the hope that it may reach you before your departure for New Orleans." Names the potential buyer as "Mr. G.W. Allen" who "first applied to me for the Timber; then for a part of the Tract; and now he proposes to give Sixteen Hundred Dollars, Cash in hand, for the whole," a price that is "something more than was given a few weeks since for a Tract of Land in the same vicinity." Explains that Allen "is a stranger to me . . . and I know nothing of his circumstances," but the buyer "intends spending the Winter here, in order 'to operate extensively in the Wood line.' " Concludes that "Should you deem it proper to accede to his proposition, no conveyance will be made until the purchase money shall be paid." ALS. DLC-TJC (DNA, M212, R14). See Clay to James Brown Clay, December 10, 1846.

George Washington Allen founded the town of Greenfield, Ill., where he became postmaster as well as a miller and merchant. *ISHSJ*, 24:553.

To HENRY WHITE Lexington, November 27, 1846

At the moment of my departure from home, which I leave to-morrow for New Orleans, I take great pleasure in the acknowledgment of the receipt of your kind favor of the 21st instant. I wish I could enjoy the satisfaction of your company on the voyage, not however, with the discomforts which we experienced in that terrible old hickory last winter.

I congratulate you on the marriage of your daughter.[1] Say to her that I wish her all possible happiness; and that, if she does not enjoy it, so far as her husband is concerned, I must say, "white man is very uncertain."

I congratulate you also on public affairs. I think light is once more beaming upon us, and light, too, from the Key stone [Pennsylvania], as well as elsewhere.[2]

Your information and explanations are very friendly and satisfactory.

As to the Tariff of 1846,[3] I think our true policy is to go for its repeal, and the restoration of the Tariff of 1842,[4] and nothing else than the repeal of the one and the restoration of the other.

My wife [Lucretia Hart Clay], and all at Ashland, unite in affectionate regards to you and all of yours.

Copy. Printed in Colton, *Clay Correspondence*, 4:537-38. 1. White's daughter Anne married George H. Bryan on Nov. 9, 1846. Philadelphia *U.S. Gazette*, Nov. 11, 1846. 2. Clay to Littell, Nov. 17, 1846. 3. Clay to Greeley, June 23, 1846. 4. See 9:628.

From the Young Men's Henry Clay Association of the City of New York, December 7, 1846. On behalf of the association, "(formed, in May 1844, of those who became in that year first entitled to vote for Presidential Electors,)" invite Clay to attend "their Third Annual Ball on the 29th of the present month, at Rathbun's Hotel in this City." Explain that their organization "(generally denominated the '*Young Guard*') have celebrated their two previous annual festivals under circumstances apparently tending to repress the ardor even of ever-hopeful youth." Insist, nonetheless, that "their devotion to you has glowed unchangeably; and their hope of the ultimate vindication of your rights and of the triumph of the principles which patriotic faith has embodied in you, has never fainted." Maintain that they "Organized to honor your name, and to promote the interests of the country by your advancement," and that "they still fondly cherish your fame, and firmly abide by their earliest pledges."

View recent Whig victories as the "now useless repentance of a vast portion of those whose suffrages brought disgrace upon the nation by the election of 1844." Hope that the "sad lessons learned by the people during the past two years will be felt in their action—when they next exercise their sovereign power in disposing of their highest honors and trusts." Wish Clay will have the opportunity to "demonstrate in your own person your favorite sentiment that '*Truth is omnipotent and public justice is certain.*' " L, draft. CtY.

On December 22, 1846, Clay wrote to Alexander Wilkin *et al.* to acknowledge the invitation, "but, waiving all other considerations, the distances from the place of my present sojourn [New Orleans] to the City of N. York will not allow me to enjoy that satisfaction." Thanks the association for "the ardor, the constancy, and the fidelity of the attachment to me which they do me the honor to entertain." After "a dark period of great discouragement," hopes that "brighter and better and happier days for our Country would yet come. And the recent events, to which you have adverted, are an assurance and a guaranty of their approach. If misconception and misrepresentation accomplished their work, we may, I trust, congratulate ourselves that their success will only be temporary. The consequences may, indeed, be more durable. These we now feel in foreign war, and in the abandonment & neglect of vital domestic interests." Warns that the recent Whig victories "should not be made the occasion of any party exultation." Believes that "If our fellow citizens, hitherto opposed to us . . . are left to an unimpassioned consideration" of the Polk administration's policies, "many of them cannot fail to bring their minds to the same conclusions at which we have arrived." ALS. *Ibid.*

To JAMES BROWN CLAY Natchez, Miss., December 10, 1846

I left Louisville in the Bunker hill on the evening of the first and arrived here on the morning of the 8h. instant. Unluckily I found Mr. [William St. John] Elliot and most of my friends absent at their respective plantations. I shall leave this place for New Orleans this evening. I find the business of the Agricultural Bank in statu quo, awaiting the decision in January or Feby of the Supreme Court of this State as to the constitutionality of the last act of the Legislature.[1] Those interested, as Creditors or Stockholders in the Bank entertain great apprehensions.

I received at Louisville the letters which you enclosed to me at that place from Mr. Benson about wine, and from [John M.] Bailhache about my Alton land.[2] Low as the price of $1600 cash is, which has been offered for it, I authorized him to take it, and to remit me the amount at N.O. to get rid of the vexation of trespasses on the timber.

I shall receive the wine at N.O. and will have it sent up, when a division of it can be made.

When you go to Ashland, I wish you would remind them of having the Cistern filled. Before I left home, I directed the pipe to be stopt, that the roof might be well washed, before the water was let into the Cistern.

I shall be glad to hear from you frequently.

My love to Susan [Jacob Clay]; and kisses for dear Lucy [Jacob Clay].

ALS. DLC-TJC (DNA, M212, R11). Addressed to J.B. Clay at Lexington, Ky. 1. Eustis & Chaplain to Clay, March 5, 1846. 2. Bailhache to Clay, Nov. 23, 1846.

From John Pendleton Kennedy, Baltimore, Md., December 15, 1846. Expresses his hopes that the Maryland legislature, which is scheduled to meet on December 28, will "adopt the most decisive measures for the complete restoration of the credit of the state, by the punctual payment henceforth of the interest on the public debt, and by funding the arrears of interest now due in six per cent stock." Views the question as important to "The honor of the Whig party in Maryland." Complains that "some of our friends in the State . . . have taken up the impression that there is no obligation of equity to compel them to *fund the arrears* at six per cent,—holding that to be a payment of interest upon interest." Adds that these are "men of honorable minds . . . who would be disposed to do what should be considered strictly just in the matter, but they are, for the most part, persons unacquainted with the usages of business relating to such transactions."

Describes the state bonds as "issued chiefly to raise money for the [Chesapeake & Ohio] Canal; are payable at a remote day; and engage the state to pay the interest either quarterly or half yearly." Explains that these bonds are not "a common debt due at a particular day, which, being unpaid, is recoverable through the Courts with interest" but were "intended as investments of money yielding an annual return to the holder . . . and when the interest has been withheld, to treat that item as principal." Is persuaded "that a word from you upon this point would do more to determine the action of our Legislature in the direction I desire it should take, than a hundred speeches from me [Clay to Kennedy, December 27, 1846]. If Clay will "express your wish that Maryland would take a high ground on this question, and no longer delay that justice which she owes to her own character, her Whig predominance, and to those to whom she is indebted," is certain that "our young members . . . would" then be able "to justify themselves to their people at home." Does not desire "any thing for publication, much less any elaborate argument," just a "letter as a casual aid to the purpose I entertain . . . or perhaps to refer to it in debate, as a matter incidentally arising out of a correspondence with you."

Concerning the 1848 presidential election, claims that "If you are to be again in the field, Maryland has no other name for the contest—nor will the Whigs here commit themselves to any one until that contingency is determined." If Clay chooses not to run, "the universal wish here . . . is to see you again in the Senate, where . . . your influence and authority would be such as no other man has ever had there." Is "almost tempted to believe that the Senate Chamber will become the only proper arena for the ambition of the greatest men of the Country." Fears that "This wretched principle of *availability* . . . is about to cast the Chief Magistracy forever into the hands of the men whose mediocrity shall shield them equally from the praise or censure of the people."

Adds in a postscript: "I am now engaged upon a Biography of Mr [William] Wirt, and find amongst his papers a good deal of correspondence with Benjn. Edwards who then lived (1805) in Kentucky at *Shiloh*, I think." Asks if Clay knew this man, and, if so, if he could "furnish me with a short sketch of his character. . . . But not if it is to cost you any labor in the noting of it." ALS. MdBP.

After the financial panic of 1837, Maryland had been unable to pay interest on its state bonds, which had been issued to finance internal improvements. In 1847 the legislature passed a resolution calling for payment of the state's debt, but resumption of interest payments did not begin until January 1, 1848. Alfred C. Bryan, "History of State Banking in Maryland," in *Johns Hopkins University Studies* (Baltimore, Md., 1899), 17:1-144, espec. 108; *Niles' Register* (January 9, 1847), 71:296.

For Kennedy's biography of Wirt, see Bohner, *John Pendleton Kennedy*, 180-85. The book, entitled *Memoirs of the Life of William Wirt, Attorney General of the United States*, was published in Philadelphia in 1849.

Benjamin Edwards, who died in Todd County, Ky., in 1826, was a native of Maryland who had served in the state legislature and in Congress before moving to Kentucky. He was the father of Illinois governor and senator Ninian Edwards. See

BDAC; Washington *Daily National Intelligencer*, December 11, 1826. See also Clay to Kennedy, December 27, 1846.

To JAMES BROWN CLAY New Orleans, December 19, 1846

I transmit enclosed, via Balto. the second number of a bill the first of which I sent yesterday by the river for the sum of $2853:30.[1] If you should have got the note discounted you had better get the Bank to forward the bill & await its maturity.

I have written to P.T. Ellicott[2] offering your Mules as mine at $300 delivered in Balto. or $250 at Ashland, and have requested him if he wants them to write to & pay you[.]

I recd. your letter with its enclosures after I wrote to you yesterday.[3]

I find that Martin Duralde [III] has only $300 in Bank. [W.C.C.] Claiborne [Jr.] is to administer on his Estate and to pay it over to me to pay his debts. His father [Martin Duralde, Jr.] is absent.

When an opportunity occurs, I will write to Henry [Clay, Jr.] as you desire.

I have enquired about Hemp here. There is little or none in the market. That of a good quality would command here $90 per ton. So [Thomas S.] Kennedy told me to day. If you can purchase in K[entucky]. a good article at $60 per ton, six months credit, you would do well with it.

My love to Susan [Jacob Clay] & Lucy [Jacob Clay].

ALS. DLC-TJC (DNA, M212, R11). 1. On Dec. 18, 1846, Clay had transmitted to James "a draft for $2853:30, and will send the other number of the draft by the Eastern mail." Sent also "your part of the profits," a sum of $436.42, from the sale of their mules by Ursin Bouligny, Jr. *Ibid.* 2. Philip T. Ellicott (1809-59) was the proprietor of a chemical works and steamblast furnace in Baltimore. *Baltimore City Directory for 1845* (microfiche). 3. Not found.

To OCTAVIA WALTON LEVERT New Orleans, December 19, 1846

I have this moment seen our mutual friend Genl. [Joseph] Bates, who told me that he bore a letter to me from Dr. [Henry] LeVert which he has not yet delivered.[1] I cannot postpone to its reception the tender to you and to the Dr. of my cordial congratulations on the event, which has happily occurred in your family. Another child! and a daughter too![2] You are too good a christian not to submit to the will of Providence, and be resigned to the sex of your infant; although I dare say, if it had been HIS pleasure, you would have prefered a son.

I am delighted to learn from Genl. Bates that your health is good, and that no apprehensions are entertained on account of it.

I reached this City a few days ago, and every day had been intending to announce to you my safe arrival, but was prevented by some unexpected engagements, or circumstances. My voyage from Louisville this winter was entirely free from the mishaps and discomforts which attended that of the last.[3]

Genl. [Charles Fenton] Mercer accompanied me as far as Natchez, where I stopt a few days; he proceeding on his voyage to this City. Poor fellow! ill during the whole voyage, he is now confined at the Verandah,[4] and I should be glad if I could speak of his recovery, with more confidence than I can.[5] He calls his complaint a bad cold—I wish it may not terminate in consumption.

Here at Dr. [William Newton] Mercer's, where I am, all are well, and every thing is in statu quo, except that Anna [Mercer] continues to advance towards womanhood.

This City is less gay, I understand, and less filled with strangers than usual. Among the latter, the military and naval officers &c constitute a large portion. Genl [Winfield] Scott arrived yesterday, and dines with us to day in Canal Street.

As I do not expect to return befor[e] March, I hope to see you, either her[e] or at Mobile.[6]

I hope that no excitement of jealousy will arise with "The Graces,"[7] in consequence of the appearance of the little stranger. They will soon learn that a Mother's heart is capaci[ous] enough to embrace all of them.

My cordial respects of Dr. Le V[ert], to your father [George Walton] and mother [Sally Walker Walton], and Kisses for all your daughters.

ALS. KyU. 1. Letter not found. Gen. Bates is probably Maj. Gen. Joseph Bates of the Alabama militia. He was a friend and supporter of Clay, and they spent much time together in Mobile in 1844. Garrett, *Reminiscences of Public Men in Alabama*, 173-74. 2. The daughter was named for Clay, Henrietta Caroline. See Clay to LeVert, April 14, 1844. 3. Clay to Lucretia H. Clay, Jan. 12, 1846. 4. The Verandah Baths and Dressing Rooms in New Orleans, N.B. Goins, proprietor. New Orleans *Daily Picayune*, March 7, 1846. 5. Mercer survived until May, 1858, when he died of cancer. *DAB*. 6. Clay did not visit Mobile during this trip. 7. Clay to LeVert, April 14, 1844.

To THOMAS B. STEVENSON New Orleans, December 19, 1846

I recd your letter of the 10th instant in respect to the approaching Senatorial Election in Kentucky.[1] The subject has occasioned some concern, not to say vexation.

I took a formal and final leave of the Senate more than four years ago. I not only have no desire but I entertain a particular disinclination to return to it. I have given no authority nor countenance to the use of my name as a candidate. I could not reappear as a member of the Senate, without at least an apparent inconsistency; and I can not concieve a state of things in which I would consent to go back.

My wish is that an election should be made from among the avowed Candidates[2] for the office; and although I regard them all as able and competent to serve the State with credit and fidlity, and all my friends, if I had myself the election in my own hands, I should give my sufferage to one of them; I need not, nor would it be proper to indicate which.

I have not said that, if elected, I would not serve, because such a prior declaration, in advance of an election seems to me unbecoming and indelicate; but if my anxious desire is regarded, and if my feelings and interests are at all consulted, the attention of the General Assembly will be wholly withdrawn from me and concentrated upon some other person.

To this effect in substance, previous to the receipt of your letter, I wrote to General [Leslie] Combs and James Harlan Esqr.

We have no news here, except the arrival yesterday of General [Winfield] Scott en route to Mexico.

Copy. OCHP. Printed in Colton, *Clay Correspondence*, 3:459-60. 1. After 26 attempts and the withdrawal of several candidates, the Kentucky legislature elected Whig Joseph R. Underwood to the U.S. Senate on Feb. 12, 1847. Ky. Sen., *Journal* . . . 1846-1847, p. 281. 2. Those considered by the legislature for senator, in addition to Underwood, were Albert G. Hawes, Robert P. Letcher, Linn Boyd, James Guthrie, Robert B. McAfee, and Thomas Metcalfe. *Ibid.*

Toast at the dinner of the New England Society of Louisiana, New Orleans, December 22, 1846. Although claiming to be "Very little in the habit of addressing assemblies of any kind [laughter]—I don't mean to say I never was, but that I am not now in the habit of addressing assemblies," remains, "not altogether unobservant of the proceedings relating to the condition, welfare and prospects of our country." Asserts that "when I saw around me to-night Gen. Brooke and other old friends, I felt half inclined to ask for some little nook or corner in the army, in which I might serve in avenging the wrongs to my country—[applause]. I have thought that I might yet be able to capture or to slay a Mexican—[applause]. I shall not be able to do so, however, this year, but hope that success will crown our gallant arms, and the war terminate in an honorable peace." Thanks them for their invitation: "It is not the first time I have met you, and the association fills me with pleasure. You do right, gentlemen, in commemorating and encouraging the spirit of liberty and opposition to oppression that brought to the shores of the New World your glorious ancestors." Copy. Printed in the New Orleans *Daily Picayune*, December 23, 1846.

The New England Society of Louisiana had been incorporated in 1842 for the purpose of fostering "among its members, friendship and good feeling, and to assist the destitute and those worthy of charity coming from the New England States of the Union." *An Act to Incorporate The New England Society of Louisiana. Approved, March 26, 1842* . . . (New Orleans, 1842), 5.

Gen. Brooke is probably Gen. George Mercer Brooke, originally from Virginia, who in 1848 was promoted from brigadier to major general for meritorious conduct in the Mexican War. Heitman, *HRDUSA*, 248.

To JOHN PENDLETON KENNEDY New Orleans, December 27, 1846
I received your favor of the 15h. inst. I believe that Mr. Benjamin Edwards, about whom you enquire of me, was the father of the late Govr. Ninian Edwards of Illinois, whom you must have known, or at least heard of. I did not know Benjamin Edwards, his residence having been near Bardstown (K.) some distance from mine. I think I have heard the Govr. speak of the intimacy of Mr. [William] Wirt in the family of his father. Either Mr. [John J.] Crittenden, or Mr. [James T.] Morehead will probably be able to communicate more information to you than I possess in respect to Mr. B. Edwards.

I saw, with much satisfaction, your election to the Legislature of Maryland.[1] There you will be able to render to your native State services of more importance than any you could perform for the Union, in the H. of Representatives, constituted as that house is at present.[2] You will doubtless direct your efforts to the object of re-establishing the financial credit of the State, and of placing it hereafter on a sure and stable footing. Proud of Maryland, as a patriotic and distinguished member of our Confederacy, and grateful for the support and confidence with which it has always honored me, I am most anxious to see it relieved from its pecuniary embarrassments by ample provision for the honorable fulfilment of all its obligations. Your debt is large, but you have a great deal to shew for it, in those noble works of Internal improvement, which must become more and more valuable & productive from year to year.[3] I presume that the great diversity of opinion among the members of your Legislature will arise out of what should be done with the arrears of unpaid interest. Shall they be funded, and thus become a new capital, bearing interest, or remain unpaid and barren? It seems to me that you can hardly avoid funding them, without exposing yourselves to the imputation of not going up to the full and just extent of your obligations.[4]

Whatever you may do, I sincerely hope that the honor and the high character of Maryland will be preserved untarnished. This is a desire, I imagine, common to every Whig in the U. States.

The agitation of the question of my return to the Senate of the U.S. has been made in K. without any consultation with me.[5] Personally I have not only no wish, but a positive disinclination, to go back to that body. Nothing but a mere sense of strict duty, arising out of a persuasion that I could be useful to our Country, would ever reconcile me to the resumption of a seat in the Senate. I see no prospect of usefulness on my part there, and therefore feel no obligation of duty to return. I have, accordingly, since my arrival here, written home, earnestly requesting that a successor of Mr. Morehead may be chosen from among the avowed Candidates for the office.[6]

This unhappy War with Mexico fills me with anxious solicitude.[7] When is it to terminate? How? If the Country is conquered what can be done with it? Can the conquest be relinquished? If not, can all Mexico, with her eight millions of inhabitants, speaking another language, obeying other Laws, differing from us in religion and race, be united or annexed to the U.S.? Can our Government extend its authority over such an immense extent of territory, and preserve the discordant population in peace and prosperity? These are very, very grave questions.

I am glad to see no eagerness, at least no general eagerness, to open the next Presidential Campaign. I think that the public mind had, for some time to come, better be left to the undisturbed and undiverted consideration of the pernicious measures of the last Session of Congress. To start now the question of the C. Magistracy might have the effect of rekindling party passions, and of preventing many who may, if left alone a little longer, be disposed to join the Whig ranks. Our prospects are good, better I think than they ever were at any corresponding periods, preceding great political changes. And I do not believe that they will be impaired by our forbearing to rush on the Presidential contest . . .

ALS. MdBP. 1. Kennedy had been elected to the Maryland house of delegates from the city of Baltimore in the election held Oct. 7, 1846. He was subsequently chosen speaker of the house. As a result of the Maryland election, Whigs controlled the state senate by 13 to 8 seats and the house by 53 to 29. *Niles' Register* (Oct. 17, 1846), 71:98; Bohner, *John Pendleton Kennedy*, 174. 2. Clay to Berrien, Dec. 12, 1845. 3. Kennedy to Clay, Dec. 15, 1846. 4. *Ibid.* 5. The Frankfort *Commonwealth* had reported on Dec. 8, 1846, that "sundry Kentucky newspapers" had been advocating Clay's return to the Senate and stated that this was done without Clay's desire or knowledge. 6. Clay to Stevenson, Dec. 19, 1846. 7. Clay to Lawrence, April 30, 1845.

From I.A. Bragaw, Hartford, Conn., December 30, 1846. Identifies himself as a hardware merchant, and sends Clay a pocket knife as a tribute for his "long exertions in behalf of the labor of your country." Notes that the knife was made in Salisbury, Connecticut, where cannon shot and shells were made during the American Revolution "and which since, thanks to legislation which has received its chief impress from you, has been able, in the refined form of cutlery, to contribute to the peaceful triumphs of American industry and skill." Asserts that if Clay were now president, "the country would not have had occasion to mourn, as it now does, the river and harbor wrecks, spoliation of citizens, and war." Copy. Printed in Washington *Daily National Intelligencer*, July 2, 1847.

Clay wrote to Bragaw at Salisbury, Conn., on June 19, 1847, acknowledging the gift. Continues: "I have been very desirous to learn the effect upon American manufactures produced by the last Tariff [of 1846; Clay to Greeley, June 23, 1846]." Since Europe "has been so occupied with supplying herself with necessary food . . . the competition between foreign and domestic manufactures has been much less unequal than it would otherwise have been." Adds: "The struggle so far has been between well-fed and ill-fed operatives; between capital diverted from purchase of the raw material to the purchase of bread, and capital greatly augmented by the sale of food; and between manufacturers working short time and full time." Wonders if "when Europe is no longer starving . . . we shall be able to sustain a successful competition." Hopes that "our manufactures have struck such deep and strong root, that they may be able to stand up and flourish against all adverse causes." Copy, extract. Printed in the Portsmouth (N.H.) *Journal of Literature & Politics*, July 24, 1847. This newspaper printed Bragaw's name as "Brigaw"; the name undoubtedly is Bragaw, as the *Intelligencer* gave it, since that was a family name in Connecticut. I.A. Bragaw has not been further identified.

The great potato famine began in Ireland in 1845 and by the following year had spread to continental Europe. It continued into the 1850s, with Ireland and Germany suffering the most. For the effects of the famine, including the dramatic increase in immigration to the United States, see Langer, *Encyclopedia of World History*, 679; David H. Bennett, *The Party of Fear from Nativist Movements to the New Right in American History* (Chapel Hill, 1988), 61-92.

To JAMES BROWN CLAY New Orleans, January 17, 1847

I recd. your letter of the 1st. inst. and was much distressed by the account you give me of dear little Lucy's [Jacob Clay] health.[1] She is one of the few links that bind me to life, and I should be quite inconsolable if we were to lose her. Tell Doctor [Benjamin W.] Dudley that I hope he will exert all his skill to restore her.

The Madeira wine goes up in the next trip of the Peytona. There are 23 dozen in 12 boxes. On its arrival, [Richard] Pindell may have Eight dozen, you seven & I will retain the other eight. He can settle with me for it on my return. It is a very superior article.

Mr. U[rsin]. Bouligny [Jr.] does not wish to continue the Mule business. I will see if I cannot make some arrangement with young Roman.[2] But you ought to recollect that, unless the Government again comes into the market for Mules, they will be low another year.

I have heard nothing as to the progress of [Ambrose] Barnett in getting out hemp. It bears now a good price here and at the Eastward. I am inclined to think that it would be a good business permanently to hackle it, selling the ton at home.

I have recd. no letter from Henry [Clay, Jr.] since I have been here; but I frequently hear that he is doing well. I suppose that he is now at Monterey.[3]

My agricultural debt is not yet decided. Great fears are entertained that the Court in Mississippi will decide unfavorably.[4]

The sale of the house and lot belonging to the Estate of Mr. [James] Brown is to take place this week.[5]

I shall send up by the Peytona about 900 lb of beautiful Sugar, as white as refined sugar, of which I intended 150 lb for Susan [Jacob Clay].

I should be glad to know what the purchasers of the Combs lot[6] intend to do.

Thomas [Hart Clay] has not written me since I left home. Has he sold any of his bricks?[7]

Give my love to Susan & kiss Lucy for me.

My health has been generally good.

ALS. DLC-TJC (DNA, M212, R11). Printed in Colton, *Clay Correspondence*, 4:538. 1. Clay to Susan J. Clay, Nov. 3, 1845. 2. Probably a son of Andre B. Roman. 3. Gen. Zachary Taylor had captured Monterey in Sept., 1846, and the troops remained there for some time. In Feb., 1847 the Kentucky legislature passed a resolution to present a sword to Taylor as a tribute to his gallant conduct at the battle of Monterey, the baptism by fire of the Kentucky Volunteers. Anderson C. Quisenberry, "General Zachary Taylor and the Mexican War," *RKHS* (May, 1911), 9:21-22. 4. Eustis & Chaplain to Clay, March 5, 1846. 5. Preston to Clay, April 26, 1844. 6. Reference obscure. 7. In Oct., 1846 Thomas Hart Clay and James B. Clay began to make bricks on the Mansfield property. Lexington *Observer & Kentucky Reporter*, Jan. 2, 13, 1847.

To JAMES BROWN CLAY New Orleans, January 30, 1847

I received today your letter of the 19h. informing me of your having purchased 30 tons of hemp, stating that you may purchase 60 or 70 tons more, and asking me to send an authority to join my name in security for the payment of the price[.]

I send the authority enclosed accordingly. Some clean hemp, altho' not hackled, sold yesterday at $95 per ton, and if your's were now here you might probably get that price, if it be a good article. You had better send it forward as soon as possible, and be sure to have it well cleaned and baled. What operates somewhat against, the article is that freights are now very high, being one cent per pound to Boston. I have authorized [Thomas S.] Kennedy to day to sell yours at $95 to be paid on delivery; but I don't think it probable he will find a purchaser until the article comes forward. I would not advise you to go beyond $60, and that only for clean good hemp. I fear the present upward tendency of hemp & all other produce cannot be sustained. If Thomas s [Hart Clay] hands hired for breaking my water retted hemp, could be employed in hackling and cleaning hemp, I think it would be profitable.

I am sorry to hear that poor little Lucy [Jacob Clay] continues unwell. Kiss the dear child for me, and my love to Susan [Jacob Clay].

ALS. DLC-TJC (DNA, M212, R11). Printed in Colton, *Clay Correspondence*, 4:538-39.

Speech in New Orleans, February 4, 1847. Although doubting "the propriety of my presence and participation" and concerned that "my motive might be misunderstood," has decided that "all considerations of fastidious delicacy and etiquette should be waived and merged into a generous and magnanimous effort to contribute to the relief of the sufferings which have excited our feelings." Considers "The appalling and heartrending distresses of Ireland and Irishmen" which are "the object of our present consultation. That Ireland, which has been in all the vicissitudes of our national existence our friend, and has ever extended to us her warmest sympathy—those Irishmen, who, in every war in which we have been engaged, on every battlefield, from Quebec to Monterey, have stood by us, shoulder to shoulder, and shared in all the perils and fortunes of the conflict." Believes that it is "the Irish nation, which is so identified with our own as to be almost part and parcel of ours—bone of our bone and flesh of our flesh," and not "a few isolated cases of death by starvation, that we are called upon to consider." Describes the famine: "stalking abroad throughout Ireland—whole towns, counties—countless human beings, of every age and of both sexes, at this very moment, are starving, or in danger of starving to death for bread. Of all the forms of dissolution of human life, the pangs and agony of that which proceeds from famine are the most dreadful." Adds that "death by starvation comes slow, lingering, and excruciating. From day to day, the wretched victim feels his flesh dwindling, his speech sinking, his friends falling around him, and he finally expires in horrible agony." Begs compassion for "the wretched Irish mother . . . her famished children clinging to her tattered garments, and gazing piteously in her face, begging for food! And see the distracted husband-father . . . tortured with the reflection that he can afford no succor or relief to the dearest objects of his heart." Argues that "Ireland, in respect to food, is differently situated from all the countries of the world. Asia has her abundant supply of rice; Africa, her dates, yams, and rice; Europe, her bread of wheat, rye, and oats; America, a double resource in the small grains, and a never-failing and abundant supply of Indian corn. . . . But the staple food of large parts of poor Ireland is the potato, and when it fails, pinching want and famine follow. It is among the inscrutable dispensations of Providence, that the crop has been blighted these last two years."

Asks: "Shall starving Ireland—the young and the old—dying women and children—stretch out their hands to us for bread and find no relief? Will not this great city, the world's storehouse of an exhaustless supply of all kinds of food, borne to its overflowing warehouses by the Father of Waters, act on this occasion in a manner worthy of its high destiny. . . . We are commanded, by the common Saviour of Ireland and of us, to love one another as ourselves. . . . Let us demonstrate our love, our duty, and our gratitude to Him, by a liberal contribution to the relief of His suffering Irish children." Copy. Printed in Colton, *Clay Correspondence*, 3:46-49.

To MARY MENTELLE CLAY New Orleans, February 8, 1847

I received your agreeable letter of the 24h. Ulto. Far from concurring with Thomas [Hart Clay] in condemning the length of the letters of women, the details in which they go are always very satisfactory. When one is a long way from home, the minutest possess an interest. I am sorry that there was any delay in the purchase of hemp as it is still high here, and would command $90 or $95 in this market. But I fear that price may not be long maintained.

Mr. [James] Erwin is better, but I fear his complete recovery will not be soon if it ever take place. It is still very difficult for him to pronounce a connected sentence.[1]

I hope you will not neglect your bacon hams. Those sent down lately by your mother have been much approved.[2]

Tell Thomas and James [Brown Clay] that if they can sell the hemp which they have purchased at an advance of $20 per Ton, and get paid for baling it, that I think they had better sell at home. When the river opens to St Louis, I fear that a quantity will be brought down on the Ohio & Mississippi rivers that will diminish the price. At present all products are high. The question is can prices be supported.

We have had very bad weather here during the month of January, and up to yesterday in February.

I shall expect to see the ground about your house very much improved on my return, and I begin to feel tired of my long absence.

My love to Thomas & your children.

ALS. DLC-HC (DNA, M212, R6). 1. James Erwin had apparently suffered a stroke. He died in Lexington on June 1, 1851, leaving his estate in chaos. See Clay to Andrew Eugene Erwin, July 19, 1851, and *RKHS*, 41:155. 2. Clay to Lucretia Hart Clay, Jan. 19, 1846.

From HENRY CLAY, JR. "Camp at Agua Nueva 20 miles in front of Saltillo," February 12, 1847

I have not received a letter from you for many weeks. The last was written before you left Ky. I have heard indirectly since that you are in New Orleans and in good health.

By a letter received from Mr. [Thomas] Smith and from other sources I learned that unfavorable reports in regard to me prevailed in Ky.[1] I replied to his letter in Monterey and sent it under an envellope to you in New Orleans. I hope you received it. The prevalence of such reports did not surprize me. You will remember that in July last I wrote you[2] from the camp on the Rio Grande near Burrita informing you of certain facts connected with the command of the Reg[imen]t which augured nothing but evil.[3] From that source these things have issued. The public rarely discriminates justly. A rgt may be likened to a limited monarchy. Every thing depends upon the head. The commander of this one [Col. William R. McKee] is a good fellow but slow in his conclusions with no capacity for organization and unfortunately addicted to excesses in a very dangerous fault. As to myself I assure you upon my honor that my own habits have not for years been so good as during this campaign and I have not for a single moment been incapacitated for my duties except by sickness and the dislocation of my arm. The Col and myself are on the best terms at present. I labor assiduously for the Regt. and endeavor to supply all deficiencies that I can: but I assure you I long heartily for the day when I shall be freed from the double responsibility which now seems to rest upon me. I am, without the hope of any distinction, only endeavoring to avoid disgrace. If the Regt is disgraced I go with it. Should it win distinction the fame devolves upon another. In a regular Regt. the office I hold is one of little labor and less responsibility. In mine as at present constituted it yields a harvest of both. These things I say only to you and in confidence. I like the Col personally and sustain him before the Regt and every body else. I am no disorganizer and every corps must have a head. I desire therefore that you will burn and not repeat what I write. To save the credit of the Regt and myself I must have the influence which I now wield. Had I my choice however I would much rather be a private than a Lt Col under the present arrangement. This condition of things is making me prematurely old. I long for a battle that it may have an end. So far I have managed to maintain a good character for the Regt. It stands here much higher than either of the other Ky Regts.[4] The cavalry under [Col. Humphrey] Marshall is badly disciplined and has lately met with losses of which you have no doubt heard which are well calculated to cast disgrace upon it. [Maj. John P.] Gaines' party ought to have maintained themselves in the house where they were until night and then cut their way out. [Capt. William J.] Heady's should never have been sent out. To send out 20 men to look after a body which had just before captured 80 was an absurdity. They went out however in obedience to an order of Wools [Brig. Gen. John E. Wool].[5]

When I wrote from Monterey we had lately arrived there from Seralvo [*sic*, Cerralvo] by a forced march in consequence of a false alarm, the same which brought Genl [Zachary] Taylor back from Monte Morelos [*sic*, Montemorelos]. Some short time afterwards a similar stampede carried us to Saltillo or rather to a camp within 5 miles of that place. We were subsequently removed to the outskirts of the town. Night after night we were annoyed by false alarms and a feverish excitement among the men was created by unceasing notifications that we might immediately expect an attack.[6] This state of things was produced by [Maj. Gen. William O.] Butler who knows little about war and Wool whom you know—the veriest petit maitre in arms that ever existed. Butler has just got a leave of absence to return home and much to our relief Taylor has arrived among us. Immediately upon his arrival he ordered the army out to this place. He has near 5.000 men at this point. The place has been selected because it is in advance and because should the enemy come T. will here meet them coming from a march of some 30 miles without water. It is besides a good open field where he may deploy and bring into action all the several arms of his force. The latter consists of about 10 field pieces of horse artillery, the Ky and Arks Regts of cavalry 3 or 4 companies of regular dragoons and the balance Vol infantry.[7]

Taylor is very sore about late proceedings at Washington. He was not mentioned in the Presidents [James K. Polk] message and has been supplanted in the command by [Maj. Gen. Winfield] Scott in a very cavalier manner.[8] He considers it the result of an intrigue between Scott, [Brig. Gen. William J.] Worth, and [Secretary of War William L.] Marcy. This Army sympathises with him. For one I must confess I consider the manner of the thing very improper to say the least. Scott without seeing or consulting with him stripped him at once of all his veterans and advised him to fall back upon Monterey.[9] This latter movement would perhaps be well enough except for the moral effect of retiring. Taylor gathering together such troops as he has left determined at once upon an opposite course namely to advance. He now awaits the arrival of 4 or 5 of the new Vol. Regts from the States, when after collecting sufficient material and stores he will advance unless he receives contrary and peremptory orders from Washington upon San Luis or Zacatecas. He will take great hazards and although not absolutely a desperate game yet he will play a very bold one. At the same time he remarks that had he been properly relieved he would merely have applied for a command suitable to his rank and remained in the field only so long as the year vol's remain—the same who came in consequence of the danger in which he was placed on the other side of the Rio Grand[e.] His movement will not take place till the 1st April at all events. In the meantime we shall remain probably at this place.

Genl T., I say it in confidence, is not free from ambition. The Presidency begins to loom before him. This though not generally known, you may set down as certain.[10] He feels his power. By the by I consider him a faithful public servant and a just man. Except yourself I know few whom I would prefer to him. He is a Whig upon principle. a man of not very warm feelings but one who has studied our early history and whose prejudices lean to the old maxims of [George] Washington. He is very much beloved by the army—due partly to his personal courage and his success.

My health is good. I have not and probably shall never recover the perfect use of my arm.[11] Present me kindly to Dr [William N.] Mercer and family. . . .

Agua Nueva, February 19, 1847

The within was written on the 12h but as many of my letters have miscarried I have postponed till now to send it. We are at the same place. I think now T. will not advance far and will probably not attempt any of the large towns should he do so. He still awaits news from Scott and does not know what force the latter will turn over to him. I predicted at Matamoros in a letter to you last August that the last campaign would terminate in disappointment to the [Polk] Administration. I now greatly fear the same result for Scotts. The season is too far advanced and his force 12000 too small to make much impression on the Mexican people after marking [*sic*, marching] on taking and holding Vera Cruz.[12]

Ten thousand rumors reach us that [General Antonio Lopez de] Santa Anna is marching with a large force, some say 20.000 on this place. What truth there is in them I cannot tell.[13]

My Monarch was badly snagged at Monterey and I had to dispose of him. I am now badly mounted. I have only horse a Mexican from Xacatecas [*sic*, Zacatecas]. [P.S.] Major [Cary] Fry has just arrived bringing me several letters from you for which I thank you.

ALS. Henry Clay Memorial Foundation, Lexington, Ky. 1. It had been rumored that the officers of the 2nd Kentucky Volunteers, which was led by Col. William R. McKee, Lt. Col. Henry Clay, Jr., and Maj. Cary Fry, "were incompetent from inebriation, and that the regiment suffered therefrom." The Frankfort *Commonwealth* refuted this statement on Nov. 17, 1846, declaring it a calumny. 2. Letter not found. 3. The Rancho de la Burrita was a wet, primative, and unhealthy area located 9 miles from the Rio Grande and east of Matamoras. Prone to disease and boredom, the inexperienced soldiers were difficult to discipline and frequently incurred problems with Mexican civilians in the region. Henry Clay, Jr., was evidently referring to some of these problems and McKee's inability to exert his authority over his troops. Rives, *The United States and Mexico*, 2:150, 251-53; George W. Smith & Charles Judah (eds.), *Chronicles of the Gringos, The U.S. Army in the Mexican War, 1846-1848* (Albuquerque, 1968), 286-87. 4. At this time, three Kentucky Regiments served in Mexico: the 1st Infantry, or the Louisville Legion, under Col. Stephen Ormsby; the 2nd Infantry under Col. William R. McKee; and the 1st Cavalry under Col. Humphrey Marshall. Collins, *History of Kentucky*, 1:53-54, 56. For Humphrey Marshall, grandson of the Humphrey Marshall with whom Clay fought a duel, see 6:1287. 5. For Maj. John P. Gaines, a Boone County lawyer serving under Col. Marshall, see *BDAC*. For Capt. Heady, see Collins, *History of Kentucky*, 1:53, 127, 180; 2:100. For Brig. Gen. Wool, see *DAB*. Gen. William O. Butler [*BDAC*] had sent Maj. Gaines and an escort of Ky. cavalry under Capt. Cassius M. Clay on a scouting mission east and south of Agua Nueva. Finding no sign of the Mexicans, they turned west and joined with Maj. Solon Borland's 50-man detachment of Arkansas cavalry to probe south from Encarnacion. On Jan. 23, 1847, all 71 Americans surrendered to a force of 300 to 500 Mexican lancers that had surrounded them during the night. Gen. Wool ordered the 1st Kentucky Cavalry to send out another patrol, commanded by Capt. Heady, which was captured about 30 miles from Encarnacion on Jan. 27. Bauer, *The Mexican War*, 207. 6. For the various false alarms—or stampedes, as the volunteers called them—see Bauer, *The Mexican War*, 204-5, 207-8; Rives, *The United States and Mexico*, 2:304-6. 7. At the Battle of Buena Vista on Feb. 23, 1847, Taylor's front line included Capt. John M. Washington's 8-gun battery of the 4th U.S. Artillery, the 1st and 2nd Illinois Infantry with Capt. P. Edward Connor's company of Texas volunteers attached to the latter, the 2nd Kentucky Infantry, with the Kentucky and Arkansas volunteer cavalry regiments on the extreme left flank. In reserve were the 2nd and 3rd Indiana Infantry, Col. Jefferson Davis's Mississippi Rifles, two squadrons of U.S. Dragoons, and two batteries of the 3rd U.S. Artillery, commanded by Captains Thomas W. Sherman and Braxton Bragg. The 5,000 American troops were pitted against approximately 14-20,000 Mexican soldiers. In a narrow victory, Taylor's army suffered 272 killed, 387 wounded, and 6 missing. Mexican casualties amounted to 591 killed, 1,048 wounded, and 1,894 missing. *House Exec. Doc.* 60, 30 Cong., 1 Sess., pp. 1098-99, 1118; Gen. Cadmus M. Wilcox, *History of the Mexican War*, Mary Rachel Wilcox, ed. (Washington, D.C., 1892), 213-14; Bauer, *The Mexican War*, 209-18; Rives, *The United States and Mexico*, 2:351-52. 8. For the political and military considerations involved in Polk's transfer of four-fifths of Taylor's men to Scott's force for the Vera Cruz campaign and the relationships between Polk, Taylor, and Scott, see Bauer, *Zachary Taylor*, 191-93; Holman Hamilton, *Zachary Taylor, Soldier of the Republic* (Indianapolis, 1941), 221-29; Paul Bergeron, *The Presidency of James K. Polk* (Lawrence, Kansas, 1987), 92-94; Singletary, *The Mexican War*, 104-15. 9. *Ibid.* 10. Greeley to Clay, Nov. 15, 1846. 11. Clay to LeVert, Nov. 6, 1846. 12. For the various proposals for an assault on Vera Cruz, see Bauer, *The Mexican War*, 86, 121-22, 202, 204, 232-53; Rives, *The United States and Mexico*, 2:285-89, 291-95, 298-300. 13. For Gen. Santa Anna's battle plans, see Bauer, *The Mexican War*, 201-2, 204-18; Rives, *The United States and Mexico*, 2:337-60; Bauer, *Zachary Taylor*, 191-206.

To EPES SARGENT New Orleans, February 15, 1847

I ought to have written to you before, and beg you to excuse my apparent neglect. I now send enclosed a memo: of which you can make use in the new edition of your work.[1] I do not think that you will have any difficulty in enlarging it to the extent desired. Beginning at the point at which the former edition stopt, subsequent events will furnish you abundant materials. There are the frauds in the last election in N. York, Pennsa. Georgia and Louisiana,[2] which should be prominently presented; the influence of the Native American question, uniting against the Whigs all the new Catholic imigrants;[3] and the strange course of the Abolitionists.[4] Then the manner in which I received & submitted to the result, as evinced by the Speech I made to the Kentucky Electors in Decr. 1844 at Ashland.[5] &c. You might draw a strong contrast between the actual condition of the Country now, under Mr. [James K.] Polk's administration, and what it would have been if the Whigs had prevailed. In the latter event, there would have been no annexation of Texas,[6] no war with Mexico,[7] no National debt, no repeal of the Tariff of 1842,[8] no Sub-treasury,[9] no imputation against us, by the united voice of all the nations of the earth, of a spirit of aggression and inordinate Territorial aggrandizement. But I forebear.

I observe what you state, in reference to the efforts of friends of Gentlemen desirous to be the Whig Candidates for the Presidency, to represent me as unwilling, under any circumstances, to consent to the use of my name again.[10] Altho' I have really formed no determination, one way or the other, on that question, they have no authority for making any such statement; and it ought to mislead no one. I have thought it most becoming me to remain passive on the subject. Whether I ought or ought not to consent to the use of my name again, if there should be a desire to use it, depends upon several conditions, as to the existance of which I shall be able to judge at the proper time. I am glad to perceive that our friends at Washington have been very discreet, in regard to this delicate question.

I have enjoyed very good health, during my sojourn here. This great City is almost exclusively occupied with the operations of Commerce. Great difficulty is experienced in finding Vessels to transport the vast amount of produce borne hither by the Mississippi.

I sent you the other day a little Speech made by me at a public meeting for the relief of the suffering Irish.[11]

Be pleased to present my respects to your brother [John O. Sargent].

ALS. MCM. 1. Clay to Sargent, August 7, 1844. The last several chapter headings in the 1848 edition follow Clay's suggestions in this letter almost verbatim. 2. Clay to Smith, June 17, 1844; Ewing to Clay, June 23, 1844; Frelinghuysen to Clay, Nov. 9, 1844; Bronson to Clay, Nov. 20, 1844; Roman to Clay, Dec. 2, 1844. 3. Ewing to Clay, June 23, 1844; Lee to Clay, Nov. 2, 1844. 4. Clay to Clayton, Dec. 2, 1844. 5. Clay to Ky. Presidential Electors, Dec. 4, 1844. 6. Clay to Crittenden, Feb. 15, 1844. 7. Clay to Lawrence, April 30, 1845. 8. Clay to Greeley, June 23, 1846. 9. Davis to Clay, Nov. 5, 1846. 10. John J. Crittenden, John M. Clayton, and possibly Willie P. Mangum, all former Clay supporters, were assuring Whigs that he would not again be a candidate. Poage, *Henry Clay*, 155-56; Kirwan, *John J. Crittenden*, 202-23; Van Deusen, *Henry Clay*, 384-87, 391; Shanks, *Papers of Willie Person Mangum*, 5:92-96. 11. Speech in New Orleans, Feb. 4, 1847.

From A.W. Davis, Charleston, Tallahatchie Co., Miss., February 20, 1847. Addresses Clay "as President of the American Colonization Society" and encloses "the will of the late Revd. Samuel Hurd of this county." Advises Clay that "the main bequest is to the colonization soc—The property is valued at some $40. or 50.000." Reports that Hurd's wife, who had died three years earlier, left "a considerable number of negroes to be sent to Africa & set free after the payment of certain debts and legacies mentioned—the bequest valued at some $15. or 20.000. Mr. Hurd was the executor of her will—And as you will perceive he has made the executor of his will executor also of the will of his late wife." Cautions that the "executor pronounces the bequest to the Am Col Society wholly invalid . . . claims the property as his own," and "intends to hold it." Notes that the executor "has employed eminent counsel *for* this region to defend his imaginary rights." Cites as the chief question the "residuary clause," which the executor "represented to the testator (who for some time declined permitting it to be inserted)" as a guarantee for "carrying out the intentions of the will." Reports that the executor "is absolved from giving security, he is worth nothing—and has taken the present crop of cotton to New Orleans & sold it,—it therefore behooves the Society to act promptly."

If Clay requires more information about the will or "my own standing," refers him to "the Revd. A.B Lawrence one of the editors of the Presbyterian Herald published at Louisville." Adds: "I have written this as the friend of the late Mr Hurd, one of the most estimable of men—And from being desirous that his property should not be divested from a public benevolent channel to the purposes of private avarice." ALS. DLC-Records of the American Colonization Society (DNA, M212, R20).

For the *Presbyterian Herald*, started in Louisville in 1831, see J. Stoddard Johnston (ed.), *Memorial History of Louisville From its First Settlement to the Year 1896*, 2 vols. (New York, 1896), 2:70, 73.

For Albert B. Lawrence (1787-1861), see E.D. Witherspoon (comp.), *Ministerial Directory of the Presbyterian Church, U.S., 1861-1967* (Doraville, Ga., 1967), 312.

On May 2, 1847, William McLain wrote Clay to inform him that "We have already taken measures to have the rights of the Soc. But we have fears as to the result." Reports that among Hurd's papers was "a letter addressed to the Trustees, which the *Executor claims*, & which he says *creates* an *actual emancipation* of the *slaves*, which is contrary to the laws of Miss. & thus invalidates the will." One trustee "is now in Miss. looking to the case." ALS. DLC-Records of the American Colonization Society (DNA, M212, R20).

To ABBOTT LAWRENCE New Orleans, February 23, 1847

An incident has occurred which has given me great pain. Several weeks ago, a young Englishman by the name of Belgrove brought me from you a letter of introduction (I cannot be mistaken as to your hand writing, although I destroyed the letter) representing him as the son of a large Manufacturer in Manchester. I paid him all the attention due to a person introduced by you. He was invited to dine with my friend Dr. [William N.] Mercer, at whose house I stay, and was accordingly entertained with other company here. Having expressed a wish to view a Cotton and a Sugar plantation, he requested me to furnish him with letters, which would enable him to gratify that natural wish. I gave him a letter to Mr. F. Conrad, a Sugar planter, residing near Baton Rouge, and another to Sam. Davis Esqr a Cotton planter, near Natchez, both gentlemen of high respectability. Mr. Conrad received and entertained him with his accustomed great hospitality.[1]

It appears that he afterwards forged a draft, in Mr. Conrad's name, on his factors in N. Orleans Messrs. Adams and McCall,[2] for about $3000 (I have not learnt the exact sum.) This Draft he made payable to a house in Baton Rouge, whose names he also forged, and negotiated the draft with a Broker in Natchez. The draft was paid on presentation to Messrs. Adams

& McCall. Such are the particulars as I have just learnt them, since my return last evening from Mobile, where I have been a few days. Belgrove informed me that his distination was Mexico and at one time he had made an arrangement to proceed there in company with & under the protection of Col. Baker[3] of the Volunteers, whom he met in this City; but by the advice of Col Baker he was induced to postpone the journey.

Measures have been taken to arrest the offender, but their result is uncertain. You will oblige me much if you can aid the injured parties in recovering what they have been robbed of, by arresting the culprit, or otherwise, or if you can afford any information concerning him.

As I shall have left this City for Kentucky, before your reply can get here, be pleased to address it to Dr. W.N. Mercer, who is acquainted with the contents of this letter, and will communicate any information you may transmit to Messrs. Adams & McCall.

ALS. MH. 1. Belgrove has not been identified. F.D. Conrad was a sugar planter near Baton Rouge and a member of the Louisiana Agricultural and Mechanics Association. Kellar, *Solon Robinson*, 2:159-60. Samuel Davis was a cotton planter near Vidalia, La. William Ransom Hogan & Edwin A. Davis (eds.), *William Johnson's Natchez* . . . (Baton Rouge, 1951), 762, *passim*. 2. The firm of McCall and Adams was located at 62 Gravier Street, New Orleans. *Michel & Company's New Orleans Annual and Commercial Register for 1846*. 3. Possibly Edward D. Baker of the 4th Illinois Volunteers, who had resigned from Congress to participate in the Mexican War. He was in New Orleans at this time. *BDAC*; New Orleans *Picayune*, Jan. 17, 1847.

To James Brown Clay, Lexington, Ky., February 24, 1847. Discusses the "dull" hemp market in New Orleans: "Unless your hemp was sold yesterday, it has not been sold. [Thomas S.] Kennedy had determined [to] take $90 per ton for it [Clay to James B. Clay, February 28, 1847]." Complains about "the high freights, and I see no prospect of their falling." Advises James to sell his last parcel through Thomas Smith at Louisville "if he can get $85 per ton for it, and if not to ship it to Philada. by the way of Pittsburg[h] and the Pennsa. Canal, if he can ship at less than 25$ per ton." Remains unsure about his departure for Kentucky, but there "will be time enough on my return to make arrangements about our land near St. Louis." Intends to travel north on "the next trip of the Peytona, after the one she is now making."

Concludes: "I have at last recd. a letter from Henry [Clay, Jr.], but he says nothing in it about his Louisville business. He is well, but writes in bad spirits, owing to his having no prospect of active service." ALS. DLC-TJC (DNA, M212, R14).

From EPES SARGENT Boston, Mass., February 27, 1847

I left New York a few days since, having been summoned here to see another beloved sister in the last stage of consumption.[1] You, who have experienced so many similar afflictions, will readily imagine the painful character of my visit.

I received your kind letter last evening,[2] and thank you for your attention to my requests, and for the useful hints, which will so much facilitate the labor of revising and expanding the Memoir. The alterations you suggest shall be duly made. As the new edition will probably be put to press some time in May, I wish, should any other improvements occur to you, that you would apprise me in regard to them before the first of that month.[3]

I had an interview this morning of a gratifying character with my old friend, Mr. Abbott Lawrence, whom I had not seen for many months. Mr. Lawrence is, as you well know, one, who, though a Bostonian, is not circumscribed in his political vision by the horizon of State street. We conversed with perfect frankness for some time upon political prospects and affairs. He told me that, he had been contemplating writing to you to learn if there were in truth any serious foundation for the assertion so confidently made in many quarters, that you would under no circumstances consent to be again a candidate for the Presidency.[4]—but a press of occupation had intervened to prevent his carrying out his intention of communicating with you. He seemed gratified by my assurances that you had authorized no person to assert directly or indirectly that you would or would not be a candidate; and he acquiesced in the judiciousness of that course, which would shun the agitation of the question for some time to come. He candidly told me, that he thought the finger of public sentiment, in New England as well as in New York, was pointing to Judge [John] McLean, but, he added "you need no assurance as to my own preferences—they *are* and always have been for Mr. Clay—I would far, far rather have him our next President than any other man in the country." He told me he was *confident* that no prominent Whig in New England was as yet committed on the subject of the next Presidency—"with the one exception of Mr. [Daniel] Webster, and he—strange hallucination!—was committed for Mr. Webster." Mr. W., he told me, had even conceived the idea of making the tour of the Southern states the coming spring or autumn with the view of strengthening his position! Mr. Lawrence thought in conclusion, that the chances lay between Mr. Clay and Judge McLean, who were in truth the only formidable candidates as yet. [Thomas] Corwin[5] had been talked of, but that could end in nothing. Many of our politicians insist that we must take our next candidate from Ohio—and that the feeling at the North on the subject of slavery will absolutely prevent our adopting a candidate from a slave state. Of course these speculations are already familiar to you. The action of Congress on the Wilmot proviso[6] and the issue of the Mexican war will have an important bearing upon the question who shall be our candidate. Mr. Lawrence fully acquiesced in my suggestion that there was a *great probability* of such a conjunction and grouping of circumstances, that all the friends of the *Union* would, a year hence, look to Mr. Clay as the only man capable of reconciling jarring interests and harmonizing sectional prejudices and distrusts.

I have given you very hastily the drift of my conversation with Mr. Lawrence. Of his strong, sincere preferences there can be no doubt. He told me that the friends of Corwin and McLean were writing to him perpetually—but he had not answered their letters.

I find I shall miss the mail if I do not close my letter here. I need not tell you how gratifying it always is to me to hear from you.

ALS. DLC-HC (DNA, M212, R6). 1. Sargent's sister Elizabeth (b. 1830) died in Roxbury, Mass., on May 13, 1847. See also Clay to Sargent, Oct. 17, 1846. Sargent, *Epes Sargent . . . and His Descendents*, 30. 2. Clay to Sargent, Feb. 15, 1847. 3. Clay to Sargent, August 7, 1844. 4. Clay to Sargent, Feb. 15, 1847. 5. Greeley to Clay, Nov. 15, 1846. 6. For the Wilmot Proviso, which would have prohibited slavery in any territory acquired from Mexico, see Charles B. Going, *David Wilmot, Free Soiler . . .* (New York, 1924), 94-105, 159-201, 211-27; Chaplain W. Morrison, *Democratic Politics and Sectionalism: The Wilmot Proviso Controversey* (Chapel Hill, 1967), 3-4, 15-20, 30-31, *passim*. For the Free Soil controversey that ensued after the acquisition of California and New Mexico, resulting finally in the Compromise of 1850, see William Henry Smith, *A Political History of Slavery* (1903; reprint ed. New York, 1966), 82-86, 97-99, 112-14; Holman Hamilton, *Prologue to Conflict, The Crisis and Compromise of 1850* (Lexington, Ky., 1964); Quaife, *Diary of James K. Polk*, 4:232-38, 254-55, 257, 287, 293, 298-300, 302-4, 308-12, 316.

To James Brown Clay, Lexington, Ky., February 28, 1847. Encloses "a draft for $612:44" to apply "to the payment of Thomas's [Hart Clay] note in bank for $600, if it arrive in time to meet that note." Sends also "another draft for $1391:75." Informs him that "W[orsley]. F[oreman]. and Kennedy. . . . sold your hemp at $90 per ton." Believes James would "have done a little better" with the sale of "the residue of your hemp" if he had sent it to New Orleans. Adds that "Freights continue high, and I do not see how they are to fall. I still think that shipments are better through the Pennsa. Canal than by this route." ALS. DLC-TJC (DNA, M212, R11).

To Octavia Walton LeVert, Mobile, Ala., February 28, 1847. Decided to present "some trifling memento to my namesake, your little infant daughter; and it occurred to me that a silver cup would be more useful to her, at present, than any thing I could offer." Arranged to have "Henrietta Caroline LeVert engraved on it," explaining that "*Henrietta* is the English name, Henri*ette* the French. I adopted the former, because it is associated with Caroline, also an English name." Hopes that "your Henrietta" may "realize your fondest hopes, and prove a blessing to her parents, and a bright ornament to her sex!" ALS. Courtesy of Historic Mobile Preservation Society. For the LeVert children, see Clay to LeVert, April 14, 1844.

From ZACHARY TAYLOR Agua Nueva, Mex., March 1, 1847

You will, no doubt, have received, before this can reach you, the deeply distressing intelligence of the death of your son [Henry Clay, Jr.] in the battle of Buena Vista.[1] It is with no wish of intruding upon the sanctuary of paternal sorrow, and with no hope of administering any consolation to your wounded heart, that I have taken the liberty of addressing you these few lines; but I have felt it a duty which I owe to the memory of the distinguished dead, to pay a willing tribute to his many excellent qualities; and, while my feelings are still fresh, to express the desolation which his untimely loss, and that of other kindred spirits has occasioned. I had but a casual acquaintance with your son, until he became, for a time, a member of my military family;[2] and, I can truly say, that no one ever won more rapidly upon my regard, or established a more lasting claim to my respect and esteem. Manly and honorable in every impulse, with no feeling but for the honor of the service and of the country, he gave every assurance, that in the hour of need, I could lean with confidence upon his support. Nor was I disappointed.—Under the guidance of himself and the lamented [Col. William R.] McKee, gallantly did the sons of Kentucky, in the thickest of the strife, uphold the honor of the State and of the country. A grateful people will do justice to the memory of those who fell on that eventful day. But, I may be permitted to express the bereavement which I feel in the loss of valued friends. To your son I felt bound by the strongest ties of private regard, and when I miss his familiar face, and those of McKee and [Col. John J.] Hardin,[3] I can say with truth, that I feel no exultation in our success.

With the expression of my deepest and most heartfelt sympathies for your irreparable loss, I remain, my dear sir, most faithfully and sincerely, Your friend . . .

Copy. Courtesy of Dr. Bennett H. Wall. 1. Henry Clay, Jr., died at the Battle of Buena Vista on Feb. 23, 1847, after being wounded in the leg and then bayonetted. See Jeffry D. Wert, "Salvation of Taylor's Little Army," *Military History* (Dec., 1985), 27-28; Wilcox, *History of the Mexican War*, 232; Frankfort *Commonwealth*, April 6, 1847. 2. Due to illness, Henry Clay, Jr., was transferred for a period in 1846 to Gen. Taylor's staff with the understanding that he would return to his regiment as soon as his health improved. This health problem may have involved an injury he had received [Clay to LeVert, Nov. 6, 1846]. Frankfort *Commonwealth*, Nov. 17, 1846. 3. At Buena Vista Col. John J. Hardin, commanding the 1st Illinois Volunteers, led a counterattack in conjunction with the Kentuckians against the Mexicans. Both he and Col. McKee of the 2nd Kentucky were killed. Anderson C. Quisenberry, "Gen. Zachary Taylor and the Mexican War," *RKHS* (May, 1911), 9:22-25; Bauer, *The Mexican War*, 210, 216.

To SUSAN JACOB CLAY New Orleans, March 8, 1847

I received and thank you for your very acceptable letter.[1] Far from finding it tedious, as you apprehended, I read every line of it with interest. Like yours, we have had a very disagreeable winter here, since the first of January, full of sudden changes, and constantly wet.

I have been very much grieved by the sad condition of my dear little Lucy [Jacob Clay]. I pray to God that she may be restored to health and preserved to us. A Mrs. Calhoun, whom I met here, tells me that she has a little son affected in the same way, for whose recovery she has travelled much in Europe and the United States, every where consulting the best physicians. She thinks the free application of cold water the best remedy she has found.[2]

The faults which Henry Clay [III] displays with you, he had developed at Ashland. I regret them extremely. We must do the best we can with him and them until his father [Henry Clay, Jr.] returns, which I suppose will be next summer, when I hope he will take some decisive course with him.

My health has been generally good this winter, with the exception of colds, which the bad weather has had too much tendency to produce.

I received James s [Brown Clay] letter of the 24h. Ulto. I wish you would say to him that I shall leave this City for Natchez the 16h. inst. There I shall remain a few days. I desire to go up in the Peytona on her next voyage. But I am afraid it will be the 25h. of this month before she can take me away from Natchez. In that case it may be the last of this month before I reach home. Tell him that I wish to be present at the trial of his suit, and that he must make some arrangement for its postponement, if it be called before my arrival.[3] I should be very sorry to be absent at the trial.

Mrs. [William C.C.] Claiborne [Jr.] has promised to get some music for you before I go, of which I will take charge. I have seen more of her this winter than the last. She is very amiable.

I have not been once to the theatre or Opera this winter. I shall for the first time go tomorrow night to hear the celebrated Irish wit Lover.[4]

Give my love to both the James's and kiss dear Lucy for me.

ALS. DLC-TJC (DNA, M212, R11). 1. Not found. 2. Clay to Susan J. Clay, Nov. 3, 1845. 3. Reference obscure. 4. Samuel Lover (1797-1868), Irish songwriter, novelist, and painter, played in Armory Hall at New Orleans. New Orleans *Daily Picayune*, March 9, 1847; *DNB*.

To LUCRETIA HART CLAY New Orleans, March 13, 1847

Enclosed, I send two bills (the first number) to guard against any accident that may befal me. I wish them kept by you until my return. I retain in my possession the other two numbers. I have been engaged to argue a cause next winter in the Supreme Court of the U.S. on account of which $2000 are to be paid me monday, and six thousand more, if I succeed. Out of this I may have to pay $1000 to another Counsel. I do not wish this matter spoken of out of the family.[1]

Mrs Marshall and Mrs Smedes[2] were down here a few days this week. They dined at Dr. [William N.] Mercer's.

I shall leave here on tuesday next for Natchez, where I shall remain a few days; and I think I shall go up in the Peytona, in which case it will be near the last of the month before I get home.

We are in anxious suspense here about news from the Army. [Zachary] Taylor has probably had some hard fighting. Rumor says he lost 2000 men, and killed 4000; but I do not believe that there have been such heavy losses. Henry [Clay, Jr.], I suppose was in the fight, as he was with Taylor.[3] If I should get any certain intelligence before I leave here I will write again.

My love to John [Morrison Clay] and Henry [Clay, III].

ALS. DLC-TJC (DNA, M212, R11). Printed in Colton, *Clay Correspondence*, 4:539. 1. The case in question was *Houston et al.* v. *The City Bank of New Orleans*, in which Clay represented Houston. This suit arose out of bankruptcy proceedings by Thomas Banks under the federal bankruptcy act of 1841 [9:408-9]. Before Banks filed for bankruptcy in 1842, his property had three mortgages against it, with the third one being held by the City Bank of New Orleans. After due notification to Thomas Banks's creditors, including the City Bank, a judgment was issued to sell the property on Feb. 15, 1843. Prior to the sale, the U.S. District Court ordered the recorder to erase the mortgages from the records. The recorder challenged this order, but it was affirmed by the Supreme Court of Louisiana. Thus, when William Houston *et al.* purchased the property, they received a clear title. Proceeds of the sale were given to the New Orleans Canal and Banking Company, which held the oldest mortgage; however, the amount fell short of what was due even on the first mortgage. The City Bank, which had been notified of every step in the proceedings, then sued the purchasers as third parties in possession of the mortgaged property. This suit was based on the contention that the highest court of the state, as well as the U.S. Supreme Court, had misinterpreted the bankruptcy act. The Louisiana Supreme Court ordered the mortgaged property to be sold and the proceeds to be paid to the City Bank. The U.S. Supreme Court reversed this decision, deciding for Clay's client. Benjamin C. Howard, *Reports of Cases Argued and Adjudged in the Supreme Court of the United States, January Term, 1848* (Boston, 1854), 6:486-507. 2. Possibly Mrs. Thomas A. Marshall and Mrs. Willian C. Smedes whose husbands were at this time partners in a Vicksburg, Mississippi, law firm. Richard A. McLemore (ed.), *A History of Mississippi*, 2 vols. (Hattiesburg, Miss., 1972), 2:386-87. Mrs. Marshall is not to be confused with Eliza (Mrs. Thomas A.) Marshall of Kentucky. 3. In the Battle of Buena Vista. Taylor to Clay, March 1, 1847.

From CARY H. FRY Camp Buena Vista, Mex., March 22, 1847

You will perhaps be surprised that I have not written to you sooner, but it has not been my fault—The deaths of my lamented friends Cols [William R.] McKee and [Henry] Clay [Jr.] left me alone in charge of the [2nd Kentucky] Regiment, and you are no doubt aware that the duties of a Commanding officer of a regiment, particularly after a battle, are by no means light—I could not write by the express who left here after the fight, and since they went, we have had no communication with the Rio Grande untill now—

I am aware that Genl [Zachary] Taylor wrote to you directly[1] after the battle informing you of the death of Henry, so I need not enter into the particulars—Sufficient to say, that no man ever fell more nobly, or more deeply regretted by his brother soldiers—

He was every inch a soldier, and had he lived, would have returned home, worthy of the praise and Gratitude of the whole Nation—I enclose you a lock of his hair, which was taken from his head as soon as he was brought into the Camp—I have taken charge of his trunk & ect—I sent his purse containing I think $76.50 by Mr Crittenden,[2] who went to the U.S. with dispatches—

He was buried near Saltillo, and it is my wish, as well as that the

Regiment, both officers and men, to take his body together with that of Col McKee and Capt [William T.] Willis[3] to Kentucky when we return—

I trust you will allow us the melancholy satisfaction, of paying this last honor to the remains of our deceased brother in Arms—Allow me to say in conclusion My Dr Sir, that no man unconnected with Henry by the ties of consanguinity, loved him more than I did, and no one suffered his loss more—Present my kindest regards to Mrs [Lucretia Hart] Clay & your friends generally, and for yourself as well as for them accept the heartfelt sympathy . . . P.S. I examined Henry's papers, and fearing that we might have another fight, and that they might fall into the hands of the Enemy I, by the advice of some of his friends, burnt all that were private, or rather all those that seemed to be of that character—

Copy. KyU. 1. Taylor to Clay, March 1, 1847. 2. Thomas Crittenden, son of John J. Crittenden, was on Gen. Taylor's staff. Kirwan, *John J. Crittenden*, 203. 3. Capt. Willis of the 2nd Kentucky Regiment was a lawyer from Jessamine County. Collins, *History of Kentucky*, 1:52; Frankfort *Commonwealth*, April 6, 1847.

To WILLIAM N. MERCER Lexington, April 1, 1847

I arrived here in safety three days ago, and found every body and every thing in a more comfortable & satisfactory state than I had anticipated, after the terrible past winter; but the very next day after my arrival the distressing intelligence reached me of the fall of my son Henry [Clay, Jr.] in battle![1] I find it extremely difficult to sustain myself under this heavy calamity. I was greatly attached to him, and he had high qualities, well known to me, entitling him to my warmest affection. How often, my dear friend, are the objects most endeared to us snatched away from us! Such has been my sad experience throughout life. The persons and the things, upon which I had most placed my heart, have one after another been taken in succession from me. How inscrutable are thy dispensations, Oh God! Perhaps the object is, to detach us altogether from this world, as possessing nothing on which we should fasten our feelings and affections, and to point to, and prepare us for, another and a better world. You, who have had so full a measure of grief and sorrow, in the loss of dear connections, will be able to comprehend the extent of my affliction, and I am sure will give me your kindest sympathy.

I hope our friend Miss [Eliza] Young has regained her composure, after the sudden and sad loss which she has recently sustained.[2] I pray you to communicate to her, to Anna [Mercer] & to Miss [Mary D.] Kemble my affectionate regards. Mrs. [Lucretia Hart] Clay found in her new bonnet brought from N. Orleans, a neat cap, for which she supposes she is indebted to Miss Young. She charges me to present to that lady both her thanks [remainder of letter missing]

AL, incomplete. LU-Ar. 1. Taylor to Clay, March 1, 1847. 2. Reference obscure.

To Josiah Randall, Philadelphia, April 2, 1847. Acknowledges receipt of "a Coppy of the bill of Mr. [Isaac] Shelby [Jr.] agains[t] the Trustees of the Penna. B.U.S, as filed by you [Clay to Bayard, May 7, 1846]," and Randall's letter "acceding to the terms on which Mr. Shelby proposed to engage your professional services." Explains that the "bull [*sic*, bill] which I sent you was prepared by me in exact conformity with our chancery practice." Although understanding that "the alterations made by you in it, had for their object to make it correspond with the rules of practice adopted in your Court," complains that the "coppy sent me is verry awkwardly made out, and I suppose to be imperfect in not containing clause in the bill, embraceing the prayer for relief &c." Transmits "authentic natorial copies of the assignments of the Judgments sued upon from G. Beech down to Mr. Shelby" to be used as "evidence, legally admissible," but adds that "in addition to the notarial certificates . . . depositions can be taken." Does not expect to visit Philadelphia soon because he is "overwhermed by a terable affliction which has just happened to me in the fall of a belovid son [Henry Clay, Jr.] in the bloody battle of Buena Vista [Taylor to Clay, March 1, 1847]. What a callamitous, as well as unjust and unnessary war is this Mexican war."

Adds in a postscript that Shelby will forward the "postnotes which formed the basis of the judgements" and "will also shortly remit to you the residue of the certain part of your fee." Copy. KyU. Endorsed on verso: "Copy of letter from H. Clay to J. Randall. dated 2. Apl. 1847."

To PETER SKEN SMITH Lexington, April 2, 1847

Your favor of the 19th ultimo, transmitting the proceedings of "The American Ratification Meeting,"[1] reached here a few days prior to my return from New Orleans. Owing to my absence and to a great domestic affliction, which has befallen me in the death of a beloved son [Henry Clay, Jr.], who fell in the battle of Buena Vista,[2] of which intelligence arrived here several days ago, a delay has arisen in my return of an answer to your letter which I hope you will have the goodness to excuse.

You inquire of me, "at the instance of the Native American Committee of the State of Pennsylvania," of which you are chairman, whether, if it be tendered to me, (and that unanimously,) I would be disposed to accept the nomination of President of the United States from the National Native American Convention to assemble at Pittsburg[h] in May next for the purpose of nominating candidates for President and Vice President of the United States.[3]

Waiving all inquiry into and the expression of any opinion on the principles and objects of your association as being unnecessary, from the conclusion to which I have come, I must frankly say that I can perceive no public good likely to result from my acceptance of the proposed nomination, and that, if tendered to me, I should be constrained to decline accepting it.

I request you, nevertheless, and the other members of the Executive Committee, to be assured that I justly appreciate the compliment intended me, and to accept my cordial thanks for the personal confidence and kindness which prompted their attention to be directed to me.

Copy. Printed in Washington *Daily National Intelligencer*, Sept. 17, 1847. 1. The Native American party held its state convention at Harrisburg, Pa., on Jan. 22, 1847, and made nominations for governor and canal commissioners. Pittsburgh *Morning Post*, Feb. 8, 1847. 2. Taylor to Clay, March 1, 1847. 3. The Native American National convention met at Pittsburgh on May 4. The delegates did not make a nomination for president and vice president, agreeing instead to meet at Philadelphia in the fall. Pittsburgh *Morning Post*, May 12, 13, 1847.

To Benjamin S. Book, April 7, 1847. Expresses his thanks "for the Compliment rendered me of naming your young Son after me," and hopes the child "may prove a blessing to his parents, an ornament to his Country, and acceptable in the sight of God." In answer to Book's request "for a few of the leading principles which should govern a Republican and a Patriot," replies that it "would be difficult . . . without writing an essay, for which I have neither time nor feelings at present." Asserts, however, "that our first public duty is to form our opinions of public men & measures, after resorting to the most authentic information in our power, and the next is, frankly to express and act upon them whenever it may be necessary. And lastly we should constantly and carefully guard against the seductions of individual interest or aggrandizement." Thanks him for "the expression of your opinion, in regard to my return to the Senate of the U.S.," but adds: "You will have probably heard, before this reaches you, that I declined returning to that body [Clay to Kennedy, December 27, 1846]." ALS. KyU.

To JOHN J. CRITTENDEN Lexington, April 8, 1847

I received, my dear Sir, your kind letter of the 6h. & thank you for the expression of sympathy and condolence, on the late melancholy occasion, which it contains.[1] Whilst I feel but too sensibly that none can heal the wound, which has been inflicted, but Him, who has permitted it, I cannot but feel grateful to those who would contribute to the assuagement of my grief.

The first letter which I recd. through your hands, was from Genl [Zachary] Taylor,[2] which I have permitted to be published, which I should not have done if it had been limited to my son, and if I did not regard it as creditable to the heart of Genl Taylor.

The last letter I recd. through you was from my son himself, written or rather closed, only four days before the fatal action which closed his existence.[3]

I also recd. Mr. [Chapman] Coleman's note,[4] with his purse found on his person in the field of battle, I have no doubt, with all its contents, after his death.

ALS. DLC-John J. Crittenden Papers (DNA, M212, R20). 1. Letter not found. Clay refers to the death of Henry Clay, Jr., at the Battle of Buena Vista. 2. Taylor to Clay, March 1, 1847. 3. Henry Clay, Jr., to Clay, Feb. 12/19, 1847. 4. Fry to Clay, March 22, 1847.

Resolutions of the Democratic Whig Young Men's General Committee of the City of New York, April 8, 1847. Have learned "that among the many distinguished heroes by whose blood the recent splendid victory . . . was purchased at Buena Vista, Lieutenant-Colonel Henry Clay Jr. has fallen [Taylor to Clay, March 1, 1847] while fighting bravely . . . giving as his last words of command to his men, an order to secure their own safety, and leave him to the fate which he soon suffered, from the bayonet of the savage and merciless foe." Resolve that "the mingled grief and admiration excited by . . . the fall of this young hero, dying (as was recorded in the Epitaph of the Spartans at Thermopylae) 'in obedience to his country's laws,' most painfully reminded us of the mighty sorrows of the illustrious Sire, of whose nobility of nature, and Eminent patriotism, he, by his life and death, proved himself so remarkably an inheritor." Resolve further to "commend to the poets and historians and artists of our country the Events and scene of our young hero's fall, as worthy of a companionship, with that of the last of the heroes of the age of Chivalry." Copy. Henry Clay Memorial Foundation, Lexington, Ky.

The resolutions were forwarded to Clay under a cover letter, dated May 8, 1847, and signed by Theodore E. Tomlinson, Alexander F. Dodge, and John Hoke. LS, apparently written by Dodge. *Ibid.*

For Tomlinson, a lawyer, and Dodge, a coal dealer, see Doggett, *New-York City Directory for 1844 and 1845.*

To Sylvester Schenck, Auburn, N.Y., April 8, 1847. Acknowledges receipt of "your official letter of the 22d February last, accompanied with the office chair and chirographical appendages, presented to me by the Whigs of Auburn." Notes that this "testimonial so very acceptable and valuable. . . . possesses exquisite beauty and contains every possible convenience for reading and writing, down to the minutest object. . . . It is quite surprising how so much accommodation and so many articles of utility and comfort could be combined in so small a space. Designed and executed by American artists, and on that account more highly valued by me, they are extremely creditable to their judgment and skill."

Concerning the "unexpected issue of the last Presidential election [Clay to Webb, February 29, 1844]," believes that "Besides being relieved from a vast responsibility, it furnished the occasion of the exhibition of testimonials and the outpouring of affection from the hearts of my friends and countrymen." Adds that these "spontaneous and disinterested manifestations are worth far more than the Presidency itself."

If he had won the election, predicts that "we should have preserved the protective policy. . . . The march of improvement in our rivers and harbors would not have been arrested, and, above all, we should have avoided this unnecessary war of aggression with a neighbor torn to pieces by internal dissensions." Is convinced that the war's "brilliant achievements" and "glorious laurels" cannot "compensate for the exceptionable manner in which it was begun, the brave and patriotic lives which have been sacrificed, and the fearful issues which I tremble in contemplating may grow out of its termination. But I have not now a heart to dwell on this painful theme. I turn from it with hope and dutiful submission to Him whose . . . wise but inscrutable dispensation has permitted this awful calamity to visit our beloved country." Copy. Printed in New-York *Daily Tribune,* August 4, 1875.

Schenck is listed in William H. Boyd, *Auburn Directory, 1859-60* (New York, 1860) as a tailor living at 99 North with his business at 75 Genessee. Information supplied by Eileen J. O'Brien, New York State Historical Association, Cooperstown, N.Y.

To Unknown Recipient, New York, April 8, 1847. Reports that he feels no personal regret over the outcome of the 1844 presidential election [Clay to Webb, February 29, 1844], because "it furnished the occasion of the exhibition of testimonials and the outpouring of affection . . . of which I had no previous conception that I ever could be the honored object."

Expresses his concern, however, about the adverse impact of the election on the future of the country. Believes that if he had won, "we should have preserved the protective policy under which we had made such rapid and encouraging advances, the march of improvement in our rivers and harbors would not have been arrested, and, above all, *we should have avoided this unnecessary war of aggression with a neighbor torn to pieces by internal dissensions* [Clay to Lawrence, April 30, 1845]. The brilliant achievements and the glorious laurels acquired during its prosecution, gratifying as they are to our national pride and character, *can never compensate for the exceptionale manner in which it was begun, the brave and patriotic lives which have been sacrificed, and the fearful issues which, I tremble in contemplating, may grow out of its termination.*" Copy, extract. Washington *Daily National Intelligencer,* April 27, 1847. Editors have concluded that this extract may be from Clay's letter to Schenck, above.

From William Preston *et al.,* Louisville, Ky., April 10, 1847. Report that the "People of Louisville, deeply moved by the circumstances attending the battle of Buena Vista, and wishing to manifest the profound esteem for the brave men who fell . . . adopted a series of resolutions expressive of their feelings." Note that "the undersigned" have "the sad yet grateful duty . . . of making the requisite arrangements to bring back to this State the remains of the brave officers & soldiers from this City, who . . . died in the service of the Nation. Among those who perished on that sanguinary battlefield, you, Sir, sustained the loss of a brave & gallant son [Henry Clay, Jr.]. . . . To the City of his adoption he was endeared in life by many virtues, and the sad story of his unyielding valor, & chivalric death, will long be remembered & treasured by her sons [Taylor to Clay, March 1, 1847]." Intend "to bring back his last remains . . . that he may peacefully repose in the bosom of his own loved Kentucky." Ask permission to do this, as well as "to administer the last sacred rites of sepulture and afterwards to erect a monument." LS. Henry Clay Memorial Foundation, Lexington, Ky. Printed in Colton, *Clay Correspondence*, 4:539-40.

For William Preston—lawyer, congressman, and minister to Spain and Mexico—see *DAB*.

Clay, writing from Lexington, replied on April 12, 1847: "I yield, gentlemen, readily, the permission requested. Louisville now contains the remains of his beloved wife [Julia Prather Clay], and was the place of his own residence at the time of his death. There is, therefore, a peculiar fitness that those who, in life, were united together by the strongest bonds of affection should sleep together in death." Extends his "profound gratitude and thanks" for their interest. Copy. Printed in *Niles' Register* (August 7, 1847), 72:363.

Henry Clay, Jr.'s, remains were interred in the state cemetery at Frankfort on July 20, 1847. A monument was erected in 1850. Collins, *History of Kentucky*, 1:55.

To RICHARD HENRY WILDE Lexington, April 10, 1847

I received, my good friend, your kind letter[1] on the subject of the death of my beloved Son [Henry Clay, Jr.].[2] The sentiments of sympathy and condolence which it expresses, on the melancholy occasion, are worthy of your heart, and soothing to mine, as far as it can be soothed by the language of friendship. But there are some wounds, so deep and so agonizing, that He only can heal them, by whose inscrutable dispensations they have been permitted to be inflicted. Such an one I have experienced in the loss of my poor son. It is some comfort to me to know that, in all the forms of death, he would himself have preferred that which has fallen to his lot.

It is true that I left N. Orleans with fearful forebodings of the fate of Genl [Zachary] Taylor's army, and of the fate of my son. I was satisfied that the desperate fortunes of [General Antonio Lopez de] Santa Anna would constrain him to risk a battle, however hazardous it might be.

I reached home, in perfect safety, and found nothing but sunshine here, every body and every thing more comfortable and in a better condition than my fondest hopes had even anticipated. But the very next day brought the sad intelligenc[e] which has filled all our hearts with grief and anguish and put my house in mourning!

ALS. CSmH. 1. Not found. 2. Taylor to Clay, March 1, 1847.

To JOHN A. DIX Lexington, April 13, 1847

I am very thankful for the kind consideration which prompted your letter of the 5h. instant, transmitting an extract from one received by you from Major [Roger Sherman] Dix,[1] your brother, in which he writes in friendly and favorable terms of his companion in battle, my lamented and beloved son [Henry Clay, Jr.].[2] I think I had heard through my son, or some other channel, of the mutual friendship which subsisted between Major Dix and himself.

I congratulate you on the success with which your brother came out of the bloody field of Buena Vista.[3] My great affliction is somewhat alleviated by knowing that my dear Son preferred, if death were to come, that he should expire on the field of battle, in the service of his Country.

ALS. NNC. 1. Roger S. Dix graduated from the U.S. Military Academy in 1827. He was breveted lieutenant colonel on Feb. 23, 1847, for gallantry and meritorious conduct in the battle of Buena Vista. He died Jan. 7, 1849. Heitman, *HRDUSA*, 375. 2. Taylor to Clay, March 1, 1847. 3. For the battle of Buena Vista, see Henry Clay, Jr., to Clay, Feb. 12/19, 1847.

To WILLIAM N. MERCER Lexington, April 13, 1847

I received, my good friend, your kind letter of the 26h. Ulto. with its accompaniments, and I have also received a very friendly letter from Bishop Oty [*sic*, James H. Otey], written at your instance.[1] If our grief could be lessened by manifestations of sympathy and condolence, it would be much abated; for they reach us from every quarter, in every form, and in the most touching and feeling manner. But alas! there are some wounds so deep and so excrutiatingly painful, that He only can heal them, by whose inscrutable dispensations they have been inflicted. And the death of my beloved son [Henry Clay, Jr.] is one of them.[2] It is, indeed, some consolation to me to know, that he himself preferred, if death must come, that his life should be terminated on the field of battle in the service of his Country. My poor wife [Lucretia Hart Clay] bears the affliction with less than her usual fortitude. She has had so much to suffer; and we have been tortured by account after account, coming to us, as to the manner of his death, and the possible outrages committed upon his body, by the enemy, whilst he had temporary possession of it.[3] But, my dear friend, I ought not to inflict my distresses on you, who have had such a large measure of your own.

With my love to dear Anna [Mercer], give her my thanks also for the pretty Spectacle case, the work of her own hands, which she sent me. And I request you to make my affectionate regards to Miss [Eliza] Young and Miss [Mary D.] Kemble.

ALS. LU-Ar. Addressed to Mercer at Canal Street, New Orleans. 1. Letter not found. For Otey, Episcopal bishop of Tennessee and provisional bishop of Mississippi, see *DAB* and Arthur H. Nall, "Bishop Otey as Provisional Bishop of Mississippi," *Publications of the Mississippi Historical Society* (Nov., 1900), 3:139-45. 2. Taylor to Clay, March 1, 1847. 3. *Ibid.*

To Unknown Recipient, Athens, Ga., April 13, 1847. Thanks him for his letter of the 5th inst. which "comes to me when I am suffering under one of the heaviest afflictions that has ever befallen me, deep as I have drunk out of the cup of domestic sorrow [Taylor to Clay, March 1, 1847]." Believes that his pain would be lessened if "expressions of sympathy and condolence" helped, but "there are some wounds too deep and too painful to be healed by any other remedy, than one which flows from Him, by whose incomprehensible dispensations they have been inflicted." Copy. Printed in *Niles' Register* (August 7, 1847), 72:363.

To Charles Lanman, New York City, April 14, 1847. Acknowledges "your kind letter on the melancholy occasion of the death of my beloved son [Henry Clay, Jr.]."

Cites his son's death [Taylor to Clay, March 1, 1847] as "one of the severest among" his many "domestic afflictions." Is consoled "knowing that he died where he would have chosen, and where, if I must lose him, I should have preferred, on the battlefield in the service of his country." Copy. Printed in Lanman, *Haphazard Personalities*, 125.

To MARY S. BAYARD Lexington, April 16, 1847

Upon my return from N. Orleans the 29h. Ulto, after an absence from home of four months, I met here, my ever dear and excellent friend, your very kind and acceptable letter of the 24h. March. I found Mrs. [Lucretia Hart] Clay and my family, and every thing here, in the most satisfactory condition, and a bright sun shine beaming all around. But the next day, whilst we were all at a family dinner, my son James [Brown Clay] entered, with grief depicted in his countenance, and related the sad and melancholy event which had befallen my beloved son [Henry Clay, Jr.] on the bloody Battle field of Buena Vista.[1]

After that, I had not the heart to write to you, all of whose generous sympathies I knew would be excited by my distressing bereavement. But I was thinking of composing myself to the task, when your friendly letter of condolence of the 4h. instant arrived. Thanks, my good friend, for both your letters. And many, many thanks for the sympathetic tears which you have shed for me to the memory of my lamented son!

If the manifestations of kindness and sympathy, which reach me [words excised from manuscript] in language the most touching, could console me [words excised from manuscript] irreparable loss, my grief would be diminished and my fortitude would be equal to the painful occasion. But alas! there are some wounds so deep and so excruciatingly distressing that HE only can heal them, through whose incomprehensible dispensations they have been permitted to be inflicted. The death of my dear Son is one of them. It is indeed some consolation to me to know that he himself preferred, as I would have chosen, that, if I were to be deprived of so great a blessing as he ever was to me, he should expire on the field of battle, in the service of his Country. I pray fervently to God that he may temper this great affliction to my heart, and enable me to fulfill whatever duties remain to me, during the remnant of my life. Among these is what I owe to three interesting and highly promising orphans (two sons and a daughter)[2] left by my son, and who had been previously deprived of their mother [Julia Prather Clay], a most lovely, amiable & accomplished lady. It will, I know, be agreeable to you to learn that, in a pecuniary point of view, they have been left in very comfortable circumstances.

I am greatly obliged to you for the friendly interest you take in the preservation of my health. It has been better than usual, during the last five or six months.

I still cling to the hope that I may be able to visit Philada. during the approaching summer. I cannot say absolutely that I shall go, but I think I will some time in July.

Do me the favor to present my affectionate regards to Mr. [Richard H.] B[ayard]. and your daughters, and to express to them my obligations for the kind sympathy which they have felt for me on the recent trying occasion.

Adieu my dear friend! May you be spared such calamities as have fallen to my bitter lot, and long live in health and happiness.

ALS. DeHi. 1. Taylor to Clay, March 1, 1847. 2. Henry III, Anne, and Thomas J. Clay.

To JOHN M. CLAYTON Lexington, April 16, 1847

Your favor of the 10h. March, addressed to me at N. Orleans, not finding me there, followed me to this place, where it found me suffering under one of the greatest afflictions which has ever befallen me, in a life which has been full of domestic afflictions.[1] I have not had a heart to write to you; and now I can hardly trust myself in the performance of the task. If I could derive any consolation from the fall of my beloved son [Henry Clay, Jr.] on the bloody field of Buena Vista,[2] it would be from the fact that, if he were to die, I know he preferred to meet death on the field of battle, in the service of his Country. That consolation would be greater, if I did not believe that this Mexican War was unnecessary and of an aggressive character.[3] My poor son did not however stop to enquire into the causes of the War. It was sufficient for him that it existed in fact, and that he thought the Nation was entitled to his services[.]

You are, my dear friend, as much entitled to know my sentiments, upon the various subjects of your letter, as any other friend I have. But I think that you greatly overrate the value of my opinions, and especially the value of any preference I might entertain, as to the person who should be the next Whig Candidate for President of the U. States.[4] I will nevertheless frankly express my views in regard to the several topics suggested by you.

And first, as to myself, only because you have commenced with me. I have remained perfectly passive, since the last election, expressing to nobody, whether I would or would not consent to the use of my name again; for really I had formed no determination one way or the other. There are conditions on which I would, more from a sense of duty than from any personal desire, consent to being placed before the Country as a Candidate for that office. These conditions are first, the continued possession of my health, and the enjoyment of my mind unimpaired. And, secondly, a perfect persuasion that my services were demanded by an unquestionable majority of the Country. The latter condition, I apprehend, is not likely to exist; possibly not the first. I had supposed the time has not arrived when it was necessary for me to form, much less announce, any positive determination.

Most certainly, I have no wish to embark in any doubtful or uncertain contest. And even under the most favorable circumstances, if I were to be brought forward, my consent would be yielded only from a conviction of duty to my Country and my friends.

Passing by me, as being very much out of the question, I should greatly prefer you, or Mr. [John J.] Crittenden, to anybody else.[5] As to Mr. [Daniel] Webster,[6] without dwelling upon strong objections which exist against him, I consider there is no possibility of his election.

Judge [John] McLean[7] will be found a heavy, I think, too heavy weight to carry, whatever may be the progress which he has made or his friends for him. 1st. He was a [Andrew] Jackson man, and there are many Whigs who will never vote for one who supported Jackson. 2dly. He did not deport himself with fidelity towards the adminstration of Mr. [John Quincy] Adams, of which he formed a part. 3dly. He is a Judge, with drawn, or who, it will be thought, ought to have been entirely with drawn from the political Arena.

4thly. His opinions on leading questions are unknown; and when he is put upon the stand, and subjected to interrogatories his responses, I am quite confident, will be found unsatisfactory. And I might add two minor objections. 1st. The known abolition principles of his wife [Rebecca Edwards McLean], and his tendency the same way. 2dy. I understand that a letter is in existence from him in Cincinnati, in which he speaks of me in a manner likely to alienate many of my friends. I am told that it can, and probably will be brought forward at a suitable time against him.[8]

If we pass from the Civilians to the Military, who are spoken of as Candidates, I decidedly prefer [Zachary] Taylor to [Winfield] Scott.[9] I do not think either of them possessed of the requisite qualifications for President of the U.S. Taylor is the most straight-forward & I believe most sincere and honest man. He has the bluntness of the Soldier, with nothing of the petit-maitre about him.

I must nevertheless own, that, looking to principle, and to the principles of the Whig party, I should regret the existence of any necessity to take up a mere Military man. What a fatal tendency would it not have, upon the future destinies of the Republic, if both of the present great political parties should concur in establishing a precedent, giving a preference to mere Military Chieftains! It would give to the Nation an irresistible impulse towards War and conquest, towards which it is already too much inclined. I do not regard the election of [William Henry] Harrison as committing the Whig party to a preference for mere military men; for he was quite as much if not more distinguished in his Civil than his military career.

Yet there may be no alternative left but to take Taylor or submit to the continuation of Locofocoism. There are already strong indications in that direction. Painful, and I fear ultimately, unhappy as the choice of such an alternative, either way, might be, I could not hesitate to give my humble suffrage to Genl. Taylor.

I have thus written in answer to your letter as fully as is probably needful; but I write in strict confidence and not for the press. A few months may bring forth important events, and I am inclined to think that it is the best course for the Whig party to avoid any premature action on the Presidential question.

I hope to be able to visit the East, in a quiet way, during the approaching summer, when I may fall in with you some where. In that case we may be able to look around with the advantage of knowing and estimating all intervenin[g] events, and with the benefit of a freedom in conversation, which cannot be enjoyed in correspondence.

ALS. DLC-John M. Clayton Papers (DNA, M212, R20). Letter marked "(Confidential)." 1. Taylor to Clay, March 1, 1847. 2. Henry Clay, Jr., to Clay, Feb. 12/19, 1847. 3. For Clay's views on the war, see Clay to Greeley, June 23, 1846; Clay to LeVert, Nov. 6, 1846. 4. Greeley to Clay, Nov. 15, 1846. 5. Although Crittenden was frequently mentioned as a possible Whig presidential nominee for the 1848 election, he steadfastly refused to become a candidate. He was an early supporter of Zachary Taylor and perhaps more than anyone else was responsible for his nomination. John M. Clayton, too, was a favorite of many Whigs, especially Thurlow Weed, but did not become a serious contender. Kirwan, *John J. Crittenden*, 218. 6. Webster made a tour of the South in 1847 but found little encouragement for his candidacy. Although he was eventually nominated by the Massachusetts Whig convention, support for him was limited to New England. Baxter, *Daniel Webster*, 392-402. 7. Greeley to Clay, Nov. 15, 1846. 8. Reference obscure. 9. For Taylor, see Greeley to Clay, Nov. 15, 1846. In the spring of 1848 Clayton and Thomas Corwin began to tout Scott, but his candidacy made little headway. Charles W. Elliott, *Winfield Scott, The Soldier and the Man* (New York, 1937), 588-92.

From James Devereux *et al.*, Philadelphia, Pa., April 16, 1847. As "members of the Commercial Room Association of this City," express their "feelings of the deepest sorrow" at news "of the death of your Son Lt Col: [Henry] Clay [Jr.] at the battle of Buena Vista whilst defending nobly the honor of his Country's Flag." Assure Clay that "We admired the Son because we loved the Father," and therefore wish to deliver their condolences "to you, and through you to her [Lucretia Hart Clay], who is the partner of all your griefs and all your joys." Commend the "Patriotism which prompted your son to take up arms in defence of his Country's rights" and agree that "the noble Gallantry which characterized his conduct upon the Field of Battle, so unequivocably attested by his Commander in chief [Taylor to Clay, March 1, 1847], must forever remain fresh in the recollection of his Countrymen." LS. Henry Clay Memorial Foundation, Lexington, Ky. Signed by Devereux and 42 others.

The letter of condolence from the Commercial Room Association was forwarded to Clay under a cover letter written by Daniel Haddock, Jr., the organization's president, and dated April 19, 1847. *Ibid.*

Devereux and Haddock were both Philadelphia merchants, the former at 89 Pine and the latter at 10 S. Wharves. *McElroy's Philadelphia Directory for 1845.*

From WILLIAM A. WITHERS[1] Cynthiana, Ky., April 16, 1847

Permit me an entire stranger but one under many obligations to your lamented son [Henry Clay, Jr.] for his many acts of kindness and attention to my son, a stranger boy,[2] to him, who left s[c]hool and volunteered and under his immediate command received that attention and kindness that has endeered him to me beyond any powers I have of description; to condol with you on this melancholly bereavement.[3] one irrepairable in time, Although he fell covered with glory—it is hard for a father to give up such a son althoug[h] his Country may demand the sacrifice,

My particular object in now obtruding on your sorrows is to enclose you an humble tribute to the character of your son by one of his officers who has shed his blood on the same field of glory [Buena Vista] that your gallant son yielded up his life, and now mourned by me as lost forever, from the last accounts I have no hope that he is living. he fell in the last charge of the gallant 2nd Ky. Reg[imen]t but fell I am informed dooing his duty. He was acting on that memorable day as adjutant to the regt.[4]

So soon as he heard of the vile and unfounded imputation against the character of the gallant commanders of his Regt.[5] wrote the inclosed and I immediately had it published as a tribute to him who had so kindly treated my boy—keep it.[6] it is the eviidence of one that knew no gile and now is numbered I am fearfull with the dead in favour of his best and dearest friend he found in the Army. althoug[h] promoted by Genl. [Humphrey] Marshall first & afterwards by Genl [William O.] Butler to the station of aid[e] he abandoned both for the society of his beloved Cols. [William R. McKee and Henry Clay, Jr.] and on resigning his place under Butler he wrote me that he had received many acts of kindness from the genl. yet he loved his own dear Regt. the best and never again would he be seperated from it only by his fall on the field of battle or on its being disbanded[.]

You will see that one of the predictions in his letter has been fulfilled literally, that Justice must & will be done them hereafter, how but but oh how dear the sacrifice . . .

ALS. Henry Clay Memorial Foundation, Lexington, Ky. 1. William A. Withers, a Virginian by birth, was a merchant in Cynthiana, Ky. William H. Perrin, *History of Bourbon, Scott, Harrison and Nicholas Counties, Kentucky* (Cincinnati, 1882), 687. 2. William T. Withers was a 2nd lieutenant, serving under McKee and Clay at the battle of Buena Vista. Anderson C. Quinsenberry, "Gen. Zachary Taylor and the Mexican War," *RKHS* (May, 1911), 9:37. 3. Taylor to Clay, March 1, 1847. 4. Withers's son survived the battle, moved to Mississippi, and served in the Confederate Army during the Civil War. A lawyer, he returned to Kentucky and raised thoroughbred horses. *Biographical and Historical Memoirs of Mississippi*, 2:1068. 5. Henry Clay, Jr., to Clay, Feb. 12/19, 1847. 6. Enclosed was a clipping said to be from the Frankfort *Commonwealth* of Feb. 19, 1847, which contained a letter from W.T. Withers to his father, dated Jan. 12, 1847, saying: "I hesitate not to say, that there are no better officers or more polished gentlemen in the volunteer service than Cols. [William] McKee and [Henry] Clay [Jr.]."

To JOHN J. CRITTENDEN — Lexington, April 18, 1847

I ought to have shown or sent to you a letter I lately received from J.L. White[1] of New York, but my late great labors have led to a neglect of my correspondence, & I cannot now lay my hand upon it. If I should recover it before you go to Washington I will send it to you. I had transmitted to him confidentially your last letter to me. His breath[e]s nothing but the most friendly sentiments toward you. My being out of the way (and that bad preference it seems he still will cherish) you are his next choice.[2]

When do you go Eastward? If not too soon I hope to see you at Frankfort.

I have finished the draft of my speech[3] & my vanity prompts me to think that I have improved it.

Copy. OHi. 1. Letter not found. Reference is to Joseph L. White, a New York City lawyer, and previously a congressman from Indiana. *BDAC*; Doggett, *New-York City Directory for 1844-45.* 2. Clay to Clayton, April 16, 1847. 3. It is unclear to which speech this refers.

From Garnett Duncan, Louisville, April 20, 1847. Encloses "a Copy of the proceedings of a Bar meeting" forwarded as "a testimonial of the high respect in which your lamented son [Henry Clay, Jr.] was held by his professional brethren." ALS. Henry Clay Memorial Foundation, Lexington, Ky.

Enclosed with this letter is a statement of the proceedings of the Louisville Bar Association in which they determined to wear mourning for 30 days in testimony of their respect for Henry Clay, Jr.

To CHARLES LANMAN — Lexington, April 22, 1847

I recd. today your friendly letter, and a number of the [New York] Express,[1] to which it refers, containing an account of the proceedings on the occasion of the celebration of my Birthday, in the City of New York, with which I was honored by my young Whig friends.[2] Filled as my heart is with grief for the loss of my lamented and beloved son [Henry Clay, Jr.],[3] I cannot but feel profoundly grateful for the enthusiastic compliment which has been thus rendered to me. I wish that I was more conscious of deserving it than I am; and that I did not feel that of all our Countrymen, [George] Washington only merits the anniversary of his birth to be commemorated.

I thank you for the interesting details, attending the celebration, which you have done me the favor to communicate.

Be pleased to give my best regards to Mr. [James] Brooks,[4] your associate.

ALS. MH. Printed in Lanman, *Haphazard Personalities*, 125-26. Letter marked "(Private)." 1. Letter and newspaper not found. 2. On April 15, 1847, nearly 700 men attended the celebration of Clay's birthday (April 12) at the Apollo Salon in New York City, with J. Phillips Phoenix presiding. Lexington *Observer & Kentucky Reporter*, April 24, May 1, 1847. 3. Taylor to Clay, March 1, 1847. 4. For Brooks, who founded the New York *Express* and later served in Congress, see *DAB*; *BDAC*.

From Charles D. Drake, St. Louis, Mo., April 23, 1847. Reports that, at Clay's request, he had contacted Judge Robert Wash [5:919] and Col. John O'Fallon [2:437] to ask their views about the selling of Clay's land near St. Louis. While O'Fallon answered in writing, Wash spoke with Drake and "expressed the opinion that it would not be advisable for you to attempt a sale of your property next month, but should sell either next Fall or very early next Spring. This he thinks best with reference to the class of persons,—gardners, who would wish to purchase, & who would object to buying at a time of year when they would lose a season." Impresses upon Clay "what I said in my last, that, if you will hold the property five years, it will sell for *double* what it would now." ALS. DLC-TJC (DNA, M212, R14). For Drake, see 6:1090.

From D.M. Craig, Lexington, April 27, 1847. On behalf of "the Bishop of this Diosess R[igh]t R[ev.] B[enjamin] B Smith," desires "to know of you If It would be agreeable and convenient for you to serve this Diosess in her next General Convention of this Church" at New York City in September. Assures Clay that "The Church does not require that her delegates be Communicants, in the Same but leaves her Temporal affairs to the Controul of her Best and Purust Men." Sends "the last Journal of the Gen Convent with the Constitution & Cannons annext for inspection." ALS. DLC-HC (DNA, M212, R6). Clay did not attend the convention in September.

To ADAM BEATTY Lexington, April 29, 1847

I received your favor of the 19h. I regretted very much to part with my Saxony Sheep, but the dogs left me no other alternative. My near residence to the City exposed me very much to their depredations.

You will have seen in the papers a statement that the demand of our Executive [James K. Polk] upon Mexico for a cession of Territory, includes all of Mexico North of 26°. degrees of N. latitude extending from the Gulph to the Pacific.[1] If that be the demand, I apprehend there is no present prospect of Peace. I presume that the capture of the City of Mexico itself would not induce the Mexican Government to part with the largest portion of its Territory, as the contemplated cession would be.

I have seen the movements, in Mason [County] and else where to which you refer, for bringing out Genl [Zachary] Taylor as the Whig Candidate for President.[2] They did not surprize me; and if we are to have a military Candidate, I should prefer him to any other of our military men. But I have never had but one opinion, and that is unaltered, in regard to the policy and propriety of elevating to the Chief magistracy a Citizen without any experience in, and who had never developed any qualities for, Civil administration, whatever might have been the splendor of his military career. In the case of [William Henry] Harrison he had great civil experience, perhaps more, than he had of military.

I beg you to consider this part of my letter confidential.

ALS. Courtesy of George J. Blazier, Marietta, Ohio. 1. Clay was referring to newspaper reports leaking information concerning the secret mission of Nicholas Trist to negotiate a treaty with Mexico. News of Trist's April 16 departure appeared in the New York *Hearld* on April 21, much to Polk's dismay. On April 22 the Washington *Daily National Intelligencer* reprinted articles dealing with the mission but gave no details. On April 24 it reported that the Polk administration had authorized negotiations for a boundary slightly south of the 36th parallel in California and at Passo del Norte in Texas, but on April 26 it revised this, writing that the administration would accept more realistic terms than half of Mexico. Actually, Trist's instructions had been to obtain a guarantee of the Rio Grande as the Texas boundary and to acquire New Mexico and the two Californias, as well as the right of transit across Tehuantepec (the latter, however, was not essential). For these terms, Trist could offer up to $30,000,000. In the Treaty of Guadalupe-Hidalgo, signed by the Mexican commissioners on Feb. 2, 1848, Mexico renounced all claim to Texas, New Mexico, and California in exchange for $15,000,000. The boundary ran up the Rio Grande to the southern boundary of New Mexico, followed the southern and western limits of New Mexico to the point nearest the Gila River; from there it ran north to the Gila which it followed to the Colorado River; it then dropped down to the boundary between Alta and Baja, Calif., which it followed to the Pacific Ocean. It did not include transit across the isthmus. Bauer, *The Mexican War*, 282-87, 384-85, *passim*; McCormac, *James K. Polk*, 491-553; J.S. Reeves, *American Diplomacy Under Tyler and Polk* (Baltimore, 1907), 309-29; Bergeron, *Presidency of James K. Polk*, 98-106. For the peace treaty, ratified by the U.S. Senate on March 10, 1848 (38-14), see Parry, *Treaty Series*, 102:29-59. 2. Greeley to Clay, Nov. 15, 1846. The Taylor meeting in Mason County, Ky., was held on April 12, 1847. Frankfort *Commonwealth*, April 20, 1847.

From Rebecca Frick, Danville, Pa., May, 1847. Expresses her sympathy for "the sad bereavement you have experienced in the death of your dear son [Henry Clay, Jr.]." Laments the loss of "Your Son your own name, your noble gallant Son [Taylor to Clay, March 1, 1847]—And O how like his father so self-sacrificing." Suggests to "My Dear brother in affliction, let us try to realize that 'Time is short' and that we will soon meet our children again in heaven where God and Christ is."

Writes that "My husband [George A. Frick] is very much grieved for his friend—You must allow him to call you friend—for he esteems you more highly than he does any other man in the United States—or out of them—He too has a son in Mexico—he is with General [Winfield] Scott—he left home and friends and a good practice as a physician to fight his Country['s] battles." Regrets that "This war has carried Sorrow and dismay into every portion of our Country—My heart is pained with every days account of the sad cruelties practiced—I could not partake in the rejoicing manifested by many in our town—by illuminations and other demonstrations of joy over the victory atchieved at Buena Vista. . . . on account of the Sorrow I felt for Mr Clay and others."

Desires to "speak to you of my own dear and only child who is now no more. . . . She was an enthusiastic admirer of yours." Reports that "when we received the New York news [Clay to Webb, September 23, 1844], My daughter wept tears of sorrow[.] My husband did not leave his doors for several days." Deplores "the wicked deception practiced upon you and upon this nation—that we are now made to mourn over the loss of friends—Who however much they might disapprove of the manner in which this war was brought about—Yet they would stand by their Countrys honour in the hour of trial and if required of them to die for her." Comments that among those fighting is "Mr Fricks son Clarence Henry," a lieutenant in the 2nd Pennsylvania Regiment, who wrote from New Orleans that "he had called on Mr Clay but could not see him . . . but afterwards he mentioned he had a shake of the hand from H Clay." Returns to the death of her daughter, "who died of an affection of the throat" and "only one month after giving birth to a still born baby," believing that Clay "can appreciate my feelings, for you too hath He afflicted."

Concludes: "Excuse me Mr Clay for *I could not refrain* from attempting to write to you your life and Character are so familiar to us. that I cannot deem you a Stranger." ALS. DLC-TJC (DNA, M212, R11).

George A. Frick was a lawyer and a banker in Danville, Pa. His son Dr. Clarence H. Frick led the Columbia Guards and rose to captain in the Second Pennsylvania Volunteers during the Mexican War. D.H.B. Brower, *Danville, Montour County, Pennsylvania* (Harrisburg, Pa., 1881), 149, 157, 176; Wilcox, *History of the Mexican War*, 686.

To Whom It May Concern, May, 1847. Introduces the "Rev. Dr. A[lexander]. Campbell" who is "about to make a voyage to Europe and to travel particularly in Great Britain, Ireland and France." Describes Campbell as "among the most eminent citizens of the United States, distinguished for his great learning and ability, for his successful devotion to the education of youth, for his piety and as head and founder of one of the most important and respectable religious communities in the United States [Disciples of Christ]." Notes also "he was a distinguished member about twenty years ago, of the convention called in the State of Virginia to remodel its civil constitution [7:576], in which . . . were ex-Presidents [James] Madison and [James] Monroe, and John Marshall, the late Chief-Justice of the United States." Adds that "Dr. Campbell, whom I . . . regard personally as my friend, carries with him my wishes and my prayers for his health and happiness whilst abroad, and for his safe return to his country, which justly appreciates him so highly." Copy. Printed in Robert Richardson (ed.), *Memoirs of Alexander Campbell*, 2 vols. (Cincinnati, 1872), 2:548.

To Robert Morris, May 6, 1847. Acknowledges receipt of "a Copy of the Pennsa. Enquirer, containing a tribute to the virtues and memory of my lamented Son [Henry Clay, Jr.], who fell at Buena Vista [Taylor to Clay, March 1, 1847]." Thanks him "and other friends, for the handsome manner in which my beloved son has been spoken of." Concludes that he could "cease to mourn for him if consolation could be drawn from any human source," but feels "that He only can heal the wound which has been inflicted, who permitted it, and to Him I strive to bow and submit, in meekness and humility." ALS. DLC-George H. Stuart Collection (DNA, M212, R22).

Robert Morris (1818-88) of Oxford, Miss., was founder of the order of Eastern Star. In 1860 he moved to LaGrange, Ky., where he remained until his death. *NCAB*, 25:395.

To DANIEL ULLMANN Lexington, May 12, 1847

I duly received your letter of the 3d. instant, and thank you for the friendly expression of your regret and sympathy, on account of the great and irreparable loss, which I have sustained, in the death of my beloved son [Henry Clay, Jr.], on the bloody field of Buena Vista.[1] It has been one of the most lamentable events of my life, which has been full of domestic afflictions. Altho' I feel some consolation in the gallant manner of my Sons death, in the service of his Country, and in the general sympathy which the public has so generously displayed, on account of it, the deep wound which I have received can only be effectually healed by Him, whose dispensations have produced it.

I approach, at this time, the other subject of your letter, under feelings, which would not allow me to touch it but at the instance of such a long tried and faithful friend, as I have ever found you to be.

And first, as to the movement in Philada., to bring out Genl. [Zachary] Taylor as the Whig Candidate for President, which you say is represented to have been made by my advice and with my approbation.[2] So far from that being the fact, it took me completely by surprize, and most certainly I neither did, nor is it probable that, at any time, I could advise or approve such a movement. Now, it appears to me to be premature, impulsive, and if generally concurred in by the Whig party must place it in a false and inconsistent position.

I have thought that any serious movement, earlier than next Winter or next Spring, to designate the Whig Candidate would be unwise. By that time, we shall have a pretty correct view of the whole ground, and of what the Whigs may be able to accomplish in 1848. The War with Mexico is yet in progress. We do not certainly know how it will terminate, nor how Genl. Taylor himself may finally come out of it. In the mean time it would be very embarrassing to him to be a recognized Candidate for the Presidency in opposition to the very party, to the orders of whose Administration he is subject.

Then there is Genl. [Winfield] Scott. Perhaps whilst I am now writing he is in possession of the City of Mexico.[3] Will he create no competition with Genl. Taylor? May we not have two Whig Generals in the field of politics?[4] And as the other party may desire the eclat of military deeds, may they not bring forward some third General?[5]

As to the inconsistency to which I have referred, it seems to me that the Whig party has been long and deliberately committeed against the election of a Military officer to the Presidency, who had never developed any capacity for civil administration. The election of Genl [William Henry] Harrison was no departure from that rule; for he was quite as much distinguished in various walks in civil life as he was in his military career. The true principle, I think, is this, that great military attainments and triumphs do not qualify of themselves nor disqualify for the President.

If Genl. Taylor, who is absolutely without any experience whatever, in civil administration, shall be elected, I think we may bid adieu to the election ever again of any Man to the office of Chief Magistrate who is not taken from the army. Both parties will stand committed to the choice of military men. Each in future will seek to bring him forward who will be most likely to secure the public suffrage. Military chieftain will succeed Military Chieftain until, at last, one will reach the Presidency who, more unscrupulous than his predecessors, will put an end to our Liberties, and establish a throne of Military despotism.

If it were highly probable or certain that we must take Genl. Taylor or submit to the continuance in power of the present dominant party, that would present a different state of things. The question then would be between the perpetuation and increase of corruption, leading certainly to the destruction of the Government, on the one hand, and the ultimate danger of Military despotism, on the other. In such a painful dilemma, it might be expedient, as an only resort, to select the Genl as the Whig Candidate. But this ought not to be done but upon the strongest necessity; and at this early day no such necessity is manifest. On the contrary, there is much reason to hope that the Whig party may be able to elect any fair & honorable man that they may choose to nominate.

As to myself, after the disastrous termination of the contest of 1844,[6] I determined to submit to my fate, and to remain passive, and I have accordingly so remained. I have never stated to any mortal whether I would consent or not to the use of my name again as a Candidate. On that question I have formed no positive determination, one way or the other. If God were to spare my life & my mind should remain in full vigor; and if there were to be such popular demonstrations of a desire to elect me as to leave no doubt of the result, I might consent to my name being again used. But the latter condition is not likely perhaps to occur, if the former should exist. Up to the battle of Buena Vista, I had reason to believe that there existed a fixed determination with the mass of the Whig party, throughout the U.S., to bring me forward again. I believe that the greater portion of that mass still cling to that wish, and that the movements we have seen, in behalf of Genl Taylor, are to a considerable extent superficial & limited. Such is the fact in this quarter. And even in Philada. I have been informed that by far the greatest enthusiasm was displayed, at the public meeting, when some allusion was made to my name.

If Genl. Scott is successful to the extent, which we may anticipate, in Mexico, most probably a party will spring up to bring him forward; and in the collisions which may arise, it is possible that the Whig public may deem it wise and expedient finally to put aside both Generals, and select some Civilian.

I am afraid that you will find this long letter a great infliction; but you must attribute it to yourself, and to the confidence and friendship which I entertain for you.

P.S. I ought to say that I have long & intimately known Genl. Taylor; and that I regard him as an honest straightforward man; but I know nothing of his opinions upon public affairs, except by inference from the fact of his preference of me to Mr. [James K.] Polk.

ALS. NHi. Printed in Colton, *Clay Correspondence*, 4:540-43. Letter marked "(Confidential)." 1. Taylor to Clay, March 1, 1847. 2. A Philadelphia city and county Whig convention met on April 10, 1847, and nominated Taylor for president. It also ratified the nominations previously made at Harrisburg for state offices. Washington *Daily National Intelligencer*, April 14, 1847. 3. Mexico City did not fall until Sept. 13, 1847. For this campaign, see Bauer, *The Mexican War*, 308-22. 4. For Taylor's candidacy, see Greeley to Clay, Nov. 15, 1846; for Scott's, see Clay to Clayton, April 16, 1847. For the political and military rivalry between Taylor and Scott, see Henry Clay, Jr., to Clay, Feb. 12/19, 1847, and Singletary, *The Mexican War*, 102-27. 5. The Democrats did nominate a general for president in 1848. By the winter of 1847-48, Gen. Lewis Cass had emerged as a serious contender; he won the presidential nomination at the Democratic convention, held at Baltimore on May 22-26, 1848, beating out James Buchanan, Levi Woodbury, George M. Dallas, W.J. Worth, John C. Calhoun, and William O. Butler. The latter, a Kentuckian, received the vice presidential nomination. Frank B. Woodford, *Lewis Cass: The Last Jeffersonian* (New Brunswick, N.J., 1950), 248-71; McKee, *National . . . Popular and Electoral Vote*, 58-62. 6. Clay to Webb, Feb. 29, 1844.

To John Bailhache, May 14, 1847. Informs Bailhache that if he has not yet sold Clay's land "in Missouri, opposite to Alton [Illinois]. . . . I will thank you to consider my proposition to take $1600 Cash for it withdrawn [Bailhache to Clay, November 23, 1846]." Has received "an application for it from Missouri, to which I have replied that I would take two thousand dollars for it, one half in hand, and the other half in equal payments at one and two years, with interest." ALS. ICHi.

To George Stone, May 15, 1847. Expresses thanks for "your friendly letter of condolence, on the occasion of the death of my beloved son [Henry Clay, Jr.], at the battle of Buena Vista [Taylor to Clay, March 1, 1847]." Remains grateful for his friends' condolences, "and the public generally has kindly manifested its sympathy." Hopes that God will help him "ultimately to bear, with becoming resignation, the infliction which His providence has permitted." ALS. ViU.

For George W. Stone (1811-94), an Alabama lawyer and judge, see *DAB*.

From Asa Kinne, New York City, May 17, 1847. Acknowledges Clay's "offer to become a subscriber to my 'Quarterly Law Compendium.' " Adds that he "shall decline taking any pay from you for said work," and will continue "to present you with the work while I publish it, and you are willing to receive it." ALS. DLC-TJC (DNA, M212, R14).

Kinne was a lawyer who lived at 230 W. Twenty-first Street. Doggett, *New-York City Directory for 1844 and 1845. Kinne's Quarterly Law Compendium for 1845; or Digest of Cases Reported in the United States and Great Britain in 1843, 1844, & 1845* was published in New York in 1845. Another edition of 2 volumes in 1, which included cases for 1844-46, was published in 1847.

To JOHN J. CRITTENDEN Lexington, May 24, 1847

I transmit you the enclosed,[1] at the request of Col. W[illiam] H. Russell. In the controversy between the two rival governors in California (with the limited means of judging which I possess) it seems to me that the right is with Col [John C.] Freemont [*sic*, Fremont].[2] Should you entertain a similar opinion, I hope you will do, whatever you may deem proper to maintain his authority[.]

Copy, by Mrs. Chapman Coleman. DLC-John J. Crittenden Papers (DNA, M212, R20). 1. Enclosure not found. 2. Clay to Mason, *ca.* June, 1847.

To Elisha W. Tracy, May 24, 1847. Declines invitation to attend the Northwestern Harbor and River convention to be held in Chicago on the first Monday in July. Concurs "in what is announced to be the object of the Convention," and hopes "its deliberations may be conducted in a spirit of harmony, and . . . lead to good practical results." Copy. Printed in Washington *Daily National Intelligencer*, July 16, 1847.

The address of the Chicago committee proposing the convention was printed in *ibid.*, May 6, 1847. The convention met July 5-7, 1847, and discussed the need for internal improvements for the western lakes, harbors, and rivers. The convention favored federal appropriations for such purposes. *Ibid.*, July 14, 1847.

To William R. Prince, Flushing, N.Y., May 28, 1847. Extends thanks for "your friendly offer to send me next fall any tree or plant which I might select from your rich and ample collection." Although he already has "as many rare shrubs plants and trees as I care about," would be thankful "if you should find it quite convenient to send me half a dozen choice Firs." ALS. ViU.

For William Robert Prince, horticulturist and son of William Prince with whom Clay had had prior dealings, see *DAB*.

To JOHN Y. MASON[1] *Ca.* June, 1847[2]

[Manuscript badly torn to this point.] Col. [William Henry] Russell[3] is descended from a distinguished Virginia family, and is the grand nephew of Patrick Henry, whose name he partly bears.

One of the objects, I believe, of his journey to Washington is to lay before the Executive [James K. Polk] the state of Upper California, at the time he left it, and especially the causes and condition of the controversy, which has arisen, between Col. [John C.] Fremont and Genl. Kearney [*sic*, Stephen W. Kearny], in regard to the Government of that Country.[4] I have not adequate means to form any judgment as to the merits of that controversy; and, if I had, my opinion would possess no value. But I cannot repress the expression of the hope that they will be found to be on the side of Col Fremont, whom I do not personally know, but who I believe has, with Commodore [Robert F.] Stockton, achieved the conquest of the Country, and in whose government of it, I should entertain more confidence than in that of almost any other man.

ALS, partially torn. ViU. 1. For Mason, who had been attorney general in Polk's cabinet before becoming secretary of the navy in 1846, see *NCAB*, 6:7. 2. Date has been torn from this letter; however, the dispute between Fremont and Kearny (see below) was first reported in late May, 1847. 3. For Russell, see 8:92. Russell accompanied Fremont to California (see below) and later defended him at his court martial. 4. Stephen W. Kearny (1794-1848) had been placed in command of the Army of the West and became military governor of New Mexico. See *DAB*. John Charles Fremont (1813-90), a captain in the U.S. Army and a noted explorer [see *DAB*], led a survey party to California with orders to turn it into a military expedition if war had broken out by the time he arrived. He established a civil government in New Mexico in Sept., 1846, and in Jan., 1847 with the help of a naval force under Robert F. Stockton he captured Los Angeles. Kearny and Stockton quarreled over command jurisdiction, and Fremont, who had been appointed civil governor by Stockton, refused to obey Kearny's orders. Stockton left for Mexico and Washington sustained Kearny's authority. Fremont was deposed, court-martialed, convicted of insubordination, and resigned from the army. Allan Nevins, *Frémont, Pathmaker of the West* (New York, 1939), 305-42.

To William Passmore *et al.*, North Wayne, Me., June 1, 1847. Acknowledges the presentation "by the Whig Scythe Smiths of North Wayne" of "half a dozen grass, and half a dozen grain scythes" which "arrived in safety yesterday, free from any charge of transportation." Notes it is "just about the commencement of the season for their use . . . I shall therefore soon test the value of their steel, which I have no doubt I shall find as good as their form and finish are excellent." Extends his best wishes to "an establishment, which grew up under the benign influence of the Tariff of 1842, and which has employed from 80 to 100 men and made 12.000 dozen of Scythes annually."

Concludes: "Yes! Gentlemen, I entirely concur with you in deprecating this Mexican War, the causes which brought it about, & the manner of its commencement. I sincerely wish that every bayonet and sword employed, in its prosecution, by both belligerents, were converted into sythes, ploughshares and axes, and they dedicated to their respective uses in the innocent and peaceful arts of life." ALS. KyU.

The North Wayne Scythe Company was organized in 1844 by R.B. Dunn and continued in operation until 1861. Henry D. Kingsbury (ed.), *Illustrated History of Kennebec County Maine 1625-1892* (New York, 1892), 815.

To ZANETTE F. RUSSELL[1] Lexington, June 2, 1847

I received your letter and the one accompanying it from Col. [William Henry] Russell.[2] I have frequently received letters from him during his absence, and from them had learnt the difficulties arising out of the collision between the American Commanders for the Government in California.[3] Believing that Govr. [John C.] Fremont and Col. Russell ought to be sustained in authority, before the receipt of your letter, I had written to that effect to a friend in the Senate.[4] And I shall take great pleasure, and be most happy, to do any thing in my power (altho' I fear that will not be much) to uphold their power and authority. I dare say, however, that they will have more efficient friends than I am, altho' more faithful and anxious they could not have. . . .

ALS. Courtesy of Henry Clay Simpson, Lexington, Ky. 1. For Mrs. Russell, see William Henry Russell entry in *DAB*. 2. Letters not found. 3. Clay to Mason, *ca.* June, 1847. 4. Clay to Crittenden, May 25, 1847.

To Richard H. Wilde, New Orleans, June 2, 1847. Explains that "The death of my dear Son [Henry Clay, Jr.] has restored to me the interest which he was to have received as one of the Counsel, in the case of the Heirs of Dubreuil [Clay to Henry Clay, Jr., March 17, 1845]. Upon that supposition, I wish you to consider yourself as entitled to one half of that interest. . . . That will make your interest three tenths, to which I regard you as fairly entitled."

Discusses the disposition of "the W[rit]. of Error in the S[upreme]. Court of Huston [*sic*, Houston] et al vs The City Bank [Clay to Lucretia H. Clay, March 13, 1847]," desiring that it be tried "at the next term of that Court, of which however there is no prospect, unless we can prevail on the Court to take it up, out of its turn."

Hopes that they can petition for a hearing "some time in February" which "would suit me best, but I will yield to your convenience." ALS. NNC.

To WILLIAM McLAIN Lexington, June 5, 1847

I have received a letter from H[arry]. I. Thornton Esq. informing me that Chancellor [William] Crawford has decreed in my favor against the Exors of the Revd. Mr. [Thomas S.] Witherspoon for the Slaves which he devised to me.[1]

Mr. Thornton informs me that the Slaves are generally unwilling to go to Liberia; and that some of them have husbands and wives not under our control, from whom they would be separated, if they were sent to the Colony. As the devise and recovery of the slaves are in my name, I have sent a power of Atto. to Mr. Thornton,[2] authorizing him to take possession of the Slaves, to collect their past hire, if there be any, and to hire them out until otherwise ordered. I hope their repugnance to going to Liberia will be ultimately overcome. If it should not be it will become my duty to consider where else I shall send them, or what I shall do with them. In the mean time, a fund may be accumulated which may be employed, if sufficient, in the purchas[e] of husbands & wives, or otherwise for the benefit of the Slaves.

I have thought it right to apprize you of what I have done, and I should be glad to receive any advice, assistance or suggestions.[3]

ALS. DLC-Records of the American Colonization Society (DNA, M212, R20). 1. Letter not found, but see McLain to Clay, Jan. 2, 1846, and Clay to Thornton, June 5, 1847. 2. Clay to Thornton, June 5, 1847. 3. On June 10, 1847, Noah Fletcher acknowledged receipt of Clay's letter to McLain, "a copy of which I have forwarded to him at *Urbana, O.* and am sure he will be much gratified to learn that Chancellor Crawford has decreed in your favor." Explains that McLain "has been absent several weeks on business of the Society in relation to African Colonization" and will probably answer personally after his return in mid-July. ALS. DLC-Records of the American Colonization Society (DNA, M212, R20).

To HARRY I. THORNTON Lexington, June 5, 1847

I received your favor informing me of Chancellor [William] Crawfords decision in my favor against the Exors of Mr. [Thomas S.] Witherspoon for the slaves which he devised to me.[1] Enclosed I transmit a power of Attorney to you,[2] authorizing you to receive possession of the Slaves, to collect the hire due, since the death of Mr. Witherspoon, and to hire them out in future; and further authorizing you to appoint a substitute. If you cannot yourself attend to it, perhaps it would be well to get the Exors to do so.

My object is to gain time to ascertain the disposition of the Slaves and finally to determine what shall be done with them; and in the mean time to accumulate a fund which can be hereafter used for their benefit. If there be any now willing to go to Liberia they might be sent at the end of the year; for I suppose they are hired out for this year. As to such of them as have husbands or wives not under our control, perhaps a fund may be accumulated by the hire of their partners to purchase them.

I should be glad to receive a list of all the Slaves, and an account of their past hire, and what they are hired for during the present year, and where they all are.

I shall write to the Managers of the A[merican]. Col[onization]. Society on the subject.[3]

ALS. KyU. 1. McLain to Clay, Jan. 2, 1846. 2. The power of attorney, dated June 5 and recorded August 5, 1847, is in Deed Book P, Greene County, Ala. 3. Clay to McLain, June 5, 1847.

To JULIA A. TOWLER[1] Lexington, June 7, 1847

I called this morning at Mr. Megowan's[2] in Lexington to see you, but you had departed for Columbia [Tennessee]. My object was to present to you in person, what I now communicate in writing, my cordial thanks for the beautiful lines which you kindly addressed to me, on the death of my beloved Son [Henry Clay, Jr.]. They are highly creditable to your heart and to your head. The advice you give to restrain my grief, for that melancholy event, is very good;[3] and certainly the generous expressions of such sympathy as you, my other friends, and the public have manifested, are calculated to alleviate our sorrows. They place under great and grateful obligations. But He only, my young friend, can effectually heal such wounds as we have received, by whose inscrutable dispensations they have been permitted to be inflicted. You have felt, in early life, the bereavement of an excellent father. May your surviving parent, and your other relatives, be long spared to you! And may you enjoy all other earthly blessings. My warm regards to your Mother.

ALS. DLC-TJC (DNA, M212, R11). Printed in Colton, *Clay Correspondence*, 4:543. 1. Julia A. Towler was possibly J. Alice Towler (Neeley) who graduated from the Columbia Female Seminary in 1847 and was the sister of Dr. J.M. Towler, a physician and elder in the First Presbyterian Church, Columbia. Information supplied by Ruth Jarvis, Tennessee State Library and Archives, Nashville. 2. Either Megowan's Hotel in Lexington, established by Robert Megowan in the late 1780s or the home of one of Megowan's sons—Robert, Jr.; David; James; Joseph; or Thomas B. 3. The poem concludes: "Weep not for thy son; / he has gone to his rest, / And the turf lies soft, on a soldier's breast. / What! weep for the brave one? bright laurels he wore, / He soared like the eagle, he died at the sword." Towler to Clay, June 2, 1847. ALS. Henry Clay Memorial Foundation, Lexington, Ky.

To Jeremiah N. Reynolds, New York City, June 11, 1847. Supplies "for your friend a letter of introduction to our minister in England [George Bancroft], and a general letter of recommendation, which my travelling friends have some times found useful." Extends thanks "to the numerous friends I have in your quarter for the warm and unshaken attachment which they continue to cherish for me." Although a "quiet & passive looker on" since his defeat in 1844, is not "less anxious than at any former period of my life for the success of the principles for which we have contended, and for the honor and prosperity of the Country." Concerning preparations for the 1848 presidential campaign, believes that "all demonstrations at present, and prior to next winter, were and would be premature and unwise." ALS. NhD.

On June 11, 1847, Clay wrote a letter to George Bancroft introducing "James Phalen Esq. of New York." ALS. NIC.

From Richard H. Wilde, New Orleans, June 11, 1847. Thanks Clay for extending one-half of Henry Clay, Jr.'s, interest in the legal affairs concerning the Dubreuil heirs [Clay to Wilde, June 2, 1847] but "yet lament[s] more than ever the fatality that places it in your power. Would to Heaven the Mint could have been sunk, and your gallant son revived!" Assures Clay that the "only palliatives of grief, are Time and Occupation, and I rejoice that the cares and duties of the world necessarily, however painfully, recall you to it."

Concerning the on-going case [Clay to Henry Clay, Jr., March 17, 1845], has arranged for John R. Grymes and W.C. Micou, "the two best heads in N[ew]. O[rleans].," to assist him. Adds that "By giving them part of my interest, and a large slice of another greater case, undertaking all the labor and appealing to their friendship I have secured their assistance, in the District & (State) Supreme Courts." Now feels "greatly encouraged" about the case, and has undertaken "a vast deal of labor & vexation in procuring nearly all the proof of heirship, which alone was wanting."

Informs Clay that "[Gustavus] Schmidt propound[ed] to me . . . to sell out his interest" in the case "to me for $500. . . . If I had had the money I would have taken him up." Has also proposed "as a mode of indemnifying me for the sacrifice I made in securing the help" of Grymes and Micou "to raise the $500 and let Schmidt retrocede his interest to you." Has "not heard from them on the topic" and "Schmidt has been for a month past, & still is in the Havanna [*sic*]."

Encloses "a Petition for the object you propose" in the City Bank [of New Orleans] case [Clay to Lucretia H. Clay, March 13, 1847]. Thinks "it best not to ask any particular time" for the hearing, as "I will attend whenever the Court will hear us," even though "I have other cases . . . which I may attend to in person, or argue on paper, according to circumstances, & principally according to the disposition made of the City Bank & Houston." Would gladly argue the case "upon printed briefs, but I fear my clients would consent with difficulty, if at all. . . . They would be very apt to believe it was suggested to save myself a journey to Washington, and as they paid for one, they will hardly think themselves well treated unless it is made, even if they gain their case." ALS. DLC-TJC (DNA, M212, R14).

On June 21, 1847, Clay expressed approval of Wilde's actions: "I am glad that you feel so much confidence" about the Villars case, now that "it has been invigorated by the opinions of the eminent gentlemen whom you have consulted." Agrees also to effecting "an arrangement with Mr Schmidt for the relinquishment of his interest" in the case, and "you may consider me pledged to pay one fifth (one hundred dollars) of the five hundred which he asks for the surrender of his interest." Approves Wilde's "petition to the S[upreme]. Court" on the City Bank case and will get John J. Crittenden or Reverdy Johnson "to present it at the assembling of the Court in December" and try "to prevail on the Court to fix the trial somewhere about the 10h. February next." ALS. ViU.

W.C. Micou was an attorney at 11 Exchange Place d. 153 Canal Street, New Orleans. *Michel & Company's New Orleans Directory and Commercial Register for 1846*.

To PHILIP R. FENDALL

Lexington, June 16, 1847

I received your favor on the subject of my claim as Exor of Col [James] Morrison against the Columbia [*sic*, Columbian] College,[1] and I am anxious to hear further from you. I am very desirous to know what a Religious Community will finally determine, in respect to a just demand, which I have foreborne to press from considerations of kindness arising out of my knowledge of its embarrassment, and of respect for those who professed the religion of my parents. No reason has been yet communicated to me for their declining to pay the debt or renew the evidence of it. I think the Revd. O[badiah]. Brown[2] must recollect my application to him many years ago, as the Agent or Treasurer of the Trustees, and his statement that they were without funds, but would provide payment for me as soon as possible.[3]

I thank you for your kind condolence, on the occasion of our late most distressing bereavement.[4] It has put in requisition all our fortitude, and that has hardly availed us. . . .

ALS. KyU. In an endorsement, it is noted: "*28 June*. Forwarded to Mr Clay Report of Treasr. to Trustees, 14 June '47, and letter from commee. to Mr. Clay 28 June." Neither the report nor the committee's letter has been found. 1. James Morrison had bought a certificate from the Columbian College in the District of Columbia in 1823, shortly before his death. This certificate was supposed to bear interest, but due to the continued financial embarrassment of the Baptist school, none had been paid. For the history of Columbian College (now George Washington University), see Norman W. Cox (ed.), *Encyclopedia of Southern Baptists*, 2 vols. (Nashville, Tenn., 1958), 1:102-3, 131-32, 300-301. 2. Brown (1779-1852) served as pastor of the First Baptist Church of Washington, D.C., for forty-three years and helped raise money to start the Columbian College in 1821. *Ibid.*, 1:202. 3. On June 21, 1847, Fendall replied that he had received no answer "to my communication to the Trustees of the Columbian College, concerning its debt to Col. [James] Morrison's estate." Has learned also that Brown is absent from Washington and "his family did not now expect him for two or three weeks." Adds in a postscript that he has discovered from "a member of the Board this wk. that they are disposed to take the ground that the advance was meant by Col. M. as a gift." ALS. KyU. 4. Henry Clay, Jr.'s death. See Taylor to Clay, March 1, 1847.

To JOHN JORDAN

Lexington, June 19, 1847

I received your letter, with the accompanying Manuscripts and printed sheets, which you forwarded to me through the Express.[1] I have given some of them a hasty perusal, and find them quite creditable to your genius and your patriotism; and I thank you for the opportunity afforded me to peruse them. You do not express a desire that they should be returned to you by mail, and I therefore retain them subject to your order. As you have requested the letters of the Revd. Dr. [George W.] Bethune[2] to be returned to you, I transmit them enclosed. Of course, I know nothing about your relations or intercourse with him further than I derive from these letters. Judging from them exclusively, I am strongly inclined to believe that you have wronged him in supposing that he was your enemy and had injured you in a delicate and tender point. And if so you may have done injury to another standing in a much nearer relation to you.[3] I am sure that, if you are sensible of this, you would hasten to repair the injustice to both parties.

ALS. PHC. 1. Letter and manuscripts not found. Jordan is probably John Jordan, Jr. (1808-90), a Quaker who maintained connections with the Moravian sect to which his grandfather had belonged. He was for many years a leader of the Historical Society of Pennsylvania, was president of the Manufacturers and Merchants Bank of Philadelphia, and founder of the Clearing=House Association of the Banks of Pennsylvania. *PMHB*, 14:V-XL, 76. He is not to be confused with John Jordan, Jr., of Lexington [1:135-36]. 2. For George Washington Bethune, a Dutch Reformed clergyman and author, as well as a prominent member of the American Colonization Society, see *DAB*. 3. Reference obscure.

To SIDNEY HOWARD GAY[1]

Lexington, June 28, 1847

The National Anti Slavery Standard[2] is occasionally sent to me, by whom or why I know not, being no Subscriber for the paper.

In No. 4 of the 8h. Vol. under date the 24h. instant, there is published in it a letter, purporting to be from the Genius of Liberty, and to be signed "Frederick Glidden," containing a tale from a person, who represented himself to Mr. Glidden as having escaped from my service, and being on his way to Canada.

I desire to assure you that there is not one word of truth, in the whole tale, from beginning to end, so far as it relates to me. I never owned, or knew, or had in my service, any such person in my life; and every statement of Tom to Mr. Glidden, in respect to his residence with me, as represented in the letter, is a fabrication, and destitute of all foundation.

ALS. NNC. 1. For Gay (1814-88), journalist, author, and abolitionist, see *DAB*. 2. *The National Anti-Slavery Standard* was published at New York City by the Anti-Slavery Society from 1840 to 1864. Gay became one of its editors in 1843. *DAB*; Mott, *A History of American Magazines*, 458.

From J.D.G. Quirk, New Orleans, June 29, 1847. Sends "a breast pin and a locket made of the hair of your lamented son, Henry [Clay, Jr.], who fell at Buena-Vista, gallantly fighting in his Country's cause [Taylor to Clay, March 1, 1847]." Expresses his "deep sympathy felt for you, who, after having devoted a long life to the advancement of the honor, welfare and renoun of the Union, gave still one more proof of your patriotism, in devoting your Son to the same cause." Asks Clay "to accept the tokens which I have sent you, and to present the locket to the honored mother [Lucretia Hart Clay] of Col. Clay." Although "of little value," feels that "from the associations connected with them, they will be more highly prized by you than rubies and diamonds." Adds in a postscript: "Presuming that it would be grateful to the feelings of the family of your lamented son, I also send, with the above, the remainder of the hair preserved from the body, here." ALS. Henry Clay Memorial Foundation, Lexington, Ky. Endorsed: "With a small package."

Quirk was an undertaker at 93 Camp Street, New Orleans. The bodies of those killed at Buena Vista had arrived at New Orleans on June 5. Quirk presented two coffins as a gift to the Second Kentucky Volunteers for the bodies of Col. William R. McKee and Lt. Col. Henry Clay, Jr. New Orleans *Daily Picayune*, June 6, 11, 12, 1847. See also Clay to Quirk, July 16, 1847.

From James H. Otey, "Mercer Hall," Columbia, Tenn., July 9, 1847. Gratefully acknowledges "your cordial and sincere sympathy in my affliction; for I knew that your heart had been wrung by a bereavement [Taylor to Clay, March 1, 1847] similar to that which has pierced my own with inexpressable anguish. . . . and no one has any just conception how it bruises & crushes the spirit, who has not had personal experiences of this calamity." Believes, however, that "the chastening I have received, is less than my sins deserve." In addition to the death of "the sweetest and loveliest flower that bloomed by my side," suffered the loss of "*Rev Ph: W. Alston* . . . the most promising man in all the South west," who "died suddenly at my house . . . after an illness of less than thirty hours."

Assures Clay that "since the year 1812 . . . your name has been enshrined in my own heart as identified with the interests, the honor and glory of my Country. No man has filled so large a space in the eye of the world, on this side of the Atlantic, since the days of our own peerless [George] Washington." Held high hopes "that with your experience of the falsity and emptiness of worldly professions, you would turn from such in loathing and disgust." Feels "in your spiritual welfare a very deep interest. The circumstances to which I have adverted above—the stirring recollections connected with my youth, and the fact that so few of our distinguished men have been known to the professions of Christ's saving name, may all have operated to create that interest for you which I have long felt, but to yourself never before expressed." Rejoiced, therefore, "upon the receipt of your letter informing me of your determination to unite yourself with the Church; and altho' the information came in the midst of the desolation of earthly hopes, for a time, I forgot my griefs."

Hopes Clay will permit "two or three suggestions" as he begins "a life which I trust & pray will make your last days your best days." First, "you must not expect to find the performance of religious duties, properly so called, very agreable & easy, at first." Urges "the reading of God's word—especially the Psalms, which exhibit similar trials in the case of David—and perseverance in prayer." Believes that "all trials, difficulties and temptations are designed in the wise providence of God to invigorate and confirm the graces & virtues of the Christian character" based on faith, virtue, knowledge, temperance, patience, godliness, brotherly kindness, and charity. Warns, however, that "no man can know that he possesses one of these graces or virtues, till it is brought into action. . . . He may trust that he has *faith*—the providence of God will give him an opportunity, (as he has to you & me,) to *exercise that faith*." Affirms that it "must be a divine and wonderful system that will convert all the trials and tribulations of life, into means or instruments of moral improvement—of spiritual peace—of abiding hope—of holy joy in God." Describes the "constant exercise" of faith as that which allows a Christian "to draw the comfortable conclusion that he is in heart & affection that which he is by name & in profession viz: *a child of God.*" Hopes this "train of reflection" will lead Clay "to comfortable & profitable conclusions." ALS. DLC-HC (DNA, M212, R6).

Written in Clay's hand in his own prayerbook was the statement: "I was christened the 22d. of June, 1847, by the Rev. Mr. [Edward F.] Berkley, of Christ Church, in the city of Lexington, in my house at Ashland, according to the forms of the Episcopal Church. I partook of the Sacrament of the Lord's Supper the fourth day of July, 1847, in the Chapel of Transylvania University, in Lexington; and on the 15th day of the same month, I was confirmed in the same chapel, by the Right Rev. Bishop [Benjamin B.] Smith." Copy. Printed in Colton, *Clay Correspondence*, 3:53.

Otey's 16-year-old daughter Sarah M. Otey had died on May 28, 1847. Green, *Memoir of Rt. Rev. James Hervey Otey*, 31, 74, 162, 211.

From Thomas B. Stevenson, Cincinnati, July 10, 1847. Forwards "a bed quilt, cloth, thread and every thing of home production, and every stitch of it wrought by Mrs. [Elizabeth] Schultz, of Pennsylvania, a venerable lady of seventy-six years of age." Remarks that the "value of the numerous testimonials presented by your countrywomen, are to be estimated not merely by their intrinsic utility" but "as the spontaneous offerings of the heart's homage" and "an appreciation, by just and disinterested minds, of your honorable career of public and private usefulness." Assures Clay that "if the highest honors of the Republic have not been bestowed in acknowledgement of such services, you enjoy what is more appreciable, the verdict of disinterested minds that you have deserved them," and that "your name is already historic." Considers this "token of respect," especially "regarding the source and character of it, though perhaps, among the least costly, as one of the most gratifying. It is the work entirely of one whose age might imply a cessation from all the thoughts and cares of time; but her pulsations are strong and quick in the display of justice and gratitude. . . . It is the product of the *Needle*—the NEEDLE, that implement and emblem of *industry* the source of all prosperty, of which throughout your whole life, you have been the recognized and unrivalled advocate, protector and champion." Copy. Printed in the Lexington *Observer & Kentucky Reporter*, August 7, 1847.

On July 15, 1847, Clay thanked Stevenson for "the bed-quilt . . . wrought by the hands of Mrs. Elizabeth Shultz, of Pennsylvania," and praised "the beauty and comfort of this present, the venerable hands which made it, the purely American materials of which it is composed," and "the friendly motives which prompted the tender of it." Cherishes "not so much the intrinsic value of these testimonials, which, however, is often not inconsiderable," but "the fact that they emanate from the heart, and touch mine with greateful sensibility." Copy. *Ibid.*

To THOMAS DUCKETT[1] Lexington, July 12, 1847

I duly received your obliging letter, addressed to me by you as the President of the Whig Convention of Maryland, recently assembled,[2] transmitting a resolution which they adopted in which, after adverting to the death of my lamented son [Henry Clay, Jr.] at the battle of Buena Vista,[3] they express their sympathy with me, and assure me of the continued affection of Maryland towards me.

I receive with profound and grateful sensibility this friendly and feeling expression of the sentiments of the Whig Convention of Maryland. The death of my beloved son was a great affliction, which has put in requisition all my fortitude and resolution. The goodness of Providence, and the kindness of my friends and countrymen, will, I hope, enable me to bear it with becoming resignation.

I have often received distinguished proofs of the attachment and confidence of Maryland,[4] and regard so many of its citizens as my personal friends, that it affords me high satisfaction to be assured that I continue to enjoy its friendly consideration. . . .

Copy. Printed in Lexington *Observer & Kentucky Reporter*, August 7, 1847. 1. For Thomas Duckett of Prince Georges Co., Md., son of Judge Alben B. Duckett, see Effie G. Bowie, *Across The Years in Prince Georges; a Genealogical and Biographical History of Some Prince Georges County, Maryland and Allied Families* (Richmond, Va., 1947; reprint ed., Baltimore, 1975), 647, 651, 709-10. 2. On June 16, 1847, the Maryland State Whig convention met at Cambridge to nominate a gubernatorial ticket. The convention passed resolutions praising the bravery of Henry Clay, Jr., and extending sympathy to Clay. Philadelphia *North American*, June 15, 29, 1847. 3. Taylor to Clay, March 1, 1847. 4. See 8:549 and 9:759.

From Daniel Ullmann, Philipsburg, Pa., July 12, 1847. Reports that "Since the receipt of your letter [Clay to Ullmann, May 12, 1847] I have corresponded with many of our friends in various parts of our country, and find their views generally to coincide with ours." Notes that one "in whose judgment I place considerable confidence" has written: " 'I have not been unwilling that Mr Clay should be left back until the last moment, as if he were not to be brought forward. *Then go it with a vengeance.*' "

Explains that "Decided symptoms are showing themselves of an impending contest between the friends of Gen.s [Winfield] S[cott]. & [Zachary] T[aylor]." Cites a Harrisburg Whig newspaper, the *Telegraph*, "which flies the name of G. Scott at the head of its columns"; the paper challenges the notion "that we know nothing of G.S's principles" and that the Whigs should take care not to be "fatally damaged by giving power to a doubtful man." Suspects that "the Convention will make them both step aside, and take you up." Notes that "Ohio Whigs are speaking out very plainly as to military Candidates." Wonders why "such gentlemen as Messrs [James T.] Morehead, [William J.] Graves &c." take part "in meetings bringing forward Gen. T.," and suspects "the Philadelphia meeting [Clay to Ullmann, May 12, 1847], was, I think, not so much to bring forward Gen. T. as to make a certain gentleman a prominent candidate for the V.P.y."

Asserts that "It will be necessary to handle the question of the Tariffs—42 [9:628] &—46 [Clay to Greeley, June 23, 1846]. It is somewhat difficult to meet our opponents before the Farmers when wheat is ranging from $1.25+ to $2. per bushel." Continues: "The famine in Europe has produced such an enormous rise in all grains, and specie has flowed in on us to such an extent that they have drowned the effects of the Tariff of—46, and somewhat neutralized the effects of the Sub T[reasur].y. Besides, the mania for Railways in Europe and this country has kept up the price of iron; and the war has called for such enormous supplies of all its material, and such immense expenditure of money that almost every branch of business has been greatly stimulated." Although "the country appears to be eminently prosperous," warns that the "tide . . . is beginning to ebb." If Europe has an "abundant harvest . . . we shall be flooded with manufactured goods; specie will leave us." The Mexican War, too, continues to demand "great supplies of the precious metals." Predicts that "we shall soon see the combined effects of those searching measures, the Tariff of—46—, the warehousing act, and the SubTreasury [Davis to Clay, November 5, 1846]." Hopes Clay will offer "Some such course of remark" to "meet the case." ALS. DLC-HC (DNA, M212, R6). Letter marked "(Confidential)."

Many Ohio Whig newspapers ran editorials in the spring and summer of 1847 opposing both the Mexican War and the nomination of a military man for president. Holt, *Party Politics in Ohio*, 267-305, 312-19.

The Philadelphia Whig convention that nominated Taylor was presided over by

John Sergeant. Ullmann presumably believed its purpose was to promote Sergeant for the Whig vice presidential nomination. Indeed, a letter to the editor of the Philadelphia *North American* previously had protested a statement issued by the Pennsylvania Whig Executive Committee recommending him for that office. Philadelphia *North American*, May 5, 7, 11, 1847.

To Philip R. Fendall, Washington, July 16, 1847. Acknowledges receipt of a "communication of the Trustees of Columbia [*sic*, Columbian] College, on the subject of the demand of Col. [James] Morrison's Estate [Clay to Fendall, June 16, 1847]." States that although "I have been, and yet am, the friend of Columbia College. . . . It was that friendly feeling, connected with a knowledge of its pecuniary embarrassments, that induced me so long and so patiently to forbear urging this demand." Assures Fendall that "I would further demonstrate my friendship, by a voluntary surrender of this demand, if it were my own . . . but it belongs to others." Explains the "error, under which the Trustees may be laboring, in supposing that Col. Morrison designed a donation to Columbia College." Notes that Morrison's will, "which I prepared for him," contains "no such intimation of his intention," and as late as "his last illness, I wrote a Codicil to his will, in which he is also silent in regard to any bequest to Columbia College." Cites "Transylvania University, situated in the City of his residence [Lexington, Ky.]," as Morrison's "residuary Legatee." Believes that Transylvania, which "has been and yet is laboring under pecuniary difficulties," does not deserve to see funds "diverted from the institution, to which it was given, and applied to the benefit of another, a distant, if not alien institution, to which it was not given." Hopes that "the Trustees of Columbia College, on giving to these views the consideration which they seem to me to deserve, will not hesitate to pay the amount of the Certificate, principal and interest, or to give a new Certificate, embracing both." Remains certain that the Trustees of Transylvania would support his actions and "will naturally conclude that a remote Provincial institution, surrounded itself by embarrassments, ought not to make a donation to another distinguished and elevated seat of learning, situated at the metropolis of the Nation, in sight of its ample Treasury, and in the midst of its assembled wisdom." ALS. NcD.

In an endorsement, Fendall noted that he "conferred with two of the trustees; &c, on their suggestion, have sent a copy of Mr. Clay's letter to the President of the Board to be laid before them." On September 20, 1847, a further note was added: "The Board not having acted, I called this day on the President, who promised to convene them by Saturday next." See Fendall to Clay, November 25, 1847.

To J.D.G. QUIRK Lexington, July 16, 1847

I this day received your friendly letter,[1] with the locket and breastpin, both containing hair of my lamented Son, Lieut. Col. Henry Clay [Jr.],[2] which accompanied it, and hasten to present an expression of the great obligations and of the cordial thanks of Mrs. [Lucretia Hart] Clay and myself for these precious presents, intended for her and for me. No tribute to the memory of my beloved Son could have been received by us more delicate and touching. They are more highly prized by us "than rubies and diamonds," and will be carefully preserved by us, and transmitted to his children, by whom they will be fondly cherished, with a lively and grateful recollection of the generous and friendly source whence they have proceeded.

I should fail, my dear Sir, to give utterance to my feelings, if I did not also convey to you my heart-felt acknowledgments for the splendid Coffin,[3] made, I understand, at your instance, which now contains the mortal remains of my dear Son, and which you gratuitously and generously presented for that melancholy purpose.

I regret that I cannot testify to you the depth of my great obligations to you by some more substantial evidence; but I am quite sure that the noble spirit, which has animated you, finds in itself its best and most appropriate recompense.

May you long live, in health, happiness and prosperity, and be favored with every blessing which Providence ever deigns to bestow.

ALS. ViU. 1. Quirk to Clay, June 29, 1847. 2. Taylor to Clay, March 1, 1847. 3. Quirk to Clay, June 29, 1847.

To THOMAS B. STEVENSON Lexington, July 23, 1847

I have to trouble you with a little friendly commission, which I am sure you will take pleasure in executing—Captain G W. Cutter of Covington[1] was among the persons who last spoke to your departed friend, my lamented son [Henry Clay, Jr.],[2] and received from him a brace of pistols which he has safely delivered to me.

I desire to present to him some memorial, which I have concluded shall be a ring, containing some hair of my beloved son. I have not been able to procure one at the Jewellers shops in Lexington. May I ask therefore the favor of you to get me at Cincinnati (at a cost of some fifteen or twenty dollars) to have the enclosed hair or a part of it placed in it, and present it to the Captain in my behalf?

I go hence tomorrow to the W[hite] Sulphur Springs in Va.[3]—and will on my return pay the cost of the ring, when you inform me of it. . . .

Copy. OCHP. Printed in Colton, *Clay Correspondence*, 3:460-61. 1. For George Washington Cutter (1801-65)—a Covington, Ky., lawyer, a captain in the 2nd Kentucky Regiment at Buena Vista, and the person who stayed with Henry Clay, Jr., as he died—see *DAB*. 2. Taylor to Clay, March 1, 1847. 3. Clay left Lexington on July 24, 1847, and arrived at White Sulphur Springs, Va. (W. Va.) on July 29. He left there on August 9 for Baltimore, arriving on August 13 and reaching Philadelphia the next day, where he stayed with Henry White. Traveling on to Cape May, N.J., on August 16, he swam in the ocean and was involved in a carriage accident. From Cape May he went to New Castle, Dela., on August 23 and spent the night with Chancellor John Jones. The next day he visited John M. Clayton's estate "Buena Vista" before going on to Baltimore late in the evening. He stayed overnight at Barnum's Hotel in Baltimore and left for White Sulphur Springs on the 25th, reaching there on August 28. He left White Sulphur on Sept. 9 and arrived at Ashland between Sept. 13 and 20. Washington *Daily National Intelligencer*, July 31, August 9, 13, 14, 18, 19, 26, Sept. 11, 1847; Lexington *Observer & Kentucky Reporter*, July 24, August 14, 28, Sept. 1, 8, 1847; Clay to White, Sept. 20, 1847.

To Philip R. Fendall, Washington, July 30, 1847. Regrets he did not get to see Fendall "after you were so kind as to proceed to Balto. to meet me. . . . I should have had much satisfaction in an interview with you." Asks that he "communicate to Mr. [Joseph] Gales [Jr.] my thanks for his kind invitation to me to stop at his house" in Washington, but regrets that it is "not a part of my arrangements to pass by the metropolis [Clay to Stevenson, July 23, 1847]." ALS. ViU. Letter written from White Sulphur Springs, Va. (W. Va.).

Endorsement, August, 1847. Attests to having "attentively perused many months the N[orth]. American, published in Philadelphia, with which the U. States Gazette is now associated." Compliments "the consummate ability with which it is generally edited" and "the soundness of the principles." Adds: "I think it eminently merits public patronage, and especially Whig support" as one of the party's "most fearless champions and enlightened supporters." ADS. PU.

The Philadelphia *North American*, founded in 1839, was a staunchly Whig newspaper. Over the years, it absorbed a number of other papers, including in 1847 the *United States Gazette*. Hudson, *Journalism in the United States*, 182-83.

To DANIEL ULLMANN White Sulphur Springs, Va. (W. Va.)
August 4, 1847

I received your friendly letter[1] prior to my departure from home ten days ago, and brought it with me to this place. I thank you for the kind tender of your friendly offices, of which, if there should be need, I shall avail myself, with the fullest confidence in your fidelity to the Whig cause, and in your personal regard to me.

I think it even now very manifest that the Locofoco party does not intend to make Genl [Zachary] Taylor its Presidential Candidate;[2] and if it should not but should designate some other Candidate, the condition of popular unanimity, on which alone he states, in one of his late letters, that he will consent to run, will not exist. I think it impossible that the General should maintain silence as to his principles. He must make some public avowal of them, in other words he must say whether he is a Whig or Democrat.[3] Such silence could not, I think, be maintained by Genl [George] Washington, if he were to rise from the dead and consented to be again run for the Presidency. Genl [Andrew] Jackson was constrained to proclaim his, altho' he did not afterwards conform to them.

But suppose him to preserve silence, and the other party to designate some other Candidate, what then are the whigs to do? Will they not only forego all their objections to a mere military man, as President, but take one haphazard, without knowing whether he holds a single principle in common with them?

I have thought for some time, and continue to think, that it is highly probable that the other party will finally settle down on Genl [Winfield] Scott, and I think I have seen some indications of this both in its conduct, and in his.[4]

You ask me what is the best mode of conducting the campaign in your State. I should think it best to rely upon the old issues, with the exception of that of a Bank of the U.S. which I believe was never pressed in Pennsa. There is 1st. the principle of protection, and the fraud practised in Pennsa. by the Kane letter.[5] In further support of this fraud I learnt yesterday from the honble Reverdy Johnson, that, during the canvass of 1844, when some interrogatories were addressed from your State to [James K.] Polk, requesting a more explicit avowal of his opinions in regard to the Tariff of 1842, Mr. [James] Buchanan[6] wrote to Tennessee that the Kane letter was working well, and begging that those interrogatories might not be answered, and Mr. Polk accordingly remained silent.

Then there is 2dly. the Mexican War, its causes, the manner of conducting it, and the great National debt, which it fastens on the Country.[7] 3dly. The alarming encrease, the Veto's,[8] and the abuses of the Executive power—The improvement of the Country &c &c. These and other topics will readily present themselves, and will be treated by you to the greatest advantage.

It is true, as you remark, that the famished condition of Europe[9] has concealed the effects of the Tariff of 46; but these will be more and more manifested, as bread & other food become there abundant. Already have the prospects of a good crop in Europe led to a decline in the prices of American food.

I shall remain here until monday next, when I purpose passing through your Native State to Cape May [New Jersey], where I desire to enjoy a Sea bath, which I have never in my life before had an opportunity of doing. You must not however infer that my health is bad. It is on the contrary very good.

ALS. NHi. Printed in Colton, *Clay Correspondence*, 4:543-45. Letter marked "(Confidential)." 1. Ullmann to Clay, July 12, 1847. 2. There was some Democratic interest in Taylor, particularly in Pennsylvania and South Carolina, but Taylor, though essentially non-partisan, was generally assumed to be a Whig. For a discussion of Taylor's support among various factions in both the Whig and Democratic parties, see Holman Hamilton, *Zachary Taylor, Soldier in the White House* (New York, 1951), 38, 40, 42; Bauer, *Zachary Taylor*, 218, 222, 226; Wiltse, *John C. Calhoun: Sectionalist*, 319-20. 3. Taylor, who had never voted in his life, attempted to maintain a non-partisan attitude, accepting nominations and endorsements from all groups and parties and generally evading specific answers on questions of policy. When pressed, however, he admitted as early as the fall of 1846 that his sympathies lay with the Whigs. Because he continued to avoid strict party ties and commitments, however, by early 1848 his popularity with Whig leaders was fading. Then on April 22, 1848, he wrote his "First Allison Letter" in which he declared: "I am a Whig but not an ultra Whig." This letter helped rally Whig support for his nomination. Hamilton, *Zachary Taylor, Soldier in the White House*, 38, 42, 44-45, 47, 52, 74-83; Bauer, *Zachary Taylor*, 215-33. 4. Scott's pronounced Whig views and frequent disagreements with and criticism of the Polk administration ruined any chance of his receiving the Democratic nomination. Moreover, there is no evidence to suggest either he or the Democrats were seriously interested in such a move. See Elliott, *Winfield Scott*, 425-32, 489-94. 5. Clay to Clayton, August 22, 1844. 6. Buchanan had corresponded in Sept., 1844 with Aaron Brown of Tennessee, urging him not to allow Polk to write anything more about the tariff. Charles G. Sellers, *James K. Polk, Continentalist, 1843-1846* (Princeton, N.J., 1966), 122. 7. Clay to Lawrence, April 30, 1845. 8. Polk made a liberal use of the veto power, a practice that added appreciably to the strength and role of the presidency. Peterson, *Great Triumvirate*, 418; Sellers, *James K. Polk, Continentalist*, 324-29, 352-55, 445-47, 473-76; McCormac, *James K. Polk*, 287, 293, 321-39, 470, 671, 679-80, 722-25. 9. Clay to Bragaw, Dec. 30, 1846.

To JAMES BROWN CLAY

White Sulphur Springs, Va. (W. Va.), August 6, 1847

I received to day your letter of the 28h. Ulto with its enclosures. Mr. Ellicott,[1] who wants the pair of Mules, is here, and I stated to him that it would be sent to him but that he would have to pay $50 more than he did for the pair which he last bought, to which he assented. I would advise that you send two or three pair, in my name, and give him the choice. I will write to Mr. Elliott [*sic*, William St. John Elliot] about the mules you purpose sending to Mississippi; but if I should omit it, you can write him & say that you did so at my instance. You will recollect that Mules are not wanted so early in that State as in Louisiana. Dr. [William N.] Mercer tells me that he will want ten, and when I told him that the price would be from $105 to $110 he did not object to it but said that he would probably see them in K[entucky]. If you buy mules for below, perhaps, your best plan will be to get the seller to keep them as long as the 20h. Sept or 1st. Oct. and then start them by land to Natchez.

The latter part of the journey fatigued me very much, but I have now recovered from it. Dr. Mercer & I go to Cape May [New Jersey] the 9h. inst, he leaving his family here. I shall return by this route on my way home.

My love to all at home, and kisses for Lucy [Jacob Clay].

Your letter is the only one I have recd. from home[.] Letters may be addressed to me at Cape May until the 18h. inst. and afterwards to this place.[2]

ALS. DLC-TJC (DNA, M212, R11). Printed in Colton, *Clay Correspondence*, 4:545. 1. Probably Philip T. Ellicott of Baltimore. 2. Clay to Stevenson, July 23, 1847.

To MARY S. BAYARD White Sulphur Springs, Va. (W. Va.), August 7, 1847

After performing the sad and melancholy duty of attending at Frankfort the Funeral obsequies of my lamented son [Henry Clay, Jr.],[1] and his slain companions, on the 20h. Ulto., I left Ashland the 24h. for this place which I reached about ten days ago.[2] It was my purpose to execute a wish, which I have long entertained, to visit, for the first time in my life, a Seabath at the Bathing season. In fulfillment of it, I shall leave here, in company with my friend Dr. [William N.] Mercer monday next, and proceed by the least fatiguing conveyances to Winchester [Virginia], and thence to Baltimore, which we cannot avoid. Our present design is to go to Cape May [New Jersey], by the route of New Castle, and in the Steamboat which descends the Delaware from Philadelphia. It will probably be friday night before we get to Baltimore, and saturday before we reach Cape May.

I should be most happy to see you and Mr. [Richard H.] Bayard and your dear family, prior to my return to Kentucky; and my object in now writing is to ascertain where you are and what are your plans. Under existing circumstances, and in the present state of my feelings, I wish to avoid the crowd and bustle of Cities, and therefore would prefer not going to Philadelphia.

Will you not favor me with a line, which, if written by the return mail, would reach me in Balto. and otherwise may be addressed to me at Cape May, informing me of your movements?

I shall return to this place, on my way home, in company with Dr. M. who leaves his family here.

My warm regards to Mr. B.

ALS. DeHi. 1. Taylor to Clay, March 1, 1847; Preston to Clay, April 10, 1847. 2. Clay to Stevenson, July 23, 1847.

To LUCRETIA HART CLAY White Sulphur Springs, Va. (W. Va.), August 9, 1847

I leave here today in company with Dr. [William N.] Mercer for Cape May [New Jersey]. He leaves Miss [Eliza] Young and his daughter [Anna Mercer] & Miss [Mary D.] Kemble behind. I expect to be gone about three weeks, and to return by this place on my way home. My health has been good since I was here, and I have met some of my old acquaintances. Judge [Francis T.] Brooke, his daughter (who is divorced and is very much brooke [*sic*, broke]), her child and two other of his grandchildren are here.[1]

We have seven Episcopal Clergymen here, two Bishops among them, Oty [*sic*, James Harvey Otey] and [John] Johns, and a son of Mr [Samuel L.] Southard.[2] I have heard both the Bishops and young Southard preach. He is quite promising, and preaches well.

(I have only received one letter from James [Brown Clay],[3] since I left home. I suppose that John [Morrison Clay] has written to me and that his letters are on the way. Tell him that I want very much to hear how he is getting along with his stable, and whether his filly is recovering. I shall direct any letters that come here for me, during my absence to follow me to Cape May.)

There is a good deal of Company, and much more expected at this place, which is greatly improved since you were here. But poor Mr. [James] Calwell is greatly in debt, and I fear it will be difficult for his family to keep the property[.][4]

My love to all at home.

ALS. DLC-TJC (DNA, M212, R11). 1. Helen, who was the daughter of Brooke's second wife Mary Champe Carter Brooke. Helen's child was named Mary Champe for her grandmother. For the divorce, see Francis T. Brooke, *A Family Narrative of a Revolutionary Officer* (Richmond, Va., 1849), 38. 2. For Samuel Southard, Jr., see Michael Birkner, *Samuel L. Southard; Jeffersonian Whig* (Rutherford, N.J., 1984), 52. For Johns, see 5:125. 3. Not found. See Clay to James B. Clay, August 6, 1847. 4. Calwell (or Caldwell) owned the White Sulphur Springs resort.

Speech in Philadelphia, August 14, 1847. From the balcony of Henry White's house, Clay addressed a "vast crowd" of Whigs who had assembled and cried with "surging waves of sound" for his appearance. He explained that he "had come to this city without any intention—certainly without any desire—of causing such a public manifestation. He had left his home for the purpose of escaping from afflicting and perpetually recurring feelings, in the hope of finding among the friends whom he might meet during his travels a portion of consolation for the heaviest affliction Providence had ever visited upon him [Taylor to Clay, March 1, 1847]; but under whatever circumstances he might have come among us, he would be void of gratitude, he would be destitute of all the finer feelings of nature, if he failed in thankfulness for the kindness so manifested. The city of Philadelphia, he was proud to say, had, during all the trials, difficulties, and vicissitudes of his chequered career, been his warm and steadfast friend." Concludes by saying that he hoped "that they would unite with him in the expression that to our country, whether it is directed in its public measures by a good government or a bad one—whether it is in prosperity or adversity—in peace or at war, we should always give our hearts, our hands, and our hopes." Copy, summary. Printed in Washington *Daily National Intelligencer*, August 18, 1847.

From Enoch C. Wines, Burlington, N.J., August 16, 1847. Expresses sympathy for the "late severe affliction, through which a mysterious but, doubtless, everwise & benignant Providence has called you to pass [Taylor to Clay, March 1, 1847]." Since he saw "an account in the public papers of your baptism, whereby you have become a member of the visible church of Christ [Otey to Clay, July 9, 1847]," feels he "cannot refrain from conveying to you my cordial congratulations on the auspicious issue of your sorrowful bereavement." Assures Clay that although the "hand of affliction is heavy . . . it is because it is filled with gold." Compliments Clay on "your self-possession, your wisdom, your calm energy & your noble heroism. . . . But never, on any other occasion, have you displayed so true a wisdom, or appeared invested with so sublime a dignity, as when receiving the baptismal waters, & seated at the communion table of our common Lord." Recalls the death several years earlier of one of Clay's "estimable & beloved" daughters [Anne Brown Clay Erwin] and remembers Clay's "declaration that Mrs. [Lucretia Hart] Clay, though deeply distressed, was yet amply sustained & solaced by her religion, & the earnest expression of your wish that you had the same source of consolation, & of your hope that you some day should possess it [8:808-9]." Hopes that "you find, in this the heaviest affliction of your life, the loss of a talented, generous, & chivalrous son [Henry Clay, Jr.],—all the consolation which the gospel is fitted to bestow, & assuredly does bestow upon all who cordially embrace it." Asks Clay to "pass a day or two with us at the Oaklands" School, located "quite in the country" in "an elevated & airy situation . . . surrounded by venerable forest trees, whose grateful shade defends us . . . from the scorching heats of the sun." Extends his "warm regard & friendship" to "your son John [Morrison Clay]." ALS. DLC-TJC (DNA, M212, R14). Printed in Colton, *Clay Correspondence*, 4:547-48.

The Oakland School, outside Burlington, N.J., was operated by Wines. *NCAB*, 1:180.

From Martin Van Buren, "Lindenwald," near Kinderhook, N.Y., August 17, 1847. "Believing it to be your intention to visit New Port [Rhode Island]," assures Clay "of the pleasure it will afford me to receive you at my House." Lives "but a verry few miles from the Depot on the Boston & Albany Rail Road & the same distance from the [Hudson] River" and "will be most happy to send my Carriage . . . to either place." Adds: "I live very retired & my advice would be that you should so arrange it as to spend your Sabbath with me, & as much longer as will suit your pleasure and convenience." Expresses his sympathy for "the severe affliction which has befallen you [Taylor to Clay, March 1, 1847]." ALS. DLC-Martin Van Buren Papers (DNA, M212, R22). Enclosed in letter addressed to "John or Smith Van Buren Esqrs at NewPort R. Island."

For Clay's itinerary, see Clay to Stevenson, July 23, 1847.

To LUCRETIA HART CLAY

Cape May, N.J., May [*sic*, August] 18, 1847[1]

I arrived here the day before yesterday, and took a Sea bath yesterday for the first time in my life. The air, the water, and the whole scene greatly interested me. The Company is much diminished, but there is quite enough for me. Mr. and Mrs. Vertner[2] and other friends are here. Dr. [William N.] Mercer went to N. York, but is to join me this evening,

They gave me an enthusiastic reception both in Philada. and elsewhere.[3] I was almost crushed by their kindness. I received today a parcel of letters sent me by James [Brown Clay], but not a line from him or any other member of my family. I presume I have letters at the W[hite]. S[ulphur]. Springs.

They want me to go back to Philada. to go to N–York,[4] &c &c, but I shall leave here on Monday or Tuesday and return by the way of Balto. to the Va. Springs. From all that I hear, there is a deep feeling still abiding towards me, and a hope in regard to the future, in which I do not allow myself much to indulge [several lines excised]

My love to all at home; and I pray God to bless and protect you.

ALS. DLC-TJC (DNA, M212, R11). 1. Clay misdated the letter May rather than August. It is postmarked August 18. 2. Probably the Daniel Vertners. 3. Speech in Philadelphia, August 14, 1847. 4. Clay to Stevenson, July 23, 1847.

From Elizabeth Booth, New Castle, Dela., August 19, 1847. Encloses a poem she wrote "on the day Mr. Clay went to Cape May." Hopes Clay "would condescend to send her a line in return, or even his autograph . . . as a valuable memorial." Directs Clay's answer "to Judge Booth, New Castle." AL. DLC-TJC (DNA, M212, R11). A 17-line poem, "To the Hon. Henry Clay," accompanies this note. Endorsed on verso by Clay: "Answd."

Elizabeth was probably the daughter of James Booth (1789-1855), who served as chief justice of Delaware from March 12, 1841, until his death. *NCAB*, 4:72.

Speech to Delegations of Citizens from New York City, Trenton, New Haven, and Philadelphia, Cape May, N.J., August 20, 1847. In an emotionally charged address, explains "the objects and motives which have brought me to the shores of the Atlantic." Recalls his return from New Orleans in March and the receipt soon thereafter of "melancholy intelligence," the death of Henry Clay, Jr., at Buena Vista [Taylor to Clay, March 1, 1847]. Reports that "I have been nervous ever since, and was induced to take this journey; for I could not look upon the partner of my sorrows [Lucretia Hart Clay] without feeling deeper anguish. . . . Every thing about Ashland was associated with the memory of the lost one. The very trees which his hands assisted me to plant, served to remind me of my loss." Despairs that "of eleven children, four only now remain. . . . Of six lovely daughters, not one is left."

Decided to leave "that theater of sadness . . . and descend to the ocean's wave" to "obtain some relief for the sadness which surrounded me." Reaffirms that he is travelling "for private purposes, and from private motives alone. I have not sought these public manifestations, nor have I desired to escape them." Points out that even "in Virginia—in every section of the state of my birth . . . I invariably refused" to stop and talk to supporters, "and only staid in each place sufficiently long to exchange one vehicle for another." Nonetheless, expresses his gratitude "that I, a private and humble citizen, without an army, without a navy, without even a constable's staff, should have been met, at every step of my progress, with the kindest manifestations of feeling—manifestations of which, at present, a monarch or an emperor might well be proud." Copy. Printed in Colton, *Clay Correspondence*, 3:56-57. Printed also in Washington, *Daily National Intelligencer*, August 26, 1847.

To Egbert Benson [Jr.], "near the City of New York," August 21, 1847. Thanks him for the "invitation to put myself under your hospitable roof," and notes that "When I left home I entertained such a pleasing thought. But I find it utterly impossible for me to travel, especially through towns, without exciting a popular movement, incompatible with my feelings and wishes." Plans now to retrace his steps home "by way of the Virginia Springs," and regrets missing "the pleasure of meeting you." ALS. NHi. Written from Cape May, N.J. For Clay's itinerary, see Clay to Stevenson, July 23, 1847.

For Egbert Benson, Jr., see Martha J. Lamb, *History of the City of New York*, 2 vols. (New York, 1877), 2:509 and Egbert Benson [Sr.] in *DAB*.

To Thomas J. Henderson, Piqua Post Office, Lancaster County, Pa., August 21, 1847. Has "been mortified . . . to learn . . . that you never received my letter expressing my thanks and acknowledgments for the plough you did me the favor to send me." Notes that the plough is "most excellent" and "highly prized at Ashland." ALS. PHarH.

To John L. Lawrence, New York City, August 21, 1847. Thanks Lawrence for "tendering the hospitality of your roof, of which I should have been very happy to avail myself, if I had visited N.Y.," but regrets "that I was constrained to decline the invitation." ALS. ViU. Written from Cape May, N.J. For Clay's itinerary, see Clay to Stevenson, July 23, 1847.

To Henry White *et al.*, Philadelphia, August 21, 1847. Acknowledges a note of the "Citizens of Phila. inviting me to partake of a public dinner . . . during my present journey to the Eastward." Although thankful for "the many proofs . . . of the attachment and friendship to me of the good people of Philadelphia," remarks that "it would be entirely incompatible with the state of my feelings . . . to accept the compliment of a public dinner." Asks instead that he be permitted "to gratefully treasure the offer of it among the numerous testimonies I have received of the affectionate regard of my fellow Citizens of Philadelphia." ALS. ViU. Written from "Cape Island."

To JONATHAN CHAPMAN[1] *et al.* White Sulphur Springs, Va. (W. Va.), August 31, 1847

On my return home, I recd. in Delaware, your obliging note,[2] addressed to me at the instance of my friends in Boston and its vicinity, inviting me to visit that City. And you are pleased to state, in flattering terms, the high appreciation of my public services which prevails in New England, and the benefits which that interesting section of our Country has derived from the policy which I endeavored to establish. It is most true, Gentlemen, that my aims, in any measures which I espoused, were the good of the whole, of which I believed all parts might avail themselves, some sooner, some later, according to circumstances, but which, at all events, would tend to the common good. I can bear witness that the adoption of the protective policy encountered serious and formidable opposition from Massachusetts. She was most unwilling that any obstacles should be interposed, in the prosecution of that Foreign Commerce, by which she had so greatly prospered. But when it was once adopted, far from making any violent or factious opposition, she quietly and patriotically submitted to the decision of the National Councils. And full of enterprize, energy, and elasticity, she quickly adapted her industry to the new state of things, and is now enjoying the rich rewards of her skill vigor and economy.[3] I rejoice in the well earned prosperity of New England. After the lapse of fourteen years since I last visited it,[4] I should be most happy again to interchange friendly salutations with its inhabitants, and to witness the intervening vast progress which it has made. The plainess & simplicity of my reception at Boston, if I could have gone there, which you delicately and kindly proposed, would have been in exact correspondence with my wishes. But, gentlemen, I left home for the purpose of visiting the first time in my life a Sea bath. I was not determined to which I should repair, but finally concluded to go to Cape May [New Jersey]. Having gratified that curiosity, I desire to return to my residence, deviating as little as possible from the most convenient and direct route.[5] There are obvious reasons for this course, which, I am sure, you will have the goodness to recognize.

I must request therefore that you will receive yourselves, and communicate to those whom you represent, my sincere regrets that I am compelled to forego the pleasure of accepting their friendly invitation. I add my fervent prayers for the constant happiness and prosperity of New England, in war and peace, and amidst all the changes which have been or may be made in our National policy.

ALS. MB. 1. For Chapman, the Whig mayor of Boston from 1840-42, see Holli & Jones, *Biographical Dictionary of American Mayors*, 64-65. 2. Chapman *et al.* had written Clay from New York City on August 21, 1847, reporting that "Your numerous friends in the city of Boston and its vicinity" learning that "you proposed to extend your present journey as far north as Newport in Rhode Island," named "a Sub-committee, to meet you in New York, and extend to you . . . personally" an invitation to their city. Since they did not meet him in New York, "we are compelled to this mode of addressing you." Note that "we in New England have always looked upon you as a part of our treasures. . . . and amidst the abundant prosperity which has crowned our New England industry, we acknowledge, under Providence, our deepest obligations to the patriotic policy, which your mind had so large a share in originating." Also express sympathy for Clay's "heavy domestic calamity" and promise that his visit would include "no idle parade or ceremony to annoy you," merely a meeting "in the simple, republican manner . . . as citizens greeting a fellow citizen. . . . to give you evidence upon the spot, that wherever you may reside in fact, you have *a home* in Boston." LS. DLC-TJC (DNA, M212, R11). 3. For the transition of Massachusetts from an economy dominated by shipping interests opposed to protection to one controlled by manufacturing interests in favor of a high tariff, see Baxter, *Daniel Webster*, 104-7, 124, 142, 184; Arthur B. Darling, *Political Changes in Massachusetts 1824-1848* (New Haven, 1925), 2, 12, 37; Taussig, *Tariff History*, 72. 4. See 8:665-66. 5. Clay to Stevenson, July 23, 1847.

To CHRISTOPHER HUGHES White Sulphur Springs, Va. (W. Va .),September 4, 1847

About to return home in a few days, after a rapid excursion to the Seaboard,[1] I snatch a few moments from the company and crowds by which I am constantly surrounded, to express my deep regrets that I had not the satisfaction of seeing you. Prior to my arrival here, I heard that you were to be at this place, but I found it was a mistake. On my passage through Balto., both going to and returning from Cape May [New Jersey], I enquired for you, intending to stop at least a short time with you, but learnt that you were in the interior of Pennsylvania.

I lament to hear that your health is not good, but I hope that the fears of your friends have exaggerated your illness.[2] Do take good care of yourself. Above all, let not your wonted good spirits flag or fail you. The mind and the body are so intimately connected that the depression of the one almost always affects the other.

Adieu my dear friend! May God preserve & bless you.

P.S. My warm regards to your daughter [Margaret Hughes].

ALS. MiU-C. Addressed to Hughes at Chester Springs, Pa., and Baltimore, Md. 1. Clay to Stevenson, July 23, 1847. 2. Hughes had "rheumatic gout." See Hughes to Clay, Sept. 14, 1847.

To Henry White, Philadelphia, September 4, 1847. Reports that "I arrived here last Saturday, less fatigued than I had feared, but with a very bad cold, of which I am getting rid, and when it passes off, my health will be, I hope, even better than it was when I left home. I take my departure hence on Thursday next. I found here and have received since my arrival very satisfactory letters from my family. The friendly attentions of the public have constantly been rendered wherever I have been." Presents his "affectionate regards to the whole of your family." ALS. ViHi. Written from White Sulphur Springs, Va. (W. Va.). For Clay's itinerary, see Clay to Stevenson, July 23, 1847.

From Joseph L. White, New York City, September 4, 1847. Regrets he was not "one of the New York party who visited you at Cape May . . . but at that time I was absent in Indiana & Kentucky." Had hoped "to learn something of the *cause* of the *movement* in your State, by leading Whigs in behalf of Genl. [Zachary] Taylor." Views John J. Crittenden's support for the movement as "a subject of regret & disappointment; yet I had a lingering hope that his object was not to go ultimately for Genl Taylor, but temporarily to divert public attention from yourself to him, & thus create an opinion among our opponents, that you would in no event be a candidate. Such a hope was natural, knowing as I did Mr Crittenden's former devotion to your interests." Has decided that "unless he has acted in the matter with your knowledge & approbation, he has separated himself from his friends in this region without warning, & I fear without just excuse." Asks: "*Is it possible that he had such approbation? And has* *the recent movement in Ky been made after consultation with & approval by you?*" Is convinced that "among the controuling spirits of the Whig party" there is "little or no interest felt for Genl Taylor, out of Kent[uck]y." Concludes that if Kentucky "would remain quiet, the flame kindled for him, with the aid of his incessant correspondence, would soon be extinguished, and the entire mass of the Whig party (excepting only [Daniel] Webster, [William] Seward, [Thurlow] Weed [Horace] Greel[e]y & C[o.], with whom we can dispense) would again rally for their first love." Asks: "Will not the Whigs of your State preserve a neutrality . . . or are they demented?" Copy. NcD. Copy also in DLC-John J. Crittenden Papers (DNA, M212, R20) under date of September 15 with minor variations in punctuation, spelling, and wording. See Clay to White, September 20, 1847.

On September 21, 1847, Clay sent a copy of this letter to Crittenden: "I think it due to our mutual friendship & the candour & confidence which have ever existed between us, that I should afford you an opportunity of perusing the enclosed letter." Assures Crittenden "that I do not endorse any of the conjectures," and asks that he return the letter after giving it "such consideration as you may think it merits." Copy. DLC-John J. Crittenden Papers (DNA, M212, R20).

Crittenden, convinced that Clay could not be elected and apparently believing that he would not be a candidate, had been advising and promoting Taylor for months. In addition, the Whig party in Kentucky had factionalized, and many of its old leaders now opposed Clay. His old enemies, such as the Wickliffes, Ben Hardin, and John Pope, were now joined by his friend Robert P. Letcher and other former supporters who opposed his nomination, believing as Crittenden did that Clay could not win. Thus, many Kentucky Whigs joined the Taylor movement chiefly to prevent Clay from running again and losing, rather than to demonstrate genuine support for Taylor. Without the Kentucky defection and especially Crittenden's aid, the success of Taylor's quest for the Whig presidential nomination was much less likely. Clay's letter of September 21 to Crittenden, enclosing the White letter, is generally considered to mark the beginning of his estrangement from Crittenden. This friendship was not completely restored until shortly before Clay's death. For further discussion, see Kirwan, *John J. Crittenden*, 200-230; Hamilton, *Zachary Taylor, Soldier in the White House*, 56, 61, 67, 142, *passim*; Mrs. Chapman Coleman (ed.), *The Life of John J. Crittenden with Selections from His Correspondence and Speeches*, 2 vols. (Philadelphia, 1871), 1:281-83.

From Elizabeth Sloan, Baltimore, September 12, 1847. Praises "your beautiful and touching address, delivered at Cape May [Speech at Cape May, August 20, 1847]." Claims to understand "that desolating, lonelyness of heart, which so well, teaches us genuine true sympathy." Sends a poem concerning death and asks Clay to accept it as "my humble offering, of little merit, and valuless, except as a slight token of my devotion to one, who well deserves the affection of all Americans!" Encloses a 56-line poem. ALS. DLC-TJC (DNA, M212, R11).

From Christopher Hughes, Yellow Springs, Chester Co., Pa., September 14, 1847. Thanks Clay for his "kind—volunteered Letter [Clay to Hughes, September 4, 1847]." Explains that he knows "how to value such marks of affectionate interest & esteem—and from such men—as you?—Why, the pride of my Life—has consisted in gaining the affection & confidence of the really Great men—with whom I have Come into Contact & Communion . . . & if I were to set about enumerating proofs of the success . . . of my honest frank—& honourable Life—of what Mr. J.Q. Adams called—(in his letters 30 years since.)—my '*Winning Ways*.' I should write a Book like Ch: J. Ingersolls War History *in Length*—& as unlike it as possible in another point. *Every word* of *my* Book—would be *True*."

Wishes he had been able to accept Clay's invitation "to Ashland & to go pass last winter—with you—at N. Orleans! I wish'd to do *both*! But—tho—I may—some day—*see you*—at Ashland, I doubt—if I ever shall see N.O.! I fear the voyage! and I have a repugnance to that part of our Great Country: if I had been—*with you*—you never should have made that speech about—'Killing a Mexican [Toast at Dinner of the New England Society of Louisiana, December 22, 1846]'! *I* should have understood yr. joke! But did *others*? *No*! I ought always to be *with you*! & you know it." Claims that "if I were to give way—at this moment to my feelings—as I did . . . when I got news of your *defeat* . . . by the election of that ignoble—obscure—& miserable Creature—[James K.] Polk [Clay to Webb, February 29, 1844]! . . . my eyes would stream with tears of affection—sympathy & devotion to you . . . and I am weeping like a child thinking of your public wrongs."

Refers to "my friend [William N.] Mercer's Letter" to illustrate "how Lookers-on,—think—feel—& express themselves—concerning the phases & phenomena of Eminent Persons," and concludes that "no earthly eminence could ever be compensation *to me*—for such sufferings—as yours—described by Mercer:—who is your Friend! and *his* account is not overstated! it accords with your Own—*to me*—in 1842—of your sufferings—in Balt[imo]re: & elsewhere, in the [William Henry] Harrison Elec.—campaign!"

Regrets having missed Clay "on your passage through Baltimore—on your way—to the North [Clay to Stevenson, July 23, 1847]" and adds that "in health & activity—I should have '*hooked on*' to you, at B.—& nothing should have separated us!"

Recalls their long friendship: "Do you suppose—that I do not *know*—how sincerely you esteem & *love me*? and—that—in your Conscience & most secret *thoughts*—you know & *feel*—that you never *had* a truer & more faithful & *constant* friend—than I have ever been to you." Feels that "I should have just taken possession of you! at *Baltimore* going & coming—you should have stopped at *my house*: & no 'Barnum's'—nor any other house—but *mine*—should have *roofed*—you! . . . and then—I'de have followed you to Philda: & after-wards—we would have 'locked arms'—& gone *a*-seeking of—'a Watery Grave'—& been *drowned* together—in the sea: *Cape Ma*[*y*.]"

Hopes that it is not "too late" for Clay to be " '*up* for President,' " but adds "I shall *insist* upon your following *my* advice—in some points; you shall neither *speak*—nor *write*: What have *you*, Sir, to *say*—that you have not already—*said*? . . . You charge me with '*jawings*.' Why a pretty Miss Boswell—of Ky. told me last Summer—'that *you* do nothing else.' but *jaw*—at Ashland!"

On page 11 of his letter, decides to "cut short & give you—a 'hasty' . . . acct—of myself—fate & state." Reports that he "bore up—pretty well—'till March (this year), & really looked—fresh—hale & *handsome*," although "I *degraded* myself by going to the President's House. . . . Would you believe—that that mean Varlet—Polk—after my 32 year's honourable service abroad" has "stupidly & unwisely" recalled him "to give my place—to a base Culprit—named *Damroc* [*sic*, Auguste Davezac]." And "never asked me—*to dinner*." Concludes: "I still *want*—to return in my old Trade—Diplomacy—to Europe."

Describes a recent bout "with Rheum[ati]c: Gout," during which the doctors practiced "*Calomel* & Bleeding I was *bled out* of the Gout—*into* the Dropsy!" When the "Philda. Drs. of fame" declared him "to be hopeless," came to Yellow Springs "(as *they* said:—) 'to die!' " Decided afterward that "Homeopathy—but especially, 'The Water *Cure*'—has recovered & renewed me & I w[ill] never again swallow a drug!"

Insists that "whenever you *do* Come to *Baltimore*—you are to lodge & live—at my House. . . . Now—this point is *settled* ! ! ! . . . I am quite comfortable & easy—indeed—*independent*—in my affairs & state; with the Certainty . . . of leaving my Daughter so" because he has resolved "*not* to espouse & pay *other person's debts*." Refuses to become like "The Model of worldly thrift & wisdom . . . Robt. Gilmor [5:163-64]—of *our* Town," who "is *now*—a Bankrupt! ay! a Beggar" because he had endorsed and paid the debts of a man "who married *Mrs. Gilmor's* Niece! & the World turns up its snout—at *old Bob Gilmor*!" Is relieved that he can claim that "After all my 'taxes' are paid—I have a clear income of—Dolls: 6.000—per Ann and live—in my *own* house" with four servants in "ease & comfort:—but not wealth."

Concludes: "My Daughter [Margaret Hughes] (a jewel of sense—& grace—& Conduct—) & sends her *love* to you." ALS. DLC-HC (DNA, M212, R6).

Charles J. Ingersoll's book was *Historical Sketch of the Second War Between the United States of America, and Great Britain* . . . , 2 vols. (Philadelphia, 1845-49).

In 1845 Polk had replaced Hughes as chargé de affaires to The Netherlands with Auguste Davezac of Louisiana. Davezac served from April 19, 1845, to February 3, 1846. Hughes had not been notified of his removal until Davezac's arrival at The Hague. Chester G. Dunham, "The Diplomatic Career of Christopher Hughes," Ph. D. dissertation, Ohio State University, 1968, pp. 226, 230; Richardson Dougall & Mary Patricia Chapman, *United States Chiefs of Missions 1778-1973* (Washington, 1973), 107.

To JOSEPH L. WHITE Lexington, September 20, 1847

I hasten, upon my return home, first to acknowledge the receipt of your friendly letter of the 4h. instant, among the many letters which have reached here during my absence.

Altho' you may not be a "very old friend," in any sense of the term, you have been a most devoted faithful and efficient one, to whom I am under great obligations, sincerely and gratefully felt, if not before expressed to you; and therefore you are justly entitled to a full and frank answer to the enquiries contained in your letter.

The movements in Kentucky to which you refer, in behalf of Genl. [Zachary] Taylor, so far from being prompted by me, have been made without my approbation, and without consultation with me.[1] I believe the Genl. to be an honest, patriotic and straightforward man, but totally without experience in civil administration. And thinking as I have always done, and as I am happy to find the young mens Comee. of N. York do, as to the impropriety of elevating to the Chief Magistracy of the Union;[2] a military commander, without civil qualifications, nothing could reconcile me to the election of him: but to escape from some greater danger. And that greater danger ought to be manifest, as well as the impracticability of the election of any Whig professing the requisite experience and civil capacity, before the alternative of resorting to the General should be embraced.

In some instances, the movements in K[entucky]. have been at the instance of doubtful or suspected Whigs, with the concurrence of a few Loco's.[3] In no instance, I believe, did any of the public meetings contain any thing like a majority of the Whigs in the respective Counties or Communities in which they were assembled. At the meeting, which you were assured was to be an overwhelming one at Lexington last monday,[4] altho' the greatest efforts were made by a few acting in concert, to render it an imposing affair, & although on the part of those opposed to any present action, there was no previous arrangement or concert, the subject of the address recommending Genl. Taylor was postponed until April next, and 97 persons, I am informed, (for I had not returned home) were all that could be mustured in support of immediate action.

I believe that the great body of the Whig party in Kentucky is unmoved, and entertain the same preference that it always did. At the same time, it is quite probable that, if Genl. Taylor should be nominated by a Whig Convention, as their Candidate for the Presidency, he would receive the vote of K. But, wherever I have been, or with whomever I have conversed, I find that his letters have produced a great abatement of the feeling which had been exerted in his favor.[5]

I am not aware that Mr. [John J.] Crittenden[6] has done any thing inconsistent with his friendship for me. If he has, it has been by correspondence; for I have not understood that he has attended any public meeting favorable to Genl. Taylor. That he would support the Genl. if nominated I have no doubt. And so he would me, and so would other Whigs, who have shared in these Taylor movements, if I were nominated and consented to the nomination.

And this brings me to say something about myself. I have taken no part in public affairs, since the disastrous result of the last P. election.[7] I have remained quiet and passive. I have said to no one whether I would or would not consent to my name being again presented to the public. That question, it appeared to me, ought to depend upon a full consideration of all circumstances existing at the time when it might be necessary, if ever, for me to determine it. Among these circumstances my own personal condition, and the general state of public feeling and wishes would be most important.

The Louisville Journal has taken its course, without any consultation with me.[8] It states my views in regard to the use of my name again, in language rather more forcible & unqualified than I employed, but it is mainly correct.

My opinion has been and still is, that no general movement of the Whig party should be made, in regard to the designation of a Candidate for the P. until towards the next Spring. By that time all the elections will be over, we shall have a further view of this Mexican War, important developments may be made in Congress, and we may be able to take a survey of the whole ground.

You speak of Messrs. [Thurlow] Weed, [William] Seward, [Horace] Greel[e]y & c. Who are they for? Mr. G[reeley]. especially has been supposed to be friendly to me.

But I must conclude. Perhaps I may shortly again write to you.

P.S. I must beg that you will regard this letter as confidential, & particularly that it is not to appear in the Newspapers.

ALS. Courtesy of Albert D. Arfin, Massapequa Park, N.Y. Letter marked "(Confidential)." 1. White to Clay, Sept. 4, 1847. 2. Young Men's Henry Clay Association to Clay, Dec. 7, 1846. 3. For instance, a meeting had been held on August 14, 1847, in Lexington to nominate a candidate for president "without distinction of party." A handbill was circulated saying this meeting was premature and in opposition to the wishes of a majority of Whigs in Fayette County. Although the meeting was intended to nominate Taylor, no such nomination was made. Lexington *Observer & Kentucky Reporter*, August 18, 1847. 4. A meeting had been held at the Fayette County Courthouse on Sept. 13, 1847, to consider Taylor for the presidency. It was attended by both Democrats and Whigs, including George B. Kinkead, Henry Johnson, Thomas Metcalfe, Leslie Combs, John C. Breckinridge, Henry Clay Pindell, and Robert Wickliffe, Sr. It was decided to postpone making a nomination until April, 1848. *Ibid.*, Sept. 15, 1847. 5. Taylor's letter of May 18, 1847, to James W. Taylor, endorsing an editorial in the Cincinnati *Signal* which urged projection of the Ordinance of 1787 to keep slavery out of the southwestern lands, was very unpopular in the South. Other letters, such as the one to Edward Delony of Louisiana—in which he refused to answer questions on the country's banking and tariff needs, writing: "I am *not prepared* to answer them"—also damaged Taylor's campaign. Hamilton, *Zachary Taylor, Soldier in the White House*, 43-47; see also Clay to Ullmann, August 4, 1847. Taylor handily carried Kentucky over Lewis Cass by 67,141 votes to 49,720. McKee,

National . . . Popular and Electoral Vote, 71. 6. White to Clay, Sept. 4, 1847. 7. Clay to Webb, Feb. 29, 1844. 8. On Sept. 1, 1847, George D. Prentice, editor of the Louisville *Daily Journal* and an early supporter of Zachary Taylor, had proclaimed in his paper that Clay did not seek and could not be prevailed on to become a candidate. Betty C. Congleton, "Contenders for the Whig Nomination in 1848 and the Editorial Policy of George D. Prentice," *RKHS* (April, 1969), 67:119-33, espec. 123.

To MARY S. BAYARD Lexington, September 22, 1847

I am quite sure, my ever true and dear friend, that you will be pleased to hear of my safe arrival at home, in good health.[1] I remained at the W[hite]. Sulphur Springs eight or ten days after my return from Cape May, and then commenced my journey homewards, in an Extra Stage, with an agreeable party of six, the number which we limited for comfort, besides servants. I found my family all well.

I will not amuse you with events after I left Philadelphia. The newspapers have anticipated me, altho' their accounts ought to be received with some abatement of their extravagance. I was not, for example, in any very imminent danger at the Cape from the oversetting of a carriage. Nor did I leap out of it, with a young lady in my arms, although after getting out of it myself I did assist her.

You know, when I left you, I had some thought of returning to the City. If I could have done so quietly, and passed a day or two with yourself, and a few other friends, I should have been most happy. The few hours which I spent with you and your dear children were by far the most agreeable of my whole journey. But I found that I was in danger of being killed by kindness, and as I was not ambitious of such a death, I concluded that it was best to return by the shortest route to the mountains of Virginia, and gave up all purpose of again visiting Philadelphia this summer.

I was extremely delighted to meet Miss Bayard[2] at the Cape. I found her the same good kind and intelligent friend, greatly improved by the operation at Paris on her eyes. Nor, since she has become an *Ironmaster*, is her head at all hardened. She almost persuaded me to make her a visit, in company with you, and to see how, in her new vocation, she succeeds in making pigs, bars &c.

Do write me and tell me every thing about yourself and family. When is the marriage of your daughter to come off?[3] Mr. [Richard H.] Bayard, I observed, was quite gay in Fancy balls &c at R[hode] Island. Present my affectionate regards to him, to your children, and to Miss B when you see her.

ALS. DeHi. 1. Clay to Stevenson, July 23, 1847. 2. Probably Richard Henry Bayard's only sister Ann Caroline. Her name appears on more than 15 deeds in the Dauphin County Court House. The Bayard family's ironworks was known as Victoria Furnace; located on Clark's Creek northeast of Dauphin in Rush Township. Ann Caroline purchased 1078 acres there in 1847. Horace A. Keeper, *Early Iron Industries of Dauphin County* (Harrisburg, Pa., 1927), 11-13; information also supplied by Constance J. Cooper, manuscript librarian, The Historical Society of Delaware, and Warren W. Wirebach, librarian, The Historical Society of Dauphin County. 3. On August 31, 1848, Elizabeth Bayard married Frederick Henry Rich of the Royal Engineers. Information supplied by Constance J. Cooper.

To JOHN J. CRITTENDEN Lexington, September 26, 1847

I hasten to acknowledge the rect. of your favor, and to relieve your mind from any impression that I shared in the views taken by Mr. [Joseph L.] White of the course, which you had thought proper to take in regard to the next Presidential election.[1] It is due to that gentleman to say, that he was not singular in entertaining those views. Repeatedly, whilst I was recently abroad, and since I have returned home, similar statements, in respect to your course, were made to me, with enquiries &c. I thought I understood you. I find I did; and to all such enquiries, I made representations of your conduct substantially corresponding with your own account of it.

As to myself, my feelings and wishes have undergone no change, since I communicated them to you, without reserve, in relation to the next P. election. It may not ever be necessary for me to decide whether I would consent to the use of my name again or not; but I declare solemnly that, up to this time, I have not brought my mind to determine that I would consent. I have remained passive, permitting, without seeking to control, the course of events. If the nomination were tendered to me, my decision would be guided by my personal condition, at the time, and by the state of the public sentiment.

But whilst this is my position, I must frankly own to you that the movements in K[entucky]. have occasioned me some mortification.[2] They wear the aspect of impatience under the tyes, which have so long bound me to the State and to the Whig party, and an eager desire to break loose from them. They were not necessary, at least so many of them, to Genl [Zachary] Taylor. It could not be doubted that, if he were the nominee of the Whig party, or of both parties, the State would give him its suffrage. It did seem to me that, without any regard to my feelings, considering the unsuccessful attempts to secure my election, made by K., her character would be best illustrated and promoted, by dignified silence, and, instead of taking the lead, to leave to other States to occupy the front & foremost rank.

Besides, I am not a stranger to the arts and to the instruments which have been employed to get up most of those meetings. They have been not unfrequently prompted or promoted by the malignity of some of my personal enemies uniting with Loco's.[3] These enemies (by the bye some times your's also) care less for Genl. Taylor than the gratification of their malevolence towards me. And as to the locos, they will generally desert as soon as their own flag is unfurled, as unfurled it will most certainly be.

But I am accustomed to adversity; and the purpose of wounding my feelings has not been accomplished to the extent designed. I thank God that, more than ever, I can look on, with calmness and composure, upon all events, whether they affect me or not.

There have been many enquiries of me concerning Genl. Taylor. I have aimed, and I think in every instance I have succeeded to do him justice. I could not say, and have not said, what opinions he entertains on public measures; for I did not know. And, as he has recently stated that he had formed none on certain leading measures, I am glad that I did not commit him.[4]

I should regret extremely any collision between his friends and mine. If such should unfortunately arise, it will not be my fault.

I would say much more, if I did not expect 'ere long to have the pleasure of seeing you, when we can talk much more fully & freely than is fit for a letter. P.S. I have no objection to your taking a copy of Mr. Whites letter;[5] of course with the restriction that no public use is to be made of it.

ALS. DLC-John J. Crittenden Papers (DNA, M212, R20). 1. Crittenden's letter not found; but see White to Clay, Sept. 4, 1847. 2. Clay to Beatty, April 29, 1847; White to Clay, Sept. 4, 1847; Clay to White, Sept. 20, 1847. 3. White to Clay, Sept. 4, 1847; Clay to White, Sept. 20, 1847. 4. *Ibid.* 5. White to Clay, Sept. 4, 1847.

To JOSHUA R. GIDDINGS Lexington, October 6, 1847

I received, my dear sir, your friendly letter[1] in all the spirit of kindness and amity in which it was dictated, and I answer it in the same spirit.

I am thankful for your friendship, which I cordially reciprocate. I hope that it will continue to be mutual between us, whatever may be the political events of the future.

You tell me that it is possible that I may be again a candidate for the Presidency by the nomination of the Whig convention, and with honorable candor, add that you are not favorable to my nomination.[2]

After the disastrous termination of the last contest, I never expected to be again a candidate. I do not now expect it, nor have I determined in my own mind that I would accept the nomination if it were offered me. It probably never will be necessary for me to decide that question; but if it should be, I should deliberately consider the circumstances which ought to influence my judgment.

I am not surprised at the progress of the anti-slavery feeling which you describe in the Free States.[3] The annexation of Texas,[4] this most unnecessary and horrible war with Mexico,[5] and the overthrow of the tariff of 1842,[6] were well calculated to produce that effect. But you, perhaps, ought to reflect that these measures could not have been carried without large Northern support; and perhaps justice would also require that it should not be forgotten that some of us were most decidedly adverse to them.

You kindly refer to the subject of the slaves I hold, and tell me what would be the good consequences of my emancipating them.

I regret as much as any one does the existence of slavery in our country, and wish to God there was not a single slave in the United States, or in the whole world. But here the unfortunate institution is, and a most delicate and difficult affair is it to deal with.

I have during my life emancipated some eight or ten, under circumstances which appeared to me to admit of their emancipation.[7] The last was Charles [Dupuy], and I am not sure that he is benefited by his freedom.[8] Of the remainder (some fifty odd), what I ought to do with them, and how, and when, is a matter of grave and serious consideration often with me. I am perfectly sure that to emancipate them forthwith would be an act of great inhumanity and extreme cruelty. I wish you would come and see me and them. Do come. You would behold among them aged and decrepit men and women and helpless children, utterly unable to gain a livelihood or support in the world. They would perish if I sent them forth in the world.

Alas, alas! my good friend, I fear you have a very inadequate idea of the duties, obligations, and relations which exist between my poor slaves and me.

But whatever I may or might do towards them must be wholly independent of all political motives or considerations; it must rest exclusively with my own sense of duty and propriety.

Nor do I believe that if it were possible for me to be influenced by the motive of my own political advancement in the emancipation of my slaves, at this time, it would tend in the smallest degree to the promotion of that end. My object and purpose would be alike assailed by the ultras on both sides, if not by others.

Copy. Printed in Julian, *The Life of Joshua R. Giddings*, 208-10. Letter marked "[Confidential]." 1. Not found. 2. Giddings had made it clear that he would not support a slaveholder for president, and this included both Clay and Zachary Taylor. James B. Stewart, *Joshua R. Giddings and the Tactics of Radical Politics* (Cleveland, Ohio, 1970), 124, 128; Stephen E. Maizlish, *The Triumph of Sectionalism: The Transformation of Ohio Politics, 1844-1856* (Kent, Ohio, 1983), 63, 89, 102, 147, 151, 155-60. 3. Largely as a result of the Mexican War and the Wilmot Proviso agitation [Sargent to Clay, Feb. 27, 1847] that fostered a growing opposition to slavery, the "Conscience Whigs" and the Barnburners of the Democratic party began to break their traditional political party ties. They eventually coalesced with supporters of the disintegrating Liberty party and in 1848 formed the Free Soil party, a harbinger of still further slavery agitation. John Mayfield, *Rehearsal for Republicanism: Free Soil and the Politics of Antislavery* (Port Washington, N.Y., 1980), 9, 30-41, 78-79, *passim*; Maizlish, *The Triumph of Sectionalism*, 15-16, 53-55, 61-70, 88-106, 113, 117. 4. Clay to Crittenden, Feb. 15, 1844. 5. Clay to Lawrence, April 30, 1845. 6. Clay to Greeley, June 23, 1846. 7. See 1:277; 7:482-83, 590; 9:52; also Richard L. Troutman, "Emancipation of Slaves by Henry Clay," *JNH* (April, 1955), 40:179-81. 8. Deed of Emancipation, Dec. 9, 1844.

To John McCracken, New Haven, Conn., October 6, 1847. Expresses his thanks "for the friendly sentiments towards me cherished in Connecticut." Finds "great delight" in Connecticut's prosperity and is "glad that it has resulted in part from the establishment of a system of policy, to which I ever dedicated the utmost of my poor exertions." Remains convinced of the "beneficial tendency of that system." Adds that "if it has unfortunately met with a check, let us hope that it will be only temporary, or that, in spite of any unwise legislation, all our great interests will continue to advance and flourish."

Regrets his inability to accept "the kind invitation to me to visit New Haven, which you were good enough to bear to Cape May; and I was grateful to my friends for admitting the sufficiency of the reasons which dissuaded me [Speech to Delegations of Citizens, August 20, 1847]." Concludes: "I should deeply regret if I thought I was never more to see New England, and yet I am wholly unable to say when, if ever, I shall again have that gratification." ALS. KyU.

To Messrs. Gibson & Farmer, Newark, N.J., October [?] 11, 1847. Thanks them for the present of "a bureau travelling trunk." Adds: "I concur entirely in the sentiment you have expressed. 'Give us protection—a fair, reasonable protection—and all the branches of the mechanic arts will prosper, the laborer will be adequately rewarded, and our country placed safe on the road to national prosperity and advancement.' I have seen nothing to change my convictions on that subject. We have enjoyed undoubtedly, in all the departments of Agriculture, and perhaps in some of those of manufactures, a high degree of prosperity this year. But the cause of it cannot be mistaken. It was the European famine [Bragaw to Clay, December 30, 1846] which threw the balance of trade so greatly in our favor, and has filled our public treasury. The circle of another year, I apprehend, will not be completed before we shall witness the sad effects of the repeal of the tariff of 1842 [9:628], and the passage of the tariff of 1846 [Clay to Greeley, June 23, 1846]." Copy, extract. Printed in Lexington *Observer & Kentucky Reporter*, November 6, 1847.

From James Brown Clay, Cumberland Gap, Ky., October 12, 1847. Writes from "4 miles this [Kentucky] side of the Gap." Reports that he and his stock "have got on perfectly well so far, with the exception of one of my Warfield horses, which was foundered from eating new corn." Left directions "at Pogues 24 miles from the Gap" to return the horse to Lexington, and asks Clay "to make Lewis [slave] take him home & fatten him as I intend him as a present to young Jacob." Assures Clay that he is "getting over . . . by degrees" the "cold I took before leaving home, which occasined me to cough very severely." Intends to go through "Abington Va . . . travelling only about 20 miles pr day."

Requests Clay that "when you have read this letter please send it to Susan [Jacob Clay]," who "can tell Mr [John J.] Jacob that if he wants a pair of carriage horses, I was offered a beautiful pair of large Bays 15 1/2 or 15 3/4 hands high for $200.00 by Wm Walker 3 miles this side of Richmond which I think would please him." If he cannot return by November 20, wants "Parker Todhunter to have my mules at McClures fed for me." ALS. DLC-TJC (DNA, M212, R11).

On October 17, 1847, Clay sent James's letter to Susan Clay, in care of John J. Jacob of Louisville, Ky. Reports that "We are all well here, and I hope that you and dear Lucy [Jacob Clay] and James [Brown Clay, Jr.] are so also." Believes "that every thing is as it ought to be at your house." ALS. *Ibid.*

James Brown Clay, Jr., Susan and James Brown Clay's son, was born in 1846 and died in 1906. "Young Jacob" may be Susan's brother Thomas P. Jacob who later accompanied them to Portugal. J.M. Armstrong (pub.), *Biographical Encyclopedia of Kentucky* (Cincinnati, 1878), 321. For a correction of John J. Jacob's middle initial, see Clay to Susan J. Clay, November 13, 1847.

To ANNA MERCER Lexington, October 16, 1847

I transmit to you, my dear Anna, a letter which has come to my hands for you, since your departure from this place. You ladies are fond of receiving letters, and you many therefore receive it with pleasure, although time and circumstances may have otherwise deprived it of interest.

I transmitted the other day one under similar circumstances to Miss [Eliza] Young.

Let me, I beseech you, some times hear from you. Next to your dear father, and to Miss Young, I will not allow that any other person takes a livelier interest in your welfare than I do.

My warm regards to your father to Miss Young and to Miss [Mary D.] Kemble. P.S. Can you keep a little secret? I saw this day a beautiful pair of slippers, worked for your father, by the fair hands of a pretty young Lady. Don't tell him of it. Let them come upon him by surprize.

ALS. LU-Ar.

From James Brown Clay, Raleigh, N.C., October 31, 1847. Reports his arrival the previous day, "all well, excepting my cold." Informs Clay that neither [Thomas P.] Devereaux, "Mr. [George] Badger or Col [Richard] Hines are here, & in fact I have met no acquaintance except Mr [Willie P.] Mangum, with whom I spent last evening." Expects to visit Hines "at [his] plantation in the neighborhood of which I [expe]ct from what he says to dispose of some [hors]es." Although he has "sold nothing so far except one [ho]rse," expects little "difficulty, this [n]ot being the region for mules." Reports that "the stock look very nearly, if not quite as well as when I left home," despite travelling 505 miles. Asks Clay to "Tell R[ichard]. Pindell that there is great scarcity of pork through this whole region & that I think it will command from $5– to $6." Requests Clay to pay a "little note of mine to Caldwell for $225—the price of a pair of the Balto. mules" if it falls due before he returns. ALS, manuscript torn. DLC-TJC (DNA, M212, R11).

From Harry I. Thornton, Eutaw, Ala., November 1, 1847. Reports that "in relation to the disposition of the negros bequeathed to you by Mr [Thomas S.] Witherspoon. . . . All of them are willing to go to Liberia at any time except two, viz, Jack, and Tena: and the only objection with them, is their marriage with slaves not embraced in the will." Describes Jack as "a very valuable young man about twenty eight years old, a good carpenter, whose wife and children belong to Dr Witherspoon the Extr. of his late brother" and who "is worth at least two hundred & forty dollars a year." Notes that Jack "is happily situated & is willing to wait and work for the money to buy his family." Describes Tena as "a very sickly woman, about thirty years of age . . . under the care of Col. Kerr," who will "liberate Tena's husband, if her health should become good." Recommends as well that "the family consisting of Moses, his wife Epra, & their two children Louisa & Charlotte" remain in Alabama, since "Moses is an excellent carpenter & will hire readily for twenty five dollars per month. His wife & her two children have been raised in the house, & can also be hired togather, for at least one hundred dollars per year." Suggests that "The remainder of the negros . . . ought to be sent as soon as practicable to Africa." Explains that the remaining 18 are a "whole family" and that "It is very difficult to employ them profitably, without hiring them to persons who will put them under overseers." Adds: "I hire them now as I can by the day, the week, or month, some times to one person & then to another. . . . they more than pay expenses, but with much trouble to them, & to me, & with some loss of time in looking out for employment." From the "entire amount of their hire" and other funds, about $1000 is available for the disposition of the slaves. Believes he can "procure a trustworthy white man" for $100 to take them to New Orleans and will pay $100 for "transportation to that city." Proposes distributing the remaining $800 to provide the "eight heads of families . . . a sufficient outfit, even if their passage money were to be paid out of it." Understands, however, that the American Colonization Society "will pay their passage over." Hopes the slaves can leave soon, because "There is a feeling of jealousy in the community always, with regard to negros situated as these are, especially towards those that have to labor out of doors, which will manifest itself." Has learned that "a Packet would leave N. Orleans for the colony in Jany next" and "if you should visit N. Orleans the agent could deliver them" or "perhaps the Col. Society may have a regular agent there, who might be authorised by you to act in the premises." Concludes: "I will cheerfully co-operate in any course you may decide upon." ALS. DLC-Records of the American Colonization Society (DNA, M212, R20).

On November 20, 1847, Clay wrote the American Colonization Society secretary William McLain that he wanted Thornton's "views and suggestions carried out in respect to the Slaves bequeathed to me by the late Mr. Witherspoon, both as to those who should immediately proceed to Africa, and those who for the present had best remain." Since "the A.C. Society would take charge of the transportation," supposes that "an Agent of its own, instead of the one suggested by Mr. T. . . . take care of them to the port of embarkation." Concludes: "I am glad that these poor creatures have means of their own, which may be applied to their comfort during the voyage, and on their arrival in Africa. I wish the whole of them so applied." ALS. *Ibid.*

From ZACHARY TAYLOR Near Monterey, Mexico, November 4, 1847

By yesterday's mail I had the gratification of receiving your very welcome letter of the 27th. September—Rest assured that nothing has transpired, nothing can transpire to impair the amicable and kindly relations which it has been my pleasure and pride for so long time to maintain with you—Hints, similar to those to which you refer, have been thrown out in letters which I have recently received;[1] but they have had no influence whatever upon me; not one word has served, in the remotest degree, to prejudice me against yourself or your friends, in either personal or political relations.

I fully agree with you in the necessity for more deliberation in the selection of a candidate for the Presidency, and I truly regret that my name should have been used in that relation. It has been permitted with the greatest reluctance on my part, and only from a sense of duty to the country—My repugnance to being a candidate before the nation for that exalted office has been frankly and sincerely made known—Most truly is it my hope that before next November, the party may select a whig in all respects worthy of the confidence of the Country—To a mutual friend of ours I have recently made this announcement, asserting my greater desire for the quiet of private occupations, as not only a more appropriate termination to my services as a soldier, & more consonant with my earnest wishes, but particularly proper in reference to my limited acquaintance with matters of civil & national policy—I stated to him specifically that I was ready to stand aside, if you or any other whig were the choice of the party, and that I sincerely hoped such might be their decision—[2]

The importance of harmony and good feeling among the opponents of the present [Polk] dynasty, is, by no one appreciated more considerably than by myself, and whatever may be the decision of the party, I shall be studiously guarded in this particular, and strive to lend my best endeavours to the preservation of unity—Permit me to repeat that whatever representations may be made to me, from any source, conveying any expression of disrespect towards yourself or your friends, or that either entertain unfriendly feelings towards me, be assured my dear Sir, they will be repelled and discredited as they justly merit—

I am much rejoiced that I have this opportunity to assure you not only of my frank and full confidence in your friendship and kindly feelings, but that I warmly appreciate your wishes for my own success and your expressed desire to contribute to it. . . .

LS. DLC-HC (DNA, M212, R6). Letter marked "Private." Printed in Colton, *Clay Correspondence*, 4:548-49. 1. Reference obscure. 2. Taylor had written a number of letters expressing the sentiment that he would gladly stand aside for Clay and did not really desire the presidency. Bauer, *Zachary Taylor*, 227.

From Peter Sken Smith, Philadelphia, Pa., November 6, 1847. Informs Clay that "In the fall of 1844 I showed your two letters (herewith returned at your request) the only letters of yours to me upon the subject of *Nativism* [Clay to Smith, June 17 and October 16, 1844], probably to certain leading *democrats* in the *Native* ranks—The consequence was a majority for Henry Clay in the 'two Philadelphias [city and county]' of between four & five thousand votes [Davis to Clay, October 4, 1844]." Assures Clay that "Not one word has ever been copied from your letters to me, nor have I ever parted with them or suffered copies." Explains that he had a "full and free conversation with Nathan Sargent Esq a mutual friend" concerning "the only use ever made of your letters." Warns that "I frequently heard in 1844 of a similar letter or letters written by you to friends in New York—Perhaps you will be able to recollect and be governed accordingly [Clay to Frelinghuysen, May 22, 1844; Clay to Webb, October 25, 1844]." ALS. DLC-HC (DNA, M212, R6). See also Clay to Smith, November 13, 1847, and Clay to Greeley, November 22, 1847.

To SUSAN JACOB CLAY Lexington, November 13, 1847

I thank you for your letter, which I should have sooner acknowledged, but that I was a week absent from home attending the trial of a Cause in Anderson.[1]

I send you the last letter I have received from James [Brown Clay]. I hope you have still later. His trip, will I hope and believe, benefit his health.[2]

I am delighted to hear from you that my dear Lucy [Jacob Clay] is better.[3] May God bless and restore to health one in whose welfare I feel the greatest solicitude.

At your house[4] every thing goes on as well as could be expected. Here we are all well, your mother[5] engaged in her Milk business, the Selling of pork, &c[.]

My best regards to your father[6] and your family[.]

Kiss dear Lucy and James [B. Clay, Jr.] for me.

ALS. DLC-TJC (DNA, M212, R11). 1. The Singleton case. See Speech in Lexington, Nov. 13, 1847. 2. James B. Clay to Clay, Oct. 12 and 31, 1847. 3. For Lucy's problems, see Clay to Susan J. Clay, Nov. 3, 1845. 4. Clay Villa. 5. Reference is to her mother-in-law Lucretia Hart Clay. 6. Susan's father has been previously identified as John I. Jacob of Louisville; however, his personal papers, located at the Filson Club Historical Society in Louisville, reveal that his middle name was Jeremiah. The confusion has arisen because of the identical way Jacob wrote a capital "I" and "J." Many published sources have, therefore, erroneously given his middle initial as "I." Information supplied by Dr. James J. Holmberg, Filson Club.

To PETER SKEN SMITH Lexington, November 13, 1847

I received today your favor of the 6h. inst. transmitting two letters of mine, addressed to you in 1844.[1] Your letter proves you to be, what I had previously believed you to be, a gentleman of honor and good faith. I shall probably never have an opportunity of demonstrating this conviction otherwise than expressing it; but should such an occasion ever occur, in my future life, I would eagerly embrace it[.]

My letters were what I supposed them to be, an expression of my belief that the Native American party was actuated by good motives, whether wrong or right in the objects at which they aimed. Such I believe to be the intention of the mass of all parties.

I believe I wrote to N.Y. letters in 1844 similar to those addressed to you.[2] I do not know that any unfair use is attempted to be made of them, none could be, if they were justly interpreted.

ALS. DNA, RG56, Customs Applications, Collectors, Entry 247, Box 195. Letter marked "(Private)." 1. Probably Clay to Smith, June 17, 1844, and Clay to Smith, Oct. 16, 1844. 2. Smith to Clay, Nov. 6, 1847; Clay to Greeley, Nov. 22, 1847.

SPEECH IN LEXINGTON, KY. November 13, 1847

The day is dark and gloomy, unsettled and uncertain, like the condition of our country, in regard to the unnatural war with Mexico. The public mind is agitated and anxious, and is filled with serious apprehensions as to its indefinite continuance, and especially as to the consequences which its termination may bring forth, menacing the harmony, if not the existence, of our Union.

It is under these circumstances, I present myself before you. No ordinary occasion would have drawn me from the retirement in which I live; but, whilst a single pulsation of the human heart remains, it should, if necessary, be dedicated to the service of one's country. And I have hope that, although I am a private and humble citizen, an expression of the views and opinions I entertain, might form some little addition to the general stock of information, and afford a small assistance in delivering our country from the perils and dangers which surround it.

I have come here with no purpose to attempt to make a fine speech, or any ambitious oratorical display. I have brought with me no rhetorical bouquets to throw into this assemblage. In the circle of the year, autumn has come, and the season of flowers has passed away. In the progress of years, my spring time has gone by, and I too am in the autumn of life, and feel the frost of age. My desire and aim are to address you, earnestly, calmly, seriously and plainly, upon the grave and momentous subjects which have brought us together. And I am most solicitous that not a solitary word may fall from me, offensive to any party or person in the whole extent of the union.

War, pestilence, and famine, by the common consent of mankind, are the three greatest calamities which can befal our species; and war, as the most direful, justly stands foremost and in front. Pestilence and famine, no doubt for wise although inscrutable purposes, are inflictions of Providence, to which it is our duty, therefore, to bow with obedience, humble submission and resignation. Their duration is not long, and their ravages are limited. They bring, indeed, great affliction whilst they last, but society soon recovers from their effects. War is the voluntary work of our own hands, and whatever reproaches it may deserve should be directed to ourselves. When it breaks out, its duration is indefinite and unknown—its vicissitudes are hidden from our view. In the sacrifice of human life, and in the waste of human treasure, in its losses and in its burthens, it affects both belligerent nations; and its sad effects of mangled bodies, of death, and of desolation, endure long after its thunders are hushed in peace. War unhinges society, disturbs its peaceful and regular industry, and scatters poisonous seeds of disease and immorality, which continue to germinate and diffuse their baneful influence long after it has ceased. Dazzling by its glitter, pomp and pageantry, it begets a spirit of wild adventure and romantic enterprize, and often disqualifies those who embark in it, after their return from the bloody fields of battle, from engaging in the industrious and peaceful vocations of life.

We are informed by a statement which is apparently correct, that the number of our countrymen slain in this lamentable Mexican war, although it has yet been of only 18 months existence, is equal to one half of the whole of the American loss during the seven years war of the Revolution![1] And I venture to assert that the expenditure of treasure which it has occasioned, when it shall come to be fairly ascertained and footed up, will be found to be more than half of the pecuniary cost of the war of our independence. And this is the condition of the party whose arms have been every where and constantly victorious!

How did we unhappily get involved in this war? It was predicted as the consequence of the annexation of Texas to the United States.[2] If we had not Texas, we should have no war. The people were told that if that event happened, war would ensue. They were told that the war between Texas and Mexico had not been terminated by a treaty of peace; that Mexico still claimed Texas as a revolted province: and that, if we received Texas in our Union, we took along with her, the war existing between her and Mexico. And the Minister of Mexico [Juan N. Almonte] formally announced to the Government at Washington, that his nation would consider the annexation of Texas to the United States as producing a state of war. But all this was denied by the partizans of annexation. They insisted we should have no war, and even imputed to those who foretold it, sinister motives for their groundless prediction.

But, notwithstanding a state of virtual war necessarily resulted from the fact of annexation of one of the belligerents to the United States, actual hostilities might have been probably averted by prudence, moderation and wise statesmanship. If General [Zachary] Taylor had been permitted to remain, where his own good sense prompted him to believe he ought to remain, at the point of Corpus Christi; and, if a negotiation had been opened with Mexico, in a true spirit of amity and conciliation, war possibly might have been prevented. But, instead of this pacific and moderate course, whilst Mr. [John] Slidell was bending [*sic*, wending] his way to Mexico with his diplomatic credentials, General Taylor was ordered to transport his cannon, and to plant them, in a warlike attitude, opposite to Matamoras, on the east bank of the Rio Bravo [Rio Grande];[3] within the very disputed territory, the adjustment of which was to be the object of Mr. Slidell's mission. What else could have transpired but a conflict of arms?

Thus the war commenced, and the President [James K. Polk] after having produced it, appealed to Congress. A bill was proposed to raise 50,000 volunteers, and in order to commit all who should vote for it, a preamble was inserted falsely attributing the commencement of the war to the act of Mexico. I have no doubt of the patriotic motives of those who, after struggling to divest the bill of that flagrant error, found themselves constrained to vote for it.[4] But I must say that no earthly consideration would have ever tempted or provoked me to vote for a bill, with a palpable falsehood stamped on its face. Almost idolizing truth, as I do, I never, never, could have voted for that bill.

The exceptionable conduct of the Federal party, during that last British War [of 1812], has excited an influence in the prosecution of the present war, and prevented a just discrimination between the two wars. That was a war of National defence, required for the vindication of the National rights and honor, and demanded by the indignant voice of the People. President [James] Madison himself, I know, at first, reluctantly and with great doubt and hesitation, brought himself to the conviction that it ought to be declared.[5] A leading, and perhaps the most influential member of his Cabinet, (Mr. [Albert] Gallatin,) was, up to the time of its declaration, opposed to it.[6] But nothing could withstand the irresistible force of public sentiment. It was a just war, and its great object, as announced at the time, was "Free Trade and Sailors Rights," against the intolerable and oppressive acts of British power on the ocean. The justice of the war, far from being denied or controverted, was admitted by the Federal party, which only questioned it on considerations of policy. Being deliberately and constitutionally declared, it was, I think, their duty to have given to it their hearty co-operation. But the mass of them did not. They continued to oppose and thwart it, to discourage loans and enlistments, to deny the power of the General Government to march the militia beyond our limits, and to hold a Hartford Convention,[7] which, whatever were its real objects, bore the aspect of seeking a dissolution of the Union itself. They lost and justly lost the public confidence.—But has not an apprehension of a similar fate, in a state of case widely different, repressed a fearless expression of their real sentiments in some of our public men?

How totally variant is the present war! This is no war of defence, but one unnecessary and of offensive aggression. It is Mexico that is defending her fire-sides, her castles and her altars, not we. And how different also is the conduct of the whig party of the present day from that of the major part of the federal party during the war of 1812! Far from interposing any obstacles to the prosecution of the war, if the Whigs in office are reproachable at all, it is for having lent too ready a facility to it, without careful examination into the objects of the war. And, out of office, who have rushed to the prosecution of the war with more ardor and alacrity than the Whigs? Whose hearts have bled more freely than those of the Whigs?—Who have more occasion to mourn the loss of sons, husbands, brothers, fathers, than whig parents, whig wives and whig brothers, in this deadly and unprofitable strife?

But the havoc of war is in progress, and the no less deplorable havoc of an inhospitable and pestilential climate. Without indulging in an unnecessary retrospect and useless reproaches on the past, all hearts and heads should unite in the patriotic endeavor to bring it to a satisfactory close. Is there no way that this can be done? Must we blindly continue the conflict, without any visible object, or any prospect of a definite termination?—This is the important subject upon which I desire to consult and to commune with you. Who, in this free government is, to decide upon the objects of a War, at its commencement, or at any time during its existence? Does the power belong to the Nation, to the collective wisdom of the Nation in Congress assembled, or is it vested solely in a single functionary of the government?

A declaration of war is the highest and most awful exercise of sovereignty. The Convention, which framed our federal constitution, had learned from the pages of history that it had been often and greatly abused. It had seen that war had often been commenced upon the most trifling pretexts; that it had been frequently waged to establish or exclude a dynasty; to snatch a crown from the head of one potentate and place it upon the head of another; that it had been often prosecuted to promote alien and other interests than those of the nation whose chief had proclaimed it, as in the case of English wars for Hanoverian interest; and, in short, that such a vast and tremendous power ought not to be confided to the perilous exercise of one single man. The Convention, therefore, resolved to guard the war-making power against those great abuses, of which in the hands of a monarch it was so susceptible. And the security, against those abuses which its wisdom devised, was to vest the war-making power in the Congress of the United States, being the immediate representatives of the people and the States. So apprehensive and jealous was the Convention of its abuse in any other hands, that it interdicted the exercise of the power to any State in the Union, without the consent of Congress. Congress, then, in our system of government, is the sole depository of that tremendous power.—The Constitution provides that Congress shall have power to declare war, and grant letters of marque and reprisal, to make rules concerning captures on land and water, to raise and support armies, to provide and maintain a navy, and to make rules for the government of the land and naval forces. Thus we perceive that the principal power, in regard to war, with all it ancillary attendants, is granted to Congress. Whenever called upon to determine upon the solemn question of peace or war, Congress must consider and deliberate and decide upon the motives, objects and causes of the war. And, if a war be commenced without any previous declaration of its objects, as in the case of the existing war with Mexico, Congress must necessarily possess the authority, at any time, to declare for what purposes it shall be further prosecuted. If we suppose Congress does not possess the controlling authority attributed to it; if it be contended that a war having been once commenced, the President of the United States may direct it to the accomplishment of any objects he pleases, without consulting and without any regard to the will of Congress, the Convention will have utterly failed in guarding the nation against the abuses and ambition of a single individual. Either Congress, or the President, must have the right of determining upon the objects for which a war shall be prosecuted. There is no other alternative. If the President possess it and may prosecute it for objects against the will of Congress, where is the difference between our free government and that of any other nation which may be governed by an absolute Czar, Emperor, or King?

Congress may omit, as it has omitted in the present war, to proclaim the objects for which it was commenced or has been since prosecuted, and in cases of such omission the President, being charged with the employment and direction of the national force is, necessarily, left to his own judgment to decide upon the objects, to the attainment of which that force shall be applied. But, whenever Congress shall think proper to declare, by some authentic act, for what purposes a war shall be commenced or continued it is the duty of the President to apply the national force to the attainment of those purposes. In the instance of the last war with Great Britain, the act of Congress by which it was declared was preceded by a message of President Madison enumerating the wrongs and injuries of which we complained against Great Britain.[8] That message therefore, and without it the well known objects of the war, which was a war purely of defence, rendered it unnecessary that Congress should particularize, in the act, the specific objects for which it was proclaimed. The whole world knew that it was a war waged for Free Trade and Sailors' Rights.

It may be urged that the President and Senate possess the treaty making power, without any express limitation as to its exercise; that the natural and ordinary termination of a war is by a treaty of peace; and therefore, that the President and Senate must possess the power to decide what stipulations and conditions shall enter into such a treaty. But it is not more true that the President and Senate possess the treaty making power, without limitation, than that Congress possesses the war making power, without restriction. These two powers then ought to be so interpreted as to reconcile the one with the other; and, in expounding the constitution, we ought to keep constantly in view the nature and structure of our free government, and especially the great object of the Convention in taking the war-making power out of the hands of a single man and placing it in the safer custody of the representatives of the whole nation. The desirable reconciliation between the two powers is effected by attributing to Congress the right to declare what shall be the objects of war, and to the President the duty of endeavoring to obtain those objects by the direction of the national force and by diplomacy.

I am broaching no new and speculative theory. The Statute book of the United States is full of examples of prior declarations by Congress of the objects to be attained by negotiations with Foreign Powers, and the archives of the Executive Department furnish abundant evidence of the accomplishment of those objects, or the attempt to accomplish them, by subsequent negotiation. Prior to the declaration of the last war against Great Britain, in all the restrictive measures which Congress adopted, against the two great belligerent Powers of Europe, clauses were inserted in the several acts establishing them, tendering to both or either of the belligerents the abolition of those restrictions if they would repeal their hostile Berlin and Milan decrees and Orders in Council, operating against our commerce and navigation.[9] And these acts of Congress were invariably communicated, through the Executive, by diplomatic notes, to France and Great Britain, as the basis upon which it was proposed to restore friendly intercourse with them. So, after the termination of the war, various acts of Congress were passed, from time to time, offering to Foreign Powers the principle of reciprocity in the commerce and navigation of the United States with them.[10] Out of these acts have sprung a class, and a large class, of treaties (four or five of which were negotiated, whilst I was in the department of State,) commonly called reciprocity treaties concluded under all the Presidents, from Mr. Madison to Mr. [Martin] Van Buren, inclusive. And, with regard to commercial treaties, negotiated without the sanction of prior acts of Congress, where they contained either appropriations or were in conflict with unrepealed statutes, it has been ever held as the republican doctrine from Mr. [John] Jay's treaty[11] down to the present time, that the passage of acts of Congress was necessary to secure the execution of those treaties[.] If in the matter of Foreign Commerce, in respect to which the power vested in Congress to regulate it and the treaty making power may be regarded as concurrent, Congress can previously decide the objects to which negotiation shall be applied, how much stronger is the case of war, the power to declare which is confided *exclusively* to Congress?

I conclude, therefore, Mr. President and Fellow-Citizens, with entire confidence, that Congress has the right either at the beginning or during the prosecution of any war, to decide the objects and purposes for which it was proclaimed, or for which it ought to be continued. And, I think, it is the duty of Congress, by some deliberate and authentic act, to declare for what objects the present war shall be longer prosecuted. I suppose that the President would not hesitate to regulate his conduct by the pronounced will of Congress, and to employ the force and the diplomatic power of the nation to execute that will. But, if the President should decline or refuse to do so, and, in contempt of the supreme authority of Congress, should persevere in waging the war, for other objects than those proclaimed by Congress, then it would be the imperative duty of that body to vindicate its authority, by the most stringent, and effectual, and appropriate measures. And, if, on the contrary, the enemy should refuse to conclude a treaty, containing stipulations securing the objects, designated by Congress, it would become the duty of the whole government to prosecute the war, with all the national energy, until those objects were obtained by a treaty of peace. There can be no insuperable difficulty in Congress making such an authoritative declaration. Let it resolve, simply, that the war shall, or shall not, be a war of conquest; and, if a war of conquest, what is to be conquered. Should a resolution pass, disclaiming the design of conquest, peace would follow, in less than sixty days, if the President would conform to his constitutional duty.

Here, fellow Citizens, I might pause, having indicated a mode by which the nation, through its accredited and legitimate representatives in Congress, can announce for what purposes and objects this war shall be longer prosecuted, and can thus let the whole people of the United States know for what end their blood is to be further shed and their treasure further expended, instead of the knowledge of it being locked up and concealed in the bosom of one man. We should no longer perceive the objects of the war, varying, from time to time, according to the changing opinions of the Chief Magistrate, charged with its prosecution.—But I do not think it right to stop here. It is the privilege of the people, in their primitive assemblies, and of every private man, however humble, to express an opinion in regard to the purposes for which the war should be continued; and such an expression will receive just so much consideration and consequence as it is entitled to, and no more.

Shall this war be prosecuted for the purpose of conquering and annexing Mexico, in all its boundless extent, to the United States?

I will not attribute to the President of the United States any such design; but I confess that I have been shocked and alarmed by manifestations of it in various quarters[.] Of all the dangers and misfortunes which could befall this nation, I should regard that of its becoming a warlike and conquering power the most direful and fatal. History tells the mournful tale of conquering nations and conquerors. The three most celebrated conquerors, in the civilized world, were Alexander, Caesar and Napoleon. The first, after overrunning a large portion of Asia, and sighing and lamenting that there were no more worlds to subdue, met a premature and ignoble death. His Lieutenants quarrelled and warred with each other, as to the spoils of his victories, and finally lost them all. Caesar, after conquering Gaul, returned, with his triumphant legions to Rome, passed the Rubicon, won the battle of Pharsalia, trampled upon the liberties of his country, and expired by the patriot hand of Brutus. But Rome ceased to be free. War and conquest had enervated and corrupted the masses. The spirit of true liberty was extinguished, and a long line of Emperors succeeded, some of whom were the most execrable monsters that ever existed in human form. And that most extraordinary man [Napoleon], perhaps, in all history, after subjugating all continental Europe, occupying almost all its Capitals, seriously threatening, according to Mr. [Adolphe] Thiers, proud Albion itself, and decking the brow of various members of his family, with crowns torn from the heads of other monarchs, lived to behold his own dear France itself in the possession of his enemies, and was made himself a wretched captive, and far removed from country, family, and friends, breathed his last on the distant and inhospitable rock of St Helena. The Alps and the Rhine had been claimed as the natural boundaries of France, but even these could not be secured in the treaties to which she was reduced to submit. Do you believe that the people of Macedon or Greece, of Rome, or France, were benefitted, individually or collectively, by the triumphs of their great Captains? Their sad lot was immense sacrifice of life, heavy and intolerable burdens, and the ultimate loss of liberty itself.

That the power of the United States is competent to the conquest of Mexico, is quite probable. But it could not be achieved without frightful carnage, dreadful sacrifices of human life, and the creation of an onerous national debt; nor could it be completely effected, in all probability, until after the lapse of many years. It would be necessary to occupy all its strongholds, to disarm its inhabitants, and to keep them in constant fear and subjection. To consummate the work, I presume that standing armies, not less than a hundred thousand men, would be necessary, to be kept perhaps always in the bosom of their country. These standing armies, revelling in a foreign land, and accustomed to trample upon the liberties of a foreign people, at some distant day, might be fit and ready instruments, under the lead of some daring and unprincipled chieftain, to return to their country and prostrate the public liberty.

Supposing the conquest to be once made, what is to be done with it? Is it to be governed, like Roman Provinces, by Proconsuls? Would it be compatible with the genius, character, and safety of our free institutions, to keep such a great country as Mexico, with a population of not less that nine millions, in a state of constant military subjection?

Shall it be annexed to the United States: Does any considerate man believe it possible that two such immense countries, with territories of nearly equal extent, with populations so incongruous, so different in race, in language, in religion and in laws, could be blended together in one harmonious mass, and happily governed by one common authority? Murmurs, discontent, insurrections, rebellion, would inevitably ensue, until the incompatible parts would be broken asunder, and possibly, in the frightful struggle, our present glorious Union itself would be dissevered or dissolved. We ought not to forget the warning voice of all history, which teaches the difficulty of combining and consolidating together, conquering and conquered nations. After the lapse of eight hundred years, during which the Moors held their conquest of Spain, the indomitable courage, perseverance and obstinacy of the Spanish race finally triumphed, and expelled the African invaders from the Peninsula. And, even within our own time, the colossal power of Napoleon, when at its loftiest height, was incompetent to subdue and subjugate the proud Castilian[.] And here in our own neighborhood, Lower Canada, which near one hundred years ago, after the conclusion of the seven years war, was ceded by France to Great Britain, remains a foreign land in the midst of the British provinces, foreign in feelings and attachment, and foreign in laws, language and [word illeg.] And what has been the fact with poor, gallant, generous and oppressed Ireland? Centuries have passed away, since the overbearing Saxon overrun and subjugated the Emerald Isle. Rivers of Irish blood have flowed, during the long and arduous contest. Insurrection and rebellion have been the order of the day; and yet, up to this time, Ireland remains alien in feeling, affection and sympathy, towards the power which has so long borne her down. Every Irishman hates, with a mortal hatred, his Saxon oppressor. Although there are great territorial differences between the condition of England and Ireland, as compared to that of the United States and Mexico, there are some points of striking resemblance between them. Both the Irish and the Mexicans are probably of the same Celtic race. Both the English and the Americans are of the same Saxon origin. The Catholic religion predominates in both the former, the Protestant among both the latter. Religion has been the fruitful cause of dissatisfaction and discontent between the Irish and the English nations[.] Is there not reason to apprehend that it would become so between the people of the United States and those of Mexico, if they were united together? Why should we seek to interfere with them, in their mode of worship of a common Saviour? We believe that they are wrong, especially in the exclusive character of their faith, and that we are right. They think that they are right and we wrong. What other rule can there be than to leave the followers of each religion to their own solemn convictions of conscientious duty towards God? Who, but the great Arbiter of the Universe, can judge in such a question? For my own part, I sincerely believe and hope, that those, who belong to all the departments of the great church of Christ, if, in truth and purity, they conform to the doctrines which they profess, will ultimately secure an abode in those regions of bliss, which all aim finally to reach. I think that there is no potentate in Europe, whatever his religion may be, more enlightened or at this moment so interesting as the liberal head of the Papal See.[12]

But I suppose it to be impossible that those who favor, if there be any who favor the annexation of Mexico to the United States, can think that it ought to be perpetually governed by military sway. Certainly no votary of human liberty could deem it right that a violation should be perpetrated of the great principles of our own revolution, according to which, laws ought not to be enacted and taxes ought not to be levied, without representation on the part of those who are to obey the one, and pay the other. Then, Mexico is to participate in our councils and equally share in our legislation and government. But, suppose she would not voluntarily choose representatives to the national Congress, is our soldiery to follow the electors to the ballot-box, and by force to compel them, at the point of the bayonet, to deposit their ballots? And how are the nine millions of Mexican people to be represented in the Congress of the United States of America and the Congress of the United States of the Republic of Mexico combined? Is every Mexican, without regard to color or caste, per capitum, to exercise the elective franchise? How is the quota of representation between the two Republics, to be fixed? Where is their Seat of Common Government to be established? And who can foresee or foretell, if Mexico, voluntarily or by force, were to share in the common government what would be the consequences to her or to us? Unprepared, as I fear her population yet is, for the practical enjoyment of self government, and of habits, customs, languages, laws and religion, so totally different from our own, we should present the revolting spectacle of a confused, distracted, and motley government. We should have a Mexican Party, a Pacific Ocean Party, an Atlantic Party in addition to the other Parties, which exist, or with which we are threatened, each striving to execute its own particular views and purposes, and reproaching the others with thwarting and disappointing them. The Mexican representation, in Congress, would probably form a separate and impenetrable corps, always ready to throw itself into the scale of any other party, to advance and promote Mexican interests. Such a state of things could not long endure. Those, whom

God and Geography have pronounced should live asunder, could never be permanently and harmoniously united together.

Do we want for our own happiness or greatness the addition of Mexico to the the existing Union of our States? If our population was too dense for our territory, and there was a difficulty in obtaining honorably the means of subsistence, there might be some excuse for an attempt to enlarge our dominions. But we have no such apology. We have already, in our glorious country, a vast and almost boundless territory. Beginning at the North, in the frozen regions of the British Provinces, it stretches thousands of miles along the coasts of the Atlantic Ocean and the Mexican Gulf, until it almost reaches the Tropics. It extends to the Pacific Ocean, borders on those great inland seas, the Lakes, which separate us from the possessions of Great Britain, and it embraces the great father of rivers, from its uppermost source to the Belize, and the still longer Missouri, from its mouth to the gorges of the Rocky Mountains. It comprehends the greatest variety of the richest soils, capable of almost all the productions of the earth, except tea and coffee and the spices, and it includes every variety of climate, which the heart could wish or desire. We have more than ten thousand millions of acres of waste and unsettled lands, enough for the subsistence of ten or twenty times our present population. Ought we not to be satisfied with such a country? Ought we not to be profoundly thankful to the Giver of all good things for such a vast and bountiful land? Is it not the height of ingratitude to Him to seek, by war and conquest, indulging in a spirit of rapacity, to acquire other lands, the homes and habitations of a large portion of his common children? If we pursue the object of such a conquest, besides mortgaging the revenue and resources of this country for ages to come, in the form of an onerous national debt, we should have greatly to augment that debt, by an assumption of the sixty or seventy millions of the national debt of Mexico. For I take it that nothing is more certain than that, if we obtain, voluntarily or by conquest, a foreign nation we acquire it with all the incumbrances attached to it. In my humble opinion, we are now bound, in honor and morality, to pay the just debt of Texas. And we should be equally bound, by the same obligations, to pay the debt of Mexico, if it were annexed to the United States.

Of all the possessions which appertain to man, in his collective or individual condition, none should be preserved and cherished, with more sedulous and unremitting care, than that of an unsullied character. It is impossible to estimate it too highly, in society, when attached to an individual, nor can it be exaggerated or too greatly magnified in a nation. Those who lose or are indifferent to it become just objects of scorn and contempt. Of all the abominable transactions, which sully the pages of history none exceed in enormity that of the dismemberment and partition of Poland, by the three great Continental Powers of Russia, Austria, and Prussia.[13]—Ages may pass away, and centuries roll around, but as long as human records endure all mankind will unite in execrating the rapacious and detestable deed. That was accomplished by overwhelming force, and the unfortunate existence of fatal dissensions and divisions in the bosom of Poland.—Let us avoid affixing to our name and national character a similar, if not worse, stigma. I am afraid that we do not now stand well in the opinion of other parts of christendom. Repudiation has brought upon us much reproach. All the nations, I apprehend, look upon us, in the prosecution of the present war, as being actuated by a spirit of rapacity, and an inordinate desire for territorial aggrandizement. Let us not forfeit altogether their good opinions. Let us command their applause by a noble exercise of forbearance and justice. In the elevated station which we hold, we can safely afford to practice the Godlike virtues of moderation and magnanimity. The long series of glorious triumphs, achieved by our gallant commanders and their brave armies, unattended by a single reverse, justify us, without the least danger of tarnishing the national honor, in disinterestedly holding out the olive branch of peace. We do not want the mines, the mountains, the morasses, and the sterile lands of Mexico. To her the loss of them would be humiliating, and be a perpetual source of regret and mortification. To us they might prove a fatal acquisition, producing distraction, dissension, division, possibly disunion. Let, therefore, the integrity of the national existence and national territory of Mexico remain undisturbed. For one, I desire to see no part of her territory torn from her by war. Some of our people have placed their hearts upon the acquisition of the Bay of San Francisco in Upper California.[14] To us, as a great maritime Power, it might prove to be of advantage hereafter in respect to our commercial and navigating interests. To Mexico, which can never be a great maritime Power, it can never be of much advantage. If we can obtain it by fair purchase with a just equivalent, I should be happy to see it so acquired. As, whenever the war ceases, Mexico ought to [be] required to pay the debt due our citizens, perhaps an equivalent for that Bay may be found in that debt, our Government assuming to pay to our citizens whatever portion of it may be applied to that object. But it should form no motive in the prosecution of the war, which I would not continue a solitary hour for the sake of that harbor.

But what, it will be asked, shall we make peace without any indemnity for the expences of the war? If the published documents in relation to the late negotiations between Mr [Nicholas] Trist and the Mexican Commissioners be true, and I have not seen them any where contradicted, the Executive properly waived any demand of indemnity for the expences of the war.[15] And the rupture of that negotiation was produced, by our Government insisting upon a cessation from Mexico, of the strip of mostly barren land between the Nueces and the Rio Bravo [Rio Grande] and New Mexico, which Mexico refused to make. So that we are now fighting, if not for the conquest of all Mexico, as intimated in some quarters, for that narrow strip and for the barren Provi[n]ce of New Mexico, with its few miserable mines. We bought all the Province of Louisiana for fifteen millions of dollars, and it is, in my opinion, worth more than all Mexico together. We bought Florida for five millions of dollars, and a hard bargain it was, since, besides that sum, we gave up the boundary of the Rio Bravo, to which I think we were entitled, as the Western limit of the Province of Louisiana, and were restricted to that of the Sabine.[16] And we are now, if not seeking the conquest of all Mexico, to continue this war indefinitely for the inconsiderable objects to which I have just referred.

But, it will be repeated, are we to have no indemnity for the expenses of this war? Mexico is utterly unable to make us any pecuniary indemnity, if the justice of the war on our part entitled us to demand it. Her country has been laid waste, her cities burned or occupied by our troops, her means so exhausted that she is unable to pay even her own armies. And every day's prosecution of the war, whilst it would augment the amount of our indemnity, would lessen the ability of Mexico to pay it.—We have seen, however, that there is another form in which we are to demand indemnity. It is to be territorial indemnity! I hope, for reasons already stated that that fire-brand will not be brought into our country.

Among the resolutions, which it is my intention to present for your consideration, at the conclusion of this address, one proposes, in your behalf and mine, to disavow, in the most positive manner, any desire, on our part, to acquire any foreign territory whatever, for the purpose of introducing slavery into it. I do not know that any citizen of the United States entertains such a wish. But such a motive has been often imputed to the slave States, and I therefore think it necessary to notice it on this occasion. My opinions on the subject of slavery are well known. They have the merit, if it be one, of consistency, uniformity, and long duration. I have ever regarded slavery as a great evil, a wrong, for the present, I fear, an irremediable wrong to its unfortunate victims. I should rejoice if not a single slave breathed the air or was within the limits of our country. But here they are, to be dealt with as well as we can, with a due consideration of all circumstances affecting the security, safety and happiness of both races. Every State has the supreme, uncontrolled and exclusive power to decide for itself whether slavery shall cease or continue within its limits, without any exterior intervention from any quarter. In States, where the slaves outnumber the whites, as is the case with several, the blacks could not be emancipated and invested with all the rights of freemen, without becoming the governing race in those States. Collisions and conflicts, between the two races, would be inevitable, and, after shocking scenes of rapine and carnage, the extinction or expulsion of the blacks would certainly take place. In the State of Kentucky, near fifty years ago, I thought the proportion of slaves, in comparison with the whites, was so inconsiderable that we might safely adopt a system of gradual emancipation that would ultimately eradicate this evil in our State.[17] That system was totally different from the immediate abolition of slavery for which the party of the Abolitionists of the present day contend. Whether they have intended it or not, it is my calm and deliberate belief, that they have done incalculable mischief even to the very cause which they have espoused, to say nothing of the discord which has been produced between different parts of the Union. According to the system, we attempted, near the close of the last century, all slaves in being were to remain such, but, all who might be born subsequent to a specified day, were to become free at the age of twenty-eight, and, during their service, were to be taught to read, write, and cypher. Thus, instead of being thrown upon the community, ignorant and unprepared, as would be the case by immediate emancipation, they would have entered upon the possession of their freedom, capable, in some degree, of enjoying it.—After a hard struggle, the system was defeated, and I regret it extremely, as, if it had been then adopted, our State would be now nearly rid of that reproach.

Since the epoch, a scheme of unmixed benevolence has sprung up, which, if it had existed at that time, would have obviated one of the greatest objections which was made to gradual emancipation, which was the continuance of the emancipated slaves to abide among us. That scheme is the American Colonization Society.[18] About twenty-eight years ago, a few individuals, myself among them, met together in the city of Washington, and laid the foundations of that society. It has gone on, amidst extraordinary difficulties and trials, sustaining itself almost entirely, by spontaneous and voluntary contributions, from individual benevolence, without scarcely any aid from Government. The Colonies, planted under its auspices, are now well established communities, with churches, schools and other institutions appertaining to the civilized state. They have made successful war in repelling attacks and invasions by their barbarous and savage neighbors.[19] They have made treaties, annexed territories to their dominion, and are blessed with a free representative Government. I recently read a message, from one of the their Governors to their Legislature, which, in point of composition, and in careful attention to the public affairs of their Republic, would compare advantageously to the messages of the Governors of our own States. I am not very superstitious, but I do solemnly believe that these Colonies are blest with the smiles of Providence; and, if we may dare attempt penetrating the veil, by which He conceals his allwise dispensations from mortal eyes, that he designs that Africa shall be the refuge and the home of the descendants of its sons and daughters, torn and dragged from their native land, by lawless violence.

It is a philanthronic and consoling reflection that the moral and physical condition of the African race in the United States, even in a State of slavery, is far better than it would have been if their ancestors had never been brought from their native land.—And if it should be the decree of the Great Ruler of the Universe that their descendants shall be made instruments in His hands in the establishment of Civilization and the Christian Religion throughout Africa, our regrets on account of the original wrong, will be greatly mitigated.

It may be argued, that, in admitting the injustice of slavery, I admit the necessity of an instantaneous reparation of that injustice. Unfortunately, however, it is not always safe, practicable or possible, in the great movements of States and public affairs of nations, to remedy or repair the infliction of previous injustice. In the inception of it, we may oppose and denounce it, by our most strenuous exertions, but, after its consummation, there is often no other alternative left us but to deplore its perpetration, and to acquiesce as the only alternative, in its existence, as a less evil that the frightful consequences which might ensue from the vain endeavor to repair it. Slavery is one of those unfortunate instances. The evil of it was inflicted upon us, by the parent country of Great Britain, against all the entreaties and remonstrances of the colonies. And here it is among [several words illeg.] us, and we must dispose of it, as best we can under all the circumstances which surround us. It continued, by the importation of slaves from Africa, in spite of Colonial resistance, for a period of more than a century and a half, and it may require an equal or longer lapse of time before our country is entirely rid of the evil.—And, in the meantime, moderation, prudence and discretion among ourselves, and the blessings of Providence may be all necessary to accomplish our ultimate deliverance from it. Examples of similar infliction of irreparable national evil and injustice might be multiplied to an indefinite extent. The case of the annexation of Texas to the United States is a recent and obvious one where, if it were wrong, it cannot now be repaired. Texas is now an integral part of our Union, with its own voluntary consent. Many of us opposed the annexation with honest zeal and most earnest exertions. But who would now think of perpetrating the folly of casting Texas out of the confederacy and throwing her back upon her own independence, or into the arms of Mexico? Who would now seek to divorce her from this Union? The Creeks and the Cherokee Indians were, by the most exceptionable means, driven from their country, and transported beyond the Mississippi river. Their lands have been fairly purchased and occupied by inhabitants of Georgia, Alabama, Mississippi and Tennessee. Who would now conceive of the flagrant injustice of expelling those inhabitants and restoring the Indian country to the Cherokees and the Creeks, under color of repairing original injustice?[20] During the war of our revolution, millions of paper money were issued by our ancestors, as the only currency with which they could achieve our liberties and independence.—Thousands and hundreds of thousands of families were stripped of their homes and their all and brought to ruin, by giving credit and confidence to that spurious currency. Stern necessity has prevented the reparation of that great national injustice.

But I forbear, I will no longer trespass upon your patience or further tax my own voice, impaired by a speech of more than three hours duration, which professional duty required me to make only a few days ago.[21] If I have been at all successful in the exposition of the views and opinions which I entertain I have shown—

1st. That the present war was brought about by the annexation of Texas and the subsequent order of the President, without the previous consent and authority of Congress.

2d. That the President, being unenlightened and uninstructed, by any public declaration of Congress, as to objects for which it ought to be prosecuted, in the conduct of it is, necessarily, left to his own sense of what the national interests and honor may require.

3d. That the whole war making power of the nation, as to motives, causes and objects, is confided by the constitution to the discretion and judgment of Congress.

4th. That it is, therefore, the right of Congress, at the commencement or during the progress of any war, to declare for what objects and purposes the war ought to be waged and prosecuted.

5th. That it is the right and duty of Congress to announce to the nation for what objects the present war shall be longer continued; that it is the duty of the President, in the exercise of all his official functions, to conform to and carry out this declared will of Congress, by the exercise, if necessary, of all the high powers with which he is clothed; and that, if he fail or refuse to do so, it becomes the imperative duty of Congress to arrest the further progress of the war by the most effectual means in its power.

Let Congress announce to the nation the objects for which this war shall be further protracted and public suspense and public inquietude will no longer remain. If it is to be a war of conquest of all, or any part of Mexico, let the people know it, and they will be no longer agitated by a dark and uncertain future. But, although I might have foreborne to express any opinion whatever as to purposes and objects for which the war should be continued, I have not thought proper to conceal my opinions, whether worth any thing or not, from the public examination. Accordingly I have stated

6th. That it seems to me that it is the duty of our country, as well on the score of moderation and magnanimity, as with the view of avoiding discord and discontent at home, to abstain from seeking to conquer and annex to the United States Mexico or any part of it; and, especially, to disabuse the public mind in any quarter of the Union of the impression, if it any where exists, that a desire for such a conquest, is cherished for the purpose of propagating or extending slavery.

I have embodied, Mr. President and fellow-citizens, the sentiments and opinions which I have endeavored to explain and enforce in a series of resolutions which I beg now to submit to your consideration and judgment. They are the following:

1. *Resolved*, as the opinion of this meeting, that the primary cause of the present unhappy war, existing between the United States of America, and the United States of the Republic of Mexico, was the annexation of Texas to the former; and that the immediate occasion of hostilities between the two republics arose out of the order of the President of the United States for the removal of the army under the command of General Taylor, from its position at Corpus Christi to a point opposite to Matamoras, on the East bank of the Rio Bravo, within territory claimed by both Republics, but then under the jurisdiction of that of Mexico, and inhabited by its citizens; and that the order of the President for the removal of the army to that point, was improvident and unconstitutional, it being without the concurrence of Congress, or even any consultation with it, although it was in session: but that Congress having, by subsequent acts, recognized the war thus brought into existence without its previous authority or consent, the prosecution of it became thereby National.

2. *Resolved*, That, in the absence of any formal and public declaration by Congress, of the objects for which the war ought to be prosecuted, the President of the United States, as Chief Magistrate, and as Commander in Chief of the Army and Navy of the United States, is left to the guidance of his own judgment to prosecute it for such purposes and objects as he may deem the honor and interest of the nation to require.

3. *Resolved*, That, by the Constitution of the United States, Congress, being invested with the power to declare war, and grant letters of marque and reprizal, to make rules concerning captures on land and water, to raise and support armies, to provide and maintain a navy, and to make rules for the government of the land and naval forces, has the full and complete war making power of the United States; and, so possessing it, has a right to determine upon the motives, causes and objects of any war, when it commences, or at any time during the progress of its existence[.]

4. *Resolved*, as the further opinion of this meeting, that it is the right and duty of Congress to declare, by some authentic act, for what purposes and objects the existing war ought to be further prosecuted; that it is the duty of the President, in his official conduct, to conform to such a declaration of Congress; and that, if, after such declaration, the President should decline or refuse to endeavor, by all the means, civil, diplomatic, and military, in his power, to execute the announced will of Congress, and, in defiance of its authority, should continue to prosecute the war for purposes and objects other than those declared by that body, it would become the right and duty of Congress to adopt the most efficacious measures to arrest the further progress of the war, taking care to make ample provision for the honor, the

safety and security of our armies in Mexico, in every contingency. And, if Mexico should decline or refuse to conclude a treaty with us, stipulating for the purposes and objects so declared by Congress, it would be the duty of the Government to prosecute the war with the utmost vigor, until they were attained by a treaty of peace.

5. *Resolved*, That we view with serious alarm, and are utterly opposed to any purpose of annexing Mexico to the United States, in any mode, and especially by conquest; that we believe the two nations could not be happily governed by one common authority, owing to their great difference of race, law, language and religion, and the vast extent of their respective territories, and large amount of their respective populations; that such a union, against the consent of the exasperated Mexican people, could only be effected and preserved by large standing armies, and the constant application of military force—in other words, by despotic sway exercised over the Mexican people, in the first instance, but which, there would be just cause to apprehend, might, in process of time, be extended over the people of the United States. That we deprecate, therefore, such a union, as wholly incompatible with the genius of our Government, and with the character of free and liberal institutions; and we anxiously hope that each nation may be left in the undisturbed possession of its own laws, language, cherished religion and territory, to pursue its own happiness, according to what it may deem best for itself.

6. *Resolved*, That, considering the series of splendid and brilliant victories achieved by our brave armies and their gallant commanders, during the war with Mexico, unattended by a single reverse, The United States, without any danger of their honor suffering the slightest tarnish, can practice the virtues of moderation and magnanimity towards their discomfited foe. We have no desire for the dismemberment of the United States of the Republic of Mexico, but wish only a just and proper fixation of the limits of Texas.

7. *Resolved*, That we do, positively and emphatically, disclaim and disavow any wish or desire, on our part, to acquire any foreign territory whatever, for the purpose of propagating slavery, or of introducing slaves from the United States, into such foreign territory.

8. *Resolved*, That we invite our fellow citizens of the United States, who are anxious for the restoration of the blessings of peace, or, if the existing war shall continue to be prosecuted, are desirous that its purpose and objects shall be defined and known; who are anxious to avert present and future perils and dangers, with which it may be fraught; and who are also anxious to produce contentment and satisfaction at home, and to elevate the national character abroad, to assemble together in their respective communities, and to express their views, feelings, and opinions.

Copy. Printed in the Lexington *Observer & Kentucky Reporter*, Nov. 20, 1847; also printed in Colton, *Clay Correspondence*, 3:60-69; resolutions also in DLC-Martin Van Buren Papers (DNA, M212, R22). 1. The number killed in action in the Mexican War was 1,192, while 529 died of wounds and 11,155 from disease and miscellaneous causes, for a total of 12,876. Bauer, *The Mexican War*, 397. 2. Clay to Crittenden, Feb. 15, 1844. 3. For the circumstances surrounding John Slidell's mission to Mexico and the movement of Taylor's army to the Rio Grande, see Rives, *The United States and Mexico*, 2:58-59, 64-73, 78-80, 128-30; Bauer, *The Mexican War*, 23-29; Singletary, *The Mexican War*, 150-51. 4. The bill, which was brought up on May 11, 1846, following the president's war message, stated in its preamble: "Whereas by the act of the republic of Mexico a state of war exists. . . . " Combining the declaration of war with an appropriation of money to support Taylor and his men as well as to pay volunteers to assist them, the bill posed a dilemma for the Whigs who had to choose between supporting the preamble or deserting the men in the field. It passed the House by a vote of 174 to 14, with

20 abstentions. In the Senate it passed with 40 yeas, 2 nays, and 3 abstentions. Bauer, *The Mexican War*, 68-69; U.S.H. of Reps., *Journal*, 29 Cong., 1 Sess., 307, 791-97, 805-6. 5. For Madison's views on declaring war with Great Britain, see Irving Brant, *James Madison, The President, 1809-1812* (New York, 1956), 42-43, 112, 356-57, 363, 406, 479. 6. For Gallatin's reluctant support of the war with Britain, see Raymond Walters, Jr., *Albert Gallatin, Jeffersonian Financier and Diplomat* (New York, 1957), 247-50. 7. See 2:222. 8. Richardson, *MPP*, 1:499-505. 9. See 1:280, 388-89, 526-27, 637, 738-47; 2:297. 10. See 4:247, 680-81, 941; 5:29, 71, 121, 143, 466-67, 469-70, 900, 909-12. 11. See Subject Index 7:724, Great Britain: Jay's Treaty. 12. Pope Pius IX, who became head of the Catholic Church in 1846, instituted a number of liberal reforms. Langer, *Encyclopedia of World History*, 701, 712-13. 13. For the various partitions of Poland, see *ibid*., 512, 517-19, 1037. 14. For the growing U.S. interest in acquiring California, see Rives, *The United States and Mexico*, 2:45-52, 164-94; Singletary, *The Mexican War*, 55-57, 63-70, 149; Graebner, *Empire on the Pacific, passim*. 15. For the Trist mission and the Treaty of Guadalupe Hidalgo which ended the war, see Clay to Beatty, April 29, 1847. 16. For the Louisiana Purchase, see Subject Index 7:742; for the Adams-Onis Treaty, see Subject Index 7:764. 17. See 1:3-8. 18. See 2:383-85; 6:84, 95. 19. The colony of Liberia had begun during the 1820s to expand its territory, annexing adjoining areas whenever possible and fighting with the "slave factories" along the coast. Staudenraus, *The African Colonization Movement*, 150-57, 166, 240-42. 20. See Indians: U.S. relations with, in Subject Index 7:735; also index entries—Georgia and Indians—in 8:920, 923. 21. Clay had been employed by Milton N. Singleton, administrator of the will of Jaconias Singleton. By an administrator's bond, dated Oct. 14, 1847, M.N. Singleton promised to pay Clay a $250 retainer that day and $750 if the will was established. AD, in Clay's hand, signed by Singleton. DLC-TJC (DNA, M212, R19). Clay and George Robertson argued in favor of the will in Anderson Circuit Court, while Thomas F. Marshall and John J. Crittenden represented a son attempting to break the will. The case was decided in favor of upholding the will. Frankfort *Commonwealth*, Nov. 23, 1847.

From Robert T.P. Allen, Kentucky Military Institute, Frankfort, Ky., November 15, 1847. Encloses two receipts for "One hundred dollars, on acct. of education of Henry Hart Clay" and for "two hundred dollars, on Acct. of education of the two sons of Jas. Erwin Esq—." Notes that "The boys are in good health, and are every thing in regard to attention to duty that could be desired of them." ADS. DLC-TJC (DNA, M212, R19).

For Allen, an 1834 West Point graduate, a clergyman, and superintendent of Kentucky Military Institute, see USMA, *Register*, 186. KMI, located near Frankfort, Ky., was founded by Allen in 1845 and was chartered by the state in 1847. Federal Writers Project, The American Series, *Military History of Kentucky* (Frankfort, Ky., 1939), 116.

Henry Hart Clay was apparently Henry Clay, Jr.'s son—referred to in this volume as Henry Clay, III, to differentiate him from others with the same name—although he generally did not use a middle name. The two Erwin boys were probably Andrew Eugene (b. 1829) and Charles Edward (b. 1835).

To John J. Crittenden, Frankfort, Ky., November 18, 1847. Writes that "I ought to have shewn or sent to you a letter I lately recd. from Mr. J[oseph]. L. White of N.Y.; but my late great labors have led to a neglect of my correspondence, and I can not now lay my hands upon it." Relates, however, that the letter "breathes nothing but the most friendly sentiments towards you. My being out of the way (and that bad preference, it seems, he will cherish) *you* are his next choice." Reports that he has "finished the draught of my Speech [Speech in Lexington, November 13, 1847], and my vanity prompts me to think that I have improved it." ALS. DLC-John J. Crittenden Papers (DNA, M212, R20). Written from Lexington, Ky. Letter from White not found, but see White to Clay, September 4, 1847.

Clay had requested that reporters not take notes on his speech against the Mexican War but rather wait for him to revise and publish it. It first appeared in the Lexington *Observer & Kentucky Reporter* of November 20, 1847, and then subsequently in other papers.

From P.S. Bush, Covington, Ky., November 20, 1847. Encloses a letter [not found] which "has been mislaid for many years" that "I could not find . . . when it might have done some good." Believes it to be "the only written acknowledgement, of your *only colleague* on that eventfull occasion that has not in the same way swept away every charge of 'Bargaining &c.' " Sends also "another letter showing Mr Johnson's address and that he corresponded with me upon that subject." Asks that before the letter is made public "that it be first shown to Mr John T Johnson or his brother H[enry] Johnson Esq (who resides in Lexington) for their acknowledgement of its genuineness." ALS. DLC-HC (DNA, M212, R6).

To HENRY HART CLAY Lexington, November 22, 1847

I received your letter communicating your desire to be taught Music, at the Franklin [Military] Institute.

I accede to your wishes, with pleasure, and request you to ask Mr. [Robert T.P.] Allen to engage a Master to teach you on such instrument as you prefer. I wish you to learn especially the characters of Music, usually taught.

We are all well here, and should be glad to see you, and your Cousins at Xmas.[1] I sent to each of you a copy of a late Speech[2] which I made.

You may shew this letter to Col Allen.

Your grand Mama [Lucretia Hart Clay], and all here unite in love to you and your Cousins . . .

ALS, signature torn. Henry Clay Memorial Foundation, Lexington, Ky. 1. Andrew Eugene and Charles Edward Erwin, who were attending school with him. See Allen to Clay, Nov. 15, 1847. 2. Speech in Lexington, Nov. 13, 1847.

To HORACE GREELEY Lexington, November 22, 1847

You are right in saying, in your favor of the 6h. inst, that you have not been a troublesome correspondent. Far from it, I receive your letters always with pleasure,

You will have seen, in my Speech,[1] and resolutions,[2] of the 13h. inst. how I have committed myself. Will they not represent me as a Western man (I protest against being considered as a *Southern* man) with Northern principles?

I did not touch eo nomini the Wilmot proviso,[3] because in my view of things, it was not necessary to touch it. And sufficient for the day is the evil thereof.

Is there not danger that Conquest of, or in, Mexico may be sought, at the North, to make it *free* territory?

I am not decided to consent to the use of my poor name as a Candidate for the next President.

I will decide next Spring, or earlier if necessary.

Standing thus aloof from that matter, I can speak with a freedom which I would not indulge, if it were settled that I should be a Candidate.

Personally, I am entirely friendly to Mr. [William H.] Seward.[4] I think that, in any Whig Administration, his name ought to stand prominent for high office at home or abroad.

Whether it would be expedient to use it for V.P. depends upon a deliberate calculation of chances. He would bring much Irish & Catholic support to the Whig ticket. Of that I am sure. Would that counterbalance the opposition to him (I regret to learn) from Whigs in N. York, and Whigs at the South? That is the question.

If it should be deemed unadvisable to run him, how would J[ohn]. M. Clayton, [Millard] Fillmore or A[bbott]. Lawrence do?[5]

My speech is received, they tell me, every where heard from in this State, with enthusiastic approbation. There has not been time yet to hear from much beyond it.

Taylorism is every where on the decline with us.[6] It was a burst of enthusiasm, which was of a nature not to last. Many now regret having yielded to it.

You have seen a Circular written by some of my friends.[7] Its candor and truth protect us against any injury from its treacherous publication.

Would it not be well, if my resolutions are approved in N.Y. to hold public meetings to Sanction them?[8]

I write in haste, but hope I have said all that is necessary.

P.S. I wrote in the autumn of 1844 to Genl. P[eter]. S. Smith some letters about Nativism, which he has most honorably returned to me.[9] They did not commit me to that cause, altho' I am glad to repossess them.

About the same time, I wrote to Col. [James Watson] Webb, perhaps to D[avid]. B. Ogden, and to Mr. Frelinghuisen [*sic*, Theodore Frelinghuysen] similar letters.[10] Are they used, or likely to be used, in any event, to my prejudice? There is nothing in them, properly considered, that ought to prejudice me with any body. Had I better take them back?

I mean, if I should be a Candidate, to write no letters, make no speeches, and be mum. I expect, if that contingency should arise, to be as much abused for my *silence*, as I have been for my speaking or writing.

ALS. NBuHi. Letter marked "(Confidential)." 1. Speech in Lexington, Nov. 13, 1847. 2. *Ibid.* 3. Sargent to Clay, Feb. 27, 1847. 4. Seward's name was frequently mentioned as a possible Whig vice presidential candidate in 1848. This idea was sometimes promoted by Greeley. Van Deusen, *Horace Greeley*, 120; Van Deusen, *William Henry Seward*, 99-112. 5. John M. Clayton was promoted more for president than vice president, and, in fact, received Delaware's 3 votes on the first ballot at the Whig National convention, even after he had asked them to vote for Taylor. R.A. Wire, "John M. Clayton," Ph.D. dissertation, Univ. of Maryland, 1971, pp. 213, 215. Abbott Lawrence had been the favorite of many, including Thurlow Weed and a number of Taylor supporters, but as a New England cotton manufacturer, he could not be placed on the same ticket with Taylor, a slaveholder and cotton planter. He did, however, receive 109 votes for vice president on the 1st ballot at the Whig convention to 115 for Fillmore. The 2nd ballot gave Fillmore 173, Lawrence 87. Lawrence's loss may be partially attributed to the fact that his support for Taylor had alienated Clay's friends. Fillmore, who had had a good record in Congress and was currently comptroller of New York State, was supposedly nominated as a peace offering to Clay and Webster supporters. Van Deusen, *William Henry Seward*, 107-9; McKee, *National . . . Popular and Electoral Vote*, 63; Robert J. Rayback, *Millard Fillmore, Biography of A President* (Buffalo, N.Y., 1959), 173-91; Kinley J. Brauer, *Cotton Versus Conscience* (Lexington, 1967), 235. 6. Clay to Ullmann, August 4, 1847. 7. In October a committee in Lexington, headed by George Robertson, had issued a confidential circular denouncing the methods and tactics of the Taylor campaign in Kentucky. The circular was published in the Louisville *Courier* following Clay's Nov. 13 speech. Poage, *Henry Clay*, 168. It was reprinted in the Lexington *Observer & Kentucky Reporter* on Nov. 20, 1847. 8. Greeley to Clay, Nov. 30, 1847; Clay to McMichael, Dec. 1, 1847. 9. See Clay to Smith, Nov. 13, 1847. 10. Clay to Webb, Oct. 25, 1844; Clay to Felinghuysen, May 22, 1844.

From Philip R. Fendall, Washington, D.C., November 25, 1847. Informs Clay that "I began this Thanksgiving day with reading your Lexington speech [of November 13, 1847]; and can imagine few stronger causes for thanksgiving, on the part of the country, than that it has pleased the Almighty to spare you to give it." Asserts that "of the numerous persons whom I have heard mention the speech, all agree that it is fully equal to any thing that can fall from you, (especially in the articles of condensation and arrangement) as well in manner as in matter." Notes that the "futile attempt of the Union to charge a historical error on it has been fully exposed in this morning's Intelligencer."

Explains that "I have not written to you about the debt of the Columbian College to Col. [James] Morrison's estate, because I have been constantly hoping for more definite action on the case [Clay to Fendall, July 16, 1847]." Although "the President of the Trustees . . . promised to convene the Board on the Saturday next following" September 20, he "omitted to take with him the copy of your letter; and so nothing was done." Reports that at the next meeting, "a committee of three . . . was appointed" but there has been "No report, so far as I can understand, though my importunity has been constant." Writes that he had urged an "amicable settlement" and warned the board "of your determining to bring suit." Concludes that although the "bringing of the suit will be a question of expediency for you," will "continue to press the subject to a conclusion." L, draft. NcD.

Clay had asserted in his speech that John Slidell was wending his way to Mexico when Polk ordered Taylor to move into the disputed territory at the Rio Grande. The Washington *Union* challenged this claim, but the Washington *Daily National Intelligencer* of November 25, 1847, argued that Slidell had to be considered "on his way to Mexico" so long as it was not known by the Polk administration whether or not he would be received by the Mexican government. The failure of the mission was not learned until three months after Taylor was ordered to the Rio Grande and twenty days after he actually started his march.

From William McLain, Washington, D.C., November 26, 1847. Informs Clay that the American Colonization Society "shall start a vessel from N. Orleans, 1st Jan. 1848, and we take the slaves of Mr. [Thomas S.] Witherspoon at that time." Estimates that "It will cost at least $1100 to pay the expenses of their transportation, & support them Six Months in Liberia." Hopes that since "the Soc. is Much pressed for funds at present . . . a part of the money belonging to these people should be paid to the Society, & that a part should be for their own use." Adds, however, that the "Soc. can furnish them a house to live in, provisions, Medicine & medical attendance for Six Months, until they have become acclimated & have time to build a house &c. for themselves." Leaves it to Clay to judge "as to what part of their Money should be paid to the Soc.," and urges that "The people should be made distinctly to understand the Amt. of money which they have" for their own expenses: "Then they will have no cause of complaint, that they have been unfairly dealt with." Learned from "Similar cases . . . the importance of having a perfect understanding of their true rights & conditions . . . before they leave their homes." Thanks Clay for "the allusion you made to Colon. in your late great speech [Speech in Lexington, November 13, 1847]." ALS. DLC-Records of the American Colonization Society (DNA, M212, R20).

From William C. Preston, Columbia, S.C., November 28, 1847. Praises Clay's Mexican War speech [Speech in Lexington, November 13, 1847] as "not only equal to your great reputation but in my judgement surpasses what you have heretofore done. The eloquence with which you have expressed yourself gave me delight while the dignity, wisdom, and lofty spirit of patriotism throughout it inspire me with a sort of awe, & fill me with solemn emotions." Assures Clay that "It gave me the more profound satisfaction as it had been preceeded by rumours of a different character." ALS. DLC-HC (DNA, M212, R6). Printed in Colton, *Clay Correspondence*, 4:550.

The rumors to which Preston refers probably resulted from Clay's "Kill a Mexican" comment in New Orleans. See Toast at New England Society meeting, December 22, 1846.

From HORACE GREELEY New York City, November 30, 1847

The hour is late (11 o'clock) the night bitter cold, and I have 4 miles yet to go home; yet if I do not write now I cannot by day, when my office is a thorough fare; and I am hurrying off to Washington to-morrow or next day. So I will hurry through a few lines in reply to your favor of the 22d.

We have had meetings of both our General Committees this evening, and Resolved, with scarcely a dissent, to hold a great public demonstration in response to your Lexington Speech[1] on the 15th of December, or two weeks hence[.] We could not get the Tabernacle sooner, and there is no other place in the City fit for such a meeting in winter. We hope to make a moral and profound impression. If John M. Clayton will come on and speak for us, we will do something the Country will willingly hear of. If not, I shall try Mr. [Thomas] Corwin.[2] Our call will be signed by nineteen twentieths of all who are entitled to speak for the Whig party of this city—senators, Assemblymen, Common Council, Lieut. Governor [Millard Fillmore], Mayor [William V. Brady], Member of Congress, General Committees, Ward Committees, &c. and we have hope to include some strong names from the opposite party.[3] If they will put their names to what they think and privately talk, we are sure of it.

Still, it is not to be disguised that we have some who doubt, and a few who oppose, but they are not more than one-twentieth of the Whigs. These are cent[e]ring on Gen. [Winfield] Scott, Gen. [Zachary] Taylor being out of the question here.[4] He will not have five Delegates in the National Convention from all North of Pennsylvania. Gen. Scott, if the great influence of Mr. [Daniel] Webster is thrown for him,[5] as now seems probable, will be quite strong with the politicians, though he has as yet no strength with the masses. But it ought to be understood your way, as it certainly is the fact, that Gen. Taylor *cannot be nominated in a Whig National Convention.* If any Military man is taken up, it will be Gen. Scott, who, at any rate, is not afraid to say he is a Whig and knows what a Tariff is. Yet it seems to me wrong and mischievous to nominate a General fresh from a war of invasion for President. The consequence will soon be wars and conquests for the sake of the Presidency. It seems to me a misfortune that we did not disband the Army, except the General Staff, ten years ago, and rely on the Militia, when any force is needed. Late events have found them very easily transformed into soldiers of very high order. Then what need of a Standing Army? I hope we shall soon abolish it.[6] As to the Vice Presidency, I think that this State may be carried with almost any Whig, Mr. [Thoedore] Frelinghuysen excepted. Mr. Fillmore is very good, but I think we shall want him for Governor next Fall. (He ought to have been the man last year, and would but for the insane folly of some who pretended to be his friends, in setting him up as the enemy of the Anti-Renters, who then held the balance of power. This year he was placed on the Anti-Rent ticket, though he never courted it, and he is in the best position to be our next Governor.)[7] But no man has any *positive* strength to bring to the Whig National Ticket—that is, strength outside of the Whig party—but Wm. H. Seward, whose name will bring votes to any ticket it is on in every State where there are Catholics or Irishmen.[8] Still, it may be best to take another man; though I think few of those who dislike him (and they are many) would refuse to vote for a Whig they loved for President because he was the candidate for Vice P. The whole matter deserves consideration. I don't think we can gain or lose any thing South of N.C. and Ky. nominate whom we may; but if we could carry N. York and Pennsylvania, retaining Ohio, there is no more to be said.

I would not interpose a suggestion with regard to your own name in connection with the Presidency; but we shall rally around it here to the last. Should you ultimately resolve to decline, we must of course think you have done what was best; but this city will send five of the most obstinate Clay men in the Convention, and the State I think mainly of the same sort.[9] I think there can be no necessity of your speaking on the subject till the Convention shall assemble; and then should you determine not to consent to be a candidate, we shall have one grand fight and probably fall to pieces. Gen. Taylor can get no vote of the People this side of the Delaware; Scott is very hard to take, and [John] McLean unloved. My second choice is Corwin; and the Taylor men never will vote for him[.][10]

I wish you would recall your letters respecting Nativism as speedily as possible.[11] No matter how unexceptionable, they will be used to our prejudice. There is a low villain named *Job Haskell*,[12] formerly an ostler, and then a charcoal dealer, elevated to a Police Justiceship by Nativism, but always a bitter Loco-Foco, who operated in 1844 with a Native letter which purported to be yours, but which I think must have been forged or altered. I never could get sight of it; he operated entirely under secrecy; but he openly boasts since Election that he made [James K.] Polk President—and he probably did. He only showed his letter where he pleased, and I cannot trace it. But the fact being, known that you had written a letter or letters to the Natives, he had a good chance to utter whatever he pleased. We must not be in such a predicament again. P.S. [Thurlow] Weed says the leading Barnburners of our State are not satisfied with your Slavery resolution[13]—say if you had said 'No more Slave Territory at any rate', they would have supported you—that is Lt.-Gov. [Addison] Gardiner, John Van Buren,[14] &c. I apprehend, however, they did not mean to do it, though they did us good service this Fall.[15]

ALS. DLC-HC (DNA, M212, R6). 1. Speech in Lexington, Nov. 13, 1847. 2. Apparently none of these men spoke at the meeting which was held at the Tabernacle on Dec. 20, 1847, to denounce the Mexican War and to support Clay's resolutions. With Dudley Selden presiding, the large assembly passed resolutions that approved the measures Clay had pronounced in his Nov. 13 speech, blamed President Polk for the war, and disavowed all desire for any land that would increase slave territory, while expressing respect for the constitutional rights of the South's domestic institutions. The meeting declared Clay unequaled as a statesman. New York *Daily Herald*, Dec. 21, 1847. 3. In the 1847 New York City charter elections, Whig William V. Brady had been elected mayor over Democrat Sherman Brownell by a vote of 20,871 to 19,136. In the election for the common council, 11 Whigs, 6 Democrats, and 1 Native American were elected as aldermen, while 12 Whigs and 6 Democrats were elected as assistants. Lexington *Observer & Kentucky Reporter*, April 21, 1847. 4. Gen. Winfield Scott, a resident of nearby New Jersey, had a long history of support in New York. The Weed-Seward faction had promoted him at the 1839 Whig convention as one tactic to defeat Clay's bid for the nomination, and they succeeded in nominating Scott as the Whig candidate in 1852. Elliot, *Winfield Scott*, 368, 373-82, 590-96, 608-13, *passim*. Zachary Taylor was not favored in New York because, as a Louisiana planter and a slaveholder, he was viewed as representing the Southern agricultural wing of the Whig party which did not support the northern Whig economic program. Rayback, *Millard Fillmore*, 182-84. 5. Webster continued to hope for the nomination himself, although he had little support except in New England, especially Massachusetts. Irving H. Bartlett, *Daniel Webster* (New York, 1978), 232-37. 6. The rising spirit of egalitarianism had been working against a professional military establishment and its military schools for a number of years. The U.S. House had established a committee in 1837 to report on West Point, and it decided that allowing the U.S. Military Academy graduates to monopolize the commissioned ranks was a gross violation of democratic principles. Even the militia came under attack for allowing the wealthy to buy their way out of service. Russell F. Weigley, *History of the United States Army* (New York, 1967), 154-57, 169. 7. Whig John Young had been elected governor of New York in 1846. In 1847 Whig Hamilton Fish was elected lieutenant governor to replace Addison Gardiner who had been elected to the court of appeals. Whigs won all other state offices in 1847; of those seats up for election in the state legislature, Whigs won 20 state senate seats to 1 for the Democrats and 31 assembly seats to 5 for the Democrats. *NCAB*, 13:181; New York *Daily Herald*, Nov. 1, 1847. In the 1848 state elections in New York, Hamilton Fish received 218,280 votes for governor to 123,360 for Free Soiler John Dix and 114,457 for Democrat Reuben Walworth. *BDGUS*, 3:1080-81. In the congressional elections, Whigs won 32 seats to 2 for the Democrats and 2 for the Free Soil party. *Guide to U.S. Elections*, 587-88. In the state legislative elections, Whigs won 105 seats in the assembly, the Free Soilers 17, and the Hunkers (Dems.) 6; in the state senate Whigs won 24 seats to 8 for the Democrats. New York *Daily Herald*, Nov. 16, 1848. 8. As governor, Seward had won the good will of Catholics, especially recent German and Irish immigrants, by calling on the New York legislature to establish schools where the children of the newcomers could be taught in their native language by Catholic instructors. He had forged an alliance with Catholic bishop John Hughes to promote the support of Catholic schools with public funds. In addition, he had attempted to thwart the Nativist/Whig association in 1844 and thus preserved at least some of the foreign vote for Clay. Van Deusen, *William Henry Seward*, 65-71, 102. 9. Ullmann to Clay, Feb. 18, 1848. 10. A number of northern Whigs were supporting Corwin in an attempt to block the nomination of the slaveholding Taylor. On the floor of the Senate in Feb., 1847, Corwin gave a lengthy and vehement speech against the Mexican War, which appealed to those who wanted to halt the Taylor candidacy. Corwin, however, refused to endorse abolitionism or take any position which he thought would endanger the Union or the Whig party. He thus declined in 1848 to allow his name to be presented as a candidate for the Whig presidential nomination. Maizlish, *The Triumph of Sectionalism*, 84-86; Norman A. Graebner, "Thomas Corwin and the Election of 1848: A Study in Conservative Politics," *JSH* (May, 1951), 17:162-79. 11. Clay to Greeley, Nov. 22, 1847. 12. Job Haskell had also served as a member of the state assembly in 1835. His occupation is listed as coal inspector or coal measurer in the 1842 New York City directory. Information supplied by Mariam Touba, The New-York Historical Society. 13. Resolution 7 of Speech in Lexington, Nov. 13, 1847. 14. John Van Buren, son of Martin Van Buren, was attorney general of New York in 1847 and a leading Free Soiler. Donovan, *The Barnburners*, 91, *passim*. 15. Between 1840 and 1850 the Democrat party in New York split, causing a general realignment of parties in that state. The term Barnburners came to be applied to the Radicals in the party who had originally wanted a severe restriction on canals and other public works and the reimposition of a direct tax. The Hunkers were the conservatives who supported the status quo and were said to want large hunks of the spoils of office. The split between these two groups was completed at the Syracuse convention in Sept., 1847, when the Radicals proposed a resolution supporting the Wilmot Proviso, but the Hunkers gained control and named the state ticket. The Radicals, or Barnburners, then met in Herkimer, N.Y., on Oct. 26. John Van Buren prepared the convention address which endorsed the Wilmot Proviso and Free Soil. This party split resulted in a total victory for the Whigs in the 1847 New York elections. Donovan, *The Barnburners*, 5, 32-33, 75-76, 91-97; Mayfield, *Rehearsal for Republicanism*, 8-33, 97-100.

To SYDNEY HOWARD GAY Lexington, December 1, 1847

I have received the enclosed letter, with the slip from your paper.[1]

I assure you, most truly, that I never was the proprietor of the Wife and child of Lewis (or, as he calls himself, Lewis Hayden)[2] or either of them. I never therefore sold one or the other of them. He is a drunken, worthless person, wholly regardless of truth. And as to Mrs. Todd, as he calls her, she lost her husband [Tom Todd] some years ago, under circumstances which greatly aggrieved me. He committed suicide, being a person of melancholy temperament. It is utterly untrue that he was maltreated at any time. He was, on the contrary, a favorite servant much indulged. The circumstances of his unhappy death were all published at the time.[3] His wife [Jane Todd],[4] now our Cook, has consoled herself with another husband, and I have no doubt is much happier, than L. Hayden, and far more respectable.

I do not write that you should publish my letter. I cannot condescend to appear in the public prints to contradict the falsehoods of such a worthless being as the fugitive Lewis, whether prompted by others or himself.

But I may be allowed to ask, whether you conscientiously think it right to publish such statements without previous verification?

ALS. NNC. 1. Letter and slip not found. Clay apparently refers to the letter of Lewis Hayden, published on Nov. 11, 1847, in the *National Anti-Slavery Standard*, in which Hayden asked an editor: "if Mr. Clay had sold his wife and child, as he has mine, would he have suffered that Kentuckian's letter to have room in any part of his paper until Mr. Clay had released them, or, at least, made some effort to do so? . . . Do you think he would say 'what the law makes property is property.' Would that be his answer? That is Mr. Clay's. Then go to his plantation; ask the widow Mrs. Todd, whose husband Mr. Clay, in 1844, tied up and left in the hand of his cruel overseer to flog." 2. Lewis Hayden, a slave who worked at the Phoenix Hotel in Lexington, his wife, Harriet, and their child had been assisted in escaping by Delia Webster and Calvin Fairbank, who were active in the Underground Railroad. Lewis used the last name of Grant after his owner Thomas Grant, until he reached Canada where he then changed his name to Lewis Hayden. He later became a prominent citizen of Boston and served a term in the Massachusetts legislature. He was a frequent correspondent of the *National Anti-Slavery Standard*. J. Winston Coleman, "Delia Webster and Calvin Fairbank—Underground Railroad Agents," *FCHQ* (July, 1943), 17:129-42. 3. Tom Todd, a well-known slave belonging to Clay, had been trained in the shoemaking business and was frequently hired out to others. Todd hanged himself on June 1, 1844. According to reports at the time, he had been suffering from ill health during the spring and had committed suicide after discovering that the money he kept in the back drawer of his bureau had been stolen. Reports that appeared in the *National Anti-Slavery Standard* in 1846 began to charge that Todd had been flogged with Clay's knowledge by the overseer, had become morose, and had never recovered emotionally from the beating. Lexington *Observer & Kentucky Reporter*, June 5, 1846; *National Anti-Slavery Standard*, May 7, 1846. 4. See Richard L. Troutman, "Plantation Life in the Ante-Bellum Bluegrass Region of Kentucky," M.A. thesis, University of Kentucky, 1955, p. 121.

To Charles Lanman, New York City, December 1, 1847. Expresses his thanks for "a copy of my late speech, on the Mexican war [Speech in Lexington, November 13, 1847] . . . as published in the [New York *Daily*] *Express*, the constant kindness of which towards me I have always felt and duly appreciated." Reasserts the "important point of the speech," that it is "the power of Congress to decide on the objects of any war" and that it must "proclaim what shall be those of a further prosecution of the existing war." Does not doubt that "If Congress will act . . . peace will speedily ensue." Copy. Printed in Lanman, *Haphazard Personalities*, 126.

To MORTON McMICHAEL[1] Lexington, December 1, 1847

I recd your favor of the 24h. Ulto. and return enclosed the rough draught of my resolutions,[2] with the endorsement on them requested, to which you and my young friend, your son, attach too much importance.

The important point of my resolutions was that suggesting that Congress has the Constitutional power, and that it is its bounden duty, to specify the objects for which the War with Mexico shall be further prosecuted. If it will fulfill that duty, I am persuaded that we shall soon have peace. If the Press concur with me in these opinions, ought it not to present them in the strongest lights? And ought not public meetings of the People every where to proclaim their concurrence?[3]

P.S. Entre nous, all Kentucky will soon come out for a Nat. Convention to nominate Candidates for P. & V.P.[4]

ALS. Courtesy of Frederic R. Kirkland, Wynnewood, Pa. Addressed to McMichael at Philadelphia. 1. For McMichael (1807-79), who edited the *Saturday Evening Post*, the Philadelphia *North American*, and other journals, see *NCAB*, 2:211. 2. Speech in Lexington, Nov. 13, 1847. 3. In addition to the meeting at the Tabernacle in New York City on Dec. 20 [Greeley to Clay, Nov. 30, 1847], between 10 and 20,000 New York Whigs met at Castle Garden on Feb. 17, 1848, to praise Clay's speech and tout him for president. Speakers included Philip Hone, chairman of the meeting, Henry Grinnell, Joseph L. White, and Dudley Selden. Lexington *Observer & Kentucky Reporter*, Feb. 26, 1848. For the Philadelphia meeting endorsing Clay's speech, see Clay to Clayton, Dec. 14, 1847. A large number of newspapers endorsed Clay's speech and resolutions; the Louisville *Daily Journal* of Dec. 9, 1847, listed 27 different papers doing so, but added that they were sure Clay would not accept the presidential nomination even if it were offered. 4. Calls for a national Whig convention began in earnest in Oct., 1847. Kentucky did not hold its state Whig convention until Feb. 22, 1848. See Clay to Unknown Recipient, *ca.* Winter 1847-48; Clay to Greeley, Dec. 10, 1847; and *Niles' Register* (Oct. 9, 1847), 73:83.

From John D'Evereux, London, December 2, 1847. Offers "this paltery profe [*sic*, proof] of my most affectionate regard and friendship." Assures Clay that "neither time nor separation can erace from my heart that sense of your worth, or of the poignant and trying affliction, with which it has pleased a great and a just God to overwhelm you [Taylor to Clay, March 1, 1847]." Adds in a postscript that "My Nephew William [St. John Elliot] still cheers me with the hope that we shall see you our next President." Compliments Clay on his "able and Statesmanlike resolutions you submitted to the meeting at Lexington [Speech in Lexington, November 13, 1847]." Encloses "a paragraph from the [London] Times of to day, reflecting on the Audacious and unprincipled [James K.] Polk and his misrule. . . . What a curse he has been to the Country, but I trust with the miserable [John] Tyler we shall soon see him consigned to the same degraded obscurity." LS. DLC-HC (DNA, M212, R6).

John D'Evereux, a native of Ireland and an officer in the English Army had lived for a short time in Baltimore, Md., before serving as a general in the Bolivian Army under Simon Bolivar. *Biographical and Historical Memoirs of Mississippi*, 2:397. See Don Juan [John] D'Evereux in 3:187.

The article in the London *Times* of December 2, 1847, criticized Polk for his prosecution of the Mexican War and implied that he was motivated more by a desire to obtain New Mexico and California than simply to settle the boundary of Texas.

On December 10, 1847, D'Evereux enclosed "the leading Article from the Times of to day, in regard to the Mexican War your distinguished self, Mr Polk and his unprincipled faction, who care not what dilemma they lead their country into." Notes that he has not heard from his nephew Elliot for some time. In a postscript, remarks that he is "delighted to perceive that their [*sic*, there] is a strong disposition evinced all over the United States, to bring you out again for the Presidency. You must be the President, and General [Zachary] Taylor, Vic[e] President, And then all will go right. well." LS. DLC-HC (DNA, M212, R6).

The London *Times* of December 10, 1847, again criticized Polk for his prosecution of the Mexican War and stated that if Clay had been president, the war would not have occurred. The article predicted that the military spirit would prevail in the U.S. and would make either Taylor or Winfield Scott the next president.

To THOMAS B. STEVENSON Lexington, December 2, 1847

An absence of a week at Louisville has delayed my acknowledgment of the receipt of your favor of the 22d ult.

I am greatly obliged by the letter of Mr. Noble,[1] which you inclosed. It is full of good sense and good feeling.

As to myself and the future, if there be not such demonstrations as I ought to respect, I may be compelled to decline any use of my name. Perhaps that is really best for the country and for me. I am most unwilling to be thought to desire a nomination for the Presidency. If better can be done without my name than with it, for God's sake, let me be passed by. But if I am to be used, I desire that I may be brought forward under the most auspicious circumstances. . . .

I write hastily. My letters, in respect to my late speech,[2] almost overwhelm me.

Copy. Printed in Colton, *Clay Correspondence*, 3:461, with the indication that a portion of the letter had been omitted. 1. Neither Stevenson's letter of Nov. 22 nor Noble's letter have been found. George W. Noble published in Louisville a pamphlet combining Clay's Nov. 13 speech against the Mexican War and an essay by Albert Gallatin entitled *Peace with Mexico* (New York, 1847), 17 pp. Frankfort *Commonwealth*, Dec. 21, 1847. Gallatin argued in his essay that the Polk administration had regarded Mexico's refusal to receive John Slidell as a just cause for war, and he attacked Polk's claims concerning the Texas-Mexico boundary. He charged that the U.S. must accept responsibility for instituting hostilities by moving troops into the disputed area. He also set forth terms which he felt should be sufficient to restore peace. On Dec. 6, 1847, Clay wrote to an Unknown Recipient in Virginia, asserting that he had perused Gallatin's pamphlet "which, without any concert between us . . . takes similar positions to those which I had previously occupied. He fortifies them by a striking array of facts and powerful arguments." Adds that "I am not surprised at the imputation of unworthy motives to me for the delivery of the speech. That has been so long my fortune that I should have been surprised if it had not been made. Will they charge Mr. Gallatin, in the publication of his pamphlet, with being actuated by the desire to attain the presidency? There is as much ground in the one case as in the other." Copy, excerpt. Printed in Washington *Daily National Intelligencer*, Dec. 30, 1847. 2. Speech in Lexington, Nov. 13, 1847.

To Charles Lanman, New York City, December 6, 1847. Extends his thanks for "the highly interesting pamphlet from the pen of Mr. [Albert] Gallatin" which, "although received only to-day, I have already perused with great satisfaction [Clay to Stevenson, December 2, 1847]." Believes that Gallatin's "strong facts strikingly arrayed, and strong arguments, which always characterize the productions of that eminent and venerable citizen. . . . cannot fail to exercise a powerful influence in behalf of the cause of peace." Wonders: "Will he also be accused of seeking the Presidency because he has counselled his country against the further prosecution of an unjust war?" Copy. Printed in Lanman, *Haphazard Personalities*, 126.

From William McLain, Washington, D.C., December 7, 1847. Announces that the "An[nual]. Meeting of the Am. Col. Society will be held in this city on the 18 Jan." Informs Clay that "the new position of the 'Republic of Liberia,' & the necessary adjustment of the relations between it & the Soc." requires "men of wise council." Adds: "Our Committee are exceeding anxious to have you present on that occasion, to deliver the principal address at the public meeting, & to lend the aid of your experience & influence at the Sessions of the Board of Directors." Reports that the Society "will defray your expenses, & do all in our power to render your visit here pleasant to yourself & profitable to this great cause." ALS. DLC-Records of the American Colonization Society (DNA, M212, R20). See Clay to McLain, December 16, 1847.

Clay did attend and made a speech at the meeting. See Speech to American Colonization Society, January 18, 1848.

In September, 1847, Liberia had adopted a constitution, and in October the new republic elected officers. James W. Smith, *Sojourners in Search of Freedom, the Settlement of Liberia by Black Americans* (Lanham, Md., 1987), 198-202.

From Roger B. Taney, Washington, D.C., December 7, 1847. Acknowledges receipt of Clay's petition for an early hearing "in the case of Houston & others vs-The City Bank of New Orleans [Clay to Lucretia H. Clay, March 13, 1847]." Regrets that "we cannot give this case a preference over the preceding cases either upon the ground that it is a writ of error to a state court or on account of the magnitude of the interests involved in it." Notes that several similar cases "brought here by writs of error to state courts . . . we shall most probably not reach during the present Term" and that there are also "many cases from the Circuit courts in which the amount of property in controversy is as great perhaps in some of them greater." Adds that "a considerable portion of these cases have been depending now for two years" because of "the mass of business pressing upon the court." Calls to Clay's attention a case "from the Circuit court of New Hampshire, in which we understand the leading questions are the same with those which arise in the case of Houston & others-vs-The City Bank of New Orleans." Since this case is expected to be heard "about the first of Feby . . . your case will then by the rules and practice of the Court be entitled to be heard immediately after it." Assures Clay that even if "our progress on the docket should be more tardy than we anticipated . . . we shall be so near" the New Hampshire case in early February "that the members of the Bar engaged in the prior cases, would upon considerations personal to yourself," allow it "and your case to take precedence. . . . early enough in the Term to ensure a decision before the Session closes." ALS. DLC-HC (DNA, M212, R6).

The New Hampshire case was *Philip Peck et al.* v. *John S. Jenness et al.* Howards Reports, series 48, 7:612-27. This case was not heard, however, until the January, 1849 term.

To HORACE GREELEY Lexington, December 10, 1847

I have duly received your favor of the 30h. Ulto. and I should address this letter to you at Washn., whither it stated that you were going but that I presume you will have returned to N. York to be present at your great meeting of the 15h. inst. I shall look for its proceedings with much anxiety.[1]

You will have remarked that there is a great abatement in this State in the fervor of the feeling for Genl [Zachary] Taylor.[2] The idea of appointing Electors to vote for him, without regard to the action of a Nat. Convention, may be considered as abandoned. The Louisville Journal, which did more than any other paper in K[entucky]. to give impulse to that feeling, has come out for a Nat. Convention, as have other papers in this State. The Journal will support me, if I should be the Candidate, and assent to it, with all the zeal which it ever displayed in my support. There is no feeling, none whatever, in K. for Genl [Winfield] Scott.[3]

Is it probable that the Legislature of N[ew]. Y[ork]. will give any expression to its wishes about a Presidential Candidate, at its approaching Session?[4] How are our friends, Govr. [John] Young, [Millard] Fillmore, [Thurlow] Weed, Seaward [*sic*, William H. Seward] &c disposed?

In presenting my resolution at Lexington,[5] about Slavery, I intended to express my own views and those of the meeting, without reference to those of any other party or persons. But I am surprized that the objection should be made to it, which you state, by certain Gentlemen in N.Y.[6] They would have been satisfied, it seems, if I had gone for "No more Slave Territory at any rate." But I have gone for no more territory for any purpose; and expressly for none for the purpose of Slavery. Ought not that to have satisfied them?

I agree with you that the affair of a Candidate for the V[ice]. P[resident]. ought to be most deliberately considered. We know what injustice to the Whig cause, and what injustice to Mr. [Theodore] Frelinghuysen, was done by his selection in the last contest.[7] And yet no more excellent person could have been selected. Besides Mr. Seawards great merits and great abilities, he has the further recommendation which you mention. Still his selection involves a full and fair consideration of the question of loss and gain, and on that I am not competent to decide.

I wrote several letters in the autumn of 1844 on the subject of Nativism; but I am quite sure that none of them committed me to that cause. Those I addressed (two) to Genl P[eter]. S[ken]. Smith he has recently handsomely returned to me.[8] They really contained nothing which could be made to operate to my prejudice. At the earnest entreaty of Col. [James Watson] Webb, I think, about the same time, I addressed a letter to him;[9] but I am pretty sure that there is nothing in it exceptionable. I have no recollection of ever having received from, or written any letter, to Job Haskell; but of course, in such a multitude of correspondents as I had in 1844, I cannot be positive.[10] You may, I think, rely upon it that if he has any letter from me it is a harmless one.

The best proof that the Natives never regarded me as one of themselves is to be found in the fact that they have nominated another.[11] You will also remember that in Decr 1844, when I was addressed by the K[entucky]. electors at this place, I advised the Whig party to stand by its own principles, without blending itself with any other party.[12]

I believe that you may freely confer and correspond with any of the members of the K. delegation (the Whigs of course) on all matters relating to me. Several of them (my own immediate representative Charles S. Morehead)[13] among them never entered at all into the Taylor movement; and those who did would, I am sure, be delighted in any encouraging prospect of the successful use of my name. Both policy and justice require that the friends of Genl Taylor should be regarded as my friends.

I observe statements in the N[ational]. papers of my intention to go to Washn. this winter. I am engaged in a highly important cause in the S[upreme]. Court from Louisiana.[14] It is not certain that it can be tried at the present term; but if it can be (of which I expect to be duly advised) I may go there towards February[.] I have also some professional business[15] in Philada. to which City I may also go, *if I should visit Washington.* But in any contingency, I hope to pass "unmolested," to use the language generally employed in passes given to Slaves leaving home.

ALS. NjP. Letter marked "(Confidential)." 1. Greeley to Clay, Nov. 30, 1847. The date of the meeting was changed from Dec. 15 to Dec. 20. 2. Largely resulting from Taylor's nonpartisan attitude and his letters. See Clay to Ullmann, August 4, 1847; Clay to White, Sept. 20, 1847. 3. On Nov. 30, 1847, the Louisville *Daily Journal* announced that while it had previously felt there was no need for a national Whig convention, it was now persuaded otherwise. Since Taylor fever had not pervaded the entire country as expected, the *Journal* feared that the general surely would be defeated if a few states appointed Taylor electors and shunned a national convention. Thus, the paper opposed a Taylor convention in Kentucky in Feb., 1848 to choose electors without waiting for a national convention. The *Journal* in the spring of 1848 subtly continued to promote Taylor, but made an attempt to appear neutral, asserting that it supported the candidate most likely to win the election. Louisville *Daily Journal*, April 13, 18, 21, 1848. 4. The New York legislature as a whole did nothing about endorsing a presidential candidate; however, the Whig legislative caucus came out in favor of a national convention and supported Clay for the nomination. Lexington *Observer & Kentucky Reporter*, Feb. 26, 1848. 5. See Resolution 7, Speech in Lexington, Nov. 13, 1847. 6. Greeley to Clay, Nov. 30, 1847. 7. Ewing to Clay, June 23, 1844; Clay to Clayton, Dec. 2, 1844. 8. Clay to Smith, Nov. 13, 1847. 9. Clay to Webb, Oct. 25, 1844. 10. Greeley to Clay, Nov. 30, 1847. 11. The Native American National convention, which met in Philadelphia in Sept., 1847, nominated Gen. Zachary Taylor for president and Gen. Henry A.S. Dearborn for vice president. Washington *Daily National Intelligencer*, Sept. 16, 1847. 12. Speech to Ky. Presidential Electors, Dec. 4, 1844. 13. See 4:463. 14. Clay to Lucretia H. Clay, March 13, 1847. 15. Relating to Isaac Shelby, Jr., and the U.S. Bank of Pennsylvania. See Clay to Bayard, Oct. 21, 1845 and May 7, 1846; Clay to Randall, April 2, 1847.

To HENRY CLAY NILES[1] Lexington, December 13, 1847

Very great and constant engagements, since the receipt of your favor of the 16h. Ulto. have delayed my acknowledgment of it. I greatly esteemed and loved your excellent father [Hezekiah Niles]. His high regard for me is demonstrated by the compliment of bestowing my name on you. He was an able, enlightened & indefatigable patriot, with whom I had the happiness to agree in opinion on momentous questions of National policy. Unsolicited by him, I once had it in my power to offer him a highly important public office, under the General Government, the acceptance of which he declined;[2] and I regretted extremely that the public would not be benefited by his services.

May you emulate his virtues, and render yourself as useful to our Country as he was! I add my best wishes for your health, happiness and prosperity.

ALS. KyU. 1. See 7:545. 2. An appointment to the Patent Office. See 7:210-11.

To WILLIAM C. PRESTON Lexington, December 13, 1847

Among the many commendations which I have received of the Speech which I felt it to be my duty to make at Lexington on the 13h. Ulto,[1] none has afforded me so much gratification as that contained in your favor of the 28h. Ulto; because I believe there is no more competent judge in our Country than you of such a production. I place myself less value on any oratorical merit which it possesses, if it has any, than upon the opinions and views which I endeavored to present. I devoutly pray to God that if, as I am fully persuaded, they are correct, they may not be lost upon our Country.

Although I do not often hear directly from you, I constantly feel the liveliest interest in your health and welfare, and avail myself of every opportunity to make enquiries about you. . . .

ALS. DLC-Campbell-Preston Papers (DNA, M212, R20). Addressed to Preston at Columbia, S.C., "Via City of Washington." 1. Speech in Lexington, Nov. 13, 1847.

To Isabella P. Butler, December 14, 1847. Thanks her for conveying "the respect and confidence with which your father has always honored me," along with the "friendly and favorable consideration of me by both of you." During the nation's "long and arduous trials," finds "great consolation & encouragement" in discovering "my humble exertions constantly cheered & sustained by so many good virtuous persons of both sexes." Prays that "an All wise Providence will deign yet to smile upon our Union, and avert all evils from it." ALS. ICHi.

To JOHN M. CLAYTON Lexington, December 14, 1847

The brief expression made by you in Philadelphia of your approbation of my recent Speech and Resolutions[1] gave me great satisfaction, as I have much confidence in your judgment. But will they do any good? Do they meet with the concurrence of our friends? Will they act upon them? The most important feature in them is that which depicts the duty of Congress.[2] I have, as yet, no where seen the principle that Congress has the right to declare for what objects the War shall continue to be prosecuted contested. I believe it to be incontestible. I had hoped that in the House there would be no great difficulty in a majority uniting in a declaration of what its objects shall be. My fears related to the Senate, and I suppose that will depend pretty much upon the course of [John C.] Calhoun, [Thomas Hart] Benton &c.[3]

It seems to me that the exceptionable character of the Message, the many distracting subjects which it recommends to Congress, and especially that of establishing Governments for conquered Countries will favor & promote the action of Congress in defining the objects of the War.[4]

Do let me hear from you often and fully. I have not heard whether the S[upreme]. Court will allow my cause to be tried at the present term;[5] and consequently I am unable to say whether I shall visit Washington or not this winter. We had yesterday and last night a fall of Snow a foot deep, which is not a very encouraging circumstance for a long journey.

ALS. DLC-HC. 1. Speech in Lexington, Nov. 13, 1847. A meeting in support of Clay's speech and resolutions was held at the Chinese Museum in Philadelphia on Dec. 6, 1847, with Samuel Breck presiding. Robert T. Combs introduced 11 resolutions; this was followed by addresses from Joseph R. Chandler and Morton McMichael. Clayton's remarks may have been made at this meeting, but, if so, they were not recorded in the news accounts given in the Philadelphia *North American* of Dec. 7, 1847, or the Washington *Daily National Intelligencer* of Dec. 9. 2. See Resolutions 2, 3, and 4 of speech. 3. Calhoun introduced resolutions in the Senate on Dec. 15, 1847, opposing the conquering of Mexico in order to hold it as a province or to incorporate it into the U.S. Such action, he argued, would be inconsistent with the avowed object of the war, would depart from settled practice, and would lead to subversion of free and popular institutions. These resolutions were ultimately tabled. *Cong. Globe*, 30 Cong., 1 Sess., 26, 53-54, 96-100. For further discussion of Calhoun's position on the war and possible territorial acquisitions, see Wiltse, *John C. Calhoun: Sectionalist*, 326-28. Benton at this time was preoccupied with the court-martial of his son-in-law John Charles Fremont and did not introduce any resolutions, etc., on the matter. Chambers, *Old Bullion Benton*, 305-12, 319. 4. For Polk's Third Annual Message of Dec. 7, 1847, see *MPP*, 4:532-64. 5. Clay to Lucretia H. Clay, March 13, 1847.

To WILLIAM N. MERCER Lexington, December 14, 1847

I was very glad to receive your kind letter, after you reached Laurel Hill,[1] and to learn that you had all safely arrived there.

I am still in uncertainty about the necessity of my going to Washington to fulfil my professional engagement. My going depends on the sole contingency of the S[upreme]. Court allowing the cause to be tried at its present term, and of that I am yet unadvised.[2] A fall of snow yesterday and last night of a foot deep, after tremendous rains, makes me shudder at the thoughts of the journey.

I transmitted to you and to my friend Miss [Eliza] Young, each, a Copy of a Speech which I recently delivered, and of resolutions which I offered at a public meeting in Lexington.[3] I suppose that they will be ill received at N. Orleans, so much benefited by expenditures arising out of the Mexican War. Every where else their reception has been enthusiastic and far exceeding my expectations. But whatever may be their effect, I have discharged a public duty, as I thought, and that is enough for me.

Some of my warm friends still indulge, probably chimerical, hopes of me for the Presidency; but I have not made up my mind to consent to such a use of my name, and my present inclination is against it. But my final decision will be governed by a profound sense of public duty.

Tell Dr. Hawkes [*sic*, Francis L. Hawks] that he is a scurvy—very scur[v]y fellow, not to have come to see me, on his way from New York. I am afraid that brilliant Speech, which he made at the Episcopal Convention,[4] turned his head, and made him forget all humble persons and things.

I sent you through Mr. [Thomas] Smith a barrel of corned beef from one of the finest beeves that ever was slaughtered.

My love to Miss Young & Miss [Mary D.] Kemble and kiss dear Anna [Mercer] . . .

ALS. LU-Ar. Addressed to Mercer at Canal Street, New Orleans. 1. Mercer's plantation near Natchez. 2. *Houston* v. *The City Bank of New Orleans*. See Clay to Lucretia H. Clay, March 13, 1847; Taney to Clay, Dec. 7, 1847. 3. Speech in Lexington, Nov. 13, 1847. 4. Francis L. Hawks (1798-1866), a former North Carolina lawyer, had entered the Episcopal ministry and had become rector of Christ Church in New Orleans and the first president of the University of Louisiana. In 1847 he made a lengthy address at the General Convention of the Episcopal Church on the subject of episcopal authority and jurisdiction and the differences between them. It bore on the subject of whether or not the Diocese of New York could elect a new bishop since their bishop had been suspended. *DAB*; also information provided by Elinor S. Hearn, The Archives of the Episcopal Church, Austin, Tx.

To WILLIAM McLAIN Lexington, December 16, 1847

I received your letter[1] expressing a wish that I would attend at the approaching Session of the American Colonization Society, at which grave and weighty matters are to be considered and decided, and that I would deliver the principal address at the public meeting.

It is possible but not yet decided that I may be called to Washington to attend to important professional business.[2] If I go, I should endeavor to attend the annual meeting of the Society; but in no event can I engage to make the principal or any other address to the Society. If present, my duty will be to preside at the meeting; and any thing, beyond what circumstance might make it proper for a presiding officer to say, would be incompatible with my situation.[3]

I think that you greatly over estimate the effect upon the interests of the Society, or the Republic of Liberia, of any thing that I could say.

AL, signature removed. DLC-Records of the American Colonization Society (DNA, M212, R20). 1. McLain to Clay, Dec. 7, 1847. 2. The case of *Houston* v. *The City Bank of New Orleans*. See Clay to Lucretia H. Clay, March 13, 1847. 3. He did make a lengthy address. Speech to American Colonization Society, Jan. 18, 1848.

To SYDNEY HOWARD GAY Lexington, December 22, 1847

I received your favor of the 10th last. I find on enquiry that Lewis Hayden is not the Lewis that I supposed. From the tenor of his (L H's) first publication,[1] I understood him to convey the idea that he and his wife were both in my service, that I sold his wife and child to go down the river or to the South; and that he witnessed the agonizing scene of their separation.

But his tale is equally untrue and unfounded. I never sold, in my life, any woman and child to go down the river or to go South. I never owned his wife and child. My invariable habit has been to bring together, if I could, rather than to separate man and wife. I do not even know Lewis Hayden. It is quite possible that I may have seen him in the streets of Lexington, but if I ever did, I have no sort of recollection of him.

The information I have obtained about him is this: that two gentlemen in Lexington purchased him,[2] at his instance, with the view of his ultimate emancipation; that his hire or earnings were to be applied to that object; that, during the existence of this arrangement, he escaped, under the auspices of Mr. Fairbanks [*sic*, Calvin Fairbank],[3] and that he carried away with him *his wife and her child*, who belonged to a Citizen of Lexington. Mr. Fairbanks was prosecuted for the abduction of Lewis Hayden his wife and child and, as is well known, was convicted.

Such I believe to be a true account of the matter. I leave it to your own sense of propriety to make such correction as you please; but I must repeat that I cannot consent, by the publication of my letters to be brought in contact with Lewis Hayden. Accustomed as I have been to traduction his calumny, if uncorrected, will be only a small addition to the mass.

ALS. NNC. 1. Clay to Gay, Dec. 1, 1847. 2. Thomas Grant and Lewis Baxter. *FCHQ*, 17:141. 3. Clay to Owsley, June 20, 1846.

To ROBERT P. LETCHER Lexington, December 22, 1847

You talked of going to Washn. Do you still think of it. I am called there by professional business, and purpose starting on saturday or sunday next.[1] Can't you come along? I should be very glad of your company.

ALS. ViU. 1. To argue the case of *Houston* v. *The City Bank of New Orleans* in the Supreme Court. See Clay to Lucretia H. Clay, March 13, 1847.

To H.R. Robinson, New York City, December 24, 1847. Acknowledges receipt "in good order, and perfect safety, the lithographic view of the Battle and Battle ground of Buena Vista [Henry Clay, Jr., to Clay, February 12/19, 1847], to which it refers, and which you have done me the favor to present to me." Praises it as "a rich and beautiful specimen of the Lithographic art, and portrays one of the most signal and decisive battles ever fought." Realizes that it "will constantly remind me of a sad loss which I sustained on that memorable occasion," but shares nonetheless "in the glory which was won by our gallant Commander [Zachary Taylor] and his brave army." Is consoled "by the consideration that my lamented son [Henry Clay, Jr.], I know, if he were to be prematurely taken away, preferred such a death as he encountered [Taylor to Clay, March 1, 1847]." ALS. CSmH. Robinson was a lithographer, located at 142 Nassau Street, New York City. Washington *Daily National Intelligencer*, January 28, 1848.

From Zachary Taylor, Baton Rouge, La., December 28, 1847. Expresses his gratitude for the "warm & hearty reception I have met with from so many of my fellow citizens . . . since my return, in addition to their manifestations of their high appreciation & approval of my conduct while in Mexico." Feels "more than compensated . . . for the dangers & toils I have encountered in the public service, as well as for the privations in being so long seperated from my family & friends," but regrets nonetheless certain "circumstances connected with my operations in that country which I can never forget."

Explains that he "left Mexico after it was determined the column under my orders was to act on the defensive, & after the Capital of the enemy had fallen into our hands [Clay to Ullmann, May 12, 1847], & their army dispersed, on a short leave of absence, to visit my family, & to attend to some important private affairs." Adds, however, that he "informed the Secretary of War [William L. Marcy], should my presence in Mexico be deemed necessary at any time, I was ready to return." Does not expect, therefore, "to have it in my power to visit Kentucky, altho, it would afford me much real pleasure to mix once more with my numerous relatives & friends in that patriotic state, to whom I am devotedly attached; as well as again to visit if not the place of my nativity, where I was reared from infancy, to early manhood." Appreciates Clay's "kind invitation to visit you at your own hospitable home, & should anything occur which will enable me to avail myself of it, I will embrace the opportunity with much real pleasure." Since "I found my family or rather Mrs

[Margaret Smith] Taylor on my return in feeble health," expects to "devote what time I can spare, or can be spared me from my public duties" to put his private affairs "in order as far as I can do so."

Warns Clay to "take every precaution to protect yourself while traveling from the effects of the severe cold weather" if he visits Washington. Reassures Clay that "altho, I had received some letters from individuals in Kentucky calculated, or perhaps intended to produ[c]e unkind feelings on my part towards you . . . their object has not been accomplished in the slightest degree." ALS. DLC-HC (DNA, M212, R6). Printed in Colton; *Clay Correspondence*, 4:550-52.

Taylor was born in Orange County, Va., on November 24, 1784, and his family moved to Jefferson County, Va. (Ky.) near Louisville in 1785. He had left Mexico on November 26, 1847, and arrived in Louisiana on the 30th. After a great welcome at New Orleans on December 3, he travelled on to Baton Rouge where he spent most of the ensuing thirteen months. Hamilton, *Zachary Taylor, Soldier of the Republic*, xv, 25, 249, 254.

To LUCRETIA HART CLAY Wheeling, Va. (W. Va.), December 30, 1847

I arrived here tonight, less fatigued than I had feared; and in good health. I came on board the Silas Wright at Maysville [Kentucky] on tuesday morning at 4. O Clock. The whole surface of the Ohio river was covered with floating ice, and I feared that I should be blocked up in the river, and be unable to reach this place; but fortunately the weather has been much milder the last two days, and we struggled through better than I had anticipated. I shall lay over tomorrow night, and avoid night travelling.

I wish you would tell James [Brown Clay] not to forget attending to the business with Stanhope for the persons in Augusta Va.[1]

My love to all at home.

ALS. DLC-TJC (DNA, M212, R11). 1. Reference obscure.

To Unknown Recipient, *ca.* Winter, 1847-48. Hopes that the meeting will deem it "premature to nominate at that time Genl. [Zachary] Taylor or any body else." Desires the meeting also "to declare in favor of a National Convention" which will choose the candidate who "will best conduce to the establishment of the principles of the Whig party." AL, fragment. DLC-HC (DNA, M212, R6).

This undated letter possibly refers to the Kentucky Whig convention which met in Frankfort on February 22, 1848. Clay was anxious that it not endorse Taylor, and it did not make any endorsement for president. It did, however, choose two delegates at large to attend the Whig National convention, provided for county delegations of the respective districts to choose the other delegates, and nominated John J. Crittenden for governor. (All but one of the Kentucky delegates who went to the national convention were Taylor supporters.) As soon as the convention adjourned, a second convention of Taylor men met and unanimously endorsed Taylor, creating the impression that Kentucky Whigs had officially nominated Taylor. Kirwan, *John J. Crittenden*, 213-14; Poage, *Henry Clay*, 171-72.

From Charles Gorr, Baltimore County, Md., January 11, 1848. Informs Clay that "you are my Favored man For the next Bresadend & I God a Blan in my Head if it was taken . . . wood kill the Loko Foko Party For Some time to com." Although "[Zachary] taylor is the Stronger man" because he "Stans Between Both Partis," hopes "he God Sans anof to Give a way & Let you have a Noter Gance" and then be "Bresaden after that." Even though "I am onley Farmar," believes that "Some of our Hard Paedishion auto talk about some think Like that." Adds that "if they take that way I will due as much as the next man if Nod I will Nod wode for a Noder man in this World for Bresadend Nor helb the Party." Hopes "the Lokos wod take Poke" again, since "aneybody Can Beed him Because they had due much of him Ready." Asks Clay to "Excuse my Bad Hand all I Can Righd I Have Larnd from my Self[.] I Can Righd a verrey God dudg [Dutch] hand put that wod nod anser your Perpos." ALS. MdHi.

To CHRISTOPHER HUGHES Washington, January 12, 1848

I have received the articles (the Cloak & Vest) which I bespoke at your house, and beautiful & most comfortable articles they are. And I have also received a most friendly letter from Messrs. John Orem &Co.[1] and what do you imagine? They propose to tender them to me as presents. Nothing was more unexpected, and I feel embarrassed by their liberality. Will you not assist me to get out of this embarrassment? If their condition in life is such as to make it at all inconvenient to them to offer me such valuable articles, I should be most unwilling to take them without an equivalent. I have written them the enclosed letter[2] which you will please read. If you think I ought not to accept of their kindness, be pleased in a delicate and respectful way to offer them payment for the Cloak & Vest, and in that case you may not deliver the letter, but express my obligations to them. On the other hand, if you conceive that, without impropriety, I can receive the articles as presents, you may deliver my letter.

I enclose an order on P[hilip]. T. Ellicott Esqr. for $196:75 which he will pay on presentation; and out of the proceeds, you can pay Messrs. Orem &Co. and make a remittance to me of the balance, or the whole, as you may finally decide. I should prefer the remittance to be in the form of a Check, or a Certificate of deposite.[3]

There is too much political fog here for me yet to see any thing clearly and distinctly. The Whig party has not settled definitively on any course in regard to the Mexican War.

My affectionate regards to your dear daughter [Margaret Hughes].

ALS. MiU-C. Addressed to Hughes at Baltimore. Endorsed "From Henry Clay. 12 Jan. 1848. Washington. wrote to him on 14th Jan. & enclosed a draft to his order for $196.75—from Mechanics Bank—on the Bank of Washington. C Hughes Baltimore." 1. John Orem & Co. were Baltimore merchant tailors located at 230 West Baltimore at corner of Charles Street. Murphy, *Baltimore Directory for 1845*. 2. On Jan. 12, 1848, Clay wrote to Messrs. John M. Orem & Co. to acknowledge receipt of "a Cloak and vest." Notes that "They fit me remarkably well, have come to me at a season of intense cold, and I find them both very comfortable." Adds: "Whilst, Gentlemen, I feel that I have no claim upon you for any presents, much less such costly and elegant ones, I tender an expression of my cordial thanks and grateful acknowledgments for the friendly feelings towards me." ALS. MdHi. 3. See endorsement above.

From Lewis Meredith, York, Pa., January 13, 1848. Sends Clay "a book styled Truth Triu[m]phant" with the request that he accept the gift "from one unknown to thy self." Since "it has been upon my mind for some time past, to present said book to thee., believing as I do that obediance to my feelings when of a pure nature brings peace of mind and quietness of soul. . . . I have taken the liberty of sending said book unto thee, without knowing thee." ALS. KyBB.

On January 21, 1848, Clay thanked Meredith for the book "which, prompted by your friendly feelings towards me, you have done me the favor to present to me." Intends to give the book's "grave and important subjects . . . the most serious consideration" at the "earliest opportunity I can command to give it an attentive perusal." ALS. Courtesy of J. Winston Coleman, Jr., Lexington, Ky.

To RICHARD H. BAYARD Washington, January 15, 1848

I found, on my arrival here, your friendly letter of the 5h instant awaiting me. I thank you for your kind invitation to me to stop at your house, in the event of my going to Philadelphia. I am sure that no where in that City should I be so happy. It is my desire and present purpose to go to Philadelphia, if I possibly can. Indeed, independent of the gratification of meeting you and other friends, I have some professional business there which makes my presence necessary.[1] But the uncertainty of the progress on the docket of the Supreme Court[2] prevents my now deciding positively, and specifying a day when I shall be able to go, if at all. I will notify you beforehand, if I can have the pleasure of putting myself under your auspices[.]

In the mean time do me the favor to present my affectionate regards to Mrs. [Mary S.] Bayard and the young ladies.[3] As she has more leisure than you, I will thank you to say to her that I would be glad to receive from her a line informing me if certain events expected in your family are to take place or not,[4] and where you sister [Ann Caroline Bayard] is.

ALS. DeHi. 1. For Isaac Shelby, Jr. See Clay to Bayard, May 7, 1846. 2. *Houston* v. *The City Bank of New Orleans*. See Clay to Lucretia H. Clay, March 13, 1847. 3. Daughters: Mary Louisa, Caroline, Elizabeth, Harriet, Louisa. 4. Possibly the marriage of Eliza (Elizabeth). See Clay to Bayard, Oct. 19, 1848.

To CHRISTOPHER HUGHES Washington, January 15, 1848

I found on my arrival here the letter which you did me the favor to address to me at this place, and I have since received both your favors in regard to the little commission, with which I entrusted you, including the draft for $176:75, being the amount of my order on Mr. [Philip T.] Ellicott.[1] I thank you for your kind attention to that affair. Yesterday I sent to the Conductor of the Carr your Cloak, which I hope will have safely reached you.

I met with your Norwegian friend[2] at Mr. [Alexandre de] Bodisco's and was highly pleased with her. She told me that you were to receive her in Balto. The wedding[3] was quite a splendid concern, where I found many old acquaintances[.]

Mr. Carroll is perfectly right.[4] I am disappointed in my lodgings, which are not what I hoped they would be.[5] I am thinking about changing them. The difficulty in going to a private house is the pressure of the crowd which I might draw there.

My affectionate regards to Miss Margaret [Hughes.]

ALS. MiU-C. 1. Hughes's letter not found, but see Clay to Hughes, Jan. 12, 1848, in which the amount is given as $196.75. 2. Reference obscure. 3. Carolina de Bodisco married Brooke Williams at her father's home in Georgetown on Jan. 11, 1848. Washington *Daily National Intelligencer*, Jan. 14, 1848. 4. Probably Maryland congressman James Carroll. 5. Clay was staying at the U.S. Hotel in Washington.

To JAMES BROWN CLAY Washington, January 16, 1848

I received this moment your favor of the 10h. and was glad to hear that all are well at home. My cause is not likely to be reached, I fear, for two or three weeks, if it be reached at all.[1] I have not changed my purpose on the subject to which you refer. I have only suspended the execution of it, in deference to some friends who fear that bad consequences to the Cause and the Country might ensue if I were immediately to execute it.[2]

Mr. Jacobs [*sic*, Richard Taylor Jacob] is to be married tomorrow and I shall go to his wedding.[3]

I send a list of some plants which Mr. [William R.] Prince [Jr.] has forwarded to me.[4]

I am sorry that you indulge in bad spirits. You are wrong to do so, and I think you have no occasion to do so. You have much to cheer and animate you. More by far than most persons.

My love to Susan [Jacob Clay] & the children.

ALS. DLC-HC (DNA, M212, R6). Printed in Colton, *Clay Correspondence*, 4:553. 1. *Houston* v. *The City Bank of New Orleans*. See Clay to Lucretia H. Clay, March 13, 1847. 2. Clay had planned to announce that he would not be a candidate for president. See Clay to Mercer, Feb. 7, 1848. 3. Richard T. Jacob, brother of Susan Jacob Clay, married Sarah McDowell Benton, third daughter of Thomas Hart Benton, in Washington on Jan. 17, 1848. Washington *Daily National Intelligencer*, Jan. 24, 1848. 4. On March 2, 1848, Clay wrote William R. Prince [Jr.] thanking him for the "plants & shrubs which you have sent to Kentucky for me, in place of a previous parcel which had been cast overboard from the ship Quebec." LS. NcD.

Speech to American Colonization Society, Washington, D.C., January 18, 1848. States that he has been prevailed upon "rather against my own wishes, and quite unexpectedly" to "say a few words," but warns that "I have come here without a solitary note, with no prepared or elaborate speech." Mentions that while he was one of those who formed the colonization society about thirty years before, it has been "some years since I had the honor of sitting in your Society" and "in all human probability this is the last instance in which I shall ever be permitted to do so."

Recalls that when the society was formed [2:383-85], its intent was to establish a colony on the shores of Africa "to which free colored persons with their own voluntary consent might go. There was to be no constraint, no coercion, no compulsory process to which those who went must submit. . . . Far, very far, was it from our purpose to interfere with the slaves, or to shake or affect the title by which they are held in the least degree whatever. We saw and were fully aware of the fact that the free white race and the colored race never could live together on terms of equality. We did not stop to ask whether this was right or wrong: we looked at the fact, and on that fact we founded our operations. I know, indeed, that there are men, many of them of high respectability, who hold that all this is prejudice: that it should be expelled from our minds, and that we ought to recognise in men, though of different color from ourselves, members of our common race, entitled in all respects to equal privileges with ourselves. This may be so according to their view of the matter, but we went on the broad and incontestible fact that the two races could not, on equal terms, live in the same community harmoniously together. And we thought that the people of color should be voluntarily removed, if practicable, to their native country, or to the country at least of their ancestors. . . . we never thought of touching in any manner the title to slave property." Notes that they wanted only to show that colonization was practical and to provide a place where those who owned slaves, if they chose, could liberate and send them.

Points out that from its establishment the society "has had to stand the fire of batteries both in front and rear, and upon both flanks. Extremes of opinion and action, which could unite in nothing else, united in assaulting us," and includes those who fear for the safety of the institution of slavery as well as the abolitionists. Argues that the abolitionists should not oppose colonization since their object "is to emancipate at one blow the whole colored race. Well, if they can do that, then our object begins. The office of colonization commences only where theirs would end. . . . our object is to carry them to a place where they may enjoy, without molestation, all the benefits of freemen."

Refers to the argument that the colonization society can never effect its object without aid from the national government or the states. Says it is their purpose to demonstrate "the power of colonization" to the American people and to convince them that if they "take hold of this great project in their State Legislatures, or otherwise, the end sought is practicable." Also takes up the argument that Africa is not the country of blacks born in the United States. Asserts that "Africa is the real home of the black man, though, as a casual event, he may have had his birth on these shores. There his race was found, and there alone, till it was torn from thence by the hand of violence." Adds that colonization may also be the means of bringing Christianity to Africa. Mentions that there are already twenty-five places of public worship in Liberia, and contends that these colonists can be more effective in spreading Christianity than all the missionaries throughout the world. Contends that there is no place to which they could be sent as cheaply as to Africa where it costs only $50 per person for transportation and maintenance for six months.

Discusses the argument that even the national government could not afford to colonize all the free blacks. States in reply to this contention that immigration from abroad during the last year into the port of New York "was fully equal to the annual increase of the free colored population of the Union [a footnote states that immigration was 200,000; the increase of free blacks 65,000], and yet all that was done voluntarily." Believes that freed slaves will voluntarily go to Africa when properly informed of the improvement they can make in their condition. Asks "why should the free people of color in these United States not have the option of removing to Africa, or remaining where they are, just as they themselves shall choose? That is all we attempt."

Disputes the contention that colonization in Africa usually results in death, citing statistics that show the mortality in the twenty-five years of Liberia's existence to be 20%, far less than the death rate in the colonies of Plymouth and Jamestown. To those who say that not much has been accomplished in Liberia, asserts that four or five thousand emigrants reside there besides "thousands more of recaptured Africans" and "many thousands more in the United States now seeking the advantages of colonization." Notes that "it requires time to accomplish great national affairs. The creation of a nation is not the work of a day or of a century." Calls for the state governments to provide aid as Maryland has done.

Continues: "I ask of this entire Union (with possibly the exception of Massachusetts) does the black man, however fair may be his character, and from however long a line of free colored ancestors he may proceed, enjoy an equality with his white neighbor in social and political rights. In none: no where. As to social rights, they are out of the question. In no city, town, or hamlet throughout the entire land is he regarded as on an equal footing with us. The laws of all the States (and, in this respect, some of the free States are even more rigorous than the slave States themselves) render it impossible. And so great is the rigor of the laws in some of the States—rendered more vigorous by the schemes and efforts of the abolitionists—emancipation, under any circumstances and with whatever purpose, is absolutely prohibited." Notes that a man in Alabama whom he did not know recently bequeathed him twenty-five or thirty slaves, giving no cause for this action [McLain to Clay, January 2, 1845]. However, "I had some belief that the design of the testator in consigning these slaves to my care was that they should be sent to Liberia." Since arriving in Washington, has heard that twenty-three of the slaves "have embarked at New Orleans for the coast of Africa." They have done this of their own accord, because in Alabama they could not be free. The colonization society thus furnishes an opportunity to states and to individuals to emancipate their slaves despite laws to the contrary.

States that he will not touch the question of slavery but wishes to conclude by asking all parties, abolitionists and "those who carry the doctrine of slavery to the extreme; . . . to look calmly and dispassionately at the great enterprise we have in view." Contends that suppression of the slave trade would be much more effective if the entire coast of Africa were populated by free men of color.

Admits that one motive in founding the society was to lessen the bad influence on slaves of free people of color who make up a large portion of the population in jails and penitentiaries. Abolitionists have focused on this single motive and ignored all the others, arguing that colonization was a scheme of slaveholders to protect the institution. This is not a fair argument, he contends, because there were many other motives.

Concludes by congratulating the society on its success to date and urging it to continue the work. Copy. Printed in Washington *Daily National Intelligencer*, January 24, 1848; excerpts printed in Colton, *Clay Correspondence*, 3:75-77.

In 1832 the Maryland legislature had appropriated $20,000 per year for ten years to pay for transferring manumitted slaves from the state to Liberia. Staudenraus, *The African Colonization Movement*, 232.

To William H. Dorsey, Baltimore, January 22, 1848. Acknowledges an invitation to address "the Mercantile Library Association of Baltimore . . . during my sojourn at the Eastward." Appreciates "the compliment of this request" but regrets his "inability to assume the execution of the task," since "Professional business only brought me from home, and to that object I must confine myself." Intends to "remain in attendance upon the Supreme Court [Clay to Lucretia H. Clay, March 13, 1847], seizing any opportunity . . . for the fulfillment of my engagements." ALS. MdHi.

The Mercantile Library Association of Baltimore was founded in 1839 by the city's clerks and merchants. The organization served its members both as a library and a club until it was dissolved in 1928 and its collection dispersed at auction. William H. Dorsey served as vice president (1845), president (1847), and as a member of the board of directors (1848). He died at Baltimore in 1854. Information supplied by Donna Ellis, Maryland Historical Society, Baltimore, Md.

From George A. Hulbert *et al.*, Cortlandville, N.Y., January 31, 1848. Write as "young men now attentively engaged in the acquisition of knowledge" who hope "to calm somewhat the wavering billows of Life, and more successfully brave its tempests," while fulfilling "the high obligations that we owe to the Divine Author of our existence." Add: "Actuated by an increasing desire for a continued advancement in intellectual cultivation, ere our youthful days the most suitable time for mental improvement shall have speedily taken their flight, we in behalf of the members of the 'Jeffersonian Lyceum,' a Society established for mutual education, solicit. . . . some questions for discussion becoming our age." ALS. DLC-HC (DNA, M212, R6).

In 1848 Hulbert was an 18-year-old student living with the Eleazer Edgecomb family in Cortlandville, N.Y. Information supplied by Eileen J. O'Brien, New York State Historical Association, Cooperstown, N.Y., is based on the 1850 census for Cortlandville.

To JAMES BROWN CLAY Washington, February 1, 1848

I received your letter informing me of the occurrence which has taken H[enry]. C[lay]. Erwin to N[ew]. O[rleans]. I am deeply concerned about it; but I cannot but think that Mr. [Seargent S.] Prentiss will not fight him.[1] If he should decline doing so, I hope Henry will let it drop there, without resorting to any measure of violence or denunciation.

I have some hope of getting my cause tried next week,[2] altho' there is not, I regret to say, entire certainty in regard to it.

I enclose a bill of lading for a barrel of Sperm [whale] oil, presented by Mr. [Jared] Coffin, which I will thank you to hand to your mother[.][3]

I adhere to my purpose communicated to you before I left home. I have suspended the execution of it for the present, in consequence of strong assurances that if I take the step now it will be ruinous to the Whig party. It places me in a state of painful embarrassment[.][4]

My love to Susan [Jacob Clay] & the children.

ALS. DLC-HC (DNA, M212, R6). Printed in Colton, *Clay Correspondence*, 4:553-54. 1. Letter not found. While arguing a case in court, Prentiss had made derogatory references to James Erwin which were embellished in the press. Henry Clay Erwin took exception to these remarks about his father and challenged Prentiss to a duel. Prentiss reluctantly accepted the challenge, but friends intervened, Prentiss apologized, and the challenge was withdrawn. George L. Prentiss (ed.), *A Memoir of S.S. Prentiss*, 2 vols. (New York, 1858), 2:435-44. 2. *Houston* v. *The City Bank of New Orleans*. See Clay to Lucretia H. Clay, March 13, 1847. 3. Not found. 4. An announcement that he would not be a candidate for president. See Clay to Mercer, Feb. 7, 1848.

From James Laurence Day, Madison, Morris Co., N.J., February 7, 1848. Addresses Clay as president of the American Colonization Society and assures him that "No friend of the colored man can read your Lexington speech [Speech in Lexington, November 13, 1847] & not acknowledge your stand in favour of African colonization, among slave holders and on slave territory, as, (next to your views on the Mexican war question) the crowning honour of this the winter of your most useful life." Describes Clay's reputation as "dear to the memory of the sons of freedom—not less to the new-born family on the West coast of Africa . . . than to us for your uncompromising opposition to executive usurpation."

Views African colonization as "one of the noblest enterprises & worthy [of] the best exertions of the ablest minds," a belief strengthened by "three and a half years residence among its people." Although "Liberia . . . has had conservative intelligence and virtue enough" in the past, "*now* . . . she needs the whole counsel of her friends to instruct her in the most enlightened political economy, that she may be led to every possible developement of the national and agricultural (as well as educational) resources of the country. Neglecting this she may prate of freedom forever and her friends here do the same and she will remain weak and defenseless Liberia still." Argues that if Liberia exports "a few hogsheads of sugar and a few bags of coffee, not as curiosities, but as commercial staples . . . the able & enterprizing free-colored man . . . will not ask the colonization society what it will give him to go, but on what terms he *may* go."

Asks Clay to invite "the Congress of the United States and the Legislature of each State . . . *to authorize the presentation to the Republic of Liberia yearly and every year, of the published proceedings of their several bodies—the public acts, and above all the chancery & supreme court reports,*" which would "form a most valuable fountain of Legal and political knowledge, the worth of which Liberia will find it in her future history fully to appreciate." ALS. DLC-HC (DNA, M212, R6).

Dr. Day had practiced medicine in Wilkes Barre, Pa., before serving as colonial physician in Liberia from 1840-43. Bell I. Wiley, *Slaves No More, Letters from Liberia 1833-1869* (Lexington, Ky., 1980), 317.

To WILLIAM NEWTON MERCER Washington, February 7, 1848

I was extremely sorry to learn from your letter just recd. (enclosing one from Mr. [F.D.] Conrad)[1] that your health and that of the Ladies of your family had not been good. I fervently hope that this letter may find it re-established. My own has been quite as good as in this Northern climate I could have expected. The amount placed in your hands by Mr. Conrad, I will thank you, at your convenience, to invest in a good N. York bill at 60 days after sight, and forward it to me at Philada. whither I purpose going in about a fortnight, and I shall remain there probably long enough to receive your letter.

I left home with a determination publicly to announce my disinclination to the use of my name as a Candidate for the P[residency]. Upon my arrival here, I have been induced, by the state of things which I found existing, to *suspend*, at least, the execution of that purpose. I found in all the Free States a great indisposition to take up Genl. [Zachary] Taylor.[2] I was assured that my withdrawal would be attended with the prostration of the Whig party in them; that I only could receive the support of the Whig votes in those States; that N. York was as certain for me, if my name were used, as any State in the Union[3]; and that even elections, now fast approaching, would be lost if I withdrew. It was not easy to resist the force of entreaties founded on this posture of affairs. In momentarily yielding to them, I reserved the right freely to act ultimately on my own convictions. To you I need not say that I should be most happy to be forever liberated from all political tyes and entanglements.

The prevalent opinion here (and it is my own) that Genl. Taylor cannot get the nomination of the N[ational]. [Whig] Convention, now absolutely determined on, nor secure his election, if he remains in his present non-committal position as to parties and measures.[4]

I shewed you a letter I addressed to him last Septr.[5] In due season, I received his answer full of the most friendly expressions, and proper sentiments.[6] I wish I could shew it to you; but I am unwilling to confide it to the casualties of the Mail.

We began today in the S[upreme]. Court the argument of three causes, of which our Friend Freeland's is one.[7] It will occupy two or three more days. I wish you would mention it to him. Mr. R[everdy]. Johnson assists me in the argument.

I will write you again before I return some time in March to Kentucky. My affectionate regards to Miss [Eliza] Young Anna [Mercer] & Miss [Mary D.] Kemble.

ALS. LU-Ar. Letter marked "(Confidential)." 1. Neither Mercer's nor Conrad's letter has been found. 2. Clay to Ullmann, August 4, 1847; Clay to Greeley, Nov. 30, 1847. 3. Horace Greeley and others were assuring Clay of this, at least partly, if not primarily, in an effort to stop Taylor's nomination. In addition, the New York City Whig General Committee on Feb. 1, 1848, adopted resolutions recommending Clay for the Whig presidential nomination in 1848. Clay to Greeley, Nov. 30 and Dec. 10, 1847; Clay to McMichael, Dec. 1, 1847; Washington *Daily National Intelligencer*, Feb. 7, 1848; Van Deusen, *Horace Greeley*, 119-22. 4. Clay to Ullmann, August 4, 1847. 5. Not found. 6. Taylor to Clay, Nov. 4 and Dec. 28, 1847. 7. Clay and Reverdy Johnson presented oral arguments in the case of *Houston* v. *The City Bank of New Orleans*. The other two cases have not been identified, since Clay made no other oral presentations. Freeland was probably John Freeland, originally of Virginia, who had settled in New Orleans and made a fortune as a cotton merchant. About 1856 he returned to Virginia and died in Richmond in 1872. Richmond *Whig and Advertiser*, Dec. 10, 1872.

From William McLain, Washington, D.C., February 9, 1848. Communicates "the following resolution" from the "*Board of Directors* of the American Colonization Society": "*Resolved*, That the grateful thanks of this Board are eminently due to the Hon. H. Clay, the venerated President of our Society for the highly interesting & able address delivered at our recent Annual Meeting in the Capitol [Speech to American Colonization Society, January 18, 1848]." Since "the address has been read by thousands who would not have read any thing on the Subject from any other Man . . . it has thus accomplished immense good for the cause." ALS. DLC-Records of the American Colonization Society (DNA, M212, R20).

To MARY S. BAYARD Washington, February 12, 1848

I am afraid you accuse me of neglect in not [words excised from text] transmitted an answer to your favor of the 18h. Ulto. I beg to assure you that none was intended. I have been kept here in a state of the greatest uncertainty about the trial of the cause which brought me here,[1] and, as my future movements depended upon that, I forebore to write until I could say what was certain as to them. At last my cause has been tried, the argument in it having been concluded by me yesterday, and I once more feel in the enjoyment of a degree of freedom.

I have to remain here next week, and the week after, I think early in it, I shall take my departure for Philada. stopping a day or two in Balto. as I do not wish to reach Philadelphia until *after* the [Zachary] Taylor demonstration.[2]

My anxious wish was to have gone directly to Mr. [Richard H.] Bayard and you, and to have placed myself under those friendly auspices, which have heretofore afforded me so much repose & happiness; but Col. [John M.] Swift the Mayor[3] has been here, and has insisted, with so much earnestness and authority, that I should first stop at his house, that I have been forced into one of those compromises, in private affairs, which I have been sometimes compelled to make in public. I have consented to remain with him two days only upon the express condition that I might freely afterwards go to your house, if you would agree to receive me. I was the more reconciled to this arrangement, because I was in hopes, that, if my arrival created any commotion, you and Mr. B. would escape the annoyance.

I hope then, my beloved friend, soon to be with you, and I reserve for that agreeable occasion all relating to public matters which I have not treated of in this. Say to the girls that I am provoked that certain interesting ceremonies are not likely to occur in the case of either of them, during my sojourn in the City of brotherly love.[4] To them, and to Mr. Bayard, I pray you to offer assurances of the warm esteem . . .

ALS. DeHi. 1. *Houston* v. *The City Bank of New Orleans*. See Clay to Lucretia H. Clay, March 13, 1847. 2. A meeting to promote Taylor's candidacy, and to celebrate both Washington's birthday and the first anniversary of the Battle of Buena Vista was held on Feb. 22, 1848, at Philadelphia. A letter from Taylor to Joseph Ingersoll was read at the meeting. Washington *Daily National Intelligencer*, Feb. 24, 1848. 3. Swift (1790-1873), a lawyer, was mayor of Philadelphia in 1832-38, 1839-40, 1845-48. Holli, *Biographical Dictionary of American Mayors*; *CAB*. 4. The daughters were Mary Louisa, Caroline, Elizabeth, Harriet, and Louisa. Reference is to possible marriages. See Clay to Bayard, Oct. 19, 1848.

To JOHN SLOANE Washington, February 12, 1848

I received your friendly letter,[1] and it affor[d]ed me very great satisfaction to find that you, who have ever been one of my truest, best and most stedfast friends, remain firm and faithful in your attachment to me.

I left home with a resolution to announce to the public, in some suitable form, my disinclination to the use of my name again as a Candidate for the Presidency. But I thought it due to friends, before I took that final step, to consult with them here. Upon my arrival, I was most earnestly appealed to, chiefly from the Free States but not exclusively, to abandon or suspend the execution of that purpose.[2] I was told, if I did not, that the Whig party would be prostrated in them; that approaching elections would be lost; and that Genl. [Zachary] Taylor, if he could be elected under any circumstances (which some doubted) could not be if he continued to maintain his present noncommittal position.[3]

I consented not to abandon but to *suspend* the fulfillment of my design, and so I remain. I feel great embarrassment in this perplexing attitude. And I think I cannot much longer delay taking a decisive step.

My belief is that a great deal in the Taylor movement[4] is artificial and manufactured; but then examples are not few of ultimate success in that process of creating public opinion.

It is my opinion that, if this Mexican War continue to the time of the Election, any Whig, who can combine the party, may be elected. But I have been so often before the public, that nothing but a conviction (which I do not feel) that a *majority* of the Nation required my services, could reconcile me to another use of my name. I am not at all surprized that many good men have become tired by the unavailing efforts to use it with success. I have no reproaches to make them, and I make none.

If we are to credit official communications from the President [James K. Polk], the rumors of peace are unfounded.[5]

I shall leave here the week after next for Philada. where some business takes me, and where I shall continue a week or ten days.

ALS. MH. 1. Not found. 2. Clay to Mercer, Feb. 7, 1848. 3. Clay to Ullmann, August 4, 1847. 4. Greeley to Clay, Nov. 15, 1846; White to Clay, Sept. 4, 1847. 5. On Feb. 2, 1848, Polk had reported to the Senate on the progress of negotiations between the U.S. peace commissioner and the Mexican commissioners during a suspension in hostilities. He noted that "the invitation from the commissioner of the United States to submit the proposition of boundary referred to in his dispatch of the 4th of September 1847 . . . was unauthorized by me, and was promptly disapproved." On Feb. 10 Polk notified the Senate that "No communication has been received from Mexico 'containing propositions from the Mexican authorities or commissioners for a treaty of peace,' except the 'counter projet' presented by the Mexican commissioners on the 6th of September . . . which . . . I communicated to the Senate of the United States on the 2d instant." *MPP*, 4:569, 572. For the peace treaty, see Clay to Beatty, April 29, 1847.

To HENRY T. DUNCAN Washington, February 15, 1848

I recd. your letter of the 9th. inst. and I was gratified with the proceedings in Bourbon, of which it gave a full account.[1] I presume through other channels you are advised of the state of public affairs here. I see no prospect of peace at present.[2] Upon my arrival here the strongest appeals have been made to me to take no step withdrawing my name from among those from which a selection is to be made of a candidate for the Presidency. I have been assured that, if I did, it would lead to a prostration of the Whig party, especially in the Free states.[3] Then they say that Genl [Zachary] Taylor cannot be supported in his present non-committal position. Some doubt, if he were to assume distinct Whig ground, whether he could obtain the whig support.[4] I have suspended any definitive action.

Great surprise exists here as to the hot haste of our Taylor friends in Ky.[5] Why is it? I am often asked, without being able to give any very satisfactory answer—What will be the issue of the two Conventions in Frankfort next week?[6] Nobody knows here. After the long period of time during which I have had the happiness to enjoy the friendship and confidence of that state, what have I done, it is enquired, to lose it? Those conventions, if they would act wisely, I think would acquiesce in the N[ational]. Convention and leave their own delegates to act freely, according to all circumstances.

My suit has been argued in the S[upreme] Court,[7] and I shall leave this place next week for Philada where some business takes me[.]

Copy. DLC-HC (DNA, M212, R6). Printed in Colton, *Clay Correspondence*, 4:554-55. 1. Letter not found. On Feb. 7, 1848, Whigs met in Bourbon County and appointed delegates to attend the Kentucky State Whig convention at Frankfort on Feb. 22. These delegates were instructed to select 2 delegates from Kentucky to attend the Whig National convention. Lexington *Observer & Kentucky Reporter*, Feb. 12, 1848. 2. Clay to Beatty, April 29, 1847. 3. Clay to Mercer, Feb. 7, 1848. 4. Clay to Ullmann, August 4, 1847; Clay to Greeley, Nov. 30, 1847. 5. Clay to White, Sept. 4, 1847; Clay to Crittenden, Sept. 20, 1847. 6. Clay to Unknown Recipient, *ca.* Winter 1847-48. 7. *Houston* v. *The City Bank of New Orleans.* Clay to Lucretia H. Clay, March 13, 1847.

From John L. Lawrence *et al.*, Albany, N.Y., February 16, 1848. On behalf of 38 additional "undersigned Whig members of the Legislature of the State of New York," who believe "that the interests of the country essentially demand the elevation to the Chief Magistracy of a third statesman of talent, learning, experience and integrity, and whose principles are known and understood by the people," inform Clay that they intend to "recommend him to the Whig National Convention [Greeley to Clay, November 15, 1846] as the favorite of the State of New York." LS. DLC-TJC (DNA, M212, R11). See Clay to Greeley, December 10, 1847.

From William G. Payne, Carrollton, Ky., February 16, 1848. Regrets he cannot "visit you at Ashland . . . as I am obliged to return to Virginia on some Court business . . . & surely I can do you more good there than here." Believes that Virginia "has Once again come to her sences & will support you so will New York & New Jersey." As a "Hanoverian . . . born in the year of Independance" and who remains "Independant in all my Political feelings," views "the Butlers here" as "Clever Men . . . but their political Creed & mine is wide apart, at all events I shall support you & no One Else." Thinks well "of Genl [Zachary] Taylor," but "Genl [Winfield] Scott . . . is my next Man after yourself." Assures Clay that if "Mr [James K.] Polk had . . . been as well known as he now is; He never could have been Elected." ALS. DLC-HC (DNA, M212, R6).

The "Butlers" probably refers to the prominent Butler family of nearby Louisville, which included Democrat William O. Butler.

To LUCRETIA HART CLAY Washington, February 18, 1848

I finished the argument of my cause this day week.[1] My friends were highly gratified with it, and I was well satisfied. I feel very confident of success; but the Court has not yet decided it. I was in hopes that the cause would be decided before I left this City, which I purpose doing to go to Philada. the 23d. instant. The Court has however a great amount of business before it, and I draw no unfavorable conclusions from the delay.

I have been excessively overrun with Company at the Tavern (the U.S. Hotel) at which I stopt, and have been very much jaded. To get a little rest, and to catch some breath, I have accepted an invitation from Mr. [Joseph] Gales [Jr.] to remain at his house, during the few days which I shall continue here. I have just removed into it, and find my quarters both quiet and elegant. It is Mr. [Matthew] St. C[lair]. Clarke's house on the Square of the Presidents. I dined at the Presidents [James K. Polk] the day before yesterday, and was entertained with the greatest civility.

I shall stop in Philada. about a week, and then returning, via Balto. proceed home. It may be the 15h. March before I get there. I expect to stop a day or two in Pittsburg[h].

I recd. a letter from N. Orleans, sent me by James [Brown Clay], with a Check for $175 the amt. of your hams then sold.[2] They proposed forwarding one or two boxes to Boston.

I still suspend the execution of the resolution in regard to the P[residency]. and may not take any decisive step until I get home.[3] This is the course strongly urged by many friends.

We have delightful weather here at present. If it be as good with you, all hands are gardening today.

Thomas [Hart Clay] wrote me about the mistake in making your ginger Cakes.[4] The effects upon whose who ate them must have been very ludicrous.

I have gone out very little to parties or dinner; and have not been out of bed after 10 O Clock more than two or three times since I have been here.

My love to all at home.

ALS. DLC-HC (DNA, M212, R6). 1. *Houston* v. *The City Bank of New Orleans*. See Clay to Lucretia H. Clay, March 13, 1847. 2. Not found. 3. See Clay to The Public, April 10, 1848, in which he announced his willingness to accept the nomination, if offered. 4. Reference obscure.

To LESLIE COMBS Washington, February 18, 1848

I received your favor this morning. I have written this winter no letters to Kentucky on public affairs but in answer to letters which I received, and of this description only three.[1] That which you thought ought to have been addressed to you was of that character.

I remain in my passive position in regard to the Presidency. To this course I have been strongly urged. It is generally approved. Whether and when I may change it depends on circumstances.[2] There is no occasion for precipitate action. Mine at least shall be deliberate; having due regard to country, party, friends. If I were to credit all I hear and see, there would be no doubt of my election, if nominated by the National Convention, with my consent; but experience has brought diffidence, and I do not lend too ready an ear to even agreeable things.

I learn from New York that there is not a particle of doubt that, if I were a candidate, the vote of that State would be given me by an immense majority. The Legislature (I mean the Whigs) have had a caucus, in which they passed a resolution, with I believe unanimity, designating me, although not naming me, and excluding our friend General [Zachary] Taylor, though not naming him.[3] Our Kentucky and other friends ought to know what an up-hill business that is of supporting the General in the free States; and yet I lose no suitable occasion to impress on all union, harmony and concord.

I am fully convinced that no preference will be expressed next week in Virginia, at Richmond,[4] for General Taylor; most probably none will be expressed for any one.

I expect to be in Philadelphia the two or three last days of this month and the first week of the next. If I can give any impulse to your business there, I shall not fail to do it.[5]

Copy. Printed in Colton, *Clay Correspondence*, 4:555. 1. One of the letters was probably Clay to Duncan, Feb. 15, 1848; however, the other two have not been identified. 2. Clay to Lucretia

H. Clay, Feb. 18, 1848. 3. Clay to Greeley, Dec. 10, 1847; Lawrence *et al.* to Clay, Feb. 16, 1848. 4. The Virginia State Whig convention met at Richmond on Feb. 24-25, 1848, and by a vote of 87 to 18, passed resolutions recommending Zachary Taylor to be the Whig nominee, but promising to support the candidate nominated by the national convention. Washington *Daily National Intelligencer*, Feb. 28, 1848. 5. Combs's business probably had to do with his suit against the Bank of Kentucky in which a Philadelphia court had awarded him $14,500 for serving as an attorney in the Schuylkill Bank case. Collins, *History of Kentucky*, 1:55.

From DANIEL ULLMANN Philadelphia, February 18, 1848

Your kind favor of the 4th Aug. last, from Virginia White S[ulphur]. Springs, was duly received, and its valuable suggestions acted upon.[1]

I have been for some time in this city and in New York conversing with numbers of our friends, observing the course of affairs, and endeavoring, in my humble way, to aid in giving them a right direction.

Oppressed as you must be by all sorts of demands upon your time, I should not venture to occupy a moment of it, were it not that I feel constrained to add my voice to those of your other long tried friends, to pray and entreat you, for our, for your own, and for your country's sake, not to say any thing to the public which shall prevent us from insisting that you shall be our leader in the coming great campaign; on whose result many of us believe will hinge the fate of our Government and nation. We feel strongly and deeply on this subject; and, I assure you, that your real friends are now in that state of mind which will cause them to put forth exertions which will eclipse all their former efforts in your behalf.

Of course I put little or no faith in the thousand rumors of the press respecting your intentions. Most of them are plainly fabrications. I know that when Henry Clay speaks it will be in a way that his friends will understand. Our position at this time is strong. Eternal right and truth are on our side. The principles of your Lexington speech[2] must sink deep into the honest heart of the nation. As to what this city and state [Pennsylvania] may do, you know that I think it of minor consequence. I am well satisfied that they cannot give the vote of the State to any Whig. They, therefore, should have no weight in our councils.

It is different with N. York. The meeting of last night at Castle Garden shows where the Whigs of the city are, and the intelligent action of the Whig members of the Legislature is a true index of the State.[3] Our "weak brethren" will be strengthened by these proceedings. The men who are now busy against us, are, with some marked exceptions, the same who defeated us at Harrisburg in 1839.[4] Their demonstration on the 22d will reveal their real strength.[5] Should Gen. [Lewis] Cass or any man of his stamp be the Loco candidate, the Barnburners section will surely throw their influence into your scale, notwithstanding the passages in the address of the Utica Convention[6] which met yesterday, that apparently conflict[s] with this view. They will either drive the Baltimore convention[7] into the adoption of their views respecting the "Wilmot proviso",[8] which I look upon as not to be thought of, or they will indirectly throw their influence in your favor. If New York[9] and Ohio[10] go for you, it ought to decide the matter with all honest Whigs. I fear that I shall tire you, and therefore will close. This much I have been forced to write, because, even if I should be so fortunate as to see you here, you will be so surrounded, that it will be impossible for me to have any conversation with you.

Until the close of next week I shall be at this House;[11] after that, my address will be No. 27 Wall Street, New York.

ALS. DLC-HC (DNA, M212, R6). Letter marked "(Confidential)." 1. Clay to Ullmann, August 4, 1847. 2. Speech in Lexington, Nov. 13, 1847. 3. Clay to McMichael, Dec. 1, 1847; Clay to Greeley, Dec. 10, 1847; Lawrence *et al.* to Clay, Dec. 16, 1847. 4. See 9:92, 116-17, 288, 455. 5. A meeting attended by an estimated 5,000 had been held at Military Hall in New York City on Feb. 15, 1848, to nominate Taylor for president. Another meeting, held outside the hall with possibly more people than the one inside, also endorsed Taylor and adjourned to meet at Niblo's Garden on Feb. 22. Speakers at the latter meeting included Henry and Moses Grinnell and Ogden Hoffman. Pittsburgh *Daily Gazette*, Feb. 28, 1848; New York *Daily Herald*, Feb. 16 and 23, 1848. 6. The Democratic (Barnburner or Wilmot Proviso) convention met at Utica on Feb. 17, 1848, and adopted a long address opposing the extension of slavery. They elected Churchill C. Cambreleng and Jared Wilson as two of the delegates to the Democratic National convention to be held at Baltimore. They did not instruct them as to whom they should support for the nomination. Washington *Daily National Intelligencer*, Feb. 21, 1848. 7. Clay to Ullmann, May 12, 1847. 8. Sargent to Clay, Feb. 27, 1847. 9. At the 1848 Whig National convention at Philadelphia, New York gave Clay fairly solid support on the first three ballots: on the 1st Clay received 20 votes, Webster 1, Scott 5, and John M. Clayton 1; on the 2nd Clay had 28, Taylor 1, Webster 1, Scott 5, and Clayton 1; on the 3rd Clay had 28, Taylor 2, and Scott 6. On the 4th ballot Clay won only by 14 votes to 6 for Taylor and 16 for Scott. Arthur M. Schlesinger, Jr. (ed.), *History of U.S. Political Parties*, 4 vols. (New York, 1973), 1:436-39. 10. At the Whig National convention, Ohio gave Clay and Taylor only 1 vote each on all four ballots, while Scott won the remaining 21 on all except the first, when he won 20 votes and John McLean 1. *Ibid.* The Whig party in Ohio was fragmented over the slavery extension issue and supported Scott primarily in the hope of stopping Taylor. Clay supporters were particularly outraged because Whig Gov. William Bebb had assured Clay that he would have Ohio's support at the national convention. See Bebb to Clay, April 4, 1848. 11. Columbia House, Philadelphia.

To Robert C. Winthrop, Washington, D.C., February 18, 1848. Because "I have been dining out and dissipating so much this week," asks to be excused from a social engagement. Assures Winthrop that if "the Ladies expected by you from Boston had arrived, I should have made a most extraordinary effort to meet them," but, since they have not yet come, hopes he can "fill the place reserved for me with some less prostrated friend." ALS. MeB.

Winthrop (1809-94), a member of the House of Representatives from Massachusetts, was Speaker of the House during the Thirtieth and part of the Thirty-first Congresses. *BDAC.*

To Sheehan and Duggan, New York City, February 19, 1848. Thanks them for their letter "with the exquisitely beautiful case of Razors which . . . accompanied it." Notes that they have given him this "testimonial . . . in consequence of some feelings I expressed, and some sympathies I cherished, for the suffering people of Ireland." Adds: "Gentlemen, I do not deserve it. I must have had a heart colder than stone, if I had been capable of listening to the sad accounts of Irish distress without the deepest emotions. My regret was, that I could do little or nothing to mitigate the suffering of a generous and gallant people."

Mentions that they have told him that the case and its contents which they have given him were made abroad. States: "They do not, on that account, command themselves less to my acceptance and admiration. I hope that I have liberality enough to recognize excellence, in Science and in the Arts, whether displayed in foreign or domestic productions. Indeed, my anxious desire to naturalize in our own country all that genius, skill and invention can contribute to the comfort, elegance and happiness of our race, has proceeded from witnessing how much has been accomplished, in other civilized countries, towards these noble ends."

Extends his "fervent prayers that Ireland, and you, and all your countrymen, may ever hereafter be happy and prosperous." Copy. Printed in Lexington *Observer & Kentucky Reporter*, March 15, 1848. See also Bragaw to Clay, December 30, 1846, and Speech in New Orleans, February 4, 1847. The Frankfort *Commonwealth* of March 7, 1848, identifies Sheehan and Duggan as Irishmen by birth, now associated with "a firm in New York." The firm, which was not further identified, was located on Maiden Lane, New York City. Lexington *Observer & Kentucky Reporter*, March 4, 1848.

An undated excerpt of a letter from two unnamed Irishmen in New York, printed by Calvin Colton, is undoubtedly Sheehan and Duggan's letter to Clay which accompanied their "handsome present of cutlery." In it, they state that one of them had "the good fortune . . . to hear your speech [Speech in New Orleans, February 4, 1847] in behalf of the famishing millions of our native land, when in New Orleans on business, during that dreadful winter of 1846-47. It has since been the fortune of the other to hear and to witness in Ireland, and elsewhere in Europe, the estimation and gratitude which that speech has excited. It is our pleasing duty to thank God that your thrilling appeal to the best feelings of our common humanity was the means, by stimulating the energies of ever-blessed charity among the American people, of saving thousands of our countrymen from a death of agony and horror." Add that "American benevolence is devoutly blessed in parlor and cabin, where even *your* name, illustrious as it is, had hardly been heard before the famine; and that thousands . . . invoke blessings on the head of HENRY CLAY."

Present him with the gift which is "the work of foreign artisans" and hope that "it may not, on that account, be unacceptable," but that it "among your many tokens of American esteem and thankfulness, a single remembrance of the tears of gratitude which, at the mention of your name, have bedewed the cheek of suffering Ireland, may not be unwelcome." Copy. Printed in Colton, *Clay Correspondence*, 3:49.

To THOMAS B. STEVENSON Washington, February 19, 1848

I have received your favor of the 11th inst for which I thank you. I have only time to express the results of my observation and opinion.

1st I think the fervor for General [Zachary] Taylor has abated.

2d That it is probably impracticable for him to get the nomination, or if he were to get it, to be elected, without a more distinct avowal of Whig principles than he has yet made.[1]

3d That the demonstrations in my favor have considerably increased of late.

Nevertheless, I maintain my passive position; neither, for the present, consenting to or refusing the use of my name.

On reaching home in March, and after a careful survey of the whole ground of my duty to our Country, to our principles and to myself—I may finally decide.[2]

I am afraid that Congress will do nothing to end the War. Its moral courage has increased since the commencement of the session, but I apprehend has not yet reached the point of decisive & distinctive action.[3] On all these matters, however, you are better advised by other friends.——On business of a private nature I go to Philadelphia next week, and hope to reach home by or before the 25th inst.

Copy. OCHP. Partially printed in Colton, *Clay Correspondence*, 3:461. Letter marked "Private." 1. Clay to Ullmann, August 4, 1847; Clay to White, Sept. 20, 1847; Greeley to Clay, Nov. 30, 1847; Clay to Mercer, Feb. 7, 1848. 2. Clay to Lucretia H. Clay, Feb. 18, 1848; Clay to The Public, April 10, 1848. 3. For instance, a bill authorizing the president to call out additional forces for prosecution of the Mexican War had been tabled in the Senate on Jan. 5, 1848. *Cong. Globe*, 30 Cong., 1 Sess., 74, 111.

To RICHARD COLLINS[1] Washington, February 20, 1848

I thank you for your letter of the 13h. inst. My correspondence with Frankfort this winter has been very limited; but through others I have been kept posted up as to the state of public affairs. I wish it was better. Before this letter reaches you, the several Conventions which were to assemble on the 22d will have acted.[2] I sincerely hope that their deliberations may be characterized by wisdom & harmony and their decisions may redound to the honor of the State.

I was induced on my arrival here to *suspend* the execution of the purpose I communicated to you at Maysville. I was led to believe that, if I did not, it might prove fatal to the Whig party in the free States, lose us probably elections in one or more of them, and possibly end in the total disorgination of the party.[3] Genl. [Zachary] Taylor is far from being a favorite in the free States, and in his present noncommittal position, I do not believe can be elected. And the difficulty is, how can he change it, after what he has deliberately and repeatedly written?[4] If I were to retire, some other Whig would spring up, who would divide if he did not carry all of the free States.

I have concluded therefore, for the present, to take no decided step, and to await until I can get a better view of the whole ground of my duty to the Country, to my friends and to myself.[5]

I hope to find you at Maysville on my return home.

ALS. OCHP. 1. For Gen. Richard Collins (1797-1855)—Maysville merchant, railroad president, and Kentucky legislator—see Collins, *History of Kentucky*, 2:587-88. 2. Clay to Unknown Recipient, *ca.* Winter 1847-48. 3. Reference is to his intent to announce he would not be a candidate for president. Clay to Mercer, Feb. 7, 1848. 4. Clay to Ullmann, August 4, 1847; Clay to White, Sept. 20, 1847. 5. Clay to The Public, April 10, 1848.

To JAMES BROWN CLAY Washington, February 21, 1848

Mr. [John Quincy] Adams was stricken to day in his seat in the H[ouse]. of R[epresentatives]. with paralysis, and, if not now dead, it is believed that he cannot live until night.[1] Both houses immediately adjourned[.]

The Court has not yet decided my cause;[2] but as it has a press of business before it, I do not draw any unfavorable conclusion from the delay. I cannot lose it.

I shall leave this City the day after tomorrow for Philadelphia on Mr. [Isaac] Shelbys [Jr.'s][3] business, and shall be detained there about a week.

Mr. [Nicholas] Trist has certainly concluded a treaty with the Mexican Comm[issio]n, which is now in this City. I understand that it cedes the boundary of the Rio Bravo [Rio Grande], all New Mexico, and Upper California; & that we are to pay 15 millions of dollars, besides assuming the payment of the debt due from Mexico to our Citizens.[4] I am told that the Treaty will be submitted to the Senate for its advice &c.

I wrote to your mother[5] that I had received the Check which you sent me from N[ew]. O[rleans].

My friends appear to increase in confidence that I will obtain the nomination if I desire it. I have postponed final action until my return home[.][6]

My love to Susan [Jacob Clay], Lucy [Jacob Clay], and your other children.[7]

ALS. DLC-TJC (DNA, M212, R11). Printed in Colton, *Clay Correspondence*, 4:556. 1. Adams suffered a stroke in the House of Representatives on Feb. 21, 1848. He lapsed into a coma and died on Feb. 23. Marie B. Hecht, *John Quincy Adams* (New York, 1972), 626-28. 2. *Houston v. The City Bank of New Orleans*. See Clay to Lucretia H. Clay, March 13, 1847. 3. Clay to Bayard, May 7, 1846. 4. Clay to Beatty, April 29, 1847. 5. Clay to Lucretia H. Clay, Feb. 18, 1848. 6. *Ibid.*; Clay to The Public, April 10, 1848. 7. James (b. 1846) and John (b. 1847 or 1848).

From William McLain, Washington, February 21, 1848. Informs Clay that he would "answer *Prof.* [Simon] *Greenleafs* letter, but *My answer* would not Meet his expectation." Explains that Greenleaf "wants the *Name* of *H. Clay* to show to some of the *Merchant Princes* in Boston to induce *them* to *contribute*." Hopes Clay will answer Greenleaf who is doing much "to check *abolition opposition* & increase our funds." ALS. DLC-Records of the American Colonization Society (DNA, M212, R20).

Greenleaf (1783-1853), a Harvard law professor and president of the Massachusetts Colonization Society, drafted the constitution which was accepted in principle by Liberia in 1847. *CAB*; Charles M. Wilson, *Liberia, Black Africa in Microcosm* (New York, 1971), 51, 57.

To THOMAS SNOWDEN & WILLIAM M. MEREDITH[1] Washington, February 21, 1848

I have received your obliging letter, transmitting a Copy of a preamble and resolution, adopted by the Select and Common Councils of the City of Philadelphia,[2] presenting their respectful salutations and cordial welcome, on the occasion of my intended sojourn in that City, and tendering to me the use of Independence Hall to meet my fellow citizens.

I am greatly honored and obliged by this distinguished proof of the friendly consideration of the Select and Common Councils of Philadelphia, and request you to present to them my cordial thanks & respectful acknowledgments. Called by private and professional business to that City, it was my wish to avoid all ceremonies, and to be allowed to sojourn in it, as a private Citizen. Should it become necessary to use the Hall of Independence, for the purpose indicated, I shall avail myself, with gratitude, of the proffered privilege.[3]

ALS. DeHi. 1. Thomas Snowden had been elected president of the common council of the City of Philadelphia on Oct. 15, 1847. *Journal of the Common Council of the City of Philadelphia . . . October 15, 1847 . . .* (Philadelphia, 1848), 4. For William M. Meredith—lawyer, former state legislator, and at this time president of the select council of Philadelphia—see *DAB*. 2. The preamble noted that Clay was to be in Philadelphia and the resolution, adopted on Feb. 17, 1848, announced that the common and select councils would welcome and wait upon him during his visit to the city. Philadelphia *North American and United States Gazette*, Feb. 18, 1848. 3. Speech at Independence Hall, Philadelphia, Feb. 26, 1848.

To CHRISTOPHER HUGHES Washington, February 22, 1848

I leave here in the Cars tomorrow evening at five O'Clock, and after stopping with you in Balto. tomorrow night, I must proceed the next morning (thursday) to the City of Philada. I had hoped to have remained longer with you, but must reserve that pleasure to my return.

By the time this reaches you, poor Mr. [John Quincy] Adams will be probably no more.[1] You will have heard that he was yesterday stricken with paralysis in his seat in the H[ouse]. of R[epresentatives]. So we go!

My affectionate regards to Miss Margaret [Hughes].

ALS. MiU-C. 1. Clay to James B. Clay, Feb. 21, 1848.

Resolution of the Common Council of the City of New York, February 22, 1848. Hopes that Clay "may be persuaded by a respectful invitation to extend his journey" from Philadelphia to New York so that "all who wish, may be permitted to offer their respects and interchange affectionate salutations—with that venerated and illustrious Statesman." Resolves, therefore, "that the Hospitalities of the City be tendered to Henry Clay by this Common Council" and instructs that "a committee of five from each Board"—the board of aldermen and the board of assistant aldermen—carry the resolution into effect. D. MiU-C.

Speech at Independence Hall, Philadelphia, February 26, 1848. Expresses gratitude to Philadelphia and her citizens for their "kindness, attention, and regard." Notes that in his "long and chequered career, his life had not been free from vicissitudes; but under every circumstance, and however situated, he had always met with kindness in Philadelphia."

Disclaims any intent to make a formal speech, and even if he "had contemplated any thing of the kind, his feelings on account of the recent death of Mr. [John Q.] Adams [Clay to James B. Clay, February 21, 1848] would reluctantly restrain him; for in this sad event he largely participated in the emotions of grief that pervaded the whole country. A great patriot had died, a bright light had gone out. He . . . had been connected with him closely, both in private and in public life, and for very many years. His relations with that great statesman and eminent patriot, in the close of the war with Great Britain and on many other occasions, were now remembered with feelings and emotions of friendship, admiration, and affection for his memory, which he should in vain endeavor to describe." Copy, summary. Printed in Washington *Daily National Intelligencer*, March 1, 1848.

Clay had left Washington on February 23, 1848, for Philadelphia. On the way, he stopped in Baltimore to visit Christopher Hughes. A committee of 100 from Philadelphia met him at Elkton, Md., and escorted him the remainder of the way to the city. He was welcomed at Wilmington, Dela., with flags, cannons, and music. Throngs awaited him at the railroad station in Philadelphia when he arrived there on February 25, and they accompanied him to the mayor's house. The next day he made his speech at Independence Hall, followed by a formal reception. He left for New York City on March 7, accompanied by a group of 100. Their party was met at Amboy, N.J., by the New York City Councils, 200 invited guests, and 400 others. This entire group then boarded a steamboat for New York City where Clay spoke to a huge crowd at Castle Garden. During his six days in New York City, Clay visited and spoke at the Rutgers Young Ladies' Institute, the Institution for the Blind, and the Institution for the Deaf and Dumb. He also made private calls on Albert Gallatin, Martin Van Buren, and John Jacob Astor. On March 13 he returned to Philadelphia via Newark, N.J.; on the 16th he went on to Baltimore; on the 18th he departed for Lexington via Cumberland, Md., Pittsburgh, Pa., and Maysville, Ky. All along the route he was greeted by crowds and treated to receptions. Sargent, *Henry Clay*, 305-14; Lexington *Observer & Kentucky Reporter*, February 26, March 4, 11, 14-15, 18, 22, 1848.

To Mrs. Morris *et al.*, Philadelphia, February 28, 1848. Is flattered by "your desire to possess a portrait of me, painted by Mr. [George W.] Conarroe." Regrets that "my time will be so fully engrossed by engagements of business [Bayard to Clay, May 7, 1846; Clay to James B. Clay, February 21, 1848], and of a public nature, that I cannot appropriate enough of it to Mr. C. to admit of his making a portrait of me worthy of your regard." ALS. Courtesy of J. Winston Coleman, Jr., Lexington, Ky.

For George W. Conarroe (1803-82), a Philadelphia artist, see Groce, *New-York Historical Society's Dictionary of Artists.*

Speech to Philadelphia Commercial Room Association, February 28, 1848. Expresses his gratitude and thanks them "for the glory of the reception he had every where met," and adds "that the recollection of it would endure while life lasted." Notes that he has "endeavored to serve his country honestly and faithfully, without any regard to himself individually. He had hoped to see established upon a firm, liberal, stable, and lasting footing, the commerce of the country,—and among his deepest regrets, were the instability and vacillation indicated by the policy of the public councils of the government." Adds that he hopes commerce will "yet be placed upon a firm and unmoveable basis." Praises the merchants of Philadelphia for their "courage and firmness" that has allowed them to maintain "the name and glory transmitted by their ancestors to commerce and would hereafter preserve them untarnished." Copy, summary. Printed in Philadelphia *North American and United States Gazette*, February 29, 1848.

The Commercial Room Association was an organization made up of "gentlemen engaged in the various branches of commerce." *Ibid.*

From John Wheeler, Enterprize, East Florida, February 28, 1848. Doubts Clay remembers him unless he recalls a day spent in Burlington, Vermont, "when you were present at the annual Commencement of the University," but believes that "I may be not so unknown, as to render it improper to speak of matters of *public* concern to you." Recommends to Clay's attention the "Hon. Geo. P. Marsh" who "left the practice of law, against his own special wishes, at the earnest solicitation of the most considerate, & best men of our state, to go into public life," and who "ought to be retained in the public service." Praises Marsh's "knowledge of law . . . of history, in its original doctrines . . . of languages most various" and his understanding of "the literature, & history, & law of the German States, & the north of Europe." Describes his "moral character" as "unblemished," and adds that Marsh's "untireing industry, great promptness & decision & punctuality" is a "rare . . . *combination* of qualities . . . not to be lightly regarded by all who seek the public good." Notes, however, that "I do not know that Marsh seeks office, or if he does what office." ALS. DNA, RG59, Applications and Recommendations, Roll 4.

John Wheeler (1798-1862), a Congregational minister who had for some years been president of the University of Vermont, spent his winters in the South after resigning from the university in 1848. Ezra H. Byington, *Rev. John Wheeler, D.D. 1798-1862* (Cambridge, 1894); and information supplied by J. Kevin Graffagnino, University of Vermont.

For George P. Marsh, who served in Congress from 1843 until 1849, when he was appointed by President Taylor as minister to Turkey, see *BDAC*.

From JOHN McLEAN Cincinnati, March 1, 1848

Your favor from Baltimore was lately received at this place, it having been forwarded to me by Mr [John M.] Botts.[1]

The manifestations of confidence and affection by your fellow citizens in your late tour[2] must be gratifying to you, as they certainly have been to your friends. No higher honors could be bestowed than those which you have received.

No one can so fully understand and appreciate the importance of your position, as connected with the future, as yourself; and this knowledge best qualifies you to determine your course of action. Standing in the advance of all your compeers in age and in renown, you owe much to yourself. But your fame is not exclusively your own. It belongs also to the nation. No one friendly to his country could desire a step to be taken or omitted by you, which might not result, as it would be designed, for the general good.

You cannot be insensible to the claims of duty, but your friends have no right to expect from you personal sacrifices. I can only repeat what I said to you in Washington, that if on a full view of the whole ground your friends believe, and your own judgment shall concur with their's, that there exists the highest probability of success, you ought not to withhold your name. But in all frankness I will say, that you ought not to enter into a doubtful contest. Your fame is of too much value to yourself and to your country to compromit it, in any degree, on a hazardous result.

Political success is no longer a test of merit or qualification. Had this been otherwise, you would long since have been at the head of the government. If your name shall be brought before the country, with your assent,[3] I shall feel the utmost solicitude for your success.

ALS. DLC-HC (DNA, M212, R6). Printed in Colton, *Clay Correspondence*, 4:556-57. 1. Not found. 2. Speech at Independence Hall, Philadelphia, Feb. 26, 1848. 3. Clay to The Public, April 10, 1848.

To William Erigena Robinson, Washington, March 4, 1848. Encloses "the Autographs which I promised." Complains that "Such are my incessant engagements here, that I have scarcely looked into a newspaper since I left Washn," but will try to "get hold of the [Philadelphia *Daily*] news," which Robinson brought to Clay's attention. Intends to visit New York City on "Tuesday next," and "I shudder in contemplation at the scenes through which I shall have to pass." LS. ViU.

For Clay's itinerary, see Speech at Independence Hall, Philadelphia, February 26, 1848.

To Beach Vanderpool *et al.*, Newark, N.J., March 5, 1848. Acknowledges "resolutions of the Common Council of the City of Newark inviting me to visit that City & tendering to me its hospitalities." This "fresh proof of the friendly Consideration entertained for me" helps Clay recall "the agreeable day" he passed through Newark "upwards of fourteen years ago." Regrets, however, "that my arrangements & engagements are such as not to allow me to accept your friendly invitation." LS. NjMoHP.

For Vanderpool (1808-84)—mayor of Newark in 1846-47, well-known businessman, and later a member of the New Jersey legislature—see *Proceedings of the New Jersey Historical Society*, 84:80.

Clay did pass through Newark, where he was enthusiastically welcomed, but he did not make a formal speech. Epes Sargent, *The Life and Public Services of Henry Clay . . .* (New York, 1855), 314. For his itinerary, see Speech at Independence Hall, Philadelphia, February 26, 1848.

To Sarah Josepha Buell Hale, Philadelphia, March 6, 1848. Extends thanks for "the purse intended for me, and the bag for Mrs. [Lucretia Hart] Clay—a kind offering from the Ladies fair." Asks her to "do me the favor to make my respectful acknowledgments to all your associates." ALS. CSmH.

For Hale (1788-1879)—writer, conservative reformer, and editor of *Godey's Lady's Book*—see *DAB*.

From Joseph Rasky, Philadelphia, March 7, 1848. Takes the liberty of addressing Clay as "one whom I believe never suffered any human kind to go unrequited of their deserts when in his power to gratify them with a token of Acknowledgement." Asks Clay to recall "on your visit to Girrard [*sic*, Girard] College . . . your apparent notice of the Orphan boy who welcomed you in a few heart felt words." Explains that "Since your departure . . . that Poor Boy's whole mind & soul has been engrossed with thoughts of you" and "his Continued expressions now are that Mr. Clay is ever before him as a model which he hopes to follow thro life." Assures Clay that if he will send "your note to Walter D. Smith, enclosed to me," it "will be duly presented and gratefully recd." ALS. DLC-HC (DNA, M212, R6).

Walter D. Smith is listed as a student at Girard College in the school's annual report of 1847-54. Joseph Rasky is not mentioned in the report. Information supplied by Jamesena W. Faulk, librarian, Girard College. Smith's speech to Clay during his visit to Girard College is in the Philadelphia *North American & United States Gazette*, March 4, 1848.

In his reply to Smith's greeting, Clay expressed his gratitude for the welcome and said that "nothing had ever afforded him so much gratification during his visit to Philadelphia." He hoped that the students "would continue to emulate each other in meritorious conduct and mental improvement; and that . . . they should obey their instructors and conform to the rules and discipline of the institution." He urged them "never to forget the benevolent author of the blessings they were enjoying, and so to act that in after life they might be an honor to the institution, ornaments to society, and acceptable in the sight of their Creator." Before leaving, Clay shook hands with each orphan. Copy, summary. *Ibid.*

Speech at New York City, Castle Garden, March 7, 1848. Wishes he could express "the feelings of a grateful heart, excited by this splendid and magnificent reception." Although thankful for the greeting, "signalized by the discharge of cannon, by the display of flags, by the sound of gay and exulting music, by the shouts and cheers of an affectionate multitude," cannot forget that "these testimonies offered to the living" are "about to be paid to the dead." Notes that on the next day, "the venerable remains of the illustrious ex-President of the United States [John Quincy Adams]" will reach New York City [Clay to James B. Clay, February 21, 1848]. Contrasts "this day's demonstrations, on the arrival of an humble individual, whose efforts in his country's service you much too highly appreciate, and the ceremonies which will follow to-morrow." Hopes the funeral ceremonies will "moderate the unworthy impulses which most men bring into the strifes of our existence here" as well as "repress and chasten the violence of party contests, and the heat and acrimony of party feeling" until "we shall all be laid low in the narrow house which our venerable and pure-hearted patriot now occupies." Copy. Printed in Colton, *Clay Correspondence*, 3:84-85.

For Clay's reception in New York City, see New York *Daily Herald*, March 8, 1848; Washington *Daily National Intelligencer*, March 10, 12, 13, 1848. For his itinerary, see Speech at Independence Hall, Philadelphia, February 26, 1848.

Speech at Rutgers Young Ladies' Institute, March 8, 1848. Thanks them for their welcome. Expresses his delight in meeting "in this place the future mothers and present daughters of my country." Does not intend to make a long speech, but wants to say that he hopes "the noble objects which the founder of this institution had in view in its establishment, may be fully attained." Adds: "I trust that the opportunities which the young ladies possess of improving their minds, cultivating their taste, expanding their understandings, by the advantages here offered, may not be lost, but that they may fulfil their high destinies, and render themselves a blessing to their parents, an ornament to their country, and acceptable to that God to whose providence I shall always pray for their prosperity fame and happiness." Copy, summary. Printed in Sargent, *The Life and Public Services of Henry Clay* (1855), 311.

Rutgers Female College was founded in New York City in 1838. *National Union Catalog Pre-1956 Imprints*, 512:58.

From Robert Kirk, New York City, March 10, 1848. Offers Clay some "little boon," and pledges to continue to aid "your elevation to the highest station in the gift of any people." Whether or not Clay decides to run for the presidency, "your friends will rejoice in the consolation that no other man living enjoys so large a share of a grateful peoples love and regard." ALS. DLC-HC (DNA, M212, R6).

Kirk is possibly Robert C. Kirk, an Ohio physician and merchant who later served in the state legislature, as lieutenant governor of Ohio, and as minister to Argentina and Uruguay. *NCAB*, 12:440-41.

From JOHN L. WENDELL[1] New York City, March 11, 1848

I would have been happy to have had a few moments private conversation with you but despairing of an opportunity I have concluded to put upon paper what I wish to say to you.

I entreat you not to authorize the declaration that you will not accept a nomination for the presidency.

Owen Webb (in the address of the [Zachary] Taylor meeting) says that you have no rival in the hearts of whigs, including of course himself Moses Grinnell *et id omne genus*, but they cannot support you because you cannot be elected.[2] Now I say that if you do not prevent it, by a declaration that you will not accept, you will not only be nominated but elected.

1. You will have the vote of New York, and if so, who can doubt of your election. You would have had that vote in 1844,[3] but for the change of *2500 whig votes effected* by the Roman Catholic Bishop ([John] Hughes) to wreak his vengeance upon [Theodore] Frelinghuysen because he did not call to order two fanatical clergymen (Coxe and Kirk) who at a meeting of the American Missionary Society at Worcester in Massachusetts, spoke of the Roman Catholic Church as "The Whore of Babylon" the lady in Scarlet &c. the complimentary epithets applied to her, tho' in bad taste, ever since the Reformation.[4] That this change would take place was well known to [William H.] Seward's clique as was evidenced by their announcement of the loss of the State on the very evening of the day of election, when of course it was impossible to speak from actual returns. The intimacy subsisting between Hughes, Seward, and [Thurlow] Weed warranted the belief that the two last were well aware of Hughes' doings,[5] and from the omission to counteract him by giving notice &c. the Suspicion of treason was so strong that to save himself from the compliment of a coat of tar and feathers the Editor of the [Albany] Evening Journal [Weed] as announced by himself was obliged to flee from the city of New York.[6]

2. You will have the vote of New York if nominated, because let who will, be the nominee of the Whig Convention, he will have the vote of New-York. The breach between the two sections of the Loco-Foco party cannot be healed previous to the next election. Mr. Van Buren (not John, but Martin,) is the Head of the Barn-Burners, and he will prostrate whoever shall be nominated at Baltimore, who had a hand in defeating his nomination in 1844. [Lewis] Cass, [James] Buchanan, and [Levi] Woodbury of course go overboard. So also the Barn-Burners will not vote for any candidate who

will not support the Wilmot proviso, which is the *Shibboleth* of their section of the party.[7] Van Buren has thrown the power of the state of New York into the hands of the Whigs, and will do the same with the power of the nation, unless a man of his dictation is nominated: which is a most improbable event.

3. The power of Seward in the State of New York is gone. So is that of *Weed* the editor of the Evening Journal. When I thanked you yesterday for setting an example in speaking out frankly upon the subject of the Mexican War,[8] and thus giving a direction to public opinion, you remarked: "Still I was not seconded in New York" and appealed to the course taken by our Governor [John Young].[9] You may recollect I observed that his course was no evidence of public opinion; and most surely it is not. He was the fruit of the whoredoms of Seward and Weed with Anti-Rentism, and a more miserable production in the shape of a Statesman cannot well be imagined. Even whilst *Weed* and [Horace] *Greeley* acted together the *controlling influence* they once possessed was destroyed. It was a long and arduous work to destroy it; but it was done. They still possess influence, but it is no longer acknowledged as High Treason to differ from the Albany Evening Journal. Besides Greeley has cut loose and is for once in the right.[10] I hope he may continue true to the end; but he wants *good looking after*.

4. Without the *controlling* influence which Seward possessed, our friend Moses [Grinnell] can do no mischief in the State of New York.

I trouble you with these remarks that you may compare them with the views and opinions of others in making up your mind upon the question of permitting your name to be brought before the Convention. Most Sincerely do I hope that you will consent to have it presented.[11] I mean not to compliment you, but as I view the state of things in our beloved country your election alone can save our glorious institutions. We want a man of elevated sentiments to fill the high station of President of the U.S. and to draw about him a body of honourable, high-minded men. The course taken by many Whigs upon the question with England as to Oregon,[12] and upon the war with Mexico[13] has alarmed me. The mean subserviency of some; the wavering independence of others; and the too general adoption of expediency instead of right as the rule of action have excited my fears. From the Loco-Focos nothing is to be hoped. The demented conduct of the administration upon both the above questions, and the unqualified support of its partizans show that nothing is to be expected from that quarter but mis-rule and ruin.

ALS. DLC-HC (DNA, M212, R6). 1. For Wendell (1785-1861)—an Albany, N.Y., lawyer, a judge, a writer of law digests, and a reporter for the New York Supreme Court—see *CAB*. 2. For the Taylor meeting, see Ullmann to Clay, Feb. 18, 1848. 3. For New York's vote in 1844, see Clay to Webb, Sept. 23, 1844. 4. Cox was probably Samuel Hanson Cox (1793-1880), a Presbyterian minister known for his intelligence, eccentricity, and arrogance. He served 36 years as director of the Union Theological Seminary and was active in missionary and Bible societies, as was Frelinghuysen. See *DAB*. Kirk was probably Edward N. Kirk (1802-74), a Presbyterian and Congregational minister who served with the American Board of Commissioners for Foreign Missions before settling in Boston in 1842. See *DAB*. For the Catholic-nativist issue in the 1844 campaign as it concerned Frelinghuysen, see Ewing to Clay, June 23, 1844. 5. For Bishop Hughes's role in the 1844 election, see Lee to Clay, Nov. 2, 1844. 6. Weed and William Henry Seward were thought by some Clay supporters to have "deliberately knifed" the Whig ticket in New York in 1844. The nativist-Catholic issue was one factor in these charges, as well as the fact that Weed had predicted a Democratic victory to Whigs who sought his last-minute advice before betting on the election. This led to threats to tar and feather Weed. Glyndon G. Van Deusen, *Thurlow Weed: Wizard of the Lobby* (Boston, 1947), 136. 7. For the origin of the Barnburners, see Greeley to Clay, Nov. 30, 1847. Martin Van Buren, although endorsing the Barnburners's stand in support of the Wilmot Proviso, had advised caution in splitting the Democratic party on this issue; however, at the Democratic National convention in Baltimore, both the Barnburners and the rival Hunker delegation (Conservatives) were seated, with New York's votes divided between them. When Lewis Cass won the nomination, the Barnburners walked out. They then held their own convention at Utica on June 22, 1848, drew up a platform endorsing the proviso, and nominated Martin Van Buren for president and Henry Dodge of Wisconsin for vice president. Van Buren reluctantly allowed the nomination to stand, but Dodge declined. Meanwhile, on June 21 in Columbus, Ohio, a pro-Wilmot Proviso "People's Convention" (also called Barnburners's Convention), attended by anti-slavery Whigs and Democrats, was held and announced their separation from both major parties, joining forces with the Free Soil advocates. On June 28 a similar convention of Conscience Whigs assembled in Worcester, Mass. Out of these meetings and many others in free states, where anti-slavery advocates were unhappy with both Lewis Cass and Zachary Taylor, came a call for a national convention, held at Buffalo, N.Y., on August 9-10, at which the Free Soil party was formed by an alliance of Democratic Barnburners, Liberty party members, and Conscience Whigs. The party platform called for "Free Soil for a Free People." The convention nominated Martin Van Buren for president and Charles Francis Adams for vice president. Donovan, *The Barnburners*, 98-109; Mayfield, *Rehearsal for Republicanism*, 101-25; McKee, *National . . . Popular and Electoral Vote*, 66-69; Schlesinger, *History of U.S. Political Parties*, 1:741-63, 871-82; Maizlish, *The Triumph of Sectionalism*, 106-7. 8. Speech in Lexington, Nov. 13, 1847. 9. Gov. Young's message to the New York legislature had been hostile to Clay's speech and resolutions on the Mexican War. New York *Daily Herald*, Jan. 5, 1848. 10. Greeley and Weed had worked together in electing Seward as governor, in supporting a revision of New York's constitution, and in most other political matters for several years. In 1848 Weed did not view Clay as an "available" candidate, while Greeley strongly supported Clay in the pages of the *Tribune* and at the public reception given to Clay at New York City in 1848; however, Greeley has been accused of promoting Clay as a means of stopping Taylor, while really favoring John McLean or Thomas Corwin. Van Deusen, *Horace Greeley*, 98-120; Greeley, *Recollections of a Busy Life*, 311-14. 11. Clay to The Public, April 10, 1848. 12. A number of Whigs, including John Q. Adams, earlier had aligned themselves with the western expansionist Democrats and insisted that the U.S. assume an "All Oregon" stance. Merk, *The Oregon Question*, 227-29. 13. Joshua R. Giddings had charged in Congress on Feb. 28, 1848, that when the Mexican War began, Whigs had opposed it, but that they now supported it; also, he argued that the party had opposed slavery and now wanted to extend it. A number of Whigs had, in fact, embraced moderate territorial expansion, and the pro-Taylor *National Whig* had even published editorials in favor of annexing all of Mexico. In addition, Southern Whigs were generally as opposed to the Wilmot Proviso as the Southern Democrats. *Cong. Globe*, 30 Cong., 1 Sess., 393; Graebner, *Empire on the Pacific*, 188-89; William J. Cooper, Jr., *The South and the Politics of Slavery, 1828-1856* (Baton Rouge, 1978), 238-43; David M. Pletcher, *The Diplomacy of Annexation—Texas, Oregon and the Mexican War* (Columbia, Mo., 1973), 551-52.

To Christopher Hughes, Baltimore, Md., March 12, 1848. Leaves New York for Baltimore, by way of Philadelphia. Pleads that while in Baltimore, "My greatest want is rest & peace. Do keep the crowd off me; and if you cannot I shall hasten away from you." ALS. MiU-C.

To Thomas Bell, New York City, March 14, 1848. Acknowledges receiving "at the N.Y. hotel the cut of beef which you did me the favour to send me." Adds: "It was most excellent[.] I ate of it frequently & never ate better beef. I congratulate you upon your success with your fine stock, and I concur with you in thinking that a cross between the Durhams & the native stock produces a better breed than either of the primitive races." LS. Courtesy of Henry T. Duncan, Jr., Lexington, Ky.

Speech to Hibernian Society of Baltimore, March 17, 1848. Speaks on this occasion, "dear to every Irish heart, as well as to all who feel a sympathy for the many afflictions and wrongs of Ireland," to the society, "the main object of which is to educate and provide for the children and orphans of the sons and daughters of Erin, and to smooth the rugged path of the poor and destitute emigrant." Notes that "I have, during a life by no means short, been honored with the respect, love, and friendship of many Irishmen . . . bonded by mutual love and esteem that still causes the fond remembrances of some that are now no more, to cling to my heart-strings with still closer fervency as life speeds on to its close. . . . Among those whom it has been my privilege and pride to claim as close and intimate friends in life was the lately deceased and much lamented [Alexander] Porter, of Louisiana, who bore in his breast a most noble and devoted Irish heart, distinguished throughout his adopted State and country as one of the great friends of man, but more especially of the poor and oppressed. I could also describe to you the unswerving friendship of a Wier, a Lacy, and hosts of others, the remembrance of whose many and oft repeated acts of kindness through a series of years can never be effaced." Mentions also the "amiable and philanthropic" Luke Tiernan of Baltimore, "a man whose character I may hold up to your view as a true exemplar of the generosity, the hospitality, and the noble devotion of Irishmen, wherever I have met them."

Offers "a sentiment in honor of one who, though he has led on a whole nation to victory, has used no weapons but the weight of his religious character and the powers of moral suasion. I allude to the great reformer of the age—Father Mathew—a conquerer without armies, who is soon coming amongst us, fresh from his gigantic labors of love among the warm-hearted Irish, about whom there will linger something of the deep political character of that people which it will be good to inhale. He comes to us with a world-wide renown, distinguished for his unbounded philanthropy, his many and unostentatious charities, which have secured to him a broad and enduring popularity with all classes and conditions, unlimited by diversity of religious opinion or sectional bounds. He will be welcomed to our shores by eager thousands of all sects, parties, and localities, and by none more earnestly and devotedly than myself. I shall hope to give him a cordial welcome, and will take delight in extending to him that hospitality and esteem due the great good man of Ireland, who in a few brief years has accomplished a century's work in the amelioration of his race; imparting new life, energy, and enthusiasm to the great cause of the physical and moral regeneration of his countrymen."

Closes because he is leaving early in the morning and must "prepare my physical faculties for the fatigue of travel." Ends by proposing the sentiment: " '*The Rev. Theobald Mathew*—A safe arrival—a generous and disinterested reception to him in the United States.' "

There followed a number of other toasts, including one given to Clay by Christopher Hughes, who was introduced as a man whose "devotion to the interests and honor of his country whilst abroad is only equalled by his devotion to Henry Clay at home." Hughes rose and said: "The sentiment just offered speaks of my love of country and my love of HENRY CLAY. Why, sirs, he continued, how were it possible for me to love one and not love the other? They are one and the same; so thoroughly identified in history that to separate them were impossible. And so you think I love Clay. Well, sirs, have I not a right to love Clay? I have loved *clay* all my life since my earliest recollections; for my father was a *brickmaker*, and that brings me to something of an hereditary descent from *Clay*."

Clay was then elected by acclamation as an honorary member of the Hibernian Society of Baltimore. He then rose and said that "During my life I have had the honor, abroad and at home, to have been elected an honorary member of various societies and associations, and . . . on no occasion have I regarded the voluntary extension of such an honor to me with more gratification than I now feel. I shall cherish the recollection of your cordial reception . . . as among the most pleasing incidents of my life." Copy, summary. Printed in Washington *Daily National Intelligencer*, March 24, 1848.

For the history of the Hibernian Society, organized in 1803 "for the relief of emigrants," see Harold A. Williams, *History of the Hibernian Society of Baltimore 1803-1957* (Baltimore, 1957).

Father Theobald Mathew (1790-1856), an Irish priest and temperance reformer, planned a trip to the U.S. in 1848 but had a stroke in the spring and was unable to come until 1849. *New Catholic Encyclopedia* (Washington, D.C., 1967). See also Clay to Grinnell, May 28, 1851.

To WILLIAM N. MERCER Cumberland, Md., March 18, 1848
I am this far on my return home. I am sure that you will be pleased to hear that I gained my Cause for Messrs. Freeland and others in the S[upreme]. Court.[1] The Judges were unanimous.

I transmit enclosed a draft on my Clients at short sight for Six thousand dollars ($6000) with the collection of which I request to trouble you. When received I will thank you to pay to our friend R[ezin]. D. Shepherd Esq Five thousand & ten dollars on account of my bond which he holds.[2] The residue of $990 I will thank you to invest in a good bill on N. York, payable 70 days after date, and forward it to me at Ashland.

I have directed the honble Mr. [Charles S.] Morehead to send to you a Copy of the Opinion and Mandate of the S. Court, in the above case, and when received I will thank you to hand it to Mr. [John] Freeland.[3]

I am returning after receiving the most enthusiastic demonstrations of affectionate attachment, of which I was ever in my life before the object.[4] I have the satisfaction to assure you, most positively, that I am not dead, which is more than at times I feared. I am filled with astonishment that I should have been able to pass through such scenes and such trials. And yet I believe I shall carry with me home as much weight in flesh as I brought from it.

I think I shall decide, shortly after I reach home, and perhaps announce to the public whether I will consent or not to the use of my name again as a Candidate for the Presidency.[5] My desire for retirement is strong; but so are the appeals and entreaties made to me to acquiesce in my being once more a Candidate. The conflict between my private wishes, and these appeals to me is painful in the extreme. It is believed by many that my retirement would lead to a dissolution of the Whig party, in the free States especially. The position of Genl [Zachary] Taylor is not satisfactory to the Whigs any where, but in the free States it is very unsatisfactory.[6] What ought I to do? I am unambitious of the honor of engaging in a doubtful contest, and at my time of life retirement is most suitable and congenial with my feelings.

My affectionate regards to the Ladies.

ALS. LU-Ar. 1. Clay to Mercer, Feb. 7, 1848. 2. Probably the bond mentioned in Shepherd to Clay, April 8, 1845. 3. Clay to Morehead, March 18, 1848. See also Clay to Mercer, Feb. 7, 1848. 4. Speech at Independence Hall, Philadelphia, Feb. 26, 1848. 5. Clay to The Public, April 10, 1848. 6. Greeley to Clay, Nov. 30, 1847.

To Charles S. Morehead, Washington, March 18, 1848. Returns "the opinion and Mandate of the S[upreme]. Court" Morehead had sent [Clay to Mercer, February 7, 1848], "with the request that you will get Mr. [William T.] Carroll to certify and authenticate them properly" before sending them to "Dr. Wm. N Mercer, Canal Street, New Orleans, without delay [Clay to Mercer, March 18, 1848]." If Carroll will not "give out the Mandate" until $159.78 in "plaintiffs Costs" are paid, "I will remit a Check for the amount immediately upon my reaching home, if not from Pittsburg[h]." Asks Morehead "to advance the amount for me" if Carroll "requires prompt payment." Requests Morehead "to ask Mr. Carroll in what way the Costs are recovered—whether by Execution from the S. Court, or through the Court below?" ALS. CtY.

William T. Carroll of Maryland was clerk of the U.S. Supreme Court from 1827-63. *Congressional Quarterly's Guide to the U.S. Supreme Court* (Washington, 1979), 761.

To CHRISTOPHER HUGHES Cumberland, Md., March 19, 1848
I arrived here in safety last evening after a fatiguing and disagreeable journey. I was glad, on your account, that you did not accompany me. I feel much recruited by a good nights sleep, and a good days rest.

I dined, en famille, with your brother in law and your sister[1] today most pleasantly. They were very kind, and pressed me to stop with them. Their boys will, I think, do credit to the blood of the two races, which runs in their veins.[2]

Tomorrow morning I depart for Pittsburg[h], and I shudder in advance at the exciting scenes which await me there.[3]

The astounding news from France has just reached me. Poor France! I fear she is destined to undergo another bloody Revolution. It is preposterous to suppose her capable of establishing and maintaining a Republic. Louis Phillipe [*sic,* Louis Philippe] must have been wholly ignorant of the consequences of his abdication.[4]

I hope, my dear Hughes, you will take good care of your health. Except your shortness of breathing, you are perfectly well. I thank you for the many, many acts of kindness you have done me, during my late visit to the Cities; and for the many objects of comfort and convenience, with which you have loaded me and my trunk. They were not needed to assure me of your long and faithful friendship for me; but will serve often to recall you to my affectionate recollection.

Remember me kindly to your dear daughter [Margaret Hughes]; and present my respectful compliments to the Baron and Baroness Tuyl.[5] Say to the latter that she won much of the respect and esteem of . . .

ALS. MiU-C. 1. Hughes's sister Juliana (b. 1798) had married Charles M. Thurston (b. 1798) in 1820. When Thurston retired after twenty years in the army, they settled in Cumberland, Md., where he farmed and served as president of the Mineral Bank. *WMQ,* series 1, 6:17-18. 2. The Thurstons had the following children: George A. (1821-74); Margaret Hughes (1822-26); Charles B. (1826-68); William S. (1828-68); May Jeanett (m. Charles P. Manning); Samuel M. (b. 1832); Julian Hughes (1834-53); Henry Scott (1837-68). *Ibid.,* 7:130. 3. On March 24, 1848, Clay wrote Hughes from Pittsburgh, saying that "My reception here has been quite as distinguished as it was in Phila & N. York, considering the difference in the extent of population." ALS. MiU-C. See Speech at Independence Hall, Philadelphia, Feb. 26, 1848, for the itinerary of Clay's trip. 4. For the abdication of Louis Philippe on Feb. 24, 1848, and the revolutions throughout much of Europe in 1848, see Peter N. Stearns, *1848: The Revolutionary Tide in Europe* (New York, 1974); George Fasel, *Europe in Upheaval: The Revolutions of 1848* (Chicago, 1970). 5. Charlotte Mansfield (daughter of Mary B. Smith and John Mansfield of England) married Baron Vincent Gildemeester van Tuyll van Serooskerken (1812-60) on August 8, 1844. Mary B. Smith was a sister of Christopher Hughes's wife Laura Sophia Smith. Vincent van Tuyll was the son of Carel Lodewijk baron van Tuyll van Serooskerken (1784-1835) and Maria Louisa Gildemeester (1790-1860) and undoubtedly a kinsman of Baron de Tuyll who was Russian Minister to the U.S. [4:141]. Vincent and Charlotte's daughter, mentioned in Clay to Hughes, Sept. 30, 1848, was Marie Louise Otteline Niagara baroness van Tuyll van Serooskerken (d. 1903), born in Niagara, Canada, on July 25, 1848. Information supplied by Donna Ellis, Maryland Historical Society, and William Reitwiesner, Library of Congress. For the ancient Dutch noble Serooskerken family, see *Nederland's Adelsboek 1923* ('S-Gravenhage, 1906), 79-82.

From A. Pierse, New Orleans, March 24, 1848. Has read "that you will withdraw your name from before the country as a candidate for the presidency," but that "you intended to wait until you reached home [Clay to Lucretia Hart Clay, February 18,

1848]." Asks "whether you have the right, considering your position in the whig party, & your duty to the country, to withdraw your name without consulting" the party that will be assembled in Philadelphia on June 7 [Greeley to Clay, November 15, 1846]. Notes that the "whigs have sustained defeats with you, & they wish to triumph with you. To vindicate you against the gross slanders & denunciations of the democratic party is a duty the whigs owe to themselves, & to their political principles." As a delegate to the national convention, begs him to "give the whigs the liberty to choose their candidate." Thinks if Mexico does not accept the peace treaty [Clay to Beatty, April 29, 1847], "I look upon your election as absolutely certain." ALS. DLC-HC (DNA, M212, R6).

An Allen Peirce was a delegate to the Whig National convention from New Orleans; however, it is possible that this spelling of the last name is incorrect in the New Orleans *Daily Picayune*, March 15, 1848.

To Z. COLLINS LEE[1] Pittsburgh, March 25, 1848

I thank you for your favor communicating an account of the [Zachary] Taylor Movement in Balto. last monday,[2] of which I have received from others concurring information. At last, some of the politicians, and some of the conductors of the press will discover that they have mistaken public opinion.

Will there be any counter movement in Balto. favoring the National Convention, and indicating any other preference?[3]

My reception here, they tell me, surpassed any thing of the kind which ever before occurred in this City,[4] which I leave monday for Ashland.

ALS. Courtesy of J. Winston Coleman, Jr., Lexington, Ky. 1. Zaccheus Collins Lee (1805-59) studied law under William Wirt after attending the University of Virginia. He practiced law in Baltimore, served as U.S. district attorney from 1848-55, and as judge of the Superior Court of Baltimore from 1855-59. Edmund J. Lee, *Lee of Virginia 1642-1892, Biographical and Genealogical Sketches of the Descendants of Colonel Richard Lee* (Philadelphia, 1894; reprint ed., Baltimore, 1974), 466. 2. A Taylor mass meeting was held at the Exchange Building in Baltimore on March 20, 1848. A majority of those present seemed to be for Clay, and Reverdy Johnson was booed and hissed as a traitor when he endorsed Taylor. The meeting broke up amid predictions that this meeting marked the end of the Taylor movement in Baltimore. New York *Daily Herald*, March 22, 1848. 3. On March 23, 1848, the Maryland Whig State Central Committee, which had previously endorsed Taylor, instead urged support for whomever was nominated. *Ibid.*, March 25, 1848. 4. For Clay's itinerary, receptions, etc., see Speech at Independence Hall, Philadelphia, Feb. 26, 1848.

To MARY S. BAYARD Lexington, March 31, 1848

I promised you, my dear friend, to inform you when I reached home. I arrived the night before the last in health and safety, and found Mrs. [Lucretia Hart] Clay and my family generally well[.]

My journey was without fatigue, every facility being afforded me to render it easy and comfortable. They gave me a most splendid reception at Pittsburg[h].[1] As I approached it in a Steamboat on the Monongahela, filled with passengers and resounding with music, one of the most brilliant scenes opened on me that I ever beheld. In front a beautiful wire bridge was gracefully suspended over the river, crowded with people. The bend of the river, from the waters' edge, to its summit, for many hundred yards, was chock full with people. The whole population of the City appeared to have precipitated itself on the Bank, rising in amphitheatrical array. All this was accompanied with the display of numerous flags, the roar of Cannon, the ringing of bells and the sound of music, and the enthusiastic cheers of the countless multitude.

At night there was a torch light procession of all the fire Companies, with them bands of music, flags, firing of rockets &c &c.

From Pittsburg[h] to Maysville, on my descent of the Belle Riviere, at all the towns and villages, the whole surrounding population seemed to have gathered together, to greet to cheer and welcome me, amidst the incessant roar of Cannon.

I dwell on these occurrences not because I am intoxicated or much affected by this pompous display, but because, I know, my dear friend, how deeply you feel interested in all that concerns me.

The very day of my arrival at home was fixed for the trial of the unfortunate case of young [Lafayette] Shelby,[2] and I am now engaged in a cause of Life or Death.

There seems to be no peace, no repose for me!

Say to Dr. Herring that I followed his prescriptions and was benefited by them on my journey and cordially thank him.

I have not seen the correspondence about the Bell[3] published, perhaps because I have looked very little into News papers. As you did me the honor to be my Secretary, will you have the goodness to ascertain if my letter of acknowledgment reached its destination?

From what I have learned, since I reached home, Kentucky retains unabated her attachment to me. They have had recently a great meeting at Louisville,[4] & passed strong resolutions in my favor.

In reviewing my late Eastern excursion,[5] I recall the days which I passed at your house as by far the most quiet & agreeable.

Present my affectionate regards to Mr. [Richard H.] Bayard, to Caroline, to Baring [Powell] and his charming little wife,[6] to Mary, to Lizzie and the girls. And do my good friend keep me constantly advised of every interesting occurrence in your dear family.

P.S. Do me the favor to remember me most kindly to your grand mother[7] and Mrs. Jackson.

Copy. KyU. 1. Speech at Independence Hall, Philadelphia, Feb. 26, 1848. 2. Clay to James B. Clay, Feb. 2, 1846. 3. On March 13, 1848, Clay had been presented by a "Committee of the Councils" of Philadelphia with a bell cast "from a portion of the . . . 'Bell of Independence.' " The committee presented the bell as a token of their esteem. Committee to Clay, March 13, 1848. Copy. Printed in Lexington *Observer & Kentucky Reporter*, April 26, 1848. Clay replied on March 14, thanking them for the bell and saying: "It adds to the many, many obligations under which, during a long series of years, I have been placed by the councils and people of Philadelphia. Other cities share in common . . . in commercial and manufacturing enterprise—intelligence in the possession of the arts and sciences, and in devotion to religion—but Philadelphia alone contains that renowned Hall, from which was first announced to a joyful world the glorious Declaration of American Independence. The bell, a part of which, in a miniature bell, you have done me the honor to present me, daily summoned together the patriot statesmen whose deliberations terminated in that memorable but perilous deed." Promises to carry it to Ashland and "preserve it amongst the most highly prized and cherished objects of my residence." Clay to W. Morris *et al.*, March 14, 1848. *Ibid.* The bell in Independence Hall had cracked in 1845, and after attempts to repair it failed, filings from it were gathered up and two smaller bells were cast—one was presented to the Historical Society of Pennsylvania, the other to Clay. 4. A group of about 1,500 Whigs met at the courthouse in Louisville on March 25 and declared Clay to be their first choice for the Whig nomination. They also pledged their support for a national convention and called for Whig harmony. Louisville *Daily Journal*, March 27, 1848. 5. Speech at Independence Hall, Philadelphia, Feb. 26, 1848. 6. Baring Powell had married Caroline Bayard, daughter of Mary and Richard Bayard, on Jan. 25, 1847. Delaware *Gazette*, Feb. 2, 1847. 7. Probably Elizabeth Oswald Chew, Mary's maternal grandmother. Kate M. Rowland, *The Life of Charles Carroll of Carrollton*, 2 vols. (New York, 1898), 2:55, 241-42; and Benjamin Chew article in *DAB*.

To SEARGENT S. PRENTISS Lexington, March 31, 1848

I seize, my dear Mr. PRENTISS, the first moment after my return home, to express to you my thanks and gratitude for the generosity and magnanimity displayed by you in the amicable adjustment of the difficulty, which had arisen between you and my grandson, H. Clay E———.[1] I was at the Eastward, when he resolved to proceed to New Orleans, and ask of you satisfaction for the injury which he supposed you had inflicted on the character of his father [James Erwin]; and he acted altogether on his own impulses, or the advice of young members of my family. When at Washington I heard of the occurrence, it occasioned me infinite pain and regret; but I concluded, from my knowledge of the chivalry and magnanimity of your character, that no hostile meeting would take place; and the gratifying event demonstrated the correctness of my judgment.

Nevertheless, during my sojourn in Philadelphia, just before I went out to dine in company, I heard that a meeting was certainly to be had, and that it had probably taken place about eight days prior to that time. I did not know, therefore, but that during the dinner, I might hear of the fall of my friend, or my grandson. Imagine what must have been the agonized state of my feelings! After the dinner was over, I was relieved by a telegraphic dispatch, announcing the honorable accommodation of the unpleasant affair.

This event, my dear Mr. PRENTISS, has added new cement to the friendship which has existed between us, and on which I have ever placed the highest value.

I request you to present my affectionate regards to Mrs. [Mary Williams] Prentiss; and how can I think of her, and your interesting children,[2] without entreating you never to hazard a life so dear to them, and so precious to all your friends . . .

Copy. Printed in Prentiss, *Memoir of S.S. Prentiss*, 2:443-44. 1. Henry Clay Erwin. For the near-duel, see Clay to James B. Clay, Feb. 1, 1848. 2. Jane (b. 1843), George L. (b. 1844), Seargent S. (b. 1847). Another child, Eunice, was born in Oct., 1848. Dallas C. Dickey, *Seargent S. Prentiss; Whig Orator of the Old South* (Baton Rouge, 1945), 200.

To R.F. Ryan, Cincinnati, Ohio, April 3, 1848. After returning home following an absence of several months, found "your obliging letter proposing to enrol my name as an honorary member of the Emmet Club, established in Cincinnati." Accepts and wishes "all success to that club in the laudable objects for which I understand it was instituted." Copy. Printed in Lexington *Observer & Kentucky Reporter*, May 24, 1848.

Ryan is identified in *ibid.* as a Democrat and a member of the Cincinnati bar. The Emmet Club was named for Robert Emmet (1778-1803), martyr to the cause of Irish independence. See *DNB*.

From WILLIAM BEBB[1] Hamilton, Ohio, April 4, 1848

Sentiments of delicacy which you can better appreciate than I express, have deterred until now from adding my humble but earnest remonstrance to that of a vast majority of our political friends against your withdrawal from the Presidential canvass.

To enumerate the facts & reasons upon which I would base this remonstrance to one familiar as you are with the whole subject and actuated by the motives which have directed your life and must determine your decision would be signally officious and unnecessary. But there are some facts and circumstances, perhaps, more apparent to one residing north of the Ohio river, & who has several times canvassed either a large portion or the whole of the State than to any one South of that river, however ample his means of knowledge or extended his vision.

1st. Gen [Zachary] Taylor, unless I have entirely misunderstood the Whigs & people of Ohio never can get her *Whig* vote.[2] Large masses of our people, question—The Western Reserve—The Miami tribes[3] never will vote to support *War*—Slavery extension—and non committal. For one of the Whig family let me say that having cast my first vote for Clay in 1824 almost alone in a corner of Old Butler[4] in the face of the Storm of Jacksonism I can at 45 vote against another Military chieftain more non committal and possessing fewer civil pretensions than even Andrew Jackson.

2d. Judge [John] McLean is a capable man of high moral character and possessing administrative qualities of no uncommon order. But he has no strong hold on the Whig heart of Ohio. Neither the old friends of Clay, nor the young friends of [Thomas] Corwin are at all likely willingly to take him. The former will remember not to forget old scores & the latter new ones.[5] Besides the Judge is not what Algebraists term a positive quantity. Few hate, nobody loves him.

3d. Ohio prefers Corwin to all living men, yet a large number of her counties have declared for you, and scarcely one for either Taylor, [Winfield] Scott or McLean. The Corwin men say give us Corwin or give us Clay.—The Clay men say give us Clay or give us Corwin.

4th. What is true of Ohio as it regards Gen Taylor is true of N York and much of N England.

5th. Can you not get all the States you got before, and N York besides? I cannot answer for the others but I believe *we can give you Ohio again—certainly* if you declare for our favorite ordinance of 87.[6]

6th. Should Gen Taylor be nominated it seems to me the Whigs of the North will be compelled in self defence to nominate a Northern Man or suffer utter dissolution. Some would vote for [John P.] Hale,[7] some for Taylor & some for any Wilmot proviso[8] democrat that should happen to run. Much better would it be for the Whigs of Ohio to throw their votes away than to eat their words abandon their principles, advocate all they have heretofore opposed & oppose all they have heretofore advocated, and thus lose their moral power & their self respect in a vain effort to give the Whig vote of the State to Gen Taylor. Should even enough of Locofocos fall into our ranks to give us a momentary victory they would abandon us whenever a civilian or avowed Whig should be our candidate. I infinitely prefer our position as a conservative minority to such shuffling and sacrifice of *true men* for accidental allies.

Pardon this plain blunt letter. I have long felt a desire to say to you the substance of what it contains, resisted by a strong aversion to appear obtrusive. This feeling or rather dilemma I communicated to our friend Mr [Thomas B.] Stevenson who determined me to write & who kindly handed me the inclosed letter.[9]

Hoping your mind may be directed to wise conclusions as I am sure it will be by the most patriotic motives . . .

Copy. OCHP. This copy is located in the Papers of Thomas B. Stevenson and is copied in the same handwriting as the Clay-Stevenson correspondence in that collection. Printed in Colton,

Clay Correspondence, 3:476-78. 1. For William Bebb (1802-73), elected as the Whig governor of Ohio in 1846, see *BDGUS*, 3:1204. In Colton, *Clay Correspondence*, 3:476-77, Stevenson relates how Bebb had exhibited to him great enthusiasm for Clay, causing Stevenson to advise Bebb to write this letter. He adds that after Clay's consent was given for the presentation of his name to the Whig National convention, but before the convention assembled, he had learned "that Bebb was actively engaged in an intrigue to supplant Mr. Clay by bringing forward General Scott." Then, after Taylor's nomination, Bebb had voiced "his displeasure at the factiousness of the 'sore-headed *Clay*-Whigs' who were dissatisfed at Taylor's nomination." Stevenson threatened to publish Bebb's letter to Clay, and concludes: "here it is, perhaps the best example in history of a treacherous document aiding in the support of an honest reputation like that of Mr. Clay." 2. Lewis Cass carried Ohio over Taylor in 1848 by a vote of 154,775 to 138,360 votes, with Martin Van Buren, the Free Soil candidate, winning 35,354 votes. McKee, *National . . . Popular and Electoral Vote*, 71. 3. Sentiment in favor of Thomas Corwin, who was strongly opposed to the Mexican War, for the Whig presidential nomination was especially strong in the Western Reserve and the Miami River Valley of Ohio. Weisenburger, *John McLean*, 110. 4. Butler County, Ohio. 5. McLean had long hoped for the Whig presidential nomination. This produced a rivalry with Clay and even more so with Corwin, another presidential contender, since McLean and Corwin were both from Ohio. Weisenburger, *John McLean*, 110, *passim*. 6. The Northwest Ordinance of 1787, among other things, prohibited slavery in the Northwest Territory and the states carved therefrom. 7. Hale had been nominated for president by the Liberty party but later stepped down and supported Martin Van Buren who was nominated by the Free Soil party. Schlesinger, *History of U.S. Political Parties*, 1:754-55, 871, 878. See also *BDAC*. 8. Sargent to Clay, Feb. 27, 1847. 9. Not found.

To Alexander W. Bradford *et al.*, New York City, April 5, 1848. Acknowledges their invitation to "the third annual festival in the City of New-York in commemoration of my birthday." Although grateful "for the distinguished mode" in which they "testify their warm attachment and confidence in me," does not "feel that I have any claim to be so highly honored." Regrets that, even "If it would be otherwise proper (as I think it would not be) . . . my remote distance from New-York would be an insuperable obstacle." Recalls his recent visit to "the Empire City [Speech at New York City, March 7, 1848]," as "an epoch in my life." Assures them that "the hospitality I enjoyed . . . the thrilling scenes of delight . . . and the enthusiastic manifestations with which I was so kindly received . . . are still fresh in my grateful recollection." Copy. Printed in the New-York *Daily Tribune*, April 13, 1848.

For more on Clay's northern trip, see Speech at Independence Hall, Philadelphia, February 26, 1848. For Bradford, a New York City lawyer, judge, and politician, see *DAB*.

To ANNA MERCER Lexington, April 5, 1848

Upon my return home, my dear Anna, a few days ago, I found here your note to Mrs. [Lucretia Hart] Clay, with the presents you had kindly tendered to her.[1] She is so out of the habit of writing that she now hardly ever writes to me, when I am from home, leaving other members of my family to perform that office. It is therefore that I have the pleasure of making to you her and my acknowledgments for your beautiful & highly acceptable presents.

I performed the journey, and passed the winter at the North far better than I feared.[2] I think I suffered less from colds (my great affliction) than usual. They almost killed me with kindness in the Cities. My hand has been so shook, and crushed, that I have often been unable to write. The work of destruction, commenced by the men, was almost completed by the Ladies. Tell your Aunt that I protest that their caresses were not sought by me, altho' I must plead guilty as to their not having been declined.

I often wished that I was in Canal Street, under your father's [William Newton Mercer] hospitable roof, with you ladies.

Well; my dear Anna the time approaches when you are to sally out into the world, and perform your part in social circles. Will you allow me to make one or two suggestions of advice? Don't allow your affections to be too easily engaged. In youth, the heart is very susceptible, and we too often mistake its first emotions for a fixed & permanent attachment. You should be in no hurry to contract such an attachment. Why should you? The advantages you possess entitle you to the choice of all the young men in the U. States. Recollect that if you should make an unhappy choice there is no remedy. A life of misery and wretchedness is before you[.] Distrust, my dear Anna, all first impressions. Examine them thoroughly. Enquire if they are founded on the virtues, talents and good qualities of their object. If merely upon his good face, form, or personal appearance, do not allow your affections to be engaged. Consult always your good father, than whom there is no better judge of men. Consult your Aunt whose opinion and advice, I am sure you may always safely trust and follow. I am almost tempted to ask you to promise me never to engage your hand, without hearing me on the merits of any person that may solicit it. And why shou[l]d not you? Next to your father and your Aunt, you have no better friend than I am.

Perhaps I have prematurely touched on a delicate topic. If so, attribute it, I pray you, to the anxious solicitude I feel for your happiness, and that of your good father.

Present me affectionately to him to Miss [Eliza] Young and to Miss [Mary D.] Kemble. Tell him that I hope he received a letter that I addressed to him from Cumberland.[3]

ALS. LU-Ar. 1. Not found. 2. For Clay's itinerary, see Speech at Independence Hall, Philadelphia, Feb. 26, 1848. 3. Clay to Mercer, March 18, 1848.

From JOSEPH L. WHITE New York City, April 5, 1848

[Requests a letter of introduction to Lord Morpeth for "My friend John Jay Esqr." who will be traveling to England soon. Continues:]

Our friends in the [New York] legislature are working manfully to accomplish what you named to me when here as a condition precedent to your consent to the use of your name. That they will succeed, I do not doubt. Such is the opinion of [James] Brooks who has just left me. The Governor [John Young], however, & his friends will make every effort to defeat the movement. But his influence now amounts to but little, & the voice of the Whigs is coming up to the whig members of the legislature from every part of the state demanding your nomination. It is felt & I am convinced it will be obeyed—In our general committee we adopted an address to the whig members, with but *one* dissenting voice, requesting them to express the preferences of their constituents for a presidential nominee. It will be presented by Brooks or [John L.] Lawrence to the joint whig caucus of both houses to night.[1]

Your visit here accomplished all & more than I had hoped from it. There is really no Taylorism left among us outside of the Conner office;[2] & I have seen many, very many, who were deluded with it, who have return[ed] to their first love & publicly express their regrets that they ever faltered. The few [Zachary] Taylor men who are left, I know are convinced of the impracticability of carrying this State for Taylor, even if nominated, & they will rally for [Winfield] *Scott.*[3] But this game will be as easily "blocked" as the other. All our true whigs have & will have but one choice, & with them it is "*aut Caesar aut nullus.*"

ALS. DLC-HC (DNA, M212, R6). 1. On April 5, 1848, the New York Whig legislative caucus met in convention to elect delegates to the Whig National convention. They passed a resolution stating to the delegates that Henry Clay was their first choice for the presidential nomination but pledging that New York's electoral vote would be given to any "reliable Whig" who might be nominated by the convention. New-York *Daily Tribune*, April 6, 1848. See also Lawrence *et al.* to Clay, Feb. 16, 1848, for an earlier Whig legislative caucus endorsement of Clay. In the 1848 presidential election, New York voters cast 218,603 votes for Taylor, 114,318 for Cass, and 120,510 for Van Buren, giving all 36 electoral votes to Taylor. McKee, *National . . . Popular and Electoral Vote*, 71-72. 2. James Conner (1798-1861) was county clerk of New York County from 1844-52. Johnson, *Twentieth Century Biographical Dictionary*. 3. For New York delegates' votes at the Whig National convention, see Ullmann to Clay, Feb. 18, 1848.

From Samuel Forrer, Columbus, Ohio, April 7, 1848. Reports the alarm of "Many, very many, of your old and sincere friends . . . that it is your intention not to permit your name to be presented to the Whig National Convention for nomination to the office of President of the United States." Asks Clay to "give to the subject the full latitude of your mature judgment . . . before you decide against the wishes, as I believe, of a larger, much larger, number of reliable Whigs than can be found to favor the claims of any one of the gentlemen yet named for that important office." Advises Clay that in Ohio "public sentiment is rapidly concentrating to one point," and his great popularity "is the *inevitable* result of the early affections and long-established confidence of the universal Whig party; and the only question of importance which at all divides us here, and, as I suppose, elsewhere, is that of availability [Bebb to Clay, April 4, 1848]."

Names John McLean, Zachary Taylor, Thomas Corwin, and Clay as "the only persons seriously thought of here for nomination. Neither of the two first will receive any support in the National Convention until all hope of success for Mr. Corwin or yourself is entirely abandoned. . . . if either of these gentlemen is forced upon us, I consider defeat as certain. Judge McLean can not possibly get the full Whig vote of Ohio," and his nomination "would cause an apathy among not only the old reliable Whigs, but also among the young working Whigs. . . . and without an enthusiastic and general movement in favor of our candidate, we can not possibly succeed." Taylor, on the other hand, "would receive but little support in the Western Reserve," and although "some who are not Whigs might be induced to support him . . . the defections among the Whigs of the 'Reserve' alone would be so great that no extraneous acquisition can possibly compensate for the loss."

While "Your friends and the friends of Mr. Corwin here are identical *almost*," feels that "in the Reserve . . . there is perhaps less doubt as to Mr. Corwin's views in regard to the introduction of slavery in newly acquired territory" and "some might vote for him who would not vote for you. The number, however, would be small." Moreover, some Whigs "in some of the counties east of the Sciota [*sic*, Scioto] River . . . have not yet forgiven Mr. Corwin for *permitting* the General Assembly of Ohio to prefer him to a seat in the Senate of the United States."

Looks to Clay as "the standard-bearer in the next campaign; and really, sir, we should feel as if all were afloat on a most tempestuous, or, at least, uncertain sea, if your name were no longer among those from whom the National Convention may select a candidate." Hopes that "no contingency may arise to prevent your remaining passive at least, and that you will permit your friends to present your name." Copy. Printed in Colton, *Clay Correspondence*, 3:478-80.

For Samuel Forrer (1793-1874), a civil engineer and surveyor for the city of Dayton, Ohio, see A.W. Drury, *History of the City of Dayton and Montgomery County, Ohio*, 2 vols. (Chicago, 1909), 1:168.

From THOMAS B. STEVENSON Cincinnati, April 8, 1848

[Encloses a letter to Clay from [Samuel] Forrer,[1] which is "worthy your consideration . . . on account of the high character and influence of the writer" and "the intrinsic importance of his suggestions and the valuable facts he states." Continues:]

I transmitted you a letter from Judge Lazelle [*sic*, John A. Lazell][2] of our State Control Committee, through Judge [George] Robertson, a day or two ago, which is worthy your attention. Gov. [William] Bebb, some days ago applied to me for a letter to you to enable him to write in the same vein as Forrer has done. Did he address you?[3] You can have no idea how I am tortured here with anxious inquiries whether you *will* withdraw. I am literally beleaguered in my office, from morn till evening. The doubt on this subject, do what we may to remove it, is extensive; and its manifestation is distressing here. It dispirits and almost paralyses your friends, and gives boldness to opponents. The bold assertions, founded in letters said to have been written by Whig members of Congress, that you would withdraw,[4] so stunned our friends here, that I was almost tempted to publish your private letter to me[5] in order to arrest the mischief; and in fact I did state its contents almost in terms as coming from you. Yet in the face of this, it is still the parrot-cry—"*he'll withdraw*." I was so annoyed at this a day or two ago, as to invent a fictitious correspondence, announcing the withdrawal of all the others spoken of for the Presidency, which threw ridicule upon the authors of that mode of electioneering, and stopped the parrot-cry for one day at least.[6]

Would it not be advisable for you to publish a line, simply saying you adhere to your passive position, neither consenting to nor refusing the use of your name, and that your decision will be communicated to some friend who will be authorized to announce it in the N. Convention when it meets?[7] I can see no reason why you should do otherwise, unless your mind is made up not to allow your name, under any circumstances, to go before the Convention; while on the other hand I do imagine some mischiefs may befall our cause by an earlier announcement. Without seeking a nomination, it should be understood that you will not refuse the use of your name.

I concur in all Forrer says, except that he omits the name of [Winfield] Scott from consideration by the Whigs of Ohio. My opinion is very strong, if yourself and [Thomas] Corwin were out of view, he would be more acceptable in Ohio than [Zachary] Taylor, and probably than [John] McLean. The genuine working Whigs of Ohio have no confidence in McLean's political principles. By the by, he is now working what he considers a deep contrivance, but I think a very shallow intrigue, to detach Whigs from their party on anti-slavery grounds, and to rope in the Liberty party to him, a scheme which contemplates either the withdrawal or sacrifice of [John P.] Hale, and I am assured that [Salmon P.] Chase and other leading Abolitionists here and elsewhere are in the plot.[8]

It is confidently believed by your friends in this State, that you will publicly declare against the extension of slavery in the new territories. This is inferred, I think logically, not only from your general opinions and public *acts* respecting slavery, but also from your resolutions at the Lexington meeting.[9] [Bellamy] Storer[10] and I both assumed this confidently in our speeches at the great meeting of your friends lately held in this city, the *regular* resolutions of which, it is hoped, meet your approval.[11] I think you can assume the ground with little hazard of losing any southern State we hope for it all, though I hold of course that it should be taken, at all hazards, because it is *right*, being myself of the faith—"*rather be right than President*". I will not bore you with any argument on a question you understand the nature and bearings of so much better; but I do beg to make a suggestion as to the principle to be laid down in taking the ground, which I am sure will be entirely satisfactory to the north, and which cannot be assailed in the South. It is the principle of recognizing the domestic relations of the inhabitants existing at the time of acquiring the territory, under which Louisiana, Florida and Texas were acquired. [Joseph] Story lays it down in his Commentaries that the transfer of the sovereignty does not affect the relations of the inhabitants to one another.[12] I think this ground, or rather this mode of taking ground against extending slavery, will shut the mouth of the South completely; for it was on this principle alone that they acquired Louisiana, &c. with slavery.[13] I make this suggestion, however, with the utmost deference to your better judgment. On the whole, I am decidedly of opinion an *early* declaration from you on this question is expedient. It would end the contest at once in the north as to the available man, in your favor, stop all intrigues instantly, and give time to argue the south into acquiescence, which with the strong and conclusive reasons in favor, I believe can be triumphantly done, at least in all the Southern *Whig* States. I can see but one reason for postponing this declaration—and that is a very dubious one—I mean the possibility of the Locos nominating a slavery-extension man. In this case, you might gain in the South by Silence; but that would probably drive off more northern Whigs to the abolitionists.

I must acquit myself fully and faithfully of a *duty* I owe to you, to myself and the Whig cause, by the declaration of my solemn conviction that we cannot carry Ohio for you, unless you take ground satisfactorily against extending slavery in new territory, or, in less exceptionable phrase, *for free soil remaining free*. There is indeed much cant and hypocrisy on this subject; but the sentiment of Ohio on this subject is resistless as the flow of the waters.[14]

Though I am sure you must be greatly harrassed with correspondence, I will urge that you write to Forrer. I take the responsibility of requesting, also, that the second and third pages of Forrer's letter be published in the [Lexington] Observer, as from an intelligent and influential correspondent at Columbus, of course speaking of you in the third person, and omitting the allusion to Corwin's election to the Senate, and omitting also that you will "excuse" the state of feeling here favorable to him. Its publication, I think will be salutary in Ky. and I am sure it will be here. I will transfer it to the Atlas.[15] The [Cincinnati *Daily*] Gazette is publishing manufactured letters (as I suspect) from New England and elsewhere, saying you can't be elected, but McLean can be; and that paper this week, in its editorials, assumes that none but a *resident* of a free State can be elected. This is McLeanism. I reviewed this unjust mode of canvassing in the Atlas this morning, in a temper rather reckless of an open warfare with McLean, whom, though I hold him despicable, I have hitherto avoided offending. Things have come to a pass, however, that Judge [John C.] Wright must submit to my lashing, or if not, I'll tomahawk McLean.[16]

I congratulate you upon the evident reaction going on in the South, and upon the cheering prospects especially in the north. Make the declaration proposed, which I am sure accords with your judgment and feelings, and your nomination and election will follow by acclamation. I *know* that Gen. Taylor has written a letter to an agent of the Barnburners, in answer to a proposition that they would vote for him if he adhered to his "Signal letter," which proposition was accompanied by their interpretation of that letter as affirming the principles of the ordinance of '87, thanking him for his friendship, saying a "*repetition*" of his sentiments was not necessary, and not contesting the correctness of the interpretation—equivalent to an endorsement of it.[17] But I hold that the [Peter] Sken Smith & Alabama letter renders Taylor ineligible[18] even for *consideration* in a *Whig* Convention; and, unless his head be perfectly turned, (which I suspect) he will be out of the field by the middle of May.

You must pardon this tedious letter from one who, if he have no other claim to your indulgence, has ever been faithful and true and will remain as ever your friend[.] P.S. I should like to have the elements of a calculation, if you have made one. I have been told you think you can be elected without a slave State. Is that possible?

ALS. DLC-HC (DNA, M212, R6). 1. Forrer to Clay, April 7, 1848. 2. Letter not found. For Lazell, associate judge of the Franklin County Court of Common Pleas and a member of the Ohio Whig Central Committee, see William T. Martin, *History of Franklin County* . . . (Columbus, 1858), 62, 157; Holt, *Party Politics in Ohio*, 282, 297. 3. Bebb to Clay, April 4, 1848. 4. Probably a reference to the activities of the "Young Indians." See Harvey to Clay, April 18, 1848. 5. Clay to Stevenson, Feb. 19, 1848. 6. The Cincinnati *Atlas* editorial of April 6, entitled "Extraordinary Correspondence and Marvelous Coincidences," facetiously claimed that six candidates for the presidency—McLean, Taylor, Corwin, Webster, Scott and Hale—had simultaneously resigned their candidacy, probably because of the "mesmeric influence in favor of Mr. Clay." The article included a bogus letter from each of the six. 7. Clay to The Public, April 10, 1848. 8. For Salmon P. Chase, Ohio abolitionist and later U.S. senator and secretary of the treasury in Abraham Lincoln's cabinet, see *DAB*. Early in 1848 Chase was courting the abolitionist vote to support McLean as either the Whig party or a third party candidate. Weisenburger, *The Life of John McLean*, 134-36. For the splits in the Whig party in Ohio which ultimately resulted in the Democrats carrying that state, see Holt, *Party Politics in Ohio*, 278-304; Maizlish, *Triumph of Sectionalism*, 84-98. 9. Speech in Lexington, Nov. 13, 1847. 10. For Storer, Cincinnati lawyer and former congressman, see *BDAC*. 11. The Cincinnati Whig meeting adopted resolutions, brought forward by a committee chaired by Stevenson, recommending Clay for president and listing reasons for choosing him. Lexington *Observer & Kentucky Reporter*, April 1, 1848. 12. Justice Story's *Commentaries on the Constitution of the United States* . . . , 2 vols. (4th ed., Boston, 1873), 2:197 states that when a territory is ceded by treaty to another country, "The relations of the inhabitants with each other do not change." 13. For the constitutional aspects of slavery in the Louisiana Territory, see Everett S. Brown, *The Constitutional History of the Louisiana Purchase, 1803-1812* (Berkeley, Ca., 1920), 107-20, 141-42. 14. The Ohio Whig State convention, which met on Jan. 19, 1848, to nominate a candidate for governor, choose delegates to the national convention, and designate presidential electors, had issued resolutions against the forcible annexation of any Mexican territory and demanding that, if acquired, any such territory should exclude slavery. Holt, *Party Politics in Ohio*, 289. 15. Publication of Forrer's letter has not been found in any prominent newspaper. 16. Wright, editor of the Cincinnati *Daily Gazette* at this time, was decidedly pro-McLean. 17. Clay to White, Sept. 20, 1847. 18. In a letter to Peter Sken Smith on Jan. 30, 1848, Taylor wrote that he would accept any nomination "provided it had been made entirely independent of party considerations." Lexington *Observer & Kentucky Reporter*, March 4, 1848. In a reply on Jan. 28, 1848, to a committee established by a "no-party" mass meeting of Montgomery County, Ala., that had nominated him for president, Taylor said he did not oppose their use of his name, as long as it was used "independent of party distinction." *Ibid.*, April 8, 1848.

To JOHN J. CRITTENDEN Lexington, April 10, 1848

I transmit you inclosed a Copy of a note,[1] the publication of which I have authorized. I can add nothing to the reasons which it assigns for the course which I have finally felt it to be my duty to adopt; but I shall be most happy if they meet with the concurrence of your judgment.

ALS. DLC-John J. Crittenden Papers (DNA, M212, R20). Addressed to Crittenden in Washington, D.C. 1. Clay to The Public, April 10, 1848.

To THE PUBLIC Lexington, April 10, 1848

The various and conflicting reports which have been in circulation, in regard to my intentions with respect to the next Presidency, appear to me to furnish a proper occasion for a full, frank and explicit exposition of my feelings, wishes and views upon that subject. This it is now my purpose to make.

With a strong disinclination to the use of my name again in connection with that office, I left my residence in December last,[1] under a determination to announce to the public, in some suitable form, my desire not to be thought of as a candidate. During my absence, I frequently expressed to different gentlemen my unwillingness to be again in that attitude; but no one was authorized to publish my decision one way or the other, having reserved the right to do so exclusively to myself. On reflection, I thought it was due to my friends to consult with them before I took a final and decisive step. Accordingly, in the course of the last three months, I have had many opportunities of conferring fully and freely with them. Many of them have addressed to me the strongest appeals, and the most earnest entreaties, both verbally and written, to dissuade me from executing my intended purpose.[2] They have represented to me that the withdrawal of my name would be fatal to the success, and perhaps lead to the dissolution, of the party with which I have been associated, especially in the free States; that at no former period did there ever exist so great a probability of my election, if I would consent to the use of my name; that the great States of New York[3] and Ohio[4] would, in all human probability, cast their votes for me; that New York would more certainly bestow her suffrage upon me than upon any other candidate, and that Ohio would give her vote to no candidate, residing in the Slave States but to me; that there is a better prospect than has heretofore at any time existed that Pennsylvania[5] would unite with them; that no candidate can be elected without the concurrence of two of those three states, and none could be defeated, upon whom all three of them should be united; that great numbers of our fellow-citizens, both of native and foreign birth, who were deceived and therefore voted against me at the last election,[6] are now eager for an opportunity of bestowing their suffrages upon me; and that, whilst there is a strong and decided preference for me, entertained by the great body of the whig party throughout the United States, they (the friends to whom I refer) at the same time are convinced that I am more available than any candidate that could be presented to the American people.

I do not pretend to vouch for the accuracy of all these representations, although I do not entertain a doubt that they have been honestly made, and are sincerely believed.

It has been moreover urged to me that the great obligations under which I have been hitherto placed, by a large portion of the People of the United States, the full force of which no one can be more sensible of than I am, demand that I should not withhold the use of my name, if it be required.

And I have been reminded of frequent declarations which I have made that, whilst life and health remain, a man is bound to render his best services upon the call of his country.

Since my return home, I have anxiously deliberated upon my duty to myself, to my principles, to my friends, and, above all, to my country. The conflict between my unaffected desire to continue in private life, as most congenial with my feelings and condition, and my wish faithfully to perform all my public duties, has been painful and embarrassing. If I refuse the use of my name, and those injurious consequences should ensue, which have been so confidently predicted by friends, I should justly incur their reproaches, and the reproaches of my own heart. And, if, on the contrary, I should assent to the use of my name, whatever the result may be, I shall escape both.

I have, therefore, finally decided to leave to the National Convention, which is to assemble next June,[7] the consideration of my name, in connection with such others as may be presented to it, to make a selection of a suitable candidate for President of the United States. And whatever may be the issue of its fair and full deliberations, it will meet with my prompt and cheerful acquiescence.

It will be seen, from what I have stated, that there was reason to anticipate that I would decline giving my consent to the use of my name again as a candidate for the Presidency of the United States. Owing, perhaps, to this, as well as other causes, many of my friends and fellow-citizens have avowed a preference for, and directed their attention to, the distinguished names of other citizens of the United States.[8] I take pleasure in truly declaring, that I have no regrets to express, no complaints, no reproaches to make on account of any such preferences, which I am fully persuaded are generally founded on honest and patriotic convictions.

Copy. Printed in Lexington *Observer & Kentucky Reporter*, April 12, 1848. 1. Speech at Independence Hall, Philadelphia, Feb. 26, 1848. 2. See, for example, Ullmann to Clay, Feb. 18, 1848; Bebb to Clay, April 4, 1848. 3. Ullmann to Clay, Feb. 18, 1848. 4. *Ibid.* 5. Clay to Mercer, April 14, 1848. 6. Ewing to Clay, June 23, 1844. 7. Greeley to Clay, Nov. 15, 1846. 8. See, for example, White to Clay, Sept. 4, 1847; Clay to Harvey, April 18, 1848.

To SEARGENT S. PRENTISS Lexington, April 12, 1848

I saw, with much satisfaction, that you were appointed one of the Delegates from Louisiana to attend the Nat. Convention which is to assemble in June next.[1] I sincerely hope that you may be able to attend it. I believe your presence there is highly important. You will take an impartial survey of the whole ground, and have it in your power to arrive at a just decision[.]

I do not pretend to occupy that unbiased position which enables me to form a correct judgment; but unless I am greatly deceived, Genl. [Zachary] Taylor cannot be elected, with the advantage of a nomination by the Whig Convention, and here are my reasons. 1st. He will obtain very inconsiderable support from the other party, which will generally go for its own Candidate. 2. There are great numbers of Whigs that will not vote for him, more I think than to counterbalance any aid which he receives from the other party. 3. I am firmly persuaded that he cannot get the vote of Ohio,[2] and probably will lose that of other free States. 4. His noparty position (which he cannot now change) will prevent the excitement of that enthusiasm, which would be elicited in behalf of any other known whig. 4.[*sic*, 5.] And his numerous letters have created great discontent in the Whig ranks.[3]

I have this day published a note to the public, yielding my assent to the presentation of my name to the consideration of the Whig Convention.[4] I can add nothing to the exposition of the motives by which I have been governed, contained in it. Here is a sample calculation as to the result in regard to myself. I believe that I should obtain the votes of all the States (105) which I received before,[5] to which add N. York (36) that may be certainly counted upon. These would leave four more votes to be obtained, if Wisconsin be not admitted, and six if she be admitted in time to vote at the next election.[6] The deficiency, if supplied, must be derived from Pennsa. Indiana, Georgia, Louisiana, Michigan & Florida. In each of those States, there is great probability of success. We can hardly lose them all. I am persuaded that from some of them more votes would be obtained than are needed.

Among the States which before voted for me, the only two as to which any doubts exist are Tennessee & Massachusetts. In the former a great reaction in my favor has taken place, and if I should be nominated I cannot doubt that it would go for me.[7] In Boston a clique, from interested motives, has been formed for Genl. Taylor;[8] but the State at large, according to my information, has no such tendency, and would be found where it has ever been.

I have given this hasty sketch not to bias or influence your judgment, but to be used, compared, & contrasted with intelligence that may reach you from more disinterested sources.

Should you attend the Convention, which I most earnestly entreat you to do, if practicable, I hope you will come by and stop with me a while. Independent of any public considerations, I shall be delighted to see & entertain you under my roof.

ALS. DLC-HC (DNA, M212, R6). Letter marked "(Confidential)." 1. Prentiss was elected as a delegate to the convention but was unable to attend. Dickey, *Seargent S. Prentiss*, 319. 2. Bebb to Clay, April 4, 1848. 3. Clay to Ullmann, August 4, 1847; Clay to White, Sept. 20, 1847; Stevenson to Clay, April 8, 1848. 4. Clay to The Public, April 10, 1848. 5. Clay to Webb, Feb. 29, 1844. 6. Wisconsin entered the Union on May 29, 1848. See 9:765. 7. A number of pro-Clay meetings had taken place recently in Tennessee, including one in Washington County and another larger one in Nashville on April 8. Lexington *Observer & Kentucky Reporter*, March 11, April 12, 19, 1848. 8. A group of Massachusetts merchants and manufacturers, known as the "Cotton Whigs," opposed slavery only with legal arguments and sought to protect their own economic interests. Abbott Lawrence and a number of other Cotton Whigs had by 1846-47 decided that Taylor was the Whig candidate with the best chance of winning the presidential election. In addition, Lawrence himself coveted the vice presidential nomination. Brauer, *Cotton Versus Conscience*, 2, 212, 214, 230, 238-39.

To KENNETH RAYNER Lexington, April 12, 1848

I received at Balto. on my return home your favor of the 10h. Ulto, and I hope you will excuse the delay in my transmitting an Answer, which has arisen from my desire to communicate my definitive decision in regard to the use of my name, in connection with the next Presidency. This I am now able to do. A note of mine, addressed to the public, is this day published in the Lexington Reporter and Observer,[1] in which I express my assent to the use of my name. You will probably receive it as early as this letter.

I perused attentively your full and interesting account of the proceedings of your Convention.[2] You will have seen what a use was made, at the Virginia Convention held at Richmond,[3] of the alleged political character of the North Carolina Convention. I wish you could go as a delegate to the Philada. Convention in June next. What will be wanted there will be bold decided and good Speakers. For the want of such, I lost the nomination at Harrisburg in 1839, and that was the original cause of all the subsequent difficulties of the Whig party.[4] I have some hopes that S.S. Prentiss Esq of Louisiana will attend that Convention.[5] I shall urge him to do so. I am told that a majority of the Louisiana delegation is friendly to me. I know most of them.

In Kentucky, you may rely, that I am prefered by an immense majority. Even among those who were disposed to support Genl. [Zachary] Taylor, a great reaction has taken place. Public and most enthusiastic meetings are being held, expressing their preference for me. At Louisville one was recently held, the largest ever assembled in that City.[6] A similar reaction is taking place in Tennessee.[7] I have letters from the Governor [William Bebb] and other eminent men in Ohio, stating that whilst that State is ready to go for me, it will in no event go for Genl T. whether nominated or not; and that if I decline, they will put up some other name, even at the hazard of the defeat of the Whig party.[8]

You ask for the cause of the course of Abbott Lawrence and Geo[rge] Evans. The former, and some others in Massachusetts have been tickled by the V. Presidency. In Boston, a small Taylor clique exists; but taking the whole State together it is sound to the core, as I am informed. I do not understand Mr. Evans course.[9]

I shall be always glad to hear from you; and altho' I have determined to write no political letters for publication, I shall be happy to communicate to you any information you may desire.

ALS. ICN. Letter marked "(Confidential)." 1. Clay to The Public, April 10, 1848. 2. The North Carolina Whig State convention had met on Feb. 22, 1848, with Richard Hines as its president. Unable to decide on a single presidential candidate, they endorsed Clay, Taylor, and Scott and elected one Clay supporter and one Taylor supporter as delegates to the Whig National convention. Joseph Hamilton, *Party Politics in North Carolina, 1835-1860* in *The James Sprunt Historical Publications* (Chapel Hill, 1916), 15:114-15. 3. Clay to Combs, Feb. 18, 1848. 4. See espec. 9:92, 117, 361, 824. 5. Clay to Prentiss, April 12, 1848. 6. Clay to Bayard, March 31, 1848. 7. Clay to Prentiss, April 12, 1848; Clay to Harvey, April 18, 1848. 8. Bebb to Clay, April 4, 1848; Stevenson to Clay, April 8, 1848. 9. George Evans of Maine was strongly supporting Taylor for president. Nashville *Whig*, March 16, 1848. See also Clay to Prentiss, April 12, 1848.

To THOMAS B. STEVENSON Lexington, April 12, 1848

Fatigued with writing ten or a dozen letters this afternoon, I have got my son John [Morrison Clay] to act as my amanuensis in acknowledging the receipt of your favor of the 8th inst. You will have seen, before this reaches you, that I have published a note in the Observer & Reporter,[1] expressing my willingness to have my name submitted to the consideration of the Whig Convention in June. I have made in that note a full and candid exposition of the motives which governed me, and I have nothing to add to it. Having taken this ground, I mean henceforward to abstain from writing any political letters for publication, whatever the consequences may be. I have adopted this resolution not from any desire to conceal my opinions, but from a perfect conviction, derived from sad experience, that all such letters, from perversion or misrepresentation, do more harm than good.[2] It is the less necessary that I should write any letters, because my opinions, upon all subjects, have been plainly expressed or are to be plainly inferred from my public acts and public speeches. This course, I am sure, will meet the general approbation of my friends, for many of them have beseeched me most anxiously to adopt it. I hope I may meet with you in the course of the Spring or Summer, in which case I think I can satisfy you of its correctness.

I received and have answered the letter from Gov. [William] Bebb;[3] and I also received and will to-morrow answer the letter from Mr. [Samuel] Forrer.[4] I never for a moment entertained the opinion that I could be elected, if elected at all, without the concurrence of any of the Slave States. If I should be the candidate my opinion is that I would obtain the votes of Kentucky, Tennessee, North Carolina, and Maryland, and there is a fair prospect of Louisiana and Florida.[5] Assuming, which I think may be fairly done, that I should obtain the votes of all the States which gave me their suffrages before, and that of New York,[6] of which I entertain no doubt, there would be still a deficiency of some five or six votes. These, if obtained at all, must be derived from Pennsylvania, Indiana, Georgia, Louisiana and Florida, and perhaps Michigan. In Massachusetts, or rather in Boston, there is an unsatisfactory state of things. Some of our friends there have been tickled with the feather of the Vice Presidency, and hence a [Zachary] Taylor clique has been formed in that City.[7] But according to my information it does not extend much beyond its limits. I have just heard that the Whigs of the N York Legislature, with only some five or six dissentients, have nominated me for the Presidency.[8]

[Robert P.] Letcher was here last night and is very well.

ALS. Courtesy of Dr. Thomas D. Clark, Lexington, Ky. Printed in Colton, *Clay Correspondence*, 3:462-63. Letter marked "(Confidential)." 1. Clay to The Public, April 10, 1848. 2. For example, his Raleigh and Alabama letters in 1844; see Clay to Editors of Washington *Daily National Intelligencer*, April 17, 1844; Clay to Miller, July 1, 1844; Clay to Peters & Jackson, July 27, 1844. 3. Bebb to Clay, April 4, 1848; Clay's reply not found. 4. Forrer to Clay, April 7, 1848; Clay's reply not found. 5. At the Whig National convention, on the first three ballots Clay received 5 of Kentucky's votes and Taylor 7. On the final ballot Taylor received 11 and Clay 1. Schlesinger, *History of U.S. Political Parties*, 1:436-39. For the convention votes of Tennessee, see Clay to Harvey, April 18, 1848; for North Carolina, see Greeley to Clay, April 28, 1848; for Maryland, Louisiana, and Florida, see Clay to Mercer, April 14, 1848. 6. For the states carried by Clay in 1844, see Clay to Webb, Feb. 29, 1844. 7. Clay to Prentiss, April 12, 1848. 8. Clay to White, April 5, 1848.

To JAMES BROOKS Lexington, April 13, 1848

I recd. today your favor of the 6h. communicating the first account I have received, in detail, of the proceedings of your Legislative Caucus,[1] for which I thank you. It is quite satisfactory[.]

Prior to the receipt of this letter, you will have seen a note addressed by me to the public,[2] yielding my assent to the submission of my name to the consideration of the Convention in June. Circumstances seemed to me to require it. I can add nothing to the motives and reasons by which I was governed.

I transmit to you inclosed a letter which I have just received from Govr. [James C.] Jones of Tennessee.[3] I have received other letters corroborating his. If you choose to publish any thing from it, I wish names to be omitted. I have received a letter from Govr. [William] Bebb of Ohio,[4] earnestly remonstrating against the withdrawal of my name, stating that under no circumstances will that State go for Genl. [Zachary] Taylor, but that it will support me.

You will I trust appoint a State Com[mitt]ee reliable & worthy of all trust and confidence.

There will be a great effort to have all the Democratic States fully represented in the approaching Convention, with the hope of their favoring the nomination of Genl. Taylor.[5] This is the game now playing at Washington and elsewhere.

As to Kentucky, the Taylor movement was always an artificial & manufacturing concern.[6] A great reaction has taken place among the Taylor men themselves; and should I be nominated Kentucky will be as enthusiastic as ever in my support. I learn that a majority of the Delegates from Louisiana[7] are friendly to me. I know personally many of them.

(How is Massachusetts? I apprehend an unsatisfactory state of things in Boston—Has any feather from the Vice Presidents plume been tickling any body there?)[8]

My opinion is unaltered. Every thing depends upon N. York pursuing a firm, decided and undoubted course.[9] So far every thing there is well. P.S. I did not receive the Telegraphic dispatch. You write an excellent hand, to which there is but one objection, that it is not very legible[.] 2P.S. A daily paper (the Lexn. Atlas) has this day hoisted the name of myself for President, and that of Genl. [Winfield] Scott for V.P.[10] I wish to say to you that it was done without my knowledge. It took me by surprize of course I have not given, and shall not give, any intimations on that subject. I should deem them improper[.]

ALS. DLC-HC (DNA, M212, R6). Letter marked "(Confidential)." 1. White to Clay, April 15, 1848. 2. Clay to The Public, April 10, 1848. 3. Not found. 4. Bebb to Clay, April 4, 1848. 5. Balloting at the Whig National convention showed that Clay's strength lay in the Whig states and Whig strongholds of the Democratic states which were fairly safe for the party regardless of the nominee, while 75% of Taylor's strength came from Democratic states and Democratic districts in Whig states. Glyndon G. Van Deusen, *The Jacksonian Era, 1828-1848* (New York, 1959), 255. 6. White to Clay, Sept. 4, 1847. For Kentucky's votes in the convention, see Clay to Stevenson, April 12, 1848. 7. For Louisiana's votes in the convention, see Clay to Mercer, April 14, 1848. 8. Clay to Prentiss, April 12, 1848. 9. Ullmann to Clay, Feb. 18, 1848. 10. Editors of the Lexington *Atlas* were N.L. Fennell and J.B. Cochran. The *Atlas* also endorsed John J. Crittenden for governor and John L. Helm for lieutenant governor.

From CASSIUS M. CLAY New York City, April 13, 1848

In the [New-York *Daily*] *Tribune* of this morning I find a letter dated Ashland, April 10th, 1848, over your signature.[1] The letter is addressed, I presume, to the American people. If I did not know you well, the intervening space of three days only between its date and its arrival here, would lead me to suspect its authenticity. If your determination to allow your name to go before the Philadelphia [Whig National] Convention[2] as a candidate for the Presidency had been in accordance merely with your wishes and individual judgment, I should have kept a respectful silence. But as your determination is based upon the supposed interest of the *Whig party*, I shall venture, unasked, to add my opinion to that of the numerous Whigs to whom you refer. When I tell you that *royalty* rarely hears the *truth*, you will think, no doubt, that I repeat a very stale dogma, if not altogether out of place in a republic. But there are parasites in republics as well as in despotisms, and of those you have a very liberal portion just now. Were I to claim to be your personal friend, I might better, perhaps, accomplish my purposes; but as I have never avowed one class of sentiments whilst in reality holding another, I tell you frankly that, although from my earliest youth I had been something more than a cold admirer of yourself, so when you started, on the 14th of August, 1845, to the Virginia Springs, leaving your friends and family to murder me in my sick bed, for vindicating those principles which you had taught me,[3] in your *speeches, at least*, I ceased to be your friend, and became, by the necessity of my nature, your enemy. What I shall say to you now, then, will have the more weight, because you will see that it comes from an honest, if not an unprejudiced man; whilst I shall attempt to divest myself of the individual and speak as the member of a great party.

I shall then take up your letter in its proper order. In saying that you had "a strong disinclination to the use of my [your] name in connection with that office," courtesy leads me to confine myself to the remark that you deceive yourself—but no one else! So soon as you were defeated in the last election, a committee of your friends from Frankfort waited upon you and condoled with you on that melancholy event. You responded in a manner[4] that led me, almost with the power of certainty, to remark to some friends that Henry Clay is a candidate again for the Presidency. Time attests my sagacity.

So strong was my conviction that you would be a candidate, when letters were read in the [Kentucky Whig] Convention of the "Whig friends of Gen. [Zachary] Taylor" in the State House at Frankfort, from the Hon. J[ohn]. J. Crittenden, Hon. Charles S. Morehead and Hon. J[ohn]. P. Gaines, begging us not to nominate Gen. Taylor, and thus push you from the track, and saying that you would on your return home retire from the canvass,[5] in the presence of the thousands there assembled I rose up and declared that although I respected these gentlemen I had not the least confidence that you would in truth withdraw. Time attests my sagacity. After you had gone on to New York, and delegates were chosen to the National Convention whilst you were the *city's guest*, and it was again asserted that you would decline on your return home, I said no, you refused to go to New York last Summer, you would not have gone now, unless you had determined to run for the Presidency.[6] Time attests the truth of the prediction. You say that your friends represent that "the withdrawal of my name would be fatal to their success." If they so speak to you, they speak a different language elsewhere. I have been told that all the members of Congress from our own State but one told you that you could not be elected, and that divers others whom I could name told you the same thing. But if these reports be untrue, allow me to tell you that I have heard almost universally that your name would again bring us defeat. In that opinion I concur, and I will give you my reasons. Because I am not guiltless myself, and because of the bad taste of the thing, I will not urge objections to your private character. Neither will I press your prestige of *ill-luck*, in saying that all the measures which you have urged upon the people, except the Missouri compromise, have been erased from the statute book. For we lament in common, the fall of the tariff, the bank, and internal improvements, under your lead![7] I shall confine myself then to the question of availability. Three times have we run you and three times your name has brought us defeat! So soon as Gen. W[illiam]. H[enry]. Harrison had brought us up from a miserable minority, where you had left us, to a large majority, you hurried on to Washington, when Mr. [John] Tyler under Mr. [Daniel] Webster's lead was doing good service to the country and party, and by attempting to force on him and us the "obsolete Bank" which we had purposely slurred in the canvass,[8] you brought us to speedy minority!

A "long time ago," being too old to perform the comparatively light duties of Senator, you gave the public a *farewell* address[9] and retired from *public life*. The democratic party by the excess of its numbers, was at once split into widely separated fragments Messrs. [Lewis] Cass, [John C.] Calhoun, [Martin] Van Buren, Tyler, [James K.] Polk, and others, were all pressing their claims with a bitterness before unknown to the party. "Whom the gods wish to destroy, they first make mad." They determined to bring Texas into the Union, *avowedly* to break down the power of the free North, and to make this nation a slave empire. The friends of liberty rallied once more, and in spite of your Missouri compromise, and your consistent denunciation of all *real anti-slavery action*, your *Raleigh* letter[10] made you by some fatality our candidate once more. The democratic feuds were at once cured up by the greater hatred of Henry Clay. Mr. Van Buren, who had taken similar ground with yourself, but who could not unite the party, was overthrown, and Mr. James K. Polk substituted.[11] Notwithstanding the claims of other Whigs, I will now restrict myself to saying your *equals*, were postponed who no one now doubts could have been elected, we, the Whig Party, all united on you. We fought with the ardor of brotherhood, and with the *moral power* of a noble cause. Our success seemed certain.—Now once more, by that fatality which attends you, you come out in your Gazette letter,[12] and disclaim any *sympathy with emancipation*. It is true there was a little inconsistency in this, inasmuch as you had always avowed just the opposite doctrine; but as you wrote to me "*go on good Cassius*," I thought at last all things would come out right. This, however, was a small affair between you and me, and our abolition friends. But all at once, you came out in your Alabama letter;[13] when you would "*not reject a permanent acquisition of territory on account of a temporary institution*!" This was a very different affair. It lay at the foundation of the whole contest. You "changed front." The Whigs of the North were disgusted. They had nothing left to contend for. The battle was lost. We felt our country's wounds in your person. We paid your debts, we condoled with you in your retirement once more, and raised monuments to your memory![14] Once more the excesses of the Democratic Party, began to exhibit themselves. The unconstitutional annexation of Texas, and the Presidential war, began to stir the souls of indignant freemen.[15] Seeing that we were in a minority, and without the sympathies of the people—having experience that a peace party can never have the confidence of a Republic during a raging war,—our *wise* Whig leaders voted supplies, and the Whigs turned out to the war, and once more we steadily brought ourselves up from a minority where you had again left us, into a majority. The Administration had all the responsibility of the loss of honor, men, and money, by the war; our Whig generals[16] reaped all the glory. The success of our party was certain. The public, with a unanimity never before seen in this country, looked to one man; a man who, growing too great for the powers at Washington, was left to perish with a handful of men before twenty thousand troops in the enemy's country. But ZACHARY TAYLOR was not the man to die, to accommodate either President Polk or his ally [Antonio Lopez de] Santa Anna! The battle of Buena Vista[17] fixed General Taylor in the hearts of this *people*! Neither you, nor the wireworkers of party, nor the President can cause him or his friends to "*surrender*"! The honest old soldier was generous enough to give a parting compliment to your name, by saying he would have preferred you to himself to lead us on once more to the battle.[18] You have taken him at his word! Immediately your friends of the "*secret circular*,"[19] under the pretence of being "the friends of General Taylor," stab him to the vitals. Then, sharp sighted patriots found out that General Taylor was not the choice of the Whigs—that this willingness of the grateful heart of the people was all a sham affair: in a word, *that you would reluctantly consent to run again*! I am a plain spoken man, sir; I tell you I know these men—they would not have ventured to take this step *with: out your consent*! It is true this is not fair play! It looks to me like political *assassination*! Nor will it be cured in the eyes of all disinterested men by the spirit of *violence*, which your friends in Frankfort—in Baltimore—in Cincinnati—and in New York, have ventured against the friends of Taylor and "*the liberty of speech*."[20] The verdict of a jury against your son lately in Kentucky,[21] ought to teach you and them, that we are not yet *slaves* even to Henry Clay.

It is true that this is in you *deep ingratitude to Gen. Taylor*; but you are just playing out your lifelong game: for when did ever HENRY CLAY *spare* an *enemy* or a—*friend*? I congratulate you upon your determination at last to denounce the Native American party, to whom you wrote encouraging letters during the last canvass; and which they were kind enough to suppress;[22] you can do so with impunity! The Native American party is dead! But whether the memory of the Irish and other foreigners will be so easy in forgetting a *wrong* as you are in not remembering a *favor*, remains to be seen! Space compels me to pass over the long roll of your self-advocacy and confine myself to two specifications. You seem to think that Ohio[23] will not go for any "one residing in the Slave States": but you; and that New York[24] would more certainly bestow her vote on you "than any other candidate."

Ohio went for you, by the Western reserve vote, which I assisted in getting for you, because you were *suspected of truth*, in declaiming against Slavery![25] I had too much respect for your *talents* to suppose that you would again attempt the same shallow game! No, your Janus-faced resolutions at Lexington,[26] deceive no longer the blindest "fanatics." Besides, if the *free* North would not take you, when the question was *Clay* and *no slave territory*, wili they take the issue which you covertly tender them, Clay and NO FREE TERRITORY?

With regard to New York, you seem strangely to have forgotten the fact that the Whig members of the legislature have declared that the State will go for "any other Whig" to close the mouths of your partizans here![27] The city election of a Democratic Mayor in New York,[28] whilst your friends put the election upon your popularity here, demonstrates that your name is indeed "all powerful" to change a Whig majority into a minority at least! If the Whig party are capable of learning, in this, they will read the *future*. I know the strength of party organization, and the desperation of those who have life estates in your person—you may succeed in pushing Webster and [John] McLean, and [William H.] Seward, and [Thomas] Corwin, and [Winfield] Scott and others from the track once more—the dagger o[f] your "secret" *committee* and your *public inquisitors* may kill off Gen. Taylor,[29] *just now*—but the deceiver may be himself deceived!—Yes, Henry Clay can never be President of these States!

Copy. DLC-Hamilton Fish Papers. 1. Clay to The Public, April 10, 1848. 2. Greeley to Clay, Nov. 15, 1846. 3. C.M. Clay to H. Clay, Sept. 25, 1845. 4. Clay to Kentucky Presidential Electors, Dec. 4, 1844. 5. Clay to Unknown Recipient, *ca.* Winter 1847-48; Clay to Bayard, June 19, 1848. 6. For Clay's trip to the East, see Speech at Independence Hall, Philadelphia, Feb. 26, 1848. 7. See espec. 8:559; 9:529, 628 and Subject Index on Missouri Compromise, 7:747. 8. See espec. 9:529. 9. See 9:691-92. 10. Clay to Editors of Washington *Daily National Intelligencer*, April 17, 1844. 11. Clay to Crittenden, April 21, 1844. 12. Clay to Wickliffe, Sept. 2, 1844. 13. Clay to Miller, July 1, 1844. 14. For one such monument, see French to Clay, Feb. 27, 1845. For payment of debts, see Tilford to Clay, Feb. 17, 1845; Clay to Tilford, Feb. 22, 1845; Lawrence to Clay, March 13, 1845; Clay to Lawrence, March 20, 1845. 15. Clay to Crittenden, Feb. 15, 1844; Clay to Lawrence, April 30, 1845. 16. Zachary Taylor and Winfield Scott. 17. Henry Clay, Jr., to Clay, Feb. 12/19, 1847. 18. Taylor to Clay, Nov. 4, 1847. 19. Clay to Greeley, Nov. 22, 1847. 20. Hecklers in New York City booed and hissed at Taylor speakers, disrupting and occasionally forcing a premature end to their political addresses. Bauer, *Zachary Taylor*, 234; Hamilton, *Zachary Taylor, Soldier in the White House*, 83-85. 21. Cassius M. Clay had sued the Committee of Sixty—James B. Clay, secretary—for $2,500, the value of his press that the committee had dismantled and moved to Cincinnati in 1845 [C.M. Clay to H. Clay, Sept. 25, 1845]. The court awarded Cassius the $2,500 he sought. Lexington *Observer & Kentucky Reporter*, April 5, 1848. 22. Clay to Smith, April 2, 1847. 23. Ullmann to Clay, Feb. 18, 1848; Bebb to Clay, April 4, 1848. 24. Ullmann to Clay, Feb. 18, 1848; White to Clay, April 5, 1848. 25. Clay to Berrien, July 16, 1844. 26. Speech in Lexington, Nov. 13, 1847. 27. Clay to Greeley, Dec. 10, 1847; Lawrence *et al.* to Clay, Feb. 16, 1848. 28. In the New York City charter elections, William F. Havemeyer, a Democrat, had been elected by a majority of about 1,000 votes. Whigs carried 10 seats on the board of aldermen to 8 for the Democrats, while each party won 9 of the assistant aldermen seats. Washington *Daily National Intelligencer*, April 14, 1848. For Havemeyer, see *DAB*. 29. Clay to Greeley, Nov. 22, 1847.

From George C. Collins, Philadelphia, April 13, 1848. Is pleased to announce the "enthusiastic manifestation of public attachment, towards you" that followed after "Mr. [Morton] McMichael read your letter to the Committee." Assures Clay that "tears flowed from my eyes, apprehending from the disinclination you manifested of being our standard bearer that you would retire from the contest." Adds that an hour later "your address to the Public was read [Clay to The Public, April 10, 1848]," and wishes that Clay could have been "present, in some obscure place, where you could see and hear, (without being seen,) the Effect that address had upon the audience. . . . it was the proudest moment of my life." When "called upon to speak," found that "I could not give utterance to my feelings," because "you had dissipated the cloud, which had so long made me miserable and the light now shining was too brilliant to see any thing." After "the bad policy of a fraction of our party" led to defeat in 1844, now sees "no doubt" of Clay's nomination and "*of your election, I am certain.*" Cites financial woes for his inability to accompany Clay to New York. Adds: "A little aid would enable me to stand erect, and I throw myself upon you for it. . . . Send from your liberal heart, and hospitable home a small loan, say $50 or $100, and I pledge my honor and my life that Six months will not pass over my head until it is paid with interest." Regardless of Clay's decision, "I shall still continue your inflexible friend—your ardent admirer and humble but devoted advocate." ALS. DLC-HC (DNA, M212, R6). Letter marked "(Confidential)."

George C. Collins had written for the previous presidential election a pamphlet called *Fifty Reasons Why the Honorable Henry Clay Should Be Elected President of the United States, by an Adopted Citizen* (Baltimore, 1844). In it, he identified himself as an Irish immigrant who had been extremely prejudiced against Clay and the Whig party when he first arrived in the U.S. He disliked the union in 1844 of some Whigs with the nativists.

McMichael read Clay's letter to The Public at the festival in Philadelphia honoring Clay's birthday on April 12. Philadelphia *North American & United States Gazette*, April 13, 1848.

To JOSEPH L. WHITE Lexington, April 13, 1848

I received your letter of the 5th inst., and take pleasure in transmitting enclosed a letter of introduction to Lord Morpeth for Mr. [John] J[ay] and his lady.

I have just heard with much satisfaction of the result of your Legislative caucus in expressing its preference for me.[1] I retain the opinion which I expressed to you in New York that a bold, decided, and unequivocal course on the part of the Empire State will exercise a controlling influence over the [Whig National] Convention in June. So far, every thing has been well done. If the other two measures, about which we conversed, could be carried out, I should feel the greatest confidence.[2] You will have seen that I have published a note, addressed to the public, avowing my willingness to have my name submitted to the consideration of the National Convention.[3] I am very happy to learn from you that my recent visit to N York has been attended with good effects, which is more than I feared.

The Lexington Atlas, a little daily paper, has this day hoisted my name as a candidate for the Presidency and that of Gen [Winfield] Scott for the second office.[4] I wish to say to you, that the step was taken without any knowledge whatever on my part, the editor acting, I believe, exclusively on his own opinion. Of course, I have not given, and shall not give, any intimations upon that subject. . . .

LS. Courtesy of Albert D. Arfin, Massapequa Park, N.Y. 1. White to Clay, April 5, 1848. 2. Reference obscure, but for New York's vote at the Whig National convention, see Ullmann to Clay, Feb. 18, 1848. 3. Clay to The Public, April 10, 1848. 4. Clay to Brooks, April 13, 1848.

To A.D. Haslett, April 14, 1848. Sends the "lock of my hair" Haslett requested, "regretting that it is not something more worthy of your acceptance." ALS. ViU.

To WILLIAM N. MERCER Lexington, April 14, 1848

I received your favor of the 31st ultimo. informing me of your having received my draft on Messrs. [John] Freeland and others for six thousand dollars and having placed it in the hands of Mr [Rezin D.] Shepherd for collection.[1] Mr [Charles S.] Morehead informs me from Washington that he has transmitted to you the mandate &c which I hope you will have safely received.[2] There ought to be therefore, and I anticipate, no difficulty in my draft being duly honored.

You will have seen a note, addressed by me to the public, in which I express my acquiescence in the submission of my name to the action of the National Convention.[3] It so fully sets forth the reasons and motives by which I have been governed that I need add nothing to it. I should have been very glad if you had been near me so that I could have had the benefit of your advice and judgment, which would have had more weight with me than that of most of my friends. If I had decided that my name should not be submitted to the National Convention, there would have been no necessity to announce my decision until it had assembled, But, having been constrained to come to a different decision, I thought it right no longer to delay letting it be known. It appeared to me that, as delegates were being appointed to the National Convention, it was right that both they and their constituents should have timely notice of my final determination[.] I was aware too that a use injurious to me was making of the uncertainty as to my wishes, in the appointment of delegates.

I sincerely entertain the opinion expressed in my note to the public in regard to the prospects in New York, Ohio, and Pennsylvania. As to the first State, unless I am utterly deceived in a vast amount of information which I have received, if I am nominated, there is no more certain State for me in the Union.[4] My information also authorizes me to anticipate that I will receive the vote of every Slave State that voted for me at the last election.[5] Tennessee, you would probably consider as the most doubtful; but Gov [James C.] Jones and other friends in that State assure me that 999 out of every 1000 Whigs in it are for me, that I am stronger there than I ever was, and that they have no doubt of the vote of the State being given to me.[6] And, as to Maryland and North Carolina, I feel entire confidence.[7] Assuming that I obtained all the votes which I got at the last election, and the vote of N York in addition, there would be still wanting some three or four votes to insure my election. These, if obtained at all, must be derived from Pennsylvania Indiana Georgia Florida Louisiana and Iowa.[8] There are hopes of them all, and we must be very unfortunate if we lose all. Of Louisiana you are a better judge than I am. I have very strong expectations of Indiana, and as to Pennsylvania I think the result will greatly depend upon the fact whether the prices of iron and food shall continue or not to be low.[9] A good deal will also depend upon the nominee of the other party. It will most probably, I think, be [Lewis] Cass, [James] Buchanan, or [Levi] Woodbury.[10] The two first I regard as the weakest, but I think either of them can be beaten. The astounding events, which are transpiring in Europe, must exercise great influence on the choice of the next President.[11] They demand at the head of our public affairs a man of much more sagacity, energy, firmness, and decision than are possessed by either of those gentlemen. But I forbear to bore you any further with politics.

I request you to present my congratulations to Mrs [William H.] Sumner (for so I suppose Miss [Mary D.] Kemble has become) upon her recent marriage.[12] I hope that she will realize all the happiness from it which her fondest wishes anticipate. Do me the favor to present my affectionate regards to Miss [Eliza] Young, and to Anna [Mercer], in which Mrs [Lucretia Hart] Clay cordially unites. P.S. Fatigued with writing, my son has acted as my Amanuensis.

LS. LU-Ar. Addressed to Mercer at New Orleans. 1. Not found, but see Clay to Mercer, March 18, 1848. 2. Morehead letter not found, but see *ibid.* and Clay to Morehead, March 18, 1848. 3. Clay to The Public, April 10, 1848. 4. For the votes of New York and Ohio in the Whig National convention, see Ullmann to Clay, Feb. 18, 1848. On the 1st ballot at the convention, Pennsylvania cast 12 votes for Clay, 8 for Taylor, and 6 for Scott; on the 2nd, 9 for Taylor, 7 for Clay, and 10 for Scott; and on the 3rd and 4th ballots, 12 for Taylor, 4 for Clay and 10 for Scott. Schlesinger, *History of U.S. Political Parties*, 1:436-39. 5. In 1844 Clay had carried the slave states of Kentucky, North Carolina, and Tennessee. McKee, *National . . . Popular and Electoral Vote*, 57. 6. At the Whig National convention Tennessee gave all 13 of its votes to Taylor on all 4 ballots. Schlesinger, *History of U.S. Political Parties*, 1:436-39. 7. On the 1st and 2nd ballots at the Whig convention, Maryland gave all 8 votes for Clay. On the 3rd ballot 5 were cast for Clay and 3 for Taylor; on the 4th all 8 votes went to Taylor. *Ibid.* For North Carolina's vote at the convention, see Greeley to Clay, April 28, 1848. 8. At the Whig National convention, Indiana cast 9 votes for Scott, 2 for Clay, and one for Taylor on the 1st ballot; on the 2nd, 8 for Scott, 3 for Taylor, and 1 for Clay; on the 3rd, 6 for Scott, 5 for Taylor, and 1 for Clay; and on the 4th ballot, 7 for Taylor, 4 for Scott, and 1 for Clay. On all 4 ballots Georgia cast 10 votes for Taylor, while Florida cast 3 votes for Taylor on each ballot. Louisiana cast 1 vote for Clay and 5 for Taylor on the 1st ballot and 6 for Taylor on the remaining ballots. On the 1st ballot, Iowa cast 2 votes for Taylor and one each for Clay and McLean; on the 2nd and 3rd ballots, 3 votes went to Taylor and 1 to Clay; and on the 4th ballot all 4 votes were cast for Taylor. Schlesinger, *History of U.S. Political Parties*, 1:436-39. 9. Reference is to the effect of the Tariff of 1846. See Clay to Greeley, June 23, 1846. 10. Clay to Ullmann, May 12, 1847. 11. The Revolutions of 1848. See Clay to Hughes, March 19, 1848. 12. Clay to Mercer, Nov. 14, 1846.

To WASHINGTON SMITH Lexington, April 14, 1848

I received your favor, explaining the circumstances under which you accidentally retained, at New Ark [*sic*, Newark, N.J.] a Cane of mine, one of the many tokens I received of the affection of my enthusiastic friends, during my late visit to N. York.[1] I beg you to give yourself no concern about it. If we ever again meet, you can return it; and if we do not I request you to keep it as a Souvenir.

I have hardly yet got fully composed, after the stirring scenes through which I passed in the Cities. They linger in my memory and imagination like some bright dreams, or fairy tales.

On my return home, I had immediately to plunge into a trial for Life or Death, and we have been occupied two weeks in endeavoring to get a Jury, without having yet completed the pannel.[2]

ALS. MCM. Addressed to Smith in New York City. 1. See Clay's Speech in New York City, March 7, 1848. For the itinerary of his northern trip, see Speech at Independence Hall, Philadelphia, Feb. 26, 1848. 2. Case of Lafayette Shelby. See Clay to James B. Clay, Feb. 2, 1846.

From Lucius J. Gartrell, Washington, Ga., April 15, 1848. Writes to ask if Clay will allow his name to go before the Whig National convention [Clay to The Public, April 10, 1848], saying that a strong effort is being made in Georgia to create the impression that he will not allow his name to be brought up. Notes that the Georgia State Whig convention will meet on the 2nd Monday in May to decide on a preference for president. Warns that "those opposed to your nomina[tion] will reiterate this old story of your withdrawal and thereby greatly preju[dic]e your claims in that Convention."

States that despite an impression to the contrary, a majority of the Whigs of Georgia prefer Clay. "In this district, at present represented by Mr [Robert] Toombs in Congress, at least four fifths of the Whigs proclaim you their first choice for the Presidency." Asserts that he and "Thousands of whigs here" do not want Clay to withdraw.

Adds that he introduced "into the last Georgia Legislature, your Lexington

Resolutions [Speech in Lexington, November 13, 1847]," and "I shall be in our state Convention in May." ALS. DLC-HC (DNA, M212, R6).

Gartrell (1821-91), a lawyer and member of the Georgia house 1847-50, later served in the 35th & 36th Congresses and as a brigadier general in the Confederate Army. *BDAC.*

The Georgia State Whig convention met at Milledgeville on May 8, 1848, and chose delegates to the national convention. Its endorsement of Taylor was not unanimous and was qualified by the promise to support any candidate of the Whig party whose views "accord with our own on the subject of the Wilmot Proviso and Southern Rights." There were some Whigs in Georgia who favored Clay for the nomination, but they were opposed by Robert Toombs, who announced he would retire from politics if Clay were nominated, and by ex-Gov. George W. Crawford. Paul Murray, *The Whig Party in Georgia, 1825-1853* in *The James Sprunt Studies in History and Political Science* (Chapel Hill, 1948), 29:132-33. For Toombs (1810-85), see *BDAC.* For Georgia's vote at the Whig National convention, see Clay to Mercer, April 14, 1848.

To SAMUEL HAIGHT Lexington, April 15, 1848

I received today your favor of the 10th. inst. Prior to this you will have received my note, addressed to the public, announcing my assent to the submission of my name to the consideration of the National Convention.[1] It so fully explains my views and feelings, that I have nothing to add to it. I do not see how it is possible for any exception to be taken to it.

I concur with you in regretting the course of the [Washington *Daily*] National Intelligencer in regard to the French revolution;[2] but I think it ought not to operate, and I hope will not, to the prejudice of the Whig party. The editors expressly disclaim being the organ of that party and the resolutions of congratulation to the French people have been passed, in both Houses of Congress, by almost unanimous votes.[3] My own opinion is, that our sympathies and congratulations were due to the French people for the revolution which they had effected. In expressing these sentiments, we should not have been committed to the sanction of any future excesses, which may be perpetrated, in the progress of the Revolution, if any such should unfortunately occur. My hope is, that the Foreign Powers, profiting by the folly of their former interference with France, will abstain from all exterior pressure upon her, and that she, profiting by the errors which were committed in the former revolution, will peacefully establish, without the spilling of blood, a free government, upon the basis of popular representation.

No one can doubt my feelings and sympathies, who has any recollection of the course which I took in regard to the Spanish American Republics, and to Greece.[4] Whilst France has my cordial and hearty wishes for the triumphant establishment of liberty, I shall be ready to express the deepest regrets if the revolution should take an unfortunate turn. . . . P.S. I dictate to an Amanuensis[.]

LS, postscript in Clay's hand. DLC-HC (DNA, M212, R11). Printed in Colton, *Clay Correspondence*, 4:560-61. 1. Clay to The Public, April 10, 1848. 2. The *Intelligencer* had expressed skepticism about the ability of the directors to govern France and feared that establishment of a republic would lead to a general European war into which the United States would be drawn. See, for example, Washington *Daily National Intelligencer*, March 27, April 3, 1848. 3. A resolution, congratulating France on its recent efforts to establish a republican form of government, was introduced in the Senate on March 28, 1848, and passed 32 to 0 on April 7. The resolution was taken up by the House on April 7 and passed on April 10, 174 to 2. *Cong. Globe*, 30 Cong., 1 Sess., 549, 558, 567, 580, 590, 592, 604. 4. See Spanish America in Subject Index 7:764-65 and Greece 7:731.

To WILLIAM PRATHER Lexington, April 17, 1848

I send you on the other side my account[1] with Henry's [Clay, Jr.] estate, and I enclose you all the receipts except for the seasons to Boston.[2] as I suppose you will wish to make the proper entries in your official account. I have not paid the seasons to Boston, but his Keeper applied to me the other day for them and I promised to pay them. My account shows a ballance of eighteen dollars due the estate which may be left in my hands to meet future payments to Mrs [Jane] Tibbatts or you may deduct it from the remittance to be made Mr [John Jacob] Astor if you prefer it.[3] Henry's stock has turned out badly and I am sorry for it, but I do not know that it could have been avoided. Blooded stock has become a great drag. I lost the filly I purchased at the sale soon after.

Has Mr [James W.] Bates purchased the theatre?[4] or is there any probability of selling it? The debt to Mr Astor becomes now due in a little more than a year and I am anxious that provisions should be made for its payment.

My warm regards to your mother [Matilda Fontaine Prather] and family.

LS. KyU. 1. The account shows that Clay had received $217 for the estate of Henry Clay, Jr., from the sale of an "old Jenny & young Jack"; "a young filly"; "note for colt"; and "for scholar admitted on H. Clay's junr scholarship for six months." Paid out for debts owed by Henry Clay, Jr., including cash paid to Mrs. Tibbatts "under H. Clay junr's contract with her for her interest in the land he owned near Lexington, being an annuity of $30. per annum as per receipts," cash for "feeding and training," and cash for two mares "going to Boston." Balance left to the estate of Henry Clay, Jr.: $18.00. 2. Boston (1833-50) had been bred by John Wickham. He was a descendant of Diomed through his sire Timoleon and was himself the sire of Lexington, one of the greatest sires America has produced. Frank Forrester, *The Horse of America*, 2 vols. (New York, 1857), 1:276-83; William H. Perrin (ed.), *History of Fayette County, Kentucky* (Chicago, 1882), 153. 3. For the debt to Astor, see espec. 9:846; Clay to Henry Clay, Jr., May 6, 1845; and Clay to Tilford, August 4, 1845. 4. James W. Bates was for many years the proprietor and manager of the Louisville Theater. Johnston, *Memorial History of Louisville*, 2:328-30; Louisville *Daily Journal*, Nov. 30, 1846.

To JAMES E. HARVEY[1] Lexington, April 18, 1848

On the very day of the date of your favor of the 13h. inst. you must have recd. my note to the public expressing my acquiescence in the submission of my name to the Whig Nat. Convention.[2] Whatever uncertainty on that point previously existed must now be dissipated. What the result will be before the Convention, I do not know that.[3] I am more competent to judge than you. I *believe* that I shall obtain the votes of the Delegates from this State, Tennessee and Louisiana.[4] Great efforts are however making to direct them otherwise, and so of other States. The organization at Washn. should be met by counter organization, to operate on the Convention.[5] Cannot that be done?

In the event of my nomination, here is my calculation: The votes of the States which I formerly recd.[6] To which add that of N. York, and I think Indiana. I have hopes of Pennsa. Georgia, Louisiana, Florida & Iowa.[7] In Pennsa. a leading and influential Locofoco told me at Pittsburg[h] that in Allegheny County, if [Lewis] Cass or [James] Buchanan were the Candidate, they would give me in that County a majority of 5000, which is about double the usual majority. I was assured by the Editor of the [Zachary] Taylor paper that there were not ten Taylor men in that County.[8] Every where, in that State, I was informed great changes had taken place, particularly among the Irish. Still I only *hope* for Pennsa. I think I am not mistaken as to Tennessee[.] Govr [James C.] Jones and other prominent men assure me that 999 out of every 1000 Whigs are for me, and that, if nominated, I will obtain the vote of that State. The Nashville Whig papers have very much changed their tone about me.[9]

I am persuaded that every where, in the Whig States, the Whig masses are for me, and that I am opposed only by some politicians. But of all this I am an interested judge.

I cannot account for the remark of [Thomas] Corwin quoted by you. From Ohio, I have recd. from Govr [William] Bebb & others the most earnest remonstrances against my retirement, accompanied by assurances that I only, of any residents of Slave States, can obtain its vote.[10]

Judge [John] McLean has acted, as far as I know or believe, a frank, manly & honorable part, and I confess that he has secured my esteem & confidence.

I wish you would write me how my note to the public has been recd. at Washn.; how it has operated upon individuals &c.

My correspondence has become very burthensome, and I hope you will excuse my brevity.

ALS. Courtesy of Willard L. King, Chicago, Ill. Letter marked "(Confidential)." Addressed to Harvey at Washington, D.C. 1. Harvey, a South Carolinian by birth, was a Washington correspondent for the Philadelphia *North American & United States Gazette* from 1844 until 1861 when he became minister to Portugal. *PMHB* (July, 1963), 87:438. 2. Clay to The Public, April 10, 1848. 3. For the Whig National convention see Greeley to Clay, Nov. 15, 1846. 4. Clay to Mercer, April 14, 1848. 5. With the backing of such people as Thurlow Weed and John J. Crittenden, a Whig Executive Committee was formed in Washington, D.C., to raise money to provide for a unified national Whig organization for the 1848 election. Congressman Truman Smith of Connecticut was prominent in the formation of a pro-Taylor congressional group made up principally, but not exclusively, of Southern Whigs. Known as the "Young Indians," this group included Alexander H. Stephens and Robert Toombs (Ga.); John S. Pendleton, Thomas S. Flournoy, and William B. Preston (Va.); Abraham Lincoln (Ill.); Henry W. Hillard (Ala.); and E. Carrington Cabell (Fla.). A number of other congressmen hovered on the periphery. Hamilton, *Zachary Taylor, Soldier in the White House*, 63-64. 6. Clay to Webb, Feb. 29, 1844. 7. Clay did not receive the nomination, but for the convention votes see: N.Y.—Ullmann to Clay, Feb. 18, 1848; Ind., Pa., Ga., La., Fla., Iowa—Clay to Mercer, April 14, 1848. 8. Probably Robert M. Riddle, editor of the Pittsburgh *Daily Commercial Journal*, who actively supported Taylor until April 17, 1848, when he switched his paper to support Clay. Information supplied by Donald L. Haggerty, The Historical Society of Western Pennsylvania, Pittsburgh. 9. The Nashville *Whig* and the Nashville *Republican Banner* were both Taylor papers and had both opposed the idea for a national Whig convention. By April they had begun to moderate their opposition to a national convention and were printing some articles in support of Clay; however, their over-all tenor appears to have remained pro-Taylor. See, for example, Nashville *Whig*, April 1, 4, 11, 22, 1848. 10. Quote not found; but see Corwin to Clay, May 3, 1848. It was not really clear who had Corwin's support for the nomination. Sometimes it seemed to be Clay, sometimes John McLean, sometimes Winfield Scott, but never Taylor. Because there was no ideal Whig candidate who could unify both northern and southern wings of the party, Corwin was very pessimistic about the election and feared the break up of the party and ultimately the Union. Weisenburger, *The Life of John McLean*, 129-31.

To JAMES LYNCH[1] Lexington, April 22, 1848

I received your favor dated at Albany. I regretted not seeing you when I was in the City of N. York.[2] Although I was constantly occupied, and had scarcely any control over my own person or time, I should have taken some opportunity to meet you, if I had been aware of your calling. I thank you for your account of the proceedings of the Whig Caucus at Albany,[3] which agrees substantially with what I have received through other friends. Taken in connection with other manifestations of public opinion in the State of N. York, I should think that the preference of the Whigs of that State, in regard to the next Presidency, could be no longer a matter of controversy.

I hope that you and my other friends approve of my recent note, addressed to the Public,[4] expressing my acquiesence in the wish that my name may be submitted to the consideration of the [Nationl] Whig Convention. It fully and truly presents the state of my feelings. Henceforward I shall abstain from writing any political letters, and submit quietly to future results.

ALS. NN. 1. See 4:111-12. 2. Speech in New York City, March 7, 1848. 3. White to Clay, April 5, 1848. 4. Clay to The Public, April 10, 1848.

To WILLIAM D. NORTHEND[1] Lexington, April 24, 1848

Your friendly letter,[2] communicating information as to the state of public opinion in Massachusetts, entitles you to an acknowledgment of its receipt, and to my thanks. It was the more acceptable, because I was really uninformed in regard to public sentiment there. Indeed I began to believe, from the course of the Press and of prominent gentlemen in Boston,[3] that I was repudiated by the Bay State; and that its vote would be cast against me in the N[ational]. Convention.[4]

I have defined my position, in my recent note to the public.[5] I have nothing to add to the faithful exposition of my feelings and views, which it makes.

One, under my circumstances, is very apt to be deceived; but unless I am very grossly so, in this state, in Tennessee, and in the South West generally, a powerful reaction has taken place in my favor.[6] That you will be able to learn from the altered tone of the Press. My great anxiety is for the success of the good cause in which I have so long labored. If that is more likely to be achieved under some other names than my own, I shall be most happy & contented.

ALS. Courtesy of Prof. Francis Benjamin, Atlanta, Ga. Letter marked "(Private)." 1. For William Dummer Northend (1823-1902) of Salem, Mass., a future state senator, see *Historical Collections of the Essex Institute* (Jan., 1874), 12:80-81; *NEHGR* (April, 1891), 45:75 2. Not found. 3. Clay to Stevenson, April 12, 1848. 4. Greeley to Clay, April 28, 1848. 5. Clay to The Public, April 10, 1848. 6. For Kentucky in the Whig National convention, see Clay to Stevenson, April 12, 1848; for Tennessee, see Clay to Mercer, April 14, 1848.

From William C.C. Claiborne, Jr., New Orleans, April 26, 1848. Writes that "it was high time" Clay made his intentions concerning his candidacy known [Clay to The Public, April 10, 1848]. Reports that Clay's announcement "has produced [varied] impressions in this latitude. Your true friends hav[e read it] with decided pleasure, but it has excited a differen[t attitude] in another class of Whigs, who had been indulging [in public] though unfounded assertions that you could not [now] be a Candidate." Feels this "exhibition of spleen" comes from only "a small squad," who have "calculated that they themselves [have] a better chance of attaining the power to which they asp[ire in] the affairs of our little State, by running their candida[te under] the [Zachary] Taylor banner, and clinging to the skirts of the [general's] military coat." Notes that Taylor was nominated as "a no party Candidate. But an immense and *true Whig* meeting . . . has designated men from this State to the Philadelphi[a] Convention [Greeley to Clay, November 15, 1846], some of whom are your friends, and all of whom will act I think, in a proper spirit [Clay to Mercer, April 14, 1848]." Regrets he cannot go to Philadelphia himself, but adds that Clay's supporters "will have much to do here," and "are prepared to [work rea]l hard on this field, and by avoiding Plaquemine frauds [Roman to Clay, December 2, 1844], [and ca]lling upon naturalized citizens to make amends for the [harm t]hey did you" in 1844. Reports that "Mss [William L.] Hodge, [Samuel J.] Peters, [Balie] Peyton,

[Alexander] Bullitt & Co. . . . continue upon their wrong scent," one of whom has been so "parti[cular]ly splenetic" that "you might well say to him if he were worthy [of it] Sir, 'et tu quoque Brutus.' " Praises "Randell [*sic*, Randall] Hunt who [did no]t act with that set" and believes that "[Judah P.] Benjamin, [Charles M.] Conrad & others, who allowed [themselv]es at first to be taken by the vertigo" will return to Clay's side. Informs Clay of the establishment of "another paper too, for the old Whig editorial corps [of this] City have so committed themselves on the other tack, that [they] would not be fit organs in case of your nomination." Expresses pleasure at "Mr. Cassius Clay's coming out violently against [you] . . . presuming that he must exercise any influence at the North, we think that he will aid you much more effectually in this way [C.M. Clay to H. Clay, April 13, 1848]." Warns that "a Committee headed by Bailie Peyton, left this City on a visit to Genl. Taylor, which resulted in another letter from the general, in which he is more explicit, takes Whig ground and continues to declare that he is not however an Ultra Whig, and would not be the President of a party &c." Requests Clay, if "you think proper," to "communicate to m[e] any thing that you may think useful. . . . in spreading proper impressions, particula[rly among] the population of the lower part of the City." AL, parts of manuscript mutilated, including signature. DLC-HC (DNA, M212, R6).

Balie [or Bailie] Peyton, James Love, and Logan Hunton were responsible for Taylor's "First Allison Letter." See Ullmann to Clay, August 4, 1847.

On January 22, 1848, a meeting of citizens of both parties in favor of Taylor for president met at the Commercial Exchange Building in New Orleans. Balie Peyton was named to a committee to make arrangements for a non-partisan convention to meet on February 22 to nominate Taylor. Delegates named from New Orleans to this convention were: Balie Peyton, Charles M. Conrad, William L. Hodge, Randall Hunt, Samuel J. Peters, and Alexander C. Bullitt. The convention with 36 parishes represented assembled in the Louisiana house of representatives on February 22, 1848, and nominated Taylor. New Orleans *Daily Picayune*, January 23 and February 23, 1848.

The "*true Whig*" meeting was held at the Commercial Exchange on March 14 to elect delegates to the Whig National convention. A number of the Whigs who had previously participated in the non-partisan Taylor meeting had become convinced that Taylor had to have the Whig party's nomination in order to win. Appeals were made for party unity, with both Seargent S. Prentiss and Randall Hunt saying they personally favored Clay but felt that a majority of Louisiana Whigs supported Taylor. The convention pledged to support whomever was nominated by the national convention. *Ibid.*, March 15, 1848.

Alexander C. Bullitt was a New Orleans lawyer and one of the editors of the *Picayune*. A Kentuckian by birth, he was a friend of John J. Crittenden and a former supporter of Clay. The *Picayune* was a strong Taylor paper. Hamilton, *Zachary Taylor, Soldier in the White House*, 64-65.

Charles Magill Conrad (1804-78) was a New Orleans lawyer and former U.S. senator who was elected in 1848 to the U.S. House. *DAB*.

Randall Hunt (1825-92), a South Carolina native, was a New Orleans lawyer who had become a professor of law at the University of Louisiana in 1847. He later served as president of the university and rector of Tulane in 1883 after it was founded from the University of Louisiana. Johnson, *Twentieth Century Biographical Dictionary*.

Samuel J. Peters, a Canadian by birth, was a merchant and civic leader in New Orleans. In 1846 he had helped raise volunteers for Taylor's army. Alcée Fortier, *A History of Louisiana*, 4 vols. (New York, 1904), 3:225, 245.

From HORACE GREELEY Washington, April 28, 1848

I received yours of the 15th some four days since in New York, but as I wished to answer it carefully and was coming directly to this city, I concluded to defer replying until this time. I am most anxious not to confound my hopes or wishes with facts, but to give the naked and impartial truth.

Thus far, New York has chosen 12 Delegates, every one of whom is informed by his constituents that they desire the same candidate as in '44, and most of them are explicitly instructed, beside being sure to be right and earnest, whether instructed or not. We know positively that a large portion of the remaining districts—Albany, Rensselaer, Erie, Monroe, &c.—will do likewise. We know there is not a district in the State which can be openly and fairly carried for Gen. [Zachary] Taylor, though a few may and probably will be carried for Gen. [Winfield] Scott, whom I have long believed the really formidable antagonist, so far as our section is concerned. I see without surprise that Wayne County has instructed for him, and this will overbid Seneca, (which is very warmly for us, and has chosen accordingly) and will elect a Scott Delegate[.] Ontario and Livingston will choose another, and there will be some more—I think not above 6 at the outside, out of 36, and only one or two of these at heart for Taylor. If the vote is taken by States, New York is solid and certain; if by Districts, 30 for us to 6 every where else. This is for the first ballot;[1] I suspect the Jefferson and Steuben Delegates, who are not expressly instructed and are not known to us as decidedly with us, may fall off if we should not succeed on the first ballot, saying "It is of no use—if half the Convention is not decidedly for Mr. Clay, he cannot be elected." But if we are not croaked down by delegates from such States as Tennessee, Indiana, and Georgia,[2] saying that their States are hopeless unless there is a new shuffle, the all but unanimous voice and vote of New York, both on the point of preference and that of availability, must lose weight with the Convention.

New-Jersey[3] is now the theatre of a spirited struggle, in which the friends of Gen. Taylor make up by zeal and activity for lack of numbers, and are greatly strengthened by a hollow pretence of Taylorism on the part of our opponents in Sussex, Warren and Hunterdon, the three darkest Counties. I think, however, there can be no serious doubt as to the result.

Pennsylvania[4] is not doing so well; our opponents boast confidently of choosing a majority of the delegates. I have been disappointed in regard to two or three Districts, and yet I cannot see how we are to be behind unless men talk one way and vote another. Surely, we have elected 1. [Samuel] Bell [Jr.] of Berks (senatorial;) 3. in Philadelphia city and county; 1 in Lancaster, 1 in Chester, 1 in Beaver & Washington, 1 in Allegheny, 1 in Bradford, Susquehanna, &c. making 9, or half those already chosen, while [Diller] Luther of Berks, [Edward M.] Biddle of Cumberland, and the Southwark delegate in Philadelphia, are said to be entirely undecided, and our friends here at least signal chances to carry the Luzerne, Erie, Crawford, and York and Adams Districts.[5] Yet there are lists circulating here claiming ten for Taylor, and others confidently claiming a majority for Scott. I have not been able to ascertain the truth in the premise.

This City is a perfect case of the winds, in which all sorts of discouraging rumors and doleful prophecies are in constant circulation. I was met here by reports that New-York had turned about, and was going for Scott or Taylor, and was soberly asked if it were true that New-York had relinquished Mr. Clay as unavailable. I had not heard a whisper of this in New-York. Even those who there say we must have a new candidate or be beaten generally admit that New York is safe enough; but they say we can't succeed even with *New York*—that Maryland,[6] Georgia, Tennessee, Indiana and Louisiana[7] will not vote for Mr. Clay. Our answer is, 'Let us hear what *the delegates* from those States say; if they say Mr. Clay cannot be carried, and the Pennsylvanians say the same for their State, your position stands good; but you not ought to ask us to believe your mere assertion.' But some of the great men here insist that the Delegates will not know about the popular feeling of their own States—that, whatever they may say, Mr. Clay cannot possibly be elected. This incessant croaking has its effect: a good many, from hearing it at every corner, come at last to believe it, and thus Washington is a great manufactory of discouragement and apprehension.[8] Should the delegates come here to take their instructions instead of going to the Convention to say, each for himself, what his constituents desire and think, we are beaten, easily. But the New-York Delegates will not come here; I can't say as to the Western men.

Perhaps I have dwelt too much on the dosile side of the picture, but I have endeavored to be faithful. I have good report from the Southern Atlantic States generally,[9] and am confident that very few Delegates on the seaboard, from Rhode Island[10] to the Gulf of Mexico, will come here to say and vote that Whig principles and measures are obsolete, and that we have no course left but to get up a new Jackson party and try to ride with power or a hurrah. The most savage Taylor man in Maryland[11] admitted to me that his State would send Clay delegates, and blamed Taylor's no-party jockeys as having ruined the whole concern by his ridiculous letters.[12] It seems to me the Taylor men here are not near so confident as they were, but they are only the more bitter. They confidently and openly declare that Gen. Taylor *shall* win, whether or no. If a Delegation comes on from Tennessee feeling and talking as Gov. [James C.] Jones does, the effect will be very good.[13] I hope, too, that [E. Carrington] Cabell will be headed off by a Delegation of old-fashioned Whigs from Florida.[14] But they will all need to be false—lightning-proof to pass uncorrupted through this City.

As to the Vice Presidency, I have no feeling and no solicitude. I only feel that a sad mistake was made last time, against my most earnest remonstrances, and I wish it avoided again.[15] We can carry New-York, I think, with any good Whig; and if Gen. Scott can give us strength, very well. Gov. [William H.] Seward has no special claims on us, and utterly detests the idea of being ours. He is an active, energetic man, and would fill in the chair of the Senate like a bear in a cage. He has a mighty force in the love and confidence of the Adopted Citizens,[16] and running him would secure New-York and help Pennsylvania—I think it would secure that also. Still, if running him would injure us in the South, he must not be nominated, for I am utterly averse to the policy of driving off Whig votes in the hope of gaining Loco-focos. It seldom works well. If Scott cannot run, perhaps [Thomas] McKennan of Pa. or [Millard] Fillmore of our State would be best.[17] I begged for Fillmore in '44, but the South would not take him; it may be less difficult now.

Boston is very hard against us; and exerts a powerfully bad influence, not only in Massachusetts but in other parts of New England. Some of our prominent men have since last fall seen new light on the Presidency through Abbot Lawrence's[18] wine-glasses, and are now shaking their heads and ruefully sighing, 'Great man—noble fellow—pity he can't be elected!' I hope this does not affect any State vitally but Massachusetts, but, in the absence of a single journal in Boston that talked in the old way, the Districts that I confidently hoped when I was there would vote with us have not done so. Massachusetts will vote for [Daniel] Webster first and dead against us to the last, carrying New Hampshire[19] with her, and trying to affect the other New-England States.

—As to our Mayor, Mr. [William] Brady made some enemies by trying to humor all parties. He is not so strong a man as [William F.] Havemeyer, whom the Barnburners made desperate exertions for while the Hunkers dared not openly oppose him. We got out of our Charter Election quite as well as we deserved to.[20] Our Council had been at once weak, inefficient and prodigal.

—The state of things at Albany was not fairly presented in the letters you received. Gov. Seward said nothing, did nothing with reference to the Caucus. Mr. [Thurlow] Weed said in substance, "I give it up. Mr. Clay is the choice of New York. I am opposed to Gen. Taylor; I am not opposed to Mr. Clay. We agree to make the expression of preference for Mr. Clay unanimous, and only ask that one of the State Delegates shall be chosen from those who have hitherto hesitated about naming Mr. Clay, but are not now hostile to him." I did not advise, but I am not sure that our friends did wisely in rejecting this overture. They answered, however, "You have resisted us as long as you had power; now *we* have the power and we will use it." And they chose two Delegates personally hostile to Mr. Weed and to Gov. Seward also. I did not object, being puzzled, but I fear this may have been unwise.[21]

ALS. DLC-HC (DNA, M212, R6). 1. For New York's vote at the Whig National convention, see Ullmann to Clay, Feb. 18, 1848. 2. For Tennessee, Indiana, and Georgia's convention votes, see Clay to Mercer, April 14, 1848. 3. For New Jersey's convention vote, see Stevenson to Clay, May 18, 1848, #1 of date. 4. For Pennsylvania's convention vote, see Clay to Mercer, April 14, 1848. 5. For the Pennsylvania delegates and their votes, see Philadelphia *North American & United States Gazette*, June 7, 1848; Washington *Daily National Intelligencer*, June 16, 1848. 6. For Maryland's convention vote, see Clay to Mercer, April 14, 1848. 7. For Louisiana's convention vote, see *ibid.* 8. For the Whig organization in Washington, which supported Taylor, see Clay to Harvey, April 18, 1848. 9. For Georgia and Florida, see Clay to Mercer, April 14, 1848. At the Whig National convention, Virginia cast 15 votes for Taylor and 2 for Clay on the first three ballots and 16 for Taylor on the 4th ballot. North Carolina cast 5 for Clay and 6 for Taylor on the first two ballots; on the 3rd, 7 for Taylor, 3 for Clay, and 1 for Scott; and on the 4th ballot, 10 for Taylor, 1 for Clay. South Carolina cast 1 for Clay and 1 for Taylor on all four ballots. Schlesinger, *History of U.S. Political Parties*, 1:436-39. 10. At the Whig National convention, Rhode Island cast 4 votes for Clay on the 1st ballot, 3 for Clay and 1 for Taylor on the 2nd and 3rd, and 4 for Taylor on the 4th ballot. *Ibid.* 11. For Maryland's convention vote, see Clay to Mercer, April 14, 1848. 12. On Taylor's letters see, for example, Clay to Ullmann, August 4, 1847; Clay to White, Sept. 20, 1847; Taylor to Clay, April 30, 1848. 13. For Tennessee, see note 2 above. 14. Cabell was a Florida delegate, but that state had 4 delegates and only 3 votes. Philadelphia *North American & United States Gazette*, June 7, 1848. 15. Reference is to Theodore Frelinghuysen's nomination for vice president in 1844. See Ewing to Clay, June 23, 1844; Frelinghuysen to Clay, Nov. 9, 1844. 16. Greeley to Clay, Nov. 30, 1847. 17. For Fillmore's nomination, see Harlan to Clay, June 2, 1848. 18. Clay to Prentiss, April 12, 1848. 19. In the Whig National convention, Massachusetts cast 12 votes for Webster on the first two ballots and 9 for Webster, 2 for Scott, and 1 for Taylor on the 3rd and 4th ballots. New Hampshire cast 6 for Webster on the first three ballots and 4 for Webster and 2 for Taylor on the 4th. Schlesinger, *History of U.S. Political Parties*, 1:436-39. 20. William Brady (1801-70), a silversmith, was mayor of New York City from 1847-48. Holli, *Biographical Dictionary of American Mayors*. For the city's charter elections, see Cassius M. Clay to Clay, April 13, 1848. The Hunkers represented the conservative wing of the Democratic party and clashed with the more radical Barnburners. For the origin of the Hunkers, see Donovan, *The Barnburners*, 9, 33, *passim*. 21. Clay to Greeley, Dec. 10, 1847; Lawrence *et al.* to Clay, Feb. 16, 1847.

From ZACHARY TAYLOR Baton Rouge, La., April 30, 1848

Your highly esteemed letter of the 4th, inst, was duly received for which you have my best thanks; it was highly gratifying to me to hear from you & to learn you had returned to Ashland after so long a travel[1] during the most inclement season of the year in good health which I flatter myself you will long continue to enjoy—Your views as regards our respective chances to succeed to the presidency at the coming election is entitled to the greatest respect & consideration, as your opportunity of knowing the opinions of the people generally throughout the Country as regards that matter, are much better than mine can possibly be, having recently made a visit to the Seat of the genl. government, to three or four of our largest cities & passed through into & along the borders of several of the strongest States in the Union; while I have since my return from Mexico for the most part remained stationary at an out of the way place where I see or hear but little of political movements or matters save through the newspapers & letters for the most part written & published by politicians, the editors & writers of the same, are sometimes mistaken in their views on the subject of president making as other people—I conceive I am owing to circumstances which I could not well avoid in rather a peculiar situation as regards my being a candidate for the presidency; it is well known to those who had my confidence that I was very much opposed when the matter was first agitated in several of the public journals, which was soon after the battles Palo Alto Alto, & Resaca de la palma,[2] to my name being used as a candidate for that office, which I resisted as far as I could well do so, stating to those around me I had no aspirations for Civil office of any kind my greatest ambition was to bring the war we were engaged in to a speedy & honorable termination; that by being considered a candidate for that situation would have the effect to make the President [James K. Polk] hostile to me even without his being aware of it, & in such a way as to impair my usefulness in the field if not to destroy it as regarded the object I had nearest my heart, which has been realized to the full extent of my expectation; for ever since the battle of Monterey until I left Mexico, the hand of the Executive was laid heavily on me—[3]

My name continued to be constantly referred to through some of the Newspapers from the time previously mentioned, as a candidate for the Presidency until the battle of Buena Vista, soon after which I began to receive many letters from some of the first political men of the nation & from several states in which they stated it was in contemplation to bring my name before the Country as the Whig candidate for the Presidency in Novr, 1848;[4] in reply I frankly stated my objections to their doing so, among others that I was no politician, & that it might be considered presumption in me to aspire to that high station when there was such statesmen who might be elevated to it as yourself, Mr. [John J.] Crittenden, Judge [John] McLean & John M. Clayton & hundreds of others unknown to me, who were I conceived much better qualified to preside over the destinies of the Country than I was; that you were my first choice, nor did I wish to be in the way of any prominent Whig who might be brought out for that office; to which they replied, some of whom were your warm political & personal friends, that you would not again permit your name to be brought before the country as a Candidate, & that they did not believe any other Whig owing to events which had taken place, was so likely to be elected in opposition to the party in power as myself; & that I owed it to the country to permit my name to be used for said object; "that I could not avoid being a candidate if I would & ought not if I could"; under this state of things I reluctantly yielded to their wishes about that time I informed a distinguished member of Congress[5] that the arrangements for the next Presidential campaign was to be made during the approaching session of that body which would shortly meet; & [if] it was found after consulting the members of both branches of the same, it was thought advisable to take up some other individual of the party who was more available, he was authorised to withdraw my name from the contest & if it was you who was fixed on so much the better; after writing said letter I received the proceedings of the people which togeth[er] in primary assemblies in several of the States nominating me as a candidate for the presidency at the next election,[6] & in several instances stating it was understood that in the event of any distinguished Whig was brought out as a Candidate I would at once withdraw my name, urging me not to do so, but to continue as a candidate under all circumstances on the grounds I had taken which w[ere] not to be the exclusive candidate of any party &c; & on reaching New Orleans many friends called on me to let it be publicly announced that my [n]ame as a candidate for the office in question would not be withdrawn let who would be in the field, which I consented to, & advised my friends in Washington of my chang[e] in that respect without delay.[7] I therefore now cons[id]er myself in the hands of the people a portion of who[m] have placed my name before the Country for the hi[gh]est office in their gift without any agency of mine [in] the matter, & if they should think proper to drop m[e] & take another, which they ought to do provided th[at] they can fix on a more available candidate & one bette[r] qualified to serve them, & cast their votes for him at the proper time, & should succeed in electing him, it wil[l] neither be a source of mortification or disappointmen[t] to me, on the contrary, if he is honest, truthful & patriotic I will rejoice at the result—and I can say in all sinceri[ty] should you receive the nomination of the Whig N. Convention, which is to meet in Philadelphia in June,[8] & should be ele[c]ted in Novr, but few of your friends will be more gratified than myself; & should you be unsuccessful, & it should be thought your being a candidate had the effect of preventin[g] my election, it will not produce the slightest feeling of unkin[dness] towar[d]s you, but will continue to cherish those kind feelings which I have entertained for you for many years which I hop[e] are reciprocal—

AL, mutilated. DLC-HC (DNA, M212, R6). Printed in Colton, *Clay Correspondence*, 4:557-60. 1. Speech at Independence Hall, Philadelphia, Feb. 26, 1848. 2. Shortly after these battles, Thurlow Weed predicted in the Albany *Journal* that Taylor would be elected president. These victories made Taylor a presidential contender, while the victory at Buena Vista made him even stronger. On May 11, 1847, the Frankfort *Commonwealth* quoted more than a dozen pro-Taylor editors. Hamilton, *Zachary Taylor, Soldier of the Republic*, 198-99; Kirwan, *John J. Crittenden*, 203. 3. Henry Clay, Jr., to Clay, Feb. 12/19, 1847. 4. For a discussion of the many letters urging Taylor to run and his replies, at first avowing no political ambitions and then gradually acceeding, see Hamilton, *Zachary Taylor, Soldier in the White House*, 38-51, *passim*.

5. Although writing Clay on Nov. 4, 1847, that he would stand aside for him and authorizing John J. Crittenden in a Nov., 1847 letter to withdraw his name if necessary, Taylor began to back away from that stance. In Jan., 1848, he withdrew that authorization from Crittenden. In a letter, dated April 20, 1848, to the Richmond *Republican*, he reaffirmed his no-party stand, announcing that he would not refuse the Whig nomination but would remain a candidate regardless of the Whig and Democratic nominations. Bauer, *Zachary Taylor*, 222-33; Kirwan, *John J. Crittenden*, 207-20; Poage, *Henry Clay*, 175-77. 6. For meetings and nominations of Taylor see, for example, Ky.—Clay to Unknown Recipient, *ca.* Winter, 1847-48; Phila.—Clay to Bayard, Feb. 12, 1848; Va.—Clay to Combs, Feb. 18, 1848; New York City—Ullmann to Clay, Feb. 18, 1848; La.—Claiborne to Clay, April 26, 1848. Also, Whig legislators in Iowa, Ga., Ala., and Ark.; Independents in Miss.; and Whigs and others in Ill. endorsed Taylor. Hamilton, *Zachary Taylor, Soldier in the White House*, 82. 7. Probably his letter to the Richmond *Republican* (see note 5 above), but possibly his letter to Crittenden of Feb. 13, 1848, which seems to lean in that direction. Kirwan, *John J. Crittenden*, 208. 8. Greeley to Clay, Nov. 15, 1846.

From DAVID M. NAGLE[1] New York City, May 1, 1848

I regret exceedingly that a large and influential delegation of Naturalized Citizens who accompanyd. me to your quarters while sojurning in this City the Saturday evening prior to your departure for Ashland were disapointed in not being able to tender you personally their profound acknowledgements for your untiring effort in behalf of our famishing and oppressed countrymen in the land of their birth [Ireland].

As an observer of passing events, and somewhat versed in the political movements of the day, I cannot refrain from informing you of the warm manifestations evinced by the leading Adopted Citizens in this city in your favour and their determination to give you their warm support. It is really gratifying to me to perceive my countrymens minds purged from the vapours that surrounded them in the disastrous campaigns of 1844[2] when I was the only Adopted Citizen in this state who had the moral courage to take the field in your behalf.

You will be somewhat surprized when I inform you that I have received communications from Washington, Baltimore, Philadelphia and other large Citys in this state assuring me of the determination of the Naturalized Citizens to send strong delegations to the Whig National Convention,[3] for to show and prove the necessity of nominating you in preference to any other candidate. The Adopted Citizens of this City and Brooklyn are confident of being well represented in the National Convention. Had I the means I would procure the names of one thousand respectable and influential Naturalized Citizens who heretofore opposed your election, and whom I could now induce to sign a Joint Communication pledging themselves to give you their support.—By presenting such a document as this by some distinguished friend before the delegates assemble at Philadelphia would in my humble opinion have great weight with those delegates who may be opposed to your nomination; particularly when we have some leading wealthy aristocrats[4] in this city who will use all sorts of deception and intrigue to defeat your nomination.

Governor [John] Young has been in this City for the last 4 days on a *special mission* as the guest of your inveterate enemy, the Native Ex. Senator [George] Folsom.[5] I doubt whether the natives can prevent him from retireing next January to the shades of Geneseeo [*sic*, Geneseo]. His War message[6] has sealed his political destiny—like John Tyler he will carry with him the execrations and contempt of every true Whig whose expressed opinions he has basely disregarded in supporting the unhallowed and corrupt War policy of James K. Polk!

It is true there is a strong clique in this state opposed to your nomination,[7] yet I am sanguine of your success, provided money influences cannot be brought to operate against you, as the great masses of the people are enthusiastically enlisted in your favour.

I shall god willing with the concurrence of others from different parts of the union, meet my Irish friends at the National Convention at Philadelphia, there to unite our efforts in pressing upon the regular delegates the propriety as well as the expediency of nominating Henry Clay.

P.S. Please acknowledge the receipt of this letter. When the proper time arrives I trust you will permit me to use to advantage your letter[8] addressed to me, last December.

ALS. DLC-HC (DNA, M212, R6). 1. While serving as a clerk in the Custom House in New York City in 1841, Nagle had worked with Gov. William Henry Seward in trying to win the Irish Catholics to the Whig party and to turn them against Tammany Hall. Jerome Mushkat, *Tammany, The Evolution of a Political Machine 1789-1865* (Syracuse, N.Y., 1971), 201, 203. 2. Ewing to Clay, June 23, 1844. 3. Greeley to Clay, Nov. 15, 1846. 4. The Taylor Club in New York City consisted of such prominent men as James Watson Webb, Moses H. Grinnell, Simeon Draper, Prescott Hall, Charles King, Edward Curtis, Hugh Maxwell, and Richard M. Blatchford. Weed, *Autobiography of Thurlow Weed*, 1:577. 5. George Folsom, a Whig who had been elected to the New York senate in 1844 as a Native American, was a strong supporter of Taylor. He served as chargé d' affaires to The Netherlands in the Taylor administration. *DAB*. 6. Wendell to Clay, March 11, 1848. 7. For example, see Ullmann to Clay, Feb. 18, 1848, and note 4 above. 8. Not found.

From James C. Rice *et al.*, Albany, N.Y., May 1, 1848. Inform Clay that he has been made a life member of the Young Men's Association for Mutual Improvement in Albany. Continue: "Added to this feeble tribute of our respect, we beg leave to assure you, is that heartfelt esteem which a long life of ardent devotion to the best interests of your country and its education merit, together with that warmth of attachment, which every where among the young you share so munificent a part." Copy. Printed in Albany *Evening Journal*, June 1, 1848.

Clay replied on May 17, 1848, thanking them for "the official certificate of my appointment" and "for these precious testimonials of their friendly regard and esteem." Hopes the organization will "realize all the laudable objects for which it was established." *Ibid.*

Rice is possibly James Clay Rice (1829-64), who practiced law in Albany in the 1850s, served as a brigadier general in the Union Army in the Civil War, and was killed in action at Spotsylvania on May 10, 1864. Ezra J. Warner, *Generals in Blue* (Baton Rouge, 1964), 400-401.

From THOMAS CORWIN Lebanon, Ohio, May 3, 1848

On my return from Cina [Cincinnati] last evening, I found your letter of the 23d. Ult. I was not greatly surprized at its contents, knowing the habits of almost all men, in such cases, to put their own favorite construction upon the sayings & acts of others, In reply to the Main point in your letter I have only to say that I never said you ought not to be the Candidate of the Whigs. I have said always & do so still, that it would become your duty, as I am sure it would be your pleasure to decline the Nomination, if at any time you should believe your election doubtful, & that either [Zachary] Taylor [John] McLean, or [Winfield] Scott, would be more likely to succeed.[1]

In the condition in which you found the Whig party last winter, I thought with many others you ought not then to decline, but leave yourself & the Whig Convention at liberty to decide, whether a great regard to your position, & the great interests at stake, should point to you, or either of the others named, as the proper Candidate. I do not see that subsequent events have set[t]led satisfactorily this point. It is certain however, that your late letter to the public,[2] has called forth expressions from the North, & some portions of the West, which I did not expect.[3] I thought your views on the subject of Slavery presented at Lexington last fall,[4] ought to satisfy, that portion of the Whigs in the free states, who are violently opposed to the further extension of slavery. In this I find I was mistaken, yet I adhere to the belief that you will command a larger vote in Ohio, than any Candidate from a slave holding state, but from what I have recently seen I cannot say that even you could carry Ohio against a Non Slave holding democratic candidate.[5]

This distracting question arising Necessarily from the annexation of Texas & probable future acquisition of territory & which we have labored so hard to avert, I am now satisfied, will create in the free states, a controlling influence in the coming election. These facts recently developed have somewhat modified my opinions as to your success, should you be the Whig Nominee.

For these reasons I have often said that if the Convention should be of opinion, looking over the whole ground, that either of the three others named, would more certainly succeed, it would be its duty to make a selection of that person, however much they might prefer you or any other who in their judgment for any reason, could not command the Undivided strength of the Whig party—I have continually urged upon the friends of each of the Candidates, to leave these questions to be determined by the Convention that I should cheerfully give my vote to the Nominee, always declaring, as I have for the last twenty five years my preference for you greatly above all others.

I dare say I may have said, *that if it should appear that McLean or Scott could command a larger vote in the free States* than you & could be equally well supported elswhere, it would be proper to select one of them, Such has been my opinion of the proper discharge of the high duty devolving on that Convention, & I dare say I have often so expressed myself.

Thus my friend (if I may still so name you) I have answered your inquiry as I would have done to my own father. I may have been indiscreet but I have thought spoken & acted under the promptings of duty to our common country, whose prosperity, if not existence, I verily believe, depends in a great degree on the issues of a few brief Months to come[.]

Necessity has determined me to take a less active part in politics, than I have for the last fifteen years. I intend soon to leave the senate, & devote myself to the repair of my almost ruined private affairs—[6] On that account, I was sorry to know that my opinions had any weight with you in determining your course. I certainly did not intend they should. I only meant to state facts as I understood them, leaving you to form your conclusions knowing that a vast field of information was accessible to you, & not open to me, or perhaps to any one, except yourself . . .

ALS. DLC-HC (DNA, M212, R6). Letter marked "(Confidential)." 1. Clay to Harvey, April 18, 1848. 2. Clay to The Public, April 10, 1848. 3. Probably a reference to the fact that many in these sections wanted Clay to embrace the Wilmot Proviso without reservation. 4. Speech in Lexington, Nov. 13, 1847. 5. Bebb to Clay, April 4, 1848.

6. Corwin remained in the Senate until 1850, when he resigned to become secretary of the treasury. *BDAC.*

From JAMES E. HARVEY Washington, May 3, 1848

Accompanying this letter, I send a republication from the Richmond Republican, containing a correspondence between its Editor & Genl. [Zachary] Taylor, to which I get leave particularly to invite your attention.[1]

While you were in this City, it being manifest to me, that the Contest between some of your friends & some of the friends of Genl. Taylor, was waxing to a dangerous point, both for the interests of the Whig party and of their respective principals, I took occasion in one of my letters to the North American, to assert, that a letter had been received from Genl Taylor, in which he expressed the kindest personal feelings towards You & declared that in the event of Your being a Candidate, he would not suffer his name to enter the canvass.[2] I also stated, that I was confident you would abide the decision of the Convention & therefore, that there was no occasion for a breach between the interests of the party. Mr Greely [*sic*, Horace Greeley] challenged this statement, under a mistaken idea that it was advanced to serve Taylor's pretensions & I reiterated the declaration very emphatically.[3]

I have reason to know that my statement produced good feeling for a while. There was immediately evinced a disposition to Confide the question of Nomination to the Convention & to abide by its determination.

This state of things however, did not suit the purposes of the *Independent* Taylor Movement[4] and they grew restive & resolved to keep him in their exclusive possession or to foment divisions in our ranks.

Under this influence Genl Taylor was addressed by the Editors of the Republican, who though professedly Whig, are worse than neutral in politics.

My general statement of the facts in reference to Genl Taylor, was derived from his letter to you,[5] which if I remember rightly, contained no qualification of Confidence. The recollections of other Gentlemen who saw it, corresponds with my own & I am fully satisfied, that it embraces the *idea* which I published.

Genl Taylor has voluntarily put himself before the country in Contradiction of his own declarations.[6] I do not challenge the motive of this movement—I hope for the sake of his vanity, he has forgotten the sentiments which he expressed in his letter to you; but at all events, it becomes me to make good what I alleged or to furnish the public with a sufficient reason, for not vin[di]cating the truth of my assertions.

This can be accomplished but in one way & that is be the testimony of Genl Taylor himself. It becomes you to determine this question between him & me & I refer it with confidence, that as my truthfulness is concerned, you will enable me to preserve it unsuspected. I consider that Genl Taylor has challenged the production of any & all evidence that may be in existence, when he says, that my statement had "No foundation on any oral or *written* remark of Mine" (his).

I feel that this is a very delicate matter, but, the indications are now unmistakeable, that the No-party men are determined to *force* Genl Taylor upon our Convention or to run him independently, at any hazard. It is evident too, that he has given in to this bad advice & that he has permitted himself to be deceived by a set of men who have no interest to serve but their own

& who look not beyond, the consideration of superior & commanding influence, in the event of his Election. It is a game to *kick* the Whig party into submission, to which I as one humble member of the party, am not disposed to submit.

I saw the symptoms of this feeling & disposition in the temper of Col [Joseph] Taylor's[7] conversations here, while on a brief visit a week since— He complained most unwarrantably of the conduct of your friends, for *presuming*, I suppose, to object to the nomination of his brother!

Simultaneously, with this letter to Richmond, another from the same source, extracted from the Picayune on general politics, appears in the Union.[8] It is designed to produce effect and may operate in some quarters. I [d]oubt its potency in the Convention, though it may have [mo]re force than I anticipate.

There is a perfect calm here. The attempt to galvanize [Winfield] Scott does not succeed or rather it flags. [William L.] Marcy's answer has chilled the warm blood which was striving in his favor.[9]

ALS. DLC-HC (DNA, M212, R6). 1. Taylor to Clay, April 30, 1848. 2. Writing in the Philadelphia *North American and United States Gazette* of Feb. 8, 1848, under the pseudonym "Independent," Harvey declared that no state of affairs would arise in which Clay and Taylor would be placed in an attitude of hostility to each other; rather, either would refuse to run if the other were nominated at the Whig convention. 3. In an editorial in the New-York *Daily Tribune* of Feb. 14, 1848, Greeley disputed "Independent's" statement and declared that he had it from Clay's own lips and from Taylor's own hand that Taylor would not withdraw if Clay were nominated. Further, he accused "Independent" of quietly working for Taylor, a charge Harvey denied in the *North American* of Feb. 17. 4. Clay to Ullmann, August 4, 1847; Claiborne to Clay, April 26, 1848. 5. Taylor to Clay, Nov. 4, 1847. 6. Taylor to Clay, April 30, 1848. 7. For Joseph Taylor, see Hamilton, *Zachary Taylor, Soldier of the Republic*, 29, 59, 76, 231, 244, *passim*. 8. The First Allison letter. See Clay to Ullmann, August 4, 1847. 9. Scott had written Marcy on Feb. 24, 1848, complaining of the War Department's "neglects, disappointments, injuries and rebukes." Marcy answered him on April 21, refuting Scott's complaints point by point. Both letters were published in the New-York *Daily Tribune*, May 6, 1848. See also Ivor D. Spencer, *The Victor and the Spoils; a Life of William L. Marcy* (Providence, R.I., 1959), 168-71.

From CHARLES S. MOREHEAD Washington, May 3, 1848

You will no doubt have seen the two letters of Genl. [Zachary] Taylor before this reaches you, one pub[lished] in the Union and the other in the [Washington *Daily National*] Intelligencer.[1] That [of] the 22d. of April is making a favourable impression, [it] has given new hopes and spirits to his friends here. The one written a few days before and published i[n] the Intelligencer, I think is a complete antidote, & y[et] the whole matters stand about *status quo*—

In the last named letter, you will observe that he say[s] "that the statements, which have been so positively mad[e] in some of the Northern prints to the effect that should Mr Clay be the nominee of the Whig National Convention I had stated that I would not suffer my name to be used are not correct" &c. I have been asked my recollection of the contents of a letter from him to you.[2] I have not felt at liberty to speak of it, and if I did I really do not remember it with sufficient accuracy to give more than the general impression it left on my mind. I write mer[ely] to suggest that it might be well to giv[e] Mr [James] Harlan the n[ote] when he comes on to the Convention, if you do not dee[m] it improper to do so. I know that the use of it in [any] way is a matter of much delicacy, and particularly considering the relation in which you now stand to [him] I do not think that it ought to be used in any manner unless a state of things should arise, which would justify it such as an attack upon you connected with the letter—[James E.] Harvey[3] has spoken of your having recd. such a letter, and given his recollection of its purport, and I can conceive of insinuations which could only be met by producing the letter itself—You will, however, be governed by your own better judgment, taking care as you ought, to act with the utmost prudence & circumspection—I do not think that I would write any thing about it to any one—In the present excited state of the public mind any thing is seized upon and perverted & misrepresented.

There are four delegates appointed from Wisconsin[4] three ar[e] said to be for you and one for Taylor. When I can ge[t] a full list, I can determine whether it will be best to vote per capita or by states—So far it makes very little difference—

I am afraid that Judge [John] McLean has not been playing fair—Perhaps I am too suspicious, a trait by no means enviable in any ones character, but when you were here, I gave you my reasons for believing that he was for himself, and on today in a casual conversation with Mr. [John M.] Clayton, he mentioned that Judge McLean in a letter written within the last three weeks, had said that if y[ou] were nominated, there was no hope whatever of your ele[c]tion—I asked him if he was sure that such a letter had been written—I do not remember the precise words he used in reply, but to the effect that he could have it produced on a days notice—His friends here are exceedingly busy in endeavouring to circulate the idea that the only hope of success is by compromising on him—Mr Clayton thinks that Genl. [Winfield] Scot[t] is very strong, and that the demonstrations in New York when he returns,[5] will make him an imposing can[di]date for the nomination—He has been so completely u[sed] up by Marcey [*sic*, Secretary of War William L. Marcy], that I do not see how he can hope f[or] the nomination—You will see Marceys letter in the Un[ion.][6] It has not been published in the Intelligencer—

I have written this just in time for the mail [to]night and have not time to look it over, or make any corrections—

ALS, manuscript damaged. DLC-HC (DNA, M212, R6). 1. Reference is to Taylor's letter of April 20 to the editor of the Richmond *Republican* and to his first Allison Letter of April 22. See, respectively, Taylor to Clay, April 30, 1848; Clay to Ullmann, August 4, 1847. 2. Taylor to Clay, Nov. 4, 1847. 3. Harvey to Clay, May 3, 1848. 4. At the Whig National convention, Wisconsin cast 3 votes for Clay and 1 for Taylor on the first two ballots and all 4 votes for Clay on the third and fourth ballots. Schlesinger, *History of U.S Political Parties*, 1:436-39. 5. For the reception for Scott at New York City on May 20, see Elliott, *Winfield Scott*, 387-88. 6. Harvey to Clay, May 3, 1848.

From JOHN J. CRITTENDEN Washington, May 4, 1848

I had the pleasure to receive your letter enclosing to me a printed copy of your published note of the 10th of the last month, announcing your course & determination in respect to the ensuing Presidential election.[1]

I hope it may turn out for the best; but you are apprised of my opinions & apprehensions on the subject, and tho' so much less competent than yourself to judge, I must confess that I still retain the same impressions. It has all along seemed to me that there was not that *certainty* of success, which alone could warrant your friends in again presenting your name as a candidate.

The whole subject of the presidential election is becoming more & more perplexed—Genl. [Zachary] Taylor's two letters of the 20th & 22nd of the last month,[2] which you will have seen, have reached here—No certain judgment I suppose, can ye[t b]e formed of their effect. The public Press is not yet heard on the subject, & I have conversed with but few about it—I understand that these letters have produced considerable sensation here.—that of the 22nd being considered as entirely satisfactory, & mitigating to a great extent the discontent produced by that of the 20th Ult:—The decleration contained in the latter that he would not withdraw from the canvass even if yourself or any other was nominated by the [Whig] National Convention, was received here with great surprise, and, 'Tho' not inconsistent with the grounds taken in his previously published letters, it seemed to give quite a shock to the Whigs[.] It was regretted by us all—

What will be [the] result of the position thus taken by Genl Taylor, I am at a loss to conjecture—It makes the future still more impenetrable, & dark—I can hardly contemplate it without despondency.

Genl [Winfield] Scott, as I learn, begins to be much spoken of as a candidate, & his friends are said to be making preperations to press & sustain him strongly in the National Convent[ion].[3] I know nothing of the extent of those preperations, nor of the grounds on which his friends rest their confidence—So far as I can see or judge, it appears to me that the General can have no great strength of his own in the Convention, & that his nomination can only take place, if at al[l], in consequence of the conflict of other interests.

Upon the whole, it seems to me, that the political prospect before us, presents only a troubled scene, from the contemplation of which we can derive no pleasure. That you may be saved from, or pass through that Scene, in safety & honor is the sincere wish of . . .

ALS. NcD; copy in DLC-TJC (DNA, M212, R11). 1. Clay to The Public, April 10, 1848. 2. For his letter of April 20 to the Richmond *Republican*, see Taylor to Clay, April 30, 1848; for his First Allison letter of April 22, see Clay to Ullmann, August 4, 1847. 3. At the Whig National convention, Scott received 43 votes on the 1st ballot, 49 on the 2nd, 11 on the 3rd, and 63 on the 4th. Schlesinger, *History of U.S. Political Parties*, 1:436-39.

To Christopher Hughes, Baltimore, May 8, 1848. Although not surprised by the "proposal to send you [as] a delegate to the Whig Convention [Greeley to Clay, November 15, 1846]" in Philadelphia, urges Hughes "to take care of your health, and I hope that you will expose yourself to no danger whatever on my account."

Feels it is too early to predict "the result of the deliberations of the Convention, the election of delegates being yet in progress." Believes he will "receive considerable support from unexpected quarters." Expects to have "a large plurality," but fears if he does not receive "a majority, there may be an attempt to combine the friends of all the other Candidates so as to exclude me from the nomination."

Wonders why Hughes wrote "nothing about my recent note to the public [Clay to The Public, April 10, 1848]." Does not understand "the cavils to which it has been exposed," especially "the last paragraph, in which I declare that I have no regrets to express no complaints, no reproaches to make on acct of preferences entertained by my friends for other distinguished names. I wonder if they would have been better pleased if I had expressed exactly contrary sentiments?" Intends "to write no more political letters for publication."

Asks: "Did you write or speak to Mrs. [Louisa Johnson] Adams about his [John Quincy Adams's] Diary?" ALS. MiU-C.

At the Maryland State Whig convention at Baltimore on May 11-12, which chose delegates to the Whig National convention, Hughes was defeated by George R. Richardson, a Taylor supporter from the 4th district of Baltimore, by 4 votes. This defeat probably resulted from convention rules that called for voting by districts, since one newspaper declared that Richardson was elected over the wishes of the entire city of Baltimore and to the surprise of the majority of the delegates to the state convention. The Maryland Whig convention passed a resolution endorsing Clay as its first choice and Taylor as its second. New-York *Daily Tribune*, May 13, 1848; Washington *Daily National Intelligencer*, May 12, 13, 1848.

To EPES SARGENT Lexington, May 8, 1848

I recd. your favor of the 1st. inst. I had not previously seen or heard of the article, to which you refer, ascribing to you an abandonment of me.[1] If I had, I should not have easily credited such a statement in regard to my best biographer. Your note, altho' unnecessary, is very satisfactory.

I have recently received a copy of your Revised and enlarged edition of my life.[2] I have not yet examined all the additions which you have made to it; but as far as I have, they are accurate, and form a great improvement to the work, which is the fullest, and best adapted to general popular use of any biography of me extant.

The election of delegates to the [Whig] Nat. Convention being yet in progress, it is too early now to form an opinion as to the result of its deliberations.[3] From information which I have received, I shall get considerable support from unexpected quarters. I regret to learn that my old friend, the Bay State [Massachusetts], is indisposed to go for me in any contingency.[4]

ALS. KyU. 1. Not found. 2. Clay to Sargent, August 7, 1844; Clay to Sargent, Feb. 15, 1847. 3. Greeley to Clay, Nov. 15, 1846. 4. For the political situation in Massachusetts, especially Boston, see Clay to Prentiss, April 12, 1848. For Massachusetts's vote at the Whig National convention, see Greeley to Clay, April 28, 1848.

To JOHN G. PROUD[1] Lexington, May 11, 1848

I received your letter of the 29h. Ulto. with its enclosure both of which I perused with great pleasure. It always gives me much satisfaction to be assured that an old friend, like yourself, remains constant, firm, and faithful in his attachment and friendship.

I was highly gratified with the proceedings in Baltimore,[2] in which my friends shewed a much greater degree of strength than I anticipated. I await, with anxiety, to learn the Presidential preferences of Maryland, which has been so long and so fast my friend.[3]

The election for Delegates to the Whig Convention in Philada. being yet in progress, it is too early to form a decisive opinion of the result of its deliberations. In some quarters, I have been a little disappointed as to the amount of support, I shall receive; whilst in others I have, most unexpectedly, received assurances of a much larger support than I ever counted upon. My present belief is that I shall obtain the nomination unless the intrigues at Harrisburg of 1839 are re-enacted.[4]

I have not the smallest apprehension that the idea of running an independent Candidate against the Nominee of the Convention will be persisted in.[5] Such an Independent Candidate would be abandoned by all Whigs before the Election, and would not obtain a solitary Electoral vote in the U. States.

ALS. ViHi. Letter marked "(Private)." 1. Proud (1776-1865), who was in the insurance business in Baltimore, presided on April 18 at the Baltimore Whig convention that had named Clay as its first choice and resolved to elect as delegates to the National convention only those who would vote for Clay. *MHM*, 7:88, 131; New-York *Daily Tribune*, April 20, 1848. 2. *Ibid.* 3. For the Maryland State Whig convention in May, see Clay to Hughes, May 8, 1848. For Maryland's vote in the Whig National convention, see Clay to Mercer, April 14, 1848. 4. See espec. 9:92, 117, 361, 824 for the 1839 nomination of William Henry Harrison. 5. For example, see Claiborne to Clay, April 26, 1848, for the Independent movement in Louisiana.

To CHARLES FRANCIS ADAMS Lexington, May 15, 1848

Ever since the lamented event of the 23d. Feb. which deprived our Country of one of its most illustrious Citizens,[1] I have been intending to address a letter to your excellent mother [Louisa Johnson Adams] or to yourself communicating my feelings & deep regret on the occasion. If I have delayed executing that intention, it has been chiefly because I have been taught, by sad experience, amidst numerous and heavy domestic afflictions, that there is no real consolation to be derived except by appealing to our duty to submit to the irrevocable will of Providence, and by the healing influence of the lapse of time. I request now however to assure you, your mother, and the whole family, that no surviving friend of your father sympathies and condoles with you all, with more sincerity and cordiality than I do.

It ought to mitigate your grief that he lived to a ripe old age; that he died, where probably he would have prefered to die, at the post of honor and duty;[2] and that his career, through his long life, was patriotic, bright and glorious. His fame was not limited to one hemisphere but was co-extensive with the Civilized world, and faithful history must transmit it, in glowing and enduring colors, to admiring posterity.

It very rarely happens that great intellectual powers are hereditary; in this or any other Country. The most remarkable instance of it, in English history, is that of Lord Chatham, and his son William Pitt.[3] The most remarkable, in our own Country, is that of your father and grandfather [John Adams]. For near a Century has the name of Adams shone out, with the brigh[t]est beams, at home and abroad, in most of the departments, the highest amongst them, of our public Councils. May its lustre, in their descendants, continue undiminished.

My remote residence from your father's family prevents my performing those friendly little offices towards it, which would be so agreeable to the feelings of my heart; but I beg to assure you, in behalf of the whole family that, if ever an opportunity present itself in which I can render to any member of it any service whatever, I shall embrace the occasion, with the greatest pleasure.

I request you to present my respectful and affectionate regards to your mother, to your brother's widow and her daughter,[4] and to accept yourself assurances of the cordial respect and esteem of . . . [5]

ALS. MHi. 1. For the death of J.Q. Adams, see Clay to James B. Clay, Feb. 21, 1848. 2. Adams was stricken in the House of Representatives and died at age 80. Adams, *Memoirs of John Quincy Adams*, 12:282. 3. For the Pitts, see *DNB*. 4. John Adams, Jr., had died in 1834, leaving his widow Mary Heller Adams and his daughter Mary Louisa. Paul C. Nagel, *The Adams Women, Abigail and Louisa Adams, Their Sisters and Daughters* (New York, 1987), 236-40. 5. On May 24, 1848, "On behalf of my Mother and the few surviving relatives of my late father, as well as for myself," Adams thanked Clay for his kindness. Confesses he was "wholly unprepared for so deep and general a manifestation of the public regard." Hopes that one "soothing influence of this result" will be "to prove to all that class of statesmen of which you as well as he are a prominent example that the most vehement opposition of rivals and contemporaries, though attended with temporary success, avails little to cloud the deliberate judgment of a later time." Recalls with pleasure when "as a very young man I had some extraordinary opportunities of acquaintance with the most distinguished men of the country," impressions he was not "anxious to alloy" with "new ones to be found in the later society of that capital." Concludes: "Had the statesmen of that day continued to guide the destinies of the country, its prospects at this time would have been somewhat different from what they are." ALS. DLC-HC (DNA, M212, R6). Printed in Colton, *Clay Correspondence*, 4:561-62.

From JOHN LEE "Needwood," Cumberland Co., Md., May 15, 1848

You will have seen by the proceedings of our Whig State Convention that we adopted a resolution, offered reluctantly by a decided [Zachary] Taylor delegate, declaring that you were the first choice of the Whigs of Maryland, & Gen. Taylor their second choice—[1]

I demanded that the sense of the Convention should be taken separately on the two branches of this resolution,—which was strongly resisted—The first proposition that you were the choice of the State was carried unanimously—& the second by a bare majority of 54 to 49—being the full vote of the Convention—

So that the eight votes from Maryland in the [Whig] National Convention are pledged to you—[2] I hope you will maintain your present position—It was stated in the private Meeting of the Convention by the same Taylor Member that one of the Kentucky Senators has written to you to withdraw your name,[3] as the chance was hopeless—I expressed my doubts of the fact, & the assertion was positively repeated—All the indications, I think, are favourable to your nomination & election—

ALS. DLC-HC (DNA, M212, R9). 1. Clay to Hughes, May 8, 1848. 2. Clay to Mercer, April 14, 1848. 3. No such letter has been found; the closest is Crittenden to Clay, May 4, 1848. The rumor was probably based on Crittenden's support for Taylor.

To Adoniram Chandler, New York City, May 16, 1848. Thanks Chandler for sending him "a pamphlet of Mr Smith on the culture of the Tea plant." Wishes "we could supply" Americans "with that article, as good as we now derive it from China; but I fear Mr. Smith, is too sanguine in supposing that can be done."

Adds that "My acquiescence, in the submission of my name [Clay to The Public, April 10, 1848] to the Philadelphia [Whig] Convention . . . relieves me from all future responsibility, whatever the result may be." ALS. NcD.

Junius Smith's *Essays on the Cultivation of the Tea Plant* (55 pp.) was published in New York in 1848.

To E. ANTHONY[1] Lexington, May 17, 1849 [*sic*, 1848]

The engraving representing the scene in the United States Senate, on the occasion of my taking final leave of it,[2] arrived here last winter, during my absence from home.

Although tardy, I request you to accept my thanks and grateful acknowledgments for this picture, illustrating a remarkable event in my life. The whole scene is represented with wonderful accuracy; and nothing can surpass the correctness of the likeness of many of the persons portrayed in the group. When I look at the engraving, Messrs. [John Q.] Adams, [William

C.] Preston, [John J.] Crittenden, [John C.] Calhoun, [Thomas Hart] Benton, [Joseph] Gales, &c, &c., and Mrs. [Dolley Payne Todd] Madison, &c, appear to be almost actually before me.

Copy. Printed in Lexington *Observer & Kentucky Reporter*, June 28, 1848. 1. Anthony's studio was located at 217 Broadway, New York City. New-York *Daily Tribune*, June 9, 1848. 2. For the engraving, see Amyx, "Portraits of Henry Clay," Special Collections, University of Kentucky Library, B:3.12.

From James Morrison Harris, Baltimore, Md., May 18, 1848. Apologizes for not writing earlier, but preferred to wait until he could resolve "all the report[s] I heard in reference to the complexion and probab[le] course of the State Delegates elect." Believes Clay supporters had "a majority of four to six, in [the Maryland state] Convention [Clay to Hughes, May 8, 1848], but the best *Managers* in [it] were avowed [Zachary] Taylor men," and they succeeded in electing three Taylor men as delegates. Reports that the final "resolution instruc[ted the] Delegates to use their best efforts to [secure] your nomination, so long as there w[as hope] of success" and "the Delegation will enforce obedie[nce to] this instruction." Concludes: "I feel con[fident] that you will be nominated." Describes the efforts of Taylor's supporters to introduce a "resolution declaring that Taylor [was the] first choice of the state." Is especially critical of "Mudd of Alleghany [*sic*, Allegany Co. Md.], now I believe a clerk in [the] House of Rep." who was "untiring in his efforts . . . and loud mouthed in his advocacy of Gen. Taylor. I regret that his Parents should have be[stowed] upon him your name, as he shewed hims[elf to] be unworthy to bear it." Although he cannot attend the Whig National convention, hopes for "an opportunity to labor more const[ructively and] perhaps effectually for you in m[y district] and the state at large." ALS, manuscript torn. DLC-HC (DNA, M212, R6). For Harris, see 3:740.

John Henry Clay Mudd (1821-66), a graduate of Georgetown University, served as clerk in the House and practiced law in the District of Columbia. Richard D. Mudd, *The Mudd Family of the United States*, 2 vols. (n.p., 1951), 1:474.

From THOMAS B. STEVENSON Cincinnati, May 18, 1848

When I was last at Ashland, I intimated that a movement was on foot here which might seriously invade the organization of the Whig party; but something at the moment interrupted the explanation and I think you were not impressed by it. I send by this mail a copy of the [Cincinnati] Herald calling a "People's Convention."[1] The signatures are not merely Abolitionists; but there are many, very many of them Whigs. You will recognize some of the old Standards of this city men who sincerely prefer you before all men, and will still go for you, if you will but say you are opposed to the extension of slavery in free territory. That such is your opinion, is plainly infer[red] from all your public declarations, and most liberal minded men [are] perfectly willing to trust you; but it is a fixed fact that there is a less number of men in this State (and others) who require an expli[cit assur]ance to satisfy them.

I am confident that nothing short of such a declaration from you, [even] should you be the nominee, will prevent a large number of Whigs of that [state] and probably others, going over to the Abolition ranks, this [issue being] held paramount. I have a letter today from Follet [*sic*, Oran Follett], of Sandusky, the most sagacious man as I told you, I have met in Ohio who gives an unpromising account of prospects in that quarter, the people in that [quarter] indicating a willingness to take [Winfield] Scott, simply because a northern man[.] Follet was beaten as a candidate for delegate to the [Whig]

Nat. Convn. solely because he was suspected of preferring you next to [Thomas] Corwin[.]

I think, however, as to Scott's prospects for this State, though they are really stronger than as yet they have appeared, that the Quaker opposition will be fatal to him.[2] [Solomon] Meredith, the Delegate from Caleb Smith's district in I[ndian]a.[3] left here today. He is of Quaker family and lives in a strong Quaker region. He says none of that persuasion will vote for [Zachary] Taylor and a large majority of them will not vote for Scott. He is for you decidedly notwithstanding Caleb Smith's desertion to [John] McLean, and his great exertions to favor his new love.[4]

[James] Harlan writes me that a leading Taylor man of Ky, not of Frankfort, told him he did not expect Taylor's nomination; but believed [John J.] Crittenden would be the man, as he would take all Taylor's friends and many more. I do not believe C. will at all allow his name to go before the Convention; for he will deem his honor involved.

Will Gov. [James C.] Jones of Tenn. go to Phila. under his instructions to vote for Taylor?[5] I should think not.

The course of the Md. Whig Convention is very gratifying;[6] and the indications from N. Jersey are cheering.[7] Scott will land in N. York in a few days;[8] and, though his arrival will produce sensation, I should think he will see the policy of dissuading any Presidential movements in his favor and of directing his influence in the right direction.

I have communicated the call of the "People's Convention," as a matter for your information and really deserving consideration. It is a movement seriously formidable. I have satisfied myself that there is a good understanding between McLean & the Abolition leaders; though I am equally well satisfied that they will go for that man, whether the Whig or Loco [candi]date, who presents the best prospect of election and who is pledged to the exclusion of slavery from free territory, to which they are willing to subordinate all other questions for the present[.]

I am still in doubt whether I can go to Phila. Advices today from my wife in Mo. (who was to have been here ere now) imply the early death of her father and she may therefore be detained indefinitely;[9] though she may return any day. I have two little daughters on my hands, with not a friend to leave them with in the city. I have made arrangements to send them to my mothers at Georgetown, on Saturday, if their mother arrive not previously, so as to leave me the more at liberty, should not other causes prevent, to attend the convention, desiring to leave here on the 27th with Harlan. I have never had any ambition to fill any office but that of Senator of the U S; but that is not half so strong as my wish to aid in your nomination on the 7th of June;[10] and nothing but duties of the most imperious nature will prevent my attendance.

I saw Corwin again on his return from Louisville. His personal feelings towards you seemed much softened. His political course regarding you, was not disturbed by the untoward event which excited him—[11] at least that is my sincere belief. He is a noble hearted man, above being influenced by personal considerations. He says, should you declare against slavery in new territory, you would sweep the north clean, except Pa. which nothing can do but saltpetre. Can't you make an exposition of the principle that the transfer of sovereignty only transfers the allegiance of the inhabitants, *but does not alter the relations of inhabitants towards one another*, which is a sound principle in natural law and thence infer that, as slavery was *thus* recognized in Louisiana,[12] so, on the same principle, it must not be in the free territories we may acquire? It strikes me this can be successfully argued and without exposing yourself to fatal assault in the south. I am sure, at all events, more will be gained than lost, by such an exposition; and that if not made, more will be lost than saved, standing as you are. I make these suggestions, however, with great deference, well aware, as I am, of the embarrassments [that] surround the question in all aspects. *I* am satisfied now; but it is friendly to tell you that many are not.

[P.S.] [Albert G.] Hodges, one of my partners, is here. He has somewhat crippled me in my notions of the policy of the Atlas towards Taylor,[13] by telling me you deprecated my course as calculated to produce schism and opposition to you, rather than conciliation and harmony. I have handled Taylor & his letters with freedom, but not with *injustice*.

ALS, manuscript partly obliterated. DLC-HC (DNA, M212, R6). No. 1 of date. 1. Wendell to Clay, March 11, 1848. 2. For Ohio's vote in the Whig National convention, see Ullmann to Clay, Feb. 18, 1848; the traditionally pacifistic and anti-slavery Quakers opposed both Scott and Taylor because they were military leaders and Taylor because he was also a slaveholder. Rufus M. Jones, *The Later Periods of Quakerism*, 2 vols. (London, 1921), 2:718-24, 938-39; Thomas E. Drake, *Quakers and Slavery in America* (New Haven, 1950), 163-200. 3. For Meredith of Wayne Co., Ind., who at this time was a member of the state legislature as well as a delegate to the Whig National convention, see Johnson, *Twentieth Century Biographical Dictionary*. For Caleb Smith, see *BDAC*. 4. For Indiana's vote in the Whig National convention, see Clay to Mercer, April 14, 1848. 5. Jones remained true to Clay. See Erwin H. Price, "The Election of 1848 in Ohio," *Ohio Archaeological and Historical Society Publications* (1927), 36:226. For Tennessee's vote at the Whig convention, see Clay to Mercer, April 14, 1848. 6. Clay to Hughes, May 8, 1848. 7. At the Whig National convention, New Jersey on the first two ballots cast 4 votes for Clay and 3 for Taylor and on the last two ballots 4 votes for Taylor and 3 for Clay. Schlesinger, *History of U.S. Political Parties*, 1:436-39. 8. For Scott's reception, see Morehead to Clay, May 3, 1848. 9. Clay to Stevenson, June 30, 1849. 10. Greeley to Clay, Nov. 15, 1846. 11. Reference obscure. 12. Stevenson to Clay, April 8, 1848. 13. See Stevenson to Clay, April 8, 1848; Clay to Stevenson, April 12, 1848.

From THOMAS B. STEVENSON Cincinnati, May 18, 1848

I mailed you a letter this morning, since when I have received a batch of letters, containing information that may be useful to you, and the substance of which I therefore make bold to communicate, acting on the faith that he is the truest friend who is not afraid to speak unwelcome truths.

I inclose a letter from Mr [Samuel] Forrer,[1] in answer to one written to him immediately on my return from Ashland, asking him confidentially to tell me who of the Ohio delegation, you might *safely* put Gov. [James C.] Jones or others, in communication with. I wrote him because of his extensive acquaintance in the state, of his sound judgment and his fidelity to you. [Peter] Odlin,[2] I thought, and told you was perhaps the safest man. He is instructed first for [Thomas] Corwin, but at the time that was *understood* for you. Since then, the [Winfield] Scott fever has arisen,[3] and the doubt of your availability increased. I should hope, however, the movements in Mich. & N. Jersey,[4] will change the current to some extent.

The other letters to which I refer, are in part a parcel enclosed [by] Corwin, for my information, with injunction to burn them. I shall return [them] to him by today's mail. But I think it justifiable to copy some of [them for] your information, in the same spirit of confidence in which Corwin [entrusted] them to me. The first I will transcribe in full as follows.

"Washington City, May 11, 1848. Dear Sir: I have just received your favor of the 7th inst. If I could have anticipated the difficulties which we are encountering I should have been opposed to a [Whig] National Convention. I accord with you fully [in the opinion that] [John] McLean or Scott would be much better for us in all the free States than [Zachary] Taylor. Mr. Clay, you may rely upon it, is wholly out of the question. The party will be disbanded the moment he is named—if it were otherwise, I should oppose his nomination. I am certain he can do nothing with the two houses of Congress. If McLean or Scott is named, I think you may calculate that Old Zach will be in the field to a dead certainty—You know there is a feud and a bitter one between Scott & Taylor—[5] The latter considers himself much abused by the former in the matter of withdrawing the troops from him before the capture of Vera Cruz—I cannot think of any one who would be likely to take Rough & Ready out of the field but John J. Crittenden[6] and therefore if we must have a 3d man I am inclined to go for him. But we may as well look the truth in the face first as last—if we must have this question of slavery mixed up with our national politics we can do nothing with the government—we must keep under the yoke of th[is] radical democracy & the country must suffer until the people are cured of such folly—It is for this reason I have ever regarded the Wilmot Proviso[7] (as it is called) with great disfavor. I feared it would prove the rock on which the Whig party [must] split. I will only add since I have commenced writing this my colleague & friend, Mr. [Samuel D.] Hubbard[8] has been with me—I have read to him your letter—[He] says that our true course is to do nothing at Phila—we of the free States to [run] McLean & let the slave States run Taylor & thus throw the election into the House of Rep. I am not certain but that he is right. Truly Yr friend

Truman Smith"[9]

The next is an extract of a letter to Corwin from RW Thompson of I[ndian]a[10] [now] on a visit to his family at Columbus, Ohio, under date the 15th. I quote so much of it as relates to politics.

"I see but little change in the condition of things at Washington since you left. Presidential stock rises and falls with the weather. Taylor's last letter[11] [warmed] up his friends, but I do not think it has *increased* them. T[he only thing it has] done is—that if he shall get the nomination it gives him some ground to stand upon[.] Maryland has struck him rather a hard blow, as I see this morning. The Whig State Convention has appointed delegates to Phila. and instructed them by a vote of 54 to 49 (I think) to support Clay.[12] This will raise Clay stock a little—but not yet enough to give him the nomination. If Scott could get another lick at [William L.] Marcy[13] before the convention meets—he might increase his prospects—but I see they intend to keep him in Mexico until it is too late. It is also threatened that a Court Martial will be called to try him for "high crimes and misdemeanors".[14] Upon the whole, my impression when I left Washington, and yet is, that neither Clay, Taylor nor Scott will be likely to get the nomination. If Clay does not get it on the first ballot he certainly will not—and I think Taylor will have enough to prevent that—he and Scott both will surely. Where will the Clay men go to?—*that's* the question? It is not probable that any very large number of them will go for Taylor. If they should divide and part go for Taylor and part for Scott, [th]en the controversy would be an angry one. Just at that point, if a pretty [good] compromise man should be brought forward by one or two States, he would [be li]kely to succeed. Taylor out of the way, his friends would prefer Crittenden—but Crittenden is now in such a condition that he is compelled to be *mum*. McLean's friends are getting more confident of success with him as the compromise candidate—because he has maintained friendly relations with all. New England, after a complimentary vote for [Daniel] Webster will be inclined to go for him—and his nomination will in all probability depend upon the course taken by Ohio & Indiana.[15] If those states shall go for him at any stage of the proceedings before the nomination is made, he will be the candidate in all probability."

Another letter from John W. Allen[16] of Cleveland, May 12, says:

"There is no excitement here about the candidate—men have their preferences but are willing to to [*sic*] yield them readily. Corwin & McLean can [carry] this region with a rush—Webster would carry it strongly & so would Scott unless his nativism of 1845 were fastened on him.[17] It would be hard work to do much for Mr. Clay & death to attempt any thing for Old Zach. The delegates from this region only desire to know who has the most strength to determine their action. Had I been a [Joshua R.] Giddings man, I suppose I could have been sent to Phi[la.] but not being of that breed, I could not be.[18] As to the free States, I think there will [be] no quarreling after the nomination—we desire to win and care less who the servant we employ may be, than that he be honest and capable and an orthodox Whig. I have written Truman Smith to this purport, indicating no preference but merely giving opinions—He thinks Old Zach must be the man and I tell *pre*-haps so, but his nomination and the re-election of my illustrious namesake [Wm Allen of the U.S. Senate][19] would be pretty nearly identical."

Now you will indulge me in a few suggestions on these letters and their topics. They seem to me to imply a pretty strong purpose in the north to seek, or at least to acquiesce in the policy of a sectional contest. I totally differ from Truman Smith that your nomination will be the signal for the disbandment of the Whig party; believing as I do, and have said to you and others for a month past, that that is the *only* means of preventing that very result. How, on such an absurd theory, can the distinctly avowed preference of N. York[20] & other States of the north for you, be reconciled? But I am sorry to tell you, as candor compels me to do, that I seriously fear there are more Whigs in this State, which is more ultra against slavery than any other, than our Whig majority, who will not vote for you if you dont declare for the exclusion of slavery, in explicit terms, subject to no equivocal construction, from free territory. Your late letter[21] has not produced the effect hoped from it, and besides, many in Ohio believed you would in it declare against the extension of slavery. Since its publication, all the other candidates, except Taylor, seem to gain strength in this State; and I do not feel comfortably confident that even this State may not be lost to you in the Convn. It would be far more mortifying to me to see you fail of a nomination now, and by a handsome majority on the first ballot, than to see you defeated in the election. In the latter case, you and the Whig party would come out of the defeat without dishonor, having fallen in a manly struggle to uphold principles, which I think should not be even put in abeyance by nominating *such* an "exponent" of our principles as Taylor. I do not mean by this to advise your withdrawal, even though I am at this moment apprehensive of your defeat in the Convention, nor to tender any advice at all, feeling as I do the delicacy and embarrassment of assuming such a position. Moreover, I see some grounds of hope that all things may tend at last to the result of the Convention seeing, as I do, that your nomination is the true solution of all the difficulties that envison the Whig party and the country in the impending crisis. But I do beg to suggest to your consideration, the propri[e]ty of sending for [James] Harlan to spend a night with you before he leaves on the 27th, to consult on the course proper on the part of your friends in Convention. He is a cool man, and, what is of great estimation when so many have failed in fidelity, *a true man*. Put a letter in his hands authorizing him to withdraw you, should not the prospect of your nomination be a reliable one.[22] I suggest this, however, out of delicacy for your feelings, and perhaps too much in view of protecting my own from mortification in a possible, if not probable contingency. You will pardon this candor and solicitude, though doubtless you may deem it gratuitous, to the account of the zeal and friendship of one who has ever been faithful and true in good and evil hours to you.

P.S. I have not enlarged here on the only move which I think can be made to arrest, if any can, the tendencies against you in Ohio and elsewhere, because I considered that treated sufficiently in the preceding letter mailed this morning. I should mention, however, that one of the malign influences in this State, which has showed head in the last month, with strong determination to be *sure* of saving *Ohio*, against all mishaps, and though a month ago it was thought Ohio could be carried for you, it is generally assumed that a northern [can]didate will more certainly.

ALS, manuscript damaged. DLC-HC (DNA, M212, R6). No. 2 of date. 1. Letter not found. 2. For Odlin—prominent Dayton lawyer, delegate to the 1848 Whig National convention, and sometime member of the Ohio legislature—see *The History of Montgomery County, Ohio* . . . (Chicago, 1882), 485-86. 3. Stevenson to Clay, no. 1 of this date, above. 4. For New Jersey see *ibid.* At the Whig National convention, Michigan cast 3 votes for Clay and 2 for Scott on the 1st ballot; on the 2nd ballot, 3 for Scott and 2 for Clay; on the 3rd, 4 for Scott and 1 for Clay; and on the 4th, 3 for Scott and 2 for Taylor. Schlesinger, *History of U.S. Political Parties*, 1:436-39. 5. Henry Clay, Jr., to Clay, Feb. 12/19, 1847. 6. Clay to Clayton, April 16, 1847. 7. Sargent to Clay, Feb. 27, 1847. 8. For Hubbard, U.S. senator from Connecticut, see *BDAC*. 9. For Smith, U.S. senator from Connecticut, see *BDAC*. 10. For Indiana congressman Richard W. Thompson, see *BDAC*. 11. First Allison letter; see Clay to Ullmann, August 4, 1847. 12. Harvey to Clay, May 3, 1848. 13. *Ibid.* 14. For the Court of Inquiry called to investigate Scott's charges against Maj. Gen. Gideon Pillow, Brevet Maj. Gen. W.J. Worth, and Lt. Col. James Duncan and the charges made by way of appeal against Scott, see Elliott, *Winfield Scott*, 576-90. 15. McLean received only 1 vote each from Ohio and Iowa on the 1st ballot and no votes thereafter. For Ohio's votes at the convention, see Ullmann to Clay, Feb. 18, 1848; for Indiana's, see Clay to Mercer, April 14, 1848. 16. For former Ohio Whig congressman John W. Allen, see *BDAC*. 17. Scott had written a long letter, decidedly nativist in tone, which was published in the Washington *Daily National Intelligencer* on Dec. 17, 1844. In 1848 he repudiated the earlier letter. Elliott, *Winfield Scott*, 591. 18. Giddings was the embodiment of the Whig anti-slavery movement that was already considering bolting the party if a slaveowner were nominated. Stewart, *Joshua R. Giddings*, 144-48, 151-55. 19. For William Allen, U.S. senator from Ohio, see *BDAC*. 20. Clay to Greeley, Dec. 10, 1847; Lawrence *et al.* to Clay, Feb. 16, 1848. 21. Clay to The Public, April 10, 1848. 22. Clay's name was not withdrawn at the convention.

To Franck Taylor, Washington, D.C., May 18, 1848. Thanks Taylor for sending him a "book shelf in good order and undefaced, free from expence." Adds: "I have never known a Bookseller, on this side of the [Appalachian] Mountains, who was not a good Whig. So that you find they do not differ from their brethren on the Seaboard."

Claims he is "unable to anticipate the results of either of the two great [Whig and Democratic National] Conventions, now nigh at hand [Clay to Greeley, November 15, 1846; Clay to Ullmann, May 12, 1847]," but explains "from all I hear, it is equally difficult at Washington to form a correct opinion." Acknowledges "that great heat and excitement exist among the members of Congress." Concludes: "I performed a reluctant duty in acquiescing in the submission of my name to the consideration of the Philada. Convention [Clay to The Public, April 10, 1848]. Whatever the issue may be, I have thereby secured myself against all responsibility and all just reproaches, and I shall be content." ALS. DLC-HC (DNA, M212, R6).

For the Whig political organization in Congress, see Clay to Harvey, April 18, 1848.

To THOMAS B. STEVENSON Lexington, May 20, 1848

After putting a letter for you in the P.O. to day I received your two favors of the 18th, but not the call for the Peoples Convention[1] in the [Cincinnati] Herald to which you refer. I regard it only as an indication of an unsettled, uneasy and dissatisfied condition of the public mind. Any such movement cannot become sufficiently general to influence materially the [Whig National] Convention at Philadelphia.[2] Some of your communications (which I shall regard as strictly confidential) greatly surprise me. Whatever I might do, if I had not consented to submit my name to the convention,[3] I am constrained now to abide by that act. I am induced to believe, or rather to hope, that things will appear not quite so bad when it assembles. So much depends on its complexion, so much on developments during its deliberations, and so much upon the Baltimore [Democratic] Convention and its nomination,[4] that it is very difficult to provide before hand for all contingencies. I shall have a long interview with [James] Harlan before he goes. I shall deeply regret if you cannot go, and sincerely hope that you may yet be able to do so.

I think our friend Col [Albert] Hodges expressed to you too many remarks of mine, which I think were general, and did not relate particularly to the Atlas.[5]

I suppose Gov [James C.] Jones will attend the Convention.[6] I understand that he was to leave home on the 25th.

If ever there should be a time when it may be necessary for me to express my opinions about the Wilmot proviso,[7] for publication, that time has not yet arrived.

Copy. OCHP. Letter marked "(Private)." Printed in Colton, *Clay Correspondence*, 3:463, with second and third paragraphs omitted. 1. Wendell to Clay, March 11, 1848. 2. Greeley to Clay, Nov. 15, 1846. 3. Clay to The Public, April 10, 1848. 4. Clay to Ullmann, May 12, 1847. 5. Stevenson to Clay, May 18, 1848, no. 1 of date. 6. *Ibid.* 7. Sargent to Clay, Feb. 27, 1847.

From THOMAS B. STEVENSON Cincinnati, May 22, 1848

I went to Lebanon [Ohio] on Saturday. [Thomas] Corwin had no instrumentality in any way with the [John] Mc'Lean move of the Star.[1] The information on which the editor relied for the assurance that N[ew]. England would go for Mc'L. after [Daniel] Webster, was in letters from Caleb Smith and David Fisher.[2]

Corwin has written to five or six of the delegates from this State advising them of his views and feelings, indicating his preference for you first and

Webster next, and, if a civilian be not deemed available, then for [Winfield] Scott. As it is strongly asserted that Scott can carry Pa. his pretensions, in such view, would look formidable.[3]

I was very happy on reading your account of your late correspondence with Corwin.[4] He had written me the day before I went out, in the best spirit and kindest feeling, saying of you—"I esteem him, revere him, love him, just as I have since I lived in his mess. I only wish it had pleased God to make one *million* of such men, instead of *one*."

Your old friend Dr. [Walter] Brashear, of La., is here and I have had a good deal of conversation with him. He says you had a right to count on his firm & faithful friendship. But he says a majority of his delegation are for [Zachary] Taylor, who *can* carry La. but he thinks you *cant*.[5] He has a very singular scheme, however, of electing you, and which he thinks is the only one feasible. It is to divide the States between you and Taylor, in the way as nearly equal as may be in electoral strength, casting lots for first choice, and that one receiving the largest number of electoral votes to take all. I think the proposition absurd; but he is in deep earnest about it and means to propose it to the [Whig] Natl. Convn.[6]

Col. [Alexander W.] Doniphan,[7] a delegate from Mo. passed up today. He is reported as expressing confidence of Taylor's carrying Missouri.[8]

McLean's schemes are not so promising now as they seemed last week. Scott, I think, will take Ohio,[9] if you are not nominated.

But my strongest conviction still is, that both Conventions, Whig & Loco,[10] will break down, without nominating candidates. In the event of ours holding together, I take a much more encouraging view of the prospects than I did last week. But under every aspect, I shall continue to do my duty to the last, and enjoy the satisfaction of thinking I deserve success, whether I attain it or not; a philosophy on which I have ever acted.

I shall not fail to make the acquaintance of Mr. Sloan [*sic*, John Sloane]. Gov. [Joseph] Vance goes on in company with [James] Harlan and me.

Brashear says Taylor *will* win, if you are nominated, and that his friends in the South *will not* withdraw him. I certainly will not sit in any Convention where any man is presented on such terms. If the Whig Convention entertain the pretensions of any candidate, or consider any one eligible for nomination, not unequivocally subject to its decision, my sense of duty and self-respect will alike impel me to withdraw and renounce its action.

If Duncan[11] gave me, as I do not doubt he did, a faithful abstract of Taylor's letter to you, he has placed himself in a very awkward dilemma by his disavowal in the R[ic]h[mond]. Republican letter.[12] The fact is, I sicken at the assumption that he is altogether modest and unambitious and has absorbed all the honesty extant. He has little more, I fear, of either quality, than he can *afford* to display—and they do not exceed in extensiveness, the sum of his qualifications for civil services, which Corwin says consist in sleeping forty years in the woods, and cultivating moss in the calves of his legs.

Judge [Jacob] Burnet, I hear, and divers others of the McLean family & clique, are going to Phila. to correct the misrepresentation of this district by L'Hommidieu [*sic*, Stephen S. L'Hommedieu] and myself.[13]

ALS. DLC-HC (DNA, M212, R6). 1. The Lebanon (Ohio) *Western Star* had come out on May 19 in support of John McLean as a second choice to Thomas Corwin for the Whig presidential nomination. Holt, *Party Politics in Ohio*, 298. 2. The *Western Star* had also announced on May 19 that New England would first vote for Daniel Webster. For David Fisher, Ohio congressman from 1847-49, and Caleb B. Smith, Indiana congressman from 1843-49, see *BDAC*. The letters of Fisher and Smith have not been found. 3. For Scott's vote at the Whig National convention, see Crittenden to Clay, May 4, 1848. 4. Probably a reference to Corwin to Clay, May 3, 1848. 5. For the vote of Louisiana in the Whig National convention, see Clay to Mercer, April 14, 1848. 6. For the Whig National convention, see Greeley to Clay, Nov. 15, 1846. 7. For Doniphan (1808-87)—lawyer, colonel in the Mexican War, and Missouri state legislator—see *DAB*. 8. Missouri gave 6 votes to Taylor on the first three ballots at the Whig National convention and 7 for Taylor on the 4th ballot. Schlesinger, *History of U.S. Political Parties*, 1:436-39. 9. For Ohio's vote at the Whig convention, see Ullmann to Clay, Feb. 18, 1848. 10. For the Democratic National convention, see Clay to Ullmann, May 12, 1847. 11. Possibly Ohio congressman Alexander Duncan of Cincinnati. See *BDAC*. 12. Taylor to Clay, April 30, 1848. 13. Jacob Burnet, a McLean supporter, had been defeated for delegate to the Whig National convention, while L'Hommedieu and Stevenson, both supposedly Clay men, were elected as delegate and alternate, respectively. Lexington *Observer & Kentucky Reporter*, May 10, 1848. For L'Hommedieu's actions at the Whig convention, see Stevenson to Clay, July 26, 1848.

To Henry White, Philadelphia, May 23, 1848. In response to White's "desire, in the event of there not being a majority of the Whig Convention disposed to nominate me, to know who, among the distinguished names before the Convention, would be my first, second and third choice," replies he has "hitherto maintained a position of ent[ire] impartiality. . . . d[ic]tated by considerations of delicacy towards them." Adds: "I do not thin[k] that I ought to deviate from it." Expresses his hopes that the Whig National convention [Greeley to Clay, November 15, 1846] will not be "stormy," but that "it will be found animated by a spirit of concord and patriotism, and seeking to do the best it can for our common Country." ALS. IGK. Printed in Colton, *Clay Correspondence*, 4:561.

From JOSEPH L. WHITE New York City, May 26, 1848

The loco-foco nominations[1] have thrown the whole party into remorseless confusion here. I am convinced from the language held by the leading Barnburners this morning that they as well as a portion of the Hunkers are determined upon the defeat of [Lewis] Cass. No one expresses a hope of reconciliation & it is not thought possible. But *who* the disaffected will vote for it is impossible to say. That [the] more ardent of them will nominate Genl [Zachary] Taylor I am convinced, if he will but write a *twenty sixth* letter pledging himself not to veto a bill to prevent slavery in Territory now free. Such is now the wish & *expressed* determination of Jno Van Buren—Benj. Butler &c if the letter can be procured.[2] Without such a pledge they will not nominate him, nor will they wish it, if he should receive the Whig nomination.

The latter event would now seem impossible unless the pressure of Congressional influence[3] upon the convention shall be so great as to coax or frighten some of our northern delegates from their propriety. That such influence is to be brought to bear I know, & upon this the Taylor men *here* mostly rely for success.

I much feared, at one time, that the Taylor Clique intended to transfer their strength to [Winfield] Scott, in the event of failure with Taylor, & such was their design *here*, but it has been frustrated by their friends in Congress, & now they are as clamorous against Scott as they are against you. The reception of Genl Scott yesterday[4] was brilliant in military display & good in numbers, but the enthusiasm was *disgracefully small*. No man I venture to say, (unless it be the Genl), regarded it as a "Presidential movement". That his vanity so construed it however, is more than probable, from his speeches yesterday & to day. He is much talked of for the *Vice*—Presidency on the ticket with you, & by your friends.[5] His old *friends* (?) who used him in 1840, are now Taylor men or [Thomas] Corwin or, [John] McLean men, & he must look to *us* for support or remain without it. This category we hope he will discover & consent, in view of future support, to abate from his pretentions to the Presidency & take a nomination for the second office. [Willis] Hall [James] Brooks & myself are going to see him on this subject & we mean to talk plainly & promise freely for the future. To take him hereafter will be but a future ill, to secure a present & indispensable benefit, & circumstances seem to render it nescessary that we should take the risk. If, however, as I fear, his judgment has stilled itself on his vanity, & he refuses to play second fiddle now to become leader of the orchestra hereafter, why then, we must hunt for another *wind instrument*, & do as we have heretofore—without him. He has no organized force with which to threaten or oppose us. Four of our delegates are for him as their first choice, *all* the others are for you.[6]

I have spoken thus freely of Genl Scott to *you*. I do not like him, & know no sensible man who has any respect for his civil abilities, but there are many like myself, who will take any thing that wears feathers for the second office to secure a harmonious nomination of you for the first.

I have written because I supposed you would like to know how the nomination of Cass was reced. here & what was the character of Scotts reception, as such may have some influence upon the action of our convention. That New York will be for you, if nominated, is now as certain as though the vote were given & counted. All we fear is cheating & cowardice in the convention; *& this we do fear*. Every thing as we think depends on the Kentucky delegation.[7] If they come for you & stand firm, the lie will be given to the slander that Kentucky is for Taylor, & will encourage every northern delegate. If Kentucky hesitates or doubts, the north will be discouraged & may yield, which God forbid.

P.S. Col. [Charles S.] Todd has been on a Taylor mission to our delegates through the state. *His* efforts are by no means alarming, nor will they be until he learns to speak English[.]

ALS. DLC-HC (DNA, M212, R6). 1. Clay to Ullmann, May 12, 1847. 2. Taylor made no such specific commitment in regard to slavery in the territories, but he had indicated as early as his First Allison letter [Clay to Ullmann, August 4, 1847] and later in his Second Allison letter of Sept. 4, 1848, that he would veto only those acts which were clearly a violation of the Constitution. Bauer, *Zachary Taylor*, 233. For the full text of the Second Allison letter which again attempted to explain away Taylor's nonpartisan statements, see Hamilton, *Zachary Taylor, Soldier in the White House*, 121-24. For actions of the Barnburners, see Greeley to Clay, Nov. 30, 1847; Wendell to Clay, March 11, 1848. 3. For the Taylor organization in Congress, see Clay to Harvey, April 18, 1848. 4. Morehead to Clay, May 3, 1848. 5. Clay to Brooks, April 13, 1848. 6. For New York's vote at the Whig National convention, see Ullmann to Clay, Feb. 18, 1848. 7. For Kentucky's vote at the Whig convention, see Clay to Stevenson, April 12, 1848.

To ADAM BEATTY Lexington, May 28, 1848

I was at Frankfort yesterday and had an interview with the Governor [William Owsley], on the subject of the temporary appointment of a Senator.[1] He told me that he had not made up his mind as to the appointment of any particular individual. He had thought of several persons and amongst others

Mr Kincaid of Lexington, but had fixed upon no one. He was inclined he said to select some person who would not be a competitor for the office before the Legislature. I then mentioned to him your name in terms corresponding with the high opinion I entertain of you. I told him that I thought you merited the office, by your long and faithful public services by your talents and by the great benefit you have rendered the cause of agriculture[2] and I also told him how much gratified I should be, if he could reconcile it to his sense of duty to confer the appointment on you. The Governor fully concurred with me in the favorable opinion I had expressed of you, and asssured [*sic*] me that he entertained for you great esteem and regard and that he would take your name into consideration. This was the substance of what passsed between us. I am a little afraid of his appointment of Kincaid who has been a sort of pet & favorite of his. I told him I thought you would fulfill the condition which he suggested of not being a candidate before the Legislature. Mr [John J.] Crittenden is expected to return about the 15th or 20th of June, and I suppose the appointment will be made shortly after his return.[3]

I do not Know my dear Sir, that I can do any thing more to promote your views, but if you can indicate any manner in which I can further serve you, I will do so with pleasure. P.S. This letter has been written by an Amanuensis[.]

LS, postscript in Clay's hand. KyLoF. Letter marked "*Confidential*." 1. John J. Crittenden had resigned from the Senate after receiving the nomination for governor of Kentucky. Owsley first offered the seat to Clay [Owsley to Clay, June 20, 1848], who declined; Owsley then appointed former governor Thomas Metcalfe who took his seat July 3, 1848. *BDAC*. Crittenden won the gubernatorial race over his Democratic opponent Lazarus W. Powell by a vote of 65,860 to 57,397, while Whig John L. Helm defeated Democrat John P. Martin for lieutenant governor by 63,664 votes to 55,936. In the election for the state legislature, Whigs carried 8 senate seats to 3 for the Democrats, giving the Whigs an overall majority of 27 to 11. Whigs won a majority in the lower house of 64 to 36. Lexington *Observer & Kentucky Reporter*, Sept. 2, 1848; Frankfort *Commonwealth*, August 29, 1848. 2. See 9:903. 3. See note 1, above.

From Charles S. Morehead, Washington, D.C., May 28, 1848. Advises Clay that Zachary Taylor's April 20, 1848, letter [Taylor to Clay, April 30, 1848] "has produced a more settled & fixed opposition to him in the minds of a portion of the Whigs, but his friends attempt to get over it by saying that he means only [to] say that he will not act personally in withdrawing [but] that he is in the hands of his friends and that [they] will withdraw him of course if not nominated." Adds: "I still think that his prospects have increase[d]."

Considered uniting "in a com[mon] movem[ent]" for Clay, but, "[disap]pointed by alleged changes of opinion . . . I would not know with whom to unite." Notes that among Clay's friends, [John M.] Botts "is sincere tru[e] and ardent, but he has no sort of tact whatever. . . . If I suggest a doubt as to a particular vote, he will swear th[at] there is not the slightest doubt."

Has decided to follow a "calm prudent and conciliatory but firm course." Reports that among some of Taylor's friends "there is a bitterness towards you, not excelled by former locofoco opposition, but this is confined I think to a narrow circle." With those Taylor supporters "I can talk to, entertaining personally the kindest feelings and highest regard for their favorite, I endeavor to impress upon them, the propriety if he cannot be nominated of throwing their influence on you." Assures Clay that "this is the feeling of many, while a few would go against you even if nominated." Endeavors to show John McLean's friends "that their true policy is so evidently to unite cordially and zealously for you, that they would be [com]mitting political homicide to act otherwise." Adds: "[With] Genl [Winfield] Scotts friends I have no patience—They are the men [ma]ny of whom were most clamorous for you while here—who [were] most urgent that you should not withdraw your name."

Concerning Whig activities in individual states, has asked Horace Greeley about "the rumour of 16 of the New York delegation being for [Daniel] Webster [Ullmann to Clay, February 18, 1848]." Fears "you are mistaken as to the vote from Ky. . . . You however ought to know best [Clay to Stevenson, April 12, 1848]." Informs Clay that "Dr [James] Ritchie. . . . is for Taylor. . . . He said he regretted it, [but] those he represented were for Taylor, and he felt bound [to vote] for him." Agrees that Clay "is right as to Indiana [Clay to Mercer, April 14, 1848]—But in [George G.] Dunns district where [Joseph] Warner was appointed a delegate, Dunn is also a delegate who is for Taylor." Of Clay's "two votes in Illinois—One of them has changed, and is clamoring for Taylor."

Concerning Democratic party affairs, doubts "S. Carolina will vote for [Lewis] Cass in any contingency." Understands "her representatives . . . have come [out] for Taylor should he be nominated" or they would "not . . . vote at al[l]."

Includes a rough calculation of the possible vote at the Whig National convention, which shows the following: Clay, approximately 116; Taylor 127; Webster 18; Scott 13; McLean 4; John M. Clayton 3. Believes, however, that Clay could receive as many as 126 votes on the first ballot, "reducing Taylors to about 120." ALS, manuscript torn. DLC-HC (DNA, M212, R6).

James Ritchie was a delegate to the Whig National convention from Louisiana. Joseph Warner was a delegate from Indiana. Philadelphia *North American & United States Gazette*, June 7, 1848. For George G. Dunn, see *BDAC*.

At the 1848 Whig convention, Illinois cast 4 votes for Taylor, 3 for Clay and 1 for Scott on the first three ballots; on the 4th ballot all 8 votes went to Taylor. Schlesinger, *History of U.S Political Parties*, 1:436-39.

All 9 of South Carolina's electoral votes went to Lewis Cass. McKee, *National . . . Popular and Electoral Vote*, 72.

On the 1st ballot at the Whig National convention, Clay received 97 votes; Taylor 111; Scott 43; Webster 22; Clayton 4; McLean 2. Schlesinger, *History of U.S. Political Parties*, 1:436.

From HORACE GREELEY New York City, May 29, 1848

Yours of the 20th came to hand two days since, yet I have wished to be better advised on some points before answering it. The fact that I became well-nigh disheartened at Washington may have already been made apparent to you, either through my letter or The Tribune. My last day in Washington was the gloomiest by far; and I cannot since shake off a feeling that the managers and general advisers of the Whig party at Washington have resolved to put Gen. [Zachary] Taylor upon us at all hazards, and that they will accomplish their purpose. My last day in W. was the day after Gen. Taylor's Allison letter was published,[1] when for the first time the strength centered upon Gen. T. was made manifest. I had previously supposed that [Winfield] Scott would ultimately be the strong man against us, and had acted accordingly. I think I was able to convince some that he would be a very unsuitable candidate. Judge [John] McLean was somewhat talked of but manifested no strength. I had hardly before deemed the nomination of Taylor a possibility; I have since hardly had spirit for any thing. I was at Trenton last week at the [New Jersey] Whig State Convention, and there we lost two delegates to which we were justly entitled by means of superior management and activity on the part of the Taylor men. We ought to have had 6 delegates out of 7; we had but 4. [Joseph] Porter and [John L.]

Stratton[2] made fair professions to secure some votes from our side, but they will vote dead against us from the start. The whole Jersey delegation in congress (with one nominal exception) was active and powerful against us. Philadelphia must exhale a poisonous influence. With Gen. Scott a resident of East Jersey, and with a Senator and two other Members of congress[3] working hard against us nearly every delegate from this side of the State was firm for us; while nearly all West Jersey went solid against us. That could not be unless Philadelphia was really hostile to us.

I believe we are doomed to be beaten, and that the men who control the counsels of the Whig party through the machinery existing at Washington[4] have resolved to throw overboard a good part of our principles so as to make a surer rush for the Spoils. This conviction renders me almost incapable of exertion.

But the defection does not and will not take effect in this quarter. I am confident there is no delegate elected from the Southern half of this State who can be induced to vote for any body but Henry Clay; I am sure not one of the four Jersey men from this side of the State will vote otherwise; and I believe Connecticut[5] will also vote with us entire, though of that I am less certain. Truman Smith told me, the night before I left Washington, (along with any amount of Taylorism) that he should feel constrained, if he went into the [Whig National] Convention, to vote the sentiment of his constituents. I hear vaguely of a number of Scott delegates in the Western part of this State;[6] but I don't know yet how it will be with them. John A. Collier[7] is here to-day, and is confident the State will be unanimous for us, on the first ballot any how. I confess I do not think so. I know of one, elected as for us, who is now openly for Scott. One of the Ohio Delegates, elected by our friends, is here to-day, after spending some time in Washington, and brings such accounts thence as I could easily anticipate. He intimated that he had understood you were abandoned! and was rather surprised when I told him we had not heard the news this way. But in fact, all manner of rumors, many of them utterly false, are constantly set afloat; and if the delegates could but reach the convention without passing through Washington, I should be less despondent.

Whatever may be the result of the Convention, I do trust that you will have no cause to regret that you permitted the use of your name.[8] The whole country knows that you did so in deference to the urgent representations of your friends, against your own original purpose, and will rest the responsibility on these friends and not on yourself. I insist, moreover, that the People are the only judges in such cases; that no man should decline that post till a nomination is tendered him; and that the range of selection should not be narrowed except for the most urgent reasons. If your friends have been unwise in this matter, I will cheerfully bear my part of the censure. I know that Mr. Truman Smith could not have been Senator from Connecticut for six years ensuing had you withdrawn when you proposed, leaving Taylorism the ruling element in our party; and it did seem to me that a struggle against the new Military fever was due to the consistency, the sincerity and the character of our party. I did not see how it could be made with a reasonable hope of success without the use of your name. I have acted from a paramount regard to public interests and permanent results; but these are some of your friends here—I will name Dudley Selden, Willis Hall, Nicholas Carroll—who have been impelled by a single-hearted personal devotion which I am sure you will appreciate even though its results may be regretted. Had there been a few more like them, the immediate event would have been different from what I now fear it must be.

This night I shake off inaction if not despair, and for the week that is left us I will make all the fight that is in me to defeat the result which I feel to be inevitable. It could be done yet, by trading off—going for a third man—but that it shall not be. It shall be victory or entire, overwhelming defeat. The Telegraph will tell you the result soon after you will have received this. Till then adieu.

ALS. DLC-HC (DNA, M212, R6). 1. Clay to Ullmann, August 4, 1847. 2. Porter and Stratton were both delegates from New Jersey to the Whig National convention. For New Jersey's vote at the convention, see Stevenson to Clay, May 18, 1848, no. 1 of date. 3. Probably Sen. Jacob W. Miller of Morristown and Congressmen John Van Dyke of New Brunswick and Dudley S. Gregory of Jersey City, all of whom were from the eastern section of New Jersey. See *BDAC*. 4. Clay to Harvey, April 18, 1848. 5. At the Whig National convention, Connecticut gave all 6 votes to Clay on the first two ballots and then split 3 for Clay and 3 for Taylor on the 3rd and 4th ballots. Schlesinger, *History of U.S. Political Parties*, 1:436-39. 6. For New York's votes at the convention, see Ullmann to Clay, Feb. 18, 1848. 7. For Collier—Binghamton, N.Y., lawyer, former congressman, and temporary president of the 1848 Whig National convention—see *DAB*; *BDAC*. 8. Clay to The Public, April 10, 1848.

From HENRY S. LEVERT & CHARLES C. LANGDON[1] Louisville, May 29, 1848

We are on our way to Philadelphia as delegates from the first Congressional district of Alabama to the Whig National Convention. It was our intention when we left Mobile to have visited Ashland, as well to pay you personally our respects, as to consult with you in frankness and confidence, on the important subject which will engross the attention of the Convention, but a longer passage than we anticipated from New Orleans, and the indisposition of Dr. LeVert which renders it imprudent for him to undergo the fatigue of stage travelling, constrain us, very [reluc]tantly, to forego that pleasure. We have therefore concluded to address you by letter, respectfully requesting, if consistent with your views of propriety, an expression of your opinions and *wishes* on the subject of the nomination of a Candidate for the Presidency.

It is perhaps proper for us to promise that the Convention from which we received our appointment as delegates, passed resolutions, unanimously, declaring "Henry Clay the first choice of the Whigs of the first Congressional district of Alabama for the Presidency", and that those resolutions were in perfect unison with our own feelings; at the same time, the delegates were left free to act in accordance with the dictates of their own judgment—that is, they were untrammelled by special instructions.[2]

The fact, it appears to us, cannot be disguised that there is great danger of discord in the Convention, and we fear it will be of a serious character. The supporters of Gen. [Zachary] Taylor exhibit much bitterness of feeling—they are active and influential and will leave no means untried to secure his nomination. They evince a spirit of illiberality and vindictiveness that must prove fatal to the harmony of the party if carried into the Convention. For ourselves, we have uniformly opposed the "Taylor movement". We doubt the qualifications of the General, we are not satisfied of his orthodoxy as a Whig, we disapprove of his position as an "independent" candidate in defiance of the Convention,[3] we have a great repugnance to the selection of a mere "Military Chieftain" for the presidency, and we feel that it would be almost impossible for us to be induced to vote for Gen. Taylor, even should he be nominated by the Convention. Many of our Whig friends advocate the policy, as you are aware, of selecting a third man, as the only means of reconciling conflicting opinions and insuring that harmony and concert which are indispensable to the success of the Whig Cause, and in this connection the names of Gen. [Winfield] Scott, Judge [John] McLean, Mr. [John J.] Crittenden and some others have been respectively suggested. Under these circumstances, we confess to you, that we have serious doubts in regard to the proper course of action, and feel extremely desirous of obtaining the aid of your counsel and advice. We trust you will so far confide in our honor and friendship as to favor us with a free expression of your own views, wishes and feelings in regard to this whole matter, under the solemn assurance on our part, that whatever you write us shall be seen by no mortal eye save our own, if you so desire it. Such an expression from you would exert a great, a controlling influence on our action in the Convention, while without it we feel that we shall be subjected to much embarrassment. Perhaps some delegate to the Convention is already intrusted with all the information we desire—if so, can you favor us with his name, with authority to consult with him on the subject? In that event; the end we have in view would in all probability, be accomplished.

We should be extremely gratified to know your feelings, respectively, toward Mr. Crittenden, Gen. Scott Judge McLean and others who have been spoken of in connection with the Presidency. What has been their course in the [pr]esent canvass for the nomination? And in case it become necessary to select a Compromise Candidate, who ought to be selected? Who would be most acceptable to you? Who in your opinion most worthy of confidence, most "available" and most entitled to the honor? Are you satisfied with the course of Mr. Crittenden recently toward yourself? Many of your friends in the South are dissatisfied at his course.[4] Can you consistently with your sense of duty and propriety, answer these inquiries?

We were exceedingly anxious to see you and talk over all these matters privately with you, but deprived of that pleasure we have resorted to this mode, and beg that you will favor us with a reply, at the earliest moment practicable, addressed to us at Philadelphia.

We trust, honored sir, that you will excuse the liberty we have taken in thus addressing you, and that you will appreciate the motives which have influenced us. We are free to say that you have ever been, and are still, our first and only choice for the Presidency, and so long as your name is before the people as a candidate we cannot support any other. We shall vote for you in the Philadelphia Convention as long as your name shall be before that body.

ALS, probably in Langdon's hand, signed also by LeVert. DLC-HC (DNA, M212, R6). 1. For Langdon (1805-89)—editor of the Mobile *Advertiser* and later mayor of Mobile and member of the Alabama legislature—see *NCAB*, 18:149-50. 2. The Alabama delegates to the 1848 Whig convention cast 6 votes for Taylor and 1 for Clay on the first 3 ballots and 6 votes for Taylor and 0 for other candidates on the 4th ballot. Schelsinger, *History of U.S. Political Parties*, 1:436-39. Although Dr. LeVert was listed in the Philadelphia *North American & United States Gazette* of June 7, 1848, as a delegate to the convention, he was not listed in the Washington *Daily National Intelligencer* of June 9 and 16 as answering the roll call or voting at the convention.

Langdon, however, according to the *Intelligencer* of June 16, 1848, voted for Taylor on all 4 ballots. 3. Taylor to Clay, April 30, 1848. 4. White to Clay, Sept. 4, 1847.

From Philip R. Fendall, Washington, D.C., May 31, 1848. Reports again "on the subject of the debt of the Columbian College," assuring Clay that the delay was not due "to want of diligence on my part [Clay to Fendall, June 16, 1847]." Explains that "only on Wednesday last" could the Board of Trustees "be brought to act definitively." Encloses a copy of the board's "acknowledgment of the principal with a promise to pay in six months with interest from the date." Has learned, however, that the "expectation is to pay the claim sooner, out of the proceeds of a sale of an interest in real estate which has been given to the College, and will shortly be sold." Is satisfied that these arrangements are "the best disposition of the subject" short of legal proceedings.

On the Democratic presidential nomination [Clay to Ullmann, May 12, 1847], believes that "Mr. [Lewis] Cass has doubtless been selected on the calculation that a majority of the people sympathise, or can be brought to do so, with his extreme opinions, and his success would be the triumph of the new school which has infused into the public mind an appetite for war, conquest, and unlimited territorial aggrandisement, to say nothing of Dorrism [9:714-16]." Fears that this "appetite, if not checked now may at the end of four years, be beyond restraint." Hopes, therefore, that the Whig National convention "will . . . meet under a due sense of their responsibility" and will "support the nominee . . . but the efficacy of the support must depend on its ardor." Since "it is not in human nature for men to be as ardent for mere expediency as for the long cherished hopes of patriotism and personal attachment," warns the Whigs not to ignore "the lessons of history, and their own history too" and "act on the old maxim, 'honesty is the best policy.' " Assumes, then, "that the event which I have from early youth looked forward to as a political certainty is now about to happen." AL, draft. NcD.

From JAMES HARLAN Washington, D.C., June 2, 1848

I arrived here the evening of the 31st. ult. and found things in a very bad condition for the true interest of the Whig party. The Palo Alto Club[1] have regular meetings and are as well drilled, as any Corps of Regular Soldiers Genl T[aylor]. ever commanded. Their military Operations are directed against raw and undisciplined militia who are without officers. It is said thay have a Committee Appointed to watch the arrival of Delegates and indoctrinate them into the belief that you are not *available*, and Genl Taylor is the only man who can be elected by the Whigs. They have succeeded to a Very great extent in making that impression on the public mind. The delegation of both Houses from Kentucky saving [Charles S.] Morehead & [Aylette] Buckner, being known to be against your nomination, has, I fear, laid the foundation of your defeat in the Convention.[2] The impression has been made here, and seems to be generally acquiesced in that Taylor will receive the nomination. His friends are holding up the Vice Presidency to Northern Aspirants,[3] and will in that way catch most of them in the Palo Alto trap.

I have not seen [John M.] Botts. He has been absent in Va. the whole week. He is expected here to morrow evening on his way to Philada—It is the intention to have a meeting of your friends Monday evening in Philada—consult and decide what is best to be done—The present intention of the Taylor men is to Tomahawk you. My intention is to take a bold, decided and dignified course. I shall regard the nomination of Genl T. as a dissolution of the Whig party and the creation on its views of a party without principles except a longing desire after the Spoils of Office. There is one matter which I wish to suggest to you for your consideration. If Genl T. received the nomination he cannot be elected without your cooperation and endorsement—and my opinion is that even with it, he will fail—How far ought you to go in submitting to and acquiescing in the movement now being made in putting up Genl Taylor as a Whig? I think you ought not to act hastily in coming to any conclusion.[4]

I cannot inform you how the Kentucky delegation will be divided. [William R.] Griffith & [George T.] Wood are very decided for you. [John A.] McClung & [Littleton] Beard are against you, the former quite active and noisy as I have been informed.[5]

It is conceded that Taylor cannot get Ohio, but his friends say he will make it up in Louisiana, Miss: & Georgia. They say moreover that you cannot get Tennessee, but that Genl Taylor can—[6] I have seen Truman Smith.[7] I think he is bitten with the Vice Presidency, and no reliance will be placed on his professions of friendship or honesty—

I will leave for Philada to morrow evening or Sunday Morning.

ALS. DLC-HC (DNA, M212, R6). 1. Reference is to those who began touting Taylor for the presidency after his victory at Palo Alto. 2. Kentucky's senators were John J. Crittenden and Joseph R. Underwood; congressmen were Linn Boyd, Beverly L. Clarke, Samuel O. Peyton, Aylette Buckner (son of Richard A.), John B. Thompson, Green Adams, W. Garnett Duncan, Charles S. Morehead, Richard French, and John P. Gaines. For all, see *BDAC*. 3. At the Whig National convention, Millard Fillmore and Abbott Lawrence emerged as the two strongest candidates for vice president. Fillmore was nominated on the 2nd ballot, winning 173 votes to 87 for Lawrence, with 6 scattered. McKee, *National . . . Popular and Electoral Vote*, 63. See also Clay to Greeley, Nov. 22, 1847. 4. Clay refused to endorse Taylor and also rejected running as an independent candidate. See, for example, Clay to Stevenson, August 5, 1848; Clay to Dean, August 24, 1848; Clay to Cincinnati Whigs, Sept. 1, 1848. Clay's sons voted for Taylor, but Clay was too ill to go the polls. Van Deusen, *Henry Clay*, 393. 5. These men were Kentucky delegates to the Whig National convention, as were James Campbell, James B. Husbands, James W. Hayes, Josiah A. Jackson, Robert Mallory, James Harlan, John R. Houston, and Benjamin F. Bedinger. Harlan was the only Kentucky delegate who voted for Clay on all four ballots. Philadelphia *North American & United States Gazette*, June 7, 1848. 6. For states carried by each candidate in the presidential election, see Harlan to Clay, June 15, 1848. 7. Smith's name was not placed in nomination for the vice presidency at the Whig convention. Schlesinger, *History of U.S. Political Parties*, 1:442.

To Edward Phalon, New York City, June 2, 1848. Thanks him for his friendly sentiments and "for the bottle of Hair Invigorator which you had the goodness to send me. I will give it a fair trial. Although in advanced age nothing can avert the appearance of gray hairs and wrinkles, and other evidences of the lapse of years, it is well enough to put on and preserve our good looks as well and as long as we can. From the favorable account of your Invigorator, I think it must contribute to that object. I hope it may also contribute to the object of your success and prosperity in life." Copy. Printed in New-York *Daily Tribune*, June 13, 1848.

Phalon's business was located at 61 Broadway, Judson's Hotel. *Ibid.*

To John A. Watkins, New Orleans, June 2, 1848. Although believing it is "useless to speculate on the results" of the Whig National convention [Greeley to Clay, November 15, 1846], feels "it will nominate Genl. [Zachary] Taylor or me, but which I consider quite uncertain." Offers his opinion that among the candidates considered at the Democratic National convention [Clay to Ullmann, May 12, 1847], "one more vulnerable or weaker than Genl. [Lewis] Cass could not have been selected." ALS. LNHT.

To PHILIP R. FENDALL Lexington, June 6, 1848

[Accepts a new note from the Board of Trustees of Columbian College which covered only "the principal of the Certificate which I held, as the ex[ecut]or of James Morrison,"[1] but wishes "the College would have paid in cash the reduced sum." Continues:]

My opinion is that the Whigs ought to be satisfied with the nomination of Genl. [Lewis] Cass.[2] His extreme opinions, in regard to the Foreign policy of the Country, His known irresolution and want of decision, when he is called upon to act, on his individual responsibility, and other circumstances in his career, render him the most vulnerable Candidate that our opponents, I think, could have presented.[3] Who will be the opposing Candidate will be settled by the [Whig National] Convention which is to assemble at Philada. tomorrow.[4] I entertain no expectation of receiving the nomination. In announcing to the public my consent to the submission of my name to the Convention, I yielded my personal desire for remaining in private life to a high sense of public duty. The motives which actuated me were truly presented—perhaps with too much frankness—in the note which I addressed to the public.[5] If I am permitted to continue in retirement, it will be precisely what best suits me. I must, however, own that I have, with painful regret, beheld so many Whigs willing to cast overboard so many of the cherished measures and principles for which we have been so long and so strenuously contending.

Whatever may be the issue of the contest, for which the two parties are now preparing, my prayers will be offered up that it may redound to the peace, prosperity and honor of our Country. . . .

ALS. CtY. 1. Clay to Fendall, June 16, 1847. 2. Clay to Ullmann, May 12, 1847. 3. During the campaign, Cass was criticized for taking advantage of Taylor's military victories in Mexico to advocate the seizure of Cuba and the establishment of a military protectorate in the Yucatan; for acting without instructions in attempting to prevent France from ratifying the Quintuple Treaty while he served as U.S. minister to that country; for opposing the Wilmot Proviso; and for supporting the doctrine of popular sovereignty to resolve the question of slavery in the territories. Woodford, *Lewis Cass*, 204-10, 248-58, 265. 4. Greeley to Clay, Nov. 15, 1846. 5. Clay to The Public, April 10, 1848.

From David Graham, New York City, June 9, 1848. Complains of the "mis-representatives of the Whig party" who just "consummated the greatest act of national injustice which it was in their power to perform." Believes the nomination of Zachary Taylor [Greeley to Clay, November 15, 1846], "who has rejected the principles and spurned the organization and discipline of the Whigs," falls "like a clap of thunder" on "the mass of the party." Although "an honorable retirement, accompanied with the heartfelt affection of the whole nation, must be more grateful than the turmoil and anxieties attendant upon office. . . . it cannot and will not be forgotten, that in your person the integrity and the hopes of the Whig party have been stricken down, and their existence as a party blasted and destroyed." Trusts that "the day is far distant, when a forgiveness will be extended to the base combination between the heartless rivals whom you have outstripped both in unexampled devotion to your country and in the favor of your countrymen, and the truckling harpies, who, like the followers of a camp, are bent upon plunder alone." As "a Whig, and a Clay Whig," begs Clay "to withhold any expression of approval of the action of this Convention." Urges Clay to let "those who have stabbed *you* and outraged *us*" elect Taylor " 'upon their own responsibility,' (to use his own words,). . . . But, by all that is just let no appeal to the generosity of your nature, to aid them, avail to disarm your friends of the power they possess and will surely exercise, to punish the corruption of those who have betrayed them [Harlan to Clay, June 2, 1848]." Apologizes for "taking a great, perhaps a unwarrantable liberty with you," but insists he offers "the sentiments of your hosts of friends in New York, who only find relief from the despondency which weighs them down, in the proud reflection that they have battled to the last, under your glorious and honored name." ALS. DLC-HC (DNA, M212, R6). Printed in Colton, *Clay Correspondence*, 4:562-63.

For David Graham (1808-52), a New York City alderman and lawyer noted for his oratory, see *DAB*.

From JOHN L. LAWRENCE Philadelphia, June 9, 1848

The results of the assemblage, I cannot say the deliberations, of the miscalled Whig [National] Convention, will no doubt have reached you prior to the receipt of this letter. The final vote for a candidate for the Presidency has just been taken, and has exhibited the total number of 171 for Genl. [Zachary] Taylor.[1] I have not the particulars of the two last canvasses, but I believe that as long as there was a hope, all that might judiciously have been calculated upon from the New York Delegation, was performed by them.[2] The unhappy complexion of the Kentucky delegation,[3] had a malign influence from the start, and was still more pernicious when, upon the very first vote, it was found to be *one* in number worse than all our fears had calculated. Ohio and Tennessee, from which so many assurances had been given, with a view to obtain your consent to submit your name to the Convention, gave us no support worth mentioning;[4] and other states failed us beyond our anticipations.

In the present temper of those most zealous for the character of the Whig party, and the preservation of Whig principles, it is difficult to say what will be the determination of themselves and those who have so long and so sincerely aided them in their honest political exertions, as to the measure of the Convention. The first impulse is to repudiate the acts of a body, which formed for the object of presenting a *Whig* candidate for the office of President of the United States, stifled, by ordering to be laid on the table, a proposition that no person should be selected, unless pledged, to abide by the decision of the Convention, to support its nomination, and to support the measures of the Whig party.[5] The treatment of such a resolution, in the manner it was disposed of by the Convention, is a virtual dissolution of the Whig party of the Union, by their chosen representatives, and absolves every honest man from being fettered by their decisions.

With a great majority of the honest and conservative population of the Country in its ranks, the party has always comprehended some of the most corrupt men to be found, so that whenever its action was sought to be perverted to unworthy purposes, instruments were always at hand, to do the dirty work. Thus its avowed principles & its honorable members have been overriden and its name and fame prostituted and debased.

I have not time amid the bustle, confusion &, I must add, the disappointment, which surround me to say more. Every true Whig will wish to hear your counsel as to the course proper to be taken in the singular State of things which exists, and personally I shall strive to prevent any movement until your wishes in the matter shall be communicated. My brother A.R.L,[6] who is with me here, desires me to accompany his best remembrances . . .

P.S. I have just received the paper from which I cut for your information the vote of each state on the several trials of number.[7]

ALS. DLC-HC (DNA, M212, R6). 1. On the 4th and final ballot, Taylor had 171 votes to 63 for Scott, 32 for Clay, and 13 for Webster. Schlesinger, *History of U.S. Political Parties*, 1:439. See also Greeley to Clay, Nov. 15, 1846. 2. Ullmann to Clay, Feb. 18, 1848. 3. Clay to Stevenson, April 12, 1848. 4. For Ohio's vote, see Ullmann to Clay, Feb. 18, 1848; for Tennessee, see Clay to Mercer, April 14, 1848. 5. Samuel Galloway of Ohio proposed such a resolution, but it was ruled out of order. A motion to suspend the order of the day so it could be taken up was defeated. Schlesinger, *History of U.S. Political Parties*, 1:441. 6. Abraham R. Lawrence. 7. Paper not found; but the vote of each delegate on each ballot appeared in the Washington *Daily National Intelligencer*, June 16, 1848.

From George C. Collins, Philadelphia, June 10, 1848. Writes with "a sorrowful heart and a trembling hand" to "communicate to you the [ne]ws of your inundation, upon the Altar of vile treachery [Greeley to Clay, November 15, 1846]." Blames Clay's defeat on the fact that "the very men who professed the greatest friendship formerly were recently your most insidious and implacable foes." Declared his "determinati[on] to be revenged" while still at the Whig National convention, asserting that "to avenge the treachery and have satisfaction upon the Traitors, I would if no better opportunity offered, vote for [Lewis] Cass and [William O.] Butler [Clay to Ullmann, May 12, 1847]." Assures Clay that "There are thousands, who will not act in any other manner, than to annihilate politically and for ever your base and cowardly assassins[.] Great God, what are we coming to—I feel disgraced that I ever was called a Whig. . . . A party no longer of principle, but of availability and expediency—A party who now denies the sincerity and admits the rottenness of their former professions." Names "Gen. [James] Irvin one of our Delegates and for whom I always entertained great respect" as one who "vilely betrayed you actuated no doubt by that envious and evil despised preceptor of mine—Josiah Randall." Adds: "on the Evening of the sacrifice . . . I took down a beautiful framed portrait of Irvin and dashed it into a thousand fragments, at the same time saying, thus let every traitor perish! he cannot at least have a place in my domicile. Randall will no longer speak to me." Believes that "This convention was packed, and every vote that was to be deposited was long since well arranged and systematically disposed of. A more conclusive bargain and sale was never effected. A more violent outrage upon the dignity of the Whig party never perpetrated." Remains convinced, however, that "your principles shall prove the best calculated to promote the happiness of our people. . . . and I cannot help still believing that you will yet be President." Castigates the "men who destroyed your brilliant prospects in '44 by catering to unprincipled and purchaseable *Nativism* [Ewing to Clay, June 23, 1844]," and who "have again been foremost in adopting *their* candidates. And let me here observe that those heartless wretches who voted for you in '44 all but overawed the Convention to sacrifice you in '48. Let me assure you, venerable patriot, that they were in thousands in the galleries of the Museum chering for old Zak . . . and in some instances their vile lips uttered hisses and imprecations at your time honor'd name." Adds: "The North American was professedly neutral but their perfidy they practiced was most foul—[Morton] McMichael & [Robert T.] Conrad in particular." Although "[John M.] Swift Henry White and the Struthers were true to the last," cites "John Lindsay for whom I voted as Delegate" as one who "betrayed us." Concludes: "Let me say dearest and most honored of men, that Gen. Taylor will be defeated, your enemies now boast that you will endorse him, and that your enemies will be respected by you." ALS. DLC-HC (DNA, M212, R6).

For Robert T. Conrad—lawyer, publisher of the Philadelphia *North American*, and later (1854-56) mayor of Philadelphia—see Holli, *Biographical Dictionary of American Mayors*.

From LESLIE COMBS Philadelphia, June 10, 1848

I doubt if there was one *true*—viz [William Garnett] Duncan friend in the Ky delegation in Congress & certainly but One—[James] Harlan—among those [sent] here—all rotten—So Harvey & [John M.] Botts & Russel[l] think—[1] With all this I think Several of them—only lacked *faith* in your Success not love & respect for you.

But Ohio played false from first to last—Their whole movement altho agt [Zachary] Taylor was *not* for you—[2] If their votes had gone for you on 1st ballot, the 2d or 3d would have nominated you—

Vermont—R. Island—Connecticut New York—Maryland & part of N.C. were Sincere—[3] & true as long as there was hope—We had a private meeting of your friends at the mayor's [John M. Swift] office every night—After the 1st 2 ballotings we hoped the [Winfield] Scott & [Daniel] Webster men would come over to you but they were obstinate & your friends nominated Taylor as you will see—

They would not take a true *ultra* Whig & a constitutional, conservative Slave holder—and they have gotten—an *Ultra* Slave holder & no particular Whig—Many of your friends have given me the kindest messages but it is useless to write what Millions feel—My own heart has been sorely bruised—more by the Vile ingratitude of the whigs than your defeat—for what is the presidency after its pollution by [John] Tyler & [James K.] Polk?—

The Committee took me out of a Sick bed to Independence Square last night. & made me say a few words which you will find in the next North American—[4] please read them—I never took So hard a pill—In 1840 it was bad enough—

of many persons who were true to the last, I will Speak when I see you—I now only name [Nathaniel] Blunt & [Thomas A.] Tomlinson of N.Y. [George S.] Bryan of Charleston—[John] Janney & Botts—of Va—[George R.] Graham of the N[orth]. A[merican].[5] [James C.] Jones of Ten[nessee]. [William C.] Bradley & [Solomon] Foote of Vermont—[James] Harlan & [Landaff W.] Andrews of Ky. [Charles T.] Russel[l] of Mass. [Walter] Brashear & [Dudley] Curle of Louisiana—& &c. Guerilleras—and Bedouin Arabs, looking out for plunder, were thick as Blackberries from every State—far & near—Parts of Several delegations met last night I was told & determined on a new move—to call a *Whig* convention to meet *North* early in August—[6]

I do not know how true this is but the *Nor*thern whigs are much excited—They deserve their fate—& especially does Ohio—

I Shall leave as soon as I can settle with Mr [Josiah] Randall—Say about tuesday or wednesday next & return by the lakes—

ALS. DLC-HC (DNA, M212, R6). Letter marked "Private." 1. Probably James E. Harvey, reporter for the Philadelphia *North American*, and Charles T. Russell, a Massachusetts Whig. For Russell, see Brauer, *Cotton versus Conscience*, 184, 213. 2. Ullmann to Clay, Feb. 18, 1848; Bebb to Clay, April 4, 1848. 3. For Rhode Island and North Carolina's votes at the Whig convention, see Greeley to Clay, April 28, 1848; for Connecticut, see Greeley to Clay, May 29, 1848; for New York, see Ullmann to Clay, Feb. 18, 1848; for Maryland, see Clay to Mercer, April 14, 1848. On the first three ballots Vermont gave Clay 5 votes and Taylor 1, and on the 4th ballot, Clay 2, Taylor 2, and Scott 2. Schlesinger, *History of U.S. Political Parties*, 1:436-39. 4. Combs's speech at the ratification meeting of the Whig National convention on June 9, 1848, praised Clay and detailed their long friendship. He then declared that Clay would rejoice if the Southern states would support Taylor and predicted that Taylor would soundly defeat Cass. Philadelphia *North American & United States Gazette*, June 12, 1848. 5. For George R. Graham (1813-94), editor, lawyer and publisher of the Philadelphia *North American*, first with

Judge Robert T. Conrad and later with Morton McMichael, see *DAB*. 6. Many disgruntled anti-Taylor "Conscience" Whigs took part in August in the formation of the Free Soil party. See Wendell to Clay, March 11, 1848.

From John Killion, Philadelphia, June 10, 1848. Informs Clay that his presidential aspirations "have been sacrificed basely perfidiously sacraficed . . . by men who professed to be your most ardent and sincere friends [Greeley to Clay, November 15, 1846]," whose "love was not for *you*, but for the offices they expected to be the recipient of." Believes that "your black hearted enemies not only sacraficed you but also sacrificed the great Whig party." Although Clay's supporters "were anxious and determin[ed] to make amends" for his defeat in the previous presidential election, "Corruption and vile Nativism [Ewing to Clay, June 23, 1844] deprived them of that chance as in 1844 when you were before defeated [Clay to Webb, February 29, 1844]." ALS. DLC-HC (DNA, M212, R6). Letter added to last page of Collins to Clay, June 10, 1848.

Killion was a deputy sheriff in Philadelphia. *McElroy's Philadelphia Directory for the Year 1845*.

From Edwin Bryant, New York City, June 11, 1848. Hopes Clay's good "judgement will not prompt you to take any personal action" concerning the nomination of Zachary Taylor [Greeley to Clay, November 15, 1846], "until you may hear from or converse with your known and *reliable* friends, who were present" at the Whig National convention, men such as "Judge [George] Robertson who . . . will I understand return to Kentucky immediately." Describes the "excitement and suppressed feeling here" after the convention, "notwithstanding the efforts of the *trading* politicians to allay it." Notes that the "*ratification* meeting called here on Friday night last would not accomplish its purposes. It was put down and was compelled to adjourn without adopting its resolutions. Another attempt . . . is to be made this week" and "will very probably meet with a similar fate [Hall to Clay, mid-to-late June, 1848]. Offers an opinion, which appears "to prevail among staunch and genuine Whigs," that "the Convention at Philadelphia, by nominating a candidate who is not *avowedly* a Whig has dishonored itself and betrayed the Whig party." ALS. DLC-HC (DNA, M212, R6).

For Edwin Bryant (1805-69), a Kentucky journalist who had traveled to California in 1846 and had written a book about his travels, see *CAB*.

From JOHN G. PROUD Baltimore, June 11, 1848

The die is cast, and we are again disappointed; I mean the Friends of their Country and Henry Clay, throughout the United States. I have returned heartsick from Phila. where I witnessed more heartlessness of pretence in an accumulated mass, than I hope to see again dispersed thro' the World. But Sir, it is me, not you, that have to lament it most, if not exclusively. You are now left to pass the residue of your life in peace & quiet, as I pray God you will and to prepare for that happy World where the righteous Man has his hope, & the Patriot his Reward.

I left Phila. as soon after the nomination[1] was over as I could get away, and there were thousands to sympathize with me—I shall not & I need not attempt to describe my feelings & those of your Friends generally. Many of them declared they would go home & do all they could to prevent the Nominees Election. So I thought at first, but as it is only a choics [*sic*, choice] of Evils we must take time to consider which is the best. A Man without political principles, by his own shewing, & without fitness on the one side, and a Man of *bad* principles on the other, presents indeed a poor choice.

What if the "Barnburners" were to give us at their Convention on the 22d. Martin Van Buren,[2] has he not Whig principle enough to justify good Clay Whigs in giving him a preference to Gen. [Zachary] Taylor, who says he is not fit for the office of President, & moreover would not be the Expositer of Whig principles?

As I have intimated some doubts as to the sincerity of the Hon'ble Mr. [Daniel] Jenifers political regard & preference for you, I take great pleasure in doing that Gentleman the justice to say that his course in the [Whig] National Convention was firm and consistent. He did not go to the support of Gen. Taylors nomination till all hope of yours was gone; & then with your most fast friends & with reluctance, I believe, yielded to instruction. [John C.] Groome, [William E.] Coale, [George] Schley, [Lloyd] Tilghman, with Colo. Jenifer[3] remained firm & exerted themselves manfully, till all hope of the Union of [Winfield] Scotts & [Daniel] Webster's Friends with yours was gone, & they then were obliged to yield.

When you have leisure I should feel honor'd & favor'd if you were to write to me. I pray God to preserve you in health & happiness many years; your advice & Counsel may in some good degree take the place of & lengthen out your eminent active Services to an ungrateful Country.

ALS. DLC-HC (DNA, M212, R6). 1. Greeley to Clay, Nov. 15, 1846. 2. Wendell to Clay, March 11, 1848. 3. All were Maryland delegates to the Whig National convention. Philadelphia *North American & United States Gazette*, June 7, 1848.

From Thomas B. Stevenson, Cincinnati, June 12, 1848. Does not regret that "circumstances of my family [Stevenson to Clay, May 18, 1848]" kept him from the Whig National convention [Greeley to Clay, November 15, 1846], because "I cannot contemplate the result with composure how then could I have witnessed, much less aided, its consummation?" Refuses to display "mawkish sensibilities" or "be guilty of the weakness of sympathising or condoling with you. I should rather expect you to console me. I know you must feel self-poised and self-satisfied. You have played your part as a Whig, a man of principle, and a patriot; and if injustice has been done to you, or the country, that is the fault or the crime of others." Adds: "To have *deserved*, what has been *denied*, is a truer gratification to a great mind, than the mere success of attainment, however just the claim, however honorable the aspiration for it."

On Taylor's nomination, "I made some remarks on the thing, which I thought called for. . . . Having advocated a National Convention, I felt bound, as a man of honor, to submit to its award, if Taylor submitted himself to the decision and was presented upon reliable assurance of his Whiggery—but not otherwise." Notes that Col. [Albert G.] Hodges was not satisfied: "my submission was to be unconditional." Announces, therefore, that "to protect my pride of personal feeling, and to preserve my consistency and independence, I withdrew from the Atlas, which is announced in a valedictory address this morning." Asserts that "The tendency of other causes, independent of the one above named, would probably have produced the same result," since "Hodges has been quarreling with me for months, on account of my opposition to Taylorism." Willingly concedes all prospects of "acquiring influence and consideration. . . . rather than allow my pride or my independence to be encroached upon. I have lost a year and a half and I know not how much money, certainly not less than a thousand dollars, in endeavoring to do right as an editor here. I go out, utterly beggared in purse; but rich in a proud spirit and an honest heart." Acts not from "any childish petulance or unmanly sense of disappointed hope," and "never was better satisfied with myself for any act of my life, than my retirement, under the circumstances, from the Atlas." May turn up next at Frankfort, "the seat of much vicious and mischievous political mousing."

Hopes that "as your glorious career commenced by efforts towards emancipating slavery in Ky. its close may be rendered still more glorious by your aid, in the Convention next year, for the consummation of that wise policy. . . . for the good and glory of Kentucky and the country, and your own fame. I could wish also, that the sage of Ashland should distinctly, (now that no electioneering motive can be ascribed) denounce the scheme of debauching this great republic into a propagandist of slavery, by extending the curse of it into free territory." ALS. DLC-HC (DNA, M212, R6).

Stevenson had worked for 18 months as editor of the Cincinnati *Atlas*, a job next assumed by William L. Callender. Washington *Daily National Intelligencer*, June 19, 1848.

Kentucky held a constitutional convention in 1849 which drafted the state's third constitution without taking any action regarding emancipation of slaves. For the convention, see Clark, *History of Kentucky*, 300-306. For Clay's position relative to the issue of slavery in the convention, see Clay to Pindell, February 17, 1849, no. 2 of date.

To JOHN SLOANE Lexington, June 13, 1848

Among the most powerful considerations which induced me to consent to the submission of my name to the recent Whig [National] Convention at Philada.[1] was that derived from the assurance, again and again made, in every form and from the highest sources, in Ohio, that I would receive the vote of a majority of the delegates, and subsequently, if nominated, the vote of the State. But for that conviction—if I had anticipated that I would in fact receive but the vote of one delegate from Ohio,[2] I never would have yielded that consent. I was informed indeed that some eight or ten of the delegates had been chosen under express instructions to vote for me; and that all who had been appointed to support Mr. [Thomas] Corwin would, if his name was withdrawn as was expected, vote for me.

Now, my dear Sir, having always regarded you not only as a true friend, but as one of the most patriotic and enlightened representatives that I ever served with, I wish to address a friendly enquiry to you, as a matter now of historical curiosity, and not of any practical use. What were the causes which induced the Ohio delegation, with one exception, to vote against me? And especially, if any of them were really instructed to vote for me, why they voted otherwise? If there be the least delicacy or difficulty with you in telling me, I request you not to do so; for, I repeat, it is only to gratify a curiosity, which perhaps I ought not to indulge. Except to yourself or Genl. [Joseph] Vance I would not venture to make this application to any other delegate; and I have not addressed him.

How will you get along in Ohio with the nominations? All my previous information had taught me to believe that Genl [Zachary] Taylor was decidedly unacceptable to the Whigs of your State.[3]

None of the Kentucky delegates have yet returned, and I have only seen the two first ballotings of the Convention.[4]

I am afraid that we are destined to remain a long time yet under Locofoco rule; for that party will make all or any concession to the South, on the subject of the extension of Slavery to newly acquired free terri[t]ory, to secur[e] the ascendancy in National Councils.[5]

ALS. MH. Letter marked "(Private)." 1. Clay to The Public, April 10, 1848. 2. Ullmann to Clay, Feb. 18, 1848. 3. Bebb to Clay, April 4, 1848. 4. Clay to Stevenson, April 12, 1848. 5. For Sloane's reply, see Sloane to Clay, June 22, 1848.

To CHRISTOPHER HUGHES Lexington, June 14, 1848

I received your letter addressed to me from Philadelphia, transmitting one from Miss Young, to which, as it related to business, and was from a lady and a *Young* lady, I immediately replied.[1]

I was inexpressibly grieved, my dear Mr. Hughes, in perusing your account of your two maladies.[2] I hope your fortitude will be equal to the occasion of your bearing them with composure and philosophy. You have an inestimable resource in your excellent daughter [Margaret Hughes] who will, I have no doubt, contribute to prolong your days, as for her sake, and for the sake of all your friends, you should do all in your power to encrease their length. There is another resource, lying beyond their termination, to which is it not time that you should be seeking to avail yourself?

I also received your letter, communicating how you were tricked out of an appointment of delegate to the [Whig] N[ationl]. Convention at Philada. Other letters which I received corroborated your's.[3] I regretted it very much on my account as well as your own.

The nominations made by that body on friday last, were received here on the same day.[4] They leave to me no other alternative but quiet submission. To say that I was greatly disappointed as to the course of some States, but as to none so much as that of Ohio, would be merely to express an unavailing feeling. As to Ohio I had the strongest and most numerous assurances, in every form, and from the highest sources, including the Governor [William Bebb], Senator [Thomas Corwin] &c, that Ohio would support me, and could not possibly be induced ever to go for Genl. [Zachary] Taylor.[5] Many of the delegates were appointed under express instructions to vote for me. Yet I got but one vote out of the twenty three! If I had been candidly dealt with, and had foreseen such a course of that delegation, I never would have consented to my name being submitted to the Convention.

But the work is done and over. It relieves me from great suspense and anxiety, during the canvass, if I had been nominated, and from fearful and painful responsibility if I had been elected. For myself I ought to feel no regrets, and I believe that there are not many men who can bear the event with more calmness and resignation than I do. Whatever wishes I had, in relation to the office, respected my Country, and my friends far more than myself.

I wish that we were nearer each other, but I fear that your afflictions will not allow you to come to me, and I, who am not without my share of bodily complaints, do not know that I shall ever again pass the mountains. But whether we are near or far distant from each other, I need not assure you that I shall ever feel the liveliest interest in and the deepest solicitude for your health & happiness, and that of dear Margaret . . .

ALS. MiU-C. 1. Hughes and Young letters not found. Miss Young not identified. 2. Hughes had complained of rheumatic gout and dropsy in his letter to Clay of Sept. 14, 1847. 3. Letters not found, but see Clay to Hughes, May 8, 1848. 4. Greeley to Clay,

Nov. 15, 1846. 5. Bebb to Clay, April 4, 1848. Corwin letter not found, but he is identified as the Ohio senator in Clay to Bayard, June 19, 1848. For Ohio's vote at the Whig National convention, see Ullmann to Clay, Feb. 18, 1848.

To THOMAS B. STEVENSON Lexington, June 14, 1848

I hasten to express my deep regret with all the contents of your favor of the 12th which relate to yourself. I had previously seen the announciation of your retirement from the Atlas, but I was uninformed of the causes. These inspire me, if possible, with more respect than ever for your independence, the purity of your principles and your character.

Are you right in thinking of returning from Cincinnati to Frankfort? In that great and growing City what may you not do; in the latter what can you? You have abilities for eminent success at the Bar; why not turn your attention to it.

Wherever you may be, or whatever you may do, you have my best wishes, and an anxious desire to serve you in any way in my power.

The less said the better about the result of the late Whig [National] Convention at Philadelphia.[1] I believe that I can bear it with less regret than my warm hearted friends. Whatever I do feel is principally on their account, and on account of the principles which were in issue, and which have been so little regarded. I have not lost one hours sleep, nor one meal of victuals. Accustomed as I have been to disappointments, and to afflictions, they disturb now, less than ever, my composure. I hope that I derive some support from a resignation to the will of the great Disposer of all events.

There is one topic connected with the late Convention in regard to which I feel a little curiosity, and that is the unexpected course of the Ohio delegation.[2] Among the considerations which determined [me] to consent to submit my name to the Convention,[3] one of the most powerful arose from assurances which I received, in every form, and from the highest sources, (The Governor [William Bebb] amongst them) that I would receive the support of Ohio.[4] Clay and [Thomas] Corwin, and Corwin and Clay, were said to be identical, and all the delegates chosen for the one or the other, making together a large majority, were to go for me, if he were to decline, as he did. Can you tell me, my dear Sir, after all their strong assurance, how it was that I got but one vote in the delegation? I was told too that Ohio could not properly go for General [Zachary] Taylor. And yet those, who probably had it in their power to secure the nomination of a Candidate whom they could carry their state for, suffered one to be nominated, for whom, agreeably to the representations made to me, there is no probability of Ohio going[.][5]

My curiosity on this subject is rather of the historical kind; for I have no complaints or reproaches to make. My only regret is that I should have been led into error. Most certainly, if I had anticipated such a vote as has been actually given by the Ohio delegation, I never would have consented that my name should be presented to the Convention.

I observe what you say as to objects which shall engage the attention of my future life. I shall give to those subjects full consideration, with an anxious wish that the remnant of my days m[a]y be so employed as to justify the confidence and friendship with which I have been so greatly and so long honored.

Copy. OCHP. Printed in Colton, *Clay Correspondence*, 3:463. 1. Greeley to Clay, Nov. 15, 1846. 2. Ullmann to Clay, Feb. 18, 1848. 3. Clay to The Public, April 10, 1848. 4. Bebb to Clay, April 4, 1848. 5. For Ohio's vote in the presidential election, see *ibid.*

To HORACE GREELEY Lexington, June 15, 1848

Before the receipt of your obliging letter of the 29h. Ulto. I was prepared to expect the event which has since happened at Philada.[1] Your letter[2] conduced to strengthen my anticipations of it. The intelligence of the nomination of Genl. [Zachary] Taylor reached me the same day it was made—

I lost the nomination from three causes 1st. the course of the Kentucky delegation.[3] 2 My very great disappointment in not obtaining, as I had every reason to suppose I should, the support of the Ohio delegation.[4] And 3dly. the persevering adherence of the Massachusetts delegation to Mr. [Daniel] Webster.[5] How such delegates came to be appointed from K. you doubtless have heard from some of our K. friends at Philada. Never was I more surprized at any occurrence of the kind than I was by the unexpected course of the Ohio delegation. I had received the strongest assurances from the most eminent men in the State, in various forms, that the support of that State would be given to me, and that it would not go for Genl. Taylor, *if nominated.* I was entreated by the Governor [William Bebb] and by several delegates to the Convention, and by various other eminent persons in Ohio,[6] not to decline the use of my name, before I addressed my note to the public.[7] I was informed that some eight or ten of the delegates were chosen expressly to sustain my nomination; and that all, who were appointed to support Mr. [Thomas] Corwin, would go for me, upon his declining. Such was the influence upon my mind of these assurances and this information that they constituted a leading motive with me in allowing my name to go before the Convention. And, if I had foreseen that Ohio would have pursued the course which she did in the Convention, I never would have consented that my name should have been presented to that body.

I dwell on this subject of Ohio not in any complaining or repining spirit, but because it is the only important fact, stated in my note to the public, which has not been subsequently sustained.

But, if I have had great cause of surprize, in respect to that State, I have abundant reason for eternal gratitude to the City and State of New York, and to my numerous faithful ardent and enlightened friends in them, for their zealous and constant support of me.[8] And to none more than to yourself for the ability, activity, energy and efficiency which you have displayed throughout the arduous struggle.

The work is done, and I have no alternative but quiet submission. I am relieved from painful suspense, and great anxiety, during the Canvass, if I had been nominated, and from fearful responsibility, if I had been elected. I ought not to regret the event, on my own account personally, and I believe there are but few men who can bear it so well. On account of my friends indeed I could have wished that it had been otherwise. I deeply regret that I have no way of testifying my great obligations to them; but I hope they will be assured that I shall ever hold them in grateful remembrance.

The nomination of Genl. T. as far as I have yet heard in K. has occasioned much disappointment and has been coldly received. The papers will tell you, perhaps, otherwise, but they greatly exaggerate. That of Mr. [Millard] Fillmore gives entire satisfaction.[9]

As for myself I shall take no active part in regard to the nomination. Of course I can never support Genl. [Lewis] Cass. The case of Genl. T. is not like that of Genl. [William Henry] Harrison. The former, is purely a military man, without any experience whatever in Civil affairs. The latter was far more distinguished as a Civilian than as a Military commander. Genl. T. is no whig, or, if he be one, a sort of non-descript Whig, a Whig in name, without the principles of the Whigs.[10] Genl. H. was an open and avowed Whig in principle, as well as in name.

I presume my residence in a Slave State lost me the nomination. And yet those who could have secured it, have allowed one to be nominated who is far more deeply imbued with the doctrines of Slavery than ever I was or shall be. Their course resembles that of the Abolitionists in 1844.[11] They complain that they have not got a thorough-going Whig, and when they had the power to select a thorough-going Whig they would not exercise it!

But I must close, with fervent prayers that you may long live, in health & happiness, and in the enjoyment of every blessing.

ALS. Courtesy of Henry Clay Moses, Bronxville, N.Y. Letter marked "(Private)." Printed in New York *Times*, May 3, 1860, reprinted from the Albany *Statesman*. 1. Greeley to Clay, Nov. 15, 1846. 2. Greeley to Clay, May 29, 1848. 3. Clay to Stevenson, April 12, 1848. 4. Ullmann to Clay, Feb. 18, 1848. 5. Greeley to Clay, April 28, 1848. 6. See, for example, Bebb to Clay, April 4, 1848; Forrer to Clay, April 7, 1848. 7. Clay to The Public, April 10, 1848. 8. Ullmann to Clay, Feb. 18, 1848. 9. The Kentucky newspapers reacted favorably to the Taylor/Fillmore ticket. See, for example, Lexington *Observer & Kentucky Reporter*, June 14, 21, 24, 1848; Frankfort *Commonwealth*, June 13, 27, 1848. 10. On Taylor's no-party stance, see Clay to Ullmann, August 4, 1847; Taylor to Clay, April 30, 1848. 11. Clay to Clayton, Dec. 2, 1844.

From JAMES HARLAN Chiles', June 15, 1848

I have just arrived in the Maysville Stage on my way home. I regret I have not time to call and give you an account of the doings of the Philada. Convention.[1] I parted with [John M.] Botts 10 Oclock Saturday night at Balto. His last words to me were "Say to Mr Clay to Stand Still and Say nothing about the nomination until he hears all that has transpired"—Your friends in the East, South & every where who witnessed the proceedings are deeply excited. Whether Genl [Zachary] Taylor can be elected will depend upon circumstances Yet to transpire in New England, New York & Ohio—[2] If Kentucky had been true you would have received the nomination. Every body, Taylor men and all in and out of the Convention were astounded when Kentucky Voted.[3] But I have not time to go into details. The nomination has been coldly received all along the route from Philada. to Maysville.

I wrote to you the triggers were all Set at Washington before the Convention met and it was impossible to counteract the movements made by Members of Congress.[4]

ALS. DLC-HC (DNA, M212, R6). 1. Greeley to Clay, Nov. 15, 1846. 2. In the 1848 presidential election, Whig Zachary Taylor received 1,360,101 popular votes and 163 electoral votes to 1,220,544 popular and 127 electoral votes for Democrat Lewis Cass and 291,263 popular votes for Free Soil candidate Martin Van Buren. Taylor carried Connecticut, Delaware, Florida, Georgia, Kentucky, Louisiana, Maryland, Massachusetts, New Jersey, New York, North Carolina, Pennsylvania, Rhode Island, Tennessee, and Vermont. Cass carried Alabama, Arkansas, Illinois, Indiana, Iowa, Maine, Michigan, Mississippi, Missouri, New Hampshire, Ohio, Texas,

Virginia, and Wisconsin. McKee, *National . . . Popular and Electoral Vote*, 71-72. 3. Clay to Stevenson, April 12, 1848. 4. Clay to Harvey, April 18, 1848.

From Willis Hall, New York City, mid-to-late June, 1848. After Clay failed to receive the nomination of the Whig party [Greeley to Clay, November 15, 1846], writes "not to condole with you. . . . The Presidency could have added nothing to *your fame* and would have detracted much from your comfort." Describes the government's "sixty years during nearly forty of which it has been guided by your counsels" as a "Glorious period! You may justly regard it with exultation!" Praises him for promoting the "prominency of popular govt." and for impressing "upon the country that high & honorable spirit in our intercourse with foreign nations that spirit of conciliation & union among the States which have preserved us at home & made us respected abroad." Cites "Three times at least" when "the car of state would have taken the wrong road, if not the road to destruction, but for your guiding hand. Once in 1810-12, once in 1819-20, once in 1830-31." Assures Clay that "As the scroll of our history unrolls itself, your time will stand out in bolder & bolder relief until it becomes the golden age of some future people. perhaps as unlike the present as the miserable herd that now defiles the streets of home are unlike the associates of the elder Brutus."

Now "on the eve of great events," views slavery as "an immediate & bitter subject of dispute & [it] will not be relinquished until it is extinguished or the Union dissolved." Believes "the slave region. . . . have brought it upon themselves" by thrusting "slavery upon us in the most offensive way. . . . The means they have taken to render themselves as they fancied more secure on this subject has precipitated the discussion accompanied with an acrimony which will not tend to a friendly adjustment." Predicts Whigs "in this quarter" will join the "barn burners ready to make the slave question the great issue in future [Clay to Giddings, October 6, 1847; Greeley to Clay, November 30, 1847]." Adds that at the next presidential election "a barn burner will be elected."

Declares "The Whig party as such is dead—The very name will be abandoned should [Zachary] Taylor be elected, for 'the Taylor party.' The last Whig convention committed the double crime of *suicide* & homcide." Reports that the ratification meeting in New York City was postponed "indefinitely, in hopes that Gen's T's letter of acceptance will place himself more distinctly upon whig ground. They will wait in vain." ALS. DLC-HC (DNA, M212, R6). Printed in Colton, *Clay Correspondence*, 4:563-65.

The Whig General Committee met on June 9 without adopting any ratification resolutions. The committee then called a city ratification meeting for June 12. This meeting was postponed for a day and then postponed again. Finally, it was held on June 27 with Philip Hone acting as president. The meeting adopted 10 resolutions, including one accepting the nominations made by the Whig National convention. New-York *Daily Tribune*, June 10, 13, 28, 1848.

Taylor's acceptance of the Whig nomination, dated July 15, 1848, made no policy statements. The long delay between Taylor's nomination and his formal acceptance resulted when the Whig National convention's official notification went to the dead letter office because postage was due on it. Washington *Daily National Intelligencer*, July 31, 1848.

To DAVID GRAHAM Lexington, June 16, 1848

I have received your friendly letter of the 9h. so full of expressions and sentiments alike honorable to head & heart. I was prepared to expect the result of the deliberations of the Whig [National] Convention in Philada.[1] and it therefore did not take me by surprize; but I did not foresee exactly how it was to be brought about, and I have been greatly surprized at some of the incidents of the drama. I have been most astonished at the course of the Ohio delegation,[2] upon a large majority of which I had every reason to count.

But it is useless to dwell on the painful subject. Personally, I am greatly relieved. I ought to have no regrets for myself; but I do feel deeply the disappointment of my friends. I lament that I have no way of testifying my gratitude to yourself and other friends but by cherishing a fond remembrance of their devotion and fidelity. To my New York friends especially, City and Country, I am under the greatest obligations of eternal gratitude.[3] An eye witness of the proceedings of the convention, in a letter before me, says: "New York, to whom the V. Presidency, and all sorts of other lures were held out, rejected all temptation, and immortalized herself by her persevering devotion to the Whig cause and to Clay."[4]

There is no alternative for me but that of quiet submission to the decision of the Convention, *so far as respects myself.* Beyond that I feel under no obligation of duty to go. I cannot be bound to support one [Zachary Taylor], who, in a reversal of circumstances, would have felt not only not bound to support me, but who was resolved to oppose me. I cannot be bound to support a nomination of one who, claiming to be a Whig in name, repudiates the principles of the Whigs.[5]

But I shall take no precipitate step. I shall endeavor fully to inform myself of all the proceedings of the Convention. And if finally there should be no other alternative, and I am reduced to the dilemma of choosing between [Lewis] Cass and Taylor, I shall make that choice which I believe to be pregnant with least evil to my Country. . . . [6]

ALS. RPB. Letter marked "(Private & Confidential)." 1. Greeley to Clay, Nov. 15, 1846. 2. Ullmann to Clay, Feb. 18, 1848. 3. *Ibid.* 4. Not found. 5. Clay to Ullmann, August 4, 1847; Taylor to Clay, April 30, 1848. 6. Harlan to Clay, June 2, 1848.

To JOHN L. LAWRENCE — Lexington, June 16, 1848

I received your friendly letter from Philada. The result of the action of the Whig [National] Convention did not take me altogether by surprize,[1] although I was greatly surprized at some of the incidents attending it[.] I was quite astonished indeed at the course of the Ohio delegation,[2] on a majority of which I had the strongest reasons confidently to count.

It is both my inclination, and perhaps my duty, quietly to submit to the decision of the Convention, *so far as I am personally concerned.* Beyond that I feel under no obligation to go. If I had been nominated, Genl. [Zachary] Taylor has declared that he would not withdraw his name, and consequently would have opposed me.[3] Am I more bound to support him than he would have been me, in a reversal of situations? I know the humbuggery that the Louisiana delegation got up; but they shewed no credentials, no instructions from the General, and I observe that their statement is already denied by his Maryland friends.[4]

Genl. Taylor professes to be a Whig in name, but disclaims all obligation to carry out Whig principles and measures.[5] In that respect his case differs entirely from that of Genl [William Henry] Harrison. And there is another wide difference between them: Genl. Harrison was a Civilian of much experience, as well as a Soldier. Genl. Taylor, at an advanced age, is totally destitute of all experience whatever in Civil affairs.

I can offer at present no advice to my friends. I shall act with great deliberation. I desire all the information I can get about the Convention, its secret movements and springs. In no event, will I take any active part in the canvass. If finally there be no other alternative, and we are reduced to the dilemma of deciding between Taylor and [Lewis] Cass, I shall be induced to make that choice which shall appear to me to be the least pregnant with evil to our Country & our cause.[6]

I ought to rejoice in being relieved from all solicitude, during the canvass, if I had been nominated, and from all responsibility, in the administration, if I had been elected. Whatever regrets I do feel are chiefly for my friends, for our cause, greatly jeoparded if not destroyed by what has happened, and for our Country.

How, my dear friend, shall I ever acquit myself of the very great obligations which I am under to you and other friends? That *does* distress me inexpressibly. I can only cherish, in silence and retirement, sentiments of eternal gratitude. I can only wish and pray that you and all of them may long live, in health and happiness, and enjoy every earthly blessing here, and every blessing in heaven hereafter. Present me affectionately to your brother [Abraham R. Lawrence]. [Charles S.] Morehead writes me from Washington: "I became acquainted with the two Lawrences of New York, and I believe I never saw two men suffer more than they did."[7]

ALS. ViU. Letter marked "(Private)." Addressed to Lawrence at New York City. 1. Lawrence to Clay, June 9, 1848. For the 1848 Whig convention, see Greeley to Clay, Nov. 15, 1846. 2. Ullmann to Clay, Feb. 18, 1848. 3. Taylor to Clay, April 30, 1848. 4. Lafayette Saunders read a statement to the Whig National convention, prepared by the Louisiana delegation, which claimed that they had been authorized by Taylor to withdraw him from the canvass if he did not receive the nomination. A report circulated after the convention that Taylor repudiated the statement, but his friends published a card asserting that he had approved it. Indeed, Taylor himself wrote a letter to a Baltimore newspaper asserting that if he were not chosen, his friends were bound to sustain and support the nominee. Schlesinger, *History of U.S. Political Parties*, 1:435; Hamilton, *Zachary Taylor, Soldier in the White House*, 92, 102-3. 5. Clay to Ullmann, August 4, 1847; Taylor to Clay, April 30, 1848. 6. Harlan to Clay, June 2, 1848. 7. Morehead's letter not found; John L. and Abraham R. Lawrence.

From Edmund Pendleton, Cincinnati, June 16, 1848. Writes as "a young Whig" who was "taught from my infancy to reverence your name." Expresses his shock at recent events: "I have seen a Statesman grow gray in the service of his Country, the acknowledged founder and builder of the Great Whig Party of the present day, a man, who fed his ardent patriotism, his tried talents, and his known devotion to principles believed by a large majority of the people of this country to constitute the principles of action of this Government, *wounded in the house of his friends*." Complains that Clay's "well earned laurels" have been "transferred to the brow of another [Zachary Taylor] . . . about whose political character and qualifications for the highest office in the Government, a singular ignorance prevails. I have seen a monument erected to Republican ingratitude." Longs for Clay's election to the presidency "as the panting hart for the water-brook." Although other statesmen "have commanded my respect and admiration," feels "invigorated and warmed by something like a personal attachment, which, stranger as I am to you, I have always felt for *you*." Adds: "I feel now as if the domestic hearth of the Whig Party had been violated by the rude hand of the destroyer, and as if a stranger occupied the familiar parental seat."

Although "In all human probability, your honored head will be reposing beneath some splendid monument erected in commemoration of your services on earth, before the . . . abandonment of the glorious banner of the whig party," regrets that probably "I shall be permitted to see the result." Worries that "the clouds are dark and portentous." Will support the Whig ticket, but hopes there will be "another opportunity of vindicating your name and showing a proper appreciation of your illustrious deeds." Apologizes for "this intrusion upon your peaceful retirement. . . . to tell you that thousands of hearts bleed for the ingratitude of their countrymen." ALS. DLC-HC (DNA, M212, R6).

Edmund Pendleton (1823-99), a Virginia native, moved to Cincinnati in 1845 and practiced law for thirteen years. He then moved to New Orleans, became colonel of the 15th Louisiana Infantry in the Confederate Army, returned to Virginia after the Civil War, and in 1869 was elected to the Virginia state senate. *The Old Dominion, A Monthly Magazine of Literature, Science and Art* (March, 1870), 4:170-71; Toby Drews, *Genealogies of Virginia Families From the Virginia Magazine of History and Biography* (Baltimore, 1981), 4:741. A comparison of handwriting has been done by E. Lee Shephard, archivist at the Virginia Historical Society, to ascertain which of the many Edmund Pendletons was the author of this letter.

To MARY S. BAYARD Lexington, June 19, 1848

I received, my ever true and dear friend, your kind letter of the 9h. instant. How good, how considerate, how faithful to the sentiments of esteem and attachment with which you have honored me, have you always proved yourself to be! Other friends come to me, in periods of prosperity; but you have never deserted me, and your kindness especially prompts you to soothe and succor me in moments of supposed or real adversity. If the number of friends like you were greater, how much more cheerily should we move along in the path of life.

I was prepared for the event, which you deplore, of the failure of the Whig [National] Convention to nominate me for the Presidency,[1] and it therefore did not take me by surprize, but I was surprized and shocked by the course of some of the delegations to it. Most of all was I disappointed in that of the Ohio delegation.[2] I had every assurance, in every form; from the most prominent men in that State (including the Governor [William Bebb],[3] Senator [Thomas] Corwin[4] &c &c) that I would receive its support. If I had not fully believed in that fact, I would never have consented to the submission of my name to the Convention. With regard to Kentucky, I was aware of the exceptionable means which had been employed to appoint the [Zachary] Taylor delegates, and although mortified I was not much surprized.[5] But it is useless to dwell on details. The work is done, and there is no alternative left to me, but that of quiet submission to it, so far as I was personally concerned.

I ought to rejoice in the event, and I should rejoice in it but for the sake of my true and ardent friends, our cause and our Country. I do deeply feel that I have no way left to testify my sense of the great obligations under which my friends have placed me but by cherishing towards them the fondest remembrance and sentiments of profound gratitude[.]

You tell me that your heart is filled with rebellion. Witnessing as you did, or as you heard, the intrigues, and the improper means by which the result was brought about, your indignation is natural. I must say however that it is fortunate for the peace of the Union that you are not of our sex. There might otherwise be danger of a Civil War.

You will excuse this badanage. Your friend will bear the event with the fortitude, the composure and the philosophy required by the good opinion which you do him the honor to entertain.

I am relieved from a vast deal of anxiety and painful suspense, during the canvass, if I had been nominated, and from an immense responsibility, if I had been elected. In all the vicissitudes of life, it has pleased God to throw in many compensations.

Among these, one great one is that I shall have more leisure to dedicate my self to Him, to my religious duties, and to the proper preparation for another and a better world.

I shall have more leisure also for intercourse with my friends, as you so justly remark. It is deeply regretted by me that some of them are so remote from me. How happy should I be, if I were always able to count, in their circle; you, Mr. [Richard H.] Bayard, your family and dear Caroline [Bayard]!

You inquire my plans for the summer. I have formed none; and yet I would be willing to go almost any where, except to the Cities, to meet you. I am distressed to hear that your health has not been good. I hope that you will neglect no means to re-establish and preserve it. You should not yield to any feelings of despondency from any cause. If all things do not go as you wish, reflect how many blessings attend you—a faithful and affectionate husband—children most devoted to you—the love and the admiration of the whole world. Ah! how happy should I be if I could be often near you to drive away your sorrows, and to augment your joys, if my presence would at all contribute to those objects.

I have been pressed by the Governor [William Owsley] and other friends to return to the Senate of the U. States,[6] but after the final & formal leave which I took of that body in 1842,[7] I have not allowed myself to think of returning to it. There is but one consideration which recommends the step to me, and that is that I should again see friends that I may never more meet; but my purpose is to decline it.

I pray you to present my kindest regards to Mr. Bayard, to all your children, to Mr. [Baring] Powell, and to dear Caroline.[8]

P.S. I transmitted a letter of introduction to you for Mrs. [Octavia Walton] Levert, and I hope you made the acquaintance of that talented but remarkable lady.

ALS. Anonymous owner; copy in KyU. 1. Greeley to Clay, Nov. 15, 1846. 2. Ullmann to Clay, Feb. 18, 1848. 3. Bebb to Clay, April 4, 1848. 4. Corwin letter not found. 5. Possibly a reference to letters read at the 1848 Kentucky Whig convention claiming that Clay would announce he was not a presidential candidate upon his return from the East. More likely, it refers to the fact that the Kentucky convention chose two delegates-at-large to the national convention, directing the county delegations of the respective districts to choose other delegates. Taylor supporters were able to dominate the choice of district delegates. Poage, *Henry Clay*, 172-73. 6. Owsley to Clay, June 20, 1848; Clay to Owsley, June 22, 1848. 7. See 9:691-92. 8. The Bayards' daughter Caroline had married Baring Powell in 1847. Richard Henry Bayard also had an unmarried sister named Ann Caroline; thus, it is not always possible to determine positively to which of the Carolines Clay is referring. Information on the Bayard family supplied by the Delaware Historical Society.

From Thomas B. Stevenson, Cincinnati, June 19, 1848. Has decided to remain in Cincinnati because he believes "here, rather than Kentucky, is my true theatre." Reports that "[Albert G.] Hodges has proposed to sell me the entire [Cincinnati *Daily*] Atlas establishment, on liberal terms," but that he may have to forego this opportunity for lack of an associate for the business department. Notes also that "Overtures are also made me by the proprietors of the [Cincinnati] Chronicle to take charge of that paper, even intimating the dismissal of [Edward] Mansfield, (the present editor) to give me more influence." So deeply loathes "the demoralized condition of the Whig party, in its present posture," however, "that nothing but my extremely unpleasant pecuniary circumstances, without a dollar in my purse, could reconcile me for a moment to the idea of editing a paper during this campaign." With a wife and six daughters "solely dependent on my personal exertions for their daily bread," and since relations with "all or nearly all of my former Kentucky friends, that once I would have applied to in time of need . . . soured at my opposition to [Zachary] Taylor's nomination," feels he must consider the editorships because "I should starve to death here, long before I could get into profitable practice at the Bar."

Expresses pride in Clay's "lofty, self-poised position" on the results of the Whig National convention [Greeley to Clay, November 15, 1846]. Regrets the disregard of principles "in the search for that new fangled thing which, in the brainless cant of the day, is flippantly termed '*availability*.' " Fears the Whigs "will not soon, if ever, recover from the evil influences of the monstrous, demoralizing precedent it has set, of preferring for the highest civil office in the government, a warrior of veiled principles and untried qualifications, to a statesman of honour and approved principles and tried and admitted qualifications!"

Feels "with poignant humiliation, the force of your 'historic curiosity,' in regard to the course of the Ohio delegates," but believes "They have surprised their constituents . . . as much as you or me [Ullmann to Clay, February 18, 1848]," and "they will have trouble about it yet. . . . they do not stand relieved from the imputation of wanting sagacity or integrity, and they certainly had too much intelligence to be deficient in the former quality." Reports [John A.] McClung's "*conjecture*—that they thought there was an anti-Taylor majority in the Convention" and hoped it might be concentrated on Winfield Scott. Also has learned that "the [Daniel] Webster men . . . distinctly assured the Ohio delegations that they would not go for Scott as they would not for you," thus "stabbing you for the benefit of Taylor, or of breeding a difficulty to favor the chances of some third man," probably Thomas Corwin. Comments that "many of your nominal friends were hypocrites. . . . many even of those who voted for you on the last ballot, really wished Taylor's nomination." To use McClung's phrase, " 'they looked one way, sowing another.' " Has heard that Horace Greeley "neither expected nor desired your nomination, but urged it as the means of knocking Taylor in the head [Wendell to Clay, March 11, 1848]," and believes that "such was the heartless policy of Gov. [William] Bebb and the Ohio delegation." Calls the Ohio governor "a man of insincerity and duplicity [Bebb to Clay, April 4, 1848]." Concludes: "I am convinced there was much down right rascality, and that Ohio and Indiana [Clay to Mercer, April 14, 1848] were made the tools or the dupes of it, and Massachusetts [Clay to Prentiss, April 12, 1848; Greeley to Clay, April 28, 1848] a prime mover in it all." Still, views Clay's defeat as "a test of men and of the integrity of sections, that may be instructive for the future."

Since "the nomination goes down very badly" in Ohio, fears the effect of the "Barnburners of Ohio (9/10 whig)," whose movement will take away "20,000 from Taylor's vote in this State. The accession from the Locos will not reimburse the loss, and I believe we shall lose both State and Presidential elections in Ohio [Bebb to Clay, April 4, 1848]." Notes that Corwin fears "the loss of not only Mass. but all New England [Harlan to Clay, June 15, 1848]" as well.

Decides to support Taylor, despite "a weak stomach for the fight," because "*first* . . . having gone into Convention, honor binds me to the result; and *second*, in any aspect, Taylor is preferable to [Lewis] Cass, and I can see no means so likely to be effective to destroy Cass as running Taylor." Although these "are narrow grounds for a man of reflection & principles to go on," they are "the best left me to stand on, and this very reflection makes me so much more resentful towards the managers who have forced the Whigs on a position so unsatisfactory."

Thinks, "however treasonable the idea, [John J.] Crittenden will not go in so easily in Ky: as is imagined; and indeed shall not be much surprised at his defeat [Clay to Beatty, May 28, 1848]." ALS. DLC-HC (DNA, M212, R6). Partially printed in Colton, *Clay Correspondence*, 3:465-66.

Edward D. Mansfield, editor of the Cincinnati *Chronicle* from 1836-48, became editor of the *Atlas* in 1849 and served in that post until 1852. Stevenson became editor of the *Chronicle* in 1848. M. Joblin & Co., *Cincinnati Past and Present* (Cincinnati, 1872), 119-20; Colton, *Clay Correspondence*, 3:492.

From Freeman Hunt, New York City, June 20, 1848. Although "a stranger to you" and "no politician," vows that "from my youth up, your name has been to my mind the personification of all that is great in statesmanship; or good in patriotism." Blasts the "miserable politicians of the Philadelphia [Whig National] Convention," whose "calculating, Selfish designs . . . have triumphed over the warm hearts and generous impulses of the many [Greeley to Clay, November 15, 1846]." Adds: "Thank God, after the election of a [James K.] Polk to the Presidency, a fitting occupant of a chair vacated by a [John] Tyler, the office cannot add to the name or the fame of the truly great man of America," whose character is "more durable, than all the pomp of power, republican or regal, and all the monuments of marble or brass, that were ever erected to the memory of ambitious heads or blood stained hands." As editor of the *Merchants Magazine*, requests Clay to "allow me the pleasure of placing your name on my free list for life, which God grant may be a thousan[d] years." ALS. DLC-HC (DNA, M212, R6).

Freeman Hunt was an editor and publisher of a number of magazines, including the *Merchants' Magazine and Commercial Review*, which he established in New York City in 1839. For a discussion of this magazine, see Mott, *History of American Magazines*, 696-98.

From WILLIAM OWSLEY Frankfort, Ky., June 20, 1848

Although official information of the fact has not reached me, I learn through the Washington papers that Mr. [John J.] Crittenden has resigned his seat in the United States Senate, and that a vacancy now exists in the Kentucky representation in that body.[1] This vacancy it is my purpose to fill as soon as practicable after receiving official information thereof, and in casting about for an individual to fill that responsible station my mind rests upon no one that would prove so satisfactory to Kentucky, and, I may add, to the whole Union, as yourself.

The settlement of the questions that will arise out of our late treaty with Mexico,[2] it is easy to foresee, will greatly agitate the country, and probably endanger, more than it has ever been endangered, the stability of our Union.

It may be, as it heretofore has been your fortune on former memorable occasions, to allay domestic strife of alarming character, and save the country from impending ruin.

But, even if there were nothing in our domestic affairs to require it, there is every thing in our foreign relations to call for the wisdom and prudence of our statesmen. These relations are any day liable to be thrown into confusion and involved in great danger. Europe is known to be deeply agitated in every quarter; revolution is pervading every Government of the old world.[3] It could not be said to be unexpected if the very next steamer should bring us the news of a general war in Europe. Such a catastrophe, if it did not involve us in collisions of arms, would inevitably bring upon us great commercial revulsions.

In such a state of affairs our country would surely be entitled to the services of her wisest and longest-tried statesmen.

Would it be a sufficient reason for *your* absence from your country's councils, in a state of things like this, for you to say "I have taken formal leave of the Senate?" A patriot is never discharged but by death. By considerations of this sort, I therefore respectfully urge you to reconsider the opinions you held when I heretofore conversed with you on the subject, and to consent to return to the Senate of the United States. Your doing so, I have no doubt, would meet with the warm approbation of a large majority of the people of Kentucky, and would be hailed with pleasure by your friends throughout the Union. By conveying to me as soon as possible your views and determination in the premises, you will oblige . . . [4]

Copy. Printed in Washington *Daily National Intelligencer*, July 3, 1848. 1. Crittenden had been nominated for governor [Clay to Unknown Recipient, *ca.* Winter, 1847-48; Clay to Beatty, May 28, 1848]. As a result, he resigned from the Senate on June 12, and Gov. Owsley appointed Thomas Metcalfe to fill the position after Clay declined it [Clay to Owsley, June 22, 1848]. Metcalfe took his seat on July 3, 1848. *BDAC.* 2. Clay to Beatty, April 29, 1847. 3. Clay to Hughes, March 19, 1848. 4. Clay to Owsley, June 22, 1848.

From HORACE GREELEY New York City, June 21, 1848

Your kind remembrance of the 19th. has just reached me, and, though overwhelmed with pressing engagements, and conscious that you can have little desire to hear from me, I must be indulged in a few words. I should have written before, but lacked the heart for it.

I think I must have apprised you that Massachusetts would behave badly in the [Whig National] Convention;[1] I had been in the State several times during the canvass, and found all the managers and influential presses against us. Yet I did hope for two votes ([Thomas] Nye [Jr.] and [Asahel] Huntington)[2] after the first two ballots, and had reason for the hope. I am sure Mr. Nye misrepresented his constituents, and virtually told him so just before the third ballot was taken. I could not move him, however: he went from [Daniel] Webster to [Winfield] Scott. A few Delegates *did* disappoint me—that Vermont man especially, though I had warning that he was not reliable.[3] The Ohio defection was more general than I supposed it *could* be—indeed, who could foresee that [Joseph] Vance, [Stephen S.] L.'Hommedieu, &c. would be dead against us?[4] If they now lose their State by an immense defection, who will pity them?[5]

—But I did not mean to fight the battle over again. It is lost, and need not have been. With ten men at Washington as true-hearted as [John M.] Botts, and a little more discreet possibly, though I couldn't have *him* any other than he is, we could have won. But there are too many there who think they will stand better with a new-candidate than with a President who knows them; and there are some to whom one head off brings them so much nearer the goal of their ambition. We were overborne by the immense influence of that central position, and by the combined power of politicians, presses and money. Four faithful journals, properly located, would have changed the result. We had Delegates from this State [New York] ready to vote for [Zachary] Taylor if they had dared.

It is worth something to know that the great mass of the Whig People were all right. There were not three thousand Taylor Whigs within sight of our Steeples and throughout the whole State, up to the hour of the nomination. Rarely has there been greater unanimity. But the Barnburners operated powerfully against us; partly from a liking to Taylor; partly because they wish to poll a large vote for their man, and thought your nomination would revive old hatreds and send their men back to [Lewis] Cass to defeat you. Yet even with this immense diversion, and delegates willing enough to yield if they dared, I rejoice that Taylor got no single vote from our State on the first ballot, but one on the second and two on the third.[6]

—But it is all over; and let it go. If you alone were interested, I should not regret the result. I know that you have done enough for the country, and are fairly entitled to refuse. I think you have endured your share of abuse and detraction. I am sure quiet and freedom from care must be more agreeable to you than the agitations of a Presidential contest. And since the Whig party is to be broken up by this struggle, after having pretty thoroughly disgraced itself, I am glad you are in no position to be held responsible for the result.

I do not like my own attitude so well. Having fought without much lookout for the contingency of defeat, I do not take kindly the necessity of going in for Taylor, under penalty of being broken up pecuniarily and otherwise. I wish I too could spend this season on some quiet farm, and see the play acted out by those interested in its result. Thus far, I stand at bay, and have resisted all the clamor of those whose coats turn easy that I ought to raise the Taylor flag. I suppose I shall have to do it in the end, but I am not in any hurry. Next week will be soon enough; perhaps next month; I am not sure about it.[7] I should like to take a trip to Europe this summer, but am not prepared; and beside, it has a cowardly look, and I think I will see it through. With many thanks for the kindness with which you have regarded me, and with a hope that I may yet sit down with you at your fireside for an hour's quiet talk, away from the sight-seers and lion-hunters . . .

ALS. DLC-HC (DNA, M212, R6). 1. Greeley to Clay, April 28, 1848. 2. Massachusetts delegates. See Washington *Daily National Intellingencer*, June 16, 1848, for votes on each ballot. 3. Putus Baxter of Vermont voted for Taylor on all 4 ballots. *Ibid.* 4. Ullmann to Clay, Feb. 18, 1848. 5. Bebb to Clay, April 4, 1848. 6. Ullmann to Clay, Feb. 18, 1848. 7. Greeley maintained a neutral position between the Whig and Free Soil parties throughout the summer of 1848. On Sept. 27, after he became a candidate to fill an unexpired congressional term, he declared for Taylor, stating that he did so out of loyalty to New York Whig leaders. Two days later, Sept. 29, the names of Taylor and Fillmore for president and vice president appeared on the *Tribune* masthead. Van Deusen, *Horace Greeley*, 122-25.

To ADAM BEATTY Lexington, June 22, 1848

I received your two last favors. I thank you for the friendly feelings and sentiments which you have kindly expressed, on the occasion of my failure to obtain the Presidential nomination at Philadelphia.[1] The event is to be attributed, among other causes, to the conduct of the majorities of the Kentucky delegations in Congress[2] and in the [Whig National] Convention.[3] I yield to it in quiet submission, so far as I was personally concerned.

My main object however in now writing to you is to correct an error under which you labored. Your last letter appeared to be written under an impression that I would accept the vacant seat in the Senate. I never had a thought of doing so. Yesterday I received a letter from the Governor [William Owsley], tendering to me the appointment, and today I shall return an answer declining to accept it. I could not learn who the Governor will appoint.[4]

Your waiver of any objection to my taking the office, on account of my unsuccessful endeavor to prevail on the Governor to appoint you,[5] is a fresh proof of your friendship and your disinterestedness, and I thank you for it.

ALS. MHi. Letter marked "(Private)." 1. Greeley to Clay, Nov. 15, 1846. 2. The Kentucky congressional delegation generally supported the Taylor organization in Washington. See Clay to Harvey, April 18, 1848; Harlan to Clay, June 2, 1848. 3. Clay to Stevenson, April 12, 1848. 4. Owsley to Clay, June 20, 1848; Clay to Owsley, June 22, 1848. 5. Clay to Beatty, May 28, 1848.

To JAMES HARLAN Lexington, June 22, 1848

I wished much to see you, and hope soon to meet you. I got your letter from Chiles's on your way home,[1] and I have received today your favor of the 20h with the news paper you sent me. Judge [George] Robertson has returned, and has given me much information; but there are some points which you can best elucidate.

I shall take no active or partizan part in the canvass, but remain quiet, submitting to what has been done so far as it relates to myself. I think this is the course prompted by self respect and personal dignity. I shall attend no ratification meetings. How can I sanction and approve what the seven delegates from K[entucky]. did in the [Whig National] Convention, without virtually condemning what the five delegates did?[2] How can I publicly and warmly support a Candidate, who declared that, in a reversal of conditions, he would not have supported but opposed me.[3] I am not misled by the humbuggery of the Louisiana delegates.[4] What credentials, what instructions had they? They shewed none, and had none.

In November, if I am spared, I shall, with all the lights then before me, go to the polls and vote for that Candidate, whose election I believe will be least prejudicial to the Country. Of course I can never vote for [Lewis] Cass.[5]

It is too soon to form any satisfactory opinion as to the issue of the contest. Neither Candidate seems to be entirely acceptable to the party which supports him. And I suppose that party will probably succeed between whose members there will be ultimately the least division and the greatest intermediate reconciliation.

P.S. The Governor [William Owsley] very handsomely tendered me the Executive appointment to the Senate, which I this day declined accepting.[6]

Copy. Courtesy of Dr. Alan Westin, New Haven, Conn. According to an endorsement in an unknown hand, the original manuscript was presented to President Theodore Roosevelt on Jan. 13, 1905. Letter marked "(Private)." Printed in Colton, *Clay Correspondence*, 4:565-66. 1. Harlan to Clay, June 15, 1848. 2. Clay to Stevenson, April 12, 1848. 3. Taylor to Clay, April 30, 1848. 4. Clay to Lawrence, June 16, 1848. 5. Harlan to Clay, June 2, 1848. 6. Owsley to Clay, June 20, 1848; Clay to Owsley, June 22, 1848.

From Charles S. Morehead, Washington, D.C., June 22, 1848. Advises Clay that the Whig party's "very critical condition" requires "A decided expression of opinion by you" which "can alone produce sufficient harmony to prevent the election of Genl. [Lewis] Cass. With your cordial cooperation Genl. [Zachary] Taylor can be triumphantly elected." Assures Clay that "I have never given you an opinion not sincerely & honestly entertained, and. . . . My deep conviction is that you ought to endorse the nomination of Genl Taylor." Adds: "There is a deep solicitude on the part of many of your truest and most genuine friends that you should take this course. The lofty magnanimity of the act would endear you still more to the hearts of the best friends that ever man had [Harlan to Clay, June 2, 1848]." ALS. DLC-HC (DNA, M212, R6).

From JOHN SLOANE Wooster, Ohio, June 22, 1848

On reaching home on Monday last, I received your kind favour of the 13th. That letter would have been answered immediately, but for the pressure of a great family bereavement, in the death of a most estimable friend, and Son-in-law Dr. [Samuel N.] Bissell, who died during my absence at Philadelphia.[1] When I have time to recover in some degree from my present affliction, it will give me pleasure to detail to you the very reprehensible means by which Ohio has in my opinion, been disgraced;[2] and the cause of genuine whigery prostra[ted.]

Of five members of the [John] Tyler cabinet, wh[o spent] the winter at Washington, more than one half were engaged in efforts to deprive you of the nomination.[3] These with certain would be great men in Ohio, have accomplished their object. The intrigue which got up and carried the State in [the Whig National] Convention for Gen [Winfield] Scott, was one of the greatest impositions ever practsed upon any people. It emanated from a Cabal at Washington,[4] and I assure you, was brought about without one twentieth whig of the State being aware that any such thing was in existence. It may seem strange to my old congressional friends, that throughout the matter my hand has been so little observed. But when they know that the whole proceedure was as secret as the scheme dveloped in Newburg [*sic*, Newburgh] letters[5] It will be more comprehensible.

In regard to the final result in Ohio my opinion founded on present appearances is, that [Lewis] Cass will succeed.[6] The whole Western Reserve where we were wont to carry 10,000 majority, is all up in rebellion[7] and the prospect is that [Zachary] Taylor will have no majority at all. A Convention is now sitting at Columbus for the purpose of organizing a formidable opposition.[8] It is attended by many who were heretofore zealous whigs[.]

Abused as we have been, I again retire from the field as in 1844, after [James K.] Polk's election, and will be a silent spectator of the passing events.

ALS, manuscript partly obliterated. DLC-HC (DNA, M212, R6). 1. Samuel Norton Bissell (1809-June 13, 1848), a medical doctor in Wooster, Ohio, had married Sloane's daughter Eliza in 1832. In 1845 he was elected associate judge of the Common Pleas Court. *Commemorative Biographical Record of Wayne County, Ohio* (Chicago, 1889), 546-47. 2. Ullmann to Clay, Feb. 18, 1848. 3. Of Tyler's first Cabinet, inherited from William Henry Harrison, the following were in Washington during at least part of the winter of 1847-48: Daniel Webster, Thomas Ewing, John Bell, John J. Crittenden, Francis Granger, George Badger. *BDAC*; Washington *Daily National Intelligencer*, Jan. 10, Feb. 29, 1848; Lexington *Observer & Kentucky Reporter*, Feb. 26, 1848. 4. Clay to Harvey, April 18, 1848. 5. The anonymous Newburgh Addresses of 1783 complained of Congress's treatment of the army and threatened insurrection. This movement was blunted by Gen. George Washington. Morris, *Encyclopedia of U.S. History*, 109-10. 6. Bebb to Clay, April 4, 1848. 7. The Western Reserve in northeastern Ohio was an abolitionist area especially opposed to Taylor. 8. Wendell to Clay, March 11, 1848.

To WILLIAM OWSLEY Lexington, June 22, 1848

I have the honor to acknowledge the receipt of your letter of the 20th inst. delivered to me yesterday by [Assistant] Secretary [of State A.S.] Mitchell, tendering me a temporary appointment as a Senator from Kentucky, in consequence of a vacancy produced by the resignation of Mr. [John J.] Crittenden.[1] Your excellency is pleased to urge me to accept the office from various reasons, which I admit possess considerable force. There is much ground to apprehend that, both in our domestic and foreign relations, grave and momentous questions may arise, the prompt adjustment of which will require all the moderation, wisdom and experience which can be placed in the National Councils.

When you were kind enough, some weeks ago, to intimate to me that you had intended, in the event of the vacancy which has since occurred, to offer me an executive appointment it is true that I observed to you that, as I had taken formal and final leave of the U.S. Senate,[2] I could not return to it without an apparent inconsistency and some personal embarrassment. But this was not the only consideration that weighed with me. My service in the two chambers of Congress had been long and arduous. I had remained in the Senate longer then I wished at the instance of the General Assembly of Kentucky. I needed retirement and repose and there were many highly competent citizens of the State, from whom an easy selection might be made to supply my place.

If there were a *certainty* that any great emergency would arise, and that I, better than another, could assist in conducting the Government safely through it, obeying the paramount duty which one owes ever to his country, I would suppress all repugnance which I feel to the resumption of a seat in the Senate, disregard all etiquette, make any personal sacrifices, and proceed, with alacrity, to the post which might be assigned me. But dark and threatening as the clouds are which overhang us, I hope that they will be dispersed without any storm bursting over our heads; but if it should come, I am persuaded that the Commonwealth has many citizens more able than I am to face and avert its effects.

I must, therefore, adhere to the resolution which I had communicated to your Excellency, and respectfully decline accepting the appointment which you have had the goodness to offer me.

If it were possible for me to reconcile to my feelings, and to a sense of public duty, my return to the Senate, there are some minor consideration[s] opposed to my acceptance of a temporary appointment, not without weight in my mind. The session of the Senate is drawing to a close. By the time that I could make preparations for the journey and reach Washington, a very short remnant of it would be left, during which I would render no essential service. And again the executive appointment terminating with the meeting of the General Assembly, that body will have to perform the duty of designating Mr. Crittenden's successor. I am unwilling to be in a position which might occasion it the least embarrassment in the choice of that successor.[3]

I request your Excellency to accept my profound acknowledgments for the distinguished proof of the confidence in me, which you do me the honor to entertain. . . .

Copy. Printed in Lexington *Observer & Kentucky Reporter*, June 28, 1848; reprinted with minor variations in Louisville *Courier-Journal*, Jan. 6, 1894. 1. Owsley to Clay, June 20, 1848. 2. See 9:691-96. 3. Thomas Metcalfe was elected by the legislature to the U.S. Senate seat to which Owsley had appointed him. *BDAC*.

From John L. Lawrence, New York City, June 23, 1848. Although "My own impression has agreed with yours [Clay to Lawrence, June 16, 1848], as to any present active interference in regard to the Philadelphia nomination," feels that "a necessity, however disagreeable, would probably compel us to choose in the approaching election between [Lewis] Cass and [Zachary] Taylor." Has said "to the faithful, that I feared our position was not dissimilar to that of parents, whose wayward and ungrateful child was intent on a marriage they warmly disapproved. The part of wisdom, generally, in such cases is to oppose, to the utmost, until the event has happened, and afterwards to make the best of it." Adds, however, "I have not found an universal admission of the justice & propriety of its application, to existing circumstances."

Calls Ohio's vote at the Whig National convention [Ullmann to Clay, February 18, 1848] "inexplicable. Had their votes been thrown, as expected, in your favour, your nomination would, I doubt not, have been secured." Reports a Virginia delegate's view "that had your votes exceeded Taylors in number, on any ballot, a majority at least of that Delegation would have gone for you," but they were instructed to give their first vote for Taylor [Greeley to Clay, April 28, 1848]. In addition, "Massachusetts [Greeley to Clay, April 28, 1848], now so querulous as to results at Philadelphia, with the other votes for Mr. [Daniel] Webster, could have produced a like issue. With dogged and characteristic selfishness, she persisted in a policy threatening the ruin of the course she professed to cherish, if her own narrow views could not be gratified. In a Similar Spirit, she adhered to a nomination of another of her own citizens, for the second office [Abbott Lawrence]. It is somewhat consoling, in reference to the proceedings at Phila., that, in favor of one of our friends [Millard Fillmore], the Convention rejected an individual [Abbott Lawrence], who owing to the policy you sustained the immense fortune he possessed, disregarded this personal obligation for the sake of expected advancement, and was among the active contributors to your defeat [Clay to Prentiss, April 12, 1848; Harlan to Clay, June 2, 1848]." Asserts, moreover, that "The course of Delaware, was little less censurable." Refuses to comment further on "the faithless—the earlier desertion of some of whom was prevented in the Convention by the open vote determined upon by that body, upon a suggestion out of doors, originating, I believe, with my brother [Abraham R. Lawrence]."

Believes that "if Genl. Taylor is to succeed [Harlan to Clay, June 15, 1848] (an event by no means so certain as some zealots imagine) the result will be owing to the votes of *the* Whigs." Predicts that if Taylor wins and is an honest man, "he cannot be insensible, in case of his election, to his obligations to support the great National measures to which the hopes and aims of the Whig party have been so long & ardently directed. If he fulfil this duty, it little matters on whom his executive favours may fall, so that the nominees can *truly* answer affirmatively, Mr. [Thomas] Jeffersons interrogatories, 'is he honest, is he capable, is he faithful to the Constitution?' These enquiries faithfully responded to, would exclude from preferment many of his interested supporters." Wonders how the nomination of Martin Van Buren and Henry Dodge at the Barnburners convention [Wendell to Clay, March 11, 1848] will "affect the mess now bubbling in the political cauldron?" ALS. DLC-HC (DNA, M212, R6).

On the first two ballots at the Whig National convention, Delaware cast 3 votes for John M. Clayton. On the 3rd ballot, she cast 1 for Scott and 1 for Clayton; on the 4th she cast 2 for Taylor and 1 for Scott. Schlesinger, *History of U.S. Political Parties*, 1:436-39.

To WILLIAM W. WORSLEY *et al.*[1] Lexington, June 27, 1848

I received your letter[2] adverting to certain reports in circulation in respect to me, and requesting information about them. Recognizing you as among my staunchest, truest, and most faithful friends, I shall ever feel the greatest obligations to you, and shall be always happy when I can command your approbation, or do any thing agreeable to you. But I should not be entitled to your esteem, if I did not continue to act, as I have ever endeavoured to be governed according to my own convictions of duty.

I submit to the decision of the late Nat. Convention at Philada[3] with out hesitation, so far as I was personally concerned. I shall give no countenance or encouragement to any Third party movements, should any be attempted. I desire to remain henceforward in tranquil retirement and private repose. I have been much importuned, from various quarters to endorse, and to oppose the nomination of Genl. [Zachary] Taylor, by sincere and ardent friends of mine.[4] How can I endorse him? Can I say that Whig principles and measures will be safe in his hands, when he refuses to pledge himself to their support? when some of his most active friends say they are obsolete? when the Whig Convention at Philada. refused to recognize or proclaim them?

Ought I to come out in the warm support of a Candidate who, in a reversal of our conditions, declared his purpose to be to oppose me?[5] Magnanimity is a noble virtue, and I have endeavored to practise it, but it has its limits, and the line of demarcation between it and meanness is not always clearly discernible.

Again; I lost the nomination, as I believe, by the course of the majorities in the delegations from Kentucky in Congress and in the Convention.[6] And I am called upon to ratify what they did, in contravention, as I believe, of the wishes of a large majority of the people of Kentucky! I am asked to smile on and approve the conduct of the seven delegates from K. who voted against me, and in effect to censure and condemn the five who voted for me!

It seems to me, Gentlemen; that self-respect, the consistency of my character, and my true fame, require that I should take no active or partizan agency in the existing contest. If it were between Locofoco principles and Whig principles, I would engage in it with all the ardor of which I am capable; but alas! I fear that the Whig party is dissolved, and that no longer are there Whig principles to animate zeal and to stimulate exertion. I am compelled, most painfully, to believe that the Whig party has been succeeded by a mere *personal* party, as much a Taylor party, as was the [Andrew] Jackson party.

Even in such a contest, there is a choice, but it is only a choice of evils; and in such circumstances my enthusiasm cannot be excited.

I think my friends ought to leave me undisturbed, in the quiet shades of Ashland. I have served the Country faithfully and to the utmost of my ability. If I have not done more for them, it has not been from want of heart or want of inclination. My race is run. During the few days which remain to me, I desire to preserve untarnished that character which they have been pleased so much to respect. They may rest assured that I will do nothing intentionally to weaken or forfeit their good opinion of me. Abstaining henceforward from all active part in public affairs, occupying myself with my private and with higher duties, I shall, if spared, go to the polls, like any other humble Citizen, and cast my vote as I may deem best and safest for the principles which I have ever sustained, and for my Country.[7] Seeking to influence nobody, I desire to be allowed to pursue the dictates of my own conscience.

Such is the view which I have of the present posture of the Presidential question. More light may be hereafter thrown upon it, and I shall be glad to receive it, and if it should point to a different course of duty to me, I shall not hesitate to follow it.

I address this letter to you from the great respect I entertain for you, and in answer to your own. I should have preferred that you had not thought it necessary to appeal to me. But I write to you not for publication but in confidence.

ALS. DLC-TJC (DNA, M212, R11). Copy in DLC-HC (DNA, M212, R6), dated June 28. Letter marked "(Private and Confidential)." Printed in Colton, *Clay Correspondence*, 4:566-68. 1. Letter addressed to Worsley, Throckmorton, Rudd, and Thurston. These are probably William W. Worsley [1:406] who had moved from Lexington to Louisville where he owned a bookstore at this time; Gen. Aris Throckmorton, owner of the Galt House in Louisville; James Rudd, Louisville lawyer and sometime member of the state legislature; and Charles M. Thurston [3:4]. For Worsley, see Collins, *History of Kentucky*, 2:180 and *History of the Ohio Falls Cities and Their Counties* . . . , 2 vols. (Cleveland, Ohio, 1882), 1:428. For Throckmorton and Rudd, see Collins, *History of Kentucky*, 1:185, 367, respectively; see also for Rudd, H. Levin, *Lawyers and Lawmakers of Kentucky* (Chicago, 1897), 263. 2. Not found. 3. Greeley to Clay, Nov. 15, 1846. 4. See, for example, Graham to Clay, June 9, 1848; Morehead to Clay, June 22, 1848. 5. Taylor to Clay, April 30, 1848. 6. Clay to Stevenson, April 12, 1848; Harlan to Clay, June 2, 1848. 7. Harlan to Clay, June 2, 1848.

From THOMAS A. BURKE[1] Athens, Ga., June 29, 1848

I have taken the liberty of addressing you in relation to the nomination lately made by the Whig party at Philadelphia.[2] To say that the Whig party of Georgia are pleased with it, is what I dare not do, believing as I do that they are not; but that they will support it there is no doubt.[3] With myself, as well as many others your name would have been much more acceptable, but it appears the wise men of our party thought differently. Placing, as I do, the most unlimited confidence in your wisdom and forethought I have addressed you this letter to know how you regard this nomination. Can you [sup]port it? Will the Whigs of the Union support i[t? In] replying to these enquiries, you may rest ass[ured] that they are made to satisfy my own mind[.]

I dislike to be familiar to one person [manuscript torn] but cannot conclude without saying that you [have a] place in the hearts of the Southern Whigs, wh[ich has] never been and never will be held by any othe[r man.]

With wishes for your future happiness and fee[lings] of the greatest respect and esteem . . .

ALS, manuscript torn. DLC-HC (DNA, M212, R6). 1. Burke published such magazines as *The Mistletoe* and *Horn of Mirth*. Ernest C. Hynds, *Antebellum Athens and Clarke County, Georgia* (Athens, Ga., 1974), 99-100. 2. Greeley to Clay, Nov. 15, 1846. 3. For Georgia's vote in the Whig convention, see Clay to Mercer, April 14, 1848. For the outcome of the presidential election by states, see Harlan to Clay, June 15, 1848.

From John M. Botts, Washington, D.C., July 3, 1848. Apologizes for not writing "since the fire was applied to the great Ephesian Whig temple," when Clay failed to receive the Whig nomination for president [Greeley to Clay, November 15, 1846]. Does not "wish precipitately to condemn: but my wounds instead of healing . . . have festered." States that "it is now more than ever manifest that if Ohio [Ullmann to Clay, February 18, 1848] had been true to you, and the Convention true to the Whig party, that your election would have been beyond all doubt—while now, everything is thrown into the highest degree, of confusion, and disorder. and I can see no reasonable probability of Gen [Zachary] Taylor's success [Harlan to Clay, June 15, 1848]." Adds: "I cannot see the likelihood of his carrying either Massachusetts, New York, or Ohio. . . . he certainly is identified with no, one principle of the party and cannot without dishonor make a Whig President." Still, "no possible state of things can exist that can induce me to lend any countenance to the success of Gen [Lewis] Cass but whether I shall take any part for Gen Taylor depends on circumstances." If the Whig party "can be preserved under his nomination (& I think appearances are now very much against it) then I shall not do anything to prevent or defeat it—but if it is to be disbanded then I do not wish to participate in any degree however remote in the work of destruction—in other words if my house is to be destroyed by fire, I wish to save as much of the furniture as I can." Is pleased "to see that you have consulted your own dignity & self respect as I knew you would, & said you would by observing a strict silence on the subject of the nomination [Harlan to Clay, June 2, 1848]—You owe that Convention nothing—& they have no right to ask you to endorse when they have virtually said to you stand aside."

Asks: "Suppose the Buffalo Convention [Wendell to Clay, March 11, 1848] should nominate you, & the Barnburners were to go in for it—with a strong show from all the Northern States—It is a mistake to suppose [Martin] Van Buren has been nominated . . . he has only been recommended—I have reason to know some of the barnburners are looking to you, & some of them say Van Buren is also." Continues: "I see there is a Clay paper just started at Albany to promote your nomination & election what does it mean?"

Understands that "[James] Harlan & Garrett Davis are both out for Taylor—& . . . all Kentucky is going with a rush [Clay to White, September 20, 1847]. is this so?" Wonders also "Will your friends generally give a hearty support to [John J.] Crittenden [Clay to Beatty, May 28, 1848]—"

Concludes in a postscript: "Your friend [Charles S.] Morehead has committed you very fully to the support of Gen Taylor both here & in Richmond—& your friend Leslie Combs wherever he has had the chance." ALS. DLC-HC (DNA, M212, R6).

To GEORGE W. CURTIS[1] Lexington, July 4, 1848

I comply so far with the request contained in your note of the 23d ult as to acknowledge its receipt, and to say that submitting to the decision of the Philadelphia Convention, so far as I was personally affected by it,[2] I cannot give my countenance or encouragement to the use of my name in connection with the Presidency, Abstaining from the expression of any opinion in regard to the nomination which was actually made, I will only observe that Ohio, Indiana Massachusetts[3] and other Northern States had it in their power to prevent it, if they had chosen to unite upon one whose attachment to the whig cause was never doubted; but they did not think proper to do so. Ought they then to complain of what was done, upon the ground that Genl [Zachary] Taylor is not pledged to the support of Whig measures and principles?

I tender my thanks to you for the friendly sentiments towards me which you are kind enough to express . . .

Copy. DLC-HC (DNA, M212, R6). Printed in Colton, *Clay Correspondence*, 4:568-69. Letter marked "(Private)." 1. George William Curtis (1824-92) was a world traveler and occasional correspondent for the New-York *Daily Tribune* during the 1840s; he later became an active supporter of the Republican party and, in 1863, editor of *Harper's Weekly*. *DAB*. 2. Greeley to Clay, Nov. 15, 1846. 3. For Ohio's vote at the Whig National convention, see Ullmann to Clay, Feb. 18, 1848; for Indiana, see Clay to Mercer, April 14, 1848; for Massachusetts, see Greeley to Clay, April 28, 1848.

To Roland S. Houghton, July 4, 1848. Acknowledges Houghton's "very kind letter of the 30h. May," in which he had "written from the heart" to express his hope that Clay would receive the Whig presidential nomination. After his loss feels that "my friends" ought to "congratulate rather than condole with me," as "I am left to that retirement which best suits me."

Explains he "shall give, no countenance or encouragement to any further use of my name in connection with the Presidency. Ought not this to be satisfactory to every body?—Yet it is not. I am appealed to again & again to endorse, as it is termed, General [Zachary] Taylor as a good Whig. He has spoken for himself and in intelligble language. I do not know more of his sentiments than he does. I never in my life had a political conversation with him. Altho' I have long known him, the theatres of our respective services being far apart and entirely different, I have but seldom met him."

Has "read some of the letters of Mr. [Charles] Lanman from the South" and requests Houghton to "present to him my warm regards." ALS. NHi. Letter marked "(Private)."

Houghton is probably the Roland S. Houghton who lived at 71 Spring in New York City and worked at 112 Broadway. Doggett's *New-York City Directory for 1848 and 1849.*

Charles Lanman wrote many books on travel and numerous other subjects. The one to which Clay likely refers is *A Summer in the Wilderness; Embracing a Canoe Voyage Up the Mississippi and around Lake Superior* (New York, 1847).

From William Jones, New Orleans, July 4, 1848. Writes on "a day interesting to yourself, in common with every true American," to ask Clay to "accept, (as coming, accompanied by the most sincere wishes, warm from the heart of an American Seaman, for the welfare of his country's ablest Statesman,) of the painting which accompanies this. It is a correct picture of the Schooner 'Whig,' a vessel which I recently commanded in the service of the Government." Claims to have taken an active part in several political contests "with the view of placing the helm of the Ship of State in the hands of the 'Father of the American System,' " and boasts of "a genuine Whig descent from the old North Carolina stock . . . born in the congenial climate (politically considered,) of Raleigh." Informs Clay that sending the painting was "suggested by the circumstance of having recently made a voyage in the 'Whig' from Vera Cruz to this port with eight passengers, volunteer Officers and Soldiers returning from the service for their country in Mexico, and who were all your fellow-citizens of Kentucky and your most devoted friends." Feels sure that the "humble memento from the breast of an old Tar must ever be cherished by the most eloquent champion of the American sailor." Adds in a postscript that "owing to the negligence of a friend and my own absence" this letter, which was to have accompanied the picture, was delayed. Asks also "to learn your views and wishes upon the subject of the nomination of Genl. [Zachary] Taylor [Greeley to Clay, November 15, 1846], feeling bound, as I do, to be guided by the patriotism and wisdom of the Sage of Ashland." LS. Courtesy of M.W. Anderson, Lexington, Ky.

For the privateer *Whig*, built in 1812 in Talbot County, Md., see William A. Fairburn, *Merchant Sail*, 6 vols. (Center Lovell, Me., 1945), 6:417.

To EDMUND PENDLETON Lexington, July 4, 1848

Your very kind letter, deploring the decision of the Whig Convention at Philadelphia,[1] and expressing in language of great warmth and eloquence the sentiments of attachment and admiration towards me, which you do me the honor to entertain, has filled me with gratitude to you, and I thank you with all my heart for it. There is no honorable alternative left to me but to submit, as I do quietly, to the decision. Perhaps it ought to furnish to my friends the occasion of congratulating me, rather than expressing their feelings of regret and condolence. I am relieved from great intermediate anxiety, if I had been nominated, and from immense responsibility, if I had been elected. And I shall probably be happier in private life than I should have been in public office.

There were some circumstances connected with the action of the Philadelphia Convention that both surprized and disappointed me, but none so much as the course of the Ohio delegation.[2] I had the strongest assurances from many of the most eminent Citizens of that State (including the Governor [William Bebb])[3] that it would support me, and could not possibly be induced to support Genl. [Zachary] Taylor. Confiding in these assurances, they constituted a leading inducement with me in consenting to submit my name to the consideration of the Convention.[4] That consent would never have been given, if I had anticipated that the delegates from Ohio would have voted as they did. I advert to this painful topic, not in a spirit of complaint or reproach, but as a justification of the course I took.

I will not indulge in any speculations upon the consequences which are likely to ensue from the proceedings of the Convention. It is greatly to be apprehended that the old measures of policy, which divided parties being pretermitted or abandoned, a new and a sectional basis for the formation of them will be found, dangerous to the harmony, if not the existence, of the Union.

Without however indulging in fears, which I hope may prove groundless, let us all unite in imploring the blessings of Heaven upon our Country.

Copy. Printed in *The Bulletin of the Virginia Historical Society* (March, 1987), 5-6. 1. Greeley to Clay, Nov. 15, 1846. 2. Ullmann to Clay, Feb. 18, 1848. 3. Bebb to Clay, April 4, 1848. 4. Clay to The Public, April 10, 1848.

To MARY HARPER[1] Lexington, July 5, 1848

I duly received and thank you for your very friendly letter. The kind sentiments towards me which you entertain are more highly appreciated because they are the result of your own reflection, have been transmitted to you by your father [Philip J. Arcularius], and are shared by your husband [James Harper]. You remind me of your visit last summer to Cape May, in the Steamboat which my friends chartered to convey me to New York.[2] I remember it with lively feelings of gratitude. I considered your presence a great compliment to me.

You express your regrets, in common with many friends, on account of the failure of the Whig [National] Convention at Philadelphia to nominate me for the Presidency.[3] Whilst I cannot but sympathise with them, I have much reason, so far as I am personally concerned, to be thankful for the escape I have made from anxiety and responsibility. Submitting as I do to the decision, excluding me from the Canvass, I shall be able to enjoy the quiet and repose in retirement, which is most congenial with my feelings and best suited to my condition. You enquire why I was not nominated? I can add nothing to the information which you can derive from the news papers and other sources.

I request you to present my warm regards to your husband, and my best wishes for his and your health and happiness.

ALS. KyU. Letter marked "(Private)." 1. Probably Maria Arcularius Harper, wife of James Harper, reform mayor of New York City from 1844-45, who had supported Clay in the 1844 presidential election. J. Henry Harper, *The House of Harper: A Century of Publishing in Franklin*

Square (New York, 1912), 24, 37-44. 2. For Clay's Cape May trip, see Clay to Stevenson, July 23, 1847. 3. Greeley to Clay, Nov. 15, 1846.

To David F. Caldwell, Salisbury, N.C., July 7, 1848. Recalls "with pleasure, having made your acquaintance and having met you on several occasions." Although thanking Caldwell for his "regrets on account of my not having recently received the [Whig presidential] nomination at Philadelphia [Greeley to Clay, November 15, 1846]," asks "ought I not to be thankful . . . for my escape from all the agitation, and anxiety, incident to the Canvass, if I had been nominated, and from all the responsibility and vexation, if I had been elected?" Intends to "hereafter remain quietly in the retirement which is best adapted to me. I can look upon the passing scenes in tranquillity, and offer up my prayers for the happiness and prosperity of our Country." ALS. NcD.

To ROBERT P. LETCHER Lexington, July 7, 1848

I can no longer submit to the conduct of Dr. Price about the rent due on the House which he occupies.[1] He has totally deceived and disappointed me.

Painful as it is, I must distrain for the rent. If you do not like to sue out and prosecute the warrant, get James Harlan to attend to it. I do not know whether you rented the house to him in my name and that of Thomas Smith, or in my name and that of Thomas A. Marshall trustee for Nan[n]ette B. [Price] Smith. I believe the lease was verbal and not in writing. The warrant ought to be in the names of the persons who leased the property.

ALS. Courtesy of Dr. Alan Westin, New Haven, Conn. 1. Dr. Douglass L. Price, member of the Kentucky house of representatives for Fayette County in 1847 and again in 1869-71. Collins, *History of Kentucky*, 2:171. See Statement of Assets of Henry Clay, July 10, 1851.

To MARY S. BAYARD Lexington, July 17, 1848

Before I received, my truest, best and faithful friend, your letter[1] advising me to accept the office of Senator of the U.S., an official tender of it had been made to me and I had declined it.[2] So that, in my consideration of the subject, I had not the benefit of your friendly counsel. If I had hesitation in forming my resolution, it sprung from my ardent desire to see and be more with my Eastern friends (and especially with your dear family) than I can expect to be in private life; but then I thought that I ought not to mix my private feelings and inclination with the sense and consideration of public duty; and, accustomed as I am to personal sacrifices, I determined not to allow my private wishes to prevail. I feared too that I could not meet some, whom I had heretofore regarded as friends, with our former cordiality. And again, in the fusion and abolition of old parties, which appears to me to be in progress, I could not foresee what new creations would arise, and what part I could take in them. In the evening of life, as I am, I thought it too late to enter upon a new career of systems & parties.

Without however knowing when, I cherish the fond hope of again passing agreeable hours with you and other Eastern friends. I think I shall not leave Kentucky this summer, and the next is too distant to form any resolutions about it.

I am not surprized at the indignant feelings you express as to the course of some of the delegations to the late Whig [National] Convention at Philadelphia. As my good friend you could not otherwise regard them. I do not allow myself to think or speak of them as they deserve. That from Kentucky, if I am to credit what I hear, is generally and severely condemned.[3] But I will quit this unpleasant topic.

I am very glad that you met with Mrs. [Octavia Walton] Levert.[4] I have a letter from her about you, as I have your's in regard to her.[5] She is full of admiration of you. As an umpire between you, I think each has formed of the other a perfectly correct judgment. She does not possess much personal beauty, but her good nature, her kind feelings towards every body, and her charming affability is very attractive.

You have not gratified a curiosity I fell [*sic*, feel] to know where you intended to pass this summer; but as you do not speak of leaving Walnut Street, I presume that you will remain in Philadelphia. I pray that the state of your health (which I was rejoiced to learn from you had improved) may not be such as to require you to go to any of the Watering places. What a dreadful event was that which recently occurred at Cape May![6]

Present my warm regards to Mr. [Richard H.] Bayard, to your good mother [Harriet Chew Carroll], to Baring [Powell] and his sweet wife [Caroline Bayard Powell], and to all your dear family. And do not fail when you see or write to Caroline [Bayard] to remember me in the kindest terms to her.

ALS. Anonymous owner; copy in KyU. 1. Not found. 2. Owsley to Clay, June 20, 1848; Clay to Owsley, June 22, 1848. 3. Clay to Stevenson, April 12, 1848. 4. Clay to Bayard, June 19, 1848. 5. Neither letter has been found. 6. On June 29, 1848, O.P. Pearse, a Philadelphia merchant drowned at Cape May when he swam too far out and was caught in a strong current. Washington *Daily National Intelligencer*, July 3, 1848.

To SUSAN ALLIBONE[1] Lexington, July 19, 1848

If I have not before written to you, my dear Miss Susan, I pray you to believe that my silence has not proceeded from any want of regard to you or from any insensibility to the kindness which you have displayed towards me, in your obliging letter of the 4h. March last, and in presenting me with the valuable writings of Archbishop [Robert] Leighton.[2]

With perfect truth and candor I say that I have rarely ever made a visit to any individual in my life that afforded me higher satisfaction than that which I derived from seeing you. Your physical misfortunes, your resignation to the will of our Maker, your gentle and intelligent countenance, and your interesting conversation, all combined to give to the short interview I had with you a thrilling interest. I have often times thought of it, and have frequently described the touching scenes to my friends.

I have looked enough into the volume which you kindly sent me to be convinced that it merits your high commendation of it; and I intend to give the whole of it an attentive perusal.

I am very thankful, dear Miss Susan, for the friendly manner in which you allude to the domestic afflictions with which it has pleased Providence to visit me.[3] I have had a large share of them. Since my return home, another has been added to the former number, in the death of a most promising grandson at N. Orleans, under circumstances which greatly aggravated our grief.[4] I am happy however to tell you, on the other hand, that the sweet little granddaughter [Lucy Jacob Clay], whose case of Spinal affection I mentioned to you, is much better, runs about with the free use of her limbs, and we hope will have her strength and health fully re established. In behalf of her, I thank you for the little book which you had the goodness to send her. She is yet too young to read it herself, but I trust that she will be spared to be able here after to peruse it. In the mean time, her excellent mother [Susan Jacob Clay] will make her familiar with its contents.

Relieved as I am now from the cares, the troubles and the responsibility of public life, I hope to profit by retirement in making those preparations for another and better world which are enjoined upon us by our highest and eternal interests. In these, your example of perfect submission and complete obedience will be constantly remembered by me, with great benefit and advantage. Instead of condoling with me, as some of my friends have, on account of my failure to obtain the nomination at the late Philadelphia Convention,[5] their congratulations on the event would have been more seasonable and appropriate.

I request you to present my respectful regards to your brothers and their families; and accept for yourself my prayers that He who has enabled you so calmly and cheerfully to bear up under the heavy privations which you suffer, may continue His watchful care over you to the end, and that we may both hereafter meet in the regions of eternal bliss.

ALS. CSmH. Printed in Colton, *Clay Correspondence*, 4:569-70. 1. The sister of Samuel Austin Allibone, well-known literary lexicographer and librarian and correspondent of Clay. See *DAB* and index references in this volume. 2. For Leighton, Archbishop of Glasgow, see *DNB*. The writing referred to was probably the new edition of *The Whole Works of Robert Leighton . . . To Which is Prefixed, A Life of the Author* . . . , published in New York and Philadelphia in 1848. 3. An allusion to the death of all six of his daughters and one son, and probably also to the mental illness of his sons Theodore and John. 4. James Erwin, Jr., had shot himself at the St. Charles Hotel in New Orleans on April 3. It was not clear whether it was suicide or an accident. Lexington *Observer & Kentucky Reporter*, April 12, 22, 1848. 5. Greeley to Clay, Nov. 15, 1846.

From WINFIELD SCOTT Elizabethtown, N.J., July 19, 1848

I have been most unfortunate in respect to your very kind note to me of May 30, addressed to this place. It followed me to Frederick, Md., then to Washington—a second time to Frederick, thence to Leonard's town [Leonardtown, Md.] (our friend John Lee's post office) & after lying there long after I had left his hospital[1] mansion, it has finally just overtaken me here, *via* Washington!

It is now 60 days since I landed on the Jersey shore,[2] with a Mexican *diarrhoea* upon me; & altho obliged to travel & to engage in the most vexatious & disgusting work I have not had the strength to walk 300 yards, at once, in the whole time. I am still very feeble, & go, tomorrow, to the sea shore to gain vigor to meet the same court (nearly) in my own case, at the beginning of the next month.[3]

I left Mexico in the comfortable belief that the choice of a whig candidate for the presidency had been narrowed down to two names—yours & that of Genl. [Zachary] Taylor, & that you would be the nominee. The day after I landed, a distinguished public man from a wing of the capitol—a friend of yours,[4] passing by, got out of the train to see me. I stated my impressions & wishes to him, & was astonished to hear him say that your friends, in Congress, with four exceptions—[John M.] Berrien & [John M.] Botts—but no Kentuckians—were two of them—had given you up on some calculation of a want of availability! I promptly said, if I could be flattered as to the belief that my name, on the same ticket (below yours) would add the vote of a single state, I might be considered as at the service of the party, & authorized him to say so on his return to Washington—notwithstanding my reluctance to change my army commission &c. In a day or two I went to Washington, visited Frederick & returned; but I was confined to a sickbed, & altho' I saw many political men, I was not in a condition to converse or to exercise the slightest influence. I believe the impression was quite general that I was not likely to recove[r.] At the end of a week, however, I got back, with difficulty, to Frederick, & there the nomination of Genl. Taylor reached me.[5]

If he shall frankly accept the nomination, as a whig, with a pledge to administer the government on the principles of the party, I shal[l] fervently pray for his success. If no[t]—I shall at least be indifferent[.]

This is my first attempt to answer a letter which makes my head swim, & I must be done.

ALS. DLC-HC (DNA, M212, R6). Printed in Colton, *Clay Correspondence*, 4:570-71. 1. Interlined above hospital is "ble." 2. For his reception in New York City, see Morehead to Clay, May 3, 1848. 3. Stevenson to Clay, May 18, 1848, no. 2 of date. 4. Clay thought this friend was Garnett Duncan [Clay to Stevenson, August 14, 1848]; but according to Stevenson in Colton, *Clay Correspondence*, 3:472, Scott wrote him on Jan. 14, 1856, that "the person referred to was neither Mr. Duncan, nor any other Western man." Charles W. Elliott, Scott's biographer, has concluded that the person was probably New York congressman Washington Hunt. Elliott, *Winfield Scott*, 592-93. 5. Greeley to Clay, Nov. 15, 1846.

To ISAAC HENDERSHOTT[1] Lexington, July 21, 1848[2]

I received your letter[3] respecting the present prospects and condition of public affairs, and I wish that I could communicate to you any light on the embarrassment which surrounds them, but I cannot. I fear that they are full of darkness doubt & uncertainty.

You do me the favor to express your regrets that I was not nominated by the Philada. Convention as the Whig Candidate for the Presidency.[4] Ought you not rather to congratulate me on the event? I believe that I should have been elected with ease, if I had been nominated; but I have escaped great suspense and anxiety, during the Canvass, and immense responsibility, if I had been elected. I was greatly disappointed as to the course of the delegation from your State [Ohio];[5] but for the strongest assurances, written and oral, which I received from many of its most eminent Citizens[6] that I would receive its support, I never would have consented to the submission of my name to the consideration of the Convention.[7] And up to this day, I am unable to comprehend the cause of the course of your delegation.

I nevertheless submit quietly to the decision; but I can take no partizan or active part in the Canvass. I see nothing in it to animate my zeal or to stimulate my exertions. Not wishing to influence others, I desire for myself more light to guide me in the path of duty. Whatever you may have seen in the Newspapers, in regard to opinions attributed to me, on the subject of the Presidential election, I have neither written nor spoken one word for the public eye or ear, since the nomination. I have remained at home, and wish to continue, in perfect retirement. I am obliged to you for the precaution which you have recommended to your friends to believe nothing as coming from me, without it has the sanction of my name.

ALS. PWbH. Addressed to Hendershott at Springfield, Ohio. 1. Hendershott, a physician, was president of the Clark County (Ohio) Medical Society, which was formed in March, 1838.

Benjamin F. Prince, *A Standard History of Springfield and Clark County, Ohio*, 2 vols. (Chicago, 1922), 1:352. 2. Clay misdated this letter 1842. 3. Not found. 4. Greeley to Clay, Nov. 15, 1846. 5. Ullmann to Clay, Feb. 18, 1848. 6. For example, Bebb to Clay, April 4, 1848; Forrer to Clay, April 7, 1848. 7. Clay to The Public, April 10, 1848.

From THOMAS B. STEVENSON Cincinnati, July 26, 1848

I send herewith a copy of the Cincinnati Herald of yesterday, containing a speech by L[ewis]. D. Campbell, at Hamilton, on the 22d, which gives the only explanation I have yet heard from any delegate of the unexpected course of the Ohio delegation in the late Whig National Convention at Phila.[1]

I have had a long interview with Mr. Campbell since the delivery of his speech, in which I gave him to understand that I did not think he had satisfactorily defended his course. His speech is a record executed by himself, showing that he acted from beginning to ending, in opposition to his own judgment, and acted in accordance with others, whose course he thought wrong at the start, wrong in progress, and wrong in results, as he himself now says the evidence proves. Yet I think him a man of honest intentions, but he is rash, impulsive & indiscreet.

A friend promises me a sight of [Stephen S.] L'Hommedieu's suppressed paper on the same subject.[2] If I see it, and find it contains any thing worth knowing, I will immediately communicate the substance of it. I wrote your son James [Brown Clay] a few days ago a letter[3] which I suppose he showed you, in which I explained the delay of my intended letter to the N.Y. Tribune.[4]

I have been very much disgusted at the newspaper speculations as to your course towards [Zachary] Taylor & [John J.] Crittenden, and still more at the inflammatory language towards you, which I hear every day from the zealot friends of both, because you do not take the field and put to flight the absurd suspicions which they allege exist, as to your intentions towards those candidates and your feelings individually in regard to them.[5] I do not see the subject in the light they profess to do. I do not perceive that either your consistency or honor demands such a course from you. The tenor of a long life speaks well enough as to what must be your general political course. And for one, I take it for granted that as a citizen, you will vote at the polls as duty to yourself, your principles and your country may dictate, when the time comes for discharging the duty. I do not desire therefore to draw you out, if I could, on this subject. I do not doubt that the course you may find it proper to take, will be entitled to approbation.

Have you examined the provisions of Mr. [John M.] Clayton's so-called Compromise bill?[6] All that I can find conceded to the North in it is, the privilege to go into a lawsuit, before Judges yet to be appointed, and who will of course be pledged, beforehand, in regard to the question. The bill, I fear, is a cowardly evasion of responsibility by Congress; and will not allay agitation nor settle the question. Mr. Clayton himself said it was not expected that it would prevent agitation. The object of a *compromise*, by which each side concedes something, is to ensure concord and satisfaction, and thus prevent future strife. The bill will probably pass the Senate, but will be killed in the House if kept off long enough to be fairly discussed before the country. If the provisions of the bill would so operate or settle the question, although it is an unmanly evasion of responsibility by Congress and a throwing it on the defenceless Judiciary, I should think better of it. But the effect of it will be to make the Courts the objects of political influence and assault; which I contemplate with indescribable repugnance; and in such case a decision cannot be had (if ever we get one at all) that will propitiate the public sentiment. According to the bill, a sort of silent permission is given to emigrants to plant slavery on free soil, as if foreseeing, that, once planted, by a process however questionable, the institution cannot be eradicated till perhaps the next century.

If you have given this bill, or the subject of it, any attention, I should be much obliged for your views of it, not for any public use of them, (unless with your approbation) but for my own instruction.

The Whigs, in their county meetings, in various quarters of Ohio, are hedging to save the State elections;[7] at least so I understand their resolutions saying that voting for or against Taylor will be deemed no test of Whiggery. This implies the extensive apprehension that Taylor will not carry the State,[8] and they want to save what they can from the wreck. It is a weak expedient, in my opinion, for I think the State & National elections will result equally for or against the Whigs. Our candidate for Govr. (Gen. [Seabury] Ford) is playing Gen. Mum as to Taylor, thinking thereby he may whip into the Executive chair of the State (of less real dignity under our constitution, than a fence viewer's office) even though Taylor lose the State. But I believe all will go down together, if Taylor fail in this State, as he will, unless a reaction be *yet* produced. If, as is talked of, the Buffalo Convention put a popular Whig on the ticket with [Martin] Van Buren,[9] nothing, I apprehend, can save Ohio for Taylor.

ALS. DLC-HC (DNA, M212, R6). 1. In his speech Campbell described the action of the Whig National convention as a wound inflicted upon "many a true whig heart" and highly embarrassing to Ohio Whigs. He explained that he had been in favor of nominating for president Thomas Corwin first, Henry Clay second, and any other civilian Whig third. Upon arriving in Philadelphia, however, he found that the Taylor organization was very strong and no one else seemed to have any organization. The Ohio delegation conferred, and, in view of the Democratic nominations of Generals Cass and Butler, concluded that only a military man could defeat Taylor for the Whig nomination. Thus, they settled on Gen. Winfield Scott. Also, since a majority of the Kentucky delegation had abandoned Clay, they questioned Clay's availability. Campbell concluded by saying he could vote for neither Taylor nor Cass, but he called on Ohio Whigs to elect a governor, legislature, and congressmen who would be true to Whig principles. The speech appeared in the weekly edition of the Cincinnati *Herald* on July 27, 1848, as well as in the daily edition of July 25. 2. L'Hommedieu had written an address to the "Whigs of the First Congressional District of Ohio," attempting to explain why he had joined the state's other delegates in voting for Scott at the Whig convention when he had been elected as a Clay man. In it, he said that he had come to doubt Clay's availability and that if the Ohio delegation had voted for Clay, enough votes from Indiana, Illinois, Iowa, Wisconsin, New England, and New York "would have wheeled about and given the nomination to General Taylor." He attempted to have this letter published in the Cincinnati *Daily Gazette*, but the paper's editors chose not to print it. Stevenson's rebuttal of L'Hommedieu's arguments, as well as the address itself, is in Colton, *Clay Correspondence*, 3:486-90. 3. Stevenson's letter to James B. Clay, dated July 19, 1848, is in Colton, *Clay Correspondence*, 3:469. 4. Stevenson wrote a letter to Horace Greeley, editor of the New-York *Daily Tribune*, defending Clay's statement in his April 10 letter to The Public that he agreed to the use of his name for the presidency largely because of the wishes of Ohio. Stevenson argued that Clay had good reason to believe he would receive Ohio's support and would not have allowed his name to go before the convention if he had anticipated the result of the vote of the Ohio delegation. He referred to letters to Clay entrusted to him from Ohio gentlemen of "the highest social and official positions" urging Clay's candidacy. He also asserted that he had evidence that Gen. Scott was willing to run for vice president with Clay but this information was withheld from the convention "by the member of Congress who was authorized to make it known [Scott to Clay, July 19, 1848]!" Stevenson's letter was published in the *Tribune* on Sept. 14, 1848; it is also in Colton, *Clay Correspondence*, 3:473-76. 5. Some of Clay's friends, as well as some enemies of both Crittenden and Clay, accused Crittenden of duplicity in depriving his fellow Kentuckian of the nomination at the Whig convention. In addition, Clay's refusal to speak out in support of Taylor, Crittenden, or other Whig candidates or positions intensified fears that Crittenden might be defeated in the gubernatorial race in September. Political opponents of both men tried to exploit the illusory split to win victory for themselves. Finally, the Lexington *Observer & Kentucky Reporter* made a special plea before the gubernatorial election for the friends of Clay to come to Crittenden's aid. Crittenden won the election by nearly 8,500 votes. Kirwan, *John J. Crittenden*, 227-30. Although Clay was ill and could not vote in the presidential election, he did vote for Crittenden and the entire Whig ticket in the Kentucky state election. Lexington *Observer & Kentucky Reporter*, August 9, 1848; Van Deusen, *Henry Clay*, 393. 6. The question of organizing the territories of Oregon, California, and New Mexico had been referred to a Senate Select Committee, chaired by Clayton, on July 13. They reported a lengthy bill on July 18 which proposed organizing Oregon, at least temporarily, on the basis of its current laws, interdicting or prohibiting slavery until a territorial legislature could be elected and could enact a law on the subject. California and New Mexico would be organized by the appointment of a governor, senator, and judges to compose a temporary legislature, which was given no power to pass laws on slavery; the right to introduce or prohibit slavery was thereby based on the U.S. Constitution as interpreted by the judges, whose decisions could be appealed to the Supreme Court. When asked whether the bill conceded the power of Congress to interfere with slavery in the territories, Clayton responded that the bill neither affirmed nor denied it, "and herein consists the compromise." The bill passed the Senate on July 26 by a vote of 33 to 22; it was reported in the House on July 28 and tabled by a vote 112 to 97. An amended version, applying only to Oregon and incorporating the Wilmot Proviso, was passed in August and signed by President Polk. Going, *David Wilmot*, 284-89; *Cong. Globe*, 30 Cong., 1 Sess., 950, 999-1005; U.S. Sen., *Journal*, 30 Cong., 1 Sess., 477, 498-503; U.S.H. of Reps., *Journal*, 30 Cong., 1 Sess., 1124-26. 7. In the closest gubernatorial election in Ohio's history, Whig Seabury Ford won 148,756 votes to 148,445 for Democrat John B. Weller. The election eventually was decided by the legislature after it resolved a number of its own contested races. The legislature, evenly divided between Whigs and Democrats with Free Soilers holding the balance of power, declared Ford the winner six weeks after the new governor was to have taken office. *BDGUS*, 3:1205. For the disputed legislative elections and the complications arising therefrom, see Weisenburger, *The Passing of the Frontier*, 471; J.W. Schuckers, *The Life and Public Services of Salmon Portland Chase . . .* (New York, 1874), 90-95. In the congressional elections, Democrats won 11 of Ohio's seats, Whigs 7, and Free Soilers 3. *Guide to U.S. Elections*, 588. 8. Bebb to Clay, April 4, 1848. 9. Wendell to Clay, March 11, 1848.

From Philadelph Van Trump, Columbus, Ohio, July 26, 1848. After "that most strange and unnatural nomination of a candidate for the Presidency by the Philadelphia Convention [Greeley to Clay, November 15, 1846]," writes "to put myself right as to what I had written you [not found], prior to the assembling of that Convention, of the true sentiments of the *Whig masses* of Ohio." Still adheres to his opinion "as to your strength in Ohio. . . . I have witnessed nothing since that nomination to change, but a great deal to confirm and strengthen it." Adds: "Whatever reason may have induced the Delegation from Ohio to cowardly abandon you in Convention [Ullmann to Clay, February 18, 1848], one thing is clear and indisputable; they committed a gross outrage upon the feelings, and misrepresented, beyond all question, the choice, of the great mass of the Whig Party of this State." Blames "the double-dealing of Ex-Govr. [Joseph] Vance; who, though professedly an anti-Taylor man in Convention, done all he could to secure his nomination. . . . he was probably associated with the clique at Washington, in favor of Genl [Zachary] Taylor [Clay to Harvey, April 18, 1848]." Still feels that "unless some great and miraculous change takes place, it is utterly out of the question for Genl. Taylor to carry the Electoral vote of Ohio [Bebb to Clay, April 4, 1848]." Describes the Whigs of "the Western Reserve and in the Miami country" as "completely disorganized." Has learned from "acquaintances from all parts of the State" that "where apathy and indifference do not prevail, the most indignant spirit pervades the Whig ranks. . . . So much for the plottings and intrigue of Messrs. [John J.] Crittenden, [Garrett] Davis, [Robert C.] Winthrop & Co." Believes that the "Old Whig Line . . . all over the Union, feel that you have been basely sacrificed . . . to a most ignoble and vindictive spirit of personal feeling" by "almost every Whig member of Congress" who voted "in favor of the Mexican bill of May, 1846 [Clay to Lawrence, April 30, 1845]," and by "the Cabinet of 1841" who "could not forgive you for having discovered and denounced the treachery of John Tyler before they did!" Cannot forget that "in the two great periods when you would have been called to the Presidential Chair by a Triumphant majority of the [Am]erican People, to wit, 1840 and 1848, you were set aside [by t]he tinsel and humbug of mere military availability." Remains "undetermined" about supporting Taylor and requires greater evidence of his "attachment to Whig principles, before I can vote for him. . . . And there are thousands of others awaiting the same thing." ALS. DLC-HC (DNA, M212, R6).

For Philadelph Van Trump, a well-known Lancaster, Ohio, lawyer and three-term congressman, see *BDAC* and A.A. Graham, *History of Fairfield and Perry Counties . . .* (Chicago, 1883), 92.

From Nicholas Dean, New York City, July 27, 1848. Two months after the Whig National convention "promulgated the result of their apostacy [Greeley to Clay, November 15, 1846]," concludes "that no name, known to the People, could have been presented for the Presidency, which would so utterly have crushed, and extinguished all Whig enthusiasm" as Zachary Taylor's nomination. Claims that if Taylor "has not fifty times more strength South and West, than he commands North and East, it is not Whig votes, but the dissensions of our opponents, that must save him. No exertion that his leading Supporters in this city have made, or can make, avails to get up even a decent shew of numbers." Reports "the incredible fact that" on a recent trip "I did not meet a *single man who expressed himself pleased*, and not one of ten Whigs who would avow an intention of voting for him." Because Clay knows the accuracy of Dean's former communications, dares "to make statements so directly at variance with the swagger and assertions of a portion of the Whig press"; his word "is entitled to the *fullest credence*." Assures Clay that "you have nothing to regret, except it be the knowledge of the treachery of supposed friends, long cherished as such, many of whom have been warmed into life, and made conspicuous through your name, and your patronage." Adds that "Ashland with Mount Vernon, will in all time to come be consecrated ground;—Mecca's to which the good, and the true will make pilgrimages of patriotism, and there offer vows of fidelity to their Country." Concludes: "Thank God we still have *Henry Clay*. . . . a living embodiment of every generous and noble sentiment." ALS. DLC-HC (DNA, M212, R6).

From Abner G. Holmes, Philadelphia, August 3, 1848. As one who "urged reasons why you should not withdraw your name as a candidate for the Predidency," glories "in the great conservative effort to induce the 'Whig National Convention' to nominate you [Greeley to Clay, November 15, 1846]." Believes "your nomination would have disarmed factions that have sprung and are springing up all over the Union." Doubts that "the 'Free Soil' feeling in New England, Ohio, and other States, and particularly among the 'Barnburners' of New York, would have attained the force and vigor, that it has," if Clay had been nominated. Blames "northern and southern Whigs," who "by an interchange of special pleading in relation to the question of availability; lost sight of the essential principles of the party and the *old* Union, and had determined to nominate Gen: [Zachary] Taylor." Blames the "Excitement of the moment, the devotion of long-tried, and heretofore, apparently faithful leaders of the Whig cause" for deluding the people, who "now look back upon their infatuation with horror and remorse." Recalls the "9th of June last" as "that day of a stretched precedent," and adds that "reflecting Whigs think of it and cannot drive it from their minds—that the man who has strengthened—by authority it is true—not the enemies of his country, but the defenders of their own soil, against the spirit of conquest of a neighboring Republic, should, without a development of his principles, and with an utter independence of all the great ideas, thoughts and tangibilities of the Whig party, be selected as its 'Standard bearer.' " Decries "the selection of the Military Cheiftian of a single campai[g]n over the civil leader of forty years." Criticizes the "spirit of availability instead of principle" that seems to offer "certain successes, and consequently the advantage arising from the spoils." Hopes that "a few of the 'old guard' " of the Whig party can be "strong enough to form a neuclus around which their children and their children's children can rally . . . and support the principles of Henry Clay." Adds that "if Zachary Taylor desires their support, he must unfold and fight under the old Whig banner, and reject no single Emblem of thought or deed, which you have inscribed upon it."

Still looks up to Clay "for these lessons of political wisdom which formed our Early education" and "shall ever and always regulate our practice. While the Union Exists, yes, even when from inordinate ambition and the effects of conquest, it shall be broken into fragments, the lessons you taught . . . will be revived, and, future ages wonder that you were unheeded." ALS. DLC-HC (DNA, M212, R6).

Holmes was born May 25, 1798, and died November 24, 1882. Information supplied from photocopy of family Bible in The Historical Society of Pennsylvania. Holmes has not otherwise been identified.

To JAMES HARLAN Lexington, August 5, 1848

I received at the Estill Springs[1] (from which I returned yesterday) your favor transmitting a sketch of Mr. [John J.] Crittenden's Speech at Versailles,[2] for which I thank you.

How derogatory is it for *politicians* to attempt to ridicule and degrade themselves in the presence of Genl [Zachary] Taylor! And how inconsistent is it to denounce party in the same breath in which the Whig *party* is called on to support the General as a Whig, that is, a party man! It is mortifying to behold that once great party descending from its lofty position of principle—known, avowed and proclaimed principle—and lending itself to the creation of a mere *personal* party, with a virtual abandonment of its old principles!

I have a letter from Genl. [Winfield] Scott,[3] in which he states that he authorized, on his landing from Mexico, a distinguished Gentleman from Washington to say that he was willing to run as a Candidate for the Vice Presidency, on the ticket with me.

But my present object in writing to you is business and not politics. Dr. [Douglass L.] Price has treated me very ill about the rent of the house which he occupies, which has been due more than four months. I wrote to Mr. [Robert P.] Letcher,[4] who rented the property to him, and requested him to get you to distrain for the rent; and he sent me word that he would do so. I have since heard nothing about it.

I own only one half of the house, the other half being held in trust in the name of the honorable Tho. A. Marshall, for the benefit of Mrs. [Nannette Price] Smith.

If it were rented in my own name only, the [warrant] of distress, I should suppose, may be issued in my name only; but if it were rented in the joint names of Mr. Marshall and myself, the warrant can be accordingly so issued. Mr. Letcher can inform you.

ALS. Courtesy of Alan Westin, New Haven, Conn. Addressed to Harlan at Frankfort, Ky. Printed in Colton, *Clay Correspondence*, 4:571-72. 1. Estill Springs, formerly known as Sweet Springs, had been in operation in the knobs of Estill County, Ky., since at least 1814. J. Winston Coleman, Jr., *The Springs of Kentucky* (Lexington, 1955), 67. 2. Crittenden's speech in reply to Lazarus Powell, his opponent for the governorship, defended Taylor against the charges made by Powell. Crittenden emphasized that Taylor had no need for "*printed principles*—and a platform to stand upon," because he had already demonstrated his bravery, his faithfulness to his word, his ability to lead, and his patriotism. He asked: "Can a committee manufacture these things?"

Coleman, *Life of John J. Crittenden*, 1:317-20; Kirwan, *John J. Crittenden*, 224-25. 3. Scott to Clay, July 19, 1848. 4. Clay to Letcher, July 7, 1848.

To THOMAS B. STEVENSON Lexington, August 5, 1848

I returned home yesterday from the Estill Springs, where I received your favor of the 26h. Ulto. with the Speech[1] of Mr. [Lewis D.] Campbell accompanying it, for which I thank you. That speech, connected with a letter[2] which I have received from Ohio from a particular friend, throws some light on the course of the Ohio delegation.[3] It appears that it was controlled by Genl. [Joseph] Vance, who was himself controlled by a clique at Washington of members of Congress. As the delegation could not be prevailed upon to go directly for Genl [Zachary] Taylor, the next best thing for him was to take it from me, throw it away upon Genl [Winfield] Scott, and thus indirectly advance the interests of Genl. Taylor.

I have received a letter from Genl. Scott,[4] in which he writes to me: "The day after I landed, a distinguished public man from a wing of the Capitol—a friend of yours—passing by got out of the train to speak to me. I stated, my impressions and wishes to him and was astonished to hear him say, that your friends in Congress; with few exceptions, [John M.] Berrien and [John M.] Botts but no Kentuckian were two of them had given you up on some calculation of a want of availability! I promptly said if I could be flattered into the belief that my name on the same ticket (below yours) would add the vote of a single State, I might be considered as at the service of the party, and *authorized* him to say so on his return to Washington." Thus you see a false suggestion as to those who were friendly to me in Congress, and the suppression of the truth as to the willingness of Genl Scott to run as a Candidate for the V.P. on the ticket with me. I believe, indeed, that it was represented at the Philada. Convention that he would not consent to run with me. I cannot conjecture who the distinguished public man is to whom he refers from the Capitol.

You ask me what I think of the Compromise bill. Its fate in the House of R.[5] supersedes the necessity of my expressing any opinion about it; but I will say that I think it merited its fate. It settled nothing; but covering the sore with a thin plaster, it left it to fester, and to break out with more alarm and violence than ever. I wish the question were fairly settled; but that cannot, perhaps, ought not to be done without a retrocession of the Territory, or the preservation of it in the condition which it now is, as to Slavery.

I observe what you say, as to the violent language of the partizans of Genl Taylor and Mr. [John J.] Crittenden towards me,[6] in consequence of my silence. It does not disturb my equanimity, nor will it drive me from the even tenor of my way. All my solicitude now, in regard to myself, is to preserve untarnished my humble fame, and I mean to be the exclusive judge of the best means to accomplish that object. Neither temporary popularity or unpopularity will shake me.

I regret extremely the effect upon the honest Whig masses in Ohio of the Philada. nomination. From all I hear the State must be lost on the Presidential election, if it be possible to save the State elections.[7] So many Whigs in that State attach a vital and absorbing influence to the question of Free territory that I do not see how they can fail to avail themselves of an opportunity to vote for a Candidate, coinciding with them, if such an one shall be presented. And the proceedings in Congress, on that subject, with Mr. [Thomas] Corwin's able and eloquent Speech must encrease that tendency.[8] How indeed can Mr. Corwin support either Taylor or [Lewis] Cass? Will he support Taylor against his own convictions?

My son James [Brown Clay] shewed me your letter to him.

I should be glad to see your letter to the Tribune,[9] and to hear what Mr. Corwin says in answer to that you addressed to him.

ALS. Courtesy of Dr. Thomas D. Clark, Lexington, Ky. Letter marked "(Private & Confidential)." Printed in Colton, *Clay Correspondence*, 3:470-71. 1. Stevenson to Clay, July 26, 1848. 2. Van Trump to Clay, July 26, 1848. 3. Ullmann to Clay, Feb. 18, 1848. 4. Scott to Clay, July 19, 1848. 5. Stevenson to Clay, July 26, 1848. 6. *Ibid.* 7. For the 1848 Ohio state election, see *ibid.*; for the 1848 presidential election in Ohio, see Bebb to Clay, April 4, 1848. 8. For Corwin's speech against the Mexican War, see Greeley to Clay, Nov. 30, 1847. 9. Stevenson to Clay, July 26, 1848.

From Thomas B. Stevenson, Frankfort, Ky., August 10, 1848. Writes Clay from "the bedside of a child [Louisiana Stevenson], five or six years old, rapidly descending to an inevitable grave," but will "write the proposed communication to the [New York] Tribune, as soon as my sad duties here are fulfilled [Stevenson to Clay, July 26, 1848]."

Believes that "[Joseph] Vance exercised a controlling influence over the Ohio delegation [Ullmann to Clay, February 18, 1848]" at the Whig National convention, and thinks his "game was determined on, long before he went to Phila. or Washington, though it is quite probable the [Zachary] Taylor clique in Congress [Clay to Harvey, April 18, 1848] strengthened his purposes. [James] Harlan believes he has been at heart for Taylor for a year; and in one of his letters to me, suggested that Vance and Truman Smith should be installed into professorships of political Chicanery."

Asserts that he is "astonished by the facts communicated to you by Gen. [Winfield] Scott as to his wishes and disposition towards you [Scott to Clay, July 19, 1848]. That the state of sentiment among the members of Congress in respect to you was misrepresented to him, was scarcely less dishonorable than the failure to make known his willingness to run on your ticket as V.P. . . . Had Gen. Scott's disposition in this respect been known, there would have been, it seems to me, not a moment's hesitation as to your nomination. In Ohio, notwithstanding the nearly unanimous vote of his delegation for Scott, there was very little feeling for him for the first office." Recalls that "many good friends of yours" hoped that Scott might consider the second place on the ticket as a way "to stop the everlasting din" about "Taylor's military deeds." Continues: "The knowledge of the fact that Scott *authorized* such a use of his name, were it proper to communicate it to the public, would have the effect to deepen the disgust of honest people every where, at the proceedings, so heartless and regardless of principle, which produced the nomination of Taylor."

Rejoices "at the fate of [John M.] Clayton's so-called Compromise bill [Stevenson to Clay, July 26, 1848]" which "was only calculated to widen the breach, and to pour oil on the flames of contention." Favors "a retrocession of the late acquired Mexican territory" as a "remedy for other disorders in politics besides the slavery agitation, if it were at all a practicable measure; and I would throw Texas into the bargain." Fears, however, that the "debauched state of public morals, which . . . certainly lent something more than a passive sanction to the siezure of those Territories by violence, affords no encouragement to hope for popular favor in behalf of a proposition of the kind." Adds that "pride and ostentation of possession, are too strong to be relaxed at the suggestion of justice, wisdom, or even self-interest. Once, the Whig party might have been confidently looked to to favor a proposition of this kind.

Philosophically, a distinction between Whigism & Locofocoism *was*, that the former dealt with man *as he should be*, while the latter appealed to him *as he is*; or in other words, the former endeavored to educate him up to noble ends, and the latter to drag him down to base uses—the one addressing the reason and the conscience, the other inflaming the wild passions." Views Taylor's nomination as a movement "for the sake of clutching *office*, not establishing principles or measures," doomed to "address the low passions of the masses."

Does not think, "considering the conspicuous stand you have so long and justly held in reference to the election of military chieftains, to Civil office, that it would be the crowning act of your life to come out now with a red hot letter for Taylor," but, whatever Clay's course, it "will be shaped by a greater regard for true principles than was displayed in the nomination of Taylor."

Encloses [not found] "a paper containing a letter" from Thomas Corwin explaining his reasons for supporting Taylor. What he writes "is consistent with what he has uniformly said to me and many others who are intimate with him. I do not doubt the integrity of his preference for you." Writes that Corwin "says the free Soil party are the most active, violent, vigilant and hopeful men he ever knew," and that they are working primarily "to succeed in '52." Corwin states that they might " 'carry N. York, which I doubt; Massachusetts, which I think probable; and Vermont; which some here (not of their party) think certain. . . . I am not sure they will not at least break down the Whig party in Ohio,' " but Stevenson believes that "Ohio must, from present tendencies, it seems to me, fall into the lap of [Lewis] Cass. . . . or otherwise, if it were not thought utterly fruitless and factious to throw away votes on [Martin] Van Buren, I should not be at all surprised at *his* carrying Ohio yet [Bebb to Clay, April 4, 1848]." Concludes that "Taylor's nomination" is "the equivalent to the disbandment of the Whig party," but will support Taylor, "not out of the least respect for him as a Whig or as a politician, but merely because I believe it will be better *for the country* to elect him than Cass." ALS. DLC-HC (DNA, M212, R6).

For the states carried by each presidential candidate, see Harlan to Clay, June 15, 1848.

Louisiana Stevenson, daughter of Thomas B. Stevenson, died at Frankfort, Ky., on August 26, 1848, aged 5 years and 5 months. *RKHS*, 40:394.

From Thomas C. Patrick, Clay's Prairie, Ill., August 11, 1848. Reports that he has "paid your taxes on your land" for 1847, and sends a receipt for $33.35. Advises that "your taxes for this year will be $35:04." Doubts that Clay's land "could be sold at any price for cash Dowun," but "my son george" will buy "80 akers of section six the south East 80 at what it was assesed at." Adds in a postscript that there will be little rent collected this year, because "there is but 12 akers in and the stock is eatin it oup." ALS. DLC-TJC (DNA, M212, R14).

To THOMAS B. STEVENSON Lexington, August 14, 1848

I was extremely sorry to learn by your letter of the 10th inst, the alarming illness of your child [Louisiana Stevenson], which I sincerely hope may be spared to you notwithstanding your fears.

My friend in Ohio (Mr [Philadelph] Van Trump of Lancaster)[1] attributes to [Joseph] Vance the controlling influence which determined the course of the Ohio delegation; he himself being gained over by the influence of the Congressional clique at Washington.[2] That is now my opinion. With that view he prevailed on the 20 delegates to go together, and to promise that none would break unless all did so. With that view also he opposed, as

Mr [Lewis D.] Campbell states any appointment of a Comee to confer with delegates from other States.[3]

I suspect that the distinguished friend of mine, as Genl [Winfield] Scott calls him, to whom he communicated his willingness to run as V.P. on a ticket with me was G[arnett]. Duncan, who was in N.Y. about the time of the Generals arrival from Mexico.[4] General Scotts letter to me is not marked private or confidential; and I think you might say in your letter to the [New York] Tribune[5] that you have had the most satisfactory evidence that Genl Scott was willing to run as a candidate for the V.P. on a ticket with me, and that fact was not declared to the members of the Philadelphia [Whig National] Convention by the member of Congress who was authorized to make it known.

The retrocession of N[ew]. M[exico]. and California, I did not suppose to be at present practicable; but as the question, to which they have given rise, should long remain unsettled & the existing excitement and agitation should continue and increase, I should not be surprised if public opinion should finally take that direction. If the South were wise, it would yield the point in dispute, even if contrary to my opinion, if it was with her. In the mean time many of the friends of the principle that Free teritory should remain Free are putting themselves in a position full of embarrassment to themselves. They think that it is the great question of the day overruling and superceeding all other questions. How then can they vote against a Peace Candidate who agrees with them, and for another who differs from them, on that paramount Question? I who do not attach the same importance to that question, feel no such embarrassment.

I am excessively bored (even from Ohio) to come out and endorse Genl [Zachary] Taylor.[6] As if he had not spoken in a way that all may comprehend him. As if it were not enough that I should submit quietly to the decision of the Philadelphia Convention.

Suppose I *could* endorse him, and being elected, he should totally disappoint Whig hopes, would I not be justly liable to the reproaches of any one that I might have misled.

North Carolina was one of the [states] which was to have gone for him by spontaneous combustion,[7] and what has she done? Gov Moorehead [*sic*, John M. Morehead] told Judge [George] Robertson that it would have given me a majority of 12000.

The Whig Clique at Washington totally mistook the character of the Whigs, as it once was. You have correctly described it. It is not a Gun powder party.

If Congress has risen without an adjustment of the Slave question, I think the future full of uncertainty.

Mr [Martin] V[an] Buren will I believe get a much larger vote than is now imagined. The Whig party at the North and in Ohio is much more embarrassed with the anti slavery feeling than the loco foco party, and of course in all the states except N York he will make upon the former the larger inroads. I should not be surprised if many of the Old Hunkers in N.Y. unite with the Barnburners and the disappointed Whigs to give the vote of that state to Mr V.B. and thereby incidentally promote the interest of General [Lewis] Cass.[8] But I cease with speculations . . .

Copy. OCHP. Letter marked "(Private)." Printed in Colton, *Clay Correspondence*, 3:471-72. 1. Van Trump to Clay, July 26, 1848. 2. Clay to Harvey, April 18, 1848. 3. Stevenson to Clay, July 26, 1848. 4. Scott to Clay, July 19, 1848. 5. Stevenson to Clay, July 26, 1848. 6. Harlan to Clay, June 2, 1848. 7. Greeley to Clay, April 28, 1848. 8. For the presidential election, see Harlan to Clay, June 15, 1848.

To James E. Harvey, August 18, 1848. On the subject of slavery in the territories acquired from the Mexican War, believes that the North is overly apprehensive. Feels that slaves could not be kept in the new territories and that the South ought to yield on the matter. Continues: "The South has had the executive government in its hands during the most part of the time since the Constitution was adopted. Its public policy has generally prevailed. The annexation of Texas [Clay to Crittenden, February 15, 1844], and the consequent war with Mexico [Clay to Lawrence, April 30, 1845], were results of Southern counsels. The very exceptionable mode of that annexation was exclusively Southern. From the commencement of the government, we had, prior to the last acquisition, obtained Louisiana, Florida, and Texas, and all these (with the exception of the least valuable part of Louisiana) were theatres of slavery, and augmented the political power arising from slavery. Large portions of the Northern population also feel and believe that their manufacturing interests have been sacrificed by Southern domination." Thus, he contends, the South ought "magnanimously to assent" to excluding slavery from the new territories. Believes if the South does not accept this, "the conflict, exasperated by bitter contention and mutual passions, will either lead to a dissolution of the Union, or deprive it of that harmony which alone can make the Union desirable. It will lead to the formation of a sectional and Northern party, which will, sooner or later, take permanent and exclusive possession of the government." Copy, excerpt. Printed in Carl Schurz, *Life of Henry Clay*, 2 vols. (Boston, 1887), 2:323-24; dated from citation in Van Deusen, *Life of Henry Clay*, 393.

From Thomas G. Clarke, Hanover, Va., August 22, 1848. Informs him that "Many known and tried Whigs, some gray with age, a portion of your school companions, and the descendants of those who were wont to . . . hear the authenticity of the Christian religion proven by your father's [John Clay] word" have met at the Slash Church in Hanover "for the purpose of *nominating yourself* as President of these United States." Describes himself thus: "the sun in his progress has performed sixty annual revolutions over my hoary head, and from early manhood I was a Whig in principle, and for many years my votes have proved me one in practice." Does not think "When life is rapidly drawing to a close," one should be expected "to give up fixed and cherished opinions and principles to follow man, vain and unconstant man!"

Asserts that Clay's life has been devoted to the common good of his country, to make it "prosperous and happy at home—honored and respected abroad." Adds: "Consequently you are the embodiment of *Whiggery*, an exemplar for the present and future ages." Believes "the history of your life" indicates he is "an 'asserter of the rights and liberties of the people.' " Because they think the Union is in danger, they "look on you as a fit person on whom to cast their votes . . . that by so doing the republic may again be saved." Copy. Printed in Washington *Daily National Intelligencer*, September 27, 1848.

Clarke (1786-1857) was the owner of "Cherry Grove," an estate on Bell Creek Road in Hanover Country, Va. Hanover County Historical Society, *Old Homes of Hanover County Virginia* (Hanover, Va., 1983), 14.

The convention which was held at the Slash Church on August 15 was organized by Samuel Perrin, and Clarke served as its president. The convention passed eleven resolutions, including those nominating Clay for president and John M. Botts for vice president and one declaring that they would not support Taylor. Richmond *Enquirer*, August 4, 26, September 23, 1848.

From JOHN M. BOTTS Richmond, Va., August 23, 1848

Yours of the 19th was not received until the 21st. in which you say that you could not disapprove of my statement that you had given no authority to Messrs [Leslie] Combs & [Charles S.] Morehead to pledge you to the support of Gen [Zachary] Taylor, but you regret that each of them should have felt a little hurt about it![1] I made the statement without reservation, because I concurred with you in the opinion & so wrote you that a due regard to your own self respect and true dignity, required you to observe the course you had marked out for yourself, & if we were right, in that opinion, then I would have been permitting that dignity & self respect to have been forfeited in the estimation of others not to have corrected the impression that prevailed, from their statements; as to their mortification I should care nothing about it—The one was your friend [Leslie Combs], & sincerely so I believe, but was ready to jump into harness on the first night for the gratification of making a speech to 20,000 people, & having a band of music to conduct him home, which satisfies me that his wounds are easily healed, his mortification will not last long—[2] as to the other [Charles S. Morehead], he never has been with you at heart, & in my opinion was much better pleased with the result as it was, than if you had been successful; if he was with us, it was strange that he should have permitted, the impression to prevail throughout the House, & the country, up to the time of the meeting of the Convention that I was the only Clay Man in the House; nothing in my opinion but his position at home, kept him from taking an open hand for Gen Taylor—and if he was a little hurt he deserved it.[3]

I have no doubt you are "pressed from all quarters, to make a public declaration in favor of Gen Taylor & to vouch for him as a Whig" and I am glad you have remained silent. how could you do it? you have been laboring for years as the head of a great party to establish a system of measures, by which the prosperity of the country was to be advanced; and when that party had it fully in its power to carry you & these measures successfully through, they basely & ungratefully abandoned you, & then, for a stranger that repudiated, & disclaimed all connexions with them. and who stands committed at this day to no one principle or measure of the party—and now they ask you to endorse him, & thus stigmatize your own cherished policy—

Yes! contrary to my expectations Mr [Martin] Van Buren was nominated at Buffalo.[4] I thought Judge [John] McLean would have been & I still think it would have been more wise in the Convention to have selected him—as they expect to operate chiefly in Whig states—& he probably would have been but for his letter declining[.][5] You ask me to inform you on what grounds I believe Tom Corwin played you false—, the reasons are as thick as blackberries; I began to suspect him at the time of our [Virginia] State Convention.[6] he made certain statements there, which he promised to put on paper, more than once, in regard to the relative strength of yourself & Taylor in Ohio, but he dodged whenever he was called on to commit himself on paper; he played the same game—in regard to the Philadelphia meeting which I addressed on you both days—[7] this first led me to suspect that he was playing a game, to break Taylor down, through the influence of your name, for some ulterior purpose of his own; at last the thing was carried so far, that no reason appeared to doubt your success; a large number of the Ohio delegation had been selected as your friends in most cases under positive instructions to vote for you: Mr Corwin started off to Ohio; & had been there but a short time before we heard of a great reaction in favor of Gen [Winfield] Scott & altogether among your friends; and there was a simultaneous movement among the friends of Mr Corwin in the Western reserve calling a Convention to be held at Columbus on the 21st of June, to ratify the Phila nomination[8] provided it should fall on any other person than Gen Taylor but if Gen Taylor should be the nominee then they were to make another nomination; who the Columbus Convention would have nominated, as the leader of the free soil party, it is not difficult to conjecture, & whoever was made the victim there would be the leader in 52.—"The blood of the Martyr, in 48, was to be the seed of the miricle in 52" & that was Mr Tom Corwin, & old [Joseph] Vance was but the catspaw in his hands; unfortunately for Mr Tom Corwin the dissatisfied Whigs in Phila determined on the Buffalo Convention;—the Barnburners Convention[9] in New York was called in the meantime; another aspirant for the favor of the free soil party appeared [Martin Van Buren], the Columbus Convention, was obliged to defer its proceedings to the Buffalo Convention, and he was permitted to drop silently down the current without even the compliment of being suggested to the Convention, but why? the artifice was too shallow, the viel [*sic*, veil] was too thin, to conceal his perfidy; it was a subject of common conversation in Washington. I charged it upon him to his friends, they did not deny it. & when he returned to Washington I charged it upon him to his face; I told him I had said it in his absence I felt it due him & myself I should say it in his presence; he received it in such a way as to leave no doubt in my mind of the accuracy of my conjecture; and in conversations after that, more than one of the Ohio delegation, confirmed it by telling me, I had not mistaken the man who had done all the mischief.

When I saw Scott I told him the Ohio delegation had voted for him, not because they wanted or respected his nomination, but in order to carry out the views of the Columbus Convention party, it was necessary to force the nomination of Gen Taylor by defeating you, & at the same time to preserve an apparent consistency by voting all the time for a citizen of a free state; he did not feel flattered by the statement, but I mentioned such circumstances as I believe persuaded him of its truth. there are many circumstances that I would relate if I were with you, too tedious to be put in a letter; but that he played false to you is certain, & that from selfish considerations;

Now in respect to your letter from Gen Scott:[10] we had a very long & full conversation on the subject in Washington; I did not understand him to say what he has written to you: he told me, that on his landing he was met by a distinguished gentleman, who either was then or had been a distinguished member of Congress. he would not say which as by that I might guess who it was, who told him of my proposition and of my anxiety to have his name coupled with yours, and of the speech I had made in Phila. that this distinguished friend had advised & urged him not to accede to it—I did not understand him to say, that he told that gentleman of his willingness to run on the same ticket with you; but he spoke in the highest & kindest terms of you, & *said to me*, that he would not have the Vice Presidency for itself, but he would have accepted the nomination or have made any other sacrafice to receive a single state for you;

I have never made any mention of it to you or any body else, because, he said, "you needn't say any thing of this, because when it is told, I wish to tell it myself." and I am glad he has told me which authorises me to say what I have in confirmation as far as it goes; What a pity for the party, such a ticket was not adopted.

I suppose you have heard of the Albany proceedings,[11] I received a telegraphic despatch yesterday giving me the result, I should have telegraphed you immediately, but I supposed they had done it. Well of course you will be quiet, & have nothing to say about it; they have not asked your acquiescence, & I hope they will not—as matters stand now, the Whig party is hopelessly lost, for four years at all events;

Now, Mr Clay there is one way, by which it can be saved, and one only as it appears to me, how it is to be brought about? is the question; for

"If it were done, when tis done, then 'twere well
It were done quickly."

No man who is not wilfully blind, & shuts his eyes to truth but must see that Gen Taylor cannot be elected; now suppose they determine in New York to vote for you; this renders his defeat the more certain, what object then can the friends of Taylor have in blasting his reputation forever as it will be if he should be badly beaten;

Let then your friends & the friends of Gen Taylor every where unite in voting for the same electors & let each voter designate on his ticket Clay & Scott or Taylor & Filmore [*sic*, Millard Fillmore] according to his preference, & let the vote of the State be cast for the one having the largest number; if there were no election made by the people it would throw you ahead of Taylor & thus bring you into the house, where you would have 12 states certain, & who can doubt, that the friends of Van Buren would vote for you in preference to [Lewis] Cass & the friends of Cass would prefer you to Van Buren, & the free soil men every where would rather see you elected than that [William O.] Butler should be the acting President[.]

If Greely [*sic*, Horace Greeley], & the [Philadelphia] North American would take this matter up & press it earnestly we might yet [save] the Whig party from utter destruction.[12]

It was a great mistake, it was a most ridiculous blunder, to suppose that two or three grey beards, back[ed] by some forty or fifty unpledged pen-feathered politicians in Washington, could wheel into line, at the word of command from a million & a quarter, to a million and a half, whi[g] independent Whig voters for one who repudiated them & their principles & who would as soon accept a nomination from one party as the other—it would be well for these politicians to learn that the legitimate purposes of a Convention are to ascertain & give expression to public sentiments & not as in Va[13] & and Phila to suppress it on the one hand & manufacture it on the other, the people have some little chance to be consulted on such subjects—

I believe a ticket for you & Scott might yet be elected by the people—Can you give me a confidential suggestion about it. I shall leave here in less than 10 days; for the North—

I will not ask you to excuse the length of this letter because it is a great deal more trouble to me to write it, than it will be to you to read it altho I am myself too lazy to read it over . . .

ALS. DLC-HC (DNA, M212, R6). Letter marked "private." 1. Morehead to Clay, June 22, 1848; Botts to Clay, July 3, 1848. 2. Combs to Clay, June 10, 1848. 3. Botts to Clay, July 3, 1848. 4. Wendell to Clay, March 11, 1848. 5. McLean had written to James A. Briggs *et al.* on July 28, 1848, stating that he would not run for president. Weisenberger, *John McLean*, 137. 6. Clay to Combs, Feb. 18, 1848. 7. Not found. 8. Wendell to Clay, March 11, 1848. 9. *Ibid.* 10. Scott to Clay, July 19, 1848. 11. Probably the Whig meeting of August 4, 1848, which had declared it would not support Taylor but would support Clay. Albany *Evening Journal*, August 11, 1848. 12. Greeley did not take up the cause of throwing the election into the House, but on Sept. 19, 1848, he printed in the New-York *Daily Tribune* a letter from Botts endorsing that idea. 13. For the Virginia convention, see Clay to Combs, Feb. 18, 1848.

To NICHOLAS DEAN Lexington, August 24, 1848

I duly received, and perused with lively interest and gratitude, your friendly letter of the 27th. Ulto. I should confidently believe that the Philadelphia [Whig National] Convention[1] committed a great error in the nomination it made of Genl [Zachary] Taylor, if I did not distrust my judgment upon a subject with which my own name was associated.

What will be the result of the nomination, I am not in possession of sufficient data to form a satisfactory opinion. The termination of Elections in six States this month, does not look very favorable to Genl Taylor. Of these Missouri,[2] Indiana,[3] Illinois[4] and Iowa,[5] have gone for the other party; Kentucky[6] for the Whigs, and North Carolina[7] also, but with a fearfully diminished majority. With a different nomination, I believe that we should have carried three, or four of those States.

An intelligent gentleman, remarked in my presence to-day, that Kentucky was the only State in the Union which can be certainly relied on for the General. I believe myself that most of the rest are contested, or against him. Still it is possible that he may be elected by the divisions of the other party.[8] We are not able here to judge of the effect of the movement at Buffalo;[9] but I suppose that old recollections, and especially Mr. [Martin] Van Buren's course formerly on the subject of Slavery,—which forms the foundation of his present hopes,—will operate against his success.[10] I have thought it however probable that the old Hunkers might conceive it more for the interest of their friend [Lewis] Cass, that the State of New York should rather go for Van Buren, than Taylor; and that, by an union between them, the Barnburners, and a portion of the Whigs, that State might be carried for Mr. Van Buren;—[11] but of this you are better able to judge than I am.

The Whig party presents an anomalous condition—Without any candidate, who recognizes his obligation to conform to their principles, the members of it are called upon *as a party*, to support the *no party* candidate; and I have been urgently, and repeatedly appealed to, to endorse as a whig Genl Taylor, who, while he adopts the name in a modified form, repudiates the principles of the party![12] I need not say that I have not done, and shall do, no such thing—[13] Self respect, consistency with deliberate opinions long ago formed, and my sense of public duty, will restrain me from taking any prominent, or active part in the Canvass. Whatever I may do, I will not expose myself to any reproaches from those,—if there be any such,—who might be misled by my opinions. I have submitted quietly to the decision of the Convention, and beyond that I feel under no obligations.

I consider my public career as forever terminated; and I am most anxious to preserve untarnished that character, around which so many warm hearted friends, have done me the honor to rally. I should, I think, justly incur their censure if, after all that I have thought and said, (confirmed as my convictions are by observation) against the elevation of mere military men to the Presidency,—could I come out in the active support of the most exclusively military candidate ever presented to the American people; one too, who has forced himself upon the Convention, or been forced upon it. One who declared that he would stand as an Independent candidate against me, or any other Whig that might be nominated. A declaration made, under his *own hand*, and which remains uncontradicted by any thing under his *own hand*, which the public has been permitted to see.[14]

I do not mean to intimate what may be my final vote, given quietly at the polls, if I vote at all;—that will depend upon a view of all existing circumstances at the time; but neither now, or then do I desire to influence any body else.

There is nothing in the contest to arouse my patriotism, or to animate my zeal. I regard the attempt to elect Genl. Taylor as one to create a mere *personal* party. How such a party may work, I cannot foresee;—possibly better than that of either of his competitors; but this possibility is not sufficient to excite any warmth or enthusiasm with me. Genl Taylor has, I think, exhibited much instability and vascillation. He will inevitably fall into the hands of others, who will control his administration. I know not who they will be; but judging from my experience of poor weak human nature, they will be most likely those, who will have fawned and flattered the most.

Standing proud and erect in the consciousness of having faithfully fulfilled all my public duties; and supported and cheered by numberless intelligent, and warm hearted friends, in all parts of the Country,—I acquiesce in the retirement in which I expect to pass the remnant of my life. Some of these friends many censure me for the inaction which I have prescribed to myself during the present Canvass; but if they do, I appeal to their "sober second thoughts," or to the impartial tribunal of posterity.

Copy. DLC-TJC (DNA, M212, R11). Printed in Colton, *Clay Correspondence*, 4:572-73. 1. Greeley to Clay, Nov. 15, 1846. 2. In the 1848 Missouri gubernatorial election, Democrat Austin A. King defeated Whig James S. Rollins by a vote of 48,921 to 43,942. *BDGUS*, 2:843. The two houses of Missouri's newly elected legislature contained 35 Whigs and 98 Democrats. Mering, *Whig Party in Missouri*, 150. Democrats also won all 5 U.S. congressional seats. *Guide to U.S. Elections*, 587. 3. In the 1848 legislative elections in Indiana, Whigs won 8 senate seats to 7 for the Democrats, while in the house Democrats won 57 seats to 36 for the Whigs. Dorothy Riker & Gayle Thornbrough, *Indiana Election Returns, 1816-1851* (Indiana Historical Bureau, 1960), 323-34. 4. In the 1848 state elections in Illinois, Democrats carried the state senate over the Whigs by 18 to 7 seats and the house by 50 to 23. Springfield *Illinois State Register*, Sept. 1, 1848. Democrats also won 6 seats in the U.S. House to 1 for the Whigs. *Guide to U.S. Elections*, 587. 5. In the 1848 state elections in Iowa, Democrats won both U.S. congressional seats. *Guide to U.S. Elections*, 587. The Whigs had a small majority in the state senate, but the Democrats had a majority of 10 on joint ballot of house and senate. Washington *Daily National Intelligencer*, August 19, 1848. 6. Clay to Beatty, May 28, 1848. 7. In the 1848 state elections in North Carolina, Whig Charles Manley defeated David S. Reid for governor by a vote of 42,536 to 41,682. *BDGUS*, 3:1132. The parties were tied in the state house of representatives, while Whigs had a majority of 2 in the state senate. Washington *Daily National Intelligencer*, August 14, 15, 1848. 8. For the states carried by each candidate in the presidential election, see Harlan to Clay, June 15, 1848. 9. Wendell to Clay, March 11, 1848. 10. Early on, Van Buren had decided that slavery was a moral blemish on American society, but through his presidency he had taken a constitutional and legalistic stance holding that slavery was a local matter for the states and their citizens to decide. In his inaugural address he condemned abolition and promised to oppose any interference with slavery where it existed or in the District of Columbia unless Virginia and Maryland consented. In 1848, however, he drafted an address which endorsed the Wilmot Proviso and stated unequivocally that Congress had the power to determine the question of slavery in the territories. This address became the first comprehensive statement of the Free Soil party. Niven, *Martin Van Buren*, 385, 388-89, 410-11, 567-71. 11. White to Clay, April 5, 1848. 12. Clay to Ullmann, August 4, 1847. 13. Harlan to Clay, June 2, 1848. 14. Taylor to Clay, April 30, 1848.

From Thomas B. Stevenson, Frankfort, Ky., August 29, 1848. Reports that his daughter [Louisiana Stevenson] "is gone whither it is the greatest purpose of my life to accomplish a preparation to rejoin her [Stevenson to Clay, August 10, 1848]." Submits with resignation "to the will of the Great Disposer of events . . . consoled by the assured belief . . . she is now enjoying a blissful immortality." Although "sensible that individual griefs should not be obtruded upon others, you, who are a father and have lost beloved children, will appreciate this unpremeditated mention of mine."

Returns letters written to Clay from Ohio Governor William Bebb [Bebb to Clay, April 4, 1848] and Samuel Forrer [Forrer to Clay, April 7, 1848], "importuning you to stand for the nomination for the Presidency before the Whig National Convention." Feels "warranted by his own defiant consent, to publish" Bebb's letter, "if occasion arise in my judgment justifying it." To support "the averments of my letter to the [New York] Tribune [Stevenson to Clay, July 26, 1848]," desires "in order to fortify myself" to obtain copies of "the letters [not found] of Judge Lazelle [*sic*, John A. Lazell] and O[ran]: Follett on the same subject." Has read a draft of his letter to the Tribune to "Chs. Anderson of Cincinnati, and Mr. [James] Harlan, of this place." While both "are pleased with it," Anderson believes "it will produce an uproar in Ohio against her Whig delegates; and the latter is apprehensive the Taylorites will be offended."

Explains that "the prospects of a reaction in Ohio, without which [Zachary] Taylor's chances of obtaining her electoral vote are very gloomy, seem to be improving. The former political course of Mr. [Martin] Van Buren [Clay to Dean, August 24, 1848], one of almost object subserviency to what, in the political cant of the day, is termed 'the slave power,' renders him extremely vulnerable to assault, and *his* nomination, by the Buffalo Convention [Wendell to Clay, March 11, 1848], has sensibly checked the inroads which the Free Soil party seemed likely to make upon the Whig party. The defection in our ranks is nevertheless quite formidable." Believes, however, that Gen. Seabury Ford, the Whig candidate for governor, will win "by a handsome majority, as it seems to be the purpose of the Barnburners and Abolitionists, if not to vote for him, to run no candidate of their own [Stevenson to Clay, July 26, 1848]."

Informs Clay that Thomas Corwin "has taken the stump" at Wilmington and Xenia, Ohio, "seats of great defection, embracing besides large bodies of Quakers residing in those neighborhoods," and "will proceed thence to the [Western] Reserve, where he expects to be encountered by [Joshua R.] Giddings." Adds that Corwin was "quite desirous of inducing me to join him in his tour," but "Not to have been victor at Buena Vista, would I have omitted the slightest of the last attentions and duties I owed my poor lost child."

Prefers "Taylor to either [Lewis] Cass or Van Buren and shall of course commend him to others in preference to either; but it is not a little curious that so many of those who charged me with ruining the Whig party because I preferred a Statesman to a Warrior for President, now prefer such advocates of Taylor's election to themselves." Besides merely committing " 'Clay men' " to Taylor's support, "the people will scarcely give patient ear to the original Taylorites, though willing to hear what can be honestly said in favor of Taylor's election."

Wrote to Corwin "that if it were not rather a matter for commiseration than merriment, I should laugh to see *him*, the author of *the* anti-war speech [Greeley to Clay, November 30, 1847] and the great moral hero of the times, sweating on the stump, grinding and compounding materials more inflammable than gunpowder, to be let off in lieu of the 'spontaneous combustion' fizzle—for so far it *is* a fizzle." Even if "after all, availability prove unavailable and we get beaten," is consoled that "it will (or should) put an end to the upstart pretensions of mere military men to the highest civil offices."

Adds in a postscript that "Your sometime friend, Amos Kendall is here. . . . the expression of his countenance excites the idea of a famished wolf. It makes one hungry just to look at his lean, lank jaws, his restless, eager eyes, and his voracious, hooked nose." ALS. DLC-HC (DNA, M212, R6). Printed in Colton, *Clay Correspondence*, 3:480-82.

Charles Anderson (1814-95), a Dayton and Cincinnati lawyer who had served in the Ohio state senate, later moved to Texas. He returned to Ohio to serve in the 93rd Ohio Volunteer Infantry in the Civil War and was elected lieutenant governor of the state in 1863 and governor in 1865. *BDGUS*, 3:1210-11.

From N.B. Meade, J.W. King *et al.*, Georgetown, Ohio, August 31, 1848. Because of the "great disaffection in the Whig party, in this State on account of the Nomination of Gen [Zachary] Taylor," express a "wish to have a candidate, who we know to be an *honest man*, one who we know will never betray our rights." Ask Clay "to become our candidate." Explain that "The Democrats, have their candidates, the Abolitionists theirs, and the *No party* have *their candidates* but sir, the *honest Whigs*, who so nobly fought for you, our gallant leader in 44, have no candidate." Feel they cannot vote for Taylor, since he has said that he would "have consented to receive the Nomination of the *Locofoco Convention* [Clay to Ullmann, August 4, 1847]." Beg Clay to "*save* our *glorious* party, from disolution," and assure him that "you will soon find, the *true Whigs*, of the Union willing to a Man, under your *glorious banner*." Assert that in addition, "There is but few Whigs in this County, who would not gladly drop Taylor, were you an independent candidate, hundreds of the third party, who say they can never support [Martin] Van Buren, declare themselves willing to unite in your support." ALS, by Meade. DLC-TJC (DNA, M212, R11).

Meade has not been identified; however, J.W. King became mayor of Georgetown, Ohio, in 1852. W.H. Beers (pub.), *The History of Brown County, Ohio . . .* (Chicago, 1883), 393.

To CINCINNATI WHIGS Lexington, September 1, 1848

I have received your letter stating that "in the present conflicting state of the politics of our beloved country, it is the honest and sincere opinion of thousands of your friends and zealous supporters that this is the auspicious time for the independent presentation of your name to the voters of this confederacy for the Chief Magistracy of our Union," and you invite me to assume that position.[1]

My name, gentlemen, was submitted, with my consent,[2] to the consideration of the Whig Convention which met in Philadelphia, in June last,[3] and the Convention did not think proper to nominate me as a candidate for the Presidency of the United States. I have quietly submitted to its decision; and I cannot consent to any further use of my name in connection with that office. I have accordingly refrained from giving, and must continue to decline giving the slightest encouragement or countenance to any such use of it.[4]

I am, nevertheless, thankful for the confidence in me which you do me the honor to entertain.

Copy. Printed in Paris, Ky., *Western Citizen*, Sept. 29, 1848. 1. Letter not found. 2. Clay to The Public, April 10, 1848. 3. Greeley to Clay, Nov. 15, 1846. 4. Clay writes to Col. [John Francis] Hamtranck on Sept. 19, 1848, expressing a similar sentiment. States: "Ever since I knew of the Philadelphia Convention having decided against my nomination as a candidate for the Presidency, I have written many letters, uniformly and explicitly, declaring that I could not consent to any further use of my name in connection with that office, and that I would not consent to accept a nomination, if it were tendered to me. To no person or association of persons, have I, at any time given the least countenance or encouragement to use my name as a candidate for the office, since the decision of that convention. I shall deeply lament if I have any friends who will not conform to my wishes on this subject." Copy, extract. DLC-HC (DNA, M212, R6). For Hamtranck, who was reared by William Henry Harrison and served in the army under Zachary Taylor, see *NCAB*, 22:33-34.

To THOMAS B. STEVENSON Lexington, September 4, 1848

I received your favors of the 10h. and 29h. Ulto dated at Frankfort, and should have written to you before but for the hope, excited by the last, that I might possibly see you here prior to your return to Cincinnati, which I regret has not been realized. Should you at any time come this way, I request that you will oblige me by coming directly to my house, and making it your own during your sojourn.

I tender you cordial condolence on your late great bereavement.[1] My own heart has so often bled from similar afflictions that I can easily comprehend the poignancy of your grief and heartily sympathise with you. Time alone, my dear Sir, and your dependence on Him who having given her to you, has seen fit to take her away, can mitigate your sorrows.

I perused, with much interest and attention, the copy which you sent me of the letter you had kindly addressed to the Tribune.[2] It is all that I wished it to be, and I most heartily thank you for it. I do not doubt that Mr. [Horace] Greeley will cheerfully publish it. I feel much solicitude that my motives and conduct, in consenting that my name should be considered by the Philadelphia [Whig National] Convention, should be rightly understood and justified before the public.[3] This friendly act of your's accomplishes all I desire in respect to this. I shall regret very much however if it should involve you in any controversy with any of the parties concerned. I doubt however if it will have that effect; for, from what I hear from Ohio, the course of its delegates to the Convention[4] seems to be severely censured,[5] and I imagine that they will be quite willing that it should not form a topic of prominent and prolonged discussion in the news papers. I am very sorry that I cannot lay my hands upon the letters of Messrs. Lazelle [*sic*, John A. Lazell] & Follet [*sic*, Oran Follett]. I am afraid that I have destroyed them, which, in consequence of the great number of letters I receive, is the mode I dispose of them. Should circumstances here after make it necessary, you may refer to the names of The honble John Sloane of Wooster (one of the best and truest men I have ever known in Ohio) and Mr. [Philadelph] Van Trump of Lancaster, as gentlemen who strongly urged me to allow my name to go before the Convention. I am sure that neither of them will take any exception to such a reference.

I am daily assailed, and have received many, many letters from all quarters making enquiries of me as to my purpose in respect to the support of Genl [Zachary] Taylor, most of them urging me to come out with a public declaration in his favor, but some expressing a contrary wish. I have answered none of them with two or three exceptions, to which I have returned confidential replies.[6] I adhere to my purpose of Silence and reserve. It is quite probable, as you inferred, that I may be constrained to vote for him, as I can vote for no body else, now before the public. But, if I do, I shall do it quietly.[7] I wish to lead or mislead no one. Should he be elected and disappoint the Whigs, I desire to be spared any reproaches for having induced any of them to vote for him. Besides, I could not, in justice to myself, come out in any Speech or letter, in his support, without assigning such reasons for my course as would operate perhaps as much against him as for him.

I have received two strange letters from Ohio, one from Cincinnati, and the other from Geo. town, inviting me to become an Independent Candidate! They were signed by several persons who were unknown to me. I scarcely need to say that I positively but respectfully declined the invitation.[8] I think it probable that one or both of my answers will be published. One of them (the letters to me) speaks in terms of strong condemnation of the Ohio delegates.

I think Mr. [Thomas] Corwin has put himself in a position of some embarrassment. After all that he has said against the Mexican War &c and in favor of Free soil,[9] he will find it, I should think, difficult to reconcile all his friends to the support of one whose attitude must necessarily render him hostile to the proposed restriction on N. Mexico & California, and whose official influence will be directed *silently* if not actively against it.[10] Having made that question of Free soil the paramount question of the day can he hereafter justify himself to those who concur with him in refusing to support one who is pledged to the principle? Can he resume the leadership of that party? Will not some body else displace him?

On the result of the existing contest I can form no satisfactory opinion. The elections of this month will throw some additional light upon it. Those of the last were far from being auspicious to Genl. Taylor. A few more such letters as those addressed by him to Charleston and to Mr. [George] Lippard will give him the coup de grace.[11]

ALS. Courtesy of Dr. Thomas D. Clark, Lexington, Ky.; copy in OCHP. Printed in Colton, *Clay Correspondence*, 3:482-84. 1. Stevenson to Clay, August 10, 1848. 2. Stevenson to Clay, July 26, 1848. 3. Clay to The Public, April 10, 1848. 4. Ullmann to Clay, Feb. 18, 1848. 5. For example, Sloane to Clay, June 22, 1848; Van Trump to Clay, July 26, 1848. 6. For example, Clay to Hendershott, July 21, 1848; Clay to Dean, August 24, 1848. 7. Harlan to Clay, June 2, 1848; Stevenson to Clay, July 26, 1848. 8. Meade & King *et al.* to Clay, August 31, 1848; Clay to Cincinnati Whigs, Sept. 1, 1848; Clay to Meade & King, Sept. 11, 1848. 9. Greeley to Clay, Nov. 30, 1847. 10. At this point in the Colton version, Stevenson placed a footnote which says: "Mr. Clay's reasoning here would be deemed logical in regard to General Taylor, but that he ignores the Allison letter, by which the General was virtually pledged not to veto any constitutional act of Congress; and his reasoning as to Mr. Corwin would be conclusive also, but that he was not possessed of the fact, known to Mr. Corwin, that General Taylor, very soon after his return from Mexico . . . assured a gentleman . . . that having examined the question, he considered the Wilmot Proviso, both as a question of power and policy, settled affirmatively by the uniform precedents of the government in all its departments, from its origin." Adds that most of the prominent Whig speakers of the North had seen a copy. Colton, *Clay Correspondence*, 3:483-84. 11. A group of dissident Democrats in South Carolina had met in Charleston on July 20 and nominated Taylor and William O. Butler for president and vice president. Taylor acknowledged the nomination in a friendly letter to W.B. Pringle, dated August 9, 1848, which disturbed some Whigs. Taylor had written George Lippard in July stating that he was not a party candidate and if elected would not be the president of a party but of the whole people. *Niles' Register* (Sept. 13, 1848), 74:165; Bauer, *Zachary Taylor*, 243; Hamilton, *Zachary Taylor, Soldier in the White House*, 120-21. For Lippard, eccentric novelist and lecturer, see Stanley J. Kunitz & Howard Haycraft (eds.), *American Authors, 1600-1900* . . . (New York, 1938), 468.

From Nicholas Dean, New York City, September 5, 1848. Reports that "We are on the very brink of a party explosion here, whether to be characterised as an *insurrection*, or to take the more dignified form of a *Revolution*, remains to be seen. The People will not go [Zachary] Taylor;—they insist upon having a Whig,—a whole Whig, and nothing but a Whig." Describes ward meetings and petitions "having already some thousands of signatures for a grand mass meeting of all the unwavering friends of Henry Clay to be held in Vauxhall Garden." Has decided, along with John L. Lawrence "and others holding the same relation to you . . . not to give these proceedings the sanction of our names, without the most indubitable evidence that the feeling is wide spread." Unless "Our State Convention for the nomination of State Officers," which will meet on September 14, responds "to these popular outbreaks," fears "these disjointed efforts, however spirited and enthusiastic, will be powerless for any good, and I can never consent to see your name again connected with a contest, in which victory is not certain to follow." ALS. DLC-HC (DNA, M212, R6).

The Vauxhall meeting of September 7, 1848, was attended by approximately 10,000 Whigs, who made enthusiastic demonstrations and nominated Clay and Fillmore for president and vice president. Willis Hall served as president, and speeches were made by Edward V. Price and Dudley Selden, while John M. Botts sent a telegram. It was so well attended that a second meeting was organized in the garden, with William S. Duke appointed as president. New-York *Daily Tribune*, September 8, 1848.

The New York Whig State convention met in Utica on September 14, 1848, and nominated Hamilton Fish for governor and George W. Patterson for lieutenant governor. James Brooks spoke, endorsing Taylor and saying that the candidate's Allison letter was a good Whig platform. The convention then passed resolutions endorsing Taylor and Fillmore, advocating protection of American industry, and disclaiming any intention of interfering with domestic institutions in other states, but opposing the establishment of slavery in any territory where it had not existed at the time of its acquisition by the U.S. *Ibid.*, September, 15, 16, 18, 1848.

From James Morrison Harris, Baltimore, September 5, 1848. Writes of recent political affairs "with unfeigned diffidence, and after long and serious thought," proclaiming "that no man in this country,—no matter how great or elevated,—loves you,—can love you,—with a more earnest and sincere heart than I do." Informs Clay that "You have been outrageously treated in connection with this Presidential nomination. You were deceived by those in whom you reposed confidence, and in a Convention of your own Party, your great name was laid aside for that of one whose greatest recommendation to the consideration of that body, was his supposed availability. The Convention at Phila, in my judgement [Greeley to Clay, November 15, 1846], was not merely ungrateful but unwise, in the choise it made, and few sensible men can now be found I fancy, even in the ranks of Gen. [Zachary] Taylor's warmest friends anterior to the nomination; who would not admit, if they spoke frankly, that they were mistaken."

Although he regrets the "issue of that Convention," feels he must "labor zealously in the canvass, and I *am* doing so," but "My heart is not in it, as it would have been in your case." After studying the issues, however, "I cannot but think them important, *vitally* important, to the prosperity of the country."

Continues: "I care nothing about Gen. Taylor individually. He has enlisted none of my sympathies. He is to me rather your opponent, than anything else, and as far as he is *personally* concerned, his election will give me no pleasure, his defeat cause me no pain. Yet I cannot fail to recognize in him traits of character rare even in *great* soldiers. His judgement, his moderation, his humanity, his simplicity of habits and life, and his unassailed purity and honesty of character, are more important, in my view, than his confessedly great qualities of soldiership." Believes Taylor's sincerity "in his declaration that his cardinal political principles are conservative, whig," that "he will obey the will of the people properly expressed," that he will oppose "extension and annexation of Territory" and "aggressive wars." Can support "Such a man," who, "with a Cabinet,—such as I am assured he will have around him,—of sound whigs; may be expected to administer the Government with safety to the Country."

Views a Lewis Cass administration as "fraught with great danger. . . . a National *Calamity*," and Cass himself as "A seeker of place; time serving and trimming; morally dishonest as is established by the record; his election would open anew the floodgate of Governmental abuse and peculation; while his ultraism in 'progressive Democracy', would give to the policy of the Government, a still more ruinous and downward tendency." Only one thing can "defeat Lewis Cass:—The interference of Henry Clay!" Only one thing can "ensure us the 'chance of a good government', for the next four or eight years:—The interference of Henry Clay!" Believes that New York, Virginia, Pennsylvania, and Maryland would respond to even "One word from you." Fears especially that without Clay's help, "the whig state of Maryland for the first time in her history, should fall into the hands of the Spoilers."

Envies Clay's position: "You can decide not merely the fate of your own Party, but the results of a contest between twenty million of freemen. . . . the election or failure of Lewis Cass, does indeed, as your friends believe rest with you." Adds: "If you should determine to express yourself upon this subject, and will so much honor me as to let me be the vehicle of your determination; I shall be exceedingly gratified." ALS. DLC-HC (DNA, M212, R6).

For Clay's refusal to endorse Taylor, see Harlan to Clay, June 2, 1848. For the states carried by each candidate in the presidential election, see Harlan to Clay, June 15, 1848.

From John L. Lawrence, New York City, September 5, 1848. Reports no great change in local political matters "except so far as Mr. Van Beuren's [*sic*, Martin Van Buren] nomination [Wendell to Clay, March 11, 1848] and the removal from office of Benjn. F. Butler, 'the Setter up' of President [James K.] Polk may have affected it. A Sullen assent is in most places given by our friends to the nomination of Genl. [Zachary] Taylor." Advises Clay of a meeting "now projected to take place in a few days, with the avowed object of presenting you as a candidate for the Presidency [Dean to Clay, September 5, 1848]." Assures Clay "I stated in Substance, that a nomination of you ought not to be made, without your consent, which I did not believe, nor they expect, could be obtained." Maintains "That the dignity of your character, and your eminence in the estimation of your fellow citizens—far higher than the office of President, could carry you—forbid a trifling with your name, through an inconsiderate, however well intended, zeal." Adds that "if a combined *revolutionary* movement was to be made in your favour, by means of a convention of States, or in any other imposing form," he would "heartily assist in it," but would not make "you the subject of partial insurrections, which without previously extended combinations would probably prove more than useless." Has heard "that an endeavour may be made to prejudice me in your opinion, by a distorted representation of my sentiments," but has "not the remotest fear of any impression being made on your mind, inconsistent with our long friendship & communion." ALS. DLC-HC (DNA, M212, R6).

Benjamin F. Butler had been removed as attorney for the southern district of New York because of his opposition to the 1848 Democratic presidential and vice presidential nominees. U.S. Sen., *Executive Journal*, 6:444; Quaife, *Diary of James K. Polk*, 4:57-58, 83, 106, 114-15.

To JAMES BROOKS Lexington, September 8, 1848

I recd. today your favor of the 2d. with an editorial of the [New York] Express enclosed.[1] And I recognize, with much pleasure and gratitude, your friendship for me.

Prior to the receipt of your letter, I had received from the State of Ohio two communications,[2] signed by several persons, inviting me to become an

Independent Candidate for the Presidency. I promptly returned an answer stating[3] that I could not comply with their request, and that I could not consent to any further use of my name in connection with that office.

Altho' the proceedings of the Philada. [Whig National] Convention[4] did not inspire me with much respect for its powers of order, deliberation and investigation, I thought it proper to submit to its decision, so far as I was personally concerned, and I have accordingly quietly submitted to it. I have not done any thing to oppose or thwart its nomination, and I have not written or uttered one word for the public eye or ear, except the answer above mentioned. I have given, and shall give, no countenance or encouragement to any movement to bring my name, as a Candidate for that office before the public.

I think that the Philada Convention has placed the Whig party in a humiliating condition. Still, out of deference to my friends who think otherwise, and because I can give no support to the competition of Genl. [Zachary] Taylor, I have made no opposition to his election. I have problems, and shall probably continue to forbear, to take any active or partizan part in promoting his election. I have adopted this course, from self respect, from consistency with long cherished opinions, strengthened by experience and observation, from a belief that his election will be to establish a mere *personal* party, and from a desire neither to lead or mislead any one. Numerous and strong appeals have been made to me to recommend him as a Whig.[5] But I have declined doing so. I know nothing of his politics beyond his own public expression of them. According to that he is a qualified Whig, who repudiates all pledges or obligations to support the measures of any party.

I could not say any thing in behalf of his election, without assigning reasons which would perhaps injure him more than my support would benefit him. I have therefore determined to remain silent, and if I am spared to go to the polls and give the vote which I may deem least injurous to the Country.[6]

This letter is not written for publication. Indeed I dislike writing at all, as uses are too often made of my letters contrary to my intentions.

But on one point I desire no secrecy, and that is, that I am utterly opposed to the use of my name as a Candidate for the Presidency.

My warm regards to your brother.[7] P.S. I ought to say that I think highly of Mr. [Millard] Fillmore. At the Extra Session of 1841 he and I, being Chairmen of Corresponding Committees of the two houses of Congress,[8] were in frequent and intimate intercourse. I found him full of zeal ability and indefatigability. I can vouch for his being a Whig both in name and in principle.

ALS. MnHi. 1. Neither the letter nor the editorial has been found. 2. Meade & King *et al.* to Clay, August 31, 1848. 3. Clay to Meade & King, Sept. 11, 1848; Clay to Cincinnati Whigs, Sept. 1, 1848. 4. Greeley to Clay, Nov. 15, 1846. 5. For example, Harris to Clay, Sept. 5, 1848. 6. Stevenson to Clay, July 26, 1848. 7. For Erastus Brooks (1815-86), journalist and politician, see *DAB*. 8. See 9:832.

From Morton McMichael, Philadelphia, September 9, 1848. Writes "to express my grief at the result of the Philadelphia Convention [Greeley to Clay, November 15, 1846]." Views Zachary Taylor's nomination as "unwise, unkind & unmerited." Remains convinced "that it will be extremely difficult to elect him. But this very conviction makes my anxiety for his success the greater, for I am persuaded that the election of Gen. [Lewis] Cass would be the greatest calamity which could befall the country." Advises Clay that "many of *your* staunchest friends here" believe that Cass can be defeated in New York only with "the use of your name in that state. . . . They think that unless this is done, not only will the vote of New York be secured to Gen. Cass [Harlan to Clay, June 15, 1848]; but that by a necessary reaction our prospects—now most cheering—of electing a Whig Governor in Pennsylvania will be greatly diminished." For this reason they "beg you . . . to disclaim the recent movement [Dean to Clay, September 5, 1848]."

Asserts that "the truest & most devoted of your Philadelphia admirers have been shocked at this N.Y. movement . . . from the conviction that it is unjust to your self." Hopes "that you will publicly disavow the course pursued in New York; as I am sure such a disavowal will be in keeping with your high character." ALS. DLC-TJC (DNA, M212, R11).

In the 1848 state gubernatorial election in Pennsylvania, Whig William F. Johnston narrowly defeated Democrat Morris Longstreet by a vote of 168,522 to 168,225. *BDGUS*, 3:1306. Whigs carried the state senate by a margin of 21 seats to 12 for the Democrats, and held a majority in the state house of representatives of 52 to 48. New-York *Daily Tribune*, October 18, 1848. In the congressional race, Whigs won 13 seats, Democrats 8, Free Soilers 2, and Anti-Masons 1. *Guide to U.S. Elections*, 588.

From Thomas B. Stevenson, Cincinnati, September 9, 1848. Acknowledges Clay's "kind condolence, on the loss of my child [Clay to Stevenson, September 4, 1848]." Expresses annoyance "at the failure of the [New-York *Daily*] Tribune as yet to publish the communication I addressed that paper, dated and mailed the 24th of August [Stevenson to Clay, July 26, 1848]," and conceives "no reason for its non appearance, unless it be the absence of Mr. Greely [*sic*, Horace Greeley] up the Lakes." Prefers to publish it in the Tribune "not only on account of its extensive circulation, but of its hitherto friendly regard for you." If they reject it, however, doubts "whether any other press of high influence would deem its publication expedient before the November election."

Reports on Stephen S. L'Hommedieu's attempt to present a "plausible apology for his defection [Stevenson to Clay, July 26, 1848]" from Clay at the Philadelphia nominating convention, writing that the Ohio delegate argued "*first*, that the arrangements of the Taylorites, backed as they were by the Clique at Washington [Clay to Harvey, April 18, 1848] and elsewhere were such that they could not possibly have been thwarted by any opposition, and second, that, if Ohio [Ullmann to Clay, February 18, 1848] had voted for you from the first, Indiana [Clay to Mercer, April 14, 1848] and Michigan [Stevenson to Clay, May 18, 1848, no. 2 of date] would have gone for Taylor from the start." While "such logic or reasoning as this could not stand examination," has had it "thrown in my teeth that *Kentucky* having deserted [Clay to Stevenson, April 12, 1848], it was impossible or rather not to be required that others should stand fast. And this is about as much of *principle* as characterised the whole of the procedure, based as it was upon the sordid and fallacious, or as [Daniel] Webster calls it with biting sarcasm, 'sagacious and wise,' calculation of *availability*." Reports that "so far from [Winfield] Scott's willingness to run for V.P. [Scott to Clay, July 19, 1848] being known at Phila. it was said there he would not." Adds that "L'H. insinuated . . . an imputation of treachery at heart against you, on the part of Greel[e]y." Advises Clay that "Schenck. . . . denied to me positively that he had any agency in promoting the Scott movement in Ohio. . . . I am afraid we shall never know the whole truth about the extraordinary proceedings, until, if Taylor be defeated, the factions quarrel as to their relative blame in bringing about such a result, or, if elected, they fight over the expected spoils."

Believes Taylor's chances in Ohio are "extremely inauspicious [Bebb to Clay, April 4, 1848]." Others feel "Taylor will squeeze through," while "some believe [Martin] Van Buren will whip through." Worries that Lewis Cass might win if "many

Whigs, though they will not go for V[an]. B[uren]., will remain at home and let the election take care of itself."

Describes Thomas Corwin's "moral influence" in Ohio as "unquestionably paralysed to some extent" as some of his "most enthusiastic former friends . . . denounce him on the stump and in the press." Understands there is already talk of Corwin's "leading the Free Soil party for the dance of 1852," but despite his "qualities to charm the masses," is "satisfied he lacks the qualities of a leader." Does not "question the honesty of his purposes nor the integrity of his principles; but he is too facile or too ductile under the hands of other men of more indomitable spirit." Believes "His influence with the separate free Soil men, is greatly impaired by his support of Taylor. Yet it is difficult to speculate upon such a topic. Though I think him much less popular in the north now than last year, the fickleness, caprice, cant, hypocrisy and fanaticism of the north, may even yet be turned to his favor. That would not be so strange as Whigs now going for Van Buren." Concludes "As to Mr Corwin," that "it was the honest hope of my heart . . . and in which I fondly dreamed Kentucky would be gladly brought to concur, that on retiring from the Executive chair at the end of the next term, your mantle would descend on him for the succeeding one. . . . I do not know but I *may* be for Corwin in '52, but certainly *now* I feel quite indifferent to the idea." ALS. DLC-HC (DNA, M212, R6).

Schenck is probably Robert C. Schenck who at this time was an Ohio congressman. *BDAC*.

From DANIEL ULLMANN New York City, September 9, 1848

I have intended for sometime to write to you. You will notice in the papers an account of a meeting held here on the 7th instant.[1] It was a great and glorious assemblage. The feeling of discontent is wide spread. I have just returned from a trip through this State and parts of New England, and every where found Whigs who were loud in their denunciations of the fraud practised upon us at Philadelphia;[2] and vehement in the expression of their determination not to vote for its nominee for the Presidency [Zachary Taylor]. Under these circumstances your friends here feel that there is nothing in the posture of affairs which requires you to express an opinion publickly, or to put a veto upon our proceedings. We pray you to let us alone. Be acquiescent and do not publish a syllable to the public.[3] Let us proceed in our own way. My own opinion is that much may be done. The means of intercourse are now so great that days only are required to accomplish that for which months were formerly insufficient. By a vigorous rush a startling result may be attained. Whatever may be the end of it, for Heaven's sake let us have a nucleus around which a Whig party may be re-organized after we shall have emerged from the smoke of the present contest. It is the only door open for us, through which we may retreat with a conservative band, which may finally rescue our beloved country from the horrors of military rule or corrupt charlatanism.

Copy, signed. NHi. 1. Dean to Clay, Sept. 5, 1848. 2. Greeley to Clay, Nov. 15, 1846. 3. Clay to Lynch, Sept. 20, 1848.

To HENRY WHITE Lexington, September 10, 1848

I received your friendly letter, and beg you to be perfectly assured of my undiminished regard & esteem.

Altho' I believed that the Philada. [Whig National] Convention[1] has placed the Whig party in a humiliating condition—one which I fear will impair its usefulness, if not destroy its existence, I acquiesced in its decision in not nominating me, and have submitted quietly to it. I have done nothing to oppose its nomination. I have given no countenance to any movements having for their object any further use of my name, in connection with the office of President. Beyond this I cannot go. Self respect, and consistency with deliberate opinions long since formed and repeatedly avowed, against the elevation to that office of a mere Military man, must restrain me from taking any active part in the Canvass. I wish to leave every body freely to act for themselves without influence from me, if I could exert any. If I were to recommend the support of Genl. [Zachary] Taylor, and if he should be elected and afterwards, in his administration, disappoint the Whigs, I should feel myself liable to reproaches.

I regret therefore that I cannot comply with your request to make a public declaration of my intention to support Genl Taylor. Without compromiting any one, I shall go to the polls when the day arrives and give such a vote as I think may be most likely to be the least injurious to the Country. . . .

ALS. PHi. Letter marked "(Private)." Printed in Colton, *Clay Correspondence*, 4:573-74. 1. Greeley to Clay, Nov. 15, 1846.

To N.B. MEADE & J.W. KING Lexington, September 11, 1848

I have received your letter,[1] in which you are pleased to say "that there is great disaffection in the Whig party in this State [Ohio] on account of the nomination of Genl Taylor; that the Democrats have their Candidates, the Abolitionists theirs, the No party theirs, but the honest Whigs have no Candi[d]ate," and you invite me to become one. You further say that "they cannot urge the Philadelphia Convention against you, since in this State ten delegates disobeyed instructions in not voting for you[.]"[2]

But gentlemen my name was submitted to that Convention,[3] with my consent.[4] It deemed it inexpedient to nominate me, and I have submitted to the decision. I have not thought myself invested with any right to look into the motives or conduct of any delegates to the Convention. If any of them violated their instructions, they are responsible to their own consciences, and to their constituents, and not to me.

I cannot, therefore, give the smallest countenance or encouragement to any further use of my name, in connection with the office of President of the U. States.

I pray you, nevertheless, Gentlemen, to accept my respectful acknowledgments for the high confidence you entertain in me.

ALS. OFH; copies in DLC-HC (DNA, M212, R6) taken from Carl Schurz Papers and OCHP. 1. Meade & King *et al.* to Clay, August 31, 1848. 2. Ullmann to Clay, Feb. 18, 1848. 3. Greeley to Clay, Nov. 15, 1846. 4. Clay to The Public, April 10, 1848.

To THOMAS G. CLARKE Lexington, September 12, 1848

I duly received your very kind official letter,[1] transmitting the proceedings of a public meeting held at the Slash Church, in Hanover County, at which they did me the honor to propose my name as a candidate for the Presidency, in terms highly flattering and complimentary.[2]

I recognise among the persons assembled on that occasion many names with which, in my youthful days, I was very familiar and extremely intimate—associates at school, playmates, neighbors, friends. The Slash Church, too, where the assemblage took place, recalls many early and agreeable recollections, as being that at which I received a large part of my imperfect education.

Regarding those proceedings as the affectionate expression of the esteem, attachment, and confidence of my old companions, or their descendants, I have never received any similar document with more gratification, or with sentiments of more profound gratitude; and I presume that it was in that sense the proceedings occurred, and were transmitted by you to me.

Considered as a serious and formal presentation of my name to the people of the United States as a candidate for the Presidential office, I am sure that you will not be surprised at my saying that it is impossible for me to accept the nomination.

My name, with my consent, was submitted to the consideration of the Philadelphia [Whig National] Convention, which assembled in June last.[3] That body thought proper to nominate a distinguished citizen of the United States, and not me. In view of the relation in which I stood to the convention, I do not think that I ought to pass any judgment upon its proceedings. It is sufficient for me to know that it did not deem it expedient to nominate me. In this decision I have entirely acquiesced. I have quietly submitted to it, and have given no encouragement or countenance to any further use or connexion of my name with the Presidency. To this effect, I have uniformly written to all associations and individuals who have addressed me on the subject. I hope that my good friends of Hanover will approve of my adherence to this resolution, dictated by my honor, by a regard to my character, and by my desire of retirement. Tell them under what great obligations they have placed me, and that I shall cherish the proof of their friendship and confidence, which you have sent me, among the most precious treasures of memory.

Nor can I conclude without tendering to you, personally, my grateful acknowledgments for the kind and flattering terms in which you have addressed me, and especially for your touching allusion to the venerated memories of my lamented parents. . . .

Copy. Printed in Washington *Daily National Intelligencer*, Sept. 27, 1848. 1. Clarke to Clay, August 22, 1848. 2. *Ibid.* 3. Greeley to Clay, Nov. 15, 1846.

To JOHN PERRIN[1] Lexington, September 12, 1848

I received your obliging letter yesterday only, altho' it bears date the 22d Ulto. I also received the letter of Mr. [Thomas G.] Clarke with the proceedings at the Slash Church.[2] They deeply affected me, and excited emotions of the warmest gratitude. I transported myself again, in imagination, among the scenes and the companions of my boyish days. I have returned by this mail an answer to Mr. Clarke which I hope will prove acceptable to my Slash Church friends.[3] I of course could not accept their nomination altho' I felt the honor of it with the liveliest sensibility. I cannot think of adding to the complication and the embarrassments of the Canvass by the use of my name. I deplore the condition of the Country, and not the less because it has been produced not only without any agency of mine, but against my solemn warnings and publicly expressed convictions. But it is still *our* Country, and is entitled to our best wishes and fervent prayers.

I request you to present my affectionate regards to all your neighbors, and to our friend [John M.] Botts, when you see him.

LS. KyLoF. Letter marked "(Private)." 1. John Perrin was the son of Isaac Perrin of "Merry Oaks" in Hanover County, Va., and brother of Samuel Perrin who organized the Slash Church convention. For Isaac Perrin's will, see *Hanover Historical Society Bulletin* (Nov., 1974), 7. 2. Clarke to Clay, August 22, 1848. 3. Clay to Clarke, Sept. 12, 1848.

To Thomas B. Stevenson, Cincinnati, September 12, 1848. Agrees that it is "probable that the absence of Mr Greely [*sic,* Horace Greeley] from home accounts for the non appearance of your letter [Stevenson to Clay, July 26, 1848]" in the New-York *Daily Tribune.* Does not doubt Greeley's "fidelity . . . up to and including the period of the Philadelphia [Whig National] Convention [Greeley to Clay, November 15, 1846], Mr H———* [Stephen S. L'Hommedieu] to the contrary notwithstanding [Stevenson to Clay, September 9, 1848]." Hopes for an opportunity to show Stevenson "some curious letters about the course of our friend [Thomas] Corwin." Concludes: "Nominations and threats of nominations of me continue to come to me. I have one answer for all, that I cannot possibly accept." Copy. OCHP. Printed in Colton, *Clay Correspondence,* 3:484.

"Mr H———" is marked with an asterisk and on the margin beside another asterisk is written the name "S.S. La Hommidieu [*sic*]."

Despite his earlier opposition to Zachary Taylor and his support for the Wilmot Proviso, Corwin was campaigning vigorously for Taylor in Ohio. See Clay to Stevenson, September 4, 1848, and Stevenson to Clay, October 2, 1848.

From GEORGE D. PRENTICE[1] Louisville, September 13, 1848

I have two or three times, sin[ce] Gen [Zachary] Taylor's nomination at Philadelphia,[2] taken up my pen to write to you, and as often, after a little painful thought, thrown it down again. I think I need not tell you how earnestly and anxiously, for more than twenty years I have desired your election to the Presidency. There has not been a period during all that time when I would not gladly, for the sake of your election, have sacrificed half of the poor remnant of my life. I should, before the meeting of the Philadelphia [Whig National] Convention, have zealously advocated your nomination, had I felt a full or even a very strong conviction, that if nominated, you would be elected. But I could not help entertaining strong doubts upon the subject. I saw none of your old opponents who avowed a willingness to vote for you, but, on the other hand, I met not infrequently with some of your old supporters who declared, that, notwithstanding their admiration of you, they were tired of hopeless struggles and would never vote for you again.[3] To be sure the number of your old friends who talked t[hus] was very small, yet the conviction that your election, [if you] should be the nominee of the convention, would be doubtful [was] deep and extensive. Nine hundred and ninety-nine [out] of every thousand Whigs preferred you for the Presidency [over an]y other man on earth, but they felt, as you yourself felt after the close of the contest of '44,[4] that you ought not again to be a candidate unless there should be an almost absolute certainty of your success. They loved you too dearly and had too high a regard for your great fame to be able to bear the thought of seeing you exposed to the hazard of another defeat. Anxious as they were to see you President, they felt that the Presidency could add nothing to your happiness or your glory, whilst another defeat would deeply mortify both you and them though it might not, in the eyes of the judicious, tarnish the lustre of your name.

The whigs believed that they could elect Gen. Taylor to the Presidency, yet they never dreamed of having to struggle to elect him without your aid and influence. They considered Gen Taylor available, but they reckoned your cordial cooperation as one of the great elements of his availability. They did not contemplate the possibility of a contest between themselves and their old foe, in which you, for whom they had shown a deeper and more lasting devotion than any other party had ever shown for any other [lea]der, could be an inactive spectator. But you [have] given them no aid or comfort in the fearful encounter, and your apparent indifference, whilst it encourages the enemy and renders the result doubtful, cuts your old, your life-long friends to the heart.[5]

I think, my dear sir, you do not doubt that Gen Taylor is a whig, and that, under existing circumstances, the interests of the country require his election. I have the best reasons for supposing that you regard him as a whig and a worthy one—or at least that you so regarded him less than a year ago. I will state those reasons—When you were at my house in the latter part of last November, you made a suggestion to Mr [George W.] Weissinger and myself which I embodied a few days afterwards in an article upon a National Convention. The suggestion, as you made it and [as] I wrote and published it, was in these words ["A] late convention at Frankfort will probably appoint the Delegates to the National Convention, and, to prevent any collision between the respective supporters of the two eminent Kentuckians, we would respectfully suggest that the delegates be instructed to consult fully with the delegations from other sections of the country and then to cast the vote of Kentucky for Mr Clay or Gen Taylor, according as the one or the other, if neither shall have declined a nomination at that time, shall be ascertained to be the favorite of the whig party of the Nation."[6] When you received my paper containing the article, you had the kindness to write me a letter alluding particularly to the paragraph I have just quoted and saying that it met your views exactly.[7] You suggested the paragraph before it was written, and you cordially endorsed it afterwards. The paragraph suggested, not that the Kentucky delegation to Philadelphia should be left free to select from among all the distinguished whigs of the Union, but that they should be limited to a choice between yourself and Gen Taylor. Surely whe[n] you made and when you endorsed this suggestion y[ou] considered Genl Taylor a good whig and worthy of the Presidency although he had not at that time written [the] Allison letter,[8] the best whig document tha[t has] ever come from his pen. The fact that you made and endorsed the suggestion in question has always emboldened me to say that you had full confidence in Gen. Taylor's Whiggism, and I trust that in this I have not spoken untruely.

Some of the Whigs of the North are now us[ing] your name as a spell of power to break up [the] party, defeat Gen. Taylor, and, as a necessary consequence, secure the election of Mr [Lewis] Cass.[9] I suppose you are as well apprised of these movements as I am, yet I take the liberty of enclosing to you an accou[nt]. . . .

AL, last part of manuscript missing. DLC-HC (DNA, M212, R6). 1. Although the signature is missing, editors have concluded from the handwriting and internal evidence that this letter was written by George D. Prentice, editor of the Louisville *Daily Journal*. For example, the author mentions Clay having made a suggestion "to Mr Weissinger and myself" which was later incorporated into an article. Prentice's partner at the *Journal* was George W. Weissinger. Clark, *History of Kentucky*, 241. 2. Greeley to Clay, Nov. 15, 1846. 3. White to Clay, Sept. 4, 1847. 4. Clay to Webb, Feb. 29, 1844. 5. Harlan to Clay, June 2, 1848. 6. This was published in the Louisville *Daily Journal* of Dec. 4, 1847. 7. Not found. 8. Clay to Ullmann, August 4, 1847. 9. Dean to Clay, Sept. 5, 1848.

From Philip R. Fendall, Washington, September 16, 1848. Reports that although "the Columbian College had held out the expectation of their taking up, before its maturity, their note given in liquidation of their debt to C[o]l. [James] Morrison's estate [Clay to Fendall, June 16, 1847]," he has so far seen "no sign of a movement to anticipate the payment." Intends to "put in bank for collection, and it will, I trust, be paid when due."

Informs Clay that "the enthusiasm which led to and accompanied the early nominations of Gen. [Zachary] Taylor" has given way to "an alarming apathy." Believes that most Whigs "will, I presume, vote, but many of them will do nothing more." Understands "the apathy of the party" but expects that most Whigs will "use the only means left open to them, to prevent the election of Genl [Lewis] Cass." If Clay had been nominated, "I should, for one, have felt ready to dedicate myself to the canvass." Adds that "though entertaining a respectful opinion of Gen Taylor, personally I have wanted spontaneous zeal—zeal enough to take an active part as formerly."

Concludes: "Mr. John O. Sargent has returned the plan of a new edition of your speeches, lent to him years ago." AL, draft. NcD. See 9:723-24, 737-38; also Clay to E. Sargent, August 7, 1844.

To Octavia Walton LeVert, [Boston?], September 16, 1848. Has received her letter [not found] from Boston. Comments on his persual of "an account of your appearance at the great fancy ball at Saratoga." Rejoices in "the distinguished reception" she received. While it "is highly creditable to the good taste of the circles in which you have moved," remains pleased that "you do not appreciate these flattering testimonies beyond their actual worth, and that you are not likely to be intoxicated by them."

Asks if Dr. Henry LeVert "safely received some letters of introduction which I sent to him to N. York" for his visit to Europe. Is sorry "that you will not return [to Mobile] by this route, as I should have been so happy to see you under my own roof." Has not yet "decided absolutely on going to the South" this winter, but if he does, "I must go to Mobile, unless you come to N. Orleans." Adds that he has left home only once all summer "to pass a quiet week at a secluded mountain watering place."

Is grateful to hear of "the Legions of my friends whom you have met," some of whom have, "I see, been making public manifestations of their abiding attachment & confidence[.] But I cannot consent to the further use of my name in connection with the Presidency, nor could I accept a nomination for me of that office, if it were tendered to me." ALS. GU.

To MORTON McMICHAEL Lexington, September 16, 1848

Before I received today your favor of the 9h. instant, I had written to N. York, to Virginia & to Ohio stating that I could not consent to accept a nomination of me for the Presidency, if it were tendered; and that I could not consent to any further use of my name, in connection with that affair.[1] Some of these letters, or authorized paragraphs from them, will have been published prior to your receipt of this letter.[2]

I have discountenanced & discouraged all movements in my behalf, since the Philada. [Whig National] Convention.[3]

Beyond this I will not go. I cannot, as I am urged to do, take any active part in the Canvass, nor can I endorse Genl [Zachary] Taylor as a Whig. I, who for more than twenty years of my life, have been honestly and sincerely opposing the elevation of mere Military men to the Presidency, am not going to give the lie to myself, and step forward to support the merest military chieftain ever presented, as a Candidate for that office, to the American people.

I think the Philada. Convention has placed the Whig party in a humiliating condition. It suffered itself to be menaced or frightened into a nomination, which it ought never to have made. It yielded to the overbearing influence of some Southern & S. Western members of Congress.[4] It proceeded upon the degrading assumption that the gullibility and not the intelligence of the people would decide the election. It had no authentic assurance, under the hand of Genl Taylor, revoking his insulting declaration that he would continue to stand as an Independent Candidate whoever the Convention might nominate;[5] and yet it caught with avidity at a mere hocus pocus explanation of his position made by the Louisiana delegation, upon an unproduced letter alleged to be from him.[6]

I believe him to be wholly incompetent to the office. I lament to say that, from circumstances which have fallen within my knowledge, I believe that he has practised duplicity that he is vascillating and instable.

I cannot recommend my friends to vote for such a person. I do not seek to shake or change their opinions of him, but they must act on their own responsibility. I will not be instrumental in deceiving or misleading them. I will not expose myself to their reproaches, if, being elected, they should be afterwards disappointed in his administration.

The success of Genl Taylor will be to establish simply a *personal* party, the head of which has no known principles, and the course of his administration will depend upon the unknown hands into which he must inevitably fall. And who they will be, according to the unfortunate weakness of poor human nature; we may conjecture that they will be those who fawn upon and flatter him the most.

I cannot lend myself to the accomplishment of such objects. Out of deference to my friends, who take a different view of the matter, I forbear to make any opposition to his election. I remain silent and passive. My great solicitude now, that my public career is terminated, is to preserve unsullied my character.

But I have another reason for my forbearance—I can give no support to Genl [Lewis] Cass. I deprecate his election. The case, as it presents itself to me, is between the frying pan and the fire. I wish to avoid both; but if I make any choice it will be of the former.

You will find, I think, that Genl T. has two characters, one his own, and the other alien, but covered by a *Bliss*.[7] This letter you will regard confidential; but I have no desire to conceal, and you are at perfect liberty to publish, that, "whilst I feel the greatest obligations and under the deepest gratitude to my friends, who still wish for my election as President, I cannot accept of any nomination for that office, and that I am not willing that my name should be further used in connection with it."

I neither think it just nor *politic* to treat them with any abusive or harsh epithets.

ALS. PHi. Letter marked "(Private)." 1. Clay to Cincinnati Whigs, Sept. 1, 1848; Clay to Meade & King, Sept. 11, 1848; Clay to Clarke, Sept. 12, 1848; Clay to Lynch *et al.*, Sept. 20, 1848. 2. For example, Clay to Cincinnati Whigs, Sept. 1 was published in the Washington *Daily National Intelligencer*, Sept. 26, 1848. 3. Greeley to Clay, Nov. 15, 1846. 4. The "Young Indians" in Congress who had been so influential in defeating Clay's nomination were primarily from the Southwest and West. For this group, see Clay to Harvey, April 18, 1848. 5. Taylor to Clay, April 30, 1848. 6. Clay to Lawrence, June 16, 1848. 7. William Wallace Smith Bliss, known as "Perfect Bliss," was Taylor's son-in-law and personal secretary. Whether correctly or not, Taylor's best campaign letters were attributed to Bliss. Hamilton, *Zachary Taylor, Soldier in the White House*, 26, 119, 136, 173.

To Mrs. M.B.O. THOMAS Lexington, September 16, 1848

I received your favor requesting my Autograph, and a lock of my hair, both of which trifling objects, I take pleasure in transmitting; and I tender you my thanks for your appreciation of my character, which prompted you to desire to possess them.

I expressed the sentiment to which you refer, that I would rather be right than be President;[1] but it has been applauded beyond its merit.

It is to be regretted that, when a stranger lady addresses one, there was not in her signature, or in some other certain mode, an indication whether she is married or single; for when the superscription is to be written, on the answer, it is necessary to know that fact. I feel this embarrassment now, and if I make a mistake I pray you to forgive it.

ALS. MWA. 1. See 9:283.

To DANIEL ULLMANN Lexington, September 16, 1848

I received your favor of the 9th instant, informing me of the movement of some of my friends in New York to bring out my name as a candidate for the Presidency.[1]

I feel under the greatest obligations and the warmest gratitude to them, for the sentiments of attachment, confidence, and friendship which they do me the honor to entertain. And to you, in particular, I owe an expression of my cordial thanks for your long, ardent, and ever faithful attachment to me.

But, my dear sir, after the decision of the Philadelphia Convention, against my nomination,[2] I have felt bound quietly to submit. I could not, therefore, accept a nomination, if it were tendered to me, nor do I wish any further use of my name in connection with the office of President.

I never would have consented to the submission of my name to that Convention, but under a conviction that I should have been elected if nominated. I firmly believe now that such would have been the result.

The Convention chose to nominate another, and I have ever since avoided giving the slightest countenance or encouragement to any further efforts on my behalf.

To bring me into the canvass now, would, I think, only have the effect of adding to existing embarrassments, and perhaps of throwing the election into the House of Representatives, at a time when parties are most exasperated against each other. Such an issue of the contest is to be deprecated.

I am glad to hear that you have finally established yourself in your profession in New York.[3] I request you to accept my cordial wishes for your success, happiness, and prosperity.

Copy. Printed in Colton, *Clay Correspondence*, 4:574-75. 1. Dean to Clay, Sept. 5, 1848. 2. Greeley to Clay, Nov. 15, 1846. 3. Ullmann was a lawyer. Johnson, *Twentieth Century Biographical Dictionary*.

From Henry Moore *et al.*, Wheeling, Va. (W. Va.), September 18, 1848. Write as "the most ardent of your friends" to express their "pain and mortification" at "recent efforts in some quarters to place you in an attitude of opposition to the election of Gen. [Zachary] Taylor [Dean to Clay, September 5, 1848]." Beg Clay "to make known to the Country, your actual position in relation to the important canvass now [in p]rogress."

View Taylor's election as "es[sential to t]he establishment of those great principles . . . to which your life has been devoted." Believing that "your sentiments are in unison with our own," condemn the actions of Clay's "ill judging f[riends]" who are "[c]onstantly and eager to use the great and deserved influen[ce of] your name for the defeat of the distinguished patriot, whom the Whigs of the union have placed in nomination."

Impressed by Clay's "lessons of patriotism" and encouraged " 'to fight on and fight ever'," intend to "turn with unabated confidence, to one whose disinterested and heroic devotion to the same high objects has been conspicuous in many a day of trial." Suggest, "in our zealous regard for your own historic renown," that Clay announce his support for Taylor to take advantage of yet "another occasion upon which you [can] render our Country [consid]erable service." LS, manuscript torn. DLC-HC (DNA, M212, R6). The letter is signed by 21 men.

Moore was on the board of directors of the Wheeling and Belmont Bridge Company. Wingerter, *History of Greater Wheeling, West Virginia*, 1:169.

To WILLIAM G. PAYNE Lexington, September 19, 1848

In answer to your letter,[1] I take pleasure in saying that I do not believe Mr. Filmore [*sic*, Millard Fillmore] is an Abolitionist, on the contrary, I believe that he would be as much opposed to any interference with slavery as it exists in the several States by Congress as you would be. In the extra session of 1841 he and I served as chairman in corresponding committees of the two Houses, which brought us often together,[2] I found him able, enlightened, indefatigable in the discharge of his responsible duties at the head of the Committee of Ways and Means, and patriotic.

Copy. Printed in Washington *Daily National Intelligencer*, Nov. 11, 1848. 1. Not found. 2. See 9:832.

To JAMES LYNCH *et al.* Lexington, September 20, 1848

I have received your official letter[1] as members of the (Whig) Democratic Genl Committee of the city and County of New York, and I take pleasure in answering it.

Never from the Period of decision of the Philadelphia [Whig National] Convention against my nomination as a Candidate for the Presidency,[2] have I been willing, nor am I now, to have my name associated with that office[.] I would not accept a nomination if it were tendered to me, and it is my unaffected desire that no further use be made of my name in connection with that office. I have seen therefore with regret, movements in various quarters having for their object to present me as their candidate to the American

People, these movements have been made without any approbation from me.[3] In the present complicated state of the Presidential Election they cannot in my opinion be attended with any public good and may lead to the increase of embarrassments, and to the exasperation of parties.

Whilst I say this much without reserve, I must nevertheless add that I feel profound gratitude to such of my warm hearted and faithful friends as continue to indulge the vain hope of placing me in the office of Chief Magistrate of the United States. And that I neither think it just or politic to stigmatize them as factionists or by any other opprobious epithets. Among them I recognize names which have been long distinguished for ability, for devotion to the Whig Cause, and for ardent patriotism.

You advert with entire truth to the zeal and fidelity with which the delegation from New York, sought in the Philadelphia Convention to promote my nomination as a candidate for the Presidency.[4] I am most thankful to them and shall ever recollect their exertions with profound gratitude.

And here Gentlemen I would stop, but for your request that I would communicate my views, this I shall do briefly, and frankly, but with reluctance, and regret.

Concurring entirely with you, that the Peace, prosperity and happiness of the United States depend materially on the preservation of Whig principles, I should be most happy if I saw more clearly than I do that that [*sic*] they are likely to prevail.

But I cannot help thinking that the Philadelphia Convention humiliated itself, and as far as it could, placed the Whig party in a degraded condition. Gen. [Zachary] Taylor refused to be its Candidate. He professed indeed to be a Whig,[5] but he so enveloped himself in the drapery of qualifications, and conditions, that it is extremely difficult to discover his real politics. He was, and yet, is willing to receive any and every nomination no matter from what quarter it might proceed. In his Letter to the Richmond Republican of the 20th April last, he declared his purpose to remain a candidate, no matter what nomination might be made by the Whig Convention.[6] I know what was said and done by the Louisiana Delegation[7] in the Convention, but there is a veil about that matter which I have not penetrated. The letter from him which it was stated one of that Delegation possessed, has never been published, and a letter on the some subject addressed to the independent party of Maryland, has at his instance been withheld from the public.[8] It was quite natural that *after* receiving the nomination he should approve the means by which he obtained it, what I should be glad to see is some revocation of the declaration in [the] Richmond Republican Letter before the nomination was made.

On the great leading national measures which have so long divided parties, if he has any fixed opinions they are not publicly known. Exclusively a military man without the least experience in civil affairs, bred up and always living in the camp with his sword by his side, and his Epoulettes on his shoulders, it is proposed to transfer him from his actual position of second in command of the army to the Chief Magistracy of this great model Republic.

If I cannot come out in active support of such a candidate, I hope those who know anything of my opinions deliberately formed and repeatedly avowed will excuse me, to those opinions I shall adhere with increased instead of diminished confidence. I think that my friends ought to be reconciled to the silence I have imposed on myself from deference to them as well as from strong objections which I entertain to the compettitor [Lewis Cass] of Gen. Taylor. I wish to lead or mislead no one but to leave all to the unbiased dictates of their own judgement.

I know and feel all that can be urged in the actual position of the present contest. I entertain with you the strongest apprehension from the Election of Gen. Cass, but I do not see enough of hope, and confidence in that of Gen. Taylor to stimulate my exertions and animate my zeal. I deeply fear that his success may lead to the formation of a mere *personal* party. There is a *chance* indeed that he may give the country a better administration of the Executive government than his compettitor would, but it is not such a chance as can arouse my enthusiasm or induce me to assume the responsibility of recommending any course or offering any advice to others.

I have great pleasure in bearing my humble testimony in favour of Mr. [Millard] Fillmore, I believe him to be able, indefatigable, industrious and patriotic. He served in the Extra Session of 1841 as chairman of the Committees of the two Houses of Congress and I had many opportunities of witnessing his rare merits.[9]

I do not desire the publication of this letter, but if you deem it necessary, you may publish the four first and the last paragraphs.[10]

Copy. DLC-TJC (DNA, M212, R11); copy in NcD. Printed in Colton, *Clay Correspondence*, 4:575-77. 1. James Lynch *et al.*, in a letter dated Sept. 13, 1848, wrote Clay as the "Executive Committee of the Democratic Whig Committee of the city and county of New York . . . on the subject of the use which has lately been made of your name . . . as a candidate to be supported at the ensuing Presidential election." Recall how the Whigs of New York faithfully supported Clay at the Whig National convention and express the belief that most New York Whigs will, nevertheless, give Zachary Taylor their "fair and honorable support." Add, however, that "A small portion of them . . . have deemed it expedient to dissent, and to place you in nomination . . . without your consent or approbation, relying on the devoted attachment of many of your friends, and, influenced by what we consider a zeal not tempered by discretion or sound judgment" to form in New York State an electoral ticket with Clay for president and Millard Fillmore for vice president. Believe this would not be to the advantage of the Whig party or agreeable to Clay. Note that they have heard he has dissented to such action and beg him "to communicate to us your views on the subject; the publication of which . . . will tend to produce union and harmony in this State, and thereby ensure triumphant success." Copy. Printed in Washington *Daily National Intelligencer*, Sept. 29, 1848. 2. Greeley to Clay, Nov. 15, 1846. 3. Clarke to Clay, August 22, 1848; Meade & King *et al.* to Clay, August 31, 1848; Dean to Clay, Sept. 5, 1848. 4. Ullmann to Clay, Feb. 18, 1848. 5. Clay to Ullmann, August 4, 1847. 6. Taylor to Clay, April 30, 1848. 7. Clay to Lawrence, June 16, 1848. 8. Taylor had written the Independent Taylor party of Maryland on June 29, 1848, approving the course of the Louisiana delegation and asserting that his friends "were . . . bound, if I were not nominated, to sustain and support the nominee." He asked that this letter not be printed, although he did not object to its being circulated among friends. The letter, however, finally appeared in the Washington *Daily National Intelligencer* on Sept. 23, 1848, preceded by letters from Reverdy Johnson and William H. Collins that explained the delay in its appearance. Johnson also stated that on August 8, Taylor had written giving his approval for publication of the June 29 letter. Hamilton, *Zachary Taylor, Soldier in the White House*, 102-3. 9. See 9:832. 10. This part of the letter was widely published in newspapers.

To HORACE GREELEY Lexington, September 21, 1848

Mr. [Thomas B.] Stevenson of Cincinnati addressed a letter to you (of which he sent me a Copy) which I should be glad might appear in the [New York] Tribune, if you see no sufficient objection against it.[1] It serves to sustain the grounds on which I was induced to consent to the submission of my name to the Philada. [Whig National] Convention,[2] and that is a point about which I feel some solicitude.

I regret the movements, made to bring out my name as a Candidate, both on my own account and that of my friends who made them.[3] I do not think that they can effect any good. After the nomination of the Convention, there was but one alternative for me, either to show that it was not the result of the "fair and full deliberations" of the Convention, or to acquiesce. Whatever I might have believed, I could not establish the first, and therefore felt that I ought to submit. I have accordingly quietly submitted; rigorously abstaining from giving to any person, on any occasion, the least encouragement to the further use of my name. But I felt no obligation to go any further. Both honor and self respect forbade that I should come out in the active support of a Candidate, who, in a reversal of conditions, had avowed his determination to oppose me.[4]

As to what the Louisiana delegation[5] said and did there is a mystery about their conduct, which has never been unravelled. Why has the letter, which one of them asserted he had from Genl [Zachary] T[aylor]., never been published? Why was that withheld from the public, which was addressed to the Independent party of Maryland?[6] His approval of what that delegation did, *after* he received the nomination was playing the safe game of "Heads I win, tails you lose."

Under this view, I feel no obligation to step forth as an active partizan of Genl. Taylor. If I saw in his election greater good that I do, I might suppress all sense of private wrong, and appear openly in his support. But besides the military objection, I fear that his success may lead to the formation of a mere *personal* party.

I have written an answer to a letter from the Executive Comee. of the Whig D[emocratic]. Comee. of N. York, expressing in strong terms my disinclination to the further use of my name as a Candidate.[7]

I feel most sensibly for my friends who made the Vauxhall movement.[8] Would it not be their best course to discontinue the use of my name, upon the ground that I am unwilling to be placed in that attitude?

What is to be the issue of the contest? I now think that Taylor will get the Whig States of N. England,[9] and that if he obtains the vote of Ohio[10] he will be elected. The contradictory accounts from the latter State render it difficult to judge; but it is favorable for him there that the election for Governor first comes on.[11]

ALS. MB. Letter marked "(Private)." 1. Stevenson to Clay, July 26, 1848. 2. Clay to The Public, April 10, 1848. 3. For example, see Dean to Clay, Sept. 5, 1848. 4. Taylor to Clay, April 30, 1848. 5. Clay to Lawrence, June 16, 1848. 6. Clay to Lynch *et al.*, Sept. 20, 1848. 7. *Ibid.* 8. Dean to Clay, Sept. 5, 1848. 9. For the 1848 presidential election, see Harlan to Clay, June 15, 1848. 10. Bebb to Clay, April 4, 1848. 11. Stevenson to Clay, July 26, 1848.

To CHRISTOPHER HUGHES Lexington, September 30, 1848

Your letter of the 25h. instant afforded me very great delight, principally because, from the playfulness of its style, it demonstrated that your health was better, your spirits good, and that Richard[1] was himself again. Long may he continue so!

I had heard unfavorable accounts of the state of your health and they had distressed me. Thanks, for your improvement to Mountain air and to your noble daughter [Margaret Hughes].

You ask if we shall ever and when again meet. I hope that we shall often before either of us goes hence. *When* I know not, but if you will not come here to see me (as you ought) perhaps I may go next year to see you, if I am spared. As for the approaching winter, possibly I may go to New Orleans, but that is an undecided point.[2] Its climate is not always good, but even with its humidity, the greatest objection to it in winter, it is not as bad as your friend represents. And when it happens to be dry, as sometimes it is, nothing can be more delightful. I think you had better risk it, especially if I do.

You appreciate [John M.] Botts justly. He is a true man, not always discreet, but always honest and patriotic.

The Philada. [Whig National] Convention is now an old affair, of which I wish to say but little, especially as I can not speak well of it. I think it humiliated itself, and put the Whig party in a false position, from which it is doubtful whether it will ever recover.

I have been so opposed to the election of a *mere* Military character to the Presidency, that I hold myself in reserve whether I shall vote at all. If I do, it will be from deference to friends, and from an invincible opposition to the election of Genl [Lewis] Cass, the only serious competitor of Taylor.

But the military objection weighs heavily with me.[3] Here is a man presented, in the actual command of one division of the Army, with his sword by his side, his epaulets upon his shoulders, bred up in the Camp, & destitute of all, the least, civil experience!

Suppose the other Commander of the other division of the Army were the opposing candidate, and each had under him a greater amount of force—might not the old drama of Pompey and Cesar be again exhibited?

I recoil from the contemplation of such prospects, even in the distant future, if indeed it be remote.

Give my love to dear Margaret. Tell her that she reasons from her good heart, about the Presidency, and I am not sure that the heart is not generally a better guide than this proud & self conceited head which we wear.

You advert to the marriage of Chancellor [Samuel Smith] Nicholas with the daughter of Genl. Smith.[4] I hope that he will make her a good husband; but, with respectable talents, he is cold, selfish and eminently conceited. This is entre nous.

I beg you to remember me kindly to the [Baron Vincent de] Tuylls & offer my congratulations on the birth of their child.[5]

This has been a year of great domestic afflictions with us. We lost early in it a favorite grandson,[6] last week a neice of Mrs. [Lucretia Hart] Clay,[7] and this week I have just heard of the death of my son in law, Mr. [Martin] Duralde [Jr.], my daughter [Susan Clay Duralde] having preceded him twenty three years ago.[8]

Ah! my dear Hughes, we must all soon follow them. We ought to be prepared for it, and I hope that you think seriously on that momentous matter.

ALS. MiU-C. Addressed to Hughes at the Astor House, New York City. 1. Shakespeare's *Richard III*. Geoffrey Cumberlege (ed.), *The Oxford Dictionary of Quotations*, 2nd ed. (London, 1953), 144. 2. Taylor to Clay, Nov. 17, 1848. 3. Clay to Clayton, April 16, 1847; Clay to Greeley, June 15, 1848. 4. Mary Mansfield Smith (1817-74) was the daughter of John Spear Smith and granddaughter of Gen. Samuel Smith, who was Hughes's father-in-law. She married her cousin S.S. Nicholas in Louisville on July 29, 1848. Information from family *Bible* of John Spear Smith, provided by Donna Ellis, Maryland Historical Society. 5. Clay to Hughes, March 19, 1848. 6. James Erwin, Jr. See Clay to Allibone, July 19, 1848. 7. Eliza Ross, daughter of Dr. Richard Pindell and Lucretia Clay's sister Eliza Hart, had died at her home in Lexington on Sept. 25, 1848. Lexington *Observer & Kentucky Reporter*, Sept. 27, 1848. 8. For Susan's death, see 4:658-60, 665-66.

From Thomas B. Stevenson, Cincinnati, October 2, 1848. After the publication of his article in the New-York *Daily Tribune* [Stevenson to Clay, July 26, 1848], informs Clay that the "Locofoco and Barnburner papers of this city promptly siezed on its statements to stir up further disaffections in the Whig ranks here; but none of the heartless men who enticed you by their fair promises and then foresook you . . . think it expedient to hazard any controversy in regard to my statements." Expresses surprise that "the fact stated in reference to Gen [Winfield] Scott's willingness to run on your ticket for Vice President [Scott to Clay, July 19, 1848]" did not induce "more commentary than it seems to have done."

Explains "Other excitements" on the "public mind": "The movements of your friends in New York [Dean to Clay, September 5, 1848] and elsewhere [Clay to The Cincinnati Whigs, September 1, 1848]; your refusal of the use of your name as a candidate for President; and Gen. [Zachary] Taylor's last Allison letter [White to Clay, May 26, 1848], have principally occupied the attention of the Whigs. That letter places Taylor, certainly on much more satisfactory ground to the Whigs; and in my opinion we have to thank, what I conceive the firmness but what the Taylorites deemed the obstinacy of yourself and your friends, for thus driving Taylor to a more acceptable position." Fears, however, that Taylor's letter "came too late to accomplish the results which an earlier publication would have promoted."

Describes Thomas Corwin's support for Taylor as "doubtless producing some effect; but certainly less than was anticipated." Since he cannot visit Clay to "see the letters you propose to show me" concerning Corwin [Clay to Stevenson, September 12, 1848], requests him to "transmit the letters by some confidential hand" so Stevenson can learn more "of the real character of the man." Adds: "Some recent circumstances have awakened unpleasant suspicions as to some of his conduct and probable motives; and I found, the other day, on a visit to his own county, that many of his old supporters there discard him."

Remains unconvinced that Taylor will carry Ohio, and reveals the "most candid opinion of our best judges" is that "[Lewis] Cass will most probably . . . secure a plurality, and, consequently, the electoral vote [Bebb to Clay, April 4, 1848]." Admits, however, that "every thing is so mixed up . . . it is almost trifling to speculate." Reports that "[Joshua R.] Giddings is stumping here and hereabout, and, I apprehend, with some effect." Notes that the Whig stronghold has been in the Western Reserve, but now Taylor's success requires "a great increase" of votes "South of the National Road. It is represented to us from Columbus that there will be; but I do not see the evidence." Writes that "[William S.] Archer . . . says Virginia will go for Cass and there is no hope for Taylor, if Ohio do not vote for him. Caleb Smith tells me Indiana is altogether hopeless for Taylor." ALS. DLC-HC (DNA, M212, R6). For the states carried by each candidate, see Harlan to Clay, June 15, 1848.

To DAVID WEBB[1] Lexington, October 2, 1848

I received and thank you for your friendly letter. I have been perfectly persuaded that the movements in New York and elsewhere, since the Philadelphia [Whig National] Convention, to present my name as a candidate for the Presidency, proceeded from the warmest regard and attachment, and the most friendly motives towards me.[2] I have felt the deepest gratitude to my friends for the sentiments which they do me the honor to entertain. And I have felt the injustice and impolicy of the attacks made upon them, by a part of the Newspaper press,[3] most sensibly.

After the nomination made at Philada. there was but one alternative for me, either to submit to it, or to contest it upon the ground that it was not fairly made. Whatever I might have thought of the conduct of the Convention itself, of that of particular delegations, or of that of particular delegates, standing as I did in an interested attitude, it did not become me to contest the decision. I therefore submitted to it. Having promptly resolved on this course, when I saw, in N. York and in other places, my name again announced as a Candidate, I could not remain silent. Silence would have been acquiescence, and that equivalent to express assent. Besides, I was formally addressed in several instances, and asked if I would consent to become a Candidate.[4]

I shall regret extremely, if any of my friends are dissatisfied with the declaration, which I have felt bound, uniformly and explicitly, to make, that I could not consent to the use of my name in connection with the Presidency.

Altho' I have not the honor of a personal acquaintance with you, the very friendly tenor of your letter entitles you to these explanations, and I shall be happy if they command your approbation.

P.S. I have no objection to your shewing this letter to any friend; but I have an invincible repugnance to appearing in the News papers.

ALS. NHi. Letter marked "(Private)." Addressed to Webb at 432 Pearl Street, New York City. 1. Webb's carpet business was located on Pearl Street, while his home address was 4 Market Street. Doggett, *New-York City Directory for 1848-49.* 2. Clarke to Clay, August 22, 1848; Meade & King *et al.* to Clay August 31, 1848; Clay to Cincinnati Whigs, Sept. 1, 1848; Dean to Clay, Sept. 5, 1848; Clay to Lynch *et al.*, Sept. 20, 1848. 3. For example, the Washington *Daily National Intelligencer* of Sept. 14, 1848, reprinted an article from the Albany *Evening Journal* that criticized Willis Hall and others for invoking Clay's name and accused them of really favoring Martin Van Buren. 4. See note 2 above.

From Nicholas Dean, New York City, October 5, 1848. Informs Clay that "steps taken . . . to induce an abandonment of the movement in your behalf [Dean to Clay, September 5, 1848]" are "now effectually accomplished, though there is still a deep current of grumbling, and dissatisfaction." Reports that "the moment it was known that *you* desired the abandonment of the organization [Clay to Lynch *et al.*, September 20, 1848], all was hushed;—even the monomaniacs (and there are a great many insane upon this subject) became quiet, and manageable, only claiming to let off their stifled zeal in one more general and tremendous shout of 'Henry Clay forever.' " Impresses upon Clay that "You are idolized!—I am quite aware how wide spread throughout the Country, are similar feelings, but . . . New York must certainly be the focus,—the only spot where the cry is heard 'give us Henry Clays boots for President rather than any living man, save himself.' " Adds that "since your name is fully, and decidedly withdrawn," Zachary Taylor's "prospects are certainly *greatly improved.*" Despite those whose "feelings of disgust, and disappointment" may "drive them over to our opponents," believes "the party as such, will no doubt generally cast their ballots for the Philadelphia nominee;—having the peculiar advantages which the schism in Loco Focoism gives him, he can hardly fail to carry the vote of this State, though by a majority much less than a truly popular name would command [White to Clay, April 5, 1848]."

Remains uncertain "whether Taylor or [Lewis] Cass is to occupy the White House [Harlan to Clay, June 15, 1848]—Which would be the better tenant, is with me so problematical that I shall be content with the negative influence of withholding my vote altogether." ALS. DLC-HC (DNA, M212, R6).

From Dudley Selden, New York City, October 9, 1848. Thanks Clay for his "very kind letter [not found]," which apparently defended the conduct of Selden, Willis Hall, and Joseph L. White [Clay to Lynch *et al.*, September 20, 1848]. Assures Clay that there is no need to make it public, adding that "Had the attack eminated from a more reliable source I might have solicited your shield, but it surely cannot be necessary to defend myself against so gross and well known a libeller as the proprietor of the [New York] Courier & Enquirer [James Watson Webb]." Intends to use Clay's letter only so much "as may be necessary if we find ourselves assailed by men of character."

Reports that "Genl [Leslie] Combs recently informed me that he had left with Mr Greely [*sic*, Horace Greeley] (and I think he said by your permission or donation) a letter written to you many years ago by Gov [Lewis] Cass [4:257], wherein he expressed his gratification at your successful defence against the charge of a bargain whereby you were to become a member of Mr [John Quincy] Adams Cabinet—With regard to the publication of this letter, it should be posthumous, or at least postponed. Now it will be considered an attempt to influence the present Presidential Canvass[,] hereafter it will become an important item in your personal history." Believes Cass's supporters "would now assail you for its publication." After the election, the letter will receive "its full value as testimony" and make "your course in withholding it an act of high magnanimity." ALS. DLC-HC (DNA, M212, R6). See also Dean to Clay, September 5, 1848; Clay to Webb, October 2, 1848.

To THOMAS B. STEVENSON Lexington, October 9, 1848

I received your favor of the 2d. I saw with pleasure, that the [New-York *Daily*] Tribune had at last published your letter,[1] the delay having probably arisen from Mr Greelyeys [*sic*, Horace Greeley] absence. It is republished in the [Lexington] Observer and Reporter,[2] and I am very glad that it is upon the record. The public mind is now so engrossed with the Presidential election that it does not attract so much attention as it would have done at any other time; but it will tell with the thinking part of the community.

I think it hardly worth while to send you by the Mail the letters to which I refered respecting our friend T[homas] Corwin.[3] I will reserve them for some cozy evening, which I hope you will ere long pass with me.

As to Genl [Zachary] Taylors last letter to Mr Allison,[4] I don't think much of it. He began with the silly if not presumtuous hope that the two parties would vie with each other in supporting him. Hence he courted both, and was to be an umpire between them. To the Whigs he said "I am a Whig and would have voted for Clay." To the Democrats "I am not a bitter Whig,[5] and will make no pledges." As the prospect of getting democratic votes has declined, he has become more Whig; and if the canvass were postponed a few months longer he would be a *bitter* Whig.[6] He gave to the Louisiana delegation no authority to withdraw his name if not nominated at Philadelphia;[7] but after he was nominated it was quite convenient and very prudent to rectify that act. But suppose another had been nominated would there have been any rectification?[8] I pause for a reply[.]

I can form no satisfactory opinion as to the issue of the contest. If Genl Taylor lose Ohio,[9] I think he will lose the election. I believe Maryland, N Jersey, Delaware, and Connecticut all doubtful. He will now I think get New

York.[10] As to Ohio, do not be too confident of Mr Corwins fine speeches. They tell better from the stump than at the polls. When were we more certain than in 1842? Besides it is impossible but that his moral power[11] has been weakened[.]

I have succeeded, and I rejoice in preventing my name from disturbing the canvass. They want me to go further, but I wont.—What do you think? I had a pressing letter from Govr [William] Bebb to attend the Hamilton Convention,[12] as the *first* of Mr Corwins friends addressed.

Copy. OCHP. Letter marked "(Private)." Printed in Colton, *Clay Correspondence*, 3:485. 1. Stevenson to Clay, July 26, 1848. 2. On Sept. 30, 1848. 3. Clay to Stevenson, Sept. 12, 1848; Stevenson to Clay, Oct. 2, 1848. 4. White to Clay, May 26, 1848. 5. The Colton version transcribes this as "an ultra Whig." 6. *Ibid.* 7. Clay to Lawrence, June 16, 1848. 8. The Colton version transcribes this as "ratification." 9. Bebb to Clay, April 4, 1848. 10. For the states carried by each presidential candidate, see Harlan to Clay, June 15, 1848. 11. Colton transcribes this word as "position." 12. The Cincinnati and Hamilton County Whig convention met at Carthage on August 26, 1848, to nominate candidates for presidential elector, Congress, and state and local offices. Lexington *Observer & Kentucky Reporter*, Sept. 2, 1848.

From Abraham M. Schermerhorn, Walnut Grove, Ontario Co., N.Y., October 11, 1848. Writes after "the most disgraceful result of the Whig Convention at Philadelphia in June last [Greeley to Clay, November 15, 1846] . . . to ask your advice as to the course it was the duty of your ardently attached and devoted friends to pursue." Although he has "seen several letters from you in the papers, forbidding the use of your name as a fourth candidate [Clay to Cincinnati Whigs, September 1, 1848; Clay to Brooks, September 8, 1848; Clay to Meade & King, September 11, 1848; Clay to Lynch *et al.*, September 20, 1848]," failed to find any further "indication of your wishes," which would "determine the course of thousands, & I proudly claim to be one of the truest if humblest of this band."

Argues that "Whigs cannot consistently vote for Mr. [Martin] Van Buren. . . . And to indirectly aid in promoting the election of Mr [Lewis] Cass, by omitting to vote, is a dreadful alternative too painful to contemplate." Considers it "a bitter pill" to vote for Zachary Taylor, "because there was no legitimate, fair or honorable reason why he should be selected as the candidate of the great Whig party, to the exclusion of one who was the first choice of nine tenths of that party, and who had done more to give character to that party & to the country than all other men together."

Adds that "It may, however, be a matter of imperious duty to swallow this pill and save the country from a continuance of . . . misrule . . . and this would be made the easier if you could find it in your heart to say to us—My friends I pray you to forget the wound which has been inflicted . . . and to do all in your power to save the country from the curse which would be inflicted upon it by the election of Gen. Cass."

Hopes Clay remembers him as "the person who arranged the matter of your receiving the calls of the ladies at his house when you was in Geneva [N.Y.] in 1839." Reminds Clay that "I saw you repeatedly in Washington, in company with my Uncle Gen Solomon Van Rensselaer" in 1841, and they met again "in New York in March last, when you introduced me to Mr. Dudley Selden," circumstances he alludes to "for the purpose of satisfying you that you are addressed by a firm and attached friend." ALS. DLC-HC (DNA, M212, R6).

To David Mundell, October 12, 1848. Thanks Mundell for the boots he has made and given Clay. Also thanks him for his friendly sentiments regarding the Whig presidential nomination and "my not receiving the nomination [Greeley to Clay, November 15, 1846] at Philada."

Regrets the loss primarily for the sake of his friends. Hopes the person who is elected president will be faithful and true. Adds: "We have had good and bad Presidents, and it is a consoling reflection that the American Nation possesses such elements of prosperity that the bad Presidents cannot destroy it, and have been able to do no more than slightly to retard the public advancement." ALS. Brooklyn Historical Society, Brooklyn, N.Y.

To NICHOLAS DEAN Lexington, October 16, 1848

I duly received your obliging letter of the 5th instant, and I have perused it with the greatest satisfaction.

The vivid picture which you have drawn of the enthusiastic attachment, the unbounded confidence, and the entire devotion of my warm-hearted friends in the city of New York, has filled me with the liveliest emotions of gratitude.

There was but one more proof wanting of their goodness, to complete and perpetuate my great obligations to them, and that they have kindly given, in deference to my anxious wishes; it was, not to insist upon the use of my name as a candidate for the Presidency, after the promulgation of my desire to the contrary.[1]

Copy. Printed in L.B. Clarke, "Henry Clay, Personal Anecdotes, Incidents, Etc.," *Harper's New Monthly Magazine* (August, 1852), 5:397. 1. Dean to Clay, Sept. 5, 1848; Clay to Brooks, Sept. 8, 1848; Clay to Lynch *et al.*, Sept. 20, 1848.

To The Palmyra New York Whigs, October 16, 1848. Has received their letter together with an account of a public meeting of his friends at which they proposed his name for president. Expresses "the liveliest gratitude" for their attachment to him, but notes that "I have already, in different forms announced to the public that I cannot accept a nomination for that office. . . . And it has been a source of inexpressible satisfaction to me to find that my friends everywhere, in deference to my feelings and wishes, have declined to press the use of it." Copy. Printed in New Orleans *Daily Picayune*, November 8, 1848.

To MARY S. BAYARD Lexington, October 19, 1848

I cannot resist the good opportunity afforded by Dr. Harris,[1] my ever dear and true friend, of dropping you a few lines. He brought me a kind letter from Mr [Richard Henry] Bayard, by which I was sorry to learn that your daughter Mary had been quite ill; but as he represented her convalescent, I hope that her health is now entirely restored. I contragulate on the marriage of Eliza, which I take it for granted was entirely agreeable to you and Mr. Bayard. I trust that you may live, and she may live, to see her husband advanced to the rank of an Admiral.[2]

This has been a year of great domestic affliction to us. In the spring we lost a favorite grandson [James Erwin, Jr.] under painful circumstances.[3] And a few weeks ago the husband of our eldest deceased daughter [Susan Clay Duralde], Mr. [Martin] Duralde [Jr.],[4] and a neice of Mrs. [Lucretia Hart] Clay [Eliza Ross], whom she dearly loved.[5]

I believe that I shall pass the approaching winter in N. Orleans altho' I have not absolutely decided on it. And the next summer, if God spare me, I hope to see you and other friends at the Eastward[.]

The issue of the Presidential election now depends, in my opinion, upon Pennsa.[6] If that State vote for [Zachary] Taylor he will be elected, and not otherwise. There is not the smallest prospect of his getting Ohio. I told the public so in April last but I was not believed.[7] Indeed all the statements contained in my note to the public are in a process of verification.

Present me affectionately to Mr. Bayard, to Mary, Baring [Powell] and his wife [Caroline Bayard Powell] and all the rest of your children and to your good mother [Harriet Chew Carroll].

ALS. Anonymous owner; copy in KyU. 1. Possibly Dr. Thomas Harris (d. 1861), a Philadelphian who entered the Navy as a surgeon on July 6, 1812, and was for many years Chief of the Bureau of Medicine and Surgery at Washington. For a time he was also in charge of the Naval Asylum at Philadelphia. *PMHB*, 7:123, 127-29; Edward W. Callahan (ed.), *List of Officers of the Navy of the United States and of the Marine Corps From 1775 to 1900* . . . (reprint ed., New York, 1969), 248. 2. Clay to Bayard, Sept. 22, 1847. 3. Clay to Allibone, July 19, 1848. 4. *Ibid.* 5. Clay to Hughes, Sept. 30, 1848. 6. For the states carried by each candidate in the presidential election, see Harlan to Clay, June 15, 1848. 7. Clay to The Public, April 10, 1848.

From George D. Prentice, Louisville, October 21, 1848. Writes: "We have been looking anxiously for the publication of the letter written to you by Gen. [Lewis] Cass in '25 [Selden to Clay, October 9, 1848]; congratulating you upon your successful vindication of yourself. Genl [Leslie] Combs says that he directed a copy of the letter to be sent to the Washington correspondent of the North American [James E. Harvey]," but it has not yet appeared. Since "The St Louis Union, the Indianapolis Sentinel, and other Locofoco organs boldly deny that Cass ever wrote you such a letter. . . . I appeal to you whether justice to yourself and your friends does not require its immediate publication." ALS. DLC-HC (DNA, M212, R6).

From Joseph Hertich, "Asylum," St. Genevieve, Mo., October 23, 1848. Sends a newspaper account from the New Orleans *Bee* containing a letter from the mayor of New Orleans [Abdiel D. Crossman] to the council of the first municipality "respecting the purchase of certain documents, in the hands of Mr Bernard Marigny, necessary it seems, for the defense, in the Suit of Villars Dubreuil's heir, vs the United States [Clay to Henry Clay, Jr., March 17, 1845]." Appears from the letter "that Marigny has documents . . . that may operate against us, which the Council wanted to purchase." Believes "if they were in our possession," they might be used "to aid our cause or we might procure others to counteract them," but worries what may happen if "it take us by a Surprise unprepared."

Has written to Samuel Judah, enclosing a copy of the mayor's letter, and informing him "that it is your desire to go to New Orleans in Decr. or Jany to make a definite disposition of the Suit pending vs the United States." Asks Clay to let him know two or three weeks before he leaves for New Orleans "so that I may be there at the same time." ALS. DLC-TJC (DNA, M212, R14). Postmarked Fredericktown, Mo.

Also on October 23, Clay wrote Samuel Judah in Vincennes, Indiana, advising that he expected to reach New Orleans in early January. States that "We met with a great misfortune in the loss of poor [Richard Henry] Wilde," and he has thought of trying to engage Seargent S. Prentiss to assist in the Dubreuil case. Notes that he attempted to engage W.C. Micou, "but he declined from the press of business, stating however that [Judah P.] Benjamin would examine and engage in the case, but I have never heard from him." ALS. Courtesy of Charles J. Bayard, Fort Collins, Colorado.

Hertich wrote again from Asylum on November 4, 1848, saying that John P. Wilde, the son of Richard H. Wilde, tells him "that Marigny's documents, have been deposited in the Archives of the Council." Wonders if "this *honorable* council, have it in their power to possess themselves of them, and to deprive us of the use of them? God forbid." LS. DLC-TJC (DNA, M212, R11).

Joseph Hertich, a Swiss immigrant, had settled in Danville, Ky., before moving to St. Genevieve, Mo. There he opened a school known as the "Asylum" which became the premier school in that area for many years. His interest in the Villars case stemmed from the fact that he married Marcelite de Villars. Weston A. Goodspeed, *History of Southeast Missouri* . . . (reprint ed., Cape Girardeau, Mo., 1955), 408, 499-500.

Abdiel D. Crossman, mayor of New Orleans, had informed the council on September 25, 1848, that he would not veto their resolution to purchase the papers from Marigny for $5,000, although he felt it might raise some doubt as to "the propriety and justice of purchasing evidence to deprive the heirs" of Dubreuil of their rights. He refrained from action because he believed the veto should be used sparingly, but he added that he saw no "actual necessity for the immediate consummation of the contract" with Marigny. The council did, however, receive the documents and they were placed in the municipal archives. New Orleans *Bee*, October 6, 14, 1848. For Crossman, see Holli, *Biographical Dictionary of American Mayors*, 85-86.

Richard H. Wilde had died of yellow fever in New Orleans on September 10, 1847. *DAB*.

From Thomas B. Stevenson, Cincinnati, October 2[5], 1848. Encloses a transcription of Stephen S. L'Hommedieu's "To the Whigs of the First Congressional District [Stevenson to Clay, July 26, 1848]" which was "written in New York and intended [for publication] in the Cincinnati Gazette" to explain "the influences that shaped his course" at the Whig National convention. Believes the paper will fall "very far short of achieving its intended purpose of vindi[cating] . . . the writer." ALS, manuscript torn. DLC-HC (DNA, M212, R6). Printed in Colton, *Clay Correspondence*, 3:485-86. The last number of date on this document is torn; however, Colton gives the date as October 25, 1848.

To JAMES BROWN CLAY Lexington, October 28, 1848

Mr. Hiram McElroy[1] of Morganfield (Union County) has written to R[ichard]. Pindell to know if the Carthage land[2] is for sale; that two men of that County, one by the name of Holcomb, and the other Brashear wish to purchase it for a Saw mill; and that they would give $4.50 per acre for the land, payable in one two and three years. The land lies, as he describes it, near the mouth of Highland Creek and not above Shawnee town.

I have written to Mr. McE. that you are now absent to view the land, and with authority to sell it; and that I cannot give an answer to his proposal until your return. If you think the offer a fair one, perhaps you had better go to Mr. M[c]E. But I should prefer a payment in hand of one third.

We are all well here; and your family pretty much as you left them.

ALS. DLC-TJC (DNA, M212, R11). Addressed to James B. Clay at St. Louis, Mo. 1. McElroy was a member of the Kentucky house of representatives from Union County for several terms. Collins, *History of Kentucky*, 2:736. 2. On Jan. 16, 1849, Clay, acting as executor of the James Morrison estate, concluded an agreement with an unnamed party for the sale of "a tract of land lying in Union County Kentucky . . . being a military survey on the Ohio river, including the town of Carthage." The 300-acre tract brought $4.50 per acre, 1/3 to be paid in land, 1/3 in one year and the other 1/3 in two years. ADS. DLC-TJC (DNA, M212, R11).

To Philip R. Fendall, Washington, October 28, 1848. Informs Fendall that "I shall be much surprized, and consider myself very ill used" if the debt due Clay as executor of the James Morrison estate from the Columbian College [Clay to Fendall, June 16,

1847] "is not paid at its maturity. After having relinquished more than half the debt, if they fail to make payment, the transaction will wear an aspect which I forbear to characterize."

Views the outcome of the upcoming presidential election "to be as uncertain as the cast of the die. I should not be surprized if there are not, in the popular vote, 20.000 difference between [Zachary] Taylor and [Lewis] Cass, and yet there may be a very great difference in the electoral vote [Harlan to Clay, June 15, 1848]." Believes "Cass will most certainly obtain the vote of Ohio [Bebb to Clay, April 4, 1848]" and that "unless Taylor is supported by Pennsa. he will probably be defeated." Fears that Taylor "may be cheated out of Pennsa., as I was in 1844," and that "deplorable consequences might ensue" if he should get "the plurality in the popular vote, and yet lose the Election. Such are the strange workings of our complicated system!" ALS. Courtesy of Elsie O. and Philip Sang, Chicago, Ill.

To THOMAS B. STEVENSON Lexington, October 29, 1848

I duly received your favor of the 23d instant. I have some intention of passing the ensuing winter at the South, and if I go, it will be between the middle and last of December.[1] In the mean time, with the exception of about a week that I may be at Louisville (but where I cannot now say) I shall be generally at home. I hope that you will make your promised[2] visit to me soon after the P[residential] election.

I regret that you have found occasion on your late excursion for increased distrust of the straight forwardness and fidelity of Mr. [Thomas] Corwin in regard to the vote of the delegates from Ohio in the Philadelphia Convention.[3] I have been painfully constrained to adopt one of two conclusions, either that he has great constitutional instability and infirmity of purpose, or that he was maneuvering to bring about his own nomination in the conflict which he anticipated might arise in the convention between the friends of the several prominent candidates. The first is the most charitable conclusion, but there are some circumstances which indicate the latter. You remember some letters, copies of which you sent me in the course of the summer from [Richard Wigginton] Thompson, Truman Smith &c.[4] Some of them held out the hope of that very state of things. I told Mr Corwin my views on the Free Soil question,[5] and he knew therefore with me, as the candidate of the party, all was safe in Ohio. He was suspected, and charged at Washington for want of fidelity to me. But enough of this for the present.[6]

I read with attentive interest your reflections on the gloomy state of public affairs and the public mind, and I share in your apprehensions of the future. Knowing, however the proneness of men of advanced age to look upon their own latter times unfavorably, and to draw disadvantageous comparisons between them, and the earlier periods of their lives, I have not allowed myself to indulge in these gloomy feelings. But the condition of age is not applicable to you. It is undeniable that the last twenty years of our public career have been marked by violence, fraud, corruption and shameful disregard of principle. In studying the history of our British ancestors, we find similar periods, and yet that Nation ultimately purified itself, at least to a considerable extent, and got right again. I entertain hopes that our country may also recover, altho' I hardly indulge any expectation of living to witness its convalescence.

I have also received your favor of the 26th transmitting Mr L'Hommadeus' [*sic*, Stephen S. L'Hommedieu] vindication.[7] I agree with you that it is most lame and impotent. That a man knowing as well as he did the wishes of the community which he represented, should allow himself to be diverted from his duty by conversations in Steam boats, Stages and Taverns proves at least that he had not any very strong sense of the obligations under which he was placed. I suspect that he had a predisposition to defeat my nomination. At all events he appears very promptly to have come into the support of the nomination unacceptable as he knows it to be to the people of Ohio. He appears also to have been a ready and willing listener to the [Zachary] Taylor arguments. Who but himself believes really that there would have been any union between the Barnburners and old Hunkers, if I had been nominated? And who can believe that *Two*[8] *hundred* of *my* friends in Cincinnati, before he left it cautioned him against voting for me? What did he expect to do with that nucleus for [Winfield] Scott of which he speaks? But I forbear. I regret extremely that your great State is now suffering from the wayward course of its delegation, and I wish that years may not elapse before it again attains the lofty eminence on which it lately stood.

Well the election is nigh at hand and fact will soon supercede all speculation. Still I will indulge in some.

1st I do not believe that there will be a difference of more than 20 000 in the popular vote, and yet there may be a very great difference in the Electoral vote between Taylor and [Lewis] Cass.[9]

2d Taylor will lose Ohio, and by fair or foul means, Pennsylvania also.

3d Vermont, Connecticut, N. Jersey, Delaware, and Maryland are all in more or less danger, and I think Taylor must have great good luck if he do not lose some of them.[10]

I am inclined to think that Cass will be elected, contrary to my wishes.

I reserve for the occasion of your contemplated visit, to which I look forward with pleasure, many things which I have not leisure now to write.

Copy. OCHP. Partially printed in Colton, *Clay Correspondence*, 3:490-91. 1. Taylor to Clay, Nov. 17, 1848. 2. The Colton version transcribes this word as "proposed." 3. Ullmann to Clay, Feb. 18, 1848. See also Clay to Stevenson, Sept. 12, 1848. 4. Stevenson to Clay, May 18, 1848. 5. No such Clay to Corwin letter has been found, but see Corwin to Clay, May 3, 1848. 6. The Colton version omits this paragraph. 7. Stevenson to Clay, July 26, 1848. 8. The Colton version reads "*five*." 9. For the election results and the states carried by each candidate in the presidential election, see Harlan to Clay, June 15, 1848. 10. Colton omits these three paragraphs, beginning with "1st."

From Susan Allibone, Hamilton, N.J., November 6, 1848. Despite her "debility which often renders me unable to use a mechanical medium for the conveyance of thoughts," desires to express her "regard for those I love by imploring for them 'the blessing of the Lord.' " Hopes that "God will grant you a double portion of His Spirit. I should not feel satisfied if any ordinary measure of conviction, faith, love, and holy obedienc[e] were yours." Thanks God "for the spiritual illumination He has granted you," and "for the desire you express to consecrate the retirement, you are at last permitted to enjoy, to the interests of 'another and a better world,' " when he can "be released forever from 'every day's report of wrong & outrage, with which earth is filled!' " Reminds Clay, however, that "whilst the believer rejoices that 'to die is gain,' he ought also to remember that 'to live is Christ.' "

Explains why she is "thankful that this glorious Redeemer is the portion of my soul": "When my earthly friends sit down and weep because their unwearied attentions cannot remove the firm purpose of disease, my Saviour draws me still more closely into the Sanctuary of His presence, and my wearied spirit reposes thus in peace." Adds that "there is an amputation of the heart, caused by the removal of her most cherished objects of affection, which requires the still more tender offices of Him, who 'came to give the oil of joy for mourning, and the garment of praise for the spirit of weariness;' and in this source also, I have been greatly comforted. If I had never known bereavement, I could not so fully sympathize with the deep afflictions to which your letter [Clay to Allibone, July 19, 1848] alludes." Since Clay's "susceptibilities of suffering are unusually acute," prays that "the consolations of the Holy Spirit, and the sanctified uses of adversity may be given you in proportionate measure." Hopes Clay can teach his family "to consecrate the energy they have inherited from their earthly Parents to the glory of their Father in Heaven" and congratulates "your children and grandchildren, that they are permitted to surround you in the evening of your days."

Continues: "Permit me to say that I do not think you suit the times, dear Sir. *Expediency* has become the watch word of our Nation, and your political vestments have never assumed a chameleon here. . . . Oh! that we had many Daniels to confess that . . . our fathers have seemed and done wickedly, and we implore that national judgments may be averted." In "the stormy elements around us," asks "is it not an unspeakable privilege to be the subject of a kingdom which cannot be moved?"

Adds that "I am truly gratified to learn that the heal[th] of your little granddaughter [Lucy Jacob Clay] has so greatly improv[ed]. . . . I shall not soon forget the arms of affection with which you made me acquainted with the character of Mrs [Lucretia Hart] Clay, to whom you will please present my respectful regards."

Concludes: "My sister . . . is my support today, as I am still unable to attempt a greater effort than the pencilship of a letter." ALS. DLC-HC (DNA, M212, R6). Printed in Colton, *Clay Correspondence*, 4:577-79.

From William McLain, Washington, D.C., November 7, 1848. Encloses a copy of a resolution of the Executive Committee of the American Colonization Society authorizing the Reverend John Miller "to speak and act for this Society, at such times and places as shall appear suitable to him, in any of the countries he may visit" on his trip to Europe and "to solicit and receive any donations in aid of the work of colonization." Explains that Miller, of Frederick, Md., is the "son of Rev. Prof. [Samuel] Miller of Princeton." Does not "anticipate that he will do much for the Soc. while in Europe—but he may be of Some use, & his good Sense & prudence will prevent him from doing any harm." Adds that "Wherever he goes *your name* will be a ready passport to the best society—"

Reports that "Our cause has been gaining ground very rapidly this Year. . . . We have sent 443 emigrants to Liberia already, & there are 567 now waiting for a passage." ALS, with enclosure. DLC-Records of the American Colonization Society (DNA, M212, R20).

For both Samuel Miller (1769-1850), professor at Princeton Theological Seminary, and his son John (1819-95), a Presbyterian clergyman and graduate of Princeton Theological Seminary, see *DAB*.

From Nicholas Carroll, New York City, November 16, 1848. Regrets "to learn through the public journals of your illness," but assures Clay that "prayers, are offered for your preservation—your peace & happiness—by the honest masses of the people."

Reports that "100 or more of your close friends . . . from Connt. this state & City N.J. Pa. Del & Md." will meet in one week to discuss entering into "an organization . . . that will not suffer the future to be as the past." Asks Clay to "preserve *for the present all* letters you may have received, during the canvass, & prior thereto, touching the action of *the June Slaughter House* [Greeley to Clay, November 15, 1846]," in case "their production may be *all* essential."

Complains that " 'The Available' is elected, having received, excluding the votes of the four new states [Florida, Iowa, Texas, Wisconsin], some 200,000 less of the people's voices than were gloriously accorded you in 1844." Adds that "The *old* Democrats manifest much *honest* interest in our future & would make *any* concession to have Henry Clay as the Independent Candidate for 1852."

Asserts that "if Genl. [Zachary] Taylor's Administration is *clean* Whig, & the interests of the country are not forgotten in a disgraceful scramble for the plunder, it will have the ardent, *honest*, & thorough support for *one* term only, of those who abominated the nomination & when made 'asked no favors nor shrunk from no responsibility' in fearlessly denouncing its villainy." Adds that "if however the accession of Taylor, in Taylor*ism*, should prove Jackson*ism* No 2—fore God we will fight." If the administration "be honest it will be sustained from motive of duty. Should it prove otherwise the war begins anew."

Informs Clay of "apparently well accredit[ed]" rumors "that you will be tendered the state & declining that the mission to St James." Wishes, however, to see Clay "a member of the Constitutional Convention of his State [Stevenson to Clay, June 12, 1848]—its Presiding Officer as of course he will be . . . and with the halo of emancipation added to his towering virtues . . . he & his friends may then in perfect trust await the issue of such a deed." ALS. DLC-HC (DNA, M212, R6).

Clay was confined to bed with an unspecified illness for much of November. For updates on his condition, see Lexington *Observer & Kentucky Reporter*, November 15, 18, 29, Dec. 6, 1848.

From ZACHARY TAYLOR Baton Rouge, La., November 17, 1848

On my return here a day or two since after a short absence, I found your highly esteemed letter of the 23d, ulto. for which accept my most cordial thanks; the one referred to written by you in May last,[1] reached me by due course of mail, & I owe you an apology for not replying to it, which I deferred doing from day to day, under the expectation that certain events would occur which I wished to refer to in my reply, but which were so long in taking place, as to induce me to give up doing so altogether; said letter was entirely satisfactory as regarded the matter alluded to. (& to put an end to the misrepresentations growing out of the same going the rounds through various newspapers, I at once caused a short article to that effect, to be published in the Picayune of New Orleans,[2] which may have met your eye, & relieved me from great a[n]xiety, as I believed the course then pursuing by certain individuals touching our correspondence, was calculated if not intended to bring about a state of distrust if not unkind feelings between you & myself,[3] as well as some of friends; which had they succeeded in doing, would so far as I am concerned, been a source of much pain & mortification to me.

There certainly could be no objection or impropriety in your permitting your friends to read any of the letters I wrote you, who ought not to have made any use of them for any purpose, without your authority, as there was an implied confidence at least, which ought not to have been violated; it is true I allowed a a [*sic*] few & very confidential friends to read yours written to me, nor am I aware that any use was made of them directly or indirectly for any purpose whatever; nor was any copy taken of any one of them & furnished to a member of Congress or anyone else, altho, I have no doubt you have been informed I had done so.[4]

The hostile course pursued by the honl, Mr. [John M.] Botts[5] towards me since I was brought prominently before the Country, as a candidate for the highest office known to our laws, has been doubtless the cause of some mortification on the part of a portion of his friends, you perhaps among the number, as I feel confident you did not approve it. Had Mr. B. or anyone else opposed my election to the presidency on the ground of want of qualifications to discharge the important duties connected with said office, in a becoming manner & proper spirit it would have been all right & proper, & would not have given me one moments concern; nor does it at any rate; but the moment misrepresentation & scurrility was resorted to whether it effected the object of defeating me or not, it must ultimately degrade those whoever may be concerned in it.

I trust I have many devoted personal friends who from various causes were opposed to my reaching the offic[e] in question & took every honorable & proper means in their power, & no other, to prevent my success, & I shall certainly would[6] never think of censuring them, much less to permit it on my part, to interrupt our friendly relations because they done what they thought right in opposing my election to an office which they thought another was better qualified to fill.

I beg leave to return you many thanks for your kind invitation to visit Ashland should I go to Kentucky before you leave for the South; which it would afforded me much pleasure to have done, & passed a few days under your hospitable roof, but I must forgo this pleasure as it will be out [of] my power to leave Louisiana or Mississippi for several months, at any rate during the present year; but should you carry out your intentions of visiting the South as contemplated,[7] & should pass the month of January in New Orleans I will try & take you by the hand at that time or during the same month . . .

ALS. CU-B. Printed in Colton, *Clay Correspondence*, 4:580-81. 1. Not found. 2. The New Orleans *Daily Picayune*, June 21, 1848, printed a letter from Taylor saying that "None but the kindest feelings exist between Mr. Clay and myself, and he is well aware should he be nominated and elected, such a result would cause me no mortification or ill feeling, but rather pleasure and congratulation." 3. Taylor to Clay, Nov. 4 and Dec. 28, 1847. 4. *Ibid.* 5. Botts continued to promote Clay after Taylor's nomination and to urge an attempt to throw the election into the House of Representatives by running Clay as an independent candidate. See Botts to Clay, July 3 and August 23, 1848. 6. The word "would" has been interlined, apparently in a different hand. 7. On Dec. 20, 1848, Clay left Ashland bound for Louisville on his way to New Orleans. He departed Louisville on the steamship *Alexander Scott* on Dec. 24 and arrived in Natchez on Jan. 5, 1849. Remaining at Natchez a few extra days because of the cholera epidemic, he reached New Orleans on Jan. 13, aboard the *Princess*. Enroute from Natchez to New Orleans, he accidently met President-elect Taylor on the *Princess* at Baton Rouge. The two reportedly had a brief but friendly talk. Clay suffered a fall in New Orleans on Jan. 20 that temporarily incapacitated him and caused him to forego a trip to Mobile as well as other planned activities. Leaving New Orleans toward the end of March, he arrived back at Ashland on March 30 after a stopover at Louisville. Lexington *Observer & Kentucky Reporter*, Dec. 20, 27, 1848, Jan. 6, 13, 24, 31, March 21, 31, 1849; Clay to Harlan, Jan. 26, 1849.

From Rezin D. Shepherd, New Orleans, November 29, 1848. Has received Clay's check for $150 which pays all interest on his bond up to October 7, 1848 [8:835-36]. Adds: "As I passed through Louisville I learnt with much regret of your Severe Indisposition [Carroll to Clay, November 16, 1848], and Since my arrival here I Understand that you are probably by the this time restored to health." ALS. DLC-TJC (DNA, M212, R14). See also Clay to Mercer, March 18, 1848.

From JOEL T. HART Lexington, December 4, 1848

I hope you will accept this head I send you, which I have finished entirely with my own hands;[1] and also another which I will finish in a day or two, as a small token of the grattitude and obligation I feel toward yourself and Family who have extended to me so much kindness.

I will call out to see you this evening or tomorrow. . . .

ALS. DLC-HC (DNA, M212, R6). Printed in Colton, *Clay Correspondence*, 4:581. 1. Hart to Clay, Sept. 26, 1845.

To James Maker, Washington, December 4, 1848. Acknowledges "your friendly feelings and kind expressions towards me." Since "Your political opposition to me was when you did not know me, and ceased when you did," assures Maker that "I have equal regard for you as if it had never existed." Concludes: "If you have continued to discharge the duties of Public Gardener as well as you did, when I had an opportunity of observing how you fulfilled them, I hope it may be the pleasure of the new Administration to retain you in that place." ALS. DLC-HC (DNA, M212, R6).

From Clement N. Vann, Fayetteville, Ark., December 7, 1848. A student at the Ozark Institute, writes to thank Clay "for your kind and benevolent defence of my wronged and oppressed nation—The Cherokee people." Asks for Clay's autograph as a "token which may serve as a memorial of your benevolent exertions on our behalf and as a constant monitor to point me to the imitation of your magnanimity." The "Cherokee-school-boy" begs Clay to "Believe not the indian character incapable of" feelings of gratitude, "though it is for true they seldom have cause for its lodgement. Yet to this yourself [8:358-59, 726-27, 759-60, 861] and Mr. [William] Wirt are noble exceptions [8:266]." Writes a 24-line poem "as a faint shadowing forth of the firmness of the foundation upon which you have based your fame as far as relates to what my little nation may be able [to] avail in the general slant."

If Clay is appointed to Taylor's cabinet, "I humbly and sincerely pray that you may lend your influence to the Cause of my oppressed nation." Reports that "a friend and acquaintance of yours" had remarked to him "that under any circumstances whatever he had ever found you a friend of the oppressed." ALS. DLC-HC (DNA, M212, R6).

Clement N. Vann later served as a state senator from the Saline district, fought in the Confederate Army in the Civil War, and was a member of the Southern Cherokee delegation at the treaty negotiations of 1870-71. *Chronicles of Oklahoma*, 32:411.

The Ozark Institute, founded in 1845 as a mission school, was located at Mt. Comfort, about three miles from Fayetteville, Ark. Hugh Park, *Reminiscences of the Indians by Cephas Washburn* (Van Buren, Ark., 1955), vi.

To CHARLES FENTON MERCER Lexington, December 10, 1848

I have delayed transmitting an answer to your friendly letter chiefly in consequence of my long confinement by indisposition and now altho free from disease, I am still so weak as to make it expedient to employ the pen of one of my sons in addressing you. I am very sorry that you did not execute your intention to make me a visit, I looked for you, having heard that you entertained such a friendly purpose. I hope if we are both spared another year, that you will come and see me. Altho you have established yourself in a position which has some advantages I fear you must be very destitute of congenial society.

The Presidential election is now over,[1] and it must be gratifying to you and other of my friends, that its results demonstrate that I could have been elected with ease, if I had been nominated at Philadelphia.[2] I should have got all the votes which Genl. [Zachary] Taylor has received, possibly Georgia[3] excepted, and in addition Ohio[4] certainly, and I believe Indiana, which last he has lost by more than double the vote that I did in 1844.[5]

You urge me to return to the Senate, and cite the example of Mr [John Quincy] Adams! Mr Adams death happened undoubtedly in a most remarkable manner, and will of itself give him a distinguished place in History.[6] But except that event I do not think that Mr Adams added anything to his fame, by his service in Congress after his retirement from the Presidency. On the contrary I think several parts of his public conduct, had the tendency to diminish instead of augmenting his reputation.

If I could be persuaded that I could materially contribute to the proper adjustment of the momentous question which has grown out of the acquisition of New Mexico and California, I should cease to feel any repugnance to the resumption of a seat in the Senate.[7] But I cannot reconcile it to myself to become a formal or avowed candidate for that office. I do not know what I might be inclined to do, if the general assembly were voluntarily to tender it to me;[8] Perhaps deference to their will, would make me hesitate before I declined it. But that is an event not likely to happen.

I am making my arrangements to go to New Orleans in the course of a week or two, and to pass the winter there.[9] I should be most happy to have you as a fellow passenger again, on the voyage, though not under the circumstances in which you were placed, during the last one, which we made together. But I fear your improvements at Fentonville will prevent your going.[10]

LS. NjHi. 1. Harlan to Clay, June 15, 1848. 2. Greeley to Clay, Nov. 15, 1846. 3. Taylor carried Georgia over Cass by a vote of 47,544 to 44,802. McKee, *National . . . Popular and Electoral Vote*, 71. 4. Bebb to Clay, April 4, 1848. 5. In 1844 Polk defeated Clay in Indiana by a vote of 70,181 to 67,867, a difference of 2,314 votes. In 1848 Cass carried Indiana over Taylor by 74,745 to 69,907, a difference of 4,838. McKee, *National . . . Popular and Electoral Vote*, 56, 71. 6. Clay to James B. Clay, Feb. 21, 1848. 7. Sargent to Clay, Feb. 27, 1847. 8. Clay was elected to the U.S. Senate on Feb. 1, 1849, by a vote of 92 to 45 over Richard M. Johnson. Collins, *History of Kentucky*, 1:58. See also Clay to Underwood, Feb. 11, 1849. Clay's election aroused the fears of the "Young Indians" in Washington who believed he would be antagonistic to the Taylor administration in revenge for his loss of the Whig nomination. It also revived the factional struggles of the Whig party in Kentucky, but it proved that his influence on Kentucky Whigs remained strong. A letter from Robert P. Letcher was read to the legislature, declaring that Clay would give his cordial support to the administration. Gov. Crittenden, among others, was convinced that Clay's election would cause no problems. Van Deusen, *Henry Clay*, 394-95; Poage, *Henry Clay*, 189-92. 9. Taylor to Clay, Nov. 17, 1848. 10. Mercer had been ill during the earlier voyage. See Clay to LeVert, Dec. 19, 1846. Fentonville was Mercer's home on the Kentucky River near Carrollton, Ky. James Mercer Garnett, *Biographical Sketches of Hon. Charles Fenton Mercer 1778-1858 . . .* (Richmond, Va., 1911), 26, 55.

To CHARLES S. MOREHEAD Lexington, December 14, 1848

During the present Session of Congress, and under the present [James K. Polk] Administration, I presume, selections will be made of Cadets for West Point Academy. I should be glad to obtain a warrant for my grandson Henry Clay Junr [III] the eldest son of Lt col Henry Clay.[1] He is now fourteen years of age, has been eighteen months at the Franklin Military Institute, and is a boy of much promise. He has lost, as you know, both of his parents [Henry Clay, Jr., & Julia Prather Clay].

If you have any difficulty in procurring the warrant, I flatter myself that, if you would mention my wishes to the President [James K. Polk], he would direct it to issue[.] I would address myself directly to him, if I did not apprehend that it might be contrary to established usage.

ALS. DNA, M688, R175, frame 521. 1. Henry Clay, Jr. (really the son of Henry Clay, Jr., designated by editors Henry Clay III to avoid confusion) entered the U.S. Military Academy in 1850 [Clay to James B. Clay, May 27, 1850]. On Jan. 19, 1853, the Academic Board of the Academy recommended his discharge to the War Department because of his "having received an amount of demerit greater than 200 (289) between the 16th of June 1852 and the 14th of January 1853." He then submitted his resignation which was accepted on Jan. 31, 1853. USMA, *Register*, 203; and information supplied by Alan C. Aimone, Asst. Librarian for Special Collections, USMA Library.

To CHRISTOPHER HUGHES Lexington, December 16, 1848

I am so far recovered from my recent illness that I purpose leaving home the 20th. instant for New Orleans.[1] I cou'd not think of taking my departure without expressing my thanks to you for the friendly interest you felt in my recovery.

I received your short note from New York, in which you promised to write me, on your return home, a long epistle, which I have not yet received. I am very anxious to hear from you and of your being in the enjoyment of good health.

Well; you were mistaken in your prediction of the issue of the Presidential election—Genl [Zachary] Taylor and not Genl. [Lewis] Cass is elected.[2] I rejoice with you in the downfall of the party which has so long afflicted our Country, and in the brighter prospect of a better administration of the Genl. Government, for which we are authorized to hope. I expect to meet the President elect at N. Orleans,[3] and, from the amicable relations which exist between us, I may possibly be then able to form an opinion whether that hope will be realized or not.

It must be a source of some gratification to you and other friends, who desired my nomination at Philada, to be now satisfied, by the results of the election, that I should have been elected with ease, if I had been nominated. Besides obtaining the votes of every State which have been cast for him (Georgia[4] possibly excepted) I should *certainly* have gotten the vote of Ohio,[5] and I believe Indiana.[6] He obtained a larger popular vote than I might have done in some of the South Western States, but, on the other hand, my popular vote would have greatly exceeded his in the Free (or as Mr [Thomas] Ritchie would have it in the non slave holding) States.

But this view of the subject has now an interest only for my friends and for history. It should not affect our desire that the new administration may honorably acquit itself, and for the advantage of our Country.

I request you to present my affectionate regards to Miss Margaret [Hughes] . . .

ALS. MiU-C. 1. Taylor to Clay, Nov. 17, 1848. 2. Harlan to Clay, June 15, 1848. 3. Taylor to Clay, Nov. 17, 1848. 4. Clay to Mercer, Dec. 10, 1848. 5. Bebb to Clay, April 4, 1848. 6. Clay to Mercer, Dec. 10, 1848.

To WILLIAM R. HERVEY[1] Lexington, December 19, 1848

On the eve of my departure for N. Orleans, and fearing that I may pass through Louisville, without the pleasure of meeting you, I cannot leave home, without an acknowledgment of your friendly letter,[2] brief though it be, and too long delayed. This delay has proceeded from a tedious illness, from the effects of which I have not yet entirely recovered. I wished particularly to thank you for your devotion to me, for the fidelity of your attachment, and for the confidence which you have reposed in me.

The reflections and remarks, which you make on the decision of the Philadelphia Convention,[3] are such as thousands of other good Whigs throughout the Land concur in. The event is however passed, and has but little other than historical interest. General [Zachary] Taylor is elected, and whilst rejoicing in the change of the administration, which that event will produce, we may indulge the hope that his will conduce to the prosperity of the Country.

My friends, who desired my nomination, must derive one gratification from the results of the election, since they demonstrate that I could have been elected with ease. I should have obtained the vote of every State which was cast for him (possibly Georgia[4] excepted) and besides these, Ohio[5] certainly, and I believe Indiana.[6] If his vote in some of the South Western States, which went for his competitor,[7] were larger than I might have obtained, my popular vote in the Free States would have greatly exceeded his.

Regretting that I have not time to reply to that part of your letter, which requests me to particularize the desirable amendments to our Constitution, I must conclude, fervently wishing that you may long live in health happiness and prosperity.

ALS. Courtesy of Dr. Holman Hamilton, Lexington, Ky. 1. Hervey, a Louisville lawyer, was the son of Philadelphia merchant Joseph H. Hervey. *RKHS*, 37:137; 41:110-11. He is listed in the *Louisville City Directory* for 1848-49 as a discount clerk at the Branch of the Northern Bank of Kentucky. Information supplied by Dorothy Rush, librarian, The Filson Club, Louisville, Ky. 2. Letter not found. 3. Greeley to Clay, Nov. 15, 1846. 4. Clay to Mercer, Dec. 10, 1848. 5. Bebb to Clay, April 4, 1848. 6. Clay to Mercer, Dec. 10, 1848. 7. Harlan to Clay, June 15, 1848.

To THOMAS B. STEVENSON Lexington, December 19, 1848

On the eve of my departure for N Orleans I have time only briefly to acknowledge the recept and cordially to thank you for your friendly letter transmitting Slips &c. The article from the Courier[1] was composed with proper caution and due consideration.

[Horace] Greeley writes me from Washington that the Free Soil question will be *certainly* adjusted at this session on the basis of admitting the newly acquired teritory as one or two States into the Union.[2]

Should that event occur it will exercise some influence on my disposition to return to the Senate, should the office be within my power.[3] It will leave none but the old questions of Tariff, Internal Improvements &c on which I have heretofore so often addressed both branches of Congress.

Copy. OCHP. Printed in Colton, *Clay Correspondence*, 3:492, with misspellings corrected. Letter marked "(Private)." 1. Here an asterisk appears in the copy, drawing attention to a note at the bottom of the page that states: "The name 'Courier' is a slip of the pen. He ment the Cincinnati Chronicle of Dec 15, containing an article on his proposed return to the U.S. Senate.—T.B.S." "*Chronicle*" appears in the Colton version, and a footnote by Stevenson says he wrote the article, which urged Clay's return to the Senate, for the *Chronicle*. 2. Stephen A. Douglas had introduced a bill in the Senate on Dec. 11, 1848, that provided for the admission of the territory including California and New Mexico into the Union as one state, thus bypassing the territorial stage. President Polk was so anxious for the admission of California that he lobbied strongly for it; however, the bill never came to a vote. U.S. Sen., *Journal*, 30 Cong., 2 Sess., 52, 67, 114, 120, 127, 148, 158; Quaife, *Diary of James K. Polk*, 4:232-38, 254-55, 257, 287, 293, 298-300, *passim*. For the controversy surrounding the more conventional bill to form territorial governments for California and New Mexico, see Going, *David Wilmot*, 342-43, 351-

52. For the Free Soil controversy, see also Sargent to Clay, Feb. 27, 1847. 3. Clay to Mercer, Dec. 10, 1848.

From Philip R. Fendall, Washington, December 21, 1848. Reports that he is "still unable to close the transaction of the Columbian College [Clay to Fendall, June 16, 1847]." Although he had urged "a punctual discharge of their engagement, giving them to understand, that if the note shd. not be paid at maturity, I might . . . sue on the original obligation," regrets that "The note has not been paid." Adds that one of the trustees of the college hoped to obtain funds "in a few weeks from a particular source, and should there be a disappointment, he promises to obtain a note from the trustees individually on which note the Bank of Washington will advance the money." If they do not follow through with this, "they will deserve, after your generosity to them, to be held to the last cent, principal and interest, of the original obligation." Draft, signed. NcD.

From John Sloane, Wooster, Ohio, December 22, 1848. Writes after Ohio gave its electoral votes to Lewis Cass [Bebb to Clay, April 4, 1848], and notes that "the State has been for a number of year[s] gradually yielding to influences hostile both to its honor and interest." Believes Ohio's downward course began with the election of 1840 when stump speaking by "enthusiastic, and to some extent reckless young men" and the "near approach to equality of numbers between the parties" began to prevent "men of reflection and prudence from taking any measures for disabusing the public mind from the influence of political empiricks." Fears Ohio has "fallen under the controul of men not remarkable for attainments in political philosophy." Now that Ohio operates under "the New York system of a central power at the seat of government under the regulation of State central committee" in Columbus, where "there is not a great deal of Statesmanship," the "central committee have assumed to regard the Whig cause of the State as entirely subject to their management and discretion." Declares, however, that "the Albany Regency or the Richmond junto were more potent in their day than is the Whig central committee of Ohio," despite "certain Whigs which the canvass of 1840 brought into notice" who courted "the good will of the Abolition party and make various concessions to insure their support." Blames all these causes for "the prostration of Ohio influence in the Philadelphia convention [Ullmann to Clay, February 18, 1848] as well as in the late election."

Accuses "our central clique (by which I mean those who govern the Central Committee)" of desiring "the prostration of yourself and all citizens of our State devoted to your support" in favor of John McLean and Thomas Corwin. Recounts the central committee's call for a "mass meeting of the whole Whig population [Stevenson to Clay, April 18, 1848]" last December "to nominate a President & Gov.," fully understanding that "the rail road and Turnpike facilities for reaching the Seat of Govt from the South and SW part of the State being so much greater than from the North & east . . . would certainly result in Gov Corwin's nomination." Recalls, however, that " 'the pistol missed fire.' The convention was refractory" and "nominated Gov [Joseph] Vance and myself" as delegates to the Whig National convention, believing that "two votes were thereby Secured in your favor." Although McLean was offered as a "free State candidate," ultimately "Twenty one of the 23 delegates from Ohio with Gov Vance at their head thought Gen [Winfield] Scott a more available free State candidate [Ullmann to Clay, February 18, 1848]."

Condemns "our friend Vance," whom "I presume you like every one else regarded . . . as your fast friend," for giving "preference to the Society of your opponents [Van Trump to Clay, July 26, 1848]." Adds that "our friend was always a little demagogual." Clay's friends "never confided in him" during the presidential campaign of 1824 because "He was always inclined to court the South & had it not been for his obligations to you, he would have gone for Mr [William] Crawford." Notes as well that Vance "as late as 1841-42 . . . was in favour of [John] Tyler's Exchequer."

Condemns the central committee's "confidential circular . . . urging the holding of Mass meetings in the several counties and congressional districts for the appointment of delegates to support" either Clay or Corwin. When "One of these circulars was directed to me . . . I denounced the whole scheme and pronounced the whigs of the Several districts as the proper authority for deciding the manner of their action with out the superintendance of the central committee." After his congressional district held two mass meetings "and resolutions passed in both with great unanimity nominating you for the Presidency," was appalled when their delegate "had the audacity to vote for genl. Scott and declare that to be the sentiments of his district." Adds: "I am fully persuaded that we fell victims to a conspiracy the object of which has been to destroy your standing and clear the way for an union with the Abolitionists at next election."

Discusses the course of Thomas Ewing, who "took occasion like gov Corwin to express his preference for you," but who "was already engaged in favour of the genl long before his nomination at Philad. . . . His feelings towards you I have no doubt were in perfect keeping with those of Mr [Daniel] Webster." Assures Clay, however, that "Apart from the Junior members of the legal profession," Ewing "has never had a Strong hold on the affections of any considerable number of the people" of Ohio.

Hopes that Taylor's victory is a victory for the Whig party and will bring about "a complete demolition of all the idol temples of Locofocoism." Knows nothing of the general's "character or disposition" and cannot "venture to conjecture whether the men who have composed the old whig guard are to receive his countenance and support." ALS. MH.

For the election of 1824-25, see Subject Index, 7:714-17.

To JAMES BROWN CLAY Natchez, Miss., January 10, 1848 [*sic*, 1849]

Hearing that the Cholera[1] has greatly abated in N[ew]. O[rleans]. and that there is no longer danger of it, I shall leave this place this afternoon for that City. I have staid with Mr. [William St. John] Elliot, where I have been treated with the greatest possible kindness. There has been no Cholera here. My health has been improved, although I do not yet feel entirely well.

I mentioned to Mr. Elliot, Liberty, Mr. [Richard] Pindells negro boy, and he requests me to enquire into his character, through you, and to ascertain at what price he may be bought. If his character is such as I heard it, and R. Pindell will sell him at a reasonable price, Mr. Elliot will purchase him. Do make these enquiries immediately and let Mr. Elliot know the result by a line addressed to him.

I hope to hear from home when I get to N.O. My love to Susan [Jacob Clay], dear Lucy [Jacob Clay] and James [Clay] & John [Clay]; and let me hear soon from you.

ALS. DLC-TJC (DNA, M212, R11). 1. Ships brought cholera from Europe to New York and New Orleans in Dec., 1848. From those cities, it spread across the country, killing as much as 10% of the population in cities such as Cincinnati and St. Louis before dying out in 1854. It caused numerous deaths in Kentucky during the summer of 1849, including in July alone 217 in Lexington, 36 in Fayette County, and 141 in Louisville. Charles Rosenberg, *The Cholera Years* (Chicago, 1962), 101, 105, 172; Bauer, *Zachary Taylor*, 268; Collins, *History of Kentucky*, 1:59.

From Rhesa B. Howard, Randolph Co., Ga., January 19, 1849. Asks Clay to "Do me favour as this is the hour of troubble and Distress with me." Wants "to borrow 700 hundred Dollars from you and I pledge my self uppon the honor of gentleman to pay you." Explains that "I am Living in the hart of the stave [*sic*, slave] country and I want to get way from it from this accursed Land of stavery that I detest sow mutch." Hopes that "the Day is not far Distant when I hope I shall bee able to quit this Land of stavery and kiss the shore of free soil Land." Recalls that "the Great Ruler of the universe brought the children of Israel out from under the task masters and I hope the Day is not far Distant when all others [are] out." Since "you was my choise of the worled" for president, wants Clay "to give your enfluance to those that advocates the Americans that I do and if they will assist me to any money I shall bee under many obbligations to them for it." ALS. DLC-TJC (DNA, M212, R11).

From J. Phillips Phoenix, New York City, January 22, 1849. Expects "that a seat in the Cabinet or the Senate will be tendered to you," and advises that "should it be so—do not decline it, except rendered absolutely necessary to do so, by the state of your health." Urges Clay not to "lose the occasion, should it be presented to you, to show, when it should be felt, that, your power had not passed from you." ALS. DLC-HC (DNA, M212, R6). Letter marked "Confidential." For Clay's return to the Senate, see Clay to Mercer, December 10, 1848.

To JAMES HARLAN New Orleans, January 26, 1849

I met with an accidental but violent fall a week ago, in carelessly descending a flight of Stairs, to receive a gentleman who bore me a letter of introduction, and I got terribly bruised. I broke no bones, but it disabled me for the present from walking without assistance, and almost from writing.

I received yesterday your favor of the 12th, and today that of the 14th. I regret extremely that the use of my name, in connection with the office of Senator, should have created any division among the Whigs, or excited any dissatisfaction with any one.[1] God knows that I have no personal desire to return to that body, nor any private or ambitious purposes to promote by resuming a seat in it. I exposed to you and to other friends, at the period of my departure from home, the exact state of my feelings when I declared that I could not reconcile it to my feelings to become a formal or an avowed candidate; and that if the General Assembly had any other person in view, I did not wish to interfere with him. I added that, if nevertheless the Legislature thought proper to require my services in the Senate, deference to their will, a sense of public duty, and the hope of doing some good, would prompt me to accept the office.

These views are unchanged. According to them, it follows that I have no desire to have my name pressed upon the General Assembly, and I hope that it will not be presented, unless it is manifestly the free and voluntary wish of a majority of that body. It would be a great mortificati[on] to me to be thought to be solicitous for that office, and to be supposed to be seeking it, from the reluctant grant of the Legislature. I hope that my friends will act in consonance with this state of my feelings, and not suffer my name to be used but on the conditions which I have stated.

ALS. Courtesy of Alan Westin, New Haven, Conn. Printed in Colton, *Clay Correspondence*, 4:583-84. 1. Clay to Mercer, Dec. 10, 1848.

To Major Anderson Miller, January 27, 1849. Hopes that Miller will be successful in obtaining an appointment as "Superintendant of the Live Oak and other public Timber, under the administration of Genl. [Zachary] Taylor." In addition to Miller's "attention, diligence and fidelity," Clay praises his "thorough acquaintance with most of the Districts of the Country in which the Timber to be protected is situated." ALS. MB. For Miller, see 2:238. He did not receive the appointment.

A bill was reported in the Senate on February 22, 1849, to amend an 1831 act entitled "An act to provide for the punishment of offences committed in cutting, destroying, or removing live-oak and other timber of trees reserved for naval purposes." This act did not pass; however, on March 3, 1849, an act was approved creating the Department of the Interior. U.S. Sen., *Journal*, 30 Cong., 2 Sess., 246; 4 *U.S. Stat.*, 472; 9 *U.S. Stat.*, 395-97.

To THOMAS B. STEVENSON New Orleans, January 31, 1849

The breaking out of Cholera[1] here prevented my meeting Genl [Zachary] Taylor in this City, as had been expected. I met him at Baton Rouge,[2] but only long enough to exchange friendly salutations, without any opportunity to converse on political affairs.

About a fortnight ago I met with a terrible accidental fall which, altho fortunately I broke no bones, has for the present confined me to my lodgings, disabled me from walking, and almost from writing.[3] To that cause is owing my not having earlier acknowledged the receipt of your friendly letter of the 25th inst.

I suppose that I shall be elected to the Senate by the General Assembly of Ky, in which case I shall hardly feel myself at liberty to decline,[4] confered as the office will be without any solicitation from me, *without my* being a candidate, and with the knowledge of my strong disinclination to return to that body. Deference to the will of the General Assembly, *a sense* of duty, and the possibility of my being able to do some good, overcome my repugnance. If I go to Washington it will be with an anxious desire that I shall be able to support the measures of the new Administration in consequence of their conformity with Whig policy.

There seems to be yet some slight prospect of a settlement at Washington of the Free Soil question;[5] but we shall see.

The Cholera has nearly entirely disappeared from the City. P.S. You can enclose the letter to Mr [Joseph] Underwood[6] to Mr [Truman] Smith or Mr [Thomas] Corwin.

Copy. OCHP. Printed in Colton, *Clay Correspondence*, 4:584. 1. Clay to James B. Clay, Jan. 10, 1849. 2. Taylor to Clay, Nov. 17, 1848. 3. Clay to Harlan, Jan. 26, 1849. 4. Clay to Mercer, Dec. 10, 1848. 5. Sargent to Clay, Feb. 27, 1847; Clay to Stevenson, Dec. 19, 1848. 6. On Jan. 31, 1849, Clay wrote Kentucky Sen. Joseph R. Underwood: "I wish through you to recommend to the President and Secretary of the Treasury the name of Thomas B. Stevenson Esqr of Cincinnati" to be Register of the Treasury. Believes Stevenson's "talents of a high order," his "unsullied honor and probity, great zeal and industry, dilligent habits of business, and a firm adherence to good principles" will "give entire satisfaction." Copy. OCHP. Stevenson did not get the position.

To Octavia Walton LeVert, Mobile, February 6, 1849. Regrets "to learn that your dear little Sallie (or Sally) had been afflicted by disease," but rejoices "that she has recovered." Is glad to hear that Mrs. LeVert plans to visit New Orleans because "it will, I apprehend, afford me the only opportunity of having the pleasure of seeing you." Despite "a firm determination to visit Mobile . . . the Cholera [Clay to James B. Clay, January 10, 1849] first and an accident [Clay to Harlan, January 26, 1848] which befel me near three weeks ago have frustrated my plans." ALS. KyU.

Mrs. LeVert's daughter Sally Walker Walton LeVert died on May 3, 1849, aged 8, and her daughter Claudia Anna Eugenia LeVert died on May 8, aged 11. Both children died of scarlet fever. Information supplied by Caldwell Delaney, Museum

Director, City of Mobile Museum Department. See also LeVert to Clay, May 19, 1849.

From R. Ross, Prairie du Chien, Wisc., February 6, 1849. Rejoices to know "that you have returned to the United States Senate [Clay to Mercer, December 10, 1848]." Prays that God will "spare your health as to enable you to render service and save this Country from its now almost downfallen condition." ALS. DLC-TJC (DNA, M212, R14).

To Henry White, Philadelphia, February 8, 1849. Is glad that "you approve of my determination not to interfere in mere local appointments, in other places, distant from me, in other States." Understands that "Such interference . . . is regarded as officious and improper by many," and believes that "the voices of the business men, who have most to do with these local appointments ought to be heard and respected."

Concerning his appointment as U.S. senator, did not feel "at liberty to decline accepting it. I was no Candidate, and really did not desire to return [Clay to Mercer, December 10, 1848]." Unless he learns that his "presence at the Call Session on the 4h. of March is necessary," will skip the proceeding, "which is one of form principally." Adds in a postscript: "Give my regards to [William D.] Lewis and tell him that altho' I can take no part in his appointment, if he be nominated to the Senate he may be sure of my vote [Clay to Lewis, February 9, 1849]." ALS. PHi. Written from New Orleans.

Lewis was appointed collector of the port of Philadelphia. *DAB*. The "called session" was a special session of the Senate called by the new president so that the Senate could approve his appointments. It lasted from March 5-23, 1849. *BDAC*.

To WILLIAM D. LEWIS New Orleans, February 9, 1849

I sent a word to you through [Henry] White,[1] but my friendship for you prompts me to address one to you directly.

I have thought that I ought not to interfere in mere local appointments, in places remote from me, and in other and distant States. I know, from experience and observation that such interference is regarded with jealousy, looked upon as officious, and is sometimes even injurious to the applicant.

I have no doubt of your ample qualifications for the office of Collector of the port of Philadelphia,[2] and, if nominated, I should take great pleasure in voting for your confirmation.

My relations with Genl [Zachary] Taylor are perfectly amicable; but I did not see him after the receipt of your letter, and I have not learned from him, further than his published letters inform us,[3] as to the principles which will regulate his administration of the public patronage.

ALS. PHi. 1. Clay to White, Feb. 8, 1849. 2. *Ibid.* 3. For instance in his Allison letters. See Clay to Ullmann, August 4, 1847; White to Clay, May 26, 1848.

To JOSEPH R. UNDERWOOD New Orleans, February 11, 1849

Although I have no official evidence of my election to the Senate from Kentucky, I presume from what I have seen that such an event has happened.[1] Under all the circumstances, I shall not feel at liberty to decline the acceptance of the appointment, altho' I really had no wish to return to the Senate, and shall go back with some thing like the feelings which the day laborer may be supposed to have, who having worked hard all day by sun shine, is sent again at night into the field to work by moon light. I do not however apprehend any danger from lunacy.

My object in now writing is to say, that, as I presume the Call Session of the Senate is [a] matter of form, and that no serious discussions or divisions will arise in it,[2] I shall not attend, unless I should hereafter receive information inducing me to believe my presence material. Besides the inclement season of the year, rendering the journey very disagreeable, I have not entirely recovered from a lameness occasioned by a late accidental fall.[3]

ALS. KyU. 1. The credential, signed by Gov. John J. Crittenden and Kentucky Sec. of State Orlando Brown and certifying to the U.S. Senate that Clay had been elected to that body by the state legislature, is dated Feb. 5, 1849. DS. DNA, RG46 (11B-B2). See also Clay to Mercer, Dec. 10, 1848. 2. Clay to White, Feb. 8, 1849. 3. Clay to Harlan, Jan. 26, 1849.

From James Kennedy, Thornton Farm, February 12, 1849. Writes to express his delight "to lern that Your Honour has accepted once more . . . a ceat in the United States Senate [Clay to Mercer, December 10, 1848]." Although "no doubt destin'd as prop to this republick," regrets that Clay did not receive the Whig presidential nomination "in consequence of a set of traitors in our rank that would take up and support the Devil if they thought he was available." Complains that "Gen [Zachary] Taylor . . . has never held a sivil office" and "nothing can be said in his behalf but his military atchievements." Because of the Whigs's "past unprinciple conduct as a party—I had forsaking all connection with the party and voted for [Lewis] Cass." First favored "Thomas Jefferson, [James] Madison and so on in the Democratic line and in 1824 I supported your Hon as the only true democrat . . . I have from that day to this been your true friend. . . . At the convention that took up Gen [William Henry] Harrison [9:92, 117, 827] I beged and expostulated with several Gentleman in your behalf" but was told "by one of the leading whigs of this State" that "you was a hackoney candidate." Reports that in private conversation with a "leading whig . . . that makes grate profession of Friendship and love for you. . . . He said you was a good souldier in the whig ranks" and "fought well," but "he all wais had some doubt about making you Commander in chief for fear you would get back to your early love for Jeffersonian politicks—my answer was that you had never lost sight of it." Encourages Clay to "return with me to the Locofoco ranks I believe they are the true Democratic ranks. and support such measures as has been tryed such as the present treasure sistom Tariff and so forth—by going with them you can lead them but they are like Swine they will not drive." Assures Clay that Democrats "from Main [*sic*] to California" will "welcom you in there ranks," now that he has "good caus for leaving the unprinsipl[ed] party." ALS. DLC-HC (DNA, M212, R6). Letter marked "private and confidential."

From JOHN SLOANE Wooster, Ohio, February 12, 1849

I rejoice at your election to the Senate of the United States[1] and most heartily congratulate you on the occasion. My feelings however are not governed so much by the honor it may be supposed to confer upon you, as I consider it impossible for any appointment to that already possessed by you, nor even by by [*sic*] the hope of any great good which the situation may put it in your power to confer upon the country or the evidence it presents of the proper spirit in the people of Kentucky to be steadfast in their attachment to a distinguished public servant. In these days of inordinate personal ambition it is cheering to see that there is one State in the union where attachment to the honor and interest of the nation prevails over all personal considerations[.]

About the time of your departure for the South I wrote you a long letter intended more particularly [to] elucidate certain Statements made in my answer to your letter June last.[2] That letter I hope you have received, because it will in some measure enable you to appreciate the present anomalous condition of Ohio, and the disgraceful scenes which daily occur in our Legislature.[3] Correct political sentiment and patriotic action, are my dear Sir suffering under a fearful paralysis in Ohio: and from the character of much of our population and the delusion now so rife in the world, I fear the day of our deliverance therefrom is far distant[.] The disease I fear will yield to no treatment, but like the Cholera must be left to waste itself by a spontaneous exhaustion of the causes which induce the susceptability[.]

I have often reflected within the last 20 years on the contrast between the members of Congress from the west who placed Mr. [John Quincy] Adams in the Presidency and every other delegation which has succeeded them. It will readily occur to you, that not one of the former was appointed to office by the administration which they brought into existence; while almost ever since with the members of the dominent party the receipt of office was as common as the mercenary engagements of the surfs during the last century: Witness the Speaker of the House of Representatives seeking the place to enable him to do the bidding of the President with assurance of an appointment to a foreign mission in his pocket.[4] I refer to this contrast for the purpose of showing the prudence which prevailed among our friends on one hand, and the self-denying principle on the other[.]

Having thus almost unconsiously wandered into a course of retrospection, I will take the liberty [for the benefit of history if you please] to furnish an item of evidence of a Somewhat analogous subject. I do this the more readily, because no other person is possessed of the facts but yourself. Indeed I have long intended to do it but never could meet with what seemed a suitable occasion. During the suspense which pervaded the public mind in 1825, as to how the members from the Western States denominated your friends would vote as between the three candidates returned to the house I had several conversations with Judge [Benjamin] Ruggles a Senator from Ohio in which he[5] very modestly urged the election of his favourite Mr. [William H.] Crawford.[6] The Judge was my particular friend as was also Judge [Jesse Burgess] Thomas a Senator from Illinois[.] Shortly after one of these conversations, I made with you an engagement to pay you an evening visit at your lodging on an evening named[.] When I entered your room I found Judge Thomas there; and after the usual salutations you observed to the Judge that the subject of conversation between you and him need not be interrupted by the arrival of a mutual friend; and proceeded to repeat it in my presence. From this it appeared that the Judge had waited on you for the purpose of soliciting your suport of Mr. Crawford. You then stated what your objections to the proposition were: among which was the imbicility into which a severe and long protracted attack of fever had thrown Mr Crawford, and from that cause his utter incapacity to discharge the duties which an election would impose upon him. To all this, Judge Thomas, offered neither objection nor argument, but by his looks, and manner, seemed very much disconcerted. When the subject seemed disposed of, I arose and took leave, and Judge Thomas left with me; and although his residence was in a contrary direction from mine he accompanied me nearly half way home: frequently expressing regret that his project had been discovered; I endeavoured to put him at ease; by refering to the intimacy and confidence that had long existed between us, and finally saying that if it had equally suited his purpose, he would have made directly to me, the same proposition he had made to you[.] To this he readily agreed, but said that he could not but regard "himself as caught[.]" You will recollect the enthusiastic attachment which obtained among the party of Mr Crawfords friends and that Judge Thomas was considered as a chief manager among them, and the impression which must have been made upon your mind (as it was certainly made upon mine) was that his proposition had the sanction of the party: although for a number of years afterwards, many of them were among the most noisy about bargain, sale &C[.]

In all the correspondence which has taken place between us I believe I have never intimated any thing personal to myself. You will therefore I hope excuse me if I shall now in some degree deviate a little from my former course. Up to the time of the Jackson controversey I had enjoyed an extraordinary degree of popularity. Indeed at one election, I received as I believe, a larger majority of votes than was ever given for a member of Congress any where. All that, and much more, I staked on that contest. The result was my utter prostration as a politician.[7] This however was not unlooked for by me, and the inducements to a contrary course on my part, was of a ten fold amount. The party was very deficient in talent, and violent in their adherence to each other: and had I chosen to go with them, I could have had a carte blanche.[8] but I knew their character, and the destructive[9] influence which their success must exercise upon the country; and I took a course as far as possible to avert it.

Of the persecutions which have followed, you can have but little conception, not being personally acquainted with the heterogeneous character of our population, made up as it is of a medley from almost every part of the world with a larger portion of the most ignorant factions [word illeg.] from Pennsylvania. These men boasting of their contempt for every thing like dignity, knowledge, and character, hold that attachment to a wild indigested notion of democratic equality is all that is requisite to qualify for any station in public affairs. It has been amongst this description of men rendered desperate by the fulmentations of a profligate press and the proper sacrifices for what they called political hersey frequent harangues of vulgar demagogues together with the daily detractions of such as regard personal character & private business that I have spent the last 20 years. In all that time I have never been a candidate for their Suffrages; but that does not seem in the least to allay their rancours[.] I know of no situation which by comparison will illustrate my condition, except that of maintaining a blockhouse in the midst of hostile Indian country[.]

Permit me now Sir in great confidence to say to you, that if you shall find that the coming [Taylor] administration will be inclined to countenance such as have kept the faith, and laboured in the cause through evil and good report; and that my conduct as a member of the whig national convention at Philadelphia[10] has not forfeited their favourable consideration, I should like to know whether it would be presumptious in me to expect some appointment evinced of their confidence. I have not before hinted any thing of the kind to any one. I have received a letter from Mr [Thomas] Corwin making an unconditional tender of his services for any thing I may want but I avoided every expression of expectation. Indeed until I had consulted you and learned something about the policy which is likely to prevail I would not think of assuming the attitude of an applicant[.] Should any thing of the kind assume a[11] practicable Shape you know me well enough to determine what it would be proper to offer; and what I ought to accept[.][12]

ALS. MH. 1. Clay to Mercer, Dec. 10, 1848. 2. Sloane to Clay, June 22, 1848, and Dec. 22, 1848. 3. The aftermath of the 1848 presidential election resulted in a transformation of Ohio politics that by 1852 had brought about the demise of the Whig party in that state. Whigs lost the support of Free Soilers in the Western Reserve, which had been their stronghold, and the Free Soilers allied with the Democrats. Maizlish, *The Triumph of Sectionalism*, 118-86. See also Stevenson to Clay, July 26, 1848. 4. Andrew Stevenson had been Speaker from 1827-34 and minister to Great Britain from 1836-41. *BDAC*. 5. The words "earnestly but" have been stricken. 6. For the election of 1824-25 and the corrupt bargain charge, see Subject Index 7:660; 8:911; 9:934. 7. Sloane had served in Congress from March 4, 1819, to March 3, 1829. He had been defeated in the 1828 congressional election by Jacksonian John Thomson. *BDAC*; *Guide to U.S. Elections*, 551. 8. "And would have stood measures" has been stricken. 9. The word "demoralizing" has been stricken. 10. For the Whig National convention, see Greeley to Clay, Nov. 15, 1846; for the Ohio delegation at the convention, see Ullmann to Clay, Feb. 18, 1848. 11. The word "tangible" has been stricken. 12. Sloane was appointed treasurer of the U.S. after Thomas Corwin became secretary of the treasury in the Millard Fillmore administration. *BDAC*; U.S. Sen., *Executive Journal*, 8:274, 285-86.

To A. PIERSE New Orleans, February 16, 1849

I received [several words missing, da]ys ago your favor of the 14th Ulto. I also received that which y[ou had t]he goodness to address to me in March last,[1] and I thank you f[or the] friendly sentiments towards me which they both evince. I regre[t y]our illness which prevented your attendance on the Philadelphia [Whig National C]onvention,[2] altho' I presume that your presence would not have altered the result. To that result I have submitted, I hope, with proper deference and respect, and I trust that it may prove to be for the advantage of the Country.

The President elect [Zachary Taylor] will not find himself at Washington on a bed of roses. His greatest difficulty will arise out of the Free soil question,[3] if it be not settled at the present Session. Should it remain unadjusted during his administration, I fear it will widen the existing breach between the South and the North. If the new President should be fortunate in the selection of a Cabinet, he may get along very well.[4] Although I had no desire to return to the Senate, the circumstances under which I was recently elected do not leave me at liberty to decline accepting the appointment.[5] If I am spared, I shall attend the regular Session with an anxious wish to find the course of the new Administration such as that I can consciously support it.

I am not surprized at your entertaining a wish to go to California. To those whose age and condition in life admit of their going there, the Country offers great inducements and attractions. With respects to the appointment of a Governor, unless it be authorized by an act of Congress, passed at the present Session, I presume no appointment will be made, and the Country will continue, I suppose, under military authority.[6] I have no person in view. There will be no doubt great competition for the office. My personal relations with Genl. Taylor are amicable, but until I possess more information than I now do, I should be unwilling to make any recommendation for that office.

As I consider the Call Session for the ensuing month, a matter of mere form, and the journey would be extremely unpleasant, I shall not attend it.[7]

ALS, manuscript torn. ViU. 1. Pierse to Clay, March 24, 1848. 2. Greeley to Clay, Nov. 15, 1846. 3. Sargent to Clay, Feb. 27, 1847. 4. Taylor's cabinet consisted of John M. Clayton (Del.)—State; William M. Meredith (Pa.)—Treasury; George W. Crawford (Ga.)—War; Reverdy Johnson (Md.)—Attorney General; Jacob Collamer (Vt.)—Postmaster General; William B. Preston (Va.)—Navy; Thomas Ewing (Ohio)—Interior. Auburn S. Cunningham, *Everything You Want to Know About the Presidents* (Chicago, 1931), 39. 5. Clay to Mercer, Dec. 10, 1848. 6. California remained under military rule when Taylor became president. In Sept., 1849, the new president sent a special agent to advise them they could form a government and adopt a constitution before applying for statehood. The Californians, already working toward that end, adopted a constitution and seated a government that took office on Dec. 20. In his first annual message to Congress, Taylor recommended California for statehood and warned Congress against introducing "exciting topics of sectional character." California applied for admission to the Union on March 12, 1850, but was not admitted until Sept., 1850, as part of the Compromise of 1850. Morris, *Encyclopedia of American History*, 210, 212; Hamilton, *Zachary Taylor, Soldier in the White House*, 176-80. See also Sargent to Clay, Feb. 27, 1847; Clay to Stevenson, Dec. 19, 1848. 7. Clay to White, Feb. 8, 1849.

To RICHARD PINDELL New Orleans, February 17, 1849

Inclosed I transmit the letter[1] which I promised before I left home, on the subject of Emancipation. It has been prepared under very unfavorable circumstances, while I have been suffering from the effects of a violent fall, which disabled me for a time from walking or writing. This is the first and only draught of the letter. I wish it published in the Observer and Reporter,[2] and as I desire it to be correctly published, if you can not attend to the revisal of the proof sheets, I wish you would ask Judge Trotter[3] to do me that favor. I do not know that James [Brown Clay] has returned home.

You will see from the concluding paragraphs of my letter that I have no confidence in any hopes of success. But notwithstanding I think I am under some obligation to give publicity to my opinions.

Copy. Printed in Colton, *Clay Correspondence*, 3:346, no. 1 of date. 1. See below, Clay to Pindell, Feb. 17, 1849, no. 2 of date. 2. Although the Lexington *Observer & Kentucky Reporter* states on March 10, 1849, that the letter was published in its last issue (March 7), it is not found in the available microfilm edition of that paper. 3. George R. Trotter was the Lexington City Court judge who, in 1845, heard the case against the Committee of Sixty that had dismantled Cassius M. Clay's newspaper office. Collins, *History of Kentucky*, 1:51; Perrin, *History of Fayette County*, 441.

To RICHARD PINDELL New Orleans, February 17, 1849

Prior to my departure from home in December last, in behalf of yourself and other friends, you obtained from me a promise to make a public exposition of my views and opinions upon a grave and important question which, it was then anticipated, would be much debated and considered by the people of Kentucky during this year, in consequence of the approaching convention, summoned to amend their present constitution.[1] I was not entirely well when I left home, and, owing to that cause and my confinement several weeks during my sojourn in this city from the effects of an accident which befel me, I have been delayed in the fulfillment of my promise, which I now proceed to execute.

The question to which I allude is, whether African slavery as it now exists in Kentucky shall be left to a perpetual or indefinite continuance, or some provision shall be made in the new constitution for its gradual and ultimate extinction?

A few general observations will suffice my present purpose without entering on the whole subject of slavery under all its bearings and in every aspect of it. I am aware that there are respectable persons who believe that slavery is a blessing—that the institution ought to exist in every well organized society, and that it is even favorable to the preservation of liberty. Happily the number who entertain these extravagant opinions is not very great, and the time would be uselessly occupied in an elaborate refutation of them. I would, however, remark, that if slavery be fraught with these alleged benefits, the principle on which it is maintained would require that one portion of the whole race should be reduced to bondage to serve another portion of the same race when black subjects of slavery could not be obtained, and that in Africa, where they may entertain as great a preference for their color as we do for ours, they would be justified in reducing the white race to slavery in order to secure the blessings which that state is said to diffuse.

An argument in support of reducing the African race to slavery is sometimes derived from their alleged intellectual inferiority to the white races, but, if this argument be founded in fact (as it may be, but which I shall not now examine,) it would prove entirely too much. It would prove that any white nation which had made greater advances in civilization, knowledge and wisdom than another white nation, would have a right to reduce the latter to a state of bondage. Nay, further: if the principle of subjugation founded upon intellectual superiority be true and be applicable to races and to nations, what is to prevent its being applied to individuals? And then the wisest man in the world would have a right to make slaves of all the rest of mankind!

If indeed we possess this intellectual superiority, profoundly grateful and thankful to Him who has bestowed it, we ought to fulfil all the obligations and duties which it imposes; and these would require us not to subjugate or deal unjustly by our fellow men, who are less blessed than we are, but to instruct, to improve, and to enlighten them.

A vast majority of the people of the United States, in every section of them, I believe, regret the introduction of slavery into the colonies, under the authority of our British ancestors, lament that a single slave treads our soil; deplore the necessity of the continuance of slavery in any of the States; regard the institution as a great evil to both races, and would rejoice in the adoption of any safe, just and practicable plan for the removal of all slaves from among us. Hitherto no such satisfactory plan has been presented. When, on the occasion of the formation of our present constitution of Kentucky in 1799,[2] the question of the gradual emancipation of slavery in that State was agitated, its friends had to encounter a great obstacle, in the fact that there then existed no established colony to which they could be transported. Now by the successful establishment of flourishing colonies on the western coast of Africa, that difficulty has been obviated. And I confess, that, without indulging in any undue feelings of superstition, it does seem to me that, it may have been among the dispensations of Providence to permit the wrongs, under which Africa has suffered, to be inflicted that her children might be returned to their original home, civilized embued with the benign spirit of Christianity, and prepared ultimately to redeem that great continent from barbarism and idolatry.

Without undertaking to judge for any other State, it was my opinion, in

1799, that Kentucky was in a condition to admit of the gradual emancipation of her slaves; and how deeply do I lament that a system, with that object, had not been then established. If it had been, the State would now be nearly rid of all Slaves. My opinion has never changed, and I have frequently publicly expressed it. I should be most happy if what was impracticable at that epoch could now be accomplished.

After full and deliberate consideration of the subject, it appears to me that three principles should regulate the establishment of a system of gradual emancipation. The first is, that it should be slow in its operations, cautious, and gradual, so as to occasion no convulsion, nor any rash or sudden disturbance, in the existing habits of society. 2d. That, as an indispensable condition, the emancipated slaves should be removed from the State to some colony. And, thirdly, that the expenses of their transportation to such colony, including an outfit for six months after their arrival at it, should be defrayed by a fund to be raised from the labor of each freed slave.

[1.] Nothing could be more unwise than the immediate liberation of all the slaves in the State, comprehending both sexes and all ages, from that of tender infancy to extreme old age. It would lead to the most frightful disorders and the most fearful and fatal consequences. Any great change in the condition of society should be marked by extreme care and circumspection. The introduction of slaves into the Colonies was an operation of many years duration; and the work of their removal from the United States can only be effected after the lapse of a great length of time.

I think that a period should be fixed when all born after it should be free at a specified age—all born before it remaining slaves for life. That period I would suggest should be 1855 or even 1860, for on this and other arrangements of the system, if adopted, I incline to a liberal margin, so as to obviate as many objections, and to unite as many opinions as possible. Whether the commencement of the operation of the system be a little earlier or later, is not so, important as that a day should be permanently *fixed*, from which we could look forward, with confidence, to the final termination of slavery within the limits of the Commonwealth.

Whatever may be the day fixed, whether 1855 or 1860, or any other day, all born after it, I suggest, should be free at the age of twenty-five, but be liable afterward to be hired out, under the authority of the State, for a term not exceeding three years, in order to raise a sum sufficient to pay the expenses of their transportation to the Colony, and to provide them an outfit for six months after their arrival there.

If the descendents of those, who were themselves to be free, at the age of twenty-five, were also to be considered as slaves, until they attained the same age, and, this rule were continued indefinitely as to time, it is manifest that slavery would be perpetuated instead of being terminated. To guard against this consequence, provision might be made that the offspring of those who were to be free at twenty-five, should be free from their birth, but upon the condition that they should be apprenticed until they were twenty-one, and be also afterward liable to be hired out, a period not exceeding three years, for the purpose of raising funds to meet their expenses to the Colony and their subsistence for the first six months.

The Pennsylvania system of emancipation fixed the period of twenty-eight for the liberation of the slaves, and provided, for so her courts have since interpreted the system to mean, that the issue of all who were to be free at the limited age were from their birth free. The Pennsylvania system made no provision for colonization.

Until the commencement of the system, which I am endeavoring to sketch, I think all the legal rights of the proprietors of slaves, in their fullest extent, ought to remain unimpaired and unrestricted! Consequently they would have the right to sell, devise, or remove them from the State, and, in the latter case, without their offspring being entitled to the benefit of emancipation, for which the system provides.

2d. The colonization of the free blacks, as they successively arrive, from year to year, at the age entitling them to freedom, I consider a condition absolutely indispensable. Without it, I should be utterly opposed to any scheme of emancipation. One hundred and ninety odd thousand blacks, composing about one-fourth of the entire population of the State, with their descendents, could never live in peace, harmony and equality with the residue of the population. The color, passions, and prejudices would forever prevent the two races from living together in a state of cordial union. Social, moral and political degradation would be the inevitable lot of the colored race. Even in the free States (I use the terms free and slave States not in any sense derogatory from one class, or implying any superiority in the other, but for the sake of brevity) that is their present condition. In some of the free States, the penal legislation against the people of color is quite as severe, if not harsher, than it is in some of the slave States. As nowhere in the United States are amalgamation and equality between the two races possible, it is better that there should be a separation, and that the African descendants should be returned to the native land of their fathers.

It will have been seen that the plan I have suggested proposes the annual transportation of all born after a specific day, upon their arrival at the prescribed age, to the colony which may be selected for their destination; and that this process of transportation is to be continued until the separation of the two races is completed. If the emancipated slaves were to remain in Kentucky until they attained the age of twenty-eight, it would be about thirty-four years before the first annual transportation began, if the system commence in 1855, and about thirty-nine years, if its operation begin in 1860.

What the number thus to be annually transported would be, can not be precisely ascertained. I observe it stated by the Auditor that the increase of slaves in Kentucky last year was between three and four thousand. But, as that statement was made upon a comparison of the aggregate number of all the slaves in the State, without regard to births, it does not, I presume, exhibit truly the *natural* increase, which was probably larger. The aggregate was effected by the introduction and still more by the exportation of slaves. I suppose that there would not be less, probably more, than five thousand to be transported the first year of the operation of the system; but, after it should be in progress some years, there would be a constant diminution of the number.

Would it be practicable annually to transport five thousand persons from Kentucky? There can not be a doubt of it, or even a much larger number. We receive from Europe annually, emigrants to an amount exceeding two hundred and fifty thousand, at a cost for the passage of about ten dollars per head, and they embark at European ports more distant from the United

States than the Western coast of Africa. It is true that the commercial marine, employed between Europe and the United States, affords facilities in the transportation of emigrants at that low rate, which that engaged in the commerce between Liberia and this country does not now supply; but that commerce is increasing, and by the time the proposed system, if adopted, would go into operation, it will have greatly augmented. If there were a certainty of the annual transportation of not less than five thousand persons to Africa, it would create a demand for transports, and the spirit of competition would, I have no doubt, greatly diminish the present cost of passage. That cost has been stated upon good authority to be at present fifty dollars per head, including the passage, and six months outfit after the arrival of the emigrant in Africa. Whatever may be the cost, and whatever the number to be transported, the fund to be raised by the hire of the liberated slaves, for a period not exceeding three years will be amply sufficient. The annual hire, on the average, may be estimated at fifty dollars, or one hundred and fifty for the whole term.

Colonization will be attended with the painful effect of the separation of the colonists from their parents, and in some instances from their children; but from the latter it will be only temporary, as they will follow and be again reunited. Their separation from their parents will not be until after they have attained a mature age, nor greater than voluntarily takes place with emigrants from Europe, who leave their parents behind. It will be far less distressing than what frequently occurs in the state of slavery, and will be attended with the animating encouragement that the colonists are transferred from a land of bondage and degradation for them, to a land of liberty and equality. And 3d. The expense of transporting the liberated slave to the colony, and of maintaining him there for six months, I think ought to be provided for by a fund derived from his labor, in the manner already indicated. He is the party most benefited by emancipation. It would not be right to subject the non-slaveholder to any part of that expense; and the slaveholder will have made sufficient sacrifices, without being exclusively burdened with taxes to raise that fund. The emancipated slaves could be hired out for the time proposed, by the sheriff or other public agent, in each county, who should be subject to a strict accountability. And it would be requisite that there should be kept a register of all births of children of color, after the day fixed for the commencement of the system, enforced by appropriate sanctions. It would be a very desirable regulation of law to have the births, deaths and marriages of the whole population of the State registered and preserved, as is done in most well governed States.

Among other considerations which unite in recommending to the State of Kentucky a system for the gradual abolition of slavery, is that arising out of her exposed condition, affording great facilities to the escape of her slaves into the free States and into Canada. She does not enjoy the security which some of the slave States have, by being covered in depth by two or three slave States, intervening between them and free States. She has a greater length of border on free States than any other slave State in the Union. That border is the Ohio river, extending from the mouth of Big Sandy to the mouth of the Ohio, a distance of near six hundred miles, separating her from the already powerful and growing States of Ohio, Indiana and Illinois. Vast numbers of slaves have fled from most of the counties in Kentucky from the mouth of Big Sandy to the mouth of the Miami, and the evil has increased and is increasing. Attempts to recover the fugitives lead to the most painful and irritating collisions. Hitherto countenance and assistance to the fugitives have been chiefly afforded by persons in the State of Ohio; but it is to be apprehended, from the progressive opposition to slavery that, in process of time similar facilities to the escape of slaves will be found in the States of Indiana and Illinois. By means of railroads, Canada can be reached from Cincinnati in a little more than twenty-four hours.

In the event of a civil war breaking out, or in the more direful event of a dissolution of the Union, in consequence of the existence of slavery, Kentucky would become the theater and bear the brunt of the war. She would doubtless defend herself with her known valor and gallantry; but the superiority of the numbers by which she would be opposed would lay waste and devastate her fair fields. Her sister slave States would fly to her succor; but, even if they should be successful in the unequal conflict, she never could obtain any indemnity for the inevitable ravages of war.

It may be urged that we ought not, by the gradual abolition of slavery, to separate ourselves from the other slave States, but to continue to share with them in all their future fortunes. The power of each slave State, within its limits, over the institution of slavery, is absolute, supreme, and exclusive—exclusive of that of Congress or that of any other State. The government of each slave State is bound, by the highest and most solemn obligations, to dispose of the question of slavery, so as best to promote the peace, happiness and prosperity of the people of the State. Kentucky being essentially a farming State, slave labor is less profitable. If, in most of the other slave States, they, find that labor more profitable in the culture of the staples of cotton and sugar, they may perceive a reason in that feeling for continuing slavery, which can not be expected should control the judgment of Kentucky, as to what may be fitting and proper for her interests. If she should abolish slavery, it would be her duty, and I trust that she would be as ready, as she now is, to defend the slave States in the enjoyment of all their lawful and constitutional rights. Her power, political and physical, would be greatly increased; for the one hundred and ninety odd thousand slaves and their descendants would be gradually superseded by an equal number of white inhabitants, who would be estimated *per capita* and not by the federal rule of three-fifths prescribed for the colored race in the constitution of the United States.

I have thus, without reserve, freely expressed my opinion and presented my views. The interesting subject of which I have treated would have admitted of much enlargement, but I have desired to consult brevity. The plan which I have proposed will hardly be accused of being too early in its commencement or too rapid in its operation. It will be more likely to meet with contrary reproaches. If adopted, it is to begin thirty-four or thirty-nine years from the time of its adoption, as the one period or the other shall be selected for its commencement. How long a time it will take to remove all the colored race from the State, by the annual transportation of each year's natural increase, can not be exactly ascertained. After the system has been in operation some years, I think it probable, from the manifest blessings that would flow from it, from the diminished value of slave labor, and from the humanity and benevolence of private individuals prompting a liberation of their slaves and their transportation, a general disposition would exist to accelerate and complete the work of colonization.

That the system will be attended with some sacrifices on the part of slaveholders, which are to be regretted, need not be denied. What great and beneficent enterprise was ever accomplished without risk and sacrifice? But these sacrifices are distant, contingent, and inconsiderable. Assuming the year 1860 for the commencement of the system, all slaves born prior to that time would remain such during their lives, and the personal loss of the slaveholder would be only the difference in value of a female slave whose offspring, if she had any, born after the first day of January, 1860, should be free at the age of twenty-five, or should be slaves for life. In the mean time, if the right to remove or sell the slave out of the State, should be exercised, that trifling loss would not be incurred. The slaveholder, after the commencement of the system, would lose the difference in value between slaves for life and slaves until the age of twenty-five. He might also incur some inconsiderable expense in rearing, from their birth, the issue of those who were to be free at twenty-five, until they were old enough to be apprenticed out, but, as it is probable that they would be most generally bound to him, he would receive some indemnity from their services, until they attained their majority.

Most of the evils, losses and misfortunes of human life have some compensation or alleviation. The slaveholder is generally a land-holder, and I am persuaded that he would find, in the augmented value of his land, some, if not full indemnity for losses arising to him from emancipation and colonization. He would also liberally share in the general benefits, accuring to the whole State, from the extinction of slavery! These have been so often and so fully stated that I will not, nor is it necessary to dwell upon them extensively. They can be summed up in a few words. We shall remove from among us the contaminating influence of a servile and degraded race of different color; we shall enjoy the proud and conscious satisfaction of placing that race where they can enjoy the great blessings of liberty, and civil, political and social equality; we shall acquire the advantage of the diligence, the fidelity, and the constancy of free labor, instead of the carelessness, the infidelity and the unsteadiness of slave labor; we shall elevate the character of white labor, and elevate the social condition of the white laborer; augment the value of our lands, improve the agriculture of the State, attract capital from abroad to all the pursuits of commerce, manufactures and agriculture; redress, as far and as fast as we safely and prudently could, any wrongs which the descendants of Africa have suffered at our hands, and we should demonstrate the sincerity with which we pay indiscriminate homage to the great cause of the liberty of the human race.

Kentucky enjoys high respect and honorable consideration throughout the Union and throughout the civilized world; but, in my humble opinion, no title which she has to the esteem and admiration of mankind, no deeds of her former glory, would equal in greatness and grandeur, that of being the Pioneer State in removing from her soil every trace of human slavery, and in establishing the descendants of Africa, within her jurisdiction, in the native land of their forefathers.

I have thus executed the promise I made, alluded to in the commencement of this letter, and I hope that I have done it calmly, free from intemperance, and so as to wound the sensibilities of none. I sincerely hope that the question may be considered and decided without the influence of party or passion. I should be most happy to have the good fortune of coinciding in opinion with the majority of the people of Kentucky; but, if there be a majority opposed to all schemes of gradual emancipation, however much I may regret it, my duty will be to bow in submission to their will. If it be perfectly certain and manifest that such a majority exists, I should think it better not to agitate the question at all, since that, in that case, it would be useless, and might exercise a pernicious collateral influence upon the fair consideration of other amendments which may be proposed to our constitution. If there be a majority of the people of Kentucky at this time adverse to touching the institution of slavery as it now exists, we, who had thought and wished otherwise, can only indulge the hope that, at some future time, under better auspices and with the blessing of Providence, the cause which we have so much at heart may be attended with better success.

In any event, I shall have the satisfaction of having performed a duty to the State, to the subject, and to myself, by placing my sentiments permanently upon record.

Copy. Printed in Frankfort *Commonwealth*, March 13, 1849, no. 2 of date; also in Colton, *Clay Correspondence*, 3:346-52. Although the Lexington *Observer & Kentucky Reporter* of March 10, 1849, claims that this letter was published in its previous number (March 7), it does not appear in the available microfilmed version of that paper. 1. Stevenson to Clay, June 12, 1848. 2. See 1:3-8.

From Philander Chase, Jubilee College, Ill., February 20, 1849. Requests Clay to support his efforts to have his son, Henry J. Chase, "appointed the Marshal . . . for the State of Illinois." Fears that Zachary Taylor "may for want of an advocate present let the name of my son slip his memory." Asks Clay's assistance because "I have nearly bereaved my Children of their inheritance by my expenditures for the Church[.] My Fathers estate was greatly impaired by his his [*sic*] zeal in support of our National independence and none of us his descendants have ever been the better for the avails of any appointments from the government of the U.S. Thus circumstanced have I not reason and a right to solicit and receive this appointment for my Son." ALS. DNA, RG59, Applications and Recommendations, R4.

Clay wrote Thomas Ewing on April 14, 1849, explaining that while he did not wish to interfere in appointments in states outside Kentucky, "I cannot withhold an expression of the high opinion I entertain of Bishop Chase, and the gratification it would afford me if his wishes in regard to his son could be realized." *Ibid.*

Jubilee College was an Episcopal Seminary founded by Chase in 1839. *DAB.* Chase's son did not receive the appointment. Benjamin Bond was appointed marshal for Illinois and confirmed on March 1, 1850. U.S. Sen., *Executive Journal*, 8:146.

From Adam Beatty, "Prospect Hill," [near Maysville] Ky., February 22, 1849. Encloses "a copy of the resolutions, adopted at a very large and respectable meeting of friends of Emancipation, in Maysville, on the 12th of february."

Advises Clay that "A claim in the 6th resolution does not meet with my concurrence." Although he agrees with their desire " 'to see some system of emancipation, accompanied by colonization, engrafted in the constitution, about to be formed,' " disagrees with the following clause, " 'We do not however, at present, deem it proper to insist upon that measure. But we do deem it indispensable to insist upon the insertion of a clause in the new constitution, by which the people will be allowed to vote upon the subject.' " Adds: "This clause seems to me equivalent to giving up the whole matter in controversy." Reports that he suggested to the chairman a modification, but although the chairman had agreed to make an amendment, "(I know not for what reason) it was not done." ALS. DLC-HC (DNA, M212, R6).

Beatty had served as president of the Maysville Emancipation convention. For the resolutions passed at the meeting, see Lexington *Observer & Kentucky Reporter*, February 21, 1849. For the 1849 Kentucky Constitutional convention, see Stevenson to Clay, June 12, 1848.

To JAMES BROWN CLAY New Orleans, March 3, 1849

I was glad to learn by your letter of the 18h Ulto. that you had returned from Missouri. Your journey must have been a dreadful one, but you will find some compensation for it, in the profits you expect to realize.[1]

My health is better, and I can again walk.[2] I hope to reach home towards the last of this month. The weather is now fine here, and I am desirous not to return until the winter breaks.

I have heard that Col. [Robert] Allen has discontinued his school, but I have not heard whether Henry [Clay III] is admitted at We[s]t point.[3] I declined going to Washn. at the Call Session.

As you were absent, I sent to Richard Pindell a [word missing] letter on the Emancipation question.[4] As I regret to hear that [it is] not popular, I suppose that my letter will bring on me some od[ium.] I nevertheless wish it published. I owe that to the cause and [to] myself, and to posterity.

I observe what you say about the Check for $600 fr[om] Mr. [Jared S.] Dawson. I wish to find in Bank when I get home enoug[h] to pay my note there. As you do not speak of the $500 w[hich] Mr. [Philip R.] Fendall was to have sent,[5] I am afraid that it is not r[eady.]

I am delighted to hear that dear little Lucy [Jacob Clay] is better.[6] Yo[u are] perfectly right to take her to the Sea bath, if it be recommended; b[ut] ought you not to think of the Arkansas Springs?

I wish you would say to John [Morrison Clay] that if he can find Store room at Ashland for our hemp, I think that he had better not be in any hurry in selling it. I think hemp will rise.

Mr. Conner has not yet paid me for the Jack, but I expect he will do so before I go home.

My love to Susan [Jacob Clay] and your children [Lucy, James, John].

ALS, manuscript torn. DLC-TJC (DNA, M212, R11). Printed in Colton, *Clay Correspondence*, 4:585, with paragraphs 5, 7, and 8 omitted. 1. Probably a reference to the sale of mules. See Clay to Susan J. Clay, April 15 and May 14, 1849. 2. Clay to Harlan, Jan. 26, 1849. 3. Clay to Morehead, Dec. 14, 1848. 4. Clay to Pindell, Feb. 17, 1849, no. 2 of date. 5. Clay to Fendall, June 16, 1847; Fendall to Clay, March 15, 1849. 6. Clay to Susan J. Clay, Nov. 3, 1845.

To LESLIE COMBS New Orleans, March 7, 1849

I received your last letter,[1] transmitting one which is returned.[2] Many thanks are due to you for various communications received during the past winter, and which afforded me much valuable information. I should have before acknowledged them, but for the consequences of my fall, which for a time disabled me from both walking and writing.[3]

The project of assuming the debt of Texas on the consideration of her relinquishment of her territorial claim beyond the Nueces, is worthy of serious examination. The difficulty in the way will be the Free Soil question.[4]

I am most anxious that you should obtain some good appointment under the present Administration.[5] You, I think, eminently deserve it. Whether I can aid you or not, I can not at present say. My relations to the President [Zachary Taylor], on my part, and, as far as I know, on his, are amicable; but I have had no proof of any desire to confer or consult with me on any subject. Some of his warm and confidential friends, I have reason to know, view me with jealousy, if not enmity. While self-respect will restrain me from volunteering any opinion or advice, unless I know it will be acceptable, public duty will equally restrain me from offering any opposition to the course of his Administration, if, as I hope and anticipate, it should be conducted on principles which we have so long cherished and adhered to.

I hope to reach home, and to see you in all this month,[6] when there will be time enough to talk over all these and other matters.

I did not go to the Call Session,[7] because, supposing that it would be short and formal, and without any serious division, I disliked encountering, in my lame condition, a journey so long in the winter.

Copy. Printed in Colton, *Clay Correspondence*, 4:585-86. 1. Not found. 2. *Ibid.* 3. Clay to Harlan, Jan. 26, 1849. 4. Sargent to Clay, Feb. 27, 1847. 5. Combs did not receive an appointment. 6. Taylor to Clay, Nov. 17, 1848. 7. Clay to White, Feb. 8, 1849.

To SUSAN JACOB CLAY New Orleans, March 10, 1849

I received your letter yesterday, and I must first express my delight at the improvement of Lucys [Jacob Clay] health.[1] I pray that it may continue, until it shall be perfectly restored.

I am sorry for the roving spirit in James [Brown Clay] of which you complain; but if his health is benefited by it, perhaps you ought to be reconciled to it, if he will not float off to California. I do wish that he had some permanent & agreeable employment. Can't you prevail on Cousin Zack. to give him some?[2] My aid shall not be wanting, if it can be of any service. But as you shew so little taste, as my private Secretary, for reading letters, I do not know that you would be pleased with his having any official position.

I am now nearly well, being able again to walk as well almost as ever.[3] And I am very anxious to return home, and once more to see you all. I intend to leave this City about the 17h instant, and proceeding up the river, on which I may stop at one or two places,[4] I hope to get to Ashland about the last of this month.

The weather here is as warm now as it is ordinarily with us in May. I find, it entirely too hot, and I can bear no other covering at night but a sheet.

Tell James that I have received his letter of the 25h Ulto and that I will think of the affair of the P.O. by the time I get home.[5]

Kiss all your children [Lucy, James, John] . . .

ALS. DLC-TJC (DNA, M212, R11). 1. Clay to Susan J. Clay, Nov. 3, 1845. 2. Clay himself appealed to President Taylor to give James an appointment. See Clay to Taylor, May 12, 1849. 3. Clay to Harlan, Jan. 26, 1849. 4. Taylor to Clay, Nov. 17, 1848. 5. Reference obscure.

To JAMES HARLAN New Orleans, March 13, 1849

I received your favor of the 3d. instant. I concluded not to attend the Call Session, which I could not have done, without much personal discomfort.

The Cabinet of Genl [Zachary] Taylor was not, it seems, exactly as you supposed.[1] Some of the appointments excited surprize. I think that he might have made one of greater strength. I am truly concerned that [Robert P.] Letcher was overlooked.[2] I had strong hopes that he would have been appointed, and I thought I had reason for them.

I think it quite likely that you may be right in supposing that neither me nor my friends will find much favor at Court. As to myself, having given no just cause for its frowns, I can bear them without difficulty; but the President will be unwise if he neglects or proscribes my friends. Without them, he never could have been elected.

Whilst I have no desire to go into the [Kentucky Constitutional] Convention,[3] I shall make no decision until my return. I leave this City on the 17th. inst. and stopping on the river at one or two places, I hope to reach home about the last of the month.

I request that you will take care that my interest in the house occupied by Dr. [Douglass L.] Price is not sold for taxes.[4]

ALS. Courtesy of Alan Westin, New Haven, Conn. Printed in Colton, *Clay Correspondence*, 4:586 with last paragraph omitted. 1. Clay to Pierse, Feb. 16, 1849. 2. John J. Crittenden had pressed Taylor to appoint Letcher to his cabinet, but Taylor believed that cabinet posts were allotted to states, not to men, and refused. Since Crittenden had refused to accept the position of secretary of state, Kentucky had forfeited its first chance for a cabinet post and would have to wait until all other states had their turn. Bauer, *Zachary Taylor*, 252. 3. Stevenson to Clay, June 12, 1848. 4. Clay to Letcher, July 7, 1848.

From Philip R. Fendall, Washington, March 15, 1849. Forwards to Clay "the proceeds of the claim of Col. [James] Morrison's estate on the Columbian College [Clay to Fendall, June 16, 1847]." Encloses "a check of the Bank of Washington on the National Bank of N. York for five hundred and twenty three dollars 58/100, being the principal of the note, $500, and the interest (as calculated at the Bank in which the note had been left for collection)." After being "put off so often," had "made up my mind that it would be necessary to bring suit." Credits "the personal exertions of one of the Trustees" for avoiding legal actions. Refuses to accept a commission for his services "because I inferred from what you said when authorising a compromise, that in doing so you were taking on yourself a personal loss; and this loss I am not willing to increase."

Expresses his pleasure to learn that Clay is "fully recovered from the severe attack which you had last fall [Carroll to Clay, November 16, 1848], and from the accident which afterward befel you [Clay to Harlan, January 26, 1849]." Believes "your recent letter to Mr [Richard] Pindell [Clay to Pindell, February 17, 1849, no. 2 of date]" will "make a deep impression on the public mind." Concludes that although "the subject . . . forbids unanimity as to the doctrine . . . there cannot be two opinions as to the structure of the argument or the style of the composition." ALS, draft. DGW.

From William Lloyd Garrison, Boston, March 16, 1849. States that he is publishing Clay's letter to Richard Pindell [February 17, 1849, no. 2 of date] on the subject of slavery and emancipation. Notes that from the time he first heard of the letter, "I felt curious to see whether any, and, if any, what changes had taken place in your views and sentiments on this grave subject since your detestable speech in the U.S. Senate [Speech in Senate, February 7, 1839; see 9:278-83]. Ten years of anti-slavery agitation have witnessed many changes, equally cheering and surprising, in the opinions of individuals and collective bodies, respecting the colored population of this country, especially that portion of it now held in the galling fetters of slavery at the

South. I supposed it to be possible, therefore,—not probable, no, sir!—that, in the Letter now under consideration, there would be at least a slight indication that you were growing less selfish, less inhuman, less cowardly, on the question of negro emancipation. But I see no evidence of this in your epistle."

Asserts that he has "watched the career of no man more narrowly than your own" for the last twenty years, and "I find we do not approximate any nearer to each other. . . . Most happy should I be to give you the right hand of fellowship, for I am not blind to your shining abilities; but either you or I must 'right about face,' before that grasp can be given."

Asserts that Clay's letter "is not what the time or the occasion demands. Nay, with a single exception, it is remorseless in purpose, cruel in spirit, delusive in expectation, sophistical in reasoning, tyrannous in principle." Believes that if Clay is sincere in his statements, "it shows that you are removed from a true sense of justice, and a clear perception of human rights. . . . no sign of repentence do you give for the countless wrongs and outrages you have inflicted, or caused to be inflicted, on an unoffending, weak and helpless race." Contends that Clay has "long stood at the head of as cruel a conspiracy against God and man as was ever contrived. . . . As the author of the Missouri Compromise, you have done more than any other to lengthen the cords and strengthen the stakes of oppression." Thus, blames Clay for the establishment of slavery in Texas, and adds that if Mexico has been deprived of the "immense territories of New Mexico and California . . . for the purpose of extending the dominion of the Slave Power, the criminality is eminently yours."

Regards "JOHN C. CALHOUN as a more honest, trust-worthy and harmless man than yourself, even on this question of slavery . . . you are more to be feared, and can do incomparably greater mischief, by your double-dealing and hypocrisy. He, by his monstrous and headlong advocasy of man-stealing, makes no proselytes, but repels rather than allures; you, by your pretended desire to see it come to an end, not now, but at a future period long protracted, and by your oily tongue and wily compromises, would deceive the very elect, if it were possible."

The one exception in Clay's letter which saves it "from utter condemnation" is "that portion . . . in which you admit, that the principle on which slavery is advocated would equally require the enslavement of the white race with that of the black; and that intellectual inferiority can in *no* instance justify the holding of any human being in bondage. True, these propositions are self-evident, but their endorsement by you . . . is of some value. You further add, that 'if indeed we possess this intellectual superiority, we ought to fulfill all the duties and obligations which it imposes, and these would require us not to *subjugate or deal unjustly by our fellow men* who are less blessed than we are, but TO INSTRUCT, TO IMPROVE, AND TO ENLIGHTEN THEM.' By this standard, then, do not complain, sir, if I measure you." Castigates Clay for owning "more than sixty slaves," and asks: "Are you not condemned out of your own mouth?"

Continues: "Sir, slavery is 'the sum of all villanies'—it is pollution, concubinage, adultery—it is theft, robbery, kidnapping . . . it . . . depraves the manners and morals of all who are infected by it! This you know; and yet you dare to affirm that its continuance *is a matter* of 'necessity'! Ah! this is ever 'the tyrants plea,' and you are a tyrant." Concludes with an extensive attack on Clay's belief that slavery may have been imposed by Providence in order to civilize and Christianize Africa. Copy. Printed in Boston *The Liberator*, March 16, 1849.

For Garrison, well-known abolitionist and editor of *The Liberator*, see *DAB*.

To REVERDY JOHNSON New Orleans, March 17, 1849

I received your letter announcing your appointment as Atto. General,[1] and kindly tendering your friendly offices.

I congratulate you on your promotion. Your official position reconciles the discharge of public duties with the professional pursuit of your private interest.

I am thankful for the offer of your friendly services, of which if necessary I will avail myself. Heretofore my family has been unfortunate with the powers that be. If Mr. [John] Tyler had fulfilled a promise voluntarily made by President [William Henry] Harrison to my son Henry [Clay, Jr.] of the mission to Brussels,[2] Col. Clay would be yet living; but he would not fulfill it. Mr. [James K.] Polk was applied to last winter for a Cadets appointment of Col. Clay's eldest son (H. Clay Jr. [III]) and Mr. Polk spoke very warmly and kindly, but my grandson did not obtain the appointment![3]

When in office myself, I made it a sacred rule never by my influence to appoint any relation of mine. And not a human being that has any blood of mine in his veins holds any Federal office. . . .

ALS. MdHi. 1. Not found. For Taylor's cabinet, see Clay to Pierse, Feb. 16, 1849. 2. See 9:507-8; Clay to Taylor, May 12, 1849. 3. Clay to Morehead, Dec. 14, 1848.

From Willis Hall *et al.*, New York City, March 26, 1849. Congratulate Clay on the "joyful occasion" of his 72nd birthday. Praise Clay's life, "every year of which has been marked by some signal service to the nation." Observe that "calmly, cheerfully have you acquiesced in the decision of the People, and at the moment that inferior minds stung with a sense of injury might have retired from public service. You have been labouring with the fearlessness and energy of youth and the wisdom of age for the advancement of your beloved country." Add: "Your example is not lost. It has taught the world how ardent how inextinguishable is the love of country in a Patriot's bosom!" LS. DLC-HC (DNA, M212, R6).

From James C. Johnston *et al.*, Louisville, Ky., March 27, 1849. Write to Clay as a committee of his friends to invite him to a public dinner at the Galt House in Louisville at any time convenient to him. Explain that this is designed as "a tribute to one whose whole career, for half a century, has been marked by untiring zeal for his country's welfare." Add that "We represent gentlemen who differ among themselves, and many with you, on questions of national and State policy: but all concur in their high estimate of your great talents, ardent patriotism, great purity of purpose, and eminent public service. Copy. Printed in Lexington *Observer & Kentucky Reporter*, April 4, 1849. This letter was also signed by Ben. J. Adams, C.M. Thruston, Geo. D. Prentice, E.G. McGinnis, and Wm. H. Field.

Writing from Louisville, Clay replied on March 28, expressing his gratitude for the invitation and their kind sentiments. Notes that "After an absence of more than three months from this State, to be thus honored and welcomed, as soon as I have again trodden its soil, is a high gratification. . . . Nor is the compliment at all diminished by the fact of diversity of opinion on public affairs. . . . Such diversity of opinion, when honorably entertained, should no more estrange or alienate us from each other than the fact of difference in our physical or mental constitutions, of which it is the consequence." Regrets, therefore, that the desire "to reach my family and home, after my long separation from them" necessitates a rejection of the invitation which comes "from some of the best friends I have in the world, both personal and political." *Ibid.*

To James B. Dodd, Lexington, Ky., April 2, 1849. Sends "my grandson H[enry]. Clay" to Transylvania University "in virtue of his father's (Lieut. Col. [Henry] Clay's) title to a Scholarship." Once it is decided which class he should enter, "My wish is to direct his attention particularly to Latin, the Mathematics and the French Language, and to the Greek language if he has time for its study." ALS. KyLxT.

For Dodd, president of Transylvania University from 1847-56, see Robert Peter, *Transylvania University: Its Origin, Rise, Decline and Fall.* Filson Club Publications No. 11 (Louisville, 1896), 171.

Clay's grandson did not enroll at Transylvania; instead he went to Lisbon with his uncle. See James B. Clay to Clay, November 27, 1849.

To N.B. Blunt *et al.*, New York City, April 6, 1849. Has received their invitation to visit New York for a celebration of his birthday. Feels "this honor far transcends any merit I possess, or the value of any public services I ever performed." While expressing his "profound gratitude and thankfulness," states that he cannot accept "your kind invitation." Copy. Printed in Washington *Daily National Intelligencer*, April 17, 1849.

From Robert Monroe Harrison, Kingston, Jamaica, April 6, 1849. Expresses his pleasure at Clay's return to the Senate and hopes he can help bring "our Government back to those principles by which the late Honorable John Quincy Adams and his administration were activated."

Desires to give up "the miserable appointment of *Consul here*" because of "the emoluments being so pitiful, that no favorite partisan of the different Administrations from General [Andrew] Jackson down would condescend to accept of the appointment." Adds that "this Colony owing to the pseudophilanthropy and insane measures of the British Government has fallen never to rise again." Desires "a Collectorship Navy Agency, or some situation to enable me to support my large family." Would also accept "an appointment as Chargé to some of the South American Republics . . . (speaking, as I do, French and understanding Spanish,)" or "any thing connected with the Naval or Merchant Service." Maintains that although he is now "seventy odd years old," he is still vigorous, and even if he were not, "I have two noble and talented young sons whom I could always call to my aid." Adds that "One of them, Richard Adams . . . speaks French Spanish, Italian, and German," while "The other William Henry . . . is not only a first rate accountant but writes a splendid bold hand." Hopes Clay will "do something for an old and faithful servant, (and his two sons,) who has served his Country with zeal and fidelity for many years, whilst ignorant uneducated persons have been appointed to missions abroad, where they were not only laughed at by our citizens, but were despised also by foreigners." LS. DNA, RG59, Applicatons and Recommendations, R4.

On June 24, 1849, Clay enclosed Harrison's letter to Secretary of State John M. Clayton, calling the consul "one of our most faithful and zealous foreign Agents" and hoping "some suitable appointment could be conferred upon him or one of his sons." ALS. *Ibid.*

On June 25, 1849, Clay informed Harrison that he had written Clayton and "testified to your merits and long service." Hopes Harrison's efforts "prove successful. I am inclined to think that the presence of yourself or of one of your sons at Washington might have a favorable tendency in the promotion of your wishes." ALS. Courtesy of Elsie O. & Philip Sang, Forest Park, Ill.

Harrison did not receive another appointment from the Taylor administration. He remained in Jamaica until his death in 1858, having served as consul there since 1831. Previously, from 1827-31, he had served at St. Bartholomew. See DNA, RG59, Cons. Disp., Kingston, Jamaica, 1858 (M-T31).

To Philip R. Fendall, Washington, April 7, 1849. Acknowledges receipt of "a Check for the amount of the debt due to the estate of Col. [James] Morrison. . . . but I should have been better satisfied if you had retained the commission ordinary in such cases." Hopes that in the Taylor administration's "arrangements for the public service. . . . If ample competency, great industry, fidelity to the Whig cause, and persecution for that fidelity, constitute any title, you will not be overlooked in the distribution of the public patronage." Assures Fendall that if "my wishes or my name can be of the least service to you . . . you are authorized to use them freely." ALS. NjP. See Clay to Fendall, June 16, 1847; Fendall to Clay, March 15, 1849, for the debt to Morrison's estate.

During a congressional recess in 1849, Fendall was appointed federal attorney for the District of Columbia. His name was presented to the Senate on May 13, 1850, and he was confirmed on September 24. U.S. Sen., *Executive Journal*, 8:177, 194, 232, 249.

To Thomas Winslow Gordon, April 7, 1849. Thanks Gordon for "the acrostic on my name, which you did me the honor to compose in 1847." Despite the "disappointment you and other friends may have felt in my not obtaining the nomination for the Presidency, at the Philadelphia Convention [Greeley to Clay, November 15, 1846], let us all unite in hopes and prayers that the success of the one which was made may conduce to the prosperity and happiness of our common Country." Copy. Printed in Ruth Winslow Gordon, "A Letter from Henry Clay," *Kentucky Progress Magazine* (October, 1931), 4:35.

To MORTON McMICHAEL

Lexington, April 7, 1849

Your very kind letter of the 13th. Ulto. addressed to me at N. Orleans, followed and reached me here. I perused attentively, and with much pleasure, the article in the [Philadelphia] N[orth]. American to which my attention was called.[1] I owe most of the praise and commendation which it bestows, with so much eloquence and liberality, to the generosity of your nature and to the fidelity of your friendship.

I regret deeply that there is no encouraging prospect of the adoption of the scheme of gradual emancipation of the African race, at the approaching Convention, as proposed by me, or any other scheme.[2] This inauspicious state of things is to be ascribed to the indiscreet and unwise interference, on the subject of slavery, by violent abolitionists in other States, to the jealousy existing between the two rival parties of Whigs and Democrats in Kentucky, each fearing that the other might obtain some advantage over it, and to the timidity of leading individuals among us, in suppressing their real sentiments.

All this I knew when I wrote the letter, which has called forth an expression of your approbation; but I could not, towards the close of my life, relinquish the inestimable privilege of freely expressing my sentiments on a great public matter, however they might be received by the public.

ALS. PHi. 1. Not found. 2. Reference is to the 1849 Kentucky Constitutional convention. See Stevenson to Clay, June 12, 1848. For Clay's suggestion for gradual emancipation, see Clay to Pindell, Feb. 17, 1849, no. 2 of date.

To JOHN SLOANE

Lexington, April 10, 1849

Having returned a few days ago from N. Orleans I found here your two favors of the 22d. December and 12th. Feb. last. I regret the delay in my receipt of them, particularly the last.

I transmit enclosed a letter to the President [Zachary Taylor], the only one I have addressed to him directly on the subject of office.[1] With what success it may be attended, I cannot anticipate. I sincerely hope that our wishes may be gratified. My relations with the President, on my part, are amicable; but great efforts have been made to prejudice him against me, and I do not know how far they have succeeded.[2] Perhaps you may not like the offices which I have suggested; but as I had not the advantage of knowing your particular wishes, I was governed by circumstances in naming them.

Your letter of Decr.[3] presents a deplorable picture of Ohio politics. I fear that it will be a long time before they are straightened again. Had I been nominated how different would have been the present condition of the Whig party in that State! I have a letter from Genl. [Winfield] Scott, in which he states that he authorized it to be known that he was willing that his name should be used as a Candidate for the V[ice]. P[resident]. on a ticket with me.[4] Yet that fact was suppressed at the Philada. [Whig National] Convention. Circumstances have compelled me most reluctantly to believe that Genl. [Joseph] Vance was the Agent or instrument in carrying off from me to Genl Scott, the twenty Ohio delegates who acted with him in the Convention.[5]

I have a perfect recollection of what passed in my room in the early part of 1825 with Judge [Jesse Burgess] Thomas, in your presence in regard to the approaching Presidential election, & it accords with your own.[6] The truth is that there were some most unscrupulous persons in the [William] Crawford party.

Excuse my brevity. I am still borne down by a burthensome correspondence, which greatly accumulated in my absence.

ALS. MH. 1. Clay to Taylor, April 10, 1849. 2. *Ibid.* 3. Sloane to Clay, Dec. 22, 1848. 4. Scott to Clay, July 19, 1848. 5. For example, Van Trump to Clay, July 26, 1848; Clay to Stevenson, August 5 and 14, 1848. 6. Sloane to Clay, Feb. 12, 1849.

To ZACHARY TAYLOR Lexington, April 10, 1849

I wish to present to your consideration for an official appointment the name of John Sloane Esqr of Wooster in the State of Ohio.[1] I served with this Gentleman some time in the H. of Representatives of the U.S. to which he was elected by perhaps the largest popular majority that any member ever obtained. He was afterwards Secy of State in Ohio.[2] I consider Mr Sloane one of the purest, most patriotic, and among the most intelligent persons I have met in the public counsels. His habits are those of great industry, and free from any taint of dissipation. I need not add, that he has been uniformly, a devoted Whig. The offices to which I think his talents well adapted, are those of Comptroller, Auditor, or Territorial Governor, in any one of which I am sure, that he would acquit himself, with honor, probity, and industry.[3] He is not rich; but has taken care of his credit and standing[.]

P.S. I regretted my inability to attend the called session of the Senate. Beside my desire to be always present, when duty calls me, I wished for opportunities of personal intercourse with you, in which I might remove unfounded impressions, if any such had been made by sinister influences.[4]

Copy. OClWHi. 1. Sloane to Clay, Feb. 12, 1849; Clay to Sloane, April 10, 1849. 2. From 1841-44. *BDAC.* 3. Sloane to Clay, Feb. 12, 1849. 4. See, for example, Taylor to Clay Nov. 17, 1848; Clay to Mercer, Dec. 10, 1848; Stevenson to Clay, April 30, 1849.

To PETER SKEN SMITH Lexington, April 13, 1849

Upon returning a few days ago from N. Orleans, I found here your letter of the 25h Decr. last, requesting me to aid you in obtaining some respectable appointment from the President[.]

I have thought it right not to interfere in mere local appointments in different and distant States from that of my residence, and I have generally foreborne to do so. Such interferen[ce] is regarded as officious & is some times injurious to the person in whose behalf it is made.

But I have no hesitation in expressing the wish that you may obtain some suitable appointment. I have known you long; chiefly by correspondence, and as an Editor,[1] and the impression of you made on my mind is favorable, altho' we have sometimes differed in opinion, especially as to the policy of agitating the Native American question.[2]

If you suppose that my name will be of any service to you, in your application at Washington, you are at liberty to use this letter with the proper department.

ALS. DNA, RG56, Customs Applications, Collectors, Entry 247, Box 195. Endorsed in Smith's hand: "*Remark*—Under date of Apl. 14. 1849, Mr. Clay in another letter to me [which letter relating to some other private matters I cannot with propriety file] says, 'Whilst I was at New Orleans, I declined recommending for the office of Collector of the Port of Philadelphia one of my best friends.' " Reference is to William D. Lewis. See Clay to Lewis, Feb. 9, 1849. 1. Smith had edited the *Native Eagle and American Advocate*, a weekly magazine. Feldberg, *The Philadelphia Riots*, 95. 2. Clay to Smith, June 17, 1844; Smith to Clay, Nov. 6, 1847.

To SUSAN JACOB CLAY Lexington, April 15, 1849

I received your letter transmitting a note of James s [Brown Clay] to which, if he does not return in time, I will attend. I am sorry that he is absent from you so much longer than you expected; and I wish that he was fairly out of and through his Mule speculation.[1]

We are all pretty well here and at Mansfield. The two last very cold days have made me a little unwell with a bad cold.

Kiss dear Lucy [Jacob Clay] and her brothers [James, John] for your affte father . . .

ALS. DLC-TJC (DNA, M212, R11). 1. Clay to James B. Clay, March 3, 1849.

To Rodney Dennis, April 15, 1849. Thanks Dennis for his "friendly sentiments," claiming that "You do me too much honor" in comparing "me & the renowned men of Antiquity. I am in one respect better off than Moses. He died in sight of, without reaching, the promised land. I occupy as good a farm as any that he would have found, if he had reached it; & it has been acquired not by hereditary descent, but by my own labor." After "more than my share" of public honors, "I am contented, & now seek for better, if not higher offices & honors, in a better world." Copy. DLC-HC (DNA, M212, R6). Printed in Colton, *Clay Correspondence*, 4:587.

For Dennis, who at this time was the owner of a grocery business in Hartford, Conn., see *NCAB*, 5:434.

To CHRISTOPHER HUGHES Lexington, April 16, 1849

I was last night, my dear Hughes, whilst lying in bed, thinking of writing to your dear daughter [Margaret Hughes] to obtain information as to the state of your health and your actual condition. Whilst I was sojourning at N. Orleans, I received indirectly such unfavorable accounts of your situation that I was unwilling to address you directly.[1] Your favor of the 9th. inst., received this morning, has afforded some relief to my anxiety about you, since it contains an assurance that you were better and that hopes of your recovery might be cherished. God grant that they may be realized! The effects of the Indian Hesop upon your system are indeed wonderful. How admirably some times, one of those simple (old womens) remedies works, and rises above skill and science!

I wish indeed my dear friend that you could come here. But as you say, and as I fear, that is impracticable[.] I hope to see you in Balto. next fall.

I returned from N. Orleans a few days ago,[2] in good health, as you may infer from the fact, that the day after reaching home I was summoned to another County, to appear as Counsel in a Jury cause, which occupied four tedious days.[3]

During my abode at N.O. I met with a terrible fall in descending a flight of steps at Dr. [William N.] Mercers. I broke no bones, but I was so bruised that I was confined to my room five or six weeks. I don't know but the fall was of service to me, in arousing some of my sleeping interior organs, and stimulating them to the performance of their duties.

You see I wrote about myself. In youth our topics of correspondence are our pleasures, in age our pains.

I pray you, my dear Hughes, to keep me advised about your health—may I not say the progress of your recovery?

Mrs. [Lucretia Hart] Clay joins me in affectionate remembrance to you. And I add my warm regards for Margaret.

ALS. MiU-C. 1. For a discussion of Hughes's ailments, see Clay to Hughes, June 14, 1848. 2. For Clay's itinerary, see Taylor to Clay, Nov. 17, 1848. 3. Clay had participated, along with Samuel Hanson, in an attempt in Clark County Circuit Court to overturn the will of Joel Quisenberry. Chilton Allen and Garrett Davis appeared for the parties in favor of upholding the will. The jury failed to reach a verdict. Lexington *Observer & Kentucky Reporter*, April 7, 1849.

To Octavia Walton LeVert, Mobile, April 17, 1849. Expresses his condolences on the "loss of your poor brother . . . a most heavy & deplorable calamity; the next greatest to that of your husband, one of your children, or one of your parents." Commiserates with her "winter of affliction. . . . But I was not without mine." Describes his fall at Dr. William N. Mercer's house which prevented him from visiting Mobile: "How cruel was fortune, when we were so near together, to deprive us of the satisfaction of meeting, by our respective afflictions." Now "entirely recovered from the effects of my fall," finds the weather in Kentucky "cool, elastic, bracing, so different from the hot, murky disagreeable winter I passed at N. Orleans." Adds, however, that "three or four days" of "intensely cold dry weather . . . has destroyed all our fruit."

Views "the calamities of life" as "dispensations of Providence, sent probably for our good, although we may not see it, but to which . . . it is our duty to submit in obedience and with resignation. If much has been taken from you, much also is left to comfort, to cheer & to console you." ALS. KyU.

Robert Watkins Walton, Mrs. LeVert's brother, had died of yellow fever at Mobile, Ala., on March 22, 1849. Information supplied by Caldwell Delaney, Museum Director, City of Mobile Museum Department.

To Jared S. Dawson, Bellefontaine, Ohio, April 18, 1849. Expresses his approval of "the sale of 200 Acres of my Logan [Co., Ohio] land at eight dollars per acre, $600 in cash, $200 to be paid the first of next month $400 the 16 Jany next and $400 the 16th. Jany 1851." Thanks Dawson for his "kind attention to my interests and for the advantageous terms on which you effected the Sale." Adds: "I am inclined to think that lands will rise this year. When you can make a Sale of the residue on fair terms,

I will thank you to do it." ALS. DLC-HC (DNA, M212, R21). See Clay to Dawson, January 17, 1844.

On June 27, 1849, Clay acknowledged receipt of $150 from Dawson "on account of the instalment of $200 due 1st. May last on the 200 Acres of my land in Logan sold by you." Informs Dawson that he had written "a person in Covington [Kentucky]. . . . that I would take five dollars per acre, cash in hand" for the residue, but "if it were sold on credit I would not vary the terms you had proposed." AL, signature removed. DLC-HC (DNA, M212, R21).

On September 21, 1849, Clay sent Dawson a receipt for "the One hundred dollars you paid me on account of my land sold by you." ALS. *Ibid.*

On December 17, 1849, Clay acknowledged receiving $250 from Dawson, adding that "I shall be glad to receive . . . further sums when your collections are made, including the $400 due 1st. proximo." AL, signature removed. *Ibid.*

To JESSE M. CHRISTOPHER Lexington, April 19, 1849

[Apologizes for the long delay in answering his letter. Continues:]

Concurring in many of your observations about the course of the Philada. [Whig National] Convention, and of particular individuals,[1] I must say, at the same time, that they are themes upon which I do not like to dwell, and which I wish to banish as much as possible from my recollection.

Since the date of your letter, the new Administration has been organized and gone into operation. We have yet to learn what will be the course of its measures of public policy. I hope it will be Whig, and such as all Whigs may be able conscientiously to support. I have some fears that a discrimination will be made between the original supporters of Genl [Zachary] Taylor, and those who preferred other Candidates, in the appointments to public office.[2] Such discrimination would be very unwise and very unjust. It is perhaps too soon to judge if there be any purpose to make it.

I suppose that, if my life be spared, I shall have to attend the next Session of Congress. I shall go there, if I do attend, with an anxious desire to establish as many of the public principles for which I have ever contended, by my co-operation, as may be practicable; and with no view blindly to oppose or blindly to support the Administration. . . .

ALS. NRU. 1. Greeley to Clay, Nov. 15, 1846. 2. Patronage was a major problem of the Taylor administration. For a discussion of the way it was managed, see Hamilton, *Zachary Taylor, Soldier in the White House*, 203-18; Bauer, *Zachary Taylor*, 259-65.

To JAMES HARLAN Lexington, April 20, 1849

Since my return home, I have recd. your friendly letter, expressing the opinion that it is inexpedient for me to go into the Convention.[1] My opinion coincides with yours. Before I left home last winter, I stated to friends here that I could not be a Candidate, and since my return I have stated that I would not be. It is a sufficient reason that the Session of the Convention will probably run into that of Congress,[2] or so near it that I should not be able to leave home and travel to Washington in good weather, if I go there, as I suppose if living I must do.

I wish again to trouble you with some business with Dr. [Douglass L.] Price; but I cannot do so unless you will charge the usual Commission, which I must insist on your doing.

Another year's rent of the house became due the first inst., $275.[3] As he purchased one half of it from Mr. Pilkington on the first of October, I am willing to credit him with one half of Mr. Ps. half, that is one quarter of the above. The other half of it, I must receive, it being necessary to replace Mr. Ps. half of the cost of new roofing the house &c, the whole of which I paid. Dr. Price owes a small bal. of the previous year's rent. Leaving that to be adjusted with me, if he is not prepared to pay the rent, I am willing to take his negotiable note, with such surety as you will approve, at four months, including int. from the first inst. The principal will be $206:25, exclusive of int.

I expect to pass through Frankfort about this day week, and shall be glad if the business be arranged by that time. I will then also pay the taxes if you will have the goodness to ascertain for me the amount.

ALS. Courtesy of Alan Westin, New Haven, Conn. 1. The Kentucky Constitutional convention. See Stevenson to Clay, June 12, 1848. 2. The Ky. Constitutional convention ran from Oct. 1 to Dec. 21, 1849; the 31 Cong., 1 Sess. opened Dec. 3, 1849. 3. Clay to Letcher, July 7, 1848.

To THOMAS B. STEVENSON Lexington, April 21, 1849

It has been a good while since I heard from you. The last letter I wrote to you was from N[ew]. O[rleans]. transmitting a letter which I hoped might benefit you at Washington,[1] but, as I have seen no announcement of your name for any appointment, I fear that my application in your behalf, if one were made, has been unsuccessful. From the general character of the appointments, which I have observed, I apprehend that they have been pretty much confined to the Taylor men to the exclusion of the friends of other Candidates. Such a course if it be adopted, will be both unwise and unjust.

I observe that the Newspapers are stating that I am to deliver an agricultural address at Cincinnati,[2] during the present year. Such a statement is without any authority from me, and I am totally at a loss to know how it came to be made. Will you do me the favor to see the managers of the society[3] and let them know, if they do not already, that I have made no such arrangement, nor can I. I have neither the time not taste, nor, perhaps, talents for compositions suited for such occasions.

I returned home in good health, which I thank God I continue to enjoy. But I have not regained entirely my lost flesh—

Copy. OCHP. Printed in Colton, *Clay Correspondence*, 3:492. 1. Clay to Stevenson, Jan. 31, 1849. 2. It had been reported in the New Orleans *Daily Picayune* of April 6, 1849. 3. On April 28, 1849, the Lexington *Observer & Kentucky Reporter* reported that, contrary to a statement in some newspapers, Clay would not be speaking at the annual meeting of the Ohio State Agricultural Society.

To Z. COLLINS LEE Lexington, April 24, 1849

I received today your letter.[1] You are right in supposing that I cherish friendly feelings towards you, and I wish I could serve you. I think that you have fair claims on the patronage of the Government. But, in relation to mere local offices, situated in different and distant States from that of my residence, I have found it necessary to adopt the rule of non interference. In respect to them, I cannot be supposed to be well acquainted with the wants and wishes of the Communities who ought to control such appointments. And I have found that such interference, by a distant person, is some times regarded as officious, and some times is even prejudicial to the person in whose behalf it is made.

I regret therefore that I cannot comply with your request for a recommendation for the office mentioned by you.

I must add, in candor, that I entertain doubts whether a recommendation from me would command any particular attention. Whilst I entertain myself only amicable feelings towards the Administration, I am not sure that those of a contrary character have not been instilled into the mind of the President [Zachary Taylor].[2]

ALS. CtHi. 1. Not found. 2. Clay to Taylor, April 10, 1849.

To Thomas B. Stevenson, Cincinnati, April 26, 1849. Acknowledges Stevenson's letter [not found] and its "expression of the feelings of the President [Zachary Taylor] in regard to me." Based on information in a letter [not found] from "Col B[uckner]. H. Payne. . . . a man of truth [Clay to Taylor, May 12, 1849]" believes that there must be "some mistake, or some insincerity on the part of high functionaries. Charity and hope induce me to think that it is the former [Stevenson to Clay, April 30, 1849]." Reasserts his refusal to "be a candidate for the [Kentucky Constitutional] Convention [Stevenson to Clay, June 12, 1848]," because "the Session of that body will run into the Session of Congress." Copy. OCHP. Printed in Colton, *Clay Correspondence*, 3:493.

From THOMAS B. STEVENSON Cincinnati, April 30, 1849

I return Col. [Buckner H.] Payne's letter.[1] I do not question the correctness of his detail of the conversations of the President [Zachary Taylor] and Secretary of State [John M. Clayton]. At the same time, there is *no* "mistake" in the truth of what I communicated. He did use expressions similar to those I repeated, and even more offensive, at Louisville, on the river, and here.[2] What I reported was avouched to me by Gov. [Joseph] Vance and R[ichard]. M. Corwine,[3] to whom the language of Taylor was addressed. Vance chuckled with evident delight at it. Corwine spoke of it with sorrow, having been an original Taylorite. I thought and said at the time, though satisfied of his ill feeling toward you, that wise men at Washington would restrain him there. The report of Payne confirms this. I despise the character of an informer and I also despise such private evil speaking as that reported by Vance and Corwine. I thought, however, it was due to you that you should know facts. I suppose the administration will be wise enough to avoid a conflict with you, because, if no other reason operated, they must know that, while they may possibly annoy or injure you, they will injure if not destroy themselves. This is a bond to keep the peace. I hope there may be peace—I hope it for the sake of the Whig cause and of the country. And as it seems to me impossible that the administration can succeed without your cooperation, I shall even yet, notwithstanding any private feelings of the President, not be surprised if he and his Cabinet will be gratified to see you take your old course at the head of the party in the Senate. As well as I can see in the future, I am inclined to the opinion that, on your appearance at Washington, they will make proper advances to you. I certainly would make none to them, further than the proprieties of position may require, and such as must show that, whatever may be the state of private feelings, you are too lofty in principle to indulge upon public questions the least factiousness of spirit. Your whole life is to me and to all candid men a guaranty for that; but all men are not candid; and, unfortunately, too many men in the Whig party, men once your ardent friends, are lately in the habit of suspecting you will be governed by vindictive rather that patriotic feelings in your Senatorial course. Hence the frequency of the impertinent and I think insolent inquiry—"will Mr. Clay support the administration?" Many of these men, actuated only by a hope of propitiating favor at Court by disparaging you, will be as ardent (though not trustworthy) friends of yours as ever when they find you have the friendship of the administration. Of the class of those who pretend to fear you will make mischief, as they flippantly talk, are Jos. Vance and Tho. Ewing. The former is more excusable, because he [is] in his dotage. But *I know* they talk so, having heard them. Yet nothing can be determined in regard to your political relations towards the administration until after you go to Washington, unless Taylor and [John M.] Clayton correspond with you on the subject beforehand,[4] as Col. Payne stated their purpose to be. Our principles and our Country are foremost considerations with me, and I shall be rejoiced if you and the administration harmonise in their support. If not, I shall stand by the party that stands by them, but certainly with every predilection in favor of my old love.

But we shall see what we shall see; and at all events, if there be a rupture, sufficient unto the day is the evil thereof.

I have not thought Emancipation can be carried now, not during this the most propitious time to propose it in Convention, though it should be discussed.[5] This lessens my regret at your determination not to go into the Convention.

ALS. DLC-HC (DNA, M212, R6). 1. Payne's letter not found, but see Clay to Stevenson, April 26, 1849; Clay to Taylor, May 12, 1849. 2. Expressions not found, but see Clay to Stevenson, April 26, 1849. 3. Corwine was a Cincinnati lawyer who at various times practiced with Caleb Smith, R.S. Holt, and Rutherford B. Hayes. *OH* (1968), 77:28; Harry Barnard, *Rutherford B. Hayes and His America* (New York, 1954), 183-84. 4. Taylor to Clay, May 28, 1849, was written in response to Clay to Taylor, May 12, 1849. 5. The 1849 Ky. Constitutional convention. See Stevenson to Clay, June 12, 1848.

To ZACHARY TAYLOR Lexington, May 12, 1849

I have recently received from a gentleman (Buckner H. Payne Esq. of New Orleans) who professes to be a common friend, a communication respecting a conversation which he had with you at Washington, concerning me,[1] from the friendly tenor of which I am induced to address this letter.

During the brief period of the Administration of Genl. [William Henry] Harrison of the Executive Government, and among the last interviews which I had with him in March 1841, he requested me to inform my son, the late Lieut. Col. H[enry]. Clay [Jr.], that the mission to Brussells [*sic*] was at his service, and to hold himself in readiness to proceed on it, if he chose to accept it.[2] No solicitation on my part, or that of any of Col. Clays friends, had been made, and the purpose of President Harrison took me by surprize. I communicated to my son the tender thus voluntarily made to him, and he expressed his willingness to accept it.

But, when Mr. [John] Tyler succeeded to the Presidential office, he thought proper to confer the mission to Brussells on Mr. [Henry W.] Hilliard of Alabama, who had been his warm friend at the Harrisburg Convention.[3] In lieu of that mission, Mr. [Daniel] Webster, the Secy. of State, proposed that the office of Secretary of Legation to Charles S. Todd Esq. Minister to Russia should be offered to my son. This was promptly declined; for, without disparagement of the one or of any exaggeration of the other, I really thought that a reversal of the respective official positions proposed for them, would have been more conformable with the dictates of justice and merit.

I have not adverted to these past incidents under any impression that they create any, the smallest, obligation with you; but for a totally different purpose. During my long connection with public affairs, I have never employed any official influence which I might happen to possess to promote the appointment to public office of any relations of mine. Nor was any one of them, at any time, ever promoted at my instance. And, at the present period, I know of no solitary human being having any blood of mine in his veins, who holds a public station.

I have referred to the preceding incidents, by way of apology or excuse for myself, in the apparent departure from a rule, which I had so long and so strictly observed, which the object of this letter may suggest.

My son James Brown Clay, now in his thirty second year, would be gratified, if it be consisent with what may be deemed for the public interests, to obtain either the mission to Brussells, or to Rome, Naples or Lisbon; and I should be glad that he could receive the appointment.[4]

It is a delicate subject for a father to speak of the qualifications of a son; but I think that I can describe those of James with perfect truth. He is entirely free from all habits of dissipation whatever, and he has great industry, with remarkable capacity for the transaction of business, in which he displays much quickness. I practised law with him several years, and in some of the departments of the profession, I found him better informed and more conversant than I was. I think he has very respectable talents. He has a wife [Susan Jacob Clay] and three children,[5] and with what he has in possession, and in fair prospect, he has reason to count upon means of independent support.

I have thus communicated his wishes and mine; but full of perplexity and embarrassments as I am quite aware you are in your present exalted station, if this application is likely to add in any degree to them, I must request that you will not think of it another moment, after perusing this letter.

ALS. KyU. Endorsed on verso: "No. IX. from hon H. Clay of Ky, on the subject of the appt, of his son as chargé to ['Naples,' crossed out]—Lisbon." 1. Not found, but see Clay to Stevenson, April 26, 1849. 2. See 9:507-8. 3. For Hilliard, chargé in Brussels from 1842-44, see *BDAC*. 4. Taylor to Clay, May 28, 1849; Clay to Clayton, June 7, 1849. 5. James, John, and Lucy.

To JAMES BROWN CLAY

Lexington, May 14, 1849

I should have written to you since my return home, now more than a month ago,[1] but that the uncertainty as to the time of your remaining at Independence rendered it doubtful where a letter might find you. We are all well here, and there is no Cholera at Lexington. I was ten or twelve days at Louisville, where the Cholera does prevail but not to a very bad extent.[2] Susan [Jacob Clay] and your children were all very well last wednesday, but, poor thing, she was greatly distressed by your absence, and the fears she entertained for you about the Cholera.

I send a Copy of the remaining note I hold for my land near Alton.[3] If convenient you may collect it; but don't put yourself out of the way for that purpose, as I retain the original and can send it to Mr. [John M.] Bailhache.

Your Mule enterprize has not realized hopes; but as it was well conceived, and you have no self reproaches to make, you ought not to let it distress you. P.S. If you get the amt of the note obtain a good Check for it on N–York.

ALS. DLC-TJC (DNA, M212, R11). 1. Taylor to Clay, Nov. 17, 1848. 2. Clay to James B. Clay, Jan. 10, 1849. 3. See 9:108; Bailhache to Clay, Nov. 23, 1846; Clay to James B. Clay, Dec. 10, 1846; Clay to Bailhache, May 14, 1847.

From Henry Stevens, Barnet, Vermont, May 15, 1849. Sends a copy of the "Twenty Ninth Annual Report of the Vermont Colonization Society." Also, a copy of Berttens [?] & Houghton's Addresses and a copy of the Burlington *Free Press* "containing my Address before the Orange County Agricultural Society. Oct last." Describes himself as "a homespun Farmer nearly fifty seven years of Age," who has "at all times been a friend to a Protective tarriff." Adds that he has studied the history of the "sheep Wool and woollen manufactures of England and other Foreign governments from the 14th Century to the present time," as well as the history of manufacturing in the United States.

States that "I have become satisfied that something more must be done to protect the producers of Cotton. and Wool[.] The improvements in machinery within the last ten or fifteen years has been greater and of more real benefit that [*sic*, than] all improvements previous to that time," but "The improvements in machinery is far in advance of public opinion, that is in advance of the knowledge the people in general have of the art of manufacturing." Believes if knowledge of these improvements became common, "within seven years . . . the whole amount of Cotton produced in our Country would be manufactured within the United States." Contends that American manufacturers could produce cotton and woolen cloth of all qualities cheaper than England, Holland, Germany, or France, while paying higher wages, if they used the most advanced machinery; but predicts that with continued use of ordinary machines, they "cannot be successful in their business with any reasonable amount of tarriff for protection." AL. VtHi.

Henry Stevens was the father of Henry Stevens, a famous bibliographer and book collector who did most of his work in London, England. See the son's entry in *DAB*.

From Octavia Walton LeVert, Mobile, May 19, [1849]. Asks Clay to "have pity for my sorrow, and give me your prayers for my heart is crushed. Both my precious ones died of scarlet fever, within the short space of five days." AL. DLC-HC (DNA, M212, R6). Enclosed is an obituary for Sally Walton LeVert and Claudia Anna Eugenia LeVert. See Clay to LeVert, February 6, 1849.

To SUSAN JACOB CLAY Lexington, May 20, 1849

I have not heard from you or James [Brown Clay] since I left Louisville. Have you heard from him?

I have been unwell since I returned home, and was confined to bed with fever two or three days. I am now up again and better, the fever having been subdued, but it left me much debilitated.

We were at your house friday, which Emilly says she airs twice a week. Things look very well in the garden on the grounds &c. We are all well here.

Kiss the children [James, John, Lucy] for me, and give my respects to your father [John J. Jacob] and family. Do come home as soon as you can.

ALS. DLC-TJC (DNA, M212, R11).

To ANDREW J. BALLARD[1] Lexington, May 21, 1849

I received and thank you for your friendly letter. When I was recently at Louisville, I think it was Mr. [Charles M.] Thruston who informed me of the existence of the letter of Amos Kendall to the late David White, now in the possession of his widow.[2] I was well aware at the time of the election of Mr. [John Quincy] Adams in 1825 that Kendall was opposed to the election of Genl. [Andrew] Jackson, and I should be glad to obtain the evidence of the fact which his letter would supply. How to get it is the question. I have some reason to apprehend that the feelings of the widow towards me are inimical.

If Mr. Shanks would procure the letter for me, I should be very thankful to him, and he would place me under great obligation. Mr. Thruston I believe told me that measures had been adopted, or were in contemplation, to procure the letter. I wish you would have the goodness to consult with him, and in concert resort to any honorable means to obtain possession of the letter. The truth, I imagine, is that the letter is not of a confidential nature; and that the publication of it has been only withheld because, subsequent to its date, both D. White and Kendall went over to Jackson.

ALS. KyLoF. 1. Ballard was a Louisville lawyer, Kentucky state legislator, and editor. Armstrong, *Biographical Encyclopedia of Kentucky*, 431. 2. Not found.

From JOHN SLOANE Wooster, Ohio, May 22, 1849

Your kind favour of the 10th Ult accompanied by your letter to the President of the United States [Zachary Taylor][1] was duly received; for which I return you my most hearty thanks[.] Your letter to the President gave me some embarrassment as to what would be the most proper manner to communicate it to him. I had to be sure heard of the *new rule* adopted by him not to receive any recommendation of any one directly made to him, but that all such should be presented to some one of the heads of Departments;[2] but as one part of your letter was of a nature personal to the President and yourself and ought therefore not therefore to be submitted to the inspection of other persons unless by his act I concluded to enclose it to my friend Mr [Elisha] Whittlesey who is located at Washington as chief superintendent of the creation of the Washington Monument[3] with a request that he would in person present your letter: giving him the substance of its contents, and the reasons why that mode of presentation was adopted which he was desired to state[.]

I have a letter from Mr Whittlesey dated 5th inst. acknowledging the receipt of my letter and enclosure; and detailing the circumstances attending his interview with the President, I make a brief extract from his letter. "Not knowing that I should be able to see the President alone, and converse with him; Yesterday I wrote a letter to him, and called with Mr. Clays letter and my own; and although he had company, I conversed with him for some time and spoke of your standing and character and of the letters mentioned which I held in my hand, and hoped he would so far relax his rule as to receive them. I was satisfied he did not intend to vary from the rule. I did not ask him to take the papers, and having made known their contents, I delivered them to Mr [William M.] Meredith Secretary of the Treasury, and requested their favorable consideration. A copy of my letter will be sent to you[.]"

How far these facts may tend to elucidate the suggestion in your letter to me of the attempt at civil influence I will not remark upon: but that such influences are sought to be applied in some instances I have reason to apprehend. I have a letter from Judge McLane [*sic*, John McLean] covering one [to] the President in which he expresses his conviction that he is an object of suspicion and dislike. The Judge's letter to the President I sent to Mr. [John M.] Clayton Secretary of State, he being the only member of the Cabinet with whom in the absence of Mr. [Thomas] Ewing (then in Ohio) I had any personal acquaintance[.]

After the receipt of Mr. Whittlesey's letter I wrote to Mr John Sergeant stating my wishes and what had been done and asking him to give his opinion of my claim to consideration[.] I have since availed myself of an offer made by Mr [Thomas] Corwin to render me any service I might ask for, and also letters to Messrs [Daniel] Webster & [John] Davis of Massachusetts and with those efforts I rest my case[.][4]

In the present condition of our Whig triumphs I forbear to make any rema[r]ks at present.

ALS. MH. 1. Clay to Taylor, April 10, 1849. 2. For the patronage practices of the Taylor administration, see Clay to Christopher, April 19, 1849. 3. The Washington National Monument Society had begun raising money in 1833. A cornerstone was laid on July 4, 1848; however, the site subsequently had to be changed. The Washington Monument was finally completed at government expense and dedicated at its present location on Feb. 21, 1885. *World Book Encyclopedia* (Chicago, 1984). See also 9:206. 4. Sloane to Clay, Feb. 12, 1849.

From ZACHARY TAYLOR Washington, May 28, 1849

Your esteemed letter of the 12th, inst. came to hand a few days since for which accept my best thanks—Sometime during the latter part of March, or early in April, a Mr, [Buckner H.] Payne the gentleman referred to, who I knew slightly in the South, presented himself here as an applicant for the Office of Collector of the Port of New Orleans,[1] at which place he resided, and in speaking of those who recommended him, as well as those he expected to do so, he mentioned your name; going on to say he had been on terms of intimacy with you previous to his leaving Kentucky for Louisiana, and from early associations had hoped you would have recommended him for the office in question, which you declined doing, and stating among other matters for not doing so, altho, you felt very kind towards me, yet you could not recommend any one for office, as you was not aware of my feelings toward you; in reply to which he Mr. P– stated he was coming here, and with your permission he would repeat to me, the conversation which had taken place between you personal towards myself, which you acquiesced in; in reply I stated, I certainly fully reciprocated your kind feelings, as well as thought from the course I had uniformly pursued towards you for many years, of which you must be aware, you ought to have entertained no doubts in relation to that matter. I did not suppose at the time the conversation in question would have been repeated to you, not being aware that Mr. Payne intended to take Lexington in his way in returning to N. Orleans; at the same time there was not the slightest objection to his doing so as there was nothing like confidence expressed or implie[d] in relation to the same—

It will afford me much pleasure to comply with your wishes as well as tha[t] of your son's, by conferring on him [James Brown Clay] the appointment referred to, and have no doubt as to his high qualific[a]tions for the station, and that he will discharge the duties apperta[in]ing to said office with advantage to the government, with credit to himself as well to the satisfactio[n] of all concerned—[2]

It may however be some three or four month[s] before a suitable place can be selected for him, in the meantime he can make his arrangemen[ts] for going abroad, so as to enter on the duties appertaining to the office in question within the period stated.

ALS. DLC-HC (DNA, M212, R6). 1. Clay to Stevenson, April 26, 1849; Clay to Taylor, May 12, 1849. Payne did not get the appointment. 2. Clay to Clayton, June 7, 1849.

From William N. Mercer, "Laurel Hill," near Natchez, June 3, [1849]. Reports that he has escaped a recent cholera outbreak which "has been almost confined to the lowlands. . . . on some of the river plantations" where "its ravages have been awfully severe. On one plantation twenty miles above Natchez, more than 4/5 of the slaves have died." On "Dr. [Stephen] Duncan's plantations near Lake Providence," of "6 or 700 souls . . . about 75 had died, and the disease continue[s] tho with abated violence." Notes that Duncan "seems to have yielded to the extent of the calamity, not so much from the pecuniary loss . . . as from the loss of human life. Many of the slaves had grown gray in his service, others had been born on his Estates, and all were attached to him and he to them, by that bond which unites master and slave, and of which only a slave holder can understand and feel, the full force."

Describes the effects of a recent flood: "The loss of property to the Sugar planters has been very great and I fear the sufferings of the poor occupying the suburbs [of] New Orleans will be much greater."

Hopes if the cholera abates to "visit the north" in the summer, and "will try and see you at least once more, either in the mountains or at Lexington. [I] cannot bear to think that our separation is final—Still the feeling will obtrude, and it was on that account that I avoided a formal parting with you in New Orleans." ALS. DLC-HC (DNA, M212, R6).

Although this letter does not bear a date for the year, editors have concluded that it was probably written in 1849, the year of a large cholera outbreak. Also, Mercer and Clay met at Saratoga and Newport in August, 1849. See Clay to Lucretia H. Clay, August 13, 1849.

To JOHN M. CLAYTON Lexington, June 7, 1849

I received your letter of the 31st. Ulto—communicating the determination of the President [Zachary Taylor] to offer to my son, James Brown Clay, the mission to Portugal.[1] We are both very thankful, and deeply penetrated with sentiments of gratitude, for this high proof of the goodness and the confidence of the President [Zachary Taylor].[2] I handed your letter to James, who has addressed you directly on the subject, stating his acceptance of the appointment, and when he will be ready to proceed on the mission.

I lament to hear that our affairs with Portugal wear a menacing aspect. I was not aware of any other claim that our Citizens had against it but that of Captain [Samuel C.] Reid, arising out of the British having, during the last British War, cut the General Armstrong out of the port of Fayal.[3]

Should the communication to Congress be made by the President, which you intimate, perhaps a strong resolution of that body, supporting him in the negotiation, may avert the necessity of resorting to stronger measures.[4]

My son James will of course present himself to you at Washington.

Although without any diplomatic experience, he has a good mind, is perfectly free from any bad habits, and is remarkable for his facility in the transaction of business. Under your instructions, I hope that he may be able to acquit himself, in his mission, in a manner satisfactory to you & the President.

ALS. DLC-John M. Clayton Papers (DNA, M212, R20). Letter marked "(Private)." 1. Not found, but see Clay to Taylor, May 12, 1849. 2. Taylor to Clay, May 28, 1849. 3. For Reid and the origins of this claim during the War of 1812, see 2:436-37. 4. U.S.-Portuguese relations were strained by claims involving six American vessels: the oldest claim, the *General Armstong*; the *Bolton*; the *Miles*; the *Colonel Blum*; the *Magoun*; and James Hall, captain of the *Shepherd*. In early March 1850, Clayton instructed James B. Clay to make a final demand for settlement. If a satisfactory answer was not given, Clay was to demand his passports and depart in a war vessel then being sent to Lisbon. Portugal refused to pay for the *Magoun*, the *Colonel Blum* and the James Hall claim and proposed submitting the case of the *Miles* to arbitration by a group of Lisbon merchants and that of the *General Armstrong* to the decision of a third power. Based on Clayton's instructions, Clay rejected the offer. On July 7 the Portuguese ministry agreed to pay all claims except the *General Armstrong* which it again proposed to submit to arbitration. Clay rejected the offer and left Lisbon a few days later. After Daniel Webster replaced Clayton as secretary of state in the Fillmore administration, the Portuguese offer was accepted. In 1851 arbitration of the *General Armstrong* went against the U.S. For the Taylor administration's policies toward Portugal, see Hamilton, *Zachary Taylor, Soldier in the White House*, 190-91; Bauer, *Zachary Taylor*, 277-78; Samuel F. Bemis (ed.), *The American Secretaries of State and Their Diplomacy*, 10 vols. (New York, 1928), 6:32-37. See especially Samuel C. Reid, Jr. (ed.), *The Case of the Private Armed Brig of War Gen. Armstrong, Containing Letters and Documents Referring to the History of the Claim. . . . with the Decision of the Court, and an Appendix* . . . (New York, 1857), xxi, xv, 238-39, *passim*; and Susan Bearss, "Henry Clay and the American Claims against Portugal, 1850," *JER* (Summer, 1987), 7:167-80. See also subsequent correspondence below.

From Henry Austin, Galveston, Texas, June 12, 1849. Announces his intention to seek the post of collector of the port of Galveston. Asks Clay's assistance in this regard. Points out that he is having economic difficulties because of "Reckless legislation, questions and and [*sic*] vague rumors about the validity of our land titles in Texas." Recalls Clay's remark "some years ago when I was in Lexington that 'if all questions about our land titles in Texas should be settled in twenty years we should do better than had been done in Kentucky.' " ALS. DNA, RG56, Entry 247, Collectors Box 226.

On June 14, 1849, W. Alexander wrote Clay from Galveston urging Captain Austin's appointment. He noted particularly that "Our Custom House is almost without business. Sometimes not a single entry from a Foreign Port occurs during a quarter. This is mentioned to show that the advanced age and feeble health of Captain A. should not be urged against his receiving an office which is almost a sinecure." ALS. *Ibid.*

On July 2, 1849, Clay wrote Secretary of Treasury William M. Meredith recommending Austin for the position. ALS. *Ibid.*

William R. Smith received the position Austin sought. U.S. Sen., *Executive Journal*, 8:236.

To EDWARD COLES Lexington, June 15, 1849

I have to thank you for your favor, transmitting a Copy of the interesting letter of Mr. [Thomas] Jefferson to you on the subject of Slavery, in 1809 [*sic*] which I have had published.[1]

I regret to inform you that the prospect is not very encouraging of adopting any plan, at present, in Kentucky, for the gradual extinction of that unhappy institution.[2] This unfavorable state of things is to be attributed to the agitation of the question by Abolitionists at the North, to the rivalry between the Whig and Democratic parties, each fearing that the other would obtain some advantage, if it espoused the cause of Emancipation, and to the interest which the owners of Slaves believe they have in preserving, undisturbed, the existing relations between them. There is nevertheless a highly respectable body, in various parts of the State, including many Slaveholders, in favor of the gradual emancipation of Slaves. . . .

ALS. NjP. 1. Coles wrote Clay on June 5, 1849, enclosing the letter from Thomas Jefferson to himself, dated August 25, 1814. Coles stated that he believed the letter's "publication at this time will promote your views, be gratifying to the people of Kentucky, and be of general utility." Copy. Printed in Lexington *Observer & Kentucky Reporter*, June 13, 1849; Washington *Daily National Intelligencer*, July 4, 1849. In his letter to Coles, Jefferson had proclaimed that "love of justice and the love of country plead equally the cause of those people [the slaves]." He declared it a "moral reproach" that no serious effort had been made to end slavery. *Ibid.* 2. Stevenson to Clay, June 12, 1848.

To MARY S. BAYARD Lexington, June 16, 1849

I received today, my dear and ever cherished friend, your letter of the 10h. instant, and was extremely sorry to learn from it that you had "been depressed and unhappy about many things." If my wishes and prayers could prevail, you would have none but bright and happy days and nothing to disturb or depress you.

I was very sorry that Baring [Powell] did not obtain an appointment in the Custom House, as he desired it; but at last it would have been no great affair and one wholly unworthy of him. Besides the letter to Mr. [William D.] Lewis, the Collector, I wrote to Mr. Henry White to aid the application of Baring. I have a long letter from Mr. Lewis[1] full of regrets &c on account of his alleged inability to bestow the appointment. I have not since heard from Baring. You tell me that he thinks of going to California. That is an adventure much more worthy of him than any situation in the Custom House. If I were a young man I do not know if I would not go there. All accounts from that Country justify the belief that a few years, well and judiciously spent there, would secure an ample fortune. If he decide to go, I would, with pleasure, send to him at Philadelphia or at San Francisco, a letter of introduction that might benefit him possibly. With such a precious pledge as he would leave behind him, as his dear Carry,[2] I am sure that he would exert himself & realize all the fondest anticipations of both of them.

I congratulate you on the cheering prospects of Mary [Bayard]. I fervently hope that she will find in her intended [William Henry Beck] a comple[te] fulfillment of all her wishes, and that the contemplated union may prove to you and Mr. [Richard Henry] Bayard a new source of happiness.

I am happy to inform you that my health is quite as good as could be expected of one who for the last five or six months has been in the midst of Cholera.[3] I am not sure that I shall leave Kentucky this summer. I have a wish to go, and possibly may go a few weeks to the Virginia W[hite]. Sulphur Springs. In Kentucky, we have another epidemic, the Emancipation question,[4] which rages with as much violence as the Cholera. For myself, I keep cool and apprehend no ill effects from either.

My present purpose is to go to the Eastward early in November and I may possibly visit Philadelphia, prior to taking my seat in the Senate. In resuming that Station, my wish will be to take no leading part, either in support of, or in opposition to, the [Zachary Taylor] Administration, but to be a calm and quiet looker on, occasionally offering a word of advice or pouring a little oil on the tempestuous billows.

You will have seen or heard that my son James [Brown Clay] has been offered the mission to Portugal.[5] The tender of it was handsomely made, and he has accepted it. His pecuniary situation in life is as good as he could wish, he has a fine wife [Susan Jacob Clay], and they think that a few years may be beneficially passed abroad in the public service. Of course, I need not say to you, that this little affair will have no effect upon my relations to the Administration, which are such as to leave me at perfect liberty to judge, with impartiality, of its measures of public policy.

Present my warm regards to Mr. Bayard and to your children; and do not omit to tender them also to Caroline [Bayard].

ALS. DeHi. 1. These three letter have not been found. 2. His wife Caroline Bayard Powell. 3. Clay to James B. Clay, Jan. 10, 1849. 4. Elections were taking place for delegates to the Kentucky Constitutional convention in which emancipation was the major question. See Stevenson to Clay, June 12, 1848. 5. Taylor to Clay, May 28, 1849; Clay to Clayton, June 7, 1849.

To John C. Vaughan & Thomas Brown, Cleveland, Ohio, June 16, 1849. Acknowledges receipt of an invitation "of the Freemen of the Reserve" to celebrate with them "the anniversary of the passage of the [Northwest] Ordinance of 1787, on the 13th of July next." Concurs "entirely in opinion as to the wisdom of that great measure, and I am glad it has secured to the states on which it operates, an exemption from the evils of slavery." Because this will be "the first time to commemorate" the ordinance in its sixty-one years, "It is impossible to disguise the conviction, that this purpose originates out of the question, now unfortunately agitating the whole Union, of the introduction of slavery into New Mexico and California." While "no one can be more opposed than I am to the extension of slavery into those new territories," is unwilling "to do anything to increase the prevailing excitement." Hopes the slave question "will be met in a spirit of calmness and candor . . . in a manner to add strength and stability" to the Union, since "we are fellow-citizens of one common and glorious country" who must "exercise mutual and friendly forbearance." Copy. Printed in Louisville *Examiner*, July 28, 1849.

John C. Vaughan, a South Carolina-born abolitionist, had edited the Louisville *Emancipator* and the Cincinnati *Gazette*. See Joseph Medill's article in *NCAB*, 1:131. Thomas Brown, a Cleveland lawyer, established with Vaughan in 1850 the *True Democrat*, which became the Free Soil organ of northern Ohio. For Brown, see Johnson, *Twentieth Century Biographical Dictionary*.

To THOMAS B. STEVENSON Lexington, June 18, 1849

I received your letter, and learn with regret tha[t] you have abandoned your trip to Kentucky.

The Mission to Portugal has been tendered to my son James [Brown Clay] in a handsome manner and very creditably to the Preside[nt Zachary Taylor.] James s situation, in a pecuniary point of view, is one of perfect independence, and he has no need of any office as a means of support; but he has determined to accept the appointment, wh[ich] he could not well decline, being unoccupied at present; an[d] there existing no impediment to his going abroad. I have rece[ived] from Genl. Taylor quite a friendly letter.[1]

My views in taking a seat in the Senate, if I am spare[d], remain the same as when I saw you. I shall go there with a dete[r]mination to support any Whig measures for which I have heretof[ore] contended, and in a state of mind and feelings prepared to judge fairly and impartially of the measures of the Administration. I shall not place myself in any leading position, either to support or oppose it. But I shall rather seek to be a calm and quiet looker on, rarely speaking and when I do endeavoring to throw oil on the troubled waters.

Many of the appointments of the Administration have give[n] much dissatisfaction,[2] in various localities; and if it be true, as asserted, that the President leaves selections for office to the respective Secretaries, it is contrary to usage, very exception[able], and I think unconstitutional. At last, however, I think that [the] true character of the Administration will be fixed & judg[ed] of by its measures of public policy.

I agree with you in believing that more difficulty will [be] encountered in fixing the boundaries of Texas than in deciding the question of the introduction of slavery in the new Territories.[3]

Whatever may be the ultimate purpose of Col. [Thomas Hart] Benton, I wish him heartily success in his effort to sustain himself in Missouri although I doubt whether he will do so.[4] This question of Slavery, in the Slave States, is one around which many strong prejudices supported by long habit, and powerful interests, real and imaginary, cluster. I have been mortified but not surprized at the course Kentucky is likely to take about it.[5] The truth is that many of our leading men, who had been favorable to gradual emancipation, have suppressed, modified, or abandoned their opinions. The Governor [John J. Crittenden] is quite dumb on the perilous subject.

Last week a distressing affair in Madison occurred between Cass: Clay and some of the Turners,[6] in which Cass. & one of his antagonists were badly if not mortally wounded.[7]

My health continues good for one who has been five or six months in the midst of Cholera. That epidemic now prevails in Lexington, but with less violence than in 1833.[8]

ALS, margin faded. Courtesy of Mrs. Kenneth W. Warren, Wellesley Hills, Mass.; copy in OCHP. Printed in Colton, *Clay Correspondence*, 3:493-94. Letter marked "(Confidential)." 1. Taylor to Clay, May 28, 1849; Clay to Clayton, June 7, 1849. 2. Clay to Christopher, April 19, 1849. 3. For the controversy over California's admission as a state, see Clay to Stevenson, Dec. 19, 1848. 4. For the successful attempt of a radical proslavery group to defeat Benton's reelection to the U.S. Senate in 1850, see Chambers, *Old Bullion Benton*, 341-52; Elbert B. Smith, *Magnificent Missourian* (New York, 1958), 243-60. 5. In the upcoming state constitutional convention. See Stevenson to Clay, June 12, 1849. 6. Thompson Burnam, an emancipationist, ran against Squire Turner, a proslavery advocate, for a seat as a member of the Kentucky Constitutional convention. While campaigning for Burnam, Cassius M. Clay became involved in a fight with Squire Turner's son Cyrus. Both men were severely injured, Turner fatally. William E. Ellis, H.E. Everman, & Richard D. Sears, *Madison County: 200 Years in Retrospect* (Madison County, Ky., 1985), 85-86. 7. This paragraph is omitted in the Colton version. 8. For the 1833 cholera epidemic, see 8:545-46; for the 1849 epidemic, see Clay to James B. Clay, Jan. 10, 1849.

To The Committee of Invitation of the Whigs of Philadelphia, June 21, 1849. Acknowledges their invitation to attend the 4th of July celebration in their city. Declines because of his "distant residence" from Philadelphia, but notes that he concurs "entirely with you in the importance to the welfare and prosperity of the Union of maintaining Whig principles, by all fair and honorable means." Expresses his best wishes for the success of their celebration. Copy. Printed in Washington *Daily National Intelligencer*, July 10, 1849.

To NICHOLAS DEAN Lexington, June 21, 1849

I received your favors of the 1st. and 4th. inst. I regret extremely that many of the appointments of the Executive are so unsatisfactory to the public; and still more that there should be just occasion for it.[1] I fear that the President [Zachary Taylor] confides that matter too much to the Secretaries, and that they have selfish and ulterior views in the selections which they make. It is undeniable that the public patronage has been too exclusively confined to the original Supporters of Genl Taylor, without sufficient regard to the merits, and just claims of the great body of the Whig party. This is both wrong and impolitic.

You tell me that it will be difficult to repress an expression of the Whig dissatisfaction, prior to the meeting of Congress. I should be very sorry if this was done so early,—if it should become necessary (I hope it may not) to do it at all. I think there ought not to be any denunciation of the *Administration*, unless it is rendered proper for its systems of public policy. If before these are developed, the Administration would be arraigned, it would be ascribed to disappointment as to the distribution of the patronage of Government. It will be different, if, contrary to what we have a right to hope and expect, the Administration should fail to support and recommend the great measures of the Whig party.

As to myself, I need not say to you, that I shall go to Washington, if I am spared, with a firm determination to oppose, or support measures according to my deliberate sense of their effects upon the interests of our Country.

Copy. DLC-HC (DNA, M212, R6). Printed in Colton, *Clay Correspondence*, 4:587-88. 1. Clay to Christopher, April 19, 1849.

To THOMAS B. STEVENSON Lexington, June 30, 1849

I received your two favors of the 25th. and 26th. instant. I tender you sincere condolence on the death of Dr. [Ennis] Combs.[1] It was distressing that he could not reach your house before his demise.

According to my recollection, Col [Thomas Hart] Benton was pleased with and approved all that was done to admit Missouri into the Union.[2] And if he ever reproached me with my agency in the matter, I have forgotten it. His nomination, in certain places, for the Presidency in 1852, may tend to his maintain[in]g himself at home, which I apprehend he will have great difficulty in doing. I do not think that, if I were in your place, I would say any thing at present to mar his present exertions.[3] As for myself I should be sorry if my name were in any way now, if ever, brought out in connection with the presidency[.]

I should deplore the event of the Administration being thrown into the minority in the H. of R.[4] It would be bad for them, bad for the Whig party and bad for the Country. And it would be a subject of nearly equal regret that parties should be so balanced as that a few members, strictly belonging to neither, could control the House. I am very apprehensive that Kentucky will make no addition to her Whig representation, in the next house, if she can maintain the ground she held the last.[5] In four or five districts, where there ought to be no doubt, great uncertainty exists.

I thank you for the information communicated about Mr. [Salmon P.]

Chase[.][6] I formerly knew him in Washn. very well & met him in Frankfort lately.

With regard to political affairs in Ohio, I fear that it will be a long, long time before the Whigs will be secure in the ascendancy. They never can be without the Western Reserve, and the problem is how is that to be reunited?[7] All this difficulty would have been avoided if Genl [Zachary] Taylor had not been nominated. What responsibility has not its delegation incurred by the strange course it pursued in the Philada. Convention![8] Among other consequences one is, that it postpones indefinitely, if it has not blighted for ever, any prospects of Mr. [Thomas] Corwin's future elevation.

I think it probable that your conjectures are correct in regard to the President's feelings towards me. I have been a little provoked by the advertisement of me in the Republic, a paper, by the bye, which I do not take. That and other circumstances demonstrate that some alarm has seized them at Washington. As for any calculation which is made upon my poor support, all that I have ever said, all that I have ever thought, was that I should take my seat in the Senate prepared to support Whig measures, prepared to oppose Locofoco measures, and in a state of mind to judge fairly and impartially of any new measures.[9] The mission to Portugal,[10] which in fact only rectifies in one son [James Brown Clay], an injustice which was done by [John] Tyler to another, Col. [Henry] Clay [Jr.], will not weigh a feather with me.[11]

The Cholera still lingers with us,[12] but it is mild & forebearing. I have as yet, I thank God, lost no one.

ALS. ViU. Printed in Colton, *Clay Correspondence*, 3:494-95. 1. Dr. Combs, Stevenson's father-in-law, had died on the Ohio River enroute from Missouri to visit his children in Kentucky and Cincinnati. Colton, *Clay Correspondence*, 3:494-95. 2. For the Missouri Compromise, see 2:669-70, 740-48, 775-77, 785-86; 3:15-22, 26-33, 46-47, 49-50. 3. Clay to Stevenson, June 18, 1849. 4. In the U.S. Senate Democrats had a majority of 10 in the 31st Congress, 1st Session. In the House Democrats held 112 seats, Whigs 105, and Free Soilers 13. The latter held the balance of power. Morris, *Encyclopedia of American History*, 210. For the difficulty this caused in the election of a Speaker, see Clay to Lucretia H. Clay, Dec. 5, 1849. 5. In the 1849 congressional elections in Kentucky, Whigs won 6 seats to 4 for the Democrats. *Guide to U.S. Elections*, 589. 6. Chase had been elected in 1849 to the U.S. Senate by a fusion of Democrats and Free Soilers. *DAB*; *BDAC*; Maizlish, *Triumph of Sectionalism*, 121-46. 7. The election of 1848 had effectively destroyed the Whig party in Ohio when the anti-slavery Whig stronghold of the Western Reserve refused to support Taylor's nomination. The growing strength of Free Soilism in 1848-49 left the traditional two-party system there in disarray. For a discussion of the demise of the Whig party in Ohio, see Maizlish, *Triumph of Sectionalism*, 149-86, *passim.* 8. Ullmann to Clay, Feb. 18, 1848. 9. Clay to Mercer, Dec. 10, 1848. 10. Taylor to Clay, May 28, 1849; Clay to Clayton, June 7, 1849. 11. Clay to Taylor, May 12, 1849. 12. Clay to James B. Clay, Jan. 10, 1849.

To THOMAS EWING Lexington, July 14, 1849

I have to thank you for your kind congratulations on my recovery from a recent attack of illness. It was not as bad as represented, and I believe had no connection with the prevailing epidemic.[1] But, as that still rages, all around me, in very great [m]alignity, there is no security for any one against it. I hope [t]hat it may not prove to be very mortal in its visit to Washington, a[n]d that you may entirely escape it.

ALS, manuscript torn. DLC-HC (DNA, M212, R21). 1. For the cholera epidemic, see Clay to James B. Clay, Jan. 10, 1849.

From Rezin D. Shepherd, Shepherdstown, Va. (W. Va.), July 17, 1849. Acknowledges receipt of "a Bank Check in New York for Four Thousand & Eighty Dollars being the balance of principal and Interest due on your note held by me for 10,000$." Since "the note is in New Orleans amongst my papers there . . . I herewith send you a receipt." ALS. DLC-TJC (DNA, M212, R14). See Shepherd to Clay, November 29, 1848.

To THOMAS B. STEVENSON Lexington, July 21, 1849

I received your favor of the 17th. and I am in arrear in acknowledging your preceding favor. I thank you for them both. The indisposition of Mrs. [Lucretia Hart] Clay and myself was slight and short, and I believe had no connection with the [cholera] epidemic, which has happily greatly abated.[1]

The conduct of the Atto. General [Reverdy Johnson], as reported by our friend Charles Anderson, was reprehensible. The solution of it is to be found in the extreme desire at Washington to advance the popularity and interests of the Administration.[2] I should have no objection to the publication of all the correspondence which has passed between the Executive [Zachary Taylor] and myself, in regard to the appointment of my son [James Brown Clay] to the mission to Portugal. It would be seen from it that, whilst the President has written to me in a perfectly friendly manner, I have made no commitment of myself, nor descended to any unmanly or unbecoming solicitation.[3]

The subject of Canada, I fear, will be forced upon the public consideration. I do not believe, now that all protection to its products is withdrawn by Great Britain, and her Navigation laws are repealed, and the Ports of the Provinces are freely opened to Foreign powers, that the Colonial connection can long remain. Those measures do substantially, if not in form, make Canada an Independent power. With a Government in the Colonies, a Legislature and a Ministry, modelled after those in the parent Country, it will I think soon be perceived that the appointment of the Governor and the Veto reserved to the Crown are inconvenient and impracticable forms.

The important question is what is to become of Canada? I adhere to the opinion that the happiness of both the U States and Canada will be best promoted by the Indepen[den]ce of the latter. But I am willing for one now to open a Free trade with her, for the same reason that G. Britain desires such Commercial intercourse with us, that is that she is behind us in skill capital and the progress of Manufactures. We should profit most by opening new fields for our Commerce and Manufactures. And our Free trade with Canada would be an exception to the principle of protection, which I still think we ought to maintain as to Europe.[4]

Such briefly are my views. What those of the people at large are or will be remains to be seen. I do not know on what data Genl [Winfield] Scott has arrived at the conclusion that a large majority of the People of the U.S. desire the annexation of Canada.[5]

I have some thought of passing through Cincinnati about the middle of next week on my way, by Sandusky and Buffalo, to a Seabath;[6] but if I do I shall not stop in your City longer than one night. My intention, if I go, is to take the Ridge route; but I hope that you will keep my secret, and give no publicity to my contemplated movement.

ALS. KyLoF. Printed in Colton, *Clay Correspondence*, 3:496. 1. Clay to James B. Clay, Jan. 10, 1849. 2. Reference is to the fact that members of the Taylor administration had publicized and apparently gloated about Clay's solicitation of a post for his son. Hamilton, *Zachary Taylor*,

Soldier in the White House, 215; Kirwan, *John J. Crittenden*, 250; Poage, *Henry Clay*, 192. Stevenson adds specifically in the note to this letter in Colton, *Clay Correspondence*, 3:496 that Reverdy Johnson was reported to have said that the appointment of Clay's son "would make him, as a senator, obedient to the Administration, or else prove himself ungrateful for a favor he had solicited." 3. Clay to Taylor, May 12, 1849; Taylor to Clay, May 28, 1849. 4. The United States and Canada concluded a reciprocity treaty in 1854 which provided for free trade of most products except manufactured items. For a discussion of the British, Canadian, and American trading issues, see John B. Brebner, *North Atlantic Triangle, The Interplay of Canada, the United States and Great Britain* (New Haven, Conn., 1945), 148-64. 5. Scott had written John C. Hamilton on June 29, 1849, asserting that he thought two-thirds of the American people favored annexation of Canada and the other one-third would soon see its benefits. Winfield Scott, *Memoirs of Lieut.-General Scott, LL.D.*, 2 vols. (New York, 1864), 2:602. 6. Clay left Ashland on July 24 and arrived at Cincinnati the following day. He reached Springfield, Ohio, on July 27, and passed through Sandusky and Cleveland on July 28. By August 4 he was at Saratoga, N.Y., where he remained until August 16. On August 17 he arrived at Springfield, Mass., and left the next day for Newport, R.I. He reached Newport on August 19 and stayed there for several days. On his return home he went through New York City on Sept. 4 and traveled on to Van Buren's home that same day, residing there until Sept. 8 when he departed for Utica. He attended the New York State Agricultural Fair in Syracuse on Sept. 11 and reached home on Sept. 18. Lexington *Observer & Kentucky Reporter*, July 25, August 1, 4, 17, 18, Sept. 8, 12, 19, 22, 1849; Clay to Hughes, August 4, 1849; Clay to Lucretia H. Clay, August 13 and Sept. 5, 1849; Clay to Bayard, August 23, 1849; John M. Clay to Clay, August 25, 1849; Clay to Grinnell, Sept. 7, 1849.

To George Upfold, Madison, Ind., July 24, 1849. Expresses thanks for the "Sermons which you did me the favor to send me." Remarks that "Amidst disease death and affliction with which the prevailing [cholera] Epidemic [Clay to James B. Clay, January 10, 1849] is visiting our Community we stand in great need of all the consolations of Religion." ALS. In.

Upfold (1796-1872) became the first Episcopal bishop of Indiana in 1849 after serving as rector of Trinity Church, Pittsburgh, since 1831. Johnson, *Twentieth Century Biographical Dictionary.*

To Levi A. Ward, Rochester, N.Y., August 1, 1849. Regrets he cannot accept an invitation to visit Rochester: "after having been in the midst of the prevailing epidemic for more than six months, I suddenly determined to visit some of the Eastern watering-places, and am now on my way in pursuit of that object. . . . Considering that Cholera [Clay to James B. Clay, January 10, 1849] is still prevailing, in a greater or less degree everywhere, and in some places raging with appalling violence, and that we are all more or less affected by it, in our feelings, sympathies or health, I have wished to pass on quietly to the places of my destination without exciting or accepting any public demonstrations." Copy. Printed in the Lexington *Observer & Kentucky Reporter*, August 22, 1849.

For Dr. Levi A. Ward, a physician, land speculator, and patron of educational projects, see Blake McKelvey, *Rochester, The Water-Power City 1812-1854* (Cambridge, Mass., 1945), 59, 68, 80-81, 124, 144, 192, 194.

On August 4, 1849, Clay declined an invitation from Samuel Haight to visit Catskill, N.Y.: "I have been breathing Cholera atmosphere and living upon Cholera diet, and partaking of all the feelings and sympathies which the presence of the Epidemic excites," and since "I have lost both strength & flesh . . . I am seeking to repair the loss at Watering places, as quietly as possible." ALS. KyU.

To CHRISTOPHER HUGHES Saratoga, N.Y., August 4, 1849

A sudden resolution to visit this place has brought me here. A long time of painful anxiety and solicitude about you has elapsed since I heard from you. Some Baltimoreans, whom I have met here, have given me, I lament to say, not very encouraging accounts as to the state of your health. But I rejoice that you are still in the land of the living, and I pray that your health may be yet re-established, and you long spared to us. If a wish could transport me to your residence, I should soon be with you; but the countless number of friends and fellow Citizens, whom I should encounter, during the whole journey, deter me from undertaking it; and my purpose is to remain here and at New Port [Newport, R.I.] a few weeks and then return to Ashland by the quietest route I can find.[1]

We have lived, my dear Hughes, many, many years in the bonds of sincere friendship; but we all know that our abode in this world is of short duration. If it be so ordered that we shall never again see each other here below, I hope that we shall meet in the realms of bliss above.

During more than six months past, I have been breathing a Cholera Atmosphere, living upon Cholera diet, and with all the feelings and sympathies, which the prevalence of the Epidemic excites.[2] The effect is, that I am somewhat reduced in flesh, and debilitated in strength, altho' my health is otherwise good. I trust that the mineral water, followed by the Sea bath will restore me.

Repeatedly interrupted since I began this letter, I am compelled by a constant stream of visitors, briefly to conclude it. I request you to present my affectionate regards to Miss Margaret [Hughes].

ALS. MiU-C. 1. Clay to Stevenson, July 21, 1849. 2. Clay to James B. Clay, Jan. 10, 1849.

From Manlius V. Thomson, Georgetown, Ky., August 5, 1849. Explains to Clay affairs in Mississippi that "might be turned to advantage in a pecuniary point of view." Reports that the state borrowed $7 million "for which she has issued her bonds, which have fallen into the hands of foreigners and are secretly held at Amsterdam," a portion of which "(say five millions) have been repudiated by the State and their payment refused [9:714, 716, 813-14]." The remaining $2 million, still "valid and binding on the State. . . . are called the Planter's Bank Bonds and I believe are held in London." The Mississippi legislature in 1848 authorized "the holders of the Planters' Bank Bonds to purchase or locate any of the public lands belonging to the state and pay for the same in those Bonds at six dollars per acre." Many of the "500.000 acres of the public lands within her limits" allotted under the Distribution Act "are quite valuable, being located in the fine cotton growing region of the Yazoo valley." Since these acres are "somewhat inaccessible" and "not likely soon to bring the price asked for them," suspects that "some of the best and most valuable lands in all that region . . . if hunted out and selected by a careful & judicious person might be found to be very cheap at the price asked for them." Believes that "it is probable that the legislature at its session in Jany next may reduce the price" still further, "rather than incur the further accumulation of interest." Suggests that perhaps James Brown Clay's stopover in London on his way to Lisbon "would afford him facilities for ascertaining the holders of those Bonds and for procuring an Agency from them to collect, compromise or otherwise arrange them as may be found most to the advantage of those interested." Proposes to "unite with him in the Agency and divide equally between us any commissions which may be realized for our services; he doing all which I have indicated above . . . and I undertaking to do all that may be necessary in this country to accomplish the desired objects." Since the "Mississippi legislature will assemble the first Monday in January next it is important that the arrangement should be consummated by that time and that I should be put in possession of the Bonds with ample powers to make such arrangement as may be found most advantageous." If James does not want to take part in this endeavor, requests "that you or he will, if convenient, ascertain for me the names & address of some of the principal holders of those Bonds, and also that you will give me leave to refer to you for information as to my qualification for the Agency spoken of." ALS. DLC-HC (DNA, M212, R6).

Clay wrote Thomson on August 29, 1849, advising him to go to London to look into the Mississippi debt matter. Adds: "I authorize you to make any reference to my name in support of your views which may be calculated to secure their success. This is due to the high opinion I entertain of your honor, probity and established character." Copy, extract. Printed in Howard L. Conrad (ed.), *Encyclopedia of the History of Missouri* . . . , 6 vols. (New York, 1901), 6:188.

The 1848 session of the Mississippi legislature had passed a bill providing for the sale of 500,000 acres of land granted the state by the federal government for internal improvements and making the Planters' Bank bonds receivable at par in payment for this land. A majority of bondholders, however, believed the state would ultimately redeem the bonds and so refused to part with them. The tangled web of Mississippi bond repudiation was not completely settled until 1875 when a newly adopted amendment to the state constitution prohibited the state from ever redeeming the bonds of the Union Bank or the Planters' Bank. Reginald C. McGrane, *Foreign Bondholders and American State Debts* (New York, 1935), 207-19.

To Nicholas Dean, New York City, August 6, 1849. Asks Dean not to travel to Saratoga to visit him: "Indeed, the friendship of those I esteem would be best displayed by forbearing, at this time, and under existing circumstances, to call on me; for, in spite of all my wishes, I am subjected continually to an amount of company, which I fear will prevent my realizing the good effects I anticipated from this journey." Laments the death of "Poor [John L.] Lawrence," which he learned of when "I reached Buffalo, having left Ashland before your letter communicating it arrived there." ALS. KyU. Written from Saratoga, N.Y.

Lawrence was comptroller of New York City at the time of his death. A delegation of the city bar association attended his funeral on July 27. New York *Herald*, July 27, 1849.

To Martin Van Buren, "Lindenwald," N.Y., August 9, 1849. Expresses his fear that he could not visit Van Buren "on this occasion . . . without coming in contact with large masses of people, which would have been incompatible with the quiet, of which I am desirous." Learning, however, that "the route by which I purpose going to Newport [R.I.] takes me within four miles of your residence," has decided "on my return from New port, about the last of this month, to accept your kind invitation." ALS. DLC-Martin Van Buren Papers (DNA, M212, R22). For Clay's itinerary, see Clay to Stevenson, July 21, 1849.

Speech to Students of the National Law School, Ballston Spa, N.Y., August 10, 1849. Feels if he expresses his true feelings after hearing their exams, "it might seem too much like the language of extravagant flattery." Explains that until now he had never understood their system "and its vastly superior advantages to the legal student." During their examinations has been "delighted and surprised" at the way they answered the most difficult questions he asked, and the manner in which they argued and summed up their cases. Asks: "Can it be, sir, that the case that has just been tried—that the minutely detailed stor[i]es of the witnesses drawn out by the rigid interrogations of the young counsellors, and their solemn appeals to the jury, are all fiction? Am I in a seminary of learning, or in a court-room, surrounded by the mature realities of professional life?" Admonishes them that "Constant, persevering application will accomplish every thing. To this quality, if I may be allowed to speak of myself, more than to any thing else, do I owe the little success to which I have attained. Left in early life to work my way alone, with no other than a common education, I saw that the pathway before me was long, steep, and rugged, and that the height on which I had ventured to fix the eye of my ambition could only be reached by toil the most severe and a purpose the most indomitable. But shrinking from no labor, disheartened by no obstacle, I struggled on. No opportunity which the most watchful vigilance could secure to exercise my powers was permitted to pass by unimproved. And, if I could have enjoyed the advantages which this institution is now conferring upon you, I should have entered upon my profession under far higher auspices and brighter hopes."

Warns that the labor is far from ended with their graduation today, because "The profession you have chosen, more than all others, imposes upon its incumbents the necessity for constant and arduous exertion." Indeed, the "law demands a life of laborious effort. But it is an honorable, a glorious pursuit. To search out truth, and to promote justice, is its great end. Truth is to be your aim, justice your guide, and the smiles of conscience, of God, and of men, your ultimate, your high reward. Let these considerations govern you from this time forward, and with skill and discipline you may lay the foundation, and finally reap the rewards, of a high standing and destiny in life." Copy. Printed in Washington *Daily National Intelligencer*, October 9, 1849.

The State & National Law School had instituted a 3-year curriculum designed "to make the student a *thorough legal scholar*, an *experienced familiar practitioner*, and an *easy, fluent, correct, extemporaneous speaker.* It granted a Bachelor of Law Degree. This system was designed to professionalize the study of law by replacing the old system of reading law in a law office. *Catalogue and Circular of the State and National Law School at Ballston Spa, N.Y.* (Troy, N.Y., 1850), 9, *passim.*

To LUCRETIA HART CLAY Saratoga, N.Y., August 13, 1849

We have been here now two weeks,[1] and I regret to say that I have not derived from the use of the water the benefit I wished. James [Brown Clay], Susan [Jacob Clay] and their children [James, John, Lucy] have been generally well, but on friday night I had one of the severest attacks that I ever experienced. It was a bilious cholick and I suffered excrutiating pain for several hours. Some fears were even entertained for my safety[.] I have been relieved, but am left very weak. We intended to go tomorrow to New port [R.I.], but in consequence of my weakness, we shall put off our departure for a couple of days. We are living not in the principal Hotel, but in a small house near it, and occupy all the apartments in the lower story. This affords us some degree of privacy and quiet.

I received a letter from Mary [Mentelle Clay], dated the monday after I left home, which I was very glad to get. It informed me that all were well at Ashland and Mansfield; but that the Cholera had the saturday before broken out with increased violence in Lexington[.][2] Since then I have not heard whether it continued or had abated. and I am very uneasy about it.

Dr. [William N.] Mercer and his family are here, and they intend also to go to New Port. He has been unwell but is now better.

I have received no letter from John [Morrison Clay], but hope to get one when I arrive at Newport. Give my love to him, and to Thomas [Hart Clay] & Mary and their children.[3]

ALS. DLC-TJC (DNA, M212, R11). 1. For Clay's itinerary, see Clay to Stevenson, July 21, 1849. 2. Clay to James B. Clay, Jan. 10, 1849. 3. Thomas Hart Clay's children were: Lucretia Hart (1838-60); Henry Boyle (d. after 1906); Thomas Hart (1843-1907); Rose Victoire; Mary Russell.

To Mary S. Bayard, Philadelphia, August 23, 1849. Regrets that he probably "shall have to return to K[entucky]. without the pleasure of seeing you. . . . Baring [Powell] I hear, is better, and I hoped that his condition could have been such as to admit of your coming" to Newport. Adds: "I have seen [Richard H.] Bayard, Mary [Bayard] & the [James] Harpers. He looks uncommonly well, and I never saw Mary looking prettier. She has promised to bring her intended [William H. Beck] to see me." Reports his "health has improved. . . . I have enjoyed more repose, during the four days of my sojourn here, than I have since I left home." His friends "have foreborne to press upon me, and I have profited by their kind and considerate forbearance. The weather, the air, and the bathing (which by the bye I have not yet enjoyed) are all delightful." ALS. DeHi. Written from Atlantic House, Newport, R.I.

To LUCRETIA HART CLAY Newport, R.I., August 23, 1849

I have been here now near a week,[1] and I think I have derived some benefit from the bracing Sea air. I have not yet taken the bath, which I have been as yet afraid to enter. Jameses' [Brown Clay] family are all well, and Lucy [Jacob Clay] has several times been in the sea. She has improved. James is now absent at Washington, but is expected back by the 25h. Thomas Jacobs [*sic*, Jacob][2] arrived last night. They wish to sail the week after next.

I have met with some old acquaintances here. Mrs Hull, Miss Hart her sister, &c. Dr [William N.] Mercer's family got here last night from Saratoga. This island is a most healthy place, and great crowds are annually gathered here. I have stopt at a very quiet and comfortable house, where I have enjoyed more repose than I have done since I left home.

I have received several letters from Thomas [Hart Clay], one from Mary [Mentelle Clay] and one from John [Morrison Clay].[3] They relieved me from great anxiety about the breaking out of the Cholera again at Lexington.[4] I am now assured that it has finally disappeared. We have much reason to be thankful to Providence that we have been mercifully spared.

I met at Pittsfield Mr. [George T.] Chapman, formerly our Clergyman in Lexn. who is stationed there and is doing well. I have seen [Leslie] Combs, who goes home with his wife early in next month.[5] They are in this neighbourhood. Frank Hunt[6] and his party left here last week.

Tell Thomas that I received his letter informing me of the payment of Vanmeter's notes, and that I shall write to Majr. [Thomas Hart] Pindell directing the application of the money.[7]

I still hope to reach home between the 10h. and 15h. of Sept. The Cholera on my route will probably have every where abated, and I shall have no danger of sickness to encounter but that of the Lake fever.

My love to John and to Thomas' family . . .

ALS. DLC-TJC (DNA, M212, R11). 1. For Clay's itinerary, see Clay to Stevenson, July 21, 1849. 2. Son of John J. Jacob and brother of Susan Clay. Armstrong, *Biographical Encyclopedia of Kentucky*, 321-22. 3. Not found. 4. Clay to James B. Clay, Jan. 10, 1849. 5. The Leslie Combs family had arrived in Newport in July. New York *Herald*, July 8, 1849. 6. Frank K. Hunt, youngest brother of Charlton Hunt, was a prominent Lexington lawyer. Levin, *Lawyers and Lawmakers of Kentucky*, 633. 7. Not found.

From JOHN MORRISON CLAY Lexington, August 25, 1849

I received to=day your Telegraph message from Newport [R.I.] mentioning your arrival there on the 19th. inst. in good health. From the papers & Susan's [Jacob Clay] letter to Mary [Mentelle Clay] we felt a considerable anxiety about you when you were taken with the bilious colic at Saratoga[1] & I was glad to learn that you had quitted that crowded place.

I wrote to you last month or early this,[2] directing my letter to New Port, since which I have been so busy with the hemp crop, I could scarcely find time to write. The hemp turns out an unusually good crop & by the help of hired hands I shall have it all stacked by the 5th. of next month. I have already nearly finished stacking all the clover field hemp & nearly half cut the new ground field. I have not been able to sow any wheat yet but before the middle of Sep. will probably have sowed the field adjacent Mr [James] Erwins. I have delivered one load of wheat (inferior) at the St. Mill in Lex.[3] for which I get 40¢ pr bus., and I think that we will be able to sell near $*100* worth of wheat reserving a sufficiency of the Mediterranean for seed, & some to be ground for our own use. We have had since you left home favorable weather both for our health & farming purposes. My race horses are doing well & the Trustee mare is promising entirely past our hopes & expectations. I have entered the bay Magnolia filly & the woodpecker mares two year old colt in separate stakes.[4] They are also very promising. The cholera & its features diarrhea & flux still lingers amongst us.[5] Mr John W Hunt[6] died of the latter complaint 3 days ago; & I doubt not that fruits & vegetables will still keep up the list of deaths till frost.

We look for you at Ashland about the 10th. proximo.[7] And I confidently believe you ought to seek repose & retirement from crowds & constant excitement in order to preserve & recuperate your health. I am afraid you will get little of either while abroad. We were pleased that you met with Dr [William N.] Mercer & family at Saratoga. They would be agreeable company out home with you—

Mamma [Lucretia Hart Clay] has been uninterruptedly well. She thinks the milk business rather slow since Chiles has not paid the last two months accounts.[8] Please present my affectionate regards to James [Brown Clay] & Susan & the children. & remind James of the English race saddle he is to get me in New York provided it is to be had & to send per Levi's[9] trunk home to win with. Mamma joins me in love.

P S. Please let James know that I do not forget he is upon the eve of a long voyage & that I fully intend writing to him at Lisbon.

ALS. DLC-TJC (DNA, M212, R14). 1. Clay to Lucretia H. Clay, August 13, 1849. 2. Not found. 3. Probably the steam flour mill in Lexington which was the first steam-powered mill in Kentucky. Perrin, *History of Fayette County*, 265, 272. 4. For Trustee, Magnolia, and Woodpecker, see *ibid.*, 146, 152-53. 5. Clay to James B. Clay, Jan. 10, 1849. 6. See 1:46. 7. For Clay's itinerary, see Clay to Stevenson, July 21, 1849. 8. Probably John C. Chiles, co-proprietor of the Phoenix Hotel in Lexington. Perrin, *History of Fayette County*, 153. 9. Levi was a slave serving as Clay's body servant. See Clay to James B. Clay, Sept. 3, 1849.

From Benjamin O. Tyler, New York City, August 29, 1849. Writing from Bellevue Hospital, thanks Clay for a small sum of money, which "is of far more value to me at this time, than One hundred dollars at another time." Continues: "You will with pleasure perceive see [*sic*] the improvement in my eyes by my hand writing. . . . I begin to see *light* with my right eye which I had reason to believe; that the sight was entirely lost. My good kind skilful Doctor Augustus Winn begins to think I will yet be able to see to distinguish one person from another. I hope to meet you in Washington next winter, when I hope to be able to distinguish you from the best *loco-foco* in the country." Intends to present the "proceedings of the joyous festival . . . on the 12th of April last, the Glorious Anniversary of the Birth Day of Henry Clay" in "handsome style next month." Includes a poem "To the Memory of Col. Henry Clay Junr. Who fell while Bravely defending his Country's Rights in the battle of Buena Vista." ALS. Henry Clay Memorial Foundation, Lexington, Ky.

To James Brown Clay, New York City, September 1, 1849. Writing from Newport, R.I., reports "I feel a little better since your departure. Today it is wet and cold, and the Bath cannot be taken. I think I shall leave this place on monday, and my present inclination is to go by New York." ALS. DLC-TJC (DNA, M212, R11).

To Guillaume Tell Poussin, Washington, D.C., September 1, 1849. Expresses his "very great pleasure to find that after so long a separation between us, you still cherished a friendly recollection of our former intimate intercourse." Assures Poussin "of my entire reciprocity" of feeling. Applaudes the announcement "that the French Republic had deputed you on a Mission to this Country. It could not have sent to us a citizen of France more acceptable and more Endeared to us." Regrets they cannot meet before Clay returns to Kentucky, but, "As I anticipate being at Washington next winter, I hope while there to have many opportunities of seeing you & renewing our former acquaintance." LS. DLC-Guillaume T. Poussin Papers (DNA, M212, R22). Written from Atlantic House, Newport, R.I.

Poussin had been appointed as the new French minister to the U.S. For Poussin, see 4:330.

To Miss R.D. Smith, Newport, R.I., September 1, 1849. Asks her to accept a small portion of "a parcel of fruit, better than we usually get here," just received from Boston. Adds: "Here we can enjoy the luxury of fruit, without that danger to which we are exposed from its use, where the [cholera] Epidemic prevails." ALS. PPL. Written from Atlantic House, Newport, R.I.

Miss Smith is possibly Rebecca Smith of Philadelphia who was reported to have attended the great ball at Newport that ended the social season. New York *Herald*, September 3, 1849.

To JAMES BROWN CLAY Newport, R.I., September 3, 1849

I think of going tonight, via N. York. If not, I shall tomorrow night[.] In either case I may not see you, and therefore enclose the last letter I have recd from home, from John [Morrison Clay]. Levi has absconded, inveigled away, I suppose, by some of his color or by some of the abolitionists. I have not ascertained what course he has gone, nor shall I take any measures to recover him. I shall have a free negro to accompany me home.[1]

If I see you, I should like to get some of your Baums Cholera drops, if you have any to spare.

I think my health has decidedly improved within the last four or five days.

God bless you all.

[P.S.] 3 O'Clock—Levi has voluntarily returned[.]

ALS. DLC-HC (DNA, M212, R6). Letter written from Newport, R.I. 1. Levi left Newport on Saturday with $300 given him by abolitionists. He returned to Clay on Monday. Peterson, *The Great Triumvirate*, 376; Lexington *Observer & Kentucky Reporter*, Sept. 12, 1849.

From Horace Greeley, New York City, September 4, 1849. Has refrained from writing because "Your restoration to health is very necessary to all, and in the moment that I saw you at Ballston I thought you were in need of other attentions than I could bestow." Having learned that "you would like to meet me somewhere on your return through this State," asks Clay "to indicate when and where . . . though my time is not always at my disposal. I go next Monday to the State Fair, and spend the week in the interior of this State at different points . . . I think I can arrange to be wherever you choose." ALS. DLC-HC (DNA, M212, R6).

On September 11, 1849, Clay attended the New York State Agricultural Fair at Syracuse. Lexington *Observer & Kentucky Reporter*, September 19, 1849.

To LUCRETIA HART CLAY "Lindenwald," N.Y., September 5, 1849

I arrived here (Mr. [Martin] Van buren's) yesterday evening,[1] having left Newport the evening before. I came through the City of New York, but did not remain half an hour there, having passed directly from the Steam boat on the East river to that on the North river. I travelled in that way 320 miles in about 20 hours. James [Brown Clay] and Susan [Jacob Clay], having been apprized of my movements, met me at the one boat and went in a carriage with me to the other. They are all well, and this is the day of their embarkation in the Canada for Europe.[2] I hope they may have a safe and agreeable voyage.

I shall remain here today and tomorrow, and proceed on friday upon my journey to Buffalo. I purpose stopping a day or two at Utica, and as the annual [state] fair at Syracuse takes place next week, tuesday, wednesday and thursday I fear I shall not be able to resist the importunities to stop there. If I do, it will delay the time of my reaching home; but in any event I hope to get there about the 16h. of this month.[3]

My health began to improve a few days before I left Newport, and immediately after I went into the sea. I am now better than I have been since I left home; and but for a cough which still hangs on me, I should be quite well. I ought to have remained a week longer at Newport and I am sorry that I did not.

Dr. [William N.] Mercer and his family left the same day that I did and went to Boston. They mean to travel in New England some days and then proceed home, by what route they have not yet determined, and I think it not certain that they will pass by Ashland.

Levi left me last saturday,[4] being carried or enticed away by Abolitionists. I supposed that I had lost him, and I had even engaged a free man of color to accompany me home; but he voluntarily returned to me on monday last, a few hours before I left Newport and is now with me. He says that they offered and paid him $300 and that he intended to get all the money out of them that he could and to have returned to me. They became distrustful of him and he of them at Boston, and he restored their money and came back to me as I have related.

I got a long and agreeable letter from John [Morrison Clay] just before my departure from Newport. I have the saddle and its appurtenances along for John.[5]

Give my love to him and to Thomas [Hart Clay], Mary [Mentelle Clay] and their children.

ALS. DLC-TJC (DNA, M212, R11). 1. Clay to Van Buren, August 9, 1849. 2. For James's appointment as minister to Portugal, see Taylor to Clay, May 28, 1849. 3. For Clay's itinerary, see Clay to Stevenson, July 21, 1849. 4. Clay to James B. Clay, Sept. 3, 1849. 5. John M. Clay to Clay, August 25, 1849.

To HENRY GRINNELL "Lindenwald," N.Y., September 7, 1849

I received here your favor of the 6h. inst. I was extremely sorry to hear of the destruction of your fine ship that bore my name; but I am glad to learn that, notwithstanding her misfortunes, she has been profitable to her owners.[1]

I am thankful for your kind offer to transmit any thing I may have to send to my son [James Brown Clay], who left you on wednesday last,[2] and I shall probably have occasion to embrace it.

I leave here tomorrow for Ashland, with my health much improved. I find that your great Fair[3] comes so directly in my way that I shall have to stop a day [at] it, 'though I would be glad to escape the crowd which will assemble there.

ALS. Courtesy of Dr. Thomas D. Clark, Lexington, Ky. 1. The packet ship *Henry Clay* burned at Maiden Lake, N.Y. Washington *Daily National Intelligencer*, Sept. 7, 1849. 2. For Lisbon, Portugal. 3. Greeley to Clay, Sept. 4, 1849.

To L. HODGES Steam Boat Queen City, September 15, 1849

I informed you by Telegraph from Cleveland that my black servant Levi was left at Buffalo last night whether voluntarily or against his wishes is uncertain. There are circumstances having a tendency both ways. If voluntarily, I will take no trouble about him, as it is probable that in a reversal of our conditions I would have done the same thing. As he left me and voluntarily returned at Newport,[1] and has had an opportunity of leaving me at any time within the last six or seven weeks without embracing it, I am inclined to think that he has been detained at Buffalo contrary to his real desire. In that case, you will oblige me greatly by furnishing him the necessary means and facilitating his return to Ashland.[2] Be pleased to inform me the result of your enquiries by a letter addressed to me at Lexington, near which I reside.

ALS. NBuHi. Addressed to Hodges "at the American Buffalo." 1. Clay to James B. Clay, Sept. 3, 1849; Clay to Lucretia H. Clay, Oct. 2, 1849. 2. Clay to James B. Clay, Oct. 2, 1849.

To A.B. Chambers *et al.*, St. Louis, Mo., September 19, 1849. Has received their invitation to a national convention to consider "the expediency of connecting the Atlantic and Pacific oceans" by a railroad. Declines attending because of other engagements; however, hopes the convention will arrive "at a proper conclusion." Feels personally no "prejudice nor predelictions which would sway my judgment." Thinks they should consider such things as the best route and the cost of the project. Copy. Printed in Washington *Daily National Intelligencer*, October 31, 1849.

The Railroad convention concluded in St. Louis on October 20 after four days of deliberation. Two things were decided: that the convention would not "have anything to do in the way of fixing upon a route or termini, or in deciding upon details" and that a survey of the ground needed to be made by skillful engineers. *Ibid.*, October 30, 1849.

Chambers (1808-54)—lawyer, state legislator, and editor of the St. Louis *Missouri Republican*—was born in Mercer County, Pa., moved to Bowling Green, Mo., in 1829 and to St. Louis in 1837. J. Thomas Scharf, *History of Saint Louis City and County* . . . , 2 vols. (Philadelphia, 1883), 1:909-11.

To MADISON CUTTS Lexington, September 19, 1849

On my return home last evening, after an absence of two months, I found here your letter of the 20h. July last, communicating an account of the last illness and the death of my highly esteemed friend, your aunt, Mrs. [Dolley] Madison.[1] I previously had heard the afflicting event, and I need not say feel it most sensibly. I sincerely sympathise with you and her other relations in this great loss, and tender my cordial condolence. I was glad to learn through the papers that she had made competent provision for her niece Anna Payne. I should have been surprized if she had not done so; for I well knew the mutual attachment which existed between them, and Miss Payne's devotion to her venerable aunt.

I hope that Mrs' Madison's will may remain undisturbed. No one can controvert it but her son;[2] and I am deceived in the justice and generosity of his character if he would seek to deprive poor Anna of the small portion of an estate, the greater part of which is left to him. . . .

ALS. DLC-Cutts Family Papers. 1. Mrs. Madison died on July 12, 1849. 2. Madison Cutts had drafted a will for Mrs. Madison in which she divided a trust of $20,000 between her son John Payne Todd and her niece Anna Payne. The remainder of her estate went to Todd. Todd attempted unsuccessfully to break this will. Katharine S. Anthony, *Dolley Madison, Her Life and Times* (Garden City, N.Y., 1949), 399-405.

To MR. & MRS. FREDERICK HOLLISTER[1] Lexington, September 19, 1849

I am sure, my dear Mr. and Mrs. Hollister that you will both hear, with pleasure, that I reached home in safety last evening, and found Mrs. [Lucretia Hart] Clay & my family well.

In reviewing the incidents of my late visit to N. York and the Eastward,[2] I should be wanting in heart & gratitude if I failed to express my great obligations to both of you for the kind and hospitable entertainment which I received at your hands and under your auspices, at your house. I can never forget it. My visit to Utica & Oneida is an epoch in my life never to be forgotten. And I shall cherish, with peculiar satisfaction, the valuable souvenirs which you presented to me.

I hope that you will be able, some day or other, to visit us in our quiet retreat at Ashland. I need not assure you of the very great pleasure it would afford Mrs. Clay and myself to receive and entertain you here.

May God preserve, prosper, and bless you!

[P.S.] Present my warm regards to Mr. Matterson. I went through some trying scenes at Syracuse, after you left me.[3] To escape the overwhelming crowd, I sought an assylum, and, for more than half an hour, was locked up with Mrs. Phillips at the Globe Hotel, the multitude thundering all the time to get in!

ALS. NcD. 1. Frederick Hollister (d. 1863)—a lawyer and businessman—had been mayor of Utica, N.Y., in 1843. His businesses failed in 1851, and he moved to New York City. David

E. Wager (ed.), *Our County and its People, A Descriptive Work on Oneida County New York* (Boston, 1896), 371, 497. 2. Clay to Stevenson, July 21, 1849. 3. Greeley to Clay, Sept. 4, 1849.

To Thomas B. Stevenson, Cincinnati, September 21, 1849. Reports a visit to "the Insurance office to enquire if any change was contemplated by the Company in their Agency at Cincinnati," but learned that "their agent there was an excellent one," and that "no change of him was wished or intended." Had asked because "I learnt that the Agency at New York which had been very profitable to the Agent, had been unproductive to the Company; and that they were not entirely satisfied with Mr Hoxie, the agent there." Has asked to be informed if "any resolution to supersede him. . . . should be adopted." Copy. OCHP.

The Lexington Fire, Life and Marine Insurance Company was possibly the firm where Clay was attempting to obtain a job for Stevenson.

From JAMES BROWN CLAY Southampton, England, September 27, 1849

I am now writing to you from on board the Steamer Montrose which will sail in two hours for Lisbon. We had not sufficient information or what we had was incorrect, when we left N York as we found the Steamer of this date the first which would sail after our arrival—We have spent two or three days in London three or four in Paris & the residue of our time has been spent in flying between these places[.] We arrived here two hours since, having left Paris yesterday morning at Eight—Notwithstanding our rapidity and all the sights we have seen, we have been all of us quite well and extremely delighted with every thing we have seen in Europe[.] Tell Mama [Lucretia Hart Clay] that Susan [Jacob Clay] will write her a long letter from Lisbon, giving her an account of our various purchases & extravagances at Paris—Among others We count dresses of brocade &c &c[.] We expect to be 5 or 6 days out on our passage & if we meet with nothing serious between this and Lisbon, will have reason to be very thankful—

All send their love to you to Mama & the family—We are very anxious to hear of your complete restoration to health & of every thing connected with you all at home[.]

ALS. DLC-TJC (DNA, M212, R11).

To MARGARET HUGHES Lexington, September 29, 1949

The newspapers announce that the stroke of death, so long menacing and suspended over the head of your lamented father [Christopher Hughes], has at last fallen on him,[1] and deprived you of one of the best of parents, and me of one of the best of friends. The melancholy event did not take me by surprize. From a knowledge of his afflictions, I knew that he could not long survive; and as he, who was so regular and punctual in his correspondence, when in health, did not answer my last letter, addressed to him from Newport,[2] I concluded that he must be near his final end.

I offer you, my dear Miss Margaret, my sincere and heartfelt condolence. Certain as the event of death is and warned as we often are of its near approach, by incurable disease, when it does come, we are nevertheless overpowered by the emotions of sorrow and grief. In your case, he was your last remaining parent;[3] and therefore your distress will be more intense. But you ought to derive some consolation from the reflection that he has escaped from excrutiating pain and suffering, and that he was unhappily laboring under more than one mortal disease. You will derive further and greater consolation from reflecting, that this great calamity proceeds from the Will of HIM, to whose irrevocable decrees we are bound implicitly to submit, with dutiful resignation.

To me the loss is very great. Your good father and I had maintained intimate friendly relations for about forty years. During that whole period, altho' we were frequently separated for a long time, and by great distances, our mutual friendship was unabated and remained bright and unbroken.

In another point of view the sad event which has happened has fallen seriously upon me. It has left me the only survivor of an important foreign commission, connected with the peace of our Country, and of which your father was a member.[4] His death, recently preceded by that of Messrs. [John Quincy] Adams[5] and [Albert] Gallatin,[6] is a solemn warning that I too must soon follow them. I pray and hope that we may all meet in that better world, in which neither sin nor sorrow nor death is found.

Surrounded as you are, my dear Miss Margaret, by affectionate friends and relations, an offer of any service of mine to you can be of no consequence; but I request you to believe that this is not a mere formal tender; and that I should be most happy if it shall ever be in my power to render any, the smallest service, to the beloved daughter of my departed friend.

ALS. MiU-C. 1. Hughes died Sept. 18, 1849. 2. Not found, but see Clay to Hughes, August 4, 1849, written from Saratoga. 3. See 9:499. 4. Treaty of Ghent. See 1:866-67. 5. Clay to James B. Clay, Feb. 21, 1848. 6. Gallatin died on August 12, 1849.

To Robert C. Winthrop, Boston, Mass., September 29, 1849. Explains a recent telegram he sent to Winthrop. On "the voyage from Buffalo to Sandusky" while returning to Ashland, "I made the acquaintance of a young man, who represented himself to me as your brother." His "various little acts of kindness . . . on the voyage, and during the run of the Cars from Sandusky to Cincinnati, interested me in him." In Cincinnati, however, "he subjected himself to suspicion." After being "received in good society" in Lexington, and "being invited, on the strength of your name, to dinner several times," made several attempts to borrow money, but with little success. He did not apply to me for any." When "Unfavorable reports from Cincinnati" arrived, "he suddenly departed from Lexington. . . . he subscribes his name 'John C Winthrop.' " Concludes: "I am truly sorry that a young man, so capable . . . should be unworthy." ALS. MHi.

This was evidently an imposter, since Robert's brother John T. Winthrop, had died in 1843. Lawrence S. Mayo, *The Winthrop Family in America* (Boston, 1948), 299-301.

To NICHOLAS DEAN *Ca.* Late September, 1849

If they had,[1] as I hope, a prosperous voyage, they will have arrived at Liverpool about the same day that I reached home. My separation from them, probably for a length of time, the uncertainty of life rendering it not unlikely that I may never see them again, and the deep and affectionate interest I take in their welfare and happiness, has been extremely painful.

I find myself now, toward the close of my life, in one respect, in a condition similar to that with which I began it. Mrs. [Lucretia Hart] Clay and I commenced it alone; and after having had eleven children, of whom four only remain, our youngest son [John Morrison Clay] is the sole white person residing with us.

Copy, extract. Printed in L.G. Clarke, "Henry Clay, Personal Anecdotes, Incidents, Etc.," *Harper's New Monthly Magazine*, (August, 1852), 5:397. 1. Reference is to James Brown Clay and his family.

To JAMES BROWN CLAY Lexington, October 2, 1849

I returned home this day fortnight in improved health which, with the exception of my cough, continues good[.] Levi again left me at Buffalo, and has again returned to Louisville, on his way home, having reported himself there to Mr. [Thomas] Smith[.][1]

I received your letter[2] dated at Sea, after you had been two days out, and I was sorry to learn that there was so much Sea sickness in your party. I calculated that you arrived at Liverpool about the time I got home. I found all well here.[3] John [Morrison Clay] attended the Versailles races last week,[4] and with the Trustie mare won a mile race in a field of seven horses, in three heats. His Woodpecker colt walked around the course no horse starting against him; and he thinks that he was cheated out of the race in which Tarsch ran by unfair riding. The races are now in progress at Lexington, but the track is wet and heavy and John is deprecating it very much.[5] He tells me that you are owing several forfeits, in cases of entries, some of which he will probably pay for your honor.

Col [John] Brand died with Cholera about four weeks ago. Johnston the saddler has purchased at private sale the whole of Mr. [John W.] Hunt's land of upwards of 1100 Acres at Sixty dollars per acre.[6] I think it would have commanded more at public auction, land being on the rise.

You will have seen that Secy. [of State John M.] Clayton has got into a difficulty with the French Minister.[7] I am sorry for it, and I think that with judgment and discretion it might have been avoided. But your course should be to defend the act of the Executive, if you can conscientiously; and if not to remain silent. The papers will also inform that the Secretary has also a difficulty with the British Chargé about the Mosquito coast.[8] I hope it is not so serious as to threaten War.

My crops of Hemp and Corn are uncommonly fine. And the influx of gold from California,[9] and the general prosperity of the Country are giving an upward tendency to prices. Hemp, I fear, will however be an exception next year, owing to its abundance.

I suppose you will hear from Louisville. I have heard nothing to the contrary, and therefore presume all are well there.

I enclose a ticket which I recd. for you enclosed in a circular, similar to one addressed to me, from the American Institute.[10]

Henry Hart[11] preseveres in going to St Louis about the middle of this month. Your horses and his are to be sold on saturday. [James A.] Grinsteads brother to Doubleoon won the great sweep stakes yesterday.[12]

Our love to Susan [Jacob Clay], and kiss dear Lucy [Jacob Clay] and the other children for me.

ALS. DLC-TJC (DNA, M212, R11). Printed in Colton, *Clay Correspondence*, 4:588-89. 1. Clay to James B. Clay, Sept. 3, 1849. 2. Not found. 3. The Colton version omits the remainder of this paragraph. 4. The Versailles races were held at the Daisy Hill Course for five days in September. Lexington *Observer & Kentucky Reporter*, Sept. 21, 22, 26, 1849. 5. The fall meet at the Association Course in Lexington was delayed in 1849 because of heavy rains. *Ibid.*, Sept. 26, Oct. 3, 10, 1849. 6. See John M. Clay to Clay, August 25, 1849. 7. For details of the diplomatic disputes between John M. Clayton and Guillaume Tell Poussin over various U.S. and French claims which escalated into a crisis that nearly caused a break in diplomatic relations, see Bemis, *American Secretaries of State*, 7:19-31. 8. Clayton was dealing with British chargé John F. Crampton pending the arrival of the new British minister Sir Henry L. Bulwer. For the complicated negotiations over the Mosquito coast of Central America and the right to build a trans-isthmian canal, which eventually resulted in the Clayton-Bulwer Treaty, see *ibid.*, 7:41-70; Hamilton, *Zachary Taylor, Soldier in the White House*, 193-98. 9. For the discovery of gold at Sutter's sawmill in Jan., 1848 and the subsequent California gold rush, see Zoeth S. Eldredge (ed.), *History of California*, 5 vols. (New York, 1914), 3:169-259, 321-63; Oscar Lewis, *Sea Routes to the Gold Fields . . .* (New York, 1949). 10. For the American Institute, see 8:856. 11. The Colton version omits this paragraph. 12. For Grinstead, owner of Walnut Hill Stud and breeder of Doubloon and other noted race horses, see Perrin, *History of Fayette County*, 154.

To ROBERT S. HAMILTON Lexington, October 2, 1849

I have received and thank you for "The Scheme of African Colonization," presented by you in a Discourse delivered at Xenia in July last, which I have perused with much satisfaction.[1] It is distinguished by eloquence, public spirit and ability, and I think most of the principles which it developes and enforces are founded in truth.

After the recent failure to establish a system of gradual emancipation in Kentucky,[2] I confess that I have not much hope that Slavery will ever be extinguished in any of the States, by legal enactment, at least for a long time to come. That failure may be attributed to the violent and indiscreet course of Ultra abolitionists in the North, to the great amount of property invested in Slaves, and to the repugnance with which a People change long established habits.

There remains in prospect the other mode, the natural extinction of slavery, treated by you. Whenever the rearing and maintenance of slaves become unprofitable, as it will be, when there is a certainty of the supply of cheaper free labor than Slave labor, the institution of slavery will decline and finally terminate. That may happen, either by the increase of the colored population, or by the increase of the white population of the U. States, or, as is most probable, by the increase of both.

You have considered the subject in the form of demand and supply of labor. That is a modification, with some variation, of [Thomas] Malthus's principle of population, founded on the quantity of human food or subsistence.

In December 1829 before the Colonization Society of K[entucky]. I pronounced a discourse, in which I treated of the natural termination of Slavery founded on the reduction of the wages of labor. I am sorry that I have not a copy of it by me to send you. It was published in Niles's Register, in the African Repository and in other periodicals.[3] If you can lay your hands upon it, you will be struck with the coincidence in our views, although we express ourselves in different terms.

It is a consoling reflection that, altho a system of gradual emancipation cannot be established, Slavery is destined inevitably to extinction, by the operation of peaceful and natural causes. And it is also gratifying to believe, that there will not be probably much difference in the period of its existence, whether it terminates legally or naturally. The chief difference in the two modes is that, according to the first, we should take hold of the Institution intelligently and dispose of it cautiously and safely, whilst according to the other it will some day or other take hold of us, and constrain us, in some manner or other, to get rid of it.

I apprehend that you are mistaken in supposing that the greater ratio of increase, in the colored race between 1800 and 1810 than in other decimal periods, was owing to the importation of slaves from Africa. It was owing to the acquisition of Louisiana, whose slaves were enumerated in the census of 1810.[4]

Copy. Printed in *The Nation* (August 6, 1896), 63:101. 1. Hamilton's *Discourse on the Scheme of African Colonization, Delivered Before the Colonization Society of Greene County, Ohio, at Zenia, July 4, 1849* was published in Cincinnati in 1849. Hamilton is identified by *The Nation* as a resident of New York State. Since many people bore that name in New York City alone, it has not been possible to further identify him. 2. Stevenson to Clay, June 12, 1848. 3. See 8:138-58. 4. For Clay's proposals on emancipation in Kentucky, see Clay to Pindell, Feb. 17, 1849, no. 2 of date.

To JAMES HARLAN Lexington, October 4, 1849

I saw in the [Frankfort] Commonwealth, with sorrow and regret, the death announced of your son, my name sake.[1] I tender to you, on the melancholy occasion, an expression of my sincere sympathy and condolence. I knew enough of him, from frequent interviews and conversations with him, to appreciate the great distress which the lamented event must have brought upon you and Mrs [Eliza Shannon Davenport] Harlan & your other children.[2] I have been, in my time, a great sufferer from the loss of beloved children, and I can justly estimate the grief which you now feel.

Time, and a patient resignation and submission to the Will of Him who, having given us our children, has the right to take them from us, when he pleases, can only treat the wounds inflicted, and mitigate the sorrows which the bereavement necessarily excites.

I hope that you and Mrs. Harlan will bear, with fortitude, and in a true spirit of Christianity, this sad and heavy dispensation.

ALS. Courtesy of Alan Westin, New Haven, Conn. Printed in Colton, *Clay Correspondence*, 4:589. 1. Henry Clay Harlan had died at his father's residence on Sept. 29, 1849, aged 19. He served as assistant secretary to Gov. John C. Crittenden. Frankfort *Commonwealth*, Oct. 2, 1849. 2. The Harlans had a total of 6 sons and 3 daughters. One son, John Marshall Harlan, became a noted justice of the U.S. Supreme Court. *DAB*.

To JOHN M. CLAYTON Lexington, October 6, 1849

Mr. [James] Heudebert of Mississippi[1] has been appointed Consul at Lyons. I doubt whether he will suit the office or the office will suit him. He has all the vivacity and enthusiasm of the French Character, & has some very good qualities, but I believe he is not much versed in commerce. The office too, I apprehend, is without emolument, and will not probably afford him bread, which is what he wants.

If you could commute the office given to him into such a situation as that of Bearer of despatches to some Foreign power, I think that the change would benefit him, and perhaps better promote the public interest.

I have taken the liberty to make this suggestion, as I learn that Mr. H. is on the eve of his departure for France.

ALS. DLC-John M. Clayton Papers (DNA, M212, R20). Letter marked "(Private)." 1. Heudebert was nominated as consul at Lyons on Jan. 31, 1850, and confirmed on April 24. U.S. Sen., *Executive Journal*, 8:134, 168.

To SOLOMON MEREDITH Lexington, October 6, 1849

I recd. today your letter with its enclosures. I am perfectly aware of your friendly attachment to and confidence in me, and of the proofs you have given of it.[1] I am grateful & thankful for it.

I was glad of your appointment as Marshall of Indiana, and hope that no opposition will be made to its confirmation.[2] Should opposition however be made you may rely upon all the support which my friendship for you can prompt, if God spare me to take my seat in the Senate.

ALS. InHi. 1. For example, he had supported Clay for president in 1848. See Stevenson to Clay, May 18, 1848. 2. Meredith was nominated for marshal on Jan. 30, 1850, and confirmed on May 1, 1850. U.S. Sen., *Executive Journal*, 8:144, 170.

To JAMES BROWN CLAY Lexington, October 15, 1849

I received your letter dated at Liverpool the 27th ultimo, and was very glad that you had all safely arrived, with so little inconvenience from sea-sickness. I hope that your excursion to Paris proved agreeable, and that you were not tempted by its many attractions to run into any extravagant expenditures.

The elections in Ohio[1] and Pennsylvania[2] have gone against the Administration, and, judging from present prospects, I do not see how it is to be sustained. If, therefore, you do not come home sooner, you may prepare to return on the expiration of its term. I understand indirectly that it is counting much on my exertions at the approaching session of Congress;[3] but I fear that it is counting without any sufficient ground. I intend to leave home the first of November, but not to go to Washington until about the opening of Congress. I expect to pass two or three weeks in Philadelphia.[4]

I suppose that you and Susan [Jacob Clay] hear regularly from Louisville, from which I have heard nothing of any interest. Here we are all in health, and things move on in their ordinary channels. Yesterday (Sunday) Thomas [Hart Clay] and Mary [Mentelle Clay] dined with us as usual. He goes down in a few weeks to his famous saw mill, from which he calculates to make a great deal.[5]

We expect H[enry]. Hart and his family here to-morrow or next day to make their farewell visit, preparatory to their going to St. Louis, for which he has made most of his arrangements.

Give our love to Susan and your children and to Henry Clay [III], and kiss dear Lucy [Jacob Clay] for your affectionate father.

Copy. Printed in Colton, *Clay Correspondence*, 4:589-90. 1. In the Ohio state elections in Oct., 1849, Democrats won 35 seats in the house, Whigs won 31, and Free Soilers 6. In the state senate Democrats controlled 17 seats, excluding disputed claims in Hamilton County, Whigs 15, and Free Soilers 4. Holt, *Party Politics in Ohio*, 416. Democrat Amos E. Wood was elected in a special election for the U.S. House. *Guide to U.S. Elections*, 589; *BDAC*. 2. In the 1849 Pennsylvania state elections, Democrats gained control of the legislature with 17 of the 33 senate seats and 59 of the 100 house seats. Mueller, *Whig Party in Pennsylvania*, 166-67. 3. It was generally viewed that from his seat in the Senate Clay would hold the key to the success or failure of the Taylor administration's proposals to Congress. Some Taylor partisans feared he would seek revenge for his loss of the 1848 Whig nomination by opposing the administration, while others believed he would support Taylor's policies, especially his plans for the new territories. For a full discussion, see Bauer, *Zachary Taylor*, 266; Hamilton, *Zachary Taylor, Soldier in the White House*, 235, 269; Poage, *Henry Clay*, 200; Peterson, *The Great Triumvirate*, 450, 452-55. 4. On Nov. 1, 1849, Clay left Ashland for Frankfort where he remained until Nov. 3 when he departed for Cincinnati. On Nov. 7 he arrived in Baltimore after suffering a stage accident near Uniontown, Pa., on the way to Cumberland, Md. He took the train from Baltimore to Philadelphia on Nov. 8, and that evening attended the wedding of one of Richard Henry Bayard's daughters. He was a guest of the Bayards in Philadelphia until Nov. 19 when he travelled to New York City where he stayed at the home of Egbert Benson until the 24th. From Nov. 24 to 29 he was again in Philadelphia. From there he went back to Baltimore on Nov. 29 and to Washington on Dec. 1. Lexington *Observer & Kentucky Reporter*, Nov. 3, 17, 24, Dec. 1, 3, 5, 8, 1849; Frankfort *Commonwealth*, Nov. 6, 1849; Washington *Daily National Intelligencer*, Dec. 3, 1849. 5. For references to the sawmill, see below Clay to James B. Clay, Dec. 4 and 29, 1849; Clay to Thomas H. Clay, Dec. 25 and 27, 1849.

To Thomas B. Stevenson, Cincinnati, October 15, 1849. Sends a copy of a "bill of lading" containing a listing of articles "all superior of their respective kinds," sent to Clay as a present from William N. Mercer. Since he is "anxious to receive them in safety," asks Stevenson "to call at the proper depot" when they arrive and forward them either to Frankfort or "through Mr. [Andrew M.] January's house at Maysville." Adds that if "any thing can be offered to you by the Insurance Company . . . worthy of your acceptance," nothing that he and Henry T. Duncan "can do will be omitted by us to secure it for you." ALS. Courtesy of Dr. Thomas D. Clark, Lexington, Ky. See Clay to Stevenson, September 21, 1849.

On October 23, 1849, Clay wrote Stevenson to acknowledge receipt "in good order" of "the box of Sugar, the box of brandy, and the bag of Westphalia hams. The bag of coffee is all that remains behind." Advises Stevenson that "Nothing has occurred at the Insurance Office, in regard to our wishes," but "Mr. Duncan has promised me to keep an eye on the object. . . . as I expect to leave home on the first of next month, for the Eastward." Assures him of "my cordial cooperation" with Thomas Corwin to do "any thing to promote your interests." ALS. Courtesy of Dr. Thomas D. Clark, Lexington, Ky.

To Hugh Maxwell, New York City, October 22, 1849. Encloses a letter from Guido Schmidt, judging that "Your heart and feelings . . . will be touched, and affected by perusing" it. Believes that if Schmidt's "morals and character are good, of which You have a better opportunity than I have to ascertain," he may become a "useful" or "distinguished Citizen." Understanding that Maxwell is "burthened & perplexed by applications for situations in the Custom Houses" and hesitant "to solicit your patronage," hopes he will give Schmidt "some little situation that would improve his condition," as "an act of humanity . . . that would promote the public interest." Copy. DLC-James O. Harrison Papers (DNA, M212, R21).

A notation in the James O. Harrison Papers (R21) states that Schmidt was a native of Hanover, Germany, and had been in New York about five years.

From John Hanson, Edina, Grand Bassa County, Republic of Liberia, October 24, 1849. Writes "upon the grave subject of Colonization of that class of people that reside in your much-beloved country, viz: the colored people in the United States of North America." Believes colonization to be "one of the most feasible plans that ever struck the senses of the philanthropists of your . . . country." Has had long experience in Liberia "where every one can aspire to those eminent stations which every one can attain to by his industry, and which God and nature design them to fill."

Explains that Liberia has "a very beautiful location" where three crops a year can be grown. Believes it can produce quantities of coffee, arrow root, ginger, cocoa, and various other things which can be traded to the U.S. for manufactured goods. States that he experienced "heartfelt satisfaction" at reading an account of a celebration in Kentucky honoring Liberia's national flag. Recalls meeting with Clay in Washington in 1827 at his office in the State Department. Notes that "there you . . . gave me some wholesome advice upon the feasibility of the plan of colonization and its object." Expresses his gratitude for Clay's devoted friendship to the cause and says he hopes to visit the U.S. "after our Government and its laws are properly arranged." Copy. Printed in Washington *Daily National Intelligencer*, January 4, 1850.

Hanson indicates following his signature that he is a member of Liberia's senate. He was a merchant-shipper from Philadelphia. Staudenraus, *African Colonization Movement*, 135, 159, 222, 237.

To LUCRETIA ERWIN Lexington, October 27, 1849

I received and read attentively your letter of the 10h. inst. The pursual of it touched and affected me very greatly, as it did your grandma [Lucretia Hart Clay]. It was full of feelings and sentiments so just, conceived in such a true Christian spirit, and marked by such affectionate attachment to us and to all your relations that we read it with the deepest emotions. Whilst we could not disapprove, we were seriously and sorrowfully concerned by your resolution to adopt the veil and dedicate the rest of your life to the service of God in a Convent. We could not disapprove it, because you say that your determination has been deliberately formed, and because you are solemnly convinced that it will be conducive to your present and future happiness. But it is a grave and serious step, resembling, in the separation from your friends and relations, which it involves, so much the awful separation which death itself brings about, that we could not but feel intense distress.[1]

Your happiness, my dear grand child, has ever been an object of extreme anxiety and solicitude with us. If it is to be promoted by the execution of the purpose you have in view, I would not, if I could, dissuade you from it. I have no prejudices against the Catholic religion. On the contrary, I sincerely believe that Catholics, who are truly religious, are as sure of eternal happiness in another world as the most pious Protestants. All that I hope is, that you will not act on any sudden impulse, or ill considered and immature resolution, but that you will deliberately and again and again examine your own heart and consult your best judgment before you consummate your intention.

Your father [James Erwin] and step mother [Margaret Johnson Erwin] have been to Nashville and are daily expected at home. [Charles] Edward [Erwin] is going to school at Mr. [Beverley] Hicks s, [Andrew] Eu[gen]e. [Erwin] is at the Woodlands, & Henry [Clay Erwin] with his father. Your uncle James [Brown Clay] & all his family are gone to Europe, and we have heard of their safe arrival in England on their way to Lisbon.[2] Your uncle Thomas [Hart Clay] & his family and all here are well.

You forgot that I am to go to the Senate this winter. I shall leave home for the Eastward on the 1st. Novr.[3] and I fear that I shall be kept at Washington until July next.

Write me at Washington; and in the event of your taking the veil let me know what provision exists for your support and comfort, and whether any and what pecuniary aid may be proper or expedient from your friends.

Adieu, my dear grand child. May God enlighten guide and direct you; and, if we never meet again in this world, may we meet in the regions of eternal bliss, and there join my beloved daughter, your lamented mother [Anne Brown Clay Erwin]. Such also are the prayers of your Grandma.

ALS. InNd. 1. Lucretia did not join a convent. In late 1850 she married Frederic A. Cowles. See Clay to Lucretia H. Clay, Dec. 26, 1850. 2. Taylor to Clay, May 28, 1849; Clay to Clayton, June 7, 1849. 3. Clay to James B. Clay, Oct. 15, 1849.

From Hugh Wallace Wormeley, Claiborne, Monroe Co., Ala., November 20, 1849. Explains "my intruding myself upon your philanthropy and goodness" from my "need to approach you. . . . to aid me in my application to Congress." As "a Midshipman in March 1801," he found duty on the *Maryland* to be "severe; four hours on and four hours off, cold and storm assailed us, consequently a violent cold attacked me through my system and fell upon my eyes and [I] became blind." Although his sight was partially restored in one eye, "the left eye was nearly gone and useless to me." A petition for a pension was twice rejected "by the Naval Committees of the Senate—in the Session 1845-6 I again presented my claim to Congress," but "the Committee of Naval affairs has not acted upon it and [it] ever since *slumbered there.*"

Despite affidavits attesting "that the imperfection of my eyes was very apparent immediately I left the Maryland," the committee apparently "supposed I had recovered in consequence of the long active service from the 25*th* of March 1802 (when I was reinstated and ordered to join the Chesapeake) to Septemb[er] 1805." The committee concluded that "I reported myself as fit for duty and therefore I could not have been an invalid." Argues that "History refutes this—I can refer to that committee many persons who have been maimed and disabled and performed valuable service to their Country." Adds that "These committees take another ground that I could not have been an invalid because I received an appointment as a Second Lieutenant in the Marine Corps" in September, 1804, after "nearly five years a Midshipman; and one year more I would have been a Lieutenant in our Navy." Asks: "Would any rational man have exchanged offices? A Lieutenant in the Navy ranks with a Captain in the Army and the Marine Corps." Explains as the "cause of the exchange" that "I was unable to perform sea service—Naval Officers have Watches day and night," and "it was these night watches and *saline doses* that inflamed my eyes and ultimately would have destroyed the remainder of *the vision of them*. . . . Marine officers have nothing to do with the ship or the Deck, nor do they have any watches to keep—I presume the committee did not know this." Laments that if it were not for "the imperfection of . . . [my] vision. . . . I would now be among the oldest Captains in the American Navy." ALS. DLC-HC (DNA, M212, R6).

Hugh Wallace Wormeley was probably the same person as the Wallace Wormeley listed in the General Navy Register as entering the Navy as a midshipman on November 24, 1800, and being discharged on August 31, 1801. Callahan, *Officers of the Navy . . . and of the Marine Corps*, 603.

Wormeley had first petitioned Congress in December, 1840. His petition received an adverse report from House and Senate committees on several different occasions over the years. See, for instance, U.S. H. of Reps., *Journal*, 26 Cong., 2 Sess., 54-55, 277; U.S. Sen., *Journal*, 29 Cong., 1 Sess., 36, 66, 207, 497; *ibid.*, 30 Cong., 2 Sess., 92; *ibid.*, 31 Cong., 1 Sess., 67; *ibid.*, 32 Cong., 1 Sess., 115, 385, 496. See also *Sen. Reports*, 32 Cong., 1 Sess., no. 206.

From Henry Clay Duralde, "Schooner St Mary, Valparaiso, Republic of Chile," November 22, 1849. In the midst of an "almost unprecedented long passage" to California from New Orleans, writes to explain to Clay "the causes, which induced me to treat you with such shameful neglect and inattention, during your stay in that city at the same time" last winter. Admits partaking "in pleasures of all kinds" at the "theatres, balls and other places of amusement," where "I, at, once gave myself up, to the gratification of my passions, making, pleasure & dissipation, my idols, neglecting to visit my relations, and almost ruining my constitution." Fearing that "you would ask me, how, I had spent my time, and knowing, I would have, to tell you the truth, or a falsehood, I thought, rather, than cause you any pain, that, it would be better for me, not to visit you."

Explains that the reason he decided to go to California was because he knew "there was no possibility for settling in business in New Orleans, and . . . I would soon be reduced to a state of beggary, by a continuance of my extravagance." Thus, he set sail, along with some acquaintances, on March 8. Describes in great detail the storms and other delays encountered so far during the journey. Despite the hardships, however, believes the "voyage has unquestionably benefitted my health, and hardened my constitution." Notes that he has not experienced any seasickness.

States that in about "a week or 10 days . . . we will again set sail for San Francisco." Asks to be remembered to the rest of the family "and be so kind, as to show them this letter, and tell them that pleasure & dissipation caused me, to forget them in New Orleans, but that I shall atone for my forgetfulness of them, by writing from California." ALS. DLC-TJC (DNA, M212, R11).

To JAMES HARLAN Philadelphia, November 26, 1849

I recd your favor of the 16th. inst.—In relation to the house occupied by Dr [Douglass L.] Price of which I am half owner,[1] I will be willing to take for my moiety $16.00 in Cash or its equivalent—That is to say that any portion of the purchase money not paid in hand, must bear interest during the time of postponement—which I am willing should be liberal. I regret that our State Convention has not proceeded with more despatch in the grave duties with which it is charged.—[2] And I yet hope, that it may present a better constitution than that which it is to supersede. I expect to reach Washn. on Saturday. My hand not having entirely recovered from an injury which I experienced by the upsetting of the Stage,[3] I am compelled to use that of a friend.

LS. Courtesy of Alan Westin, New Haven, Conn. 1. See Clay to Letcher, July 7, 1848. On Oct. 30, 1849, Dr. Price had paid $157.21 for rent, interest, and taxes on the house. He had purchased 1/2 of the house on Oct. 6, 1848, for $68.75. James Harlan signed a receipt on Oct. 30, 1849, for the $157.21 "Which closes the whole business to 1 April 1849 except the Balance of $30.17 which Dr Price owes and against which he claims a Sett Off for repairs." ADS. *Ibid.* 2. Stevenson to Clay, June 12, 1848. 3. Clay to James B. Clay, Oct. 15, 1849.

To John G. Proud *et al.*, Baltimore, November 26, 1849. In reply to an invitation to a public meeting in his honor to be held when he passes through Baltimore, responds that "Whilst it is always gratifying to me to see and exchange salutations with my friends and fellow-citizens in an informal manner, I should regret that my momentary presence in Baltimore should be made the occasion of any public meeting or public demonstration, on my account." Adds, however, that when he reaches the city, "I shall be glad to see, in a quiet and unceremonious way, those who may entertain any desire to see me." Copy. Printed in Lexington *Observer & Kentucky Reporter*, December 5, 1849. Written from Philadelphia.

The letter of invitation, *ca.* November 24, 1849, signed by upwards of a hundred leading citizens of Baltimore, stated that they "rejoice that you have consented to continue your patriotic service, at a time when vital measures and principles of action so deeply agitate the country and remain unsettled." Copy, excerpt. *Ibid.*

The newspaper reported that upon arriving at the railway depot in Baltimore on November 29, 1849, Clay was greeted by a large crowd which had gathered "without preconcert or arrangement." Amid "loud and continued cheering," he boarded a carriage for Barnum's City Hotel. The crowd followed him to the hotel and continued cheering until he appeared at the second floor window of the hotel. When cries for him to speak were made, he replied "we are too far apart, my friends, to do that" and stated that he would take them all by the hand the next day. Accordingly, at 11:00 a.m. on November 30 he took a position between two parlors on the first floor of the hotel where he proceeded to make some remarks.

Clay then stated that the gentlemen who had written him had referred to "great, threatening and alarming questions, which had arisen out of the war with Mexico, and the annexation to our Republic of territories formerly belonging to that country." Notes that he believes others must have reached the same conclusions he has "that under no possible circumstances was slavery likely to be introduced into the territories of California and New Mexico. The climate, the character of the country and its inhabitants, and their industrial pursuits all forbade the likelihood of slavery ever being introduced there." Adds that the question has "created animosities to a most lamentable degree," indeed "so far has the excitement . . . arisen as to threaten dissolution of the Union." Asserts: "I stand pledged under all circumstances and in all storms . . . TO STAND BY THE UNION. . . . In its dissolution I cannot see the remedy for any evil, whether real or imaginary—nothing, nothing, could be gained—all would be lost by it. By the dissolution of the Union I see introduced with it all the calamities, all the misfortunes, and all the horrors of civil war. . . . Entangling foreign alliances by the severed portions of the Union would follow dissolution, and wars—bloody, desolating and continued wars" until "We should then need no history of our country, but all that had been written in that of Greece . . . might be read as applicable to us." The conclusion of his talk was marked by nine cheers from the audience. Copy, summary. *Ibid.*, December 8, 1849.

From JAMES BROWN CLAY Lisbon, Portugal, November 27, 1849

I was happy to receive your letter of the 15th. Ulto. on the 23rd of this month & to learn that you all continued in good health at Ashland. Your letters have been the only ones to this time that we have received from our friends, in the United States. The last that Susan [Jacob Clay] has heard from her family was brought by her brother [Thomas P. Jacob] to Newport.

Susan and the little Harry[1] both continue to be remarkably well, indeed she has never had a confinement which has given either so little pain or trouble. Lucy [Jacob Clay] continues to be in good apparent health—I have consulted a Portuguese Surgeon, with whom I am very much pleased, about her condition. I was surprised to find him recommending precisely the same medicine, as that which was advised by Dr. [Elisha] Bartlett, & whose efficiency we were satisfied of—the oil of the liver of the Cod fish—He is also having made some stays for her & I entertain hopes that she may finally outgrow the deformity, which has not increased.[2]

Not having been able to find a Tutor to please me, I have to day, put Henry [Clay III] to a school, which from all I hear of it, is just the thing for him—I have directed him to be taught French—Portuguese—Mathematics, drawing & music—& it now rests with himself, to improve such opportunities as he could not have had at home—He has been obedient to me so far but I am sorry to say that he continues to be inert, lazy, and excessively selfish. His expences now he is here, will not be greater if so great, as they would have been at home.

Since I have been here my office has been very sinecure. I found some half dozen important claims against this government, in reference to which I have written several long notes to the Minister—[3] but I have no hope, that the claims will be adjusted without the intervention of a stronger power than negotiation—Indeed such is the feeble tenure by which the Ministers retain their power & the government itself, its existence, that I think they would hardly dare to pay the claims, without special authority from the

Cortes—The only good which I have so far been able to do, has been to obtain a remission for the future of a tax heretofore imposed upon granting Exequaturs to our Consuls.

I am in hopes that the President [Zachary Taylor] will bring the subject of our claims before Congress, which may have an effect upon the Cortes which assembles in January.[4] Some of the claims are of a very aggravated nature & all of them from the testimony appear just.

I fear you will not find affairs at Washington very agreeable to you—I hope it may not be necessary for you to make such exertions as you have always done there—Indeed with new men & with new parties, I think your position is above all—It seems to be the fate of the Whig party, if there any longer is such a party to achieve only barren victories—for even should the President desire he can do nothing with Congress opposed to him.[5]

I shall have no wish to remain here longer, certainly, than the time of Genl. Taylor, if so long—and I know my family will hail with joy, the time when we can return to our friends—God grant they may all be living to meet us.

The sale of the horses was better than I expected—I wonder John [Morrison Clay] did not buy the filly from Heads or Tails. I am glad to hear of his success & hope that his horses may continue to amuse him. I hope Thomas [Hart Clay] has before this time sold Richard[6] & reimbursed the money you have paid for me. I have written to him & Susan to Mary [Mentelle Clay], but we have had none from them.

We all send love to you and to the family at Ashland.

ALS. DLC-TJC (DNA, M212, R11). 1. Henry "Harry" Clay was born in Lisbon on Nov. 17, 1849. As an adult he practiced law in Louisville, Denver, and San Francisco. He died in Louisville on Sept. 22, 1884. Kerr, *History of Kentucky*, 3:8-9. 2. Clay to Susan J. Clay, Nov. 3, 1845. 3. Probably the Minister of Foreign Affairs Joao Gualberto de Oliveira, Conde do Tojal. See Susan Bearss, "Henry Clay and the American Claims Against Portugal, 1850," *JER* (Summer, 1987), 7:173. 4. Clay to Clayton, June 7, 1849; Clay to James B. Clay, Dec. 29, 1849. 5. For party make-up in the 31 Cong., 1 Sess., see Clay to Lucretia H. Clay, Dec. 5, 1849. 6. Reference obscure.

To JAMES BROWN CLAY Washington, December 4, 1849

I left home the first of last month, which throughout was a most delightful one, and, after passing two or three weeks in Philada., N. York, and Balto. arrived here last saturday, the first inst. My presence in those Cities excited the usual enthusiasm among my friends,[1] and the customary fatigue &c to myself; but I rejoice that my health is good, with the exception of a bad cold, which I hope is passing off. I have not yet seen the President [Zacahary Taylor], altho' I called yesterday and left my Card. I have seen Mr. [Thomas] Ewing and other members of the Cabinet have left their Cards. Up to this time there is no organization of the House, which is in a very curious state. Neither party has a majority, and divisions exist in each; so that no one can foresee the final issue.[2] The elections of this year have gone very unfavorably to the Whigs, and without some favorable turn in public affairs in their favor, they must lose the ascendency.

I recd. Susan's [Jacob Clay] letter of the 19h. Oct. and yours of the 5h. Novr. and the persual of them afforded me satisfaction. I observe what you both say about Mr. [George W.] Hopkins's[3] kind treatment of you. He has gone home, but if I should ever see him, I will manifest to him my sense of his friendly disposition towards you. I am acquainted with him as a former member of the H. of Representatives. I shall seize some suitable occasion to examine your despatches at the Department of State, and I am glad that you entertain confidence in your competency to discharge the duties of your official position.[4] That is a very proper feeling, within legitimate bounds; but it should not lead to any relaxation of exertions to obtain all information within your reach, and to qualify yourself by all means in your power to fulfill all your official obligations. How do you get along without a knowledge of the French language? Are you acquiring it?

I have heard from home frequently since I left it. John [Morrison Clay] had taken a short hunt in the mountains, but returned without much success. Thomas [Hart Clay] had gone down the Ohio to see about his Saw Mill and is still there. All were well. Dr. Jacob[5] is now here from Louisville. His brother with his wife[6] have gone to Missouri, where he has purchased another farm. You have said nothing, nor did Susan, about Henry Clay [III] or Thomas Jacobs [*sic*, Jacob].

Give my love to Susan and all your children, and to the boys. I will write to her as soon as I am a little relieved from company &c.

I hope you will adhere to your good resolution of living within your Salary. From what you state about your large establishment, I am afraid that you will exceed that prudent limit. How did your predecessor in that particular? I believe he was not a man of any wealth.

ALS. DLC-TJC (DNA, M212, R11). Printed in Colton, *Clay Correspondence*, 4:590-91. 1. Clay to James B. Clay, Oct. 15, 1849. 2. Clay to Lucretia Hart Clay, Dec. 5, 1849. 3. For George W. Hopkins (1804-61)—lawyer, Virginia congressman, and J.B. Clay's predecessor as chargé d'affaires to Portugal—see *BDAC*. 4. Clay to Clayton, June 7, 1849. 5. According to the Jacob Family Papers, located at the Filson Club Historical Society in Louisville, Susan's brother William R. Jacob was a physician. However, family genealogies list his birthdate as 1829, making it unusual for him to have been a doctor at this time. He practiced in Louisville most of the time until his death in 1867. Information supplied by Dr. James J. Holmberg, curator of manuscripts, Filson Club. 6. Richard T. and Sara Benton Jacob. See Clay to James B. Clay, Jan. 16, 1848.

To LUCRETIA HART CLAY Washington, December 5, 1849

I transmit you the enclosed letter from James [Brown Clay] which I thought you might like to read.[1]

I am still stopping at the Nat. Hotel, where I shall probably remain.

Two days have passed without any choice of a Speaker,[2] and no one can foresee when or how the house is to be organized.

I wish, my dear, that you or John [Morrison Clay] would keep a registry of the Calves that may drop from my blooded Cows. The Durhams are again getting up in value at the Eastward as well as with us. I am anxious about Io,[3] and I hope she will not be neglected.

My love to John.

ALS. DLC-TJC (DNA, M212, R11). 1. Enclosure not found. 2. In the 31st Cong., 1st Sess., Democrats controlled the Senate by a margin of 10. The House was composed of 112 Democrats, and 105 Whigs, with 13 Free Soilers holding the balance of power. Southern Whigs, led by Alexander Stephens and Robert Toombs, opposed the Whig candidate for Speaker, Robert C. Winthrop, because the Whig caucus had refused to pledge opposition to the Wilmot Proviso. Free Soilers opposed Winthrop because they thought he had not given adequate recognition to antislavery spokesmen during his previous tenure as Speaker. After three weeks and 63 ballots, Democrat Howell Cobb (Ga.) was finally elected Speaker on Dec. 22, 1849. These debates were marked by threats of disunion which further divided the Northern and Southern wings of the Whig party. Morris, *Encyclopedia of American History*, 210; Hamilton, *Zachary Taylor, Soldier in the*

White House, 244-52. For Cobb, see *DAB*; *BDAC*. 3. Io was a Durham cow imported by Henry Clay, Jr. Perrin, *History of Fayette County*, 185.

From JOHN M. CLAYTON Washington, December 6, 1849

I think you will be pleased as I have been, with the persual of the accompanying despatch to Count Tojal[1] by our Minister at Lisbon [James B. Clay]. Is it not a conclusive argument on the [*General*] Armstrong question?[2]

I have been so much engaged that I have not been able to call even for a minute. P.S. Please, Return the despatch as soon as you have had full time to read it.

ALS. DLC-TJC (DNA, M212, R11). Letter marked "(Confidential)." 1. For Count Tojal, Portugal's minister of foreign affairs, see Bemis, *American Secretaries of State*, 6:34. 2. Clay to Clayton, June 7, 1849.

To Robert G. Scott *et al.*, Richmond [?], Va., December 8, 1849. Regrets that his public duties will not allow him to attend the annual meeting of the Virginia Colonization Society. Asserts that he feels "the liveliest interest in the African colonization of the free people of color in the United States" and has had "all my original impressions in favor of the scheme strengthened and confirmed by successful experience." Believes the program is "susceptible of an expansion so as to colonize, in reasonable time, all the colored people of the United States now free, or who may be hereafter emancipated." Copy. Printed in Washington *Daily National Intelligencer*, December 31, 1849. For Scott, see 5:637.

To LESLIE COMBS Washington, December 10, 1849

I am very sorry to learn by your letter of the 5h. inst. that the Smallpox exists in Lexington;[1] and I shall be very uneasy until I hear more about it, and hear from home, which I have not done.

I send for your Son in law a general letter of recommendation.[2] I have occasionally given to others similar letters, which they have found useful. They are better than particular letters of introduction, because these are delivered to their respective addresses, whilst those are retained.

You were not more surprized than I was at the nomination of James W[atson]. Webb to a foreign mission.[3]

There is much and general complaint against the Administration by the Whig members who have arrived here.[4] I cannot say whether it is well or ill founded.

No Speaker. Two ballots today gave similar results to those of saturday.[5]

ALS. InHi. 1. The smallpox epidemic in Lexington had reached such severity that on Dec. 1, 1849, Mayor O.F. Payne issued an ordinance declaring that a hospital had been established to receive those infected, and if any of the ill refused to go to the hospital, guards would be posted around their houses to insure a quarantine. Lexington *Observer & Kentucky Reporter*, Dec. 8, 1849. 2. Recommendation not found; Combs had several sons-in-law. 3. Webb was appointed chargé d'affaires to Austria, but he was not confirmed by the Senate. *DAB*. 4. Complaints concerned patronage. See Clay to Christopher, April 19, 1849; Clay to Bayard, Dec. 14, 1849. 5. Clay to Lucretia H. Clay, Dec. 5, 1849.

To Charles Lanman, New York City, December 12, 1849. Thanks him "for the volume of his letters from the Alleghany [*sic*, Allegheny] Mountains, and for the assurance . . . of his continued esteem and regard." Copy. Henry Clay Memorial Foundation, Lexington, Ky.

Lanman's book, *Letters From the Alleghany Mountains*, had been published in New York in 1849.

To MARY S. BAYARD Washington, December 14, 1849

I received, my dear friend, with great pleasure your kind letter of Tuesday evening. And I am glad that you derived gratification from the demonstrations of attachment to me, on the part of the public, which accompanied me on my journey from Philada.[1] and greeted my arrival here. Too much accustomed to these things, I receive them without much emotion, and perhaps exhibit too much sensibility to the personal inconvenience to which they sometimes expose me.

I look back with great satisfaction to the quiet and agreeable days I passed in Walnut Street. I should be most happy if I could go back to Walnut Street or could bring it here. You appear to fear that all was not done to promote my comfort, during my sojourn with you. I assure you that there was no omission in that respect, and that I could not have been more comfortably or agreeably provided for and entertained.

I am afraid, my dear friend, that you allow yourself to be too much affected by the condition of Mr. and Mrs. [Baring] Powell.[2] That you should feel much on account of it; and that she should be greatly distressed, is quite natural; but neither she nor you have any cause of self-reproach. It is a great misfortune, if you please, but one which he has brought on himself, and for which the remedy is in his own hands. I hope that he will have the resolution and the fortitude to apply it. I have seen him several times, and Mr. Preston, who seems to take a deep interest in him, gives me encouraging accounts of him. But, if he will not reform, if the great attractions of his charming wife will not prompt him to render himself worthy of her, let the worst come that can come, I hope that there is yet in reserve for her many years of happiness.

In every other respect you have abundant cause of congratulations and felicity—in your husband [Richard H. Bayard], in your children, in your warm friends, and in the esteem and admiration of a wide circle of acquaintances. I am afraid that I might make you vain if I were to tell you all the fine things that are said of you, whenever, as often, you are the subject of conversation between our common friends and me.

I am, perhaps, permanently located at the Nat. Hotel, where I have a good parlour and bedroom opening into each other. I miss my Secretary very much, and should be very glad if I could occasionally have the benefit of her official services. I am to have as some of my near neighbours the British Minister & his family, who have engaged apartments in this Hotel.[3]

I wrote to Mr. Bayard yesterday, but as it was a business letter I did not touch on public affairs; and therefore you will communicate to him what I may now say on that subject.

There is great and general complaint, among the Whigs from all parts, against the Administration.[4] It is founded chiefly on the character of appointments. I dined with the President [Zachary Taylor] yesterday and I found an opportunity, although the Company was large, to tell him of this dissatisfaction. He appeared to be aware of it, and thought it arose out of an inordinate pursuit of office. I spoke of [James W.] Webbs appointment[.][5] He said it was forced on him by N. York &c. I do not think that he has any thought of a change in his Cabinet. He is to inform me when we can have a long interview. Owing to my Cold, I have declined dining with [John M.] Clayton and Reve[r]dy Johnson. I called at the Department of State on an official matter, and I thought the Secretary [Clayton] would never let me get away, telling me of all his official troubles and difficulties, professing to want my advice &c. I finally had to break away from him. I have seen [Thomas] Ewing and [William] Meredith, and had some confidential communications from the latter. I have not yet been here long enough to explore the whole ground. Upon the whole there is a very uncomfortable state of things here both for the Whig party, and I fear for the Country. From both parties, or rather from individuals of both parties, strong expressions are made to me of hopes that I may be able to calm the raging elements.[6] I wish I could, but fear I cannot, realize their hopes.

I request you to send the enclosed to Dr. Herring. . . .

ALS. DeHi. 1. For Clay's itinerary to Washington, see Clay to James B. Clay, Oct. 15, 1849. 2. Reference obscure. 3. William Henry Lytton Earle Bulwer, usually known as Sir Henry L. Bulwer, was minister to the U.S. from 1849-52. His wife Georgiana Charlotte Mary Wellesley was a niece of the Duke of Wellington. *DNB*. 4. Clay to Christopher, April 19, 1849. 5. Clay to Combs, Dec. 10, 1849. 6. Reference is to the issue of slavery in the territories. For Clay's attempts to initiate a compromise, see espec. Clay to Combs, Jan. 22, 1850; Speech in Senate, Jan. 29, 1850.

To SUSAN JACOB CLAY Washington, December 15, 1849

I received and read with great pleasure your letter of the 19th. Oct. All its details of information were agreeable to me, and I hope you will continue to write to me and to communicate every thing, the minutest circumstance concerning yourself or your dear family. I have taken apartments at the National Hotel (a parlour & bed room adjoining) for the winter. I have an excellent Valet, a freeman [James Marshall], and I am as comfortable as I can be. No advance has been yet made in Congress, in the public business, owing to the House, from its divided condition, being yet unable to elect a Speaker.[1] When that will be done is uncertain; but I suppose from the absolute necessity of the case there will be before long one chosen.

I have been treated with much consideration by the President [Zachary Taylor] and most of his Cabinet; but I have had yet no very confidential intercourse with the President. I dined with him this week, and I have been invited to dine with two members of the Cabinet, but declined on account of a very bad cold.[2] Mr. [John M.] Clayton sent me James's [Brown Clay] diplomatic note to the Portuguese minister [Count Tojal] on the case of the Genl Armstrong, with the enclosed note from himself.[3] James's note has been well spoken of by the Atto. General [Reverdy Johnson] to me, and I think it creditable[.] There are some clerical inaccuracies in it, which ought to be avoided in future Copies of his official notes. James might have added, in respect to the practice of impressment that "the Portuguese Secretary, in volunteering a sanction of it, has extended the British claim, now become obsolete, beyond any limit to which it was ever asserted by G. Britain herself, she never having pretended that she could exercise the practice within the Territorial jurisdiction of a third or neutral power, or any where but on the High seas or in her own ports."

I understood from Clayton that it was intended by the President to submit to Congress the conduct of the Portuguese Government, without recommending, at present, any measure of coercion. It is desirable to get the answer to James s note, as soon as practicable, if one be returned.

I have heard from Ashland as late as the 10h. instant. All the whites were well; but there had been a number of cases of small pox in Lexn.[4] and one of our black men had caught it, but he was getting well. Think of your present enjoyment of a delightful climate and tropical fruits, when there fell at Lexington on the 10h. inst. a snow six or eight inches deep!

Your brother, the Dr. [William R. Jacob] has returned to Louisville.[5]

You said nothing in your letter to me about Thomas [Jacob], Henry Clay [III], or my dear Lucy [Jacob Clay] and your other children. Is Henry going to school and where?

I believe I did not mention in my former letters to James that Lucretia Erwin has determined to take the Black Veil.[6]

I send herewith a letter from Mary Anne's husband[.][7]

My love to James and to all the family[.]

ALS. DLC-TJC (DNA, M212, R11). Printed in Colton, *Clay Correspondence*, 4:591-93. 1. Clay to Lucretia H. Clay, Dec. 5, 1849. 2. Clay to Bayard, Dec. 14, 1849. 3. Clay to Clayton, June 7, 1849; Clayton to Clay, Dec. 6, 1849. 4. Clay to Combs, Dec. 10, 1849. 5. Clay to James B. Clay, Dec. 4, 1849. 6. Clay to Erwin, Oct. 27, 1849. 7. Letter not found. Mary Anne possibly refers to Susan's sister Mrs. John W. Tyler, whose first name was Mary; however, the middle name has not been confirmed. Information supplied by Dr. James J. Holmberg, Filson Club, Louisville, Ky.

Remark in Senate, December 18, 1849. Just prior to the election of committee chairmen, although "ready to perform any share of the labor which must attach to me as a member of this body," would be "highly gratified if the Senate would have the goodness to excuse me from serving on any of the committees." Supposes, however, that "there is not much danger" that he would be assigned "a laborious post . . . such as chairman of a committee." *Cong. Globe*, 31 Cong., 1 Sess., 39-40. Clay was not appointed to a standing committee. *Ibid.*, 45.

Remark in Senate, December 20, 1849. In response to Sen. Jeremiah Clemens's opposition to a resolution extending the privilege of the floor to Father Theobald Mathew [Speech to Hibernian Society, March 17, 1848], temperance and anti-slavery advocate, wonders "in a spirit of the most perfect kindness, to the honorable Senator from Alabama, whether this pushing the subject of slavery in its collateral and remote branches upon all possible occasions . . . is not impolitic, unwise, and injurious to the stability of the very institution which I have no doubt the honorable gentleman would uphold." Although he has "seen something in the papers upon this subject of Father Mathew's having expressed some opinions years ago, in Ireland, upon the subject of slavery," points out, with satisfaction, that "when he came to this country, and got a nearer and more accurate understanding of the state of things, he refused to lend himself to the cause of the northern abolitionists," and therefore has "incurred their severest animadversions." Hopes that the compliment will be extended to Father Mathew as "due to him for his great services in the cause of humanity" and "as an Irish patriot." *Cong. Globe*, 31 Cong., 1 Sess., 51. Printed in Colton, *Clay Correspondence*, 6:392-93. For Sen. Clemens (Dem., Alabama), see *BDAC*.

Both houses of Congress extended Father Mathew the privilege of the floor on December 20. The following day he left Washington for a trip to the South. Washington *Daily National Intelligencer*, December 21, 1849.

To THOMAS B. STEVENSON Washington, December 21, 1849

I received your favor of the 13th inst. I abstain from making any expression of sympathy in your present unemployed situation. *You* know that it is not necessary. Before & since I recd. your letter I conversed with Mr [Thomas] Corwin about you & assured him of my readiness to cooperate with him in serving you. He informed me, contrary to your expectations that he had no *specific* office or place in view; but meant to embrace the first occasion that presented itself. I told him to let me know if any thing occurred, and that I too would keep a look out. Such is the exact state of the matter. I am sorry that it is not more encouraging.

My relations to the President [Zachary Taylor] & his Cabinet are Civil and amicable, but with all of them not very confidential.

There is great and bitter complaint against the Adm"on from all the Whigs, or nearly all.[1] I do not know what is to come of it.

My health, my spirits, and my position, all are very good. Much deference and consideration are shown me by even political opponents. I shall by a course of calmness, moderation and dignity endeavor to preserve these kindly feelings.

At present I have no plans or projects to offer.[2] I shall seize however any exigency that may arise to do good if I can. . . .

Copy. OCHP. Printed in Colton, *Clay Correspondence*, 3:497, with first paragraph omitted. 1. Clay to Christopher, April 19, 1849; Clay to Bayard, Dec. 14, 1849. 2. See below espec. Clay to Combs, Jan. 22, 1850; Speech in Senate, Jan. 29, 1850.

To Daniel Ullmann, New York City, December 21, 1849. Asserts his belief that "the objection to the Collr. of Wilmington is not so much to him as to the manner that his immediate predecessor was constrained to resign." ALS. NHi.

President James K. Polk had nominated Henry Hicks to be collector at Wilmington on December 29, 1845, to replace Arnold Naudain. Hicks was confirmed on January 3, 1846, and served until President Taylor nominated William P. Brobson on January 9, 1850. Brobson died, however, and on February 21 Taylor nominated Charles Polk who was confirmed on March 1. U.S. Sen., *Executive Journal*, 7:12, 24; 8:115, 143, 146.

To LESLIE COMBS Washington, December 22, 1849

I received your favor of the 17th inst. and thank you for its details. It seems that I have lost my negro man [Edward] by the smallpox. I hope the measures taken will arrest its progress.[1]

My object in writing you now is one of great importance, and *I wish you to lead off in it.* It will do the country good and do you good.

The feeling for disunion, among some intemperate Southern politicians, is stronger than I supposed it could be.[2] The masses generally, even at the South, are I believe, yet sound; but they may become inflamed and perverted. The best counteraction of that feeling is to be derived from popular expression at public meetings of the people. Now, what I should like to see is such meetings held throughout Kentucky; for you must know that the di[s]unionists, count upon the co-operation of our patriotic State. Can't you get up a large, powerful meeting of both parties, if possible, at Lexington, at Louisville, &c., to express in strong language their determination to stand by the Union?[3] I hope the Legislature and the [Kentucky Constitutional]

Convention also, if it has not been adjourned, may do the same.[4] If you remain silent and passive, there is danger that the bad feeling may reach you. Now is the time for salutary action and *you are the man to do it.* I inclose some resolutions[5] which, or some similar to them, I should be happy to see adopted.

Prudence and propriety will suggest to you that too free a use of my name should not be made in getting up this movement. You will know the persons to counsel with, and I wish you to keep me advised of what you do.[6]

Copy. Printed in the Louisville *Daily Journal,* July 21, 1860; also in Colton, *Clay Correspondence,* 4:593. 1. The last two sentences of this paragraph were omitted by the Louisville *Journal* but appear in Colton. For the smallpox epidemic, see Clay to Combs, Dec. 10, 1849. 2. A movement was underway to hold a convention of slave states in 1850 to promote Southern unity and declare their rights in the territorial controversy. The Nashville Convention, held in June 1850, endorsed extension of the Missouri Compromise line of 36 degrees 30 minutes to the Pacific Ocean and provided for another session of the convention to meet after the ending of the current session of Congress. By the time the second session met, the Compromise of 1850 had been adopted, dampening the fires of the extremists. See Thelma Jennings, *The Nashville Convention, Southern Movement for Unity, 1848-1851* (Memphis, 1980). 3. Numerous unionist meetings were held around the state during the next several months, including one at Lexington on June 1. Lexington *Observer & Kentucky Reporter,* Feb. 9, 23, March 16, 1850; Lexington *The Kentucky Statesman,* June 5, 1850. See also Comment in Senate, June 6, 1850. 4. Although the Kentucky Constitutional convention had adjourned on Dec. 21, 1849, it reconvened after voters accepted the new constitution. On June 10, 1850, resolutions supporting the compromise proposals pending before the Congress were submitted by the delegates to the constitutional convention. Frankfort *Commonwealth,* June 18, 1850. The Kentucky legislature successfully resisted efforts to get it to endorse the Nashville Convention. Jennings, *The Nashville Convention,* 77; Arthur C. Cole, *The Whig Party in the South* (Washington, D.C., 1913), 61. See also Remark in Senate, June 20, 1850. 5. These resolutions were: "1. *Resolved,* That this meeting is firmly attached to the union of these States, and that they go for it, one and indivisible, now and forever. 2. *Resolved,* That whilst this meeting would be most happy that the controverted question of slavery within the Territory recently acquired from Mexico, should be settled in a manner satisfactory to all parts of the Union, no settlement of it, whatever it may be, will create any just occasion for dissolving the Union. 3. *Resolved,* That this meeting beholds, in the dissolution of our glorious Union, no remedy for any alleged evils, real or imaginary, but a great aggravation of them all, and contemplate that deplorable event as the parent of other calamities, far transcending in magnitude and fatal consequences any of which complaint is now made. 4. *Resolved,* That, as far as depends upon us, we will stand by, support, and uphold the Union, against all attacks from without or within, and against all ultraism, whether at the North or the South." Printed in Louisville *Daily Journal,* July 21, 1860. 6. Colton adds: "[This advice was acted on and carried out.]" See also Clay to James B. Clay, March 6, 1850.

From Sylvester Schenck, Auburn, N.Y., December 24, 1849. As "a delegate" who "voted twice for your nomination as a candidate for president," discusses "the secret agencies and underhanded plotting against you . . . by certain aspiring politicians in this state." Offers "tangible proof of the precise acts, and precise language, which has been used in reference to yourself, by one who has at last secured a seat by your side in the United States Senate [William Henry Seward]."

As a "friend of yours . . . I was named by your friends and mine as a candidate for delegate" to the Whig National convention in 1848. Reports that "Gov [William H.] Seward . . . tried to defeat my nomination, by urging leading politicians, and among others our County Clerk, to go against me, for no other reason than because I was known to be in favor of your nomination." After Schenck's election, "Seward came personally . . . to converse with me upon the subject of my vote." He informed Seward "that I was a Clay man, and that the convention that appointed me, expected me to vote for you." Reports Seward's reply: " 'If Clay should be nominated, and elected, he will be under the control of Willis Hall and that class of politicians and it will be no better for us than if the opposite party should succeed.' " Adds that "Seward went on to develop his feelings in regard to you in a manner that satisfied me, that he was not only hostile to you then, but that the charges made against him in 1844, of want of fidelity to you were true." Believes that since Seward is now "an aspirant himself for the Presidency, and is now engaged in divising ways and means to reach it . . . you ought to have the evidence at command, of his conduct towards you." Wishes this letter to remain confidential, "but should the remark in quotation find its way into the public prints, and be denied, I will attest the truth of it by my sworn affidavit." ALS. DLC-HC (DNA, M212, R6).

See Greeley to Clay, November 30, 1847; Wendell to Clay, March 11, 1848. Seward had been elected to the U.S. Senate in 1849. *BDAC*.

To THOMAS HART CLAY Washington, December 25, 1849

I received a letter from you while you were with Henry Wilkins [*sic*, Henry Watkins],[1] at your saw-mill, but none since. I expected to have heard of your return home, and to have gotten a letter from you, ere now; but I suppose that you have been detained below longer than you expected. I shall be glad to hear from you, the prospects of your mill, etc.

I am afraid that your mother [Lucretia H. Clay] and John [Morrison Clay] have had much trouble and anxiety at Ashland. The loss of my man [Edward] by the small-pox, and the fear of its spreading must have given them much uneasiness.[2] It has become necessary to purchase or hire two additional hands for the farm. I should prefer the latter, and I have so written to John. I wish you would give him all the assistance you can in procurring them. His mill, too, has got out of order; but I hope that he has been able to get a millwright to repair.

Give my love and the compliments of the season to Mary [Mentelle Clay] and the children.

Copy. Printed in Colton, *Clay Correspondence*, 4:594. 1. Subsequent manuscript letters concerning the sawmill give the name as Henry Watkins. He was the son of Clay's half-brother John Watkins and his wife Caroline Milton Watkins. Henry was born in Woodford County, Ky., on Jan. 4, 1813, and died in Florida in 1888. Jane McMurtry Allen, *Henry Watkins of Henrico County, His Descendants and Their Allied Families* (Baltimore, 1985), 38. 2. Clay to Combs, Dec. 10, 1849.

To Henry Grinnell, New York City, December 25, 1849. Intends to vote for confirmation "of the appointment of Mr. [Hugh D.] Maxwell, as Collector of your port. . . . unless I should hereafter hear something against him, which ought, in my judgment, to change that intention." Regrets Maxwell's "appointment of his son to an important place under him, meritorious as I suppose that son to be. For nepotism is carried, in this Country, by some public functionaries, too many, to a reprehensible extent." ALS. Courtesy of Dr. Thomas D. Clark, Lexington, Ky.

Hugh Maxwell was officially nominated for collector for the port of New York on January 16, 1850, and was confirmed on September 26. U.S. Sen., *Executive Journal*, 8:122, 211, 253.

To THOMAS HART CLAY Washington, December 27, 1849

I received you letter of the 18h. inst. and I am glad that you have got home. The cost of your Saw Mill &c has greatly exceeded your expectations; but I hope that it may notwithstanding realize your calculations.

I send you, by way of loan to you, a check on N. York for $450, which is worth at least half per Cent advance in Lexington. I shall want the money next summer or fall.

I have not heard from John [Morrison Clay] lately. If you hire out Charles Lilly[1] I should like to get him, and would give for him as much as you can get from any body else[.] John could make a foreman of him; and you may tell Charles that I will give him some thing liberal.

My love to Mary [Mentelle Clay] & your children.

ALS. DLC-HC (DNA, M212, R6). 1. A slave.

To LUCRETIA HART CLAY Washington, December 28, 1849

I have been disappointed in not hearing from John [Morrison Clay]. I remitted to him two Checks, one for a $100 and the other for $150 and I have not heard of the receipt of either. The last letter I received from him mentioned the death of Edward by the Small pox,[1] and I have been afraid that it would extend and be caught by some of the young negroes at Ashland; but I hope that the measures of precaution which you adopted will prevent its spreading.

I wrote to Thomas [Hart Clay] yesterday,[2] and sent him a Check for $450 on loan, which I hope will assist him out of his difficulties. I now enclose a check also for $450 which I have made payable to John. I wish it sold in Lexington, where it ought to bring $452:25 at the least, and the proceeds deposited to my credit at the N[orthern]. Bank in Lexington. These two sums, making together $900 I received from Illinois on account of my land sold there.[3]

I have written to Thomas that I wish to get Charles Lilly[4] for the ensuing year. If he be obtained, we shall want but another man for the farm, and he can be hired. If however a good one can be purchased the funds I have sent, and now send, will enable him to be purchased. I think, from my pay this Session, I shall be able to save one thousand dollars, as I am resolved to practice all the economy I can with propriety.

There[5] is a bundle of papers in my office upstairs, enclosed in a paste-board paper and tyed up with Tape, containing the letters from Genl [Zachary] Taylor to me. Among them is one from him to me, dated at Monterey in Mexico, I think, in Septr. 1847.[6] He and I differ about the contents of that letter, and I wish you would find it, and get Thomas to make and send me a neat copy of it, and put up the original back again where you find it.

I[7] have bought, since I came Eastward, half a dozen shirts, and half a dozen pocket handkerchiefs. I find James[8] a very good servant. He has left me for a few days to go to Virginia to see his relations.

I am still staying at the Nat. Hotel, where I have a good parlour and bed room, for which and my board I pay thirty dollars per week. The British Minister [Henry L. Bulwer] occupies rooms near mine, and I yesterday dined with him. He has his wife [Georgiana Wellesley Bulwer] with him, a niece of the Duke of Wellington, a plain, but sensible person.

I have dined with the President, but declined to dine with [John M.] Clayton & Reverdy Johnson, on account of a bad Cold. These people are all civil with me but nothing more. From every body, of both parties, I receive friendly attentions and kind consideration.

My love to John.

ALS. DLC-TJC (DNA, M212, R11). Partially printed in Colton, *Clay Correspondence*, 4:594-95. 1. For the smallpox epidemic, see Clay to Combs, Dec. 10, 1849. Edward was a slave. See Clay to Combs, Dec. 22, 1849. 2. Clay to Thomas H. Clay, Dec. 27, 1849. 3. Clay to Bailhache, May 14, 1847. 4. Clay to Thomas H. Clay, Dec. 27, 1849. 5. Colton's version begins with this paragraph. 6. Taylor to Clay, Nov. 4, 1847. See also Clay to Thomas

H. Clay, Jan. 12, 1850. 7. Colton omits this paragraph. 8. James Marshall was a free black Clay hired to be his bodyservant.

To JAMES BROWN CLAY Washington, December 29, 1849

I received your letter, communicating an account of Susan's [Jacob Clay] confinement, and I was delighted to hear that she had given birth to a Son [Henry "Harry" Clay], with so little of pain and suffering.[1] I hope that she has continued to do well, and that the new comer has also been hearty. In the fine climate where you are, I trust that all your family enjoy good health.

I hear from home but not as often as I could wish. John [Morrison Clay][2] is lazy, and his mother [Lucretia Hart Clay] never writes. They have had in Lexington several cases of Small pox, which was caught by my negro man Edward,[3] whom you bought for me last year and he has died.

Thomas [Hart Clay] after six or seven weeks absence from home to set his Saw Mill at Trinity[4] has returned to Mansfield, full of hopes but finding that it had cost him nearly double as much as he had expected. He seems to be in good spirits.

After three weeks, Mr [Howell] Cobb of Georgia,[5] a democrat, was elected Speaker, and it was so much more important that the house should be organized than that whether Whig or Democrat should be chosen, that I was glad an election was made. Nothing of importance has yet been done in Congress[.]

The Portuguese Minister[6] called on me to day, and I had a long, long interview with him, both on matters personally relating to you, and on public affairs, the latter of course confidentially.

He tells me that you have a fine house and a delightful situation on the Tagus, with a beautiful prospect &c, but that they made you pay too much rent for it.

I endeavored to impress him very seriously about our claims on Portugal,[7] and that their rejection might lead to very grave consequences. I authorized him, to communicate what I said to him to the Minister of Foreign affairs [Count Tojal].[8] He read to me a very ingenious and plausible argument in the case of the Genl. Armstrong,[9] but I told him that I thought it only ingenious and plausible, and that I thought the American claim was well founded. One of his points was that the Genl A. *began* the conflict. To which I replied that the British boats approached the A. in hostile array; and that, when hailed, refusing to name whether their purposes were amicable or hostile, the A. was not bound to wait until they struck the first blow, but being authorized to conclude that their purpose was to board & capture her, she had a right to defend herself and anticipate the fall of the blow. Exactly as, when an assault is made on a man, not yet followed by a battery, he is not bound to await the battery but may defend himself forthwith.

As to the weakness of Portugal. Since the treaty of Methuen,[10] she has been an ally, and somewhat dependent on G. Britain. Her feelings and sympathies were with the British and against the Armstrong. She not only did not protect the A. which as a Neutral power she ought to have done but she did nothing to repel the British violation of her jurisdiction. She did worse, when the crew of the A. was brought on shore, she (Portugal) suffered and connived at their being mustered by or in presence of British officers that they might select from the array those whom they chose to consider British

Seamen! Never was such an indignity before offered! Never before or since did G. Britain attempt to exercise her pretended right of impressment within the jurisdictional limits of a neutral or third power, or anywhere but in her own ports or on the high seas.

The Portuguese Minister cited certain provisions of our treaty with G.B. in 1794[11] and other treaties, making provision for the case of captures within the waters of the respective parties by a belligerent of either of them &c. To all which I replied, that those treaties took the case from without the operation of the general public law; but did not affect the condition of powers (of which Portugal was one) having no such treaties with us; that as to these powers the National law furnished the rate; and that in cases like the A. that rule required either protection or indemnity. Protection had not been afforded and indemnity was therefore justly due.

My manner was intentionally very earnest; and I sought to impress the Minister with the belief I entertain that if satisfaction of our claims be withheld it will be sought for by coercion. And I told him that I should be grieved if we had any war with Portugal, especially when my son was the accredited representative of the U.S. at Lisbon. I told him that I hoped he would impress his Government with the gravity of existing circumstances. He was hurt at the reference in the Presidents [Zachary Taylor] message to this affair;[12] but I informed him that I had reason to believe that, at one time, it was contemplated to refer to it much more seriously, and I supposed this had not been done in consequence of a hope entertained that your despatches might soon bring the welcome intelligence that our claims had been admitted & provided for.

He spoke of a proposition before the Portuguese Cortes to elevate the grade of the mission to this Country. I told him that the adjustment of our claims would be an agreeable, if not indispensable preliminary to a similar elevation of the rank of our Minister to Portugal &c.

I presume that they will send you from the Dept of State the P[residential] message and all other public documents.

My love to Susan, to dear little Lucy [Jacob Clay] and all your children and to H. Clay [III] and Thomas [Jacob].

ALS. DLC-HC (DNA, M212, R6). Printed in Colton, *Clay Correspondence*, 4:595-97. 1. James B. Clay to Clay, Nov. 27, 1849. 2. The remainder of this paragraph and the next are omitted by Colton. 3. Clay to Combs, Dec. 10, 1849. 4. Clay to James B. Clay, Oct. 15, 1849. 5. Clay to Lucretia H. Clay, Dec. 5, 1849. 6. For J.C. de Figaniere e Morao, Portuguese minister to the U.S., see *Grande Enciclopedia Portuguesa e Brasiliera* (Lisbon, 1940). 7. Clay to Clayton, June 7, 1849. 8. In an undated note, written in Dec., 1849, Clay suggested to James that he read to the Minister of Foreign Affairs "passages from my letter to show the serious apprehensions entertained here." He is also warned that "you should observe the greatest courtesy, and speak gravely with[ou]t threatening." AN. DLC-TJC (DNA, M212, R11). Dating based on Clay to Susan J. Clay, Dec. 15, 1849. 9. Clay to Clayton, June 7, 1849. 10. In the Methuen Treaty of Dec. 27, 1703, England agreed to admit Portuguese wines at duties 1/3 less than those imposed upon French wines and Portugal agreed to import all woolens from England. Parry, *Treaty Series*, 25:37-43. 11. For the Jay Treaty, signed on Nov. 19, 1794, at London, see *ibid.*, 52:243-72. 12. In his first annual message on Dec. 4, 1849, Taylor had announced that the mission to Portugal to do justice on American claims had "assumed a character so grave and serious" that he would soon make it the subject of a special message to Congress. *MPP*, 5:12-13.

From "Georgia Pen," Washington, D.C., December 29, 1849. On the subject of slavery, writes to refute the idea claimed "by some of the great men of the South . . . that the Bible tolerates slavery." Notes that the "very essence of slavery, is that the slave shall produce by his labor so much more than he receives for his own maintenance as to support the master and his family. . . . The advantage of the system is supposed to be that the master is not obliged to work at all. The amount which the slave receives is not presumed to be what is a fair equivalent for what he does, or what a freeman could be hired for." Thus, the system is contrary to the book of James, chapter 5, verse 4: " 'Behold, the hire of the laborers who have reaped down your fields,' " because "He who hires a freeman to reap down his fields pays what the freeman regards as a fair equivalent for what he does; he who employs a slave does not give . . . an equivalent." Therefore, "the very essence of slavery . . . is fraud."

Asks that this letter be sent to some newspaper editors so that it can be "spread before the American people." Adds: "Ere this reaches you, I shall be in the South, where the slave-whip will be heard instead of morning prayers to summon me to the field of toil. While I march up and down the long rows in the cotton fields, the American Congress will be passing laws to bind us faster. . . . P.S. If your should ever hear from my wife and children, bid them farewell for me." Copy. Printed in Boston *The Liberator*, January 11, 1850.

From John J. Jacob, Louisville, December 30, 1849. Reports receiving "a letter from yr son James [Brown Clay] . . . informing me of Susan's [Jacob Clay] confinement and safe delivery of a grand Son [James B. Clay to Clay, November 27, 1849]." Expresses concern over "My letters from Lisbon," which "complain very much of not hearing from any of us at home altho' a half a dozen letters at least have been written. . . . Yet my Son Th[oma]s. [Jacob] says in his last letter to me that not one letter has been recd." Although he has followed instructions "to forward all letters and communications . . . thro the department of State W[ashington]. City," asks Clay to ensure that the enclosed letter to James is forwarded "thro' the Dep. of State or in any other manner you may think proper—so that it will reach its destination." ALS. DLC-TJC (DNA, M212, R11).

To JAMES BROWN CLAY

Washington, January 2, 1849 [*sic*, 1850]

I received your letter of the 27h. Novr and I was happy to hear of the continued health of Susan [Jacob Clay] and your children, and especially that she had so easy an accouchement.[1] That was the result of her previous exercise & the climate of Lisbon.

I am sorry to hear of the bad prospect of your getting our claims satisfied. I wrote you a few days ago, giving a long account of an interview which I had with the Portuguese minister [J.C. de Figaniere e Morao] &c about the case of the Genl Armstrong[.][2] In the course of it he told me that he thought some of our claims were just, and so did the Minister of F[oreign]. affairs [Count Tojal], and that they would be paid. If we are to come to any appeal to force, perhaps, it will be as well that they should reject them all, those which are clearly just, as well as those which are contestible. But, as it would be a feather in you cap, I should like that you would get them allowed or as many as you can.

The Minister told me that the owners of the Genl Armstrong demanded \$250.000. That sum strikes me to be enormous. If they agree to admit the claim you might stipulate to have the amount fixed by some commission; or, which would be better, if the owners have an agent at Lisbon, you might get him to fix the very lowest sum which they would be willing to receive, which might not exceed one fifth of the sum demanded.

I mentioned confidentially to Sir H[enry]. Bulwer, the British Minister, my apprehensions of a difficulty with Portugal, and he said that he would write to Lord Palmerston,[3] and suggest to him to interpose his good offices &c[.] He told me that a brother of Lord Morpeth was the British Chargé at Portugal.[4] If he resembles his brother you will find him a clever fellow.

No certain developements are yet made of what Congress may do on the vexed subject of slavery. I think there is a considerable majority in the House, and probably one in the Senate, in favor of the Wilmot Proviso.[5] I have been thinking much of proposing some comprehensive scheme of settling amicably the whole question, in all its bearings but I have not yet positively determined to do so.[6] Mean time some of the Hotspurs of the South are openly declaring themselves for a dissolution of the Union, if the Wilmot Proviso be adopted. This sentiment of disunion is more extensive than I had hoped, but I do not regard it as yet alarming. It does not reach many of the Slave States[.]

You complain of not hearing from K[entucky]. I have the same complaint. I have not recd. a letter from John [Morrison Clay] for a long time. My last was from Thomas [Hart Clay] of the 18h. Ulto. They were then all well.

I am glad to hear that Henry [Clay III] is placed at school, but am sorry that his defects continue to display themselves. We must hope that he will correct them as he grows older, and in the mean time console ourselves that his faults are not worse than they are.

My love to Susan, the boys [Thomas P. Jacob; Henry Clay III] and your children [James, John, Henry, Lucy].

ALS. DLC-TJC (DNA, M212, R11). Printed in Colton, *Clay Correspondence*, 4:582-83 under date 1849. 1. In the birth of Henry "Harry" Clay. 2. Clay to Clayton, June 7, 1849. 3. For Henry John Temple, Lord Palmerston, see *DNB*. 4. For Baron Howard de Walden (Charles Ellis), see Jasper Ridley, *Lord Palmerston* (London, 1970), 108, 112, 183, 185, *passim*. 5. For the Wilmot Proviso, see Sargent to Clay, Feb. 27, 1847. For the territorial/slavery controversy, see Clay to Stevenson, Dec. 19, 1848. 6. Clay to Combs, Jan. 22, 1850; Speech in Senate, Jan. 29, 1850.

To LUCRETIA HART CLAY Washington, January 2, 1850

Enclosed I send you the last letter I received from James [Brown Clay].[1] He complains that he gets no letters from Kentucky, and I have the same complaint. It is near a month since I received any letter from John [Morrison Clay]. I remitted him two checks one for $100 & the other for $150 and I have not heard of his receiving either. I sent to you a few days ago a check for $450, of the receipt of which I shall be glad to hear.

I attend yesterday (New year's day) at the Presidents Leveé. There was a vast throng. I shook hands with hundreds, and found myself an object of as much attraction as the President [Zachary Taylor] himself.

My general health is good; but colds still annoy me. I do not go out at night, and decline whenever I can invitations to dinner. I have been only to one formal one and that was at the Presidents.[2] I go to bed regularly at 10 OClock.

I am most anxious to hear from home. If John won't write, I wish Mary [Mentelle Clay] would. My love to him.

ALS. DLC-TJC (DNA, M212, R11). 1. James B. Clay to Clay, Nov. 27, 1849. 2. Clay to Lucretia H. Clay, Dec. 28, 1849.

To Henry Grinnell, New York City, January 2, 1850. Encloses a "letter to my son [James Brown Clay] which you will oblige me by forwarding." Comments that "The motives which led to the appointment of Mr. [Hugh] Maxwells son are strong. If the case stood alone, it would not provoke perhaps any animadversion; but unfortunately the instances of nepotism are shockingly numerous. Too many public functionaries seem to regard public office as a private estate, out of which they are to provide for members of their family [Clay to Grinnell, December 25, 1849]." ALS. Courtesy of Dr. Thomas D. Clark, Lexington, Ky.

Clay wrote Grinnell again on January 6, 1850, asking him to forward "a packet of letters from my son's wifes [Susan Jacob Clay] relation's, which I hope will arrive in time for the vessel bound for Lisbon." *Ibid.*

To JAMES PRATT

Washington, January 3, 1850

In answer to your letter,[1] I have to express my fears that the person to whom you refer, calling himself John Randolph, is an imposter. Like you, I believe, I subscribed for his promised Biography[2] of the late John Randolph of Va but a number of Circumstances induce me to apprehend that he is not worthy of confidence.

ALS. KyLoF. 1. Not found. 2. No such work appeared.

From Unknown Correspondent, Richmond, Va., *ca.* January 3, 1850. Suggests an "Amendment to the Constitution of the U.S." that contains two clauses. The first states that "Congress shall not abolish slavery in the District of Col. without the consent of Va. & Md." or "prohibit the transportation of slaves, from one slave state to another." The second clause requires Congress to pass laws "to prevent & punish the formation of any society, association, or assemblage of persons, in any state or territory, for the purpose of effecting the abolition of slavery, in any other state or territory," to punish "any attempt or act, made or done, by writing, printing or otherwise, in any state &c. to excite the slaves in any other state &c. to insurrection," to stop "the transmission by mail, or the delivery from post offices, of any printed paper, which may tend to excite servile insurrection," and to enable slaveowners "more effectually to recover slaves, which may have absconded from them and be found in another state." AD. OHi.

Comment in Senate, January 7, 1850. Responds to Sen. Lewis Cass, who had submitted a resolution to instruct the Committee on Foreign Relations "to inquire into the expediency of suspending diplomatic relations with Austria" in consequence of its war on Hungary, and had expressed "in very confident language, his expectation of my support." Wonders why such a "grave and serious proposition," which proposes not only "the recall of a minister of our own . . . but the sending out of the country the minister of Austria who is here [Chevalier Hulsemann]," requires "the shape of an inquiry. . . . All the facts upon which the honorable Senator bases his proposition are. . . . of an historical nature, not requiring the investigation of a committee."

Believing that "the question ought to be treated as if it were a direct proposition to suspend diplomatic intercourse" with Austria, explains why he cannot support such a move. If Cass's suggestion for "the recall of a little chargé d'affaires we happen to have at Vienna" is approved, fears that "the natural conclusion would be to declare war immediately against Austria." Finds, however, "another mode that is much more congenial, much more compatible with the course we ought to take. The exiles from suffering and bleeding Hungary are now scattered through all quarters of the globe; some have reached our hospitable shores, some are now wending their way hither, and many are scattered throughout Europe. Let the honorable Senator bring forward some original plan for affording succor and relief to the exiles of Hungary . . . something that shall be worthy of a country which is the asylum of the wretched and oppressed from all quarters of the world. . . . then he may call on me, and not in vain" for support.

Points out the great "incongruity between the premises of the honorable Senator and his conclusions." To recall the U.S. chargé would only "close the door of intercourse with Austria, by which we shall gain nothing in behalf of the suffering Hungarians." Reminds Cass that the British Parliament also determined "to keep open the door, and not suspend all intercourse with Austria." Moreover, since "the object of a foreign minister" is "to take care of our commercial affairs; to take care of our seamen; to see that the treaties existing between those countries and ours are faithfully observed and executed," worries that the recall of the U.S. chargé would only "deprive our merchants and the sailors of our country of what benefits might redound from having a minister at Vienna."

While honored that Cass had quoted some "remarks made by me for the recognition of South American independence," denies that "the course which I marked out for myself on that occasion necessarily calls upon me to cooperate with him on this." Then, "the object was to introduce into the family of nations those who had been gallantly and gloriously establishing their independence"; now, "it is to blot out of existence, so far as this suspension of intercourse can accomplish it, an ancient nation." There might have been some analogy "if Hungary had maintained her independence, if the Hungarians were still fighting and struggling for their liberty," but "unfortunately, Hungary fell suddenly, and to the surprise of the American world. She is subdued; she is crushed."

Expresses his concern that Cass's resolution "involves the principle of assuming on the part of this Government a right to pass judgment on the conduct of foreign Powers. . . . We are directing at present the exercise of that power towards a nation on account of the manner in which they have conducted a war. . . . But where is to be the limit? You begin with war. You may extend the same principle of action to religion or politics." Agrees with Sen. John P. Hale's condemnation of Russia's interference in the war: "She was afraid of the contagion of liberty in Hungary, lest it might affect her coterminous possessions," but "She had no such pretext or ground for" interfering "as Austria had, in endeavoring to subjugate . . . rebellious subjects." Wonders why Cass "has permitted Russia to pass," while directing his resolution toward "Austria, the least offending party of the two." Asks again, "Where, then, is the limit?" Chides Cass about his visit to the Sultan of Turkey and his many wives, and suggests that if we may, indeed, investigate the conduct of foreign nations, "We may say, in reference to Turkey, Your religion tolerates polygamy; unless you change your religion, and your habits of social life, we will cease all intercourse with you." Pleads with Cass: "Where . . . is to be the limit?"

Expresses an additional objection to Cass's resolutions: "the assumption of the right of interference in the internal affairs of foreign nations." Since the "independence of Hungary has been destroyed, has been crushed by a union of Russian and Austrian power," Cass's resolution calls for the U.S. "to interfere between Austria and a portion of her empire; and we are called upon to do this, in direct contradiction to the whole policy of this Government, first laid down by [George] Washington and pursued by every successor he has had." Adds: "Sir, if we are to become the defender of nations, the censurers of other Powers, I again ask the honorable Senator where are we to stop, and why does he confine himself to Austria alone?"

In answer to Cass's stated "apprehension that I was one of those stationary politicians," while "he was in favor of progress," retorts that "the progress which the honorable Senator seems so desirous of making. . . . is progress in foreign wars."

While "this is a great country . . . that very greatness draws after it great responsibilities . . . to avoid unnecessary wars, maintaining our own rights with firmness, but invading the rights of no others." *Cong. Globe*, 31 Cong., 1 Sess., 115-16.

Cass's resolution was finally tabled on December 12, 1850. U.S. Sen., *Journal*, 31 Cong., 2 Sess., 35. For Sen. John P. Hale (Free Soil party, N.H.), see *BDAC*.

In 1848-49 Hungary virtually gained independence from Austria, with the Hungarian Diet proclaiming a republic on April 13, 1849. In June Austrian Emperor Francis Joseph I accepted the help of Russia in suppressing this revolution, and by August Hungary was decisively defeated and forced back into the Austrian empire. Langer, *Encyclopedia of World History*, 720, 722-23.

James Watson Webb had been appointed chargé d'affaires to Austria on November 1, 1849, during the congressional recess. He presented his credentials in Austria on February 6, 1850, but was forced to leave after the Senate rejected his nomination. Charles I. McCurdy was appointed to the post on September 18, 1850, and confirmed on September 27. U.S. Sen., *Executive Journal*, 8:137, 231, 258; Dougall & Chapman, *United States Chiefs of Missions*, 7.

Also on this day, Clay presents the memorial of John D.D. Rosset, asking indemnity for French spoliations. Also offers a memorial from "Ether Shepley and others, citizens of Portland, Maine, asking that the Republic of Liberia, in Africa may be acknowledged as an independent nation," especially since it already "has been acknowledged by some of the governments in Europe, and is now in successful progress." *Cong. Globe*, 31 Cong., 1 Sess., 108.

Because Southern states opposed having diplomatic relations with a black republic, the United States did not recognize Liberia until October 22, 1862, when a treaty of recognition and commerce was signed in London. C. Abayomi Cassell, *Liberia: History of the First African Republic* (New York, 1970), 229.

To JAMES BROWN CLAY Washington, January 8, 1850

I had a long, long interview last night again with the Portuguese Minister [J.C. de Figaniere e Morao] on the subject of our claims against, and our relations with his Country.[1] He had just received despatches, transmitting Mr. Hopins's [*sic*, George Hopkins] diplomatic notes, and your first one, which I had previously seen. The P[ortuguese]. F[oreign]. Minister [Count Tojal] and he complained of certain phrases used in those notes. Such as the expression "Stultify" used both by Mr. H. and you in application to Portugal; & the words "sarcasm," and 'insult' employed in your note; & the intimation of a threat by you, as to the consequence of their not complying with your request for a Copy of the correspondence between the British & Portuguese Govts. relative to the case of the [*General*] Armstrong.[2] Of course, I made the best defence I could for both Mr. H. and you. Still I should have been glad if the same ideas had been conveyed in more diplomatic and less offensive language. The word 'Stultify' belongs rather to the common law than to diplomacy[.]

I contended with him that, as G[reat]. B[ritain]. the U.S. & Portugal were all mixed up in the affair of the Armstrong, we had a right to ask for what had passed between the former and the latter; and that, altho' as a general rule one Government had no right to ask for what had passed between *two* other Governmts, this case formed an exception & entitled us to ask for the correspondence. He admitted the exception, but still thought (and so do I) that you had better have abstained from intimating the inference you would draw from their failure to furnish the correspondence. That might have been reserved for the occasion of the occurrence of the failure.

He continued to admit the justice of two of our claims ([James] Hall's and another) and I understood him to own that his Secy of Foreign affairs also admitted them. But he thought that as the controverted claim of the Armstrong had been constantly kept in the foreground, and the others less urged and brought into view, that this was the cause that they had not been provided for.

He told me, confidentially, that he had advised his Governmt. to agree to an arbitration of the case of the Armstrong. Now, that I should think decidedly better than any resort to force. If you have no instructions on that subject, if it be proposed, you would have to refer it to your Government, & await its instruction as to the Arbitrat[io]n.

If the Portuguese Govr. would satisfy the claims that are just & not contested, and agree to refer the Armstrong case to Arbitration, I should think it a happy disposition of the whole matter. But I repeat that you cannot agree to refer without instructions.

Nothing of much public interest has occurred here. A proposition has been made by Govr [Lewis] Cass to suspend Diplomatic intercourse with Austria, in consequence of its barbarities towards Hungary. I spoke in the Senate against it yesterday and I feel sure that it will not pass.[3]

My latest letter from home is from Thomas [Hart Clay] of the 2d inst. Milly (Kelsey's mother)[4] had taken the Small pox; but the rest were all well. I am informed that John [Morrison Clay] has difficulty in getting two or three hands that he wants, owing to the reluctance of hirelings to come under his management—

Thomas is in good spirits.

I sent the other day through Mr. [Henry] Grinnell letters from Louisville for you.[5]

My love to Susan [Jacob Clay] & all the children.

ALS. DLC-TJC (DNA, M212, R11). 1. Clay to Clayton, June 7, 1849. 2. *Ibid.* 3. Comment in Senate, Jan. 7, 1850. 4. Probably slaves. 5. Clay to Grinnell, Jan. 2, 1850.

To THOMAS HART CLAY Washington, January 8, 1850

I received your favor of the 2d instant, and I was glad to learn from it that you had placed your pecuniary affairs on a satisfactory footing; but I hope that you had not agreed to pay to Mr. Hart[1] exorbitant interest. You tell me that, not wanting the check I sent you for $450, you handed it to R[ichard]. Pindell to deposit the amount to my credit with the B[ranch]. Bank.[2] I wish you would see that it is done, and let me know the fact.

I am greatly concerned about your poor mother [Lucretia Hart Clay]. I am afraid that she has too much suffering and trouble for one person to bear. John [Morrison Clay] promised me to do all in his power to promote her comfort and happiness. I wish you and Mary [Mentelle Clay] would do all in your power to lighten her burdens as much as possible. I do not think that I will leave her again another winter.

I wrote yesterday to John to send our mules to Greensboro', in Georgia, where I have a prospect of a good sale of them.[3] Indeed, I consider them all already engaged at fair prices. I wish you would assist him in getting them off. It would be well to have them washed. And I desire the person in whose charge they may be placed should inform me, from time to time, as he makes progress on the journey.

I am very sorry that John has so much trouble in hiring slaves.[4] You will, of course, continue to assist him; and I hardly know what advice to give from this place. He and you must be the best judges, being on the spot. If there be no better alternative, I suppose that I shall be obliged to purchase one or two young men, if good ones can be bought.

Give my love to Mary and your children.

Copy. Printed in Colton, *Clay Correspondence*, 4:598. 1. Possibly Thomas P. Hart. 2. Lexington branch of the Bank of Kentucky. 3. See also Clay to Lucretia H. Clay, March 7, 1850. 4. See also Clay to James B. Clay, Jan. 8, 1850.

To LUCRETIA HART CLAY Washington, January 11, 1850

I have been quite concerned and unhappy about the troubles and vexations which I fear you have had to encounter at home, on account of the Small pox,[1] the difficulty of hiring hands, the bad weather &c. I have often regretted that I was not at home to share them with you, or to lighten them as far as I could. I hope that John [Morrison Clay] has done all in his power as a substitute for me. He promised me to do so, and his duty and his love for you ought to prompt him to do so. I have written to him to send the Mules to Greensboro, and any vexation arising from them will be removed by their going to Georgia. I expect to get for them there a price that will repay what I advanced for them and indemnify us for the care and expense of keeping them. I sent by the Telegraph the day before yesterday a message to John to have them in readiness to start to Georgia. As to hands, if he should be disappointed in hiring now, I hope he will be able to get some later in the winter, or if we cannot do better that we shall be able to purchase one or two. I was in hopes that he might get Charles Lilly from Thomas [Hart Clay], who might have acted as a foreman; but I am sorry to learn that there is some obstacle to his obtaining him.[2]

Thomas informs me that not wanting the check for $450 which I sent to him, he had the amount deposited to my credit with the B[ranch]. Bank in Lexington.[3] I sent to you a check also for $450, and I had previously remitted to John checks for $100 and for $150; but I have not yet heard whether he received the $100 check.

From these several sources, all the money which you or John or the farm may need can be derived, unless he should purchase two hands, in which case I must make up the deficiency.

We have so far had a bad winter here; and I have had my customary colds; but they have not been as bad as I have had, nor laid me up.

I made a Speech a few days ago in the Senate, of which you will see the notice taken in the papers.[4] My friends seemed pleased with it. It is not however my purpose to speak often.

I have received since I last wrote to you several letters from home. I am glad to see Thomas in such good spirits, and so satisfied with the prospects which his [saw] Mills afford, and I hope he will not be disappointed.

My love to John.

ALS. DLC-TJC (DNA, M212, R11). 1. Clay to Combs, Dec. 10, 1849. 2. Clay to Thomas H. Clay, Dec. 27, 1849. 3. Clay to Thomas H. Clay, Jan. 8, 1850. 4. Probably Comment in Senate, Jan. 7, 1850.

To James Brown Clay, Lisbon, Portugal, January 12, 1850. Advises James that "I remitted to Mr. C. Johnson for you $110 being your part of the joint note in which you were bound with him for George. You may consider it an advance for Henry." ALS. DLC-TJC (DNA, M212, R11).

To THOMAS HART CLAY Washington, January 12, 1850

I received a letter from you enclosing a Copy of a letter from Genl [Zachary] Taylor to me, dated at Monterey in November 1847.[1] It was the Copy I wanted. I was only mistaken as to its date.

I also received the letter for Henry Clay Junr. [III] and I have forwarded it to him.

We have a May day to day.

ALS. DLC-HC (DNA, M212, R6). Printed in Colton, *Clay Correspondence*, 4:599. 1. Taylor to Clay, Nov. 4, 1847; Clay to Lucretia H. Clay, Dec. 28, 1849.

Speech to American Colonization Society, Washington, D.C., January 15, 1850. Expresses his "very great satisfaction" on this "the thirty third year of our existence as a Society." Notes that the society has "met with every species of difficulty and obstruction. We have been in the attitude of a person standing between two fires, the ultraism of the North, and the ultraism of the South. The great masses, however . . . in both of these sections are, I believe, impartial."

Finds encouragement when looking to Africa, where "we have brought into existence a State—a Commonwealth—a people self-governed, and that of a race which many have supposed were truly incapable of self-government; for, I understand, that there is not a solitary white man concerned in the administration of the government of Liberia." Praises the state papers he has seen from Liberia.

Is also encouraged by the society's progress at home where "Public opinion is becoming more and more sound every day in regard to the solution of the great problem . . . of the practicability of the redemption of Africa from barbarity, and the transportation from our own country of an unhappy race, which it is impossible to amalgamate with the larger portion of the people of this country. It is no longer a debateable question, whether colonies can be successfully planted upon the shores of Africa. It is no longer a debateable question whether it is practicable, with the application of adequate and sufficient means, to transport, from time to time, free colored persons of the United States, those now free, with their issue, and those who may become free by the acts of their owners, who may hereafter think proper to emancipate them."

Notes that in the report following his speech, they will learn that 6-700 applicants are already registered "desiring to be transported to Africa." Copy. Printed in *The African Repository* (February, 1850), 26:44-45.

To SOLOMON STURGES[1] Washington, January 16, 1850

I received your letter stating your willingness to advance $1000 towards raising a sum to enable the Republic of Liberia to purchase additional territory from the natives of Africa; and inquiring as to the character and capacity of Govr. [Joseph Jenkins] Roberts.[2] Our information, on both points, is perfectly satisfactory, and such as to induce us to believe him worthy of all confidence. The Revd Mr. [Ralph Randolph] Gurley has just returned from that Republic, and bears high testimony in favor of him.

Although I am the President of the [American Colonization] Society, I have very little agency in the transaction of its current business. That is under the control of a Board of Managers, whose agent is the Revd. W[illiam]. McLain of this City. To him I have handed your letter, and with him you will be pleased to correspond on the subject of the liberal donation, which your benevolence and humanity prompt you to offer.[3]

ALS. ICHi. Addressed to Sturges at "Putnam near Zanesville Ohio." 1. Sturges (b. 1796 in Fairfield, Conn.) was one of the founders of the firm of E. Buckington & Co. in Zanesville, Ohio. Henry Howe, *Historical Collections of Ohio in Two Volumes* (Cincinnati, 1907), 2:339. 2. On Jan. 14, 1850, Sturges explained to Clay that he had seen "a statement that Gov. Roberts of *Liberia* was negotiating for the Purchase of additional Territory, including, (if I remember right) some 700 miles of Coast, and some Large Slave Markets." If Clay can certify that Roberts is "*Honest* & *Capable*," then Sturges will "Pledge such sum as may be necessary" to complete the purchase, "*if not Exceeding One Thousand dollars*." ALS. DLC-Records of the American Colonization Society (DNA, M212, R20). For Roberts, see *DAB* and for his negotiations to acquire the Gallinas territory, see Cassell, *Liberia*, 161, 165-66, 170, 177-78. 3. On Jan. 25, 1850, Clay sent William McLain a draft from Sturges for $1,000 which was deposited in the Bank of Washington on Jan. 26. ADS. DLC-Records of the American Colonization Society (DNA, M212, R20).

Remark in Senate, January 17, 1850. Interrupts an exchange between Sen. Stephen A. Douglas and Sen. Truman Smith to request a clarification of their point of contention. Asks "whether this is the state of the case: That a resolution has passed the House of Representatives calling for certain information" concerning alleged coercion by the Zachary Taylor administration in the formation of a state government in California, "that the information has been communicated, but has not yet been made public," and that a Senate resolution "calls for precisely the same information," thereby subjecting "the Executive Department to double labor in copying the same papers twice."

Douglas expresses support for the Senate resolution, which "contains more extended interrogatories" than the House's request for information. Clay suggests that Douglas "wait until the call of the House is answered," and if it "shall be found insufficient . . . I will with pleasure go with him for obtaining additional information." Adds "a single remark": "if there has been this Executive interference in California to produce a premature birth of a State and a constitution, why, I think my worthy friend from Illinois, instead of censuring this Administration, ought to be profoundly grateful for its liberality; for, if I understand aright, it has produced a Democratic child. . . . an event which the honorable Senator cannot fail to hail with pleasure." *Cong. Globe*, 31 Cong., 1 Sess., 178. Resolution is adopted. *Ibid.*, 185. For Stephen A. Douglas (Dem., Ill.), see *DAB* and *BDAC*.

To LUCRETIA HART CLAY Washington, January 21, 1850

I am very sorry to hear that you have had a very bad winter in Kentucky. Here too it has been amongst the most disagreeable I have ever known. I have had my usual portion of colds, but otherwise my health has been good.

I have received a late letter from James [Brown Clay] (which I will hereafter send you) in which he informs me that he has been obliged to send H[enry]. Clay [III] home, on account of his obstinacy, and his refusal to submit to his authority; and I am in daily expectation of his arrival. I am very sorry for it, as I shall be embarrassed to know what is best to do with the boy. James also informs me that poor little Lucy [Jacob Clay] had fallen down the steps and broke her left arm in two places. It had been set, and she was doing as well as could be expected[.]

I transmitted a letter to you early in the Session from Lucretia Erwin, in which she wrote to me to know her age and requested me to send her some money.[1] I have heard nothing from home about her. I wanted to know her age, and also to know from her brother[2] whether her father [James Erwin] did or did not supply her with money.

I have received from John [Morrison Clay] his letter of the 13h. in which he informs me that he had received my directions to send the Mules to Greensboro in Georgia, where I had made arrangements for the Sale of them. I hope shortly to hear from John that he has been able to send them, and to get rid of that annoyance.

John informs me that he has purchased of Mr. Headley[3] two fresh cows for you, which I am glad of, as you will take an interest in that Milk business.

I regret extremely that you should have been so much disturbed & concerned by the illness of the negroes.[4] I trust that, after this Session, if God spare us, that we may be able to do something to lighten your burthens and to enable you to live an easier life. John I hope will, in my absence, do all he can to assist and relieve you. He promised me so, and his duty & affection should so prompt him.

I am still remaining at the [National] Hotel, where I have two very good rooms, but I like not the crowd which daily assembles at the Ladies' ordinary, where I get my meals.

The British Minister, Sir Henry Bulwer & his Lady [Georgiana Wellesley Bulwer] are staying at the same house, and occupying apartments near me. I have dined three or four times with them, and they appear intelligent & agreeable. At their earnest entreaty I am sitting for my portrait to a young Italian artiste, a protegeé of theirs.[5] Give my love to John.

ALS. DLC-TJC (DNA, M212, R11). 1. Not found. 2. Either Henry Clay Erwin, Andrew Eugene Erwin, or Charles Edward Erwin. 3. Probably John Headley, Clay's former overseer. See 8:676. 4. Clay to Combs, Dec. 10, 1849. 5. Probably Giuseppe (Joseph) Fagnani (1819-73) who came to the U.S. from Naples at the urging of Bulwer. Amyx, "Portraits of Henry Clay," Special Collections, University of Kentucky, vol. A:1.35a.

Remark in Senate, January 21, 1850. Presents a petition from New York citizens that describes the advantages to England of cheap postage and requests Congress to "extend the same benefits, by fixing a maximum of two cents on all prepaid letters." *Cong. Globe*, 31 Cong., 1 Sess., 196.

Later that day, supports a bill to appropriate funds to repair and improve a dam on the Ohio River at the head of Cumberland Island. Knows firsthand "of this particular obstruction. It was my misfortune or fortune to pass down the Ohio river, on board the *Old Hickory*—a steamboat bearing a name rather ominous, I confess," for "about four weeks in a voyage from Louisville to Natchez, which, under ordinary circumstances, would not have taken us more than four days, and a considerable portion of the delay arose from the very obstruction" that is the object of this bill. Recalls "the dam particularly well," especially the "seventy or eighty head of cattle, that somebody was carrying for consumption in New Orleans, that had to be thrown out of the boat, some drifting down the river, and others making their way through floating timber and ice to the shore on the other side, where they were afterwards taken up and brought on board the steamer again." After Sen. William R. King questions the propriety of repairing an improvement to navigation that itself had to become a hazard, Clay argues that "artificial objects of this kind require occasional reparation. This dam. . . . has been neglected for several years. . . . If there had been a timely application of money for the repair of the dam, it would now be performing" as it should. After more discussion, the bill is tabled. *Ibid.*, 197-98.

To LESLIE COMBS Washington, January 22, 1850

I received your favor of the 15th, and I previously received other favors. I do not write often, because really I have nothing positive to communicate, and I have neither time nor inclination to write merely speculative letters.

Every thing here is uncertain—the Slavery question in all its bearings, California, New Mexico, Texas, etc.[1] Of course, provision for your debt,[2] and all other debts of Texas, is among the uncertain things.

My relation with the President [Zachary Taylor] and his Cabinet is amicable, but not remarkably confidential with them all. I neither sought nor declined confidential intercourse. I do not go out at night, and in the day time both they and I are too much engaged to see much of each other.

Are you not pushing subscriptions to railroads too far?[3] We want one to the Ohio river; two would be better, and three better yet. But we ought not to go too fast.

I am awaiting with anxiety for popular expressions in Kentucky in favor of the Union, let what come that may.[4] Is there not danger from delay that the contagion of disunion may seize you?

Copy. Printed in Colton, *Clay Correspondence*, 4:599; partially printed in Louisville *Daily Journal*, Jan. 8, 1861. 1. The slavery and territorial controversy had become so heated that Clay felt the Union itself was threatened. At this time he was formulating a set of resolutions to resolve all of the matters in question. On Jan. 29, 1850 [Speech in Senate], he introduced a series of resolutions which provided for (1) admission of California as a free state; (2) organization, without restriction on slavery, of the remainder of the territory acquired from Mexico; (3) adjustment of the Texas-New Mexico boundary; (4) assumption by the U.S. of the Texas debt acquired before annexation; (5) noninterference with slavery in the District of Columbia; (6) abolishing the slave trade in the District of Columbia; (7) a more effective fugitive slave law; and (8) a statement that Congress had no right to interfere with the interstate slave trade. These resolutions were referred to a Senate Select Committee of Thirteen, chaired by Clay. On May 8 the committee reported an "Omnibus bill" covering the territorial matters and a bill to prohibit the slave trade in the District of Columbia. After the failure of the Omnibus bill on July 31, Sen. Stephen A. Douglas broke up the proposals into several bills which were passed separately in August and September. Known collectively as the Compromise of 1850, these acts were: (1) admission of California as a free state; (2) Texas and New Mexico Act which organized a territorial government in New Mexico without restriction on slavery, adjusted the Texas-New Mexico boundary, while the U.S. assumed the Texas debt of $10,000,000 in return for abandonment by Texas of all claims to the New Mexico territory; (3) Utah Act which established a territorial government without restriction on slavery; (4) Fugitive Slave Act which placed fugitive cases exclusively under federal jurisdiction, denied fugitives a trial by jury, provided that citizens aiding a fugitive could be fined or imprisoned, and included several other provisions making it easier to reclaim fugitives; and (5) an act abolishing the slave trade in the District of Columbia. For the Compromise of 1850, see Hamilton, *Prologue to Conflict*; Allen Nevins, *Ordeal of the Union*, 8 vols. (New York, 1947-71), 1:219-344; Peterson, *The Great Triumvirate*, 449-76; Poage, *Henry Clay*, 199-264; Elbert B. Smith, *The Presidencies of Zachary Taylor & Millard Fillmore* (Lawrence, Kan., 1988), 91-194. 2. Combs was one of the many holders of Texas bonds who had a strong desire for the U.S. to assume that debt. He ultimately received $96,393 for his bonds. Hamilton, *Prologue to Conflict*, 126, 131, 179; Smith, *Presidencies of Taylor & Fillmore*, 111. 3. There were many railroad projects being proposed in Kentucky during 1849-50. One of the largest of these, a proposal to build a railroad from Louisville to Nashville, received a charter from the state legislature in March, 1850. For railroad development in Kentucky, see Maury Klein, *History of the Louisville & Nashville Railroad* (New York, 1972), 3-5; William B. Graham, "Railroads in Kentucky Before 1860," M.A. thesis, University of Kentucky, 1931, pp. 31-59. 4. Clay to Combs, Dec. 22, 1849.

From George W. Crawford, Washington, January 22, 1850. Acknowledges Clay's "recommendation in behalf of Colonel Cary H. Fry for the office of Paymaster or Inspector General in the Army." Assures Clay that "whenever a vacancy occurs in the Pay Department," Fry will be considered. Adds that the "office of Inspector General is still vacant" and does not believe that "the President [Zachary Taylor] will nominate a successor to Colonel [James] Duncan immediately," but will "present the name of Colonel Fry to his consideration." Copy. DNA, RG107, Military Books, vol. 30, p. 27.

James Duncan of New York, who had become Inspector General on January 26, 1849, died on July 3, 1849. Cary Fry became a paymaster on February 7, 1853. *HRDUSA*, 387, 439.

Comment in Senate, January 24, 1850. Presents two petitions: one in behalf of "the widow of a revolutionary officer Mrs. Merebah Chandler," whose husband had "received little or no pay for his services, save the satisfaction of having served his country faithfully"; and one in behalf of John McAvoy, "an old soldier—not very old either, but one that served in the Mexican War, and I believe for four or five years in the United States army," who seeks "the small sum of twenty dollars" which the Treasury Department refused to authorize "for want of the strict legal proofs required."

Later in the day, comments on "a most remarkable coincidence." After presenting yesterday a petition to purchase the manuscript copy of Washington's Farewell Address, received "a petition from Pennsylvania, numerously signed, requesting Congress to purchase Mount Vernon. The petitioners state that . . . that property should be national; that it is less accessible in the hands of private individuals than it should be; but that if it belonged to the Republic all could repair to it as to a political Mecca." Remarks that this subject "has often been discussed," and if the site is "not unhealthy, it might be made use of as a situation for a marine hospital, accompanied with botanic gardens." Asks that the petition be "received and referred to the Committee for the District of Columbia." *Cong. Globe*, 31 Cong., 1 Sess., 225.

In 1847 John A. Washington had offered to sell Mount Vernon to the U.S. government for $100,000, but the offer was refused. In 1856 the Mount Vernon Ladies' Association of the Union was chartered for the purpose of buying and restoring Mount Vernon as nearly as possible to the state it was in during Washington's lifetime. The association bought the house and 200 acres in 1860 for $200,000 and began restoration. *The Encyclopedia Britannica*, 11th ed. (Cambridge, Eng., 1911).

Later in the day states his motives for presenting the resolution to purchase the original manuscript of Washington's Farewell Address. Had hoped "to accomplish the object . . . without the formality of the passage of a resolution," but since the Joint Committee on the Library "had never heretofore applied the funds intrusted to them to the purchase of manuscripts without the sanction of Congress," felt it necessary to submit this resolution.

Explains that "about fifty-three years ago . . . General Washington, the Father of his Country, by universal consent," selected the Philadelphia *Daily Advertiser* for the publication of the Farewell Address. The editor "an extremely respectable and intelligent gentleman, Mr. [David] Claypoole. . . . proposed to return the original document to General Washington . . . but being extremely desirous to possess it," received permission to keep it; "the paper from that day to this has been in the hands of Mr. Claypoole or some of his descendants."

Recently spotted a newspaper advertisement advising that the "original manuscript of General Washington's valedictory address. . . . in the handwriting and bearing the signature of Gen. Washington" was to be sold on February 12, 1850. Fearing that it might "be perhaps transferred out of the country, and made the ornament of the parlor of some of the distinguished men of Europe," decided that " 'here—here in this Capitol—in the Library of this nation, ought this document to be deposited'. . . . although we may derive great pleasure from tracing the narratives of the glory of our ancestors . . . yet some physical memorial of them, some tangible, palpable object, always addresses itself to our hearts and to our feelings."

Provides an example: "Sir, in my own humble parlor at Ashland, I have at this moment a broken goblet which was used by General Washington, during almost the whole of the revolutionary war. . . . there is nothing in that parlor so much revered, or which is an object of greater admiration to the stranger who comes to see me. This feeling of attachment to these objects, associated with the memory of those we venerate . . . is not merely a private feeling of attachment; it is a broader, more comprehensive, and national feeling. . . . these are feelings which are worthy of being countenanced and cherished by public authority."

Asks: "who is there that would not find refreshment and delight behind the Farewell Address of Washington? . . . Who is there that would not trace the paternal and patriotic advice with pleasure which was written by his own hand—that hand which, after having grasped the sword that achieved the liberties of our country, traced with the instrument of peace the document which then gave us that advice, so necessary to preserve and transmit to posterity the treasure he had bestowed on us?"

After comments in support of the resolution by Sen. Henry Foote and from Daniel Webster, who corroborated Clay's sentiments about the importance of national relics, the joint resolution is engrossed for a third reading. Sen. Jefferson Davis then expresses his objections to what amounts "nearly to a mandate" to purchase the manuscript, which "is but a corrected copy . . . known not to have been entirely the result of his own mind. . . . There is nothing to be gained by the purchase of this manuscript any more than there would be in the purchase of a walking stick which Washington used." Sen. Solon Borland also fears that this action would "only put money in the pockets of various speculators, who, under color of professions of patriotism, come here and ask the Senate to purchase" historical relics.

Clay responds that the Farewell Address was not "hawked about the Capitol . . . and offered for sale with a view to speculation." When Borland retorts that "the manuscript has been exhibited here" to promote its sale, Clay insists that he "certainly had no knowledge of it." *Cong. Globe*, 31 Cong., 1 Sess., 226-28.

For Davis (Dem., Miss.) and Borland (Dem., Ark.), see *BDAC*. David Claypoole was editor of the *Pennsylvania Packet and General Advertiser*, the first truly successful daily newspaper in the U.S. The Farewell Address was issued in that paper on September 19, 1799. Pollard, *The Presidents and the Press*, 2, 24.

To JAMES HARLAN Washington, January 24, 1850

If I have not written to you often, it is because of my perpetual involuntary engagements, and because I have really nothing to write about of a practical nature, and I don't like indulging in speculation. Slavery here is the all engrossing theme; and my hopes and my fears alternately prevail as to any satisfactory settlement of the vexed question. I have been anxiously considering whether any comprehensive plan of adjustment can be devised and proposed to adjust satisfactorily this distracting question. I shall not however offer any scheme unless it meets my entire concurrence.[1]

I do not know whether any thing will be done about the Marshall in Kentucky. All our Whig delegation concurred in the propriety of a change; but when we came to designate the man, there was unfortunately much division. The Executive [Zachary Taylor] may not, under these circumstances, deem it expedient to remove the present incumbent.[2]

My relations to the President are civil & amicable but they do not extend to any confidential consultations in regard to public measures.

ALS. Courtesy of Alan Westin, New Haven, Conn. Printed in Colton, *Clay Correspondence*, 4:599-600. 1. Clay to Combs, Jan. 22, 1850; Speech in Senate, Jan. 29, 1850. 2. John Lane was the incumbent marshal, nominated by Polk on Jan. 15, 1849, and confirmed on Jan. 26. On Feb. 2, 1850, Taylor nominated James S. Speed for the post, and he was confirmed on April 25. U.S. Sen., *Executive Journal*, 8:24, 28, 137, 170.

From Unknown Correspondent, Buckingham C.H., Va., January 25, 1850. Although unknown to Clay, writes to suggest a modification of the constitution of the American Colonization Society. Admits that it may seem "visionary," but believes it is "*possible.*" Notes that while the colonization society "is a friendly, but very imperfectly efficient institution, in the great cause of emancipation," asks if it might not be made efficient enough to eradicate slavery within a few years from Virginia and ultimately from the whole country. Suggests a detailed system whereby the society would purchase the whole number of infants born to slaves in one year and emancipate them. Provides statistics to show that by procuring $700,000 as a loan, the society could purchase the infants born each year, pay off the loan, and complete the whole work in sixty years.

Discusses possible obstacles to this plan, but asks why it should not be possible. Wonders how slavery can be ended unless this system, or a similar one, is used. Adds that "the people never can let them go, unless for charity's sake or pecuniary compensation. The former has failed, and if the compensation scheme will not effect it, here slavery remains for ever, or be removed by force." Warns that "No man can tell when the institution of slavery will burst from under us like a volcano, and bury us beneath its ruins." Copy. Printed in *The African Repository* (May, 1850), 26:141-44.

From Noah Fletcher, Washington, January 26, 1850. Thanks Clay for forwarding "two letters from T[homas]. Kirkman, Esq., one addressed to yourself, the other to the Executive Committee of the Am. Col. Soc." They will be considered by "the Committee as soon as Mr. [William] Mc.Lain returns from Norfolk, Va. where he has gone to attend the sailing *to-day* of the Liberia Packet with Emigrants for Liberia." Also acknowledges "the letter you enclosed from Solomon Sturges, Esq. covering his draft for one thousand dollars to be appropriated towards the purchase of additional territory adjoining Liberia [Clay to Sturges, January 16, 1850]." ALS. DLC-Records of the American Colonization Society (DNA, M212, R20).

Kirkman had written to Clay from Florence, Ala., on February 13, 1850, forwarding a letter to the American Colonization Society concerning his claim against the estate of Samuel Hurd who had left most of his assets to the society [Davis to Clay, February 20, 1847]. ALS. DLC-Records of the American Colonization Society (DNA, M212, R20).

For Kirkman, a native of Ireland who had opened a dry goods business in Florence, Ala., in 1821, see Smith & DeLand (pub.), *Northern Alabama Historical and Biographical* (Birmingham, 1888), 313.

To BOYD McNAIRY Washington, January 26, 1850

I send with great pleasure, according to your request, a letter of introduction of your son[1] to my friend Mr. [William N.] Mercer, who does not like to be addressed as Dr.

We are here in the midst of great excitement on the Slavery question. I do not yet see land, but hope for the best, whilst fearing the worst.

The Mission filled by Mr. Donelson remains vacant,[2] and I believe for the present is intended not to be filled. If it should be determined to fill it, I adhere to what I said in a former letter in regard to it and yourself. My relations to the present [Taylor] Administration are not hostile, but I have no reason to feel that it has any particular disposition to oblige me. . . .

ALS. DLC-HC (DNA, M212, R6). 1. John Sims McNairy, first noted in 5:922, but not otherwise identified. 2. Probably Andrew Jackson Donelson who had served as minister to Prussia 1846-49; however, he had been succeeded by Edward A. Hannegan in 1849. Hannegan was recalled in Jan., 1850, and in August President Millard Fillmore nominated Daniel D.

Barnard for the post. He was confirmed on Sept. 2, 1850. U.S. Sen., *Executive Journal*, 8:60, 214, 226; Dougall & Chapman, *U.S. Chiefs of Mission*, 59.

To THOMAS B. STEVENSON Washington, January 26, 1850

I thank you for your two last favors. Your political speculations are interesting and will be attentively considered; but I regret that I have not time to interchange views with you.

I addressed some days ago as strong a letter of recommendation of you for the office of Assistant Secrty of the Treasury (vacated by Mr. [Charles B.] Penrose) to *Mr* [William M.] Meredith as I could make it, or as I ever wrote.[1] [Thomas] Corwin in person took it to him, and as he informed me supported it. I am sorry that it did not succeed, but that another was appointed.[2] We shall continue our exertions for you, and I wish I could add with better prospect of success. Candour obliges me however to advise that you should not indulge in any very sanguine expectations. Corwin told me that he had written to you, which was the cause of my not doing so before.

There is a bad state of things here on the slavery question. My hopes and fears alternate. *Probably I may* attempt some adj*ust*ment of it.[3]

Copy. OCHP. Printed in Colton, *Clay Correspondence*, 3:497. 1. Letter not found. 2. No one was appointed as assistant secretary of the treasury to replace Penrose; however, George Harrington was appointed chief clerk, a position that had been vacant under Penrose. *The American Almanac and Repository of Useful Knowledge For the Year 1850* (Boston, 1849), 100; *The American Almanac . . . For the Year 1851* (Boston, 1850), 104. 3. Clay to Combs, Jan. 22, 1850; Speech in Senate, Jan. 29, 1850.

Speech in Senate, January 29, 1850. Submits a series of resolutions, which, "Taken together, in combination . . . propose an amicable arrangement of all questions in controversy between the free and slave States, growing out of the subject of slavery." Hopes that "at least some portion of the long time which I have devoted, with care and deliberation, to the preparation of these resolutions, and to the presentation of this great national scheme of compromise and harmony, will be employed by each Senator before he pronounces against the proposition embraced in these resolutions."

Clay's first resolution calls for the admission of California to the Union "without the imposition by Congress of any restriction in respect to the exclusion or introduction of slavery within those boundaries." Although acknowledging the "irregularity in the movements which have terminated in the adoption of a constitution by California [Clay to Pierse, February 16, 1849]" which "was not preceded by any act of Congress authorizing the convention and designating the boundaries of the proposed State," cites historical precedent in the case of Michigan's admission to the Union [Speech in Raleigh, April 13, 1844]. Since Michigan "now forms one of the bright stars of this glorious Confederacy," hopes that "California . . . if she also shall be admitted, as is proposed by this first resolution, with suitable limits . . . too will make her contribution of wisdom, of patriotism, and of good feeling to this body." Adds: "The resolution proposes her admission when she applies for it."

The second resolution states "That as slavery does not exist by law, and is not likely to be introduced into any of the territory acquired" from Mexico in 1848, "it is inexpedient for Congress to provide by law, either for its introduction into or exclusion from any part of the said territory," and calls for the establishment of territorial governments outside the "proposed State of California, without the adoption of any restriction or condition on the subject of slavery." Justifies his opinions in this resolution by pointing to "California herself, embracing, of all other portions of the country acquired by us from Mexico, that country into which it would have been most likely that slavery should have been introduced; that California herself, has met in convention [Clay to Pierse, February 16, 1849], and by a unanimous vote, embracing in that body slaveholders from the State of Mississippi, as well as from other parts, who concurred in the resolution—that California by a unanimous vote has declared against the introduction of slavery within her limits." Considers it "a dereliction of duty" to allow the territories outside California to remain "without government, leaving them to all those scenes of disorder, confusion, and anarchy which I apprehend . . . there is too much reason to anticipate."

Argues that the third and fourth resolutions, "having an immediate connection with each other, should be read and considered together." The third resolution calls for fixing the western boundary of Texas on "the Rio del Norte [Rio Grande], commencing one marine league from its mouth, and running up that river to the southern boundary of New Mexico, thence with that line eastwardly, and so continuing in the same direction to the line established between the United States and Spain, excluding any portion of New Mexico, whether lying on the east or west of that river." Clay's fourth resolution proposes in respect to Texas that "the United States will provide for the payment of all that portion of the legitimate and *bona fide* public debt of that State, contracted prior to its annexation . . . and for which the duties on foreign imports were pledged by said State to its creditors," if the Texas legislature will formally "relinquish to the United Sates any claim which it has to any part of New Mexico."

Acknowledges the complexities of "the question of what are the true limits of Texas." Believes "Texas has not a good title to any portion of what is called New Mexico," but agrees that in "the grounds which her representatives assumed . . . there is plausibility. . . . I do not think they constitute or demonstrate the existence of a good title, but a plausible one." Outlines a boundary settlement that would embrace "a vast country abundantly competent to form two or three States," which "her greatest men ought to be satisfied with as a State and member of this Union." Feels his proposition to assume Texan debts "is founded upon principles of truth and eternal justice." Texas had "invited loans to be made to her to prosecute the then existing war between her and Mexico." The money "was expended in the establishment of her liberty and her independence," and now, after Texas annexation, the United States owes "to the creditors who thus advanced their money . . . the reimbursement of the money." Asserts that it is not asking too much to require "the further condition that Texas shall relinquish . . . any claim that she has to any portion of New Mexico. . . . for the sake of that general quiet and harmony, for the sake of that accommodation which ought to be as much the object of legislation as it is of individuals in their transactions in private life."

Links his fifth and sixth resolutions, as he had connected the third and fourth. His fifth resolution declares that "it is inexpedient to abolish slavery in the District of Columbia" while it still exists in Maryland "without the consent of that State, without the consent of the people of the District, and without just compensation" to slaveowners in the District. His sixth resolution admits, however, that "it is expedient to prohibit within the District the slave-trade," allowing no slave "to be sold therein as merchandise, or to be transported to other markets without the District of Columbia."

Comments that his fifth resolution "asserts substantially no other principle than that which was asserted by the Senate of the United States twelve years ago, upon resolutions which I then offered, and which passed . . . by a majority of four-fifths of the Senate [9:123-26]." In calling for the abolition of the slave trade in the District of Columbia, explains that he does not mean to interfere with "the transfer of slaves from the inhabitants within the District—the sale by one neighbor to another of a slave which the one owns and the other wants, that a husband may perhaps be put along with his wife, or a wife with her husband." Describes his target as the "slave trade . . . pronounced an abomination more than forty years ago, by one of the most gifted and distinguished sons of Virginia, the late Mr. [John] Randolph." Claims that few "gentlemen living in the slave States look upon one who is a regular trader in slaves with any particular favor or kindness. They are often—sometimes unjustly, perhaps—excluded from social intercourse." Wishes to stop the slave trader from entering the District to "establish his jails and put on his chains, and sometimes shock the sensibilities of our nature by a long train of slaves passing through the avenue leading from this Capitol to the house of the Chief Magistrate."

In a seventh resolution, calls for "more effectual provision . . . for the restitution and delivery" of escaped slaves to their owners, a problem "so evident" that Clay declines "to add another word."

Clay's final resolution states that "Congress has no power to prohibit or obstruct the trade in slaves between the slaveholding States; but that the admission or exclusion of slaves brought from one into another of them, depends exclusively upon their own particular laws." Believes this resolution "merely asserts a truth, established by the highest authority of law in this country," and that it is useful "occasionally to resort to great fundamental principles, and bring them freshly and manifestly before our eyes, from time to time, to avoid their being violated."

Hopes his series of resolutions "may prove acceptable to both or either of the parties on these questions. . . . I think it ought to be acceptable to both. There is no sacrifice of principle, proposed in any of them, by either party. The plan is founded upon mutual forbearance, originating in a spirit of conciliation and concession; not of principles, but of matters of feeling."

Although he believes "this project contains about an equal amount of concession and forbearance on both sides," explains why he may "have asked from the free States of the North a more liberal and extensive concession": "You are numerically more powerful than the slave States. . . . not that there is any difference in valor, in prowess, in noble and patriotic daring, whenever it is required for the safety and salvation of the country, between the people of one class of States and those of the other. You are in point of numbers, however, greater; and greatness and magnanimity should ever be allied together." Describes the "sentiment of humanity and philanthropy on your side. . . . honestly and earnestly cherished, with a disposition to make sacrifices to enforce it" as "a noble and beautiful sentiment." But it is "a sentiment without sacrifice, a sentiment without danger, a sentiment without hazard, without peril, without loss." On the other side, however, "there is a vast and incalculable amount of property to be sacrificed, and to be sacrificed, not by your sharing in the common burdens, but exclusive of you. . . . The social intercourse, habit, safety, property, life, everything, is at hazard . . . in the slave States." Adds: "In the one scale, then, we behold sentiment, sentiment, sentiment alone; in the other property, the social fabric, life, and all that makes life desirable and happy."

Holds up "a fragment of that coffin in which now repose in silence, in sleep, and speechless, all the earthly remains of the venerated Father of his Country," George Washington which had just been presented to him by the man who had delivered the memorial calling for Congress to purchase Mount Vernon [Comment in Senate, January 24, 1850]. Describes the relic as "a warning voice, coming from the grave to the Congress now in session to beware, to pause, to reflect before they lend themselves to any purposes which shall destroy that Union which was cemented by his exertions and example." Asks that the resolutions be taken up for discussion on "any early day which the Senate in their pleasure may decide upon."

Sen. Thomas J. Rusk of Texas rises to challenge Clay's resolutions concerning Texan boundaries, and Sen. Henry S. Foote adds a "few remarks by way of *protest*," chiefly against the propositions concerning slavery in the District of Columbia. Clay asserts that "I differ in *toto*" with Rusk, but "I honor the Senator's watchfulness . . . as one of the representatives of the State of Texas, when he found that her garments were to be touched, to rise and make his protest against it." Reaffirms to Foote that the resolutions concerning slavery in the District are on "a firm footing with regard to the constitutional question," and that "*inexpedient*. . . . is as strong ground as can be assumed. I would not use the word unconstitutional."

Clay's resolutions meet still more criticism from Senators Foote and James M. Mason. Sen. Jefferson Davis challenges Clay's recollections "of the position of the Senate . . . twelve years ago" and asserts that he would never accept "less than the Missouri compromise line extended to the Pacific ocean, with the specific recognition of the right to hold slaves in the territory below that line. . . . I can never consent to give additional power to a majority to commit further aggressions upon the minority in this Union."

Clay deplores this "premature, and . . . unnecessary discussion." Clarifies "a mistaken representation" of his 1838 position on slavery in the District of Columbia. Regrets that Davis desires "the extension of the Missouri compromise line to the Pacific," because "no earthly power could induce me to vote for a specific measure for the introduction of slavery where it had not before existed, either south or north of that line." If citizens of New Mexico and California "choose to establish slavery, and if they come here with constitutions establishing slavery," declares he will support their admission, "but then it will be their own work, and not ours, and their posterity will have to reproach them, and not us for . . . allowing slavery to exist among them." Believes that "leaving the subject unacted upon with regard to slavery . . . is a much better proposition, as far as the South is concerned, than that of extending the Missouri line to the Pacific." Adds: "I consider it is much better for the South that the whole subject should be open on both sides of an imaginary line—for instance, the line of 36° 30′—than that slavery should be interdicted positively north of 36° 30′."

Davis maintains "that it is the right of the people of the South to carry this species of property to any portion of the Territories," but that "we are willing, in a spirit of compromise, and in compliance with past acquiescence of the States, to restrict" slavery "by the parallel of 36°30′ north."

After extensive comments by Senators Davis, William R. King, Thomas J. Rusk, and Solomon W. Downs, Clay states: "I did not intend these resolutions as abstract resolutions. I propose now that they should be made the order of the day for Tuesday next," which is agreed to. *Cong. Globe*, 31 Cong., 1 Sess., 244-52.

Clay's resolutions, setting forth his various proposals for compromising the territorial and slavery issues which were threatening the Union are printed in *Sen. Misc. Docs.*, 31 Cong., 1 Sess., vol. 1, no. 36, pp. 1-2.

For Solomon W. Downs (Dem., La.), Thomas J. Rusk (Dem., Tx.), and James M. Mason (Dem., Va.), see *BDAC*. For John Randolph's opposition to the slave trade in the District of Columbia, see Bruce, *John Randolph of Roanoke*, 1:437.

From SUSAN JACOB CLAY Lisbon, Portugal, February 2, 1850

I received your kind letter of the 16th ultimo by the last steamer from England, and began to answer it to send by the return steamer of last Tuesday, but I was obliged to leave off because of my eyes, which have been very weak since the birth of Harry,[1] and the glare of the lights at the palace on Sunday night made me suffer so much for three or four days that I was obliged to wear a green shade & could neither read nor write, and now I am not able to use them long at a time so I begin early that I may not be disapointed in getting my letter ready for the next mail[.]

I was last Sunday evening presented to the Queen—[2] On the Thursday before, as is the etiquette I wrote a note to the Duchess of Ficalho in french, telling her that I desired to be presented to *Her Most Faithful Majesty*, and beging that her Excellency would have the goodness to inform me when it would be agreeable to her Majesty to receive me. The next day I received an answer that Her Most Faithful Majesty would receive Madame James B

Clay at 8 oclock on Sunday evening at the Palace of the Necessidades. The Queen's receptions are every other Sunday evening and this was one so (not without some compunctions of conscience I assure you) I dressed myself in a beautiful rose coloured Moire antique silk trimmed very double. She was dressed very simply, an embroidered pink crepe dress, with a bouquet of Camelias in her bosom, & I think one in her hair—After leaving her presence I went with the Countess of Ogenhansen into the second drawing room which soon became filled with company, each person having of course first been in to pay their respects to the Queen. This was the first time I had been out in Lisbon and I received a great deal of attention, and I have since heard that the Queen complimented my appearance very highly—There are only three Ladies besides myself in the deplomatic corps, and I find them very kind and agreeable. Madame Colombé the Spanish minister's wife, Madame Barrot, the wife of the French minister [Theodore-Adolphe Barrot] & Madame de Bantzon the wife, of the Sweedish Chargé[.] About 11 oclock the King[3] who speaks English very well came into the room and went around it having something to say to each lady who stood while conversing with him, and af[ter] he bowed and went on to the next Lady resumed her seat[.] He is just the opposite of the Queen in every respect, being very tall and thin, and very affable in his manners while she is very haughty, particularly to her Portuguese subjects. Of the features of the King I can only say that his eyes were brown, the rest of them were so covered with hair that I could scarcely see them. His voice is very singular, he speaks through his nose, and does not emphacise any of his words which makes it extremely monotonous—After he got through with his conversation, he certainly made a very extraordinary exit for a King he walked very quickly until he got near the centre of the room, and from there with a hop skip and jump he was through the oposite door—

Feb 8th—Day before yesterday I was presented to the Infanta at Benifica, who is Aunt to the Queen, & was regent in the reign of Don Miguel—[4] Yesterday the deplomatic Corps were again at the Palace, to be presented to the Prince & Princess de Joinville who have just arrived in Lisbon and are to reside in one of the Queens palaces at Belem—The prince looks very old, at least ten years older than my husband although they are the same age, he is quite deaf and looks sad—The princess is about my size perhaps a little thinner, brown hair and eyes, and although not beautiful she has a very distingué air and graceful manners—She also looks sad. Last Evening at 6 oclock we dined with the *Nuncio* the Popes delegate. There were 36 who dined—the 4 ladies of the Deplomatic corps and the rest gentlemen; Dukes Counts Marquis's etc. The Duke of Terceira is as much like Dr [William N.] Mercer as if they were brothers, and his wife like Mrs Ashley—The dinner was very fine, course after course until ten oclock—The platean and Candelabras were very splendid—The ladies always attend these dinners with bare neck and arms—We are leading a very different life to what we led at home, now it is very gay here because it is during the carnival, but I do assure you my dear father that both Mr. Clay & myself much prefer our own fireside—with any friend who may drop in upon us to take their cup of tea, for I am happy to say that, we have not only a fireside but some kind good friends whom we shall regret to leave—So far from becoming fond of these dinners, & balls & soirees & operas I dislike them more and more every day—

The Climate agrees with all of us—I am better than I have been since my marriage, even gaining some flesh. Our dear children are all well and grow finely[.] Lucy's [Jacob Clay] arm is entirely well and her health seems perfect[.][5] as to her spine we are doing all we can, but God only knows whether she will ever recover. Johnny [John Clay] I am sure you would not know, he is so big and fat—Jimmy [James B. Clay, Jr.] grows finely, but is perfectly crazy to get home, nearly every Gallego he sees pass he calls them to take his trunk to the ship—As for my little Harry he is as fine a baby as you ever saw, and he has his right name for he is the image of you—and I shall do all my dear father that is in my power to prevent his disgracing the name illustrious in Europe as well as in our own country—

I would like for you to send this letter to Mother, that she may know of my presentation. I am going to write to one of my sisters in Louisville[6] and will tell her all about it—Tom [P. Jacob], Mr Clay & myself are taking french lessons and are progressing rapidly—I am sorry that poor Henry [Clay III] threw away such great advantages as he had,[7] when he is older I am sure he will never cease to regret it—And now my dear father all join me in love to you all all [*sic*] the family and believe me your affectionate daughter . . .

ALS. DLC-TJC (DNA, M212, R11). 1. James B. Clay to Clay, Nov. 27, 1849. 2. Maria II, formerly Maria da Gloria. See 5:310. 3. Ferdinand of Saxe-Coberg. 4. See 5:310. 5. Clay to Lucretia H. Clay, Jan. 21, 1850. 6. Either Mrs. Curran Pope or Mrs. John W. Tyler. 7. Clay to Lucretia H. Clay, Jan. 21, 1850.

To DANIEL ULLMANN Washington, February 2, 1850

I received your favor,[1] and I am very glad to find that my movement to compromise the Slavery question is approved.[2] The timid from the North hesitate, and the violent from the South may oppose it, but I entertain hopes of its success. From another quarter (the Administration) there may be a gentle breeze of approbation.

I shall need, therefore, popular support. Large public meetings (one at New York especially),[3] indorsing my plan substantially, would do much good. Perhaps the last of next week or the week after may be early enough.

Copy. Printed in Colton, *Clay Correspondence*, 4:600. 1. Not found. 2. Clay to Combs, Jan. 22, 1850. 3. A meeting of several thousand people of all parties gathered at the Castle Garden on Feb. 25 and endorsed the Union and Clay's compromise resolutions. Speakers included Gen. Winfield Scott, Nicholas Dean, and Joseph L. White. An earlier meeting at Tammany Hall had been broken up by thugs. New York *Herald*, Feb. 12, 17, 18, 19, 23, 26, 1850.

To JAMES RYDER[1] Washington, February 5, 1850

I send my grandson H[enry]. Clay jr. [III] to the Geo. Town College, according to what was understood on the sabbath.

I have to request that he may be furnished with the requisite books and I will pay as soon as you will have the goodness to inform me of the usual charges.

ALS. DGU. 1. For James Ryder (1800-1860), president of Georgetown University in the District of Columbia, see Johnson, *Twentieth Century Biographical Dictionary*.

Speech in Senate, February 5 and 6, 1850. Speaks in support of his resolutions to reach an amicable arrangement of "all questions in controversy between the Free and the Slave States, growing out of the subject of Slavery."

Clay asserts that "never, on any former occasion, have I risen under feelings of such deep solicitude. . . . I have never before arisen to address any assembly so oppressed, so appalled, so anxious. And, sir, I hope it will not be out of place to do here what again and again I have done in my private chambers—to implore of Him who holds the destinies of nations and individuals in his hands to bestow upon our country his blessings—to bestow upon our people all his blessings—to calm the violence and rage of party—to still passion—to allow reason once more to resume its empire."

Traces "other anxious periods in the history of our country" to "the violence and intemperance of party spirit. We have had testimony of this in the progress of this session" over "the subject of the institution of slavery." As the parties "catch at every passing and floating plank, in order to add strength and power to themselves. . . . the parties of the North have . . . wooed and endeavored to obtain the assistance of a small party called Abolitionists, in order that the scale in its favor might preponderate." Indications "of the existence of the spirit and intemperance of party" have grown so strong that "One whole week—I think it was an entire week—[was] exhausted in the vain endeavor to elect a Doorkeeper of the House," the chief qualification being "whether the Doorkeeper entertained opinions upon certain great national measures coincident with this or that side of the House!"

Although "I took my leave finally, and—as I supposed—forever of this body [9:691-96]" eight years ago, "I have come here in obedience to a sense of stern duty, with no personal objects. . . . if there be in or out of this Capitol—any one who is running the race for honor, and for elevation—for higher honor, for higher elevation, than that which he may enjoy—I beg him to believe that I at least will never jostle him in the pursuit of these honors. . . . if my wishes prevail, my name shall never be used in competition with his."

Points out, however, that "It is impossible for us not to perceive that party spirit and future elevation mix more or less in all our affairs." When "the White House itself is in danger of conflagration . . . we are contending about who shall be its next occupant." It is this "passion, passion—party, party—and intemperance" that "I dread in the adjustment of the great questions which . . . divide our distracted country." In Congress there are "twenty-odd furnaces in full blast in generating heat, and passion, and intemperance" who, in the last two months, have created "uproar, confusion, menace to the existence of the Union and to the happiness and safety of this people." Asks Senators "by all that they expect hereafter, and by all that is dear to them here below, to repress the ardor of these passions" and to "listen to the voice of reason."

To put these compromise resolutions together, "I have cut myself off from the usual enjoyments of social life. . . . my thoughts have been anxiously directed to the object of . . . proposing some mode of accommodation, which should once more restore the blessings of concord, harmony, and peace." Since he is "not vain enough to suppose that I have been successful," hopes that if senators "find in it any thing which is worthy of acceptance," they will follow the "true and patriotic course," which "is not to denounce it, but to improve it; not to reject, without examination, any project of accommodation . . . but to look at it, and see if it be susceptible of alteration or improvement, so as to accomplish the object which I indulge the hope is common to all and every one of us."

Describes "two or three general purposes" he hopes to accomplish. One "was to settle all the controverted questions arising out of the subject of slavery; and it seemed to me to be doing very little. . . . if we stopped one leak only in the ship of State." Therefore, he has turned "to every subject connected with the institution of slavery, and out of which controverted questions have sprung, to see if it were possible or practicable to accommodate and adjust the whole of them." His second object "was, to endeavor to frame such a scheme of accommodation as that neither of the two classes of States into which our country is unhappily divided should make a sacrifice of any great principle." Understanding that "a portion of the Union was pushing matters, as it seemed to me, to a dangerous extremity," while "another portion of the Union was pushing them to an opposite, and perhaps to a no less dangerous extremity," he also hoped for an adjustment that would be "successful and effectual by exacting from both parties some concession—not of principle, not of principle at all, but of feeling, of opinion, in relation to the matters in controversy between them. I believe that the resolutions which I have prepared fulfill that object." Believes each purpose "is susceptible of clear, satisfactory demonstration, by an attentive persual and critical examination of the resolutions themselves."

The first resolution "declares that California, with suitable limits, ought to be admitted as a member of this Union, without the imposition of any restriction, either to interdict or introduce slavery within her limits." Even though "gentlemen who come from the slave holding States say that the North gets all it desires," points out that "If slavery be interdicted in California. . . . the interdiction is imposed by California herself [Clay to Pierse, February 16, 1849]. And has it not been the doctrine of all parties, that when a State is about to be admitted into the Union, that State has a right to decide for itself whether it will or will not have within its limits slavery?" This had been established firmly with Missouri's admission, when supporters had argued "that she had as much a right to decide upon the introduction of slavery, or upon its abolition, as New York" had a right to decide "and that she stood among her peers equal." Points out to "those contending with so much perseverance for the Wilmot Proviso" that "even if they carried their object . . . it would cease the moment any State to whose territory it was applicable came" into the Union. Describes this "first resolution" as "a case where neither party concedes; where the question of slavery . . . is silent as respects the action of this Government."

Asks senators to consider "candidly" his second resolution that calls upon Congress to establish territorial governments in the land acquired from Mexico, but to provide no laws for either the introduction or exclusion of slavery in those territories. Although aware "that every one of the free States of the Union—I believe without exception—had, by its legislative bodies, passed resolutions instructing its Senators and requesting its Representatives" to get the Wilmot Proviso "incorporated into any territorial bill. . . . I call upon them to waive persisting in it" and "to see, if their eyes are open, the dangers which lie under it, if they persevere in insisting upon it." As compensation "for the surrender of that favorite measure of theirs," offers "a declaration of what I characterize and must style . . . indisputable truths": first, "that by law slavery no longer exists in any portion of the acquisition made by us from the Republic of Mexico"; and two, "according to all the probabilities of the case, slavery never will be introduced into any portion of the territories so acquired from Mexico."

Argues that these "two truths" are not "equivalent to the enactment of the Wilmot proviso," which would be "a positive enactment, a prohibition, an interdiction as to the introduction of slavery" in the territories. Hopes proviso supporters will not require "the form of a positive enactment" and will "be satisfied with the simple expression of the opinion of Congress" as part of "a scheme of arrangement and compromise" that will not require "a surrender of their favorite measure" without "some compensation for that surrender or sacrifice."

Explains at length why these "two truths" should satisfy free state senators. To validate his opinion that "slavery does not exist in the territories ceded to the United States by Mexico, I can only refer to the fact of the passage of a law by the supreme Government of Mexico abolishing it, I think in the year 1824, and the subsequent passage of a law . . . by which they propose . . . a compensation to the owners of slaves for the property of which they were deprived by the act of abolition." Adds that

"Mexico, upon this subject, showed to the last moment her anxiety," and quotes one of Nicholas Trist's dispatches as evidence that "the diplomatic representatives of the Mexican Republic urged the abhorrence with which Mexico would view the introduction of slavery into any portion of the territory which she was about to cede to the United States." Takes it for granted, then, "that slavery does not exist there by law, unless slavery was carried there the moment the treaty [of Guadelupe Hidalgo; Clay to Beatty, April 29, 1847] was ratified by the two parties to the treaty, under the operation of the Constitution of the United States," a notion he considers "irreconcilable with any comprehension or any reason which I possess." Asks how, "amidst this conflict of interests, of principles, and of legislation, which prevails in the two parts of the Union—can you come to any other conclusion than that which I understand to be the conclusion of the public law of the world, of reason, and of justice, that the *status* of law, as it existed at the moment of the conquest or acquisition, remains unchanged until it is altered by the sovereign authority of the conquering or acquiring power? That is a great principle, and you can scarcely turn over a page of the public law where you will not find it recognized."

Notes that "the institution of slavery presents two questions totally distinct . . . slavery within the States, and slavery without the States." Congress can interfere with slavery in the states only in "three specified particulars . . . to adjust the subject of representation, to impose taxes on slaves when a system of direct taxation is made, and to perform the duty of surrendering, or causing to be delivered up, fugitive slaves." If Congress makes any further move for "the overthrow or the extinction of slavery," then " 'my voice would be for war.' " In such a case, "resistance on the part of the slave States" would be called for "in defence of our rights, of our domicils, of our property, of our safety, of our lives." If "civil war should break out" over this "violation of the Constitution," then the slave states "should have the sympathy and good wishes, and desire for our success, of all men who love justice and truth."

If, however, "we should be led into war, into civil war . . . in order to carry slavery into new territories," we would "present to the astonishment of mankind . . . an effort, not to propogate rights, but—I must say it, though I trust it will be understood to be said with no design to excite feeling—a war to propogate wrongs," in which "we should have no sympathies, no good wishes; in which all mankind would be against us; in which our own history itself would be against us; for from the commencement of the Revolution down to the present time, we have constantly reproached our British ancestors for the introduction of slavery into this country." Concludes that the question of slavery in the territories is "one upon which men may honorably and fairly differ; and however it may be decided, furnishes, I trust, no just occasion for breaking up this glorious Union of ours."

Believes, however, that "there are two sources of power, either of which is sufficient, in my judgment, to authorize the exercise of the power either to introduce or keep our slavery, outside of the States and within the Territories." Describes first the ability of the Constitution "to make governments for Territories in their infant state," as was done for the Northwest Territory. Since the region was "unpeopled" in 1787, asks "how was it possible that Congress, to whom it had been ceded, for the common benefit of the ceding States and the other States of the Union, had no power whatever to declare what description of settlers should occupy the public lands?" Argues that it was "within the contemplation of the Constitution, that Congress, who owned the soil," could "regulate the settlement of the soil, and govern the settlers in those infant colonies until they should reach a sufficient degree of consideration, in respect of numbers and capacity for self-government, to be constituted into more regular municipal organizations."

The second "source of power equally satisfactory in my mind. . . . is the treaty-making power—the acquiring power." Argues that there is "a power somewhere existing either to admit or exclude slavery from the territories acquired from Mexico. . . . a substantive, actual, existing power" that existed "in Mexico, prior to the cession of those territories. Mexico could have abolished slavery or have introduced slavery either in California or New Mexico. Now, that power must have been ceded." Since "Mexico has parted with the territory, and with it the sovereignty over the territory," the "Government of the United States, therefore, possess all the powers which Mexico possessed over those territories" and can do "within, I admit, certain limits of the Constitution—whatever Mexico could have done." Asserts, then, that "the powers of Congress are coextensive and coequal with the powers of Mexico prior to the cession."

Although "there is no grant of power in express terms, in the Constitution, over the subject of slavery," points out that the "general grant of power comprehends all the particulars of which that power consists. The power of acquisition by treaty draws with it the power to govern all the territory acquired. If there be a power to acquire, there must be a power to govern." To these two sources, then, Clay traces "the power of the Government of the United States to act upon the territories in general." More importantly, "the extent of the power" is "adequate either to introduce or to exclude slavery."

With respect to the second part of his second resolution, "I propose to admit and announce that slavery is not likely to be introduced into any of those territories." Cites the case of California, where, "more than in any other portion of the ceded territories, was it most probable, if slavery was adapted to the industrial habits of the people, that slavery would be introduced; yet within the last three months, slavery has been excluded by the vote—the unanimous vote—of the Convention, against its introduction—a vote . . . not confined to men from the non-slaveholding States." Adds that New Mexico's "soil, its barrenness, its unproductive character . . . must necessarily lead to the conclusion . . . that slavery is not likely to be introduced there."

If "by law slavery does not now exist in the territories" and "if it is not likely to be introduced into the territories," asks free state senators to reconsider their inflexible stand on the Wilmot Proviso. When it was first disseminated, "did you not fear, whatever may have been the state of the facts—did you not at that time apprehend the introduction of slavery there? You did not know much in relation to the country or its inhabitants" and "It was in this state of want of information that the whole North blazed up in behalf of this Wilmot proviso." Wonders if "two years ago it had been known in the free States" that California would adopt a constitution prohibiting slavery, or if the North "had foreseen the excitement, the danger, the irritation, the resolutions which have been adopted by Southern Legislatures [Clay to Combs, December 22, 1849]" excited by the Wilmot Proviso, whether "your constituents would not have told you to come here and settle all these questions without danger to the Union." Explains to free state senators that "You have got what is worth more than an thousand Wilmot provisos. You have nature on your side—facts upon your side—and this truth staring you in the face, that there is no slavery in those territories." Asks them to "elevate yourselves from the mud and mire of mere party contentions," to act "as responsible men, and as lovers of liberty, and lovers, above all, of this Union," and work for "peace, concord, and harmony."

Moving to the third and fourth resolutions, notes that "there are none so difficult and troublesome" as those questions that relate to Texas, "because Texas has the question of boundary to settle. The question of slavery, or the feeling connected with the institution of slavery, runs into the question of the boundary of Texas. The North are, perhaps, anxious to contract Texas within the narrowest possible limits, in order to exclude all beyond them, and to make it free territory. The South, on the contrary, are anxious to extend their limits to the source of the Rio Grande, for the purpose of obtaining an additional theatre for slavery; and it is this question of the limits of Texas, and the proper settlement of her boundaries, which embarrass all others." Notes that "a third question" adds to the difficulty: "By the resolution of annexation, all territory north of 36° 30′ was interdicted from slavery. But of New Mexico, all that which lies north of 36° 30′ embraces about one-third of the whole of New Mexico east of the Rio Grande; so that free and slave territory, slavery and non-slavery, are mixed up together."

Believes further that the boundary question must be settled because of "the state of things that now exists in New Mexico. . . . there is a feeling approximating to abhorrence, on the part of the people of New Mexico of any union with Texas." Unless the question is resolved, New Mexico "will but tend to agitation, confusion, disorder, and anarchy there, and agitation here," and "we do nothing, or next to nothing, if we do not provide against these difficulties, and the recurrence of these dangers."

Asks Sen. Joseph R. Underwood to read the act of the New Mexico convention to illustrate "what they say of their situation." The act requests "the protection due to us as citizens of our common country," especially against Indian attacks: "Many of our citizens, of all ages and sexes, are at this moment suffering all the horrors of barbarian bondage, and it is utterly out of our power to obtain their release from a condition to which death would be preferable." This, Clay asserts, "is a vivid and faithful exhibition of the actual condition of things there."

Reiterating that "there is scarcely a resolution in the series I have offered that did not contain some mutual concession, or evidence of mutual forbearance," asks senators to remember that "the question of what is the western limit and the northern limit of Texas, was an open question—has been all along an open question—was an open question when the boundary was run in virtue of the act of 1838 marking the boundary between the United States and Texas," which "specifies no boundaries—it could specify no boundary. It assumes the state of uncertainty which in point of fact we know existed." Notes, however, that "the Government of the United States retained to itself the power to settle with any foreign power," and "it seems to mc that no one can resist the logical conclusion that the United States now has the power to do what the United States and Mexico conjointly could have done."

Urges that this "delicate power" be used "with a spirit of justice, generosity, and liberality." Hopes that the boundary issue can be resolved without bringing it before the Supreme Court, "because I am not of that class of politicians who believe that every question is a proper question" for the high court. "There are questions too large for any tribunal of that kind to decide—great political, national, and territorial questions, which transcend their limits, and to which they are utterly incompetent."

Challenges Sen. Thomas J. Rusk's assertion that "we had no more right to touch the limits of Texas than we have to touch the limits of Kentucky. . . . I agree with him that, when the limits are certain and ascertained, they are undisputed and indisputable. The General Government has no right or power to interfere with the limits of a State whose boundaries are fixed, known, ascertained, and recognized—no power, at least, to interfere with it voluntarily." But the boundary of Texas is "unfixed, and remains unfixed to this moment, with respect to her western limits and north of the head of the Nueces." Moreover, since the Unites States paid $15 million for the ceded territory, asks "can Texas justly, fairly, and honorably claim all she has asserted a right to, without paying any portion" of that sum.

Argues that "Texas involved the United States in a war with Mexico," and "it was not a war of Texas and Mexico—it was a war of the whole thirty States with Mexico—a war in which the Government of the United States" served "as much the trustee and agent of the twenty-nine other states composing this Union as she was the trustee and agent of Texas." Therefore, respecting "all circumstances on which Texas relies to make out a title to New Mexico, such as the map annexed to the recent treaty with Mexico, and the opinions of . . . highly respectable and eminently elevated individuals" such as James K. Polk, "I must say . . . that he had no right, as President of the United States, or in any other character, otherwise than as negotiating with Mexico—and then the Senate had to concur with him—to fix a boundary."

Believes, nonetheless, that "the power has been concentrated in the Unites States to fix upon the limits of Texas." His resolution displays the "liberality and justice" with which this power must be exercised. Texas would receive "a vast country, equal in amount nearly, I repeat, to what she indisputably possessed before—a country sufficiently large, with her consent hereafter, to carve out of it two or three additional States." In addition, a "second resolution proposes to pay a certain amount of the debt of Texas," a sum that has been estimated at not "less than three millions of dollars." Explains in detail "the principles, out of which, I think, spring our obligations to pay the debt for which the duties of foreign imports were pledged while Texas was an independent State."

Concludes that "were you to give Texas the large boundary that is assigned to her . . . and when you take into view the large amount of money, liberating and exonerating Texas from a portion of her public debts . . . I confess, I should be greatly surprised, if the people of Texas themselves . . . should hesitate a moment to accede."

At this point, the Senate adjourns for the day.

[February 6, 1850]

Reminding senators that he does not intend "to attempt any display, or to use any ambitious language, any extraordinary ornaments or decorations of speech," takes up "the relation of Texas to the Government of the United States, in regard to that portion of the debt of Texas for which I think a responsibility exists upon the part of the Government of the United States." With the "proposed grant of three millions . . . to Texas, in consideration of her surrender of her title to New Mexico," believes "we merely discharge the obligation which exists upon the part of the Government of the United States in consequence of the appropriation of the imports receivable in the ports of Texas while she was an independent Power." Nonetheless, "there is . . . no obligation on the part of the United States to discharge one dollar of the public debt of Texas." Indeed, the resolution of admission states "that in no event are the United States to be liable or to [be] charged with any portion of the debt or liabilities of Texas." But there is "a third party, no party to the annexation whatever . . . the creditor of Texas, who advanced his money upon the credit and faith of a solemn pledge made by Texas to him to reimburse the loan, and by the appropriation of the duties receivable upon foreign imports," and it is these creditors "to whom we are bound." Feels that "other creditors of Texas" cannot complain about "leaving the residue" of the debt "unprovided for," because "we shall contribute . . . by leaving the funds of the public lands held by Texas, and what other sources she may have applicable to the payment of those other debts." Moreover, "Texas has all the resources which she had when an independent Power . . . and she is exempted from certain charges, expenditures and responsibilities which she would have had to encounter if she had remained a separate and independent Power. . . . and of course those entire revenues may be applied to the payment of her debts, except those only which are applicable to the support of the Government of Texas."

Moves on to the fifth resolution, which asserts that the abolition of slavery in the District of Columbia is "inexpedient" unless the state of Maryland and the people of the District of Columbia consent to it and slaveowners in the District are compensated for the loss of their slaves. Maintains, however, "that the power to abolish slavery in the District of Columbia has been vested in Congress by language too clear and explicit to admit, in my judgment, of any rational question whatever." If slavery were abolished in all the states in the Union, there must be power to abolish it in the District of Columbia, "or is slavery planted here to all eternity." Such power "is here" in Congress, "or it is nowhere."

While admitting "the power to exist in Congress, and exclusively in Congress, to legislate . . . in the case of the abolition of slavery within this District," contends that "it was a power which Congress cannot, in conscience and good faith, exercise while the institution of slavery continues within the State of Maryland." Virginia, too, has expressed concern about "the exercise of the power; but, in the retrocession of the portion of the District which lies south of the Potomac," she is no more interested in the question of abolition in the District "than any other slaveholding state in the Union is interested in its abolition," so the "question is now confined to Maryland."

Notes that "the great, paramount, substantial object of the grant" of land from Maryland and Virginia was "to create a suitable seat of government" for the entire United States. Believes "it is not necessary, in order to render it a proper and suitable seat . . . that slavery should be abolished" in the District. Additionally, Maryland and Virginia made this grant "when all was peace, and harmony, and concord—when brotherly affection, fraternal feeling, prevailed throughout this whole Union," and it would not be right now, "after the agitation of this unfortunate subject," to have "their generous grant, without equivalent . . . turned against them, and the sword . . . to be lifted, as it were within its own bosom, to strike at their own hearts." Feels the force of the "implied faith, this honorable obligation" to keep in "constant view the object of the cession," and argues that "Congress cannot, without forfeiture of all those obligations of honor which men of honor, and nations of honor will respect . . . interfere with slavery in this District."

Explains that his resolution "neither affirms nor disaffirms the constitutionality of the exercise of the power of abolition in the District"; it is instead "inexpedient to do it but upon certain conditions." If Maryland releases Congress "from the obligation of that implied faith. . . . I consider that that would remove one of the obstacles to the exercise of the power . . . but it is only removing one of them."

The resolution also requires "the consent of the people of the District," a people who live in "a condition in violation of the great principle which lies at the bottom of our own free institutions"—they "are acted upon by legislative authority, and taxed by legislative authority, without having any voice in the administration of affairs. The Government of the United States, in respect to the people of the District, is a tyranny, an absolute Government." Hopes that its powers "will never be so exercised, tyrannically or arbitrarily." Since the abolition of slavery would affect them "in all the relations of life which we can imagine—of property, society, comfort, peace—I think we should require . . . the consent of the people of the District of Columbia."

Raises his third condition, "that of making compensation to the owners of the slaves within the District." Cites "an amendment of the Constitution of the United States, which provides that no property—no private property—shall be taken for public use, without just compensation to the owners. . . . I think, that in a just and liberal interpretation of that clause, we are restrained from taking the property of the people of the District of Columbia in slaves . . . without full and complete compensation." On "principles of eternal justice it is wrong" to do otherwise. Adds that no European powers that abolished slavery in their colonies "have ever ventured to do it without making compensation to the owners," and "They were under no such constitutional obligation as I have referred to." Realizes that some have argued that the clause to which he alludes "would not apply to the case of abolition of slavery, because the property is not taken by the Government *for* the public use. . . . By a liberal interpretation of the clause, it seems to me, however, that slave property would be so far regarded—that it *ought* to be so far regarded—as taken for the use of the public, or at the instance of the public, as to entitle the owners . . . to a compensation."

Explains the "mutual concession" contained in this resolution: "the North has contended that the power exists under the Constitution to abolish slavery here. . . . the South, or a greater portion of the South, have contended for the opposite doctrine." The resolution asks "both parties to forbear urging their respective opinions the one to the exclusion of the other." It even concedes "all that the South . . . ought in reason to demand, inasmuch as it requires such conditions as amount to an absolute security for the property in slaves in the District."

Points out that "Congress has a power within the District equivalent to and coextensive with the power which any State possesses within its own limits." No one doubts "the power and right of any State in this Union—of any slave holding State—to forbid the introduction as merchandise of slaves within its own limits." Such a law exists in Kentucky, Mississippi, Maryland, Virginia, and "most of the slave holding States." Believes that the resolution that proposes to abolish the slave trade in the District should not be "considered as a concession by either class of States to the other class. I think it should be regarded as an object, acceptable to both, conformable to the wishes and feelings of both." Fears hearing "new and terrible tidings upon this agitating subject—I have seen, sir, that . . . delegates are to be sent to a famous Convention, to assemble in Nashville in June next [Clay to Combs, December 22, 1849]—amongst the substantive causes for which delegates are to be sent . . . is, if Congress abolishes the slave trade within the District of Columbia. That is to be the cause . . . for considering whether this Union ought to be dissolved or not. Is it possible to contemplate a greater extent of wildness and extravagance to which men can be carried by the indulgence of their passions?" Since "there has been no time in my public life that I was not willing . . . to cooperate in any steps for the abolition of the slave trade in the District of Columbia" and finds "still less ground for objection now that a large portion of the District has been retroceded to Virginia," wonders why "the feelings of those who are outraged by the scenes that are exhibited, by the *corteges* which pass along our avenues of manacled human beings—not collected in our own District, nor in our own neighborhood, but brought from distant portions of the neighboring States—why should the feelings of those who are outraged by such scenes—who are unable to contemplate such a spectacle without horror—why should they be thus outraged by the continuance of a trade so exceptionable, so repugnant, as this?" Views this resolution as one "which one set of States as well as the other should rejoice to adopt" in the hope that "we shall have peace and quiet for thirty years, such as followed the disposition of the same exciting and unhappy subject after the Missouri compromise."

Regarding the seventh resolution, which calls for more "effectual provision" for the "restitution and delivery" of fugitive slaves, Clay asserts that "upon this subject, I go with him who goes furthest in the interpretation of that clause in the Constitution which relates to this subject." Believes that Congress, every state and "the officers of every State," and "every *man* in the Union" has the "obligation to assist in the recovery of a fugitive slave from labor, who takes refuge in or escapes into one of the free states." Since this clause "is one of the general powers . . . it addresses itself to all who are bound by the Constitution of the United States," and therefore "if he is present when the owner of a slave is about to assert his rights and regain possession of his property . . . every man present, whether officer or agent of the State Governments, or private individuals, is bound to assist in the execution of the laws of their country." Notes that "the terms used in regard to fugitives from criminal offences and fugitives from labor are precisely the same," so the "performance of this duty" as "enjoined in the Constitution" is required.

Cites "some confusion, and I think misconception, upon this subject, in consequence of a recent decision of the Supreme Court. . . . There is a vast difference between imposing impediments, and affording facilities in the way of recovering the fugitive slave." The Supreme Court "have only decided that the laws of impediments are unconstitutional. . . . any laws of impediment enacted by the States were laws forbidden." Notes, however, that "The court had no right to decide whether the laws of facility were or were not constitutional" because to do so "would have transcended their authority." Asserts that "the whole class of legislation" of Northern and some Western states "by which obstructions and impediments have been thrown in the way of the recovery of fugitive slaves, are unconstitutional, and have originated in a spirit which I trust will correct itself when these States come to consider calmly upon the nature of their duty." Adds that "I do think we have just and serious cause of complaint against the free States. I think that they have failed in fulfilling a great obligation. . . . it is a mark of no good brotherhood, of no kindness, of no courtesy, that a man from a slave State cannot now, in a degree of safety, travel in a free State with his servant, although he has no purpose of stopping there any longer than a short time." Most Northern states until "the last twenty or thirty years, had laws to benefit 'sojourners,' as they were called, passing through or abiding for a time in the free States with their servants. . . . Now, sir, all these laws in behalf of sojourners in the free States are swept away, I believe, in all the States except Rhode Island. . . . And in New Jersey." This "is unkind, unneighborly, it is not in the spirit of that fraternal connection existing between all parts of this Confederacy."

Deplores especially the "seduction of family servants from the service of their owners. Servants in the families are treated with all the kindness with which the children of the family are treated." Servants so seduced "have been rendered wretched and unhappy." Recounts "an instance in my own family" in which "the seduced slave addressed her mistress, begging and imploring her to furnish her the means of getting back from the state of freedom into which she had been seduced, into the state of slavery, in which she was much more happy."

Since "the existing laws for the recovery of fugitive slaves" is "often inadequate and ineffective," feels "it is incumbent upon Congress . . . to assist in allaying this subject. . . . It is our duty to make the laws more effective; and I will go with the furthest Senator from the South in this body to make penal laws, to impose the heaviest sanctions upon the recovery of fugitive slaves, and the restoration of them to their owners."

Adds, however, that "I do not think that States, as States, are to be held responsible for all the misconduct of particular individuals. . . . fanatics, if you choose to call them so—who are for dissolving the Union—(and we know there are some at the North who are for dissolving it, in consequence of the connection which exists between the free and slaveholding States)."

Moves on to his final resolution, which declares that Congress has no power to obstruct the slave trade between the slaveholding states and that its conduct "depends exclusively upon their own particular laws." Considers this to be "a concession—of what is understood, I believe, by a great number at the North to be a constitutional provision—from the North or the South," although "I know there is a great deal that might be said on both sides of the subject in relation to the right of Congress to regulate the trade between States." Hopes the resolution "will forever put an end to the question whether Congress has or has not the power to regulate the slave trade between the different States."

Presents these resolutions as an "olive-branch to both parts of this distracted, and, at this moment, unhappy country." Claims to be ready "to surrender any thing which I have proposed, and to accept in lieu of it, anything which is better." Asks opponents not to limit themselves "to objections to any one or two of the series of resolutions" unless they can "Let us see a *contre projet*. Let us see how all the questions that have arisen out of this unhappy subject of slavery can be better settled, more fairly and justly settled, to all quarters of the Union" than is proposed in Clay's resolutions. Considers the Missouri Compromise "less worthy of the common acceptance of both parties of this Union than the project which I offer to your consideration [2:699-70, 740-48, 775-77, 785-86; 3:15-22, 26, 33, 46-47, 49-50]."

Wishes "to correct a great error . . . in respect to my agency in regard to the Missouri compromise. . . . I do not know whether anything has excited more surprise in my mind as to the rapidity with which important historical transactions are obliterated and pass out of memory, than has the knowledge of the fact I was everywhere considered the author of the line of 36° 30′, which was established upon the occasion of the admission of Missouri into the Union." Notes that "so far from my having presented as a proposition the line 36° 30′ . . . it did not originate in the House of which I was a member. It originated in this body." Recalls that the initial bill to permit Missouri to hold a constitutional convention "failed by a disagreement between the two Houses; the House of Representatives insisting upon, and the Senate dissenting from, the provision contained in the ordinance of 1787; the House insisting upon the interdiction of slavery, and the Senate rejecting the proposition for the interdiction of slavery."

In the next session, "There was a majority—not a very large one, but a very firm and decided majority—in the Senate for coupling" Missouri and Maine's admission. After much discussion in committee, the two bills we disconnected, and it was agreed to "insert in the Missouri bill a clause . . . restricting the admission of slavery north of the 36° 30′ line, and leaving the question open south of 36° 30′. . . . Mr. [Jesse Burgess] Thomas . . . presented the proposition of 36° 30′ and it was finally agreed to." Adds that "as I was Speaker of the House, and as the journal does not show which way the Speaker votes, except in cases of a tie, I am not able to tell with certainty, how I actually did vote; but I have no earthly doubt that I voted, in common with my other southern friends, for the adoption of the line 36° 30′."

After Missouri included in its constitution "a provision to prevent the migration of free people of color into that State. . . . northern members" of the Congress "took exception to it" and "got in motion to keep out Missouri." To settle it, "I asked for a committee of thirteen, and a committee of thirteen was granted to me, representing all the old States of the Union." When this committee could not resolve the problem, "I brought forward another proposition, and a new one, perfectly unpracticed upon in the country. . . . I proposed a joint committee of the two Houses . . . and that this committee be appointed by ballot." When two of the 23 members of the House committee refused to serve, "to my regret, and somewhat to my annoyance, the lamented Mr. [John] Randolph" was appointed and quickly "made a suggestion which I knew would be attended with the greatest embarrassment and difficulty." Randolph wanted "the chairman of the committee of the House, who was myself," to preside at joint committee meetings. Clay "thought the chairman of the committee of each House should preside over his own committee," and this was agreed to. Taking care to put together "something practical, something conclusive, something decisive upon the question," the House committee reported a proposition that Clay was certain would carry. It declared that "if there be any provisions in the constitution of Missouri incompatible with the Constitution of the United States, the State of Missouri shall forbear to enforce that repugnant provision . . . and that she shall by some solemn authentic act, declare that she will not enforce any provision in her constitution incompatible with the Constitution of the United States." After trying to convince "our brethren from the North" that no "tribunal upon earth . . . but would pronounce the Constitution of the United States paramount," the resolution was passed. In the end, "all parties were satisfied with a declaration of an incontestable principle of constitutional law. . . . They wanted something for a justification of the course which they took."

Hopes that "Now, as then, if we will only suffer our reason to have its scope and sway, and if we will still and hush the passion and excitement which have been created by the occasion, difficulties will be more than half removed in the settlement, upon just and amicable principles, of the question which unhappily divides us at this moment."

Contrasts his own "plan of accommodation" with "that which is offered by the Missouri line, to be extended to the Pacific ocean" to ascertain which is "most proper . . . most just." Asks "gentlemen from the South" if they "are prepared to be satisfied with the line of 36° 30′, interdicting slavery north of that line, and giving them no security for the admission of slavery south of that line," reminding them that Sen. Davis had said that "he was not prepared to be satisfied with anything short of the. . . . positive recognition of slavery south of the line of 36° 30′." Points out that "if I offer the line of 36° 30′, to interdict the question of slavery north of it, and to leave it unsettled and open south of it, I offer that which is illusory to the South—I offer that such will deceive them, if they suppose that slavery will be received south of that line. It is better for . . . the south, that there should be non-action as to slavery both north and south of the line." Otherwise, "What is there gained by the South, if the Missouri line is extended to the Pacific, with the interdiction of slavery north of it?" Indeed, "if you adopt the Missouri line . . . you do legislate upon the subject of slavery, and you legislate for its restriction without a corresponding equivalent of legislation south of that line for its admission," and "I insist . . . the principles of equality would require that there should be legislation admitting slavery south of that line." Admits, however, "that I could never vote . . . to spread slavery over territory where it does not exist."

Argues, then, that "Non-action by Congress is best for the South, and best for all the views which the South have disclosed to us." Understands that many have said "with regard to California, that non-legislation upon the part of Congress implies the same thing as the exclusion of slavery. That we cannot help. That Congress is not responsible for. If nature has pronounced the doom of slavery" there, "who can you reproach but nature and nature's God. Congress you cannot. Congress abstains. Congress is passive. Congress in non-acting, south and north of the line; or rather if Congress agrees to the plan which I propose, extending no line," leaving "these territories untouched by legislative enactments."

Sen. Willie P. Mangum offers to move for adjournment, but Clay continues, asking the Senate "to look back upon the career which this country has run from the adoption of the Constitution to the present day." Discusses the "sway in the councils of the nation, whether of the North or of the South," during the past 60 years: "During the first twelve years of the administration of the government, northern counsels rather prevailed," but their measures—"the Bank of the United States; the assumption of state debts; bounties to the fisheries" and others—were not "carried exclusively by northern counsels."

Southern counsels have prevailed "for the last fifty years," but their "preponderíng influence" required cooperation, "and large cooperation, in some instances, from the northern section." Cites measures during "the fifty years that southern counsels have preponderated," including the embargo, the War of 1812, reestablishment of the Bank of the United States and "the same bank put down," acquisition of Florida, Texas, and Louisiana, Indian removals, and the Mexican War.

Finds no "just cause of reproach to the one side or the other," but admits "in all candor and sincerity, that least of all ought the South to reproach the North . . . when we reflect that even opposite doctrines have been prominently advanced by the South and carried at different times." Cites the fate of the Bank of the United States as a prime example. Also looks at "the territorial acquisitions made by this country, and to what interests have they conduced?" Points to the introduction of slavery into Florida, much of the Louisiana territory south of the 36° 30′ line, and Texas, the last gained by "a war made essentially by the South." Ironically, this war brought "the ultimate acquisition of these territories, which now constitute the bone of contention between the members of the Confederacy [Clay to Beatty, April 29, 1847]."

Another senator proposes to adjourn, but Clay continues: "I begin to see land." Asks senators to imagine "that the Union has been dissolved. What remedy does it furnish for the grievances complained of in its united condition?" Claims it would not promote the extension of slavery into New Mexico and Texas nor protect slavery in the District of Columbia. Moreover, if the Union were dissevered, "Slaves taken from the one into the other would be there like slaves now escaping from the United States into Canada. There would be no right of extradition—no right to demand your slaves—no right to appeal to the courts of justice to demand your slaves which escape, or the penalties for decoying them. . . . hundreds and thousands would escape if the Union were severed in parts."

Maintains "there is no right on the part of one or more of the States to secede from the Union. War and the dissolution of the Union are identical and inseparable. There can be no dissolution of the Union, except by consent or by war" and "No one can expect . . . that that consent would be given." Believes that in "*less* time than sixty days, I believe, our slaves from Kentucky would be fleeing over in numbers to the other side of the river, would be pursued. . . . they would be repelled, and war would break out." Suggests as well that dissolution would create "at least three confederacies"—the North, the Atlantic slave states, and the Mississippi Valley—and "other Confederacies would spring up, from time to time, as dissatisfaction and discontent" grew.

Restates his primary beliefs: "I am directly opposed to any purpose of secession, of separation. I am for staying within the Union. . . . and fighting for my rights—if necessary, with the sword—within the bounds and under the safeguards of the Union. I am for vindicating these rights; but not by being driven out of the Union rashly. . . . Here I am within it, and here I mean to stand and die." In addition to believing there is no right to secession, "I think that the Constitution of the thirteen States was made, not merely for the generation which then existed, but for posterity, undefined, unlimited, permanent and perpetual. . . . It is to remain for that posterity now and forever. Like another of the great relations of private life, it was a marriage that no human authority can dissolve or divorce the parties from; and, if I may be allowed to refer to this same example in private life, let us say what man and wife say to each other: We have mutual faults; nothing in the form of human beings can be perfect; let us, then, be kind to each other, forbearing, conceding; let us live in happiness and peace."

The only alternative is war. If we "search the pages of history . . . from the wars of Greece down, including those of the Commonwealth of England, and the revolution of France . . . none of them raged with such violence, or was ever conducted with such bloodshed and enormities as will that war which shall follow" dissolution of the Union. An "exterminating" war would follow—"not a war of two or three years, but of interminable duration . . . until some Philip or Alexander, some Caesar or Napoleon, would rise to cut the Gordian knot, and solve the problem of the capacity of man for self-government, and crush the liberties of both the dissevered portions of this Union." Fears that "the final result will be the extinction of this last and glorious light which is leading all mankind . . . to cherish hope and anxious expectation that the liberty which prevails here will sooner or later be advanced throughout the civilized world." Implores Northerners and Southerners "by all their love of liberty—by all their veneration for their ancestors—by all their regard for posterity . . . to pause—solemnly to pause—at the edge of the precipice, before the fearful and disastrous leap is taken into the yawning abyss below."

Prays that "if the direful and sad event of the dissolution of the Union shall happen, I may not survive to behold the sad and heart-rending spectacle." *Cong. Globe*, 31 Cong., 1 Sess., Appendix, 115-27.

To LUCRETIA HART CLAY Washington, February 7, 1850

I have been yesterday and the day before making a Speech of near four hours and three quarters, in the Senate, on my propositions to compromise the Slavery questions.[1] It has exhausted me very much, but I hope to recover my strength in a day or two. Whether my specific propositions will be adopted or not is uncertain, but all agree that my movement and Speeches have done good.

H[enry]. Clay Junr [III] joined me in good health a few days ago, and for the present I have placed him at the College in Geo. Town.[2] I do not know whether I could get him in at West point or not,[3] if it were desirable;

but he does not seem anxious to go there, altho' he says that he will conform to my wishes and do whatever I may require.

I wrote you that I had sent by Adams's Express line[4] last week a package which ought to reach you a little after this letter does. I have heard nothing yet from Mr. Evans about the progress of the Mules.[5]

I continue at the N[ational]. Hotel and with the exception of colds my general health is good.

My love to John [Morrison Clay].

ALS. Courtesy of Mrs. Robert P. Clay, Greenville, Miss. 1. Speech in Senate, Feb. 5-6, 1850. 2. Clay to Lucretia H. Clay, Jan. 21, 1850. 3. Clay to Morehead, Dec. 14, 1848. 4. Adams & Co. Express was located at 16 Wall Street in New York City. *Wilson's Business Directory of New-York City* (New York, 1848). 5. Clay to Thomas H. Clay, Jan. 8, 1850.

To James W. Simonton, Washington [?], February 8, 1850. Expresses his thanks for arranging a meeting with Thomas Ritchie: "I will see Mr. R. with great pleasure at my lodgings on Sunday next, between the hours of 1 and 3. . . . Or, if, on further reflection, he should prefer it, I will attend Mr. [Smith] Pyne's Church on Sunday next, and immediately after the conclusion of Divine service, I will go to Mr. R.'s private residence." Copy. Printed in Richmond *Enquirer*, September 10, 1852.

For Simonton (1823-82), who at various times was a reporter for or owner of newspapers in New York, California, and Washington, D.C., see *DAB*. The Rev. Smith Pyne was rector of St. John's Episcopal Church at 16th and H Streets N.W. in Washington, D.C. Information supplied by Jack D. Brewer, The Historical Society of Washington, D.C.

In a meeting arranged by Simonton, Ritchie, accompanied by Gen. Thomas H. Bayly of Virginia, called upon Clay in his hotel room on February 10, 1850. Ritchie had already come out in favor of compromise in an editorial in the Washington *Union* and had suggested to Sen. Henry S. Foote the idea of proposing a special Senate Committee of Thirteen to consider the problems involving slavery and the territories. Foote then brought forward the resolution to that effect. After negotiations with Clay, Ritchie became an ardent supporter of the compromise proposals. Charles H. Ambler, *Thomas Ritchie, A Study in Virginia Politics* (Richmond, Va., 1913), 280-82; Richmond *Enquirer*, September 10, 1852.

At a dinner in March, 1850, at John T. Sullivan's, Clay and Ritchie made a public reconciliation of their differences. After some badinage about the old charge of "bargain and corruption" in which Clay reportedly said: "shut your mouth, Tom Ritchie; you know perfectly well that there never was a word of truth in that charge," Ritchie promised to plant a sprig of laurel on Clay's grave if he succeeded in saving the Union. Clay then addressed the assembly, saying that "I feel it to be due to such an occasion as the present one to make a frank confession. Though I never doubted the propriety of my own conduct, in voting for Mr. [John Quincy] Adams myself in 1825 and advising my friends to vote for him, yet, were I to live this part of my public life over again, I should not deem it judicious to accept at his hands the Secretaryship of State. By doing so I injured both him and myself . . . and often have I painfully felt that I had seriously impaired my own capacity for public usefulness." Henry S. Foote, *Casket of Reminiscences* (1874; reprint ed., New York, 1968), 27-28. For Foote (Dem., Miss.), see *BDAC*.

From John P. Kennedy, Baltimore, February 9, 1850. Writes in behalf of Edward B. Bailey of Lewisburg, Va., who desires "employment under the General Government." Although aware of Clay's "necessity of keeping aloof from an active participation in matters relating to applications for office," hopes he will assist Bailey "to find some service in the Territories" consistent with his "good education" and "respectable position at the bar of Virginia."

Congratulates Clay on "your noble speech—so full of patriotism and wisdom [Speech in Senate, February 5-6, 1850]. It is the language of Nestor in our councils." Hopes "it will so touch the national heart as to bring all discord back to harmony." ALS. MdBP. No appointment for Bailey shows up in the U.S. Sen., *Executive Journal*, vol. 8.

Remark in Senate, February 12, 1850. In his speech on slavery in the territories, Sen. John M. Berrien challenges Clay's view that Congress has the power to abolish slavery in the District of Columbia but its exercise "was forbidden by the honorable obligation incurred by the acceptance of the cession" of land from the slave states of Virginia and Maryland.

Clay warns that "this implication of good faith . . . was limited. If, for example, the only ceding States now existing should consent, and, moreover, if the people of the District should consent, and compensation were made, then there would be no implication resulting from the implied faith . . . it is a thing temporary in its existence, lasting only while slavery lasts in Maryland, and terminating when consent is given. . . . That is the view I intended to take." *Cong. Globe*, 31 Cong., 1 Sess., Appendix, 209.

Remark in Senate, February 13, 1850. Presents the memorial of "a committee of the revenue bond-holders in the late Republic of Texas, praying for the payment or adjustment of the bonds which they hold." Notes that the petition "is founded upon . . . the responsibility of this Government for at least that portion of the debt of Texas contracted prior to her annexation," a view propounded by Clay in his recent resolutions on the slavery question [Speech in Senate, January 29 and February 5-6, 1850]. Proposes that the memorial be sent to the Committee on the Judiciary "because there are important questions arising under it of public and international law."

Later, when Sen. William R. King raises the question of "carrying into effect the convention between the United States and Brazil" of January 27, 1849, Clay notes that "We have now in this city a commission acting under the Mexican treaty" whose linguist "understands both the Spanish and Portuguese languages." Wonders if it "would not be better, instead of creating a new board, to assign to the existing board the duty of passing upon the claims arising out of this treaty. . . . it seems to me that the matter would be finished much sooner than if a new board, or new commission were appointed." Clay's suggestion is rejected.

Zachary Taylor had forwarded to the Senate an authenticated copy of California's constitution, and Sen. Thomas Hart Benton expresses his expectation that Clay "would make a motion for a select committee on the President's message." Clay states that he has "no desire to take the lead upon the subject," but "if it were the pleasure of the Senate to direct me to act in conjunction with any select committee on the subject, especially as it had had the kindness heretofore to exonerate me" from duty on the standing committees [Remark in Senate, December 18, 1849], he would "obey that wish." No immediate action is taken, but later that day Sen. Henry S. Foote submits a resolution calling for "a special committee of fifteen, to be chosen by ballot" to consider California's bid for statehood and "the various propositions now before the Senate relating to the same subject, in connection with the question of domestic slavery." *Cong. Globe*, 31 Cong., 1 Sess., 353-55.

For the 1849 convention between the U.S. and Brazil, see Parry, *Treaty Series*, 102:453-58.

Comment in Senate, February 14, 1850. Since Sen. Stephen A. Douglas had moved to refer President Zachary Taylor's message on California to the Committee on Territories before Sen. Henry S. Foote proposed a special committee of fifteen [Remark in Senate, February 13, 1850] to look into California statehood "in connection with the question of domestic slavery," the Illinois senator's motion receives first consideration. Clay rises in support of Douglas: "I do not think it would be right to confound or to combine all these subjects" in Foote's resolution. "I think the subject of the admission of California ought to be kept separate and distinct." Since "three or four members of Congress . . . have come here all the way from the Pacific with a constitution" for California, asks if it is "right to subject them to all the delay, the uncertainty, the procrastination which must inevitably result from the combination of all these subjects. . . . I think not. . . . it seems to me that we should decide, and decide as promptly as we can consistently with just and proper deliberation. I think the question of the admission of California is one which stands by itself."

Foote expresses his "unbounded astonishment" at Clay's stand, since "That senator some weeks ago [Speech in Senate, January 29 and February 5-6, 1850] took the lead in urging upon this body and the country the consideration of a *general scheme of pacification and compromise*," resolutions "so drawn as to cover the *whole* ground of controversy understood to be occupied by the pro-slavery and anti-slavery disputants of the country." Adds: "I am grieved—I am mortified" by Clay's reversed course. "The persecuted South has looked to him as one of her safest, most influential and distinguished sons," and unless California is admitted to statehood as part of "some liberal and equitable plan of pacification and compromise" like the one Clay had originally suggested, "the vessel of State will certainly be found to have sprung a new leak."

Clay retorts that if he "were disposed to retaliate at all" upon Foote "in reference to the supposed change of opinion," he would point out that Foote "was in favor of the admission of California a year ago, when she had no constitution; but he is opposed to her admission now, when she comes here with a constitution in her hands [Clay to Pierse, February 16, 1849], precisely in the manner in which Florida, Arkansas, I believe, and Michigan did."

When challenged by Sen. Hopkins L. Turney, who believes Florida was authorized by "a law of Congress" to write its constitution, Clay closes discussion of the issue as "not a matter of much importance." Responds instead to Foote's "sort of omnibus speech, in which he introduces all sorts of things and every kind of passenger, and myself among them. [Laughter.] And I have risen rather to vindicate myself from the charge of inconsistency." Describes Foote as "a gentleman of fine imagination and of great fancy" who totally "misconceived me." Insists that although he presented a series of resolutions at the same time, "It is impossible that anybody can conceive that I intended to embrace all this variety of subjects in one bill, and propose the passage of them all at once."

Foote responds that "all or most of these matters could be embraced in one bill." Asks Clay how "*a Senator from the State of Kentucky, within whose limits the system of domestic slavery exists, can . . . increase the number of adversary votes against us upon all the pending questions, without first receiving some compensation therefor?*"

Clay retorts: "I know no South, no North, no East, no West to which I owe any allegiance. I owe allegiance to two sovereignties, and only two; one is to the sovereignty of this Union, and the other is to the sovereignty of the state of Kentucky." If Foote and others seek "from me an acknowledgment of allegiance to any ideal or future contemplated confederacy of the South, I here declare that I owe no allegiance to it." Offended by Foote's insinuations, expresses his hope that "gentlemen will not transcend the limits of legitimate parliamentary debate in using any language towards me; because I fear I could not even trust myself if they were to do it." Senators should demonstrate "a reciprocity of parliamentary dignity and propriety."

Repeats his desire that "the Senate should express its sense upon each" of his resolutions. "If they should be affirmatively adopted" and if "some of the subjects . . . may be perhaps advantageously combined," then "I hope they can be combined in one bill." Adds, however, "beyond that," he never intended "to combine all these subjects in one bill of fifty or a hundred sections or pages." If one resolution "might be matured in the shape of a bill a little earlier than others" and if it is "a little more favorable to one section of the Union than to another," believes that "that part of the Union which had been favored by the adoption of that measure" would maintain the spirit of compromise and "would not fail to do what was right and proper when a measure came forward advantageous . . . to another portion of the Union."

Foote comments that Clay "could scarcely have been as happy in the enunciation of his views as he usually has been, else so general a misinterpretation could hardly have occurred." Denies he has been "discourteous" to Clay, since some Democrats "accuse me of being even too deferential" to him. Is "startled" by Clay's insinuation "that some persons in the South are aiming to establish a Southern confederacy."

Clay responds that "the language as used here again and again is 'treachery to the South,' 'abandoning the South,' 'failing to uphold the interests of the South'. . . . I meant to say . . . that I knew of no South in the shape of a confederated Government; no South to which I owed allegiance. I did not mean to say that there was a solitary individual in the South in favor of a dissolution of the Union."

Douglas's motion to refer Taylor's message to the Committee on Territories is amended by adding an instruction "to report a bill for the admission of California unconnected with any other subject." *Cong. Globe*, 31 Cong., 1 Sess., 365-69. Printed in Colton, *Clay Correspondence*, 6:394-409.

For Sen. Hopkins L. Turney (Dem., Tenn.), see *BDAC*.

Remark in Senate, February 15, 1850. Sen. Andrew P. Butler speaks against separating the California question from the rest of Clay's grand scheme of compromise [Speech in Senate, January 29 and February 5-6, 1850] for resolving the slavery question. "Feeling that I am identified with the weaker but the wronged party," wonders why "the Senator from Kentucky said he knew no *South* in his allegiance [Comment in Senate, February 14, 1850]" without adding " 'nor to the North, nor to the West, nor to the East, but to the Union' "; because, "to single out the *South* as not claiming his allegiance gave me pain."

Clay responds: "I think I did say the North. . . . I meant then, and I mean now, that I owe no allegiance to any one section—East, North, West, or South. And I know, I repeat, of but two sovereignties to whom I owe allegiance—the one the Union, and the other my own State." *Cong. Globe*, 31 Cong., 1 Sess., 371.

For Andrew P. Butler (States Rights Dem., S.C.), see *BDAC*.

To DANIEL ULLMANN Washington, February 15, 1850

I received your favor of the 12th inst. I am glad to hear of the contemplated popular movement in the city of New York, on the subject of the questions concerning slavery which are producing so much unhappy division and distraction.[1] It will do much good, if it be large, imposing, and be attended without distinction of party. But I must think that its beneficial effects will depend much upon its being conducted and regarded as a local and spontaneous assemblage, without any ground for the imputation of its being prompted from any exterior source. And I therefore think it would be best that there should not be any distant intervention from Congress or from any remote quarter. It would indeed be very difficult, putting that consideration aside, to prevail upon members of Congress, at the moment of so much interest and excitement, to quit Congress and repair to New York to address the meeting. At all events, motives of delicacy and propriety would restrain me from addressing any member of Congress to leave his official position with such purpose. I should hope that it was not necessary, and that gentlemen from New York, the fresher from the masses the better, could be induced, from patriotic considerations, to attend and address the meeting.

My accounts of the reception of my scheme of adjustment and accommodation of the slavery questions are encouraging.[2] There is some holding back in each quarter, from a purpose of not committing itself, until the views of the other are known. But, in spite of this reserve, there are outbreaks of approbation and sanction of the scheme. And although I can not positively say so, I entertain strong hopes that it will furnish the basis of concord and a satisfactory accommodation.

Copy. Printed in Colton, *Clay Correspondence*, 4:600-601. 1. Clay to Ullmann, Feb. 2, 1850. 2. Clay to Combs, Jan. 22, 1850; Speech in Senate, Feb. 5-6, 1850.

To John M. Clayton, Washington, February 17, 1850. States that "According to the letter of the Constitution, assuming the existence of a vacancy during the recess of the Senate, which was filled by the President, the Commission granted, on the occasion, may endure until the end of the succeeding Session. But if the President sends to the Senate the nomination of a person so appointed, and the Senate rejects the nomination, considering that the Senate is a component part of the appointing power, I think that, according to the spirit of the Constitution, such person ought officially to act no longer than during the period which would be necessary to communicate to him the fact of his rejection. And this course would manifest a deference to the judgment of the Senate calculated to preserve good feelings and harmony between the two branches of the appointing power." ALS. DeHi.

From W.E. Whitfield, Camden, Ark., February 17, 1850. On behalf of the Masonic Lodge of Camden, encloses a copy of their resolutions mourning "the death of our Brother Porter Clay . . . one of the brigh[t]est pillar[s] of the Order—one whose life of usefulness & honor has given evidences that his Work in the Lodge below will meet the approbation of & receive a rich reward at the Hands of the Great Master above." DS. DLC-TJC (DNA, M212, R11).

Porter Clay had died on February 16, 1850. Smith & Rogers, *The Clay Family*, 90.

From JAMES BROWN CLAY Lisbon, Portugal, February 18, 1850

Your letter of the 8th January was received by the last Steamer on the 15th inst.

I regret that the Portuguese Minister [J.C. de Figaniere e Morao] has not been pleased with some expressions contained in my note to his M[inister]. of F[oreign]. affairs [Count Tojal], to which you refer, but my regret is somewhat lessened by the approval which my own government gave to that note—[1] The truth is that I made use of no word which I did not consider perfectly appropriate and deserved. Mr. Figaniere could not have shown you the note of his minister to which mine was in reply—In several parts of it he had most unjustly & indiplomatically caracterised the arguments of Mr. [George W.] Hopkins as *Specious*, and had made use of sarcasms wholly unauthorised by the facts of the case or by courtesy—I intended and I think did no more than pay him fairly in his own coin—indeed he thought so himself, for his brother made excuses to me more than once, on account of the language I had censured. As to the expression "insult" I meant just what I said, I felt that my country was insulted, and determined that he should know it—As to the request for the correspondence with the British Government,[2] I was authorised to make it, by his having introduced that Govt. into the discussion, and by his reference to testimony which he had no situation to introduce—Perhaps you are right as to the inference I threatened—But you cannot understand this people! they will do nothing except upon compulsion[.] And I was verbally advised or instructed by Mr. [John M.] Clayton to take a threatening attitude. As to the other claims which Mr. Figaniere states would long ago have been provided for, but for the [*General*] Armstrong case[3] being kept in the foreground &c &c. the truth is entirely different; they have been as much and as strongly pressed as that case. The fact is the conduct of his Government has been inexcusable. Note upon note for months and even years unanswered or answered evasively, upon Claims which they neither could nor pretended to controvert, has made it quite as bad as that of the Greeks, which has recently forced the English to a grain blockade of the Pirius [*sic*, Piraeus], in which they have set us an example worthy of all imitation.[4]

You must also understand the position of Mr. Figaniere, from which his chagrin is easily deduced[.] He came here to Portugal from America with the sole purpose of having his rank advanced to that of Minister Plenipotentiary—Whether he deceived his government as to the importance ours would give to our claims, I do not know, but I do know, that he spoke freely and frequently out of doors about them, stating that we would not insist upon them &c &c. He returned to America with assurances that the Govt. would use its efforts to have the appropriation made for his increased rank & I fully understand how distasteful, the correspondence of Mr. Hopkins & myself must have been to him.

I am well satisfied that I have pursued the right course with this Government; When I arrived here I found note upon note unanswered[.] Mr. Hopkins will tell you that he had sometimes to wait weeks and even months for a simple order for things for the use of his family! The Queen [Maria II] at her audiences had the constant habit of passing him, without the slightest recognition of his presence, which was even noticed to the M. of F. Affairs [Count Tojal] by the French Minister [Theodore-Adolphe Barrot] as he himself told me; this she commenced too with me. My course has effected a change—they are now prompt in small matters, if no more. The Queen is more polite, and I am upon the most friendly terms with the Minister.

As to the claims—Count Tojal informed me last week that he should have a council of Ministers last Sunday, upon them I thot he intended soon to reply to my note—More than a week has past & I have heard nothing further—I am inclined to believe that he is endeavoring to transfer the negociation to Washington, as I have heard they have been writing buisily in the Foreign office. I have no idea that they will come out fairly & offer to pay, all but the Armstrong—I have already informed Mr. Clayton that I believed I could get them to consent to an arbitration—but I advised strongly against it—because many of the claims are too just & in none could we get a perfectly impartial arbitration[.] I should be willing, if they would agree to pay all the rest & admit the justice of the Armstrong claim to agree to refer the amount to a commission, because if they admit its justice—the value of the vessel is the least amount & it would carry interest of course, unless they gave a compromise reward—which they ought not to have power to do.

If a vessel of war had been sent shortly after the Presidents Message,[5] with instructions to me to demand passports or answers, I think the claims would now have been settled, and I think it is still the right course.

I would be glad to have your advice as to the propriety of my resignation at the end of the year if the claims are settled![6] I think we shall be satisfied with Lisbon—the salary is not more than enough if sufficient; because a Chargé is treated here as Minister & if we go to the Continent, as we wish we will be long enough from home. besides if the claims are settled the life will be very idle, & there is nothing to repay the loss of time.

Susan [Jacob Clay] and the children are quite well[.] We are all taking French lessons. She joins me in affectionate love to you.

ALS. DLC-TJC (DNA, M212, R11). 1. Clay to James B. Clay, Jan. 8, 1850. 2. *Ibid.* 3. Clay to Clayton, June 7, 1849. 4. Don Pacifico, a Moorish Jew and British subject, held large claims against the Greek government which he pressed with vigor until an anti-semitic mob burned his house in Athens in Dec., 1849. Lord Palmerston then ordered a British squadron to the Piraeus to force a settlement of this and other British claims. The British laid an embargo on all Greek vessels in the Piraeus and finally seized them in Jan., 1850. After an abortive attempt at mediation by the French, the Greeks were forced to comply in April, 1850. Langer, *Encyclopedia of World History*, 662. 5. Clay to James B. Clay, Dec. 29, 1849. 6. Clay to Clayton, June 7, 1849.

Remark in Senate, February 18, 1850. Sen. Solomon Downs, speaking on Clay's resolution relating to the admission of California, expresses concern over the phrase " 'suitable boundaries.' I thought that in it might be found some guarantee of compromise and settlement of the matter," but cannot find it.

Clay explains that when he wrote the resolution he was under the impression that California's new constitution contained "a provision that if Congress was not satisfied with the boundaries which she proposed, it might alter those boundaries so as to make them conformable to what might be deemed right." He believed California's "Representatives coming here" would bring "some instructions expressive of her consent to the modification of her boundaries. . . . and under that impression, I employed those words." Since "I do not to this moment possess the geographical knowledge which I would desire as to the nature of the country, the soil, and what portion is desert, and what capable of cultivation," he is not "absolutely committed to the admission of California even now, with the precise boundaries which she has proposed." *Cong. Globe*, 31 Cong., 1 Sess., Appendix, 165.

To LUCRETIA HART CLAY Washington, February 19, 1850

I have reason to be thankful for a pretty good share of health. I eat and drink, perhaps too much, I sleep well, going to bed regularly about 10 O'Clock, and I never worked harder. I still have bad colds, but without any fever. I think I have grown fatter. James [Marshall][1] proves to be a faithful and attentive servant, behaving very well.

Henry [Clay III] continues at Geo. town and seems quite contented.[2] He comes to dine with me every Sunday[.]

Tell John [Morrison Clay] that I have at last heard from Evans. On the 13th. of this month he had still 140 miles to travel before he got to Greensboro.[3] Tell him also that I wish if my young Jack intended for [Wade]

Hampton cannot be broke at Ashland to perform his duty that he would get Toddhunter [*sic*, Parker E. Todhunter] or Wright to have him proved.

I send you a letter from James [Brown Clay] that I ought to have forwarded before.

My love to John [Morrison Clay].

ALS. DLC-TJC (DNA, M212, R11). 1. His free bodyservant. See Clay to Lucretia H. Clay, Dec. 28, 1849. 2. Clay to Ryder, Feb. 5, 1850. 3. Clay to Thomas H. Clay, Jan. 8, 1850.

Comment in Senate, February 20, 1850. After a heated exchange between Sens. Jeremiah Clemens and Stephen A. Douglas during debate on the admission of California to the Union, Clay decries the " 'ultraism' of which this country, at this moment, stands in so much danger." Immediately lightening the mood, notes that Clemens alluded to the unlikely cooperation of Clay and Sen. Thomas Hart Benton by remarking that "the lion and the lamb had got together. I do not know to which of these quadrupeds he assigned me; I should make a very poor lamb I am afraid, and I am very far from being ambitious of claiming prowess of the lion." Clemens retorts "the lion," and worries that the cooperation of two "who had always heretofore been the antipodes of each other" meant that "the South was menaced with danger."

Clay denies "that there has been any cooperation whatever" between Benton and himself, and makes clear that although there had been several years of "no very friendly social intercourse . . . we came together again, and restored relations, at least of civility and amity." Recalls "no interchange of opinion" but only discussions "of the disposition of the [California] question before the Senate. . . . has it come to this, that one Senator cannot commune with another about the disposition of the public business of the country without incurring suspicion, without subjecting himself to animadversion, and in such language as is tantamount to a formal accusation" of collusion? Adds that "if the Senator from Missouri had been the worst enemy, the bitterest enemy I had in the world . . . I would have gone to him as to the best and most affectionate friend I had on earth, in order to produce such a great and glorious result as that would be of harmonizing the different portions of this at present unfortunate country."

Believes, however, that "on the occasion of preparing these resolutions, I consulted with too few," and "Those I did consult were generally my friends from the South; with one solitary exception, I consulted no northern gentlemen." Recalls learning a lesson in 1833 when "I consulted too many; the effect of which was to endanger the fate" of the Compromise Tariff of 1833.

Asserts that in regard to California, the North got what it wanted "not by the action of Congress, but by the action of the people of California themselves, who had a right to decide whether they would admit or exclude slavery [Clay to Pierse, February 16, 1849]." Disagrees with Clemens's view that "if Congress now admits California, Congress will be responsible for that clause in the constitution of California which interdicts slavery." Argues that "no matter how her constitution may be formed, whether with or without the consent of Congress, when that constitution is presented to us, our consideration is limited to the inquiry whether it is republican." Despite the fact that "the constitution has been formed with some degree of irregularity. . . . Congress is no more responsible for the interdiction of slavery which exists in the constitution of California now, than Congress would be responsible for it if there had been a prior act of Congress authorizing the people of California to consider for themselves, and to determine whether they would or would not come into the Union as a member of it." California had "had an excuse which did not exist in the case of other States that have been admitted into this Union. . . . She was abandoned by Congress" which "failed to discharge its parental duty towards California at the last session." To head off a "state of profound and perfect anarchy," she formed "a very excellent constitution" in which "She chooses herself, of her own free will, to refuse to admit slavery within her limits." Admonishes Clemens: "You abandoned your child, and now, when that child comes to you, having shifted for itself as well as it could in the absence of your parental authority, you reproach it with usurpation, with impudence; and are ready . . . to repel her from your doors, and send her back without any suitable government." Compares the "case of Michigan and that of California" as "the difference between government and no government; between government and anarchy; between the exercise of parental authority on the part of Congress towards Michigan, and the abandonment of all duty, constitutional, natural, and parental, on the part of Congress towards California."

Warns against an oft-repeated sentiment "that upon certain contingencies, upon the occurrence of certain events, the South must take a particular, a specified course, regardless of consequences. *Regardless of consequences*! . . . I know of no condition where a religious, moral, rational, responsible being can take a step regardless of consequences." Adds that "it is because I do look to these consequences . . . that I am led to the conclusion of making an exertion, of making every effort . . . to avert the greatest of all human calamities, not only that could befall this country, but that could befall the whole race of civilized men."

Extended comments are made by Clemens, Sen. Jefferson Davis, who criticizes Clay's "past history in connection with the subject of slavery," and Sen. Henry S. Foote, who points to the reception of Clay's speeches in the Northern press as proof that "the influence of his character and intellect has been exerted with most deadly effect against the South. . . . I do not now speak of the honorable Senator's intentions; but the *consequences* of his acts here are too palpable to be denied."

Clay asks Foote to "tell me what sort of intention is implied," and asks "how I, as a man of honor could listen to his language" concerning possible collusion between Benton and Clay. "There was a Senator came to me this morning, (I will not tell whom—that is a matter between the Senator and myself). . . . we had a very long and interesting conversation upon the most important topics of the day. . . . Now, suppose that some northern man had watched the motions of the honorable Senator from Miss—ah! I beg pardon, I was just going to name him. [Laughter.]" Asks pointedly, however, "Is it not improper for the private intercourse . . . between any two Senators" to "compose a part of the animadversions which Senators may choose to throw into their speeches?"

Regarding Foote's "reference . . . to a letter of mine addressed to a Free-Soil Convention in Ohio" last summer, explains that although "I was invited to attend the celebration of the anniversary of the passage of the ordinance of 1787 . . . I think I gave a very delicate rebuke to the parties sending me an invitation" to such a celebration [Clay to Vaughan & Brown, June 16, 1849]. Cannot understand why Foote and Davis accuse him of inconsistency in his stand on slavery over the past fifty years: "I have made no change. . . . I shall go to the grave with the opinion, that" slavery "is an evil, a social and political evil." Nonetheless, after Kentucky's recent constitutional convention [Stevenson to Clay, June 12, 1848] rejected his "practicable plan for the gradual emancipation of slavery" in the state [Clay to Pindell, February 17, 1849, no. 2 of date], "I acquiesce in her decision. . . . and no man hereafter will see me making any efforts there, or anywhere else, to disturb the deliberate decision of the Commonwealth." Even if Foote "may deem me an Abolitionist. . . . if I were to endeavor to find out the man above all others the most abused by Abolitionists, it is the humble individual who is now addressing you." Although "in these resolutions, I intend, so help me God, to propose a plan of doing equal and impartial justice to the South and to the North. . . . how has this effort been received by the ultraists? Why, at the North they cry out . . . 'It is all concession to the South,' " while in the South, "They say, 'It is all concession to the North.' " Regrets that "the ultraists, on the one hand and on the other, equally traduce the scheme I propose for conceding everything to their opponents." Concludes: "I consider us all as one family, all as friends, all as brethren. I consider us all as united in one common destiny; and those efforts which I shall continue to employ will be to keep us together as one family, in concord and harmony; and above all, to avoid that direful day when one part of the Union can speak of the other as an enemy." *Cong. Globe*, 31 Cong., 1 Sess., 399-405.

To Brantz Mayer, Baltimore, February 20, 1850. Expresses thanks for "the Memoir on New Mexico. . . . full of Historical interest" that Mayer has sent him. Regrets that "you, who are so conversant with Mexican laws and history, and otherwise are so well qualified to serve the public, have not been employed abroad in its diplomatic service." ALS. KyU.

Mayer's *Mexico As It Was and As It Is*, first published in 1844, ran through three editions. *DAB*.

To JOHN PENDLETON KENNEDY Philadelphia, February 24, 1850

Desirous to breathe a little more pure air before my return to Washington where I am compelled to listen to the grating and doleful sounds of dissolution of the Union, treason, and War, I shall remain here until wednesday,[1] when I will join you at dinner, unless in the mean time I shall hear from Washn. that I can prolong my furlough, without prejudice to my duties, in which case I will notify you. In the interval be pleased to present me respectfully to Mr. Grey [*sic*, Edward Gray][2] and the Ladies.

ALS. MdBP. 1. Clay had left Washington on Feb. 21 to spend a few days in Philadelphia. Lexington *Observer & Kentucky Reporter*, March 2, 1850. 2. Gray was Kennedy's father-in-law. Bohner, *John Pendleton Kennedy*, 63.

From JAMES BROWN CLAY Lisbon, Portugal February 28, 1850

I have shipped by the Brig Harald Haarfiger which sailed a few days since, two pairs of pigs to the care of Grinnell Minturn & Co N. York. I have informed them that perhaps you would give some directions as to the mode of conveyance to Ashland. I hope they may reach their destination—They are of the finest race of Portugal and I do not know that I have ever seen better—They are remarkable for great uniformity in size, which I think a desideratum & are all of red coulour. I am sure they will make a fine cross. I have also sent Thomas [Hart Clay] a box of grape vines & am gathering information as to the culture. I have shipped too for Ma [Lucretia Hart Clay] & the family of Mr [John J.] Jacob some boxes of sweatmeats, which I am sure they will find good.

I find Port wine extremely cheap—I buy the best of some 15 or 16 years old for $27.00 the quarter cask, of some 15 or 16 dozens—about 17 cents the bottle. Will you inform me whether I can send some home now, without the duty, or whether I must wait till I return myself. They cheat us too abominably in Madeira[.] The price of fine Madeira is only about $60.—the qr. Cask of 14 dozens. I have rect. a present of a few dozen very superior from Manche,[1] which I shall take home with a qr cask or two, which I intend to buy.

I have nothing now in reference to public affairs to communicate. I advise Mr. [John M.] Clayton by this mail, that in my opinion the Govt.

ought to proceed with any measures they intend, without reference to any expectations not founded on positive action by this Govt. I am convinced they will do nothing unless compelled & then only at the last moment.[2]

I have heard of a fine speech which you are said to have made,[3] but the last Steamer brought us nothing from America.

We often regret that you cannot enjoy the fine winter we have had. There has been really no cold & not more than 10 or 12 days rain the whole winter.

All are well & join in love to you.

ALS. DLC-TJC (DNA, M212, R11). 1. Probably a reference to the LaManche region of Spain. 2. Clay to Clayton, June 7, 1849. 3. Speech in Senate, Feb. 5-6, 1850.

To Thomas Hart Clay, Lexington, February [28], 1850. Sends "an authority to Tho. H. Pindell to sign my name as your surety or indorser upon any note not exceeding $2000." Adds: "I am quite well. Nothing done definitely for a settlement of the Slavery question." ALS. DLC-HC (DNA, M212, R6). Printed in *RKHS*, 50:310. The ALS version is headed as "Feb. 1850"; in the *RKHS* copy the date is given as February 28, 1850.

Remark in Senate, February 28, 1850. Since the ailing John C. Calhoun had been advised against attempting to address the Senate on his views concerning Clay's compromise resolutions, Sen. Andrew P. Butler requests "the privilege of having his [Calhoun's] remarks read by some friend." Clay concurs and hopes that "the request of the eminent and distinguished Senator, whose absence from the Senate is cause of the most unfeigned regret, is at once accorded." *Cong. Globe*, 31 Cong., 1 Sess., 439.

Sen. John C. Calhoun died on March 31, 1850. Wiltse, *John C. Calhoun: Sectionalist*, 475.

From Unknown Correspondent, Fairfax County, Va., February 28, 1850. Presents Clay with a cane made "from a piece of a gum copal tree cut for fire-wood on the coast of Madagascar, and the head is formed out of the tooth of a sperm whale captured by myself, with the assistance of my boat's crew." Adds that "It was shaped and fashioned by myself during some of the leisure moments of a late whaling voyage." Hopes it will be many years before Clay needs the assistance of the cane. Copy. Printed in Washington *Daily National Intelligencer*, March 14, 1850.

To JAMES BROWN CLAY Washington, March 6, 1850

I have been so excessively occupied that I have written less to you than I wished. Henry Clay [III] came safely to me, and I have placed him, for the present, at the Geo. town College, where he seems contented.[1]

Nothing has occurred since I last wrote to you on your Portuguese affairs.[2] And I presume that no communication will be made to Congress, in respect to them, until we settle, if we ever do settle, the Slavery subject.[3] On this subject I made a Speech[4] and offered a plan of compromise, of which I send you a Copy. The Speech has produced a powerful & salutory effect in the Country and in Congress. Whether the plan will be adopted or not remains to be seen. I think if any is finally adopted it will be substantially mine.

The K[entucky]. Legislature has passed moderate resolutions, given me no instructions, and refused to be represented in the Nashville Convention.[5] All this is well.

My relations to the Executive are civil but not very cordial or confidential. There has been much talk all the Session about changes in the Cabinet, and the retirement of Mr. [John M.] Clayton especially.[6] I am inclined to think that there is some foundation for the rumors.

All are well at home—

My love to Susan [Jacob Clay], Lucy [Jacob Clay] and the rest of the children[.]

ALS. DLC-TJC (DNA, M212, R11). Printed in Colton, *Clay Correspondence*, 4:601-2. 1. Clay to Ryder, Feb. 5, 1850. 2. Clay to Clayton, June 7, 1849. 3. Clay to Combs, Jan. 22, 1850. 4. Speech in Senate, Feb. 5-6, 1850. 5. Clay to Combs, Dec. 22, 1849. 6. Clay to Stevenson, April 25, 1850.

Remark in Senate, March 6, 1850. During discussion on trade reciprocity with Great Britain, expresses his "very great regret at the language" that Sen. James Cooper "has thought proper to apply to the British Minister [Sir Henry L. Bulwer], here at the seat of this Government." Fears Cooper has confused "the great interest he is desirous to protect"—the tariff policy—with "what he supposes to be the erroneous conduct of a representative" of a foreign government. Sees not "the slightest deviation from the most correct diplomatic practice and usage" in Bulwer's making known the British government's "wishes and expectations upon the subject of a tariff." Notes that Bulwer "has proposed no action. He has said that which has been read to us; and I suppose he had a right to say it, in prosecuting the interests of his own country. . . . he proposes to open no negotiations. And is it not an advantage even to us, when this subject comes up—if it should come up—to know what will be the feelings of all foreign Governments upon our action."

On the other hand, hopes that "the very object which the British Minister aims at accomplishing, will not be attained." Although Bulwer desires no increase on duties on British iron, Clay wishes to look into "a proper protection on iron . . . examined in fairness, and calmly adjusted upon principles of equity and of sound policy," during which he "shall be uninfluenced by the wishes of the British Government" and "I should hope, by any other consideration than those which belong to my own country, and all parts of it, and all its great interests." *Cong. Globe*, 31 Cong., 1 Sess., 471-72.

For Sen. James Cooper (Whig, Pa.), see *BDAC*. Sir Henry L. Bulwer had written Secretary of State John M. Clayton on January 3, 1850, saying that Britain had heard the U.S. was considering an increase in duties on British iron. He implored the U.S. not to take such action, saying it would adversely affect British public opinion at a time when Britain was facilitating commerce between the two countries. *Cong. Globe*, 31 Cong., 1 Sess., 470.

To LUCRETIA HART CLAY Washington, March 7, 1850

I have just heard of the death of my brother Porter Clay. The intelligence was brought me in the Resolutions which I enclose,[1] and I suppose is undoubted. He has gone, poor fellow, where we must shortly follow. He had but little to attach him to this life, but much, in faith and hope, to reconcile him to death, and I trust that he is now in the full enjoyment of that bliss which I hope awaits us.

My health continues quite as good as I ought to expect. Colds I constantly have, but they are not attended by fever, and in all respects are less inconvenient than usual.

I have heard only of the sale of a part of my Mules. They reached Greensboro in very bad order, owing I suppose to the disagreeable journey and weather—Mr. Nicholson hopes to sell them at my limits.[2]

We have had generally good weather in March, and I hope you have had it also. We are making slow progress in Congress. There is a better feeling prevailing and so far we may hope; but there is no specific mode of settling the matters in controversy yet discernable.

My love to John [Morrison Clay].

ALS. DLC-TJC (DNA, M212, R11). 1. Whitfield to Clay, Feb. 17, 1850. 2. Clay to Thomas H. Clay, Jan. 8, 1850.

To Boyd McNairy, Nashville, Tenn., March 7, 1850. Reports that the executive branch shows "no disposition to oblige me, or to pay respect to recommendations of mine." Suggests, therefore, "that if Govr [Neill Smith] Brown would signify his wish that your son should be appointed his Secy in the Russian mission, that would be the most likely way to gratify your wishes." Adds: "Ah! my friend how often I am pained that I am powerless in ability to serve my true & faithful friends." ALS. Courtesy of Dr. Gregg M. Sinclair, University of Hawaii. Letter marked "(Private)."

For Brown—governor of Tennessee (1847-49) and minister to Russia (1850-52)—see *BDGUS*, 4:1475-76. Colin M. Ingersoll, rather than McNairy's son, received the appointment. *The American Almanac . . . 1850.*

From John Smith, D. Keyes *et al.*, Clinton, Mich., March 8, 1850. As "humble individuals firmly attached to the Democratic faith & the Democratic party" who "can not endorse many things in your political creed," believe that "the preservation & harmony of our beloved Union are far above all party considerations." Feeling that "your eminent abilities & patriotic devotion to the Union are not only the property of Kentucky but of the *whole Union*," extend "our heart felt thanks for your conciliatory resolutions [Clay to Combs, January 22, 1850]." ALS, by Smith. DLC-TJC (DNA, M212, R11). Letter is signed by 28 others. Printed in Colton, *Clay Correspondence*, 4:602.

To A.D. CHALONER *et al.* Washington, March 9, 1850

I thank you for your kind letter,[1] expressing your approbation of my humble endeavors, in the Senate of the United States, to avert from our country that greatest of all public calamities, a severence of the Union of these States.[2] In the order of consolation which I derive in the discharge of arduous public duties, that which I most highly appreciate, is a perfect consciousness of the purity of my intentions and the convictions of my own judgment—I need not say that I enjoy that in its full sense. Next to that is the public approbation. You have done me the favor, unsolicited, to express yours. And I value it the more, because coming from you, who differ from me in other measures of public policy, it is not likely that you have been at all biased by the partiality of personal or political friendship.

I wish that I could assure you that all danger had disappeared. I think it is greatly diminished, and that a much better spirit prevails; but I shall continue to feel a lively solicitude until all matters of controversy are amicably adjusted.

Copy. Printed in Lexington *Observer & Kentucky Reporter*, March 27, 1850. 1. Dr. A.D. Chaloner *et al.* had written from Philadelphia on Feb. 22, 1850, stating that although "differing from you in politics, members of the Democratic and Native American parties," they admire "your manly fearless and patriotic stand against Dis-union in any shape." Believe that "our Countrymen" who fell "on the plains of Texas and Palo Alto, as well as at Germantown and Bunker Hill," died "fighting for the 'Union, the whole Union and nothing but the Union.' " Intend to "frown down Dis-Unionists, come they from any section of our Country," and as "Pennsylvanians, Sons of the 'Keystone' State," always will rally "under the 'Stars and Stripes,' for the Union, the Constitution, and for 'Virtue, Liberty and Independence!' " Praises Clay's pronouncement that "his allegiance, is due to the 'Union first and Kentucky last [Comment in Senate, February 14, 1850]!' " LS, probably in Chaloner's hand. DLC-HC (DNA, M212, R6). Chaloner was a physician, located at 317 Spruce Street in Philadelphia. *M'Elroy's Philadelphia Directory for the Year 1849.* 2. Clay to Combs, Jan. 22, 1850.

To Reuben Townsend, Cape May, N.J., March 9, 1850. After expressing thanks for a recent friendly note [not found], adds: "We are here in the midst of great excitement [Clay to Combs, January 22, 1850], and of great dangers; but I have strong hopes, not however free from all apprehension, that the Union will be preserved." ALS. NRU.

Although the Townsend family had long been prominent in Cape May, the only Reuben Townsend found in county histories is the one who served in the New Jersey general assembly in 1795-96. It seems unlikely that he was Clay's correspondent in 1850; however, the Reuben Townsend to whom Clay wrote is undoubtedly from the same family. See Lewis Townsend Stevens, *The History of Cape May County, New Jersey . . .* (Cape May, 1897), 451.

From Octavia Walton LeVert, Mobile, March 10, 1850. Praises Clay's "noble speech [Speech in Senate, February 5-6, 1850]," and can "find no words, wherewith to express my admiration of it. All that is most sublime in Patriotism—all that is most exquisite in language are there. That Speech will stand as the grand Land Mark, in the Ocean of the Past, and speak to Future Time of the great spirit which animated your noble bosom." Adds: "If your noble efforts avail not, then nought human can save the Republic." Copy. Printed in "Madam LeVert's Diary," *AHQ* (Spring, 1941), 3:35.

To N.L. FARRIS Washington, March 11, 1850

I received your obliging letter,[1] communicating the melancholy event of the death of my brother, Porter Clay. Prior to its receipt, I had received the proceedings of the Masonic Lodge in your city, testifying its respect to his memory.[2] I am very grateful and thankful for the kindness extended by you and others to my lamented brother in his last illness, and for the respect paid to his remains in Camden, by the Masonic Order, and other citizens. My greatest consolation in the loss which I have sustained, arises out of the fact that my brother had long been a sincere, pious, and zealous Christian.

For your kind and friendly expressions towards me personally, I beg your acceptance of my respectful acknowledgment.

Copy. Printed in the Salisbury (N.C.) *Carolina Watchman*, May 9, 1850, taken from the Ouachita (Ark.) *Herald.* 1. Not found. 2. Whitfield to Clay, Feb. 17, 1850.

To REUBEN H. WALWORTH[1] Washington, March 11, 1850

I received and thank you for your friendly letter, in respect to the adjustment of the exciting questions concerning Slavery, and I agree in many of the views you express.

There is a better spirit prevailing here, and that encourages me to hope that there will be, finally, adopted an amicable settlement of those questions, altho' the precise form of it cannot be stated.[2] I think California will be admitted, without alteration of its boundaries. Our information does not coincide with your's as to the quantity of arable land, which they contain. On the contrary, altho' the extent of surface be large, according to our information, its capacity to sustain population is quite restricted.

There is a pretty general conviction, even among Northern members, that wrong has been done to the Slave states in regard to fugitives. But the difficulty, in passing a more stringent law, is in reconciling the just rights of property with the security due to freedom, in cases where the question of Slave or no Slave arises. No one defends the Slave trade in this District[.]

ALS. DLC-Richard Rogers Bowker Papers (DNA, M212, R20). 1. For Walworth (1788-1867)—congressman, jurist, and last chancellor of New York—see *DAB* and *BDAC*. 2. Clay to Combs, Jan. 22, 1850.

Remark in Senate, March 12, 1850. After Sen. Henry S. Foote moves for the formation of a select committee of thirteen—"six members from the South and six from the North, and one to be by them chosen"—designed "to mature some scheme of compromise" to resolve the slavery question, Vice President Millard Fillmore reads a Senate rule that requires all members of special committees to be selected by ballot. Foote agrees to modify his motion.

Clay approves of the modification, being "extremely unwilling, in the constitution of a committee, or in any other act of this body, to give them a sectional aspect of any sort." Asserts, in response to Sen. John P. Hale's criticism that only a select group of Senate leaders had been consulted before Foote advanced his proposal, that "I had nothing to do with it." States that when Foote asked "if I would concur in such a measure," he replied that "I considered an amicable adjustment of all the questions which unfortunately divide and agitate this country, as of such great and paramount importance, that I will vote for any proposition, coming from any quarter, which looks to, or proposes such an adjustment. . . . I am, I must add, at the same time, however, far less sanguine than he is, that such a committee will be able to present to the Senate a scheme of adjustment and arrangement of this unhappy subject, which will command the majority; still I would make the experiment."

After describing several previous occasions on which the rules concerning committee membership were circumvented, expresses his belief that "our conversations in social intercourse, about the constitution of a committee, our arrangements about the disposition of the public business, and especially arrangements about the disposition of the great and momentous subject which now engages our attention, ought not to be caught at, criticised, and examined, for the purpose of injuring the great work which we all have at heart, and about which we ought all to cooperate." *Cong. Globe*, 31 Cong., 1 Sess., 510. Printed in Colton, *Clay Correspondence*, 3:356, under date March 13.

For the Compromise of 1850, see Clay to Combs, January 22, 1850.

To JAMES BROWN CLAY Washington, March 13, 1850

I have just recd. your favor of the 8h. Ulto. I suppose that the bad state of things here has prevented [John M.] Clayton from writing to you, and probably prevented the Executive [Zachary Taylor] from calling the particular attention of Congress to Portuguese affairs.

You will do well, if any arrangement can be effected of any of our Claims,[1] to obtain the *written* concurrence of the Agents of the Claiments, if they have any Agents near you. And if none, and a real doubt & difficulty occur, not covered by your instructions, you had better take the matter ad referendum to your own Governmt.

We are still in the Woods here, on the Slavery questions, and I don't know when we shall get out of them. Bad feelings have diminished, without our seeing however Land. All other business is superseded or suspended. I do not absolutely despair of a settlement on the basis of my resolutions[.][2]

My information from home is good. All are well there. Thomas [Hart Clay] continues to be encouraged by the prospects of his Saw Mill, and other prospects.

Tell Susan [Jacob Clay] that I read her letter with great interest, and I have sent it to her mother. Her interview with the Queen [Maria II] with all its attending circumstances, was quite imposing.[3] As her health is so good at Lisbon, I do not think that you should be in a hurry to return home, although whenever you do come we shall be most happy to see you. H. Clay jr. [III] remains at the Geo. Town College.[4]

John [Morrison Clay] has Eight Colts & Fillies, he writes me, in training, under the care of Edgar.[5]

I have seen a good deal of Sir H[enry]. Bulwer and his Lady [Georgiana Wellesley Bulwer], both of whom are intelligent & agreeable. He promised me, as I believe I informed you, to write to Lord Palmerston on our affairs with Portugal.

Give my love to Susan, to Lucy [Jacob Clay] & all the children. Tell Susan that I will write to her when I can.

P.S. Your uncle Porter Clay died in Arkansas the 22d. Ulto.[6]

ALS. DLC-TJC (DNA, M212, R11). Partially printed in Colton, *Clay Correspondence*, 4:602-3. 1. Clay to Clayton, June 7, 1849. 2. For the Compromise of 1850, see Clay to Combs, Jan. 22, 1850. 3. Susan J. Clay to Clay, Feb. 2, 1850. 4. Clay to Ryder, Feb. 5, 1850. 5. Colton omits this sentence. 6. The postscript is omitted by Colton. Actually Porter Clay died on Feb. 16. See Whitfield to Clay, Feb. 17, 1850.

From Gardner Jones, near South Bend, Indiana, March 14, 1850. States that the "President and Faculty of the Catholic Institution" of Notre Dame "cannot resist the impulse created by the recent reading of your great compromise speech [Speech in Senate, February 5-6, 1850] . . . to address you a brief letter of thanks for *their* share in that rich treat." Continues: "Professing a creed widely different from your own, and which is generally, though falsely, supposed to be anti-American and hostile to civil liberty, they yet partake with you in all those just, wise, and moderate views which you advance in the noble document referred to, and in all that patriotic and trembling solicitude for the continuance and pe[r]petuity of this glorious Union." Notes that the group addressing Clay believes the "integrity, stability, and unchecked progress of this land of religious liberty" is identified with "the highest interests of the church of Jesus Christ, and the highest hopes of humanity." Concludes: "While you are assailed by the violent and insane of both sections of the Union, we thought it might be agreeable to you to know that in a secluded religious house, whose inmates have their citizenship and conversation in Heaven, who commune more with the mighty past than the present, and whose invisible companions are the noble army of saints, your kindling oratory has warmed and cheered many a heart inflexibly and altogether American." Copy. Printed in Washington *Daily National Intelligencer*, April 2, 1850.

Gardner Jones was at various times professor of logic, metaphysics, ethics, Hebrew, and rhetoric at Notre Dame. During a portion of the 1850s he also served as editor of the Chicago *Tablet* and the Detroit *Catholic Vindicator*. Joseph A. Lyons (comp.), *Silver Jubilee of the University of Notre Dame, June 23rd, 1869*, 2nd ed. (Chicago, 1869), 156; and information supplied by Peter J. Lysy, associate archivist of the University of Notre Dame.

From Edward Coles, Philadelphia, March 15, 1850. Sends a copy [not found] of a manuscript written by Dolley Madison containing "the advice to his Country of the great and good [James] Madison." Thinks Clay may use this "with good effect, during the present diseased state of the public mind" brought about by the "ultra politicians of the day" who are "endeavoring to destroy our hallowed Union." Calls the ultras "political quacks & madmen." Copy. NjP.

On March 21, 1850, Clay expressed his thanks for the manuscript, promising that if "a suitable occasion offer, I shall be glad to embrace it to lay the document before the public." Adds: "There is less violence and more calmness prevailing in the Congressional mind, and so far I feel encouraged. But we do not yet clearly see land." ALS. *Ibid.*

To JAMES HARLAN Washington, March 16, 1850

I have been very thankful to you for the information you have, from time to time, communicated to me during the session of Congress. While on the other hand you have found me an inattentive correspondent. My apparent neglect proceeded merely from the cause that I had nothing certain or definite to communicate.

The all-engrossing subject of slavery continues to agitate us, and to paralyze almost all legislation. My hopes are strong that the question will ultimately be amicably adjusted, although when or how can not be clearly seen.[1]

My relations to the Executive [Zachary Taylor] are civil but cold. We have very little intercourse of any kind. Instead of any disposition to oblige me, I feel that a contrary disposition has been sometimes manifested. In the case of a Marshal for our State,[2] four of the Whig members, of which I was one, united from the first in recommending Mr. Mitchell. Two others of them (making six) informed the Secretary of the Interior [Thomas Ewing] that they would be satisfied with Mr. Mitchell; yet [James S.] Speed was nominated, and his nomination is now before the Senate. It was the act of the President, against the advice of Ewing.

I have never before seen such an Administration. There is very little co-operation or concord between the two ends of the avenue. There is not, I believe, a prominent Whig in either House that has any confidential intercourse with the Executive. Mr. [William Henry] Seward, it is said, had; but his late Abolition speech[3] has, I presume, cut him off from any such intercourse, as it has eradicated the respect of almost all men for him.

I shall continue to act according to my convictions of duty, co-operating where I can with the President, and opposing where I must.

I congratulate you on your appointment as one of the Revisers.[4]

Copy. Printed in Colton, *Clay Correspondence*, 4:603-4. 1. Clay to Combs, Jan. 22, 1850. 2. Clay to Harlan, Jan. 24, 1850. 3. Seward's speech of March 11 became famous because of his statement that there was a "higher law" than the Constitution. *Cong. Globe*, 31 Cong., 1 Sess., Appendix, 260-68. 4. Harlan had been appointed to a commission for revising the code of conduct for courts and codifying the laws of Kentucky. Frankfort *Commonwealth*, March 12, 1850.

To JAMES BROWN CLAY Washington, March 17, 1850

I was at the Department of State yesterday, and some of your last despatches were shown to me, and important Instructions to you were also read to me. These instructions are to be sent to you in duplicate, one copy by the mail, and the other Copy through Commodore [Charles W.] Morgan,[1] who is to proceed to Lisbon in one of the Ships of the Line, and to deliver the Copy to you which he bears. He is there to await your orders. It is not understood that you are to act finally on these instructions until the arrival of the Commodore, but that you should, in the mean time, go on with the negotiation for our claims and conclude if you can a Convention for their payment.[2]

This course of proceeding will impose on you a heavy responsibility, and you should act with great care caution & discretion. If you could prevail on the Portuguese Governm[en]t. to pay a sum in black, or in gross, for the amount and in full satisfaction of all our claims on that Governmt. it might save its honor in contesting the Armstrong case.[3] It might stipulate to pay a specified sum, and leave the distribution of it, among the claimants, to our Government. I do not know whether you have a knowledge of all the claims and the means of fixing on their just amount. I was surprized to hear at the Department that it was much greater than I had supposed. I would not insist upon extravagant or extreme allowances. I should think that if the owners of the Armstrong got Fifty thousand dollars they might be satisfied.

If after the arrival of Commodore Morgan, and after you have ascertained that no arrangement of our claims can previously be made, the Portuguese Govert. should persist in refusing to do us justice, as I understand the instructions, you are to notify that Governmt. of your purpose to leave Lisbon, demand your passports, and come away. The Commodore is not to employ force, which w[oul]d. be an act of War which the Presid[en]t [Zachary Taylor] has no power to authorize.

I suppose that this measure of sending a public vessel into the port of Lisbon has been adopted upon your advice, at least in part. I hope it may succeed; but, if the P. Govt. has the promise of British succor it is not so likely to be successful. In the present distracted state of this Country, and the weak condition of the Admon in Congress, it is much to be feared, that your departure from Lisbon, without the settlem[en]t. of our Claims, after the contemplated display of Naval force, will not be followed up by the employment of the coercion, which the serious steps you are authorized to take would seem to require. Hence the great importance of an amicable settlement if one can be made. And hence also I think our claims should be brought down to their minimum amount.

If your negotiation should finally fail, I suppose that we may see you back in the U.S. before the close of this year.

My last accounts from home represented all well.

Give my love to Susan [Jacob Clay] & the Children.

ALS. DLC-TJC (DNA, M212, R11). Printed in Colton, *Clay Correspondence*, 4:604-5. 1. Morgan was commander of the U.S. Squadron in the Mediterranean. *The American Almanac . . . 1850.* His identification in 8:810 incorrectly states that he retired from the Navy in 1842. 2. Clay to Clayton, June 7, 1849. 3. *Ibid.*

To JAMES HARLAN Washington, March 22, 1850

I received your favor of the 15th inst. What you have stated, in answer to those who have inquired of you, whether under any contingency I would consent to be a Candidate for the Presidency in 1852, is pretty much what I should have said myself, if I said any thing; but I have great repugnance to saying any thing about it. It would be great folly in me, at my age, with the uncertainty of life, and with a recollection of all the past, to say now that I would, under any contingencies, be a Candidate. I can scarcely conceive any, there are none in the range of probability, that would reconcile me to the use of my name. I have already publicly declared that I entertained no wish or expectation of being a candidate; and I would solemnly proclaim that I never would be, under any circumstances whatever, if I did not think that no citizen has a right thus absolutely to commit himself.

I[1] thank you for the information on Kentucky matters which you have kindly given me. Thinking that the State had an abundance of Banking Capital, in successful operation and well managed, I was in hopes that neither of the new Banks would be put in motion.[2]

We can not yet see clearly how or when our Slavery difficulties are to be settled.

Copy. CtY. Partially printed in Colton, *Clay Correspondence*, 4:505-6. 1. Colton omits this paragraph. 2. The Kentucky legislature had recently passed an act to encourage the organization of the Southern Bank of Kentucky and extending its charter to 1880. Also, it had chartered the Farmers' Bank of Kentucky with several branches and a capital stock of $2,300,000. Collins, *History of Kentucky*, 1:59-60.

To JAMES BROWN CLAY Washington, March 25, 1850

I recd together today your two favors of the 18h.[1] and 28h. Ulto. I am obliged to you for the articles you have shipt for your mother and me. I shall give directions about the Pigs, but I am afraid there will be great difficulty in getting them home. You cannot ship home any Port wine, without paying duties here. It must come back with you, and as a part of your luggage it will not be liable to duty.[2] I should be glad to get 6 or 8 dozen.

I have no doubt that you may return at the end of the year, if you wish it. Whether you do so or not, ought to depend on your estimate of what will most conduce to the health and happiness of your family & yourself. I should be sorry if you allowed your expences to exceed your Salary. Public functionaries are too apt to think themselves more bound than they really are to dispense hospitality. He acts wisest who limits himself to his Salary. Remember how your poor brother Henry [Clay, Jr.] burthened himself by going abroad with a debt, which is not yet all paid.[3]

My last letter and the despatches from Government will have apprized you that a display of Naval force is to be tried as an experiment in aid of your Negotiations.[4] If it fail to induce the Portuguese Governm[en]t. to pay our claims, you may have to return even sooner than you wish. I suppose it will not reach the port of Lisbon before May.

The Senate confirmed your nomination to day as soon as it was taken up, and without any opposition.[5] At no time was there danger of any.

I wish you were honorably and safely through your negotiation. The employment of a Naval force imposes on you a delicate and heavy responsibility, of the success of which I am more anxious because I understand you advised it. You may be officially interrogated as to the object of the presence of such a force. In that case, you will pursue your instructions, and I suppose have to say that the Ship is intended to take you away, if our claims are not adjusted. Commodore [Charles W.] Morgan is a particular friend of mine & a very clever fellow. You may tell him all about Yorkshire, his get,[6] &c.

I have got through the Winter better than I expected, but I find the colds of this month very bad.

I am glad to hear that you are on good terms with the Foreign Minister [Count Tojal]. Certainly it would be a good arrangement to get them to recognize the *justice* of the [*General*] Armstrong claim[7] and leave the amount to Arbitration, but that they won't agree to.

Give my love to Susan [Jacob Clay], dear Lucy [Jacob Clay], and your other children. All well at home when I last heard.

I believe I mentioned the death of your uncle Porter [Clay] in Arkansas in Feby.[8]

ALS. DLC-TJC (DNA, M212, R11). Partially printed in Colton, *Clay Correspondence*, 4:606-7. 1. The Colton version erroneously has the "15th." 2. James B. Clay to Clay, Feb. 28, 1850. 3. This sentence is omitted by Colton. For Henry Clay, Jr.'s, trip to Europe, see 8:810-11. 4. Clay to Clayton, June 7, 1849. 5. He had been nominated for the post of chargé d'affaires on Jan. 4, 1850, and was confirmed March 25. U.S. Sen., *Executive Journal*, 8:111, 137, 489. 6. Yorkshire, a famous race horse and stud, had been presented to Clay by Commodore Morgan. Clay later gave him to John M. Clay. Perrin, *History of Fayette County*, 140, 152. 7. Clay to Clayton, June 7, 1849. 8. Whitfield to Clay, Feb. 17, 1850.

To Grinnell, Minturn & Co., New York City, March 25, 1850. Hopes that the "two pair of Portuguese Pigs and some boxes" sent by James Brown Clay [James B. Clay to Clay, February 28, 1850] through Grinnell "shd. be sent in safety, but have fears about the pigs, which I am more anxious should securely reach their destination." Suggests that the items be sent "by the Erie Canal to Buffalo, thence to Cleveland, thence by the Ohio Canal to Portsmouth & thence to Thomas Smith at Louisville," but worries that the pigs may not be sufficiently fed & watered on the route." Asks to be advised "of the arrival of these Portuguese dignitaries" and "the best mode of transporting them." ALS. KyLoF.

Comment in Senate, April 1, 1850. After the formal announcement of the death of Sen. John C. Calhoun [Remark in Senate, February 28, 1850], Clay rises to second Sen. Andrew P. Butler's resolutions calling for the appointment of a special committee to superintend the funeral and for the extension of other honors. Describes their earliest years in Congress "upwards of thirty-eight years ago. We entered at the same time, together, the House of Representatives. . . . amongst whose deliberations and acts was the declaration of war against the most powerful nation" in the world. During these discussions, "no member displayed a more lively and patriotic sensibility to the wrongs which led to that momentous event" than Calhoun. "Of all Congresses with which I have had any acquaintance . . . in none, in my humble opinion, has been assembled such a galaxy of eminent and able men as were in the House of Representatives of that Congress which declared the war . . . and amongst that splendid assemblage none shone more bright and brilliant than the star which is now set."

Although later in life "it was my fortune to differ from him as to measures of domestic policy, I had the happiness to agree with him generally as to those which concerned our foreign relations, and especially as to the preservation of the peace of the country." As Calhoun's one-time messmate, Clay had formed an "estimate, not merely of his public, but of his private life": "no man with whom I have ever been acquainted, exceeded him in habits of temperance and regularity, and in all the freedom, frankness, and affability of social intercourse, and in all the tenderness and respect and affection which he manifested towards that lady [Floride Colhoun Calhoun] who now mourns more than any other." Adds "that, if at the end of his service [as secretary of war] in the executive department under Mr. [James] Monroe's administration," Calhoun had been elected president, "I should have felt perfectly assured that under his auspices, the honor, the prosperity, and the glory of our country would have been safely placed." But "No more shall we witness . . . the flashes of that keen and penetrating eye of his" or "that torrent of clear, concise, compact logic . . . which, if it did not always carry conviction to our judgment, commanded our great admiration." Compliments Calhoun's "enlightened mind," his "elevated genius," his "felicity of generalization," and "the charm and captivating influence of his colloquial powers." Adds: "I was his senior . . . in years—in nothing else." Calhoun's death causes Clay to reflect "How unbecoming, if not presumptuous, it is in us, who are the tenants of an hour in this earthly abode, to wrestle and struggle together with a violence which would not be justifiable if it were our perpetual home!" After several more eulogies, the resolutions are approved and the Senate adjourns as a mark of respect. *Cong. Globe*, 31 Cong., 1 Sess., 624-25. Partially printed in Colton, *Clay Correspondence*, 3:453-54. Clay served as a pall bearer for Calhoun. *Cong. Globe*, 31 Cong., 1 Sess., 626.

Clay and Calhoun had both entered the U.S. House for the first time in the 12th Congress which convened on November 4, 1811.

To G.G. FOSTER[1] Washington, April 2, 1850

I beg you to believe that my failure hitherto to acknowledge the receipt of your friendly letter[2] has not proceeded from any want of respect towards you, or any ingratitude for the sentiments of attachment and confidence you entertain in regard to me. My correspondence is very oppressive, and besides that one topic of your letter is not free of embarrassment, and is one on which I have great repugnance to saying or writing one word. That topic relates to the use of my name as a Candidate for the next Presidency. Considering my age, the uncertainty of human life, and the circumstances of my past career, I should regard it as a great weakness, if not folly, if I were to cherish any hopes or expectations of my name being employed in such a relation. Accordingly I have not given the slightest countenance to such a use of it. At the same time, I am fully aware that I have many ardent, if not enthusiastic, friends, who guided more by their warm feelings than calm judgment will not relinquish the hope that I may be yet elevated to the place where their hearts desire to see me put. My difficulty arises out of a conflict between their friendly wishes and the dictates of my own judgment. If I thought any man were at liberty to take such a step I would, like the son of the famous General of Carthage,[3] go to the altar and swear that, with my own consent, I would never be again a Candidate for the Presidency. But such a solemn obligation I have believed no Citizen was at liberty to contract. I have thought therefore that, abiding by the public declarations and public avowals, which I have sincerely made, it was best and most proper that I should remain passive, taking no measures to promote my own elevation, and looking on with calmness, if not indifference, to any that may be prompted by others.

Whilst this is the exact state of my views & feelings I am not insensible, nor ungrateful, to those good & true friends who flatter themselves with what I can but regard as a vain and impracticable hope. And to you, among those friends, I offer an expression of my thanks for the kindness and confidence which have induced you to place my name at the head of your paper. I must however add, in all sincerity, that I am always animated by a painful apprehension lest any one, who may espouse my cause, should suffer in purse or otherwise by such a course. And I hope that, whenever you may feel yourself in danger of incurring any loss, on my account, you will not hesitate a moment to with draw from my support.

ALS. PPRF. Letter marked "(Private)." 1. George G. Foster wrote a column called "City Items" for the New-York *Daily Tribune.* He also published a number of articles on New York and the gold regions of California. Van Deusen, *Horace Greeley*, 131; *NUC*, 178:691. 2. Not found. 3. According to legend, Carthaginian General Hamilcar Barca compelled his son Hannibal to swear at the altar his undying enmity to Rome. Hannibal later led Carthage against Rome in the Second Punic War (218-201 B.C.). Richard M. Haywood, "Hannibal," *Collier's Encyclopedia* (New York, 1985).

To Chapin A. Harris, Baltimore, April 3, 1850. Acknowledges Harris's "note [not found] communicating your wish to possess my portrait, and asking me to give one or two short sittings to an Artiste whom you have engaged to take it." While "I have lately generally declined doing so," agrees to "the Sittings desired at my rooms in the National Hotel" where "I sat for the last portrait of me taken for Sir Henry Bulwer [Clay to Lucretia H. Clay, January 21, 1850]." ALS. KyU.

For Harris (1804-60), a doctor and dentist in Baltimore, see *DAB*. The artist engaged by Harris was probably Edward Dalton Marchant whose portrait of Clay is dated April 20, 1850. Amyx, "Portraits of Henry Clay," typescript, Special Collections, University of Kentucky, vol. A:1.60b.

From William McLain, Washington, April 3, 1850. Asks Clay to sign "the accompanying *certificates* of *Life Memberships*" in the American Colonization Society. Since the society is "in great need of *Money*," hopes that Clay will "have the bill granting our claim for Supporting the re-captives of the *Pons*, hastened thro' the Senate." ALS. DLC-Records of the American Colonization Society (DNA, M212, R20).

The American Colonization Society had petitioned Congress for remuneration for the support of certain Africans recaptured from the slaver *Pons* by the *U.S.S. Yorktown*. A bill providing for such remuneration was introduced in the Senate on December 31, 1849, and passed on September 12, 1850; however, it did not pass the House that session. It did pass at the 2nd Session of the 31st Congress and was approved March 3, 1851. U.S. Sen., *Journal*, 31 Cong., 1 Sess., 36, 625; *Sen. Reports*, 31 Cong., 1 Sess., no. 14, p. 565; 9 *U.S. Stat.*, 812.

To Powell Stackhouse, Jr., Philadelphia, April 3, 1850. Although generally refusing to answer "letters, applying for my autograph, being of opinion that the collection of them is an unprofitable consumption of time," complies now because "you are a member of the Society of friends, towards whom I have always cherished sentiments of respect and regard." ALS. MnHi.

Powell Stackhouse was a stove manufacturer in Philadelphia. This letter was addressed either to him or to his grandson, also named Powell Stackhouse (1840-1927), who by the 1890s was one of the foremost independent steel manufacturers in the U.S. *NCAB*, 22:371; *M'Elroy's Philadelphia Directory for 1848.*

To THOMAS B. STEVENSON Washington, April 3, 1850

I received your favor of the 26th. I should write you oftener and longer; but really, company, correspondence, and my public duties engross all my time. I have been compelled, indeed, to decline answering the greater part of the letters I receive, or neglect my public duties.

I think, perhaps I ought rather to say that I strongly hope, that the slavery question is approaching an amicable adjustment. I believe a bill combining the admission of California, and the government of the Territories, without the [Wilmot] Proviso, could now pass.[1] But there is diversity of opinion whether the subject shall be separated and put in different bills, or be combined together. In the former case, there would be a strenuous minority opposing California, and more doubt about the passage of the Territorial bills without the Proviso.

I do not know what will be Mr. [Thomas] Corwin's final course. Although our friendly intimacy continues, he has not communicated it to me. He told me that he did not mean to speak on the subject.[2]

I am glad to see that your paper is conducted with spirit and ability.[3]

You will have seen that Mr. [John C.] Calhoun is dead.[4] The event, although expected, has created much sensation.

The [Zachary Taylor] Administration is without power. There is not much confidential intercourse between the two ends of the Avenue. My own relations to the members of it are civil, but cold.

Copy. Printed in Colton, *Clay Correspondence*, 3:498. Copies also in CHi and OCHP. 1. Clay to Combs, Jan. 22, 1850. 2. Corwin did not speak against the Compromise but was thought to favor President Taylor's plan. He did not vote on the omnibus bill or the separate bills which finally passed, because on July 20 he resigned his Senate seat to become secretary of the treasury in Millard Fillmore's administration. *BDAC*; Frankfort *Commonwealth*, July 30, 1850. 3. Stevenson was proprietor and editor of the Maysville (Ky.) *Eagle*. Colton, *Clay Correspondence*, 3:498. 4. Remark in Senate, Feb. 28, 1850.

Comment in Senate, April 5, 1850. Presents the petition of Ralph Bulkley, who has discovered "an effective method of extinguishing fires on steamers, vessels, or buildings" through the "almost instantaneous decomposition of the air" which reduces "the oxygen of the air into water." The fire dies "for want of oxygen to support combustion." Notes that "insurance companies in the city of New York . . . certify that they have witnessed experiments" that at least partly support Bulkley's claims. The inventor desires "a small sum of money" from Congress "to try the experiment, under the supervision of some officers of the navy, upon a larger scale." If the invention can do what "the inventor imagines it will accomplish," then very little "that has been made by the ingenuity of man . . . will exceed it in the benefits it will confer." Although "There are always some doubts attending the success of any new enterprise of this kind" as there were with "the invention of the immortal [Robert] Fulton," hopes that Congress will at least consider "its use for the benefit of the Government steamers and vessels." The petition is referred to the Committee on Naval Affairs.

Clay then presents the memorial of "Henry Grinnell, a merchant, who is now fitting out in the port of New York two or three vessels, which he purposes to send out in search of Sir John Franklin and his companions." Grinnell requests "the services of certain seamen belonging to the United States, and also the command of some subordinate officers, now in the employment of the United States, to give the vessels something like a naval and military discipline." Since Grinnell's "expenditure . . . is so great, it is but a small matter to ask the authority of the Government to grant the small number of seamen" he requests. Fears that Franklin and his men "will be found to be no more," but that "some useful discoveries may be made . . . and amply repay any expenditure that may be incurred by granting the prayer of the petition." The memorial is referred to the Committee on Naval Affairs.

Later, discusses a proposal "for the relief of James Robertson" who had been imprisoned by the orders of the presiding officer of the Senate. Robertson had claimed that he was jailed unjustly "for the purpose of getting rid of him as a political rival," since he was "perfectly satisfied that he controlled the elections of 1844 and 1848" and would also determine the winner in 1852. After much laughter, Clay expresses the hope that the resolution will be approved, adding that "I believe that this individual has some connection with myself." Indeed, the vice president [Millard Fillmore] recalls that the sergeant-at-arms reported to him that "there was a person here who had . . . a design on the life of Mr. Clay." Clay believes, however, that "the poor fellow had no evil intent whatever." A $100 payment to Robertson is approved by a vote of 22 to 18. *Cong. Globe*, 31 Cong., 1 Sess., 644-46.

Sir John Franklin had set sail from England for the Arctic in 1845 and had disappeared. President Taylor had asked Congress to appropriate money for a search expedition. This they refused to do, but they did approve providing men and supplies for Grinnell's ships. The remains of Franklin and his crew were not found, however, until 1859. *DNB*; Smith, *The Presidencies of Taylor & Fillmore*, 75; Bauer, *Zachary Taylor*, 277.

On December 8, 1849, James Robertson was overheard in the Senate gallery expressing his determination to kill Henry Clay. He was arrested, taken before a judge, and then placed in jail for two weeks. He later petitioned the Senate to "make him such compensation as may be just and equitable." On January 29, 1850, Sen. Joseph R. Underwood presented the report of the Committee on Claims. Washington *Daily National Intelligencer*, December 8, 1849; *Sen. Reports*, 31 Cong., 1 Sess., no. 25.

Later in the day during discussions on an amendment that would separate California statehood from the other compromise issues to be referred to a Senate Committee of Thirteen, Clay deplores "the manifest state of feeling and relation of parties at this time." Regrets that recent "agitations have engendered feelings of distrust of the honor and fidelity with which, one portion of the common subject being disposed of, the other portions of the same subject may be finally disposed of." Asserts that he does "not partake of these feelings." Since "my anxious desire has been to see these great questions settled and adjusted amicably . . . I have favored every proposition which has been offered. . . . Less confident, perhaps, than others may be, in regard to particular modes of adjusting the question, I have been in favor of embracing them all, no matter from what quarter they might come—every one which looked toward restoring union and harmony." Claims that "I am ready to vote for" California's admission "at any time, and under any circumstances, separately or conjointly," adding that "it ought to have been done instantly" following receipt of President Zachary Taylor's executive message communicating California's constitution [Clay to Pierse, February 16, 1849]. Now that "a degree of opposition" has "produced procrastination," however, believes that "the most rapid mode" of admitting California to the Union "is by combining in the same bill provisions for her admission and provisions for the government of the new territories." Although "I have heard it said that it was disrespectful to California," sees "no more disrespect in putting her in a bill with other kindred measures, than there would be in placing a bill for her admission exclusively, on the statute books. . . . There is no disrespect in this; it is imaginary." Since "we are aiming at a compromise . . . that shall lead to the restoration of peace and harmony," suggests that while "you may put into the bill as many kindred subjects as it is practicable to insert," he does not "wholly concur" in the proposal to insert a "provision for the restoration of fugitive slaves." Only "the whole subject and all parts of the subject, in reference to propriety and concurrence, and common character and sympathy between them, should be treated in combination." California now must be considered with related issues: "Why, sir, when you constitute a committee of thirteen . . . to arrange all these subjects, will you manacle them, will you tie their hands in regard to one of the most important branches of the subject?" *Cong. Globe*, 31 Cong., 1 Sess., 652.

To Committee of Clay Festival Association, New York City, April 5, 1850. Citing public duties, declines an invitation to a celebration of his birthday to be held at Niblo's Saloon in New York City on April 12. Conveys his gratitude, especially "because I understand it to be your intention 'to seize the occasion to express your devotion to the *Union* and *Constitution* of these States.' " Believes "That sentiment should be the strongest and uppermost in every American bosom." Copy. Printed in Washington *Daily National Intelligencer*, April 15, 1850.

Speech in Senate, April 8, 1850. The Senate takes up Sen. Henry S. Foote's motion to refer Sen. John Bell's compromise resolutions to a Committee of Thirteen [Remark in Senate, March 12, 1850], with special attention to Sen. Roger S. Baldwin's amendment to separate the admission of California from the remaining issues. After extended comments by Sen. Thomas Hart Benton, who agrees that California's case merits separate consideration, Clay rises to respond.

Reiterates that although "I have on various occasions stated, that, for one, I was ready to vote for the admission of California separately . . . or in conjunction with other measures," now believes "that the most speedy mode of accomplishing the object . . . is by combining some of these measures in connection with California, and by this combined bill presenting subjects, which I shall presently show are fairly connected in their nature, to the consideration of Congress at one and the same time [Speech in Senate, February 5-6, 1850]." Since "We all know perfectly well that there are large majorities in both Houses in favor of the admission of California," and since "We know at the same time that there are great difficulties with reference to the passage of territorial governments unconnected with the Wilmot proviso," views the attempt to consider California separately as a Democratic party tactic to satisfy "its own wants" while "holding back in reference to other subjects equally important in the great object which I trust animates the breasts of all—the great object of quiet and pacific action to the country." Regrets that "I did hear . . . that if it was attempted to force on the minority" of the House of Representatives "a measure which is unacceptable to it, and abhorrent to its feelings," it would resort "not I trust to acts of violence," but to "parliamentary rules and modes of proceeding" most likely to promote a stiff resistance. Hopes that the Senate will agree to the "trial of mind against mind, of argument against argument, of reason against reason," instead of "resorting to adjournments, calls for the yeas and nays, and other dilatory proceedings, in order to delay that which, if the Constitution has full and fair operation, must inevitably take place."

Finds "some unfairness" in Benton's argument "when he endeavored to show that the pending proposition was to combine California, the territorial governments for the two proposed territories, the fixation of the line of Texas, the fugitive slave bill, the bill of abolishing the slave-trade in this District [of Columbia], abolition, and God Almighty knows how many other subjects, which his imagination depicted as contemplated to be introduced in our omnibus bill, and to be considered in that way. The Senator from Missouri knows perfectly well that no such purpose existed, and he has no right to infer any purpose of the kind." Moreover, while "nobody has gone further in this proposed combination of subjects than the admission of California, the establishment of territorial governments, and . . . a suitable boundary for Texas, with the offer of an equivalent for the surrender of any territory," asks Benton to "admit how unfair, how improper, at least, it is to suppose that, by such a combination as I have indicated, the result would be to give Texas a veto on California." While the sections in relation to the settlement of the boundary of Texas depend on "the consent which Texas might or might not give," if "Texas does not give her consent, does anybody say that the other parts of the bill would become dead or nugatory?" Clay believes that "Each portion of the bill is of force and affect according to the object in view, and each might stand" alone.

Does not agree with Benton that "it is wrong to make those who might be in favor of the admission of California, and against the establishment of territorial governments, or *vice versa*, vote on such a combination . . . because they would have to vote against both, not liking a portion of the bill, or for both, still disliking a portion of the bill." Finds "little practicability in this idea of total separation of subjects." Tariff bills, for example, contain "five hundred items usually, and we have never passed a tariff bill, or given a vote upon it, without some parts of it being objectionable to some." Senators face a similar question here: "You may vote against it if you please in toto, because of the bad there is in it, or you may vote for it, because you approve of the greater amount of good there is in it. The question for the time is, whether there is more of the good than of the bad in the bill."

Argues, in addition, "that there is a perfect connection between the subjects proposed to be united." California, New Mexico, and Utah "all were component parts of the Mexican Republic" and were ceded "together in association, under the treaty by which we acquired them [Clay to Beatty, April 29, 1847]. They came here at the last session together, all imploring the establishment of territorial governments." But "Congress failed to devise and establish governments which it was called upon to do by all the solemn obligations of treaty stipulations," because of "irreconcilable differences of opinion between the two large parties in Congress; and their convictions, their consciences, restrained them from yielding the one to the views of the other." Asks: "Well, how does this matter stand? The three sisters came here at the last session of Congress; New Mexico the eldest, California next, and Utah the youngest. They came here all soliciting territorial governments. Attempts were made to give them all territorial governments, but they failed. In the mean time, Miss California has made a runaway match of it—and she has not only done that, but she has taken as large a portion of the common patrimony as she pleases. She comes here now with her two sisters—the one older and the other younger—and cocks up her nose, and asks if you will associate her with those two girls, [laughter]." Cites "the fact of their community of existence heretofore" and "the fact that we propose government for the one, matured, it is true, in the form of a State government, and for the others, governments also adapted to their peculiar condition" as "ample reason why they should be combined" now.

Challenges Benton's assertion that "in every instance of the admission of a new State the question of admission has stood by itself, unconnected with any measure whatever." Notes that Missouri, "the very State of which he [Benton] is such an able and efficient Senator. . . . was not admitted alone [2:669-70, 740-48, 775-77, 785-86; 3:15-22, 26-33, 46-47, 49-50]." Adds that "In most of the cases to which the honorable Senator has referred, Vermont, Kentucky, Tennessee, and others, there was but one single Territory to be admitted, and that was clearly defined."

Admits he is "equally anxious with" Benton "for the admission of California." Regrets, however, that Benton requires California, "who treats with so much contempt the other poor members of her family—not only . . . that her superior honor and dignity shall be recognized, but he exacts from us that she shall be kept separate and alone; that she shall not be contaminated by any sort of connection with her sisters, lest she might contract some contagious and fatal disease. The honorable Senator is not satisfied that she should stand alone, but she must lead off in the dance; she must precede all the others."

Repeats his desire "to keep these subjects together." Since "Every member of this body is desirous of restoring once more peace, harmony, and fraternal affection to this distracted people," suggests that the Committee of Thirteen be permitted "to settle, if they can, the causes of difference which exist in the country by some proposition of compromise." Even though some "will reject all propositions of compromise," points out that "All legislation, all government, all society, is formed upon the principle of mutual concession, politeness, comity, courtesy. . . . Compromise is peculiarly appropriate among the members of a republic, as of one common family. . . . if you concede anything, you have something conceded to you in return." Concludes: "Let him who elevates himself above humanity, above its weaknesses, its infirmities, its wants, its necessities, say, if he pleases, I never will compromise, but let no one who is not above the frailties of our common nature disdain compromises." *Cong. Globe*, 31 Cong., 1 Sess., 660-63. Printed in Colton, *Clay Correspondence*, 6:410-18.

For Roger S. Baldwin (Whig, Conn.), see *BDAC*.

Remark in Senate, April 10, 1850. After Sen. John P. Hale presents a number of petitions urging the prohibition of slavery and the slave trade in the territories, Clay asks if the memorials are "printed" or "in manuscript." Upon learning that the signatures were entirely in writing but that some of the headings were printed, Clay immediately accuses "these disturbers of the peace, these abolitionists . . . the [William] Jays, the [Wendell] Phillipses, and others in other quarters" of establishing "a concerted and ramified plan of operations, and I want to expose it to the Senate." Holds up the printed petition, copies of which have been "scattered throughout the whole country. Some of them found their way into my own State." Believes they were printed "at a common centre, and dispersed throughout the country, in order to make a common effect."

After Hale rises to a point of order, Clay hopes that "the honorable Senator . . . will not manifest any very great impatience at my calling the attention of the Senate to this ramified and concerted plan of the Abolitionists to circulate their little bits of printed petitions adapted to . . . every shape and mode in which they can bring up the question of slavery" in their attempt to "manufacture a sort of public opinion." Continues: "Sir, of all the bitterest enemies toward the unfortunate negro race, there are none to compare with these Abolitionists, pretended friends of theirs; but who, like, the Siamese twins, connect themselves with the negro, or, like the centaur of old, mount not the back of a horse, but the back of the negro to ride themselves into power; and in order to display a friendship they feel only for themselves, and not for the negro race. No, sir; there are not worse enemies in the country of the negro race than the ultra abolitionists. To what sorts of extremity have they not driven the slaveholding States in defence of their own rights, and in guarding against those excesses to which they have a constant tendency."

Presents several petitions of his own: two from Philadelphia recommending congressional assistance to Henry Grinnell's "search for Sir John Franklin and his companions [Comment in Senate, April 5, 1850]"; a request from William Tell Zollickoffer for a pension for his Mexican War service; and a memorial from "citizens of Indiana" asking that veterans of the War of 1812 and the Indian Wars "may be allowed bounty land."

Sens. Thomas J. Rusk, Andrew P. Butler, and Henry S. Foote reopen discussion on the "incendiary" practices of Northern abolitionists. Rusk especially expresses deep concern over a recently received petition that asked Congress "to enroll the slaves of the slave States in the militia." He asks "what would be the consequence of placing arms in their hands?" Answering his own question, he fears "the effect of this course is to appeal to the slaves which I have at home, to rise and burn my house and massacre my wife and children."

Clay expresses his conviction "to receive petitions generally," even when they "connect the subject of abolition to the right of petition." Views this memorial, however, as "a very different thing," and moves that the Senate take it up immediately. Calls for "the yeas and nays . . . that this petition will be rejected by the decisive, and indignant, and unanimous vote of the whole body."

Sen. William H. Seward objects to rejecting the memorial, as it would be tantamount to trampling a citizen's right of petition. Clay clarifies that he moved to "reject the PRAYER of the petition. . . . The petition, be it remembered, has been received. There can therefore be no reproach against the Senate for not receiving it." Asks the Senate simply to reject "what no man can conceive or dream of without horror or dismay. . . . the abominable prayer of the petition." *Cong. Globe*, 31 Cong., 1 Sess., 684-86.

The motion to reject the prayer of the petition to enroll slaves in the state militia is carried unanimously.

Remark in Senate, April 11, 1850. During discussion on Sen. John Bell's resolutions on the slavery question, Sen. Thomas Hart Benton again argues for separating the admission of California to the Union from the remaining issues, reviewing "sixty years of legislation" and "the admission of seventeen States" to prove that "there has been no example of mixing up any other matter with the admission of a State."

Clay responds that "each of those cases depended upon a particular state of circumstances." Moreover, in Missouri's case "there was that species of agitation and division" that called for "a course somewhat similar to that now proposed" for California. Into the "very act" that admitted Missouri into the Union "was inserted a clause on the subject of slavery north and south of the line of 36° 30′." Admission "was made to depend on a condition relating to the African population of the United States," that Missouri "should, by a solemn and effective act of her Legislature, declare . . . that if free negroes had the right by the Constitution of going to Missouri, that she should not exclude them under the provisions of her constitution [2:669-70, 740-48, 775-77, 785-86; 3:15-22, 26-33, 46-47, 49-50]." Now "a great subject" is again "agitating and distracting the country, and it is proposed, in the spirit of compromise and concession, to connect together two or three analogous subjects—perfectly analogous," in considering California for admission to the Union. Urges Benton to stop "intrenching himself behind various precedents" that are irrelevant to this case and to answer a "simple question": "whether it is an indignity or not on California to connect her in a great scheme of national compromise, the object of which is the restoration of harmony, peace, and concord to this people?" Clay himself sees no such indignity.

Much discussion follows, including an unsuccessful attempt by Sen. Stephen A. Douglas to table Sen. Henry S. Foote's motion to refer Bell's resolutions to a Select Committee of Thirteen. Benton then offers an amendment to Bell's resolutions stating that "nothing in this instruction shall be construed to authorize" the committee to consider anything relating to four specific points: the abolition of slavery in the states; the suppression of the slave trade between the states; the abolition of slavery within the forts, arsenals, dockyards and navy yards of the United States; and, the abolition of slavery in the District of Columbia. Benton would also disallow consideration of any other slavery question not "specially referred to it by order of the Senate." Sen. Daniel Webster protests, however, arguing that the addition of these instructions would only open another "great field for discussion." To stave off further debate and perhaps reduce the need for such instructions, Foote expresses his willingness to modify his original motion by submitting Bell's fairly comprehensive resolutions in conjunction with Clay's more concrete resolutions to a Committee of Thirteen, "leaving them, in the exercise of their discretion, to make such a report as they may deem best." Benton quickly adds an amendment to keep California's admission to the Union out of the committee's deliberations, but this is rejected by a vote of 28-26. Benton's earlier amendment to prescribe specific aspects of the slavery question that were to remain outside the committee's authority then comes up for consideration.

Clay moves to amend Benton's amendment to eliminate an ambiguity in its language. Hopes to make it clear "that Congress has no power to touch slavery as it now exists in the States" and "no power to arrest the slave trade between the States," and "I want Senators to affirm" this. Fears that if senators "vote against the instructions as proposed by" Benton, that "it would be an implication that Congress has the power to act" on slavery in the states. At the request of Sen. Lewis Cass, Clay withdraws his amendment.

Benton then modifies his amendment's wording to offer "not the least foundation in the world for supposing that the Senate is going to interfere" with slavery. Webster again expresses his fear that Benton's amendments would "be the subjects of debate for many days," thereby leaving consideration of "the main question of admission of California . . . in abeyance." Sen. John P. Hale attempts to end further debate by moving to refer both Bell's and Clay's resolutions to the standing Committee on Territories, rather than to a select committee. Hales's motion is defeated by a vote of 31-23.

Returning to discussion of Benton's modified amendment, Clay reads part of its text to point out again the opportunity for "erroneous implication." A vote against the amendment still "will be an implication that we supposed there was some power, for instance, over the abolition of slavery in the States, when there is not a member in this body, I hope, who thus thinks." Proposes several additional modifications that state specifically that "nothing in this reference shall be construed to assert or imply the existence of any power whatever in Congress for the abolition of slavery within the States" as "an amendment to the amendment" of Benton. Benton believes that he and Clay agree in principle and views his own amendment as the stronger one. Nonetheless, he accepts Clay's amendment and it is presented for a vote. Webster opposes a vote on Clay's amendment for the same reason he opposed Benton's earlier; it "introduces topics of a very grave nature" which require much deliberation. Clay "would not press any gentleman to vote upon any subject to which he has not given a full consideration," but asks Webster to remember that "I should be glad to get rid of all these obstructions if I could." Regrets that Benton's instructions in their present form "would lead to embarrassment and misconception," leaving Clay no alternative but to offer his modifications.

Foote rises to say "I am wholly disappointed in the course of proceeding," and moves for adjournment. *Cong. Globe*, 31 Cong., 1 Sess., 705, 709, 711, 713-14.

Remark in Senate, April 12, 1850. Taking up the unfinished business from the previous day, Sen. Daniel Webster asks "those gentlemen who feel most interested in that course of proceeding, whether it is worth while further to press for a committee and a reference" of the resolutions of Sens. John Bell and Clay since "all these things must be discussed in the Senate, sooner or later." He opposes any further effort to form such a committee. Sen. Daniel S. Dickinson moves to lay the question on the table.

Clay rises "to make a suggestion" to those who oppose the formation of a special committee: "Now, what I suggest is this, that we shall proceed to the appointment of the committee . . . if no good no harm can come from it." Believes that "A report from such a committee as is contemplated . . . will be productive of much good. I do believe that such a committee should take up the subject in a comprehensive point of view. . . . making suggestions and recommendations, and exhibiting a general plan for the settlement and compromise of all those troubles which now annoy and afflict us, and presenting to the country in one collective view . . . bills and amendments where necessary, and where they are not, recommending a course of action for the Senate." Otherwise, "we may go on from day to day, and week to week, in this struggle to avoid a committee, and in the attempt to take up the California bill, and it will result in nothing but delay. Sooner or later we must arrive at the question whether we will or will not unite California and the territorial bills; for I, for one, if nobody else does, mean to propose as an amendment to it the territorial bill. . . . The union or non-union of the bills is a proposition from which there is no escape—no evasion. I pledge myself, if my life is spared, if no other Senator moves it, to move when the California bill is taken up, the addition of the territorial bill." Argues, therefore, that "nothing but a great and useless waste of time will result from this unprofitable struggle to avoid the committee." Notes that 33 to 35 senators are prepared to vote for the committee, and asks Sen. Thomas Hart Benton, who inspired these remarks, "whether it is not better to waive all impediments to the constitution of the committee." *Cong. Globe*, 31 Cong., 1 Sess., 722.

For Daniel S. Dickinson (Dem., N.Y.), see *BDAC*.

To Joseph Holt, Louisville, April 16, 1850. Acknowledges receipt of a cane, cut from a special "spot of the habitable earth" that "commended such an article to my acceptance . . . that tumulus which covers the remains of Leonidas." Sends letters of introduction for Holt's use during his upcoming second "voyage to the old parts of the world." ALS. DLC-HC (DNA, M212, R21).

For Joseph Holt (1807-94), a lawyer and later postmaster general and secretary of war, see *DAB*. For Leonidas (d. 480 B.C.), King of Sparta, see *Encyclopedia Britannica*, 11th ed.

Remark in Senate, April 16, 1850. After Sen. Henry S. Foote again renews his motion for raising a special Committee of Thirteen [Remark in Senate, March 12, 1850], Clay hopes "there will be a decision promptly upon the question of committee or no committee. Let the thing be disposed of absolutely and finally." Wants a decision made today, because "if I have been rightly informed . . . to-morrow a committee composed of six members of this Chamber will depart from this city with the remains of the lamented [John C.] Calhoun [Remark in Senate, February 28, 1850]." Adds that "it would be very discourteous towards those gentlemen, and perhaps improper . . . to take up the subject in the absence of that committee."

Clay is informed that the escort for Calhoun's remains is not leaving the next day. After more discussion, Clay calls for the yeas and nays on Foote's motion. He then withdraws the motion when Foote moves to make his resolution for the formation of a special Committee of Thirteen the special order of business in the Senate on the following day. *Cong. Globe*, 31 Cong., 1 Sess., 747-48.

Comment in Senate, April 17, 1850. The Senate takes up Sen. Henry S. Foote's motion to refer the resolutions of Sen. John Bell and Clay to a special Committee of Thirteen. Sen. Thomas Hart Benton's amendment to Foote's motion, further modified by Clay to make clear that Congress has no power whatever to abolish slavery in the states, comes up for deliberation first.

Clay then offers another "amendment to the amendment proposed by" Benton, who had already accepted Clay's first modification. Desires to strike out the wording of Benton's amendment "after the word 'provided,' " and to "insert the following: 'That the Senate does not deem it necessary to express or advance any opinion, or to give any instructions, either general or specific, for the guidance of the said committee.' " Declares that Benton's amendment, in present form, "is wholly unnecessary, as the Senate would, by a unanimous voice, declare the belief that Congress has no power to abolish slavery in the several States. . . . I think it, therefore, useless as it at present stands."

Benton compliments Clay as one of the "most skilled parliamentarians . . . in America or Europe." Nonetheless, resubmits his original amendment because Clay "is not proceeding parliamentarily" by offering a resolve which "I do not think . . . can come under the name, style, or description of an amendment. . . . An amendment is to improve a thing, to make it better," but what Clay designs is to "obtain a resolution from the Senate declaring that they will not act upon the subject at all." Fears there will be "a great deal of lost time, if the proposed committee is raised," and hopes that the Senate instead will take up the matter of California's admission "unincumbered with questions which do not belong to it."

Clay ignores Benton's "parliamentary objection." Notes that Benton "wants California admitted. So do I. He regrets the lapse of time before her admission can take place. So do I. But it is a little singular" that Benton "is one of the causes which prolong the admission of California into the Union." Wants the committee to "be appointed without future opposition" that might "be productive of no consequence but that of an additional consumption of time." Warns Benton that his California bill "in the shape in which it is" will not pass. Argues that Benton's previous references "to early precedents for the admission of new States" are not appropriate here, for "we shall violate all of them if California be admitted" the way the Missouri senator desires. Points out that "from Ohio upward," states were admitted only after "the passage of a previous law proposing certain articles of compact to the new States, which were to be assented to by a convention of the people of the new States, and brought here in the shape of a compact, binding and obligatory forever upon both parties." Notes that Benton's bill lacks a "suitable provision to protect the rights and interests of the United States in California," and asserts that "she can only be admitted by annexing the condition to the act for her admission, that nothing in that act shall contravene or impair the rights of the United States in the public domain." Unlike Benton, Clay does not believe that "we may get through with this in two or three days." Hopes that Benton will come to understand that "he is prolonging the admission of California in thus continuing to oppose the appointment of this committee" to help resolve these questions. Argues further that even if the Senate could pass "a bill for the admission of California with suitable guards and protection to the public property . . . then, we must turn our attention to the condition of things in the other House. . . . If they consume anything like the amount of time in electing an officer to supply the place of the lamented individual who has died, as they did in organizing at first [Clay to Lucretia H. Clay, December 5, 1849], it may be weeks before that body will even be prepared to act upon any bill." In the meantime, "Let us go to work and act like men, talk less and act more," and decide on the formation of the special committee before taking up the California question.

Benton calls Clay's "specious amendment. . . . a resolve to govern the conduct of the Senate," and describes the proposed committee as a "jury of the distinguished and leading members of the Senate," who would dictate to "those perhaps who would necessarily fall into the category of led members," a "new proceeding in the Senate of the United States" that Benton opposes. Asserts that he is not arguing the question of California's admission to the Union. "The question is now as to the delay, the almost indefinite delay, with the chance of eventually losing the admission between the two Houses."

After Sen. Stephen A. Douglas attempts to reduce the apprehensions Clay had raised concerning the public domain, Clay insists "as a precautionary measure, that some clause be inserted declaring the retention by the Government of the United States of the public lands in California." Benton offers a motion to table Clay's amendment, but it fails by a vote of 28 to 24.

Douglas triggers extended debate on parliamentary procedure by insisting he has the right to defend his committee's bill on the admission of California against Clay's challenges. Clay explains this "very simple case" of Senate procedure. The only question before the Senate at this moment is "the amendment of the Senator from Missouri and my amendment to that amendment," neither of which "refers to the condition of California at all, or to the mode in which she should be admitted into the Union." Douglas continues to insist "that I have a right to discuss the amendment itself, as well as the amendment to the amendment, and indeed to discuss the original resolution of reference." He finally withdraws his appeal. A second procedural question, this one raised by Sen. Jacob W. Miller, concerning whether or not an amendment can "declare that no other or further instruction shall be made to a committee," is taken under consideration and declared out of order.

Benton again calls Clay's amendment "a rule of action" and clarifies his opposition by making "the point of my objection intelligible." Clay had asked the Senate to "cut itself off from its parliamentary rights," and if his amendment passes, it will "mark . . . an epoch in our parliamentary history." Launches another attack against the formation of a special Committee of Thirteen, saying "if this great number of political doctors are to sit on the body of the Republic, what will the country suppose but that the poor Republic is at the last gasp, and that it takes thirteen doctors to sit upon the case and save the patient. . . . I tell you, from this proceeding there must be an alarm, or there must be a laugh." Benton does not "believe the Republic is in danger to-day."

Clay points out that just as senators have rights, "the Senate has its rights." After Benton's original amendment with its four propositions, "he shells out eight or ten others, and speaks of having others yet in reserve. . . . has not this body a right to protect itself?" Describes the effect of Benton's amendments as "delay, procrastination, embarrassment" that prevent the "distinct and emphatic expressions of the opinion of the majority of this body." Warns that "not many years will elapse before you will find the indispensable necessity of this valuable mode of terminating a useless and unnecessary debate in this house." Adds that "we create a committee without giving that committee instructions . . . every day, and sometimes two or three times a day." Believes it best to leave a committee "untrammelled, unshackled, to the exercise of its best judgment," since "when it does anything, it is reported back to you, subject to your decision, to your power, to your control."

Considers the present case, noting that "a certain portion" of the Senate demands "California, California, and nothing but California." Another portion, including Clay, is "willing to give you California, but we want something more than California; we want to establish governments for a people thrown by the vicissitudes of war and of political events under our care." Criticizes the "Whigs who denounced the existence of the military government" established in New Mexico and Utah by the Polk administration, who "now, in a state of profound peace," propose "to pass California, pass California, pass California, and leave New Mexico and Utah to take care of themselves." Asserts that "It is contrary to every obligation of duty" to "leave New Mexico and Utah without government. . . . The error of those Senators who talk of leaving Utah and New Mexico to their fate, is exactly this: they begin where they ought to end." Sees "not the slightest evidence of disrespect to California or to any one else" in combining the two issues. Repeats that he "framed this resolution deliberately" to get rid "of the unnecessary instructions which the Senator from Missouri has proposed, and to dispose of any other instructions which his ingenuity . . . might suggest to be brought before this body."

After more remarks on procedure from Benton, Douglas, and several other senators, Clay again attempts to clarify the question: "The original motion is to raise a committee and refer certain subjects to it. The amendment [of Benton] is, to restrict that committee. My proposition is, that we will not adopt the restrictions proposed, or any other, but leave the committee free and untrammelled."

Daniel Webster and John P. Hale express further opposition to Clay's amendment. Clay asserts that "If the Senate had expressed any opinion, as the Senator from New Hampshire seems to suppose, upon the various questions that are proposed to be referred to this committee, and it should now refuse to give that committee any instructions in regard to them, there might be some incompatibility in our proposed action," but since "the Senate has expressed no opinion upon any of the resolutions offered by the Senator from Tennessee or myself," finds nothing inappropriate in his amendment.

Hale again argues that the Senate's refusal to instruct the committee intimates "that we do not know what to do" and "that we are in such a perilous condition . . . that we feel compelled to . . . proceed entirely upon the principle of implicit faith; trusting that the wisdom of thirteen men" can steer "the ship of State . . . clear of the rocks which lie before us." Asserts that "the sole serious objection that exists in the minds of Senators" to California's admission is "that she has in her constitution embodied the principle of freedom." Foote considers Hale's accusation "a very serious imputation upon myself." Hale responds, however, "that the North will be beaten, as she always has been," adding that "slavery will triumph. . . . because the North allows it."

Clay replies to Hale that "There is no destiny of defeat on the part of the North, but there is a destiny of triumph on the part of the Union of these States," which "will be the defeat of your ultra abolitionists." Recalls "the famous Missouri question," when "men who wished to defeat the adjustment and compromise of this great question were predicting that the representatives of the North who had assisted in making this adjustment would go home and find their effigies had been burnt, and would meet with a very warm reception. What was the fact, sir? Why, more exultation, more joy, and more gladness were not manifested by the people of the United States upon the annunciation of peace with Great Britain . . . than that which animated them on the compromise of that question." Repeats his belief that "It will be a triumph, not of the South over the North, or of the North over the South, but of the patriotism of the Union, of the best interests of mankind and of the world, over faction—yes, over the ultra abolitionists," who recognize that "their aliment for agitation will be cut off" by "such a compromise as I believe it is within the power of this Congress to effect."

Sen. Willie P. Mangum proposes adding flexibility to Clay's amendment, stating that while the Senate "may not deem it necessary" to instruct the committee "at this instant . . . an hour hence there may be a change of opinion." Clay agrees to the modification. Clay's amendment to Benton's amendment is voted on and approved by a vote of 29 to 22.

After extended discussion on Sen. Hannibal Hamlin's amendment (to Foote's original resolution) to except from the reference anything that relates to the admission of California as a state—and Benton's fourteen-point amendment to Hamlin's amendment—Sen. Joseph R. Underwood protests that these actions are "points of instruction" and the Senate has "already decided that they will not instruct the committee." Clay concurs: "when the Senate has decided that it will not do a given thing, it is out of order for that thing to be proposed to be done," and appeals the Chair's decision that Hamlin and Benton's amendments are in order.

Benton defends his amendments: "I intend . . . to cut up the whole address of the southern members, by which the country was thrown into a flame. . . . there has been a cry of 'wolf,' when there was no wolf . . . the country has been alarmed without reason, and against reason." Adds that the Congress has "no design . . . to encroach upon the rights of the South, nor to aggress upon the South, nor to oppress them upon the subject of their institutions." Foote attacks Benton for denouncing Calhoun's Southern Address "as fraught with mischief, and as supplying food for the agitation and excitement which has involved our institutions in dangers from which they had to be rescued by the efforts of others hostile to the propositions of that address." Referring to Benton, asks, "by whom is this extraordinary denunciation hurled against all those individuals who subscribed to this address." During Foote's speech, Benton comes down the aisle toward him. Foote retreats to the vice president's chair and pulls a pistol. In the ensuing chaos, Benton is restrained by Sen. Henry Dodge, and Sen. Daniel S. Dickinson takes away Foote's pistol. Clay, among others, calls for a restoration of order. Benton, however, proclaims: "We are not going to get off in this way. A pistol was brought here to assassinate me." Foote retorts that "If my presenting a pistol here has been understood as anything except the necessary means of self-defence, after threats of personal chastisement, it is doing me a wrong."

When Sen. Mangum offers a resolution calling for the formation of a committee "to investigate the disorder of to-day in the Senate," Clay concurs but does not believe the resolution goes "far enough. I think the two Senators who have been placed in an unpleasant relation towards each other ought to be placed under an obligation to keep the peace, and for that purpose that they should either voluntarily or otherwise go before some magistrate of this city, or that both of them in their places here should pledge themselves—which would be more gratifying to me—not to pursue the matter . . . further than what occurred to-day."

Benton protests that "I have done nothing, and I will rot in jail before I will give a promise which admits, by implication, that I have been guilty of a breach of the peace." Clay responds that "My observations did not relate to the past, but to the future." Desires merely that "the two Senators should come under some legal or personal obligation not to push this matter further."

Although Clay attempts to reopen discussion on the resolution to submit his and Bell's resolution to a special committee, the Senate adjourns. *Cong. Globe*, 31 Cong., 1 Sess., 747-64.

For Jacob W. Miller (Whig, N.J.); Hannibal Hamlin (Dem., Me.); and Henry Dodge (Dem., Wisc.), see *BDAC*. Thomas Jefferson Campbell, clerk of the House, had died on April 13. On April 17 Richard M. Young was elected to succeed him. U.S. H. of Reps., *Journal*, 31 Cong., 1 Sess., 788-89, 799, 805; Washington *Daily National Intelligencer*, April 15, 1850.

John C. Calhoun had acted as spokesman for a caucus of Southerners in Congress which met on December 22, 1848, and January 15 and 22, 1849, to formulate a response to the Wilmot Proviso as well as other matters involving slavery. The "Address of the Southern Delegates," drafted by Calhoun and signed by 48 senators and representatives, listed "acts of aggression" committed by the North against Southern rights. Wiltse, *John C. Calhoun: Sectionalist*, 378-88.

Remark in Senate, April 18, 1850. When Sen. Thomas Hart Benton moves to postpone other Senate business to take up the admission of California to statehood, Clay reminds him that "the Senator from Mississippi [Henry S. Foote] was on the floor. . . . You cannot get rid of that business" with a motion. Clay moves to table Benton's motion, and the Senate agrees by a vote of 27 to 24.

The Senate takes up Foote's motion to refer the resolution of Clay and Sen. John Bell to a special Committee of Thirteen, first considering Sen. Hannibal Hamlin's amendment and Benton's amendment to it. Benton attempts to table consideration of the question, but his motion is defeated, 28 to 24. Each subdivision of Benton's amendment is then voted upon and rejected in turn. Hamlin's amendment, excepting anything that "relates to the admission of California as a State" from the consideration of the special committee is also defeated by a vote of 25 to 20.

Sen. Isaac P. Walker proposes an amendment excepting such parts of Clay's and Bell's resolutions that "relate to the recapture and return of fugitives from service or labor." Clay objects: "I do not think it necessary . . . to give instructions to the committee on this or any other subject." Hopes Walker "will see the propriety of leaving the subject to the committee, open and untrammelled." After more discussion, Walker's amendment is rejected by a vote of 27 to 17.

Sen. John P. Hale offers an amendment to refer all the "petitions and remonstrances received this session on the subjects mentioned" in Clay's and Bell's resolutions to the committee. Clay hopes "the motion will prevail," but supposes that "the committee will not feel bound to read them all, but perhaps one or two of a class." Sens. William R. King and Jefferson Davis protest the reception of all such petitions, but Sen. Jeremiah Clemens agrees with Clay that these "great humbugs" should be sent to the committee. Laughter erupts when Clemens reads parts of a recently received petition for "the absolute necessity of establishing a United States lunatic asylum for the immediate treatment of some worthy Senators and Representatives now in Washington," especially one abolitionist senator whose head should be "shaved and blistered" and who should "be at once bled and placed on a water diet."

Clay comments that "This proposition is totally different from those we have been voting upon to-day. Those we have been voting on to-day were those of restriction. The proposition now is one of enlargement of the powers of the committee without restriction." Since he is "disinclined to give a chance to any portion of the country to reproach Congress for the non-reception of petitions," hopes now that "the opposition to the reference of these petitions may be withdrawn." Wants no man "to go home and endeavor to excite the people by using such language as this: 'Your petitions were treated with the utmost indignity. They were laid on the table, unread, unconsidered; and when I proposed to send them to the committee to which all the subject-matters of the petitions were referred, and with which, therefore, they had a necessary connection, even that was opposed.' I am no great hand at making a stump speech, but I think I could take up that theme in such a way as to exasperate and excite the populace . . . .I do fear that the non-reference of these petitions would tarnish the prospect of a general amity."

The whole question of referring these petitions to the special committee is declared out of order. The Senate then votes on Foote's resolutions to form the special Committee of Thirteen; the motion is approved by a vote of 30 to 22. Balloting for members is postponed until the next day. *Cong. Globe*, 31 Cong., 1 Sess., 770-74. P. 774 is printed in Colton, *Clay Correspondence*, 6:419-20.

For Sen. Isaac P. Walker (Dem., Wisc.), see *BDAC*.

From "Ondine," *ca.* April 19, 1850. Writes as "A lady who feels a deep interest in the result of the agitation of the subject of slavery which now pervades . . . this country." Notes that "Thou art called a great man, and hast many admirers; but I have never yet been able to discover any trace of generosity or justice in any of thy *great* speeches, compromises, or resolutions." Asks: "But wherein hast thou ever shown any sympathy for the colored race, or any desire or design to treat them with justice? In thy scheme for (emancipation, I cannot say) ridding Kentucky of her slaves [Clay to Pindell, February 17, 1849, no. 2 of date], thou didst admit that a wrong, a *great* wrong had been done them; but that slavery had become so interwoven with all the great interests of society, that it had now become one of those stupendous wrongs and evils which it was *impossible to redress*! Hadst thou said *inconvenient*, thou wouldst have said truth."

Quotes at length from the *Bible* to prove that God requires repentance for sin, adding "I am speaking to one who admits slavery to be a sin." Contends: "Hadst thou one-half the love of God in thy heart thou hast for the Constitution or the Union—one-half the love of thy neighbor thou hast for thyself . . . thou wouldst glory in setting thy slaves at liberty." Argues that if he would do this, he would "be honored as a *good* as well as a *great* man." Notes that Clay "would fain make it appear that every individual is bound by law . . . to assist" in the return of fugitive slaves. Admits: "True, the Constitution (shame to those who framed and more shame to those who uphold it) requires the return of fugitives." Insists that "I utterly repudiate whatever is in the Constitution that requires me to violate my duty to God and man." Copy. Printed in Boston *The Liberator*, April 19, 1850.

Remark in Senate, April 19, 1850. The members of the Committee of Thirteen are elected. Clay receives 28 votes in a separate ballot to name the chairman; there are also four blank ballots, and Sens. John Bell, Willie P. Mangum, and Thomas Hart Benton each receive one vote. The remaining twelve members include Bell, Mangum, Lewis Cass, Daniel S. Dickinson, Jesse D. Bright, Daniel Webster, Samuel S. Phelps, James Cooper, William R. King, James M. Mason, Solomon W. Downs, and John M. Berrien.

The bill for the admission of California then comes up for discussion. Clay warns against haste and hopes for "some understanding between the Senate and the member charged with this bill [Sen. Stephen A. Douglas] . . . that, in the event of the number of six going with the remains of our lamented colleague [Sen. John C. Calhoun], in-their absence this business shall not be urged to a vote [Remark in Senate, February 28, 1850]. It is highly improper, it seems to me, that it should be taken up during their absence." After Douglas assures Clay that he does not "feel authorized to ask the Senate to take a vote on any test question during the absence of six members of this body on a duty like that," Clay approves Douglas's "liberal, manly course," and urges that discussions begin on the California bill. Sen. Andrew P. Butler expresses his "surprise that the California bill is to be taken up and discussed in this Senate, whilst all other matters in relation to slavery, and the admission of California herself, have been referred to a Committee of Thirteen. The great end of that committee will be defeated if this course of proceeding shall be taken." Clay assures Butler that he is "mistaken if he supposes that that bill, standing by itself and alone, is to pass this Senate without a struggle, and, I trust, a successful one. I have got amendments now in my hand, attaching to it the territorial bills. . . . I have also prepared amendments providing for the settlement of the Texas boundary question, which I may, or may not, think proper to offer." In any case, he will add the territorial bills, hoping "from all the demonstrations that have been made, that there can be but little doubt that the majority of the Senate favor such a proposition."

When Benton challenges Clay's amendments as "flagrantly illegal, and violative of parliamentary law," Clay warns him against "dwelling on parliamentary law." Douglas intervenes and Clay urges the printing of the "ordinance of the Convention of California." Further consideration of California is then postponed for two weeks. *Cong. Globe*, 31 Cong., 1 Sess., 781-82.

For Jesse D. Bright (Dem., Ind.) and Samuel S. Phelps (Whig, Vt.), see *BDAC*.

To William G. Brownlow, Knoxville, Tenn., April 20, 1850. Regrets that he cannot "comply with your request to obtain the admission of your young friend John W. McNutt into West point as a Cadet." Explains that "The members of the H. of Representatives have the designation of the youths who are received in that institution, each member designating one. Ten are reserved for the President[']s designation," and "Cadets to enter next June are already selected." Notes that Zachary Taylor "did not think proper to select, among his ten, the eldest son of Col. H. Clay [Jr.] [Henry Clay III] . . . and I am indebted to my representative [Charles S. Morehead] in the House for his obtaining a place [Clay to Morehead, December 14, 1849]." ALS. Courtesy of Dr. Holman Hamilton, Lexington, Ky.

Brownlow had moved his newspaper to Knoxville, Tenn., in 1849. McNutt received an appointment to the West Point class of 1855 but did not graduate. USMA, *Register*, 204.

Comment in Senate, April 22, 1850. When Sen. Thomas Hart Benton moves to take up his motion of instruction to the Committee of Thirteen against "tacking any other bill or any foreign matter," to the bill for the admission of California, Clay feels it "incumbent upon me to object to taking up this resolution now." Until the six senators who accompanied the remains of John C. Calhoun to South Carolina [Remark in Senate, February 28, 1850] return to Washington, believes that "it would not be right . . . to take up a subject in which that committee might feel as great an interest as I feel." Moreover, "a majority of this Senate has declared that it will give no instructions, general or special, to that committee." Does not want "the minority, in consequence of the temporary absence of a portion of that majority" to "give instructions, and do the very thing which a majority of the Senate have refused to do."

When Benton protests that he only desires discussion, not a vote, on his motion, Clay interprets the move "merely as a peg on which to hang a speech. . . . The Senator, the other day, held up four tremendous quarto volumes which I believe he threatened to read from beginning to end, [laughter] and I confess I had no anticipation of submitting to that without offering some objections. [Renewed laughter.]" Nonetheless, he waives his objection, and Benton's motion is taken up. Benton speaks at length "to establish the parliamentary law, and to show that the tacking of any bill to the California bill would be a flagrant violation of that law."

Although not intending to reply to Benton's argument on "what is called 'parliamentary law,' " Clay hopes that "his speech to day would prevent the necessity of his speaking again on the same point." Adds that "if I had made notes of a parcel of authorities, in order to show the power of the Senate to connect together" various subjects, "I should have gone to the precise authorities which the learned Senator on the other side brings forward." Announces that when Benton "comes on with his war of words, which is terrible enough, when not accompanied by any emphatic use of terms, I shall come on for peace. And if the Senator's object is war against any proposition to connect together subjects which I shall show to be perfectly coherent, it is directly the reverse of mine, which will be peace." Intends to show that Benton's argument "that all the subjects contained in the resolutions presented by" Clay and Sen. John Bell, "or any considerable number of them, were to be associated together" is "totally unfounded." Will also show that "this business of 'tacking,' as it is technically called, has been carried to an extent much greater in Great Britain than in any other country," thereby refuting Benton's lengthy diatribe. Will demonstrate "that it is a question of sound discretion, to be exercised upon high considerations of State and public policy, to unite one or more measures; and I will show that even in the case of incongruous subjects, it may be done, and that if the subjects before the Senate were to be united, it would be a union of perfectly congenial, congruous, and coherent subjects." Moreover, "according to the practice of Congress . . . subjects infinitely a thousand times more incongruous than the subjects now proposed to be united, have been combined together" at other sessions. Since any further discussion would be "two or three weeks ahead of any practical result," will reserve his comments on Benton's speech until "that period of adjournment, when he threatened us with such a terrible war of words, and when I shall resort to all the laws of peace that I can." *Cong. Globe*, 31 Cong., 1 Sess., 793-94, 796-98.

From William McLain, Washington, April 23, 1850. Reminds Clay that previously "we availed ourselves of the visit of the Rev. John Miller to Europe, to circulate there Some correct information about our operating [McLain to Clay, November 7, 1848]." His influence was such that "Some three hundred pages of the *Blue Book* are filled with his testimony" before a Committee of Parliament. Now Rev. William Ives Budington of Charlestown, Mass., a life member in the American Colonization Society, will be visiting Europe "& is willing to Make himself useful to us in any way in his power." Encloses resolutions for Clay's signature that authorize Budington to speak for the society and "if you would write a few lines as a letter of general introduction" as "a ready passport to the best Society." ALS, with resolutions enclosed. DLC-Records of the American Colonization Society (DNA, M212, R20).

For Budington (1815-79), at this time pastor of the First Congregational Church in Charlestown, Mass., see *NCAB*, 10:16-17.

To LUCRETIA HART CLAY Washington, April 25, 1850

I have been suffering with bad colds for a fortnight, and they have debilitated me. I am going tomorrow to Mr. Calverts[1] (which you know is near to Bladensburg [Maryland]) to remain until monday next; but I shall take out work with me, and important work too; for it is materials to prepare a report for the Comee. of Thirteen.[2]

My hopes are strong that we may settle the Slavery questions; but all difficulties are not yet obviated.

I send you the two last letters I have recd. from James [Brown Clay].

At these dates he was not advised that a Ship of the Line had been ordered in May to bring him away, if Portugal does not allow our claims.[3] So that he may possibly leave Lisbon for [*sic*, before] he has been there a year. This will not be to be regretted as he seems to wish to return home. I am sorry that his health and that of poor Lucy [Jacob Clay] is not good.

We have had a most disagreeable April—cold, damp, and rainy[.]

Tell John [Morrison Clay] that all our Mules are at last sold but I have not yet recd all the proceeds.[4] It is the last Mule speculation that I will engage in.

My love to John.

ALS. DLC-TJC (DNA, M212, R11). 1. For Charles Benedict Calvert (1808-64)—Maryland legislator, congressman, and promoter of agriculture—see *DAB* and *BDAC*. 2. Clay did much of his work composing the Report of the Committee of Thirteen at Calvert's estate "Riverdale." Hamilton, *Prologue to Conflict*, 94. For the report, see Speech in Senate, May 8, 1850. 3. Clay to Clayton, June 7, 1849. 4. Clay to Lucretia H. Clay, Jan. 21, 1850.

To THOMAS B. STEVENSON Washington, April 25, 1850

I received your favor of the 14th inst. In respect to your desire to engage some of the letter-writers to write occasionally for your paper,[1] I regret that my acquaintance with that class of persons is very limited. Mr. J[ames]. E. Harvey and Mr. Francis J. Grund[2] stay at the same hotel that I do. The former you know as "Independent" of the [Philadelphia] North American, and I presume the latter, too, by reputation. He is admitted to be one of the best letter-writers; and he (Mr. Grund) has just now taken a wonderful liking to me. He offered to write to [*sic*, for] you for nothing, but I told him that would not do, and that you and he must adjust the terms, etc., etc. And there I leave it.

The rumors so rife of Cabinet changes a week or two ago have ceased, and at present there is no talk of any.[3] It is said that the President [Zachary Taylor] told the Cabinet that he liked them very much, and they told him that they liked him very much, and so they agreed that they would not dissolve that union. Most people believe, however, that ere long a change will be made. In the mean time there is very little concert & cooperation between the Capitol and the White House.

Copy. Printed in Colton, *Clay Correspondence*, 3:498-99. Copy in OCHP. 1. The Maysville *Eagle*. 2. For Grund, a Philadelphia journalist and later U.S. consul at Antwerp and Le Havre, see *NCAB*, 23:131. 3. Rumors were indeed rife that there would soon be changes in Taylor's cabinet. On April 16, 1850, the Washington *Daily National Intelligencer* denied a story printed in another newspaper that the Whigs in Congress were hostile to the cabinet and that President Taylor had intimated a disposition to follow their suggestion and form a new cabinet. Numerous other newspapers printed stories saying specifically that Secretary of State John M. Clayton was about to resign. See Louisville *Daily Journal*, Feb. 23, 1850; Frankfort *Commonwealth*, March 5, 1850; Lexington *Statesman*, June 8, 1850. Clayton, in fact, threatened to resign at least twice before Taylor's death. According to Thurlow Weed, Taylor was on the verge of replacing his whole cabinet when he died. The entire cabinet did resign upon Fillmore's ascension to the presidency. Bauer, *Zachary Taylor*, 310; Bemis, *American Secretaries of State*, 6:71; Hamilton, *Zachary Taylor, Soldier in the White House*, 382; Smith, *Presidencies of Taylor & Fillmore*, 156, 167-68.

Comment in Senate, April 29, 1850. The Senate takes up Sen. Stephen A. Douglas's bill that calls for the granting of the right of way and the making of a donation of land to the state of Illinois to aid the construction of the Illinois Central Railroad. Sen. William R. King offers an amendment that would permit the continuation of that railroad from the mouth of the Ohio to Mobile, giving the same rights to the states of Alabama and Mississippi. Debate centers on the bill's proposition to grant the necessary lands to the states "in alternate sections" and increasing the price of the intervening sections "to double the minimum price." A number of senators, most notably Isaac P. Walker, complain that such a practice would tax the "man whose enterprise leads him to the West." Sen. Andrew P. Butler argues that Congress should not become "the instrument of diverting the natural currents of trade and travel in favor of certain localities" by promoting an inequitable distribution of the public lands.

Clay entertains "no doubt about the general power, under proper guards and appropriate restrictions, to make the species of appropriations of the public lands which is here contemplated; and I hope to see a portion of that power extended to our lakes, and our rivers, and our harbors. I am ready, for one, to concur in any cautious, but liberal measures for the improvement of those lakes, and rivers, and harbors. The Ohio river—the greatest thoroughfare in this country, with the exception of the Mississippi—has depended almost for the possibility of navigating it upon the same general power, which I believe the Government possesses. I have no doubt . . . of the right of the General Government, as one of the greatest—the very greatest—of landholding proprietors, to appropriate a portion of that land for the purpose of making the remainder more valuable and available."

Believes that "The Government is a trustee for the purpose of administering the affairs of the nation according to its best judgment for the good of the whole, and all the parts of the whole." Describes that portion of Illinois "through which the road will run" as "a succession of prairies, the principal of which is denominated the Grand Prairie" which extends "about three hundred miles in length, and but one hundred in breadth." Explains that "the land in it is utterly worthless for any present purpose—not because it is not fertile, but for the want of wood, and water, and from the fact that it is inaccessible, wanting all facilities for reaching a market, or for transporting timber, so that nobody will go there and settle while it is so destitute of all the advantages of society, and the conveniences which arise from a social state." Building this railroad "will bring millions of acres of land immediately into market, which will otherwise remain for years and years entirely unsaleable." In "the Pine Barrens" of Mississippi and Alabama, the "soil there . . . is entirely valueless, though it is covered with timber which is intrinsically very valuable, but now worthless, because it is unapproachable, and not available for the want of some means of transport to a market." With a railroad, "you will again bring in to market an immense amount of lands, increasing their value to the benefit of the treasury of the United States." Wonders: "Is there a man even in Georgia, Alabama, Mississippi, Tennessee, Kentucky, Illinois, or the adjoining States, who will not, in one way or another, avail himself of the advantages of such a road" that will "furnish a continuous route from Chicago to Mobile," noting that "Georgia has already her iron arms stretching" to form "junctions with the Alabama road."

Downplays Butler's fears: "It is impossible, in the administration of the great interests of this country, to distribute the advantages of the administration equally amongst all the States." This railroad "is not for the sake of Illinois. . . . It is for the sake, in the first place, of the public lands, and for the sake of the commerce, and travel, and intercourse, between the people of this great republic, which, the more the facilities of intercommunication are augmented, becomes the more harmonious and homogeneous in all its parts."

Expresses some concern about the need for restrictions on the sale of public lands "so far from the road on either side of it—a distance of six miles. To go away off where the making of the road will create no additional value to the land" disturbs Clay. Concludes by voicing his support for the measure, since "I can have no doubt as to . . . the propriety of applying a portion of the public land in order to increase the value of the rest." *Cong. Globe*, 31 Cong., 1 Sess., 850-51. Printed in Colton, *Clay Correspondence*, 6:421-23.

Sen. Stephen A. Douglas had introduced Senate Bill no. 22 on January 3, 1850. It provided for making a donation of land to Illinois in aid of construction of a central railroad. The bill was referred the same day to the Committee on Public Lands. It passed the Senate on May 2 by a vote of 26-14, Clay not voting. It had been amended to give a right of way and land grants to the states of Illinois, Mississippi, and Alabama for construction of a railroad from Chicago to Mobile. It passed the House on September 18 by a vote of 88-80 and the president approved it on September 20. U.S. Sen., *Journal*, 31 Cong., 1 Sess., 52, 321, 646, 652, 659; U.S. H. of Reps., *Journal*, 31 Cong., 1 Sess., 1491; George R. Taylor, *The Transportation Revolution, 1815-1860* (New York, 1964), 95-96. See 9 *U.S. Stat.*, 466-67.

Surveys for the Illinois Central Railroad were completed by 1852 and by the end of the following year 175 miles of track had been laid. By 1855 the main line from Chicago to Cairo, Ill., and most of the branch from Chicago to Galena, were in operation. Clarence W. Alvord, *The Centennial History of Illinois*, 5 vols. (Springfield, Ill., 1919), 3:42.

Remark in Senate, May 1, 1850. Speaks in support of a joint resolution that would authorize President Zachary Taylor "to receive from Henry Grinnell, of the city of New York, the two vessels prepared by him for an expedition in search of Sir John Franklin and his companions, and to detail from the navy such commissioned and warrant officers and so many seamen as may be necessary for said expedition. . . . for a period not exceeding three years [Comment in Senate, April 5, 1850]."

Since Franklin "went on his perilous expedition not merely for the sake of his own country [Britain], or his own fame, but for the general good of mankind, and of the commercial world of all mankind," feels it is "peculiarly proper and expedient, that the interest which is taken in his fate should not be confined merely to the country from which he went, but that it should be coextensive with christendom, and all those parts of the world which could possibly be benefited, if he had succeeded." Although he concurs "in the expression of opinion urged against the union of a public and individual enterprise generally," hopes such attitudes "would not be permitted to prevent the passage of this resolution." Believes that "when anyone of our merchants displays a spirit of enterprise and humanity" as Grinnell has done, "it is very proper on the part of the Government to encourage such efforts on the part of commercial men, all over the country, and sanction them, and aid in carrying them out." Although "I am amongst those who despair of the recovery of this lost navigator, it will be a matter of satisfaction to know, if possible, what his fate has been; and it may turn out, too, that in carrying out this enterprise, other discoveries may be made, which will benefit our country and the world." Hopes that "the Senate will not hesitate to give its sanction" to the enterprise. *Cong. Globe*, 31 Cong., 1 Sess., 884. Printed in Colton, *Clay Correspondence*, 6:424-25.

From Horace Greeley, New York City, May 4, 1850. Writes in behalf of "Lewis Benedict, Postmaster (unconfirmed) at Albany" to refute "certain calumnies on his character as a Whig which he is informed have been transmitted to you, with the purpose of inducing you to oppose his confirmation." Doubts Clay is "influenced by considerations purely personal," and cites as the "only charge I have heard of that I would notice at all is that which accuses certain active Whigs of this State with conspiring to defeat the Whig ticket in 1844," an indictment he lets "pass for what it is worth—which is nothing." Praises Benedict as "a business man of rare industry and energy." Explains that New York City's mail to the north and west is funneled through Albany, but it often arrives "too late to be sent forward the same day at all," usually reaching the town "between 7 o'clock and the starting of the Express Train West at half-past 7." Adds: "I have known Mr. Benedict [to] have the Mail all assorted and sent forward when he had but twenty minutes to do it in between the arrival of the boat and the starting of the train. . . . To us newspaper men, this quality appears invaluable," and "we have sorely suffered for the want of it in former Postmasters at Albany . . . I for one should regard Mr. Benedict's displacement as a public calamity." ALS. NHi.

For Lewis Benedict, see *NCAB*, 5:361-62. President Taylor had nominated Benedict to be deputy postmaster at Albany, N.Y., on January 16, 1850. On September 30, 1850, President Fillmore withdrew Benedict's name and substituted that of James Kidd who was confirmed the same day. U.S. Sen., *Executive Journal*, 8:124, 266, 272.

Speech in Senate, May 8, 1850. Presents a report from the Committee of Thirteen, recently appointed [Remark in Senate, April 19, 1850] to consider "various resolutions relating to California, to other portions of the territory recently acquired by the United States from the Republic of Mexico, and to other subjects connected with the institution of slavery." Since most of these matters have been discussed in "a debate in the Senate itself, singular for its elaborateness and duration," the committee "will, therefore, restrict themselves to a few general observations, and to some reflections which grow out of those subjects."

Concerning "our recent territorial acquisitions" and their "connection with the institution of slavery," the committee "believe it to be highly desirable and necessary speedily to adjust all those questions, in a spirit of concord, and in a manner to produce, if practicable, general satisfaction. They think it would be unwise to leave any of them open and unsettled, to fester in the public mind, and to prolong, if not aggravate, the existing agitation."

Taking up the subjects in Sen. John Bell's resolutions first, the committee reviewed a provision in the act of Congress annexing Texas to the United States that would entitle " 'new States of convenient size, not exceeding four in number, in addition to the said State of Texas' " to admission into the Union under the provisions of the Federal Constitution and the Missouri Compromise. While the committee "are unanimously of the opinion" that these states "formed out of the territory of Texas" are "entitled to admission beyond all doubt, upon the clear, unambiguous and absolute terms" of the resolution of annexation, "the committee do not think that the formation of any such new States should now originate with Congress. The initiative . . . should be taken by a portion of the people of Texas themselves, desirous of constituting a new State with the consent of Texas. And . . . it will be for the people composing it to decide for themselves whether they will admit or will exclude slavery." And although the committee is aware that the constitutionality of the resolution of Texas annexation has been challenged, feels that when "grave national transactions . . . have been decided by a constitutional majority, and are consummated, or are in a process of consummation, there can be no other safe and prudent alternative than to respect the decision already rendered." The committee, therefore, "do not think it necessary or proper to recommend at this time or prospectively, any new State or States to be formed out of the territory of Texas," but if any such state desires admission, does not doubt that "Congress will, under a full sense of honor, of good faith, and of all the high obligations arising out of the compact with Texas, decide . . . with or without the institution of slavery, according to the constitutions and judgments of the people who compose them, as to what may be best to promote their happiness."

Regarding the question of California's admission to the Union, "the majority of the committee conceive that any irregularity by which that State was organized without the previous authority of an act of Congress ought to be overlooked [Clay to Pierse, February 16, 1849], in consideration of the omission by Congress to establish any territorial government for the people of California," which forced them "to create a government . . . best suited to their own wants." Since the U.S. Constitution's "sole condition . . . in respect to the admission of a new State is, that its constitution shall be republican in form," as California's is, California meets the requirements for acceptance into the Union. Concerning the boundary question, "It might have been, perhaps, better to have assigned to California a more limited front on the Pacific" to offer an "approach to the ocean" to any other state or states that might be organized in that region; but this is not "of any very great importance." A majority of the Committee of Thirteen recommends the passage of the bill for the admission of California and the amendment that will "leave uncontestable the right of the United States to the public domain and other public property in California."

The committee agrees that it is "necessary and proper to establish governments for the residue of the territory derived from Mexico, and to bring it within the pale of the Federal authority." The territory's remoteness, its dispersed population, its "variety of races," the people's "ignorance of our laws, language, and habits," their exposure to Indian wars, and treaty obligations require "providing for them government and law suited to their condition." Since "They are not now, and for a long time to come may not be," ready for statehood, "The territorial form, for the present, is best suited to their condition."

The committee recommends that the bill to establish these governments "be incorporated in the bill for the admission of California, and that, united together, they both be passed." The majority of the members rejects the idea that "the combination of the two measures" is "incongruous" or that the two matters "have no necessary connection with each other." Believes that "The object of both measures is the establishment of government suited to the conditions, respectively, of the proposed new State and of the new territories." Since "They are common in their origin, common in their alienation from one foreign Government to another, common in their wants of good government, and coterminous in some of their boundaries, and alike in many particulars of physical condition, they have nearly everything in common in the relations in which they stand to the rest of this Union."

In response to members "who may be willing to vote for one and unwilling to vote for the other," a majority of the committee agrees that "a spirit of mutual concession enjoins that the two measures should be connected together; the effect of which will be, that neither opinion will exclusively triumph, and that both may find in such an amicable arrangement enough of good to reconcile them to the acceptance of the combined measure." Such a course "is not at all unusual. . . . The Constitution of the United States contained in it a great variety of provisions." If "these various parts and provisions" had been "separately acted on in the Convention, or separately submitted to the people of the United States, it is by no means certain that the Constitution itself would ever have been adopted or ratified." For "the sake of that harmony so desirable in such a Confederacy as this, we must be reconciled to secure as much as we can of what we wish, and be consoled by the reflection that what we do not exactly like is a friendly concession." The committee recommends a bill for establishing the two territories that "omits the Wilmot proviso" but also "makes no provision for the introduction of slavery." Concludes that since the "proviso has been the fruitful source of distraction and agitation," and since "it would cease to have any obligatory force as soon as such territory were admitted as a State," then "There was never any occasion for it, to accomplish" its "professed object." Since California, where "the introduction of slavery was most likely to take place," has "expressly interdicted it," believes that "There is the highest degree of probability that Utah and New Mexico will . . . follow the example." Feels it is "high time that the wounds" the proviso "has inflicted should be healed up, and closed," and that "the true principle which ought to regulate the action of Congress, in forming territorial governments for each newly-acquired domain is to refrain from all legislation on the subject in the territory acquired . . . leaving it to the people of such territory" to decide the question of domestic slavery.

Turning to "the subject of the northern and western boundary of Texas," the committee admits that "a great diversity of opinion has prevailed" and has chosen to "abstain from expressing any opinion as to the true and legitimate" border. Reports a bill, "with inconsiderable variation, the same as that reported by the Committee on Territories," that proposes "to Texas that her boundary be recognized to the Rio Grande, and up that river to the point commonly called El Paso, and running thence up that river twenty miles, measured thereon by a straight line, and thence eastwardly to a point where the hundredth degree of west longitude crosses Red river; being the southwest angle in the line designated between the United States and Mexico, and the same angle in the line of the territory set apart for the Indians by the United States." Hopes that "in consideration of this concession by the United States," Texas will "relinquish any claim she has beyond the proposed boundary: that is, any claim to any part of New Mexico." If Texas will comply, "a majority of the committee recommend the payment of the sum of——millions of dollars to Texas, to be applied . . . to the extinction of that portion of her debt for the reimbursement of which the duties on foreign imports were pledged." If Texas declines "these liberal propositions . . . it is to be distinctly understood that the title of the United States to any territory acquired from Mexico east of the Rio Grande will remain unimpaired and in the same condition as if the proposals of adjustment now offered had never been made." A majority of the committee recommends that "these proposals to Texas shall be incorporated into the bill embracing the admission of California as a State, and the establishment of territorial governments for Utah and New Mexico" since the "establishment of the boundary between New Mexico and Texas has an intimate and necessary connection with the establishment of a territorial government for New Mexico." Hopes that by uniting "the three measures, every question of difficulty and division which has arisen out of the territorial acquisitions from Mexico will . . . be adjusted, or placed in a train of satisfactory adjustment."

The committee then considers "the subject of persons owing service or labor in one State escaping into another." Points out that "Nothing can be more explicit" than the language of the Constitution on this point: citizens have "the right to demand, and the obligation to deliver up to the claimant, any such fugitive." Notes, moreover, that "If, indeed, there were any difference in the duty to enforce this portion of the Constitution between the States and the Federal Government, it is more clear that it is that of the former than of the latter. But it is the duty of both." Recapturing fugitive slaves "often leads to most unpleasant, if not perilous, collisions," and a situation when the "owner of a slave . . . cannot pursue his property, for the purpose of its recovery, in some of the States, without imminent personal hazard" is "a deplorable state of things, which ought to be remedied." Although some states have refused cooperation and "a decision of the Supreme Court of the Unites States has given countenance to them," the committee believes that the "court merely meant that laws of the several States which created obstacles in the way of the recovery of fugitives were not authorized by the Constitution, and not that State laws affording facilities in the recovery of fugitives were forbidden by that instrument." Fears that "If some States may seek to exonerate themselves from one portion of the Constitution, other States may endeavor to evade the performance of other portions of it," thus rendering important provisions "inoperative and invalid." Feels that "Congress ought, while on one hand securing to the owner the fair restoration of his property, effectually to guard on the other against any abuses in the application of that remedy." The Constitution makes clear that a fugitive's fate is "determined *by the laws of the State from which he fled.*"

The committee has prepared and reported "a section to be offered to the fugitive bill now pending before the Senate" which will establish the legal procedure that will facilitate recovery "and will leave nothing more to be done than to identify the fugitive." Acknowledges receipt of "Numerous petitions . . . praying for a trial by jury, in the case of arrest of fugitives," but this would be "entirely contrary to practice and uniform usage" and "a complete mockery of justice, so far as the owner of the fugitive is concerned." Such trials in non-slaveholding states would lead to "continuance from time to time, to bring evidence from distant places; of second or new trials, in cases where the jury is hung, or the verdict is set aside; and of revisals of the verdict and conduct of the jurors by competent tribunals." In slaveholding states, however, "full justice is administered, with entire fairness and impartiality, in cases of all actions for freedom." The committee recommends for insertion into the fugitive bill pending in the Senate that "the claimant is placed under bond, and required to return the fugitive to that county in the State from which he fled, and there to take him before a competent tribunal, and allow him to assert and establish his freedom, if he can, affording to him for that purpose all needful facilities." The committee hopes that if this remedy does not work, owners of fugitive slaves "will have a just title to indemnity out of the Treasury of the United States."

Reporting on the resolutions concerning slavery and the slave trade in the District of Columbia, the committee is "of the opinion that it ought not to be abolished" within the District. Believes that "It could not be done without exciting great apprehension and alarm in the slave States. If the power were exercised within this District, they would apprehend that, under some pretext or another, it might be hereafter attempted to be exercised within the slaveholding States." While "all such power is almost unanimously disavowed and disclaimed in the free States . . . experience in public affairs has too often shown that where there is a desire to do a particular thing, the power to accomplish it, sooner or later, will be found or assumed." Moreover, the declining number of slaves in the District precludes making "the abolition of slavery an object of any such consequence as appears to be attached to it in some parts of the Union"; the 1830 census showed 4,505 slaves, but the 1840 census listed only 3,320.

On the other hand, "a majority of the committee" agrees that the slave trade, "the introduction of slaves from adjacent States into the District, for sale, or to be placed in depôt for the purpose of subsequent sale or transportation to other and distant markets," ought to be abolished. Northerners and Southerners alike have complained of "a trade sometimes exhibiting revolting spectacles." Since most, "if not all, of the slaveholding States have, either in their constitution or by penal enactments, prohibited a trade in slaves as merchandise within their respective jurisdiction," the Congress, "standing in regard to the people of this District on this subject, in a relation similar to that of the State Legislatures to the people of the States, may safely follow the examples of the States." The committee reports a bill for the abolition of that trade.

After recapitulating the committee's chief "views and recommendations," expresses the hope that "all controversies to which our late territorial acquisitions have given rise, and all existing questions connected with the institution of slavery, whether resulting from those acquisitions or from its existence in the States and the District of Columbia, will be amicably settled and adjusted, in a manner, it is confidently believed, to give general satisfaction to an overwhelming majority of the people of the United States." By acting on these recommendations, "Congress will have fulfilled its whole duty in regard" to the land ceded by Mexico, and it "will escape the unmerited reproach of having, from considerations of doubtful policy, abandoned to an undeserved fate territories of boundless extent."

The committee reiterates its hope that this "compreshensive plan of adjustment" will remove "all causes of existing excitement and agitation," leaving "none open to divide the country and disturb the general harmony." Although "The nation has been convulsed . . . by questions of a sectional nature" which are "more dangerous and more to be deprecated," finds it "gratifying to witness the outbursts of deep and abiding attachment to" the Union "exhibited in all parts of it, amidst all the trials through which we have passed and are passing."

Clay does not feel it is necessary to read in their entirety the bills and amendments to bills presented by the Committee of Thirteen. Sends to the clerk's table "A bill to admit California as a State into the Union, to establish territorial governments for Utah and New Mexico, and making proposals to Texas for the establishment of her western and northern boundaries," a bill of 39 sections. Three amendments to the fugitive slave bill are also offered. A bill to abolish the slave trade in the District of Columbia is also read. Clay hopes that "by to-morrow the bills may be printed" and feels that "the order to print them need not interrupt action on the bill to-morrow, if it be desired."

Sen. Samuel Phelps then rises to explain that while he would not go so far as to file a formal minority report, "it was my misfortune to differ with the committee on most of the prominent features of their report," especially "the construction to be given to the resolutions of annexation by which Texas came into the Union."

Clay declares that he intended to "forbear at present, and make no additional exposition" on committee deliberations at this time. Hopes to forestall future internal dissent: "I have never been associated with gentlemen on any great and momentous occasion in which a spirit of more kindness, more conciliation, and more of a disposition to listen and to give effect, as far as possible, to any opinions entertained by the members of the committee, though not entertained by all of them, than was presented during the whole of our session. Though on a few subjects there was a diversity of opinion, and although members holding diverse opinions maintained their own views of what they thought public policy required, especially in the quarters from whence they came, it was always done in the spirit of conciliation and kindness." Nonetheless, Sens. Solomon Downs, John M. Berrien, and Willie P. Mangum offer minority viewpoints on several issues.

Sen. Jeremiah Clemens, who had not served on the committee, then rises to announce his intention to vote against all of its measures. "I had no expectation that any good would result" from the formation of such a committee, and "I expected it to result as it has resulted." Clemens objects especially to the "irregularities" in the proposed admission of California to the Union.

Clay asks: "is it right to pounce upon the report unheard, or, if heard at all, heard only upon its first presentation to the Senate?" Asks senators who had not served on the committee "whether they do not owe it to themselves to look at it deliberately, to consider it dispassionately, and to form such a judgment as will not only reconcile them to their consciences and to their sense of duty but which the country itself will say is a mature judgment." Points out that "the report of a committee. . . . in the course of ordinary and parliamentary proceedings, is not acted upon, but the measures reported on the subject are acted on." Concludes: "I have enlisted myself in the great cause of this Union, and of harmony among its distracted parts; and I stand here, and here I mean to stand, to vindicate what has been done, and to vindicate this report, too, if necessary, from beginning to end, and to show that it is founded in reason, in fact, and in truth.

After much discussion by a number of senators the Senate adjourns. *Cong. Globe*, 31 Cong., 1 Sess., 944-51; *Sen. Reports*, 31 Cong., 1 Sess., no. 123.

Writing for the majority of the Supreme Court, Justice Joseph Story had ruled in *Prigg* v. *Pennsylvania* that the federal government had exclusive jurisdiction over fugitive slaves; thus, states could neither give aid nor interfere in the process of capturing runaways. Carl B. Swisher, *The Taney Period, 1836-64* (New York, 1974), vol. 5 in *History of the Supreme Court of the United States*, Paul A. Freund (ed.), 535-46.

To Henry Clay, Jr. [III], Georgetown, D.C., May 9, 1850. Requests his grandson to "come over to the City on wednesday next, with your luggage, to proceed to Kentucky" and to ask for "your a/c at the [Georgetown] College and bring it with you." ALS. MWA.

From Elizabeth Washington Wirt, Annapolis, Md., May 12, 1850. Presumes on "your friendship for my lamented Husband [William Wirt] as to ask your kind offices in behalf of his Son." If Clay and Daniel Webster will provide letters of recommendation in addition to those already written by Commodore Voorhees and Captain Upshur "to lay before the Secretary of the Navy [William B. Preston], I shall desire no other credentials—no weightier influence to be brought to bear upon the 'powers that be.' " ALS. DNA, RG45, Naval Records Collection.

This letter was addressed directly to Daniel Webster, but contained the following request: "Will you do me the additional favor to hand this letter, with its accompaniments, to Mr Clay as a joint appeal to him and to yourself for what I shall consider an inestimable favor from you both." The recommendation is for her son Dabney Carr Wirt to be appointed purser in the Navy. Wiltse, *Papers of Daniel Webster, Correspondence*, 7:423.

Commodore Philip F. Voorhees was commander of the American squadron in the East Indies in 1850 with the rank of captain. George P. Upshur is listed as having the rank of commander. *American Almanac . . . for 1850*, pp. 116-17.

Speech in Senate, May 13, 1850. Speaks at length on the bill reported by the Committee of Thirteen for California's admission to the Union, the creation of territorial government for New Mexico and Utah, and the settlement of the western and northwestern boundaries of Texas [Speech in Senate, May 8, 1850]. Admitting that "no one member of the committee concurred in all that was done, or omitted to be done," asserts that there was "a majority upon most of the subjects, indeed upon all of the subjects . . . reported by the committee to the Senate." Understanding that not all senators "agree exactly to what was done," hopes that "no one of them is so irrevocably committed against the measure as to induce him, upon the question of its final passage, to vote against it." Believes that "if these unhappy subjects which have divided the country are to be accommodated by an amicable adjustment, it must be upon some basis as that which the committee has reported," and urges senators who find "some matters in it objectionable" to allow "a fair contrast between it and all other plans" and "ultimately give it a general concurrence."

On the first measure, "the true exposition of the compact between the United States and Texas upon the occasion of the admission of that State into the Union. . . . I am happy to say there was an undivided opinion." According to this compact, "a number of States not exceeding four, with or without slavery, having the requisite population, and with the consent of Texas, were to be admitted to the Union from time to time, as they might be matured and present themselves for admission." Not all senators pledged themselves actually to vote for the admission of these new states, however.

On the subject which "created the most anxiety of all the measures upon which the committee have reported—I mean, the admission of California into the Union. . . . there are various objections." First, some argue "that there is not sufficient evidence . . . that it has a population entitling it even to one representative." Agrees that "It is impossible . . . that any such evidence could be furnished—she having become a part of this empire eight years after the last census." Points out, however, that during "the first apportionment of representation" there was "no Federal enumeration of the people of the United States on which that apportionment was made." Then, "the Congress, or rather the Convention that allotted those representatives to the various States, went upon all the information which they possessed, whether it was perfectly authentic or not." In the case of Georgia, "a larger number of Representatives was allowed to her than the exact state of her population would authorize; but it was said Georgia is a new State rapidly filling up." When Texas was admitted, "Nobody believed, I think, that Texas had a population entitling her to two Representatives," but "she was rapidly filling up" and "before the next enumeration . . . She will have a population not only entitling her to two, but probably to more than two Representatives." Explaining that under current law, California "would only be required to have a population of 106,021" to entitle her to two representatives, produces "an extract from a memorial of the Senators and Representatives from the State of California" containing details "partly conjectural, it is true, but partly, and I believe the larger portion of them official" asserting that "the population . . . on the 1st of January, 1850, was 107,069, exceeding the amount" required for two representatives. Is satisfied "in my own mind—that . . . there is at this moment a population in California that would entitle her to two Representatives." Notes that the people there "are fresh population. Sir they are bone of our bone, and flesh of our flesh, for the greater part. They have lost none of their intelligence or capacity for self-government by passing from the United States to California." They "ought to be represented somewhere" and "they are not represented now." Believes there is "no serious ground" for objecting to giving California two representatives, "precisely the same number as in the case of Texas."

Takes up the question of "the limits of Texas." The "line of 35° 30′ " was suggested in committee, but "a majority was found to be against it." The 36° 30′ line was also considered. Notes that "The North . . . does not seek such a division. It is from the South that the opposition to acceding to the limits of California, as proposed in her State constitution, comes." Concedes that while some Southerners "propose that there should be an express recognition of the right to carry slaves south of that line," most "do not ask for the recognition or a positive enactment" to allow slavery there. Considering the recent vote of the California constitutional convention against slavery, presumes Southerners understand that there "cannot . . . ever be slavery within her limits, or upon the Pacific at all." Feels that the South's real fears are based on "the apprehensions which they entertained from that preponderance and influence of northern power," but since "the thing is not very unreasonable in itself," does not think there should "be any hesitation on the part of our southern friends in Congress in acceding to these limits." Despite its "six or seven hundred miles of coast on the Pacific ocean," there are also "deserts of sand which never can be inhabited" and "successive chains of mountains." Therefore, "There seems to me to be no adequate motive for the curtailment of the limits" of California "with the view to the accommodation of future States."

Discounts the argument that California's case "was different from that of other new States that have been admitted without the previous authority of Congress," since "Michigan, Arkansas, and Florida, if not other States, came in without any other act of Congress. . . . They laid off limits for themselves." But things had been "So much the better for them; they had a good . . . territorial government." California, on the other hand, "has no government. You have deserted her; you have abandoned her; you have violated your engagement contained in the treaty of Guadalupe Hidalgo [Clay to Beatty, April 29, 1847], and left her to shift for herself." Nonetheless, "she chose to form for herself a constitution" and we do not have "sufficient motive to reject her, and to throw her back into the state of lawless confusion and disorder from which she has emerged." The committee calls upon Congress "to admit California as a State, and to sanction what she has done."

Turning to the question of creating territorial governments for Utah and New Mexico, "we fail to fulfill an obligation, a sacred obligation, contained in the treaty with Mexico" if no action is taken. Although they still "had all the benefits resulting from their own local laws" established while still part of Mexico, "the additional benefit and security resulting from the laws of the Supreme Government. . . . were transferred from that sovereignty to this sovereignty." Moreover, "we stipulated . . . that we would extend to them protection to their persons, security to their property, and the benefit of pursuing their own religion according to the dictates of their own consciences."

Expresses his concern about "oppressive and tyrannical treatment by the Mormons towards citizens of the United States": "I care not whether they are as bad as they are represented, or as good as they are represented by their friends; they are a portion of the people who we are bound by treaty as well as by other high obligations to govern." Does not think it is "right to say to the people of Utah, comprehending the Mormons, and to the people of New Mexico, deprived as they are of the benefit of the government they once had" that "we will leave them to themselves."

Realizes there had been apprehensions early in the session that "it was impossible to pass any measure for the territories, without producing in Congress scenes of the most painful and unpleasant character." But "a most gratifying change has taken place. The North, the glorious North, has come to the rescue of this Union of ours. She has displayed a disposition to abate in her demands." Continues: "The South, the glorious South—not less glorious than her neighbor section of the Union—has also come to the rescue. The minds of men have moderated; passion has given place to reason everywhere." Now there is a demand "for an amicable adjustment of those questions."

Feels that if Zachary Taylor recommended a course of action now, he would not leave "the territories to shift for themselves as they could or might" as he did in his message five months earlier. Then, Taylor had asserted that "at least New Mexico, might possibly form a State government for herself" and present herself for admission. Doubts that Taylor now would leave such "questions unsettled, and open to exasperate the feelings of opposing parties." To leave New Mexico and Utah to act "locally to protect the citizens who come there to settle, or to protect those who are in transitu through the country, without any authority connected with the supreme Government here" is to "abandon . . . our obligations contained in the treaty of [Guadalupe] Hidalgo" and to leave "the door of agitation . . . wide open."

Learning that "Texas has sent her civil commissioners to Santa Fe, or into New Mexico for the purpose, of bringing them under authority," fears that "before we meet again next December, we shall hear of some civil commotion, in the contest between New Mexico and Texas with respect to the boundary." Asks: "Is it right, then, to leave these territories unprovided for. . . . to produce possibly the fearful consequences to which I have adverted?" The committee "all thought we should establish governments" for the territories, "and if we failed . . . we should stand irreproachable for any voluntary abandonment or neglect of them on our part." When questioned about "the amount to be paid to Texas" to settle its boundary problems with New Mexico, explains that the "committee . . . thought it best not to fill up that blank until the last moment, upon the final reading of the bill" to avoid "improper speculation in the stock markets."

Although the union of these related measures in one bill "has been objected to" and "already very much discussed" in the Senate, the Committee of Thirteen recommended this course of action. Challenges Sen. Thomas Hart Benton's argument designed "to show that it was improper to connect them together [Remark in Senate, April 11, 1850; Comment in Senate, April 17, 1850]." Since "parliamentary law in this country" consists only of the U.S. Constitution, the "rules adopted by the two Houses of Congress . . . the practice and precedents of Congress," and Thomas Jefferson's manual, argues that "We have no such thing as tacking in the English sense of the term." Explains in detail that "The practice of tacking in England is confined to money bills." The real question, Clay asserts, is "whether there is any incongruity in" combining measures for California's admission, a territorial government for Utah, and another for New Mexico. This determination "rests in the sound discretion of Congress."

Cites examples to show "what has been done by Congress from time to time in the annexation of different subjects in the same bill." Notes that acts incorporating the phrase "and for other purposes" are especially likely to contain "incongruous" subjects. Points to "an act providing for the support of the Military Academy of the United States for the year 1838, and for other purposes," including "thirty or forty appropriations" for such projects as "the Documentary History of the Revolution," purchasing machinery for three branch mints, salaries for officials of the Territory of Iowa, and "contingent expenses . . . for the purpose of founding . . . the Smithsonian Institution," as evidence that there is no "non-conformity to the practice of Congress" in uniting the "three measures of the same character" proposed by the Committee of Thirteen.

Comments on "an amendment introduced by the committee into the territorial bill" that he opposed. It would prohibit the territorial legislatures from passing "any lay [*sic*, law] in respect to African slavery." Although they could still pass laws "on any other condition of slavery—'Peon' or 'Indian' slavery," they "will not be allowed to admit or exclude" African slavery. Since "My opinion is, that" according to "the law of Mexico . . . slavery has been abolished there," finds it "altogether unnecessary" to discuss the question, so long as "by law and by fact, there is no slavery there." Feels no slave owner would take his slaves to New Mexico "where he could only get three or four dollars per month" for their labor.

On the question of fugitive slaves, the Committee of Thirteen offered two amendments. The first provided that "the owner of a fugitive slave, when leaving his own State, and whenever it is practicable . . . shall carry with him a record from the State from which the fugitive has fled; which record shall contain an adjudication of . . . the fact of slavery, and . . . the fact of an elopement; and . . . such a general description of the slave as the court shall be able to give upon such testimony as shall be brought before it." This record "shall be carried to the free State, and shall be there held to be competent and sufficient evidence of the facts which it avows." The expense will be "very trifling. . . . only two or three dollars for the seal of the court, and the certificate and attestation of the clerk, &c," and the slaveowner "has got a security which he never possessed before for the recovery of his property." Expects that "county courts and courts of probate" and not necessarily a judge in chambers "could give the required record."

The Committee of Thirteen's second amendment concerning fugitive slaves requires legal authorities in free states to take a bond without surety from a slaveowner who desires to take his recovered slave back to the state from which he fled. If a black person so recovered wishes to establish his right to freedom, he may be granted a trial by jury in the state to which he is returned.

Believing that "Kentucky is the most suffering State" in terms of slaves escaping to free states, still feels "there are feelings, and interests, and sympathies on both sides of the question." The attitude of many people has changed "from what it was in 1793, nearly sixty years ago, when the fugitive slave law passed. There were, then, comparatively few free persons of color. . . . By the progress of emancipation in the slaveholding States, and the multiplication of them by natural causes, vast numbers of them have rushed to the free States." In Boston, Philadelphia, and New York, there are "eight or ten to one in proportion to the number there were in 1793." These great numbers increase the difficulty of recovering a fugitive slave, because "the rule of law is reversed in the two classes of States. In the slaveholding States the rule is, that color implies slavery, and the *onus probandi* of freedom is thrown on the person claiming it. . . . On the contrary, when you go to the non-slaveholding States, color implies freedom, and not slavery. The *onus* is shifted, and the fact of slavery must be proved."

Asserts that the "practical operation" of the proposed amendment will be "attended with not the least earthly inconvenience to the party claiming the fugitive. The case is bond without surety. That bond is transmitted by the officer taking it to the district attorney of the State from which he has fled. That officer sees that the bond is faithfully fulfilled, and that the slave is taken before the court. Perhaps, before the slave reaches home, he will acknowledge that he is a slave; there is an end of the bond and an end of the trouble about the matter. Is this unreasonable?" Contends that "our rights are to be asserted; our rights are to be maintained. . . . And in requiring such a bond as this amendment proposes to exact from the owner, I do not think there is the slightest inconvenience imposed upon him, of which he ought to complain."

Realizes this proposal will not conciliate those in the free states who assert "that there is a higher law—a divine law—a natural law—which entitles a man, under whose roof a runaway has come, to give him assistance, and succor, and hospitality. Where is the difference between receiving and harboring a known fugitive slave, and going to the plantation of his master and stealing him away?" Decries their "Wild, reckless, and abominable theories, which strike at the foundation of all property and threaten to crush in ruins the fabric of civilized society." These are people who "we do not propose to conciliate by any amendment, by any concession which we can make."

Nonetheless, "in considering this delicate question," the committee "thought it best to offer these two provisions—that which requires the production of a record in the non-slaveholding States, and that which requires a bond to grant to the real claimant of his freedom a trial by jury, in the place where that trial should take place." Believes it is true that "the greatest facilities are always extended to every man of color in the slaveholding States who sues for freedom," and that such a person usually won his case "if there were even slight grounds in support of his claim." Notes that he himself "never appeared but once in my life against a person suing for his freedom, but [I] have appeared for them in many instances, without charging them a solitary cent."

Turns to the question of "the abolition of the slave trade in the District of Columbia," asserting that "There is, I believe, precious little of it." Feels there "has been no time in the past forty years, when . . . there would not have been found a majority—perhaps a majority from the slaveholding States themselves—in favor of the abolition of the slave trade in this District." Admits that once "it would have been thought a great concession to the feelings and wishes of the North to abolish this slave trade," but regrets that now "some of the rabid abolition papers denounce it as amounting to nothing," and support instead "that offensive proviso, called the 'Wilmot proviso.' "

Hopes that "the operation of causes upon the northern mind friendly to the Union" will make "a sufficient portion of the North . . . willing to dispense with the proviso." Offers "by way of compensation" a resolution that "stated two truths, one of law and one of fact . . . to satisfy the North that it ought no longer to insist on the Wilmot proviso." Notes, however, that "some of our southern brethren. . . . say that there is yet the Wilmot proviso, under another form, lurking in the laws of Mexico, or lurking in the mountains of Mexico . . . when I hinted that the law of nature was adverse to the introduction of slavery there." Regarding the proviso as "an abstraction always—thrust upon the South by the North against all the necessities of the case," asks "Why do you of the North press it?" Argues that "You are likely to accomplish" your objects "without pressing this obnoxious measure." Explains that Southerners oppose the proviso because "when once legislation on the subject of slavery begins, there is no seeing where it is to end. Begin it in the District of Columbia; begin it in the Territories of Utah and New Mexico and California; assert your power there to-day, and in spite of all the protestations—and you are not wanting in making protestations—that you have no purpose of extending it to the southern States, what security can you give them that a new sect will not arise with a new version of the Constitution . . . which shall authorize them to carry their notions into the bosoms of the slaveholding States."

Concludes: "The cases, then, gentlemen of the North and gentlemen of the South, do not stand upon an equal footing. When you, on one hand, unnecessarily press an offensive and alarming measure on the South, the South repels it from the highest of all human motives of action, the security of property and life." After "this Wilmot proviso has disappeared, as I trust it may," hopes to get rid of the "Matters of form" still preventing progress on important questions, such as "whether we shall combine in one united bill three measures, all of which are necessary and homogeneous, or separate them into three distinct bills passing each in its turn if it can be done." Trusts that "the feelings of attachment to the Union, of love for its past glory, of anticipation of its future benefits and happiness" will "animate us all . . . to dismiss alike questions of abstraction and form, and to consummate "the act of concord, harmony, and peace" that will "heal not one only, but all the wounds of the country." *Cong. Globe*, 31 Cong., 1 Sess., Appendix, 567-73; *Cong. Globe*, 31 Cong., 1 Sess., 986. The Appendix portion is printed in Colton, *Clay Correspondence*, 6:426-51.

Taylor had first indicated his plan for dealing with the newly acquired territories in his First Annual Message on December 4, 1849, when he had stated that California would soon apply for statehood, as would New Mexico "at no very distant period." He urged that they be promptly admitted to the Union, provided their constitutions conform to the requirements of the U.S. Constitution. He had also urged that "we should abstain from the introduction of those exciting topics" of a sectional character. He hoped thus to avoid a congressional debate over territorial slavery and the Wilmot Proviso by allowing California and New Mexico to determine the status of slavery when they drew up their own constitutions. In a special message to the House on January 21, 1850, and to the Senate on January 23, Taylor said he was in favor of early statehood for California and New Mexico, but that he had not advocated the establishment of any government without the assent of Congress; rather, he believed the slavery and boundary problems could be more easily settled if all parties were states. Taylor then submitted the constitution of California to Congress on February 13 [Remark in Senate, February 13, 1850]. This position ultimately put Clay and Taylor at odds over the plan for settling the sectional controversy. *MPP*, 5:18-19, 26-30; Hamilton, *Zachary Taylor, Soldier in the White House*, 257, 264-69, 270-76, 287-92; Smith, *Presidencies of Taylor & Fillmore*, 101-4, 133-36, *passim*.

Comment in Senate, May 15, 1850. Sen. Jefferson Davis offers an amendment to the Committee of Thirteen's bill, intending to "prevent the territorial legislature from invading the rights of the inhabitants of the slaveholding states [Speech in Senate, May 8, 1850]."

Clay believes that Davis "accomplishes nothing by striking out the clause now in the bill" which states "that the territorial legislation shall not extend to anything respecting African slavery within the territory." States that "The effect of retaining this clause . . . will be this: that if in any of the territories slavery now exists, it cannot be abolished by the territorial legislature; and if in any of the territories slavery does not now exist, it cannot be introduced by the territorial legislature." The clause was inserted by the committee "for the purpose of tying up the hands of the territorial legislature in respect to legislating at all, one way or the other, upon the subject of African slavery" and to "leave the legislation and the law of the respective territories in the condition in which the act will find them." Clay "did not, in committee, vote for the amendment to insert the clause" because he "attached very little consequence to it" and finds it "of no practical importance whatever." Guesses that Davis's measure "aims at the same thing. I do not understand him as proposing that if any one shall carry slaves into the territory—although by the law of the territory he cannot take them there—the legislative hands of the territorial government should be so tied as to prevent its saying he shall not enjoy the fruits of their labor."

Davis interrupts: "I do mean to say it."

Clay responds that if Davis is moving "that slaves may be introduced into the territory contrary to the *lex loci*, and, being introduced, nothing shall be done by the legislature to impair the rights of owners to hold the slaves thus brought contrary to the local laws, I certainly cannot vote for it." Asserts that "I cannot vote to convert a territory already free into a slave territory. I am satisfied, for one, to let the *lex loci*, as it exists, remain." Asks "what will be the effect of this in that portion of New

Mexico east of the Rio Grande," noting that "Three opinions prevail upon that subject in the Senate." According to Clay, "the laws of Mexico still prevail in that country, because Texas never had possession of that country." A second viewpoint, held by Sen. John M. Berrien and others, argues that "the Constitution of the United States, by its own necessary operation, abrogated that local law, and invested the owners of slaves with the power of carrying their slaves into an operation of the territories acquired by us from Mexico." Still others believe that "all the territory this side the Rio del Norte, from its mouth to its source, is Texas, and that the laws of Texas consequently extend over it." Explains that "if the Supreme Court shall be of opinion either that the laws of Texas stretch over New Mexico this side of the Rio Grande, or, as maintained by my friend from Georgia, that the Constitution of the United States abolished the Mexican laws by which slavery was abrogated, in either case the owners of slaves in New Mexico would have a right to enjoy the possession of his property. But if, on the contrary, as I believe, the Constitution did no such thing, and Texas, not having actual possession, did not extend her laws there, then it would follow that the right to maintain and carry slaves there would not prevail."

Sens. Davis and Thomas J. Rusk continue to challenge Clay's interpretation, Davis asserting that "in common with most southern men, I hold that the law of Mexico was repealed" and that "no political laws exist" in New Mexico "except those resulting from the legislation of Texas."

Clay rejects Davis's accusation that "there is some inconsistency between my present course and that which I took the other day on the subject of non-action," explaining that "Non-action, as respects legislation on the subject of slavery, is one thing—and for that I go; but non-action, so far as to giving to these people, separated from their connection with the Republic of Mexico and brought under our jurisdiction—non-action as to giving them a suitable government, is a totally distinct thing. I am in favor of action as respects government for the territories, but I am in favor of non-action as respects the question of slavery."

Clay notes that Davis bases his amendment on a belief that "there is a right on the part of the slaveholder, in any of the slave States of the Union, to carry his slaves into Utah and New Mexico . . . that the Constitution of the United States has abrogated or abolished the laws of Mexico, and that, therefore, in virtue of the operation of the Constitution, this right exists." Clay is sure, however, that "when the question comes before the Supreme Court of the United States, to which it will be carried, the right to carry slaves there will be disavowed." Concedes that "Texas has a good title" to New Mexico, "yet she had not the possession *de facto*," and assures Davis that "I can put it to nobody more confidently, that there is a difference between a title without possession, and the obligations of the local law, or the obligations of the government *de facto* to maintain its authority, notwithstanding it is not connected with the title." Repeats that "I am willing to stand aside and to make no legislative enactment, one way or the other—to lay off the territories without the Wilmot proviso on the one hand, with which I understand we are threatened, or without an attempt to introduce a clause for the introduction of slavery into the territories—while I am for rejecting both the one and the other, I am contented that the law as it exists shall prevail, and if there be any diversity of opinion as to what it means, I am willing that it shall be settled by the highest judicial authority of the country."

Asks Davis and other Southern senators why "they can think it right that Congress, by an express enactment, should authorize its introduction into these territories? Does not that power, in virtue of which you would expressly provide for the introduction of slavery, imply the converse of the proposition, and the right to pass a law for the prohibition of slavery?" Fears that the adoption of Davis's amendment would recognize "by an irresistible conclusion, the power of Congress to prohibit as well as to introduce slavery into these territories." Asks Davis if "it is worth while for us to be disputing about—what? The right to carry slaves where no man on earth would ever think of carrying them—the right to carry slaves north of the line delineated in the bill for the adjustment of the territorial question with Texas; to carry them where they cannot go, where they would not be held as a gift, and where labor at this moment, as I learned from authorities the other day, may be obtained at the rate of from three to four dollars per month?" Urges the Senate "to dispose of" this matter "in such a manner as will show that we are anxious to consummate the great object we all so earnestly desire." *Cong. Globe*, 31 Cong., 1 Sess., 1003-5. Printed in Colton, *Clay Correspondence*, 6:452-57.

Earlier in the day, when Sen. Hopkins L. Turney asks that "the bill to promote the progress of the useful arts" be made the special order for discussion at 12:30 the next afternoon, Sen. Henry S. Foote objects to diverting the Senate's attention away from "the grave matters before us." Clay concurs with Foote's "opinion of the absolute necessity which exists for the consideration of those measures of a grave public character." Still, he considers Turney's request "so moderate and so reasonable" that "I shall not be disposed to object" so long as Turney keeps his promise "that it shall be further postponed if it shall not be got through with by one o'clock." *Cong. Globe*, 31 Cong., 1 Sess., 1001.

To J. Morrison Harris, Baltimore, May 18, 1850. Expresses his thanks for "your official letter informing me that the Maryland Historical Society, by a unanimous vote, had appointed me an honorary member." Feels that he is now "connected with an Association whose labors have already commended it to the public approbation." ALS. ViU.

Speech in Senate, May 21, 1850. Replies at length to various criticisms of the report of the Committee of Thirteen [Speech in Senate May 8, 1850], and regrets that senators have digressed from any single point under discussion and "launched out upon the broad ocean, and embraced in the course of their arguments, the entire subject."

Challenges Sen. Pierre Soule, who "finds himself unable to concur in the scheme of compromise," to "present a contre projet" of his own: "this finding of fault, and, with the aid of a magnifying glass, discovering defects, descrying the little animalculae which move upon the surface of matter . . . is an easy task, and may be practiced without any practical benefit or profitable result." Feels Soule "has done great injustice to the acts of this committee."

To Soule's comments on "the recovery and restitution of fugitive slaves," which he had made "with an air of great dissatisfaction, if not of derision," Clay wonders why "the greatest objections to the amendment . . . come from States which are not suffering under the evil of having to recover fugitive slaves." Reasserts his view that "the slave owner, in pursuit of his property, has to carry with him a record! . . . That, I say, is an advantage and a protection to the slaveholder . . . for that record will command respect in the free States," and will leave him "free to employ the provisions of the act of 1793." The "trial by jury . . . in the State from which the fugitive has fled" will not "incommode the slave owner, since the fugitive will" most likely "be found to have asked for it as a mere pretext." In any case, it guarantees a slave's right "of resorting to their tribunals of justice to establish his claim to his freedom, if he has one."

Regrets to "find myself assailed by extremists everywhere." Only a few days earlier, Northerners had attacked Clay "for conveying an alleged calumny of their institutions by saying that the trial by jury" in Northern courts "could not be relied upon as a remedy to the master who had lost his slave." Explains that he only meant "that distant and foreign courts" should not "be called upon to administer the unknown laws of a remote commonwealth." Moreover, "when you sum up the expenses and charges at the end of the case" in a distant court, even if the owner recovers his property, "the contest to regain it would have cost him more than it is worth." While

Northerners accuse him "of casting unmerited approbrium" on their "administration of justice," Southerners, "in another and last extreme," object to Clay's course "as creating embarrassment to the owners of fugitive slaves."

Returning to Soule's objections, points out that "the clause which prohibits the territorial legislatures from passing any law in respect to African slavery. . . . was voted for by every southern member" on the Committee of Thirteen "except myself." If Soule and others are so opposed to this measure, "tell us what you want; put it down in black and white . . . and do not restrict yourselves, in this unstatesmanlike manner, to the mere finding of fault."

Soule had objected to "this clause of prohibition" because "no police regulations can be made." Clay responds that "If there be slavery" in the territories, "then the necessary police regulations exist already. . . . if there is no slavery, then none are required." The sole purpose of his committee's resolutions is "to declare that the territorial legislatures should have power neither to admit nor to exclude slavery."

Turns to Soule's objections "to the clause interdicting the slave trade in the District of Columbia," which he bases "on two grounds." First, "the committee do not affirm in their report that there is no constitutional power in Congress to pass upon the subject of slavery in this District." Since "probably a majority of the Senate, believes that Congress has the power" and other members do not agree, "how does the honorable Senator expect to arrive at a compromise. . . . without asking Senators, on the one side or the other to repudiate their fixed and deliberate opinions." Adds: "I thought that the committee were on that subject as happy as they could be," since their "report neither denies nor affirms the power of Congress to abolish slavery within the District of Columbia." By "asserting that the power ought not to be exercised, I say it is a compromise with which all ought I think to be perfectly satisfied." Noting that the "bill for abolishing the slave trade. . . . is a mere adoption of the law of Maryland," a slave state, warns Soule "that we shall be much more likely to arrive at a satisfactory and harmonious result," by taking into account the opinions and interests of all parts of the country "than by attaching ourselves to a single position, and viewing from that point everything, and seeking to bring everything to the standard of our own peculiar opinions, our own bed of Procrustes."

Soule is also "mistaken in saying that a resident of the District cannot go out of the District and purchase a slave and bring him here for his own use." Soule interrupts, "I have merely stated that the effect of this section . . . will be to preclude the introduction into the District of any slave for the purpose of being sold, even if it were for the purpose of supplying the necessities of those inhabiting the District." Clay sees no inconvenience: "A slave cannot be brought within this place for sale and be here sold, but a man who wants a slave here may go to the distance of five miles and purchase one, and bring him here, not for sale, but for his own use." The bill does not prohibit this.

Complains that "No part of this compromise seems to receive the commendation of" Soule. He took up "the greater portion of the time in which he has so ably and eloquently addressed us" to refute Clay's belief that the law of Mexico abolished slavery in the territories. Even after all the Senate's deliberations, however, there is still "one question which is left unsettled, that of the *lex loci* in regard to slavery in these territories . . . Will he or anybody else tell me how it can be settled, otherwise than by the Supreme Court of the United States, whether the law of Mexico did or did not abolish slavery within the limits of those territories? That is what the committee proposes to do."

Soule again interrupts: "I expressly admitted that slavery was abolished by Mexican law. . . . if Mexican law prevails, slavery is already abolished and utterly eradicated."

Still, Clay retorts that Soule "contends for that which is the equivalent to the non-abolition of slavery by the Mexican law—that the right to carry slaves into the ceded territories was restored by virtue of the Constitution of the United States." If, as Soule believes, this right exists, Clay wonders "what more does the Senator want? . . . Would he recommend the introduction of the Wilmot Proviso into the bill, or a legislative enactment to admit slaves, because the plan of the committee is silent upon that subject?"

Soule answers that he "will be satisfied with this section of the bill," if the "amendment proposed by the Senator from Mississippi [Jefferson Davis] . . . be adopted [Comment in Senate, May 15, 1850]."

Clay concludes that Soule "may yet vote with us." Admits that "I really thought that . . . he was a gone case; that he was hopeless." But noting that Soule, "in announcing what would satisfy him, restricts himself to *this section*," Clay asks what "other law the Senator wants upon the subject of slavery than the paramount law of the Constitution." Soule answers, "Protection." Clay believes "the Constitution affords that protection," but agrees to his committee's bill "being so modified as to declare that the territorial legislature shall neither admit nor exclude slavery, which will leave it open to police regulations," if this will satisfy Soule. Clay will not agree to any modification that "by any implication" will "assert either that slavery exists now in that Country; or that it is lawful to carry it there under the Constitution."

After more discussion, and a plea to test "the question of the validity of the laws of Mexico" in the Supreme Court, Clay turns away from Soule's criticisms to discuss other subjects. Although he has not "believed that there was any present actual danger to the existence of the Union," feels that "if this agitation is continued for one or two years longer, no man can foresee the dreadful consequences. . . . the body politic cannot be preserved unless this agitation, this distraction, this exasperation . . . between the two sections of the country, shall cease." Fears that "unless this measure of compromise" passes, then "nothing will be done for California, nothing will be done for the Territories, nothing upon the fugitive slave bill" and other issues. If nothing is done, "instead of healing and closing the wounds of the country, instead of stopping the effusion of blood, it will flow in still greater quantities." If Congress "fails to furnish a remedy to any one of the evils which now afflict the country" and then "we separate and go home under those mutual feelings of dissatisfaction and discontent," expects the "reproach and opprobrium" of "all christendom." Wonders if the Republic can survive after "six or seven months" of "vainly endeavoring to reconcile the distracted and divided parts of the country" and doing nothing to quell "feelings of rage and animosity."

If the Compromise bill fails and the California bill passes, fears that the South "will say to the North, 'You got all you wanted; you got the substitute for the Wilmot proviso . . . you have got the interdiction of slavery into the constitution of California . . . and have refused us everything; you . . . mean to appropriate the whole of our acquisitions to your exclusive benefit.' " Asks how, "with a heated press, with heated parties, with heated lecturers, with heated men," can further deliberation "settle difficulties which six months of earnest and anxious labor have not enabled you to adjust?"

Addresses the complaint that "in this measure of compromise" there is "nothing done for the South." Asks how this could be true "when there is a total absence of all congressional action on the delicate subject of slavery; when Congress remains passive, neither adopting the Wilmot proviso, on the one hand, nor authorizing the introduction of slavery on the other." The South's "great effort, their sole aim" for several years has been "to escape from that odious proviso," and "The proviso is not in the bill." Asserts that "The bill is neither southern nor northern. It is equal; it is fair; it is a compromise, which any man, whether at the North or the South, who is desirous of healing the wounds of his country, may accept without dishonor or disgrace. . . . Neither the North nor the South has triumphed; there is perfect reciprocity. The Union only has triumphed."

Takes on "a very painful duty. . . . of contrasting the plan proposed by the Executive of the United States [Speech in Senate, May 13, 1850] with the plan proposed by the committee of thirteen." Hopes that any "friend of the Executive who supports his measure *to the exclusion of that of the committee*, will . . . meet us face to face. . . . here, and not in the columns of newspapers" for a "fair, full, and manly interchange of argument and opinion."

Describes the plan of the President "by a simile. . . . Here are five wounds—one, two, three, four, five—bleeding and threatening the well being, if not the existence of the body politic." Taylor's plan "is only to heal one of the five, and to leave the other four to bleed more profusely than ever, by the sole admission of California, even if it should produce death itself. . . . His recommendation does not embrace, and he says nothing about the fugitive slave bill or the District bill," and he "recommends that the other two subjects, of territorial government and Texas boundary, remain and be left untouched, to cure themselves by some law of nature." Thinks "that in the spirit of compromise, the President ought to unite with us." Although "He recommends the admission of California" and "We are willing to admit California. . . . I did hope and trust there would have been a reciprocation from the other end of the avenue, as to the desire to heal, not one wound only, which being healed alone would exasperate and aggravate instead of harmonizing the country, but to heal them all." Had looked for "some signification in some form or other, of the Executive contentment and satisfaction with the entire plan of adjustment," but, instead, "we have an authentic assurance of his adherence exclusively to his own particular scheme."

Examines the condition of the territories, making clear that "To refrain from extending to them the benefit of government, law, order, and protection, is widely different from silence or non-intervention in regard to African slavery." Taylor's plan leaves Utah "Without any government at all. Without even the blessing or curse . . . of a military government. There is no government there, unless such as the necessities of the case have required the Mormons to erect for themselves." Taylor's message leaves New Mexico with "a military government which, administrated as it is proposed to be, is no government."

At Clay's request, Sen. Joseph R. Underwood reads portions of an address from the territorial delegate in Congress [Hugh N. Smith] to the people of New Mexico, which complains of "a virtual abandonment" by the government of the United States. Clay then expresses his outrage that a "lieutenant colonel [Brevet Col. John Munroe]—a mere subordinate of the army of the United States—holds the governmental power" in New Mexico "in a time of profound peace! Stand up, Whig who can—stand up, Democrat who can, and defend the establishment of a military government in this free and glorious Republic, in a time of profound peace!" New Mexico has a population of "about ten thousand . . . composed of Americans, Spaniards, and Mexicans; and about eighty thousand or ninety thousand Indians, civilized, uncivilized, half civilized, and barbarous people." If New Mexico applied for statehood "to-morrow. . . . I, for one, would not vote for it," because "She has no population, in sufficient numbers, morally capable of self-government." Questions the ability of the lieutenant colonel to carry out his duties to protect, defend, and repel invasions, and finds his administration unsatisfactory as well. In the boundary dispute between Texas and New Mexico, the officer "says he means to be *neutral*, and has instructions from headquarters to be neutral. . . . he means to take no part with those whom he governs, but to leave them to fight it out as well as they can with the power of Texas!" Reminds the Senate of "the sacred obligations of the treaty of [Guadalupe] Hidalgo [Clay to Beatty, April 29, 1847]. . . . staring us in the face, requiring us to extend the protection of government" to these territories. Wonders what will happen to the people of New Mexico and Utah if Congress adjourns without settling the issue and persists in the view that "They have got a government good enough for them!"

This clashes with "my conception of my duty as an American legislator. My duty tells me to perform what we have promised to perform" and extend "the benefits of that supreme authority residing in the city of Mexico" which Utah and New Mexico "had when they constituted a part of the republic of Mexico." If he cannot accomplish this, at least "I shall stand acquitted in the sight of God and my own conscience; I shall be irreproachable as to any deliberate neglect."

Summarizes his arguments by comparing and contrasting Taylor's plan and the proposals of the Committee of Thirteen, asking reporters to publish them "in parallel columns." Repeats that "the President's plan is confined to a single measure," California's admission, and proposes "no plan of settlement of the agitating questions which arise out of this subject." Asks "any man who can . . . in the Senate of the Unites States" to show that Taylor's plan "is such a one as is demanded by the necessities of the caşe and the condition of the country."

Calls attention to "a floating idea in the southern mind . . . of the necessity of an equilibrium of power between the two sections of the Union—of a balancing authority. However desirable such a state of political arrangement might be, we all know it is utterly impracticable." Considering the "rapid growth and unparalleled progress" of the North, "unless the order of all republics shall be reversed, and the majority shall be governed by the minority, the equilibrium is unattainable." Asks if "it therefore follow that the southern portion is in any danger with respect to" slavery. "I think not, I believe not. All apprehensions of danger are founded on flagrant abuses of power," and there are "securities for the maintenance of southern rights." These include "that sense of truth, that sense of justice, which appertains to enlightened man, to Christian man. . . . there is the Constitution of the United States. . . . there is a necessity for the concurrence of both branches of Congress before any act of legislation, inflicting a wrong upon that southern portion of the country, could take place. . . . then there is the veto of the President. . . . there is the Supreme Court of the United States, ready to pronounce the annulment of any unconstitutional law which might unconstitutionally impair such right; and there is also a sense of responsibility on the part of Senators and Representatives to their constituents. But last, though I trust in God the occasion for its exercise will never arise, there is that right of resort to arms and to make forcible resistance when oppression and tyranny become insupportable."

Notes that the South's "great interest" in slavery is the "only one to be affected by the fact that it is a minority." In fishing, navigating, manufacturing, commerce, "every interest . . . except that great and all-pervading interest of agriculture. . . . We must be reconciled to the condition which is inevitable." Just as we cannot "stop, in its onward course, the flowing of the Mississippi river, and compel it to turn back to its sources in the Rocky and Alleghany [*sic*] mountains," it remains "utterly vain" that we "can acquire that equilibrium . . . between the slaveholding and the non-slaveholding portions of the Union. . . . And to oppose the immutable and irrevocable laws of population and of nature is equivalent to a demand for the severance of the Union."

Concludes "by repeating that here are five wounds which, by the committee of compromise, are proposed to be closed." Knows that "agitators will, even after the passage of all these measures . . . still cry out for their respective favorite measures; that the Wilmot proviso . . . will be pressed." Looks back to the time of the Missouri Compromise—"and I have been unable to determine in my own mind whether more solicitude and anxiety existed then than now"—when "the whole country was in an uproar." Recalls "the tranquillizing consequences" of that compromise "throughout this distracted country." Those "who would have dared to interrupt the universal, and deep-felt, and all-pervading harmony which prevailed throughout the country . . . would have stood rebuked, and repudiated, and reproached by the indignant voice of his countrymen." If this compromise gives "to a country bleeding at every pore" peace and happiness, "I venture to say that the agitation will be at an end." Agitators of both parties "will be hushed into silence, by the indignation they will meet everywhere, in their vain and futile attempt to prolong that agitation which has threatened this country with the most direful calamity which, in all the dispensations of God, could befall it." *Cong. Globe*, 31 Cong., 1 Sess., Appendix, 612-16. Printed in Colton, *Clay Correspondence*, 6:458-78.

The Washington *Daily National Intelligencer* of May 22, 1850, published in parallel columns Taylor's plan and the proposals of the Committee of Thirteen. Brevet Col. John Munroe had become military governor of New Mexico in October, 1849. For the boundary dispute between Texas and New Mexico and Munroe's role in it, see Hamilton, *Zachary Taylor, Soldier in the White House*, 374-80, 383.

Earlier on this day, during discussion of Sen. David L. Yulee's resolution calling upon President Taylor to deliver to the Senate copies of any correspondence concerning "an alleged military expedition against the Island of Cuba," Clay rises to declare any debate on the subject "premature." Unlike Yulee, who "goes on with a denunciatory speech in regard to the character of the information he expects to receive," Clay expresses "the hope that while we are engaged in the discussion of grave and important subjects with regard to California, we will not be diverted from our purpose by an expedition against Cuba." Proposes that the resolution be placed upon the table, and the motion carries.

Clay then moves to take up the special order of the day, the bill for California statehood, territorial governments for Utah and New Mexico, and the Texas boundary [Speech in Senate, May 8, 1850]. *Cong. Globe*, 31 Cong., 1 Sess., 1034.

For Pierre Soule (Dem., La.) and David L. Yulee (Dem., Fla.), see *BDAC*.

Certain Southern slaveholders who favored the annexation of Cuba supported Narciso Lopez who gathered together an expedition to invade Cuba and gain its independence from Spain. The force left New Orleans in April, 1850, disembarked at Cardenas on May 19, and proclaimed a revolt. The populace refused to join them, and they fled to Key West, leaving 52 Americans as prisoners. For this expedition and the U.S. government's actions to secure the release of the Americans who were captured, see Samuel F. Bemis, *A Diplomatic History of the United States* (New York, 1936), 315-16; Smith, *A Political History of Slavery*, 149-52; Hamilton, *Zachary Taylor, Soldier in the White House*, 368-71; *LHQ*, 22:1095-1167.

Remark in Senate, May 24, 1850. Sen. Pierre Soule responds to Clay's criticisms of his stand on the Compromise bill [Speech in Senate, May 21, 1850], commenting that "I would take care that it were something that would not speak to the *eye* what it meant not to the *sense*; that would not deceive by a mere trickery of words, doubtful in import because duplex in meaning."

Clay interrupts later in Soule's speech: "I understood the Senator to say that the committee had held to the eye one thing, intending at the same time another and a different thing—intending to cover the question with a 'drapery' or 'trickery.' " Soule denies this: "Speaking of the measures . . . I said . . . that they were so worded that a careless reader might be led to imagine that they imported something which, in fact, they did not import." Clay accepts Soule's personal compliments, "but that does not satisfy me if, as I supposed, he intended to cast reflections on the motives of the committee by intimating that it was their purpose to practice any deception on the Senate."

Soule begs indulgence, "considering that I was wrestling with the peculiarities of a language not my own." Clay declares himself satisfied, explaining that he "certainly would not have allowed without suitable explanation any remarks reflecting upon the purposes or intentions of that committee." Thinks Soule is wrong to compare "these resolutions of mine" with the "report of the committee. . . . The resolutions [Speech in Senate, January 22, 1850] were the resolutions of an individual; the report of the committee [Speech in Senate, May 8, 1850] is the report of an aggregate. . . . To bring, therefore, the report to the test of the resolutions is to suppose that I, who was alone responsible as the author of these resolutions, constituted the Committee of Thirteen to act upon the whole of the subject." To Soule's dissatisfaction with the failure of the bill to repudiate explicitly the Wilmot Proviso, Clay replies that "it is not there, and all that the South has been struggling for for years has been to avoid its being put there. But he wants more. He wants an argument against it; he wants it denounced as unconstitutional." Expresses disappointment that Soule had concluded his remarks "by saying that he did not consider disunion so great a calamity as others did."

Soule and several other senators object, but Clay repeats: "I understood the Senator most distinctly to say that he did not see anything in the calamities which would result from a dissolution of the Union." Soule again objects in no uncertain terms: "What I did say is this: that if the South was to be crushed to the ground, at least she should be suffered to fall with dignity, and so as to command the respect and not to attract the insulting pity of her adversaries."

Clay is "happy to hear these sentiments" from Soule, although he fears that "the course which he may happen to take may possibly lead to such a consequence at no distant day. He said he did not like this compromise." Complains that instead of limiting himself to specific subjects under debate Soule took up "every topic in the report" and commented upon, and criticised, and rejected it. Hopes that when the measures "have received all the improvements of which it is capable . . . the Senator may yet find it in his power to concur" with the committee's report. *Cong. Globe*, 31 Cong., 1 Sess., Appendix, 788-89. Printed in Colton, *Clay Correspondence*, 6:479-81.

Also on this day during discussion of a bill to establish a branch mint of the United States at New York City, Clay announces that "I am very much inclined to favor" the motion "so far as my vote goes." Observes that Sen. Thomas H. Benton "proposes to attach to it a provision for the establishment of a mint at San Francisco," which Clay also would support. Asks Benton, however, "if this would not be 'tacking,' [laughter,] and whether it will not be in violation of parliamentary law to bring together two subjects of the same kind in this bill?" Since "one is a State—the proud 'Empire State,' " and "the other, I am sorry to say it, yet I am obliged to say it, is yet a territory," points out that while "There are some points of resemblance . . . there are some points of discord." While "I do not mean to insist strenuously upon these incongruities," proposes to Benton "that if he will waive all objection to the compromise bill, and the association which is contained in that bill of certain measures, I for one will with pleasure waive all objection to the incongruity which seems to me to be rather apparent between the two measures now under consideration." *Cong. Globe*, 31 Cong., 1 Sess., 1065.

From JAMES BROWN CLAY Lisbon, Portugal, May 26, 1850

You cannot imagine in what a state of uncertainty uneasiness and expectation, we have been during this entire month. I had been informed by Mr. [John M.] Clayton that it was the opinion of the Secretary of the Navy [William B. Preston] that the Ship from the Mediterranean, with my final instructions, would reach here by the 1st. of this month, & it is now nearly the last, and it has not arrived. I have seen by the English papers that the store ship Erie[1] which I presume took Commodore [Charles W.] Morgan his orders, was lying, with the Commodore in the harbour of Naples on the 27th. last month; in 15 days after he ought to have been here; why he is not, God only knows.[2] I have been constantly uneasy for fear that his non arrival might prejudice the settlement of our affairs, and if this Government had a grain of common sense it would have done so very much. Their true policy, having determined not to pay, was most certainly to offer an arbitration of all the claims, and I have been every instant fearing that such an offer would be made, a rejection of it, which I would have to make, would of course have put us in a worse position before the world.

The English Chargé Mr. Howard [de Walden], the brother of the Earl of Carlisle [George Howard, Lord Morpeth], told me the other day, that Mr. [Henry L.] Bulwer had written to Lord Palmerston, as he promised you, to advise these people to pay all the claims which were just, & to offer to arbitrate the others,[3] and I presume he did so, for Mr. Howard told me at the same time that Count Tojal had informed him that he had offered to arbitrate all. This impression he has been for some time trying to create, through the papers & otherwise; you may have seen an article in the London Times speaking of my rejection of the offer &c, this I know was derived from Tojal, who shows every thing to the correspondent of that paper.[4] Lord Palmerston has very little influence here—he has been always opposed to the Cabral Ministry[5] & there is no good will between them. I took occasion to inform Mr. Howard, that it was wholly untrue that Count Tojal had offered to arbitrate all our claims, & said that I had no objection to his so informing his government.

I cannot predict what will be the effect produced by the coming of the Ship, if ever she does arrive, or of my demand for my passports, if they dont pay—Our action has throughout the affair been so dilatory, that I am sure it cannot have so great influence as promptness would have done; It has always been my opinion, that I ought to have been sent here in a ship of War with the same instructions, given at last; our position at the time of my arrival, was by all odds better than it is now.

Should we be suffered to go away, I am undetermined whether we shall go to Naples & to Paris through Italy & Switzerland, or go at once to Paris, I shall be determined by Commodore Morgans course; If he offers to take us to Naples, as it will not be out of his way, I shall accept. If we go that way we will still reach America in November.

As the season has arrived for Southerners to be in Kentucky, perhaps my house could now be sold—I should like it to be, as on our return home if you wont sell me Ashland, I am determined to try and buy [James Stapleton] Crutchfield's place on the Ohio—[6] Can you write to [George R.] Trotter or Pindell[7] about the house?

28th. Commodore Morgan has not arrived, and I am in hourly expectation of receiving what I feared I should receive, a proposition to arbitrate all the claims. I dined last night with the Duke of Leuchtenburg, the son in Law of the Emperor of Russia [Nicholas I], at the Russian Legation, where the Minister asked if I had received such a proposition, as Count Tojal had told him he intended to make it; he seemed surprised when I told him I had not. I shall regret to receive it because I think my instructions will oblige me to reject it, and I know it will place us in a worse position before the world. Either Come. Morgan has had orders of which I was not informed or he has not been as active as he might, and ought to, have been.

9 oclock at night—I have just recd. a note from the Minister [Count Tojal] stating the willingness of his Government to arbitrate all the claims, but as he rejects the last of them in the same note & as his language is not a distinct proposition to arbitrate, I shall not so Consider it.

We are all well, and Susan [Jacob Clay] joins me in affectionate love to you.

ALS. DLC-TJC (DNA, M212, R11). Printed in Colton, *Clay Correspondence*, 4:607-9. 1. The *Erie* was a ship of the line, commanded by Lt. William D. Porter. *American Almanac . . . for 1850,*

119. 2. Clay to Clayton, June 7, 1849; Clay to James B. Clay, March 17, 1850. 3. Clay to James B. Clay, Oct. 2, 1849. 4. The article, which appeared in *The Times* on May 6, 1850, stated that apparently James B. Clay had rejected a Portuguese offer to arbitrate the claims without waiting for a decision from his government, and that he had hinted that the squadron would be coming to enforce the claims. It concluded that "I am, however, inclined to hope that the explanation sent by this Government direct to Washington will prevent the necessity of such extreme measures." 5. Antonio Bermudo da Costa Cabral, Count of Thomar, was the dictatorial prime minister of Portugal. He was overthrown in 1851. See "Portugal" in *Encyclopedia Britannica*, 11th ed. 6. James Stapleton Crutchfield (1800-1872), the first sheriff of Oldham County and also at one time a member of the Kentucky legislature, did not sell his farm on the Ohio River. Perrin, *Kentucky*, 6:782. 7. Either Thomas Hart Pindell or Richard Pindell.

To JAMES BROWN CLAY Washington, May 27, 1850

I have written to you less of late than I wished, owing to my perpetual public occupations. We are yet in the midst of our Slavery discussions, with no certainty of the final result. I have hopes of the final success of the Compromise reported by me of the Comee of Thirteen,[1] but with less confidence than I desire.

By this time, I presume that your public duties at Lisbon are brought to an unsuccessful close.[2] I fear that the display of force in the port of Lisbon has not been attended with the benefit anticipated from it.

The[3] two pair of pigs and other things you sent us, with the exception of one pair of the pigs have arrived in safety at N. York,[4] and have been forwarded to K[entucky]. The vessel had a long voyage, and provisions getting scarce, that pair was eaten[.]

According to my last accounts from home all was well. John [Morrison Clay] won last week with the Glencoe filly by Yorkshire the Ph[o]enix stake, and the next day he also won the two mile stakes with the Yorkshire colt from the Zinghanie mare. I have not heard from home. You see that I did not judge so erroneously about Yorkshire. I have got Henry Clay [III] admitted as a Cadet in West point, and he has gone home to see his relations and to return to me next week to enter the Academy.[5]

You will see in the papers that I have spoken a great deal (much more than I wished) in the Senate. In my last Speech I had to attack the plan of the Administration for Comprising our Slavery difficulties.[6] Its course left me no other alternative. My friends speak in terms of extravagant praise of my Speeches, and especially of the last.

Since I began this letter I recd. your letter of the 27h. April, with Susan's [Jacob Clay] long and interesting letter to her mother [Lucy Robertson Jacob] which I have read & forwarded this moment.

I do not entertain much hope of the effect of the display of Naval force in getting our claims allowed, and consequently I expect you will leave Lisbon soon after you receive this letter. Should they be allowed, and should Portugal raise the rank of her representative, I suppose the measure would be reciprocated by our Executive.

I am delighted to hear that you are all so happy and that dear Lucy [Jacob Clay] has some good prospect of recovery.

I send a letter from Mary [Mentelle Clay] to Susan, and I am to blame for some delay in its transmission. My love to her and to all your dear children.

ALS. DLC-TJC (DNA, M212, R11). Partially printed in Colton, *Clay Correspondence*, 4:609-10. 1. Clay to Combs, Jan. 22, 1850; Speech in Senate, May 8, 1850. 2. Clay to Clayton, June 7, 1849; James B. Clay to Clay, May 26, 1850. 3. Colton omits this paragraph and the first 4 sentences of the next paragraph. 4. James B. Clay to Clay, Feb. 28, 1850.

5. Clay to Morehead, Dec. 14, 1848. 6. Speech in Senate, May 21, 1850. For Taylor's plan, see Speech in Senate, May 13, 1850.

Remark in Senate, May 27, 1850. During Sen. James M. Mason's speech on the Compromise bill [Speech in Senate, May 8, 1850], Clay interrupts to ask for clarification: "I understand him to propose the extension of the line 36° 30' from Texas, where it now terminates by the resolution of annexation, to the Pacific ocean. Did I understand him as requiring that there shall [not] be any legislation on the part of Congress, to recognize the right of slaveholding States to introduce their slaves south of that line, by the abrogation of any local law . . . which forbids the introduction of slavery? Is he content . . . with the line 36° 30' extended to the Pacific ocean, with nothing being said on the subject of slavery either on the right or left of that line—north or south of it?"

Mason declares "most distinctly" that this is what he meant.

Clay replies that "I could not think of offering to the South the line 36° 30', because without an express recognition of the recognition of slavery south of that line, it was offering to the South a mere ideal line, without carrying along with it any practical benefits whatever." Asks Mason "whether all the Senators from the South will be satisfied with that line, and silent as to the legislation south of that line?"

When Mason replies that he speaks only for himself, Clay notes that "any change or variation in the existing proposition, without a knowledge of some practical result, would be, perhaps, losing time unnecessarily," and wonders if other southern senators would support Mason's view. Admits that "the proposition this morning struck me with great surprise—with agreeable surprise," but "I would not say that I would go into California to disturb her limits." Will consent "to run the line 36° 30', without any recognition of the right to carry slaves south of that line, leaving *lex loci* and the Constitution of the United States to operate there. . . . through Utah and New Mexico."

After more discussion, Clay remarks that since Mason is unable "to produce credentials of authority. . . . to answer for a solitary Senator from the South," he "may accomplish his object" by making an amendment "to extend the line 36° 30' to the Pacific, and call for the yeas and nays on it." Then "we can see how many southern Senators will concur in his proposition." *Cong. Globe*, 31 Cong., 1 Sess., Appendix, 653-55.

To Jared S. Dawson, Bellefontaine, Ohio, May 28, 1850. Wonders why he has not "received a remittance from you of what you ought to have received for my land [Clay to Dawson, April 18, 1849]; or at least some explanation about it." Wants to hear from Dawson immediately, because "I am really in much want of the money." ALS. KyU.

Remark in Senate, May 28, 1850. During discussion on the Compromise bill [Clay to Combs, January 22, 1850; Speech in Senate, May 8, 1850], Sen. Jefferson Davis offers an amendment which states that territorial legislatures cannot be prevented from passing laws for the protection of "property of any kind" in conformity with the Constitution and the laws of the United States.

Clay hopes "that the question will be taken now. . . . I think it is high time that we had made some progress in this measure." Reports that he read "last night a newspaper from San Francisco, giving an account of a public meeting there, which had been convened upon the propositions which were submitted by me to the Senate, I think in February last [Speech in Senate, February 5-6, 1850], and echoing the sentiments of San Francisco, upon the subject of these propositions, back to the

Capitol. Those propositions were submitted nearly four months ago, and this is the first amendment which has been offered. . . . I hope we shall take the question now."

Sen. Salmon P. Chase amends Davis's amendment, essentially by adding the Wilmot Proviso. Clay reiterates his support for Davis's amendment "because, if there be a local law abolishing slavery, and there be in the Constitution and law of the United States authority given to carry slaves into the territory, then those laws and that Constitution abrogate the local law." Since Davis's amendment merely asserts "a fact which would follow without the introduction of the amendment, I have no particular objection to it." Disagrees with senators who believe that Davis's amendment "will authorize, under the Constitution and laws of the United States, the introduction of slavery into the ceded territory." If Chase "will modify his amendment so as to declare that it is not the intention of Congress to assert, one way or the other, the operation of the Constitution and laws of the United States as to the introduction of slaves . . . I shall have no objection to his amendment." Will vote for it if Chase will clarify the wording so that the purpose of his amendment "is merely to guard against the implication that there may be authority, by the Constitution and laws of the United States, to introduce slavery."

The Senate adjourns, after lengthy discussion, before a vote is taken. *Cong. Globe*, 31 Cong., 1 Sess., 1083-84.

Remark in Senate, May 29, 1850. Presents a petition from citizens of Berks Co., Pa., "irrespective of party, representing that, under the present tariff law, their iron, coal, and other industries are unprofitable, and that many of their laborers are thrown out of employment, and consequently are unable to earn the means of subsistence; that labor is depreciated in value, and that destitution and distress prevail; and praying for a modification of the tariff and a change from a system of *ad valorem* to specific duties, sufficient in amount to afford protection."

While concerned "that a great number of their furnaces are out of blast" and understanding that "a great deal of distress is prevailing" in other manufacturing interests, believes that "until this unhappy question of slavery is settled in some way or other [Clay to Combs, January 22, 1850], Congress will not, Congress cannot look to any other of the great interests of the country. . . . so completely has my mind been engrossed and monopolized by the importance of this subject, by the consequence of a failure on the part of Congress to settle this question, that I have been utterly unable to look at any other subject of national interest. . . . I have not felt an emotion, I declare solemnly, I have not felt an emotion connected with party politics since the commencement of the present session." Asserts that "if we can make such an adjustment, for one, I shall be disposed to look with care into these interests, and, without attempting to introduce any extravagant system of protection for any of them." Adds that "in my anxiety to settle the questions connected with the institution of slavery," he has enjoyed "a free intercourse with many Democratic friends. I have known them better, and appreciated them more, than when looking at them through the eyes of party; and I am strongly inclined to believe that they . . . will be disposed to look into these distressed portions of the manufacturing intere[s]ts; and if there is a real necessity for doing something, moderate and not extravagant—something to save them from ruin—I am persuaded that all parts of the House will come up to the rescue."

Later, during discussions concerning the establishment of branch mints of the United States, Clay expresses support for Sen. Thomas H. Benton's proposal for a mint and assay office at San Francisco [Remark in Senate, May 24, 1850]. Hoping that "we shall come to a vote on this subject as soon as we can," explains that "Before I left home, and while in conversation with distinguished men, I came to the conclusion—which has been strengthened rather than weakened by subsequent events—that a mint at San Francisco was necessary, was highly proper, and should be established without any delay." The other proposed branch mint at New York City also "ought to be established. When I was last in New York I went to the Sub-Treasury office and saw the amount of gold there, and I talked with merchants and men of most intelligence, on this subject; and I think it is necessary." Adds, however, that "there are two mints in existence that ought not to be in existence. One of them is in North Carolina and the other in Georgia," but "I shall make no proposition to discontinue them." *Cong. Globe*, 31 Cong., 1 Sess., 1097-99.

To THOMAS HART CLAY Washington, May 31, 1850

I received your favor of the 25th. I was rejoiced to hear of the successes of John [Morrison Clay] on the Turf.[1] The Locomotive paper[2] stated that John's third days entry was the Woodpecker's mare's colt. You say it was Maria Woods. Which is right? I think that John ought to sell his winners, if he can get a good price for them, which I suppose he can do. Perhaps it would be well for him to take them to Louisville & after running them there sell them. Yorkshire's reputation is now firmly established,[3] and if well taken care of he may make a great deal.

I am sorry to hear of the interference of high water in your Sawing operations. Mr. [Charles Benedict] Calvert has a Circular Saw operating in this neighbourhood, impelled by steam, which he tells me can do ten times as much as a straight saw. It costs about $500 with its fixings. I wish Henry [Watkins] could come & see it. I will go and see it, and get more particulars about it.

The fate of our Compromise is uncertain. I think it will pass the Senate.[4] The [Zachary Taylor] Administration, the Abolitionists, the Ultra Southern men, and the timid Whigs of the North are all combined against it. Against such a combination, it will be wonderful if it should succeed.

I have written to John to pay off a note of mine in the Northern Bank & sent a Check for $450 to him.

I shall go to Annapolis this (friday) afternoon, and return Sunday evening.

I think it probable that James [Brown Clay] will be at home this fall. I sent a long letter from Susan [Jacob Clay] to her mother [Lucy Robertson Jacob].[5]

My love to Mary [Mentelle Clay] and her children[.]

ALS. DLC-HC (DNA, M212, R6). 1. Clay to James B. Clay, May 27, 1850. 2. *The Daily Locomotive, A Telegraphic, News, and Commercial Reporter* was a weekly newspaper published for a short time on Broadway in Lexington by John Atkinson. It was discontinued in June, 1850. Frankfort *Commonwealth*, June 25, 1850. See extant copies at KyU. 3. Clay to James B. Clay, March 25, 1850. 4. Clay to Combs, Jan. 22, 1850. 5. Clay to James B. Clay, May 27, 1850.

Speech in the Senate Chamber of the Maryland State House, Annapolis, June 1, 1850. Since "a much lamented occurrence occasioned an adjournment of the Senate," visits "these scenes, hallowed by many interesting recollections and sacred historical associations." Expresses his thanks for "the rites of hospitality" which "you have thought proper to associate . . . with the discharge of duties which you deem preservative of our glorious Union." Claims that the "pure spirit" of George Washington "was not breathed in vain—it exists and is felt in every part of our beloved country. . . . in the good work of adjustment, conciliation and compromise" done "by the patriotic men of all parties—those who call themselves whigs and those who call themselves democrats, with equal purity, devotion, and patriotism." Deems "the occasion and the place not inappropriate to the uttering of a sentiment cherished by me, and deserving of being entertained by all men. It is this, and I assert it with great confidence, that that party, whether whig or democrat, which at the present time gives the greater support to the peaceful adjustment of the difficult and delicate questions at present distracting the national councils, and seriously threatening to disturb the harmony of the Union, will be entitled to and most assuredly will receive the lasting confidence and gratitude of the country, (great and long continued applause)." Copy. Printed in Baltimore *The Sun*, June 3, 1850.

The Senate had adjourned because of the death of Sen. Franklin Elmore (Dem., S.C.) on May 28. Elmore had been appointed to the seat left vacant by John C. Calhoun's death [Remark in Senate, February 28, 1850]. *Cong. Globe*, 31 Cong., 1 Sess., 1107. For Elmore, see *BDAC*.

Remark in Senate, June 3, 1850. During discussion on the California bill [Clay to Combs, January 22, 1850; Speech in Senate, May 8, 1850], Sen. Pierre Soule offers four new sections to substitute for the third section of the bill. These sections set down conditions for California's admission to statehood, the disposition of revenue collected at her ports, payment of her senators and representatives, and the formation of a territory named South California.

Clay thanks Soule for presenting "to the Senate and the country a *contre projet*. . . . he acts much more in conformity to the duty which every member owes to this body" by presenting "a *projet* rather than to . . . say 'We are in the minority, and we are not bound to offer any proposition.' " When it is taken up, "I dare say that every Senator will be found to express his opinion or give his vote according to his sense of duty." *Cong. Globe*, 31 Cong., 1 Sess., 1113-14.

Comment in Senate, June 6, 1850. Submits "a series of resolutions, adopted by a large meeting, embracing both parties, in a town in Kentucky, (Lexington,) in the neighborhood of which I live [Clay to Combs, December 22, 1849]," a region of the state that is "the paradise of that portion of the world." The resolutions are "in favor of that Union to which no portion of the people of the United States are more devoted than the people of Kentucky." The resolutions state that the Union is "the only guarantee" of Kentucky's "future safety, prosperity, and liberty, as it has most assuredly heretofore been the great promoter" of the state's "happiness and glory," adding that "we should consider its dissolution as the greatest calamity, not only to ourselves but to mankind." They assert as well that "the same fraternal feelings and love of freedom which controlled the immortal framers of" the Constitution "ought always to guide us, and we doubt not influenced the committee of thirteen in agreeing to their report [Speech in Senate, May 8, 1850] on the slave question." Add that they rejoice "to learn that our Senators and Representatives from Kentucky are perfectly united on this disturbing question, and we hope soon to see an amicable settlement effected on the basis of that report."

Clay believes that "nineteen-twentieths, if not ninety-nine out of a hundred of the people of the United States, desire most anxiously a settlement of this question" and the "restoration once more of peace, and harmony, and fraternity." Feels that "an immense majority . . . is in favor of that particular mode of settlement" reported by the Committee of Thirteen. While he hopes that the "Union will be shortly gratified by some measure reasonably satisfactory . . . in every quarter," warns that "To suppose that it will be entirely so to one side or the other, exclusively, is to suppose what is impossible. We must, upon subjects of this kind, as upon all human subjects, recollect the frailties, defects, and diversities of opinion which prevail in the constitution of our natures, and take things, and men, and government, and measures as we find them."

Hopes that Sen. George E. Badger's resolution "to meet hereafter at eleven o'clock, might be taken up and adopted at once, and that for the three ensuing days, including Saturday, we will meet at eleven o'clock, and in the course of that time come to a vote upon the report of the Committee of Thirteen, so that its fate may be known. . . . whatever it be, let its fate be known."

When Sen. Jefferson Davis recommends consideration of a bill for the increase of the army, Clay objects and the report is laid over.

Clay asks for the yeas and nays on Badger's resolution, but Davis and Sen. John P. Hale object to having their reports shunted aside to take up this question. Clay asks: "we have now been six months in session, and what have we done?" Explains that "It is with no unfriendly spirit towards any measure that I have desired the passage of this resolution. . . . It is to give time, and a due hearing to every thing. I think by meeting at eleven o'clock, we can, at all events, dispose of those subjects which stand in our way, and which now prevent us from doing anything with regard to the great public interests of the country till we have disposed of them." After more discussion, Badger's resolution passes by a vote of 30 to 19. *Cong. Globe*, 31 Cong., 1 Sess., 1139-40.

The Senate then turns to the Compromise bill, taking up Sen. William L. Dayton's amendment to Sen. Isaac P. Walker's amendment to abolish peon, or Indian, slavery in the territories. Dayton had inserted the phrase "growing out of or connected with any future contract" after the words "peon slavery" in Walker's amendment.

Clay complains that after "six months, in some form or other, engaged in the consideration of African slavery . . . as if we had not enough of that, peonage has sprung up at the end of these six months, about which I myself know but little, and perhaps the Senate generally do not know much." Knows little about "its effects upon the Indians themselves, or its tendency to civilization or otherwise, in those countries in which it exists," and therefore claims "no such amount of information upon the subject as to authorize me to legislate upon it." Asks Walker to withdraw his resolution "as we are evidently not in a position to legislate on the subject now." Considers it "a much more fitting subject for those local legislatures, which we propose by this bill or some other bill to establish. . . . We have never been among them; we know nothing of them; but the legislatures of the localities will be particularly informed of its operation, and if it is oppressive, or tyrannical, or injurious, they will doubtless repeal it." If Walker will not withdraw his amendment, however, Clay agrees with Dayton that "We cannot violate contracts"; peonage "appears to me to be a description of servitude springing out of contracts, and if they are contracts, it is an infringement of the Constitution of the United States to violate them." After much discussion, Dayton's amendment to Walker's amendment is defeated by a vote of 26 to 23. A vote on Walker's amendment quickly follows and it also is defeated by a vote of 32 to 20.

Sen. David L. Yulee then rises to discuss his amendment to extend the force of the Constitution and the laws of the United States over the territorial governments "to put this bill . . . upon the basis of the Clayton compromise [Stevenson to Clay, July 26, 1848]." Such a motion seems necessary since many believe that the Supreme Court has ruled that "the Constitution of the United States did not extend, *proprio vigore*, to the territories, but only so far as it was extended there by the legislation of Congress." Clay points out that the 38th section of the bill states essentially all that Yulee wants, but Yulee responds that only the laws, not the Constitution, are specifically mentioned in that section. Clay attempts to simplify matters by suggesting that Yulee merely "move to amend the thirty-eighth section by inserting the words 'Constitution and,' so as to make it read 'Constitution and laws of the United States.' "

Sen. Henry S. Foote, arguing that no Southerner doubts "that the Constitution of the United States was carried to these territories by the treaty," agrees to vote for Yulee's motion but regrets "the disposition manifested to overload the bill with unnecessary amendments." Clay concurs "that by the passage of this law the Constitution of the United States would be incidently, or by implication, carried over those territories." Concludes, then, that "the amendment could do no harm, because, if the Constitution of the United States is there already, why our putting it there by another enactment will not alter the case."

When Yulee determines that the 21st section of the bill, which concerns Utah, is the proper place to make the changes he desires—and not the 38th section that Clay suggested—Clay replies that he is "really indifferent about it." Argues, nonetheless, that the advantage of following the course he has advanced is that it can be "taken literally, not from the Clayton bill which did not pass Congress, but from repeated acts of Congress passed in the case of Arkansas, and, I think, of Illinois, but certainly of several other States." Continues to "think it would be better just to add it to the existing clause of the bill."

After more debate, Clay expresses the hope that "we shall not prolong the discussion as to whether the Constitution is or is not there. . . . If the Constitution is there, well and good; if it is not there, this enactment will carry it there." Asks that Yulee be "gratified by having his own language introduced into the bill. I always give way, whenever the question is simply as to the form of expression, both forms meaning the same thing, to that which will please most the gentleman who insists on his particular phraseology." Yulee's amendment is adopted by a vote of 30 to 24.

Sen. Roger S. Baldwin then offers an amendment to state in specific terms that Mexican laws prohibiting slavery in the territory ceded by Mexico to the United States shall remain in force until altered or repealed by Congress. Such a clarification is needed so that the Senate does not "pass a law which shall be understood in a different sense by those who cooperate in its passage."

Clay objects, noting that Baldwin "is talking of what emigrants going to the new territories want, and he wants to give them that by another form of the Wilmot proviso. Now, that has been voted upon and rejected." Sees no purpose in "prolonging our sessions and our debates day after day, by bringing forward the same things, only in a different shape," adding that if the amendment prevails, "it will be exactly equivalent to the Wilmot proviso." Disputes Baldwin's view that it "was a conceded point that the Mexican law is the local law in existence. Why, this is disputed on all sides of the Senate." Many others believe "that the Constitution of the United States, the moment it came to operate on these territories, abrogated the local law." If the Constitution has abolished local law and Baldwin's amendment prevails, then "The Constitution would say one thing, and the honorable Senator's amendment would be in direct violation" and "will be unconstitutional." If it is constitutional, Clay repeats, "it is precisely the Wilmot proviso in another and different form of expression." Asks senators "who have so much at heart the subject of the abolition of African slavery, whether a little difference is not due to the opinion of the Senate, which has been expressed over and over again." Baldwin's amendment is rejected by a vote of 32 to 23. *Cong. Globe*, 31 Cong., 1 Sess., 1139-42, 1144-47.

For a discussion of whether the Constitution extended *proprio vigore* to the territories, or whether legislative action was needed to make it so, and the various court rulings on the subject, see Von Holst, *Constitutional and Political History*, 3:444-51. For William L. Dayton (Whig, N.J.), see *BDAC*.

Speech in Senate, June 7, 1850. Rises to object to Sen. Jeremiah Clemens's amendment to the Compromise bill that would "strike out the proposition made to Texas for the purchase of the portion of her territory which is designated in the bill; that is to say, the territory claimed by her, embracing New Mexico; to strike out all the propositions, if I understand the amendment, made to Texas for settling the question of her title to the territory which I have described, and in lieu of them to recognize and confirm her rights, as claimed by her, from the mouth to the source of the Rio Grande."

Cannot consent to "leave the whole territory ever claimed by Texas, including

New Mexico, in the possession of Texas, sovereignty and all, and consequently to place New Mexico under the permanent dominion of Texas." Since he considers this "to be far the most important amendment which has been, or which probably will be offered to this bill," and conceives that "there is a good deal of misunderstanding on this subject," desires to present "a few considerations to the Senate."

Describes the section Clemens hopes to strike out as one that "amounts to nothing more than a proposal, on the part of the Government of the United States to the Government of Texas, to settle and quiet a disputed title," a "mere overture" to resolving territorial claims.

Acknowledges that many believe that "the proposals involved a great concession of slave territory to the principle of free territory," but intends to show "that, upon a certain hypothesis . . . there is a great conversion of free territory into slave territory, indeed, "a concession of three-fourths of the disputed territory to slavery by the terms of the proposals to Texas." Realizes that the question "of the validity of the title of Texas to all that portion of the territory conceded to us by Mexico lying east of the Rio Grande" has not been resolved, and warns "those who believe in one state of the title, and . . . those who believe that the opposite state of title exists, not to draw from any observations which I am about to make, conclusions favorable or unfavorable to the one side or the other."

Understands that the question "whether the western boundary of Texas was or was not the Nueces" River has divided the American people. Notes that "one great party in the United States, without, as far as I know, any exception were of opinion, a few years ago, that the *Nueces* was the western limit of Texas," and Clay agrees "generally in the conviction." Believes that "Texas would be unwise, extremely unwise,. if she desires to increase the sphere of slave territory" too far. As it stands, "assuming the Nueces was the western limit of Texas—and that is the hypothesis to which I have referred—upon that predicate, there is a cession of free territory to slavery of the country extending from the Nueces to the Rio Grande, and from the mouth of the Rio Grande up to the 36° 30′ of north latitude," an extent of land along the Rio Grande of about 1,250 miles, "about three-fourths of which are conceded by the partisans of free territory to slavery."

If, on the other hand, "the Rio Grande, from its mouth to its source, be the western limit of Texas," as "some gentlemen of each party" believe, then "Texas has no title whatever to any portion of New Mexico." Thus, "this question of disputed boundary presents exactly one of those cases which are eminently suitable for accommodation and amicable arrangement," with one side contending "for the Nueces and the other for the Rio Grande, according as the one or the other wish the theatre for slavery to be contracted or enlarged." Believes that "gentlemen from the South ought to be content in withdrawing from all future controversy a large extent of territory, stretching nine hundred and twenty miles on the Rio Grande, and dedicating it to slavery, if its future population shall so decide." Northerners should concede "the portion of the territory comprehended within the boundaries of New Mexico, between twenty miles beyond El Paso, on the Rio del Norte, up to 36° 30′ of north latitude," a concession of "about three hundred and twenty or three hundred and thirty miles." Asks "if there be cause for complaint on either side, which is the side that ought to complain?"

Turning from "El Paso, or from Texas proper, to the limits of New Mexico," asks how purchasing the right of Texas, "whatever it may be, to this territory" would amount "to a conversion of slave territory into free territory." Points out that "the principle of non-intervention is applied by the bill." Many believe that Texas, "being a slave country, established slavery where its law extended, and gave slaveholders the right to carry their slaves to New Mexico." If so, then "the right of the slaveholder remains unaffected by the bill, because there is no prohibition of that right, no abrogation of the law of Texas. The Texas laws will remain in force." But "if the Texan authority and Texan law never reached New Mexico, which is my private opinion, it follows that New Mexico continued, notwithstanding the passage of the act of 1836 by the Texan Congress, to be a part of the Mexican republic, and if it were never detached from that republic by the arms of Texas, and the Texan laws never stretched over New Mexico, it follows that, up to the moment of the cession of that territory by the republic of Mexico, the laws of that republic having, according to my humble conception, abolished slavery, slavery does not exist there, and the territory will be appropriated to the principle of free soil." Urges those on both sides of the issue to "leave the question of slavery or no slavery to be decided by the only competent authority that can definitely settle it forever, the authority of the Supreme Court of the United States."

Concludes by describing "the present condition of New Mexico": "there has been a conflict between the people of Santa Fe and some persons—according to the account which I saw, about a hundred—in the employment of the quartermaster's department of the General Government, under the direction and control of that military government, that lieutenant colonel [Brevet Col. John Munroe], who now holds in his hands perhaps the destinies of Santa Fe and New Mexico. He looks on wholly indifferent, and is neutral in the struggle about to arise between the people of Santa Fe, composed, I understand, of American citizens, Mexicans, and Spaniards, this side of the Rio del Norte, and the authorities of Texas. And this neutrality is to be kept by . . . the lieutenant colonel, who has the dealing out of civil commissions, acting . . . as if he were the Autocrat of the Russias." The lieutenant colonel [Speech in Senate, May 21, 1850] "looks with cold indifference upon that struggle already begun in the streets of Santa Fe" between "some one hundred men on each side, those in the service of this Government taking part with Texas!" Even if there were no questions about boundaries, titles, and concessions of slave and free states, "I submit, if you do not know that there is a most insuperable antipathy existing between the people of Santa Fe and those of Texas," then "the inevitable result of doing nothing will be to lead to civil war. . . . I ask if our obligations with regard to the people of Santa Fe do not impose on us the obligation to make some effort to dissever them from the authority of Texas, to which they are so unalterably determined not to be attached?"

After Sen. Thomas J. Rusk asserts that "there is no State in the Union that will make more sacrifices to bring about good feeling and preserve that Union" than Texas, he asks Clay "to point out how and in what manner, consistently with the Constitution of the United States, under which we act, this question can ever come before the Supreme Court without the consent of Texas?"

Clay replies: "By referring to the controversy between Rhode Island and Massachusetts, the Senator from Texas will see how this matter can be brought before the Supreme Court. . . . Let New Mexico be admitted as a State. She will then be a State—a peer, and equal with Texas. New Mexico, then being a State, the question would arise as to the title to this territory between New Mexico, as the new State, and Texas the prior State. That question can be brought before the Supreme Court by a bill *in equity*, the mode of proceeding which is generally carried on. That was the mode of proceeding adopted in the dispute between New York and New Jersey, and between Illinois and some other State."

While continuing to abstain "from all discussion on the title of Texas," does not "mean to say that there was nothing in that title." Reports that "If the committee did not think there was something in her title, they would not propose a large and liberal equivalent to Texas for the surrender of whatever title she has beyond El Paso. . . . If Texas had not any sort of title at all, how could we propose an equivalent for her title?" Compliments Rusk on his willingness "to make great sacrifices in order to bring about a good state of feeling between the two sections of the Union." Hopes there will be no more "boundless discussion—almost as boundless as the territory claimed by Texas herself—of what is the exact state of the title of Texas," but understands that Rusk "will support what he believes to be the just rights of his State, at every hazard, and to the last extremity."

In the discussion that follows, Sen. Stephen A. Douglas suggests designating the ridge that separates the watershed of the Mississippi from that of the Rio Grande as the eastern limit of New Mexico. Clay notes that "in the Committee of Thirteen I proposed myself substantially that limit. I proposed that we should run the eastern line of New Mexico by beginning at El Paso and thence running to the uppermost source of the Red river and thence to the 42d degree of north latitude, or the ancient line between the United States and Mexico," but the committee did not concur with this plan.

Sees some merit in Douglas's "suggestion of enlarging the Indian territory, by making to it an addition from what would be ceded by Texas, if this bill pass," but wonders if Douglas perceives "that if the proposition made by the committee should be acceded to by Texas, it will always be in the power of the Government of the United States to take such part of New Mexico as it pleases and assign it to the Indians there?"

Comments also on Sen. Clemens's proposition "to confirm the title of Texas from the mouth to the source of the Rio Grande, and to declare it to be a part of Texas," asserting that "it is impossible to do that." Also challenges Clemens's suggestion that Texas undertake "to remove the Indians and place them north of the line of the 34th parallel of latitude, still within Texas; how can we do that? By what authority can we do it?" When Clemens charges that Clay has misunderstood the proposals, Clay simply retorts: "I shall not quarrel with that; but the question is, whether it is not better to take the line proposed by the committee, in which will be contained the power of the United States to take any portion of it, from the head-waters of the Arkansas river—for really, sir, it is a country not worth disputing about, only fit for Indians to hunt upon—take it at any time and assign it to the Indians." Asks for a quick vote on Clemens's amendment. After more discussion, the amendment is rejected by a vote of 37 to 17. *Cong. Globe*, 31 Cong., 1 Sess., 1154-57, 1162-63. Partially printed in Colton, *Clay Correspondence*, 6:482-85, 503-8.

Comment in Senate, June 8, 1850. During debate on the Compromise bill [Clay to Combs, January 22, 1850], Sen. Henry S. Foote offers three amendments: first, to make the northern boundary of Texas the 34th degree of north latitude; second, to allow Texas to retain her title to all territory embraced by her boundary of 1836 if Texas rejects the compromise's proposition to cede a portion of that territory; and third, to reaffirm the validity of the Texas resolution of annexation.

Clay "cannot agree . . . to any of his amendments. I think two of them are, according to my conception, wrong, and the third is unnecessary." The Committee of Thirteen considered "making the 34th degree of north latitude the northern boundary of Texas," and notes that "we considered it, discussed it, decided against it, and determined on a line twenty miles above El Paso, and thence across to the Indian territory." One reason for this was "to deviate as little from what we supposed to be the eastern boundary of New Mexico as possible. I was extremely desirous myself that El Paso should have been retained as the northern boundary of Texas . . . believing that that was the point of the ancient boundary of New Mexico." States that he yielded because "it was said that there were some settlements between El Paso and twenty or thirty miles above, which had no necessary intercourse with New Mexico, but had intercourse with Texas." This territory is "inaccessible to New Mexico" because of "an intervening desert," called "the Desert of Death" which renders impossible "any connection by commerce or traveling between Santa Fe and El Paso." Although conditions proved not to be quite so severe, the committee took into account "the alleged antipathy of the inhabitants immediately above El Paso, and within thirty miles of it, to be connected with New Mexico, and their desire to be attached to Texas."

The "inevitable effect" of Foote's first amendment "would be to diminish, very materially, the pecuniary equivalent which it is proposed to offer to Texas for the surrender of territory. It gives her land which she does not want, and takes away from her money which she does want." Hopes Foote "will waive this amendment. . . . If you begin to disturb it, where is it to end?"

Finds Foote's second amendment "unnecessary, but at the same time I have no objection to it. . . . There is a provision in the bill retaining to the Government of the United States all its rights unimpaired" because "we are the parties acting, proposing, making overtures. The other party could not be affected, if it chose to reject our proposals," so "the amendment is not necessary, in my opinion, but still I have no objection to it."

With respect to Foote's third amendment, "I really think our southern friends ought to be satisfied with what we have done." The committee has proposed "to adopt the principle of non-intervention in New Mexico, leaving the state of law there as it exists, merely declaring that slavery shall not be admitted or excluded. Is not that sufficient?" Asks "what necessity is there for the reaffirmation of the binding and obligatory force of the resolution of annexation? . . . No practical proposition is made, but merely to put an abstract assertion in this bill of a principle which is already sufficiently secured by the action of Congress." Reasserts that "the first and third amendments ought not to be adopted, and that the second is unnecessary, but I have no objection to it."

After much more discussion on the Texas boundary question, Sen. Stephen A. Douglas discounts both the 34th parallel and "this desert, or Journey of the Dead, as it is called" as a suitable boundary between Texas and New Mexico. Suggests instead "that the northern boundary of the State of Texas shall be a line drawn due east from the Rio Grande through the centre of this Desert of Death to the Red River."

Clay announces that "I regret extremely this obstruction to the bill on the subject of a few miles more or less on the Rio Grande." Thinks that "after the full consideration given to the subject by the committee, that there ought to be some disposition to acquiesce in the decision to which they came." Repeats the alternatives the members considered and the lack of "satisfactory information concerning the people of this country, or their disposition to be annexed to one party or the other." Although "Texas has her two Senators [Sam Houston; Thomas J. Rusk] upon this floor entirely disposed in negotiating for their State, to get all they can," and "I make no reproach against them for it," complains that "the information which I get from the Delegate from" New Mexico [Hugh N. Smith] "is very different from that which we derive from the Senators from Texas." Asks "in fixing the boundaries of States—of empires perhaps—is it of any importance whether there are a few inhabitants above or below the line? Now, we do not hear from these people. The honorable Senator from Texas states, as he no doubt believes, that they desire to be attached to Texas. The Delegate from New Mexico behind me states directly the reverse."

Discounts the arguments of Texas senators who complain of the inaccessibility of Santa Fe to inhabitants of the El Paso region. Argues that "the same objection applies to Austin. Besides that, I am told that there is a fine natural road, a great commercial highway . . . and the only difficulty is the want of water." Adds that "wells can be sunk. Why, I have had half of dozen ponds made at Ashland, and we have hundreds and thousands of them in Kentucky . . . there will be no difficulty in forming depots of water for the accommodation of travelers over these ninety or one hundred miles of fine natural highway, without any obstruction of mountains or even very inaccessible hills, and with the finest grass pasturage on every side." Asks Sen. Thomas J. Rusk not to "persevere in this desire to go to the line of 34°" or "a much less amount of pecuniary equivalent must be offered to Texas."

Rusk makes a plea "that these people may not be required to pass through where they would be liable to be scalped by Indians." Does not feel it is right that "Texas is charged with factious opposition if she asks to have the line extended so as to include these people. . . . if you will take away your political missionaries, and withdraw your influences from among the people of Santa Fe, they will quietly organize under the authority of Texas."

Clay accuses Rusk of being "unnecessarily excited," admonishing him that "it is useless to talk of bravery, and resorting to conflict, and the 'degradation of Texas.' " Repeats that "towards Texas I have the kindliest feelings, and amongst other considerations which urged me to oppose the taking of thirty-four as the boundary line between Texas and New Mexico . . . was that we shall not be at liberty, on establishing that line, to offer to Texas any such pecuniary equivalent as, for one, I feel strongly disposed to do."

Complains that "this matter has been already more discussed than was necessary. . . . Of all the topics connected with this arrangement, the one that gave me most trouble and anxiety has been the proper adjustment of this territorial line." Although desiring to resolve it "in an amicable manner," found it "impossible to agree in all respects with the gentlemen who represent the State of Texas." Remains "so anxious . . . for the adjustment in an amicable and satisfactory manner of these great and troublesome questions, that there is scarcely any thing I would not be willing to do; but I repeat that I think it would be better to adhere to the line proposed by the committee."

After more discussion, Clay interrupts to say he is "very anxious . . . to get a vote upon this subject" of amending the committee's boundary proposals. Rejects Sen. Jefferson Davis's insinuations that " 'the whole object sought in this part of the bill is to give slave territory to the control of the free States.' " Also discounts Davis's "argument of a want of power. . . . What is there in the Constitution or anywhere else—what provision is there, either expressed or implied, in the Constitution, which restrains the United States on the one side and Texas on the other from accommodating this difficulty?" Hopes for a quick vote on the amendment, since "it is not for us in a momentous question like this to be disputing about a few inhabitants, or whether they live in a village, or are scattered through a portion of country."

During further considerations, when Sen. Rusk raises the question of compensation to Texas for her territorial concessions, Clay urges that the topic not be taken up at this time: "We shall most probably have a full discussion upon it when the question comes up for filling in the blank," and Rusk "is weakening his argument by bringing up this question now." *Cong. Globe*, 31 Cong., 1 Sess., Appendix, 789-90, 792-94, 797. Pp. 792-93 printed in Colton, *Clay Correspondence*, 6:500-502.

To THOMAS O. LARKIN[1] Washington, June 10, 1850

I received by Mr. Carter the beautiful Watch chain made, in California, of specimens of native gold from the Placers,[2] which you have done me the favor to present to me. They are curious in themselves, and curiously combined in the Chain which they form. I thank you cordially for this highly acceptable present.

I regret the delay in Congress in the admission of California as a State in the Union, and hope it will not be much longer prolonged.[3] Ready always to vote for her reception, either as a separate measure, or in combination with other measures, I satisfied myself that the most certain and most speedy way of accomplishing the desirable object, was to unite a provision for the admission of California with other measures, also desirable, and on that conviction I have been proceeding.[4] The result will be known in a short time.

ALS. CU-B. 1. For Larkin (1802-58)—merchant, diplomatic agent, and U.S. consul at Monterey when California was acquired by the U.S.—see *DAB*; John A. Hawgood (ed.), *First and Last Consul, Thomas Oliver Larkin and the Americanization of California*, 2nd ed. (Palo Alto, 1970). Larkin had written Clay from New York on May 27, 1850, praising Clay's work for the admission of California as a state, sending Clay the gold watch chain, and mentioning the eighteen years he had spent in his "adopted country" of California. Copy. Printed in New York *Herald*, June 7, 1850. 2. Placer came to refer to any place or mine where mineral deposits might be found. There were different kinds of placers depending on topographical position—hill, flat, bench, bar, river-bed, gulch. Rockwell D. Hunt (ed.), *California and Californians*, 5 vols. (New York, 1926), 2:157. 3. Clay to Pierse, Feb. 16, 1849; Clay to Combs, Jan. 22, 1850. 4. Clay to Combs, Jan. 22, 1850; Speech in Senate, Jan. 29 and May 8, 1850.

To FRANCIS T. BROOKE Washington, June 11, 1850

I recd. my dear friend your kind letter, and it would afford me the greatest pleasure if I could accept your invitation to visit St. Julien.[1] Its quiet hospitality would be the greatest relief to me, from cares and anxieties of pub[lic] life, and the storms of the Senate Chamber. But I cannot now abandon my post, we are in the midst of the Slavery contest,[2] and I can get no discharge until it has terminated.

ALS. ViU. 1. Near Fredericksburg, Va. 2. Clay to Combs, Jan. 22, 1850.

Comment in Senate, June 12, 1850. On Sen. Thomas H. Benton's motion to postpone further discussion on the Compromise bill until March 4, 1851, Clay hopes "that we shall be allowed to take the vote on the proposition. . . . If the vote shall be against the postponement, we can resume the consideration of the amendments which are before us. If the bill shall be so fortunate as to reach its third reading, at that time, I will, so far as it becomes me, pay attention to what has been said on the one side and on the other. My object is to save time, and to arrive at practical conclusions as soon as possible." After two calls for the yeas and nays, Clay withdraws his call "for the present," to allow Sen. William L. Dayton to take the floor.

Later, when Benton offers to withdraw his motion for a postponement, Clay requests him to do so, "to avoid what I regarded as useless consumption of time. . . . we have lost two days in consequence" already. Asks "that he will allow us to vote on this question." Benton withdraws his motion.

Sen. Stephen A. Douglas's amendment, in part setting the New Mexico boundary at "the range of mountains or dividing ridge separating the waters flowing into the Rio Grande from the waters flowing into the Arkansas and Red rivers," is then taken up. Clay feels "constrained to vote against this amendment," largely because "the waters which empty into the Rio Grande, so interlock that it will be impossible to ascertain where any ridge does separate them."

Informed that this part of the amendment was to be stricken out, Clay responds: "Very well. Of course that obviates the objection." Repeats his "desire to see substantially the position which the committee proposes to make to Texas for the relinquishment of her title." If "gentlemen will be contented with the bill as it stands at present. . . . I will present a separate section, limiting, circumscribing the boundaries of New Mexico to what is understood to have been her ancient eastern boundary, reserving all east of that ancient boundary for the extension of our Indian territory."

After more amendments to the amendment are discussed, the practicability of the final measure is questioned. Clay sees "no sort of difficulty if the Senate choose to adopt the amendment. . . . the difference between the report and amendment is simply this: The committee propose to run from a point twenty miles above El Paso to the terminus which the amendment proposes," the point where the one hundredth degree of west longitude crosses Red River. "The form of the portion between the two bills will be a triangle, having this difference for its base, and will not embrace a large extent of country. You will therefore take less from New Mexico, according to the report of the committee, than by this amendment. That is the whole of it. It is simply extending the base of the triangle about forty miles."

When Sen. Thomas J. Rusk comments that the southern boundary of New Mexico also has long been a matter of great uncertainty, Clay agrees that "there has been some variation of that boundary in different epochs of the Spanish or Mexican history." Since "the Congress of Mexico, in 1824, recognized El Paso as the boundary of New Mexico, and so does the treaty of [Guadalupe] Hidalgo [Clay to Beatty, April 2, 1847]," believes that El Paso must be "recognized as the southern limit of New Mexico. That is the state of the fact."

After much more discussion, Clay attempts to clarify the question: "There are three points of departure proposed for our consideration. The first is El Paso, the second a point twenty miles above, and the third sixty miles above. All the lines running eastwardly from these points are to have the same *terminus*, in the . . . Indian country." Whatever may be taken from New Mexico, "she is more than compensated for by the addition of territory on her eastern line, and west of the Indian territory." Although initially inclined "to begin, as the Senator from Illinois has proposed, at El Paso," when the committee agreed upon "a line twenty miles above," decided to "vote for that; not because it was what I first preferred, but because the committee is in favor of it." *Cong. Globe*, 31 Cong., 1 Sess., Appendix, 852-56; *Cong. Globe*, 31 Cong., 1 Sess., 1192.

Also this day, during discussion on the Texas boundary and compensation questions, Sen. Dayton complains of "part of the scheme connected with it. . . . the recapture and restoration of fugitive slaves." Fears the compromise proposal would make "the free states, the mere executive, the mere ministerial officers of the slave States," whose statute books require "nothing beyond the oath of the claimant himself to entitle him to the possession of the runaway." In a free state, this practice "would be an outrage upon law and evidence."

Clay challenges Dayton's finding "that the oath of the owner of a slave was everywhere deemed sufficient evidence to establish the fact of slavery." Avers that "there is not such a law, within my recollection, in any slave State in the Union. But in every case where the question of freedom or slavery is at issue, the master can be no more a witness in that case than in any other to which he was a party." Dayton insists that Clay has misinterpreted his comments, and, after further questions raised by Sen. James M. Mason, he continues at length this digression from the Texas issue. *Cong. Globe*, 31 Cong., 1 Sess., Appendix, 816.

Comment in Senate, June 13, 1850. During discussion on the amount of compensation to be offered to Texas as part of that state's boundary settlement with New Mexico, Clay hopes that "the blank will not be now filled, and that any proposition to that effect will be voted down." The committee had decided against setting a sum, partly because "it might lead to stock speculations" and partly because "the committee could not know what extent of territory Texas would yield her claim to." The "proper time for filling the blank was . . . upon the third reading of the bill . . . when the whole subject will be open to discussion and full consideration."

Responds to Sen. William H. Seward's accusation that "the effort to get these measures passed had arrested the progress of the public business, and prevented Congress from discharging its duties." Since there is no compromise measure before the House of Representatives, asks how "has the proposition . . . in this branch of Congress interrupted the public business in the other?" Blames Seward "and those who cooperate with him" for being "the true and legitimate cause of the interruption of the public business" of the Senate. If the Committee of Thirteen [Remark in Senate, March 12, April 12, 18, and 19, 1850] "had been appointed according to the ordinary course of legislative proceeding . . . as it ought to have been, for such an object as national reconciliation, without opposition; if, as an experiment to settle the distraction of the country, every Senator had voted for it, as . . . they ought to have done, three months ago we might have had a report and a definitive settlement of the question." The minority, including Seward "are the true cause of the interruption of the public business—not of Congress, but of this branch of Congress. . . . The gentlemen who were not satisfied with the expression of the opinion of the majority once, twice, thrice, and four times, but who resorted to every possible means of thwarting the declared and known wish of the majority, I charge them with being the cause of the obstruction." This week "a motion was made on which to hang speeches, and three days after the motion was made, and when the speeches have been delivered, a withdrawal takes place of the proposition. And yet we, the majority, are to be charged with impeding the progress of the public business! . . . To postpone, to delay, to impede, to procrastinate, has been the policy of the minority in this body, and yet they rise up here and charge us . . . with causing delay." The committee had worked with "As little delay . . . as was proper on a subject of such vast complication" and "have taxed our physical powers, and required the meeting of the daily sessions to be fixed an hour in anticipation . . . and yet we are to be charged with delaying the public business." Feels "the horrible injustice" done to his committee "with such a degree of sensibility, that I forgot the weak and feeble, and, I might almost add, the trembling limbs with which I have come to this body to-day."

Contrasts Sen. Hopkins L. Turney's amendment "to strike out all that relates to a compromise of the title of Texas to the country of New Mexico . . . and to leave the question as it now is" with the committee's proposal "to preserve New Mexico entire . . . to detach it from Texas, to define its limits, give it the benefit of a civil government, and put it into a position to become a State, when the amount and the intelligence of its population shall authorize it." Although Seward and other northern men profess to "have so much at heart the preservation of New Mexico, detached and separated from Texas," the senator "tells us he is against the whole bill, and therefore against any part of the bill." Asks him, however, "if the bill is to pass, would you not rather it should pass with the preservation of New Mexico and the adjustment of the boundary of Texas than without it?"

Later, after Sen. Thomas H. Benton blames all the delays on Clay's insistence on combining all these elements into a single bill, Clay "thought once or twice of calling the Senator from Missouri to order. . . . The Senator read my speech three times, which would have been out of order if the same rule applied to speeches that applies to bills." Has "never sought to fill" the office of lecturer to the Senate, as Benton has charged: "In giving a lecture, the person lecturing ought to have some ability to impart instruction, and the person to whom it is addressed should have the capacity of receiving it. In this case, as between the Senator and myself, both of these conditions are wanting. [Laughter.]" Moreover, "this dispute as to who caused the delay. . . . did not originate with me."

Benton had also accused Clay of inconsistency in his stand on California statehood. Clay retorts that he had heard that Benton "last summer . . . denounced the admission of California as an unconstitutional and highly improper measure. . . . If that was the opinion of the Senator last summer, the change of opinion in him is certainly quite as remarkable a change as that which he has attributed to me." Adds that Benton also had "pronounced that the admission of Texas by a resolution of Congress would be unconstitutional. And yet the honorable Senator changed his opinion on that point afterwards" as well. Given Benton's own course, "ought he not to have some regard for those who may find it necessary to change their opinions in regard to some subjects?"

Vindicates his own course on California. When he had learned that "California had formed a State constitution [Clay to Pierse, February 16, 1849] . . . I own that I was for her immediate admission." Trying "throughout life to be a practical man, and to give and take, to yield in all cases not involving essential principles," decided "the speediest mode of admitting California was by a combination of these several measures. . . . I did it in reference to practical legislation, and the condition of the other House and of this House. There is no great difference of principle involved in the two modes [Clay to Combs, January 22, 1850]."

Returning to the immediate question of the amount to be paid to Texas, argues that the sum will not "leak out and affect speculation" because "the committee has not absolutely fixed any sum to be paid to Texas. The sum will be determined according to the shape which the bill may finally take."

When Benton takes issue with Clay's comments, Clay says he does not "wish to engage in any controversy with the honorable Senator." Although he has heard "from two or three different quarters" that last summer Benton "did not think California ought to be admitted," feels he has not stated "the matter as a matter of fact which I knew or could vouch for" and leaves it to Benton "to disprove it, if he might think it proper." Nonetheless, "for my own vindication," reads a letter from one John W. Reid to a member of the House of Representatives from Missouri reporting that Benton had indeed opposed California's admission to statehood under Zachary Taylor's scheme to skip the territorial phase. Does not "pretend to say that this is at all important. . . . I made the illusion incidently" in answer to Benton's charges that Clay changed his "opinions as to the speediest course of admitting California."

Benton hopes Clay would have Reid's letter entered "upon the journal." Clay does not "think that would be right." Benton retorts "nobody gets off from me in that way," and intimates that Clay is in fact the author of the Reid letter. Clay answers: "I repel with scorn and indignation the imputation that I am the author of that letter. I hurl it back to him, that he may put it in his casket of calmunies, where he has many other things of the same sort." *Cong. Globe*, 31 Cong., 1 Sess., Appendix, 861-62, 865-67. Printed in Colton, *Clay Correspondence*, 6:485-93.

Also this day, Sen. Salmon P. Chase presents a memorial signed by many of "the most respectable and influential citizens of northern Ohio," who "ask for the admission of California, and earnestly remonstrate against making that admission at all dependent upon any other question whatever. They also emphatically protest against the establishment of governments for the territories without an express interdiction of slavery therein." Sen. Jesse D. Bright understands Chase to say that this is the opinion of "nineteen twentieths of the people" of Ohio, and cannot understand why Ohio and adjacent Indiana "should differ so widely in reference to the unsettled political questions of the day."

Clay comments: "With regard to the people of Ohio, I know something of them; I have the highest possible respect for them, and am very grateful to them. But I shall be greatly disappointed if, in some instances—I will not say what—gentlemen, when they go home, shall find themselves without constituencies, so far as a conformity of will creates a constituency. . . . I have risen to present some resolutions from a portion of the 'frantic people' of the United States—frantic on behalf of the compromise everywhere, if not in Ohio." Presents resolutions from St. Louis, "that city which is going to vie, in a few years, perhaps some twenty or thirty years, with the empire city of the country." The resolutions "were passed at a meeting of both political parties, and they speak—as any man would confess, who knows anything about the sentiment of Missouri—the sentiment of that State" and of that "great city, great in fact, and greater still in embryo." The resolutions support the spirit of compromise, through which "peace and harmony will speedily be restored, sectional jealousies allayed" and "the union of the States more firmly cemented." The resolutions are then ordered to lie on the table. *Cong. Globe*, 31 Cong., 1 Sess., 1202-3.

From Edmund Dillahunty *et al.*, Columbia, Tenn., June 14, 1850. Report that "At a recent term of the Circuit Court of Maury County. . . . A Committee was appointed, containing an equal number of leading & influential Whigs & Democrats, which reported a preamble & series of resolutions that were unanimously adopted." Express their appreciation for "The services of the Committee [of Thirteen] of which you are the chairman [Remark in Senate, April 12 and April 19, 1850]. . . . The time has arrived when the question of slavery should be settled, and settled forever." Add that "it is very evident that the only way to settle it is by compromise [Clay to Combs, January 22, 1850]." Argue that "the people of the south are not against honorable concession for the adjustment of a question involving the peace, harmony & perpetuity of our excellent form of government," and assure Clay that he and his committee have deserved "the confidence and regard of enlightened patriots & philanthropists throughout the Country." ALS. ViW.

Dillahunty served as circuit judge of Maury County, Tenn., from 1836-52. Weston A. Goodspeed, *History of Tennessee* . . . (Nashville, 1886), 763.

Remark in Senate, June 14, 1850. During discussion on the Compromise bill, Clay objects to Sen. Jeremiah Clemens's amendment to fill in the blank in the 39th section with the sum of $1,000,000, the proposed price of the territory to be purchased from Texas. Clay prefers to "leave the blank as the committee proposed, to fill it up after the ascertainment of the extent of territory which may be proposed to be purchased from Texas." Since "We do not know the exact amount of territory which it is proposed to purchase from Texas," except "what it is, according to the present expression of the opinion of the Senate. . . . The committee, therefore, thought it right to forebear, for this as well as other reasons which I have stated, to make any proposal to fill the blank till the bill arrives at the period of its third reading, when, according to the parliamentary usage, blanks are most generally filled up." After more discussion, the amendment is defeated by a vote of 30 to 8. *Cong. Globe*, 31 Cong., 1 Sess., 1209-12.

From J.W. MORROW[1] Jefferson City, Mo., June 15, 1850

Although it may be almost like the voice of one Crying in the wilderness, yet I feel it to be the duty of every patriot to cheer with his voice, how feeble so ever it may be, those who are nobly and gallantly devoting their great energies to the adjustment of the only question that can endanger the Union, and to the restoration of peace and concord to the country. I regard the compromise bill[2] as the rock of our political salvation. The masses of the people of this state so regard it—and it is opposed, so far as I know or believe by those who follow Col. [Thomas Hart] Benton in his eccentric course, and by them alone. The leading organ of Col. Benton's party has denounced it in the language and spirit of an Abolitionist. That you may see how all efforts to adjust the slavery question are treated by those who continually cry *disunion* and *nullification*, I enclose a slip from the Republican which explains itself. The Union and publications of that cast oppose the compromise bill because they are Abolitionists, and a great many others oppose it because Col. Benton opposes it. It may strike you as a strange fact, but it is still quite true that, there are those who have professed all their lives to be Whigs who are following Col. Benton in his eccentric movements.[3]

It would not be quite candid to allow you to infer that I act with the Whig party—and although it is true that on all the great points of party politics I differ widely and radically from the whig party—Yet I am not one of those who will withhold a just homage to whig patriotism for fear of having my party fealty questioned:—and I feel assured that the Democratic party of this state, I mean all those who have not wandered away with Col. Benton in the worship of strange gods, will stand by you and that noble phalanx of patriots who act with you in this crisis with unfaltering firmness. *The people trust to the Compromise bill to save the Country*, and you may infer with what disgust, the intelligent, thinking and patriotic men of the Democratic party contemplate the Course of Col. Benton, and the paltry pretences under which he attempts to cover his very unsatisfactory—not to say, factious, opposition:—and I venture the prediction that unless the President [Zachary Taylor] and his Cabinet change their course, especially in relation to the omnibus bill,[4] they will retire with less of the respect and confidence of the masses than did Mr. [John] Tyler and his cabinet.

God speed the compromise bill.

ALS. ViW. 1. Morrow was judge of the county court of Butler County, Mo., from 1855-58. Goodspeed, *History of Southeast Missouri*, 377. 2. Clay to Combs, Jan. 22, 1850; Speech in Senate, May 8, 1850. 3. Benton wanted California admitted to the Union without any other measures "tacked" to the bill. See, for example, Speech in Senate, April 8, 1850; Remark in Senate, April 11, 1850; Comment in Senate, April 17, 1850. Benton, in effect, became a leader of the forces supporting the Taylor administration's position in opposition to Clay's compromise proposals. The St. Louis *Missouri Republican*, the leading newspaper in Missouri, opposed Benton on this issue while the St. Louis *Union*, which had been formed in 1847 by a combination of the *Reporter* and the *Missourian*, supported him. Hudson, *Journalism in the United States*, 202; Chambers, *Old Bullion Benton*, 316-17, 348, 357-72. 4. Clay to Combs, Jan. 22, 1850.

Remark in Senate, June 15, 1850. When Sen. John P. Hale offers an amendment to the Compromise bill to put the appellate power of the Supreme Court on the same footing in the territories as in the states, Clay declares that "there is no well-founded objection" to Hale's amendment, and "I am glad to see arising in him a spirit of improvement of the bill. At first, he and some of his cooperators wanted to make the bill as bad as possible, and voted against it piecemeal or as a whole. But this is an effort to improve it, and I think the Senator ought to be encouraged in it. [A laugh.]"

After much negative discussion, including Sen. Daniel Webster's comment that "we have never treated the judicature of the Territories the same as the judicature of the States," Clay announces that "I am inclined still to think that the amendment is a proper one." Understands that Hale's object "is to give a jurisdiction by way of writ of error and appeal from the territorial courts to the Supreme Court, to the same extent, and that only, which exists in the courts of the United States. . . . In the original bill, as it stands, there is a limitation to the writ of error and appeals to a certain amount of money—$1,000." If the bill is not amended, a question that arises "under the Constitution, or laws, or treaties of the United States, that the party is entitled, under the [Federal Judiciary] act of 1789," cannot be brought before the Supreme Court "unless there is an amount of $1,000 involved."

When Sen. Daniel Webster points out that the "law of 1789 limits appeals from the circuit court to the Supreme Court, to cases in which the amount in controversy exceeds $2,000, let the question be what it may," Clay agrees he is "certainly right," but asserts that Hale "is right as to the object, though he has not used the proper phraseology to embrace his object." Now, if "a constitutional question arises before the territorial courts, unless the amount in value is $1,000, you cannot bring that constitutional question to the Supreme Court of the United States." Suppose "a slave carried into the Territories . . . sues for his freedom there" and "His value is not a thousand dollars. You could not settle the question of constitutional right, under the bill as it now stands." Hale's object "to make the right of appeal and writ of error coextensive in the territorial courts with what they are in circuit courts of the United States" is one "I think . . . should be accomplished—to secure the power of testing in the Supreme Court of the United States the right, under the Constitution, to carry slaves into the Territory."

After disposition of Hale's amendment, Sen. Pierre Soule wishes to ascertain the views of the Committee of Thirteen and other supporters of this measure concerning "the condition in which this [Compromise] bill will place the Territories about to be organized," especially Utah and New Mexico, "when they shall present themselves for admission." Wonders if they will "be admitted, whatever the people of the same decide about slavery." Clay asserts that "the committee has expressed itself upon that subject—the majority of the committee, I mean. I am not able to recollect whether it was a unanimous vote of the committee, with sufficient exactness." Clay then reads that section of the committee report that declares the Wilmot Proviso to be " 'Totally destitute . . . of any practical import' " and asserts that " 'the true principle which ought to regulate Congress in forming territorial governments for each newly-acquired domain is to refrain from all legislation' " on slavery, " 'leaving it to the people of such Territory, when they have attained to a condition which entitles them to admission as a State, to decide for themselves the question of the allowance or prohibition of domestic slavery.' " Does not support Soule's amendment to specify that Utah and New Mexico be admitted "with or without slavery, as their constitutions may prescribe at the time of their admission," because Soule "assumes that Utah, with the limits assigned to the Territory of Utah, is to be admitted as a State," which may "be expedient or not." Additionally, Clay objects to "incorporating in the bill a mere obstruction," questioning the "practical utility of urging any formal expression by the Senate of such an opinion at this time, with a view to control the legislation of the Congress of that distant day."

Later, when Sen. David R. Atchinson urges that a vote be taken on Soule's amendment, Clay expresses the hope that "there will be no protraction of the debate. I think we can get a vote." If Soule's amendment seems to "meet with general favor, I should, individually, have made no objection to it. There is a class of amendments, on one side and on the other, which I should neither advocate nor oppose on my own account. I am only anxious that they should be disposed of. I do not attach to them the value which those who advocated them do, nor do I attribute to them the pernicious effects which their opponents attribute." *Cong. Globe*, 31 Cong., 1 Sess., Appendix, 897-99, 902-3. For Sen. David Atchinson (Whig, Mo.), see *BDAC*. For the Federal Judiciary Act of 1789, see 1 *U.S. Stat.*, 73-93.

From JAMES BROWN CLAY Lisbon, Portugal, June 18, 1850

At last, after a month and a half of suspense and expectation, and after having had the duplicate of instructions to be brought by him, for more than two months, I have advice from Gibraltar that Commodore [Charles W.] Morgan with the Frigate Independence & Steamer Mississippi, will certainly be here today or tomorrow.[1]

The proposition to arbitrate all our claims[2] which I informed you was not distinct enough, upon a reperusal (in Portuguese) I found to be sufficiently so; I answered that I had no authority to accede to it; in fact my instructions I consider positively against such a mode of settlement, and even were they not so, I should not consent to that course after [J.C. de] Figaniere [e Morao] had told you that he & the M[inister] of F[oreign]. Affairs [Count Tojal] considered some of the claims just—it would be ridiculous to arbitrate claims which both they & I regard as just.

My final note I have already long since prepared; in it I recite the efforts we have made to have justice done & the result of them, and temperately but firmly & in strict accordance with my instructions, demand to know for the last time whether they will pay or not, & inform them that if I do not receive a satisfactory answer in 20 days I am ordered to demand my passports.

This government is acting upon these false hopes. First, that ours will accede to the proposition to arbitrate. Second that there will be a change in the Ministry at Washington,[3] and third that Congress will not support the Executive in causing payment of the claims.

Before transmitting my final note, it is my intention as soon as the Ships arrive, to request a private interview with the Minister, in which I shall endeavour, to remove his false impressions, to do which I shall shew him parts of your several letters,[4] and will give him a last opportunity to propose to settle with some little grace. If I am not able to convince him of the utter futility of his hopes, then I look upon it as certain that they will let me go away; I do not despair of being able to do this. The Government has got itself into a scrape with the Cortes, by denying that there is any serious difficulty with us, and insisting on the demotion of their Minister at Washington to the Second grade, so that if I am suffered to go away, and our Govt. orders either blockade or reprisals, it would be a death blow to the [Antonio Bermudo da Costa] Cabral Ministry, and in my opinion might endanger the crown itself.

I shall be greatly relived when it is all over as I assure you, I would not again undergo the anxiety and suspense I have had for the last six weeks, for a years salary.

We have just received news of the Cuba invasion, which has created here a great sensation. I understand that the Spaniards are sending a force of some 6000 men in steamers from Cadiz to Cuba. I am sure that our Govt. will do all it can to control our people, but I do not believe it can prevent the loss of the island to Spain.[5]

We hear very seldom from you, and none from Ashland; Mary [Mentelle Clay] & Thomas [Hart Clay] have each written once in the last ten months, and except from George Trotter, I do not think we have heard from Lexington this year.

I wrote you something about the sale of my house in one of my last letters! I wish it could be made on good terms, as when we return to America I am determined on a farm.[6]

If the Commodore arrives this evening I will open my letter to inform you.

Susan [Jacob Clay] joins me in affectionate love to you.

ALS. DLC-TJC (DNA, M212, R11). 1. Morgan arrived in Lisbon on June 19. Bemis, *American Secretaries of State*, 6:36. 2. Clay to Clayton, June 7, 1849. 3. For rumors of a change in Taylor's cabinet, see Clay to Stevenson, April 25, 1850. 4. For example, Clay to James B. Clay, Dec. 29, 1849, Jan. 2 and 8, March 13, 17, and 25, 1850. 5. Speech in Senate, May 21, 1850. 6. James B. Clay to Clay, May 26, 1850.

From Elijah F. Nuttall, New Castle, Ky., June 18, 1850. Describes the feelings "of the people of this County [Henry] upon the subject of the compromise proposed by the committee of thirteen [Speech in Senate, May 8, 1850]." Assures Clay that "We have taken great pains, to ascertain whether patriotism has, in this hour of trial and perhaps peril got to so low an ebb as that one single man could be found who would raise his voice against the adjustment of this disturbing question, and I declare to you upon the Honor of a man that out of the nineteen hundred and sixty voters in this County not one is opposed to your plan of adjustment." Believes that "Politicians who desire to keep up excitement" to promote their presidential aspirations "are preparing for themselves an unenviable but certain doom," while "the people who at last are most interested, will rejoice when they learn that this great question is settled in peace and brotherly love." Admires "a great party Struggle involving great cardinal principles when conducted upon elevated grounds," but loathes the "low and contemptible political *Huxtering* that would endanger a government that the chances of a party to administer it might be increased." Those who hope to rule "ought in the true spirit of patriotism to make it certain that we will have a government to be administered." Worries about the influence of "Northern & Southern Ultraisms." Believes that "The south ought to be satisfied with the committees plan—They can never get more. The north ought to concede it because I am well satisfied the south will never Take less." Asserts that if it were not for the political machinations of presidential hopefuls, "The report of the committee would be adopted in twenty four hours." Praises Clay's noble exertions in behalf of our country . . . you will be hailed by your admiring countrymen as you were after the Missiouri Compromise." ALS. ViW.

Elijah F. Nuttall, a Henry County lawyer, served at various times in both houses of the Kentucky legislature. Maude Johnston Drane, *History of Henry County Kentucky* (n.p., 1948), 239, 241, 244.

Remark in Senate, June 18, 1850. In discussions on the Compromise bill, Sen. Jefferson Davis offers an amendment that would declare as repealed "all laws or parts of laws, usages or customs, preexisting in the Territories" acquired from Mexico that "restrict, abridge or obstruct the full enjoyment of any right of person or property" guaranteed by the U.S. Constitution. Sen. John P. Hale amends the amendment by adding "That the laws abolishing slavery in the said Territories are excepted from the repealing clause."

Clay asserts that he "shall vote neither for the proviso nor for the amendment to which the proviso is proposed to be attached." The proviso "is exactly equivalent to the enactment." Says he had thought "there had been a clear understanding . . . that the Senate would not decide itself upon the *lex loci* as it respects slavery; that the Senate would not allow the territorial legislature to pass any law upon that question; in other words, that it would leave the operation of the local law or of the Constitution of the United States upon that local law to be decided by the proper and competent tribunal—the Supreme Court of the United States." The amendment's effect is "to declare that the *lex loci* shall be abrogated. . . . that is to say, if there be any local law contravening the Constitution of the United States, such local law shall be abolished; but if there be any such local law, the Constitution by its own operation *per se* abolished that law." Is willing to leave the entire question "to the Judiciary of the United States itself; but I am not willing to abolish the local law before that decision is given," because it may be "unnecessary, if the Constitution does entitle any man to carry any description of property into these Territories." *Cong. Globe*, 31 Cong., 1 Sess., Appendix, 916.

To JAMES O. HARRISON Washington, June 19, 1850

I duly received your favor of the 6th inst. transmitting two letters, one addressed to Mr [Daniel] Webster and the other to Gen [Lewis] Cass. From the former of these gentlemen I have received an answer which is herewith transmitted.[1] I have not yet received the reply of Gen. Cass, but when I obtain it I will forward that also. I am afraid that the great length & labor of this session will prevent his acceptance of your invitation.

I am very glad to hear that you have organized an agricultural association whose exhibitions are to take place at Lexington.[2] The great difficulty of our people, is the want of perseverance & also too much disposition to be dissatisfied with the distribution of prizes. If these difficulties can be surmounted great good may be accomplished. The location of Lexington is admirable for the purpose & the accommodations which it affords are fully adequate to any number of strangers & visitors that may choose to attend the fair. In the event of the non-compliance of Gen. Cass with your wishes, I am afraid it will be very difficult to prevail on any other member of Congress to visit Lexington in September.[3]

We are still almost exclusively engrossed by the consideration of questions connected with slavery. I wish I could speak with more confidence of the result of any of the measures pending before Congress. I have not relinquished the hope of the ultimate passage of the Compromise Bill reported by the committee of thirteen.[4] But it has to encounter a powerful opposition, first from the Abolitionis[ts] & Free-Soilers of the North—secondly from the ultra Southern men & last, though not least, from the Administration.[5] They charge the measure as containing elements of incongruity, but it is not half as incongruous as the elements of opposition to it.

I beg you to make my warm regards to Margaret . . . [6]

LS. DLC-James O. Harrison Papers (DNA, M212, R21). 1. In a letter to James O. Harrison and Henry T. Duncan, dated June 14, 1850, Webster declined their invitation. Wiltse, *Papers of Daniel Webster, Correspondence*, 7:397. 2. A new agricultural society had been formed in Lexington. Officers, elected on April 13, 1850, included Benjamin Gratz as president and James O. Harrison as one of the directors. Perrin, *History of Fayette County*, 120-21. The agricultural fair was held Oct. 1-5, 1850. Lexington *Kentucky Statesman*, Sept. 18, Oct. 5, 1850. 3. Cass did not attend. 4. Clay to Combs, Jan. 22, 1850; Speech in Senate, May 8, 1850. 5. For the Taylor administration's plan for dealing with the slavery/territorial issue, see espec. Speech in Senate, May 13, 1850. 6. Harrison's wife, Margaretta Ross Harrison, was the daughter of Lucretia Hart Clay's sister, Eliza Hart Ross. Armstrong, *Biographical Encyclopedia of Kentucky*, 140.

Remark in Senate, June 19, 1850. During consideration of the Compromise bill, Sen. Isaac P. Walker offers an amendment that would strike out of the 10th section a clause that would prohibit the lands and property of non-residents from being taxed at a higher rate than that belonging to residents.

Clay believes the amendment "if adopted, would be in violation of the uniform principle and practice of the Government. As far as I recollect, the Government has never made any discrimination, in the imposition of taxes, between the lands of residents and non-residents." If, in fact, "there is some inconvenience, some hardships, on the part of the residents," they "derive also the principle benefit of the government in the protection which it affords." Points out that a non-resident is subject to a " 'road-tax,' " yet "he derives no benefit. The benefit is derived by those who travel over the road." Since "The advantages which the non-resident derives are altogether incidental and indirect . . . he ought not to be taxed for these more than the resident is for his direct and positive advantages." The amendment is defeated, but no vote is recorded. *Cong. Globe*, 31 Cong., 1 Sess., 1255.

Also on this day, Sen. Joseph R. Underwood offers an amendment to allow "for a suit to be instituted by the State of Texas against the United States, in the Supreme Court of the United States. . . . in the event that Texas rejects these propositions" in the Compromise bill for the settlement of her boundary with New Mexico. Sen. Daniel Webster objects, arguing that "if any provision shall be made, it . . . should depend only upon the action of this Government," and not Texas, "to take some other mode of settling the question."

Clay attempts to suggest an adjustment "so that Texas may, if she pleases, institute the suit; but the Government, in the event of her not doing it, shall bring a bill at a required time. . . . If put in this form—in the alternative—I should have no objection to it."

After much more discussion, Clay wishes "to make two or three observations." First, "I do not think the amendment proposed by my colleague will be found to be necessary. It provides for a contingency, and is a contingency upon a contingency." Favors "the principle of the amendment" but would prefer "a joint resolution afterwards as a distinct measure" that would "accomplish everything, without . . . obstructing the course of the bill itself" any further.

Complains that "a hundred times almost . . . I have been quite ready to yield, and say, for one, I withdraw from all further efforts for the passage of this bill. I never have seen a measure so much opposed—so much attempted to be thwarted. We exhibit a spectacle of a *see-saw*, putting the least weight on one side, while there is an obstruction of the balance on the opposite side." Instead of seeking harmony, "difficulties almost insuperable, upon points of abstraction, upon points of no earthly practical consequence . . . discourage the stoutest heart." Hopes all further amendments can be completed quickly, and "I hope by Thursday next we may come to a final decision of the bill."

When Sen. John M. Berrien objects to Clay's complaint, claiming that he had not presented "any measure which I did not conceive to be incumbent on me in the discharge of my duty," Clay assures him that "there is no necessity for the observations he has made." Nonetheless, regrets that Berrien's "great name, throughout the whole progress of this bill, has been everywhere in the country exhibited in opposition to this measure." Does not doubt Berrien's "determination to do what, in his judgment, he may deem right," nor does he believe Berrien has any intention "of thwarting this measure or prolonging it." Did hope, however, that Berrien had "abandoned the idea of restricting the representatives of California to one, or of objecting to her admission as a State." Desires only to "come to some conclusion upon the bill, which has already occupied two months of the . . . session." *Cong. Globe*, 31 Cong., 1 Sess., Appendix, 922-23, 929.

Remark in Senate, June 20, 1850. Presents the resolutions of "a Convention [Stevenson to Clay, June 12, 1848] in the State of Kentucky. . . . composed of one hundred delegates, representing all parts of the State. They formed a constitution, which was submitted to the popular voice" and reassembled "after the people . . . passed upon" it. The convention, "composed of rather a large portion of Democrats, and the residue Whigs," adopted resolutions [Clay to Combs, December 22, 1849] earnestly deprecating "whatever threatens the integrity of that venerated charter of our liberties" and approving "the patriotic endeavor of the Committee of Thirteen to reconcile the existing differences between the northern and southern sections of our Confederacy." Expresses his "great pleasure" in noting that "during a life which is not very short, I have never known the people of Kentucky so united, to a degree almost amounting to unanimity, as they are in favor of the report of the Committee of Thirteen of this body." The resolutions are received and laid upon the table. *Cong. Globe*, 31 Cong., 1 Sess., 1263-64.

SPEECH AT ELLICOTT'S MILLS, MD. June 23, 1850

The ringing of that bell, (the bell of the Catholic Church was then ringing for vespers,) admonishes us that this is no time for a speech, if I had the wish to make one, or you to hear it. Respect for the day forbids it. But I have sometimes had the character attributed to me of a peace-maker. In that character I trust I may make a few not unwelcome remarks on a subject that, I am sorry to learn, has caused some of you to loose [*sic*, lose] your temper, and to hold an indignation meeting.

I understand that you censure Mr. [Robert] Hare because I did not stop on my way through your town, to receive your friendly greetings.[1] Now, for this omission I am to blame, and against me must your indignation be directed, and not against Mr. Hare.

I left Washington and reached the Relay House on Friday morning, jaded and exhausted with the exciting duties in which, as you know, I have been engaged.[2] I was on my way to Col. [Charles] Carroll's [III] by his kind invitation, where I desired to enjoy quiet and the air of the country. I desired to pass through without attracting notice. At the Relay House I accepted a seat in Mr. Hare's carriage, and learned from him afterwards that some arrangements had been made by you to express those sentiments of confidence and respect for which I have been indebted to you on former occasions, and which, under other circumstances, it would be most pleasant to me to receive. I requested Mr. Hare to avoid such a meeting, and said to him: Mr. Hare, if I am to be taken to an exciting meeting, I request that you will turn back your carriage to the Relay House. So if any one is to blame it is myself; and on me must your displeasure fall, and not on my friend, Mr. Hare.

Copy. Printed in the Boston *Daily Advertiser*, June 28, 1850. 1. Clay had stopped in Ellicott City, Md., on June 21 to have breakfast with Mr. Hare while enroute to visit Charles Carroll III. The citizens of Ellicott City had determined to give him a reception which he avoided with Hare's help because of his health. *Ibid.* 2. Reference is to work on the Compromise of 1850. See Clay to Combs, Jan. 22, 1850.

To WILLIE P. MANGUM Washington, June 25, 1850

Come back to us forthwith, if you possibly can. We shall be hard run, if not defeated in the Senate without your vote.[1] [William K.] Sebastian[2] has come over to us, as is confidently asserted, and as I believe. On the other hand, [John M.] Berrien has left us, and [Jackson] Morton[3] cannot be relied on for the Compromise.

ALS. NcD. Printed in Shanks, *Papers of Willie Person Mangum*, 5:178. 1. Mangum was in North Carolina. For his role in supporting the Compromise of 1850, see *ibid.*, 5:179. 2. For William K. Sebastian (Dem., Ark.), who favored the compromise, see *BDAC*. 3. For Jackson Morton (Whig, Fla.), who opposed the compromise, see *ibid.*

To HENRY CLAY, JR. [III] Washington, June 26, 1850

I received your letters by Lieut. Pearse,[1] and I was glad to hear directly from you. Genl [Winfield] Scott and Majr Glover[2] had both written to me about you, and spoken of you in favorable terms. I hope you will strive to merit their good opinion. You will find the life of a Cadet a little hard at first but you will come to like it after a while. Upon finishing your course at the Academy,[3] it will be at your option whether you enter the Army or not.

I will send by another letter today or tomorrow a check for $75 of which you will deposite a part & retain a part.[4]

My last accounts from home represent all well. Your uncle John [Morrison Clay] had won two more races at Covington.

I heard as late as the last of May from your uncle James [Brown Clay]. They were all well, and he expected to return home by November.[5]

ALS. Henry Clay Memorial Foundation, Lexington, Ky. Addressed to Henry Clay, Jr. [III] at West Point, N.Y. 1. Possibly Nicholas B. Pearce of Ky. who graduated from West Point on July 1, 1850, and later became a brigadier general in the Confederate Army. USMA, *Register*, 199; *HRDUSA*, 778. 2. Probably a civilian employee at West Point with a militia commission, since there is no record of his having a commission in the regular army or a military position at the academy. Information supplied by Alan C. Aimone, Asst. Librarian for Special Collections, United States Military Academy. 3. Clay to Morehead, Dec. 14, 1848. 4. On June 27,

1850, Clay again wrote, noting that "I send you, according to my promise . . . a Check on N. York for $75, of which you will retain $25. for your personal expences, and place the other fifty in deposite to your credit at the Point." ALS. Henry Clay Memorial Foundation, Lexington, Ky. 5. Clay to Lucretia H. Clay, Dec. 14, 1850.

Remark in Senate, June 26, 1850. Moves "that when the Senate adjourn it adjourn to meet to-morrow at 11 o'clock, and at that hour every day thereafter, until otherwise ordered." Feels that "out of respect for ourselves, out of respect for the country, out of respect for the duty which we owe to the other public business of the country, we should ascertain what is to be the fate of this [Compromise] bill." Makes a telling comparison: "Upon a question as to the organic law of the Government of France, limiting and restricting, to a great extent, the elective franchise, a body composed of upwards of 700 members decided the question in less than ten days, passed the bill, and submitted it to the proper authority to be acted upon. And here we have been nearly two whole months upon a single bill, and if any man can see when the question is to terminate, I own, for one, that I am in utter darkness." Asks for the yeas and nays.

Sen. John P. Hale hopes that "we will not be very quick" to follow the French example since the bill to which Clay referred is an "infamous measure . . . that disfranchises three fourths of the voters of France." Adds that "If the common and ordinary course of legislation had been taken upon this [Compromise] subject, without attempting to force the judgments of individuals to take measures which they looked upon to be reprehensible, for the purpose of obtaining others which they deemed proper, we would have had none of this delay; we should have passed upon these measures months and months ago."

Clay accuses Hale of being "in his usual vocation. There has not been a proposition for dilatory proceedings in relation to this bill, since its origin to this moment, to which he has not lent his aid, his countenance, and his support." Criticizes Hale for his "great perversion of the purpose for which I cited" the French proceedings. Disagrees with Hale that the delay "has resulted from the fact of the connecting together of measures, contrary to the usual mode of parliamentary proceeding. . . . I vindicated the conjunction of the measures in a manner which no one has yet ventured to answer [Speech in Senate, April 8, 1850; Remark in Senate, April 11, 1850; Comment in Senate, April 17, 1850]." Asserts that "upon the final passage of any such combined measure every man must decide for himself, and according to his own conscientious convictions, whether he will vote for the combined measures or not; just as in the case of a tariff, combining thousands of items, with some of which he is satisfied, and to others of which he is opposed." Urges the country to "decide, and decide it by the yeas and nays upon propositions for adjournment, who has procrastinated this measure. . . . I trust that a majority, a large majority, of the Senate will be found in favor of restoring the 11 o'clock hour for meeting and going on with this business until we can arrive at a conclusion." After more discussion, Clay's motion is approved by a vote of 30 to 17. *Cong. Globe*, 31 Cong., 1 Sess., 1298-99.

Remark in Senate, June 28, 1850. Sen. William L. Dayton resumes his comments on his amendment concerning "the sum to be paid to Texas, specifying that for the sum that may be paid she shall relinquish all her public lands." He does not propose "to move it until the sum shall have been fixed upon," however.

Clay reasserts "that I do not intend to fill the blank in the bill until it is on its third reading. On reaching that stage, I will move to fill the blank with the amount to be paid to Texas, and then the question will be open."

Later, before the Senate proceeds to its executive business, Clay hopes "that it will meet the general concurrence of the Senate, on both sides of the Chamber—and I have had a consultation with several gentlemen opposed to the bill, and they have concurred in the suggestion—that we should now indicate a day when we shall decide the final question on the engrossment of the bill." Suggests a date four business days from now. When Sen. John Bell argues that "neither I nor other gentlemen who desire to address the Senate will have sufficient time to express themselves," Clay then suggests an extension of one day: "There would be great propriety in taking the vote on that day," the Fourth of July. No further action is taken, however, and the Senate adjourns after its executive session. *Cong. Globe*, 31 Cong., 1 Sess., 1314.

From Brantz Mayer, Baltimore, July, 1850. In gratitude for Clay's willingness "to foster those who were following the humbler and quieter walks of literature," presents "as the only tribute I can tender . . . a work designed to illustrate the history and resources of one of those American States which were summoned into the brotherhood of nations by your sympathy and eloquence." Copy. Printed in Brantz Mayer, *Mexico; Aztec, Spanish and Republican: A Historical, Geographical, Political, Statistical and Social Account of That Country* . . . , 2 vols. (Hartford, Conn., 1851), 1:iii. Letter written to dedicate the book to Clay. See also Clay to Mayer, October 4, 1844, and February 20, 1850.

From James A. Bayard, Wilmington, Delaware, July 1, 1850. Acknowledges receipt of "the letters of introduction you were kind enough to favor me with." While hoping Clay "will be gratified in the success of the last and greatest effort you have made for the peace and welfare of our common country," regrets that Delaware's senators [Presley Spruance & John Wales] "are the mere tools of the Secretary of State [John M. Clayton], an able perhaps but certainly not a high principled politician.—That they will misrepresent their constituents, in voting against the Compromise Bill [Clay to Combs, January 22, 1850], they will find to their Cost, should such be their course."

After a meeting held in favor of the Compromise bill in which "no thought or feeling connected with party" existed, another meeting was "held in support of what is called the President's plan [Speech in Senate, May 13, 1850], & generally to sustain the administration." Explains that "on first taking the question the votes were so equally divided that it was impossible to tell whether the resolutions were carried or defeated, & even on a second trial the majority was very small—No citizen of Delaware addressed the meeting, but it was instructed in its action by a Mr. [Aaron] Clark of New York & Clayton's drill sergeant—Morton McMichael of Phila. They were ashamed of McMichael as much from his known subserviency to Clayton, that I see . . . his name has not been noticed in the publication of the proceedings." Adds, however, that "our Senators will find that in questions involving hazard to the Union, the people of Delaware know nothing of parties."

Expresses his opinion in favor of "the adoption of the Missouri line extended to the Pacific [Clay to Combs, December 22, 1849], but believing that to be unattainable, I would sacrifice any opinion which did not require an abandonment of principle," and views "the bill as report[ed] by you [Speech in Senate, May 8, 1850]" as the "only hope of amicable adjustment." Confesses that since the slavery question "rent asunder the ties which bound the Methodist Church in 1844 [Clay to Unknown Recipient, June 26, 1844], I have dreaded the time . . . it should be brought into the National Legislature—My hopes now rest on your exertions, and influence, & if you fail in arresting the spirit of disunion I shall indeed despair." Regrets he is "not now a representative from my State" so he could help sustain Clay's measures "against the fanatical madness of men of extremes," and deplores the "policy of an administration which in the mere spirit of selfishness treats with levity questions involving the future happiness of millions.—I have no patience with a set of politicians, who following politics as a trade for its power & emoluments are insensible to dangers, which when upon them they are the first to shrink from." Reminds Clay that even "if the result is disastrous . . . there is no evil so great, that it cannot be borne if one is sustained by the consciousness of fully performed duty." ALS. DLC-Thomas Francis Bayard Papers (DNA, M212, R20).

Bayard was, in fact, soon elected to the U.S. House as a Democrat and served from March 4, 1851, to January 29, 1864. *BDAC*. For Spruance (Whig) and Wales (Whig), see *ibid.*

Bayard had given a speech at the non-partisan Wilmington meeting, held on June 22, in support of the compromise. Washington *Union*, June 28, 1850. Sen. Wales presented the resolutions of this meeting to the Senate on June 26, asking that they be printed. On July 3 Wales presented the proceedings of the Wilmington meeting "expressing their approval of the plan recommended by the Executive for the adjustment of the slavery question" and moved that these too be printed. The Committee on Printing to whom both were referred reported on July 6 against printing them. U.S. Sen., *Journal*, 31 Cong., 1 Sess., 420, 436, 438. See also Comment in Senate, July 3, 1850.

To THOMAS HART CLAY Washington, July 1, 1850

I send by this mail a pamphlet, containing a full account of the Circular Saw, and Mr. [Charles B.] Calverts letter.[1]

I think you had better consult with H[enry]. Watkins about it. If he has never seen one in operation it would be very well for him to come if he can and see Mr. Calverts.

Your letter has filled me with uneasiness about John [Morrison Clay], from whom I recd. a short letter dated the day after yours. I wrote him a long letter last week & again to day.[2] I wish you would relieve me by a Telegraphic despatch, if you can, as to the state of his health.[3]

I advised him, besides training his horses, to put some of his young stock in good condition for exhibition at the Lex[i]n[gton] Agric[ultura]l fair in September[4] and I suggested that perhaps you might be able to assist him with some of them, which I wish you could do. I am a good deal debilitated but still struggling for the Compromise.[5] Its fate will I think be decided next week, and I regret to say is uncertain, but I still have hopes.

My love to Mary [Mentelle Clay] & the children[.] P.S. You never informed me if Allegrante[6] had a colt—

ALS. Henry Clay Memorial Foundation, Lexington, Ky. 1. Enclosures not found. 2. Letters not found. 3. Probably a reference to John's recurrent mental problems. See Clay to Henry Clay, Jr., March 17, 1845; Clay to James B. Clay, July 18, 1850. 4. Clay to Harrison, June 19, 1850. 5. Clay to Combs, Jan. 22, 1850. 6. See 8:757; 9:150, 184.

To FRANCIS BOWEN[1] Washington, July 2, 1850

I wish to express my thanks to you for the July number of the North American Review, which you did me the favor to send to me. I have read the 10th. Article with uncommon satisfaction.[2] It is able, liberal and patriotic. If the sentiments, which it expresses so well and so clearly, prevailed more extensively in New England, we should have no difficulty in effecting a satisfactory adjustment of the Territorial & Slavery questions.

I lament that Congress has, during the present Session, justly incurred the rebuke which the Author[3] of the article so severely administers.

ALS. CSmH. 1. For Bowen (d. 1890), editor of the *North American Review* from 1843-53, see *NCAB*, 6:452. 2. The 10th article was entitled, "The California and Territorial Question," *North American Review* (July, 1850), 71:221-68. It praised Clay and Daniel Webster as statesmen and criticized Congress for its failure to pass the Compromise bill. It also castigated Congress for debating at great length bills it then killed and in the last two or three days of a session, passing bills it had not discussed. 3. No author's name was given in the *North American Review*.

Remark in Senate, July 2, 1850. After Sen. David L. Yulee offers a resolution for adjournment *sine die* on August 1, 1850, Clay protests: "There are questions in relation to the formation of territorial governments in our recently-acquired acquisitions from Mexico; there are questions relating to the subject of slavery within the United States and in these Territories; and I do trust that Congress will not think of an adjournment, without some final and decisive adjustment of these questions, or at least the ascertainment of the utter impracticability of settling any of these questions." Believes that "nothing would be more inexpedient than for the Senate at this time to commit itself to any day of adjournment. . . . There is no member of this body more anxious than I am that this session of Congress should come to a termination. But I would as soon quit the field of battle at the moment when our arms were directed against a foreign enemy, and when it was my duty to expose my life to the utmost hazard—I would as soon, aye sooner, flee from such a field of battle, than I would quit my post here." Complains that "we have not had the assistance of the honorable Senator in our endeavors to settle these agitating questions."

Although "There is an idea that, when there is a fixed day of adjournment, some moral or parliamentary coercion will operate upon members, and compel them to accelerate the dispatch of business," believes "that it would be altogether improper and highly imprudent . . . to fix such an early day" and moves that further consideration be postponed for two weeks. After further discussion, the motion to postpone is approved. *Cong. Globe*, 31 Cong., 1 Sess., 1329-30.

Comment in Senate, July 3, 1850. In debate on the Compromise bill [Clay to Combs, January 22, 1850], Sen. John Bell defends Zachary Taylor's plan for California's admission [Speech in Senate, May 13, 1850] as "influenced . . . by the highest and noblest motives of duty and patriotism." Regrets that "that simple point of view, unembarrassed by any considerations of a party or political nature" has been used by the Committee of Thirteen "in a way to present the issue as one between the Executive and Congress."

Clay defends the actions of the committee, reminding Bell that even before speaking in support of the Compromise bill, "I made a speech as conciliatory towards the Administration as it was possible for me to find language to put it in." Notes that "the editor of the *Republic*, the organ of the President," first declared that "the President adhered to his own plan," but then "those editors were dismissed, among other reasons, because they approved of the plan of the committee." Claims that "my speech of the 21st of May was defensive against a prior attack, and a meditated attack, on the part of the Administration and its friends, against the compromise proposed by the committee, and not an attack upon the Administration, further than was necessary to defend our measure and to contrast the two measures." Would have been pleased if Taylor "had adopted one of two courses—either to recommend silence, permitting Congress to act according to its own judgment, or had signified his pleasure in the adoption of the plan of the committee, or any other plan. . . . But war, open, war, undisguised war, was made by the Administration and its partisans," and the May 21st speech merely "was a vindication of the plan of the committee."

When Bell persists in his charges, Clay asserts that "I came here with the most anxious desire to cooperate with the Administration in all public measures, and that desire remains, so far as I can cooperate with them" consistent with his "firm and unshaken determination to act upon my own judgment and convictions of duty." Given "the determination of the Executive to oppose any measure but his own," as well as "the subsequent dismissal of the editors" of the *Republic* "the influence which the Administration had exerted outside of Congress, and inside of Congress, and in both Houses of Congress," knowing that "Secretaries and heads of departments have denounced the measure, and that the President himself in derision had called it the omnibus bill," Clay concludes "that I would defend the measure, and I would defend it against a thousand Presidents, be they whom they may. [Applause.]"

Bell continues to chastise Clay for his "exercise of this moral despotism." When Bell considers the great differences between Taylor's plan and that of the Committee of Thirteen, he wonders "whether Mahomet will go to the mountain, or the mountain shall come to Mahomet." Clay interjects, "I only wanted the mountain to let me alone. [Laughter.]"

After Bell argues that any significant change of policy by Taylor might have furnished his detractors "with the last evidence . . . of his utter unfitness for the high station he occupied, the sacrifice of his own self-respect," Clay notes that "there were two courses" Taylor could have followed. He could "come out in support of the measure"; or, the other course "with which the committee would have been satisfied . . . was a course of forbearance—to say nothing, to do nothing against the measure . . . to leave to Congress its undisturbed and free deliberations upon a great measure, involving the peace and harmony of the country." If Taylor had remained silent, "if war had not been made upon it by all the influences of power, the measure would have passed both Houses without the slightest difficulty. That is the universal opinion." *Cong. Globe*, 31 Cong., 1 Sess., Appendix, 1091-93.

Alexander C. Bullitt and John O. Sargent, editor and assistant editor of the administration newspaper the Washington *Republic*, had printed editorials favoring the Compromise bill and praising Clay. This led to their being forced out and replaced by Allen A. Hall, a supporter of Taylor's plan. Since Bullitt's resignation came on May 14, it is generally assumed that this accounted for the change in Clay's attitude toward the administration from a relatively conciliatory stance in his May 13 speech to one of attack in his May 21 speech. Nevins, *Ordeal of the Union*, 1:319-20; Hamilton, *Zachary Taylor, Soldier in the White House*, 332-33.

Also this day, Sen. John Wales presents the resolutions "of a large public meeting which has been held at Wilmington, in the State of Delaware, of those who are unfavorable to the compromise bill."

Clay responds: "I have received a letter from one of the most eminent citizens of Delaware [Bayard to Clay, July 1, 1850], by which I am informed that upon the question of the adoption of these resolutions, the meeting was so nearly equally divided, that it could not be ascertained on which side the majority lay." Complains that the resolutions "endeavor to assail the bill before the Senate upon the ground of its being, in the popular language of the country—but I hope the term will not be applied in the Senate—an 'omnibus' bill," but the resolutions, "which have a diplomatic odor about them, are much more incongruous in their character." Disagrees with Wales's assertions that the Compromise bill "has not yet produced the concord which its authors hope for," and that "the Senators from the South are not united, or that there is considerable division between them." Adds: "If I know anything of the people of Delaware—and my heart is full of gratitude towards them . . . if influences are not brought to bear upon them, I venture to say they will stand alongside of the vast majority of the States of the Union in favor of this compromise—a majority so great that in some States, Maryland for example, the neighbor, the nearest neighbor of Delaware, and in my own State, it approximates almost to unanimity." Going "beyond the slaveholding States . . . the States of Indiana and Illinois, are almost unanimous in favor of the bill" as well. Disputes the charge that "compromises of former times have failed, as they will fail now"; "When the Missouri compromise [2:699-70, 740-48, 775-77, 785-86, 788; 3:15-22, 26-33, 46-47, 49-50] was proposed, it was everywhere said, and in both Houses of Congress, 'it will bring no peace to the country.' And yet everywhere throughout this nation there was a degree of joy and exultation almost unparalleled in its existence. So it was said when the compromise of the tariff of 1833 [8:604, 619-22, 626-27] was adopted," after which "the manufacturing interest never enjoyed seven years of more profound peace and prosperity than it did during the prevalence of the compromise tariff of 1833." Asserts that "the nation wants repose" and that any "healing measure. . . . will be hailed with a delight which the disturbers of the peace will find themselves wholly unable to destroy or impair."

When Wales claims that his evidence came from an "eye-witness . . . who partook in the proceedings," Clay retorts that his information, too, came "from a citizen of Wilmington." Wales presses his assertion that "these resolutions passed almost unanimously; that the persons who cried 'nay' were the editors of papers in opposition," and rejects Clay's remark "that these resolutions partook of a 'diplomatic odor.' "

When Clay asks—several times—"Who drew them up?" Wales explains only that "petitions favorable to the 'compromise' were got up . . . in Wilmington, and sent into the county of Kent for signature, and not one signature has yet been presented from that quarter." Clay praises Wilmington as "an extremely respectable city, full of industry and energy," but charges that "There was an editor, if I am rightly informed, from the 'North American' press of Philadelphia [Morton McMichael], who went to Wilmington to assist the good people of Delaware in framing these resolutions." Therefore, "with respect to the 'diplomatic odor' which these resolutions emit, I did not locate the diplomacy in Wilmington." Complains, however, that the resolutions "are so comprehensive. . . . Why, their 'omnibus' bill is ten times as large" as the Compromise bill and "covers the foreign diplomacy of the country and the entire Administration." Since "Their 'omnibus' contains matter vastly more incongruous than" the Compromise bill, cannot understand why "they oppose this bill because of the incongruity of the measures of which it is composed." *Cong. Globe*, 31 Cong., 1 Sess., 1332-33. Printed in Colton, *Clay Correspondence*, 6:509-14.

Comment in Senate, July 5, 1850. Sen. John Bell continues [Comment in Senate, July 3, 1850] to attack the Compromise bill, questioning how well it serves Southern interests. Clay notes that he opposed the clause that Bell has particularly criticized, one that prohibited "the local territorial legislature from passing any law to establish or prohibit slavery," and expresses his surprise "that it [was] pressed upon us by southern votes." Does not attach "to that clause any importance as an equivalent," or concession "to the South" for the admission of California as a free state. "The equivalents to the South are to be found . . . in the forbearance of Congress to exercise any power over the subject of slavery; a forbearance to enforce the Wilmot proviso in the Territories; and the advantages resulting to the South from the settlement of the question of the Texan boundary, giving to the South indisputably nine hundred miles on that river, and leaving the whole subject of the Territories open on the subject of slavery, and to be decided when the States shall come to act for themselves."

Later in the deliberations, Bell discounts the notion that the residents of New Mexico are suffering under the "arbitrary sway of a 'lieutenant colonel [Col. John Munroe]' of which we have heard so much." In response Clay reads "a passage from the address of the Delegate from that Territory [Hugh N. Smith] to the people of the Territory" that reminds residents " 'that you have no other than a military government to administer the civil laws with which you came into the Union.' " The delegate had also complained, " 'Is there a civil officer but holds his office by commission from the military officer during his will and pleasure?' " Clay notes that there are other documents as well that "have declared against this military government, and denounced it as a most odious and despotic institution."

When Bell complains that Clay and other compromise supporters have "assumed a position from which they cannot be moved" and that "a distracted country protests, the cause of freedom throughout the world protests, against that position," Clay asserts that "I have never said that this plan, and this plan only, could command my approbation." Insists he will aid "any plan that will pacify the country and give peace and harmony." Rejects Bell's comment that "I would not vote for" California's "admission if this plan were not adopted," but favors some kind of "combination of measures, as containing equivalents and concessions" as "more likely to pass the two Houses of Congress." Having "no attachment to any plan," affirms that "If I saw in the plan of the President [Speech in Senate, May 13, 1850] a plan which would settle these great questions, I would embrace it" or "any plan, come from what source it may" to "accomplish the great objects of peace and concord." Still, believes "that this plan is only likely to succeed." Regarding the separate admission of California, Bell should know "what has been threatened and what is likely to occur in the other House," and it was "upon that information that I avowed that this plan was more likely to pass the House, and be well received at the South and in all parts of the country. . . . if it fails, no other comprehensive scheme is likely to succeed." *Cong. Globe*, 31 Cong., 1 Sess., Appendix, 1095, 1097, 1100-1101.

Also this day, presents two petitions from Pennsylvania, "on the subject in which she feels so deeply interested, and about which there is so much prevailing distress, especially in that State." The citizens of Pittsburgh pray for "an alteration in the tariff of 1846 [Clay to Greeley, June 23, 1846], so as to substitute specific for ad valorem duties" and for "such other modifications as will conduce to give vigor and encouragement to the industrial pursuits of the country." Reads from a letter which states that " 'The suffering of our iron-men is beyond parallel, and unless some relief is afforded soon, the manufacture of iron, I fear, will cease altogether in Clarion and some of the other counties north of this." The petitions are received and tabled. *Cong. Globe*, 31 Cong., 1 Sess., 1341.

To LUCRETIA HART CLAY Washington, July 6, 1850

I am waiting in a state of painful anxiety to hear from home as to John's [Morrison Clay] condition.[1] I have written twice to him lately,[2] and I hope to hear favorable accounts of him.

The weather here is intensely hot, the Thermometer yesterday having been at 92. My health is good, except the debility produced by the heat. I go to Riversdale [*sic*, Riverdale] (Mr. [Charles B.] Calverts) whenever I can and breathe the Country air.

When Congress will adjourn is still uncertain. The distracting Slavery question continues to be the all absorbing subject.[3] When and how it will be decided, God only knows. I hope for a decision, & a favorable decision in the Senate next week, but it is not certain. The breach between the [Taylor] Administration and me on that matter, is getting wider and wider.[4] Their conduct is generally condemned. They seem utterly regardless of public feeling and opinion, and blindly rushing on their own ruin, if not the ruin of their Country.

I think it probable that by this time James [Brown Clay] has left Lisbon.[5] He expects to be at home in Novr. I send you the last letter from him[.][6]

Do tell John to let me know how your money affairs at home are. I hope you will not allow yourself to want for any thing. If there be any deficiency, let him draw on me. My love to him . . .

ALS. DLC-TJC (DNA, M212, R11). 1. Clay to Thomas H. Clay, July 1, 1850. 2. Letters not found. 3. Clay to Combs, Jan. 22, 1850. 4. Speech in Senate, May 13 and May 21, 1850. See also Comment in Senate, July 3, 1850. 5. Clay to Clayton, June 7, 1849. 6. Possibly James B. Clay to Clay, June 18, 1850.

From John Winthrop, Boston, Mass., July 11, 1850. Encloses a statement from "our consul at Havana [Robert B. Campbell] . . . to be communicated to the president

[Zachary Taylor]," but "Since the sad Event which has occurred at Washington, I have been somewhat doubtful where to address myself." Believing Clay "to be the pilot, under whose guidance, we are to weather the storm which now lowers over us; I have taken the liberty of fulfilling my promise to Gen. Campbell by placing his communication in your hands."

Campbell's statement concerned his inability "to ascertain, with any degree of certainty, Either the position, or condition of the prisoners captured on board of the American vessels Georgiana & Susan Loud [Speech in Senate, May 21, 1850]." Has learned from "the Captain General, that the prisoners were 'all alive & would live,' " contradicting the "common rumor of the death of nine of their number." Reports that "the trial of the prisoners was proceeding under a sort of admiralty Court, consisting of the General of Marines (supposed to be very hostile to the Americans,) the 'Fiscal,' a sort of Judge Advocate, or procureur, & one or two other functionaries" who did not allow the prisoners "to go into any defence." Explains that "*the Capt. Genl. had the absolute power to discharge them instanter* without reference to courts, however, Constituted," and that he had acknowledged "that the capture & detention of the prisoners *was illegal*; but, that all access to them or interference in the matter had been peremptorily prohibited." Adds that the Captain General would "receive no demand or message from our Government through the consul . . . looking upon him purely as a commercial agent, & not invested with any diplomatic functions whatever." ALS. DNA, RG45, Miscellaneous Letters Received.

John Winthrop (b. 1809, Boston, Mass.; d. 1886, Newport, R.I.)—the last of the male line of Gov. John Winthrop of Massachusetts—practiced law for a number of years in New Orleans. Mayo, *The Winthrop Family*, 411-13. The "sad event" to which he refers was the death of President Zachary Taylor on July 9. Hamilton, *Zachary Taylor, Soldier in the White House*, 386-99; Bauer, *Zachary Taylor*, 314-20.

To MARY MENTELLE CLAY Washington, July 13, 1850

I received your letter with its inclosure.[1] I wish you would tell your mother not to pay the Abion's account,[2] or any other account against me, without my direction. I will arrange these matters myself.

My health is reasonably good. Mrs. Brand,[3] of Lexington, and her party are now here, and will to-day witness the funeral ceremonies of General [Zachary] Taylor, about which the whole city is in a commotion.[4]

Tell Thomas [Hart Clay] that I think the event which has happened will favor the passage of the Compromise bill.[5]

I can not tell you, my dear Mary, how anxious I am to be at home with your dear mother, my wife [Lucretia Hart Clay], and all of you.

Copy. Printed in Colton, *Clay Correspondence*, 4:610-11. 1. Not found. 2. Reference obscure. 3. Probably Henriette Holley Brand, widow of William M. Brand of Lexington. 4. Winthrop to Clay, July 11, 1850. 5. Clay to Combs, Jan. 22, 1850.

Comment in Senate, July 15, 1850. Sen. William L. Dayton formally offers his amendment to provide a specified sum of money to Texas, in return for which Texas would transfer to the United States "all her right, title, and interest in and to the vacant and unappropriated lands lying within her limits."

After demanding proper parliamentary procedures—"the reading of the clause . . . to be stricken out; the reading of the clause intended to be inserted; and the reading of the clause as it will be if the amendment should be adopted"—Clay reiterates that he "entertained the purpose not to fill in the blank" with the amount "to be paid to Texas until the third reading of the bill, if it should reach that point." Although it is "proper then to fill in any blank that might, to that time, have been left in the bill," he concedes that "there has been a modification of the parliamentary law" in the Senate, "that is, as to filling up blanks." Finding that "no amendment can be made on the third reading of a bill without unanimous consent," now intends "to fill the blank as one of the last amendments that it will be in order to make to the bill before it is ordered to an engrossment." Dayton withdraws his amendment. *Cong. Globe*, 31 Cong., 1 Sess., 1378-80.

Also on this day, Sen. Isaac P. Walker offers an amendment to the Compromise bill, the effect of which would be "to bring the question on the separate admission of California," Clay asks "whether all the labor bestowed by the Committee of Thirteen, and by the Senate, upon this great work of pacification is now to be lost." Views the question as "whether we will take California . . . without compensation: or whether, rejecting the motion, we will take California, with the compensations that are provided in this bill. If the motion prevail, the effect of it will be to bring up instantly the question of the admission of California," for which "there is a large and decisive majority in the affirmative; of which majority . . . I am one." Even if "reduced to the necessity of voting separately and distinctly upon the question of the admission of California, with her whole limits . . . without any compensation, without any equivalent, without any rejection of the principle of the Wilmot proviso, I am prepared to give the vote." But urges senators to consider "whether or not they will take the admission of California with the compensation contained in this bill as it is, or as it may be hereafter modified by subsequent amendments, in preference to what is otherwise inevitable—the separate admission of California. I hope and trust the proposition will be rejected." Would seek a postponement, "But, as I presume the proposition will be rejected by a large majority, I shall not ask this." After more discussion, Walker withdraws his amendment. *Ibid.*, 1379.

Remark in Senate, July 16, 1850. Sen. Thomas J. Rusk challenges those parts of the Compromise bill designed to settle the Texas-New Mexico boundary question, urging the Committee of Thirteen to "Withdraw your claim," and give Texas "the boundaries which properly belong to her."

Clay argues that "It is extremely difficult to reconcile the conflicting opinions prevalent on the subject" of reciprocal cessions between Texas and the United States. The Committee of Thirteen had omitted "to express opinion as to the title" to the land under consideration, because "the object of the bill was to propose a compromise, an adjustment, a settlement of the controverted question." Turns from Rusk's comments to berate Sen. Thomas H. Benton for speaking of the committee's actions with "language to this effect: 'The bill is caught *flagrante delicto* . . . in the very act of perpetrating its crime, in the very act of auctioneering for votes to pass itself.' " Clay asks: "Who auctioneered? . . . the bill, or the Senate, or the committee? . . . I repel the charge as a groundless and unfounded imputation," and declares Benton's language as "remarkable to be used in a deliberative body."

Asks the secretary of the Senate to read a bill introduced by Benton on January 16, 1850, concerning a reduction of Texan boundaries in exchange for "a consideration to be paid her by the United States." Notes that both Benton and the committee used "the very same language" and wishes "to know what is the difference in principle between the bill of the Senator and the bill reported by the committee." Although "more land is purchased by the bill proposed by the Senator. . . . In principle they are all the same." Feels "ashamed . . . when any one will get up and suppose any amount of money offered in the shape of an appropriation for legitimate purposes . . . can be supposed capable of operating on the cupidity of members" of either House. Repels "any charge of the kind" and expresses his pride in his association with the Committee of Thirteen, which shall be vindicated "from any aspersion which may be made against the purity of their motives or purposes."

Challenging Benton's assertions concerning the southern boundary of New Mexico and the northern boundary of Texas, "I contend that it is at *El Paso,* or possibly about a league above it." Benton's sources of information, including "the maps of [Alexander von] Humboldt and General [Zebulon] Pike" and "the journals of the travels of American officers" are "imperfect, loose, and unsatisfactory," in part because "the boundaries of the various provinces and subdivisions of Mexico . . . were scarcely ever marked with any certainty."

Presents "authentic and incontrovertible documents as to the fact of the true line of New Mexico crossing at El Paso," including a "copy of a decree made by the Congress of Mexico" in 1824 "before any question could arise." Notes that the Treaty of Guadalupe Hidalgo [Clay to Beatty, April 29, 1847] "contains an express allusion to the line of El Paso, as being that which constitutes the southern boundary of New Mexico." There is also "corroborative proof of El Paso being the true boundary, furnished by the present military government of New Mexico." The committee required no "further argument or evidence" and believed that "the testimony is complete that the basis of El Paso . . . is the true line—a line running east and west from El Paso being the true southern boundary of New Mexico."

Feels that the committee's deviations from the true boundary are also justifiable. While Texas desired "to bring within her limits some towns or settlements above El Paso" that wish "to be attached to Texas rather than to New Mexico," the latter "is most abundantly indemnified and compensated by the territory proposed to be included within her limits by the committee's bill." Hopes Benton's amendment will not be adopted and the committee's bill will be accepted.

Benton again challenges Clay's views on the New Mexico boundary, but takes even more serious objection to Clay's personal attack on "my language," asking "which is the worst, the acts or the words—the bill or my language." A sharp exchange ensues, Clay calling Benton to order "for the words that this bill, framed by the Committee of Thirteen, has been caught 'in the very act of auctioneering for votes to pass itself,' " and then adding "the previous words used by the Senator, 'the crime of the bill is that.' "

Clay determines that "I shall not speak of the epithets which have been applied to this bill." Benton "says the boundary runs down to the mouth of the Puerco," while "I say the boundary of New Mexico stops at El Paso. He says that by the proposition we make to Texas we give up 70,000 square miles which belongs to New Mexico, lying south of the line which we have proposed. I say we give up not an acre south of the line. This is the point which is in contest between the Senator from Missouri and myself." Benton "says we cut off New Mexico at the hips—I think that was the classic expression he employed—and gave half to Texas below, and retained the other half above El Paso. I say we do not cut off a foot below El Paso." *Cong. Globe,* 31 Cong., 1 Sess., Appendix, 1261-65. Printed in Colton, *Clay Correspondence,* 6:493-99.

Also on this day after Sen. William H. Seward moves for the reception of resolutions in support of California's immediate admission to the Union and the prohibition of slavery in the territories, approved at a public meeting at Utica, N.Y., Clay inquires "if it was the request of the members of this meeting that these proceedings should be submitted to Congress." Explains that he has "received twenty sets of resolutions from my own State, expressive of opinions in behalf of this compromise; but, none of them expressing a wish that they should be brought before us, I have foreborne to present them." Wants to know if resolutions can be legally received "unless there is the expression of such a request on the part of the meeting that offers them." Informed by the presiding officer that "the rule if rigidly enforced" is "that no Senator is at liberty to present resolutions simply sent to himself and colleagues," Clay hopes others will note "the point with reference to future action; because I have heretofore acted according to the understanding of the rule I have stated" by not presenting numerous resolutions. *Cong. Globe,* 31 Cong., 1 Sess., 1390.

Remark in Senate, July 17, 1850. In debate on the Compromise bill, expresses his wish that "the amendment now pending, and others which I hear are to be proposed, might be acted upon, so that the measure now under consideration might be matured and perfected as far as possible," so it can "be judged of by the Senate . . . and by the country afterwards." "[I]n this oppressive state of the weather, and considering all the anxieties, the pressure, the physical, and mental exertion which this measure has imposed on many of us—and to myself perhaps more than to many others—it is for no personal gratification and with no ambitious subject" that Clay desires "at some suitable time once more to address the Senate." Reminds the Senate that "except in the consideration of incidental questions of amendments. . . . I have cautiously forborne to enter at large into the general subject; but it is my wish yet to do so." Notes that "It is my duty" to do so, but if the Senate "wish, without determining upon all the amendments proposed, to arrive at once at a test question, and to decide upon the fate of the bill, either rejecting its further consideration or continuing it until perfected. . . . I will not address the Senate to-day, but seek an opportunity on some future occasion."

Later, after Sen. Henry S. Foote submits two amendments concerning the Texas and New Mexico boundary and the establishment of the Territory of Colorado, Clay rises for "perhaps a word or two on each" of them. Foote's amendment "proposing an alteration of the line which separates New Mexico from Texas, from twenty miles above El Paso to the 34th degree of north latitude. . . . makes a difference . . . of about two degrees." While preferring "the bill pretty much as it has been reported by the committee . . . I am ready to conform to such a course as will be likely to produce a favorable result." Claims that if such amendments will "reconcile any of those who have heretofore opposed the bill to the bill, I should not only have no objection but should be very glad to go for" them. Also will support Foote's amendment for the establishment of a territory of Colorado, if "California consent to the formation of such a territory" carved out of the "lower part of California . . . south of the thirty-fifth degree of north latitude," especially if such action will "gain any friends to the bill." *Cong. Globe*, 31 Cong., 1 Sess., Appendix, 1270-72.

To JAMES BROWN CLAY Washington, July 18, 1850

I have received several letters from you of late, the last dated about a month ago, when you were hourly expecting the arrival of Commodore [Charles W.] Morgan.[1] I hope that the presence of his Squadron in the port of Lisbon may facilitate the success of your negotiations, 'tho' I fear it will not.[2]

You will have heard of the death of Genl [Zachary] Taylor.[3] President [Millard] Fillmore succeeds him. The old Cabinet has resigned, and a new one will be announced in a few days.[4] My relations to the new Chief are intimate and confidential.

The Compromise bill is yet undecided[5] and its fate is uncertain but will [manuscript torn; lines missing] about a fortnight & return to Washn.

Every thing is pretty much in statu quo at home. I was alarmed about John [Morrison Clay] some days ago,[6] but later accounts have relieved me. He had won four or five races with Yorkshire's get, and the excitement, I fear, was too much for him. Yorkshire has made quite a good season at $30.

I have frequently sent to you letters from home, and I am surprized that they should not have reached you[.]

I do not hear of any chance of selling your house and lot—[7]

I shall be very glad when you get back; and I feel at a loss where to direct this letter; but I will give it a chance to reach you.

My love to Susan [Jacob Clay] and all your [manuscript torn.]

AL, manuscript torn. DLC-TJC (DNA, M212, R11). 1. James B. Clay to Clay, June 18, 1850. 2. Clay to Clayton, June 7, 1849. 3. Winthrop to Clay, July 11, 1850. 4. For Taylor's cabinet, see Clay to Pierse, Feb. 16, 1849. Fillmore's new cabinet consisted of Sec. of State Daniel Webster; Sec. of the Treasury Thomas Corwin; Sec. of War Charles M. Conrad; Attorney General John J. Crittenden; Postmaster General Nathan K. Hall; Sec. of the Navy William A. Graham; Sec. of the Interior Thomas M.T. McKennan (briefly), followed by interim Daniel C. Goddard, and then Alexander H.H. Stuart on Sept. 12, 1850. Rayback, *Millard Fillmore*, 242-46. 5. Clay to Combs, Jan. 22, 1850. 6. Clay to Thomas H. Clay, July 1, 1850. 7. James Brown Clay to Clay, May 26, 1850; Clay to James Brown Clay, Oct. 27, 1850.

To Charles B. Calvert, "Riverdale," Prince Georges County, Md., July 19, 1850. Thanks Calvert "for your kind offer of Tomatoes," but explains that the Washington market" is well supplied, and there is no occasion of drawing on the resources of Riversdale [*sic*]." Wishes he knew "when I shall be able to make my contemplated Speech [Speech in Senate, July 22, 1850]. . . . I may deliver it tomorrow or next da[y.]" Complains of the "very oppressive" heat and envies Calvert "the pleasant breeze[s] of Riversdale." ALS, manuscript torn. Prince Georges County Historical Society.

Comment in Senate, July 19, 1850. After Sens. William R. King and Andrew P. Butler express their deep concerns about the Compromise bill, Clay undertakes the "very painful duty" of making "some response to the argument of the two Senators." Feels "no mortal man has ever before, in any deliberative body, been placed in such a condition as I have been in connection with this subject" and cannot decide "whether the embarrassments which I encounter from the open enemies of the bill, or those which have arisen from gentlemen disposed to be friendly to it, are greatest."

Advises King that "the power of Congress to reject the admission of California *in toto*, to treat the country as a Territory, without the organization or form of a State, to reject it in whole or reject it in part, to remit the Senators and Representatives who have been deputed to this Congress by California" is "incontestable." Considers King's difficulty with accepting the Compromise bill not "as a question of power . . . but a mere question of expediency." While the power to grant statehood should be "exercised and regulated . . . by a sound discretion," asserts that "there is no limitation upon the power to admit a State into the Union."

Informs Butler that his supposition "that it was a constitutional prerequisite that there should be a territorial government. No such thing." This requirement "is not to be found in the Constitution," only "in the practice of the Government."

Butler interrupts to say that he had only contended that people residing in the territories or on the public domain had no "faculty to form for themselves a constitution, without the previous assent of Congress."

Clay agrees that such people "have not . . . the power or the right to do it; but, if they do it, and Congress chooses to waive the irregularity of their doing it and to admit them, the act of admission retroacts upon the fact of the organization and makes it legal." No matter "what sort of people they are . . . if Congress chooses, upon the presentation of the constitution framed by such people, to admit them, Congress has the power to do so."

Since the "question recurs, then, to a ground of expediency in the exercise of an indisputable power," asks King to give up his resistance to California because of her large size. The state of Texas "even with the reduction of her limits proposed by this bill . . . has an extent of territory far exceeding that of California." Population is not a useful measure either, for who "would make a State so small as Rhode Island or as Delaware? We go by facts, by circumstances, and by the condition of the country" in statehood decisions.

To those who believe "that if you admit California with her proposed limits, you create a danger as to the continuation of the Union," advises that "cut her up as you may, if there is a disposition upon the Pacific to fly off from this Union. . . . that disposition would be common to every State on the Pacific, though that number should be two, three, or four." Moreover, this danger would be "equally applicable to Texas," but it is "not quite so imminent, because of the proximity of Texas to the residue of the Union."

Describes himself as "the guardian, not merely of the rights, and honor and interests of one section, but of all sections," and finds it "perfectly incomprehensible . . . to perceive how the rights or the honor of the South can be appeased by a greater or less extent of territory given to California." Believes that "If the rights—I should rather have said the wishes—of any section of the Union are concerned in the creation of a new State out of the present limits of California, those wishes" would be found "in the North," because "as certainly as the sun rises in the east and sets in the west . . . so surely will the formation of a new State on the shores of the Pacific . . . result in the formation of another free State." Cannot understand, therefore, how "the rights and honor of the South" are to be affected by "the limits of California."

If the issue of California's borders was "an original question and a single question, I might be disposed to look much more carefully into the question than I think it now" deserves. Suspects, however, that "when you come to deduct her mountains and deserts and unprofitable and uncultivatable lands, there will not be left more . . . actual arable land, than is now included in the State of Illinois."

Explains "what commends to my acceptance the limits of California as she presents them. Sir, we are engaged in a great work of compromise. . . . I am now considering the admission of California . . . as a part of a system, as part of a whole, as part of a scheme of accommodation and settlement of these great questions, to restore harmony and to put an end to this discord and division." Is disposed "even to admit the State with her extensive limits, considering it as a part of a great whole, which whole is to carry the balm of peace and contentment to a distracted country." Moreover, if a new territory is created "by cutting off all south of 35° 30′," the "Representatives from California cannot be admitted" because "one State will have sent Senators and Representatives, and another state, distinct from that which has sent them, is admitted." Separating the California issue from the other questions in the Compromise bill "would destroy the completeness and harmony and perfection of the whole system of measures comprehended in the bill before the Senate."

Turning to Sen. John M. Berriens's observation of "my disposition to judge of amendments without regard to their merits," claims "he did me an injustice." Explains "that there have been some amendments made to this bill which I should not care the pinch of snuff I hold in my fingers, whether I vote pro or con upon. . . . some of these amendments had no merit, and therefore I was indifferent about their fate."

Controverts entirely another of Berrien's positions, "That if Congress admits California, it admits California with her restriction as to slavery, and that admitting California, with her constitution restricted as to slavery, is equivalent to the passage of the Wilmot proviso. I deny it. . . . I am not now speaking of consequences, of effects, but of power, of authority." The "doctrine of the South, and of the Senator from Georgia amongst them, has been, that Congress has no power . . . to impose the interdiction" of slavery, "and that, if Congress does impose it, it is a usurpation of power." Asks, "Now, sir, with regard to admitting a State having of itself inserted an article prohibiting slavery. Does Congress pass upon that article? . . . If there are provisions of a local and municipal character, provided they do not impair the republican form of the Government, Congress is not responsible for them one way or the other; it is their own affair." Reminds Berrien that "one among the wisest and most eminent southern men," John C. Calhoun, "not three years ago . . . declared the doctrine to be that a State, when forming for herself a constitution, and proposing to come into the Union, had exclusive power to decide for herself whether she would or would not have the institution of slavery." Puts no faith in the argument "that when Congress admits a State, and that State has interdicted slavery, that therefore Congress has interdicted slavery." Berrien has "confounded usurpation and lawful authority."

Admits "I am, as might be well supposed, anxious for the passage of this measure," but does not care for "any credit or honors which might accrue from its passage. . . . Man or mankind have no honors or offices in their gift which I expect, which I want, which I desire." Wishes "whilst I linger yet a few years here, to perform all the duties and all the obligations which result from my connection with that society of which I am an humble member." Will accept "these measures in any form—yes, willing to take them in the conjoint form in which they are presented, or in a separate form, or in any mode." Cites "the God-like object of restoring peace and contentment and harmony" as the end that "animated me, without any desire at my time of life to add any thing whatever to the reputation which I may have acquired by any former public services."

While he cannot vote for his friend's amendment, believing that "the interests of the country require that the bill should be kept as it is," claims that "As to the fate of the measure, I am prepared for it, whatever it may be. . . . I have hoped and believed throughout that it would carry, and I have believed that it ought to carry, because of my perfect conviction of the beneficent effects which would result from the adoption of the scheme. But . . . if defeat awaits it, I will not yet despair of the country. I will still hope that others under better auspices, with more good fortune than may have attended the labors of the committee and myself, will bring forth some great, comprehensive, healing measure."

Sen. Butler challenges Clay on California once more: "If she is not a State at this time we do not *admit* her as a State, but we *make* her one. That is my proposition."

Clay argues that "California is a State, at this moment, but not a State in this Union. That is my answer. . . . she is a State out of the Union asking for admission as a State into the Union." Admits that "no people have a right to take possession of any portion of the public soil or domain of the United States, and to erect themselves into a commonwealth," but if they do so "and we waive all these irregularities on their part, the moment she is admitted she is a perfect and complete State."

Berrien then admits that Congress has unlimited power to admit new states, but asks Clay "where in the Constitution is found the power of Congress to create new States?" Clay asserts that "the power of Congress to regard California either as a Territory or as a State was incontrovertible. . . . But I say again that she is a State, organized as a State out of the Union, and to be legitimatized or illegitimatized, according to the action and discretion of Congress."

Later, after the amendments under consideration are rejected and the Senate prepares to adjourn for the day, Clay repeats his desire to make "a general reply, in conclusion" to the debate on the Compromise bill. Has reserved this "general summary . . . to the last moment; and I had hoped that there would have been no objection to indulging me in the exercise of that common courtesy, which is accorded on all occasions in legislative bodies to him who has charge of an important measure. Still . . . if it is the pleasure of the Senate to come to a vote at once, I shall acquiesce." If the bill is to be defeated, asks "that it should be by indefinite postponement, rather than by laying it on the table, whence it may be taken up at any time; for really, the state of my health is such as to render it absolutely necessary for me to repair to some sea-bathing place, so as to invigorate it a little." Means to propose an amendment "to fill up the blank in regard to the amount to be paid to Texas," but still believes "we may arrive at a definite conclusion by Tuesday next." *Cong. Globe*, 31 Cong., 1 Sess., Appendix, 1398-1402, 1404. Printed in Colton, *Clay Correspondence*, 6:516-28.

California had designated William M. Gwin (Dem.) and John C. Fremont (Free Soil Dem.) as her U.S. senators and Edward Gilbert (Dem.) and George W. Wright (Indep.) as her representatives. *BDAC*.

To WILLIAM N. MERCER Riverdale,[1] Prince Georges County, Md., July 21, 1850

I have intended and wanted, for some time past, to write to you, but I have been almost afraid to approach you on a subject upon which I am sure all your anxiety is painfully excited, and in regard to which I feel the deepest solicitude—I scarcely need say it is the state of the health of dear Anna [Mercer].[2] I had heard through Mr. [Rezin D.] Shepherd & others such accounts of it as to create in my mind great alarm and the most serious apprehensions. But as, in a letter which I received from her several months ago,[3] she said nothing about it, and as you too had been silent in regard to it, in the letters I recd. from you, I hoped that there was exaggeration in the intelligence which had reached me; and I was more disposed to confide in this hope, because, if her condition had been really what it was stated to me to be, I did not suppose that the White S[ulphur]. Springs were suitable to her. I sincerely hope that it may turn out that I was misinformed; but I pray you to relieve my anxiety if you can, by transmitting to me more favorable information.

My own experience in life has unhappily been that, in the dispensations of an inscrutable Providence, those cherished objects, on which the greatest amount of my affection was placed have, one by one, been taken from me. I am afraid that, in this sad experience, I do not stand alone. I have felt it nevertheless to be my duty to bow with resigned submission to irreversible decrees, and to trust that what has been ordered by an Allwise and Merciful God has been designed for the best, afflicting and incomprehensible as it may be to me.

I have borne the seven months toil and arduous labor through which I have passed far better than I could have anticipated; but I begin to feel the debilitating effects of incessant and anxious exertion; and as soon as the compromise measure is disposed of,[4] without waiting the adjournment of Congress, I purpose passing two or three weeks at New Port [*sic*, Newport, R.I.][5] where my health derived so much benefit last summer.[6]

That measure will, I think, be definitively decided in the Senate during the current week. Its fate is not entirely certain; but I have all along hoped and believed, and still hope and believe that it will pass. The event of the death of Genl. [Zachary] Taylor, however lamentable it may be in its private aspects, will not be unfavorable to the Compromise.[7]

The new President [Millard Fillmore] has commenced his administration under some good auspices. I believe him to be eminently patriotic, honest and intelligent. And he has wisely dispensed with all the old Cabinet, whose unpopularity, whether merited or not, would have greatly endangered the success of his Administration. The new Cabinet I think on the whole well composed.[8]

I request you to present my affectionate regards to Anna and Miss [Eliza] Young.

ALS. LU-Ar. Addressed to Mercer at White Sulphur Springs, Va. 1. Charles B. Calvert's estate. 2. Clay to Mercer, Nov. 14, 1846. 3. Letter not found. 4. Clay to Combs, Jan. 22, 1850. 5. Clay to Mercer, August 1, 1850. 6. Clay to Stevenson, July 21, 1849. 7. Winthrop to Clay, July 11, 1850. 8. Clay to James B. Clay, July 18, 1850.

Speech in Senate, July 22, 1850. Desires to make "a rapid review of some of the objections that have been made to the adoption of the" Compromise bill. Since "some rather impatient anxiety has been manifested to arrive at the conclusion of this important subject . . . I have risen this morning to perform a duty toward the committee and to the subject which my position prompts me to endeavor to execute." Refers to the efforts of Sen. John P. Hale, who "has upon two occasions moved to lay this bill on the table . . . perfectly secure not merely of the general result" but of "his being cooperated with by all opponents of the bill." Clay appreciates Hale's withdrawing the motions on his request, but does not "desire again to place myself in any attitude of solicitation with regard to the progress and the final disposition of this bill."

Discounts arguments heard "again and again . . . that perfect tranquillity reigns throughout the country, and that there is no disturbance threatening its peace . . . but that which was produced by busy, restless politicians." Claims "I am no alarmist; nor . . . am I very easily alarmed by any human event," but "the tendencies of the times, I lament to say, are towards disquietude, if not more fatal consequences." How can this be a time of "profound peace," when there has been "a convention [Nashville Convention; Clay to Combs, December 22, 1849] representing a considerable portion of one great part of the Republic," which met "to deliberate about measures of future safety in connection with great interests of that quarter of the country." A number of legislatures have already solemnly resolved "that if any one of these measures—the admission of California, the adoption of the Wilmot proviso, or the abolition of slavery in the District of Columbia—should be adopted by Congress, measures of an extreme character . . . would be resorted to." The subject of the "recovery of fugitive slaves . . . has given rise to more irritation . . . through the slaveholding country," which views it as "a great evil, a great wrong, which required the intervention of Congressional power." These subjects, however, "are nothing in comparison to those which have sprung out of the acquisitions recently made from the Republic of Mexico."

Even "minor circumstances of the day intimate danger ahead," such as the establishment of "a sectional paper . . . here to espouse, not the interests of the entire Union, but the interests of a particular section." This paper made "a departure from the truth" by asserting that in Kentucky "there was existing great diversity of opinion upon the subject of the adoption of this measure, and that the Constitutional Convention [of 1849; Stevenson to Clay, June 12, 1848; Clay to Combs, December 22, 1849] . . . had unanimously, or nearly unanimously, rejected a proposition in favor of the compromise. Why, directly the reverse is the fact. . . . for fifty years I have never known so much unanimity upon any question in that State." The Kentucky Constitutional convention "instead of opposing it by a unanimous vote of the body, expressed its approbation of this pending measure, by a unanimous vote [Clay to Combs, December 22, 1849]."

Another one of the "misfortunes of the times is the difficulty in penetrating the northern mind with truth; to make it sensible to the dangers which are ahead; to make it comprehend the consequences which are to result from this or that course." Describes, on the other hand, a pamphlet "containing an exposition of political economy, written in a style well calculated to strike the mind of the masses, but full of errors and exaggeration . . . setting forth in the strongest terms the supposed disadvantages resulting from the existence of this Union to the southern portion of the Confederacy, and portraying in the most lively hues the benefits which would result from separating and setting up for themselves." Many other "concomitant causes" exist, but hopes that those who are "desirous of preserving this Union" will be made aware of the "dangers which really exist, without underrating them on the one hand, or magnifying them upon the other."

In this state of things, Sen. Henry S. Foote's proposal "something more than four months ago" for a Committee of Thirteen [Remark in Senate, March 12, 1850] as "An experiment to restore the harmony of the country met with the most determined and settled resistance." When the committee was finally appointed [Remark in Senate, April 12 and 19, 1850], "among the reproaches which were brought forward" by Sen. John Davis was that "that committee was organized and created by only a bare majority of the Senate." Clay's "sense of duty" prompted him to point out that "upon the constitution of this committee, only about thirty or thirty-one members of the Senate voted at all," because Davis "and others who concurred with him in opposing the constitution of the committee, chose to sit by in sullen silence . . . without voting, as it was their duty to do."

Of the committee's "composition it does not become me to speak. . . . The country, the Senate will judge of that." Nonetheless, describes its members as "men of ripe experience, and whose large acquaintance with public affairs entitled them at least to respectful consideration when they were engaged in the holy office—if I may use the expression—of trying to reconcile the discordant parts of this distracted country." After they submitted their report, "all sorts of epithets were applied" to them. "They were called the thirteen doctors, not in kindness," by Sen. William L. Dayton, who "seemed not only disposed to deny their healing powers, but to intimate even that they were thirteen quacks, [laughter;] that, instead of bringing forward a measure to cure and heal the public disease, they had brought forward a measure that only aggravated the disorders of the country." Leaves it "to the Senate and to the country" to decide "whether a measure intended, at any rate, as an olive branch," or the committee that prepared it, "ought to have been so treated."

Will confine most of his remarks to the three measures "now under consideration—the admission of California, the establishment of territorial governments for Utah and New Mexico, and the adjustment of the boundary between New Mexico and Texas," and will leave discussion of the fugitive slave law and abolition of the slave trade in the District of Columbia until later. Considers it "most remarkable . . . that that feature of the bill which was supposed to be less likely to encounter objection—that measure which it has been asserted would draw after it, by the force of its own attraction, the other measures contemplated by the bill . . . the admission of California has encountered the most of the difficulties which have been developed in the progress of the bill." Accuses Sens. Pierre Soule, John M. Berrien, and William R. King of "directing your energies mainly to the subject of the boundaries of California." Since "it is California which we have been charged with introducing into this bill for the purpose of conciliating support for other measures," hopes that the three senators' judgment and "proper sense of duty" would not allow them to "reject the whole measure because there is something in it dissatisfactory to them in respect to California." Even if it is defeated, the Committee on Territories will take up the California bill and "it will be passed as it is—with all its exceptionable features . . . by a considerable majority." Asks the senators to reconsider their stand and desist in their opposition, unless they find "difficulties of a constitutional nature." Maintaining that "there is no constitutional ground for objection—that it is altogether a matter of expediency," hopes that when the senators "perceive it is a part of a great system of reconciliation and harmony to the country, they will not be disposed to reject the benefits and compensations to be found in other parts of the bill." The alternative, "the admission of California alone, without any measure accompanying it, will have the unavoidable tendency of aggravating the sense of wrong and injury" that exists in the slaveholding States.

Concerning the New Mexico and Utah questions, "scarcely a Senator who has risen upon this floor has failed to acknowledge the duty of Congress to provide territorial governments. . . . some wishing for the Wilmot proviso, and others objecting to the proviso." First, makes "a few brief observations" on the recently deceased President Zachary Taylor's plans for resolving this problem [Speech in Senate, May 13, 1850]. Praising Taylor as "an honest man—he was a brave man" whose conduct of "the foreign affairs of our Government . . . met with my hearty and cordial concurrence," assures the Senate that what "I shall have to say . . . upon the plan proposed by the late President . . . will be with the most perfect respect to his memory, without a single feeling of unkindness abiding in my breast." Taylor's plan "was that New Mexico should come in as a State, as soon as she had organized a State, adopted her constitution, and presented it here." Asserts that "I should be utterly unwilling to receive New Mexico as a State in her present immature condition." Expects a census to show that "there are not perhaps one thousand American citizens" in New Mexico, and "perhaps not above eight thousand or ten thousand of Mexicans and mixed breeds, exclusive of Pueblo and other Indians, and they [are] certainly not in a condition to comprehend the duties and attend to the rights and obligations which belong to the exercise of the government of the people of the United States." Moreover, New Mexico, "conscious of her own imperfect condition," desires a territorial government. The push for immediate statehood "has only been in consequence of her extreme necessity, pressing her to despair upon her part of obtaining any territorial government."

In addition, "We all agree about the necessity of an adjustment of the Texas boundary" with New Mexico. If it is not adjusted, "there is imminent danger of . . . one, if not two civil wars—the civil war between the people of New Mexico, in resistance to the authority of Texas, to which they are utterly averse, and the civil war lighted upon the upper Rio Grande, which may, in time, extend itself to the Potomac."

Rejects the notion that this Compromise bill is "a compromise of principle, or of a principle." A compromise "is a work of mutual concession—an agreement in which there are reciprocal stipulations—a work in which, for the sake of peace and concord, one party abates his extreme demands in consideration of an abatement of extreme demands by the other party . . . a measure of mutual sacrifice." Each side "should be reconciled to the concession which he has made, in consequence of the concession which he is to receive, if there is no great principle involved, such as a violation of the Constitution of the United States. . . . such a compromise as that ought never to be sanctioned or adopted." Dares any senator "to point out . . . a solitary provision in this bill which is violative of the Constitution of the United States."

Insists that this compromise need not produce "any such consequences as have been apprehended. There may be a mutual forbearance." If the North will "forbear . . . to insist upon the application of the restriction denominated the Wilmot proviso," there is no "violation of principle there." Even if Congress had "the power to pass the Wilmot proviso, which is denied," considers "a forbearance to exercise" it is "not a violation of, the power to pass" it. Argues that forbearing to exercise a power "is no violation of the Constitution, any more than the Constitution is violated by a forbearance to exercise numerous powers that might be specified that are granted in the Constitution, and that remain dormant until they come to be exercised by the proper legislative authorities." Disagrees that "the bill presents the state of coercion—that members are coerced in order to get what they want, to vote for that which they disapprove." Points to numerous treaties "and other questions from time to time" settled "upon the principles of mutual and reciprocal concession" and finds no "more coercion in this case than in the passage of a bill containing a variety of provisions, some of which you approve and other of which you disapprove." To Northerners who feel coerced into voting for the bill without "the Wilmot proviso incorporated in the territorial part" because of their "wanting California, as they do, so much," asks them to imitate the example of Sen. James Cooper of Pennsylvania: simply "say to your constituents, if you choose to do so, 'We wanted the Wilmot proviso in the bill; we tried to get it in, but the majority of the Senate was against it.' " Since California "has got an interdiction in her constitution, which, in point of value and duration, is worth a thousand Wilmot provisoes; we were induced . . . to take the bill . . . whatever omissions may have been made, on account of the superior amount of good it contains."

Does not think this " 'omnibus,' as it is called, contains too much. I thank, from the bottom of my heart, the enemy of the bill who gave it that denomination. The omnibus is the vehicle of the people, of the mass of the people." Moreover, "it contains all that is necessary to give peace and quiet to the country." Far from being "too heavily freighted" or containing "incongruous matter," argues that "according to the congressional law, this bill is in conformity with practice in innumerable instances." Concludes that this "ostensible objection . . . is not the real one." If any senator "would attach to the territorial bills the Wilmot proviso," would he have seen "the incongruity or felt any intolerable burden? Would not the Senator even from Massachusetts [John Davis] have voted for the whole of this incongruous bill with pleasure, if it had only contained the Wilmot proviso? It is not that the bill has too much in it: it has too little according to the wishes of its opponents: and I am very sorry that our omnibus cannot contain Mr. [David] Wilmot, whose weight would break it down." On the other hand, Sen. John Bell "wants to put in it two or three more States from Texas, provisionally, upon the event of their becoming applicants for admission to the Union."

Argues that "this measure has not half the incongruity of the elements of opposition to the bill." Criticizes Sen. John P. Hale's "argument delivered with all possible self-complacency" concerning a closed door meeting between Clay and Sens. Lewis Cass, Henry S. Foote, and Daniel Webster: "May I ask to what keyhole he applied his ear or his eye—in what curtain he was ensconced—to hear and perceive these astonishing circumstances, which he narrated with so much apparent self-satisfaction? [Laughter.]" Admits to repeated consultations with "Democratic friends" and wishes these meetings "had been more numerous and of longer duration." Insists that "there is not a solitary instance in which a subject connected with party politics" was discussed, since they spoke only "of that measure which absorbed all our thoughts . . . the subject of pacifying, if possible, the distracted parts of this country—a subject upon which, between us, there was a perfect coincidence of opinion." Also criticizes "the extremes who are united against this measure. . . . Upon the very subject under consideration there is among them no union of sentiment, no coincidence of opinion, and yet a most cordial and confidential cooperation." While more moderate Democrats and Whigs "threw aside, as not germane, and as unworthy of their consideration, all the agitating party politics of the day" to work together on the Compromise bill, opponents of the measure "are as wide apart as the north and south poles," despite their "quite as frequent consultation." Admits, however, that if "in the consultation between these ultra gentlemen from the South there was any mixture of the abolitionist element . . . that I could not say."

Although Sen. William L. Dayton interrupts to disclaim all knowledge of discussions among the bill's opponents, Sen. James M. Mason admits there had indeed been "frequent consultations" between Southern senators "upon questions involving the dignity, honor, and safety of the southern States."

Clay responds, "And so, undoubtedly, did our consultations relate to the dignity, honor, and safety of the Union, and the Constitution of our country. [Loud applause from the gallery.]" The president of the Senate threatens to have the sergeant-at-arms clear the gallery if order is not restored.

When calm prevails, Clay resumes: "there is neither incongruity in the freight nor in the passengers on board our omnibus. We are all heartily concurrent upon the only topic which brought us together. . . . We have no Africans or Abolitionists in our omnibus—no disunionists or Free-Soilers, no Jew or Gentile. Our passengers consist of Democrats and Whigs, who . . . have met together," forgetting political differences, to take up "this great measure of reconciliation and harmony." In light of the great conflicts of opinion on such questions as California's statehood and Texas's boundaries, asks if they can be adjusted otherwise "than by meeting in the spirit of amity and conciliation, and reconciling the great interests to be preserved and promoted by union and concord?"

Rejects Sen. Davis's assertion that "there are no parties who can make a compromise." Even in the writing of the Constitution of the United States, "that greatest of all compromises," although "there were no technical parties to that instrument . . . there were great and conflicting interests pervading all its parts" that were "compromised and settled" by "ample concession, and in the spirit of true patriotic amity." This "magnificent compromise . . . indicates to us the course of duty when differences arise." Has heard "that a different temper prevails at this time—that it is possible to carry these measures if they are presented in succession." Although the committee is not "wedded to any given system of arrangement," they "preferred combining them in one measure because we thought it most practical and most likely to lead to an auspicious result." If "a series of successive measures" promises greater success, no committee member will utter "a murmur of complaint. . . . It is not the means, it is the great specific end we have in view" that is important. Still, feels a combined bill is better to prevent "one party" from getting "all that it immediately wanted," while "the other would obtain nothing which it desired."

Hopes that "in the spirit of our revolutionary sires" who tried "conciliating and reconciling as much as possible opposing and conflicting interests," that Northern senators might tell their constituents after this measure's passage, " 'We have got California; she is secure; there is a prohibition of slavery in her constitution that will last perhaps forever; whereas the Wilmot proviso would have had a limited and an evanescent duration, existing while the territorial form of government remained. . . . We have secured California for you; she is dedicated now and forever to that free-soilism which you so much prize.' " If constituents protested that Northern senators had not obtained enough, "might you not add, with propriety, that you endeavored to reconcile the distracted and disunited portions of this great empire, and you thought that no imposition or restriction was necessary to any object which you desired to attain, and in a spirit of conciliation, therefore, you forebore to vote against the final measure, because it secured so much of what the North wanted?"

Cannot understand why "a united Senate almost in favor of all the measures in detail" opposes them when they are "presented unitedly to be acted on." Concerning the Wilmot Proviso, so much of an obstacle in these proceedings, Clay cites Sen. John Davis's own opinion that "the proviso is not, in itself, a principle, but a means to accomplish an end." Sees no need for insisting on the proviso, since "the existence of African slavery depends upon the character of the climate and of the soil. The nature of the soil of New Mexico forbids the expectation that slavery will ever be planted there. . . . Slave labor has been found . . . utterly valueless" in states where cotton, sugar, rice, hemp, tobacco, and other staples are not cultivated. "Does anybody pretend that the soil of New Mexico or Utah is adapted to the cultivation of these articles?" Particularly deplores Davis's "expression which filled all of us with profound regret" when he "spoke of New Mexico being adapted to the *breeding* of slaves."

When Davis interrupts to claim he had spoken "of the capacity of the country for 'traffic' in slaves," Clay retorts that "That is the language of the gentleman's speech, as printed; but the word 'breeding' was used by the gentleman, or I never heard a word of the speech." Will not accept it as "a *lapsus linguae* from the heat of debate." Considers this talk "about the cotton power, the lords of the loom, and the breeding of slaves" as suitable for "the bar-rooms of cross-road taverns; but I never hoped or expected to hear upon the floor of the Senate such epithets applied to the great manufacturers of the North and the cotton growers of the South." Points to the slave states of "Maryland, Delaware, North Carolina, Kentucky, and Tennessee, which have generally stood by the principle of protection to northern interests." Notes that it was not the South, "but it was the North and South combined," that "repealed the [tariff] act of '42 [9:628] by the passage of the act of '46 [Clay to Greeley, June 12, 1846] and prostrated the principle of protection." Feels "it would be as near the truth of history to say that the North itself has governed the country through the South. . . . Unquestionably, without the concurrence and support of the North, none of these great measures which are charged to the account of southern domination—the 'slave power' or the 'cotton power' could have passed."

Returning to Davis's comments, declares that his "charge upon the slaveholding States of breeding slaves for market is utterly false and groundless." Slaveholders "take care of their slaves; he fosters them, and treats them often with the tenderness of his own children." When they "multiply on his hands" and "he cannot find employment for them," he is "reluctantly and painfully, compelled to part with some of them. . . . But to say that it is the purpose, design, or object of the slaveholder to breed slaves, as he would domestic animals, for a foreign market, is untrue in fact, and unkind to be imputed, or even intimated, by any one." It is not through "such reproachful epithets as 'lords of the loom,' 'lords of the plantation,' 'the slave power,' and 'the money power,' that this country is to be harmonized."

Turning to "vindicate the measures proposed in this bill" from the attacks of Southern senators, believes "amongst our southern friends two or three great errors are occasionally committed. They interpret the Constitution according to their judgment; they ingraft their exposition upon it; and, without listening to or giving due weight to the opposite interpretation . . . they proclaim their own exposition of the Constitution, and cry out, 'All we want is the Constitution!' " Since "infallibility is not the lot of mortal man," feels that "for any section or set of gentlemen to rise up and say the 'Constitution means so and so, and he who says otherwise violates the Constitution,' is, in itself, intolerant" and lacking in "mutual forbearance and respect."

As a case in point, considers the Southern position that "the Constitution confers no authority upon Congress to impose a restriction upon the very subject of slavery in territorial governments." When a state about to enter the Union chooses to exclude slavery, doubts that "such an exercise of authority on the part of the State—a conceded power" can be "confounded with the unconstitutional exercise of it by Congress." Believes that Southerners who equate "an interdiction to the introduction of slavery in the California constitution" with "an interdiction exercised unlawfully by Congress" are mingling "truth and falsehood, black and white, things totally dissimilar. . . . The question is one of power; and I say the exercise of such a power," which Southerners consider a "usurpation by Congress, is totally distinct from the lawful exercise of a similar power by the State forming" her own government.

Praises, by contrast, the "change of public opinion, a modification of public opinion, at the North," especially in the old Northwest, concerning the Wilmot Proviso. Lauds Sen. Lewis Cass "who came here with his hands tied and bound by a restriction which gave him no alternative than a violation of his conscientious convictions of duty, or a resignation of his seat" until Michigan "nobly released and untied the hands of her Senators . . . to pursue their own best judgment." Also praises Sen. Henry Dodge, "whose grave and Roman-like deportment in this body has filled me with admiration," assuring him "that there is nothing wanting to a consummation of his glory . . . there is *nothing* wanting but to cap the climax of renown by contributing to carry triumphantly through this important measure of conciliation."

Explains "what has been gained and lost by each" section if the Compromise bill passes. "The North gains the admission of California as a free State, and the high probability of New Mexico and Utah remaining or becoming free territory; avoids any introduction of slavery by the authority of Congress; sees New Mexico detached from Texas, with a high degree of probability . . . that New Mexico will ultimately become a free State; and secures the abolition of the slave trade in the District of Columbia." The South "avoids the assertion by Congress of the dangerous principle, as they regard it, contained in the Wilmot proviso; places beyond controversy nine hundred miles of the territory of Texas on the Rio Grande . . . gains an efficient fugitive slave bill, and silences agitation about the abolition of slavery in this District." The South "will get no territory in Utah, New Mexico, or California, adapted to slave labor, in which slaves will be introduced"; however, "she cannot blame Congress, but must upbraid Nature's law and Nature's God!" Since it is "inevitable" that slavery will not be introduced here, asks Southern senators "why contend for it? . . . Two hundred years hence, if not much sooner, our posterity will read the history of the present times, agitating and threatening the country as they do, with as much astonishment as we pour over the leaves of the historian in which he recounts the witchcraft, and the persecution and punishment of witches in former times." Reminds those who desire "the greatest extension of the theatre of slavery . . . that if Texas includes all the territory now claimed by her . . . I venture to say that, in some thirty, forty, or fifty years, there will be no slave State in the limits of Texas at all. . . . the northern population—the population upon the upper part of the Rio Grande—will in process of time greatly outnumber the population holding slaves upon the Gulf and the lower waters of Texas; and a majority will be found to be adverse to the continuance of slavery." Notes that he presented the same sentiment "some six years ago from Raleigh," when "I said that if two, three, or four States were formed out of Texas, they would ultimately become free States [Clay to Editors of Washington *Daily National Intelligencer*, April 17, 1844]." Therefore, "it should be the inclination of the South, to look at the facts and nature as they exist, and to reconcile themselves to the fact that it is impossible . . . to carry slaves to the countries which I have described."

After outlining what each section gains from this compromise, asks again "is there anything of which the South can justly complain?" Cites "one provision which did not meet with my approbation . . . that is, the provision which does not permit the Government of the Territories to establish or prohibit slavery. But it was introduced at the instance of some southern gentlemen." A second amendment "provides that if any States from this Territory shall come here, with a constitution admitting slavery, such State is to be admitted." The South cannot complain because she "gains a virtual abandonment of the Wilmot proviso." Since the South resists submitting disputable questions to the Supreme Court, the only way it can be "satisfactorily done" is "by compromise, and by the compromise proposed in this bill."

Contrasts the committee's measures with "what has been contended for by some southern Senators during the progress of this bill, viz: the line of 36 degrees 30 minutes to be run to the Pacific—to cut that much off, of course, from the State of California." Some Southerners believe "that, in virtue of the Constitution, the right to carry slaves south of that line already exists," an opinion Clay views as "one of the most extraordinary assumptions, and the most indefensible position that was ever taken by man." Notes that "There are but three provisions in the Constitution which relate to the subject of slavery. There is that which subjects slave property to taxation; that which makes it a component part in the estimation of the population in fixing the ratio of representation; and that which provides for the recovery of fugitive slaves." It is not responsible for slavery's "continuance or its protection for a moment." True, "upon the high seas, a vessel, of whose cargo slaves compose a part, would be under the protection of the Constitution and the Government of the United States," but "the moment it gets into a separate territorial jurisdiction, the flag and the ship, and the cargo become subject to the territorial jurisdiction. . . . Thus, if a vessel leaves the port of Charleston with a cargo of slaves, and enters into the port of Boston or New York, the moment she casts anchor within the harbor . . . the laws of Massachusetts or New York . . . operate upon the slaves, and determine their actual condition," if "they are voluntarily carried there" and are not fugitives. Describes Louisiana and Mississippi state laws that act in much the same way. "If, therefore, it be true that, according to the laws now in force in California, New Mexico, and Utah, slavery cannot be introduced . . . the Constitution of the United States is as passive and neutral upon the subject" of slavery "as the Constitution or Government of any other country upon earth." Therefore, Southerners' supposition that "the Constitution of the United States carries slavery into California, supposing her not to be a State, is . . . totally unwarranted." If that were true, "no State could pass an enactment in contravention of the Constitution." Adds that "My rules of interpreting the Constitution are the good old rules of '98 and '99. . . . Amidst all the vicissitudes of public life, and amidst all the changes and turns of party, I never have in my life deviated from these great, fundamental, and I think undisputably true principles of interpreting the Constitution of the United States." If there is a power "which gives you a right to carry your slaves to California. . . . You must resort to some such general power as the Federalists did in the early history of this country, when they contended for the doctrine of 'general welfare.' "

Realizes that some senators merely wish "to run a line of 35 degrees or 36 deg. 30 min. through California, without declaring what the effect of that line shall be, either north or south of it," which impresses him as "running a line in the sand—a line without motive, without purpose, without accomplishing any end whatever." Others who "have contended for an express recognition of the right to carry slaves south of that line, have contended for something much more perfect and efficient than to run a naked line without any such declaration. But, then, there are two considerations which oppose insuperable objections to any such recognition." First, "you cannot do it without an assumption of power on the part of Congress to act upon the institution of slavery," which would be "a usurpation, according to the southern doctrine." Second, the proposal is "impracticable and unattainable." Neither house could muster a majority "to affirm any right of transporting slaves south of 36 deg. 30 min."

By contrast, the committee's proposal would "admit California forthwith, and New Mexico as soon as she presents a constitution, and Utah to follow on some time after New Mexico . . . all to be permitted to decide the question of slavery for themselves." Believing that in both California and New Mexico "slavery will be prohibited," asks "What advantage to the South? Sir, it is a one-sided measure. . . . It is all North, and looks not at all towards southern interests." It would be worse, however, "if you admit New Mexico with the boundary between her and Texas unadjusted," because "Texas by the assertion and successful prosecution of her claim," can take "all the territory and all the people that would have constituted any ground for the admission of the State of New Mexico."

Considers the consequences of the defeat and the success of the bill. If it is defeated, "and no equivalent measure be passed," Texas will be left in "danger . . . of two civil wars. There is danger in the first place, of the resistance of the people of New Mexico to the authority of Texas." Also, "if New Mexico goes on to organize herself into a State government . . . there is danger of a servile civil war, originating between Texas and—if you please—the troops of the United States that may come in in aid of New Mexico."

Does not mean "to magnify the power of Texas" or "of any single State," and deplores hearing "individuals in States talking as they occasionally do, with so little respect as to the power and justice of the General Government." Tells of a delegate to the Nashville Convention proposing to a South Carolina crowd "to hoist the standard of disunion," unsure "which most to admire, the gravity and possible consequences which may ensue from carrying out the views of the delegate . . . or the ridiculous scenes which occurred during the public meeting."

Although impatient with "this bravado," is not "disposed to undervalue its importance," since "There are certain great interests in this country which are contagious, sympathetic." In an armed conflict between Texas and the United States, believes that "we might not come off second best in a contest with Texas alone. But, sir, Texas will not be alone . . . there are ardent enthusiastic spirits of Arkansas, Mississippi, Louisiana, and Alabama, that will flock to the standard of Texas, contending, as they believe, for slave territory. And they will be drawn on, State by State . . . from the banks of the Rio Grande to the banks of that river which flows by the tomb of Washington. . . . If there should be a war, even of all the southern States with the residue of the Union, I am not going to say that in such a contest, such a fratricidal contest, the Union itself, the residue of the Union, might not prove an overmatch for southern resistance." Warns that "all history teaches, that the end of war is never seen in the beginning of war, and that few wars which mankind have waged among themselves, have ever terminated in the accomplishment of the objects for which they were commenced."

Offers "two descriptions of ties which bind this Union and this glorious people together. One is the political bond . . . and the other is the fraternal commercial tie." Hopes "to see both preserved. I wish never to see the day when the ties of commerce and fraternity shall be destroyed, and the iron bands afforded by political connections shall alone exist and keep us together." Considering the possibility that "thousands of gallant men will fly from the States which I have enumerated" as well as the "valiant population" of Missouri will "flock to the standard of the weaker party, and assist Texas in her struggles," hopes that senators will not "content yourselves with going home, and leaving it to be possibly realized before the termination of the current year." Explains that "this bill, which separates a reluctant people about to be united to Texas, a people who themselves, perhaps, will raise the standard of resistance against the power of Texas," will guard "against the possibility of a sympathetic and contagious war" between the slave states and the "General Government, which I regard as almost inevitable, if Congress adjourns with the admission of California alone, stopping there, and doing nothing else." Such an act "will enrage the South, and make them rush on furiously and blindly, animated, as they believe, by a patriotic zeal to defend them against northern aggression."

Turns to the "reconciling and salutary consequences" of passing the Compromise bill. Disagrees entirely with Sen. John P. Hale's view "that if you pass this bill you do not hush agitation; you even increase it." While "I detest his abolition principles, I admire his . . . good humor, his power of ready debate, the promptness with which he can carry on a guerrilla fight in the Senate." Wonders, however, if "the Abolitionists conceive that more agitation will spring out of this measure than exists now? They live by agitation. It is their meat, their bread, the air which they breathe; and if they saw, in its incipient state, a measure giving them more of that food and meat, and bread, and air, do you believe that they would oppose themselves to its adoption? Do you not believe that they would *hail* [Hale] it as a blessing? [Great laughter.]"

Notes that "there is not an Abolition press . . . that is not opposed to this bill—not one of them. There is not one Abolitionist in this Senate Chamber or out of it, any where, that is not opposed to" it. Believes they oppose it because "They see their doom as certain as there is a God in Heaven who sends his providential dispensations to calm the threatening storm and to tranquilize agitated man." Turning toward Hale, announces that "your business, your vocation is gone. . . . What! increased agitation, and the agitators against the plan! It is an absurdity."

"Let us . . . see how there could be greater agitation after the adoption of this general system of compromise." Finding little to cause agitation in the admission of California, the creation of territorial governments, the settlement of the Texas boundary, the passage of a "constitutional fugitive bill," or the abolition of the slave trade in the District of Columbia, asks "Then what can they agitate about?" Admits they might "agitate a little about not getting the proviso fastened upon the bill; and might agitate a little about not getting the abolition of slavery itself in the District of Columbia." But with the passage of "a scheme or system which brings into fraternal harmony those whose hands were about to be raised against each other as enemies," asks "whom will they agitate?" Suspects that "that fanatic, desperate band who call themselves, I don't know what—liberty men, or something of the kind . . . who have declared that this Union ought not to exist—those who would strike down the pillars upon which stands the most glorious edifice that was ever erected by the arm of man—self-government. . . . *they*, perhaps, might agitate." Remains certain that the "great body of the people of the United States will be satisfied and acquiesce in this great settlement of our national trials." The agitators, however, "will be stigmatized, and justly stigmatized, as disturbers of the peace."

Clay's convictions about the "healing effect of this great plan of compromise" are "supported by the nature of man and the truth of history. . . . after perturbing storms a calm is sure to follow. The nation wants repose." Consistent with "the universal desire which prevails throughout the wide-spread land . . . the acceptance of this measure, in my opinion," will "lead to a joy and exultation almost unexampled in our history." Refers to "historical instances occurring in our Government," especially the Missouri Compromise [2:669-70, 740-48, 775-77, 785-86; 3:15-22, 26-33, 46-47, 49-50], to verify his convictions in the "healing and tranquilizing consequences" of the passage of this bill. "Then, as now, when it was approaching its passage, when being perfected, it was said, 'It will not quell the storm, nor give peace to the country.' " But when it was approved, "bells rang, the cannons were fired, and every demonstration of joy" was made. Nor did Northern congressmen "incur the displeasure of their constituents," as Hale has threatened them "to make them swerve from the patriotic duty which lies before them." Neither the Treaty of Ghent [7:727] nor any other event in Clay's public life has given "such unabounded and universal satisfaction as the settlement of the Missouri compromise. We may argue from like causes like effects."

Warns, however, that "Now, more than then, are the dangers which exist, if the controversy remains unsettled, more aggravated and more to be dreaded. The idea of disunion then was scarcely a low whisper. Now, it has become a familiar language in certain portions of the country." Fears that "People begin to contend that this is not so bad a thing as they supposed." Hopes now "from the greater amount of agitation, from the greater amount of danger, that, if you adopt the measures under consideration, they, too, will be followed by the same amount of contentment, satisfaction, peace, and tranquillity which ensued after the Missouri compromise."

During debate on the Compromise Tariff of 1833 [8:604, 619-22, 626-27], "half a dozen Senators" said "that there would be agitation still. . . . It was said: 'You have adopted the measure which will ultimately prostrate the principle of protection.' " But "the great mass of the people of the United States, and . . . the manufacturers themselves" met Clay on a tour of New England "with more demonstrations of cordial affection and confidence" than he had enjoyed in his life. Blames the Martin Van Buren administration for undoing the good of the compromise tariff, and points out that it was "the North, it was New York, it was Pennsylvania, unintentionally, aided by other free States, that led to the adoption of the tariff of 1846, by the results of the contest of 1844 [Clay to Webb, February 29, 1844]."

His lack of "physical power" forces Clay to "hasten towards a conclusion." Urges senators to consider the committee report "with a just conception and a true appreciation of its magnitude, and the magnitude of the consequences that may ensue from your decision one way or the other." Believes "from the bottom of my soul, that the measure is the reunion of this Union. I believe it is the dove of peace, which taking its aerial flight from the dome of the Capitol, carries the glad tidings of assured peace and restored harmony to all the remotest extremities of this distracted land." Asks senators to "discard all resentments, all passions, all petty jealousies, all personal desires, all love of place, all hoaning after the gilded crumbs which fall from the table of power. . . . Let us go to the limpid fountain of unadulterated patriotism . . . and think alone of our God, our country, our consciences, and our glorious Union."

Describing an "individual man" as "An atom . . . a mere speck . . . a drop of water in the great deep," and a mere "grain of sand," asks "Shall a being so small, so petty, so fleeting, so evanescent, oppose itself to the onward march of a great nation, to subsist for ages and ages to come?" Exhorts "Forbid it God! Let us . . . elevate ourselves to the dignity of pure and disinterested patriots. . . . What are we—what is any man worth who is not ready and willing to sacrifice himself for the benefit of his country when it is necessary?"

Makes personal appeals to senators. Of Sen. James M. Mason he says, "I have thought of the revolutionary blood of George Mason which flows in his veins—of the blood of his own father—of his own accomplished father. . . . can he, with the knowledge he possesses of the public sentiment" of Virginia "and of the high obligation cast upon him by his noble ancestry. . . . put at hazard this noble Union" for "abstractions and metaphysical theories—objects unattainable, or worthless, if attained" when the honor of Virginia and the South "are preserved unimpaired by this measure."

To the senators from Rhode Island [Albert C. Greene; John H. Clarke] and Delaware [Presley Spruance; John Wales], "my little friends, which have stood by me," urges them to prevent "a breaking up of the waters of this Union," or they will "be swallowed up in the common deluge."

Warns those dreaming of "the idea of a great Southern Confederacy" that would "take possession of the Balize [*sic,* Belize] and mouth of the Mississippi, I say in my place never! *never*! NEVER will we who occupy the broad waters of the Mississippi and its tributaries consent that any foreign flag shall float . . . upon the turrets of the Crescent City—never—never!" Calls upon Southerners to sacrifice their "bitter words, bitter thoughts" and with the rest of the nation swear that "we will preserve her Union, and that we will pass this great, comprehensive, and healing system of measures, which will hush all the jarring elements."

If we "go home, doing nothing to satisfy and tranquilize the country," asks "What will be the judgment of mankind? . . . Will not all the monarchs of the Old World pronounce our republic a disgraceful failure?" What will your constituents think if you cannot tell them that "all the seeds of distraction or division" are "crushed and dissipated?" What will you tell your wife, "the partner of your fortunes, of your happiness and of your sorrows, when in the midst of the common offspring of both of you, when she asks you, 'Is there any danger of civil war?' " Asserts that "The contentions and agitations of the past will be increased and augmented by the agitations resulting from our neglect to decide them. . . . We shall stand condemned in our own consciences, by our own constituents, and by our own country."

Admits "I have been aware that its passage for many days was not absolutely certain." Hopes it will pass "because from the first to the last I believed it was founded on the principles of just and righteous concession—of mutual conciliation. . . . it deals unjustly by no part of the Republic," it "saves the interests of all quarters of the country." Realizes that "its fate depended upon four or five votes" which "we could not count upon the one side or the other with absolute certainty." The bill may "be defeated. It is possible that, for the chastisement of our sins or transgressions, the rod of Providence may still be applied to us." A defeat will be "a triumph of ultraism and impracticability . . . a victory won by abolitionism; a victory achieved by free-soilism; a victory of discord and agitation over peace and tranquillity." Prays "in consequence of an inauspicious result," the defeat will not "lead to the most unhappy and disastrous consequences to our beloved country. [Applause.]"

When Sen. Robert W. Barnwell takes exception to Clay's comments about "a friend whom I hold very dear" and about the South at large, Clay claims to have "said nothing about the character of Mr. [Robert Barnwell] Rhett, for I might as well name him. . . . But, if he pronounced the sentiment attributed to him of raising the standard of disunion and of resistance to the common Government, whatever he has been, if he follows up that declaration by corresponding overt acts, he will be a traitor, and I hope he will meet the fate of a traitor. [Great applause in the galleries, with difficulty suppressed by the Chair.]"

Hopes the "sentiment of disunion. . . . is confined to South Carolina." Proclaims that "If Kentucky to-morrow unfurls the banner of resistance unjustly, I will never fight under that banner. I owe a paramount allegiance to the whole Union—a subordinate one to my own State." If Kentucky calls me "to support her in any cause which is unjust to the Union, never, *never* will I engage with her in such a cause." Respects South Carolina, "but I must say, with entire truth, that my respect for her is that inspired by her ancient and revolutionary character, and not so much for her modern character." Warns Barnwell that "there are as brave as dauntless, as gallant men . . . in every other State of the Union, as are to be found in South Carolina," and if she should "hoist the flag of disunion . . . tens of thousands of Kentuckians would flock to the standard of their country to dissipate and repress their rebellion."

Sen. Hale challenges Clay's assertion that Northern legislators who supported the Missouri Compromise did not find their political careers damaged by their stand, noting that many who did "have never recovered from the odium with which they were overwhelmed from that day." Clay responds that if Hale "says they were all sacrificed, I am sure he is mistaken." Admits few of the Northerners who voted for it were New Englanders like Hale, but "if you were to look over the list of northern members who voted for the Missouri compromise, you would find that a majority of them were sustained." If any of these men "were sacrificed in the cause of their country, I would write upon their tombstone this epitaph: 'Here lies a noble patriot, who loved his country better than himself'—an epitaph which I would never be able to write, I am afraid, on the tomb of the Senator from New Hampshire. [Laughter.]" Advises Hale that "there are two kinds of sacrifices which men make for office. . . . a sacrifice to power here" and "a sacrifice to constituents at home." While Hale "may not be ready to sacrifice himself to the gifts of power and authority here," fears "he has exhibited too much readiness to minister to local and unfounded prejudices, and to inflame sectional animosities among the people whom he represents." If Hale "talks about the sacrifice of northern rights and power. . . . Let him specify" which ones. Does he "hug that precious 'Wilmot' so . . . that nothing but that will do?" Will he not be satisfied by anything "but Wilmot, *Wilmot*, WILMOT? Is that a sacrifice?" Is he not "satisfied with every real security for the accomplishment" of this wish, or does he need to inflict wounds "regarded as derogatory to the honor and feelings of the South?" Rejects as well Hale's assertion that Northern congressmen who voted for the Missouri Compromise were rewarded with official appointments by President James Monroe. Dares Hale to "tell me if the North does not get almost every thing, and the South nothing but her honor. . . . I do not want general broadcast declamations, but specifications. Let us meet them, like men, point upon point, argument upon argument." *Cong. Globe*, 31 Cong., 1 Sess., Appendix, 1405-15. Printed in Colton, *Clay Correspondence*, 6:529-67.

For Senators James Cooper (Whig, Pa.); Albert C. Greene (Whig, R.I.); John H. Clarke (Whig, R.I.); Robert W. Barnwell (St. Rights Dem., S.C.); Robert Barnwell Rhett (St. Rights Dem., S.C.), see *BDAC*. The "sectional newspaper" to which Clay refers had been established in May, 1850, in Washington, D.C., with Elwood Fisher and Edwin DeLeon as editors. It was supposed to be under the guidance of 63 members of Congress, was non-partisan, and was to be a defender of Southern rights. The first issue of *The Southern Press* came out on June 14, 1850. Richmond *Enquirer*, May 15 and June 19, 1850; Ambler, *Thomas Ritchie*, 283.

Remark in Senate, July 23, 1850. When Sen. John W. Davis claims that he has not described New Mexico as ideal for the "*breeding* of slaves [Speech in Senate, July 22, 1850]," Clay offers to "call up a dozen Senators here whose recollection of it is coincident with my own. I was struck with the term; I was wounded by it, because the placid and quiet manner of the honorable Senator did not lead me to expect the use of such an expression upon a subject so delicate, and with regard to which the public mind of the slaveholding States is so sensitive." Notes that upon looking at printed copies of the speech, however, "I found instead of the term which gave me so much pain, the idea of a traffic of slaves in New Mexico was substituted for it. Now, I beg the Senator himself to consider how there could be a traffic in slaves in

New Mexico, without their being there or being carried there." Knowing "how liable we are, in the heat of debate, to use expressions which afterwards occasion regret to others and to ourselves," still intends to "stand by the term, with the conviction on the part of the Senator that he did not use the term to which I took exception, and with an equally strong conviction on my part that he did it."

Later, when Sen. Jefferson Davis offers an amendment to an amendment that would repeal territorial laws that "deny or obstruct the right of any citizen of the United States to remove to and reside in said Territory, with any species of property legally held in any of the States," Clay reiterates that "the great principle which pervades throughout this bill is the principle of non-intervention by Congress upon the subject of the institution of slavery." Asks then, if by this amendment, "Congress can repeal existing laws prohibiting slavery, could not Congress enact laws authorizing the introduction of slavery, or if slavery was existing there abolishing slavery? What, in other words, is the difference between the direct action of Congressional legislation upon the subject of slavery, to introduce it or to prohibit it, and the exercise of this power by Congress to repeal existing laws within the Territory, which existing laws have declared the abolition of slavery? If that is so, the great principle of non-intervention seems to me as clearly violated." *Cong. Globe*, 31 Cong., 1 Sess., Appendix, 1416.

Also on this day when Sen. David L. Yulee extensively quotes the views of John C. Calhoun on the subject of slavery in the territories, Clay rises to a point of order: "I contend that it is out of order to take up the opinions of any gentleman not with us," especially since it was not merely "a simple allusion," but "a continued discussion as to what those opinions were." *Ibid.*, 1139.

From Ed[.] Hall, Washington, July 24, 1850. Since "Mr. [John M.] Botts name has been mentioned" to Millard Fillmore for a cabinet position, complains of the objections raised against his nomination: "Virginia, had a member in the late cabinet [Sec. of the Navy William B. Preston], that she has a full minister abroad [William C. Rives, France], and that she is and always has been a democratic state." In answer to these objections asserts: "Maryland had a member in the last cabinet [Attorney General Reverdy Johnson], that Kentucky has a full minister abroad [Robert P. Letcher, Mexico], that the son of the present Atty. Genl. [John J. Crittenden] holds the most lucrative office in the gift of the government, and that Missouri has always been democratic." Argues in support of Botts: "His ability is universally admitted. His devotion to & efficient service for the Whig party are preeminent—his appointment" would help "unite the Whig party . . . particularly . . . in Virginia," where "a union of the Whigs . . . will insure the State to the Whigs next spring, & will secure beyond a doubt the election of six perhaps ten members of the next House of Representatives." With Virginia Democrats split "upon the compromise bill & other matters, particularly the struggle that is going on between the eastern & western sections of Virginia. . . . Mr Botts more than any other man, has the confidence of all parties in Virginia." Believes, therefore, that "no appointment has been made or can be made, that will accomplish so many objects dear to the Whig party." ALS. DNA, RG59, Applications and Recommendations.

Thomas Crittenden had received the appointment of U.S. consul in Liverpool which, with its private business opportunities, was said to be worth $20,000 per year. Kirwan, *John J. Crittenden*, 251-52.

Virginia was split over the Compromise of 1850 in much the same way she had split over nullification and would permanently split in 1861, with the western section being strongly Unionist and the eastern section identifying with Southern interests. This division was evident in the Virginia Constitutional convention of 1850-51 in which the major controversy was over how to count slaves for the purpose of representation. Charles H. Ambler, *Sectionalism in Virginia From 1776-1861* (New York, 1964), 248-72.

In the 1851 state elections in Virginia, Democrat Joseph Johnson defeated Whig George W. Summers by a vote of 67,427 to 60,286. Johnson was elected under the new constitution, becoming the state's first popularly-elected governor and the only pre-Civil War governor from the trans-Allegheny region. *BDGUS*, 4:1643-44. In the congressional race, Democrats won 13 seats to 2 for the Whigs. *Guide to U.S. Elections*, 593-94. Democrats also won a majority in both houses of the state legislature, with approximately 34 seats in the senate to 16 for the Whigs and 1 contested and 89 seats in the house to 55 for the Whigs and 1 vacant. Richmond *Enquirer*, January 6, 1852.

Remark in Senate, July 25, 1850. Sen. John P. Hale offers an amendment to an amendment that requires "the rights and claims" of Texas and the United States to "remain as they were at the date of the execution of the treaty of Guadalupe Hidalgo [Clay to Beatty, April 29, 1847]" and that "neither party should take any steps to extend their possession, or should be precluded from doing so hereafter, by anything which has occurred" since the treaty's ratification. Clay believes it is "not worth while to make any alteration, or raise any question on this point." Since the Compromise bill seeks only to effect "a mutual understanding between Texas and the United States . . . no man can hesitate as to our power to pass a bill of mutual forbearance until a final settlement" is reached.

Later, when a number of senators seek to adjourn, Clay makes clear that "I have got the floor before any motion to adjourn is made, and I have a right to make what remarks I desire to make." After "eight months in coming to a vote on this measure . . . the Senator from Massachusetts [John Davis] wants to postpone it still further" in hope of defeating it. Adds that "we too have friends absent" who would vote for the bill, but "if we are to put off the vote till these Senators can be here, I shall have to go away. I cannot stay here. My physical powers are failing. I cannot remain much longer. If you put the question off from day to day in order to accommodate one absentee, you will create others." Hopes "the motion to adjourn will not prevail." *Cong. Globe*, 31 Cong., 1 Sess., Appendix, 1429, 1435.

Earlier on this day, interrupts Sen. Sam Houston's comments on a motion to prohibit unauthorized exercise of civil authority by army officers and urges him to "postpone to another day the remainder of his remarks." Moves to take up the Compromise bill with the hope "that we may be able to draw this subject to a conclusion this day. Whatever may be its fate, and whichever side may have the majority, I hope the day will not close until we have decided absolutely upon it." *Cong. Globe*, 31 Cong., 1 Sess., 1456.

Remark in Senate, July 26, 1850. Suggests an amendment that would require the commissioners resolving the Texas boundary question with the United States to make their joint report to Texas on January 1, 1851, and to Congress on February 1, 1851. It is not deemed appropriate to the amendment to which Clay wishes to attach it.

Later, offers an amendment "for the appointment of commissioners to settle the boundary—to fix upon a line." If they fail, each party will "remain with their rights precisely as before." Introduces this amendment only "to satisfy scruples which are entertained by some gentlemen, although I have none myself."

When debate is diverted from the topic, Clay hopes that "the sense of propriety of gentlemen or the Chair would confine the discussion to that." Reaffirms that the amendment is "not necessary," merely making clear in order to satisfy the members from Texas an implication "that the rights of the United States shall remain unaffected if the proposition be not accepted by Texas." Restates that "It was a mutual reservation of rights." The amendment is soon withdrawn with the consent of the Senate. *Cong. Globe*, 31 Cong., 1 Sess., Appendix, 1436, 1440-42.

From WILLIAM G. BROWNLOW Knoxville, Tenn., July 27, 1850

For 12 years I have edited a Whig paper,[1] and for 15 years I have battle[d] in the Whig cause. I never applied for office, and never recived any patronage. I am poor and in debted for my new Printing Office. The State Department will have $500 to pay to a Press in this city for advertising the Laws, Treaties, &c. at the close of each Session. The Knoxville Whig has the largest circulation of any Whig paper in this end of the State, or any paper ever published here. I was denied the job by the late Secretary of State,[2] expressly on the ground, as I believe, that I was opposed to the nomination of Gen. [Zachary] Taylor by the Philadelphia Convention.[3] We learn here, that Mr. [Daniel] Webster is Secretary of State. Could you feel free to say one word to him in my favor? I hate to trouble you thus, but I know not who else to apply through.[4]

ALS. DNA, RG59, State Dept. Misc. Letters Recd. Regarding Publishers of the Law, July, 1850. Endorsed by Clay: "Mr. Brownlow is a firm, decided & thorough going Whig, eminently meriting what he is desirous to obtain." 1. Brownlow had started his *Whig, and Independent Journal* in Elizabethton, Tenn., in 1838, moved it to Jonesborough in 1839, and to Knoxville in 1849. *BDAC*; Hudson, *Journalism in the United States*, 575. 2. John M. Clayton, who had resigned following Taylor's death. 3. Greeley to Clay, Nov. 15, 1846. 4. Brownlow accepted the appointment to publish the laws in a letter to Daniel Webster of July 8, 1852. Wiltse, *Papers of Daniel Webster, Correspondence*, 7:576.

Remark in Senate, July 29, 1850. Desiring "some practical mode adopted for the purpose of giving quiet and rest to the country, especially upon the subject of the title of Texas," has "no objection" to voting for Sen. James W. Bradbury's amendment "proposing an arbitrator, or, if you please, a commission [Comment in Senate, August 1, 1850]." Although there is "a clear right to resort to a court of justice" to settle the question, the Supreme Court "does not supersede the resort by individuals having a conflict to any other mode more amicable, more speedy, more satisfactory." Describes three ways suggested to settle the question: "a direct offer to Texas"; "an adjustment by arbitration or a commission" as was done in Georgia and elsewhere; or by "resorting to the Supreme Court." Since "the Constitution opens the court for this purpose," wonders "Why, then, put in a bill a provision for doing that which, under the Constitution, can be done without any such enactment." Singles out Sen. William L. Dayton, who had amended Bradbury's amendment, for his obstinance: "He objects to everything that proposes a settlement of the question with Texas, and he declares that, although this amendment is offered here to the Senate to improve the bill, yet, if adopted, the bill would not be in a form which could commend itself to his acceptance." Ultimately, both Bradbury's amendment and Dayton's amendment to it are defeated, but Bradbury's amendment is revived in a slightly different form. *Cong. Globe*, 31 Cong., 1 Sess., Appendix, 1449.

For Sen. Bradbury (Dem., Maine), see *BDAC*.

Comment in Senate, July 30, 1850. During discussion on the Compromise bill, Sen. William K. Sebastian attempts to strike out words in Sen. James W. Bradbury's amendment [Remark in Senate, July 29, 1850] in order to "remove all kinds of restrictions upon the power and discretion of the commissioners in the settlement of" the Texas boundary question.

Clay opposes Sebastian's move. "The truth is, that, after all, there is quite ample discretion left to the commissioners, and my only regret is, that we cannot determine something more than we are able to do, to submit to the commission in establishing a conventional line." Wishes to "leave the whole thing afloat in relation to the conventional line." Sebastian's motion is defeated.

Sen. William C. Dawson offers an amendment to prohibit the territorial government from operating east of the Rio Grande until the Texas boundary question is settled [Clay to Fillmore, August 10, 1850]. Clay finds the proposition to be "characterized by great fairness." It restrains "the United States from treating the disputed territory as its own property until the dispute is settled." Believes "an antecedent adjustment of the question of disputed territory was essential to peace, and essential even to government there," until a commission can "agree upon a conventional line and recommend it to the Legislature of the State of Texas and to Congress." Since the case does not depend upon "documents, maps, history, or travel," hopes the dispute can be resolved by a commission "in five or six weeks after opening their session." Asks "every man who wishes to see this question settled pacifically, if there is not prudence, propriety, fitness, justice, in abstaining from acting upon the territory east of the Rio Grande within the boundary of New Mexico, until it is decided whether it is ours or belongs to Texas."

When his views are challenged by Sen. Stephen A. Douglas, Clay says that "Nothing is further from my intention than in any contingency to concede to Texas all the territory this side of the Rio Grande, in the fair adjustment of this question." Indeed, "if Texas chooses, with military force, to move upon the territory while this process of adjustment is going forward, I hope she will be repelled . . . with all the force requisite to accomplish that object." The effect of Dawson's amendment "will be that Texas will forbear." Feels, however, that Dawson's amendment can be improved "so as to fix the time (say the 1st of January) for the commission to report to the Texan Legislature, and the time (say the 1st February) for them to report to Congress," an amendment Clay intends to propose, along with a stipulation that "the territorial government shall not go into operation until the 1st of April or May next, leaving the intervening time for the adjustment of the territorial dispute."

Later, in response to a motion by Sen. Moses Norris to strike out the words " 'establishing or prohibiting African slavery' " from an amendment on the establishment of territorial governments, Clay hopes "that if my southern friends, and my northern friends, too, will only listen . . . they will concur in the motion." Explains that the "clause is an interdiction imposed by Congress upon the local Legislature either to introduce or to exclude slavery. . . . Congress has no such power according to the southern doctrine. That doctrine is one of clear and clean non-intervention." Since "The amendment in the bill" that Norris seeks to amend "assumes the power to exist in Congress," which would give it "the power to impose the Wilmot proviso," feels that "southern gentlemen . . . ought to oppose the exercise of power by Congress to interdict the local Legislature." Understands that Northerners "should be for retaining the clause" as it stands because, if "there is at this moment an abolition of slavery in the Territories, this clause serves to continue that abolition of slavery." Notes, however, that "my northern friends, who are anxious to exclude this clause by the adoption of this amendment, go upon a higher principle than mere interest." Perceptive Northerners realize that the clause "is in contravention of the principle for which they have contended on behalf of southern interests, and that is the principle of non-intervention on the subject of slavery. . . . upon which they are willing to stand with their southern friends." The principle "pervades the entire bill, running through it from first to last." Moreover, if the "Constitution is paramount and supreme, and if the Legislature of the Territory were to pass any law in violation of the Constitution, that law unquestionably would be null and void from the moment of its passage. . . . It appears to me, therefore, that upon the very principle for which southern gentlemen have stood up, they should strike out this clause from the bill, and leave it a clear and indisputable bill of non-intervention, from the enacting clause to the end." *Cong. Globe*, 31 Cong., 1 Sess., Appendix, 1458-59, 1465.

For Senators William C. Dawson (St. Rts. Whig, Ga.), William K. Sebastian (Dem., Ark.) and Moses Norris (Dem., N.H.), see *BDAC*.

To Ferdinand Campbell Stewart, Staten Island, N.Y., July 30, 1850. Expresses his thanks for Stewart's invitation "to enjoy the Sea Air and the Sea bath of your pleasant locality." Although "most anxious to leave" Washington because "My health requires that I should do so," regrets "I cannot say when." Hopes to return to "New Port [Newport, R.I.] . . . having derived great benefit from my visit to that place last summer [Clay to Mercer, August 1, 1850]." ALS. DLC-HC (DNA, M212, R6).

Stewart was a physician at the Marine Hospital on Staten Island and one of the founders of the New York Academy of Medicine. *CAB*.

Remark in Senate, July 31, 1850. Sen. James A. Pearce, describing the portion of the Compromise bill dealing with the territorial government of New Mexico as "cranky, lop-eared, crippled, deformed, and curtailed of its fair proportions," moves to strike out all these provisions until he can offer another proposition [Comment in Senate, August 1, 1850].

Clay cannot "repress the expression of my regret and surprise at this motion." It will "destroy one of the most valuable features of the bill, the object of which is the adjustment of this troublesome boundary question." Even "in the shape in which" the bill is, "I do not think it is liable to the objections which the Senator has offered." Hopes Pearce "will withdraw his amendment until he sees the result of an effort to make the bill consonant with his own peculiar views," since contemplated amendments will "prevent the effect which is apprehended of a surrender to Texas of all that she claims."

Complains that now that "light was beginning to break upon us," it is "possible, upon slight and unimportant amendments—amendments which will not affect the great object of this bill, upon mere questions of form and punctilio—that we shall now hazard the safety, the peace, if not the union of the country." Hopes senators will waive "slight objections" and instead "act upon the great principles which led our fathers to adopt the Constitution," overcoming "difficulties and objections" by embracing "a spirit of conciliation and peace." Decries all the efforts to forestall "imaginary difficulties" that "should not affect the great principle and soul of the measure. Our object is to settle this question of boundary as soon as possible—in half a dozen months" and then "We shall know whether we shall go on blind folded or with our eyes open, looking to all the consequences."

Pearce responds that Clay "entirely mistakes me," and that his amendment merely delays the territorial government of New Mexico from going into operation until March 4, 1851. *Cong. Globe*, 31 Cong., 1 Sess., Appendix, 1473-74; *Cong. Globe*, 31 Cong., 1 Sess., 1490.

For Sen. James A. Pearce (Whig, Md.), see *BDAC*. For the final wreck of the omnibus bill on this day, see Comment in Senate, August 1, 1850.

Comment in Senate, August 1, 1850. After the Compromise bill "met with a fate not altogether unexpected [Clay to Combs, January 22, 1850]," Clay blames "the extremists on the other side of the Chamber and on this." He and his committee "stand free and liberated from any responsibility of consequences." Blames Sen. James A. Pearce for making the proposition that was "the immediate cause" of the defeat [Remark in Senate, July 29, 1850; Comment in Senate, July 30, 1850; Remark in Senate, July 31, 1850].

Still feels that there is "no fear in regard to the admission of California," but cannot support Sen. Henry S. Foote's proposition to admit the state with certain restrictions, because it is not "a part of a general pledge or plan of compromise," but "a separate measure, detached from any compensating measures contained in a combined bill, and relates only to California itself."

Although "unawed by any threats, whether they come from individuals or from States. . . . if any one State, or a portion of the people of any State, choose to place themselves in military array against the Government of the Union, I am for trying the strength of the Government. [Applause in the galleries, immediately suppressed by the Chair.]" Will not be "alarmed or dissuaded from any course by intimations of the spilling of blood. If blood is to be spilt, by whose fault is it to be spilt? . . . I maintain it will be by the fault of those who choose to raise the standard of disunion." Proclaims that "so long as it pleases God to give me a voice to express my sentiments, or an arm, weak and enfeebled as it may be by age, that voice and that arm will be on the side of my country, for the support of the general authority, and for the maintenance of the powers of this Union. [Applause in the galleries.]"

As the presiding officer restores order with warnings to the gallery, Clay repeats his former willingness "to take the measures united. I am willing now to see them pass separate and distinct," but "without that odious proviso which has created such a sensation in every quarter of the Union." Repeats his hope that no "blood is to be shed," but if it is, "I will be among the last to give up the effort to maintain the Union in its entire, full, and vigorous authority." Continues to believe "these threats are not so alarming and so dangerous" as they may seem. During the Whiskey Rebellion, the U.S. Army "moved forward for the purpose of subduing it. . . . But the insurgents then—as disunionists and traitors always will—fled from the approach of the flag of the Union."

Contradicts Sen. William C. Dawson, who had used the language of a resolution Clay had offered early in the session to imply "a willingness on my part to circumscribe the limits of California." Explains he had introduced the "word 'suitable,' implying nothing in particular . . . in order to allow the Senate and the country a discretion to be applied to the whole subject. . . . It was not a restriction."

Pearce defends his course which had brought about the defeat of the Compromise bill, but Clay simply notes that it now "belongs to the history of the country." Intends to say nothing about Pearce's "motives and his ready and fearless encounter of the responsibility," but insists "that the immediate cause of the loss of the bill was" Pearce's amendment. Clay, Stephen A. Douglas, and others had offered amendments that accomplished "substantially the very object which he" desired, but Pearce "persisted in his own," which led to the bill's defeat. Nonetheless, does not doubt Pearce "acted upon conscientious motives."

Later, Sen. James M. Mason says that Clay had declared "that it is the duty of the Federal Government to take no further account of State resistance than they would do of the resistance of individuals or private citizens." Clay denies this: "I said, and I repeat—and I wish all men who have pens to record it—that if any single State, or the people of any State, choose to raise the standard of disunion and to defy the authority of the Union, I am for maintaining the authority of the Union."

Senators Mason and Andrew P. Butler continue to criticize the Compromise bill for giving so little to the South, while giving the North nearly everything it had demanded. Clay refuses "to be drawn into a discussion of the exploded doctrines of nullification. I hoped they had expired with the illustrious individual [John C. Calhoun] whose recent death we all so sincerely lament [Remark in Senate, February 28, 1850]." Protests against these two senators' claim to speak for " 'the South, the whole South.' Sir, I should think it would be very fortunate if Senators were always confident that they were able to represent the sentiment of their own States." Tells Mason that "I believe that if the people of Virginia had been here, four fifths of them would have voted for that compromise measure." Asks the senators if they "expect to be able to have the sword drawn against the Union" when their constituents had not supported the "rejection of this compromise."

Rejects the doctrine of nullification, asking "whether we are bound together by a rope of sand, or an effective, capable Government, competent to enforce the powers therein vested by the Constitution of the United States." Believes the latter to be true, because "I denied the doctrine twenty years ago—I deny it now—I will die in denying it. There is no such principle. If a State chooses to assume the attitude of defiance to the sovereign authority, and set up a separate nation . . . Shall the other twenty-nine yield to the one, or the one yield to the twenty-nine?" If the "force of a State is put in array against the authority of the Union, it must submit to the consequences of revolt." Although Southerners believe the "flattering unction that the army is composed of officers from Virginia, South Carolina, and other southern States, and the army will not draw their swords," warns that under Gen. Winfield Scott's command the army will do its duty.

Clay notes that for Virginia he has had "always feelings towards her which are inspired in the filial bosom towards its parent," yet if "any State chooses to array itself in authority, and give orders to set themselves in military or hostile array toward the Union, the Union is gone, or the resistance must cease." Mason "speaks of Virginia being my country. This Union is my country; the thirty States are my country; Kentucky is my country, and Virginia no more than any other of the States of this Union." His "obligations and feelings and duties towards her in my private character" would cease if Virginia "lawlessly, contrary to her duty, should raise the standard of disunion against the residue of the Union. . . . I would go against Kentucky herself in that contingency, much as I love her." *Cong. Globe*, 31 Cong., 1 Sess., Appendix, 1486-87, 1489-91. Printed in Colton, *Clay Correspondence*, 6:568-75.

Sen. James W. Bradbury had introduced an amendment to entrust the Texas-New Mexico boundary to a U.S.-Texas commission, but on July 29 this failed to pass. It was revived by Sen. William C. Dawson on July 30 when he offered an amendment that the New Mexico Territory would not have jurisdiction east of the Rio Grande until a boundary commission established the boundary. This provision, which would leave Texas in control of many New Mexicans until the commission acted, was supposed to insure the support of the two Texas senators for the Compromise bill. The Dawson amendment passed 30 to 28. On July 31 Sen. James A. Pearce attacked the Dawson proposition, apparently with President Fillmore's approval, and offered three amendments to the Omnibus. A 33-22 vote did away with the New Mexico territorial part of the Compromise bill in order to get rid of the Dawson amendment. A 29-28 vote struck from the bill everything related to Texas. Next, by 3 votes Pearce failed to restore the Bradbury proposal without the Dawson provision. The Omnibus was finally wrecked by a 34-25 vote removing California statehood from the bill and leaving only the portion creating the Utah Territory. Hamilton, *Prologue to Conflict*, 108-12; Rayback, *Millard Fillmore*, 249-53; Smith, *Presidencies of Taylor & Fillmore*, 171-81. See also Clay to Fillmore, August 10, 1850.

To ANNA MERCER Washington, August 1, 1850

On the eve of my departure from this City, for Newport,[1] I cannot go without expressing to you the very high gratification I derived from the perusal of your letter,[2] which Lady like had no date. It relieved me from deep anxiety on your account, as it did our friends, the Elliotts,[3] to whom I shewed it last night.

I hope that your health will continue to improve,[4] and that you will take the greatest care of it. You must yourself attend to it, and not trust the discretion of your fond father [William N. Mercer]. Dance less, go to fewer parties, and avoid all excesses in your amusements. I have not forgotten how much you suffered at Newport last summer by wearing at the Fancy ball too tight shoes.

My love to your father and to Miss [Eliza] Young.

ALS. LU-Ar. 1. Clay left Washington on August 5 and arrived the same day in Philadelphia where he made a speech. On August 7 he left for Newport, R.I., via New York City by boat, accompanied by Mr. & Mrs. Charles B. Calvert. When their boat stopped in New York City, followed by a large cheering crowd, they took a carriage to Pier 3 where they boarded the Fall

River boat *Empire State*. In a short address to the crowd Clay asked to be excused from making a speech, because "I am fatigued and broken down endeavoring to serve you in the councils of the nation and am now on my way to recruit my health and strength." Concludes: "Now, gentlemen, I have a compromise to propose to you. . . . I want you to let me alone; I am fatigued and want rest; I would like to go to my stateroom, if you will let me. By and by, if God spares me, I will return and see you all again; and as to my Omnibus, you had better all get into it and ride home as fast as you can." Despite this plea, the police had to be called in to prevent his being "killed with kindness." The boat reached Newport during the night of August 7-8. On the 8th he held a large levee at Bellevue House where he was staying. He left Newport and arrived in Philadelphia and Baltimore on August 26 and was back in Washington on the 27th. New York *Herald*, August 8, 9, 13, 27, 1850; Washington *Daily National Intelligencer*, August 12, 14, 21, 1850. 2. Not found. 3. Possibly the William St. John Elliots of Natchez. 4. Clay to Mercer, July 21, 1850.

To CALEB CUSHING Washington, August 3, 1850

I received your letter[1] and thank you for the approbation which you have kindly expressed of my exertions, during the present Session of Congress, to settle the existing difficulties, on the Slavery subject, and to restore harmony to the Country. Those exertions have not been attended with the success which the good intentions, which prompted them, merited. But hopes are entertained that the several measures, which were combined in one bill, may be passed in separate bills.[2] Should that be the happy result, all at which I aimed will have been substantially accomplished.

ALS. DLC-Caleb Cushing Papers. 1. Not found. 2. Clay to Combs, Jan. 22, 1850.

Speech at Philadelphia, August 5, 1850. Appreciates the "friendly salutation" and "cordial welcome" to Philadelphia. When an omnibus tried to force its way through the crowd and was stopped, comments "That omnibus is like the omnibus I left at Washington—it didn't get through [Clay to Combs, January 22, 1850]." Explains that he would be much happier "could I have congratulated you on the doings of the body of which I am a member; but I regret to say they have done nothing, absolutely nothing of moment. . . . But we must never despair of the Republic." Hopes that "the best acts of that body are to come, and . . . that hereafter they will redeem themselves, and their latter days in the session will be their best." Copy. Printed in New-York *Daily Tribune*, August 6, 1850.

To THOMAS HART CLAY Philadelphia, August 6, 1850

I am here on my way to Newport, for which place I proceed to-morrow, and hope to reach it during the night.[1]

I received your letter of the 28th ultimo, and I was gratified to learn that your prospects from the saw-mill were so good.

My relations with Mr. [Millard] Fillmore are perfectly friendly and confidential. In the appointment of Mr. [John J.] Crittenden I acquiesced.[2] Mr. F. asked me how we stood? I told him that the same degree of intimacy between us which once existed, no longer prevailed; but that we were on terms of civility. I added that, if he thought of introducing him into his Cabinet, I hoped that no considerations of my present relations to him would form any obstacle.[3]

I shall be very glad if any thing can be done for Carroll,[4] and I will see on my return to Washington.

As to the post-office in Lexington, my wishes will, I anticipate, finally prevail.[5]

I am very much worn down, but I hope that Newport will replace my health and strength.

My love to Mary [Mentelle Clay] and the children.

Copy. Printed in Colton, *Clay Correspondence*, 4:611. 1. Clay to Mercer, August 1, 1850. 2. As attorney general. See Clay to James B. Clay, July 18, 1850. 3. White to Clay, Sept. 4, 1847. 4. Reference obscure. 5. Joseph Ficklin, long-time Lexington postmaster, continued in that office until Oct. 4, 1850. President Fillmore nominated Clay's choice, George R. Trotter, for the office, and he was confirmed on March 6, 1851. U.S. Sen., *Executive Journal*, 8:292, 311-12; Thomas L. Walker (comp.), *History of the Lexington Post Office From 1794 to 1901* (Lexington, 1901), 23, 26-27.

From John R. Thomson *et al.*, Saratoga, N.Y., August 8, 1850. As 102 "Citizens of the United States," regret "the failure of the Bill introduced by you as Chairman of a Committee of the Senate of the United States for the settlement of the difficulties and embarrassments which have recently threatened the harmony if not the existence of the Union [Clay to Combs, January 22, 1850]." As men "from every section of the Country" and as "Members of both of the great political parties," they desire "to express their hearty thanks and gratitude for the patriotic exertions and unsurpassed ability which have distinguished the friends of Compromise in the Senate of the United States and in an especial manner its great advocate and defender." Hope that "the Bill as originally reported by you . . . or a series of Bills embracing the same objects may still be passed" to quiet "the agitation of the public mind." Agree with Clay's sentiment "that 'when shadows, clouds and darkness are gathering around the Ship of State he is a recreant and a traitor that will not stand by her to the last.' " LS. MoSW.

For Thomson (1800-1862)—former consul in Canton and later a U.S. senator from New Jersey—see 4:261; *BDAC*. See also Clay to Thomson, August 14, 1850.

To MILLARD FILLMORE Newport, R.I., August 10, 1850

I have seen and perused, with much satisfaction, your message to Congress on the subject of the Texas boundary question.[1] I think the grounds you have taken are just and proper, & such as the Country will support. Still I hope that, by some settlement of the dispute, on fair & honorable terms, during the present Session of Congress, all danger of any collision of arms may be averted.[2]

I send for your perusal (you may afterwards destroy it) a letter from Mr. Apperson,[3] one of our State Senators, and otherwise one of the most distinguished & meritorious Citizens in K[entucky]. to shew with what satisfaction your accession to power is hailed in that State.

My trip has already benefited me very much, and I hope to return to Washn. in about a fortnight with my health & strength entirely recruited by the invigorating air and Seabathing at this place.[4]

ALS. NBuHi. 1. On August 6 Fillmore had sent a message to Congress urging a speedy settlement of the Texas-New Mexico boundary dispute and outlining the alarming conditions which existed there. He threatened to use military force if the Texas militia marched into any other state or territory and attempted to "enforce any law of Texas." Rayback, *Millard Fillmore*, 251-52; Smith, *Presidencies of Taylor & Fillmore*, 181-83; *MPP*, 5:67-73. 2. The Texas boundary bill passed the Senate on August 9 and was approved by Fillmore on Sept. 20. It conceded to Texas 33,000 square miles of territory but denied the other 70,000 which she claimed. 9 *U.S. Stat.*, 446-52; Rayback, *Millard Fillmore*, 250-52; Hamilton, *Prologue to Conflict*, 136-38. 3. Richard Apperson, Sr. (*ca.* 1799-1864), a lawyer from Montgomery County, Ky., served in the state legislature and as a member of the 1849 Kentucky Constitutional convention. His son, Richard, Jr. (1829-78), was also a lawyer and judge. Armstrong, *Biographical Encyclopedia of*

Kentucky, 26; Kerr, *History of Kentucky*, 3:531-32. The latter combines the careers of the father and son as one person. Apperson's enclosed letter has not been found. 4. Clay to Mercer, August 1, 1850.

To Gentlemen of Saratoga Springs, N.Y., August 14, 1850. Has received their invitation of the 9th to visit Saratoga Springs. Explains that he has experienced "very great benefit, from the invigorating air and the sea bath of this locality [Newport, R.I.]," and has, therefore, "concluded to remain here until my return to Washington." Notes that his health and strength have already improved on this short trip [Clay to Mercer, August 1, 1850].

Thanks them "for the kindness of the expressions contained in your letter, in respect to my public career and public service." Appreciates them especially since they come from men of both political parties. Regrets that the Compromise bill [Clay to Combs, January 22, 1850] has not met with the success it merited, but "I unite with you in hoping that the same object may be accomplished by the passage through Congress of the separate bills of which that measure was composed." Copy. Printed in New York *Herald*, August 19, 1850. Written from Newport, R.I.

To JOHN R. THOMPSON [*sic*, THOMSON] *et al.*

Newport, R.I., August 14, 1850

I have very great pleasure in acknowledgeing the receipt of your obliging letter, dated at Saratoga on the 8th instant, in which you are pleased to express feelings of regret on account of the failure of the Compromise Bill in the Senate of the United States.[1] That Bill contained a provision for the admission into the Union of the State of California, a provision for the establishment of Territorial Governments in Utah, and New=Mexico, and propositions for the amicable settlement of the disputed boundary between New=Mexico, and Texas. Besides that bill, the Senate's Committee of Thirteen reported two other bills, one for the more effectual recovery of fugitive slaves, and the other to abolish the Slave trade in the District of Columbia.

These several bills, taken together, composed a system of healing measures, which, if adopted, the Committee and myself firmly believed would restore concord and harmony to the Union. With you, gentlemen, I regret extremely the failure of the first mentioned bill. That event was namely owing to one of the most extraordinary co=operations of Ultras, from the North and South, which was ever witnessed in a deliberative body. There were other minor causes of the defeat of the bill, relating to the course of individual members, upon which it would be unpleasant for me to dwell.[2] If the bill could have been submitted to the suffrages of the people of the United=States, I am fully persuaded that an immense majority of them would have been in favor of it. And I am equally convinced that, if every Senator had voted in conformity to the wishes of his State, the bill would have been carried by a majority of more than two thirds of the body.

I thank you, gentlemen, for the expression of your approbation of the exertions of the friends of the Compromise in the Senate.

Assembled as you are, at Saratoga, from all parts of the Union, and belonging, as you do, to both the great political parties of the Country, the testimony which you have thus spontaneously rendered, possesses a high and in=appreciable value. Among the friends of the Compromise=Bill, I think the public gratitude is eminently due to the exertions of Mr [Daniel] Webster, General [Lewis] Cass, General [Henry S.] Foote, Mr [Daniel S.] Dickinson, Mr [James] Cooper, Mr [Jesse D.] Bright Mr [Solomon W.] Downs and Mr [Willie P.] Mangum, all members of the Committee of Thirteen,[3] except General Foote, who declined that service from considerations of delicacy.[4]

An attempt is making at Washington to carry through Congress, substantially, the various measures reported by the Committee, in the form of distinct bills.[5] I sincerely hope that the attempt may prove successful. Some of those measures were united together, in the same bill, under the belief that, in that form, they would be most likely to be carried. The great object of the Committee was the peace and tranquility of the country; and, if that can be secured, by the separation of the measures they recommended, far from feeling their pride or sensibility wounded or affected, they will heartily rejoice in the consummation of the patriotic end, at which they aimed.

But, gentlemen, whatever may be the result at Washington, let us cling, with ardent fidelity, to that Union, which we have inherited from our ancestors; and let us firmly resolve to stand by, support and maintain it, against all efforts to destroy it, whether made in the form of forcible resistance, or in exercise of any pretended right of secession[.]

LS. MoSW. 1. Clay to Combs, Jan. 22, 1850. 2. Comment in Senate, August 1, 1850. 3. Remark in Senate, April 19, 1850. 4. Foote later recalled that he had made the motion to refer the territorial/slavery problem to a Committee of Thirteen on condition that he not be made a member of it. Foote, *Casket of Reminiscences*, 26. See also Speech in Senate, April 8, 1850. 5. Clay to Combs, Jan. 22, 1850.

To JAMES BROWN CLAY Newport, R.I., August 15, 1850

I am here where we were together last summer. I left Washington a good deal jaded with the long session, and arduous labors, and I have already derived much benefit from my sojourn at this place. I received at Washington your letter of the 8th ultimo, and I have received here your letter of the 18h ultimo, with the despatches you sent by Lieutenant Drayton.[1] Aaron [Dupuy] has gone to Washington, where I suppose I shall find him on my return.[2]

You conducted the negotiation in which you have been engaged at Lisbon, with credit and advantage. But I could wish that you had received payment of all the claims but that of the General Armstrong,[3] and either had accepted the proposal to refer that to arbitration, or had taken it ad referendum to your government. You would have then acquired all the eclat of a successful negotiation. I have no idea that in the actual posture of affairs, our government will resort to any measure of coercion against Portugal. It is probable the proposal made at Lisbon, will be renewed and accepted at Washington. In that case you will not receive as large a share of the merit of placing our claims on the eligible ground on which they now stand, as you really deserve.[4] In the face of such a proposal from a weak power, the U States would hardly be justifiable in resorting to reprisals, or going to War. Then, ought the other claims to be postponed or jeoparded on account of the Armstrong, with which they have no connection, and which is the most disputed among them.

I write without any knowledge of views entertained at Washn. Of these I shall probably be informed when I go back, and if I should I will communicate them to you.

My relations to the new [Fillmore] Administration remain and are likely to remain amicable. They have agreed to turn out old [Joseph] Ficklin and appoint Geo. R. Trotter at Lexington.[5]

If you should want to return to Europe, I should ask that you should be sent on some other mission.

My information from home is all good & encouraging[.] I send a letter from Mary [Mentelle Clay] to Susan [Jacob Clay]—I was glad to hear that Susan & little Harry [Clay] had recovered from their illness. My love to her & all the children.

ALS, partially in Clay's hand. DLC-TJC (DNA, M212, R11). Sent in care of Baring Brothers & Co., London. 1. Letter and dispatches not found. There were at this time two Lieutenant Draytons in the U.S. Navy—Percival, a South Carolinian who was a Unionist during the Civil War, and William S., who resigned from the Navy in 1851. For Percival, see *NCAB*, 4:219; for William S., see Callahan, *Officers of the Navy . . . and of the Marine Corps*, 170. 2. Clay to Thomas H. Clay, August 15, 1850. 3. Clay to Clayton, June 7, 1849. 4. Remainder of letter is in Clay's hand. 5. Clay to Thomas H. Clay, August 6, 1850.

To THOMAS HART CLAY Newport, R.I., August 15, 1850

I received your two last letters, the last inclosing one from Mary [Mentelle Clay] to Susan [Jacob Clay], which I have forwarded.[1] James [Brown Clay] will return in October or November; he has closed his negotiation, and although he has concluded no convention with Portugal, he has succeeded in placing our claims with that Government on a much better footing than they ever stood before.[2] He has sent old Aaron [Dupuy] home, and he is now in Washington. I have been benefited by my visit to this place, and shall remain here about a week longer. It is so cool here as to require the use of fires.

They are passing through the Senate, in separate bills, all the measures of our Compromise, and if they should pass the House also, I hope they will lead to all the good effects which would have resulted from the adoption of the Compromise.[3]

I have seen Henry Pindle's [*sic*] wife[4] here, and I was very glad to hear from her that your mother [Lucretia Hart Clay] is in good health, and that she has been enjoying more of society than she has been accustomed to do.

Give my love to Mary and the children.

Copy. Printed in Colton, *Clay Correspondence*, 4:611-12. 1. Not found. 2. Clay to Clayton, June 7, 1849. 3. Clay to Combs, Jan. 22, 1850. 4. Probably Henry Clay Pindell, whose wife was J. Ann Pearce, daughter of James Pearce of Louisville. G. Glenn Clift, *Kentucky Marriages, 1797-1865* (Baltimore, 1966), 118.

To Baring Brothers & Co., London, England, August 17, 1850. Recommends "to your friendly offices, The Honble Joseph L. White, an eminent member of the Bar of the City of New York, and formerly a member of the H. of Representatives." Explains that White is going to England "in connection with the great work of uniting the Pacific and Atlantic Oceans, by means of a Ship Canal, in which the whole Commercial world is so largely interested." Does not doubt the project's "practicality and ultimate success." Adds that "American Capalitsts, being unwilling to monopolize so great an achievement, are desirous to afford to those of England an opportunity of sharing in the noble enterprize." ALS. NjP. Written from Newport, R.I.

The American Atlantic and Pacific Ship Canal Company, of which Joseph L. White, Cornelius Vanderbilt, and a number of associates were owners, had obtained a contract from Nicaragua in 1849 to build a canal across the isthmus. White and

Vanderbilt sailed for London, arriving there on October 5, 1850, where they met with the firms of Rothschild and Baring Brothers in an effort to obtain capital for the project. These firms promised financial aid as soon as the Americans could substantiate their statements. David I. Folkman, Jr., *The Nicaraguan Route* (Salt Lake City, 1972), 16-21, 24; Miles P. DuVal, Jr., *Cadiz to Cathay, The Story of the Long Diplomatic Struggle for the Panama Canal*, 2nd ed. (Stanford University, 1947), 39, 54.

From JAMES BROWN CLAY Naples, August 17, 1850

I wrote to you from Gibraltar en route from this City giving you an account of the events which immediately preceded my leaving Lisbon. My despatches to the Government would only arrive in Washington after the death of poor Genl. [Zachary] Taylor,[1] (of which event we heard on our arrival here for the first time) & perhaps after the formation of the new Cabinet, at the head of which I perceive is Mr. [Daniel] Webster.[2] As I have so often repeated to you, I believe that I faithfully executed the duties committed to my charge, in strict obedience to my instructions; it is impossible for me to form any opinion as to the course which the new [Fillmore] administration may think proper to take; I can only speak of my own instructions. I do not know whether in any case I should be continued in office, but as to a return to Lisbon my mind is fully made up; I will not return there unless my course is fully sustained & then only in the event of the Mission being advanced in Grade.[3] You know very well that I have never been an office seeker, and I have come to this conclusion from motives, in which the dignity of the country is as much concerned, as any private or personal considerations whatever. Should my course at Lisbon be entirely approved of & should Mr. [Millard] Fillmore choose to offer me a similar appointment to another Court, I should be willing to accept it, for the residue of his term.[4]

We had a long, but a very pleasant voyage from Gibraltar being varied by a squall on the coast of Africa; we reached here on the 9th. instant & will be forced to remain, because there is no good way to get from Naples, until the 24th. when we shall go to Rome for a few days; from thence we expect to go to Florence &c &c. The health of every member of my family was improved by the sea voyage; we are all now very well & enjoying ourselves very much. The trip will be expensive but if we never see Europe again, I do not know that I shall regret the money. Commodore [Charles W.] Morgan was very kind; I shewed him letters about the Yorkshire colts with which he was perfectly delighted.[5] I fear that many persons in his squadron are dealing very unfairly by him by writing letters & making reports full of falsehood about him; indeed one case concerned ourselves & was a most outrageous thing.[6] I expect to reach Florence about the 4th. of Sept. but I will keep the Barings[7] advised of my movements & you had better write through them.

I hope my dear Father that your health continues good & that we may all be spared to meet once more. Susan [Jacob Clay] joins me in affectionate love to you.

ALS. DLC-TJC (DNA, M212, R11). 1. Winthrop to Clay, July 11, 1850. 2. Clay to James B. Clay, July 18, 1850. 3. Clay to Clayton, June 7, 1849; Clay to Webster, August 22, 1850. 4. He did not receive another appointment. 5. Clay to James B. Clay, March 25, 1850. 6. Reference obscure. 7. Baring Brothers & Co. in London.

To MILLARD FILLMORE Newport, R.I., August 17, 1850

Our negotiations with Portugal having terminated by my son's [James Brown Clay] demand of his passports,[1] I take the liberty of making a few suggestions. My son has left our claims upon far better ground than they ever before occupied. And I regret that his instructions, according to his, which was probably, the just, interpretation of them, did not admit of his accepting the Portuguese proposal. That was to pay all the claims, but that arising out of the case of the Genl. Armstrong, and to refer that to Arbitration. Portugal, being a weak power, in the face of such a proposal, Congress would hardly authorize a resort to measures of coersion. And then, it does not seem to me to be right that the other claims, which have no connection with that of the Genl Armstrong, should be postponed or put in jeopardy, on account of that, after an offer to pay them.

I suppose that the Portuguese proposal will be renewed at Washington, or that an official intimation will be made of a willingness to conclude a Convention on the basis of it at Lisbon. If the arbitration of the Armstrong case be agreed to, I suppose it might be well to obtain the assent of the owners of that claim to that mode of determining it.

Should you decide to accept the Portuguese offer, and it should be compatible with the public interests, I should be glad that my son might be allowed, by convention, to conclude a negotiation which, I hope, he has with credit, as he has with some success conducted. Mr. [John M.] Clayton expressed himself to me very highly satisfied with his diplomatic correspondence.

I suppose that he has communicated to the Department of State his wishes and where he may be found. Despatches would reach him in Paris, where he will be in Septr & Octr.

If you deem it proper to renew the negotiation, I suppose that the call of the H. of R. for the correspondence will be answered by saying that it is not thought proper at present to communicate it.[2]

I hope to reach Washn. by monday the 26h. inst.

ALS. NBuHi. Letter marked "(Confidential)." 1. Clay to Clayton, June 7, 1849. 2. See also Fillmore to Clay, August 20, 1850; Clay to Webster, August 22, 1850.

To JAMES BROWN CLAY Newport, R.I., August 20, 1850

I wrote you a few days ago a letter encloseing one from Mary [Mentelle Clay] to Susan [Jacob Clay], and sent it to the care of Baring Brothers & Co.[1] and Lieutenant Drayton[2] now offering to take charge of this, I address you again. The Portuguese affair will be settled I think upon the basis of their proposal. Indeed there is a rumour that it has already been done in Washington.[3] I wrote a letter a few days ago to the President [Millard Fillmore], advising a settlement upon that basis, but expressing a wish that if convenient, you might be allowed to consummate a work which you so well begun.[4] I expect to return to Washington on the 26th. instant, and then shall know, and write you all about it.

Mr Goodloe of Lexington has offered me to exchange his store=house in that City, for your house and lot, and to give you Twenty five hundred dollars to boot.[5] I answered to him that I would take Three thousand dollars to boot, cash in hand and his Store=house, for your house, and that part of the ground, which is enclosed around it, excluding what was outside. I have received from him no answer to my offer, but I believe I shall not conclude the bargain if he is willing to make it, until your return[.] I thought his Store=house would rent for as much as your house, and as you desired to sell that, the exchange might be beneficial to you. I have been much benefitted in my health, by my sojourn here, and I hope shortly after my return to Washington to be enabled to set out very soon for Ashland[.] My last accounts from there represent every body and every thing favorably.

The Slavery question is still un=adjusted in Washington. After the defeat of the Compromise bill, all our measures have been taken up, and passed in the Senate in detail, and sent to the House.[6] Their fate in that body is very uncertain[.] It will probably in part, be decided this week[.]

Give my love to Susan, and kiss dear little Lucy [Jacob Clay], and the other children for me[.]

LS. DLC-TJC (DNA, M212, R11). 1. Clay to James B. Clay, August 15, 1850. 2. Either Percival or William S. Drayton. See *ibid.* 3. It had already been settled in principle by August 17. New York *Herald*, August 19, 1850. See also Clay to Clayton, June 7, 1849; Clay to Webster, August 22, 1850. 4. Clay to Fillmore, August 17, 1850. 5. Possibly Thomas W. or David K. Goodloe, who are both listed in the 1850 census as living in Fayette County. Also a D.S. Goodloe operated a bookstore in Lexington. Lexington *Kentucky Statesman*, June 29, 1850. For the sale of James's house to Harvey Miller, see Clay to James B. Clay, Oct. 27, 1850. 6, Clay to Combs, Jan. 22, 1850.

From MILLARD FILLMORE Washington, August 20, 1850

Your note[1] in reference to your son James [Brown Clay], came to hand yesterday, and on consulting with the Secretary of State [Daniel Webster], we both agreed that your request was reasonable, and such as it would give us pleasure to comply with. But after Mr. Webster returned to his office, he sent me the enclosed copy[2] of a letter from your son, of which he thought it possible you were not appraised. I therefore enclose it with his note. We had previously concluded to close our negotiation here much as you suggested.[3]

ALS. DLC-TJC (DNA, M212, R11). 1. Clay to Fillmore, August 17, 1850. 2. Not found. 3. Clay to Webster, August 22, 1850. See also Clay to Clayton, June 7, 1849.

To Common Council of Buffalo, N.Y., August 21, 1850. Says he has not determined on the route by which he will return to Kentucky, so he cannot say whether or not he can accept their invitation to visit that city. Notes that there "are occasions when the great interests of our country require an oblivion of all party differences, and a united devotion of our best exertions to the security and preservation of our Union." Believes "We are in such a crisis at this moment [Clay to Combs, January 22, 1850], and I am happy to be able to declare, that I have witnessed among my democratic fellow citizens, as pure and patriotic disinterestedness as has been manifested by any other party in the country." Copy, extract. Printed in New York *Herald*, August 29, 1850. Written from Newport, R.I.

To JAMES BROWN CLAY Newport, R.I., August 22, 1850

I transmit letters which I have just recd. from the President [Millard Fillmore]. You will perceive that they have determined to close with Portugal on the basis of the proposal made to you.[1] I wanted you to give the finishing stroke to the work you began, and the President kindly acceded to my wishes; but what may prevent it is your absence both from Lisbon and the U.S.[2] I will see about it when I return to Washn. I wanted you to have the credit of completing your own work.

I had letters from home to day. All well.

My love to Susan [Jacob Clay] & the children.

AL. DLC-TJC (DNA, M212, R11). 1. Fillmore to Clay, August 20, 1850, is undoubtedly one of the letters to which he refers. 2. Clay to Fillmore, August 17, 1850; Clay to James B. Clay, August 20, 1850; Clay to Webster, August 22, 1850.

To DANIEL WEBSTER Newport, R.I., August 22, 1850

I received a letter from the President [Millard Fillmore], in which he kindly expressed his willingness, that my son James [Brown Clay] might give the finishing stroke to the negotiation which he had conducted at Lisbon, by concluding a suitable convention, and that you had concurred in that arrangement.[1]

I am much obliged by this friendly disposition on the part of the President, and yourself.

Whether the object can be attained or not, ought to be, and I desire to be regarded entirely subordinate to convenience, and the public interest.

My son left Lisbon on the 18th of July, and I transmit enclosed, a letter from him, dated the 17th[2] which describes his intended movements, and where dispatches may find him.

I do not know if he would like to return to Lisbon, which would be somewhat awkward, as under his instructions, he has closed his mission there, and new Credentials might be necessary.[3]

It has not been usual for any other person to conclude a Convention in the U. States, but the Sec'y of State.

Whether a case of exception might not be presented under the circumstances of the negotiation, and James might not be directed by you to conclude here, with the Portuguese Minister [J.C. de Figaniere e Morao], what was begun in Lisbon, is suggested for your consideration.[4]

I shall be entirely content with any decision you may make.

I send my son's letter also,[5] for the purpose of your seeing confidentially, what serious consequences sometimes result from the free conversations between Members of Congress, and foreign Members.

I hope to reach Washington early next week.[6]

LS. ViU. 1. Probably Fillmore to Clay, August 20, 1850. 2. James B. Clay to Clay, July 17, 1850. 3. *Ibid.*; Clay to Clayton, June 7, 1849. 4. Although Webster wrote James B. Clay on August 23, 1850, asking him to return to Lisbon to negotiate the agreement, the letter did not reach him in Europe until he had already decided to return home. When James arrived in Washington in late 1850, he tendered his resignation as chargé. Wiltse, *Papers of Daniel Webster, Correspondence*, 7:174, 408, 415, 431. 5. James B. Clay to Clay, August 17, 1850. 6. Clay to Mercer, August 1, 1850.

From Francis W. Hawks, New York City, August 26, 1850. Realizing that "It is sometimes very inconvenient to have a character, and however justly, to be possessed of influence," hopes Clay will "forgive me if I add to the annoyances you have experienced from this cause." Writes in behalf of his son, "a civil engineer. . . . at present employed near Memphis." Has learned from the "European engineer" who has been his son's "master and instructor for a couple of years" that "the place of assistant engineer at the Navy yard of Memphis is vacant at this time, and that my son is qualified to fill it." While "gratified and surprised to hear of his proficiency," advises Clay that "the boy is nearly nineteen years old," which may "of itself be an obstacle to his appointment." Wonders if "such appointments are conferred only on those who have been educated by the government at West Point, and hold commissions from the U. States." Although he knows his son "has brains & honesty. . . . I am sure I need not say to you that if he is not qualified for the position, I do not wish him to have it; but if he be, may I ask of you to see the proper authorities and further his appointment?" Asks Clay to consider his request "part of the penalty you must pay for greatness to listen to the applications of the weak for help." ALS. CtHi. Endorsed by Clay on September 3, 1850: "H. Clay will thank [Secretary of the Navy] Mr. [William A.] Graham (to whom Dr. Hawks is supposed to be well known) to peruse the within; and if it be compatible with the public interests Mr. Clay would be very glad that young Mr. Hawks could receive the appointment requested."

On September 5, 1850, Graham replied that the "appointment of an Assistant Civil Engineer at the Memphis Navy Yard is not deemed necessary at this time," but if such a position opens up, "Mr Hawk's will receive respectful consideration." Copy. DNA, RG45, General Letter Books, vol. 44 (1850-51), p. 102.

To LUCRETIA HART CLAY Washington, August 27, 1850

I returned this morning from New Port [Newport, R.I.], after an absence of about three weeks.[1] I have been much benefited by the Sea bath & air of that place. I bathed in the Sea every day last week but saturday and sunday. Upon my return, I find that a vast amount of important business remains to be finished by Congress. Such is the extent and magnitude of it that no one can foretell when Congress will adjourn.[2] Unless the Session is brought to a close by the breaking out of some pestilence, or the occurrence of some other great calamity, I doubt if it will adjourn before October. It certainly will not if indispensable public business is despatched. Never have I been so tired of a Session of Congress or so anxious to get home. If I can possibly get away without danger of the imputation of neglect of duty I will not remain here more than a week or two longer.

James [Brown Clay], as you will have heard, left Lisbon and went to Naples, from whence he means to visit other parts of Europe and return to the U. States in November.[3] He acquitted himself very well in his mission. But for his instructions, he might have made an advantageous treaty for the settlement of American claims. They required him to reject a liberal proposal made by the Portuguese Government, on the basis of which the Government here will conclude a treaty.[4] I should have been glad if James could have concluded the treaty himself and so have acquired the merit of the negotiation, which he deserves. The President [Millard Fillmore] is very kindly disposed towards him.

He has sent old Aaron [Dupuy] home,[5] in advance of his family, and I have him here on my hands, which I am sorry for. But I shall send him off to Lexington in a day or two.

John [Morrison Clay] has kindly written to me of late, and I hope that he will continue to do so.[6] After my long absence from home, every thing that I get or hear from there interests me very much.

I have returned to the same lodgings at the National Hotel, which I left when I went to New Port.

Give my love to John & to Thomas [Hart Clay] & Mary [Mentelle Clay] and their children.

ALS. DLC-TJC (DNA, M212, R11). 1. For an itinerary of the trip, see Clay to Mercer, August 1, 1850. 2. The 1st Session of the 31st Congress adjourned on Sept. 30, 1850.

3. James B. Clay to Clay, August 17, 1850. 4. Clay to Clayton, June 7, 1849. 5. Clay to Thomas H. Clay, August 15, 1850. 6. Letters not found.

To William A. Graham, Washington, August 28, 1850. Recommends George Ross Harrison, son of James O. Harrison, "whose wife [Margaretta Ross Harrison] is a grand niece of Mrs. [Lucretia Hart] Clay" for appointment as midshipman in the Navy. ALS. ICHi.

On August 29, 1850, Graham replied that "there is not, at this time, an opportunity to appoint young Harrison," because "the 8th Con[gressional]: Dist: of Kentucky, of which he is a resident, having now 4 Midshipmen in the service, the Law prevents it." Copy. DNA, RG45, General Letter Books, Naval Records Collection, vol. 44, p. 75.

Clay wrote James O. Harrison on August 30, 1850, explaining that "George cannot be appointed . . . unless some of the other Kentucky Districts, which have not their quota, will through their representatives, agree to adopt him." Adds that "This I shall attempt to get them to do." ALS. DLC-James O. Harrison Papers (DNA, M212, R21).

On September 3, 1850, Clay again wrote William A. Graham, saying that George A. Caldwell, "the member of the House of Representatives from Kentucky, whose District is entitled to a Midshipman, has kindly consented that Geo Ross Harrison . . . may receive the appointment." ALS. PHi. Endorsed on verso: "Appoint him as from the 4h Dist. Ky Geo Ross Harrison 861 appointed from 4th Dist though a resident of the 8th Dist. Appd Sept 5. '50."

Clay informed James O. Harrison of his son's appointment on September 6, noting: "I recd. important aid in procuring it from Mr. Caldwell our member in the H. of R. from Kentucky, and I think you would do well to make your acknowledgments to him." ALS. DLC-James O. Harrison Papers (DNA, M212, R21).

George Ross Harrison failed his examinations and was forced to leave the Naval Academy in 1851. See Clay to Henry Clay, Jr. [III], June 27, 1851. For Congressman George A. Caldwell of Columbia, Ky., see *BDAC*.

To Messrs. Smith *et al.*, Warrenton, Va., August 29, 1850. Acknowledges an invitation to "a public dinner, proposed to be given, in honor of Genl. Henry S. Foote, at Warrenton on the 31st. instant." Wishes he could meet his "many highly esteemed friends, of both political parties, in the County of Fauquier" and "testify . . . to the very high merits of the distinguished Senator from Mississippi." Although "I had only a casual and limited acquaintance with him" previously and "came to Washington with impressions somewhat unfavorable towards him," now concludes from "his course and conduct, during this long protracted and arduous Session . . . that he is an ardent able and enlightened patriot," who "no one has surpassed . . . in firm devotion to that Union." Praises his "untiring industry, and patriotic zeal, to heal and adjust the agitations and dissentions which unhappily afflict our common Country." Regrets that he cannot attend the dinner at Warrenton, "in that State, which gave him, you and . . . me our birth" due to the press of "my public duties." ALS. DLC-Curry Autograph Collection (DNA, M212, R20).

To JAMES BROWN CLAY Washington, August 31, 1850

I wrote you two letters from Newport,[1] & since my return to this city, I have had interviews, both with the President [Millard Fillmore] & Mr [Daniel] Webster about your conduct of the negociation with Portugal.[2] They both spoke of it in terms of high praise, that of Mr Webster bordering even on extravagance. I had intimated to him a wish, from Newport, that you might be allowed to consummate the work that you had begun, by concluding a convention with Portugal.[3] He promptly assented to my wish, but the difficulty is, when to complete the work. If you were now at Lisbon, or had no repugnance to going back, I suppose you would be directed to agree upon a treaty. Or if you were now in the United States, I suggested to Mr Webster, that under his direction you might be authorized to agree with the Portuguese Minister [J.C. de Figaniere e Morao] upon a Convention[.] Mr. Webster thought the business might take that course, but you are not here to enter upon it. I am apprehensive that unless you are instructed to go back to Lisbon, (which I suppose, you would be hardly willing to do,) and there sign a treaty, the work will fall into other hands. I have been desirous that you should enjoy the *eclat* of finishing what you had so successfully begun. Should that not be the case, I have no doubt that in the next Annual Message, the President will notice your services in terms of suitable commendation.[4]

Mr Goodloe has been with me this morning and has been quite urgent to close the exchange of property with you, upon the terms I stated in my last letter, that is that you should give your house and lot, without the ground outside of the enclosure, for his storehouse in Lexington and three thousand dollars cash.[5] He seemed disappointed that I would not conclude the bargain, which I told him I did not like to do, as I expected you so soon at home. His house you know, is not in one of the best business situations; but he thinks it would rent for $600. per annum. That I doubt; but if it brought only $500. it would be better than to keep your own dwelling house & be rented out. You must decide for yourself. If you wish me to complete the bargain, I can do so. One cause of Mr Goodloe's urgency, was, that he has an opportunity now, of selling his own house & lot, which he may lose, if the exchange with you is long delayed.— Congress is yet in Session & no one can tell when it will adjourn.[6] If it performs, what I think is its indispensable duty, it cannot get away before the 1st of October. Hopes & fears alternately prevail as to its adjustment of the Slavery questions.[7]

My late accounts from Ashland, make favorable representations of every body & every thing, there. Wearied out with this long Session, & having now been absent ten months from home, I never have been, in my life, so anxious to be there. Present my love to Susan [Jacob Clay] & kiss dear little Lucy [Jacob Clay] & the rest of your children for me. I have heard that you had a great christening of my little namesake [Henry "Harry" Clay] at sea.

LS. DLC-TJC (DNA, M212, R11). 1. He wrote three letters to James B. Clay from Newport: August 15, 20, and 22. 2. Clay to Clayton, June 7, 1849. 3. Clay to Fillmore, August 17, 1850; Fillmore to Clay, August 20, 1850; Clay to Webster, August 22, 1850. 4. In his First Annual Message, Dec. 2, 1850, Fillmore announced that the U.S. had accepted the offer made by Portugal to settle the claims, although no formal treaty had yet been concluded. He continued: "It gives me pleasure to say that Mr. [James B.] Clay, to whom the negotiation on the part of the United States had been intrusted, discharged the duties of his appointment with ability and discretion, acting always within the instructions of his Government." *MPP*, 5:82. 5. Clay to James B. Clay, August 20, 1850. 6. It adjourned on Sept. 30, 1850. 7. Clay to Combs, Jan. 22, 1850.

To William Hickey, Washington, September, 1850. Expresses his pleasure to learn "that you intend to publish a fourth edition of the volume, compiled and prepared by you, containing the Constitution of the United States, and other highly useful and interesting matter." Believes that Hickey's "residence at the city of Washington" has afforded him "an opportunity of access to the original text of the Constitution," and "Your work, therefore, deserves perfect confidence in its entire authenticity." Does not doubt "the existence of a constant and large demand" for the work among American citizens at home and those "who are going abroad," as well as among "foreigners who are coming among us." Copy. Printed in William Hickey, *The Constitution of the United States of America, with an Alphabetical Analysis; the Declaration of Independence*, 4th ed. (Philadelphia, 1851), xix.

For William Hickey (1798-1866), who at various times was clerk of the War Department, executive clerk of the Senate, reading clerk of the Senate, assistant secretary and acting secretary of the Senate, see *Records of the Columbia Historical Society* (1935), 35-36:109-23.

To George L. Prentiss, September, 1850. Acknowledges "your friendly letter in respect to the death of your lamented brother, S.S. PRENTISS," whose demise stirred "emotions of sorrow and grief, which have been rarely exceeded in my breast by any similar occurrence." Expresses his gladness to learn "that you have resolved to prepare for publication some memorials of your noble brother," whose "memory is fully worthy of it." While "I should be very happy to comply with your wish that I would supply some estimate of your brother's character and talents," admits that "it so happened that I never heard him, except on three occasions" and "We had but few opportunities of personal intercourse." Although "Several letters reciprocally passed between us," all concerned public affairs except one "that related to a painful affair which he had with a grandson [Henry Clay Erwin] of mine [Clay to James B. Clay, February 1, 1848]" and its "honorable and amicable termination [Clay to Prentiss, March 3, 1848]." Describes, nonetheless, "your brother's mental character, as a public speaker": "he was distinguished by a rich, chaste and boundless imagination, the exhaustless resources of which, in beautiful [l]anguage and happy illustrations, he brought to the aid of a logical power, which he wielded to a very great extent. . . . his conceptions seemed to me almost intuitive. His voice was fine, softened and, I think, improved, by a slight lisp, which an attentative observer could discern." On "The great theatres of eloquence and public speaking in the United States"—the "Legislative Hall, the Forum and the Stump, without adverting to the Pulpit"—proclaims that "Your brother was brilliant and successful on them all." Copy, extract. Printed in Prentiss, *Memoir of S.S. Prentiss*, 2:580-81.

For George L. Prentiss—theologian, brother, and biographer of S.S. Prentiss—see Dickey, *Seargent S. Prentiss*, 1-5. S.S. Prentiss had died on July 1, 1850. *Ibid.*, 400.

Speech in Senate, September 3, 1850. Speaks in support of the bill to suppress the slave trade in the District of Columbia. "By the slave trade, is meant a foreign slave trade, as it respects the interests of the District. It consists of the introduction within the District of slaves from adjoining slave States, and their being placed in a depôt here, not for the purpose of finding a market at all in the District—for I am told that scarcely a case has ever occurred of the purchase by an inhabitant of the District of a slave deposited in one of these places of confinement—but for subsequent transportation to different markets by land or water—generally by water—to the southern cities, particularly to Mobile and New Orleans. It is a trade in which the inhabitants of the District have no sort of interest and no sort of connection, and which only brings upon the District a degree of obloquy on the part of all those—of whom I profess to be one—who regard this species of trade as a thing to be abhorred, and to be avoided wherever it can."

Notes that the bill "does not propose to interfere in the slightest degree with the right of one inhabitant of the District to sell a slave to another inhabitant of the District, nor does it interfere with the right on the part of the inhabitant of the District to go out of it and purchase for his own use a slave, and to bring the slave within the District for his own use."

Explains that the bill is "merely a revival of the law of Maryland, as that law existed at the time of the cession of this District." There are "only two sections, the first of which is a prohibition of the right of any owner of a slave, or any person with the consent of the owner bringing a slave into this District for sale, or to be placed in depôt for the purpose of being transported as merchandise for sale to a distant market. . . . the second invests the local authorities of the District with the power to prohibit all depôts being established within the District for the confinement of slaves." Describes the depots as "nothing more than private jails, subject to no inspection of public authority, under the exclusive control of those who erect them . . . and all the prisoners or slaves confined in them are subject to the police regulations which may be established . . . by the owner of the jail."

Hopes the bill will force the slave trade to "go somewhere else—either to Virginia, if slaves can be deposited there, or to Maryland, if they can be deposited there, but to exclude a traffic within the District." Does not feel he needs to "go into any elaborate argument on the subject to prove the propriety of abolishing a trade thus foreign to the people of the District," since it has been denounced for at least the last forty years.

Suggests three "unimportant" amendments to clarify the language of the bill, and all are adopted.

After Sen. Henry S. Foote offers several modifications, Sen. R.M.T. Hunter speaks at length in opposition to the bill. Clay refuses "to follow that Senator in the wide range which he has taken, particularly where he dwelt upon the blessings which he supposes to be imparted to the African race by that African slave trade, which, I believe, has met with the almost unanimous detestation of mankind." Hunter has decried " 'sentimental legislation,' " but Clay feels "that all just legislation should be the result both of the head and of the heart," and should be "adopted to the use and benefit of mankind." Regrets that Hunter sees in this bill "the foundation of abolition within the District. Directly otherwise was the object of the" Committee of Thirteen, which had included this proposition in its Compromise bill. Realizes that "Two complaints" constantly arise "in respect to the existence of slavery within this District, one having for its object the abolition of slavery here, the other the abolition of the foreign slave trade," both of which are "topics of agitation . . . at the North." Therefore, "the committee propose to abolish this foreign slave trade within the District," which is clearly within the power of Congress "unless gentlemen carry themselves into the regions of metaphysics and abstractions." Believes that the abolition of this slave trade "will satisfy, to a great extent, northern feeling, and I add with pleasure, southern feeling too; for I have shared in the horror at this slave trade in this District, and viewed it with as much detestation as any of those at the North who complain of it."

Recounts the court case of "Groves and Slaughter. The argument urged in that case was, that, by the Constitution of the United States, the regulation of trade between the States, and consequently, the regulation of the trade in slaves between the States, was vested in the Congress . . . and that no State can undertake to prohibit within its own limits the introduction of slaves—they being an article of commerce—from other States." The state of Mississippi, on the other hand, "had provided by her constitution that slaves should not be introduced within her limits as merchandise." The court decided "that it was a power which every State had a right to exercise, and that every State in the Union might forbid the introduction of slaves within her limits as merchandise, from any other State." Since "the power of Congress over this District is perhaps equal to the power of the several States within their limits, and as every State has the power to prohibit the slave-trade within its own limits," it seems "necessarily to follow that Congress possesses this power here." Claims that the "power of Congress to regulate the slave trade between the States depends upon a general grant contained in the Constitution to regulate trade. But that grant does not extend to the case of slaves, on account of principles of police, which appertain to each State, and of which it is the exclusive judge." Repeats his assertion that "there cannot be the least particle of doubt" that Congress has the power "to break up this detestable slave trade within the District of Columbia."

Describes his specific target as slave-traders who find it "convenient to erect their depôts within this District. . . . I am very glad to learn, from . . . the Mayor of the city," that there is "but one depôt remaining where slaves are found to be constantly for sale. I have heard that no inhabitant of the District was ever known to have purchased slaves from these depôts." Slaves are only brought here until "it suits the persons engaged in the trade . . . [to] transport them to New Orleans, Mobile, or some other southern market." It seems best, then, to abolish the slave trade in the District "thereby giving greater security against the agitation of the question of the abolition of slavery itself within the District."

Suggests that if the South did not "take alarm upon the slightest circumstance, and not be dreading every occurrence lest it touch the particular institution which they cherish so much," then "they would add safety and security to that institution itself; and I am sure there would be less of agitation throughout the country at large." Since "the owners or traders are the jailers, and the subjects of this imprisonment are slaves brought from a distance," Congress should be able to "put an end to this traffic without creating sensations of alarm from the shores of the Potomac to the Rio Grande."

Disapproves of amendments that would detract from "the bill as reported by the Committee of Thirteen, and I feel it my duty to insist upon it." The committee's bill is "direct, straight forward, appropriate to its object" and employs "the requisite and proper means to carry that object into effect." Especially dislikes Sen. Henry S. Foote's amendment which takes into account "the abduction of free persons of color and the seduction of slaves from their owners." Also criticizes the amendment of Sen. James A. Pearce which would "impose a very heavy penalty for the seduction of slaves from their masters." Hopes such matters "will be introduced in a separate bill" so that "At this late period of the session," we can "confine ourselves to the consideration of this one." Noting also that the language of Foote's proposal is "indefinite, and liable to a different interpretation," announces that "I shall . . . vote against these amendments, and for the bill as it was reported by the Committee of Thirteen." Since "we have had this bill before us for six months" and "are ready to act on it," urges that "the subject be finally disposed of." The Senate should "do its duty and its whole duty" regardless of the actions of the House of Representatives, and vote on "the last one . . . of a series of measures looking to the restoration of harmony and concord" in the United States. The yeas and nays are then ordered.

Before the vote is taken, however, Pearce offers still another amendment to impose greater regulations on free negroes in the District, who are often a "disorderly, riotous, and troublesome population," and "are becoming every day more and more depredators upon the property and peace of the community."

While believing Pearce offers "very proper objects," Clay still urges him to "introduce a bill separately to accomplish" them. Does not want to be called upon at this time "to pass a code of laws for the colored population, free and bond, in this District." If, as Pearce argues, "the free colored population in this District has increased" and "ought to be diminished," asks that "grave, serious, and humane consideration" be given to the questions "What will you do with them? . . . Where are they to go?" Feels Pearce's proposed penalty to "punish, by suitable punishment, those who attempt to entice slaves away" is "rather too severe. It proposes to subject a person to not more than ten nor less than two years' imprisonment, for persuading a negro to elope from his master." Would punish "a free person, parent of a child in slavery," who persuades "the child to run away," but believes "the punishment should be moderate. But I would punish much more severely one of those Abolitionists who come here for the purpose of enticing away slaves." Repeats his unwillingness to vote for amendments "amounting almost to a code for the black race here, bond and free," but admits that "I should be inclined to vote for them in another form."

After more discussion on Maryland's state laws on the slave trade, Clay argues that "slaves may be lawfully introduced into this District from Maryland and put in depôt here and subsequently transported. That is the law of Maryland" and "the same thing can yet be done in Virginia. . . . This bill will break up the nuisance."

When Sen. Solomon W. Downs moves to postpone further consideration of the bill for one week, Clay objects. The motion to postpone is defeated 27 to 23. *Cong. Globe*, 31 Cong., 1 Sess., 1743-44; *ibid.*, Appendix, 1633-34, 1636-37. Partially printed in Colton, *Clay Correspondence*, 6:576-83.

For the case of *Groves* v. *Slaughter*, see Swisher, *The Taney Period*, 207, 334, 364-70, 373, 388, 535, 567. The bill to suppress the slave trade in the District of Columbia was approved on September 20. 9 *U.S. Stat.*, 467-68.

Remark in Senate, September 5, 1850. During discussions on compensation due the Cherokee Indians "for subsistence," Clay claims not to "have a very clear understanding of the subject." But "if the Indians agreed with the Government to constitute this body an umpire" and if the Senate "has referred the subject to a committee" which undertook a "tedious investigation of a vast amount of papers," then "I am for standing by what the committee has done. It is one of those cases in which we must have confidence in a committee," and "I shall therefore vote for what that committee recommend" and "against anything that proposes to change the result of their action." *Cong. Globe*, 31 Cong., 1 Sess., Appendix, 1340.

Resolutions for compensating the Cherokee Indians in the amount of $189,422.76 plus 5 percent interest were passed. U.S. Sen., *Journal*, 31 Cong., 1 Sess., 601.

To THOMAS HART CLAY Washington, September 6, 1850

I have recd. your letter of the 31st. Ulto. I congratulate Louisa [Mentelle] and her family upon her marriage,[1] which I hope and believe may prove a happy one—

We can see no end yet of this fatiguing Session. So far nothing is definitively decided on the Slavery question.[2] Perhaps there may be today or tomorrow. In the mean time I am again getting very much exhausted. I wish that I had remained longer at Newport [R.I.],[3] where I was much benefited. I shall [as soon] as possible return home, where I desire to be more than I ever did in my life.[4]

I am sorry you lost your purse, the contents of which you can so ill spare.

Tell John [Morrison Clay] that I have heard nothing of late about the prospects of his stable; and that I hope to receive week after next week two or three Telegraphic accounts of his winnings.

My love to Mary [Mentelle Clay], & the children.

ALS. DLC-HC (DNA, M212, R6). Partially printed in Colton, *Clay Correspondence*, 4:612. 1. Griffin P. Theobald married Louisa Mentelle at the Episcopal Church in Lexington on August 29, 1850. Louisa was probably a sister of Thomas Hart Clay's wife. Clift, *Kentucky Marriages*, 151. 2. Clay to Combs, Jan. 22, 1850. 3. Clay to Mercer, August 1, 1850. 4. The Colton version omits this paragraph and the next.

From Ladistano Ujhazy, Decatur County, Iowa, September 8, 1850. Writing from "our new establishment," informs Clay that "my family and I, and several of my compatriots are now situated in the Western part of Iowa, on fertile soil, and under healthy skies." Assures Clay that "our new existence, which only aspires to the liberty of our souls and the basic necessities of life. . . . will be fulfilled if the magnanimity of Congress will deign to assign us a piece of land." Sends through a friend "an address by the governor [Ansel Briggs] and my friend [Louis] Kossuth, directed at the generous American people and which was entrusted to me for publication." ALS, in French. DLC-HC (DNA, M212, R6). Translated by Mrs. Siglinde Couch, Lexington, Ky.

For Kossuth and his role in leading the Hungarian Revolution [Remark in Senate, January 7, 1850], see Langer, *Encyclopedia of World History*, 720, 723, 744. Count Ujhazy and a small group of Kossuth's followers founded New Buda in Decatur County, Iowa. The Hungarians and the Iowa legislature petitioned Congress to make a land grant to the exiles, but nothing was done. Ujhazy and his immediate followers eventually moved to Texas. Cyrenus Cole, *A History of the People of Iowa* (Cedar Rapids, Iowa, 1921), 230-31. For Iowa Governor Ansel Briggs, see *BDGUS*, 2:429.

To HENRY CLAY, JR. [III] Washington, September 10, 1850

I suppose that you have now gone into Barracks, and that you find yourself more agreeably situated than when you were Camping out.[1] I hope that you will apply yourself, with diligence and contentment to your studies, as I am satisfied that it will conduce to your credit and respectability in future life.

I hear frequently from home where all are well. Louisa Mentelle is married to Mr. Griffin Theobalds [*sic*, Theobald] the dumb man, & it is a good event.[2]

I have not heard since July from your uncle James [Brown Clay], whom I look for home this fall. Old Aaron [Dupuy] has already returned.[3]

Congress will adjourn the 30h. inst. and I wish you to write me immediately. I send you two News papers.

ALS. Henry Clay Memorial Foundation, Lexington, Ky. 1. For the West Point curriculum which included summer camp with fall and spring classroom sessions, see Stephen E. Ambrose, *Duty, Honor, Country: A History of West Point* (Baltimore, Md., 1966), 71-75, 90, 94-97, 134-35, 148-50, *passim*. 2. Clay to Thomas H. Clay, Sept. 6, 1850. 3. Clay to Thomas H. Clay, August 15, 1850.

Remark in Senate, September 10, 1850. When Sen. Stephen A. Douglas presents the credentials of William M. Gwin and John C. Fremont as senators from the new state of California, Sen. Jefferson Davis objects that "the constitutional provisions for the election of Senators could not have been complied with in this case," and offers a resolution to refer their credentials to the Committee on the Judiciary with instructions for the committee to report on the law and the facts. After comments by several other senators, Clay argues that "Prior to yesterday, California was a State *de facto*, out of the Union. Upon the approbation of the President of the United States of the bill for her admission into the Union, she became, and now is, one of the States of the Union, having equal and all the privileges which belong to any State in the Union." Notes that "Among those privileges is that of being represented on this floor by two Senators." Contends, therefore, that the Senate cannot "make any reference of those credentials not made in the case of any other State. If we do, then she does not in all respects . . . stand on that equal footing which the constitution has prescribed."

Davis's resolution is defeated, Clay voting with the majority. Following the vote, the oath of office is administered to Gwin and Fremont. *Cong. Globe*, 31 Cong., 1 Sess., 1792.

Both the bill admitting California as a state and the bill organizing the Utah Territory were approved on September 9. See 9 *U.S. Stat.*, 452-58.

Also on this day, when Sen. James M. Mason seeks to strike out the "first two sections" of the bill to end the slave trade in the District of Columbia [Speech in Senate, September 3, 1850], in other words, those sections "which constitute the bill as it was reported by the Committee of Thirteen," Clay protests that the bill "will become one of a totally different character, providing only for the punishment of persons enticing slaves from the District, and investing a power in the Corporation to prohibit free persons of color from coming into the District." If Mason's amendment prevails, "there is an end to the attempt to abolish the slave trade in the District of Columbia."

Rejects Mason's charge that "I was mistaken in the law of Virginia, and in the law of Maryland. . . . The prohibition of the introduction into Virginia and Maryland of slaves for sale existed, accompanied with denunciation of the penalty that if they were introduced they should become free." All that the Senate is asked to do now is "that we should do what each of those States did, with the further object of abolishing the depôts" in the District. "This has been done by numerous of the slave States. It has been done by the State of Mississippi by her constitution," and Kentucky did it as well, "though the law has recently been altered."

Although Mason "says he makes this motion in conformity to some resolutions passed by" the Virginia legislature, reminds Mason that that body "subsequently modified" their views and "does not insist on it as a *sine qua non* in the arrangement of these slavery subjects." Hopes "this amendment will be rejected."

Sen. James A. Pearce points out that many other senators do not object to abolishing the slave trade in the District but do not like the provision that allows for "the manumission of the slave thus brought in in violation of this law," and offers an amendment calling for a fine instead. Clay prefers "the bill as it stands, though I am indifferent to the fate of the amendment which is proposed; except that I think a much larger fine ought to be imposed" than the $100 to $400 that Pearce suggests. States his reasons for supporting the "bill as it stands": it "is the law of Virginia and Maryland as it existed at the time of cession of this District, forbidding the introduction of a slave, and declaring that, if introduced contrary to law, he shall be free"; second, freeing a slave thus introduced "is the appropriate penalty. . . . Where contraband articles of merchandise are introduced there is a forfeiture, and so there ought to be in a case of this kind"; and, finally, "it is much more likely that the law will be efficacious, if the person introduced is entitled to his freedom" rather than having a mere "pecuniary penalty inflicted upon" the party introducing him. However it is effected, "my great object is the abolition of the trade."

Sen. George E. Badger fears that freeing slaves in these cases is the equivalent of "punishing the District of Columbia for the misconduct" of others, especially since "the coming of free negroes into this District" is already considered "a kind of nuisance." Clay feels that "if this bill is passed and duly promulgated, there will not be one slave in twenty years introduced in violation of the law." With "a pecuniary penalty . . . there is difficulty in inciting the prosecution." Moreover, if "an insolvent agent, or a person worth nothing," is caught bringing slaves into the District, "you can get nothing out of him." *Cong. Globe*, 31 Cong., 1 Sess., Appendix, 1638-39.

In February, 1850, the Kentucky legislature repealed an 1833 law forbidding the introduction of slaves into the commonwealth from other states. The new Kentucky constitution also prohibited the legislature from taking any direct action against slavery. Harry A. Voltz, III, "Party, State and Nation: Kentucky and the Coming of the American Civil War," Ph.D. dissertation, University of Virginia, 1982, pp. 73, 77, 304, 306.

From Isaac Owen, Sacramento, Calif., September 11, 1850. Reports that he had performed "the funeral services of your grand son Mr Henry Clay Duralde. who was drowned in the Sacramento River about eight miles above this City on last thu[rs]day night." Regrets that "a young man of his talents, promise, and moral worth should be taken from among us in the morning of his life," but rejoices "to know he sustain[ed] a good moral character." Although "it becomes necessary to communicate this melancholy intelligence," is gratified "to know that you are acquainted with that Gospel which has brought life and immortality to light [Otey to Clay, July 9, 1847]." ALS, manuscript mutilated. Josephine Simpson Collection, Lexington, Ky.; ALS, draft, in CBPac.

Isaac Owen, a native of Vermont and a Methodist minister, was one of the founders of the College of the Pacific. John W. Caughey, *Rushing for Gold* (Berkeley, Ca., 1949), 90-92.

Remark in Senate, September 11, 1850. During discussions on the bill for the abolition of the slave trade in the District of Columbia [Speech in Senate, September 3, 1850], Clay expresses again his desire "that this question should be brought to a speedy termination." Restates his position that "under the language of the Constitution," Congress has the power of "exclusive legislation over this District in all cases whatsoever." Maintains, however, in reference to the abolition of slavery in the District, that "while the institution exists in Maryland now, or while it existed in Maryland and Virginia before the retrocession, it would be a gross violation of good faith to exercise this power."

The current question, however, "is not the abolition of slavery in the District." The committee only intended that this part of the original Compromise bill "should give peace and security to the maintenance of slavery within this District, until it exhausts itself by the process of time." Admits there are "some limitations contained in the Constitution which operate upon the exercise of the power of Congress, when applied to this District"; these "restrictions . . . are contained chiefly in the amendments." Insists there "is no restriction, and I challenge the production of a restriction if there be one, which restrains the exercise of the power of Congress over a trade, foreign, alien to the District, and in which the District has not a particle of interest." If there "are to be found . . . limitations of the Constitution," then "those limitations must be produced and shown to be applicable to the power. But there are no limitations in this case. . . . the power of Congress over the slave trade in the District cannot be questioned." The slave trade "stole into this District" by congressional enactment, and it is impossible to "maintain that Congress is incompetent to repeal its own laws."

Repeats his view "that, in good faith towards Maryland, we ought not, while the institution exists there, to disturb" slavery in the District. But, in the case of "introducing slaves for sale within the District," in "prohibiting and suppressing it," we make a change to come into "precise conformity" with Maryland's policy.

To Southern senators who "yesterday spoke of the embarrassment which they felt in determining whether to vote for the bill abolishing the slave trade in the District" or for Sen. William H. Seward's amendment "abolishing slavery in the District," Clay points out the crucial difference. Seward's proposition "has for its object the entire and immediate abolition of slavery within the District of Columbia. The bill reported by the Committee of Thirteen does not touch slavery in the District of Columbia. It does not deal with it at all." The bill states "that it would be a violation of law to introduce a slave here to be sold here," and if a slave is illegally introduced here to be sold he "shall be free." Some Southerners "choose to regard this as a species of emancipation; but it is no such thing; it is a penalty inflicted on the owner of the property for violating the law of the land." It is the preferred punishment because "it is more suitable because it is more appropriate, because it is more effectual in preventing that slave trade which it is the object of the bill before the Senate to interdict." Since "the law of Virginia and Maryland was, that any slave brought into these States should be and was free from the date of his introduction," then "we can do the same thing under a power which I contend is equal to that in respect to this District." Hopes that Sen. James M. Mason, who has raised these questions, "will confide a little more in his own powers of discrimination" and "perceive the great difference between the two measures." *Cong. Globe,* 31 Cong., 1 Sess., Appendix, 1647-48. Printed in Colton, *Clay Correspondence,* 6:585-87.

Remark in Senate, September 12, 1850. In discussion of the bill to abolish the slave trade in the District of Columbia [Speech in Senate, September 3, 1850], Clay interrupts debate on amendments to repeat his hope that the Senate "will leave the bill in the state in which it was originally reported." Since the House of Representatives has just passed the Fugitive Slave bill, "This is the only one remaining, and its object was known, too, throughout the session as being simply to abolish the slave trade in this District; a trade consisting of the traffic in slaves not belonging to the District, but brought here." If the proposed amendments are adopted, "I apprehend that the effect will be that we shall pass no bill at all. . . . we shall neither suppress the slave trade in the District, nor provide those additional laws which are supposed to be necessary to prevent the enticement away of the slaves, or the increase of free people of color in this District." This will be "the consequence of those gentlemen who are opposed to the interdiction of the slave trade concurring in the vote with those gentlemen who are opposed to the other provisions of the bill." Believes that "if the two measures were separately introduced . . . they would both pass." For the bill "to prevent the enticement away of slaves and to regulate the conditions of free persons of color, there would be an undivided southern vote . . . and for the bill to suppress the slave trade we shall have, I believe the undivided northern vote." If the measures are combined, "the effect will be to lose both, to lose all."

Hopes that "slavery will itself pass away in the District," and notes happily that the slave trade "is said to be less active than it was formerly." But to Northerners, "the enormity of the slave trade here is the leading theme of conversation. . . . the idea of the existence of such a trade within the District" is "more calculated to agitate and excite, and produce those feelings which we are all desirous of allaying at once, than almost any other subject connected with these agitating questions." Any new matters introduced now will only give rise to "protracted debate, and . . . may give rise to still further debates." Objects to the introduction of any further additional provisions "when the effect will be to prevent the passage of any law" on these subjects. *Cong. Globe,* 31 Cong., 1 Sess., Appendix, 1664-65. Printed in Colton, *Clay Correspondence,* 6:587-88. The Fugitive Slave bill was approved on September 18. 9 *U.S. Stat,* 462-65.

Also on this day, during discussions on the Deficiency bill, Sen. Thomas Hart Benton submits an amendment that would compute mileage for congressmen from California and the delegate from Oregon traveling to and from Washington "according to the most traveled route within the limits of the United States." Clay argues that "the question of mileage, in consequence of discrepancies in the mode of charging" has produced "a great number of irregularities, not to say abuses." This can be remedied by "a general law," but "I do not think it right to apply a particular rule to new members." Benton had insisted that there was at least one well-traveled overland route from the Pacific to the East, but other senators pointed out that it took far less time and wear to sail to the East by way of Cape Horn. Benton's amendment, then, in Clay's view, proposed to pay California congressmen and Oregon's delegate who "travel by one route . . . for traveling by another route which they have never traveled, and which perhaps they never will travel." The current law "does not limit the route. . . . by whatever route a member may come to Washington, by that route he shall be paid." Since the word " 'route' undoubtedly means a water route as well as a land route," it "applies as well to the ocean as to the Mississippi River." Insists that "it is a vested right of every member to receive his pay by whatever route he follows." *Cong. Globe,* 31 Cong., 1 Sess., Appendix, 1342-43.

From John Sloane, Wooster, Ohio, September 12, 1850. Writes "on the subject of a suitable situation," understanding "the difference of situation, between the present [Fillmore] administration and that of the preceeding one [Taylor's]. The former had the full range of all the offices of all the Departments whereas the other is probably limitted to a few objectionable incumbents." Agrees "to be satisfied with a place which is less important" than he "might have aspired to [Sloane to Clay, February 12, 1849]." States that "the lowest amount of compensation which would induce me to go to Washington," considering his experience as "ten years a member of Congress and 3 years Secretary of State in Ohio," is "$2,000 annually." Suggests that if "the appointment of Assistant postmaster Genl. made from Iowa" does not continue to be satisfactory . . . I would accept that place." Has learned that "Gov [Thomas] Corwin . . . is in contemplation to make a change in the office of commissioner of Pensions," but since such a vacancy "must be filled with a lawyer," can lay no "claim to that place on my part." Desires "to have any place" due to "the desperate character of the persecution which I have suffered from 1824 to 48 and the relief" such a "reputable sojourn . . . would give to a wearied but unsubdued Spirit." ALS. MH.

On September 19, 1850, Clay wrote Sloane saying he had called on Thomas Corwin, who "expressed warm regard for you, and agreed with me in a high appreciation of your services and merits. I understood him to say that he had tendered the office of Treasurer [of the U.S.] to you [Sloane to Clay, February 12, 1849]. Should that not be acceptable, I think he will propose some other suitable place." Copy. KyU.

To F.R. BACKUS Washington, September 13, 1850

In reply to your letter,[1] I have to say that the statement that I am engaged in the preparation of a new Tariff to be presented at the next Session is not true. Some of us are considering the propriety of attempting at this Session some modification of the existing Tariff,[2] but nothing has been yet absolutely determined on.

ALS. KyLoF. 1. Not found. 2. For the Tariff of 1846, see Clay to Greeley, June 23, 1846. For Clay's subsequent request for modification, see Remark in Senate, Dec. 23, 1850.

To RICHARD H. BAYARD Washington, September 13, 1850

I have just returned from an interview with the President [Millard Fillmore] and Mr [Daniel] Webster, the principal object of which related to yourself in connection with the Portuguese Mission.[1] I first saw the latter, with whom my conversation terminated by my enquiring if he would interpose any obstacle to your appointment, should the President be disposed to confer it. He promptly, and with apparent satisfaction, replied none whatever.

I next saw the President to whom I remarked that, in consequence of Mrs. [Mary] Bayards delicate health,[2] rendering her residence in a Southern climate desirable, and in consequence also of some other family considerations, you were willing to accept the Portuguese mission, on the return of my son [James Brown Clay] altho' it was, in my opinion, below your merits. The President said that, if he now had to make the appointment, he would appoint you; that he was not in the habit of making pledges or promises in advance, because he ought not to preclude himself from a consideration of the actual state of circumstances when he acted; and that therefore he could not *pledge* himself to make the appointment at a future day. I told him I thought the rule he had adopted was correct, that it was satisfactory to me for him to have said what he had done, and that I would confidentially communicate what had passed between us to you, to whom I had no doubt it would be also satisfactory[.]

I have not heard from James since he left Lisbon in July.[3] He is now somewhere in Italy. I have no doubt that he will not return to Lisbon to reside. It is possible he may (altho' I am inclined to think he will not) go back to conclude a Convention in conformity with instructions from Mr. Webster.[4] Should he do so, I feel quite confident that he will not remain a longer time than may be necessary to the accomplishment of that object. His wish was to return to the U. States in November. If I should hear from him, prior to the adjournment of Congress, I will inform you.

You will perceive the propriety of regarding the contents of this letter as strictly confidential.

I feel quite sure that, unless some thing extraordinary and unexpected arises, the President will appoint you.

ALS. DLC-James Asheton and Richard Henry Bayard Papers (DNA, M212, R20). Letter marked "(Confidential)." 1. Bayard was offered his choice of the post in Portugal or in Belgium. He decided on the latter and served as chargé d'affaires in Belgium from 1851-53. See Clay to Richard H. Bayard, Sept. 18, 1850; Clay to Mary S. Bayard, Sept. 26, 1850. Daniel Webster's nephew Charles B. Haddock of New Hampshire received the appointment to Portugal. Both men were nominated on Dec. 9, 1850, and confirmed on Dec. 10. U.S. Sen., *Executive Journal*, 8:273-74; Baxter, *Daniel Webster*, 282. 2. The nature of her ailment is not known. 3. James B. Clay to Clay, June 18, 1850. 4. Clay to Webster, August 22, 1850.

Comment in Senate, September 14, 1850. During debate on the bill to abolish the slave trade in the District of Columbia [Speech in Senate, September 3, 1850], Clay is bothered that Sen. George E. Badger persists in his motions for heavy penalties to be imposed on those who help slaves to escape. Of all the measures designed "to restore that concord and harmony throughout the country," only this one remains to be passed. In passing the Fugitive Slave bill in the House of Representatives [Remark in Senate, September 12, 1850], Clay believes that "our northern friends have behaved on that subject . . . with liberality—some of them with great liberality." But the "northern portion of the people of the country attach much more importance" to this measure. If we do not pass a bill on this subject "and our northern friends return home and are interrogated . . . 'the fugitive bill passed, all the other measures passed, how does it come that the measure which we have heretofore more anxiously desired than almost any other thing connected with the subject was defeated?' " They will have to be told that the amendments of Sens. Badger and James A. Pearce were the reason.

Does not object "to the principle of the amendments to increasing the penalty for enticing away slaves," but, as he has "repeatedly remarked," wishes to see these measures in a separate bill. For "fifty years there has been no complaint about the inadequacy of the law to prevent the enticement of slaves" until a recent case brought it to the nation's attention, and Congress should not "act precipitately after an occurrence which is calculated to excite irritation." Asks, therefore, "cannot the subject lie over until the next session."

Complains that the amendment blends together two different offenses. Admits that those who are caught "enticing or attempting to persuade" a slave to escape even "without a consummation of the crime. . . . ought to be punished, but certainly not punished in the same measure as inflicted on the man who aids, assists, or abets the runaway, or who, after his escape, harbors and conceals him from his master."

Also asserts that "the fact of persuading a slave . . . is susceptible of much loose proof." A man "may say carelessly, and not with any intention, why do not you leave your master . . . and that before a jury may be considered as an attempt to persuade him to run away, and subject the man to a penalty of not less than two nor more than ten years' imprisonment." An important "principle of the penal law" is "the proportioning of the penalty or punishment to the crime according to its nature . . . for the effect of extreme, harsh, and cruel punishments is to prevent any punishment being inflicted from the reluctance which juries feel to inflicting such punishments."

Concerning "free people of color," whose "number has increased," feels that "whatever should be done should be carefully done, and in a spirit of justice and humanity towards this unfortunate class." Asks "Where are they to go? There are as many of the free States, as well as the slave States, who prohibit their entry into them." Cannot "sanction the expulsion, by force if necessary, of these human beings, these free people of color, from a residence within the District, without making any provision for an asylum for them." Declares: "I admit the evil, and I admit there ought to be some remedy applied; but I think the remedy, whatever it is, should be carefully and deliberately considered. . . . Whether it be, as I hope it may, with the consent of the colored man to send him to Liberia, or some other place, some provision of the kind ought to be made."

Repeats his fear that "I am . . . apprehensive that their retention would cause the defeat of the bill, in this or the other House, and our northern friends, perhaps would have some cause to reproach us, after having consented to the passage of all the other measures, if we should refuse to pass an act to which, perhaps, they attach the most importance."

In regard to amendments proposed by Sen. Pearce, argues that if the original bill is combined with the amendments Pearce proposes, then "both will fail." Asks that the senator not insist on this "unconsidered subject, crudely presented to us, and with respect to which there ought to be careful consideration, both as to the object and the phraseology to accomplish the object."

Complains of vagueness in "the third section" of the amendments. Pearce "thinks the actual running away with a slave is to constitute the crime. . . . As I understand it, the mere enticing or inducing a slave to run away, whether he runs away or not, is liable to the punishment which is provided." Every slave state "has graduated the punishment of these offenses according to their nature. . . . But here it proposed to make the mere conception of a crime liable to the same penalties as the consummation of it." Also insists on "a trial by jury, with punishment graduated according to the opinion of the jury." Still, "at this late period of the session," thinks Pearce "should be satisfied with the avowal of purpose to redress grievances" at the next session "when we should have time to deliberate."

Allays fears that these measures will "not produce that healing effect which their authors and advocates were calculated to effect. . . . There must be a little time allowed." While "a few of the ultra Abolitionists" will "continue to agitate," it would be only natural for them to "show some signs of dissatisfaction" after being defeated by this bill. "The defeated party are always mortified, vexed, and irritated; and the successful party should bear with a great deal." Remains convinced that "the great mass of the people everywhere rejoice and are glad that these questions have been solved."

Comments on the so-called "penalty of emancipation which this bill affixes to the bringing of a slave here for the purpose of selling him. There is no attempt to touch slaves within the District. Nor is there any attempt to emancipate any one. It is merely a penalty to be inflicted upon a man living out of the District who brings a slave within the District contrary to the law. . . . That is all. It is not intended as emancipation, but as a penalty. If emancipation follows, it is a consequence, and not the object and principle design of legislation."

Later, Clay asks for the yeas and nays on the 3rd, 4th, and 5th sections of the bill, admitting "that the amendments adopted in committee, have been somewhat improved by the amendments made in the Senate," but still thinks "the subject is so unnecessarily introduced into the bill that I shall be constrained to vote against the amendments."

After the amendments are defeated, Clay asks that "the bill may have its third reading." On September 16 the bill was engrossed and passed. *Cong. Globe*, 31 Cong., 1 Sess., Appendix, 1665-66, 1672-74. Partially printed in Colton, *Clay Correspondence*, 6:589-91.

The recent case regarding the enticement of slaves to escape had occurred on August 8, 1850, when Washington police captured a white man, William L. Chaplin, who was transporting slaves Allen and Garland out of the District of Columbia and away from their masters. Allen was captured with Chaplin, but Garland, though wounded, escaped. Washington *Daily National Intelligencer*, August 9, 1850. See also Remark in Senate, September 18, 1850.

Remark in Senate, September 16, 1850. During discussion on the bill to suppress the slave trade in the District of Columbia, Sen. Thomas H. Benton expresses his delight that his stand on the Compromise or "omnibus" bill [Clay to Combs, January 22, 1850] was completely vindicated: "I am one of those who insisted that certain bills, commonly called the omnibus, should be separated and treated on their own merits [Speech in Senate, April 8, 1850; Remark in Senate, April 11, 1850]. . . . I was right in everything that I said. We have had votes upon every subject, and when separated every subject passed, passed quickly, without a struggle, and by a great majority."

Clay responds: "The events of the last few weeks are not, in my opinion, a proper subject for individual triumph or for indulgence of a spirit of egotism. They are the triumphs of the country, the triumphs of the Union, the triumphs of harmony and concord in the midst of a distracted people." Whether these bills should have been combined or separated "was the merest question of form that ever occurred" and "if there had been no opposition to the combination, these measures would have all passed three or four months ago." Has heard that "there was a majority of some thirty or forty" in the House "ready to pass these bills in their combined form," but that is "only conjectural." Nonetheless, the "measures have passed. I am rejoiced at it, and I have no doubt that the beneficial effect intended to be produced by them, whether in a combined or separate form, will, at no distant day, be fully realized." *Cong. Globe*, 31 Cong., 1 Sess., 1829.

To Millard Fillmore, Washington, September 16, 1850. If Fillmore intends "to appoint a Chargé des Affaires from Virginia" and "the competition is confined to Genl. Cock and Mr. Pendleton," believes that "Genl Cock will give most public satisfaction, especially to the Whigs in Virginia." ALS. NBuHi. Letter marked "(Private & Confidential)."

John S. Pendleton of Virginia was nominated as chargé des affaires to the Argentine Republic on February 6, 1851, and was confirmed on February 25. U.S. Sen., *Executive Journal*, 8:288, 298. "Genl. Cock" possibly refers to John Hartwell Cocke (1780-1866) who rose to the rank of brigadier general in the War of 1812 and served for many years as a vice president of the American Colonization Society. Clement Eaton, *The Mind of the Old South* (Baton Rouge, 1964), 4-20. No Cock or Cocke received any appointment from Fillmore.

To RICHARD H. BAYARD Washington, September 18, 1850[1]

I had an interview with the President [Millard Fillmore] yesterday, at his instance. He asked me if you would not prefer the Belgian Mission, stating that Mr [Daniel] Webster wished one of the missions, either to Portugal or Belgium, for a friend of his [Charles Haddock], who would like to go to

Lisbon, on account of the great cheapness of the place.[2] I informed the President that I had confidentially communicated to you what had passed between him and me, at our last interview, that I had received your answer, expressing your satisfaction &c, that I should myself decidedly prefer the Belgian mission, but that I did not know if the state of Mrs. [Mary S.] Bayards health would not induce you to prefer the other. He requested me to see Mr. Webster and make an amicable arrangement of the two missions between you and his friend.

I have this moment returned from Mr. Websters. After talking the whole matter over he consented, with cheerfulness, that you might have your choice of the two missions. I think that to Belgium will be filled next week, or immediately after the adjournment of Congress. The President inclines to the former. That to Portugal will not be filled until my son [James Brown Clay] is heard from.

You must now decide for yourself. I should like to have a conversation with you on the subject, but for that there is no opportunity.

My affectionate regards to Mrs Bayard and the family.

P.S. You need not hurry your decision, which will be sufficiently early recd. next week.

ALS. DLC-James Asheton and Richard Henry Bayard Papers (DNA, M212, R20). Letter marked "(Private and Confidential)." 1. Letter is not dated but is endorsed "Hon. Henry Clay Sep 18h. 1850." 2. Clay to Bayard, Sept. 13, 1850.

Remark in Senate, September 18, 1850. When Sen. Salmon P. Chase asks to introduce a bill to prohibit slavery in U.S. territories, Clay opposes the request: "There is, I believe, peace now prevailing throughout all our borders. I believe it is permanent." Trusts the Senate to "put its face against any further disturbance of this country." Chase disagrees with Clay's opinion "that these questions are settled," but withdraws his proposition.

Later, when Sen. Thomas G. Pratt's bill to prevent the enticing or assisting of slaves to escape from the District of Columbia comes up for a second reading [Comment in Senate, September 14, 1850], Sen. John P. Hale teases Clay by stating his hope that "the Senate will not take up and debate another of these distracting and aggressive measures, to wound the sensibilities of gentlemen here." Clay responds: "I consider the passage of this bill as part of that great system of policy which has for its object peace and quiet." Explains that "This bill proposes to put an end to an aggression," and adds in retort to Hale that "if he will enter into bond and security that no more slaves shall be stolen from the District," then "I presume gentlemen will not ask for the passage of this bill."

Chase objects to taking up Pratt's bill after his own—"which I consider as infinitely more important"—was withdrawn in deference to the Senate's wishes. If Pratt's bill "is a part of the scheme of adjustment," as Clay argues, "it has recently been adopted as such" and "received no consideration . . . from the Committee of Thirteen."

Clay reminds Chase that "the question is on the second reading of the bill—a mere matter of form." If Chase introduces his bill, "the whole subject was fully open for discussion. The motion now is simply to take up a bill as a matter of form to give it its second reading," an "almost invariable custom." The bill is then taken up.

Clay proposes "to strike out the third section, which excludes free persons of color from this District." Although "they have been increasing" and "something ought to be done," feels that first "we should ascertain where they are to go, and where they can go." When Pratt explains that the bill only prevents "free negroes coming into the District hereafter," Clay withdraws his motion. *Cong. Globe*, 31 Cong., 1 Sess., 1858-59.

Pratt's bill died at the end of the session without coming to a vote. U.S. Sen., *Journal*, 31 Cong., 1 Sess., 636, 647, 651. For Pratt (Whig, Md.), see *BDAC.*

From Charles Buford, Lexington, Ky., September 19, 1850. Writes in behalf of "John Adair of Kentucky" who "was appointed Collector of the Port of Astoria in Oregon" during James K. Polk's administration. Explains that after Adair and his family went to Oregon, "the expences of the voyage consuming all, and more than all, he was worth," only "a very short time" later "before there could be any proof of his incompetency, he was removed from office by Genl [Zachary] Taylor's cabinet." Describing the removal as "an act of wanton cruelty," asserts that there "was no difference of opinion upon the subject" among Kentucky Whigs and Democrats. Has just learned that Adair "is still acting Collector his rival, having failed, to execute the required bonds," and therefore desires "his restoration to office. The salary is small, but still of consequence to him, without means, and with a large family to support." Hopes Clay "will present the hardness of the case to those in power, and endeavour to have him reinstated."

Adds in a postscript: "your son John [Morrison Clay], has won two races today viz the mile heats race with Yoric [*sic*, Yorick]; and the 2 year old stake with his Boston colt; both good races and won in fine style." ALS. DNA, RG56, Entry 247, Collectors, Box 183.

On September 23, 1850, Clay sent Buford's letter to Secretary of the Treasury Thomas Corwin, commending the case "to your consideration & justice." *Ibid.*

Yorick was sired by Clay's stallion Yorkshire. Charles Buford was one of the leading horsebreeders in Lexington. Perrin, *History of Fayette County*, 144, 152, *passim.*

John Adair remained collector at Astoria until August 15, 1852, when he was replaced by George Gibbs. The following year, however, he was appointed collector of the port of Umpqua. Charles H. Carey, *A General History of Oregon Prior to 1861*, 2 vols. (Portland, 1936), 2:467, 496, 741, 762, 769.

To JAMES BROWN CLAY Washington, September 20, 1850

I recd. your letter dated at Naples the 17h. Ulto. That from Gibraltar, to which it refers, has not been received.

I have written so fully to you of late that I do not know that I have much now to add. There will not be at present any attempt to elevate the grade of our mission to Portugal, and already the subject of your successor has been matter of consideration.[1] From most of your letters, I supposed that you had no desire to remain in Europe in the Diplomatic line, unless you had a position of higher rank. If I had believed that you were desirous to be transferred, in the same rank, to another court, perhaps I could have had it done.

I do not know whether you will determine or not to go back to Lisbon to complete the work you began there.[2] It will be, I apprehend, inconvenient to do so, and I do not think it would be important if you do not wish to return.[3] If you [go] back, your salary will continue, I presume, without regard to the fact of your having formally quit Lisbon. And indeed, whether you go back or not, I am inclined to think that it ought to continue up to the time when you may decline, if you do decline to go back, and that you ought to make out your account accordingly, as your remaining in Europe has been, among other objects, to hear from Washington.

All our Slavery troubles are now supposed to be adjusted. Every measure which I proposed in Feby last has substantially passed;[4] and the Country seems to be disposed generally to give me quite as much credit as I deserve.

I keep moving about, but my health is not as good as I could wish. I expect to leave this City on the 28h instant for home, which I never in my life so much wanted to see. I received Telegraphic dispatch the day before yesterday that John [Morrison Clay] had won two races that day, one with Yorrick [*sic*, Yorick], and the other with the Boston Colt from Margaret Woods. His best horse Zampa[5] was lame and did not run.

We are at a loss when to expect you, as we do not know whether you will return to Lisbon. I informed you that the President [Millard Fillmore] and Mr. [Daniel] Webster both entertain very favorable opinions of the manner in which you have acquitted yourself in your mission[.][6]

My love to Susan [Jacob Clay] & the children.

ALS. DLC-TJC (DNA, M212, R11). 1. Clay to Bayard, Sept. 13, 1850. 2. Clay to Clayton, June 7, 1849. 3. Clay to Webster, August 22, 1850. 4. Clay to Combs, Jan. 22, 1850. 5. Zampa had been sired by Yorkshire. Perrin, *History of Fayette County*, 152, 154. 6. Clay to James B. Clay, August 31, 1850.

Remark in Senate, September 21, 1850. During discussion on appropriations for hydrographical and topographical surveys to improve navigation on the Ohio River, Clay speaks in support of a proposition to set aside $20,000 for a system of river improvements "to consist of the erection of reservoirs of water towards the head of the river, to be let out to supply the channel of the river during the dry season." Explains that "in seasons of freshets, at high water, a vast surplus is thrown through the channel, leaving a deficiency for the space of some two months. . . . The principle is to retain the surplus. . . . by the erection of dams upon the headwaters of the river." The system "has been reviewed by scientific men. . . . who have arrived at the conclusion that it is practicable." Admits "that it is said that it is a humbug," but recalls "[Robert] Fulton's great attempt to apply the power of steam to the navigation of the waters," the steam-powered railroad, and the new "telegraphic communication," all of which were "pronounced to be a humbug," but succeeded spectacularly. Moreover, "Congress appropriated $30,000 for . . . ascertaining the practicability of communications by means of electricity."

Points out that eight states, including "four of the largest States of the Union: New York, Pennsylvania, Ohio, and Virginia" are "directly interested in this project." The $20,000 sum will cover "those surveys and examinations . . . necessary to ascertain certainly the practicability and probable expense of the object. The engineer, who has made these calculations, assures us that a sum less than half a million of dollars will be sufficient to render the Ohio river navigable all the year, with an amount of water sufficient at least for the secondary if not the primary class of steamboats." Asserts that "For less than the cost of a custom-house in New York or Boston, we may effect an object" that would be "profitable" and "just" for a "national appropriation of money." For "less than we appropriated the other day for the erection of a custom-house at Bangor," the Senate can sanction "an object in which all the western States are so deeply interested."

While not "sufficiently skilled in scientific requisites to arrive at a just conclusion on these subjects," feels that this "is one of those projects which is commended to me by no aversion to Nature herself, for I do not consider . . . that rivers were only made for canals. I think we adopt what Nature herself points out to us, by constructing reservoirs to supply a deficiency of water in the channel of the river at certain seasons of the year." *Cong. Globe*, 31 Cong., 1 Sess., Appendix, 1380-81.

To HENRY CLAY, JR. [III] Washington, September 24, 1850

I received your letter of the 17h. inst. I am sorry that you find your confinement disagreeable; but my dear child it is impossible that you should ever become distinguished and worthy of your lamented father [Henry Clay, Jr.] and worthy of me, without study, close study, and some sacrifices of ease and comfort. These I hope you will cheerfully make. The longer you remain the more will your studies become light and agreeable. Such was your father's experience.

I was sorry to see so many demerits affixed to your name by the last official report, which was communicated to me.[1] I hope that you will exert yourself constantly to lessen the number of them, until none shall be attached to you.

I shall leave here in a few days for home, and I will write to you, and get others to write to you when I get there. In the mean time, I hope my dear Grandson that you will resolutely meet all your studies and all your duties, and do not bring any reproach on me or discredit on yourself. I will send you some Washn. papers.

AL. Henry Clay Memorial Foundation, Lexington, Ky. 1. Clay to Morehead, Dec. 14, 1848.

Remark in Senate, September 24, 1850. In discussion on the Mexican Indemnity bill, Clay argues that "the bill ought to pass. It is the duty of Congress to make appropriations to furnish ways and means; and it is the duty of the Executive to make remittances to pay debts; and we ought to aid the Executive in making these payments in the most advantageous manner to the country."

Feels obligated to live up to "a verbal contract . . . made with the former Administration," so Congress should "make the appropriation." If there is "one point of objection . . . that is, that we are asked to make an appropriation now which is to be paid on the last day of May next," but the "mode of exchange," requiring dealings with European bankers, "requires time." Also, "the state of the market in relation to exchange in Mexico" is such that "By giving time," bankers can "give you better terms than they would do if they drew only within a month of the 30th May, pressing an amount on the market which it could not absorb, and consequently sustaining great loss, both on the part of the Government and the bankers." Thus, it is best "that the eight or nine months may be employed in this process . . . to place the money on the best terms we can get where the creditor is to receive it, in the city of Mexico." *Cong. Globe*, 31 Cong., 1 Sess., Appendix, 1379.

The so-called Mexican Indemnity bill (HB388) provided for "carrying into execution . . . the twelfth article of the treaty . . . [of] Guadalupe Hidalgo." The 12th article provided for the payment of $15,000,000 to Mexico, $3,000,000 up front and the remainder in instalments of $3,000,000 per year plus an annual interest rate of 6 percent. HB388 passed the House on September 18 and the Senate on September 24. It was signed by the president on September 24. U.S. Sen., *Journal*, 31 Cong., 1 Sess., 650, 662, 669, 686; U.S. H. of Reps., *Journal*, 31 Cong., 1 Sess., 1437, 1494, 1520, 1548.

Also on this day, presents a petition from "all the practical printers in the city of Washington, in every office, and without regard to polititical predilections or preferences," who ask Congress "to dispense with the contract system in the printing for Congress." Since "it operates disadvantageously to the public and also to the petitioners, who appear to be a very respectable class of people. . . . they think some other system ought to be adopted," because "those who contract do not receive anything like remunerating prices, and are utterly unable to give liberal wages to those whom they employ." Adds that "My own personal opinion is that it would be better to establish a Government printing office and put it under suitable management." The petition is referred to the Committee on Printing. *Cong. Globe*, 31 Cong., 1 Sess., 1959.

To MARY S. BAYARD Washington, September 26, 1850

Intending to take my departure saturday morning for Ashland, I wish before I go to say a few words to you, and they can only be a few, altho' if I had time, as I have inclination, they should be many. I thought it best to address Mr [Richard H.] Bayard directly instead of answering your two last letters, as contingencies might possibly arise, in which it might be expedient to use my letters,[1] considering the subject of which they treated.

His hopes and yours, I trust, will be realized, in respect to the mission to Europe;[2] and I sincerely hope also that your health will be re-established by it, and that you may derive from it all other anticipated advantages[.]

Considering the accidents of human life, especially those which are incident to my advanced stage of it, we may never meet again. This to me will be a great privation; cheerfully however submitted to, from the hopes that it may redound to your health & happiness. But truth & friendship compel me to say that a large portion of my own satisfaction & enjoyment in life has been, during the last seventeen years, derived from your society & friendship. My affectionate regards to Mr Bayard and every member of your family.

ALS. DLC-James Asheton and Richard Henry Bayard Papers (DNA, M212, R20). 1. Clay to Bayard, Sept. 13 and 18, 1850. 2. On Sept. 26, 1850, Richard H. Bayard advised Clay that "I have decided in conformity with your opinion and that of Mr. [Daniel] Webster in favor of Brussels," and asks that he communicate to President Fillmore "suitable acknowledgements for his kindness in offering this particular Mission." Copy. DLC-James Asheton and Richard Henry Bayard Papers (DNA, M212, R20).

To Common Council of Detroit, Mich., September 26, 1850. Thanks them for their letter praising his efforts in Congress to preserve the Union and inviting him to visit their city. Declines their invitation because of his desire to return home as speedily as possible.

In respect to the way Congress had dealt with the sectional controversy, states that the adjustment "was attended with great difficulty, and that difficulty was augmented by an amount of ultraism, from both sections of the Union, which I have never before seen in the National Councils. I think the adjustment would have been effected considerably earlier but for objections which were taken to the form in which it was proposed." Warns that there will still be "discontent and passions in different quarters," but believes "these discontents will find no sympathy with the great mass of the people . . . and that they will soon die away and disappear." Copy. Printed in Washington *Daily National Intelligencer*, October 23, 1850.

Remark in Senate, September 27, 1850. When Sen. Joseph R. Underwood makes a motion to print 5,000 additional copies of Rev. Ralph Randolph Gurley's report on his mission to Liberia, Clay voices his support: "I know the person who was sent by the Executive Government to Liberia to collect information contained in this report, and I believe he is worthy of confidence and regard. I believe this report will be . . . read with great satisfaction." Since the cost of this printing is estimated at only $200, the motion is quickly "agreed to—ayes 25, noes not counted." *Cong. Globe*, 31 Cong., 1 Sess., 2033-34.

Gurley had gone to Liberia in September, 1849, as a special agent of the American Colonization Society to observe developments there since it had attained independence. On his return home, he wrote a comprehensive report addressed to the secretary of state who then submitted the report to the Senate. Cassell, *Liberia*, 161.

To BENJAMIN GRATZ *et al.* Lexington, October 10, 1850

I have received, with the liveliest feelings of thankfulness and gratitude, the friendly note which you did me the honor to address to me,[1] inviting me to attend a Free Barbecue[2] which my neighbours and other fellow Citizens of Kentucky, Whig and Democratic, are preparing to give the 17th. instant, as a testimony of their approbation of the public services of myself and other members of Congress, during the late protracted Session, in the adoption of measures, intended to heal the divisions existing in the Country, and to restore harmony & concord.[3]

During the arduous struggle in Congress, it was a source of great satisfaction and encouragement to me to learn from Kentucky that my fellow Citizens in this State, without distinction of party, were almost unanimous in favor of those measures, so long discussed, which were designed to reconcile Sectional differences, and preserve the Union free from all danger. I am rejoiced, upon my return home, to find that I was not mistaken as to the state of public opinion in Kentucky. My Democratic fellow Citizens have met and welcomed me with a cordiality and warmth not surpassed by the Whigs, and both parties have united in gratifying demonstrations of their attachment and confidence.[4] It is highly honorable and consoling to the patriotism of our Country that, on such great and perilous occasions, as that which occurred during the late Session of Congress, parties will lay aside all their divisions and strifes, and heartily co-operate in the preservation of that glorious Union, without which we have no sure guarranty for the enjoyment of Liberty, or any other political blessing.

I cherish the hope, and entertain the confident belief that the system of measures, passed by Congress, will finally be acquiesced in by the great body of the People of the U. States, and lead to quiet and tranquillity. Malcontents, at the North and in the South, may seek to continue or revive agitation, but, rebuked and discountenanced by the Masses, they will ultimately be silenced generally, and induced to keep the peace.

Having returned home, Gentlemen, in delicate health, and greatly wanting repose, I should have preferred to avoid the ceremonies and excitement incident to the Barbecue, especially as that was not needed to assure me of the kind and friendly feelings towards me, entertained by my neighbours and fellow Citizens of all parties. But as I understand that extensive arrangements have been made, and invitations sent out, which would occasion much disappointment if the Barbacue were not served up, I accept your invitation with great pleasure. And, in behalf of those patriotic members of Congress who co-operated in the measures of Adjustment, and for myself, I tender an expression of profound acknowledgments for the approbation of our joint exertions which you, and those you represent, do us the honor to entertain.[5]

ALS. DLC-James O. Harrison Papers (DNA, M212, R21). 1. On Oct. 4, 1850, Benjamin Gratz *et al.* had written Clay from Lexington, inviting him to "a free Barbecue, to be given in this city on the 17th inst." by "Democrats and Whigs alike" who want to express their "feelings of admiration and gratitude" for his services in preserving the Union and the Constitution. Note that "During your long and eventful career, they have never welcomed your return with such unanimous and affectionate manifestations of their regard as now. Kentucky, as you know, has been for many years divided into two great parties, each struggling for the ascendency. Now her people are, for the time, standing side by side upon the same glorious platform. . . . The cry that 'the union was in danger,' obliterated . . . the old party issues and animosities, and Kentucky, animated by the loftiest patriotism, rallied all her sons to the rescue. Her Whigs and her Democrats stood shoulder to shoulder in the fearful crisis. The triumph that followed is the most glorious in our annals." Add that "in this great struggle, you were a great actor. The courage and patriotism and eloquence displayed by you in adjusting those fearful questions which threatened to dissolve the Union, have not only extorted the admiration of the country and of mankind, but placed you above and beyond the region of party. Upon this lofty eminence may your fame rest forever." Copy. Printed in Frankfort *Commonwealth*, Oct. 22, 1850. 2. The Barbecue was held at the fairgrounds on Oct. 17, 1850. Six resolutions praising Clay and the Compromise of 1850 and declaring Kentucky's support for the Union were passed, ten toasts were offered, John C. Breckinridge gave a speech and Clay responded, and letters from politicians who could not attend were read. Breckinridge's, but not Clay's, remarks are recorded in the Lexington *Kentucky Statesman*, Oct. 19, 1850. 3. Clay to Combs, Jan. 22, 1850. 4. When Clay arrived back in Lexington from Washington on Oct. 2, 1850, he was met by a large contingent and escorted to the Phoenix Hotel. After making some remarks and declaring that the Union was safe, he pointed his finger in the direction of Ashland and stated: "But there lives an old lady about a mile-and-a-half from here, whom I would rather see than any of you." Lexington *Kentucky Statesman*, Oct. 5, 1850. 5. In an undated letter, probably written *ca.* Oct. 10, 1850, Clay informed James O. Harrison that "it would be very well to address invitations to the proposed Barbacue" to prominent political leaders, including Stephen A. Douglas, Lewis Cass, Henry S. Foote, and Jesse D. Bright. Doubts that any, except possibly Bright, might attend, "but they might all regard the invitation as a compliment." ALS. DLC-HC (DNA, M212, R21).

To JAMES BROWN CLAY Lexington, October 18, 1850

I recd. here two letters from you in Italy,[1] and was glad to learn by the last that you had recd. my letters addressed to you from New port [Newport, R.I.].[2] I do not think that the Executive at Washn. thought that you had departed from your instructions in demanding your passports at Lisbon. At least no such idea was expressed to me. On the contrary both the President [Millard Fillmore] & Mr. [Daniel] Webster spoke to me in flattering terms of your conduct of the negotiation.[3] Mr. Webster drew a very advantageous comparison of you with another Foreign minister of the U. States of the highest grade.[4]

The case which occurred at Lisbon was strictly within your instructions. The only question was whether they ought to have been given. Perhaps if Mr. [John M.] Clayton had foreseen the offer of Portugal to pay all the claims but that of the [*General*] Armstrong,[5] and a proposal to arbitrate that, he would not have given them. The only doubt I have is whether you might not have presumed that & acted accordingly. Perhaps you took the wiser course in pursuing your instructions strictly. At all events, no mischief but a little delay has happened.

I think it is optional with you whether you return or not to Lisbon.[6] If entirely agreeable and convenient to you I think it would be best, and in that case I think that Susan [Jacob Clay] will do well to return with her brother [Thomas P. Jacob] & children from Paris, as I understand you to contemplate.

Whether you go back or not, I think your Salary ought not to be limited to the time you left Lisbon, but should run on until the time that you finally decide to return home. The govt. too ought to pay you for any losses you sustained in House rent, and by the sale of your furniture, in consequence of your sudden departure from Lisbon, under its orders.

I inferred from all your letters that you did not wish to remain in Europe, in the same diplomatic grade. If I had supposed otherwise, perhaps I might have procured your transfer to another court, in the same grade. Of that we will talk on your return—

Your house is not sold. I shall not accept Goodloes offer.[7] His store house is not worth, I am told, more than four or five thousand dollars & is difficult to rent. In the mean[time] [George R.] Trotter, appointed p. master,[8] is about to return to Town, and I shall have some trouble in having your house suitably taken care of. He it is feared is in the last stage of consumption. If you were at home I believe that I would now sell you Ashland, and take your house in part.[9]

Henry C. Hart now here says that your St Louis land has advanced $10.000 since you left us.[10]

John [Morrison Clay] won the week before the last Three days races, the only ones he ran, in Louisville.[11]

The health of all here and at Mansfield is good except my own. I have fears for myself, which I hope may prove unfounded.

My love to Susan [Jacob Clay], Lucy [Jacob Clay] and the other children.

ALS. DLC-TJC (DNA, M212, R11). 1. Not found. 2. Clay to James B. Clay, August 15 and 20, 1850. 3. Clay to Clayton, June 7, 1849. 4. Reference obscure. 5. Clay to Clayton, June 7, 1849. 6. Clay to Webster, August 22, 1850. 7. Clay to James B. Clay, August 20, 1850. 8. Clay to Thomas H. Clay, August 6, 1850. 9. Clay to James B. Clay, Oct. 27, 1850. 10. See 9:303. 11. The races in Louisville ran from Oct. 8-11. John entered Maria Wood on both the 10th and 11th and Yorick also on the 11th. Louisville *Daily Journal*, Oct. 7, 10, 11, 1850. Maria Wood had been sired by Yorkshire. Perrin, *History of Fayette County*, 152, 154.

From Hamilton Fish, Albany, N.Y., October 18, 1850. Acknowledges Clay's recommendation [not found] of "Mr Graves to be appointed a Commissioner for this State," but regrets "that I cannot evince my appreciation of any recommendation from you, by returning forthwith a Commission," because "I have already appointed Mr Graves. His Commission bore date on 1 July last." Desires "the names of Gentlemen in different parts of your State, & especially in the larger Cities & towns, suitable to be appointed as such Commissioners. Our Statute limits the number of these officers to five for any County."

Informs Clay that "our Whig friends who took exception to the proceedings at the State Convention at Syracuse" held their own meeting "yesterday at Utica," marked by a "spirit of toleration & devotion to the interests of the Whig party." Adds that "I hope that in November we shall be able to give a good account of this State." ALS. DLC-Hamilton Fish Papers (DNA, M212, R21).

The New York Whig State convention had met in Syracuse on September 26, 1850, with Francis Granger acting as chairman. The convention nominated Washington Hunt for governor but then split into two factions over whether the resolutions adopted by the convention should accept the Compromise of 1850, even though it did not embrace the Wilmot Proviso, or should recommend that Congress explicitly prohibit slavery in New Mexico and Utah and should thank Sen. William Henry Seward for representing New York's views in the U.S. Senate. When substitute resolutions providing for the latter passed, Granger led the conservatives, dubbed the "Silver Greys" because of Granger's long hair, out of the convention. The Silver Greys, who had President Fillmore's support, held another convention at Utica on October 17 and at Fillmore's insistence nominated Washington Hunt for governor, thereby keeping the Whig party intact. Alexander, *Political History of New York*, 2:153-57; Smith, *Presidencies of Taylor & Fillmore*, 202-4.

In the 1850 New York State elections, Washington Hunt defeated Democrat

Horatio Seymour for governor by a vote of 238,421 to 238,159. *BDGUS*, 3:1081. Whigs also won 81 seats in the state assembly to 47 for the Democrats, and 1 for the Free Soil party. New York *Herald*, November 8, 1850. Whigs won 17 congressional seats to 16 for the Democrats. *Guide to U.S. Elections*, 591. In New York City Whigs won 12 seats on the board of assistant aldermen to 7 for the Democrats. New York *Herald*, November 7, 1850. Whig Ambrose C. Kingsland was chosen as mayor over Democrat Fernando Wood by 22,546 votes to 17,993. Holli, *Biographical Dictionary of American Mayors*.

On October 29, 1850, Clay wrote Hamilton Fish that Mr. Graves "had not recd. your Commission. . . . You may therefore deem it necessary to send to him a duplicate." Recommends "Thomas Smith of Louisville (K.) as a suitable person to be appointed Commr. &c for N. York in that City." ALS. KyU. There were several Graveses in Lexington, and it is not clear which one received the commission. See also Fish to Clay, November 8, 1850.

To HENRY CLAY, JR. [III] Lexington, October 22, 1850

I got home about three weeks ago,[1] and found all well here. I have recd. from Washington an offic[i]al report of your Demerits the last month, representing the number at 15.[2] This I believe is less than the preceeding months averaged; and I hope you will exert yourself to diminish them, until none remain to be charged to you.

Nanny and Tommy[3] are now up at Mr. [Thomas A.] Marshall's having come to see me. She has been very well, but he has had a fever, from which he has recovered.

Geo R. Harrison has been appointed a Midshipman and is now at Annapolis, preparing for his profession, of which he appears very fond.[4]

I shall expect you to write to me when ever you can. Your Grandma [Lucretia Hart Clay] & Uncle John [Morrison Clay] send their love.

ALS. Henry Clay Memorial Foundation, Lexington, Ky. 1. Clay to Gratz *et al.*, Oct. 10, 1850. 2. Clay to Morehead, Dec. 14, 1848. 3. For "Nanny," or Anne Clay (1837-1917), Henry Clay III's sister, see 9:31 and Melba Porter Hay, "Madeline McDowell Breckinridge: Kentucky Suffragist and Progressive Reformer," Ph.D. dissertation, University of Kentucky, 1980, pp. 4, 176, *passim*. For Henry's brother "Tommy," or Thomas J. Clay, see 9:389, 391, 393. Thomas J. Clay died Oct. 12, 1863, of typhoid while serving in the Confederate Army. Henry Clay III had died on June 5, 1862, of typhoid fever while serving in the Union Army. Smith & Rogers, *The Clay Family*, 179. 4. Clay to Graham, August 28, 1850.

To Alexander H.H. Stuart, Washington, October 22, 1850. Expresses his disappointment that "Col. William Henry Russell of California" had not been named to "an Indian Agency in that State." Has learned "that he failed to obtain it, in consequence of an objection interposed by Mr. [John J.] Crittenden, founded upon some passionate expressions used by Col. Russell, towards him in reference to the nomination of Genl [Zachary] Taylor." Complains that "a Mr. [George] Barbour of this State was appointed, who, as I am informed, has used quite as exceptionable language towards me, as any which Col. Russell could have employed in regard to Mr. Crittenden," but adds that "for this I did not care a straw."

Describes Russell as "a blood connexion of Patrick Henry," who "was a member of the Kentucky Legislature . . . and altho' a Whig was chosen from a Democratic County." As "one of the Pioneers to California," who "had much intercourse with the Civilized Indians in that State," brought several back to Missouri, one of whom "remained with me several months." Praises his "prominent part in the Whig party" of Missouri. In behalf of this "interprizing, brave, intelligent and honorable" man, who has been "a most zealous & faithful friend," takes "the liberty to ask the President

[Millard Fillmore] and you to reconsider the case of Col Russell," since Barbour declined the appointment. ALS. KyLoF. Written from Lexington.

George W. Barbour of Trigg County, Ky., had served in the state senate 1848-50. Collins, *History of Kentucky*, 2:731. Fillmore nominated Barbour for Indian agent on September 28, 1850, and he was confirmed on September 30. When he declined, Fillmore on May 4, 1852, nominated Pearson B. Reading of California in his place. Reading was confirmed on May 11. U.S. Sen., *Executive Journal*, 8:268, 272, 384, 387. For Russell's subsequent appointment, see Clay to Fillmore, Early March, 1851.

To JAMES BROWN CLAY Lexington, October 27, 1850

I sold your house and lot, and the ground which you are to get on Megowan's death, on the 24h. inst. to Harvey Miller at Nine thousand dollars, one third payable in a draft endorsed by E.P. Johnson at N[ew]. O[rleans]. on the first of January next, one other third on the 24h. Oct. 1851 and the remaining $3000 on the 24h. Oct 1852, without interest, and with the same endorser. Possession immediately delivered. Considering your anxiety to sell, the sale is a good one, property being very low in Lexn.[1] The only regret I have is that, if you had been at home, perhaps I might have sold you Ashland & taken your property in part.

Your mother [Lucretia Hart Clay] has had all your furniture &c brought to Ashland, except the bed stead & looking glasses, which I will try to sell to Mr. Miller.

I repeat what I said in a former letter[2] 1st. that the Governmt ought to indemnify you for losses occasioned by your sudden departure from Lisbon, and 2dly that your Salary ought to continue until your final departure from Europe, as you had to remain there for instructions from Washn. after you left Lisbon—

We are all tolerably well. H[enry]. C. Hart and his family dined with us today on their return to St Louis.

My love to Susan [Jacob Clay] & the children.

ALS. DLC-TJC (DNA, M212, R11). 1. James B. Clay to Clay, May 26, 1850. 2. Clay to James B. Clay, Oct. 18, 1850.

To Griffith Owen, October 30, 1850. Expresses his sympathy after "the destruction of the Church in Southwark," in Philadelphia and admires "the motives which prompt the desire to have it rebuilt." Regrets he cannot accept an invitation to deliver a "discourse or lecture . . . in order to promote it," because he is already too "burthened with engagements, public and private . . . to contract any new one." ALS. Wv-Ar.

This Griffith Owen was probably a descendant of Griffith Owen, a Quaker preacher who served in William Penn's proprietary government in the early 1700s. *DAB*.

From George W. Jones, Dubuque, Iowa, November 2, 1850. Complains that "Coln. F[itz]. H[enry] Warren, the second asst P.M. Genl, who prevented the appointment of your friend Mr Wm Gilliam to the Land Office at Iowa City . . . has co-operated with Mr [William H.] Seward in the appointment of Free soilers & abolitionists to Office & . . . warmly opposed the Compromise & adjustment Bill [Clay to Combs, January 22, 1850]." Now Warren "has written to this State that our Sur Genl. Coln Caleb H. Booth is to be removed . . . & that Mr Springer a Free-soil friend of his is to be appointed." Claims that the "leaders of the Whig Party in this state . . . have always been opposed to Coln. Warren, know that he coincides in feeling & in actions with Seward, [John P.] Hale & other of the Abolition party & will, by the opening of the next Session of Congress address you & the President [Millard Fillmore] for the purpose of procuring his removal." Until then, however, "Warren has & still does controul all removals from and appointments to Office in this state, whilst . . . other whigs of equally high character, have no influence. I was not surprised at this during the admn. of Genl [Zachary] Taylor but I am now that Mr Fillmore is at the head of the Govt." Believes Fillmore will not consent to Booth's removal but might be pressed upon to do so by "Mr Stewart [*sic*, Alexander H.H. Stuart]" who "is unacquainted with the *real* character of Warren & will again be controuled by him." Asks Clay to "address Mr Stewart in reference to Coln Warren & if not asking too much of you may I, also, request you to say a word in fav. of the retention of Coln Booth as Sur Genl." Adds that Booth was recommended "by whigs as well as by democrats," has never been "a violent partizan" and has conducted himself to the entire satisfaction of "all liberal minded & just whigs." ALS. ViU.

Fitz Henry Warren (1816-78), newspaper editor and in 1844 chairman of the Iowa Whig state committee, had been appointed in 1849 first assistant postmaster general in the Taylor administration. *NCAB*, 12:228. Caleb H. Booth had been nominated and confirmed as surveyor general for Wisconsin and Iowa in January, 1849. He held that office until George B. Sargent was nominated for it in January, 1852. Sargent was confirmed on May 1, 1852. U.S. Sen., *Executive Journal*, 8:23, 358, 386. The Mr. Springer to whom Jones refers is probably Francis Springer who had served in the Iowa house and was nominated in January, 1852 as register of the land office at Fairfield, Iowa. He was confirmed on August 31, 1852. *Ibid.*, 8:358, 452. William Gilliam was nominated to be receiver of the public moneys for the Chariton district in Iowa on August 21, 1852, but his name was withdrawn for the position on August 30 when he was nominated for the post of register of the land office for the Chariton district. He was confirmed on August 31. *Ibid.*, 443, 446, 448. Caleb H. Booth was subsequently mayor of Dubuque. For Booth and Springer, see also *Iowa Journal of History and Politics*, 2:485; 4:509; 12:242; 54:335.

To Thomas B. Stevenson, Cincinnati, Ohio, November 3, 1850. Expresses his pleasure when he learned that "Mr [Thomas] Corwin had tendered to you the head of a Bureau." Feels Stevenson's "decision not to take it" was "wise if you have reasonable prospects of an independent support where you now are." Because of "its uncertain tenure," considers officeholding "as a means of obtaining a livelihood . . . not very desirable."

Fears that "Mr [Joseph] Gales [Jr.] of the [Washington *Daily National*] Intelligencer is . . . on his last legs."

While he would like "to render any friendly service in my power to Mr R.M. Corwin [*sic*, Richard M. Corwine]," regrets there are circumstances "not necessary to mention, which prevent my recommending him for the Judicial Station in California." Copy. OCHP. Partially printed in Colton, *Clay Correspondence*, 3:499.

Stevenson notes in Colton, *Clay Correspondence*, 3:499 that the offer to him of an appointment was "an unsolicited kindness" which resulted from "the unavailing exertions to procure me an appointment under the Administration of President [Millard] Fillmore's immediate predecessor [Zachary Taylor]." For earlier attempts to obtain a government appointment for Stevenson, see Clay to Stevenson, December 21, 1849, and January 26, 1850.

Joseph Gales, Jr., did not die until 1860. *CAB*. Corwine is not listed in U.S. Sen., *Executive Journal*, vol. 8 as receiving the appointment in California.

To ALEXANDER H.H. STUART Lexington, November 7, 1850

I recd. your kind friendly & satisfactory letter of the 30th. Ulto. and I am thankful for it. The information which I received,[1] that the Atto. General

[John J. Crittenden] had prevented the appointment of Mr [William H.] Russell to an Indian Agency was from Dr [William M.] Gwin.[2] He stated that the President [Millard Fillmore] was willing to appoint him, but referred him to Mr. Crittenden, who was inflexibly opposed to the appointment, and that it was therefore not made. I am very glad to receive your correction of that statement.

If there are well founded objections to Col Russells appointment (of which I am altogether ignorant) of course I should not desire it to be made. But I hope that you will not readily listen to them, unless clearly sustained; for I have known him long and well, and I have ever regarded him as a high minded gentleman, of truth honor and probity.

I was much gratified with your appointment of Mr. Crutchfield, who I am sure you will find capable, trust worthy, religious and entitled to all confidence.[3]

I see it announced in the public papers that Mr. [William L.] Hodge is appointed Assistant Secy of the Treasury.[4] If the appointment be not actually made, I wish you would say to the Secy of the Treasury [Thomas Corwin] that I think he would do well to make full enquiries about Mr. H before he is appointed. He is in bad odor in N[ew]. O[rleans]. & in Philada. and his appointment will prejudice the Administration in both those Cities. He has failed in Commercial business, I have understood, three times, once in Marseilles in France, once in Philada. and again at N.O. and under circumstances which brought reproaches on him. I have known him several years. He has talents, a good deal of plausibility, and is somewhat visionary. The establishment of the Bulletin in N.O (of which he was an Editor) was thought at the time to be a mere political speculation.[5] In making this communication about him, I have no other wish than to guard the Administration against an unpopular appointment.

ALS. ViU. Letter marked "(Confidential)." 1. Clay to Stuart, Oct. 22, 1850. 2. For Gwin (1805-85), an 1828 graduate of Transylvania University who had subsequently moved to Mississippi, New Orleans, and California, and was at this time U.S. senator from California, see *BDAC* and *DAB*. 3. Possibly James S. Crutchfield of Kentucky. There is no record in the U.S. Sen., *Executive Journal*, vol. 8 of the appointment of anyone named Crutchfield to any office requiring Senate ratification during the Fillmore administration. 4. Hodge received the appointment and, in fact, served as acting secretary of the treasury for a time in the spring of 1851 when Thomas Corwin was ill. Washington *Daily National Intelligencer*, March 13, 1851. 5. The New Orleans *Bulletin*, was established in 1847. Hudson, *Journalism in the United States*, 492.

To JOHN EWING

Lexington, November 8, 1850

I recd. your letter,[1] and I perused the narrative which it contains of your sufferings sacrifices & misfortunes with all the sympathy which my friendly regard for you, long entertained, could prompt. I would have prevented or relieved them, if I could.

Until I received your letter, I did not know that your nomination had been before the Senate, & had been rejected.[2] I, of course, was not present when the rejection occurred, and do not know the grounds of it. Had I been present, unless something had been established to your prejudice, of which I have no knowledge, I should have supported your nomination.

You ask my advice as to what you should do. I would give it, with pleasure, if I knew of any to offer. All that I can say is, that I shall be very glad if the President [Millard Fillmore] would nominate you for any suitable office, that I would advise him to do so,[3] and that I would support any such nomination, unless there should be objections to it, well founded, of which I am unaware.

ALS. In. 1. Not found; for Ewing, see 4:863. 2. Ewing was nominated for register of the land office at Crawfordsville, Ind., on May 20, 1850, and his nomination was rejected by the Senate on Sept. 26. U.S. Sen., *Executive Journal*, 8:183, 254. 3. Apparently, Fillmore did not appoint Ewing to any other post.

From Hamilton Fish, Albany, N.Y., November 8, 1850. Forwards a new commission for Graves [Fish to Clay, October 18, 1850] to replace that "issued . . . on 1[s]t July last but by mistake it was made as though his residence had been at Louisville & was sent to him at that place." Sends another commission for Graves to Lexington. Encloses a second commission "for Mr [Thomas] Smith of Louisville . . . together with a Set of the printed instructions issued by the Secretary of State" so he "may receive it through the hands of the Gentleman to whom he is indebted for it."

Reports that the result of recent New York elections "is yet in doubt as to our State Ticket [Fish to Clay, October 18, 1850]." Hopes that "our Governor is Elected, but . . . the official returns may be necessary to decide." Believes that "A majority of the delegation in the next Congress from this State will be Whig—& we have a large majority in the Legislature, & thus may count among the fruits of the victory a Whig Senator, who I trust will be a sound Conservative Whig—'a Northern man,' not 'with Southern,' but with *National* principles." ALS. DLC-Hamilton Fish Papers (DNA, M212, R21).

Hamilton Fish himself became the new Whig senator in 1851. See Fish to Clay, February 18, 1851; Clay to Fish, February 23, 1851; Clay to Maxwell, February 15, 1851.

To Josiah Randall *et al.*, Philadelphia, November 8, 1850. Has received their invitation to a "Union meeting of the people in Philadelphia." Would have been glad to attend, but "the necessary attention to my private affairs forbids my leaving home so soon after my return from the late protracted session of Congress." Notes that "I rejoice in the proposed public sentiment of the North. The question before the nation is, (it would be folly to blind or disguise it,) whether agitation against slavery shall put down the Union, or the Union shall be preserved, and that agitation be put down. There is no other alternative. And is there any patriot that can doubt or hesitate on such an issue?" Copy. Printed in Frankfort *Commonwealth*, December 3, 1850.

The Union meeting was held at the Chinese Museum in Philadelphia on November 21, 1850, John Sergeant presiding. The resolutions adopted affirmed their allegiance to the Constitution, the laws (specifically the Fugitive Slave law), and the Union. Washington *Daily National Intelligencer*, November 22, 23, 1850.

From JAMES BROWN CLAY London, England, November 15, 1850

I received your favor of the 18th. Ultimo, some days since, and am happy to know that the view you take, of my demand for my passports at Lisbon, coincides perfectly and precisely with my own.[1] I thought that I might perhaps have taken the responsibility of accepting the offer made, or of referring it home; I thought too that instructions so positive ought never to have been given by Mr. [John M.] Clayton. In determining to follow strictly my instructions (respecting which Susan [Jacob Clay] will tell you I had great struggles to make up my mind) I was mainly influenced by my position and yours. I had been sent to Lisbon not because I was known to possess talent, nor yet from love of you; I saw through the whole winter accounts of the opposition of the Cabinet to you & your great measure,[2] and I was determined to give Mr Clayton, who sometimes in his foreign intercourse, if I may believe what I am told acted as though cracked or drunk, no pretext to wound you through me.[3] If his instructions were wrong, or ought not to have been given, it was his own fault & I was determined that he should bear the burden of it; in short I felt myself placed in a position of antagonism at least to the degree of making me very cautious.

Susan will, I hope before this, have reached home[4] & presented to you our last boy [Henry "Harry" Clay], your little namesake; I have waited for Mr. [Daniel] Websters reply to my letter, informing him that I wished to return to Lisbon to conclude a convention, according to his desire which letter reached Washington on the 12th. October, until I am tired waiting;[5] if I do not receive it by the mail of next Monday, I shall sail for America on the Arctic, Wednesday next.[6]

I notice what you say about letting me take Ashland;[7] when I return we can talk it over; you know my desire has always been to relieve my mother [Lucretia Hart Clay] from the care and trouble of so many negroes, which, I think she ought not at her age to continue; if I were to take Ashland, it seems to me it might be done in such a way, that the purpose would be known only to us.

Give my love to my mother and to all at home . . .

P S. I hope you wont give yourself any trouble about my house—[8] if [George R.] Trotter leaves it let it be locked up & the gates fastened until my return.

ALS. DLC-TJC (DNA, M212, R11). 1. Clay to Clayton, June 7, 1849. 2. Clay to Combs, Jan. 22, 1850. 3. Rumors abounded about Clayton's supposed drinking habits, and he was often criticized for inefficiency, absentmindedness, and a lack of organization in his management of the State Department. Smith, *Presidencies of Taylor & Fillmore*, 53. 4. Susan Jacob Clay, her children, and two servants arrived in New York City on Nov. 13, 1850, aboard the steamship *Atlantic* from Liverpool. New-York *Daily Tribune*, Nov. 13, 1850. 5. Clay to Webster, August 22, 1850. 6. James arrived with a servant in New York City in the *Arctic* from Liverpool on Dec. 5, 1850. New-York *Daily Tribune*, Dec. 5, 1850. 7. Clay to James B. Clay, Oct. 18, 1850. 8. Clay to James B. Clay, Oct. 27, 1850.

Speech to the General Assembly of Kentucky, Frankfort, November 15, 1850. Thanks them for "the distinguished honor" they have shown him and others in Congress "who co operated at the late session of Congress in the adoption of measures having for their object the harmony, tranquility, and preservation of the Union [Clay to Combs, January 22, 1850]." Notes that "Heretofore I have frequently received gratifying testimonies of the confidence and attachment of my countryman, but they were principally confined to the party of which I was a member. What gives extraordinary and inexpressible value to this occasion is that it has been dictated by no party feelings, but is the voluntary offering of . . . both political parties, who unanimously passed the resolution which has brought us together."

Recalls how, when the last session of Congress opened, "The public mind had been greatly agitated, distracted, and divided upon subjects connected with the institution of slavery." Refers to the Missouri controversy in 1819-21 [2:669-70, 740-48, 775-77, 785-86; 3:15-22, 26-33, 46-47, 49-50] and the "opposition of South Carolina to the tariff, in 1832, 1833 [8:604, 619-22, 626-27]" in which "there was great danger of a civil war with that State which might . . . have spread to surrounding States." Feels, however, that "what peculiarly distinguished the late struggle was that . . . we heard in various quarters, an open and undistinguished declaration of a necessity and desire for" a dissolution of the Union; also, "we had never before seen in a time of peace, the assemblage of a sectional convention of delegates, the tendency of which was to break up the Confederacy [Clay to Combs, December 22, 1849]."

Asserts that the principal reason he returned to public life was the "perhaps presumptuous hope that I might" be able to allay the gathering storm. Explains that in the resolutions he presented to the Senate in February, 1850 [Speech in Senate, February 5-6, 1850], "My desire was to embrace all the subjects of agitation arising out of the institution of slavery, and to leave none open for future agitation, and . . . to settle them in a just and honorable manner." Adds that the subsequent measures recommended by the Committee of Thirteen [Speech in Senate, May 8, 1850] differed little from his original proposals. Also explains that when President Zachary Taylor recommended the admission of California into the Union [Speech in Senate, May 13, 1850], "not entertaining myself a particle of doubt as to the propriety of its admission, and not being aware of the great and extensive opposition existing amongst the Southern members of Congress against it, I was in favor of its immediate admission as a separate and distinct measure. But, when I became acquainted with that opposition, and considering that it was a mere question of form, I thought it best to unite it with other kindred measures in one common bill."

Discusses the various objections made to California's admission to statehood. Claims the South won a victory in the organization of territorial governments for Utah and New Mexico even though they may never enjoy the privilege of transporting slaves there [Remark in Senate, September 10, 1850]. The Wilmot Proviso was not applied to California, New Mexico, or Utah. Congress adopted non-intervention, leaving them "perfectly free . . . to admit or exclude slavery as they shall deem best." Notes that California "by her constitution, and not Congress," has excluded slavery and that "The vote of her Convention interdicting it was unanimous, nearly one-third of the Delegates themselves being from slaveholding States." Moreover, believes "nature and nature's God" have given an "irreversible decree" against slavery in Utah and New Mexico.

Believes the most "difficult, complicated, and embarrassing question . . . was that of the boundary of Texas [Clay to Fillmore, August 10, 1850]." Discusses at length the various boundary claims and concludes that "if ever there was a case upon earth in which a disputed boundary should be settled and amicably adjusted by compromise, that of TEXAS was one." Explains that the $10,000,000 given Texas "for the exclusion of New Mexico from her limits" is really only $5,000,000 more than the U.S. was already bound to pay "in consequence of . . . having, in virtue of the resolution of annexation, appropriated to themselves all the duties on foreign imports receivable in the ports of Texas whilst independent, which had been previously pledged to those creditors." Wishes the U.S. government had "legitimate ground . . . to advance to every debtor State in the Union a sum sufficient to pay all its debts, and to restore its credit wherever that credit has been tarnished."

Remarks that he will "at present say nothing . . . in respect to the fugitive slave bill [Remark in Senate, September 12, 1850], except that it was the aim of the provisions which are embodied in it to give fair, full, and efficacious effect to the constitutional provision for the surrender of fugitives." Notes that "No one was hardy enough, on the floor of the Senate, to deny the right of the owner of the fugitive slave . . . to have his property restored to him," for "the moment the constitutional right is conceded, everything is yielded." In regard to the last measure—abolishing the slave trade in the District of Columbia [Speech in Senate, September 3, 1850]—notes that it had already been reduced "I think . . . to a single prison or depot in which slaves were deposited." These slaves were "brought chiefly from Maryland and Virginia" and "the inhabitants of the District had no sort of interest, on the contrary they wished it abolished." Adds that "It sometimes exhibited the institution of slavery in one of its most painful and unpleasant forms. I have myself seen . . . gangs of slaves chained together driven through Pennsylvania avenue. And what humane person can contemplate such a spectacle without painful feelings? The existence of the trade gave rise to great clamor and great exaggeration at the North." Points out that Kentucky, Mississippi, and many other slaveholding states had already abolished such trade.

In regard to the combination of the compromise measures into one bill, says that "The friends of the compromise were in favor of all the measures, either in the aggregate or in detail. . . . they were animated with no other desire than the peace and harmony of the whole country. The opponents . . . with some exceptions, were against the measures in the aggregate and in detail, and their objection . . . to their union was not the true and real objection. But for their indiscreet and bitter opposition the omnibus would have passed months before the separate bills passed."

Asks: "Will this system of measures allay excitement and agitation, and pacify, tranquillize, and harmonize the country? I hope, trust, and believe it will. At all events, the field of excitement and agitation has been greatly circumscribed." Concludes that of all the "threatening topics connected with slavery at the commencement of the late session of Congress, one only remains . . . and that is the fugitive slave bill. Narrowed down to that single ground, the slaveholding States will occupy the vantage position. The constitution is with them, the right is with them; and, if its execution shall be opposed or . . . thwarted by force, that State which makes such an opposition will place itself clearly, manifestly, and indisputably in the wrong."

Asserts that he did not expect the compromise to lead to immediate acquiescence of the ultras of the North and South. Thus, "we perceive that at the South a second edition of the Hartford Convention has again assembled [Clay to Combs, December 22, 1849], and is laboring to stir up" the spirit of discord and disunion. Believes these will be put down "by the intelligence, the patriotism, and the love of union of the people of the various slaveholding States."

Considers what would happen if the Union were dismembered. Points out that the slaveholding states would have no right to demand the return of fugitive slaves. This is a well-established principle between foreign powers which do not have an extradition law; by contrast, now "we have the constitution, the law, and the clear right on our side."

States that when he is asked "when I would consent to a dissolution of the Union, I answer, never—never—never; because I can conceive of no possible contingency that would make it for the interests and happiness of the people to break up this glorious Confederacy and to separate it into bleeding and belligerent parts." Adds, however, "I would yield to it if Congress were to usurp a power, which I am sure it never will, to abolish slavery within the limits of the States; for in the contingency of such a usurpation we should be in a better condition as to slavery, bad as it would be, out of the Union than in the Union."

On apprehensions regarding the "want, in future time, of territorial scope for the slave population," predicts that "at a very distant day, not very likely to occur in the present or the next century, whenever the vast unoccupied wastes in Mississippi, Arkansas, Louisiana, Alabama, Florida, and Texas shall become fully peopled, slavery will have reached its natural termination." Then, it will be "much cheaper to employ free than slave labor, and slaves, becoming a burden to their owners, will be voluntarily disposed of and allowed to go free." Hopes at that time "Africa . . . will be competent to receive from America all the descendants of its own race."

Also predicts that "If the agitation in regard to the fugitive slave law should continue and increase and become alarming, it will lead to the formation of two new parties, one for the Union, and the other against the Union." Continues: "And the platform of that Union party will be, the Union, the Constitution, and the enforcement of its laws. And if it should be necessary to form such a party . . . I announce myself, in this place, a member of the Union party." Warns if the Whig party "is to be merged into a contemptible abolition party, and if abolition is to be engrafted on the Whig creed, from that moment I renounce the party and cease to be a Whig. . . . if I am alive, I will give my humble support for the Presidency to that man, to whatever party he may belong, who is uncontaminated by fanaticism, rather than to one who, crying out all the time and aloud that he is a Whig, maintains doctrines utterly subversive of the Constitution and the Union."

Announces that "I want no office, no station in the gift of man" except "a warm place in your hearts." Contends that one of the benefits of the crisis has been that Democrats and Whigs "have been more thrown together in free and friendly intercourse. . . . For myself, I say . . . I was in conference and consultation quite as often, if not oftener, with Democrats than Whigs; and I found in the Democratic party quite as much patriotism, devotion to the Union, honor, and probity, as in the other party."

Details Kentucky's crucial position in the Union, and concludes that "Whilst the Northwestern States, and Pennsylvania, and Virginia, and Tennessee, and Kentucky remain firm in their attachment to the Confederacy, no presumptuous hand will dare to attempt to draw successfully a line of its separation." Copy. Printed in Washington *Daily National Intelligencer,* November 27, 1850.

To Daniel M. Grissom, Owensboro, Ky., November 18, 1850. Advises Grissom "that if your object and that of your friends is the practice of law in the Western States . . . study in some Western school." Suggests "a very good school in Lexington of which the late [Ephriam M. Ewing] & present [Thomas Marshall] Chief Justice of Kentucky are professors aided by Madison C Johnson." Concerning "the school at Balston [*sic,* Ballston Spa, N.Y.]" mentioned by Grissom, reports that he "thought favorably of it" on his only visit there [Speech to Students of the National Law School, Ballston Spa, New York, August 10, 1849], but has "received less flattering accounts from it since." LS. MoSHi.

Grissom, a native of Owensboro, moved to St. Louis in 1853 where he worked on the *Evening News* (1853-63), the *Union* (1863-68), and the *Missouri Republican* (1869-88). William Hyde & Howard L. Conrad (eds.), *Encyclopedia of the History of St. Louis* . . . , 2 vols. (St. Louis, 1899), 2:949.

To William Kinney *et al.*, Staunton, Va., November 18, 1850. Has received their letter of the 6th instant, inviting him to attend a meeting at Staunton, Va., on November 25 in support of "the measures adopted at the recent session of Congress, for tranquillizing the country and re-establishing concord and harmony [Clay to Combs, January 22, 1850]." Although concurring "in the patriotic object of the proposed meeting," regrets he cannot attend, because "my private affairs require an attention which will not allow me to leave this place [Lexington, Ky.] for Washington until early in next month." Extends his "hopes and good wishes and prayers for the success of your proposed meeting." Copy. Printed in Washington *Daily National Intelligencer,* December 6, 1850.

For William Kinney (1795-1863)—lawyer, politician, and president of the Central Bank of Staunton—see *VMHB* (April, 1897), 4:439; Hugh M. McIlhany, Jr., *Being the Genealogies of the Kinney . . . and Other Families of Virginia* (Staunton, Va., 1903), 12-20.

The Union meeting at Staunton on November 25 approved the Compromise of 1850. Kinney, chairman of the committee on invitation, read Clay's letter, as well as others from compromise supporters such as Daniel Webster and Lewis Cass. Washington *Daily National Intelligencer,* December 6, 1850.

To ALEXANDER H.H. STUART Lexington, November 18, 1850

I transmit to you enclosed a letter from my friend the Hon Senator [George W.] Jones of Iowa.[1] Although he is a democrat, I have a great respect & regard for him and entertain great confidence in him. I cannot say that I have the same confidence in the deputy post master to whom he refers, but your better opportunities of judging of him, than I have, will enable you to appreciate his character better than I can. I think you may confide in the representations of Gen Jones. I was sorry that Mr [William] Gilliam was not appointed to the land office in Iowa City owing, as I understood, to the interference of Mr [Fitz Henry] Warren. Mr G was a person long known to me as a true Whig and a man of great worth. Of course I am not acquainted with all the considerations which should govern the question of the removal or retention of the surveyor general, but I shall be very glad if Gen Jones' wishes in regard to him can be gratified.

LS. ViU. Letter marked "(Private)," in Clay's hand. 1. Jones to Clay, Nov. 2, 1850.

To SUSAN JACOB CLAY Lexington, November 21, 1850

I was rejoiced, my dear Susan, to have seen by the News papers, that you and your children had arrived safely at N. York,[1] and by the Telegraphic dispatch which you sent me from Pittsburg[h] that you had reached that City. Not knowing whether you will first come here or go to Louisville I address this letter to you at the latter. I expect to leave home on the first or second of next month. Will you come here before I go? If not I must try to go by Louisville to see you and the children. I have sold James's [Brown Clay] house for Nine thousand dollars, one third to be paid at N. Orleans the first of January next, one third in Oct. next, & the other third the October following, all well secured.[2] Harvey Miller was the purchaser. Considering James's anxiety to sell, & the low price of Town property, the sale is considered a good one. But if he had been at home & could have made an arrangement with me for the purchase of Ashland, I would have allowed him $10.000 for his house. Mr. [George R.] Trotter had left the house & I could get no good tenant. So you see you are without house & home; but I hope you will pass as much of your time as you can at Ashland. John [Morrison Clay] expects to go to N. Orleans in two or three weeks. We are all well here and at Mansfield.

Write me immediately about your movements[.]

My love to Lucy [Jacob Clay] & the other children.

ALS. DLC-TJC (DNA, M212, R11). Printed in Colton, *Clay Correspondence*, 4:612-13. 1. James B. Clay to Clay, Nov. 15, 1850. 2. Clay to James B. Clay, Oct. 27, 1850.

To HENRY CLAY, JR. [III] Lexington, November 22, 1850

Your brother Tommy [Thomas J. Clay] has had a serious and protracted illness at Judge [Thomas A.] Marshalls.[1] We feared we should lose him, but thank God he is spared to us and is now convalescent. Mrs. [Nannette Price] Smith has been unremitting in her kind attentions to him. Your aunt Susan [Jacob Clay] with her children has, I suppose arrived by this time at Louisville, having left your uncle James [Brown Clay] to follow her this winter or next Spring.[2]

I have had no letter from you since my return; but I received yesterday the official report of your conduct for the month. I was sorry to see the number of 36 demerits put down against you. I am afraid, my dear child, that you do not sufficiently appreciate the great advantages you have in your position at the [U.S. Military] Academy, nor the disgrace that you would have attached to your name if you should be compelled to leave it from neglect or incompetency.[3] How would poor [Andrew] Eugene Erwin rejoice if he had your situation! I pray you to redouble your efforts and act a part worthy of your poor fathers name [Henry Clay, Jr.] and mine. Imagine him to be looking down on you! How would his spirit be mortified if you dishonored him or me. Your cousin Geo. R. Harrison is at the Naval School at Annapolis and is delighted with his studies and with his prospects as a Midshipman.[4] [Charles] Edward Erwin is staying with us and going to School in Lexington.[5]

Your grandma [Lucretia Hart Clay] joins me in love to you.

P.S I expect to be in Washn from the 8h to 10h. of next month.

ALS. Henry Clay Memorial Foundation, Lexington, Ky. 1. Clay to Henry Clay III, Oct. 22, 1850. 2. James B. Clay to Clay, Nov. 15, 1850. 3. Clay to Morehead, Dec. 14, 1848. 4. Clay to Graham, August 28, 1850. 5. Charles Edward Erwin may have been attending Beverley A. Hicks's Lafayette Seminary in Lexington where his Duralde cousins had earlier gone [9:89-90]. Edward married Hicks's daughter Evaline A. Hicks in Oct., 1857. *FCHQ* (April, 1929), 3:113-16.

To William R. Turner, Marysville, Calif., November 24, 1850. Thanks Turner for "communicating an account of the death of my poor grandson Henry C. Duralde [Owen to Clay, September 11, 1850]." Although gratified to learn "that he so conducted himself as to command the esteem of those who knew him," still views his "migration to California" as an "unadvised measure" and "an unnecessary adventure."

Is pleased to learn that "my nephew [Humphrey Marshall] is District Attorney in your Judicial District, and is doing well."

Praises "the propriety of your official conduct, in the trying riotous proceedings" in California "in which you had to act a prominent part." ALS. CHi.

Turner, a Mississippian by birth, was judge of the 8th judicial district court in California. While trying a case in June, 1850, Turner had become involved in a controversy with Stephen Field, the defense attorney in the case and later justice of the U.S. Supreme Court, had found Field in contempt of court, had fined him, and had ordered him to jail. This action aroused great controversy and is probably the "riotous proceeding" referred to by Clay. Field subsequently won a seat in the state legislature where he was able to get the judicial districts changed, thereby removing Turner as judge. William H. Chamberlain, *History of Yuba County, California* (Oakland, Calif., 1879), 51-52.

On December 27, 1850, Clay wrote Alexander H.H. Stuart recommending "Humphrey Marshall of California as Atto. for the U. States in the Southern District of that State." Identifies Marshall as "the son of The Honble Thomas A. Marshall Chief Justice of Kentucky, the grand nephew of the late Chief Justice [John] Marshall, and the cousin of Mr. Humphrey Marshall of the H[ouse]. of R[epresentatives]. from the Louisville District. He is also the grand nephew of Mrs. [Lucretia Hart] Clay." Notes that Marshall has lived in San Francisco for two years and practiced law there. ALS. DNA, RG59, Applications and Recommendations (R4).

To LUCRETIA HART CLAY Washington, December 14, 1850

I arrived here last night, without any accident, and with the exception of a bad cold in good health. We passed the mountains on wednesday and thursday last in delightful weather. I never passed them more comfortably. And yesterday, altho' cold, it was clear and fine travelling weather.

I unfortunately missed James [Brown Clay].[1] He passed me in the stage wednesday night, whilst I was asleep in the mountains, twelve miles East of Union town [*sic*, Uniontown, Pa.]. I was very sorry for it. We tried to

Telegraph him at Lexington, at Maysville & at Pittsburg[h], but could not do it, the wires being every where out of order.

[Andrew] Eugene [Erwin] and Mr. Ewing[2] whom I joined at Maysville, travelled the whole journey with me, and are now stopping at the same tavern (the Nat. Hotel) with me.

I am very anxious to hear whether John [Morrison Clay] undertook or abandoned his contemplated trip to N. Orleans.

Give my love to James, Susan [Jacob Clay] & their children. Tell them that I hope to hear often from them.

ALS. DLC-TJC (DNA, M212, R11). 1. James B. Clay to Clay, Nov. 15, 1850. 2. Probably Thomas Ewing, who was in the Senate at this time.

From Gabriella S. Page, Newport, Ky., December 16, 1850. Asks Clay's assistance "in procuring a Cadets Warrant for my son, Legh R. Page, whose name at present stands upon the 'list at large' as an Applicant for admission to West Point, among the *Ten* to be appointed by the President [Millard Fillmore]." Explains that she and her husband, an Episcopal clergyman, are burdened with "the usual accompaniments of his vocation, *poverty* & a *large family*" and must "make every lawful exertion to give our children . . . a useful education, sound principles & the blessings of God." Reminds Clay that in Louisville two years ago she acted "as instructress to your lovely & interesting grand children, Nannie [Anne Clay] & Thomas Clay," who will "ever be remembered with deep interest, not only for their own sakes, but also for that of their noble Father [Henry Clay, Jr.] & venerated Grandfather." ALS. DNA, M688, R182, frames 479-81.

Mrs. Page was the wife of Charles H. Page who, upon coming to Kentucky, had first served as rector in the St. Matthew's parish where he had operated a girls' school and later as rector at St. Paul's parish, Newport, Ky. While at Newport, he supplemented his income by serving as chaplain of the U.S. Army Barracks located there. Frances K. Swinford & Rebecca S. Lee, *The Great Elm Tree, Heritage of the Episcopal Diocese of Lexington* (Lexington, 1969), 157, 198-200. Their son did not receive an appointment to the U.S. Military Academy.

To HENRY GRINNELL Washington, December 19, 1850

I am very desirous to place a grandson of mine, [Andrew] Eugene Erwin, now with me here, in a respectable Mercantile house, to acquire the requisite knowledge in the honorable calling of a Merchant. He is 17 years of age, well grown, being nearly as tall as I am, free from all dissipation, and as amiable and as much beloved, by all who know him, as any young man I ever knew. His education has been well attended to.

I know of no friend in the City of New York, to whom I can apply with more propriety than to yourself, to ascertain for me if a situation can be obtained for him, in some establishment which you can recommend, and on what terms. You will greatly oblige me by making the requisite enquiries & informing me the result.[1]

ALS. Courtesy of Dr. Thomas D. Clark, Lexington, Ky. 1. Clay to Lucretia H. Clay, Dec. 26, 1850; Clay to Unknown Recipient, Dec. 27, 1850.

To HENRY CLAY, JR. [III] Washington, December 23, 1850

I have not had a letter from you since the adjournment of the last Session of Congress; but they send me the monthly official reports of your conduct at the [U.S. Military] Academy. I was glad to see that in the last the number of marks of demerit against you was diminished; but how much should I have been gratified if there had not been one![1] I hope that I shall soon see a report without any. If we economise our time well, rise early, do not waste it, there is enough for every thing. I want to hear from you, to know if you do not like the school better than you did, and if you are not resolved to strive for the first honor of your Class.

I wrote you that Susan [Jacob Clay] and her children had returned home. James [Brown Clay] followed her a few weeks ago, and they were all at Ashland last week.[2] He and I missed each other as [we] were proceeding in opposite directions on the mountains.

I brought [Andrew] Eugene Erwin with me.[3] I wish to place him in one of the mercantile establishments at Boston or N. York, to learn the business of a merchant. You will have heard of the death of your grandmother [Matilda Fontaine] Prather, about four weeks ago.[4] Your brother Tommy [Thomas J. Clay] had got well when I left home.[5]

ALS, signature removed. Henry Clay Memorial Foundation, Lexington, Ky. 1. Clay to Morehead, Dec. 14, 1848. 2. James B. Clay to Clay, Nov. 15, 1850. 3. Clay to Unknown Recipient, Dec. 27, 1850. 4. Mrs. Prather died Thanksgiving Day, Nov. 28, 1850. Louisville *Daily Journal*, Nov. 30, 1850. 5. Clay to Henry Clay, Jr. [III], Oct. 22, 1850.

To JAMES BROWN CLAY Washington, December 23, 1850

Prior to the receipt of your letter dated at Ashland the 17h. inst. I had addressed a letter to you containing some things not necessary to be repeated here.[1] I have not yet had a good opportunity of conversing with either the President [Millard Fillmore] or Mr. [Daniel] Webster about you or your late mission;[2] but the other night at Jenny Linds concert,[3] sitting by Mr. Webster, he broke forth in extravagant praises of you. I do not think that you ought to put an unfriendly interpretation upon any thing which occurred, about your return to Lisbon. Your letter from Geneva of Sept. did not contain an *unconditional* offer to return.[4] You submitted some point of honor to Mr. W. I think he might have sent earlier instructions to you; but I suppose his absence from Washn. & his indisposition formed his excuse.[5] In his letter of the 5h. Novr (which I hastily read) he seems to have been undecided whether you wished to return or not, but left it to you to determine. After you returned to the U.S. I do not think that you ought to have gone back to Lisbon for the temporary purpose of concluding the convention. And, upon the whole, I have no regrets about it, considering how well & how strongly the President speaks of you, in his annual message,[6] and in what favorable terms, officially & privately Mr. W speaks of you, and that the public ascribes to you the success of the negotiation. I wrote you that I think you are entitled to your salary up to the 20h. Novr and a quarter beyond, and to indemnity for any loss in furniture &c in consequence of your sudden departure from Lisbon—[7] I believe it is usual also to charge for Stationary, postage &c. If you will send me your a/c I will endeavor to have it settled.

I was in hopes that you would stay with your mother [Lucretia Hart Clay] until my return, and that we would then talk about your future. As to your purchase of Ashland,[8] I never desired that you should make it, unless prompted by your own interests and feelings. When I go hence, it must be sold, and I have never feared that it would not command a fair & full price.

I should regret deeply to see you sit down doing nothing. You must engage in some occupation, or you will be miserable. The Law, Farming, or the Public service are the only pursuits which I suppose present themselves to you. You don't like the first, which is moreover no where in K[entucky]. profitable; and your decision must be between the two others.[9] I had inferred that you were tired of diplomacy, unless you could get a higher grade than that which you lately held. At present, there is none that I know of; but perhaps some vacancy may occur. As to elevating the mission to Lisbon, I have heard here of no proposal to that effect. It does not depend, you know, exclusively on the Executive; Congress must sanction it. Possibly after the conclusion of the Convention, if Portugal should desire to increase the rank of her minister, it may be proposed to reciprocate it by the President; but I do not apprehend that a higher rank would be thought of than that of Minister Resident.

You did not say whether you were satisfied or not with my Sale of your house and lot.[10] I would not have sold it but for your great anxiety to sell. It was a good house, but I never liked its external appearance. The situation was one of the finest in Lexn.

You will direct what I shall do with the draft for $3000. when I receive it from N[ew]. O[rleans.]

My love to Susan [Jacob Clay], Lucy [Jacob Clay] and the other children.

ALS. DLC-TJC (DNA, M212, R11). Printed in Colton, *Clay Correspondence*, 4:613-14. 1. Not found. 2. Clay to Clayton, June 7, 1849. 3. Swedish soprano Jenny Lind had given a concert in Washington on Dec. 16. Lind also attended the Supreme Court to hear Clay present a case, and he subsequently called on her. Washington *Daily National Intelligencer*, Dec. 18, 1850; New York *Herald*, Dec. 19, 20, 1850. For Jenny Lind (1820-87), see Gladys Shultz, *Jenny Lind: The Swedish Nightingale* (Philadelphia, 1962). 4. Clay to Webster, August 22, 1850. 5. Webster suffered from a condition described as catarrh or asthmatic cough and was away from Washington much of the time. George T. Curtis, *Life of Daniel Webster*, 2 vols. (New York, 1870), 2:472, 478. 6. Clay to James B. Clay, August 31, 1850. 7. Clay to James B. Clay, Oct. 18, 1850. 8. James B. Clay to Clay, Nov. 15, 1850. 9. James bought a farm and moved to Missouri where he lived until after his father's death. He then returned to Kentucky and purchased Ashland. He later served one term in Congress. *BDAC*. 10. Clay to James B. Clay, Oct. 27, 1850.

To LUCRETIA HART CLAY Washington, December 26, 1850

I received a few days ago a letter from James [Brown Clay][1] in which he tells me that all are well at Ashland, and that John [Morrison Clay] had reached Louisville safely. I have not since heard from him. I was in hopes that James and his family would, remain with you the greater part of the winter, but he says they are going to Louisville. I have a prospect of placing [Andrew] Eugene [Erwin] at Boston or N York,[2] and he will leave me in a day or two for those Cities[.]

Mrs [John] Bell speaks favorably of the man [Frederic A. Cowles] who was to marry, and I suppose has been married to Lucretia [Erwin].[3] He is a Cousin of her aunt Susan,[4] with whom she was staying.

I send you a letter which I have received from W[illiam]. [C.C.] Claiborne [Jr.], according to which, it seems, that the first mortgage which was made to secure Annes [Brown Clay Erwin] children is valid & in full force.[5] If that be true, with the Woodlands, they may be able to get what belongs to them, in right of their mother. Claiborne says that he will send you some Silver Goblets &c which belonged to H[enry]. C Duralde. By the by, an account has been rendered against me from California for between three & four hundred dollars for money advanced to him and for his funeral expences.[6]

I am suffering with one of the worst colds I ever had. I mean to stay within doors as much as I possibly can to try and get well of it. Miss [Mary D.] Kemble, now Mrs. [William H.] Sumner is stopping at this hotel with her husband, and desired me kindly to remember her to you.

My love to all at Ashland & at Mansfield. Tell Mary [Mentelle Clay] that she is my principal dependence to hear from home, and that I wish she would write me often and minutely. Old Mr. Coffin is here, and says that he is going to send you another supply of Cotton cloth.[7]

ALS. DLC-HC (DNA, M212, R6). Printed in *RKHS* (Oct., 1852), 50:312. 1. Not found. 2. Clay to Unknown Recipient, Dec. 27, 1850. 3. Clay to Erwin, Oct. 27, 1849. 4. A note to this letter in the *RKHS* identifies "Aunt Susan" as Susan Jacob Clay, wife of James Brown Clay; however, Lucretia had apparently been living with her father's relatives in Tennessee and not with James and Susan Clay, who had just returned from Portugal. 5. Cowles to Clay, Nov. 17, 1851. 6. Owen to Clay, Sept. 11, 1850. 7. Possibly Jared Coffin, a good friend of Clay's. A note in the *RKHS* identifies this man as Levi Coffin, a leader in the Underground Railroad, but this seems unlikely.

To UNKNOWN RECIPIENT[1] Washington, December 27, 1850

I recd and thank you for your letter of the 23rd inst in relation to my Grand-Son [Andrew] Eugene Erwin. Although his parents[2] have been wealthy, that is not their present condition, and he is convinced that his success and prosperity in life depend upon his own exertions. He is therefore resolved to work diligently and laboriously to advance his fortunes[.] He would prefer being placed in a large Commission House, or Wholesale Grocery, but if a suitable place cannot be obtained in one of them, he would go into a Dry Good Store. He will leave here the last of this week, for New York, where he will confer and advise with you.[3] This letter affords a Specimen of his handwriting, which is not as good as I could wish, but which he promises to improve.

LS. Courtesy of Dr. Thomas D. Clark, Lexington, Ky. 1. Possibly Henry Grinnell. See Clay to Grinnell, Dec. 19, 1850. 2. Anne Brown Clay Erwin and James Erwin. 3. Although Andrew Eugene Erwin went to work for a firm in New York City, he did not remain there long. He soon left for California, arriving in San Francisco in May, 1851. While in California he met and married Josephine Russell, daughter of Clay's long-time friend William H. Russell, and they settled in Missouri in 1853. Eugene served as a colonel in the Confederate Army during the Civil War and died during the siege of Vicksburg. Josephine later visited Kentucky and married her husband's uncle, John Morrison Clay. See Clay to Lucretia H. Clay, Jan. 4, Feb. 11, April 11, 1851; Clay to Erwin, Sept. 14, 1851; Louisiana Wood Simpson, *The Colonel's Lady* (Lexington, 1981), *passim.*

Remark in Senate, December 30, 1850. During discussion of the relations between the United States and Austria, Clay asserts that "it is important that every branch of the Government should proceed with great caution and great delicacy." Although we regret Hungary's "inability to establish her own separate national existence upon a firm and solid basis, her fate is sealed [Remark in Senate, January 7, 1850]." While "Our sympathies . . . were naturally extended to her struggling people," wonders if it is "worth while to continue to irritate either Austria or Russia" on "a subject which is past and ended?"

President Millard Fillmore's communication of papers concerning the response of the American government to Austrian actions "is marked by great ability as everything which emanates from that source generally is." Doubts, however, that there is any need for "a diffusion of this paper among the people of the United States" as has been moved. The extra copies "are not wanted by the people of the United States," because "To a man, they are satisfied with the principles first laid down by the immortal Father of his Country, and to which there has been a general adherence from that day to this."

Any diplomatic interference is a matter "of great delicacy." If a state in this Union "was in a state of revolt against the General Government, and any European power should send an agent here for the purpose of obtaining information, even such as that which our agent was sent to Hungary to procure," there would certainly be "a great deal of feeling throughout the United States." We should "place ourselves in their position" before we take any further action concerning the Hungarian situation.

Suggests that while he approves of the general tone of the papers communicated by the president, there are some things which should "be received with limitation and doubt." While it "is a domestic document," it nonetheless "is transmitted to every corner of the globe" once it is published. There are "unquestionable precedents where foreign Governments have been called to account for acts which were somewhat if not wholly of a domestic character," and wonders if it is wise to "say anything in that document which another Government must feel as a reproach."

Believes, then, that "there is no necessity for printing the great number of copies which has been proposed." The American people "have never heard anything about this correspondence. . . . The principles contained in that paper are fastened and fixed in the American heart and mind," and its publication will only "continue the irritation which may exist between a foreign Government and this." Instead, "we should in such a delicate matter move with caution and circumspection, establishing no principles which may in the future history of the country react disadvantageously to us."

The motion to print extra copies of the papers is defeated by a vote of 21-18. *Cong. Globe*, 31 Cong., 2 Sess., 136.

President Fillmore had communicated the correspondence between Secretary of State Daniel Webster and Chevalier J.G. Hulsemann, the Austrian chargé d'affaires to the U.S. This correspondence related to the secret mission of A. Dudley Mann who had been sent by the Taylor administration to Hungary to determine the status of the revolution there in order to determine whether or not the U.S. should extend recognition to Hungary's independence. The correspondence is printed in *Cong. Globe*, 31 Cong., 2 Sess., Appendix, 45-48. See also Bemis, *American Secretaries of State*, 6:15, 84-91.

To George P. Burnham, Boston, 1851. Acknowledges receipt of four "splendid Cochin-China fowls." Praises "their enormous size . . . their fine proportions and beautiful plumage." Adds "It has been my aim, for many years, to collect at this place [Ashland] the best improved breeds of the horse, the cow, the sheep, swine and the ass." Views Burnham's gift as "a congenial and valuable addition" to Ashland's stock. Copy. Printed in George P. Burnham, *The History of the Hen Fever* (Boston, 1855), 86-87.

Burnham (1814-1902) was a prolific writer who sometimes used the pseudonym "Young 'un." *NUC Pre-1956 Imprints*, 86:35-37.

"H. Clay's List of Taxable Property," 1851. Lists taxable property valued at $62,200, including Ashland and its 510 acres @ $40,800; Mansfield and its 125 acres @ $6,250; 33 slaves @ $9,600; half ownership of house and lot in Frankfort @ $1,500; 35 mares and mules @ $1,750, 2 jennies @ $200; 16 head of cattle @ $100; and "17 Black tith[e]s" @ $2,000. Also listed, but no value given, are: "1 Stud horse, Yorkshire"; 2 carriages; 3 gold watches; 2 pairs of gold spectacles; and "Two Tythes (H. Clay & J.M. Clay)." ADS. Courtesy of J. Winston Coleman, Jr., Lexington, Ky.

From "A True Whig," New York City, January 2, 1851. Feels it is "my duty even tho' it be in the Shape of an anonymous letter" to urge passage of "a protecting Tariff—One that will enable American Manufacturers, American Labor & American Industry to live, instead of Supporting & giving encouragement to foreign competition." While "not Surprised you should be Somewhat indifferent to that question in Your advancing Years," although it has "heretofore engrossed So much of Your attention," still hopes "you will yet declare your valuable opinions & exert yourself to give us protection." Condemns "the ad. valorem duty System . . . in existence [Clay to Greeley, June 26, 1846]" in the U.S. Complains that "we are constantly making & adjusting our Laws to Serve Great Britain & her manufactures—which Country has been built up by the protection the manufacturers received from her Govt and which has not been a little aided & fostered by the great mind of Sir Robt Peel, to the injury & Sacrifice of her Colonial interests abroad [9:597, 685]."

Although the high price of cotton the previous two years has given "us so much more Sterling to draw on England for," fears "the result when our Cotton prices come down to the old rates. . . . a general Bankruptcy among all those who are extended in their business . . . a closing up of all the Cotton Mills & Ironworks—a Money Crisis—and ruin throughout the Country." Warns that "When you cripple the great manufacturing enterprize . . . you strike at the bone and Sinew of trade." When "you leave them unprotected against foreign competition . . . you bring ruin amongst us" and leave the South "at the mercy of the Manchester Capitalist." Describes the U.S. as England's "best and largest Customer by far and well may the Manchester Spinner say 'America is one of our Colonies.' "

Points out that "within the Short Space of two Years Europe has taken of American Securities enormous amount of Stocks," including many "issued for the carrying on the Mexican War." Wonders "what would be the present Situation of our Banks had we not had these Stocks to give in return for their Supply of goods and had been obliged to Send them Sterling remittances."

Expresses "the Sentiments of every true Whig" in asking Clay to "not lose a moments time, but take up the Subject of the Tariff." If Clay will use "only one tenth part the exertion you did on the California Compromise question [Clay to Combs, January 22, 1850], you will Succeed in Extricating a large proportion of the North & East from ruin."

Will visit Clay in Washington in March to "explain to you my reasons for having made this letter anonymous." Copy. DLC-Thomas Corwin Papers.

To LUCRETIA HART CLAY Washington, January 4, 1851

I had a letter today from Thomas [Hart Clay] in which he informs me that you had been called on for Theodores [Wythe Clay] board which would diminish the money I left with you.[1] I expected that Genl Dudley[2] and Mr [James] Harlan at Frankfort would have sent you some money as I directed. I now send you a Check for $200, which ought to bring in Lexington $201.

[Andrew] Eugene [Erwin] left me some days ago for the North with a prospect of getting a suitable situation either in Boston or N. York as he might prefer.[3] There has not yet been time to hear from him. Tell Thomas that the contract with the Mill wright is in the Portfolio on the stand in the dining room. But as he has so long delayed beginning the repairs, if the Overseer[4] can get along with the Mill, the work may be postponed until my return, unless the Mill Wright now insists on proceeding with it. I advanced him $7 to pay for Cogs.

I wish you would request the Overseer to have set up in the Locust grove on the Road any Trees that have fallen.

I have heard nothing from John [Morrison Clay] since he left Louisville.

I shall continue to feel quite uneasy about him 'till he returns. How does [Charles] Edward [Erwin] behave? Henry Clay [III] never writes to me, but his marks of demerit, I am told, are not for any serious faults.[5]

Give my love to Thomas, Susan [Jacob Clay] & the children.

ALS. DLC-TJC (DNA, M212, R11). 1. Not found. For Theodore's hospitalization, see 8:442-43. 2. Probably Jephthah Dudley. 3. Clay to Unknown Recipient, Dec. 27, 1850. 4. A Mr. Wheeler. 5. Clay to Morehead, Dec. 14, 1848.

To JAMES BROWN CLAY Washington, January 7, 1851

I recd. your two last letters[1] in reply to two which I had addressed to you. I was extremely sorry to hear of the return of your Sore throat, which I hope will not prove serious or last long. But you ought to lose no time in applying proper remedies.

There is no difficulty in the settlement of your account, but before closing it, the [State] Department waits the a/c of the American Bankers at London.[2]

I have heard from Dr. [William N.] Mercer that he had recd. the bill I sent him for $3000, the first payment on your house, due the 1st. inst.[3] As soon as I receive the remittance on N. York in which I directed the proceeds to be invested, I will inform you. I have no occasion for any part of it.

I do not know the position of the farm of [James S.] Crutchfield,[4] whether above or below the mouth of the K[entucky]. river, nor in what County. You are aware that there is a great difference in the fertility of Ohio bottoms—I once thought more favorably of them than I now do; but I dare say that there are some of them very good—

As you are averse to owning Slaves, have you thought of Indiana bottoms on the Ohio? I know nothing of them myself. What I think you ought to well consider is whether both you and Susan [Jacob Clay] can be happy on a farm. For myself, I believe that the chance of happiness is greater there than in public life.[5]

I am and shall continue anxious about John [Morrison Clay] until he returns in safety. I yielded to his wishes not without many misgivings.

My love to Susan & all the children.

ALS. DLC-TJC (DNA, M212, R11). 1. Not found. 2. Clay to James B. Clay, Feb. 13, 1851. 3. Clay to James B. Clay, Oct. 27, 1850. 4. James B. Clay to Clay, May 26, 1850. 5. Clay to James B. Clay, Dec. 23, 1850.

To JOHN MORRISON CLAY Washington, January 13, 1851

I have been glad to receive your letter dated at Mobile the 3d. inst. the first information I have recd. from you since you left Louisville. I wrote two letters to you which I addressed to you at N. Orleans,[1] and which I hope you will get, if you have not already.

All were well at home, when I last heard from there; and Yorkshire and the Colts were doing remarkably well. They have sent Edgar to join you.[2] He left Louisville the first of this month.

I am afraid that Dr [William N.] Mercer, who is going to the Havannah [*sic*, Havana, Cuba], will be absent from N.O. when you may have occasion, if you should have occasion to use the letter of credit I gave you to him. I will therefore send you such a letter addressed to Mr. [Rezin D.] Shepherd. I wish you would keep me advised of all your movements, your health &c. I am sorry that you have suffered with your teeth.

ALS. Henry Clay Memorial Foundation, Lexington, Ky. 1. Not found. 2. A slave. See Clay to James B. Clay, March 13, 1850.

To Simon Greenleaf, January 13, 1851. Hopes that "the favorable change, which you describe as having taken place, in respect to the abolition of slavery and the American Colonization Society, will endure and increase." Adds that "the Board of Managers" will consider fully "your suggestion of the expediency of sending an Agent to New England." Copy. Courtesy of James S. Leonardo, Des Moines, Iowa.

Abolitionist James G. Birney had written a letter which was later published as a pamphlet, advising free blacks to go to Liberia as their best hope of escaping racial prejudice and attaining true equality. He was immediately falsely accused of backing away from abolition and was once more claimed by the Colonization Society. This may be the "favorable change" to which Greenleaf had referred. Fladeland, *James Gillespie Birney*, 278-81.

Remark in Senate, January 15, 1851. Presents two petitions "signed by a large number of citizens of the State of Indiana," who are "anxious to remove from our land the greatest cause of discord," and therefore hope "Congress will pass a bill providing means to remove from our country all that portion of the African race who are both willing and ready to emigrate to Africa." This bill should include "suitable provision . . . for their wants for one year after their arrival" and "a bounty of land [to] be given them on their arrival."

Presents a petition "from Rhode Island," which "is signed by a large portion of the *elite* of that State," including the governor [Henry B. Anthony], lieutenant governor [Thomas Whipple], present and past State legislators, "and by many of the *literati* of that State, heads of colleges," and many other citizens. It asks for "more effectual suppression of the African slave trade," since "the measures which have been adopted by the three great Powers, the United States, Great Britain, and France, to suppress that trade by means of keeping stationary squadrons upon the coast of Africa, have totally failed." They support "the establishment of colonies upon the western coast of Africa," because "wherever they have been planted there is an entire and absolute suppression of the African slave trade, so far as that coast is concerned." They desire "that a line of steamers may be established, or a line of sailing packets, for the purpose of augmenting the inhabitants of the colonies."

Calls to the Senate's attention a recently-received document "containing correspondence between our public functionaries at Rio [de] Janeiro and the Department of State" that "deserves the careful pursual of every member of this body." Despite "all that has been done by the three great Powers . . . the slave trade is perhaps carried on to as great extent in the empire of Brazil as it ever has been." The Rhode Island petitioners disclosed that the Brazilian slave trade "is chiefly carried on by American vessels," at least 93 of which "have cleared from the ports of Brazil to the coast of Africa" in the past four or five years. How they do this "is worthy of some notice. The American vessel is bought in some of the Brazilian ports, but she is to be delivered in an African port. She sails under American colors, and is laden with provisions and other appliances adapted to the prosecution of the African trade, and passes over the ocean without molestation, because we have . . . refused to the British the right of search, and have not allowed it to be exercised by any foreign Power. . . . In a few days after her arrival" in Africa, "the captain goes on shore, meets the agent who is to receive the vessel, and returns and proclaims to the crew that the vessel has been sold—that her crew is to be changed—that her American flag is to be pulled down and another one hoisted, in order to carry a cargo of slaves back to Brazil; and these poor American seamen are often left to perish on the inhospitable coast of Africa . . . and are often compelled to engage in the navigation of the slave vessel" as the only way to get home.

The Rhode Island petitioners hope that "the grant of sea letters" will be "withheld from vessels clearing from Brazil to the African coast," since "there is no trade whatever" with Africa "other than that connected with the slave trade." They also call for other regulations "for the purpose of exempting our navigation from any participation in that odious traffic."

Believes that both the American and British public feel "that the keeping of squadrons upon the coast of Africa with a view to the suppression of the slave trade is a failure, or, at all events, that it is attended with an enormous amount of expense, and with a vast and inhuman sacrifice of health and life, which is not justified." We currently "keep up, by the eighth article of the treaty of Washington, a squadron amounting to at least eighty guns on the coast of Africa, but we also keep up . . . a large and extensive squadron upon the coast of Brazil." This costs "not less than, perhaps, half a million of dollars." While, "I will not say . . . that it has been a total failure," doubts "whether there would not be less loss of African life, if there were no attempt whatever to suppress the slave trade by means of these squadrons than there is in consequence of keeping them; the result of which is merely to multiply adventurers to send out more ships, to run more chances, to take more risks, in order to "transport slaves from Africa to Brazil and Cuba."

Believes there "is no effectual remedy to the suppression of the slave trade by the occupation in Africa of the coast itself, and stopping it at the threshold when it begins." Since treaty obligations to maintain a squadron off the African coast expired in 1847, feels "it is worth considering whether we shall expose the lives of our gallant seamen in such an inhospitable climate, at such a vast expense, and reaping so little benefit from the operation."

Colonization "commends itself to my mind by some additional considerations. . . . of all the projects of the age there is none to compare with that great project of transporting the free people of color in the United States with their own consent to the coast of Africa." Here, many "States are passing the most rigorous laws to exclude them from their territory." Therefore, "I see no other remedy than that of sending them back to the land whence their ancestors were taken. . . . The whites at the North would be benefited, the whites at the South would be benefited, the slaves would be benefited—the poor creatures themselves would be benefited; for, instead of remaining in a country where they never can be elevated to high social and political condition with the whites," it is better that they be "carried to the country of their ancestors" where "they may rise to an importance which they can never attain here." Commerce, religion, and civilization will all be promoted by the "transfer of the free people of color with their own consent from the United States to Africa."

Concludes that "if we would only renounce those unhappy subjects of agitation which have distracted our country too long. . . . and unite all our energies in directing the free people of color from the shores of America to that place where they can enjoy real freedom, and pursue their own happiness, what a glorious result would it be for our country!"

The petitions are referred to the Committee on Commerce. *Cong. Globe*, 31 Cong., 2 Sess., 246-47.

On January 20, 1851, Clay submitted a resolution to instruct the Committee on Commerce to "inquire into the expediency of making more effectual provisions by law to prevent the employment of American vessels and American seamen in the African slave trade." *Ibid.*, 285.

For the Treaty of Washington, better known as the Webster-Ashburton Treaty, see 9:405, and Betty Fladeland, *Men and Brothers, Anglo-American Antislavery Cooperation* (Chicago, 1972), 336-37, *passim.*

Remark in Senate, January 16, 1851. During discussions about British interference in Central America, during which Sen. James Shields offers a resolution requesting

President Millard Fillmore to provide information on the subject, Clay announces that "I concur entirely in the call." Still, feels that "upon this as upon all other questions relating to our foreign affairs," we should "proceed with the greatest deliberation" and "get the information" before "we venture to pronounce a judgment animadvertently on the conduct of a foreign Power." Having confidence in both President Fillmore and "the present enlightened representative of Great Britain at this Government [Sir Henry L. Bulwer]," hopes that "we will refrain from discussing and animadverting upon these public matters until we get the truth, the whole truth, and nothing but the truth." *Cong. Globe*, 31 Cong., 2 Sess., 264.

For a discussion of British activities in Central America, the problems resulting from ambiguities in the Clayton-Bulwer Treaty, and the response of President Millard Fillmore and Secretary of State Daniel Webster to these events, see Bemis, *American Secretaries of State*, 6:95-100 and Clay to James B. Clay, October 2, 1849. For James Shields (Dem., Ill.), see *BDAC*.

Remark in Senate, January 17, 1851. Presents the petition of Cornelius Vanderbilt of New York City who "has been for thirty years past extensively engaged in the business of building and running steam vessels." It must be "well known to every Senator . . . that Mr. Vanderbilt has been one of the most successful and enterprising persons engaged in that description of navigation." Vanderbilt "proposes to build six steamers of the largest burden, from one to two thousand tons," to navigate "between New York and Chagres, and between San Francisco and Panama," giving the United States "the privilege of purchasing these steamers at their cost in the event of any war or threatened war. . . . He also proposes to carry the mail, whenever the Government, and only when the Government desires it, at thirty thousand per annum for each of these steamers, which is less than the sum now paid." Vanderbilt offers this "without asking one dollar of present appropriation." The petition is referred to the Committee on Finance. *Cong. Globe*, 31 Cong., 2 Sess., 268. See also Clay to Baring Brothers, August 17, 1850.

To HENRY CLAY, JR. [III] Washington, January 18, 1851

I received your letter of the 10th. from which I was glad to perceive that you had a good standing in your Class[.] But still it is not as good as I could wish, or as I am sure you can make it, and I hope that you will exert yourself to improve it by the next examination.

You say that you do not like the confinement of West point &c. What would you do if you were not there? You must be employed, or you would be in the greatest danger from idleness and dissipation. When you shall have completed honorably your course at West point, you will in after life be very glad of it; as I am sure you would be then greatly mortified if you did not avail yourself of the opportunity for improvement which you now have, and which thousands of young lads would rejoice to get.

You speak of [Andrew] Eugene Erwin's liberty &c.[1] Do you know that he is going into a Counting house, where he will have to rise as early as you, sweep out the Store, perform menial offices &c. Eugene would be very glad to exchange situations with you.

I send you five dollars. All well at Ashland on the 10h inst.

ALS. Henry Clay Memorial Foundation, Lexington, Ky. 1. Clay to Unknown Recipient, Dec. 27, 1850.

To Representatives of Union Meeting, Tarrytown, Westchester County, N.Y., January 20, 1851. Declines an invitation to a meeting to be held on January 30 in

Westchester County by people "without respect to party, to express their determination to abide by the compromises of the last session of Congress [Clay to Combs, January 22, 1850], and to manifest their devotion to the Constitution and the Union." Rejoices at their plan to assemble, however, and predicts it will "do a great good," adding that "in heart, in spirit, and in soul I am with" such meetings.

Believes that "Two classes of disunionists threaten our country. One is . . . open and undisguised in favor of separation; the other . . . disavowing a desire of dissolution of the Union, adopts a course and contends for measures and principles which must inevitably lead to that calamitous result. Of the two I think the latter more dangerous, because it is deceptive and insidious. I hope both will be defeated." Copy. Printed in Washington *Daily National Intelligencer*, February 7, 1851.

At the Tarrytown meeting, letters from Clay, Daniel Webster, and other supporters of the Compromise of 1850 were read and applauded. The group attending the meeting approved resolutions endorsing the Compromise and calling for preservation of the Union. *Ibid.*, February 4, 1851.

From John Salter, Portsmouth, N.H., January 21, 1851. Suggests that if Clay will investigate "the course taken to get the bill through Congress that passed & was approved 3d. August 1848" concerning "wooden Docks with basins & Railways," he "will find corruption to the core." Informs Clay that he had sent Millard Fillmore "a copy of a communication . . . directed to John Y Mason then Secretary of the Navy, condemning" these docks. Assures Clay that he is "a wig but never vote for such men as John P Hale of the Senate or A[mos] Tuck of the House although they owe their seats to the wigs of this state." ALS. NhHi.

Although there were a number of John Salters living in Portsmouth at this time, it seems most likely that this correspondent was Captain John Edward Salter (1816-74), a successful shipmaster and shipowner. William M. Emery, *The Salters of Portsmouth, New Hampshire* (New Bedford, Mass., 1936), 43. For Amos Tuck (Indep., N.H.), see *BDAC*.

For the act making appropriations for the naval service for the year ending June 30, 1849, which was passed August 3, 1848, see 9 *U.S. Stat.*, 266-73.

Speech to Annual Meeting of the American Colonization Society, Washington, D.C., January 21, 1851. Notes that he is "the sole, or almost the sole survivor" of the group that assembled thirty-four years before to found the American Colonization Society. Is encouraged that "all the operations of the Society during the past year have been unusually successful and . . . greatly blessed." Points out that the number of emigrants to Africa has been greater than in any preceeding year; also, the amount of money contributed to the society, and public favor in all parts of the Union has been greater than ever. Believes, in fact, that "some of the very causes which have led to great agitation, to uncommon excitement, and to serious apprehension in respect to the institutions of our country,—those very causes themselves, a happy termination of which I hope has taken place—have conduced to the advantage of the Society," in that "many abolitionists of the North . . . have become satisfied that to agitate the subject of slavery with a view to the extinction of slavery within . . . the various States in which it is tolerated and exists by law, is vain, fruitless, and a failed effort . . . and that their exertions hereafter, if governed by motives of humanity and benevolence, should be directed . . . to the great purpose of colonization [Clay to Greenleaf, January 13, 1851], which in its ultimate consequences will lead to the final separation of the two classes of persons that now inhabit this country."

One auspicious occurrence is the proposition being considered in Congress for the government to establish a line of steam packets which would ply between the U.S. and Africa, as well as other points. Believes these could "furnish the means of transporting emigrants . . . to Africa." Announces that even if it fails in this session of Congress, "I shall never despair; for . . . 'despair' is a word not in the vocabulary of the Colonization Society." Asserts that "Colonization is a common object for the common benefit of the whole country"; that it has "nothing sectional in it, nothing selfish in its aims," nor does it deal with "property or the rights of property." Because all are beneficiaries of it, thinks the Constitution "grants ample authority for the performance of this common duty."

Another positive force for the society is the report of the Rev. Ralph R. Gurley [Remark in Senate, September 27, 1850] which, based on information collected in Liberia, offers "nothing but hope and encouragement . . . as to the prospects of the Republic of Liberia." As a result, colonization can no longer be considered "an idle, visionary, and impracticable scheme." Also encouraging is the bequest to the society of John McDonogh of New Orleans which amounts to $25,000 per year for forty years.

Contends that "of all the projects of the existing age," colonization is the greatest. Predicts that Africa will receive great blessings from the civilization and Christianity brought back to that continent by the return of so many of "the African race" from America. Predicts that at a "distant, very distant, perhaps . . . day" there will be an end to slavery in the U.S.: "It may by law. It may by the sword. It may by the operation of natural causes, and it is the operation of natural causes to which I look for its ultimate extinction. As to the sword, nobody I trust would think of the employment of that to put an end to slavery. And as to law, I believe I have had some experience on that subject in the State to which I belong. The question was very much agitated there during the year before last, and I am very reconciled to the decision of my State although it was contrary to my wishes [Stevenson to Clay, June 12, 1848; Clay to Pindell, February 17, 1849, no. 2 of date]; in that decision I acquiesce, for I believe that no safe mode of gradual emancipation by the operation of law can terminate in any one of the States the existence of slavery much, if any sooner than it will be terminated by the operation of natural causes." Explains that by natural causes he means when free labor can be procurred at a cheaper rate than slave labor, and contends this will happen when the "population shall be three or four times as great as it is." Although he cannot predict how long this will take, believes "It may take some two centuries to carry them back" to Africa "to such an extent as no longer to create any solicitude or anxiety about the few who may linger and remain behind."

Referring to the free blacks, says he does not want "to wound their feelings . . . for it is not their fault, that they are a debased and degraded set. . . . more addicted to crime, and vice, and dissolute manners than any other portion of the people of the United States. It is the inevitable result of the law of their condition." Thus, "the free people of color" would benefit by a return to Africa, because "from the nature of our feelings and prejudices . . . they can never be incorporated, and stand upon an equal platform." So, too, will white laborers, slaves, and commerce benefit from colonization.

Asserts that in the past the slow, gradual emigration promoted by the colonization society has been beneficial, because it has enabled Liberia to avoid the disruption, famine, and confusion which too rapid settlement would have produced. Concludes, however, that "the time has now arrived when some considerable acceleration may be given to the transporting of emigrants from the United States to Africa."

Turns to the question of suppression of the slave trade, noting that maintaining French, English, and American squadrons along the coast of Africa has failed to stop this "odious traffic [Remark in Senate, January 15, 1851]." Contends that the best method of suppression is colonization, because on the 350 miles of African coast now occupied by colonists, "not a single slave *depot*" exists. Wishes Britain's Queen [Victoria] were present as the president of the U.S. [Millard Fillmore] is so that he could try to persuade them both to divert the money spent on maintaining the squadrons to the cause of colonization. Copy. Printed in *African Repository* (April, 1851), 27:105-14.

Clay had presented in the Senate two petitions [Remark in Senate, January 15, 1851] asking that provision be made to transport to Africa all blacks who were willing to go. Thomas Ewing also presented a memorial from Ohio requesting the establishment of a line of steamers between the U.S. and Liberia. These were referred to the Committee on Commerce, but no further action was taken. U.S. Sen., *Journal*, 31 Cong., 2 Sess., 84, 117. For John McDonogh (1779-1850), a wealthy New Orleans merchant and philanthropist, see *DAB*.

Remark in Senate, January 22, 1851. Presents the petition of James Stoddard, who desires "compensation for his services and the use of a wagon and horses" during the War of 1812. Endorses him as "a person of great merit," deserving of "an allowance of bounty land or . . . a pension." The petition is referred to the Committee on Pensions.

Presents the petition of "certain temporary clerks in the Second Auditor's office asking an increase of compensation," since "the amount allowed to clerks in the General Land Office and other bureaus is $4 per day, while the pay allowed them is only $3 per day." The petition is referred to the Committee on Finance. *Cong. Globe*, 31 Cong., 2 Sess., 303.

Also on this day, during discussions on the slave trade, after Sen. John P. Hale disparages Clay's resolution to prevent the employment of American vessels and seamen in this traffic [Remark in Senate, January 15, 1851], Clay reminds the Senate that he had based his motion on "a public document, communicated to this body at its own request, in relation to the prosecution of the slave trade from the coast of Brazil to Africa." Our public agents in Brazil for years have apprised "this Government as to the extent to which that trade is carried on in American vessels, and occasionally by American seamen," and "all recommended some more stringent measures in order to put a stop to it [Remark in Senate, January 15, 1851]." Explains again how it is arranged so that even though a "vessel sails from the Brazils," it flies the American flag and has an American captain and crew, noting that "our flag protects them during their outward passage." Once in Africa, the ship is delivered to a purchaser, and "the crew is changed, a different flag is hoisted, and a Brazilian, or Portuguese, or some other foreign commander put in charge of the ship." American seamen "are left to perish . . . or compelled to take a part in navigating a slaveship back to the coast of Brazil." If "sea-letters shall be no longer granted to American vessels clearing out from the ports of Brazil to the coast of Africa," it "will put a stop to the abuse of our flag." Moreover, "None of the flags of other nations can be used for that purpose, because, in regard to most of them, the right of search has been secured to the British."

Admits there are also other suggestions "such as making it penal for the owner of an American vessel to sell it for the purpose of prosecuting the slave trade." These are "mere objects of inquiry" based on years of information, and not, as Hale had implied, "an occasion for the continuance, the renewal of that unhappy agitation which we have witnessed throughout the country."

Proclaims that "slavery is of two descriptions—the domestic, and foreign or African slavery, the slave trade." Domestic slavery, "and that alone, has been the cause of the agitation." Has heard of "nobody anywhere, no matter to what party he may belong . . . who was not in favor of the suppression of the African slave trade." Yet Hale "supposes that we cannot act upon this uncontroverted subject, about which there is a unanimous opinion, without leading to all the agitation and discussion of the" problems of domestic slavery.

Repeats his support for the American Colonization Society, whose colonies occupy "the extent of three hundred and fifty miles" of the African coast, where "there is a complete and absolute suppression of the slave trade." Suggests that "if the entire margin of that coast was colonized, we should hold the door to Africa, and no slave could get out to be carried to Brazil or any other country." Although he believes "that colonization is the most effectual method of suppressing the African slave trade, I do not mean to say that there are no other modes by which, to a certain, to a beneficial extent, there might not be some suppression of it." The "squadrons on that coast have done some thing, but not enough . . . to justify the great expense," but "withholding sea-letters" might "repress to a very great extent that portion of the slave trade . . . between the Brazils and Africa." *Ibid.*, 305.

Later, when Clay addresses Sen. Jefferson Davis's question, which "was, whether we had a right, and whether it was proper, to put an end, if we could, to the slave trade between the Brazils and the coast of Africa," he notes that there is "no such object indicated" by his resolution. Nonetheless, the policy of suppressing the African slave trade "is not the policy of this country alone, but of all Christendom." Therefore, we should have "a right to restrain the shameful abuses of our flag when it has been employed in the prosecution of the trade." We also have "a duty, to protect our seamen against being inveigled into the trade and left to perish upon the coast of Africa." While "unwilling . . . to interfere in the policy of any foreign Government upon the question of the slave trade, odious as I regard it," still considers it "an imperative duty, to impose all proper restraints upon our own people in prosecuting this trade under our flag, in our own vessels, and in part with our own seamen." *Ibid.*, 308.

Still later, during discussions about a bill to satisfy American claims for spoliations committed by the French before July 31, 1801, Clay notes that he had "some familiarity with the subject of this claim when I occupied a different position in the Government of the country [7:665]." Denies arguments that "from the nature of the claim, it was not assignable," because "It was . . . perfectly in the power of the owner of any one of these claims against France, or on our Government when they were virtually assumed by us, to transfer his right in equity to any person and for any purpose he pleased."

Also argues that "All . . . we are responsible for to the claimants against France, in consequence of the . . . treaty of 1808, is to pay the value of the claims which the claimants had upon France; in other words, the prospect which they had of recovery of these claims upon France." Admits that the amount of indemnity "is a question of difficulty," but adds that "it has been settled down at five millions of dollars" which is 1/2 or 1/3 "of the nominal amount of the claims."

Points out that in many instances the insurers "were utterly destroyed," and notes that these insurance offices were composed "Of individuals—widows, orphans, and persons in every condition of life." They were injured "in consequence of not getting the indemnity to which they were entitled, either from France or from this Government." Cannot "see any propriety whatever in withholding from the hands of individuals composing those companies that benefit" which this bill will secure. Will, therefore, vote for the bill. *Ibid.*, 310-11.

After additional debate, Sen. Thomas J. Rusk's amendment to the bill that would exclude any payment under the bill to any assignee or insurer is defeated 25 to 30, Clay voting nay. *Ibid.*, 312.

The bill to provide for the ascertainment and satisfaction of claims of American citizens for spoliations committed by the French prior to July 31, 1801, passed the Senate on January 24, but did not pass the House. U.S. Sen., *Journal*, 31 Cong., 2 Sess., 68, 110.

To Lewis Cass, Washington, January 24, 1851. Since "I am a little indisposed," asks Cass "or my friend [Henry S.] Foote . . . to pair off with me on the Spoliation Bill [Remark in Senate, January 22, 1851]." Copy, extract. Printed in Robert F. Batchelder, Catalog 57, Item 216, Autographs, Ambler, Pa.

From George R. Harrison, Annapolis, Md., January 24, 1851. Writes from the Naval Academy to explain that "The Ship St, Lawrence will [sa]il in a short time for the worlds fair at London," and "I would like [very muc]h to be ordered to her." Although "much pleased with the [Scho]ol & Professors," is convinced "of what benefit a cruise [of] a few mont[h]s would be to me." ALS, partially illegible. DLC-HC (DNA, M212, R21). Endorsed by Clay: "I wrote to Geo. that I did not think that the permission would be given, and therefor had better not be applied for," and that "no advantage [was] to be derived by him from a voyage in the St. Lawrence" if it were "to the neglect of his studies."

The World's Fair, known as "The Great Exhibition," opened at the Crystal Palace in Hyde Park, London, on May 1, 1851, and ran into November. London *The Times*, May 1-2, 1851.

From Jordan L. Mott, New York City, January 24, 1851. Writes to protest against a bill "introduced by Mr. [Hopkins L.] Turney, Chairman of the Committee on Patents." Believes that passage of the bill "would paralize Ingenuity, and render Letters Patent of little or no value." Provides "a brief history of the movements of Inventors," especially recalling the actions of a convention of "Patenters throughout the United States" held during the "Fair of the American Institute" in 1845. Reports that the convention "acknowledged insufficiency of the existing Laws relating to Patents," desired "to have these laws amended," and offered at least six proposals for government consideration. Complains, however, that only the propositions "that would insure to the benefit of the Infringer" or that were "non-important to the Patenter" have "received the consideration of Congress." Describes similar meetings in Philadelphia, Boston, and Baltimore, but regrets that "the party who controlled the doings of this last Convention" were the "Men who have so much sympathy for the defendant in Patent Suits." Explains that "Agents representing themselves to be Inventors or Inventors friends . . . go from Shop to Shop soliciting signatures" on memorials to the Senate, a movement that "is a gigantic fraud attempted to be perpetrated to promote the Interested view of certain defendants." Argues that a plea from a "gang of Smugglers" who employed $500,000 so "that the Laws might be so framed that they could escape its penalties. . . . would be considered honest compared with the one now before the Senate." Praises inventors—"a very small part of the Community"—as men "endowed with the Heaven born gift of Creating. . . . The wonderful effect produced by creative genius during the half Century just closed have proved their power to do good." Concludes: "We therefore appeal to *you*, as the known Champion of the rights of every American Citizen . . . to cause the bill now before the Senate to be postponed to the next Session of Congress" to prevent passage of "a hasty ill, digested Law, paralising the Best Interests of the people." Since "Invention is the Parent of Manufactures. . . . He who would 'Rather be right than be President' cannot will not refuse" to help. ALS. DLC-HC (DNA, M212, R6).

For Mott (b. 1799), owner of Mott's Gold Medal Stove and Range Depot in New York City and who incorporated the J.L. Mott Iron Works in 1853, see *NCAB*, 7:117-18.

A "bill giving further remedies to patentees" had been introduced in the Senate on December 10, 1850, but did not pass. U.S. Sen., *Journal*, 31 Cong., 2 Sess., 31.

The meeting of inventors to which Mott refers was held on October 22, 1845. The meeting, which decided to resolve into the "National Society of Inventors," proposed a 10-point plan to improve legal and congressional support of patents and patentees. New-York *Daily Tribune*, October 23-24, 1845.

To Elizabeth Harrington, January 27, 1851. Explains that the "Government of the U.S." would not fund the purchase "of an estate in Loudon County Virginia, for the purpose of establishing a Female Seminary on it." Adds: "If the Estate is to be acquired and dedicated to the object you wish, it can only be done by private means and individual enterprize." ALS. CSmH.

Remark in Senate, January 27, 1851. During debate on a bill "to make good to Missouri the two per centum of the net proceeds of the public lands heretofore withheld from that State," Clay inquires "whether this is the bill for paying to Missouri the two per centum which was reserved for making roads leading to Missouri." When informed that it was the same bill, Clay states that "I shall be able to prove to the Senate that Missouri is not the creditor of the General Government," but "the General Government is greatly the creditor of Missouri in reference to that fund." Notes that he has been "confined a day or two" and was not aware that the bill would be taken up today. Asks, therefore, for a postponement so that he can present his views, as "I am rather too feeble to go into a discussion of the question at this time." The bill is laid on the table until the next day. *Cong. Globe*, 31 Cong., 2 Sess., 345.

This bill, which was first read on December 9, 1850, did not pass. U.S. Sen., *Journal*, 31 Cong., 2 Sess., 29. See also Speech in Senate, February 6 and February 14, 1851.

Remark in Senate, January 30, 1851. Presents a memorial of H.A. Frost, a British subject who has lived in Michigan but now resides in Canada, asking for an amendment to the patent laws which would allow a foreigner who has resided in the United States for five consecutive years "at any time previous to his application" to pay the same fee as a citizen and to be allowed "to file a *caveat* on payment of the same fees as citizens." Notes that Frost claims to have made "some very important inventions, which tend to cheapen very much the erection of . . . buildings," and that "he is very poor, and cannot pay the price of $500, which is required by our laws to be paid by a foreigner, in order to obtain a patent." The memorial is laid on the table. *Cong. Globe*, 31 Cong., 2 Sess., 384.

Later on this day debate centers on a bill to ascertain and settle the private land claims in California on which the question pending is an amendment offered by Sen. Pierre Soule. This amendment states "That possession in good faith, within determined metes and boundaries, during twenty years, shall be deemed *prima facie* evidence of a complete grant, even against the Government." Clay opposes "any proposition which will introduce a new and distinct rule of property from that which is presented in the treaty [of Guadalupe Hidalgo; Clay to Beatty, April 29, 1847]." Agrees that the U.S. is bound "to carry the treaty into full effect" and ought to give it "a liberal and generous interpretation; but we are not bound to go beyond it. We are not to introduce new rules of property in behalf of the inhabitants of California, extending their land and enlarging their possessions." Believes the proposition before the Senate "is . . . a new rule. . . . that . . . is not required of us by good faith, in the execution of the treaty." Argues that this amendment would "extend the titles and . . . possessions of the old settlers" in California "to the prejudice not only of the Government itself, but of the new settlers who have gone to California." Concludes that "it would be unwise and incautious to adopt the amendment." *Ibid.*, 390-91.

To George Vandenhoff, Washington, D.C., January 30, 1851. Ask him to repeat his "readings of [Richard B.] Sheridan's dramatic writings" or "of such parts of Shakespeare as you may select" and request that he do this "before the adjournment of Congress." Copy, signed by twelve members of Congress in addition to Clay. Printed in Washington *Daily National Intelligencer*, February 1, 1851.

Vandenhoff replied on January 31, 1851, saying he would "be proud" to comply with their request. Sets "Tuesday, Thursday, and Saturday, of next week, for the repetition of my three 'Evenings with Sheridan,' the admirable wit of whose sparkling comedies may perhaps be felt as an agreeable relief to your severer duties of the day." *Ibid.*

George Vandenhoff (b. 1820, England) was an actor who came to the U.S. in 1842. He subsequently studied law and wrote a number of books. *NCAB*, 1:427.

Remark in Senate, January 31, 1851. In response to a resolution offered the previous day by Sen. James M. Mason to inquire into the propriety of paying certain Spanish claimants for the loss of their slaves in the *Amistad* case, Clay asserts that while he is inclined to think the claim is not well-founded, he has "no fixed and determined opinion on the question." However, he thinks "it right to make the investigation."

Notes that "I have chiefly to notice the solicitude with which certain members of this body recur to the compromise [Clay to Combs, January 22, 1850], and seize hold of everything they can to reagitate the country in reference to that subject." Referring to Sen. John P. Hale, asks if the Senate does not remember that last year "during the progress of that compromise through this body . . . the very member who last addressed us, and others who concur with him, in their general opinions, declared that if they wanted a subject of agitation, continued, increased, exaggerated agitation, they would desire the passage of those compromise measures? That was their prediction. And what was the prediction made by myself and the other friends of that compromise? That if the measures passed they would bring tranquility and peace to this entire country; they would settle agitation; they would silence the agitation." Insists that the agitators are silenced on the subject of domestic slavery, "but whenever the foreign African slave trade is brought up they seize on it with a desperate grasp to find if they cannot make out of that some cause for agitation."

Points out that the other day Hale voted "in a small minority against an inquiry in relation to the suppression of the foreign slave trade. That and that only, can be the theme of agitation." Believes that even the "hopeless effort" to excite agitation "in certain localities . . . is dying away," and Hale "will find even a great portion of the party of which he was a leader [Free Soil], ultimately to acquiesce in what has been done." *Cong. Globe*, 31 Cong., 2 Sess., 402. Following more debate, the resolution to conduct the inquiry is approved. *Ibid.*, 403.

To Messrs. Fauntleroy, Hastings, & Drigan, Brownsville, Texas, *ca.* February, 1851. Replies to a letter from them [not found] expressing their approbation of his career, and states that it is "gratifying to me to know that, when I go I shall leave behind me the friendly and favorable opinion of many of my country men. . . . With respect to the measures of compromise brought forward at the last session of Congress [Clay to Combs, January 22, 1850] . . . I was anxious for their adoption and indifferent whether that was done by separate bills, or by one general bill. Finally, they all did pass, and substantially as originally proposed." States that he was pleased to concur in the liberal proposals to Texas and is also glad "she has acceeded to them" by a decisive majority. Hopes that tranquility will prevail, and does not believe agitators of the Fugitive Slave Law will "be able to effect anything, or to disturb the deliberations of Congress." Copy, extract. Printed in Frankfort *Commonwealth*, February 25, 1851.

Fauntleroy was probably Thomas T. Fauntleroy (1796-1883), a former Virginia lawyer who spent most of his career as a U.S. Army officer. In 1849 he was sent to the Texas border, was commissioned a colonel in 1850, and subsequently became a brigadier general in the Confederate Army. *CAB*. Hastings was possibly David H. Hastings, also an Army officer. *HRDUSA*, 510. Drigan has not been identified.

Speech in Senate, February 6, 1851. Recalls that when the bill "to make good to the State of Missouri the two per centum of the net proceeds of the sales of Public

Lands heretofore withheld from that State" had been called up a few days ago [Remark in Senate, January 27, 1851], he had stated that instead of Missouri's being the creditor of the general government, "she was largely the debtor." Rises now to show that "every cent of the two per cent. fund reserved in the compact between Missouri and the General Government has been expended, and a great deal more." Moreover, this was done "with the silent acquiescence . . . of the State of Missouri, and with the positive votes of her Senators and Representatives."

Points to the construction of the Cumberland Road from Cumberland, Md., to Vandalia, Ill., which was stopped because of a dispute between St. Louis, Mo., and Alton, Ill., concerning the terminus of the road. Asserts that "between seven and eight hundred miles of the Cumberland [R]oad have actually been constructed, at a cost for nearly" $6,000,000 and "upon a pledge of reimbursement to the Government . . . of the amount expended from the two per cent. fund," first from the state of "Ohio, then from Indiana, then from Illinois, and then from Missouri." But instead of being reimbursed $5,800,000, the general government has received "about $1,230,000 or $1,300,000."

Recalls how he had "contributed in some degree . . . to the passage of laws" in session after session which were to continue construction on the road [2:187-90, 310; 3:23, 56, 189-90, 581; 7:94; 8:20, 470, 831-33; 9:27-28, 167, 251-52, 273, 331, 400-402, 761]. For this reason he feels honor bound to show that Ohio, Indiana, Illinois, and Missouri are not due "one single cent of the two per cent. fund." States that the law which authorized Missouri Territory to form a state constitution [3 *U.S. Stat.*, 545-48] provides "That five per cent. of the net proceeds of the sale of lands lying within the said territory or State, and which shall be sold by Congress, from and after the 1st day of January next, after deducting all expenses incident to the same, shall be reserved for making public roads and canals, of which three fifths shall be applied to those objects within the State, under the direction of the Legislature thereof, and the other two fifths in defraying, under the direction of Congress, the expenses to be incurred in making of a road or roads, or canal or canals, leading to the said State." Points out that the two percent fund "was all to be made outside of her limits" and that "the whole amount of this fund has been expanded specifically upon the Cumberland road," the benefits of which "have been incalculably great."

Asserts that when the Cumberland Road reached Wheeling, Va. (W. Va.), opposite Ohio, "every obligation towards the State of Ohio resulting from the expenditure of the two per cent. fund was completely fulfilled. . . . But then the States beyond Ohio—Indiana, Illinois, and Missouri—having the same two per cent. fund pledged in the respective articles of compact . . . had a right to ask the continuance of the road."

Next, discusses various bills of appropriation which have been passed to expand this fund. Believes "the Senate will find, from the appropriations to which I have called their attention, that vastly more than $230,000 has been expended, without making Missouri at all chargeable for any part of the [Cumberland] road outside the State of Illinois." Since the "deficit of reimbursement for the construction of the whole road from Cumberland to Vandalia is about four millions and a half, and if Missouri is liable for her portion of that . . . it would be perhaps twenty or thirty times the amount of $230,000." Even "if you charge to Missouri only what has been expended within the limits of Illinois, it will exceed three or four times the amount claimed" for her by this bill. Concedes that the road has not been completed up to the state line of Missouri, but argues that "the literal interpretation . . . is not the true and just interpretation of the act. The question is whether Missouri has or has not derived benefit" from the road. "As I have already stated, every Western State has derived benefit." Adds that the "fund may hereafter accumulate, if unappropriated, perhaps to an amount sufficient to carry the road to the line of Missouri," but argues that the general government "was not limited as to the time when the road should be constructed" or the type of road to be built. Concludes, then, that the "bill ought not to pass."

Sen. Thomas Hart Benton responds, attacking Clay's arguments and insisting that the reserve fund from public land sales was divided "into two parts—three fifths to be applied in making the road to the State, and two fifths within and through it. . . . I lay stress upon those words 'to' and 'through.' " Further, Missouri has postponed asking for the two percent until it became evident "that the road was given up by Congress, and was never to go to Missouri."

Clay responds that "the Senator from Missouri has not controverted several positions which I assumed. . . . He has not denied that there is not a single cent of the two per cent. fund in the Treasury of the United States. He has not denied that the whole has been expended on the Cumberland road. He has not denied that it was expended under the express provisions in the several acts declaring that the reimbursement of the General Government should be made out of that two per cent. fund. He has not denied that . . . Missouri, during the progress of these various acts, never intervened to protest against an appropriation of the money to advance the road." Admits that in "the original terms of the compact between Ohio and the General Government, the stipulation with respect to the application of the five per cent. was, that it was to be applied to make roads to and through the State; the words 'through the State' have been rejected in every other instance." Moreover, believes a "road leading to it or near it substantially complies with the stipulations contained in the compact"; also, the road has not reached Missouri because "the fund was exhausted when it reached Vandalia." Points out that the road could never literally have reached to Missouri anyway, but only to the bank of the Mississippi River in Illinois, and there is such a road from Vandalia to the banks of the Mississippi, opposite St. Louis. Adds, that "if Missouri . . . will wait until there is an accumulation from the sales of land in Missouri to make another road they may have another road, if they insist upon it, upon the top of the one they have already." *Cong. Globe*, 31 Cong., 2 Sess., Appendix, 138-43; *Cong. Globe*, 31 Cong., 2 Sess., 451. Printed in Colton, *Clay Correspondence*, 6:592-603. See also Speech in Senate, February 14, 1851.

Remark in Senate, February 7, 1851. Presents the petition of John Buneff asking to be given bounty land in consideration of the services of his father in the War of 1812. The petition is referred to the Committee on Pensions. *Cong. Globe*, 31 Cong., 2 Sess., 459.

Later in the day following Sen. Robert C. Winthrop's presentation of the credentials of Robert Rantoul, Jr., to be his successor as senator from Massachusetts, Clay rises to say he does not agree with one of the conclusions reached by the Committee on the Judiciary in its report on this matter, "and if the Senate will not concur in it, the retiring member [Winthrop] will be entitled to retain his seat until there is some acceptance by competent evidence known on the part of the person elected." Therefore, moves to take up the committee's report "with the view of deciding whether the retiring member is entitled to his seat."

After considerable discussion as to whether or not Mr. Rantoul has accepted the position, the motion to take up the report is agreed to and the report is read. The report states, in part, that a sitting member under Executive appointment to the Senate "has a right to occupy his seat until the vacancy shall be filled by the Legislature of the State" during its "next meeting. . . . To fill such vacancy, it is not only necessary to make an election, but that the person elected shall accept the appointment. . . . and when his credentials are presented in his absence, his acceptance may be fairly implied."

Clay again rises to say that he agrees with the report except its conclusion on what indicates acceptance: "If the newly-elected Senator presents himself with his credentials and offers to take the oath" there is an express acceptance, or "if he transmits the credentials" to the Senate, there is "a strongly-implied acceptance." But when the governor of the state transmits the credentials, as in this case, in the absence of the person elected, "I think it is no evidence whatever of acceptance." Suggests from what he has read in newspapers that Rantoul, who is absent from Massachusetts on a speaking tour in the West, "may not yet have heard of his election." Contends that in the absence of any proof of his acceptance, "the Senator who holds by Executive appointment has a right to hold the seat." *Ibid.*, 460-61.

Following additional discussion, a motion by Sen. John P. Hale to table the matter is defeated 22 to 25, with Clay and Sen. William Henry Seward pairing their votes. After still more discussion, the Senate adjourns without resolving the matter. *Ibid.*, 462-67.

Rantoul took the oath and was seated on February 22, 1851. U.S. Sen., *Journal*, 31 Cong., 2 Sess., 208. For Rantoul (Dem., Mass.), see *BDAC*.

To James Harlan, Frankfort, Ky., February 8, 1851. Writes to ask if Harlan would accept a position as one of the commissioners of the board to settle land claims in California. Notes that the salary is $6,000, and "I am not *authorized* to say, but I *think* you can get it if you wish it. Write me by return Mail." ALS. Courtesy of Dr. Alan Westin, Yale University. Harlan did not serve as a commissioner. *BDAC*.

In an undated letter with endorsement "Mar./51," Clay wrote President Millard Fillmore, saying "If you should not deem it proper to appoint Mr. N[athan]. Sargent Commr. of P[ublic]. buildings, I can not forbear saying that I should be glad to see Mr. Geo[rge]. C Washington appointed, and that I believe no more popular appointment could be made." ALS. NBuHi. Letter marked "(Confidential)."

William Easby was nominated by Fillmore on March 3, 1851, to be commissioner of public buildings. His appointment was approved on March 12. U.S. Sen., *Executive Journal*, 8:310, 318, 332. Nathan Sargent had been nominated for recorder of the General Land Office in 1850, but his nomination had been rejected by the Senate. On December 20, 1851, Fillmore nominated him to be register of the treasury, and he was confirmed on February 10, 1852. *Ibid.*, 8:240, 264-65, 338, 367.

Remark in Senate, February 10, 1851. During debate on the bill "to supply deficiencies in the appropriations" for 1851, an amendment is proposed to pay the Cherokee nation "the amount due under article 9 of the treaty of August 6, 1846 . . . and on amount paid to agents and others employed by the Government in carrying out the provisions of the treaty with the Cherokees of 1835-'6, $724,603.37" and interest at 5 percent; "*Provided, however*, That the sum now appropriated shall be considered as a final settlement of all claims under the treaties with the Cherokees of 1835-'6 and 1846." Sen. Isaac P. Walker of Wisconsin moves to amend this amendment to provide "That the money appropriated in this item shall be paid in strict conformity with the treaty with said Indians of August 6, 1846"; that is, that the money be paid to the Indians per capita rather than through agents.

After considerable discussion on this issue, Clay rises to say "If the treaty is to be taken strictly, that is to say, if the payment is to be made per capita, to every individual entitled under the appropriation, the consequence would be that these Indians would come here to receive out of the public Treasury their respective portions of the fund." Points out that the treaty does not provide for sending the money out to the Indians, so "how is it to be carried out? Two modes are suggested. One is by agents of this Government; the other is by agents whom the parties themselves have chosen. A delegation of the Indians are here with full powers, representing their whole nation, and prosecuting this claim with authority to receive the amount. Now, sir, shall we not trust these agents whom the Indians themselves have trusted, rather than an Indian agent who may happen to be at some one of the posts near the Cherokee Indians? I think it is evidently the most proper." *Cong. Globe*, 31 Cong., 2

Sess., 494-95, 497-98. Following more discussion, Walker's amendment to the amendment is defeated 21 to 25, Clay voting nay. Later in the day, the original amendment to pay the Indians is passed 31 to 13, Clay voting yea. *Ibid.*, 499-500.

For the December 29, 1835, treaty between the U.S. and the Cherokees, see Parry, *Treaty Series*, 85:409-20; for that of August 6, 1846, see *ibid.*, 100:149-54.

To LUCRETIA HART CLAY Washington, February 11, 1851

The Session of Congress[1] is passing off and drawing to a close, and I [am] extremely glad of it; for I long to be at home. My health, with the exception of colds (and a distressing exception they are) is tolerably good. I am able of late generally to attend the Senate[.]

The last accounts I had from John [Morrison Clay] were good, but I have no very late one, and I am all the time uneasy about him. I shall be glad when he returns back to Ashland, without any disaster.[2]

W[illia]m. [C.C.] Claiborne [Jr.] has written to me that he has sent to you some articles of plate, which belonged to Henry C. Duralde,[3] but what they are he does not state. Probably only some that we gave to his poor mother [Susan Clay Duralde]. I enclose a letter which I received from Col [William Henry] Russell,[4] respecting Henrys death & burial.

[Andrew] Eugene Erwin is here. He has made some arrangement with a New York firm by which they agree to take him into their service, and to pay him good wages.[5] I am not entirely satisfied with it, but if they comply with it, in a pecuniary point of view it looks and I hope may turn out very well.

Thomas [Hart Clay] writes me that our Overseer[6] is getting on very well. I wish you would tell him that I desire the Wheat field adjoining Clarke[7] and the Tates' Creek road sowed in Clover. Thomas [Hart Clay] also says that you are quite satisfied with Phillis.[8] I hope that she may continue to please you, but I am afraid that she will give out about the time of my return home.

I sent you a few days ago by the Express Mail the bale of Cotton goods which Mr. Coffin[9] presented to us.

I have not received any letter from Mary [Mentelle Clay] for a long time.

ALS. DLC-TJC (DNA, M212, R11). 1. The 31st Congress, 2nd Session ended on March 3, 1851, but was immediately followed by a called session of the Senate. See Clay to James B. Clay, Feb. 18, 1851. 2. Clay to Lucretia H. Clay, Dec. 14, 1850. 3. Owen to Clay, Sept. 11, 1850. 4. Not found. 5. Clay to Unknown Recipient, Dec. 27, 1850. 6. Mr. Wheeler. 7. Probably John Clarke. MacCabe, *Directory of the City of Lexington . . . 1838 & '39.* 8. There was a family of Short-horn cattle known as Phillis; a cow from this family is probably the Phillis to which Clay refers. Perrin, *History of Fayette County*, 186. 9. Probably Jared Coffin.

Remark in Senate, February 11, 1851. Presents a memorial from Pennsylvania citizens asking for a modification of the tariff. The memorial is referred to the Committee on Finance. *Cong. Globe*, 31 Cong., 2 Sess., 503.

Later in the day, Clay supports a motion to reconsider a bill for the relief of the captors of the frigate *Philadelphia* which had narrowly been rejected by the Senate on the previous Saturday. Points out "that the Senate was very thin" when the vote was taken and the vote "was against the repeated decisions of the other House and this. . . . I think it is due to the parties interested, due to the memory of the gallant officer [Stephen] Decatur, who, whilst he lived . . . was my favorite in the Navy. . . . It is due to all parties concerned to give it a full and fair consideration when there is something like a full Senate." Hopes the Senate will vote to take it up and then lay it on the table so that it can be taken up "at this session, and if not, at some other session, without any prejudice arising from the decision of Saturday." *Ibid.*, 505.

The motion to reconsider is approved 27 to 13. Clay then moves to lay it on the table. This, too, is approved. *Ibid.*

Still later in the day, the Senate considers a bill making a grant of public lands to the several states "for the relief and support of indigent insane persons." A motion to table the bill is defeated, 17 to 33, Clay voting nay. Clay then rises to say that "I voted against laying the bill upon the table, although I am not now fully prepared to vote for the bill." Believes its object "is a benevolent one," but wonders if "so large a portion of the public domain should be placed under the direction of a single individual."

Sen. James A. Pearce of Maryland corrects him, saying that the 10,000,000 acres appropriated by the bill would be distributed to the states and the states rather than an individual would have control of the land. Clay responds: "The fact is, I have not considered this measure with all the attention which it deserves." Would like more time to study the bill, but will not ask for its postponement unless that is the general will of the Senate. After consideration of several amendments, the bill is engrossed for a third reading. *Cong. Globe*, 31 Cong., 2 Sess., 506, 511. This bill passed the Senate on February 12, 1851, but did not pass the House. U.S. Sen., *Journal*, 31 Cong., 2 Sess., 172.

To S. WATERMAN[1] Washington, February 11, 1851

I received your favor on the subject of the Treaty recently concluded between the United States and the Swiss Confederation.[2] I disapprove entirely the restriction limiting certain provisions of the Treaty, under the operation of which a highly respectable portion of our fellow-citizens would be excluded from their benefits. This is not the country nor the age in which ancient and unjust prejudices should receive any countenance.

When the Senate acts on the Treaty, the matter will be fully considered and I hope justly disposed of.

Copy. Printed in Henry Samuel Morais, *The Jews of Philadelphia* (Philadelphia, 1894), 261. 1. Dr. Sigismond Waterman (1819-99), a Bavarian, received a medical degree from Yale in 1848 where he also served as instructor. He later practiced medicine in New York City. *The Universal Jewish Encyclopedia* (New York, 1943). 2. The "Convention of Friendship, Reciprocal Establishment, Commerce and for the Surrender of Fugitive Criminals between Switzerland and the United States" had been signed at Berne on Nov. 25, 1850. Parry, *Treaty Series*, 104:447-60. It apparently was not ratified by the Senate.

Remark in Senate, February 12, 1851. During debate on a "joint resolution authorizing the President to confer the title of Lieutenant General by brevet, for eminent services," Clay rises to say the "resolution has, I think, not been treated exactly right." Points out that "It does not name any individual. . . . It proposes to invest the President of the United States with the power, by and with the advice and consent of the Senate, if I understand correctly, to grant the rank of brevet lieutenant general for services actually performed." Notes that at a time when war was raging, the Senate rejected a similar resolution by a small majority, but adds that in "that case it was understood that a particular individual was designed to be placed in the office of lieutenant general and commander-in-chief of our armies in the field." That individual, he says, "had rendered no such meritorious services as would call upon the country to bestow the rank of lieutenant general"; this resolution, however, "proposes to create that rank only for actual brilliant services performed." Thus, "the difference is too marked . . . to admit of a comparison between the two cases."

Asserts that he is fully ready to grant this honor to a man who is entitled to the rank because of his "achievements and laurels won in service. . . . And so, sir, with regard to the office of admiral." Believes the U.S. is a "competitor for supremacy of the ocean. And do we ever expect to acquire an actual supremacy, to beat down our great commercial and naval rival, without granting the rewards and without bestowing the high honors which are bestowed in all other countries, and nowhere more freely than by that Power whose naval supremacy we would supplant?"

Adds that in regard to "the individual whom it is supposed is to be rewarded here; the whole country, the whole world, rings with his praises in a military point of view." Concludes it is "the duty of a nation to offer its sentiments of gratitude . . . by bestowing this rank . . . to the individual who may receive it, the case of the conqueror of Mexico." *Cong. Globe*, 31 Cong., 2 Sess., Appendix, 149.

The resolution authorizing the president to confer the title of lieutenant general by brevet for eminent services passed the Senate 31-16 on February 13, 1851. It did not pass the House. U.S. Sen., *Journal*, 31 Cong., 2 Sess., 114, 175. A resolution specifically to confer upon Maj. Gen. Winfield Scott the brevet rank of lieutenant general had been introduced on February 24, 1849, but had not passed either the Senate or the House. *Ibid.*, 30 Cong., 2 Sess., 256. An earlier attempt by the Polk administration to secure a bill creating the rank of brevet lieutenant general with the purpose of appointing Thomas Hart Benton as supreme commander in charge of the Mexican War effort had been killed by Congress in January, 1847. Smith, *Magnificent Missourian*, 217-20.

To THOMAS HART CLAY Washington, February 12, 1851

After I wrote to your mother [Lucretia Hart Clay] yesterday, I recd. last night Marys [Mentelle Clay] letter, for which I thank her.[1]

Considering what is best to be done with Yorkshire, we must either keep him at Ashland, and in that case under the direction of the Overseer, or if you have a suitable stable for him at Mansfield, he may be taken there. I am afraid that he would interfere too much with the operations of Mr Wheeler[2] on the farm to admit of his proper attention to him. I should therefore prefer his standing at Mansfield, if you can have him properly attended to. But in that case, Harvey[3] must be left in the care of the Stock at Ashland and you must get some other groom for Yorkshire. Indeed if he remain at Ashland, it may be necessary to get some assistance for Harvey.

John's [Morrison Clay] absence[4] during one half of the Season of the horse ought to satisfy him with the arrangement of placing the horse under your care. If he goes to Mansfield, your pastures must be relied on for the mares sent to him, and I suppose you have corn enough to feed the mares, requiring grain, of which you should make a charge against the horse[.]

I wish you to say to your Mother that I desire her to engage a White gardener, and I shall be satisfied with any terms she agrees to, and with his going to the Garden house near town.

ALS. DLC-HC (DNA, M212, R6). 1. Clay to Lucretia H. Clay, Feb. 11, 1851; Mary Mentelle Clay's letter not found. 2. The overseer. 3. A slave. See Bayless to Clay, August 31, 1844. 4. Clay to Lucretia H. Clay, Dec. 14, 1850.

To JAMES BROWN CLAY Washington, February 13, 1851

I send herewith your account with the public as audited, exhibiting a bal. against you of $9 8/100.[1] This is owing to the disallowance of your charges for two English papers. Mr. Pleasanton [*sic*, Stephen Pleasonton] suggests that you are entitled to have made good any loss, if you sustained any loss, on exchange, that is, I suppose, by receiving your money in London, instead of the U.S. How that was, I do not know; but if you have any such a/c and will send it to me I will endeavor to have it passed. Otherwise, I will if you wish it pay the Nine dollars 8 Cents.

I had deposited the draft from N[ew]. O[rleans]. with Corcoran & Riggs[2] for collection, and as it had some time to run, and as I presumed you had not returned from St. Louis, I have omitted to take it up; but will do so in a day or two and send it to you.

My love to Susan [Jacob Clay], dear Lucy [Jacob Clay] & the children . . .

ALS. DLC-HC (DNA, M212, R6). 1. Pleasonton had written Clay from the "Fifth Auditor's Office" of the Treasury Department on Feb. 12, 1851, stating that the adjustment of James Brown Clay's accounts as chargé d'affaires to Portugal reveals "a small balance of 9.08/100 dollars is due from him." LS. DLC-TJC (DNA, M212, R11). 2. William W. Corcoran (1798-1888) and George W. Riggs had formed the banking firm of Corcoran & Riggs in Washington, D.C., in 1839. For Corcoran, see *NCAB*, 3:153; for Riggs, see *NCAB*, 15:229.

Speech in Senate, February 14, 1851. Sen. Thomas Hart Benton rises to reintroduce his bill, defeated the previous week, to pay to Missouri the two percent that had been withheld from the sale of her public lands. As he proceeds to defend the bill, Sen. Henry S. Foote makes a point of order, that it is not in order to discuss the merits of a proposition upon a motion to be allowed to introduce a bill. The question of allowing the reintroduction of a bill already defeated during the session is also brought up. After considerable discussion over parliamentary procedure, an exception is made and Benton is allowed to continue.

Following Benton's speech, Clay rises to say that "I took no part in the preliminary proceedings this morning, either to express any sentiment or to vote, because, on the one hand, I did not desire to deny to the Senator from Missouri the benefit of a new trial for his bill, nor on the other hand did I wish to seem to be anxious to violate an established principle and usage of parliamentary law." Notes that the Senate has given "the Senator from Missouri the privilege of an exposition of the motives which led him to ask leave to introduce the bill again, and at the same time to accord to any other Senator the privilege of reply." Wishes to avail himself of this privilege without going into "the long and elaborate argument of the Senator from Missouri."

First of all, corrects Benton's assertion "that the speech recently made by me in opposition to this bill [Speech in Senate, February 6, 1851], and published in the papers of this city, was revised by me. . . . I never saw it from the time it was delivered until I read it in the morning papers. . . . I very rarely, even in former years, revised the speeches which I made: perhaps too seldom for the poor reputation which I may have in the country."

Elucidates the issue: "A compact was made with various States, pledging, in the instance of Ohio, the two per cent. fund to carry the road to the State, and through it, but in all the other instances pledging the General Government to supply the two per cent. fund at its own discretion in roads leading to those States—Indiana, Illinois, and Missouri. The argument of the Senator is, that, although the Cumberland road has been extended some seven or eight hundred miles, it has not been carried directly up to the line of Missouri. My argument, on the other hand, was, that the whole two per centum was to be expended under the direction and according to the judgment of Congress, in constructing roads leading to those States, and that Congress was to be the judge of where the road should commence; and that from the terms of the compact it was manifest that it was not intended the road should begin at the State or from the State, but it was to begin somewhere else and lead to the State. I contended that the General Government, in the faithful execution of this stipulation, had exhausted the whole two per cent. fund of all the four States, and that the exhaustion took place even before the road reached Vandalia, the seat of government of Illinois. I have contended, therefore, that the General Government has honestly endeavored to carry out its contract, and that if it has failed to carry the road to the line of Missouri, it has been not because of an indisposition to fulfill the contract, but because of the exhaustion of the fund out of which the object was to be accomplished."

Believes that if "there is an imperative obligation . . . to carry the road up to the line of Missouri," Benton should not ask "to be refunded an exhausted fund" but rather should "introduce a bill to compel the General Government to extend the road from Vandalia to the eastern bank of the Mississippi." Asserts also that "in the compacts with the several States" the two percent fund was "to be applied to the construction of a road leading to the State, without specification as to the character of the road." Denies it was specifically to extend the Cumberland Road; rather, "it was any road which Congress chose." Denies, too, Benton's contention "that the General Government was under obligation to carry the road to Jefferson City, the seat of government of Missouri."

Complains that Benton "has looked up an old speech of mine made in 1825 [4:19-33], which I have never read since it was made, and has brought that speech into contrast with the one which I made the other day; and he contends . . . that a different interpretation is given to the compact by the two speeches." Points out that the 1825 speech "was made before there had been any application of the two per cent. fund, to any considerable extent, if to any extent whatever, of the three States of Indiana, Illinois, and Missouri." Explains: "I was arguing then that Congress was bound to apply that fund in execution of the compact. I was arguing against the position . . . that the compact was fulfilled when the Cumberland road reached the Ohio river. I contended upon that occasion, as I contended the other day, that our obligation to Ohio ceased when the road reached the Ohio river; that the fund out of which the object was to be accomplished was exhausted, and therefore that Ohio had no claims upon us for the extension of the road further; but that Indiana, Illinois, and Missouri had claims upon us to carry the road through Ohio, not for the sake of the benefit of Ohio, although she might incidentally derive benefit from it, but for the sake of the States to which it was to be carried, or towards which it was to lead." Now, "There is no State, and there will be none for a long time, west of Missouri, to which, in the execution of a compact, we should carry the road through Missouri as it was carried through Ohio. . . . If it is to be carried there, it is clearly not within the compact, and it must be carried under the general power . . . to make internal improvements." Has "never denied that if the fund existed in abundance . . . you should carry the road as far as you could. . . . But I contended . . . that the General Government . . . had carried the road as far as the money would enable them to do." Thus, there is no incompatibility between the 1825 speech and the one of a few days ago.

Turns next to the practicability of making a paved road through Illinois. Notes that when the Senate considered such a proposal in 1836 and 1838 [8:831-32, 834; 9:167], the idea "was abandoned because of the enormity of the expense of making it, the materials not being at hand, and having to be drawn from such an immense distance. . . . Hence Congress only contemplated to make a road that was not macadamized through the State of Illinois."

Sums up his argument by saying that "Missouri has had the application of the two per cent. fund to more than three times its amount, even if you limit her liability to that only expended in the State of Illinois, and there is no money out of which she can be paid. That two per centum was positively and expressly pledged to the reimbursement of the expenditure which the General Government had made, but that reimbursement has not yet been effected, and, until it is effected, Missouri has no claim on the Government." Concludes that "leave to introduce the bill should be granted, and a day set aside for its consideration and discussion," if the Senate and the House have "one of those fourteen precious days" left in the session to spare for such a bill. *Cong. Globe*, 31 Cong., 2 Sess., Appendix, 177-79. For Benton's speech, see *ibid.*, 173-77. Following Clay's speech the Senate votes 13 to 31 against allowing the bill to be introduced, Clay voting nay. *Cong. Globe*, 31 Cong., 2 Sess., 544. Clay's speech is printed in Colton, *Clay Correspondence*, 6:603-8.

To HUGH MAXWELL Washington, February 15, 1851

I received your letter transmitting one addressed to you by Mr [James W.] Beekman[1] which I have read with much attention and interest. I had previously been aware of the course which he had pursued in the Senate of New York, on the occasion of the recent attempt to elect a Senator of the U. States,[2] but the motives of his conduct were only matters of conjecture—these are fully developed in the letter with the perusal of which you have favoured me, and I take pleasure in saying that with his views of public duty (and they are my own) I think he is entitled to great praise for his firmness, resolution and patriotic determination. He was about to elect a Senator of the U.S. Whether the person to be chosen would or would not support the system of compromise measures adopted at the last session of Congress[3] was a question of high importance to the State of N. York and to the union. If he were opposed to that system he would come here as an agitator, if in favor of it as a friend to the Union[.] I think Mr Beekman had a right as an elector to know in which of those characters the new Senator would appear at Washington. Of Gov. [Hamilton] Fish I entertain personally very favorable opinions; and I am utterly unable to comprehend why he should not make an open explicit and undisguised avowal of his sentiments on the important question which I have stated.[4]

These, my dear sir, are my sincere views; but I cannot consent to any publication of them, as that would be inconsistent with a rule, to which I have endeavoured always to adhere not to interfere in elections in States other than that of my residence. I return the letter of Mr Beekman, and assure you of my constant and great respect & regard.

Copy. NRU. 1. Letters not found. Beekman had been a student at Columbia with Hamilton Fish, who was responsible for persuading him to enter politics. Allan Nevins, *Hamilton Fish: The Inner History of the Grant Administration*, 2 vols. (New York, 1957), 1:41. 2. Hamilton Fish was the candidate for U.S. senator in 1851. Because of his friendship with Thurlow Weed and the fact that he had written a number of letters and made statements criticizing the Fugitive Slave Act of 1850, conservative Whigs became alarmed and demanded assurances that, if he went to Washington, he would support the entire Compromise of 1850. This he declined to do, instead writing a letter to Washington Hunt affirming his support for the Fillmore administration and for the compromise except the Fugitive Slave Law. The moderate Whigs remained unsatisfied with this response, and Beekman joined with Democrats in the New York state senate to cause a 16 to 16 tie in the vote on Fish's election. Fillmore wrote a letter supporting Fish, while Clay responded with the above letter. On March 18, with two Democrats absent, Fish's friends in the state senate sprang a resolution to go into an election and after fourteen hours finally triumphed in electing Fish to the U.S. Senate. *Ibid.*, 1:41-42. 3. Clay to Combs, Jan. 22, 1850. 4. See also Fish to Clay, Feb. 18, 1851; Clay to Fish, Feb. 23, 1851.

To LUCRETIA HART CLAY Washington, February 15, 1851

I recd. a letter from Mary [Mentelle Clay] about the employment of a Gardner.[1] I had before written to Thomas [Hart Clay] about engaging one,[2] and stated to him that I should be satisfied with any arrangement you would make. I think the terms proposed by the one you wish to employ are well enough. As to our keeping that or pasturing and feeding his cow and horse for $20, I think we had better to do it, as whether we agree to do so or not, they will be kept on our pastures &c. It is to be understood that all the fruit and ornamental trees are retained by us, except that he may have the peaches gathered from the trees, strawberries &c. If he will graft the apple trees that have not been budded or heretofore engrafted, he may have one half of them; but I do not wish him to pull up and throw away any trees until I get home[.]

I should be glad if Mary would tell me how Adam[3] has attended to the Cows, whether you have any Durham Calves &c. The blooded Stock are looking up very much at the Eastward, and I would not now sell Diana's heifer and her calf for any thing like the price I would have taken last fall.

Mary tells me that you have filled one of the Ice Houses and the other partly, & I am glad of it.

I am very glad that you are pleased with Mr. Wheeler.[4] I suppose he takes care of every thing. The hemp that he breaks out might be put in the Corn Crib. How has Adam taken care of the Portueguese Pigs?[5]

I have not heard lately from John [Morrison Clay].

ALS. DLC-TJC (DNA, M212, R11). 1. Letter not found. 2. Clay to Thomas H. Clay, Feb. 12, 1851. 3. A slave. 4. The overseer. 5. James B. Clay to Clay, Feb. 28, 1850; Clay to James B. Clay, March 25 and May 27, 1850.

To John Morrison Clay, February 16, 1851. Reports he has just received John's letter [not found] "informing me of your Sale of Magic & Zampa at $3000. and think it an excellent one. I wish you may be able to sell the rest of your stock as well." Explains that he would not have suggested sending Yorkshire to Mansfield if John had been at home, but "In your absence I thought it the best arrangement." Hopes John will see Mrs. Octavia Walton LeVert while he is in the South. States that "My Brazil case is in a course of preparation for submission . . . and I have great hopes of it." Mentions that he will not leave Washington until March 10, and adds that Andrew Eugene Erwin is with him. AL, signature removed and manuscript mutilated. Courtesy of M.W. Anderson, Lexington, Ky.

Magic was one of the horses sired by Yorkshire. Perrin, *History of Fayette County*, 152, 154.

The Brazil case to which Clay refers is a legal case in which he was acting as attorney for Margaret Ray, who was attempting to obtain from Brazil money owed her husband Joseph in a claim. Ray to Clay September 12, 1850. DS. DNA, RG76, Boundary and Claims Commissions and Arbitrations (R1). For Joseph Ray, see 4:562, 597.

On September 16, 1850, Clay had given Philip R. Fendall his power of attorney to act in the Ray case. ADS. *Ibid.*

On June 23, 1851, Clay writes Fendall sending him a statement [not found] "in respect to Ray's claim against the Government of Brazil." Characterizes the case as "quite complicated," and feels the Rays "have reposed perfect confidence in the justice of their claim, without making any exertions to furnish proof to establish it." ALS. KyU.

Clay sends Fendall on August 6, 1851, his "statement of facts and of argument in the [Ray] case," which he hopes will "aid you in the preparation of a more complete exhibition of his case." Thinks, however, "It is very imperfect," because he did not have possession of all the documents in Washington and Rio de Janeiro relating to the matter. Believes that he has proved "that the original wrong done Mr. Ray was his violent expulsion from the Brazilian Empire," but concludes that "arriving at a just amount of indemnity due to Mr. Ray" is a difficult problem. LS. NcD.

To FRANCIS LATHROP[1] *et al.* Washington, February 17, 1851

I have received your letter, informing me of the intention of the Union Safety Committee of N. York[2] to celebrate the approaching Anniversary of the Birth day of [George] Washington by a public dinner, and inviting me to attend it. And you express the motives which prompt the desire to distinguish the occasion by unusual demonstrations. I heartily concur in all of them. It is highly refreshing to recur, some times, to the great principles on which our Union has been founded, and to the great men who have founded it. Among these, the Father of his Country stands out in bold prominent and unrivalled relief. To his counsels we may, with perfect confidence, repair to invigorate our patriotism, and to stimulate our highest exertions in the support of that Union, which it was his greatest ambition to achieve and perpetuate.

In surveying the actual condition of our Country, we ought not to shut our eyes, to the dangers which it presents. On the one hand, in the Free States, it should not be disguised, that there is a spirit of opposition to the Constitution and Laws existing which, if it be not checked and discountenanced, may lead to the most dangerous consequences.[3] On the other, in the single state of South Carolina, there is a like spirit from opposite causes prevailing, to a great extent, threatening more immediately the safety of the Union, so far as it depends on the proceedings of a single State.[4]

In favor myself of the supremacy of the Constitution the laws and the Union, I am alike opposed to all attempts to violate or endanger them, from whatever quarter they may proceed. I hope that the opponents of the General Government will pause before they venture to make forcible resistance to its lawful operation. No one living would more deprecate than I should the shedding of blood in a Civil War. But if, regardless of all consequences, the standard of resistance to the Laws and of rebellion, against the common government should be raised, I have no doubt that it will be promptly & effectually put down, and that the moral effect would be to add greater strength & stability to our glorious Union.

Of that Union, gentlemen, I have not time, if the occasion were fit, to say all that I feel & think. It embodies all that is grand, and great & glorious. All the hopes of the enlightened friends of Liberty throughout the whole Civilized world. Destroy it, and break us up into petty, jealous and belligerent fragments, and there is a melancholy annihilation of all the bright and animating anticipations of Mankind.

Gentlemen, you have devoted yourselves to the noble cause of the Union, and to the compromises on which it depends. Go on, fearlessly move on. Triumph and the gratitude of the world await your patriotic exertions[.]

I should be most happy to be with you on the ever memorable 22d. of Feby.; but my public duties here will not allow me the enjoyment of that high satisfaction.

ALS. NcD. 1. For Lathrop (1806-82), an insurance and railroad president, as well as associate judge of the New Jersey Court of Errors and Appeals in 1869, see New York *Times*, March 5, 1882. 2. The Union Safety Committee of New York was composed of wealthy merchants dedicated to the preservation of the Compromise of 1850. Smith, *Presidencies of Taylor & Fillmore*, 206. 3. Reference is to resistance to the Fugitive Slave Law in the North. See, for example, Remark in Senate, Feb. 17, 1851; Comment in Senate, Feb. 18, 1851. See also Nevins, *Ordeal of the Union*, 1:350-52, 380-404. 4. In opposing the Compromise of 1850, South Carolina, led by such fire-eaters as Robert Barnwell Rhett and Gov. Whitemarsh B. Seabrook, was openly considering secession, either separately or in cooperation with other Southern states. By the fall of 1851 when it became obvious that no other Southern state would cooperate in secession, Unionists and cooperationists combined in South Carolina to defeat those in favor of separate secession. Throughout the deep South the Whig-versus-Democrat rivalry gave way to a new alignment of Southern Rights extremists versus Unionists. Although secession sentiment was strongest in South Carolina, other Southern states particularly Georgia, Mississippi, and Alabama also experienced a struggle between those who supported the compromise and those who opposed it, with disunionists losing out for the moment in state elections. The South uniformly insisted, however, that the Fugitive Slave Law must be strictly enforced. Nevins, *Ordeal of the Union*, 1:346-79; White, *Robert Barnwell Rhett*, 103-34.

Remark in Senate, February 17, 1851. Submits a resolution asking the president "to lay before the Senate, if not incompatible with the public interest, any information he may possess in regard to an alleged recent case of a forcible resistance to the execution of the laws of the United States in the city of Boston, and to communicate . . . what means he has adopted to meet the occurrence, and whether . . . any additional legislation is necessary to meet the exigency of the case, and to more rigorously execute existing laws. *Cong. Globe*, 31 Cong., 2 Sess., 580.

On February 15, 1851, a slave from Norfolk, Va., Frederick Jenkins (known as Shadrack) was arrested and taken to federal court for arraignment. A crowd of blacks burst into the courtroom, overpowered the guards, and rescued Shadrack, enabling him to escape to Canada. Richard Hofstadter, *American Violence* (New York, 1970), 85. For Fillmore's response which promised to enforce the law, see *Cong. Globe*, 31 Cong., 2 Sess., Appendix, 292.

To JAMES BROWN CLAY Washington, February 18, 1851

I enclosed yesterday one, and now send the other number of the draft of Cochoran [*sic*, Corcoran] & Riggs, substituted for that from N[ew]. O[rleans].[1]

I think you do your mothers [Lucretia Hart Clay] heart wrong in supposing it engrossed by John [Morrison Clay]. His great misfortunes undoubtedly deeply affect her;[2] but I believe that she affectionately feels for all her children. Her manner does not always truly indicate the intensity of her actual feelings.

I have no doubt that the plan you marked out for yourself at and near St. Louis, persevered in and vigorously pursued, will be highly profitable. The only fear I have is that you may not be contented with it.[3]

As Slaves are selling, I do not think that Thomas [Hart Clay] asks too much for the two you want. To him they are worth fully the price. I forget whether the time has elapsed, within which the man of whom I bought them was at liberty to repurchase them.

I hope to return home immediately after the adjournment of Congress on the 4h. But it is possible that I may be detained a few days beyond it to try a cause in the Supreme Court.[4]

I wish you, Susan [Jacob Clay] & the children would meet me at Ashland on my return. Whilst you are building & preparing at St Louis, you had better remain with us. Judging from the letters of John, he has been very prudent & unexcited at Mobile.[5] If the three horses which he has retained should acquit themselves well on the turf, he will be probably able to sell them advantageously . . .

ALS. DLC-TJC (DNA, M212, R11). 1. Clay to James B. Clay, Feb. 13, 1851. 2. Reference is to John's mental problems. See Clay to Henry Clay, Jr., April 5, 1845; Clay to Thomas H. Clay, July 1, 1850. 3. Clay to James B. Clay, Dec. 23, 1850. 4. Clay delayed his departure from Washington until March 10 because of a special called session of the Senate. See Clay to James B. Clay, March 5, 1851. The called session of the 32nd Congress ran March 4-13, 1851, and was ordered by the president so that the Senate could transact executive business, especially in regard to nominations which had not been acted on in the regular session. See *MPP*, 5:110.   5. Clay to John M. Clay, Feb. 16, 1851.

Comment in Senate, February 18, 1851. Presents a memorial from Philadelphia asking for a modification in the bounty land law that would grant to soldiers of the War of 1812 one hundred sixty acres of land; also a memorial from Clarion County, Pa., asking for a modification of the tariff. The 1st is referred to the Committee on Public Lands, the 2nd to the Committee on Finance. *Cong. Globe*, 31 Cong., 2 Sess., 595.

Later in the day, Clay moves to table a resolution by Sen. Jefferson Davis to instruct the secretary of the Senate "to require the proprietors of the daily papers employed to print the current debates of the Senate, to publish the same as furnished by the Reporters, without alteration being made by any other person . . . and that so much of the resolutions of the 11th of August, 1848, and the 24 of February 1849, as authorizes the publication of speeches revised or written out by Senators, shall be . . . rescinded." After some debate the motion is agreed to, 26 to 13, and the resolution is tabled. *Ibid.*, 596.

Still later during discussion of his resolution submitted the previous day [Remark in Senate, February 17, 1851], Clay rises to say that the resolution "embraces three objects": 1st, to ascertain from the president the actual facts relating "to the obstruction to the execution of the [Fugitive Slave] law" which occurred in Boston last Saturday; 2nd, to learn what measures the president has used to support the authority of the law; and 3rd, to ascertain from the president whether or not there are "defects in the existing law which ought to be cured by other laws, in order to secure their supremacy throughout the country." Until the information is received, believes it would be premature to enter into a lengthy discussion of the resolution, but does want to say "that I have been shocked, distressed, astounded by the occurrence" in which the law and officers of justice "have been insulted, threatened, beaten down, and the prisoner in their custody seized and carried away with exultation and triumph." Asks "By whom was that mob impelled onward? By our own race? No, sir, but by negroes; by African descendants; by people who possess no part, as I contend, in our political system; and the question which arises is, whether we shall have law, and whether the majesty of the Government shall be maintained or not; whether we shall have a Government of white men or black men in the cities of this country." Hopes this action "will be effectually and immediately punished, and that the authority of the law will be maintained in every part of our common Republic."

Sen. John Davis rises to say that he believes the majority of the people in Massachusetts, though they find the Fugitive Slave Law offensive, are yet willing that it, like other laws, shall be enforced. Believes, however, that they have a right to ask for a modification or repeal of this law and that any attempt "to suppress freedom of debate and freedom of thought" on this subject "is unwise."

Clay asserts in response that "A law [Remark in Senate, September 12, 1850] was passed at the last session to enforce a clear and explicit article of the Constitution. . . . We have acted upon it; we had discussed it, debated upon it, and decided upon it. We will not now, especially when there are indications of violence and a forcible resistance to the law, listen to any attempt to repeal or modify the law. Let the authority of the law be maintained; let it be executed; let the defects, if there are any defects, be developed during the progress of its execution, and when there is a spirit of obedience pervading . . . the whole country, then and not till then will the time arrive when we should look into the law and ascertain whether there be any grounds of objection calling for further legislation."

Insists that he has not said anything against the people of Boston or of Massachusetts and hopes "it is not deemed unkind by the Senator from Massachusetts, or offensive, to speak of that negro mob that dared to lay their sacrilegious hands in the sanctuary of justice, upon the very sword of justice itself, and to wave it over its officers and ministers, threatening them with its application. . . . I denounce such resistance, whether made by white men or black men." *Ibid.*, 596-97.

To Committee of Invitation for Celebration of Washington's Birthday by Friends of the Union in Macon, Ga., February 18, 1851. Reports receiving their invitation [not found] to attend the celebration of Washington's birthday in Macon, Ga. States: "To no place in the States would I go, if I could, on such an occasion, with more satisfaction than to Macon; with no friends of the Union, anywhere, would I more gladly unite than with those who shall assemble at Macon, in feelings and demonstrations of joy and gratulations for the safety of the Union. To that safety, Georgia has greatly and gloriously contributed."

Compares the Compromise of 1850 [Clay to Combs, January 22, 1850] to George Washington's statement concerning the Constitution: " 'That it will meet the full and entire approbation of every State is not, perhaps, to be expected; but each will doubtless consider that, had her interest alone been consulted, the consequences might have been particularly disagreeable or injurious to others; that it is liable to as few exceptions as could reasonably have been expected, we hope and believe; that it may promote the lasting welfare of that country, so dear to us all, and secure her freedom and happiness, is our most ardent wish.' "

Recalls that when the Compromise passed last year, "all eyes were turned to Georgia, and all hearts palpitated with intense anxiety as to her decision. Ultraism had concentrated its treasonable hopes upon that decision. I never doubted it. I knew many of her eminent citizens, their patriotism, and their devotion to the Union." Notes that when Georgia "announced her deliberate judgment. . . . It diffused inexpressible joy among the friends of the Union, throughout the whole . . . land. It crushed the spirit of discord, disunion and civil war."

Concludes: "Gentlemen, it requires only perseverance, concert and co-operation, among the friends of the Union, to secure the fruits of the great victory which has been won. Whatever others may do, for myself, I am firmly resolved never to cast my vote for any man whose fidelity to the Union admits of the least doubt." Copy. Printed in New York *Herald*, March 10, 1851.

Georgia was generally considered to be the most pro-Union of the cotton states. Indicative of this was the Georgia Platform adopted at a state convention in Milledgeville in December, 1850. These resolutions pledged Georgia to abide by the Compromise of 1850 as a permanent settlement for the sectional controversy. However, they warned that Georgia would resist, even to the point of breaking the Union, any effort to weaken the Fugitive Slave Law, suppress the interstate slave trade, or abolish slavery in the District of Columbia. On this platform Robert A. Toombs and Howell Cobb established the Union Rights party. William J. Cooper, Jr., *The South and the Politics of Slavery 1828-1856* (Baton Rouge, 1978), 307-9, 313, 317-18.

From Hamilton Fish, New York City, February 18, 1851. Regrets that Clay has allowed his influence to be "brought to bear upon the pending Election for U.S. Senator from this State," noting that "a letter from you addressed to a personage in this City [Hugh Maxwell] holding a high office under the Federal Government is being circulated & shewn for the purpose of producing prejudice against me [Clay to Maxwell, February 15, 1851]." While acknowledging that Clay's letter admits "to a want of propriety in the interference on the part of a Senator from a remote state" and "contains some kind expressions toward myself personally," believes it also creates "the impression . . . that I have refused to express opinions upon certain leading public questions" and challenges "the propriety of my election."

Criticizes "the character of W Hugh Maxwell," who would consider it "no betrayal of your confidence, if he barely keeps your letter from being printed in the newspapers" in order to proclaim "your desire that I should not be Elected." Since "for reasons very sufficient I have been compelled to withhold all respect or regard for him," fears that "the whole patronage & influence of the Custom House is brought to bear against me, instigated & stimulated by all the malice & envy of its principal officer." Warns Clay against accepting Maxwell's profession of friendship: "The Devil, they say, sometimes quotes Scripture."

Asserts that "I have desired no concealment of my opinions upon the various important measures of the last Session of Congress nor . . . has there been any concealment." Although "I have had no occasion for a *public* or *official* expression of opinion. . . . I have, both in conversation, & in correspondence, expressed my opinions very freely" on the "several measures of the last Congress, and upon the imperative & absolute importance of the enforcement of all laws however distasteful they may be to sectional feelings." Presumes that "letters of mine could be found in nearly every County of this State," and notes that "Public reference has been made to a correspondence between Mr [Millard] Fillmore & myself" that supported the view "that Gov Fish would be 'patriotic, national, & independent if elected.'" Although "I certainly did decline being interrogated" by "persons holding the extremes of antagonist opinions" who sought "to entrap & embarrass," considers "the position entirely too elevated & dignified to be the object of even seeming personal interference, or solicitation on the part of the Candidate." Prefers to "refer all enquiries, to what I had *previously* said, and written, & to let them judge me by my past action & life." Believes that "the repetition of five lines from either of many letters written before the Legislature met . . . would have secured my election. . . . The State may be left with but one Senator," and "possibly a Free Soil Democratic Legislature may next year send one of their faith. But high as I estimate a seat in the United States Senate, I hold my own honor & character too high to obtain that seat by what I should deem a sacrifice of consistency, or of self respect." Hopes that Clay will see "that your confidence has been abused, & your name & influence is being used for a purpose which you did not design." ALS. DLC-HC (DNA, M212, R6).

To EDDA de N. MIDDLETON[1] Washington, February 20, 1851

I received your note.[2] From the conversation I had with you, in this City, at your instance, in relation to the unhappy alienation between your husband and yourself, I felt much interest and sympathy for you. Confiding in your positive and strong assurances that you had given no just cause for that alienation, I felt anxious for a reconciliation between you. I afterwards had an interview with Lieut. Middleton, and he left an impression on my mind that he also was persuaded of your innocence. I hoped therefore that your former affectionate relations would be restored. I still trust that such a desirable event may happen, and that you will demonstrate, by your exemplary conduct, and your devotion to him, that you are worthy of all his love & confidence.

I am thankful for the sentiments of esteem and admiration, which you have done me the honor to express.

ALS. KyU. Addressed to Middleton at the "Merchants' Hotel" at Philadelphia. 1. Possibly the wife of Lt. Edward Middleton, USN (later commodore). See *NCAB*, 7:259. 2. Not found.

Remark in Senate, February 20, 1851. During debate on the bill for the relief of the East Tennessee and Georgia Railroad Company, Clay argues that "the principle is of extremely doubtful propriety"; that is, "It is to give a credit of four years upon duties which are properly payable upon large importations of iron for railroads, and the reimbursement of those duties is to take place by four different installments, without interest." Contends that "here the Treasury is to be invaded; we are not satisfied with distributing with lavish hand the public lands, but we are called upon in fact to distribute the public revenue; or divert it from its proper course." Since the Committee on Finance has reported adversely on the bill already, believes "the proper course is to recommit the bill, in order that the Committee on Finance may examine into the effect of the bill, as proposed to be amended by the Senator from Tennessee [Hopkins L. Turney] and the Senator from Maryland [James A. Pearce]." Moves to recommit the bill to the Committee on Finance. Following more discussion concerning possible amendments, the bill is tabled, 29 to 21, Clay voting yea. *Cong. Globe*, 31 Cong., 2 Sess., 626. This bill had been introduced on December 17, 1850, by Hopkins L. Turney of Tennessee. It did not pass at a later date. U.S. Sen., *Journal*, 31 Cong., 2 Sess, 42.

Also on this day during discussion of the Post Office bill, Clay comments on the amendment proposed by Sen. Jacob W. Miller of New Jersey: "The bill, as it now stands, proposes to reduce the rates of postage to three cents on prepayment, and five cents where there is not a prior payment. The Senator from New Jersey proposes to strike out the option, and requires a prepayment from everybody." When Miller replies that no prepayment is required, Clay responds that, in that case, "I am disposed to go along with the committee, and with the estimates which that committee has derived from the proper Department." Notes that "We have heard a great deal about the universal demand for cheap postage. Amidst the millions who cried out 'Give us cheap postage,' has there been anyone who has looked at the financial effect upon our revenue. It is our business to see to the consequences; and whether the Post Office Department, which has hitherto relied upon its own resources, shall be made to depend upon a tax upon the people, in order to relieve them from a slight amount of postage." Urges "caution and prudence" in "every step."

Notes that the proposed amendment would reduce rates "from five and ten cents to three and five." Continues: "We know that the reduction of a tax sometimes increases the revenues which are derivable from it. That takes place to a certain point, beyond which you cannot go; for if the argument is to be pushed to the extreme, take off all tax and you will have a greater amount of revenue. The great difficulty is to strike the point which will give the requisite revenue, and at the same time afford the required facilities to the community at large. . . . I think it is a great thing, in giving facility to the business, when you come down to the rates proposed by the committee. Let us pause and see what the effect will be upon the country and its correspondence, and if hereafter we find we can safely and justly make other reductions, do it." *Cong. Globe*, 31 Cong., 2 Sess., 273.

The "act to reduce and modify the rates of postage . . . and to provide for the coinage of a three-cent piece" passed the Senate on February 26, 1851, and was approved by the president on March 3. U.S. Sen., *Journal*, 31 Cong., 2 Sess., 95, 222, 261.

To A. Merwin, February 21, 1851. Expresses his appreciation for "my appointment as an honorary member for life of the American Board of Commissioners for Foreign Missions; and I am indebted for this compliment to Mr. Anson G. Phelps, who generously contributed the requisite sum to accomplish the object." Copy, extract. Printed in Paul C. Richards, *Autographs, Catalogue 235* (Templeton, Mass., 1988), entry 264.

Although the printed extract of this letter gives the name "A. Merwin," it seems likely that the letter was really addressed to Orange Merwin (1777-1853), former congressman from Connecticut. See *BDAC*. Anson G. Phelps (1781-1853), a Connecticut manufacturer and philanthropist, was active in the American Bible Society, the American Board of Commissioners for Foreign Missions, the American Home Missionary Society, and the Connecticut Colonization Society. *DAB*.

The American Board of Commissioners for Foreign Missions had been founded by New England Congregationalists in 1810 and was the first foreign mission society in the U.S. See Charles K. Whipple, *Relation of the American Board of Commissioners for Foreign Missions to Slavery* (1861; reprinted ed., New York, 1969).

Speech in Senate, February 21, 1851. President Millard Fillmore's response to Clay's resolution of February 17 [Remark in Senate, February 17, 1851; Comment in Senate, February 18, 1851], asking for information concerning the rescue of a fugitive slave in Boston, is presented to the Senate. Clay responds that he feels "great satisfaction" in the president's message. "Its general tone and firm resolution announce that he will carry into effect the execution of the laws of the United States." Believes "the marshal of Massachusetts ought to be dismissed" and does not doubt that the President is scrutinizing his conduct to see if "he should or should not dismiss him."

Expresses a "high degree of satisfaction . . . in seeing the general and faithful execution of this [Fugitive Slave] law" in Indiana, Ohio, Pennsylvania, and New York. "It has been executed everywhere except in the city of Boston and there has been a failure there upon two occasions to execute the law." In respect to this recent event, "I stated upon a former occasion, that the mob consisted chiefly, as is now stated by the President, of blacks. But, when I adverted to that fact, I had in my mind those, wherever they may be, in high or low places, in public or private, who instigated, incited, and stimulated to these deeds of enormity, those poor black, deluded mortals. They are the persons who ought to be reached. . . . I believe—at least I hope—the existing laws will be found competent to reach their case."

Notes that in President Fillmore's message "two or three doubts or defects in existing laws" are suggested. One is the requirement in the Fugitive Slave Law of 1795 which requires a proclamation commanding insurgents to disperse before force can be applied. Since this presupposes a preexisting insurrection, it does not apply to an incident such as that in Boston in which the "first evidence of opposition and obstruction to the law arises from the fact that a party suddenly burst into the courthouse, dispersed the officers, violated the sanctuary of justice, and committed those enormities of which we have recently heard. To make a proclamation beforehand is therefore impossible. The President suggests, among the legal remedies which these cases may call for, that of dispensing with the proclamation in such cases." Therefore, moves to refer the message and accompanying document to the Committee on the Judiciary which will then report upon the recommendations in the message.

Sen. John P. Hale states "that the President . . . is rendering his Administration ridiculous" by his proclamation calling out all the naval and military forces of the country "to defend this great Republic against a handful of negroes in Boston!"

Clay responds that Hale's statement "is perfectly in keeping and congenial with his general course upon subjects of this kind." Continues: "But I must take occasion to say that on scarcely any occasion have I risen to speak in this body when that Senator has not followed me, as if his great object was to compete with me the palm of elocution. I yield to the Senator. I know the self-complacency with which he generally rises, and I hope he will receive this surrender on my part of any ambition between him and me to contend for the palm of oratory, with the complacency with which he usually rises in this body and presents himself before us. [Laughter.]" Asks, "what is the aim of this Senator? . . . Is there any other man in the Senate who believes that it originated among these negroes? Do we not all know the ramified means which are employed by the Abolitionists openly, by word and by print everywhere, to stimulate these negroes to acts of violence, recommending them to arm themselves, and to slay, murder, and kill anybody in pursuit of them, in order to recover and call them back to the duty and service from which they had escaped? . . . Does not everybody know that it is not the work of those miserable wretches, who are without the knowledge and without a perfect conciousness of what became them or what was their duty? They are urged on and stimulated by speeches, some of which are made on this floor and in the House of Representatives, and by prints which are scattered broadcast throughout the whole country. The proclamation, then, has higher and greater aims. It aims at the maintenance of the law; it aims at putting down all those who would put down the law and the Constitution, be they black or white."

Alludes particularly to a man named Thompson, "said to be a member of the British Parliament," who has come to this country to subvert one of its institutions. States that he has been received in a number of places in Massachusetts "and the police on one occasion assembled to protect him when they had not the heart to assemble around a court of justice to maintain the laws of their country." Adds: "And yet the member from New Hampshire would have the Senate believe that it is nothing but a few negroes collected together in a court-house, of whom it is unbecoming the dignity and character of the Government to take any notice!" Concludes: "I call upon the Senate to stand by the President, and stand by the Constitution; to uphold their laws, and to prostrate all opposition."

Sen. James M. Mason of Virginia rises to say the Fugitive Slave Law passed at the last session [Remark in Senate, September 12, 1850], "if not a dead letter, has not answered the ends for which it was designed." Doubts the president can execute the law. Clay interjects to ask if there is "any instance other than in Boston where the law has not been carried into effect when it has been attempted?" Mason replies that he knows of no other instance in which it has been "successfully resisted by violence," but claims many instances in which it is successfully opposed by "evasion and illusion."

Following a long statement by Sen. Daniel S. Dickinson of New York, Sen. Hale replies to Clay's earlier statements concerning him: "The honorable Senator says that I have seemed every time he got up to follow him, and he intimates that I have such a vaulting ambition that I want to contend with him for the palm of oratory. No, sir; I know myself better than that; but I am glad he has made that remark, for it has explained to me a slander which I had been utterly at a loss to explain. It has been said by him that I have sometimes taken occasion to get up and make speeches when the gallery was full of ladies. This suggestion of the Senator explains it."

Clay asks: "Does the Senator mean to say that I have propogated any such slander?" Hale replies: "No, sir." Clay asks: "What then do you mean, sir; I should like to know." Hale answers: "I do not answer questions put in that style, here or elsewhere." Proceeds, nevertheless, to "explain a remark which I think did not need explanation by anybody else except the Senator from Kentucky. I have said that I had heard the slander that I had sometimes taken occasion to speak when the gallery was full of ladies, and that that fact was explained by what the honorable Senator from Kentucky has now said—I always followed him, he selecting such occasions himself." Hale also accuses Clay of undertaking "to magnify this negro mob by connecting it with the efforts of what he pleases to style Abolitionists, which is a pretty comprehensive term all over the country. The old song has been raised, 'England is at the bottom of it.' There is an English emissary, one George Thompson, and it is not improbable the insinuation will spread . . . that this great negro mob of Boston, against which the public is preparing itself, was actually instigated by the emissaries of Great Britain." Describes the event instead as "one of the simplest and most isolated affairs that ever occurred; a momentary impulse to successful resistance to law."

After several other senators speak, Clay again rises to say that he regrets the remarks made by Sen. Mason. Doubts "whether there is any man in Congress who has watched with more anxious attention the operation of the fugitive act of the last session than I have, and in every instance which has come within my knowledge the law has been executed. . . . except in the city of Boston." Refers at length to various cases to prove this contention and asks: "Now, what does the Senator from Virginia expect? He has mentioned no case in which there has been a failure on the part of the claimant that has pursued his slave to recover him. Did he expect, upon the passage of the law, that, without diligence on the part of the master, the slave was to be returned to him at no expense whatever?" Believes there is no way to prevent individuals from aiding and harboring runaways, "and that law, above all others, will be most evaded where the object is to recover a human being who owes service as a slave to another; because, besides the aid and sympathy which he will excite . . . he has his own intellect, his own cunning, and his own means of escape at his command." Argues that "before the law can be charged with any violation of duty to the slave-holding States; before the President can be arraigned for any violation of his duty, a case should be made out where, by the exercise of proper diligence and vigilance on the part of the executive authorities, the case of evasion could be prevented."

Contends that in this case in Boston, the marshal has "failed to execute a law of the United States," and says if he were president, "I would remove him." Does not know what President Fillmore will do, but "I am perfectly satisfied, from all I know of the President and his Cabinet, that there is a most perfect and immovable determination to carry into execution the laws of the land, and to employ all the means in their power in order to accomplish it."

Turning back to Sen. Hale, denies he wishes "to suppress the freedom of debate in his own particular case," as Hale has intimated, because "There are some works too gigantic for me to attempt, and one of them is to stop the Senator from debate in this body. . . . He must, as George Canning once said, come into the Senate every now and then 'to air his vocabulary.' But the Senator made an observation with respect to a high officer of this Government that I thought unbecoming the dignity of the Senate, or the dignity of the Senator. He spoke of the message of the President as a contemptible and ridiculous message."

Hale responds: "The Senator is mistaken; I referred to the proclamation." Clay states: "I thought the Senator alluded to the message; however, I think the proclamation is one of the best parts of the message." Concludes: "It has been said that this is an isolated case. Do you ever, sir, see the papers from Boston; I mean the abolition papers from that city, and not only from that city, but from other portions of the country? Do you not see this Union denounced? Do you not see a declaration that within the limits of Massachusetts the fugitive slave law never can be executed? Do you not see advice given to the blacks to arm themselves and kill the first person that attempts to arrest them and take them back to the service from which they fled? When you see this, and when you hear of the blacks and whites mixing together in public assemblies in Boston, can you think that the blacks never heard the advice to arm themselves with revolvers and bowie knives and put down any attempt to carry them away? If you have read it, can you fail to believe that it must have operated on their minds, and that they have thought with what impunity they might rush into that court-house and commit the atrocious scene which has been depicted?" The Senate is adjourned without deciding on Clay's motion to refer the president's message to the Committee on the Judiciary. *Cong. Globe*, 31 Cong., 2 Sess., Appendix, 293-98; *Cong. Globe*, 31 Cong., 2 Sess., 660. Printed in Colton, *Clay Correspondence*, 6:609-16.

For the recent Shadrack case, see Remark in Senate, February 17, 1851. The earlier case in Boston to which Clay refers is that of William and Ellen Craft, a slave couple who had escaped from Georgia, and openly lived in Boston as fugitives. In the fall of 1850 when two Georgians representing their owner arrived in Boston to reclaim the couple, a vigilance committee headed by Theodore Parker harassed the Georgians, who were briefly jailed, and ultimately caused them to leave the city empty-handed. On November 7, 1850, the Crafts were legally married by Parker and embarked the same day for England. Nevins, *Ordeal of the Union*, 1:388; Smith, *Presidencies of Taylor & Fillmore*, 211-12.

George Thompson (1804-78) was a member of Parliament from 1847-52. He visited the U.S. in 1851 and cooperated with the American Anti-Slavery Society. *DNB*.

Remark in Senate, February 22, 1851. The Senate resumes consideration of Clay's motion [Speech in Senate, February 21, 1851] to refer to the Committee on the Judiciary President Millard Fillmore's message on the rescue of a fugitive slave in Boston [Remark in Senate, February 17, 1851; Speech in Senate, February 21, 1851]. When Sen. Thomas J. Rusk moves to postpone further consideration of this matter until the following day, Clay rises to oppose the motion, because "the question before us is the maintenance of the laws of our country, and I know of no business more important, more urgent, more demanding the attention of the Senate"; also, "it is proposed to refer the message . . . to a committee, and that committee must have some time to consider and report." Hopes "that the motion of the Senator from Texas will not prevail, but that we shall proceed to vote upon it."

Sen. Robert M.T. Hunter suggests that before discussion of the fugitive slave matter, the bills lying on the table should be referred to the proper committees. Clay does not object, but Sen. William H. Seward does object unless he is allowed also to present a petition. Hunter then suggests that if Clay will agree to postpone discussion of the president's message until Monday, much other important business can be completed today.

Clay "cannot agree," because "I know of no subject of more importance than action upon that resolution. None of the other questions comprehend the existence of the Government and the enforcement of the law." Predicts that if this matter is postponed, "When Monday comes, there will be other subjects demanding attention."

Finally, Rusk withdraws his motion to postpone and asks Clay to agree that his motion be made the order of the day for 2 p.m. this afternoon. Seward withdraws his objection, and Clay says he hopes "the bills upon the table will now be taken up and disposed of."

Later, however, after discussion resumes on his motion, Clay states: "I have reason to believe that we cannot get through with this question to-day. If there can be a general concurrence that it shall be taken up at two o'clock on Monday, whatever may be the state of business at that time . . . I will accede to the arrangement." Then, moves that the Senate meet at 11:00 on Monday. The motion is approved. *Cong. Globe*, 31 Cong., 2 Sess., 660-62.

To HAMILTON FISH Washington, February 23, 1851

In acknowledgeing the receipt of your letter of the 18th inst. I must begin by declaring with perfect sincerity, my very high personal regard and esteem for you, which existed before I had the pleasure of your personal acquaintance, and which has been strengthened and confirmed by our friendly intercourse. I must also add, that I was totally unaware of any such unfriendly relation between Mr [Hugh] Maxwell and you as that which you describe.

I received a letter[1] from that gentleman on the subject of Mr [James W.] Beekmans vote in the Senate of your State, writing [*sic*, wanting] an expression of my opinion as to his course. I had also previously heard that Mr Beekman had been bitterly denounced and violently assailed, especially by the Abolition and free soil prints. In my reply[2] to Mr Maxwell I stated that I had always acted upon the rule, of not interfering in an election in another and distant state from that of my residence. I gave no authority for the publication of my letter, of which I retained no copy, nor did I expect any use of it equivalent to a publication. I expressed the opinion that the conduct of Mr Beekman exhibited manliness, firmness and independance, and I must still adhere to that opinion. I believe from all I had understood, that he did violence to his feelings of private attachment to you, in consideration of his sense of a high public duty[.] The times my Dear Sir, are sadly out of joint, I believe that the substantial preservation and vigorous enforcement of the Fugitive Slave law,[3] involve the safety, if not the existence, of the Union. The election of a Senator of the United States from New York,[4] without any explicit public declaration, constituted as the Legislature of that State is, and declining as it hitherto has done to make any public avowal of its opinion of that law, would have been regarded as a virtual triumph of the opposition to its execution and the political effect throughout the whole country, would have been injurious. I appreciate fully the motives of delicasy which have restrained you, pending the election, from making any public annunciation of your opinion, but I think that, although that course generally ought to be pursued, an exception, arising out of the present state of our country, might with propriety be made. And could you not, my dear Sir, have availed yourself of your answer to the invitation from Tareytown [*sic*, Tarrytown],[5] to express your opinion of the law, without the danger of any imputation of indelicasy? My confidence in you is so great that I have repeatedly expressed the opinion that, if elected to the Senate of the United States, your course would be patriotic and uninfluenced by factionists or fanaticks. I have been indeed reminded of your concurrence in a testimonial given to Mr [William H.] Seward at the commencement of Gen: [Zachary] Taylor's administration, by which that Senator was enabled to controul a large amount of the public patronage.[6] I regretted it, although it did not destroy my confidence in you. If, under existing circumstances, you should be elected to the Senate of the United States, do you not expose yourself to the dilemma of being hereafter reproached by the Free Soilers if you do not act with them, or by the friends of the Constitution, the Union and the laws, if you should not, as I am sure you would, act with them?

I should my dear Sir, deeply lament that anything which I have heretofore written or anything in this letter, should have the tendency of impairing, in the slightest degree, the friendship between us, which I value so highly and under the impulse of which I subscribe myself . . .

LS. KyLoF. 1. Not found. 2. Clay to Maxwell, Feb. 15, 1851. 3. Remark in Senate, Sept. 12, 1851. 4. Clay to Maxwell, Feb. 15, 1851. 5. Clay to Representatives of the Union Meeting, Tarrytown, N.Y., Jan. 20, 1851. 6. In the struggle between Vice President Fillmore and Sen. Seward over patronage in New York State in the Taylor administration, Fish, who was then governor, signed a letter along with a number of other Whig leaders in the state saying that the wishes of Seward on patronage were the wishes of the Whig party and the state administration. Van Deusen, *William Henry Seward*, 115.

To RICHARD G. PARKER[1] Washington, February 23, 1851

I have received your letter informing me that you are preparing a series of reading books,[2] for a house in New York, and wishing to embody in some of them, extracts from some of my speeches, you desire me to indicate those from which I should prefer to have them taken. Whilst I am thankful for the compliment you wish to pay me, I regret that my numerous engagements here do not allow me time to comply, specifically, with your request. If I were to make a hap-hazard suggestion, I would say that from my speeches in January 1812, on the War,[3] on South American Independence,[4] on Greece,[5] on the removal of the deposits, during Gen [Andrew] Jackson's Administration,[6] in answer to Mr. [William C.] Rives, in 1841, on [John] Tyler's Veto of the Bank,[7] and my speech of September last on the Compromise,[8] portions from some or all of them might be taken, which would answer your purpose.

LS. MBAt. 1. Parker (1798-1869), a grammar master at various schools in Boston, was best known as a writer of textbooks and readers. *DAB*. 2. Parker collaborated with James M. Watson in producing the National Series of Readers, published by A.S. Barnes & Company in New York City. The most popular of these was *The National Fifth Reader*, which contains a selection from Clay on "Public Virtue" (pp. 420-21). *DAB*. 3. See 1:613-16, 618-27. 4. See 7:764-65, Subject Index entry on Spanish America. 5. See 7:731, Subject Index entry on Greece. 6. See 8:684-85. 7. See 9:528-29, 543-44, 553, 556-57. 8. Speech in Senate, Sept. 3, 1850.

Speech in Senate, February 24, 1851. During debate on the Post Office bill, Clay rises "to say that if the friends of free debate and free postage will only come to some conclusion to settle this conflict between the two freedoms, I am willing that the question should be taken. If not, I must call for the special order of the day." Shortly thereafter the Senate resumes consideration of Clay's motion [Speech in Senate, February 21, 1851] to refer to the Judiciary Committee the president's message relating to the rescue of a fugitive slave in Boston [Remark in Senate, February 17, 1851; Comment in Senate, February 18, 1851; Speech in Senate, February 21, 1851].

Following considerable discussion by other senators, Clay rises to say that "I came to the Senate to-day under a feeling of indisposition" because of a "high sense of duty connected with one of the most important questions, which has arisen." Hopes the subject will be terminated today. Reviews the development of this matter from the mob action in Boston, to his own motion to ask the president for the facts and for recommendations for "any amendment to these laws which he might deem necessary in order to enable him to carry out . . . his duties," through the president's response, and the Senate's debates on the issue.

Turns first to the arguments of Sen. Robert Barnwell Rhett, saying that Rhett "has . . . laid down what are the true rules of interpreting the Constitution. But he has told us nothing new; he has given us only commonplace matter. Everybody knows that . . . no powers can be exercised by Congress but such as are granted, or are necessary and proper to carry into effect the granted powers. . . . The whole difficulty with the Senator and his school is, that they undertake to say what are the granted powers, and what is and what is not necessary to carry into effect the granted powers. And if all others do not concur with them they are consolidationists, Federalists, Whigs, precipitating the country into ruin." Opines that members of this group renounce all legal precedents and shelter themselves "behind the opinion of the illustrious and lamented Senator from South Carolina, (Mr. [John C.] Calhoun,). . . . So it is with the whole school. They will tell you that the Supreme Court of the United States know nothing about the Constitution; that Congress has been violating it from 1793 down to this day. But if they can find an opinion of the lamented individual to whom I have referred, sanctioning their views, why it is worth all the precedents and the opinions of the Washingtons, Jeffersons, Madisons, Monroes, and all other Presidents of the United States." Notes that Rhett "has contended that there was no power in the Government . . . to pass the fugitive slave law [Remark in Senate, September 12, 1850]" and that it is remarkable "that there are certain coincidences between extremes in this body and in the country." For example, Rhett, "who I believe holds extreme doctrines upon the subject of slavery, and considers that institution as a blessing, and the honorable Senator from Ohio, [Mr. (Salmon P.) Chase] who holds directly opposite opinions, both unite in expressing the opinion that there is no power in the Congress . . . to pass the fugitive slave law, and that Washington, and all of us, from the commencement of the Government down to this time, have been wrong. . . . How does the matter stand now? The honorable Senator from South

Carolina and the honorable Senator from Ohio, *versus* the Supreme Court of the United States, the Congress of the United States of 1793, and the Congress of 1850, and all the members of the Senate and House of Representatives; for I never heard any one else doubt the power of Congress to pass this law."

Discusses his own view of the Constitution, saying that "From my birth, or from my knowledge of conscious existence as a human being, and since I have turned my attention to political affairs, I have been emphatically in the true, legitimate, full sense of the term, a State-rights man. But look at that school to which I have referred. They want you to exercise no power but what is to be found in the Constitution. I should like some of those strict State-rights men to point out to me what part of this Constitution gives to any one State the power of nullification of the acts of all the other States? What part of the Constitution gives to any one of the States the power of secession from the membership of the Union? Where are they to be found? Why, you find that whenever you press them on these points, they fly from the Constitution and talk about the mode of its formation, its compact character, its being formed by the States. Whenever it suits their purpose, or for any improper purpose they wish to deduce power, either of nullification or secession, or any other, they can find it without the least difficulty, limited and circumscribed as they would have all others in the interpretation of the Constitution."

Rhett interjects to say that he assumes Clay "will not at all object . . . if I should think proper to reply to the observations he is now making." Clay replies: "Of course I have no right to object to it. If the gentleman chooses, I will sit down now, if he has anything to say. . . . But it is a mere passing notice upon nullification and secession which I have been making, and I will meet the Senator, or any of his school in debate, whenever they choose to bring up this point on a proper occasion."

Argues against Rhett's contention "that the clause which relates to the recovery of fugitive slaves vests in Congress no power whatever to enforce that provision of the Constitution." Reads from the Constitution: "No person held to service or labor in one State, under the laws thereof, escaping into another, shall in consequence of any law or regulation therein, be discharged from such service or labor, but shall be delivered up on claim of the party to whom such service or labor may be due." Continues: "I hold that, when it is said a thing shall be done, and when a Government is created to put this Constitution into operation, and no other functionary or no other Government but the United States is referred to, the duty of enforcing the particular power . . . appertains to the General Government, to the Government created by the Constitution of the United States. The Constitution declares that a slave shall be delivered up. It says not how or by whom, whether by the State, or by the General Government, or by any officer; but it grants authority to Congress to pass all laws necessary or proper to carry into effect the powers granted by the Constitution."

Next, considers the charge that the Fugitive Slave Law "has not been fully executed; that there are fifteen or thirty thousand slaves in the free States, and only a few of them have been recaptured." Wonders "upon what authority" this number can be stated. Believes that it is possible that "from the commencement of the Government" that many slaves might have escaped, "But when it is asserted that at this moment there are fifteen or twenty thousand fugitive slaves in the free States, and that only half a dozen have been recaptured, and that therefore the law has not been of any practical utility, I should like to know the statistics or the facts on which the statements are founded."

Rhett responds that he got those statistics "from the published proceedings of an abolition society or convention held in . . . New York."

Clay exclaims: "Ah! exactly such an authority as the gentleman ought to take. . . . I do not believe the statement of the abolition society. No man knows how many fugitive slaves there are in the North. . . . But why are they not given up? I venture to say that in a majority of cases their former owners do not choose to put themselves to the trouble of pursuing them." Adds that "many of them die, and hundreds, perhaps thousands, escape into Canada," but it is not the duty of the government "to bring the dead back to life, or to bring the fugitives in Canada back to the United States." Admits there is inconvenience and expence involved in attempting to apprehend fugitives.

Views the principle involved in the Boston case as a question of "whether the laws shall be violently and outrageously opposed by force, or shall [they] be executed? If to-day the law upon the subject of fugitive slaves is obstructed by violence and force, and its execution prevented, what other law on our statute-book may not to-morrow be obstructed by equal violence and its execution prevented? . . . The question, then, is not the recovery of the fugitive slave. The question is, shall the Government be maintained? Shall the law be enforced?"

Recalls that a few days ago Sen. Salmon P. Chase stated that the compromises of the last session [Clay to Combs, January 22, 1850] were supposed to have brought peace and tranquility, but that they have not done so. Disputes this contention, saying that "so far as relates to the Wilmot Proviso, agitation is quiet." Also, there is no agitation on "the admission of California. . . . the settlement of the Texas boundary. . . . the abolition of slavery in this District. . . . Then those measures have worked wonders. At least, the honorable Senator, and others who concur with him in opinion. . . . have themselves been reduced to peace. Nay, more: the Senator himself, who was at the last session an agitator, cries out for peace, and reproaches me with being an agitator." Points out that no abolitionist in either the House or Senate has moved "a repeal of the measure; which . . . the Senator from South Carolina ought forth with to do, if he thinks the fugitive slave law unconstitutional."

Chase inquires if Clay means to number him "among those who ever expressed a wish for the dissolution of the Union?" Clay replies: "No, sir; I only mean to say that the Senator is in bad company. [Laughter.]" Chase responds that "if I am in bad company I do not know it." Clay retorts: "I mean in the company of the Abolitionists. If the Senator will disavow and repudiate the Abolitionists of all shades and colors, I should be truly happy to hear him." Chase says he disavows "most emphatically all association or connection with any class of persons who desire the dissolution of the Union. . . . But if the Senator, when denouncing Abolitionists, means to include . . . all those citizens who, within the limits of constitutional obligation, seek to rescue this Government from all connection with slavery, I can claim no exemption."

The two men continue wrangling over the meaning of the term "abolitionist." Finally Clay states: "Upon my word, if the Senator does not know what an abolitionist means, when he has practised the doctrine for so many years, I am sure I am unable to instruct or inform him. . . . I am very happy to hear him avow that he is not a disunion abolitionist." Nevertheless, believes that "If those who disavow extreme abolition . . . array themselves on the side of the [extreme] abolitionists . . . the inevitable consequence . . . is dangerous to the Union itself." Recalls when Chase recently rose in the Senate "to make out that I was an agitator and he a tranquil Senator," because "I called the attention of the Senate" to a document from the president "showing that, to an atrocious and nefarious extent, the slave trade was carried on, under the flag of the United States from the coast of Brazil to the western coast of Africa [Remark in Senate, January 15 and 22, 1851]." Asserts that "My object on that occasion was to enforce the laws of the country, as on this occasion my object is to clothe the Executive . . . with power sufficient to remove forcible obstruction to the execution of the laws." Exclaims: "I who, all the last session and all this session, have stood on the side of peace, of the Constitution, and of the laws and union of my country, I am an agitator! . . . and the Senator a dove of peace! [Laughter.]"

Contends that in the Boston case, except for the Whiskey Rebellion, "there has been no instance in which there was so violent and forcible obstruction to the laws of the United States since the commencement of the Government." Mentions a matter referred to earlier by Sen. John P. Hale in which "A namesake of mine [Cassius M. Clay] attempted to establish a paper in the town of Lexington . . . in a county [Fayette] where there are the greatest number of slaves of any county . . . in Kentucky [Clay to Buckingham, March 31, 1845; Cassius M. Clay to Clay, September 25, 1845]. There were some intemperate and supposed to be incendiary articles in the paper. The editor was requested to stop his paper; he refused to do it. The people of the surrounding counties—the *elite*, the men of wealth and highest respect, the most prominent men in society—I was not there myself, and do not suppose me to be approving even of that apparently orderly proceeding, for, on the contrary, I condemn all violent interference with the due and regular execution of the laws—assembled in the town of Lexington to the amount of thousands. That public meeting appointed a committee of sixty or eighty persons to request the editor again to remove his paper. He declined. They then removed it themselves. It was taken out without the employment of force and without resistance. The types were carefully put up and sent to Cincinnati, the city in which the honorable Senator from Ohio himself resides. But now for the sequel. This editor was himself exceptionable to that meeting. But he brought his suits in the courts and actually recovered damages for the injury done to his property by its being seized and removed, contrary to his wishes and in violation of his rights. He recovered a verdict and judgment, and received every cent to the full amount of injury he had sustained."

Points out two acts passed on March 3, 1807, empowering the president to use military force to carry out the laws, adding that "No man on earth would deprecate more than myself the occasion of any occurrence in which it might be necessary to employ force. . . . to enforce the laws of the United States. But a Government without power . . . without means to enforce the authority, and decrees, and judgment of its courts of justice would be the most ridiculous that ever presented itself to the contemplation of a human being. . . . I go for all the means with which we are invested by the Constitution of the country in order to maintain, at the North and at the South, and everywhere, the authority of the laws of the Government inviolate; to carry them out in full and complete execution."

Notes that the act of 1795 which "declares that Congress shall have power to pass laws to call out the militia to enforce the execution of the laws" also "required that a proclamation . . . be issued by the President calling upon the insurgents to disperse." Likewise, the act of March, 1807, "declares that the President shall have the power to call out the navy and army . . . as he is authorized . . . by the act of 1795. Proclamation, therefore, is necessary by the act of March, 1807." Since this is not practical in a case such as that in Boston, "It is proposed to invest the President with power to call out the militia, to call on the army and navy in case where he shall have just cause to apprehend, either in the arrest or after the arrest of the fugitive, a rescue of the slave." For this reason alone, "I hope the message will be referred, and I call for the yeas and nays on the question." The yeas and nays were taken with 34, including Clay, voting yea. *Cong. Globe*, 31 Cong., 2 Sess., 675-76; *Cong. Globe*, 31 Cong., 2 Sess., Appendix, 320-23; the latter is printed in Colton, *Clay Correspondence*, 6:616-28.

For the Whiskey Rebellion of 1794, which erupted in Western Pennsylvania in opposition to a excise tax on whiskey, see Morris, *Encyclopedia of American History*, 126. For the "Act to provide for calling forth the Militia to execute the laws of the Union, suppress insurrection, and repel invasion . . . ," approved on February 28, 1795, see 1 *U.S. Stat.*, 424-25. The two acts of March 3, 1807, to which Clay refers are: "An Act authorizing the employment of the land and naval forces of the United States, in cases of insurrection," and "An Act to prevent settlements being made on lands ceded to the United States, until authorized by law." See 2 *U.S. Stat.*, 443, 445-46, respectively.

To LUCRETIA HART CLAY Washington, February 27, 1851

I received a letter from Mary [Mentelle Clay] last night, which gave me a very satisfactory account of all things at home; except the loss of the Woodpecker mare, which I suppose could not be avoided.

I have received no letter from John [Morrison Clay] since that which I last sent you. I hope he is continuing to do well, I wish I could give you a good account of my own health. The cough with which I left home sticks by me, and I am never free from colds. And what distresses me is that Nature seems less & less competent to carry them off, or to resist them. Expectoration is tough and difficult, and I have frequent fits of coughing at night. I am strongly tempted to return home by Cuba, which I should not hesitate to do, if it were not that it would prolong my absence from you so long.[1] I believe it would be of great service to me, and I tremble at the prospect of passing the mountains and down the river in the month of March.

If mares are sent to Yorkshire early, and are required to be fed, the Overseer[2] must have them fed. I think that they had better be kept, in the Woodland pasture back of our house, and that none of our Stock be allowed to run with them.

[Andrew] Eugene [Erwin] is still here, and he has made as yet no permanent arrangement.[3] He has made one, on his own hook not entirely such as I could have wished, altho' in a present pecuniary point of view it is better, if carried out, than any I expected. A few days will determine.

Richard Pindell is also here; and if I abandon the Cuba trip, will accompany me home. I shall determine in a few days, and if I give it out, I hope to be at home the week after next.[4]

My love to Tho[mas]. [Hart Clay], Mary & the children[.]

ALS. DLC-TJC (DNA, M212, R11). 1. Clay to James B. Clay, March 5, 1851. 2. Mr. Wheeler. 3. Clay to Unknown Recipient, Dec. 27, 1850. 4. Clay to James B. Clay, March 5, 1851.

To William W. Groesbeeck, New York City, February 27, 1851. Expresses his thanks "most cordially . . . for the compliment of giving my name to your beautiful Yacht, and for your generous offer of a passage in it to England to attend the Great Fair [Clay to Harrison, January 24, 1851]." Regrets that the burden of his "official labors . . . prompt me to desire other and far different repose from that which I should enjoy in England. . . . I must seek it at my home." ALS. PWbH.

Groesbeeck was a New York City importer. Doggett, *New-York City Directory for 1848-49.*

To MILLARD FILLMORE Early March, 1851

Will you allow a sincere & ardent friend to say to you a few things on paper which he may not have an opportunity of expressing to you verbally?

In the distribution of patronage, complaints exist that too much is given to Massachusetts, to Virginia and Georgia. I make none as to Kentucky.

As to Virginia, what claims has she that have not been more than satisfied?

In regard to Georgia, her delegation, in both houses, has been far from supporting your Administration.

Massachusetts has got by far more than any other State, and she is going on.

As to another State, Alabama, I have been urgently requested to say to you that Mr. [Henry W.] Hilliard has no just pretentions on you.[1] He has been on all great questions, the Tariff, the Organization of the House,[2] the River & Harbour bill[3] &c opposed.

To see foes promoted & friends overlooked has a discouraging effect.

Should you not exercise more control in the patronage of the several Departments? An intimation of your wish to any of them ought to be decisive.

I present no complaints of my own. You have been very kind, and I am thankful. I could have desired that something should have been done for N[athan]. Sargent,[4] for Col [John M.] Swift of Philada.[5] & for Col W[illiam]. H. Russell of California,[6] and I hope it yet may be.

I desire to see & pay my respects to you, before my departure; but as circumstances may prevent me, I pray you to excuse these suggestions.

ALS. NBuHi. Letter marked "(Private & Confidential)." 1. Hilliard had not been a candidate for reelection to Congress in 1850; hence, his term ended in March, 1851. *BDAC.* 2. Clay to Lucretia H. Clay, Dec. 5, 1849. 3. Speech in Senate, March 1, 1851; Comment in Senate, March 3, 1851. 4. Clay to Harlan, Feb. 8, 1851. 5. Swift did not receive an appointment. 6. Clay to Stuart, Oct. 22 and Nov. 7, 1850. On March 7, 1851, Russell was nominated to be collector of customs at Monterey, Calif. He was confirmed on March 8. U.S. Sen., *Executive Journal*, 8:323-24.

Speech in Senate, March 1, 1851. During debate on a bill to amend an act "allowing compensation to the members of the Senate, members of the House . . . and to the Delegates of the Territories," Sen. James A. Pearce explains why he introduced this bill. That is, the act passed in 1818 [3:404-5] allowed compensation to members of Congress, in addition to the per diem allowance, of eight dollars for every twenty miles traveled from their residence to Congress at the beginning of each session. For many years no member of the Senate received mileage compensation at the called session of the Senate at the beginning of a new administration, then, during the 1840s this changed, causing "great jealousy" in the other House. Thus, this bill "simply provides that the compensation Senators receive at these called sessions shall be no other than the ordinary per diem allowance, except in cases of a Senator taking his seat . . . for the first time."

Clay rises to ask "will the Senate do me the favor to listen to a few words of advice from an old man?" Has a "profound respect for the Senate" and thinks "It ought to preserve inviolate the public confidence." Believes nothing will impair public confidence so much "as the assumption or presumption that the body or the individual acts from selfish, interested, or sordid motives." Recalls that he was the presiding officer of the House when the act passed in 1818, and "not a solitary member of that body ever supposed that that act was susceptible of the construction which has been subsequently given to it, by which, without traveling at all . . . large allowances have been made out of the public Treasury." Thinks the Senate ought to act to recover public confidence if it has been lost because of the interpretation of that law. For this reason, "I agree with the mode that has been proposed by" Pearce. Urges: "let us show the House, let us show the country, that we are not animated by the selfish and sordid motives which have been attributed to this body." Subsequently, the bill is read a third time and passed. *Cong. Globe*, 31 Cong., 2 Sess., 812.

Later in the day, Sen. George E. Badger moves to postpone the Appropriation bill and to take up the River and Harbor bill. During debate on this motion, Clay rises to say that "the real friends" of the River and Harbor bill "will insist upon immediate action." Indeed, "It is now or never for the bill. If we should take up the civil and diplomatic appropriation bill, we would soon have the Navy bill up, then the Army bill, and this bill will not be taken up." Ultimately, the Senate votes 31 to 25 in favor of taking up the River and Harbor bill. *Ibid.*, 813.

After considerable debate and the introduction of several amendments to the River and Harbor bill, Clay rises to say: "There are three modes of killing a bill. One is by meeting it boldly, straight-forward, coming up to the mark, and rejecting it. Another is by amendments upon amendments, trying to make it better than it was. Of course I do not speak of the motives in offering the present amendment. I speak of the effect, which is just as certain, if these amendments are adopted, as if the bill was rejected by a vote against its passage. A third mode is to speak against time when there is very little time left." Urges the friends of the bill to "vote with me against all amendments, and come to as speedy and rapid action as possible." Is himself "willing to take" the bill "as a man takes his wife, 'for better or for worse,' believing we shall be much more happy with it than without it."

Asserts that there have been no appropriations for this purpose "during the last three or four years, and, in consequence of this delinquency and neglect . . . because some $2,300,000 are to be appropriated by this bill, we are to be startled by the financial horrors and difficulties which have been presented." In respect to his own part of the country, "the great Valley of the Mississippi—I will say that we are a reasoning people, a feeling people, and a contrasting people; and how long will it be before the people of this vast valley will rise *en masse* and trample down your little hair-splitting distinction about what is national, and demand what is just and fair, on the part of this Government, in relation to their great interests? The Mississippi, with all its tributaries—the Red, Wabash, Arkansas, Tennessee, and Ohio rivers—constitute a part of a great system, and if that system be not national, I should like to know one that is national." Points to various appropriations in other parts of the country, saying "everywhere we pour out . . . the treasure of the United States . . . but none to the interior of the West, the Valley of the Mississippi," where "We have all sorts of commerce. . . . greatly superior in magnitude and importance to all the foreign commerce of the country for which these vast expenditures are made." Mentions the boats, lives, and property destroyed by "snags in the Mississippi which can be removed at a trifling expense," saying the people of this area "will not endure much longer" the appropriation of money to the "margin of the country, without doing anything for the interior." *Ibid.*, Appendix, 329-30. Printed in Colton, *Clay Correspondence*, 6:629-31.

See also Comment in Senate, March 3, 1851.

Comment in Senate, March 3, 1851. When Sen. Jesse D. Bright moves to take up a resolution, which had been tabled the day before, to suspend the 26th rule of the Senate requiring every bill to have three readings, each on different days, in order to allow an opportunity to pass the bills from the House, Clay objects and moves to table the motion. "I must insist on disposing of the unfinished business," he says. The Senate votes 28 to 18 to table the motion. Shortly thereafter Clay moves to dispense with all prior business and to proceed to the immediate consideration of the River and Harbor bill [Speech in Senate, March 1, 1851].

In support of his motion, Clay states that "there is a majority in this body in favor of the passage of that bill; and I wish to appeal to the justice, to the generosity, to the fairness of the minority, to say whether they will, if they have the power—as I know they have the power—defeat the bill by measures of delay and procrastination?" If they have such a determination, avows that "I will myself vote for the laying this bill on the table," but "I trust that we shall take up the bill and vote upon it; and I implore its friends . . . to say not one word, but come to a vote upon it."

After considerable discussion about taking up the bill, Clay rises again to call for the yeas and nays, saying "I at least will not be guilty of losing this or any other measure by speaking today." Ultimately, the Senate votes 30 to 25 to take up the River and Harbor bill.

From time to time Clay interjects brief comments and questions as various amendments are considered, stating at one point, "This is a waste of time." He also objects to a motion for a recess until 6 o'clock in the evening. The recess motion is defeated 23 to 30. After Sen. Pierre Soule asks to have a report read which presents "an able, comprehensive, and most luminous report on the practicability of the work for which this appropriation is asked," and the secretary has read a portion, Sen. John Davis moves to dispense with the reading of it. A debate ensues on whether or not this motion is in order. The Senate votes 22 to 23 against dispensing with the reading. The secretary proceeds until Sen. Samuel S. Phelps makes another motion to dispense with the reading. The president of the Senate rules that this motion is in order and his decision is appealed by Sen. Jefferson Davis, who argues "that as only a part had been read when the Senate ordered the reading of the whole, the decision was not parliamentary."

Clay responds: "I think it was a parliamentary decision," because "there was no positive order to read the report, but the Senate overruled the motion to dispense with the reading," and, having done that, "has not the Senate a right to say at any time during the progress of the reading of the report that they will dispense with the further reading?"

Davis charges that Clay "for the second time in this debate, assumes to lecture members of the Senate, because of a course of opposition to this bill, in which I participate." Debate continues, and Clay rises again to state the matter "as it actually exists": "The reading was refused to be dispensed with, and it was commenced; and, after about an hour had elapsed, a Senator moved to dispense with the further reading. Now, I am sure I have witnessed such a proceeding a hundred times in the House of Representatives, where the reading had been commenced, and it was agreed to suspend the further reading." Refers to Davis, saying he "has undertaken to say that I have endeavored to lecture this body. I appeal to the Senate, who most often endeavors to fill the lecturers chair, that Senator or myself? Why, sir, what have I done? I came to the Senate this morning, and I said that I would move to take up the bill now under consideration, but that if the minority who oppose the bill would say that in the exercise of their parliamentary rights they intended to resist the passage of the bill, I would not insist upon it. I wanted an avowal; no such avowal was made. We have gone on to this time, and in what manner the journal of our proceedings will show. The question which this day's proceedings present is, whether the majority or the minority shall govern? No one has attempted to deprive the minority of any rights appertaining to them. I hope the other portion of this body, the majority, have their rights also, and the great question, that question which lies at the bottom of all free institutions, is, whether the majority or minority shall govern?"

Finally, the further reading of the report is dispensed with by a vote of 27 to 19, Clay voting yea. Several attempts to table the bill are voted down. Ultimately the bill is postponed to be made the special order for 8 o'clock; however, it is not again taken up. *Cong. Globe*, 31 Cong., 2 Sess., 815-16; *ibid.*, Appendix, 353, 355-56, 359-60, 363, 367-68, 372, 381. Printed in Colton, *Clay Correspondence*, 6:631-32.

Also on this day, during discussion of an amendment to the Naval Appropriations bill that would strike out $84,000 for a naval depot at New Orleans, Clay announces that although he is "as favorably disposed towards that great city as any man in the Union," he "must vote to strike out the appropriation." The amendment is approved.

When Sen. David L. Yulee later offers an amendment to the Naval bill that would straighten the boundaries of the navy yard in Brooklyn, Clay points out that "the time-piece of the Senate tells us that no further amendments to this bill ought to be offered," and asks him to withdraw the amendment. He does so in the hope of saving the bill. Clay later announces, "I shall vote against every amendment to every bill which I do not deem absolutely necessary."

Yet when Sen. James Pearce attempts to renew an amendment concerning the Collins shipping line which had been rejected in committee, Clay supports him. Argues that he considers the competition between the Collins and Cunard lines "as a competition between the nations, in which I consider the honor of our flag concerned." Warns that if this appropriation is not made, "we surrender to the superiority of British liberality, which has been extended to the Cunard line." When the chair rules that this amendment is out of order since it had already been decided by the committee, Clay appeals the decision of the chair. The Senate, however, sustains the chair by a vote of 26 to 24, Clay voting nay. *Cong. Globe*, 31 Cong., 2 Sess., 833, 835-37.

When the Lighthouse bill is taken up, Clay wishes "to make one single observation. I hope the Senate and the country will take notice with what facility, with what unanimity, the power to regulate commerce on the seaboard is exercised, and what opposition is made to the exercise of the same power in the valley of the Mississippi." Later, moments before this session of the Senate adjourns *sine die*, Clay says in respect to a resolution under consideration that it "can be adopted in executive session." *Ibid.*, 840.

The "act making appropriations for the improvement of certain harbors and rivers" had passed the House on February 18, 1851, but did not pass the Senate. U.S. Sen., *Journal*, 31 Cong., 2 Sess., 193.

Edward Knight Collins (1802-78), who had organized the United States Steamship line, which was known as the "Collins Line," wanted to drive the Cunard line out of business. In 1845 Congress had authorized government aid through mail contracts to lines which would build potential warships. Collins had built five steamships under contract with the postmaster general, and the Collins Line started operation in 1850. The amendment, considered and rejected, to the Naval bill in 1851 would have authorized the payment of $600,000 per annum to Collins for future conveyance of the mails. The Collins Line prospered for a few years but was disbanded in 1857. *DAB*; *Cong. Globe*, 31 Cong., 2 Sess., 834.

The "act making appropriations for light-houses, light-boats, buoys, &c. . . . " was received by the Senate on March 3, 1851, after its passage by the House. It passed the Senate unanimously on March 3 and was approved by the president the same day. U.S. Sen., *Journal*, 31 Cong., 2 Sess., 271, 278; 9 *U.S. Stat.*, 627-29.

To Organizers of Tammany Hall Ball in Honor of Lewis Cass, New York City, March 3, 1851. Notes that "so highly do I appreciate the patriotism, the merits, and the public services of" Cass "that it would afford me much satisfaction if I could attend and assist in rendering him the proposed honor," but regrets he cannot do so. Praises their "liberality and magnanimity" in rising above party differences "to express yourselves in most flattering terms in regard to my recent exertions to avert a great calamity to our common country." Feels "it is most encouraging and gratifying to have witnessed with what zeal and alacrity Whigs and Democrats" worked [on the Compromise of 1850] "shoulder to shoulder to uphold the threatened existence of the Union." Points out "if the Union was gone, nothing would have remained" for the parties "to contend for." Adds that "Among those who stood up most prominently in defence of the Union, was the Senator in whose honor the ball . . . is to be given." Copy. Printed in Washington *Daily National Intelligencer*, March 10, 1851.

To JAMES BROWN CLAY — Washington, March 5, 1851

I transmit enclosed an official rect. for the balance against you at the Treasury:[1]

A called Session of the Senate for Executive business has been made,[2] and I shall be detained here several days in consequence.

I have been thinking but have not decided to return by Cuba,[3] on account of a cough which has hung by me too long. My detention here may prevent me, as the Boat may previously take her departure. I would certainly go if I had not been so long absent from your mother [Lucretia Hart Clay].

My love to Susan [Jacob Clay], Lucy [Jacob Clay] and the other children.

ALS. DLC-TJC (DNA, M212, R11). 1. Clay to James B. Clay, Feb. 13, 1851. 2. Clay to James B. Clay, Feb. 18, 1851. 3. Clay left Washington on March 10 and arrived in New York the same day. On March 11, following a dinner and ball at Niblo's, he embarked on the steamship *Georgia* for Havana, Cuba, which he reached on March 17 and where he remained for about three weeks. Leaving Havana, he arrived in New Orleans on April 5 where he stayed until April 11 when he departed for Louisville. He reached Louisville on April 19 and arrived back at Ashland on April 20. Washington *Daily National Intelligencer*, March 10, 13, April 2, 12, 18, 26, 29, 1851; Allan Nevins (ed.), *The Diary of Philip Hone 1828-1851*, 2 vols. in 1 (New York, reprint ed., 1970), 915; Clay to Lucretia H. Clay, March 18, 1851.

To JOHN MORRISON CLAY Washington, March 7, 1851

I recd. last night your two letters of the 26h. Ulto. I was sorry that you displayed so much feeling about the project of sending Yorkshire to Mansfield, which I thought of only because you were absent from home, and because I feared that Mr. Wheeler[1] could not give the requisite attention to the horse and mares sent to him, without neglecting the farm. Thomas [Hart Clay] however declined to take him, and he remains at Ashland. To this effect I telegraphed you today.

I am glad that you have sold another of your Colts, and hope that you may be able to sell the two remaining on equally advantageous terms.[2] All of them are or can be replaced except Hampton, which if you keep any I would retain because Boston is dead.[3]

We have an Extra Session of the Senate[4] which will detain me here yet some days.

ALS. Henry Clay Memorial Foundation, Lexington, Ky. 1. The overseer at Ashland. 2. Clay to John M. Clay, Feb. 16, 1851. 3. Hampton had been sired by Diomed, and Boston, sired by Timoleon, was the great-grandson of Diomed. Col. John Hoomes had imported Diomed, who proved to be one of the best sires ever brought to America. Forrester, *The Horse of America*, 1:137; Perrin, *History of Fayette County*, 133. 4. Clay to James B. Clay, Feb. 18, 1851.

To LUCRETIA HART CLAY Washington, March 7, 1851

An Extra Session of the Senate has been called on Executive business,[1] and we are now in the midst of it. I am afraid that it may run into next week. If it should do so, it will be decisive against my going home by Cuba, as the Steamer in which, if I went, I wished to go, leaves N. York next monday.[2] Altho' I believe the trip would have materially benefited my health, it is perhaps of not much importance, as in any event, I cannot live a great while longer.

I send you the last letter I have recd. from John [Morrison Clay]. He has sold another of his colts for $1000 and he has really done much better than I feared or expected.[3] He seems to have taken at more heart than, I think, he ought to have done, the subject of the care of Yorkshire. It turns out very well that Thomas [Hart Clay] declined taking charge of him at Mansfield, & John will now be gratified by his remaining at Ashland.[4] Upon the arrival of Mr. Bartlett, the horse had better be put under his management.

If, contrary to my present expectations, I should return by Cuba, I will inform you by letter and perhaps by Telegraph.

[Andrew] Eugene [Erwin] has finally determined to go to California, in the employment of the Aspinwalls,[5] large Capitalists and largely engaged in the Steamboat navigation. I think this arrangement not a bad one. His plan is to leave here tomorrow for Lexn. & to embark at N. Orleans for Chagres about the last of this month. You will see him, when he will explain his views.[6]

My cough continues, and if I ever get rid of it, it will not be before warm weather.

My love to Thomas's's family.

ALS. DLC-TJC (DNA, M212, R11). 1. Clay to James B. Clay, Feb. 18, 1851. 2. Clay to James B. Clay, March 5, 1851. 3. Clay to John M. Clay, Feb. 16, 1851. 4. Clay to John M. Clay, March 7, 1851. 5. William Henry and Lloyd Aspinwall had founded the Pacific Mail Steamship Company in 1848 and had built a railroad across Central America in 1849. *DAB*. 6. Clay to Unknown Recipient, Dec. 27, 1850.

To S. De CORDOVA[1] Washington, March 7, 1851

In the midst of my public engagements here, I have not had time fully to answer your letter,[2] and now I can briefly only say,

1st. That I know of no obstacles, arising out of our Laws, to the emigration of the Free persons of color to the West Indies.

2. That I have preferred Africa, as a place of destination to them, to any other for many reasons.

3. But that the scheme of African Colonization is not at all inconsistent with that to the West Indies, there being an amount of that description of population in the U.S. sufficient for both.

4. That as to the disposition of the blacks to emigrate to the West Indies, and their inclination to engage in Agricultural labor, you have near you in Philada. the means of acquiring as much information as I could possibly communicate.

ALS. CtY. 1. On April 17, 1851, the Washington *Daily National Intelligencer* reported that the Kingston, Jamaica, *Journal* contained correspondence between Clay and S. De Cordova, editor of the *Mercantile Intelligencer*. 2. Not found.

Passport of Henry Clay, March 8, 1851. Describes Clay as 73 years of age, 6 feet tall, forehead "high," eyes "blue," nose "large," mouth "wide," chin "not remarkable," hair "Grey," complexion "Fair." The passport states that Clay is to be accompanied by "his servant James Marshall, a free colored person," and is signed by Secretary of State Daniel Webster. DS, partially printed. KyLoF.

To LUCRETIA HART CLAY Washington, March 8, 1851

I have finally concluded to return by Cuba and N. Orleans.[1] The great difficulty I have felt in coming to this conclusion has been my long absence from you and my desire to be with you. But my cough continues, altho' I do not lay up, my health is bad, and the weather has been the worst of March weather. The road too by Cumberland, I am told, is almost impassable. I hope that I may be benefitted by the softer climate of Cuba. I expect to go on the 11h. from N. York in the Steamer Georgia. And I think my absence from home will not be prolonged beyond a month, that is the middle of April. On settling my bank account, I will either from here or N. York make a remittance to you.

I send herewith a Check on [New] York for $400 which I have endorsed to you, and of which you will make any use you may think proper.

I have written to John [Morrison Clay],[2] and Telegraphed him to put him at ease about Yorkshire, and I hope all will go well at home until my return.

God bless and preserve you, my dear Wife[.]

ALS. DLC-TJC (DNA, M212, R11). Printed in Colton, *Clay Correspondence*, 4:615. 1. Clay to James B. Clay, March 5, 1851. 2. Clay to John M. Clay, March 7, 1851.

To LUCRETIA HART CLAY Havana, Cuba, March 18, 1851

I arrived here last evening, after a most delightful voyage of six days from N. York.[1] I was Sea sick the first day and was glad of it. I shall remain here until the 2d. or 3d. of April, and then proceed to New Orleans, where I hope to arrive about the 6th.

I found Dr. [William N.] Mercer and his family here very much to my gratification, and they will remain and return with me to N. Orleans. His daughter's [Anna Mercer] health is much improved. My own, I think, is a little better, and I hope much from this climate in regard to my cough, which if I do not get relieved from it, will be very serious.

Poor Mrs Gibson died here a few days ago. Her brother was with her, but not her husband.

I remitted to you from Washn. a check for $400 drawn by the Bank of Washn. and from N. York a check for $300 on Philada. procured for me by Mr. Marshall Roberts of N.Y.[2] I have spent nothing of consequence since I left Washn. Every where they refused to let me pay any thing.

I have not yet seen much of this island, but enough to see that it is different from any thing I had ever before seen.

My love to Tho. [Hart Clay] & family. John [Morrison Clay] I suppose has not yet reached home.

ALS. DLC-TJC (DNA, M212, R11). 1. Clay to James B. Clay, March 5, 1851. 2. Marshall Owen Roberts (1814-80) organized the United States Mail Steamship Company in 1850. His steamships ran mail from New York to New Orleans and made connections with the steamship lines of William Henry Aspinwall to take mail to the West coast. *DAB*.

To Clay Festival Association of New York City, March 31, 1851. Has received their invitation to attend a celebration of his birthday on April 12. Expresses his "grateful feelings" and "very great obligations" for "the strength, ardor, constancy, and fidelity of their attachment to me." Adds that in his "recent public service" he has been encouraged by the knowledge "that whatever differences of opinion might elsewhere exist, between my friends and me there was none, there could be none; for the question involved was the integrity and harmony of that Union to the preservation of which we stood voluntarily and unanimously pledged." Suggests that if there are "any remaining in our country . . . who would seek or desire to overthrow it, let them go abroad and contrast our numberless blessings and our wonderful advancement and prosperity with the condition of any other people on the habitable globe; and if they do not return with profound gratitude for our admirable institutions, they must have hearts not derived from the common parent of mankind. . . . Temporary as is my absence from the United States, during my short sojourn on this delightful island [Cuba], almost in sight of the shores of our own country, I feel that sentiment in full force."

Regrets that he cannot attend their celebration since he will be enroute home

[Clay to James B. Clay, March 5, 1851]. Copy. Printed in Washington *Daily National Intelligencer*, April 16, 1851. Written from Havana, Cuba.

Willis Hall presided at the meeting in honor of Clay's 74th birthday, with Joseph L. White, N.B. Blunt, and other notables in attendance. *Ibid.*

To LUCRETIA HART CLAY New Orleans, April 7, 1851

I arrived here yesterday from Havana, where I remained upwards of a fortnight.[1] I hope, but am not perfectly sure, that my health has been benefited. My cough continues, but I think is better. I found Dr. [William N.] Mercers family there and they returned with me, and I am now stopping at his house. I purpose remaining here only a few days, the time depending in some degree on my being able to get a good and safe boat. I prefer the Peytona and she is expected here the last of this week.

John [Morrison Clay] called to see me immediately on my arrival and looks well. He sent up his boys and two of his horses the evening before I got here in the Belle Key. He is a little disappointed in his two horses and Zampa, which he sold, not being in a condition to run.[2] Of the only two that did run (Maria Woods) won at Mobile a fine race, and the other, Magic, got beaten. Maria is to run here again to day.

I have got Miss [Eliza] Young to purchase some articles for you, and a dress for each of our daughters in law.[3] I ascertained that they could be obtained here better than at the Havana.

I am very anxious once more to be at home, and think I shall not be easily tempted to leave it again. My love to Thomas's [Hart Clay] family and to James s [Brown Clay] if with you.

ALS. DLC-TJC (DNA, M212, R11). 1. Clay to James B. Clay, March 5, 1851. 2. Clay to John M. Clay, Feb. 16, 1851. 3. Mary Mentelle Clay and Susan Jacob Clay.

To RANDALL HUNT New Orleans, April 9, 1851

A notice has this moment (2 oClock) caught my eye of an intended public meeting this evening, for the purpose of tendering some compliment to me, on the occasion of my presence in this City.[1] I am infinitely obliged for the kind and friendly intentions of those who concur in that object. But I must frankly say to you, my good friend, that I am in no condition at present to attend or to receive a large assemblage of my fellow Citizens. Yesterday I was confined to my bed; and altho' Dr. Hunt[2] has relieved me from the indisposition, which occasioned my confinement, I have not deemed it prudent, and indeed have been too feeble, to leave Mr. [William N.] Mercer's house today. I should seriously apprehend the consequences of the excitement of a public meeting.

[2] I have been so often the honored object of public demonstrations of attachment and confidence in this City, that the omission of any ceremony connected with my arrival here, at this time, would occasion me no regret, nor I hope any to my fellow Citizens.

I have taken the liberty to address this note to you, as I observed, in the notice to which I have referred, that you would probably be the organ of the meeting, if it assembled.

ALS. LNHT. 1. The New Orleans *Daily Picayune* of April 10, 1851, announced that many citizens had gathered the previous evening with the intention of going to Dr. Mercer's house on Canal Street to pay their respects to Clay. When they reached Dr. Mercer's, Randall Hunt, who was to have made a salutatory address, appeared and informed them that "in consequence of indisposition," Clay could not appear. The crowd then dispersed. 2. Probably Dr. Thomas Hunt (1808-67), one of the founders of the University of Louisiana and the Medical College of Louisiana. Johnson, *Twentieth Century Biographical Dictionary*; Albert Fossier, *New Orleans the Glamour Period 1800-1843* (New Orleans, 1957), 204, 206, 212-14.

To ADAM BEATTY Lexington, April 28, 1851

I received your favor transmitting two letters, one addressed to yourself and the other in reply to it, and I thank you for the opportunity afforded me of perusing them.[1] If the course of Genl Metcalf [*sic*, Thomas Metcalfe] affords cause of regret,[2] I am grateful for the firmness and fidelity with which you remained attached to me in 1848 as upon all former occasions[.]

The nomination made of Genl [Zachary] Taylor in Philadelphia[3] has now no other than an historical interest. It has long ceased to affect me. I fear indeed that it has had a pernicious influence upon the Whig cause, but of that we shall her[e]after be able better to judge. I concur entirely in the views presented in your reply to Genl. Metcalf. Had I been nominated, I am perfectly confident that I should have obtained every electoral vote which he received, and besides them the vote of Ohio certainly, and that of Indiana probably. I should have got the Irish and the Catholic vote to an extent greater than any presidential candidate ever received them. And my majority in Pennsylvania would have been greater than that which was given to him. But the thing is passed and no one has more quietly submitted to the event than I have.

I was very sorry that circumstances were such as not to admit of my calling to see you on my return home, but I hope we may yet live to meet each other. I returned by the route of Cuba and New Orleans and was highly gratified with my visit to that delightful Island.[4]

LS. Courtesy of Earl M. Ratzer, Highland Park, Ill. Printed in Colton, *Clay Correspondence*, 4:615-16. 1. Not found; however, in Beatty's endorsement on page 3 "made soon after Mr. Clay's letter was recd.," explained that the letters to which Clay referred were Metcalfe's of July 7, 1848, and Beatty's reply of July 13, which "throw historical light, in relation to the nomination of Genl. Taylor for the Presidency, and the ground upon which Ky. gave the preference to him over Mr. Clay. This correspondence was unknown to Mr. Clay until near three years after it took place." 2. Metcalfe had written that no living man would have been happier than he to see Clay elected president, but he was convinced by 1848 that Clay could not win and joined forces with Crittenden to promote the nomination of Taylor. Kirwan, *John J. Crittenden*, 209. 3. Greeley to Clay, Nov. 15, 1846. 4. Clay to James B. Clay, March 5, 1851.

To D. Simmons & Co., New York City, April 28, 1851. Thanks them for the "two axes and the hatchets" which they have presented to him. Is glad to know "that this branch of American manufacture is carried on with such success as to need no protection." Fears that England, with her doctrine of free trade exercises "too large an influence upon our councils by her example." Notes that conditions in England are very different from those in the United States; there manufacturers need no protection but agriculture does, while in the U.S., the reverse is true. Copy. Printed in Washington *Daily National Intelligencer*, May 28, 1851.

To PETER V. HASTED Lexington, April 29, 1851

I received your letter[1] requesting me to communicate some particulars of a marble bust of me, sculptured by Mr [Mahlon J.] Pruden,[2] of Lexington, and I take pleasure in complying with it as far as I can.

I was not aware that Mr Pruden was engaged in such a work until it was completed. It was made about two years ago, when I was Seventy-two years of age, from the bust previously made of me by Mr [Joel T.] Hart,[3] and it has all the merit of that artist's work, which I had thought the best likeness of me in marble or plaster that had ever been made. There are some who think it an improvement upon the bust of Mr Hart; of that however, I am not competent to judge. My friends and myself were perfectly satisfied with Mr Hart's. I did not see Mr Pruden's untill after it was finished; and *according to my judgment, it is perfectly true to Nature and the original.* I did not sit to him at all, but he availed himself of the *frequent opportunities he had of seeing me, to make such deviations from Mr Hart as he thought would make his more perfect.* Mr Pruden is a young man of great merit, who, like Hart, Stevenson [*sic*, Peter Stephenson][4] and [Hiram] Powers,[5] has taken to the sculpture of busts without any other experiance than that which he obtained from working in stone and marble.

He has made some other busts of gentlemen in Lexington, which are greatly admired for their accuracy and beauty[.]

Copy, by Hasted. Italics attributed to Hasted. ICU. 1. Not found. 2. Pruden became the owner of Doyle's stoneyard in Lexington where Joel T. Hart once worked. He may have learned the use of Hart's pointing machine for making plaster duplicates; hence, many busts attributed to Hart may be Pruden's duplicates. Amyx, "Portraits of Henry Clay," Special Collections, University of Kentucky, A:1.74a. 3. Hart to Clay, Sept. 26, 1845. 4. For Peter Stephenson (1823-60), a noted sculptor, see *NCAB*, 8:455. 5. Hiram Powers (1805-73) was a sculptor who trained in Cincinnati and Italy. A bust of Clay, said to be by Powers but not authenticated, is now at the Kentucky Historical Society. Amyx, "Portraits of Henry Clay," A:1.74.

To BENJAMIN B. MINOR[1] Lexington, May 3, 1851

I duly received your favor of the 21st ult., in which you inform me that one of the Richmond booksellers intends to publish a new edition of the reports of the lamented Chancellor [George] Wythe, and you express a wish that I would furnish a brief memoir of the illustrious author.[2] It would be a most pleasing and grateful task to comply with your request, if I possessed the requisite authentic materials, and the requisite capacity to prepare the work. But the first condition does not exist, and it is therefore unnecessary to dwell upon the second. My acquaintance with the Chancellor commenced in the year 1793, in my 16th year, when I was a clerk in the office of the court over which he presided,[3] and when I think he must have passed the age of three score years and ten. I knew nothing personally of his career at the bar or his ancestry, or of the part which he had taken in public affairs. I understood that he was born in Elizabeth City, that he was taught the Greek letters by his mother[4] and afterwards by her assistance, and by his own exertions, he became an accomplished Greek scholar. How he learned the Latin language I do not remember to have heard, but probably at William & Mary college, or at some other college in lower Virginia. When I first knew him, his right hand had become so affected with the rheumatism or gout that it was with difficulty he could write his own name. Owing to that cause he engaged me to act his amanuensis and I attended him frequently, though not every day, to serve him in that capacity for several years. Upon his dictation, I wrote, I believe, all the reports of cases which it is now proposed to republish. I remember that it cost me a great deal of labor, not understanding a single

Greek character, to write some citations from Greek authors, which he wished inserted in copies of his reports sent to Mr. [Thomas] Jefferson, Mr. Samuel Adams, of Boston, and to one or two other persons. I copied them by imitating each character as I found them in the original works.

Mr. Wythe was one of the purest, best, and most learned men in classic lore that I ever knew. Although I did not understand Greek, I was often highly gratified on listening to his readings in Homer's Illiad and other Greek authors, so beautifully did he pronounce the language. No one ever doubted his perfect uprightness, or questioned his great ability as a Judge. I remember an incident which occurred in my presence which demonstrated with what scrupulous regard he avoided the possibility of any imputation upon his honor or his impartiality. A neighbor of his, Mr. H——who had the reputation of being a West India nabob, and who at the time had an important suit pending in the Court of Chancery, sent him a demijohn of old arrack,[5] and an orange tree for his niece, Miss Nelson, then residing with him. When the articles were brought into Mr. Wythe's house, with the message from the donor, Mr. Wythe requested the servant to take them back to his master, and to present to him his respects, and thanks for his kind intentions, but to say that he had long ceased to make any use of arrack, and that Miss Nelson had no conservatory in which she could protect the orange tree. I was amused at another scene, which I witnessed between him and the late Justice [Bushrod] Washington of the Supreme Court, then practising law in the city of Richmond. He called on the Chancellor with a bill of injunction in behalf of General——, to restrain the collection of a debt. The ground of the application was that the creditor had agreed to await the convenience of General——, for the payment of the debt, and that it was not then convenient to pay it. The Chancellor attentively read the bill through, and deliberately folding it up returned it to Mr. Washington, enquiring with an ineffable smile upon his countenance, "do you think, sir, that I ought to grant this injunction?" Mr. Washington blushed and observed, that he had presented the bill at the earnest instance of his client.

Mr. Wythe's relations to the Judges of the Court of Appeals were not of the most friendly or amicable kind, as may be inferred from the tenor of his reports. Conscientiously and thoroughly convinced of the justice and equity of his decrees, he was impatient when any of them were reversed, and accordingly evinces that feeling in his reports. Mr. [Edmund] Pendleton, from what I have heard, and the little I knew of him, I suppose was more prompt and ready, and possessed greater powers of elocution than his great rival. Mr. Wythe's forte, as I have understood, lay in the opening of the argument of a case, in which for thorough preparation, clearness and force, no one could excel him. He was not so fortunate in reply. Mr. Pendleton, on the contrary, was always ready both in opening and concluding an argument, and was prompt to meet all the exigencies which would arise in the conduct of a cause in court. The consequence was that Mr. Pendleton was oftener successful than Mr. Wythe in their struggles at the bar. On one occasion, when Mr. Wythe, being opposed to Mr. Pendleton, lost the cause, in a moment of vexation he declared, in the presence of a friend, that he would quit the bar, go home, take orders, and enter the pulpit. You had better not do that replied his friend; for, if you do, Mr. Pendleton will go home, take orders, and enter the pulpit too, and beat you there. Mr. Pendleton was far less learned than Mr. Wythe, but he possessed more versatile talents, was an accomplished gentleman, and better adapted to success in general society and in the busy world. Although not so finished a scholar as Mr. Wythe, he had a much more pleasing style of composition. The high consideration in which Messrs. Pendleton and Wythe were both held was often evinced by the distinguished honors and eminent offices which they received from their parent state. It was particularly exhibited in the organization of the Convention which adopted the Constitution of the United States, when Mr. Pendleton was appointed to preside over the body, and Mr. Wythe to preside over the Committee of the Whole, which he did during, I believe, the entire sitting of the Convention, the Constitution having been considered and discussed in Committee of the Whole.[6]

Mr. Wythe's personal appearance and his personal habits were plain, simple and unostentatious. His countenance was full of blandness and benevolence, and I think he made, in his salutations of others, the most graceful bow that I ever witnessed. A little bent by age, he generally wore a grey coating. And when walking carried a cane. Even at this moment, after the lapse of more than half a century since I last saw him, his image is distinctly engraved on my mind. During my whole acquaintance with him he constantly abstained from the use of all animal food.

It is painful and melancholy to reflect that a man so pure, so upright, so virtuous, so learned, so distinguished and beloved, should have met with an unnatural death. The event did not occur until several years after I emigrated from Richmond to the State of Kentucky, and, of course, I am not able from personal knowledge to relate any of the circumstances which attended it. Of these, however, I obtained such authentic information as to leave no doubt in my mind as to the manner of its occurrence. He had a grand nephew, a youth scarcely I believe of mature age, to whom, by his last will and testament, written by me, upon his dictation, before my departure from Richmond, after emancipating his slaves, he devised the greater part of his estate.[7] That youth poisoned him, and others,—black members of his household, by putting arsenic into a pot in which coffee was preparing for breakfast. The paper which had contained the arsenic was found on the floor of the kitchen. The coffee having been drank by the Chancellor and his servants, the poison developed its usual effects. The Chancellor lived long enough to send for his neighbor, Major William DuVal,[8] and got him to write another will for him, disinheriting the ungrateful and guilty grandnephew, and making other dispositions of his estate.[9] An old negro woman,[10] his cook, also died under the operation of the poison, but I believe his other servants recovered. After the Chancellor's death it was discovered that the atrocious author of it had also forged bank checks in the name of his great uncle, and he was subsequently, I understood prosecuted for the forgery, convicted and sentenced to the penitentiary; but whether that was the fact or not, can be ascertained by a resort to the records of the proper criminal courts of Richmond.[11]

I have written this hasty sketch, not as a memoir of the illustrious man of whom it treats, but for the purpose of contributing some materials, which may be wrought by more competent hands, into a biography more worthy of his great name and memory. I conclude it by an acknowledgment, demanded of me alike by justice and feelings of gratitude, that to no man was

I more indebted, by his instructions, his advice, and his example, for the little intellectual improvement which I made, up to the period, when, in my twenty-first year, I finally left the City of Richmond.

Copy. Printed in Thomas J. Michie (ed.), *Virginia Reports* . . . (Charlottesville, Va., 1903), 94-95. 1. For Minor (1818-1905)—lawyer, editor, and educator—see *DAB*. 2. Benjamin B. Minor, "Memoir of the Author," in George Wythe, *Decisions of Cases in Virginia, by the High Court of Chancery* . . . , 2nd ed. (Richmond, 1852), 94-95. 3. Virginia High Court of Chancery. 4. Margaret Wythe. 5. Arrack is a strong distilled liquor. 6. In 1788 Wythe was chairman of the Committee of the Whole of the Virginia convention to ratify the U.S. Constitution. Joyce Blackburn, *George Wythe of Williamsburg* (New York, 1975), 116-17. 7. George Wythe Swinney (or spelled alternately Sweeney; Sweney), aged 16 or 17, was living with Wythe in 1806 when he supposedly used arsenic to poison his granduncle. In 1803 Wythe had changed his will to leave the bulk of his estate to Swinney; thus, it was not the will which Clay remembered writing. The 1803 will also left the rent from his Richmond house and interest from his bank stock to "my freed woman Lydia Broadnax, and my freed man Benjamin and freed boy Michael Brown" during the lives of the first two and after their deaths in trust for Michael Brown. Codicils in early 1806 provided that Brown was to have no more than half the bank stock and Swinney the other half. Also, "If Michael die before his full age, i give what is devised to him to George Wythe Sweeney." Julian P. Boyd, *The Murder of George Wythe, Two Essays* (Williamsburg, Va., 1955), 20-21, 26, *passim*. 8. For DuVal (1749-1842), a lawyer and neighbor of Wythe, see *ibid.*, 46-47; *NCAB*, 11:376; *CAB*. However, Edmund Randolph was the lawyer who wrote the new codicil. 9. The codicil of June 1, 1806, revoked the bequest to Swinney and to Michael Brown, who had already died that morning from the poison, leaving the estate to be divided equally among Swinney's brothers and sisters. Boyd, *The Murder of George Wythe*, 20-21. 10. Lydia Broadnax, although poisoned, did not die. *Ibid.*, 27. 11. Edmund Randolph, who had written the codicil disinheriting Swinney, and William Wirt served as Swinney's defense attorneys. They won an acquittal for Swinney on the charges of murder and forgery. *Ibid.*, 54-64.

To JAMES BROWN CLAY Lexington, May 9, 1851

I recd. y[our] letter of the 28h. Ulto. From Susan [Jacob Clay] I had learnt your plans for the future. Altho' they involve a separation of you and your family from me, [I shall] not complain of them and think them judicious.[1] I am afraid that we did not explain ourselves mutually fully to each other[.][2] It was my anxious wish that you should have succeeded me in the possession of Ashland if it had suited your inclination and interest and if you had been at home I think we could have made some arrangement by which you could have come into the immediate possession of it and I could have taken your house. But you were not here and before you went to Europe and in your letters from Lisbon you displayed so much anxiety to sell the house that I concluded to take the offer of Mr. [Harvey] Miller.[3] Mr. [George R.] Trotter too was about to give it up,[4] and as I was on the eve of my departure for Washington [and] knew of no tenant that I could get, I did not well know what to do with it. I think it ought to have brought ten thousand dollars, which is what I should have been willing to have allowed for it, but I obtained the best price I could get, and the sale of it was far better than that to Mr. Goodloe which you appeared willing to make[.][5]

My health is not good, a troublesome and inconvenient cough has hung by me for six months past; it has reduced and enfeebled me very much. Dr [Benjamin W.] Dudley thinks that my lungs are unaffected, and that it proceeds from some derangement in the functions of the stomach. Be that as it may I must get rid of the cough or it will dispose of me. My hopes rest upon the effects of warm weather[.]

Susan and the children are well and appear to be contented and satisfied. They are a source of g[reat] happiness to me, and I look forward to their leaving us with painful anticipations. Your mother [Lucretia Hart Clay] and

John [Morrison Clay] are both quite well, and so are Thomas [Hart Clay] and his family. John is constantly occupied with our numerous horses and those which are sent to Ashland. He is in good spirits and appears much encouraged with prospects, and I think has reason to be so. My overseer [Wheeler] is doing admirably well and your Mother is better pleased with him than she ever was with any of his predecessors. I have a [gr]eat many things to say to you and to talk to y[ou] about, but among the inconveniences of my present indisposition one is that it is less agreeable to me than [several words missing] write or even to dictate as I am now doing. [I] must therefore reserve for the occasion of your return to us to say whatever I now omit. Susan gets your weekly letter regularly and I hope you will contin[ue t]o write as in that way I can learn your progress and prospec[ts.]

LS, partly ALS, manuscript torn. DLC-TJC (DNA, M212, R11). Printed in Colton, *Clay Correspondence*, 4:616-17. 1. Clay to James B. Clay, Dec. 23, 1850. 2. The portion written by Clay ends here. 3. Clay to James B. Clay, Oct. 27, 1850. 4. Clay to James B. Clay, Oct. 18, 1850. 5. Clay to James B. Clay, August 20, 1850.

To Thomas Hankey, Jr., London, England, May 10, 1851. In reply to a letter requesting his opinion on whether or not free blacks from the United States could be used to supply the needed agricultural labor in the British West Indies, states with "great pleasure" his opinion. Notes that there are about half a million of "free colored population" in the United States, concentrated primarily in Virginia and Maryland. Believes they tend to prefer life in the cities and villages "where they perform the menial offices of life and the lower departments of labor." Does not know what proportion engages in agricultural pursuits, but estimates about half. Continues: "Taken as an entire class, they are an improvident and thoughtless race, addicted to habits of vice much more extensively than any other portion of our population. There are, however, many gratifying exceptions. Their condition . . . is, perhaps, partly owing to the physical and intellectual constitution of the African race, but mainly to the degraded position which they occupy in the United States, where they do not, and probably never can, enjoy equal privileges, social and political, with the whites."

Has long believed that "it would conduce to the happiness of both races if the blacks were removed from the United States by colonization or expatriation," but that "object is unattainable . . . whilst their bondage continues to exist" and "will cease" only when "by the increase of white population free white labor can be procured cheaper than that of blacks." Explains how he helped found the American Colonization Society and discusses its success in establishing Liberia. Notes, however, that "although . . . I have a decided preference for Africa . . . for colonizing the free blacks of the United States, there is no incompatibility between the object of transporting them to Africa and that of sending them to the British West India colonies." Adds that "There are no laws, as far as I know, of any of the States opposing obstacles to the removal of those people to the West India colonies." Notes that abolitionists have opposed colonization in Africa and try to persuade free blacks from emigrating. Believes "the same source of opposition ought to be anticipated" in attempting to get them to go to the West Indies. Further, "I think considerable difficulty would be encountered" in persuading them to emigrate there, because "Degraded as their condition is in the United States, the means of subsistence here are so great that if their physical wants are generally well supplied they are apparently contented and happy, and many of them are unwilling to leave the country of their birth and the scenes to which they have always been accustomed."

Suggests that "If the attempt be made to induce these people to go to the West India colonies, it would be proper, I think, that suitable agents should be sent to the United States to explain to the free blacks the advantages and privileges they would enjoy by removing to the West Indies, and to offer to them the means of their transportation." Believes the general government would not oppose and some states, possibly Virginia, "might afford some assistance . . . in their removal."

Asks if "you ever turned your attention to China as a source of labor." Reports that on his recent trip to Cuba he heard of a planter who had 70-80 Chinese employed for seven years at four dollars per month. Reportedly, "he found them laborious and trustworthy, and . . . greatly preferred them to the blacks." Copy. NcD.

Hankey became a member of the House of Commons from Petersborough City in 1852 after the election of George H. Whalley was declared void. *Return. Members of Parliament*, 2 vols. (London, 1878), 1:part 2.

To JAMES BROWN CLAY Lexington, May 13, 1851

I promised Thomas [Hart Clay] to advance for him $600 to purchase a circular saw. Henry Watkins may come to St Louis for that purpose and if he does I wish you to assist him in negotiating his draft upon me for that sum payable at sight[.] Or perhaps he may write to you to make the purchase for him—in which case you may draw upon me. They tell me that they have logs enough to purchase $10000 if sawed up and their present saw operates so slowly that I thought they had better get one that would work better. We are all here pretty much as when I last wrote you except that Harry [Clay] has some fever from teething.

LS. DLC-TJC (DNA, M212, R11).

To THOMAS B. STEVENSON Lexington, May 17, 1851

I received your favor of the 15th. There is no significance whatever to the article to which you refer in the Reporter,[1] it was put there without my authority or knowledge, and I regretted when I saw it.

You ask what is to be done if South Carolina secedes?[2] I answer unhesitatingly that the Constitution and laws of the United States must continue to be enforced there, with all the power of the Union, if necessary. Secession is treason, and if it were not, if it were a legitimate and rightful exercise of power, it would be a virtual dissolution of the Union. For if one State may secede every State may secede, and how long in such a state of things could we be kept together? Suppose Kentucky were to secede, could the rest of the Union tolerate a foreign power in their very bosom? There are those who think the Union must be preserved and kept together, by an exclusive reliance upon love and reason. That is not my opinion. I have some confidence in this instrumentality, but depend upon it that no human government can exist without the power of applying force, and the actual application of it in extreme cases. My belief is, that if it should be applied to South Carolina, in the event of her secession, she would be speedily reduced to obedience, and that the Union instead of being weakened would acquire additional strength.

Writing as you perceive, by Amanuensis, I must be brief, and conclude with assurances of my constant regard—

LS. Courtesy of Dr. Thomas D. Clark, Lexington, Ky. Printed in Colton, *Clay Correspondence*, 3:499-500. 1. Reference obscure. 2. Clay to Lathrop *et al.*, Feb. 15, 1851.

To HENRY CLAY, JR. [III] Lexington, May 19, 1851

Your first year at the [U.S. Military] Academy is now nearly expired and I feel very anxious to know how you will stand upon its close. I have not had any letter from you since my return home[.] You are a very negligent correspondent. I received your last month's report,—and I was glad to perceive from it, that the number of marks against you was a good deal reduced from what they had been in previous months. If you should, not have them greatly increased this month, I hope you will escape the number which would lead to your dismission.[1] That event would fill us all with the deepest mortification and regret, and I sincerely hope that you will spare us such an infliction. I should be very glad to get a letter from you. We are all well here except myself, and at Louisville your sister [Anne Clay, "Nannie"] is well, but little Tommy [Thomas J. Clay] is slightly indisposed. I forget whether this is the year in which by the regulations of the Academy you are permitted to return home to visit your friends.[2] If it is let me know—

ALS. Henry Clay Memorial Foundation, Lexington, Ky. 1. Clay to Morehead, Dec. 14, 1848. 2. Clay to Henry Clay III, June 26, 1851.

To J.D.B. DeBow, New Orleans, May 20, 1851. Endorses DeBow's *Review of the Southern and Western States* because of "the great amount of valuable and useful information in respect to political economy, agriculture, commerce and manufactures and other statistics." Adds that "Without concurring in all the speculative reasonings of the work, I think it eminently entitled to public patronage." Copy. Printed in *DeBow's Southern and Western Review* (December, 1852), 13:652.

For James D.B. DeBow (1820-67)—editor, head of the Louisiana Bureau of Statistics, and subsequently Confederate cotton agent, see *DAB*. *DeBow's Review* became increasingly political and became a factor in the coming of the Civil War.

To William A. Graham, Washington, May 23, 1851. Intercedes with the secretary of the navy in behalf of Wilmer Shields, who had obtained "a furlough of six months" with the promise "that, at the end of the six months, a further term of six months would be granted him." Describes Shields as the protégé "of my friend Dr. [William N.] Mercer, one of the best of men" and "a large Cotton planter." As Mercer "is about making a voyage to Europe" for his daughter's [Anna Mercer] health, hopes that "Shields would not be ordered into service" so he could act as Mercer's "Agent to superintend his estates." Since "it appears that Mr. Shields is ordered to Pensacola," requests that if "the public wants in the Naval service . . . should admit of Mr. Shields being indulged with the additional term of six months, which he solicits, it will afford me much gratification." ALS. Nc-Ar.

Wilmer Shields was a midshipman in 1835 and a lieutenant in 1851. He resigned his commission in April, 1852. Callahan, *Officers of the Navy . . . and of the Marine Corps*.

From JOHN LUTZ[1] Lexington, May 23, 1851

Some time ago in selecting my lots in the Lexington Cemetery,[2] I added one set which I intended for you,[3] as a token of that high esteem in which I am proud to participate with your countrymen. I have learned through Mr A[braham] T Skillman[4] that you have lately spoken for a Cemetery lot and I take this opportunity to request your acceptance of lots No 37, 38, 54, and 55 of Section "I" which you will find transferred to your name on the books of the Company, and be assured that the honor which you will confer on me by your acceptance, will make me greatly your debtor.

ALS. KyLoF. Printed in Lexington *Leader*, May 30, 1933. 1. Lutz, a civil engineer who served as mathematics professor at Transylvania University, laid out the tract for the Lexington Cemetery. He later changed his name to John Lutz Mansfield. Perrin, *History of Fayette County*, 285, 304-5; Lexington *Leader*, May 30, 1933. 2. The Lexington Cemetery was incorporated by an act of the legislature in Feb., 1848. The original 40 acres were purchased for $7,000 from Thomas E. Boswell. Perrin, *History of Fayette County*, 285. 3. Clay's body was first interred on the plot given him by Lutz but was later moved to its present site when the monument was erected. Lexington *Leader*, May 30, 1933. 4. Skillman was the first president of the board of trustees of the Lexington Cemetery Company. *Ibid.*

To JOHN LUTZ Lexington, May 26, 1851

I received your very obliging letter,[1] kindly tendering to my acceptance some lots in the Lexington Cemetery, which you had reserved in the distribution of the ground. It is true, as Mr. [Abraham T.] Skillman told you, that I was thinking of purchasing a place in that Cemetery for the use of myself and family. My age, and other circumstances, admonished me that the day could not be very distant when I should have occasion for it. Your friendly offer is, therefore, very opportune, and I accept it with thankful and grateful feelings.

I have often been the favored recipient of presents, tendered by some of my many good friends. Their object was to minister to my ease, comfort and pleasure, during my life. But your friendly forecast looks farther, to the period when that must terminate; and, by your generous gift, you have provided a beautiful spot for the repose of my mortal remains. I tender to you an expression of my profound acknowledgments for your kindness.

ALS. KyLoF. Printed in Lexington *Leader*, May 30, 1933. 1. Lutz to Clay, May 23, 1851.

To HENRY GRINNELL Lexington, May 28, 1851

I have enjoyed the high satisfaction of meeting with Father [Theobald] Mathew, and entertaining him at my house. On his return to the City of New York, from the prosecution of his noble works of humanity and benevolence, in the valley of the Mississippi, he did me the honor to call to see me. During his sojourn in the U. States he has been again stricken with parallysis,[1] which, altho' it has not affected the expression of his bland and benign countenance, has materially impaired his articulation, disqualifies him from making those great exertions, to which he was accustomed in earlier life and in robust health. Nevertheless his labors, with but little relaxation and repose, have been unremitting, and been attended with the most encouraging success. Upon descending the Mississippi, he administered, in one of the towns, situated on its banks, the [temperance] pledge to seven hundred persons. He ascended it, after an interval of some months, and, stoping at the same town, he had the gratification to find that among the converts there were but three instances of relapse.

I have had an opportunity of obtaining accurate information, from an authentic source (not from himself, his extreme delicacy would restrain him from making such a communication) as to the condition of the pecuniary affairs of this good man. It has deeply interested me, and excited my warmest sympathies. During his long and brilliant career in Ireland, among the millions of persons, the victims of Intemperance, or in danger of becoming addicted to it, to whom he gave the pledge, he often met, in the poorer classes, persons in great indigence and want. To some of those he supplied, from his own purse, money to afford them immediate relief which, tho' small in particular cases, in the aggregate amounted to a considerable sum. To aid him in these laudable charities, he was under the necessity of borrowing largely from his friends, which he did under full conviction that he would be able to reimburse them from resources, which he had entire confidence in counting upon receiving from a rich Maiden Aunt, who had promised to make an ample provision for him. Her will to that effect was actually prepared, is now in existence, a short day was assigned for its execution, and before it arrived she died suddenly with the gout, and was found dead in her bed.

The consequence is, that this great Benefactor of Mankind, this true Friend of the poor, is left in a state of great pecuniary embarrassment, threatened by creditors on his return to Ireland, and exposed himself, in old age and under the influence of disease and infirmity, to that pinching want, which, in better days, and in more prosperous times, he so generously releived in others.

The British Government granted him a pension of three hundred pounds sterling. But he has not received one cent of it, having scrupulously dedicated the whole of it to the payment of his debts. To enable him to defray unavoidable expences, during his present tour in the U. States, he was supplied with the requisite means by the liberality of a public-spirited gentleman in Liverpool.

This most excellent and extraordinary man is about to depart from among us, after having, it is to be hoped, with the aid of Providence, redeemed near half a million of inhabitants of these States from one of the most debasing of all pernicious habits. Shall he return without any substantial manifestation of the public gratitude towards him? Shall even no effort be made to put him at ease, and to smooth and soften the pillow of his declining years? I think I am not deceived as to the generous hearts of my Countrymen, nor as to the warm Irish hearts of his, in believing that, if his actual condition were generally known, thousands would readily, and with the greatest alacrity, rush to his relief. His fame and a just appreciation of his signal merits are secure, and will be transmitted to the admiration of the remotest posterity. He will be regarded as one of the wonders of this remarkable age. But what will that posterity think of the present generation, if he be permitted to pine and languish in poverty and want and suffering during the remnant of a life which has been worn out by an exclusive devotion to its service? And such a glorious service! What reproaches will not be made for culpable insensibility to the value of the greatest moral reform ever achieved by one man? Shall not we, in the United States, endeavor not to merit any part of them?

Knowing well your public spirit, and your generous impulses, my object in addressing you is to ascertain if something cannot be done for Father Mathew worthy of him, and worthy of us, before he leaves our shores. On all occasions of munificence, we naturally turn our attention to our great Cities, and to yours [New York City] as the first of them. We ought to do something, we can do something in the interior. I am ready, from my limited means, to contribute my mite. But it is in the large Cities, where concert and co-operation are so easy to be brought about, that most can be effected.

It has occurred to me that a few liberal and enlightened gentlemen in your City, favorable to the object, might have an informal meeting to consult together; that they might organize a Committee of subscription and collection, correspond with other places, and thus accomplish the desired end. The pleasure of making the requisite contribution should be diffused among as many as may be convenient and practicable, without allowing that pleasure to be monopolized by only a few.[2]

Will you my dear Sir, turn these suggestions over in your fertile mind, and if you approve their object, give it your powerful aid?

Copy. DLC-William W. Corcoran Papers (DNA, M212, R20). 1. Speech to Hibernian Society, March 17, 1848. 2. On May 28, 1851, Clay sent a copy of the above letter to William W. Corcoran in "the hope that you might co-operate with Mr. Grinnell and others in the accomplishment of the benevolent end in view. Washington, I am aware, is not one of our large Cities; but, with your patronage and exertions, I trust that some thing may be done there." ALS. DLC-William W. Corcoran Papers (DNA, M212, R20). See also Clay to Corcoran, Sept. 14, 1851.

From THOMAS J. CLAY Louisville, June 3, 1851

I acknowledge the receipt of Kitty Clover by the Sea Gull and must inform you that the very sight of her surprised me as she was so fat[.]

I awoke yesterday morning with the intention of going to the boat for her when I was told she was at the stable.

In your last letter to Uncle[1] you told him to tell me that my poney was in tolerable good order, I think your horses are very fat if that is the case for I beleive if she had been fed on custard plum puding and tarts (as she will eat any thing) She would not have been fater.

Uncle received the hams yesterday the bill of lading said "Boxes in bad order" but they looked very safe[.]

Uncle received yesterday a small lot of hemp to be proved.

I am very much obliged to you for the halter which you sent with the poney and also for paying her fare down as my purse was not bountifully supplied[.]

My sincere love and affection to Grandma [Lucretia Hart Clay], you, and Uncle John [Morrison Clay].

ALS. Henry Clay Memorial Foundation, Lexington, Ky. 1. Possibly Thomas Smith, whose wife Nannette Price Smith sometimes took care of Thomas J. and Anne Clay. Thomas Smith often acted as an agent for Clay in selling hams, hemp, etc.

From B.L. Posey, Abbeville, S.C., June 13, 1851. Informs Clay that "An old woman of this district, lately deceased, (a religious fanatic,) has devised about seven likely negroes to the use of the [American] Colonization Society, and has named yourself trustee." Explains that the man who has the will "as well as, the devisor are of the sect of seceders, or associate reformed church," whose members "are all opposed (with few exceptions) to slavery, and many of them have emigrated to hireling States on that account. The man in possession of the will has excited public indignation against himself, by his talk, and may be run off." Realizing Clay "may wish to take some action in the matter," warns that "The colonization society is regarded with no favour here and those interested intend making a stubborn defense." ALS. DLC-Records of the American Colonization Society (DNA, M212, R20).

B.L. Posey was a journalist who in 1853 founded the *Independent Press* in Abbeville, S.C. *SCHM* (April, 1962), 63:88.

On June 27, 1851, Clay forwarded Posey's letter to William McLain, advising him that "As I cannot attend personally to the matter I hope you or the Board of Directors will give it the attention which it merits." ALS. DLC-Records of the American Colonization Society (DNA, M212, R20).

To DANIEL ULLMANN Lexington, June 14, 1851

I duly received your favor of the 29th ultimo, stating that some of my friends in New York have it under discussion, to make a movement to bring forward my name for the Presidency; and inquiring, in entire confidence, what my own views and wishes are, upon the subject. I have delayed transmitting an answer to your letter, from a desire to give to its important contents the fullest and most deliberate consideration. That I have now done, and I will communicate the result to you.

You will recollect that the last time but one that I was in the city of New York, I had the pleasure of dining with you and a number of other friends at the house of our friend M———[1]; that we then had a frank, full, and confidential conversation on the connection of my name with the next Presidency; and that I then declared that I did not wish ever again to be brought forward as a candidate. From that declaration, I have never since deviated in thought, word, or deed. I have said or done nothing inconsistent with it; nothing which implied any desire on my part to have my name presented as a Presidential candidate. On a review and reconsideration of the whole matter, I adhere to that declaration.

Considering my age, the delicate state of my health, the frequency and the unsuccessful presentation of my name on former occasions, I feel an unconquerable repugnance to such a use of it again. I can not, therefore, consent to it. I have been sometimes tempted publicly to announce that, under no circumstances, would I yield my consent to be brought forward as candidate. But I have been restrained from taking that step by two considerations. The first was, that I did not see any such general allusion to me, as a suitable person for the office, as to make it proper that I should break silence and speak out; and the second was that I have always thought that no citizen has a right to ostracise himself, and to refuse public service under all possible contingencies.

I might here stop, but I will add some observations on the general subject of the next election. I think it quite clear that a Democrat will be elected, unless that result shall be prevented by divisions in the Democratic party. On these divisions the Whigs might advantageously count, if it were not for those which exist in their own party. It is, perhaps, safest to conclude that the divisions existing in the two parties will counterbalance each other.[2]

Party ties have no doubt been greatly weakened generally, and, in particular localities, have been almost entirely destroyed. But it would be unwise to suppose that, when the two parties shall have brought out their respective candidates, each will not rally around its own standard. There may be exceptions; but those, on the one side, will probably be counterpoised by those on the other. I believe that no one in the Whig party could obtain a greater amount of support from the Democratic party than I could; but in this I may be deceived by the illusions of egotism. At all events it would be unsafe and unwise for a candidate of one party to calculate upon any suffrages of the other. While I do not think that the hopes of success on the part of the

Whigs at the next Presidential election are very flattering or encouraging, I would not discourage their putting forth their most energetic exertions. There are always the chances of the war. The other party may commit great blunders, as they did recently in your State, in the course of their Senators, who opposed the enlargement of the Erie Canal;[3] and as they are disposed to do in respect to the lake, river, and harbor improvements.

No candidate, I hope and believe, can be elected who is not in favor of the Union, and in favor of the Compromise[4] of the last Congress (including the Fugitive Slave bill),[5] as necessary means to sustain it. Of the candidates spoken of on the Democratic side, I confess that I should prefer General [Lewis] Cass.[6] He is, I think, more to be relied on than any of his competitors. During the trials of the long session of the last Congress, he bore himself firmly, consistently, and patriotically. He has quite as much ability, quite as much firmness, and, I think, much more honesty and sincerity than Mr. [James] Buchanan.[7]

If I were to offer any advice to my friends, it would be not to commit themselves prematurely to either of the two Whig Candidates who have been prominently put forward. Strong objections, although of a very different kind, exist against them both. They had better wait. It will be time enough next winter to decide; and I am inclined to believe that both of those gentlemen will find, in the sequel, that they have taken, or their friends have put them in, the field too early.[8]

Besides pre-existing questions, a new one will probably arise at the next session of Congress, involving the right of any one of the States of the Union, upon its own separate will and pleasure, to secede from the residue, and become a distinct and independent power.[9] The decision of that momentous question can not but exert some influence, more or less, upon the next Presidential election. For my own part, I utterly deny the existence of any such right, and I think an attempt to exercise it ought to be resisted to the last extremity; for it is, in part, a question of union or no union.

You inquire if I will visit Newport [R.I.] this summer, with the view of ascertaining whether it might not be convenient there, or at some other Eastern place, to present me a gold medal which I understand my good friends are preparing for me.[10] I have been absent from home fifteen out of the last nineteen months, and I feel great reluctance to leaving it, during the present summer. If I were to go to the Eastward, I should have to return early in the autumn, and soon after to go back to Washington, unless I resign my seat in the Senate of the United States. Under these circumstances, my present inclination is to remain at home and attend to my private affairs, which need my care.

Should my friends persevere in their purpose of presenting me the proposed medal, some suitable time and place can be hereafter designated for that purpose.[11] Surely no man was ever blessed with more ardent and devoted friends than I am, and, among them, none are more or perhaps so enthusiastic as those in the City of New York. God bless them. I wish it was in my power to testify my gratitude to them in full accordance with the fervent impulses of my heart.

Copy. Printed in Colton, *Clay Correspondence*, 4:617-20. 1. Reference obscure. 2. Both parties were divided on the slavery and sectional issues which would soon destroy the Whig party and in 1860 split the Democratic party. See, for example, Nevins, *Ordeal of the Union*, 1:174,

190-91, 202-3, 251, 399; Richard H. Sewell, *Ballots for Freedom: Antislavery Politics in the United States, 1837-1860* (New York, 1976), 163, 236-39, 257-58, *passim*; Smith, *Presidencies of Taylor & Fillmore*, 235-48, *passim*. 3. The New York assembly passed an act authorizing a loan of nine million dollars for enlargement of the Erie Canal. When the bill came to the state senate on April 17, 1851, eleven senators resigned. In the election of May 27, 1851, to fill the vacancies, six of the eleven were defeated. In an extra session called by Gov. Washington Hunt, the canal bill then passed. Alexander, *A Political History of . . . New York*, 2:163. 4. Clay to Combs, Jan. 22, 1850. 5. Remark in Senate, Sept. 12, 1850. 6. A movement for Cass had started in New York City in early 1851. Woodford, *Lewis Cass*, 289-94. He subsequently was considered at the 1852 Democratic National convention, held in Baltimore on June 1-6, 1852. Other contenders were James Buchanan, Stephen A. Douglas, William R. Marcy, and Franklin Pierce. On the 49th ballot, Pierce, who had not received a single vote on the 1st ballot, was nominated. William R. King received the nomination for vice president. McKee, *National . . . Popular and Electoral Vote*, 74. 7. Buchanan made his opening bid for the Democratic presidential nomination in Philadelphia in Nov., 1850. While not opposing the Compromise of 1850 outright, he expressed some doubt about its efficacy, noting that popular sovereignty gave no protection for slavery in the territories. He also expressed a hope that the Fugitive Slave law would be enforced. Thus, he gained support for the nomination from Southern Democrats. Philip S. Klein, *President James Buchanan* (University Park, Pa., 1962), 214-16. 8. Probably a reference to Winfield Scott and Daniel Webster, who were both being promoted for the nomination. At the Whig National convention held at Baltimore on June 16-19, 1852, the candidates were Winfield Scott, Daniel Webster, and Millard Fillmore, who had reluctantly agreed to be a candidate. Scott received the nomination on the 53rd ballot, and William A. Graham received the vice presidential nomination. McKee, *National . . . Popular and Electoral Vote*, 78. 9. Clay to Lathrop *et al.*, Feb. 17, 1851. 10. Clay to Ullmann, Sept. 26, 1851. 11. Clay to Citizens of New York, Feb. 9, 1852.

To John Cleves Short, Cincinnati, Ohio, June 16, 1851. Refers to payment of $200 which Short has given him for a legal opinion, saying "If I had made formal charge, it would not have been half the amount you have kindly sent to me."

Continues: "Yes! my dear Sir, your father [Peyton Short] was one of my earliest and best patrons. Valuable and beneficial as his patronage was, I esteemed more his society. Many nights have I passed under his hospitable roof near Versailles. It was a great treat to me to go from the bustle and turmoil of the Court house, at Versailles to his quiet and comfortable residence, and enjoy his sprightly, intelligent and delightful conversation. I never missed visiting him any term of the Court, and not unfrequently two or three times during its continuance. By the bye, I was, rather accidentally, at the old place ["Green-field"; 1:26] last month. Every thing is totally changed. Not a vestige remains of the old buildings. I should hardly have been able unassisted to recognize the spot. But, to do the present proprietor justice, he has built an excellent dwelling house and made a capital grazing farm out of it." ALS. DLC-Short Family Papers (DNA, M212, R22).

To William A. Graham, Washington, June 25, 1851. Although "George Ross Harrison [Clay to Graham, August 28, 1850] has returned from Annapolis . . . full of mortification and regret at his failure to pass successfully the recent examination" at the Naval Academy, assures the secretary of the navy that the "young man seems to be fired by an ardent ambition to serve in the Navy and still entertains the desire, notwithstanding what has occurred." Believes that "if he should be again restored to the position he has just left. . . . he shall apply himself diligently to his studies." Offers testimonials that speak "in very high terms of the general conduct of the young man and of his peculiar qualifications for the Navy." Adds: "I do not know what may be the rules of the service, but unless they are inflexibly opposed to his reinstatement I should be glad, if another opportunity is afforded him to supply the deficiency in question." Understanding that "two thirds of the young men in the school were found deficient," wonders if "the examination was too rigorous" or if "the time . . . allowed for study and preparation was too short." Hopes Graham "can reconcile it to a sense of public duty to reinstate young Harrison." LS. DNA, RG45, Misc. Letter Rec., 1851, June, p. 127.

On July 8, 1851, Graham replied to Clay that "the Regulations of the Naval Academy under the operation of which Mr Harrison has come, were drawn up by a Board of experienced and intelligent officers of the Navy, after freely canvassing the system prevailing at the Military Academy at West Point." Regrets to inform Clay that he has concluded that "the Regulations should be enforced until experience shall shew them to be erroneous. . . . I have been obliged to refuse all applications to relax the Regulations and restore the young gentlemen found deficient or admit them to a re-examination at the commencement of the next Academic term." L. DNA, RG45, General Letter Books, vol. 45 (1851), pp. 342-43.

To HENRY CLAY, JR. [III] Lexington, June 27, 1851

I have received your two letters, the one dated the 1st. instant, and the other the 18th. by Cadet Hood,[1] whom I had not the satisfaction to see. Your letters have relieved me from much of the great anxiety I felt about you, but I am still desirous to know what was the number of your demerit marks,[2] made during the current year. I hoped and believed that you could not incur the disgrace of dismissal by having two hundred of them in one short year, affixed to your name, but they had swelled up to such an amount, as to create with me considerable alarm. I did hope that your own self pride, his memory and his name,[3] as well as my own, which you bear would protect you against any disgrace at West Point, and I am happy to find that I have not been deceived. I shall soon get the official report, which I hope will shew, as intimated in your last letter, that your standing now will be better than it was in January last. I should have been glad if the rules of the Academy had admitted of your visiting us this summer, but we would much rather hear of your good health, and of your doing well, than even to see you.

Your three remaining years will soon run round, and next year you will be able to visit us. I shall watch the future monthly reports, with great interest, hoping to find in them, no more marks of demerit. And I trust my dear grand child that as those you have received heretofore have been, I understand, all venial, you will hereafter so conduct yourself, as not to incur any new ones. Your brother Thomas [J. Clay] and your Sister [Anne Clay], have come up from Louisville to pass a few days at Lexington, and they were both at Ashland to day, and are both well. Your Uncle James [Brown Clay] and your Aunt Susan [Jacob Clay] and their children, are all with us, and all enjoying good health.

George Ross Harrison returned from Annapolis a few days ago, where he had been the last nine months at the Naval School, to qualify himself as a Midshipman[.][4] He could not stand the test of an examination and has returned greatly to his own and his fathers mortification; his general conduct was very good, but his attainments not sufficient.[5] Your brother and sister as well as myself complain of your negligence in writing to us, Nanny[6] has written two or three letters to you without getting any reply; Cant you get up a little earlier in the morning, and write us oftener.

I transmit to you enclosed Ten dollars[.] All here unite in love to you.

ALS. Henry Clay Memorial Foundation, Lexington, Ky. 1. John Bell Hood graduated from West Point on July 1, 1853. USMA, *Register*, 202. 2. Clay to Morehead, Dec. 14, 1848. 3. Reference is to Lt. Col. Henry Clay, Jr. 4. Clay to Graham, August 28, 1850. 5. Clay to Graham, June 25, 1851. 6. Nickname for Anne Clay.

To SAMUEL AUSTIN ALLIBONE[1] Lexington, June 30, 1851

I recd. your friendly letter of the 23d. inst. I have been so much from home during the last eighteen months that it is not my purpose at present to leave it this summer.

I have no doubt, with you, that many of the quiet and well disposed Citizens of So. Carolina are opposed to the measures of violence which are threatened by others.[2] But the danger is, as history shews too often happens, that the bold the daring and the violent will get the control and push their measures to a fatal extreme. Should the State resolve to secede, it will present a new form of trial to our System, but I entertain undoubting confidence that it will come out of it with the most triumphant success.

I thank you for your friendly tender of your services. Should any occasion for the use of them arise, I will avail myself of them, with great pleasure.

Do me the favor to present my warm regards to your good sister [Susan Allibone]; and I reciprocate your kind wishes and prayers, with all my heart.

ALS. CSmH. Printed in Colton, *Clay Correspondence*, 4:620. 1. Clay to Allibone, July 19, 1848. 2. Clay to Lathrop *et al.*, Feb. 17, 1851.

LAST WILL AND TESTAMENT OF HENRY CLAY Lexington, July 10, 1851

In the name of God, Amen! I Henry Clay of Ashland do make, ordain and publish the following as and for my last Will and testament: hereby revoking and annulling all former and other Wills by me heretofore made.

I give and devise to my Wife [Lucretia Hart Clay] during her life, the use and occupation of Ashland with the exception of the piece thereof hereinafter divised to my son John [Morrison Clay], and also during her life all my slaves except those heretofore or hereinafter otherwise disposed of without her being liable to any account for the profits thereof. I also give to her in fee all my furniture, plate[,] paintings, library, Carriages and Horses, and such of my other horses, mules, working beasts Milch Cows and other live stock as she may select and choose to retain but upon this Condition nevertheless that either during her life, or by her last Will and Testament she dispose of the same among our children and our other descendants in such way as she may think Proper according to her own sense of their Kindness, affection and obedience to her. If she die without making such disposition the same is to be considered as part of my residuary estate.

Should my Wife not desire to reside at Ashland after my death I will and direct that a house and lot be purchased, built, or rented for her wherever she may prefer to dwell.

Upon the death of my Wife or if she shall determine to remove from Ashland, I will and direct that the Sale of that estate and of all my slaves bequeathed to her except such as she may choose to retain during her life, and also of all the above mentioned personal property which is bequeathed to her and which she may consent to be sold shall be made by my Executors, upon such terms as they may prescribe and publish.

I invest my Executors with full power and authority to sell and convey any part of my Estate, real or personal wherever situated not herein specifically devised and bequeathed including that given to my wife and not disposed of by her, after her death, or before, if she require it, or if as above mentioned she determine to remove from Ashland. But I require the concurrence in any such sale of all my Executors who may qualify or be in being when it is made.

In the event of the removal of my wife from Ashland and a consequent sale of that Estate and other property as herein provided for, I direct that the proceeds of sale be loaned out upon good and sufficient security and that the accruing interest thereon be regularly paid to my wife during her life to be disposed of as she may think proper. And upon her death out of the principal such pecuniary legacies as are herein directed are to be paid and the remainder to pass to my residuary estate. If either of my sons should purchase Ashland two thirds of the purchase money may, during my Wife's life, remain in his hands, he paying annually interest thereon, and the estate continuing bound for the said two thirds and the interest thereof.

I give and devise to my son Thomas [Hart Clay], Mansfield, where he at present resides In trust however that it shall be retained free from all debts or incumberances, as a home for the residence of himself his wife [Mary Mentelle Clay], and the Children that he has or may have by her, and of any other wife or children that he may have by such other wife and the produce thereof to be applied to their support and maintenance. And upon the death of my said son Thomas, I give and devise Mansfield to such of his Children or their descendants as he may by his last Will and Testament direct and appoint, and in default of such last Will and testament to be divided between them according to the statute of distributions. If there be any defect in the creation of this trust I desire it may be remedied by a Court of Chancery with the concurrence of that Court, Mansfield may be sold and the proceeds of sale invested in other real estate, to be subject to the same trust as Mansfield is above made subject to.

I also give to my said Son Thomas Five thousand dollars to be paid to him without interest as soon as my Executors can conveniently raise the same. I discharge and acquit my said Son from any debts which he owes me. I confirm the Gift of any slave I have made and delivered to him.

I give and devise to my son John two hundred acres of Ashland to be taken off the south side thereof on the Tates Creek road by beginning on the said road at the corner of Clark[1] and myself thence running with Clark's line to the corner of my land and the parcel of land formerly belonging to Coyle[2] purchased by the said Clark, thence with the said Coyle or Clark's line and continuing from the end of it paralel with the general course of Tates creek road so far that by running a line to the said road and thence to the beginning the quantity of Two hundred acres shall be obtained exclusive of the contents of the road. But if, as thus described, the said Two hundred acres should include the brick negro quarters now in my use, then there must be an extension of the sum by running so far on the second, or West line of the said Clark's land bought of Coyle as by running the lines in the courses above mentioned will give the quantity of Two hundred acres excluding these from the said Brick quarters.

I also give to my said Son John the slaves Harvey, Milton, Henry and Bob.

My said Son is the proprietor by my Gift of Margaret Woods, and her Herold filly and Rally and their increase and I have given him One half of Yorkshire, of Magnolia, of the Zinganee mare and of the brown imported mare and their increase. He is also the owner of Flounce[3] and I give him one half of the produce of my Jeannettes.

I direct that during my son Theodores [Wythe Clay] unhappy alienation of mind,[4] he shall be decently and comfortably supported in whatever situation it may be deemed best to place him. If it should please God to restore him to reason, I will and direct that after the death of my wife, out of the proceeds of the sale of Ashland and other property herein directed to be sold, the sum of Ten thousand dollars be paid to him without interest; but from the time of such restoration I direct that the sum of Six hundred dollars be annually paid to him until he receives the said legacy when the annuity is to cease.

I give to the Children of my lamented Daughter Anne [Brown Clay Erwin][5] in addition to what I have heretofore given their Mother the sum of Seven thousand five hundred dollars equally to be divided between them to be paid without interest after the death of my wife, out of the proceeds of the estate and property herein directed to be sold. If one or more of them die without issue prior to the payment of this legacy I direct it equally to be divided among the survivors.

I give to the Children of my lamented Son Henry [Clay, Jr.][6] the sum of Seven thousand five hundred dollars, in addition to what I have heretofore given to their father equally to be divided between them, to be paid without interest after the death of my wife out of the proceeds of the estate and property herein directed to be sold. If one or more of them die without issue prior to the payment of this legacy, I direct it to be equally divided among the survivors.

I give to my son Thomas my stock in the Lexington and Richmond Turnpike Road Company.

I give to my grandson Henry [Clay III], Son of Henry, my breast pin containing his Father's hair.

I give to my grandson Henry Boyle [Clay], son of my son Thomas, the gold watch which I wear presented to me by my friend Dr. [William N.] Mercer.

I give to my friend Dr. B[enjamin]. W. Dudley the gold snuff box presented to me by Dr. Hewitt, late of Washington City.

I give to my friend Dr. W[illiam]. N. Mercer my snuff box inlaid with gold said to have belonged to Peter, the Great Emperor of Russia.[7]

I give to my friend Henry T. Duncan my ring containing a piece of the Coffin of General [George] Washington.

I give to my granddaughter Lucy [Jacob Clay], my diamond gold ring.

I give to each of my sons Thomas, James [Brown Clay], and John one of my walking canes to be chosen by them in the order in which I have named *them*. My Wife may distribute the residue of my walking canes and snuff boxes among such of our descendants or friends as she may think proper.

In the sale of any of my slaves I direct that the members of families shall not be separated without their consent.

My Will is and I accordingly direct that the issue of all my female slaves, which may be born after the first day of January 1850 shall be free at the respective ages of the Males at twenty eight and of the females at twenty five and that the three years next preceeding their arrival at the age of freedom, they shall be entitled to their hire or wages for those years or the fair value of their services to defray the expense of transporting them to One of the African Colonies and of furnishing them with an outfit on their arrival there. And I further direct that they be taught to read, to write and to Cipher, and that they be sent to Africa, I further will and direct that the issue of any of the females who are so to be entitled to their freedom at the age of twenty five shall be deemed free from their birth; and that they be bound out as apprentices to learn farming or some useful trade upon the condition also of being taught to read to write and to Cipher. And I direct also that the age of twenty one having been attained, they shall be sent to one of the African Colonies, to raise the necessary funds for which purpose, if they shall not have previously earned them, they must be hired out a sufficient length of time.

I request and enjoin my Executors and descendants to pay particular attention to the execution of this provision of my Will. And if they should choose to sell any of the females, who or whose issue are to be free, I especially desire them to guard carefully the rights of such issue by all suitable stipulations and sanctions in the Contract of sale. But, I hope that it may not be necessary to sell any such persons who are to be entitled to their freedom but that they may be retained in the possession of some of my descendants.

All the rest and residue of my Estate not hereon Specifically devised and bequeathed and not necessary to the payment of any debt I may leave unpaid (I hope to leave none) including after the death of my wife the proceeds of the sale herein directed to be made, the principal of which she will leave, I vest in my Executors and the survivor of them in trust, first to pay to Theodore W. Clay the ten thousand dollars given to him in the event of his restoration to reason, and if he should not be so restored to pay such expenses as may be annually necessary to his Comfortable support; and secondly to pay the residue of the annually accruing interest upon this trust fund after paying what is necessary for Theodore, to my sons, Thomas and James in equal portions, during their lives, and to their respective heirs upon their death. And for the purposes of this trust my acting Executors are directed to invest the above mentioned residuum of my Estate in some good fund or in loans upon good security so that they may apply the annually accruing interest or dividends as hereinbefore directed. Or they may upon proper security lend the said fund to my sons Thomas and James. It is my Will and intention that the said fund, in equal portions shall finally pass to such persons as each of my said sons as to his part shall finally direct by his last Will and testament. And in default of said Will to their respective heirs, according to the Kentucky statute of distributions. My Executors may relieve themselves at any time from this trust by conveying the trust fund to some other trustee to be agreed on between them and my said two sons, or be appointed by a Court of Chancery. If my son Theodore shall not be restored to his reason, within five years after my death, the trustees are not required to retain the ten thousand dollars bequeathed to him beyond that time. And unless and until he is so restored, I direct that all of the annually accruing interest or dividends upon the fund shall be paid in equal portions to my Sons Thomas and James or their respective heirs until the Capital of the fund itself is paid as herein before directed.

I direct that no security be required of my Executors having full confidence in their faithful performance of their duty. And I direct that no inventory of my estate be made until after the death of my wife.

Lastly I do nominate Constitute and appoint my Wife Executrix, and my friends The Honble Thomas A. Marshall and James O. Harrison Executors of this my last Will and testament all written in my own proper hand writing on five pages of two sheets of fools cap paper. In Testimony Whereof I have hereunto subscribed my name and affixed it also in the Margin of each of the five pages this 10th day of July 1851.

[November 14, 1851]

I make this Codicil in my own handwriting to the previous last will and testament Sally Hall[8] has a note of James Erwin for eight hundred dollars with interest which Henry C. Erwin has given his note to pay. I will and direct that if he should not pay it that it shall be paid out of his proportion of the bequest made in this Will to the Children of my daughter Anne, when according to the terms of the bequest it becomes payable whether he then be dead or living.

I give to my grandson Harry Clay—son of James B. Clay my scotch pebble seal which has on it the initials of my name.[9]

Copy. Fayette County Will Book T. 1. John Clarke. See Clay to Lucretia H. Clay, Feb. 11, 1851. 2. Cornelius Coyle. See 3:886. 3. For Flounce, given to Clay by Dr. William N. Mercer, and Zinganee, a great sire, see Perrin, *History of Fayette County*, 149, 153. 4. See 8:442-43. 5. Her surviving children at this time were Henry Clay, Andrew Eugene, and Charles Edward Erwin and Lucretia Erwin Cowles. 6. Henry [III], Anne, and Thomas J. Clay. 7. See Clay to Lester, Sept. 26, 1845. 8. Long-time Clay housekeeper, Sarah Hall. See 1:309. 9. This will was probated in Fayette County on July 12, 1852, and was proved by the oaths of Benjamin Warfield and Madison C. Johnson.

Statement of Assets of Henry Clay, July 10, 1851. Lists the following: Ashland, containing "about five hundred & fifteen acres of land (of which 200 are given by my will to John [Morrison Clay])" @ $31,500; furniture, plate, paintings, wines, & library @ $7,500; stock of all kinds at Ashland @ $3,000; 27 or 28 slaves estimated at @ $9,000; Mansfield, "given by my will in trust to Thomas [Hart Clay] Due on my Illinois land next Xmas the sum of $2000 & Xmas after $2000, secured by lease of the land recorded in Ill." @ $4,000; due from the Agricultural Bank in Natchez—$2,000 [Eustis to Clay, March 5, 1846]; Frankfort Bridge stock @ $4,500 [9:451]; Maysville Road stock @ $1,900; Lexington & Richmond Turnpike, "given to Thomas $1000," @ $4,000; Lexington & Frankfort Railroad @ $10,000; Lexington & Louisville Railroad @ $500; Winchester & Danville Railroad @ $400; one half of house and lot in Frankfort (the other half owned by Dr. Douglass L. Price) @ $1,600 [Clay to Letcher, July 7, 1848]; due from the Blantons on Combs lot @ $2,600; city bond @ $300. Total: $65,500.

In addition to these specific assets, Clay mentions "an interest perhaps not very valuable in Little Sandy Salt works (see contract with the late John Breckinridge in a bundle of contracts in my press up stairs marked B"; "an interest with Mounts heirs in land on Red river"; "10000 Acres in the name of Franklin on the waters of the Kentucky [River] &c. patented to me and which Theodore [Wythe Clay] once explored"; plus, "various little sums due me evidenced by my papers." ADS. DLC-James O. Harrison Papers (DNA, M212, R21).

To The Rev. Mr. Bullock, July 15, 1851. Regrets that he cannot "attend the examination of your school tomorrow. . . . having witnessed, with much pleasure, the Lady-like bearing of the young Ladies under your charge." Although slowed by "my present feeble state of health. . . . Yesterday, in answer to an inquiry from Memphis,

I took pleasure in strongly recommending your excellent institution." ALS. Henry Clay Memorial Foundation, Lexington, Ky.

The Rev. Mr. Bullock is probably the Rev. Joseph J. Bullock, a Presbyterian minister who served (1837-39) as Kentucky's first superintendent of public instruction. He was principal of Walnut Hills Academy, a girls' school located seven miles from Lexington. Collins, *History of Kentucky*, 1:42, 507; John M. Gresham Company (compilers), *Biographical Cyclopedia of Kentucky* (Chicago, 1896), 536.

To Committee of Invitation to Dinner in New York City Honoring Bishop John Hughes, July 15, 1851. Acknowledges an invitation to a dinner on July 21 in honor of Archbishop John Hughes on his return from Europe, and thanks them. Notes that while "Entertaining a high opinion of the great ability and eloquence of the Archbishop," the "great distance of my residence from the city of New York will not allow of my acceptance of your invitation." Adds: "I should have been glad, by my presence, to demonstrate my conviction that, whilst all sincere Christians are aiming to arrive at the same state of future bliss—no matter by what different roads they may pursue their journey in this life—nothing could prevent those of one denomination from manifesting all proper courtesy and honor to eminence, piety, and devotion, in another denomination." Copy. Printed in Frankfort *Commonwealth*, August 4, 1851.

To JOHN H. HOPKINS[1]

Lexington, July 17, 1851

I duly received your favor of the 3d. inst. in which a request is contained for my consent to the publication of my former letter to you.[2] It was written, upon my dictation to an amanuensis, when I was much debilitated, and the first draught was sent to you, without my retaining any Copy. I have only a general recollection of its contents. I remember that it was a principal object with me to express my great satisfaction with your admirable lecture.[3] I am not aware that the publication of my letter would do any good, unless it should tend to the circulation of that lecture. In the present excited state of the public mind, it is very difficult to say any thing that would be satisfactory both at the South and at the North. Upon the whole I must leave it to your discretion to publish my letter or not, as you may think proper. Perhaps an extract of that part of it which relates to your discourse might be sufficient.

I did not intend to express any opinion of my own on the power of Congress to appropriate the public domain to the purchase and emancipation of slaves. My purpose was to advert to the doubt, I might have stated the denial, of the power by others. I forbear now to examine the question, because we both agree that, if the power were uncontested, it could not be exercised in the existing state of the public mind. And, if hereafter a better condition of public feeling should arise, the power may not be controverted, or the Constitution may be amended. In the meantime what you have said on the subject may do good and can do no harm.

I wish that I could enlarge more on the interesting topic of our recent correspondence; but I regret that I am prevented by my continuing debility. I thank you for your friendly wishes, and prayers in my behalf, and cordially reciprocate them.

ALS. DLC-HC (DNA, M212, R6). 1. Hopkins (1792-1868) had been a superintendent of an iron works in Pennsylvania, then a Pittsburgh lawyer, and finally an Episcopal clergyman. In 1832 he became the first Episcopal bishop of Vermont. *DAB*. 2. Letter not found. 3. In Jan., 1851, at Buffalo, N.Y., Hopkins delivered a lecture entitled "Slavery: Its Religious Sanction, Its Political Dangers, and the Best Mode of Doing It Away." Published later that year, the lecture argued that while slavery was not a sin, since it was not forbidden in the Scriptures, its abolition was urgently important and should be effected by fraternal agreement. *Ibid.*

To ANDREW EUGENE ERWIN Lexington, July 19, 1851

I received your letter of the 30th. of May, and I was glad to hear of your safe arrival in good health at San Francisco,[1] and that you were pleased with the country and with your prospects. I was also much gratified to perceive that you had a due sense of the great responsibility of your present condition. You are at a great distance from all your friends. You are very young, and you will be constantly exposed to temptations which if you have not the firmness to resist them may lead to your ruin. Let me entreat you to avoid all dissipation, and above and beyond all the vice of gambling. It is always attended with loss of character, loss of health, and often the loss of fortune. Those who indulge in it most, and if apparently successful in the hazards of the game, are nevertheless finally losers. Let me also entreat you to avoid all bad company, and to seek the society of those who are respectable intelligent and upright. This advice is given you by one who has lived long in the world, and who has had extensive opportunities of witnessing the ruin and desolation produced by dissipated habits and bad company. Remember the fate of your poor brother James [Erwin, Jr.].[2] Your father [James Erwin] left no will, and left his estate in the greatest possible embarrassment. Nobody has administered upon it, and nobody probably will. Your brother Henry [Clay Erwin] is understood to have some property under his control, but what it is I do not know. Your step mother [Margaret Johnson Erwin] and her children remain at the Woodlands and I believe are all well. She had an infant son a few days after your father's death.[3] The Woodlands, slaves and other property there will be sold either this Fall or next Spring.[4] I am paying some attention to your interests. and I hope there will be saved to each of you out of the wreck of your fathers estate some seven or eight thousand dollars apiece. I think it will be very well for you in your next letter to inform me who you would like to be appointed your guardian during your minority. My age and infirmities are too great for me to act in that character.

All are well here except myself, and I consider my situation quite delicate if not critical. All are well too at Mansfield, and your aunt Susan [Jacob Clay] who has just had her fifth child[5] is staying here for the present with her children. James [Brown Clay] left us a few days ago in good health for St Louis. All of us feel great solicitude for your welfare, and write in love to you . . .

LS. Courtesy of Henry Clay Simpson, Lexington, Ky. 1. Clay to Unknown Recipient, Dec. 27, 1850. 2. Clay to Allibone, July 19, 1848. 3. James Erwin died on June 1, 1851. The son who was born after his father's death was named James William Erwin. *JAH* (March, 1983), 69:938. 4. The "Woodlands" was sold at auction on June 7, 1852, to Benjamin Tilford for $25,600. The sale also included slaves and other items, bringing the estimated total to more than $40,000. James O. Harrison to Thomas Hart Clay, June 8, 1852. *RKHS* (Oct., 1952), 50:317. 5. Apparently a daughter named Lucretia Hart Clay. Kerr, *History of Kentucky*, 3:7.

From John A. Lynch, Cincinnati, July 22, 1851. Since Clay has "on many occasions taken opportunities of expressing a favorable Sympathy for my native Land 'Ireland' & for its People, in that Eloquent Strain of Language so natural to you," feels free "to take the Liberty of trespassing on your Valuable time." Reports that although "a member of the Legal Profession in Ireland," during the "dreadful Calamity of

Famine" he went "for three years without being able to earn any thing" to support his "three helpless little children." While "entertaining with many others no hope" for Ireland's "resuscitation but thro' one general & final Struggle for Liberty I took part in the Effort made by a few but true and Sterling self sacrificing Patriots to arouse the People from their Lethargy and by a decisive blow rid themselves of the great cause of all their Misfortunes." After "a fruitless Effort my Friends were torn from their loved Land in Chains," but "I . . . have been more fortunate in obtaining footing and Liberty on this soil under the Glorious Flag of the Republic" and escaping "the surveillance of spies & Police" in Ireland. Although employed as a clerk in a Cincinnati law office, "I cannot attempt to practice my profession without a course of Study & being duly naturalized and admitted as a Lawyer." Hopes Clay will help "in procurring me a Junior Clerkship in the Postoffice or any other of the Public Departments of the State in Washington," assuring him that even on "the lowest salary given for such services . . . $400 a year," he could "get along thro Life with some happiness." ALS. DLC-HC (DNA, M212, R6).

On October 13, 1851, Clay wrote to U.S. Postmaster General Nathan K. Hall recommending Lynch for "a Clerkship in the General P[ost] Office Department." Having had "the advantage of a personal acquaintaince with him," believes "the public service would be promoted by his employment." ALS. *Ibid.*

Lynch had apparently taken part in the "Rising of 1848" led by a group called Young Ireland. Tom Ireland, *Ireland Past and Present* (New York, 1942), 250-62.

To WILLIAM N. MERCER Lexington, August 1, 1851

I received your short letter[1] addressed to me from New York, announcing your intended departure in the Asia for Europe on the 18th June. I have been intending ever since its receipt to write to you; but from my having nothing material to communicate, and from an encreased repugnance to the exertion of writing, augmented by my continued indisposition, I have delayed executing my purpose until I have received your kind letter dated at London the 10th. Ulto.

When I wrote to you at N. York, I supposed that our friend [William St. John] Elliot would accompany you to Europe, and it was not until some time after you left our shores that I heard of his remaining behind. He is now, I learn, at a Water cure establishment on the Connecticut river, and will visit us in September. Altho' some of the letters of introduction which I forwarded to N. York were of both of you, that will not prevent your using them.

Nothing very important has occurred in the U.S. since your departure. There is apparently no abatement in the violence of South Carolina, nor any abandonment of her purpose of Secession.[2] Nothing but the folly and extravagance of that measure would lead one to suppose that she could never adopt it. I am sorry to inform you that our late intelligence from Mississippi is less favorable to the election of Mr. [Henry S.] Foote.[3] The disunionists have assumed a new garb, pretending now to be opposed to Disunion or to secession. Unfortunately, they will derive some collateral aid from an important event which has recently occurred in Cuba. It appears that early last month an insurrection broke out at Principe in that island, and that it was followed by several encounters between the insurgents and some of the troops of the Governm[en]t, in which the former are alleged to have been successful. The accounts as yet are however so vague, contradictory & unsatisfactory, that no safe judgment can be formed either as to the extent or the probable issue of the Rebellion. The most alarming fact to the Spanish Governmt., if it be true, is the infidelity of at least a portion of the Army.[4] Some companies are said to have deserted to the insurgents, and in consequence, the Regiment to which they belonged has been disbanded at Havana. In the mean time, many of our heedless young men, from various parts of the U. States, have started and are making their way to join the insurgents.[5]

I was delighted to hear the Ladies had made the voyage with such little inconvenience and suffering, and that dear Anna's [Mercer] health, altho' momentarily affected at Liverpool, had been reinstated at London. Ah! My dear friend, I cannot express to you the deep anxiety and profound solicitude which your friends (and none more than myself) entertain for you and for her, on account of her health. I hope and pray that she may be long, long preserved to you; but should it unhappily be otherwise decreed,[6] I trust that you will recognize the duty of submitting with resignation to the will of Providence.

Speaking of the much more important subject of her health, reminds me that you may like to know something of mine. I am sorry to tell you that it is no better than when I last saw you. My cough continues, perha[p]s a little abated, but my debility encreases. I have tried in vain all the old womens remedies; taking care however only to use those which can do no harm if no good, and still I cough and spit. The only redeeming hope is that the lungs are yet sound. But I must frankly own that my feelings indicate that the machine is nearly worn out, and that not one screw only but several are out of place. Some times and (within a few days) I am a little encouraged by the effects of a new regimen, which I am now pursuing. We shall see. At the advanced age of past 74, when many of the tyes to life are broken, and when the source of one taste and pleasure after another have been dried up, it is of little consequence whether one remains here below a few months more or less. I should be happy to be spared long enough to witness the return of yourself, Anna & Miss [Eliza] Young to our Country in the full enjoyment of health and good spirits.

Owing to the delicate state of my health, to my age, and to the unsuccessful and frequent use of my name, as a Candidate for the Presidency, heretofore, I have written to some friends that I can not consent to the further use of my name for that office.[7] Who will be the Candi[d]ate of either party, still less who will be the successful Candidate cannot now be asserted. Genl. [Winfield] Scott is apparently the most prominent Whig Candidate;[8] but it will be a fatal objection to him, if not removed, that he is brought out under the auspices of the abolitionists and free soilers.

I reserve the consideration of the question whether I shall return to the Senate for the period when it may be necessary to decide it. . . .

ALS. Lu-Ar. 1. Not found. 2. Clay to Lathrop *et al.*, Feb. 17, 1851. 3. Foote had resigned his seat in the U.S. Senate to run for governor of Mississippi on a Union ticket of Whigs and Democrats who supported the Compromise of 1850. Foote's original opponent withdrew on Sept. 16 and Democrat Jefferson Davis, Foote's arch-rival, also gave up his seat in the Senate to enter the race. In the election on Nov. 3, 1851, Foote defeated Davis by a vote of 29,358 to 28,358. *BDGUS*, 2:811; Clement Eaton, *Jefferson Davis* (New York, 1977), 77-79. 4. Under the leadership of Joaquin de Aguero, a cry for Cuban liberty was raised at the public square of Puerto Principe on July 3, 1851. The 15 Cuban patriots were routed by Spanish forces, but the following day at a nearby town Aguero read a declaration of independence to a group of several hundred. When Spanish troops attacked, the Cuban patriots drove them back. Optimistic messages were sent off to Narciso Lopez in the U.S., encouraging him to embark on another expedition to Cuba. By the time he reached Cuba, however, Aguero's forces had been defeated and executed. Basil Rauch, *American Interest in Cuba: 1848-1855* (New York, 1948), 154-56; Charles E. Chapman, *A History of the Cuban Republic* (New York, 1927), 36-38. 5. Gen. Narciso Lopez led an expedition which sailed from New Orleans in early August and landed about 60 miles from Havana on August 12. Col. William L. Crittenden, nephew of Attorney General John J. Crittenden, was second in command. Col. Crittenden and 50 other Southerners were captured on August 13 and executed at Havana a few days later. Lopez was captured on August 28 and publicly garroted. A number of American prisoners who were sent to Spain were eventually released after Congress appropriated $25,000 as indemnity for the wrecking of the Spanish consulate in New Orleans, which occurred when news of the executions reached there. Bemis, *Diplomatic History of the U.S.*, 316-17. 6. Anna Mercer died in Europe in the fall of 1851. See Clay to Mercer, Nov. 14, 1846. 7. Clay to Ullmann, June 14, 1851. 8. *Ibid.*

From GEORGE GRISWOLD[1] *et al.*

New York City, August 5, 1851[2]

There are periods in the history of nations, when the bold and manly counsel, the sagacious foresight, and the timely and persevering efforts of the firm and patriotic statesman can succeed in averting a fearful crisis; at the same time the warning voice of the wise and the good may require to be repeated and uplifted, until it shall resound throughout the land.

Your introduction of the Compromise measures[3] into the Senate of the United States, and their passage by Congress, marked an epoch in our history; they arrested the nearer approach of national calamity, and, as was fondly hoped, laid the foundation for returning harmony.

It has since, however, become but too apparent, that continued and unremitted efforts in favor of Union sentiments are necessary to resist the current of error, and secure the maintenance of sound principles of attachment to the Constitution, in order that our country may reap the blessed fruits that were expected from the Compromise of peace.

Several of your noble coadjutors in the cause of the Union have already addressed the people, and are now addressing them, in words of truth and patriotism, of eloquence and power; and we have thought it right to appeal to the senator from Kentucky, and entreat, that one whose voice has been so often raised in defense of the people's rights, may not be silent now.

We have a well-founded conviction that the great body of the American people are in favor of maintaining and enforcing the Compromises of the Constitution; nevertheless, in the resolutions and addresses adopted at conventions lately assembled around us, we have seen with regret, as well as alarm, that the question of adherence to the Compromise measures is avoided or evaded, that modification and amendment are declared to be requisite, and repeal, itself, admissible; as if the requirement of the Constitution, in carrying out an integral part of our national compact, was of no higher obligation than any ordinary act of legislation.[4]

It is evident, therefore, that there required to be more generally diffused a spirit that will not tamper with politicians whose course must inevitably lead to the destruction of the Constitution—a spirit that will not hold communion with those who advance and support doctrines, in relation to the great national adjustment, fatal to the future peace and harmony of the Union; who merely acquiesce because they have no alternative, while, on all important occasions, they too plainly disclose, under a flimsy vail of apparent contentment, a determination to resist and oppose the efforts of the friends of the Compromise and the Union.

We feel confident that you will not favor the abettors of such doctrines, but rather reprove and denounce them. We therefore respectfully but earnestly ask of you to leave, for a time, your retreat in Kentucky, to appear among us at New York.[5]

The people are profoundly grateful for your past efforts, and are proud and willing to acknowledge your timely and efficient services. They know and honor your Union principles and your national sentiments; and none are more deeply penetrated by these feelings, nor more desirous to acknowledge these obligations, than your fellow-citizens generally of this commercial emporium; and did we not think that the present crisis required your warning voice, your presence and your name, to arouse your countrymen to a sense of their duty and their danger, we would not attempt to disturb the repose of the sage of Ashland.

Copy, signed also by Stephen Whitney, Daniel Ullmann, and 338 others. Printed in Colton, *Clay Correspondence*, 3:400-402. 1. Griswold was a wealthy New York City businessman active in the export-import trade, insurance, banking, and real estate. *NCAB*, 3:355. 2. This letter is dated in Colton as autumn, 1851; however, it is given the date of August 5 in the New York *Herald*, Sept. 4, 1851. 3. Clay to Combs, Jan. 22, 1850. 4. Clay to Lathrop *et al.*, Feb. 17, 1851. 5. Clay to Fellow Citizens of New York City, Oct. 3, 1851.

To HENRY CLAY, JR. [III] Lexington, August 15, 1851

I have not heard from you since you went into Camp,[1] how you liked the real life of a soldier &c. I have received the official Register of the [U.S. Military] Academy, and liked your standing in your Studies much better than that of your general conduct.[2] I hope that you will exert yourself to improve in both particulars.

Your grandmama [Lucretia Hart Clay] laid her hands on the enclosed letter[3] from your father [Henry Clay, Jr.] to her, which I send to you, as I thought you might like to read & preserve it.

All are well here, except myself, and I hope that my health is improving.

ALS. PHC. 1. Clay to Henry Clay III, Sept. 10, 1850. 2. Clay to Morehead, Dec. 14, 1848. 3. Not found.

To N.W. Pollard, September 6, 1851. Acknowledges receipt of "a copy of the Baltimore *Clipper*, containing your address on the subject of the emigration of blacks from the United States to Trinidad." Believes that "the city of Baltimore had been well chosen by you as the theatre of operations." Warns, however, that "in dealing with these free blacks, you will have difficulties to encounter that will take all your patience and will render necessary all your perseverance." Suspecting that "most of those who reside in cities will be reluctant to go" to Trinidad to take up agricultural pursuits, advises Pollard to consider giving "some of the more intelligent and decent blacks a favorhood. And if you can prevail upon them to go, then their persuasion might induce others to follow." Doubts that "Kentucky will make any contribution toward defraying the expense of the deportation of any free blacks from the state. . . . and the attention with those at the helm has been directed exclusively toward Africa." Copy. Printed in Mary Elizabeth Thomas (ed.), "Henry Clay Replies to a Labor Recruiter from Trinidad," *RKHS* (Autumn, 1979), 77:263-65.

Pollard was a West Indian planter who had been sent to the United States by his government to recruit agricultural laborers. He was to encourage them to emigrate to Trinidad where they would have work and social status. He chose Baltimore as the center of his activities, because it had the largest free black population (74,823). *Ibid.*

Pollard had written Clay on August 28, 1851, asking him if Kentucky would be willing to pay transportation costs for free blacks who wished to emigrate from Kentucky. ALS. Public Record Office CO 295 174, packet no. 8264.

To WILLIAM W. CORCORAN Lexington, September 14, 1851

I received your favor informing me of your having charitably advanced to Father [Theobald] Mathew Five hundred dollars, in consequence of a letter which I addressed to you commending him to your benevolence.[1] It was not my intention to occasion such a heavy draught upon your purse; but in making the contribution you have acted in conformity with your accustomed generosity, and I have no doubt that you have experienced an amount of personal satisfaction far surpassing the value of your liberal donation.

I have not heard from Mr. [Henry] Grinnell;[2] but I do hope that, before the reverend Fathers return to Ireland, some general popular contribution will be made, to render easy his declining years, and to acquit our race of a small portion of the great obligation under which he has placed the whole of us. You have more than nobly discharged your duty.

ALS. DLC-William W. Corcoran Papers (DNA, M212, R20). 1. Clay to Corcoran, May 28, 1851, used as note to Clay to Grinnell, May 28, 1851. 2. On Oct. 9, 1851, Clay wrote Henry Grinnell, noting "that you have put in motion a plan for the relief of Father Mathew" and enclosing "a check for fifty dollars, my 'mite' which I request you to apply to the fund which is being raised for him." ALS. Courtesy of Dr. Thomas D. Clark, Lexington, Ky.

To LUCRETIA ERWIN COWLES Lexington, September 14, 1851

I have delayed answering your letter of the 5th. of August from time to time under the hope of being able to communicate the day of the sale of the woodlands and other property, but the sale could not take place without the consent of all parties this fall and it cannot now be ordered before the meeting of the Court in February next. The consent would not be given of Capt. Johnson and Mrs. [Margaret Johnson] Erwin and hence the delay until February.[1] Your brother Henry [Clay Erwin] seemed also disinclined to an earlier sale. If it be ordered in February it will be some weeks thereafter before the sale can be made. You expressed a wish in your letter to raise a couple of thousand dollars upon your interest in your mothers [Anne Brown Clay Erwin] estate. I would gladly have advanced the money if I could but it was not in my power and I really did not know to whom to apply to get it.

I think your prospects are better now than I thought when I last wrote to you. I think you will recover the land from Mr. Higgins;[2] and that your brother James's [Erwin, Jr.] part of it will be decided to have been inherited by your brothers and yourself and not by your father [James Erwin] because the property proceeded from your mother. Mr. [James O.] Harrison will bring a suit against Mr. Higgins for the land which he expects will be decided in February next. I think your interest in that land is worth not less than twenty five hundred dollars. Mr. Harrison with my advice in consequence of your great want of money, offered it to Mr. Higgins for two thousand, but he was not then inclined to give that sum. He may think better of it and be willing to give it; and I wish you to write to Mr. Harrison or to me and inform me whether you are willing to take it.

I send you herewith an unofficial copy from an official document which I have recently received from New Orleans.[3] From that document it appears that the amount of fifty odd thousand dollars which is mentioned in the deed of trust which I drew at New Orleans, besides interest is the true amount due to you and your brothers from your mothers estate. It also appears from the same document that five or six pieces of property were mortgaged to secure the payment of what is due to you from your mothers estate. But I apprehend that all those pieces of property except one were released by subsequent official proceedings at the instance of your father in New Orleans. If they were so released the records there will show, and if they were not, so much the better as they will add to your security of what you are entitled to—I hope and believe that you will receive not less than ten thousand dollars on account of your interest in your mothers estate; besides what you may get on account of the Higgins land[.]

We are all here in good health except myself, mine continues to be delicate. I had a letter to day from [Andrew] Eugene [Erwin] of the 11th. July; he was then in good health and spirits but had not heard of the death of his father.[4] [Charles] Edward [Erwin] left us some weeks ago without my consent, but with his brother Henry's to join the Cuban expedition.[5] I have not heard from him since, but suppose that he did not get further than New Orleans and that he will shortly return. Your Aunt Susan [Jacob Clay] and her children are all with us and in good health. I must request that on affairs of business you or Mr. [Frederic] Cowles will address Mr. James O Harrison, who is worthy of all your confidence, and who will keep you fully and accurately informed. I am so old and so full of engagements that writing is very irksome to me. All here join me in love and affection to you and Mr. Cowles. P.S. Your brother Henry has since gone to New Orleans, and in speaking of the Woodlands expressed a desire to retain them that he might have a home.

LS. DLC-John Brown Papers (DNA, M212, R20). 1. Clay to Andrew E. Erwin, July 19, 1851. Capt. Johnson is probably Margaret's father Henry Johnson. 2. Probably Richard Higgins. 3. Not found. 4. Clay to Andrew E. Erwin, July 19, 1851. 5. Charles Edward Erwin was not one of the casualties of the expedition of Narciso Lopez. For the expedition, see Clay to Mercer, August 1, 1851.

To ANDREW EUGENE ERWIN Lexington, September 14, 1851

I recd. to day your letter of the 11h. of July. I had previously written to you communicating the death of your father [James Erwin] on the 1st of June.[1] Since then measures have been adopted to produce a sale of the Woodlands and other property, in behalf of yourself, brothers [Henry Clay Erwin; Charles Edward Erwin] and sister [Lucretia Erwin Cowles], to pay the amount to which you are entitled from your mother [Anne Brown Clay Erwin]; but the Sale has not yet been ordered, and will not be until some time next year.[2] I think that each of you will get not less than $10.000. In the mean time your mother in law[3] and her family continue to occupy the Woodlands. It may be necessary for a guardian to be appointed for you until you arrive at full age, and for you to signify to me who you wish to be appointed. I would serve you but for my age and the uncertainty of life. I think you had better designate Mr. J[ames]. O. Harrison or Mr. Tho. A. Marshall to act as your guardian. As to Henry [Clay Erwin], I am sorry to say that I am afraid that he is too selfish and devoted to the gratification of his sensual appetites to be relied on; and he has I think shewn himself more inclined to the interest of others than to that of his own brothers and sister.

[Charles] Edward has not behaved well. He left here some weeks ago, without my consent, but with his brothers, to join the expedition to Cuba.[4] I have not heard from him, but I suppose that he did not get further than N. Orleans, and that he will return from that City. His conduct has given me great pain and anxiety, and I know not what will become of him.

I am glad to hear that you are pleased with California; and I think that you had better remain there than come home, if you see any fair prospect of doing well. I am sure that if you come home shortly, you will find nothing here to gratify or encourage you. If you remain there a few years, and accumulate a respectable sum, on your final return with that, and with what you may get from your mothers Estate, you may be able to engage in some profitable business.

I hear frequently from Lucretia [Erwin Cowles], who expects soon to be a mother; but poor girl she is very much in want of what is due to her on account of her mother; her husband [Frederic Cowles] being very poor, altho' a very good person.

I am sorry that you should have reason to complain of the neglect of your relations in writing to you. I am now old and writing is rather irksome to me.

We are all well at Ashland, at Mansfield, and I believe at the Woodlands, except myself. My health continues delicate.

All here join me in love to you.

ALS. Courtesy of M.W. Anderson, Lexington, Ky. 1. Clay to Andrew E. Erwin, July 19, 1851. 2. *Ibid.* 3. Actually a reference to his step-mother Margaret Johnson Erwin. 4. For the expedition of Narciso Lopez, see Clay to Mercer, August 1, 1851.

To Unionists of Mississippi, September 20, 1851. Has received their invitation [not found] to attend a "mass meeting of the friends of the Union at Jackson" on October 9-10. Explains that he would like to accept, "But the delicate state of my health, the low stage of water in the Ohio river, and my desire, if I can, to attend the next session of the Senate, interpose insuperable obstacles."

Expresses congratulations for "the auspicious issue of your late election of delegates to the convention," noting that "With one noble exception [Henry S. Foote], their Congressional leaders had abandoned them, or sought to involve them in all the calamitous consequences of civil war—for secession, if it has any meaning, is revolution, and revolution is war. But the people would not allow themselves to be deceived and misled; they became their own leaders; they proved true to themselves, to their country, and to the precious inheritance of the Union, which they have derived from the wisdom of their fathers, and they have signally triumphed."

Continues: "Your opponents, driven by the force of public opinion from the ground of practically exercising at this time the right of secession, have sought a refuge under the cover of theoretic or abstract right, to secede, and are endeavoring to pursuade the people to go along with them. But why assert that right if it is not to be exercised? If there be no existing exigency which requires secession, would it not be better to await until such an exigency shall arise. The assertion of the right now, by a contested majority, would not establish the right of secession, so as to bind future generations, who would form their own opinions, and act for themselves. I hope there is no covert design entertained of pledging the people to the doctrine of secession, and then, shortly after uniting upon them, to co-operate with another State, in a contingency which may happen there, in the support of that doctrine."

Wishes that their "Barbecue may realize all your anticipations, and that Mississippi may continue to manifest her fidelity to the Union." Copy. Printed in New York *Herald*, October 23, 1851.

The Unionist victory in the Mississippi gubernatorial election in November, 1851 [Clay to Mercer, August 1, 1851] was foreshadowed in the September 1-2 election for delegates to a state convention on federal relations. The Union ticket was victorious in the delegate election by a margin of 28,402 to 21,241. Nevins, *Ordeal of the Union*, 1:372-74.

To DANIEL ULLMANN Lexington, September 26, 1851

I received your favor of the 19th instant, with the memorial inclosed. On the subject of the next Presidency, my opinions and views have undergone no change since I last wrote to you.[1] Should I be able, as I now hope to be, from my slowly improving health, to attend the next session of the Senate, we will confer more freely on that subject. In the mean time, I am glad that my friends in New York have foreborne to present my name as a candidate.

I have looked at the list of events and subjects which are proposed to be inscribed on the medal.[2] I have made out and sent herewith a more comprehensive list, embracing most of the important matters, as to which I had any agency, during my service in the National councils. As to the Cumberland Road,[3] no year can be properly fixed. Appropriations for it were made from year to year, for a series of years, which were violently opposed, and the support of which chiefly devolved on me. So in regard to Spanish America,[4] the first movement was made by me in 1818, and my exertions were continued from year to year, until the measure of recognition was finally completed in 1822.

The list now sent may be too large for inscription on the medal. Of course it is my wish that is should be dealt with, by abridgment, or omission as may be thought proper. The two reports, made by me in the Senate, which gave me much credit and reputation were, 1st. That which proposed an equal distribution among the States of the proceeds of the public domain;[5] and 2d. That which averted General Jackson's meditated war against France, on account of her failure to pay the indemnity.[6] I carried both measures against the whole weight of Jackson; but he pocketed the Land Distribution bill, which was not finally passed until 1841. He could not, however, make war against France, without the concurrence of Congress, and my report preserved the peace of the two countries.

My Panama instructions[7] were the most elaborate (and if I may be allowed to speak of them), the ablest State paper that I composed while I was in the Department of State. They contain an exposition of liberal principles, regulating Maritime War, Neutral Rights, etc., which will command the approbation of enlightened men and of posterity.

I was glad to see that you were nominated for Attorney-General at Syracuse, and I heartily wish for your election.[8]

The address to me from New York, although published in the papers has not been received officially by me.[9] What is intended? I have had some correspondence about it with Mr. James D.P. Ogden, who sent me a copy informally. I can not venture to encounter the scenes of excitement which would attend me, if I were to go to New York; but in anticipation of the reception of the address I have prepared a pretty long answer, in which I treat of Secession, the state of the country, in regard to the Slavery question, etc.[10] If this answer be capable of doing any good, the sooner it is published the better.

Copy. Printed in Colton, *Clay Correspondence*, 4:620-22. 1. Clay to Ullmann, June 14, 1851. 2. The medal, which was presented to Clay on Feb. 9, 1852, was made "of pure California gold, massive and weighty, and is inclosed in a silver case." Clay's face appeared on one side and on the other the following list of his accomplishments: "Senate, 1806. Speaker, 1811. War of 1812 with Great Britain. Ghent, 1814. Spanish America, 1822. Missouri Compromise, 1821. American System, 1824. Greece, 1824. Secretary of State, 1825. Panama Instructions, 1826. Tariff Compromise, 1833. Public Domain, 1833-1841. Peace with France Preserved, 1835. Compromise, 1850." Colton, *Clay Correspondence*, 4:622. For further description of the medal, see New York *Herald*, Feb. 10, 1852. See also Speech to Citizens of New York, Feb. 9, 1852. 3. See American System: internal improvements, in Subject Index, 7:694. 4. See Spanish America in Subject Index, 7:764-65. 5. See 8:494, 539-41. 6. See 8:448, 754-56. 7. See 5:314-44. 8. Levi S. Chatfield defeated Ullmann for attorney general in the Nov., 1851 New York state elections. Unofficial results from 45 counties gave Chatfield a 502-vote lead. New York *Herald*, Nov. 13, 14, 1851. 9. Griswold *et al.* to Clay, August 5, 1851. 10. Clay to Fellow-Citizens of New York City, Oct. 3, 1851.

To ABRAHAM MORRISON Lexington, September 30, 1851

I duly received and have attentively read your letter of the 22d instant.[1] You suggest a plan of raising a fund of half a million dollars for the establishment of a permanent academy or institution for the thorough education of African youth to be sent to Africa, after the completion of their education to promote the cause of Colonization and Christianity. You propose that this fund shall be created by voluntary subscription of $500 each, by a thousand individuals, and with great liberality you offer to head the list. I have no doubt that if the scheme could be carried into practical execution, it would effect much good, but I have strong fears that the sum could not be raised with the facility you suppose. It would not be practicable to obtain from Congress an act of Incorporation for such an association for the want of constitutional power to pass it, but an act of Incorporation might be got from one of the State legislatures which would answer all purposes. In the meantime, Liberia offers us much encouragement. Her schools are well attended to, and measures are, I believe in successful progress in New England to raise a liberal fund to establish a High School or schools in Liberia. If you have had occasion, as I have, to observe the proceedings and progress of that colony, you must have been gratified with the amount of intelligence and common sense which they have brought into operation in the conduct of public affairs. It is a mistake to suppose that the colonists are chiefly recently emancipated from slavery. Many of them were born free, some are educated, although without book learning, have that not inferior knowledge which is derived from the intercourse and business of life.

What is now, I think, most needed for Africa, for her race in this country and for our race, is a greater amount of pecuniary means and other facilities to transport colonists to Africa.

I am glad that you have directed your attention to this interesting subject. If the recent decision of Indiana,[2] excluding the blacks from her borders, is to be followed, as I have no doubt in process of time it will be, by most if not all of the States, what is to become of these poor creatures. In the name of humanity, I ask what is to become of them—where are they to go?

Copy. Printed in *The African Repository* (Nov., 1852), 29:348. 1. Morrison had written Clay from Johnstown, Pa., on Sept. 22, 1851, asking his support in establishing "an institution for the education and instruction of all" free blacks "as would be found capable of receiving an education and instruction in all the mechanic arts, in agriculture, science, and Biblical literature, who would be bound, after such education, to emigrate to Africa, as missionaries to that country." Feels that the "agitation and excitement kept up in the free States on the subject of emancipation evidently interferes with "the judicious legislation" which could implement this plan. Is himself willing to put up $500, "provided one thousand other persons contribute a like sum," and requests Clay to introduce in the Senate "an act of incorporation for such an institution, with power to solicit the subscription necessary." *Ibid.*, 29:347-48. 2. A number of antislavery activists had hoped that Indiana would liberalize her Black Laws when the 1850 constitutional convention met. Instead, the convention not only refused to modify discriminatory provisions already in effect against free blacks but also added an article which prohibited all Negroes or mulattoes from entering the state and hinted at the removal of those already settled there. Sewell, *Ballots for Freedom*, 181-83.

To FELLOW CITIZENS OF NEW YORK CITY Lexington, October 3, 1851

I have the honor to acknowledge the receipt, yesterday, of the address which you transmitted to me, from a number of gentlemen in the city of New York.[1] Emanating from a source so highly respectable and imposing, from friends and fellow-citizens so numerous and intelligent, and to whom I am under such great obligations, I have perused it with profound attention and deference. After adverting to the present state of public affairs, to the spirit adverse to the measures of compromise[2] adopted during the last Congress, which prevails in certain quarters,[3] to the necessity of unremitted exertions to preserve our glorious Union, and to what has been so reasonably and well done, with so much ability, eloquence and patriotism, by some of our eminent countrymen, you invite me to leave, for a time, my quiet abode here, to appear in your great city, and to address my fellow-citizens on the actual condition, and menacing danger of our country.

I feel, gentlemen, with the greatest interest and the deepest solicitude, the full force of all that you have expressed; and I would gladly comply with your wishes, and even dedicate the remnant of a life, the largest and best part of which has been spent in the public service, to the cause of the Union, if the state of my health would allow me, and if I believed that any fresh exertions of mine would be useful. But ever since the long session of the last Congress, during which my arduous duties were greater than I was well able to encounter, my health has been delicate, and it has remained so throughout the past summer. I hope that it is improving, but it still requires the most assiduous care; and I entertain serious apprehensions that if I were to accept your invitation, and throw myself into the scenes of excitement incident to it, my strength might fail me, and my present debility might be much increased. There is no place, I am fully aware, where I should find more ardent and enthusiastic friends in one party, and more courtesy and respect in the other, than in the commercial metropolis of the Union. While I am constrained, with much regret, respectfully to decline the meeting you propose, I avail myself of the occasion to present some views which I have taken of public affairs, and which I trust may be received as a substitute for any oral exhibition of them, which I could make before a large concourse of my fellow-citizens in New York.

It was not supposed by the authors and supporters of the compromise, in the last Congress, that the adoption of the series of measures which composed it, would secure the unanimous concurrence of all. Their reasonable hopes were confined to the great majority of the people of the United States, and their hopes have not been disappointed. Everywhere, north, south, east and west, an immense majority of the people are satisfied with, or acquiesce in, the compromise. This may be confidently asserted in regard to thirteen of the slave-holding States, and to thirteen, if not fourteen, of the free States. In a few of both classes of the States, and in some particular localities, dissatisfaction exists, exhibiting itself occasionally in words of great violence and intemperance; but this feeling is, I trust, where it has most prevailed, gradually yielding to an enlightened sense of public duty. I will present a rapid survey of the actual state of things, as it appears to me, both at the North and the South, beginning at the former.

In all that region, there is but one of the various compromise measures that is seriously assailed, and that is the law, made in strict conformity with the Constitution, for the surrender of fugitives from lawful service or labor.[4] But the law itself, with two exceptions, has been everywhere enforced;[5] opposition to it is constantly abating, and the patriotic obligations of obeying the Constitution and the laws, made directly or indirectly by the people themselves, are now almost universally recognized and admitted. If, in the execution of the law, by the public authority, popular discontent is sometimes manifested, it has, with the exceptions mentioned, been invariably repressed, or prevented from obstructing the officers of justice in the performance of their official duties. If I am correctly informed, a great and salutary change has been made, and is yet in progress, at the North, which authorizes the confident anticipation that reason and law will finally achieve a noble triumph.

The necessity of maintaining and enforcing that law, unrepealed, and without any modification that would seriously impair its efficiency, must be admitted by the impartial judgment of all candid men. Many of the slave-holding States, and many public meetings of the people in them, have deliberately declared that their adherence to the Union depended upon the preservation of that law, and that its abandonment would be the signal of the dissolution of the Union.[6] I know that the abolitionists (some of whom openly avow a desire to produce that calamitous event), and their partizans deny and deride the existence of any such danger; but men who will not perceive and own it, must be blind to the signs of the times, to the sectional strife which has unhappily arisen, to the embittered feelings which have been excited, as well as the solemn resolutions of deliberative assemblies, unanimously adopted. Their disregard of the danger, I am apprehensive, proceeds more from their desire to continue agitation, which augments it, than from their love of the Union itself.

You refer, gentlemen, to "resolutions and addresses adopted at conventions lately assembled around us, in which we have seen with regret as well as alarm, that the question of adherence to the compromise is avoided or evaded,"[7] and you justly deprecate the tendency of these resolutions. I have not been an inattentive or indifferent observer of them, and with you I deeply regret their adoption. I wish that these respectable bodies could have been less ambiguous, and more explicit, in declaring their determination to acquiesce in, and abide by, a great measure of peace and compromise, which, forming an epoch in the progress of our country, was intended to reconcile and restore concord and fraternal feelings among our divided countrymen. There was no necessity to reserve a right to discuss, to modify and to repeal the obnoxious law. Such a right existed without any express reservation, not only as to that law, but as to all laws, and as to the Constitution itself, which has incorporated in it the right of amendment, and consequently that of discussion. But there are occasions when a spirit of moderation should prompt a forbearance to exercise that right. If more were intended than meets the eye, more than to proclaim the theoretic right of discussion, if it were designed to announce the right of unremitted agitation, to continue the distractions of the country, and, finally, if possible, to repeal the fugitive slave law, patriotism and harmony must condemn the unwise course, as fraught with the most mischievous and perilous consequence.

But we must make some allowance for human frailty and inordinate pride of opinion. Many persons at the North had avowed an invincible hostility to the fugitive slave law; and even declared their intention forcibly to obstruct its execution, and had appealed to a higher law,[8] which, as they contended, was paramount to all human legislation. These untenable positions were wholly irreconcilable with patriotism, or even with the existence of regular government itself. Obeying the dictates, it is to be hoped, of wiser and purer, and more social counsels, the parties who, under the impulses of passion and fanaticism, had assumed, have now abandoned them, and acknowledged their unquestionable duty to submit to the law, until it is modified or repealed by competent authority. In descending from the high and perilous ground which they could not safely occupy, to that of conceding the obligation of submission to the law, we discern, I hope, a just homage to the dictates of civilization, and to the duties of established government. If they have coupled with this proper concession the useless reservation of a right of discussion, and of insisting upon a repeal or amendment of a law to which they had taken exception, may we not hope that their purpose was only to secure a decent retreat, with a secret and patriotic determination to forbear from disturbing that return to harmony and tranquillity, so necessary to the safety and prosperity of the Union? Should it turn out otherwise, should the reckless spirit of agitation continue to disturb and distract our country, to array section against section, and to threaten the stability of the government, my confidence is unshaken in the great body of our Northern fellow-citizens, that they will, in due time, and in a right manner, apply an appropriate and effectual corrective.

In turning our attention to the South, and to the slave-holding States, we behold enough to encourage the friends of the Union, and but little to excite solicitude and alarm. In all those States, except three, there is acquiescence in the terms of the compromise, and a firm attachment to the Union. In two of those three (Georgia[9] and Mississippi),[10] we have much reason to hope, from their known patriotism and intelligence, that the same attachment exists, on the part of large majorities of the people. At all events, those among them, of whose devotion and fidelity to the Union serious apprehensions were entertained, have been constrained, in deference to public opinion, materially to change their principles, and to go to the polls upon a new issue. They have renounced and denounced the practical right of secession at present, and taken shelter under the convenient mask of the mere abstract right. Whether this shifting of position will satisfy the people of those two States, remains to be seen. They will doubtless seriously consider, that there is but a short step between the theoretic assertion, and the practical exercise of that right; and in a contingency, neither remote nor improbable, if they affirm the right, they may be soon called upon to involve themselves in all the calamitous evils of a civil war.

South Carolina alone furnishes at present occasion for profound regret and serious apprehension, not so much for the security of the Union as for her own peace and prosperity. We are compelled, painfully and reluctantly, to yield to the force of concurring evidence, establishing that there exists in that State general dissatisfaction with, and a general desire to withdraw from, the Union; and that both parties—that which is for separate State action, and that which insists upon the necessity of the co-operation of other States—equally agree as to the expediency of secession,[11] and differ only in the degree of rashness or prudence which characterizes them respectively.

Nullification and secession have sprung from the same metaphysical school; and the latter is the ally, if not the offspring of the former. They both agree that a single State is invested with power to nullify the laws of all the other States, passed by Congress; but nullification claims a right to accomplish that object, and to remain at the same time in the Union; while secession asserts a right to attain it, by withdrawing from the Union, and absolving the State from all obligation to the Constitution and laws of the United States. They both maintain that a resort to either process is peaceful and legitimate. Nullification derived an ambiguous but contested support from the memorable resolutions of the States of Virginia and Kentucky, adopted in 1798-99;[12] but those resolutions afford no color or countenance to the pretensions of secession.

The doctrine of secession assumes, that any one of the thirty-one States composing the Union, wherever or however situated, whether in the interior or on the frontier, has a right, upon its own separate will, and according to the dictates of its exclusive judgment, to withdraw from the Union whenever it pleases; that this act of secession is peaceful, and not to be controverted or obstructed by the rest of the States, or by the application of any force, within the limits of the seceding State, to execute the laws of the United States; and that, thereupon, the State and its citizens are absolved from all obligations and duties to the United States, and become a power as independent and sovereign as any of the nations of the earth. The doctrine maintains that this right of secession may be exercised whenever the State deems it has sufficient cause; at all times—in a state of profound peace and prosperity, or in the midst of a furious war, raging in all our borders; and that, in the latter case, transforming itself into a distinct and independent nation, it may escape the calamities of war, make a separate treaty of peace with the common enemy, become neutral, or even ally itself with that enemy, and take up arms against the United States. It asserts this right, although it may lead, in process of time, to the promiscuous dotting over, upon the surface of the territory of the United States, of petty independent nations, establishing for themselves any form of government, free or despotic, known to mankind, and interrupting the intercourse and violating or menacing the execution of the laws of the dismembered confederacy. It contends for this right, as well for Louisiana as for South Carolina, although the province of Louisiana cost us so much money, and was nigh involving us in a foreign war; for Texas, although it occasioned us a war with Mexico,[13] the payment of ten millions of dollars to arrange its boundaries,[14] and to acquire it, many were willing to risk a war with England; and for distant California, although that was acquired by the double title of conquest and the payment of an ample pecuniary consideration.[15]

If, indeed, the Union, under which we have so long, and generally so happily lived, be thus fragile, and liable to crumble into pieces, we must cease to boast of the wisdom of our forefathers who formed it, tear from our hearts the sentiments of gratitude and veneration with which they had inspired us, and no longer expect an enlightened world to bestow the unbounded praise which it has hitherto lavished on them. A doctrine so extraordinary and indefensible, fraught with the destruction of the Union, and such other direful consequences, finds no encouragement or support in the Constitution of the United States. It has none under the articles of confederation which formed, in terms, a perpetual Union, however otherwise weak and inefficient the government was which they established. That inefficiency arose out of the fact, that it operated not on the people directly, but upon the States, which might, and often did, fail to comply with the requisitions made on them by Congress. To correct that defect, and to form a more *perfect* Union, the present Constitution was adopted. It had been alleged, that the Union of the States, under the articles of confederation, was held together only by a rope of sand; but it was a rope of adamant, compared with the cord which now binds us, if the right of secession is sanctioned and sustained.

The Constitution of the United States establishes a government, and, like all governments, it was to be perpetual, or to have unlimited duration. It was not restricted to the existing generation, but comprehended posterity. The preamble declares, that "We, the people of the United States, in order to form a more *perfect Union*, establish justice, ensure domestic tranquillity, provide for the common defense, promote the general welfare, and secure the blessings of liberty to ourselves and our *posterity*, do ordain and establish this Constitution for the United States of America." It makes provision expressly for the admission of new States into the Union; but from the beginning to the end of it, not a clause is to be found which gives any authority or color to the right of secession of a State once admitted into the Union.

The partisans of this novel and strange doctrine attempt to support it on two grounds: First, they contend that by an express amendment of the Constitution, as all powers not granted to the government of the United States are reserved to the States, or to the people, the power or right of secession is not granted, and that it is therefore retained by the States and the people, and may be exercised at their pleasure.

This argument is refuted by either of two sufficient answers. The contested power can not be retained, if its reservation be incompatible with the obligations of the constitutional compact. But the Constitution was intended to be perpetual, or which is the same thing, to be of unlimited existence, subject only, from time to time, to such amendments as might be made, in the mode which it specifies. It created a more *perfect Union*, which was to secure the blessings of liberty to the generation which formed it, and to their *posterity*. The obligation which each State voluntarily assumed to the other States, by being admitted into the Union, was, that it would remain perpetually bound with the other States to preserve that union, for their own benefit, and to inure to the benefit of posterity. To assert in the face of that obligation, that a State may retire from the Union whenever it pleases, is to assert that a party, bound by a solemn compact to other parties, may cancel or violate the compact whenever it thinks proper, without their consent. In order to secure respect and submission to the Union, the Constitution expressly provides, "that this Constitution, and laws of the United States which shall be made in pursuance thereof, and all treaties made, or which shall be made, under the authority of the United States, shall be the supreme law of the land; and the judges in *every* State shall be bound thereby, any thing in the Constitution or laws of any State to the contrary notwithstanding."

Thus each and every one of the States has agreed, not only that its ordinary legislation, but that its Constitution, the higher law made by the people themselves in convention, shall, in any cases of conflict, be subordinate to the paramount authority of the Constitution, laws made in pursuance thereof, and treaties of the United States. If, therefore, any State were, either in its legislature, or in a convention of delegates of the people, to declare, by the most formal act, that it had seceded from the Union, such act would be nugatory and an absolute nullity; and the people of that State would remain bound by the Constitution, laws, and treaties of the United States, as fully and perfectly as if the act had never been proclaimed.

But there is another view also, conclusive against the pretension of secession being a power reserved to the States under the amendment of the Constitution referred to. The reservation of a power implies its existence in the party reserving it, prior to such reservation. But when a State existed in its independent, separate and unassociated character, it could have had no right of secession, there being no confederacy or other party from which to secede. Secession is incident to union or confederacy, without which it can have no existence, and, unless it is clearly provided for in the compact of the Union, out of which it springs, and still more, if it be utterly irreconcilable with that compact, it can have no constitutional or legitimate foundation.

It is contended, however, in the second place, that the right of secession appertains to the States, under and in virtue of their sovereignty. This argument scorns any reliance upon the reservation of powers in the Constitution, cuts loose from all the obligations in that instrument, defies the power and authority of the general government, and finds a solution of the authority for secession in the sovereignty of the States. What that sovereignty is, it does not deign to define or explain, nor to show how one of its attributes is to disregard and violate grave compacts.

The sovereignty of the States, prior to the adoption of the present Constitution, was limited and qualified by the articles of confederation. They had agreed among themselves to create a *perpetual* Union. When, therefore, the thirteen original States passed from under those articles, to the Constitution, they passed from a less to a more perfect Union, and agreed to further limitations upon their sovereignty.

Under the present Constitution, among the limitations and prohibitions upon the sovereignty of the States, it is expressly provided, that "no State shall enter into any treaty, alliance or confederation, grant letters of marque and reprisal, coin money, emit bills of credit, make any thing but gold and silver coin a tender in payment of debts; and no State shall, without the consent of Congress, lay any duty of tonnage, keep troops or ships of war in time of peace, enter into any agreement or compact with another State, or with a foreign power, or engage in war, unless actually invaded, or in such imminent danger as will admit of no delay." It may be affirmed, with entire truth, that all the attributes of sovereignty which relate to peace and war, commerce, navigation, friendship and intercourse with, and, in short, all that relate to foreign powers, and several of those attributes which relate to the internal administration of the States themselves, are voluntarily surrendered to the general government, and can not be exercised by the States. The performance of any of the forbidden acts would be null and void, no matter in what solemn and authentic form, nor by what State authority, the legislature, a convention, or the people themselves of the State, in an aggregate mass, it might be performed. The Constitution of the United States would instantly intervene, vacate the act, and proclaim the overruling, supreme and paramount authority of the Constitution, laws and treaties of the United States.

It is clear, therefore, that no State can do any thing repugnant to the Constitution, laws and treaties of the United States. What it might do, if it were in possession of all its absolute sovereignty, and had never entered into this Union, is a different question. But if we suppose, contrary to the historical fact, that the States were absolutely sovereign, when the existing Constitution was adopted, could they circumscribe and contract their attributes of sovereignty, by the stipulations and provisions which are contained in it? All history is full of examples of the total annihilation of sovereignty or nationality, oftener by the power of the sword and conquest, but sometimes by the voluntary act of one nation, merging itself into another, of which we have a striking instance in the case of Texas, in our own country.[16] Assuming that the Constitution is a mere compact between independent nations, or sovereign States, they are, nevertheless, bound by all the obligations which the compact creates. They are bound to abstain from all forbidden acts, and to submit to the supremacy of the Constitution and laws of the United States. But, it will be asked, have they not also the right to judge of the fidelity with which the common government has adhered to the common compact? Yes, most certainly. They have that right, and so has every citizen of the United States, and so has the general government also. The alleged violation of the Constitution may be exposed and denounced by all the weapons of reason, of argument, and of ridicule; by remonstrance, protest, appeals to the judiciary, and to the other States; by the press, public opinion, and all legitimate means of persuading or influencing it. If, after the employment of all or any of these peaceful methods, the government of the United States, sustained by a constitutional majority of the nation, persist in retaining the obnoxious law, there is no alternative but obedience to the law, on the part of the minority, or open, undisguised, manly and forcible resistance to its execution.

The alleged right of secession is, I apprehend, sometimes confounded with a right of revolution. But its partizans mean a totally different thing. They contend that it is a peaceful, lawful, and, if not constitutional remedy, that it is not forbidden by the Constitution. They insist that it is a State right, to be recognized and respected; and, that whenever exercised by a State, far from being censured or condemned, the State, if necessary, is entitled to the co-operation of other States. The prudent valor of these partizans, in imitation of the previous example of the friends of nullification, disclaims the purpose of using themselves, and protest against the application to them of any physical force.

The right of revolution is that right, which an unjustly oppressed people, threatened with, or borne down by intolerable and insupportable tyranny and injustice, have, of resorting to forcible resistance, to prevent or redress the wrongs with which they are menaced, or under which they are suffering. It may aim simply at the removal of grievances, or it may seek totally to change the existing government, or to establish within its limits a new government. It is a right not confined by the boundaries of States, (although being organized political bodies, they may be capable of giving greater effect to revolutionary efforts), but it belongs to oppressed man, whatever may be his condition. In all revolutions, however, there are two parties, those who revolt, and the government which they forcibly resist. There are generally two opposite opinions also, entertained of the cause of resistance: that of those who rise in rebellion, believing themselves to be wronged, and that of the existing government, which denies having inflicted any oppression or injustice. It is incumbent upon wise and considerate men, before they hastily engage in a revolution, deliberately to consider the motives and causes of revolt, and carefully to calculate the probable consequences of forcible resistance. If unsuccessful, they know that they will be guilty of treason, and incur the penalty inflicted upon traitors.

I have thus, gentlemen, presented an imperfect sketch of some of the views which I have taken of the existing topics of the day. It would admit of much enlargement and additional illustration, but I have already given to this paper an inordinate length. In contemplating that sketch, we behold much more to animate the hopes and to encourage the patriotism of the country, than to create regret and apprehension. After such a political storm as that which violently raged during the last Congress, it was not to be expected that the nation would instantly settle down in perfect quiet and repose. Considering the vast extent of our territory, our numerous population, the heated conflicts of passion, of opinion, of interests and of sections, pervading the entire Union, we have great reason to be thankful to Providence for the degree of calmness, of tranquility, and of satisfaction, which prevails. If there are local exceptions at the North and at the South, of rash and misguided men, who would madly resist the Constitution and laws of the United States, let us not despair of their return, in seasonable time, to reason and to duty. But suppose we should be disappointed, and that the standard should be raised of open resistance to the Union, the Constitution and the laws, what is to be done? There can be but one possible answer. The power, the authority and dignity of the government ought to be maintained, and resistance put down at every hazard. Government, in the fallen and depraved state of man, would lose all respect, and fall into disgrace and contempt, if it did not possess potentially, and would not, in extreme cases, practically exercise the right of employing force. The theory of the Constitution of the United States assumes the necessity of the existence and the application of force, both in our foreign and domestic relations. Congress is expressly authorized "to raise and support armies," "to provide and maintain a navy," and "to provide for calling forth the militia, to *execute* the laws of the Union, *suppress insurrections* and repel invasions." The duty of executing the laws and suppressing insurrections, is without limitation or qualification; it is coextensive with the jurisdiction of the United States, and it comprehends every species of resistance to the execution of the laws, and every form of insurrection, no matter under what auspices or sanction it is made. Individuals, public meetings, States, may resolve, that they will forcibly oppose the execution of the laws, and secede from the Union. While these resolutions remain on paper, they are harmless; but the moment a daring hand is raised to resist, by force, the execution of the laws, the duty of enforcing them arises, and if the conflict which may ensue should lead to civil war, the resisting party, having begun it, will be responsible for all the consequences.

Since the adoption of our present Constitution, and the Union which it created, by the blessing of Providence, we have advanced in population, power, wealth, internal improvement, and national greatness, with a degree of rapidity which, unparalleled in ancient or modern nations, has excited the astonishment and commanded the admiration of mankind. Our ample limits and extensive jurisdiction, more than tripled, have been made to embrace all the provinces of Louisiana, the two Floridas, Texas and New Mexico; and passing the Rocky Mountains, have reached the Pacific Ocean, comprehending Oregon, and California, and Utah. Our population has risen from four to twenty-three millions; our revenue, without onerous burden, has grown from less than three to near fifty millions of dollars; our revolutionary debt is extinguished; our mercantile marine is not surpassed by that of the greatest maritime power; the abundant products of our agriculture, satisfy all our wants, and contribute to the subsistence of other nations; our manufactures are rapidly tending to the supply of all we essentially need from them, and to afford a surplus for the prosecution of our extended foreign commerce; the surface of our land is striped over with railroads and turnpikes, and our sea lakes and navigable waters resound with the roar of innumerable steam vessels. Your own great city illustrates our surprising progress. After the commencement of the operation of this Constitution, in 1790, its population was 33,131. By the census of 1850, it was 515,394, and our other cities have increased in scarcely a less ratio. The problem of the capacity of representative government to maintain free and liberal institutions, on an extensive territory, has been triumphantly solved by the intelligence of the people, and the all-powerful agency of steam and lightning.

Such are the gratifying results which have been obtained under the auspices of that Union, which some rash men, prompted by ambition, passion and frenzy, would seek to dissolve and subvert! To revolt against such a government, for any thing which has passed, would be so atrocious, and characterized by such extreme folly and madness, that we may search in vain for an example of it in human annals. We can look for its prototype only (if I may be pardoned the allusion) to that diabolical revolt which, recorded on the pages of Holy Writ, has been illustrated and commemorated by the sublime genius of the immortal [John] Milton.[17]

In conclusion, gentlemen, let us enjoy the proud consolation afforded by the conviction that a vast majority of the people of the United States, true to their forefathers, true to themselves, and true to posterity, are firmly and immovably attached to this Union; that they see in it a safe and sure, if not the sole guaranty of liberty, of internal peace, of prosperity, and of national happiness, progress and greatness; that its dissolution would be followed by endless wars among ourselves, by the temptation or invitation to foreign powers to take part in them, and finally, by foreign subjugation, or the establishment of despotism; and that "united we stand—divided we fall."

Copy. Printed in Colton, *Clay Correspondence*, 3:402-12. 1. Griswold *et al.* to Clay, August 5, 1851. On Oct. 3, 1851, Clay wrote Griswold *et al.* saying he had received their official letter inviting him to visit New York City and would like to accept but could not "for the reasons assigned in my answer to the address." Copy. Printed in Colton *Clay Correspondence*, 3:402. 2. Clay to Combs, Jan. 22, 1850. 3. Clay to Lathrop *et al.*, Feb. 17, 1851; Clay to Committee of Invitation, Feb. 18, 1851; Clay to Unionists of Mississippi, Sept. 20, 1851. 4. Remark in Senate, Sept. 12, 1850. 5. Remark in Senate, Feb. 17, 1851; Speech in Senate, Feb. 21 and 24, 1851. 6. Clay to Lathrop *et al.*, Feb. 17, 1851; Clay to Committee of Invitation, Feb. 18, 1851; Clay to Mercer, August 1, 1851; Clay to Unionists of Mississippi, Sept. 20, 1851. 7. Many areas of the North experienced a virtual frenzy as anti-slavery spokesmen advocated resistance to the Fugitive Slave Law. See Nevins, *Ordeal of the Union*, 1:380-81. 8. See Clay to Harlan, March 16, 1850, for William Henry Seward's "higher law" speech. 9. Clay to Committee of Invitation, Feb. 18, 1851. 10. Clay to Mercer, August 1, 1851; Clay to Unionists of Mississippi, Sept. 20, 1851. 11. Clay to Lathrop *et al.*, Feb. 17, 1851. 12. For the Kentucky and Virginia resolutions, see Morris, *Encyclopedia of American History*, 130. 13. Clay to Crittenden, Feb. 15, 1844; Clay to Lawrence, April 30, 1845. 14. Clay to Fillmore, August 10, 1850. 15. Clay to Beatty, April 29, 1847. 16. Clay to Crittenden, Feb. 15, 1844. 17. In "Paradise Lost."

To BENJAMIN COATES[1] Lexington, October 18, 1851

. . . I have thought for years that the independence of Liberia ought to be recognized by our Government, and I have frequently urged it upon persons connected with the Administration, and I shall continue to do so if I have suitable opportunities.[2] The best form of accomplishing the object would be by the conclusion of a treaty of commerce with the Republic. What has hitherto dissuaded the Executive branch of the Government from acting, I apprehend, is the repugnance which is felt at having a black man in a diplomatic character at Washington. But the recognition of the independence of the Republic does not necessarily imply the reception of a diplomatic representative. Nations not unfrequently recognize each other without the usual exchange of diplomatic representation. For the present, I believe the Rev. Mr. McLean [*sic*, William McLain] is empowered to present himself as the diplomatic representative of Liberia, and he being a white man, the objection on account of color would not exist.

I am afraid that you are too sanguine in anticipating the possibility of establishing a system of gradual emancipation of the slaves of the United States. After the failure of the experiment in Kentucky two years ago,[3] I confess I despair of obtaining the object by legal enactment. I nevertheless confidently believe that slavery will ultimately be extinguished when there shall be a great increase of our population, and a great diminution in the value of labor.

Copy. Partially printed in *Tyler's Quarterly Historical and Genealogical Magazine* (Oct., 1950), 32:95; reprinted from *National Republican*, April 28, 1862. 1. Coates (1808-87)—merchant and philanthropist—was active in both the Pennsylvania Abolition Society and the American Colonization Society. Johnson, *Twentieth Century Biographical Dictionary*. 2. Remark in Senate, Jan. 7, 1850. 3. Stevenson to Clay, June 12, 1848; Clay to Pindell, Feb. 17, 1849, no. 2 of date.

To BENJAMIN COATES Lexington, October 20, 1851

I received your favor of the 14th inst transmitting some letters from President [Joseph J.] Roberts for my perusal, I have taken great pleasure in reading them, and they show him to be a man of excellent sense and good capacity.

I return them herewith according to your request,[1] I had previously written to you expressing my regret that I did not feel at liberty to sign the address to the Legislature of Liberia on the subject of the testimony which you suggested to the memory of Governor [Thomas] Buchanan,[2]

I am extremely desirous, as stated in that letter that the independence of the Republic of Liberia should be recognised by our Government, and I will do all in my power to promote that object.[3] But I am only an individual possessed of no authority to decide the question, which can only be determined by our own Government.

Copy. DLC-John J. Crittenden Papers (DNA, M212, R20). Addressed to Coates at Philadelphia. Partially printed in *Tyler's Quarterly Historical and Genealogical Magazine* (Oct., 1950), 32:95; reprinted from *National Republican*, April 28, 1862. 1. Enclosures not found. 2. Buchanan was the first governor of the Commonwealth of Liberia when it was proclaimed in 1839. He died of a fever in 1841. Staudenraus, *The African Colonization Movement*, 241. See Clay to Coates, Oct. 18, 1851; however, the portion referring to Buchanan was omitted in *Tyler's Quarterly* and the *National Republican*. 3. Remark in Senate, Jan. 7, 1850.

From William McLain, Washington, D.C., October 23, 1851. Urges Clay not to answer any letter he may receive from "Mr. A. McCaslin of S.C." concerning "some slaves left for Liberia by a Miss Robinson." Notes that "His desire is to get something from the Col[onization]. Soc[iet]y which will help him break the will. I will thank you to send me the letter, that I may show a Copy of it to our Council [*sic*, counsel] in the case." Adds: "Our Cause is gaining fame in all parts of the Country." ALS. DLC-Records of the American Colonization Society (DNA, M212, R20).

McCaslin was probably planning to use an act passed by the South Carolina legislature in 1841 which "made void all bequests, deeds or trusts of slaves made with the stipulation that they be removed from the state and emancipated." H.M. Henry, *The Police Control of the Slave in South Carolina . . .* (New York, 1914), 173.

To LUCRETIA ERWIN COWLES Lexington, October 24, 1851

Mr. [James O.] Harrison informed me today that Mr. Higgins[1] proposed to give Two Thousand dollars cash for your interest in the land which he purchased of your Father [James Erwin], to which you and your brothers [Henry Clay, Andrew Eugene, and Charles Edward Erwin] are entitled.[2] I think it is worth more than that, but as you would have to go through a law suit, and finally when you recovered it, to sell it upon instalments, I think it would be better for you to accept Mr. Higgins s offer, if Mr. [Frederic] Cowles thinks he can make more use out of $2000.00 in hand, than by awaiting the event of the suit, and ultimately getting a larger amount. I shall advise Mr. Harrison to send you a deed, to be executed by you and Mr. Cowles, if you think proper to accept Mr. Higgins s offer.

There is some difficulty about ascertaining the amount of what is due to yourself and your brothers from your fathers estate. I had hoped and believed that it was not less than $52,000.00 and upwards with interest, but some doubt arises from the transactions of your father, before the Courts in New Orleans. I have written to Mr. G[ustavus]. Schmidt, a lawyer in whom I have confidence in that City, to investigate the matter, and to report to me. But I would advise Mr Cowles to come by New Orleans in January next, and see and consult Mr. Schmidt about the matter, and to be here at the Court in February, when I hope an order will be obtained to sell the Woodlands and other property.[3] If I should go to Washington, as I wish to do, the presence of Mr. Cowles at Lexington may be very necessary. I apprehend that Mrs. [Margaret Johnson] Erwin and her father [Henry Johnson], may interpose all the difficulties in the way which they can. It would be very advisable to obtain a sale of the property at New Orleans, which is bound, to secure to yourself and your brothers what is due, devised from your mothers [Anne Brown Clay Erwin] estate. Your brother Henry may be there, but how far he may co operate with you I am not able to say. If the property there, is not sold, an objection may arise to the sale of that which is here, until that in New Orleans is disposed of. Your husband, if he goes there would do well to consult with both Mr. Schmidt, and W[illia]m. C C Claiborne [Jr.]. My own opinion is that you and your brothers are entitled to the $50 000.00 odd thousand dollars with interest, but the case is not free from difficulties.[4]

We are all well except myself.

LS. ICH. 1. Probably Richard Higgins. 2. Clay to Lucretia H. Clay, Dec. 26, 1850; Clay to Erwin, July 19 and Sept. 14, 1851; Clay to Cowles, Sept. 14, 1851. 3. Clay to Erwin, July 19, 1851. 4. Schmidt to Clay, Dec. 13, 1851.

To HENRY CLAY, JR. [III] Lexington, October 26, 1851

I received your letter,[1] which I was glad to get, as I was to learn that you are better satisfied this year than you were the last with the [U.S. Military] Academy. But I was alarmed yesterday on reading the enclosed letter from Genl [Joseph G.] Totten.[2] 45 marks of demerit in one month! 88 since the commencement of this Academic year! Why at that rate you will soon be dismissed.[3] My dear Grand child, I do hope that you will be more particular in your conduct. I should feel that your dismissal would disgrace both you and me. Your pride as a man and as a soldier ought to prompt you to comply with the regulations of the institution. I think you cannot be aware of the marks against you. We are all well here but myself. My health continues feeble.

Your uncle James [Brown Clay] and his family are still with us; but they go monday next to St Louis where they mean to live.[4]

All here join me in love to you.

ALS. Henry Clay Memorial Foundation, Lexington, Ky. 1. Not found. 2. Enclosure not found. For Brig. Gen. Totten, see *HRDUSA*, 966. 3. Clay to Morehead, Dec. 14, 1848. 4. Clay to James B. Clay, Dec. 23, 1850.

To LUCRETIA HART CLAY Louisville, October 31, 1851

I came from Ashland on monday to this City without stopping at Frankfort, and bore the journey with less fatigue than I had feared. Dr [William N.] Mercer is expected here tonight or tomorrow evening and I shall wait to see him. I do not expect therefore to reach home until sunday or monday[.] The change of weather prevented I suppose the killing of any hogs at Ashland; and I think you had better purchase some bacon to last a few days.

James [Brown Clay] and his family are well. He will go next week to St. Louis,[1] leaving Susan [Jacob Clay] and the children here a fortnight longer, in consequence of Mr. Jacobs [John J. Jacob] ill health.[2] He is quite feeble and confined to his house.

I have directed the purchase of some Buck wheat flour, if it can be had.
All are well at Mr [Thomas] Smiths[.]
My love to John [Morrison Clay].

AL, signature removed. DLC-TJC (DNA, M212, R11). 1. Clay to James B. Clay, Dec. 23, 1850. 2. John J. Jacob died on April 1, 1852. Armstrong, *Biographical Encyclopedia of Kentucky*, 321.

To J.D.H. Lexington, November, 1851

My political life is ended; but I wish once more, and for the last time, to visit Washington;—and yet, I hesitate, for I do not like to go there to be *brought* back!

Copy, extract. Printed in the Cherry Valley (N.Y.) *Gazette*, July 7, 1852.

To Dr. JAMES A. BENNET[1] Lexington, November 1,[2] 1851

I recd. and thank you for your friendly letter.[3] I should be happy if I have committed but one error in my public course in the Senate, as suggested by you. In regard to the signers of the Address to me from New York,[4] which I recently answered,[5] I knew many of them, and they I knew to be patriots and men of honor. With the major portion of them I was unacquainted. I know nothing of collisions, jealousies and enmities between them and other Citizens of N. York, and, if I did, I would not take any part in them. Are you sure that I could address any Citizen of that City, without exciting feeling in some other of its large population, if it were known? I indulge no thought or wish, not the remotest, of ever again consenting to the use of my name, in connection with the Presidential office; but I am thankful for what you kindly say on that subject.

I shall look with interest for the work on political economy, to which you refer.[6]

ALS. ICH. 1. Dr. Bennet, a native of Ireland, was both a doctor and a lawyer in New York City. Beach, *The Wealth and Biography of the Wealthy Citizens of the City of New York*, 4. 2. Only the "1" is now visible on the day's date; however, since Clay wrote this letter in Lexington and he was in Louisville on Nov. 1, another number probably followed it originally. All his other letters written during the period Oct. 31 to Nov. 2 are headed "Louisville." 3. Not found. 4. Griswold *et al.* to Clay, August 5, 1851. 5. Clay to Fellow-Citizens of New York City, Oct. 3, 1851. 6. Possibly Bennet's book *The American System of Practical Book-Keeping, Adapted to the Commerce of the United States, in its Domestic and Foreign Relations; Comprehending all the Modern Improvements in the Practice of the Art* . . . (New York, 1820).

To WILLIAM N. MERCER Louisville, November 2, 1851

I have remained here two days longer than I intended when I left home for the sole purpose of seeing you; but as your arrival is uncertain, and as my presence at Ashland is necessary, I am compelled to return without having that satisfaction.

I wished much to see you, and yet I must own that, after the recent terrible event, I was, on my own account and your's, almost afraid of the interview.[1] I rejoice however to hear from Mr. Jackson and from Mrs. Duncan[2] that you bear generally your great affliction better than I apprehended you would. I heard of it, through Gallaghane's Messenger in less than three weeks after it had occurred. I desired much to address you on the melancholy occasion, but I did not know where to direct a letter. About ten days ago I forwarded a letter for you under cover to Mr. [William St. John] Elliot.[3]

My wish was to express my own feelings and profound sympathy, rather than to attempt to offer any topics of consolation. These I well knew you could only find in your own reason, philosophy and religion, and in the lapse of time. May god grant you fortitude and strength to sustain yourself, and to preserve you for your friends! I expect to start for Washington in about twelve days, although my health is far from being good.

Present my affectionate respects to Miss [Eliza] Young . . .

ALS. LU-Ar. 1. Reference is to the death of Mercer's daughter Anna. See Clay to Mercer, Nov. 14, 1846. 2. Probably Catherine Bingaman (Mrs. Stephen) Duncan. Mr. Jackson has not been identified. 3. Not found.

To JAMES BROWN CLAY Lexington, November 5, 1851

I got home on monday,[1] but was thrown into the night and took a bad cold. All well here and at Mansfield.

The Bank yesterday discounted our note payable the first of May next.

If (as I still think) I shall go to Washn. I shall leave home the 15h. inst.[2]

ALS. DLC-TJC (DNA, M212, R11). 1. That is, he arrived in Lexington from Louisville on Nov. 3. 2. Clay left home on Nov. 15 and reached Maysville, Ky., on Nov. 16. On the evening of the 16th he left Maysville by boat. He arrived at Pittsburgh, Pa., on Nov. 19 and left that same day for Cumberland, Md., by way of West Newton, Pa. He reached Washington on Nov. 23. See Clay to Lucretia H. Clay, Nov. 16, 19, and 23, 1851; Clay to LeVert, Nov. 14, 1851.

To HENRY GRINNELL Lexington, November 5, 1851

I received your two letters respecting the efforts which you and other gentlemen have so generously made to relieve the wants of Father [Theobald] Mathew.[1] I regret extremely that they have not been more successful, and I lament the influence of those religious prejudices which interpose obstacles in their accomplishment. If he were a Mahometan, and had done as much good to mankind as he has, he should have my sympathy and my succor. There is not, I believe, the slightest foundation for the assumption that contributions to him are to enure to the benefit of the Catholic Church. If there were why have not the Catholics come forward to assist him with more zeal and promptness than they have done? All religions are interested in the cause of temperance; and I had hoped that all would have cordially united in testifying their sense of the great merits of him who, under the smiles of Providence, has done most to promote and advance it.

Whatever may be the final issue of the experiment to relieve the good father, you, and the gentlemen associated with you, have nobly responded to the appeal made to you.

ALS. Courtesy of Dr. Thomas D. Clark, Lexington, Ky. 1. Not found, but see Clay to Grinnell, May 28, 1851, and Clay to Corcoran, Sept. 14, 1851.

From Cornelius R. Mahony, New York City, November 8, 1851. Extends his "most grateful thanks . . . for your noble appeal on behalf of our dear Father [Theobald] Mathew [Clay to Grinnell, May 28, 1851]." Regrets that "the demon of religious Bigotry had been invoked . . . too successfully, to defeat your benevolent intentions." Sends "a Copy of 'The Journal of Commerce [not found],' and a Number of 'The Herald [not found],' in which you will find a refutation of the base slander with which our dear friend was assailed, yet the poison (as is mostly the case,) circulated where the Antidote will never reach." Asks for "an *autograph* letter accepting the dedication of my forthcoming work," which he will treasure "as an heirloom, to be transmitted to my posterity." ALS. DLC-TJC (DNA, M212, R11).

Mahony's forthcoming work has not been identified; however, he had published in Dublin, Ireland, in 1846 *Everyman His Own Landlord*. . . . Although the number of the New York *Herald* refuting a slander against Father Mathew has not been found, the *Herald* ran many articles supporting the relief activities being carried out on his behalf. For example, see New York *Herald*, September 25 and 29, October 1, 23, and 25, November 4, 1851.

To WILLIAM CAMPBELL[1] Lexington, November 13, 1851

I received your favor,[2] with the accompanying copy of the [Washington *Daily*] Nat[ional]. Intell[ingence]r. containing the communication signed Uncle Peter, which I have perused with much interest. The story of the African Funty Munty,[3] formerly a slave of Genl. [George] Washington, is well told, and cannot be read without much sympathy for the poor old negro. Whether, as you suggest, a pension could be obtained for him or not, from Congress, I am not able to say. Generally, in the grant of pensions, that body has acted on principles or rules none of which would include Funtys case; but they have some times departed from them. The two facts which could be urged in his behalf are his great age and that he once belonged to Genl Washington. It would aid his application, I think, if he could shew that he ever attended the General in any of his military campaigns.

If a petition should be presented, it should be accompanied by the proofs on which it depends, in the form of affidavits &c. I will present it with pleasure, if after what I have said, you think it worth while.[4]

ALS. PHi. 1. Campbell, a Quaker, owned the house in Fayette County, Pa., which Funty Munty had helped build for George Washington in 1774. Washington *Daily National Intelligencer*, Oct. 17, 1851. 2. Not found. 3. The article on Oct. 17 in the *Intelligencer* explained that Funty Munty, born in 1753 in Upper Guinea, had been captured in 1767 and brought to the U.S. He was purchased directly by George Washington and became his house servant. Washington sold him in 1784 and his third owner eventually set him free and gave him an acre of land located a mile from Cookstown, Pa., on the Monongahela River. 4. No such petition has been found.

To ROBERT TRIPLETT[1] Lexington, November 13, 1851

I received your two favors, with the essay which you have prepared on the subject of an amendment of the Constitution of the United States.[2] I will take it with me to Washington, and give it a consideration corresponding with the importance of the object, and my high respect for you. But I can hardly hold out the expectation, with any certainty of my moving in the matter, owing to the state of my health. It has been delicate throughout the present summer, and, although somewhat improved, remains in such a state as to have made me seriously hesitate about returning to Washington. Unless it should improve much more, I shall be unfit for much labor.

Copy. Printed in Robert Triplett, *Roland Trevor: Or, the Pilot of Human Life* (Philadelphia, 1853), 302-3. 1. For Triplett, who used the pseudonym Roland Trevor, see 2:237-38. 2. Letters not found. Triplett wanted an amendment which would abolish the office of president and substitute for it a 5-member national council chosen by certain states selected in a drawing weighted by the number of electoral votes of each state. Triplett, *Roland Trevor*, 303-16.

To Leslie Combs, November 14, 1851. Informs Combs that "I concluded to take with me to Washn. the Texas bonds deposited with the N[orthern]. Bank [of Kentucky] as indemnity for our liability for you." Does not want to "put them beyond our control, so as to deprive us of the security which they may afford, nor to impair our right to sell them" while in Washington. "If . . . Cochran [*sic*, Corcoran] & Riggs would advance and pay to me, on their faith, Ten thousand dollars, I would immediately remit it to the N. Bank to be applied to the debt for which we are bound, and hand over the bonds to them, if you desire it." ALS. KyU. Endorsed by Combs: "From H. Clay. Rd & ansd as desired. Nov. 16/51." See Clay to Combs, January 22, 1850.

To OCTAVIA WALTON LeVERT Lexington, November 14, 1851

I should long ago, my beloved friend, have written to you and acknowledged the receipt of your obliging favor of the 2d Septr if I had had any thing agreeable to you or to myself to communicate. But I have been rusticating here all the summer and fall struggling with precarious and delicate health, and not certain of the final issue. I am still debilitated, and with much hesitation purpose starting tomorrow for Washn.[1] I write now more for the purpose of keeping myself in your friendly recollection, and to assure you of my unabated regard than to transmit any thing interesting.

I am delighted to hear of your being safely established in your beautiful mansion. If I am ever permitted again to visit Mobile, I shall eagerly look out for the apartment, which your kindness has allotted to me.

Well, will you believe it? I have not yet been able to lay my hands on the book of your friend Lady Emmaline.[2] It has not reached our remote quarter. I promise myself a great treat from the perusal of it this winter, altho' I observe that some of our fastidious critics condemn its praise of America as much as they did the censures which we received from other Travellers. They are hard to please and satisfy.

With you I deprecate the cold-blooded massacre of our Country-men at Cuba, altho' their engagement in the [Narciso] Lopez Expedition was highly culpable.[3] It is not yet time for us to get Cuba. It will come to us in due season if we are wise, prudent and united.

My affectionate regards to the Dr. [Henry LeVert], to your dear children and to your father and mother [George & Sally Walker Walton].

Poor Anna Mercer! does not your heart bleed as mine does for her death. The Dr. [William N. Mercer] her father is inconsolable, and I fear will never recover from the terrible shock.[4]

ALS. NBuHi. 1. Clay to James B. Clay, Nov. 5, 1851. 2. Lady Emmeline Stuart-Wortley, daughter of the Duke of Rutland and widow of Stuart Wortley, had travelled through the United States, Mexico, and Canada and had written a book entitled *Travels in the United States, etc. During 1849 and 1850* (London, 1851). See New York *Herald*, Sept. 17, 1850, which contains an excerpt. The *Herald* gives her 1st name as Emmeline while Clay gives it as Emmaline. 3. Clay to Mercer, August 1, 1851. 4. Clay to Mercer, Nov. 14, 1846, and Nov. 2, 1851.

To LUCRETIA HART CLAY Maysville, Ky., November 16, 1851

I got here[1] safely about 4 O'Clock this afternoon, with good weather, and no other inconvenience than my bowel complaint, which was not so bad to day as it was yesterday. I shall be able to get up in a small boat, which Mr. Bryan[2] has Telegraphed me from Cincinnati will be here at 6, that is I expect 9 Oclock this evening.

Tell John [Morrison Clay] that most of the Hemp I saw on the road was spread down, and I think half at least of ours had better be put down pretty soon—

If the Warfield cow is *not* in calf, she must be fat and had better be sold to the Butcher.

Thornton[3] ought to get home by dinner time tuesday.

My love to John [Morrison Clay] & Mary Watkins[.][4]

AL, signature removed. DLC-TJC (DNA, M212, R11). 1. For an itinerary of Clay's trip to Washington, see Clay to James B. Clay, Nov. 5, 1851. 2. Probably Edwin Bryant of New York City. Clay spells it "Bryant" rather than "Bryan" in Clay to Lucretia H. Clay, Nov. 19 and Nov. 23, 1851. 3. Probably a slave or hired servant who had accompanied Clay to the river. 4. Clay refers to Mary Watkins as a cousin of John Morrison Clay in Clay to John M. Clay, Feb. 28, 1852. She was most likely a daughter of Clay's half-brother John Watkins; however, she does not appear in Watkins genealogies.

From James G. Blaine, Drennon Springs, Ky., November 17, 1851. Writing from the Western Military Institute, informs Clay that for four years "I have held a chair in this Institution but intend resigning next month, with the view of settling in the South & practising the Profession of Law." Hopes it will not be "presumptive in me to request from you a letter of introduction to some one of your countless friends in the South," especially those "in Natchez or New Orleans." Assures Clay "that I do not make this request with the mere selfish view of obtaining any direct advantage . . . but I earnestly desire in time to come to have some momento of the 'Patriot Statesman,' whom from my earliest years, I have been taught to honor & reverence." ALS. DLC-HC (DNA, M212, R6).

Blaine (1830-93)—Speaker of the House, U.S. senator, secretary of state, and 1884 Republican presidential nominee—resigned from the Western Military Institute in 1852. *DAB*.

From LUCRETIA ERWIN COWLES Gainstown, Ala.,[1]
November 17, 1851

I received by last Monday's mail your very welcome letter accompanied by one for Mr. [Frederic] Cowles from Mr Ja[me]s. O. Harrison,[2] relative to the disposition of the Higgin's land.[3] We have in concert this day executed a deed according to your advice,[4] which will be forwarded to Mr. Harrison together with this in the same mail—Mr Cowles will go to New Orleans in January, at which time he will confer with Mr. [Gustavus] Schmidt according to your directions, it is his intention to dispose of the property in that City at the earliest period practicable. He would be glad for the cooperation of Brother Henry [Clay Erwin] in the sale, but, if upon being advised of it, he chooses to withhold it Mr. Cowles will proceed to sell, my share under an order of court, or if a division cannot be made, the whole property will be sold. By a letter received from Henry a short time since we are informed that should a sale be effected at present the property would not bring its full value, and that a good title cannot be given by us until the arrival of [Andrew] Eugene [Erwin] & [Charles] Edward [Erwin] at full majority[.] Mr. C____ however differs in opinion, and thinks there is no question of good titles being given & a sale effected. Henry adds that he is endeavoring to collect debts on the Real Estate and thereby, pay Dr. [James] Ritchie's claim and prevent the sacrifice of the Texas Lands, which it seems there is a great probability of our losing.

I wrote to GrandMa [Lucretia Hart Clay] by last mail—assure her of my continued good health—We regret much to hear of your protracted indisposition and trust that it may prove nothing serious.

Your acquaintances around us are enjoying good health—Col Darrington & Lady desire to be particularly remembered to you. Mr. Cowles writes in kind regards to yourself, Grand-Ma family and all enquiring friends—

We shall be most happy to hear from you at any time . . .

ALS. DLC-TJC (DNA, M212, R14). 1. Gainstown, Ala., was a post-village of Clarke County on the Alabama River sixty miles NNE of Mobile. *Lippincott's Gazetteer of the World* (Philadelphia, 1922), 692. 2. Not found. 3. Clay to Lucretia E. Cowles, Oct. 24, 1851. 4. Not found, but on May 2, 1851, Frederic and Lucretia Cowles had by legal document named James O. Harrison as their attorney "to ask, demand and receive from James Erwin and Andrew Erwin . . . such part of the estate of Anne B. Erwin deceased as the said Lucretia is by law entitled to." Witnessed by Henry Clay and Susan Jacob Clay. DS. DLC-James O. Harrison Papers (DNA, M212, R21).

To LUCRETIA HART CLAY Pittsburgh, November 19, 1851

I arrived here this morning at eleven O'Clock.[1] Mr. [Edwin] Bryant met me, as he had promised, in a Stern wheel boat, and we ascended the river as comfortably as could be, in a small boat and with a large crowd of passengers. Fortunately the weather has been good during the whole voyage, and we met with no accidents. I have borne the journey so far as well as I could have expected, but as usual I have caught a cold this morning[.] I spit up more blood than I have done for many weeks. I hope the Alum water will relieve me.

Mr. Bryant has been very kind and attentive. We leave here this afternoon, by a new route, going up the Monongaheld [*sic*, Monongahela] and up the Youghioghany [*sic*, Youghiogheny] by Steamboat to West Newton [Pennsylvania], and thence to Cumberland [Maryland] by a Turnpike and plank road. We thus avoid the Cumberland road, and we are promised to be put down at the town of Cumberland by 6 O'Clock tomorrow evening[.]

My love to Thomas [Hart Clay] and family, John [Morrison Clay] and Mary Watkins[.]

ALS. DLC-TJC (DNA, M212, R11). 1. For an itinerary of Clay's trip to Washington, see Clay to James B. Clay, Nov. 5, 1851.

To LUCRETIA HART CLAY Washington, November 23, 1851

I arrived here last night from Cumberland [Maryland], which I left on yesterday (saturday) morning.[1] We reached that place on thursday night, after the most fatiguing day of my journey, during which we passed the mountains in a snow storm. I thought it best to remain friday at Cumberland to recruit, and accordingly did so. Upon the whole, I have borne the journey as well as I could expect; but I am sorry to say that I experience no improvement in my cough, which has probably been increased by cold. Mr. [Edwin] Bryant remained with me all the time, slept in Cumberland with me, and has been very kind and attentive to me throughout the whole journey. He left me this afternoon, and expects to leave New York for California the 26th. inst.

I have stopped at the Nat[ional]. Hotel (Gadsbys old stand) where I remained last Congress. Whether I shall remain here or go to a private boarding house will depend on the state of my health. I have remained indoors all this day, and have seen but few persons, and heard no news.

My love to John [Morrison Clay], Thomas [Hart Clay] & family & Mary Watkins.

ALS. DLC-TJC (DNA, M212, R11). 1. For an itinerary of Clay's trip to Washington, see Clay to James B. Clay, Nov. 5, 1851.

From Jared S. Dawson, Bellefontaine, Ohio, November 23, 1851. Encloses "a statement of our account, the best I can make out" since his memorandum book "must have been taken out of my pocket or state room on a steam boat between St Louis & Louisville Ky." Hopes "this account will be satisfactory to you although I had thought I was entitled to a receipt of about $200. which I cannot find." ALS, copy. DLC-TJC (DNA, M212, R14).

The account, dated November, 1851, indicates "a balance in my hands of $184.73" with a "*Balance due* on *notes* in my *hands*" for Clay of $782.00. D. *Ibid.*

To LUCRETIA HART CLAY Washington, December 1, 1851

I received a letter from John [Morrison Clay] on the very day but after I had written to him,[1] in which he informs me of what had occurred at Ashland subsequent to my departure from home. He tells me that no letter had been received from Mr. [Jared] Dawson at Bellefontaine.[2] Fearing that you might be in want of Cash, I now enclose a check for $150 which I have made payable to John, and which he can cash at Lexington, and which you can apply to any wants at Ashland.

The Gardner had behaved so well up to the time of my leaving home, that I was very sorry to learn that he had so misconducted himself as to oblige you to dismiss him; and I wish if you could meet with another good one that you would employ him. I am afraid that you will miss one very much.

My health continues as it was without any material improvement. Nevertheless I attended the Senate today, and even made a short speech;[3] but I returned very weak. Dr [William W.] Hall, a good physician, is attending me.[4]

If I get about Xmas my money from Illinois,[5] I shall have plenty; but if I am disappointed in that, and also in that from Bellefontaine, I will send you from time to time out of my pay. My love to John and all at Mansfield and to Mary Watkins.

ALS. DLC-TJC (DNA, M212, R11). 1. Neither letter found. 2. Dawson to Clay, Nov. 23, 1851; Clay to John M. Clay, Dec. 3, 1851. 3. Remark in Senate, Dec. 1, 1851. 4. William W. Hall (1810-76) was a specialist in diseases of the throat and lungs. *DAB*. 5. Clay's Illinois land had been sold to the Hunters. See Clay to John Hunter, Feb. 4, 1852; Memo, late June, 1852.

Remark in Senate, December 1, 1851. Sen. Jackson Morton presents the credentials of Stephen R. Mallory and of David L. Yulee, both of whom claim to have been elected to the U.S. Senate from Florida. Mallory's credentials had been signed by the governor of Florida and Yulee's, which included proceedings of the joint meeting of the Florida legislature, had been signed by the secretary of state of Florida. After the chair rules that "It is . . . a proper subject for the Senate to decide, as to whether they will admit either gentleman previous to an investigation by a committee, or exclude both until after an investigation," Sen. Jesse D. Bright moves to submit the credentials of both men, along with extracts from the journals of the Florida legislature, to a Select committee.

Clay rises to oppose Bright's motion, saying that "the case is perfectly clear, according to the usage existing in every deliberative body of which I have any knowledge. Mr. Mallory comes here with a credential in due form, affording *prima facie* evidence of his right to the seat which he claims." Contends that the "proceedings behind the credentials which took place in the legislative body" of Florida "could only be legitimately offered at the time when the gentleman contesting the seat of Mr. Mallory should choose to present a petition claiming that seat." But for the motion of Sen. Bright, "I should move at once that the oath of office be administered to Mr. Mallory."

Debate continues on the proper procedure for the Senate in deciding this issue. Clay rises again to say: "Feeble as I am, I cannot refrain from making a few additional observations." Argues that it is "the duty and right of this body to determine all questions of elections of its members. The question is as to the method of doing this." Outlines the method: "the party having the return takes the seat, and the other party presents his petition claiming it; that petition is referred to a committee; it is reported upon by the committee and acted upon by the body."

Disputes the argument made earlier by Sen. William H. Seward that each candidate has presented *prima facie* evidence of election. Contends, rather, that the legislative journal presented by Yulee is not a valid credential; instead, "The only evidence of any election which we have, is the certificate of the Governor." Discusses the appropriate time to consider the validity of an election, reiterating that it is only after the oath has been administered to the one "having in his pocket the return." Then, "let him who contests the seat come forward . . . and claim it." Nevertheless, points out that "if you go into the journal of the Legislature of Florida, which I think is entirely out of order and informal, it proves there was no election [of Yulee] in the first instance, and therefore no credentials. . . . The Legislature afterwards proceeded to make an election; and the Governor has given the certificate of it. The only question . . . is whether you will overrule the decision of the Legislature, and declare, contrary to their judgment, that an election was made of Mr. Yulee, when they declared that there was no election, and proceeded to elect."

Eventually, Bright withdraws his motion, and Clay moves that Mallory be sworn in. The motion is approved. *Cong. Globe*, 32 Cong., 1 Sess., 2, 4.

Stephen R. Mallory (Dem.), subsequently Confederate secretary of the navy, retained the seat in the Senate over Yulee's challenge. *BDAC*.

This day marked Clay's final appearance in the U.S. Senate.

To JOHN MORRISON CLAY Washington, December 3, 1851

The day on which I last wrote you, I recd your first letter, and I have this day recd. yours of the 27th. Ultimo transmitting a copy of Mr. [Jared] Dawson's letter and a copy of his a/c.[1] He has made two wrong charges against me, one of $250 which I never I think recd. and the other a charge of commissions on money not yet collected. Be pleased to take care of his letter and a/c. I wrote to your mother [Lucretia Hart Clay] the day before yesterday, and enclosed to her a check for $150 on N. York made payable to your order.[2]

If when you make your last killing of hogs, you could buy butchered 9 or 10 in the market, weighing from 160 to 180 lb, it might be well enough to buy them. Otherwise we can buy bacon in the Spring.

There is no essential improvement in my health. I attended the Senate on the first day,[3] which was fine, but did not yesterday or to day, because it is very blustering.

It was very well to get rid of wintering the old brown mare. My love to your Mama, Mary [Mentelle Clay] & Thomas [Hart Clay] & his family.

ALS. Josephine Simpson Collection, Lexington, Ky. 1. Neither Clay's nor John M. Clay's letter found, but see Dawson to Clay, Nov. 23, 1851. See also Clay to Dawson, April 18, 1849. 2. Clay to Lucretia H. Clay, Dec. 1, 1851. 3. Remark in Senate, Dec. 1, 1851.

To JAMES BROWN CLAY Washington, December 6, 1851

I have not heard from or of you, or Susan [Jacob Clay] or the children since I parted from you at Louisville; and they write me from Ashland that nothing has been heard from you. I suppose that on the rise of the Ohio Susan and your children joined you at St. Louis; and I hope all are well in your house.

I passed the Mountains[1] with as little fatigue & discomfort as I could expect; but since my arrival here on the 22d Ulto. my strength, my flesh, and my appetite have continued to decline, and I feel weaker than I did when I left home. I regret now that I ever left it at all, and my utmost wish is to live to return.

Mr. [Daniel] Webster shortly after my arrival here called to see me, and very soon launched out in praises of you, your ability, and capacity for business &c.[2] He inquired for your post office as if he wished to write to you. I told him that you had removed to the neighborhood of St. Louis; built yourself a comfortable dwelling house, and that I believed you had not much ambition. You will be able to appreciate these remarks of Mr. W.

My love to Susan and all the children.

ALS. DLC-TJC (DNA, M212, R11). 1. Clay to James B. Clay, Nov. 5, 1851. 2. Clay to Clayton, June 7, 1849; Clay to James B. Clay, August 31 and Oct. 18, 1850.

To LUCRETIA HART CLAY Washington, December 9, 1851

After my attendance on the Senate the first day,[1] I thought it best to remain at my lodgings, and I have not been there since; but I rode out two or three good days. My cough has been worse here than it was before I left home. It has been better however within the two or three last days. I should feel more encouraged, if it were not for the loss of my flesh and strength. I have determined to go out to no dinners, and declined one to the Presidents [Millard Fillmore] this week.[2] He called to see me last evening,[3] and a great deal of kindness is shown to me here.

I beg that you will not allow yourself to be alarmed by any reports or rumors that may reach you as to my health. I will try to keep you informed as to my actual condition by letter or by Telegraph. This day being very fine I have just returned from a drive of six or seven miles in a close carriage.

I recd. a letter today forwarded by John [Morrison Clay] from Lucretia [Erwin Cowles].[4]

I write with great difficulty. My love to John [Morrison Clay] & Mary [Watkins].

ALS. DLC-HC (DNA, M212, R6). 1. Remark in Senate, Dec. 1, 1851. 2. Clay wrote President Fillmore on Dec. 7, 1851, expressing "his sincere regrets that he cannot have the honor of accepting his invitation to dinner," and citing his "feeble state of health" as the reason. ALS. MB. 3. Defying the rules of etiquette, President Fillmore called on Clay at the National Hotel at least three times in the ensuing months. Rayback, *Millard Fillmore*, 350. 4. Possibly Cowles to Clay, Nov. 17, 1851.

To George Washington Anderson, Louisville, December 11, 1851. Questions the practicality of Anderson's proposal to sell "the house and lot in Louisville, held in trust for the benefit of your wife &c and to vest the proceeds in a farm of Genl,

[Charles Fenton] Mercer at the mouth of the Kentucky, to be held in similar trust." As a trustee of the will of Thomas Hart [3:117-18], "by which the Trust property has been secured" to Anderson's wife Eleanor Hart Anderson and her children, wants to "be better satisfied than I am that the conversion of the house and lot into the farm would be advisable. Suppose you were to die, leaving Eleanor on the farm, what could she do there? What could you do, without hands to work it? Hiring would be of very doubtful profit." Adds that "You have no friend who has felt more for you than I have. . . . If I can not now comply with your request, it is because of duties to others." ALS. KyU.

From Gustavus Schmidt, New Orleans, December 13, 1851. Although he has "employed every leisure moment . . . to obtain such information as would enable you to defend the rights of your grand children," regrets that "my efforts have not been so successful as I hoped, owing chiefly to the complicated nature of the transactions of the late Mr. James Erwin [Clay to Erwin, July 19, 1851], the various means employed by him, at different periods, to conceal his fortune, or to give himself the appearance of a man of wealth, according to his advantage to represent himself to the world in one or other of those aspects." Explains that before his wife's [Anne Brown Clay Erwin] death "in 1836 [*sic*, 1835; see 8:808-9]. . . . Mr E was . . . generally esteemed as a man of wealth, enjoyed extensive credit, and was regarded as a shrewd business man" and was "prompt and honorable in fulfilling . . . his obligations." Still, during that time, "Mr E bought a great deal of property in the name of other persons. . . . to enable him to dispose of it without requiring the renunciation of his wife" and "to enable him to buy property without giving any endorser on his notes, the agent he employed being the ostensible purchaser, & Mr Erwin, whose solvency was undoubted, being the endorser."

When his wife died, "one half of the property owned by Erwin vested absolutely in his children as heirs of their mother," and "a new relation was created between him and his children, which until distinctly ascertained and determined, would greatly embarrass his speculations." Readily available evidence proves indisputably that Erwin "owes his children $37000 with 5 pr. ct interest from the year 1836." Questions remain about "other property, acquired during the lifetime of their mother and of which they, as her heirs are entitled to claim the half." The chief difficulties concern "ascertaining the amount of property so bought by Erwin prior to the death of his wife" and "finding out who now holds said property." Fears that "only by examining the different notorial offices, searching the records of the courts &c," can he "expect to acquire some light which may eventually guide us in dispelling the obscurity which now surrounds the affairs of Mr E."

Concludes: "Doctor [William N.] Mercer has returned. . . . Time and sorrow have stamped their impress on his noble features, and though he evidently strives to hide an aching heart under a smoothe brow, it is apparent that the loss of his beloved child [Anna Mercer], has deeply wounded his sensibilities [Clay to Mercer, November 14, 1846]." ALS. DLC-HC (DNA, M212, R21).

To ELIZA NEWPORT Washington, *ca.* December 15, 1851

I am obliged to you, Madam, for this visit and for the kind interest you have manifested in my behalf, and I also appreciate the feeling that impelled you to pay the visit. Your advice I acknowledge to be of the highest magnitude and I shall endeavor to give it that consideration which it so justly merits and demands at my hands. I am aware that when one like myself has arrived at the age of three score years and ten and who is in as feeble health as I am now cannot expect to remain here much longer. Yet Madam when it pleases God to take me hence, I am willing to go; and if Dr Jackson of

Philada[1] who is expected here this evening should not be able to afford me that relief for my cough that is sought for, I care not how soon that period may arrive. I do not pretend to say that I have a full assurance that all will be well (and I suppose very few if any have this assurance) yet Madam I have faith in the mercy of God and am not afraid to *die*.

Copy. PSC. 1. Historians have generally assumed this to be the famous Dr. Samuel Jackson of Philadelphia; however, in a Memo, late June, 1852, Clay gives instructions that his bill to Dr. Francis Jackson of Philadelphia be paid. Yet, no Dr. Francis Jackson appears in the Philadelphia city directories for this time period. Information supplied by William Handley, The Free Library of Philadelphia. For Samuel Jackson, see *DAB*.

To THE GENERAL ASSEMBLY OF KENTUCKY Washington, December 17, 1851

When you did me the honor to confer on me the appointment of a Senator from Kentucky,[1] which I now hold, in accepting it, I did not intend or expect to serve the entire term of six years. I had previously retired finally, as I supposed, from that body.[2] But out of the Territorial acquisitions, resulting from the war with Mexico, momentous questions arose, seriously menacing the harmony and peace, if not the integrity, of the Union. I felt it to be my duty to return again to the Senate, and to contribute my humble aid, by an amicable settlement of those questions, to avert the calamities with which we were threatened. Such a settlement was attempted, during the last Congress,[3] is now in a progress of execution, and I trust and hope will accomplish all the good that could be expected from any great measure, adopted to heal National divisions and animosities which had risen to such an alarming height.

On the approach of the present Congress, it was with much hesitation, proceeding partly from my feeble state of health, that I concluded to return, for the last time, to the Senate. But I have no thought of ever again taking a seat in that body, after the close of the present Session. Having come to this determination, I consider it encumbent on me to place it in the power of the General Assembly to appoint my successor, during its present Session.[4]

I do, therefore, hereby resign the office of a Senator of the United States from the State of Kentucky, this my resignation to take effect on the first monday of September 1852.

In dissolving this official relation, in which I stand to the General Assembly, I cannot forbear renewing an expression of my great obligations, and my profound gratitude, for the many distinguished and gratifying proofs which it has given to me of its confidence and attachment.

ALS. KyLoF. 1. Clay to Mercer, Dec. 10, 1848. 2. See 9:691-96. 3. Clay to Combs, Jan. 22, 1850. 4. Archibald Dixon was elected by the General Assembly on Dec. 30, 1851, as Clay's successor for the next Congress. However, when Clay died in June, 1852, David Meriwether was appointed to finish the session. Dixon's credentials were presented on Dec. 6, 1852, and he took his seat on Dec. 20. *BDAC*.

To LUCRETIA HART CLAY Washington, December 18, 1851

Since I last wrote to you, I have not attended the Senate, partly owing to my feeble health, and partly to bad weather. I rode out in a carriage on several fine days. I sent for Dr. Jackson[1] an eminent physician of Philada to come and consult with Dr. [William W.] Hall, my attending physician, on my case. He accordingly came, and remained here two days. They thoroughly examined my condition, and pronounce my cough not consumption, but bronchitas. They think that they can so far check or abate it as to make life more comfortable than it is, and I am now pursuing the system of treatment which they adopted. My hopes are not as strong as theirs, but I do not believe that I am in any immediate danger, and I trust that I shall be permitted to return home, and expire in the bosoms of you and my dear family, for whom I feel a degree of affection greater than ever.

Dr. Jackson wanted me, and I was inclined to go to Philada. and remain nigh him some weeks; but the weather was too bad to undertake the Journey. Possibly I may hereafter go there.[2]

I was glad yesterday to receive letters both from Thomas [Hart Clay] and John [Morrison Clay].[3] Tell them that I hope they will continue to write to me, without expecting much regularity in my replies. I am so feeble that I write very slow and with difficulty.

John's letter was business like and full of interesting details about his operations at Ashland, which I was very glad to get. I have not heard from [Jared] Dawson of Bellefontaine but I have written to him objecting to one charge of $250 that he makes in his account against me.[4]

Yesterday I transmitted to Frankfort a letter resigning my seat in the Senate of the U.S. on the first monday in Septr next.[5] So that if I should live, I should come here no more[.]

I experience the greatest kindness from every body and Mr. [Charles B.] Calvert does not allow me to suffer for any thing.

My love to Thomas and his family and to John [Morrison Clay] & Mary Watkins[.]

ALS. DLC-TJC (DNA, M212, R11). 1. Clay to Newport, *ca.* Dec. 15, 1851. 2. Clay remained in Washington until his death. 3. Not found. 4. Dawson to Clay, Nov. 23, 1851; Clay to John M. Clay, Dec. 3, 1851. 5. Clay to General Assembly of Ky., Dec. 17, 1851.

To ELISHA WHITTLESEY Washington, December 20, 1851

I am greatly obliged to Dr. Banning for the offer of his brace which he supposes would relieve me from any complaints which he supp[os]es I may have and to you for your Kind Communication of the same.

I am in the hands of two Phisicians[1] who possess my entire confidence; and without their approval should not deem it proper to use any remedies other than those they prescribe.

I will consult with them and if they advise the use of Dr Bannings invention I will inform you but if you do not hear from me you may conclude they do not recomend its use.

My case is that of a chronic cough of long duration proceeding from the Bronchal tubes and I confess I should not think I should derive any benefit from D Bannings machine[.]

LS. OClWHi. 1. Drs. Hall and Jackson. See Clay to Newport, *ca.* Dec. 15, 1851.

To JOHN NEAGLE Washington, December 22, 1851

My indisposition has delayed the acknowledgement of the receipt of your letter of the 15th. Ultimo.

You inform me that you have offered to the General Assembly of Kentucky, a full length portrait of me which you had taken:[1] And, also the portrait of the late Col. [Richard M.] Johnson—[2]

I appreciate the delicacy towards myself which prompted your Communication: but whilst I am unable to afford you any assistance at Frankfort I sincerely wish that you may obtain from the Legislature a liberal Compensation for your paintings—

As that body is not remarkable for its generous patronage of the fine arts, I am afraid that you may be disappointed—I have heard nothing from Frankfort myself on the subject. I always thought favorably of your portrait of me. And should you fail in you present application where an event shall occur in regard to myself which Cannot be very distant, I think it probable that your application to the Legislature would meet with more favor—

LS. DLC-Ainsworth Rand Spofford Papers. 1. See 9:789, 822-23. 2. The portrait of Johnson (25″ × 30″) was painted at Frankfort in March, 1843. The price requested for Clay's portrait was $1,060 and for Johnson's $150. This proposal was introduced in the Ky. house on Nov. 19, 1851, and was referred to the Committee on Libraries. No further action was taken either at this or the next session. Ky. H. of Reps., *Journal* . . . 1851-1852, pp. 104-6.

To MARY MENTELLE CLAY Washington, December 25, 1851

I received to day, your letter of the 19th inst. and I was very glad to get the details contained in it about yourself, your family, and affairs at Ashland. And I am under very great obligations to you and to Thomas [Hart Clay], for the kind offer which you have made, to come, either one or both of you to Washington, to attend me during my present illness. If there were the least occasion for it I should, with pleasure, accept the offer, but there is not. Every want, every wish, every attention which I need is supplied. The [National] Hotel at which I stay, has a bill of fare of some thirty or forty articles every day, from which I can select any for which I have a relish, and if I want anything which is not on the bill of fare, it is promptly procured for me. The state of my case, may be told in a few words. If I can get rid of this distressing cough, or can materially reduse it, I may yet be restored to a comfortable condition. That is the present aim of my physicians,[1] and I have some hope, that it has abated a little within the last few days. But if the cough cannot be stoped or considerably reduced, it will go on, untill it accomplishes its work. When that may be, it is impossible to say, with any sort of certainty. I may linger for some months, long enough possibly to reach home once more. At all events, there is no prospect at present of immediate dissolution. Under these circumstances, I have no desire to bring any member of my family, from home when there is not the least necessity for it. With regard to the rumors which reach you from time to time, and afflict you, you must bear with them, and rest assured of what I've already communicated to your Mother; that if my case should take a fatal turn, the telegraph shall communicate the fact.[2] I occupy two excellent rooms, the temperature of which, is kept up during the day at about 70°. The greatest inconvenience I feel is from the bad weather, which has confined me nearly a fortnight to my room, and I can take no exercise untill the weather changes. My love to Thomas and all your children, to your Mother and to all others at Ashland.

LS. DLC-HC (DNA, M212, R6). Printed in Colton, *Clay Correspondence*, 4:623. 1. Drs. Hall and Jackson. Clay to Newport, *ca.* Dec. 15, 1851. 2. Clay to Lucretia H. Clay, Dec. 9, 1851.

From John Pendleton Kennedy, Baltimore, December 25, 1851. Regrets to learn "that the severity of the season has affected your health and compelled you to withdraw from the labors of the Senate. Mrs [Elizabeth Gray] Kennedy and her sister [Martha Gray] both beg me to say to you, that as they have great faith in the efficacy of good nursing, they would be very happy to . . . minister in that way to your comfort, and . . . to have you here at our house." Adds that if "you intend to visit Philadelphia with a view to the medical aid which your case requires. . . . let me entreat you to put yourself under our charge, at least in passing, and to remain with us whilst in Baltimore." Copy. MdBP.

From Father Theobald Mathew, Cork, Ireland, December 29, 1851. Writes "From the south of that Green Island, which you have often, in your own eloquent . . . inspired Language, made the subject of your warmest eulogy" to present his "heartfelt wishes" for the New Year. Implores: "Blessed be the remainder of your brilliant, and useful Life, and may the prospect of future glory, gild it with felicity." Concludes "With endearing remembrance of your exceeding Kindness in the day of my distress." ALS. DLC-HC (DNA, M212, R6). Printed in Colton, *Clay Correspondence*, 4:624.

For examples of Clay's pro-Irish speeches, see Speech in New Orleans, February 4, 1847, and Speech to Hibernian Society, March 17, 1848. For his efforts to assist Father Mathew, see Clay to Grinnell, May 28, 1851.

To JOHN PENDLETON KENNEDY Washington, December 31, 1851

I am very thankful for your kind invitation for me to sojourn under your hospitable roof for a while And to the ladies of your family for their friendly offer to nurse me.[1]

If I had any purpose of going to Baltimore I should accept your invitation with pleasure—but I have no thought of going there unless I should pass through it on my way to Philadelphia; to which place I have some thought of paying a visit—

Should I do so I may stop a night at Baltimore, and ask the shelter of your roof—

Be pleased to present my best respects with the Compliments of the Season to Mr. [Edward] Gray Mrs. [Elizabeth Gray] Kennedy & Miss [Martha] Gray; and tell the ladies that I am perfectly sure of the tenderness with which they would kindly nurse me, if I were under their happy auspices—

LS. MdBP. 1. Kennedy to Clay, Dec. 25, 1851.

To JAMES ROBB[1] Washington, December 31, 1851

There are epochs in our country when the safety of the Republic is supposed to be in danger. We have passed and are passing through one of them, perhaps the most perilous which has occurred since the establishment of our Government. On those great occasions, the sympathy and friendly feeling are formed between those who act in concert to avert impending calamities. I confess I cherish that feeling and sympathy towards all those with whom I had the honor of acting during the last Congress and I confess that to no one are they entertained in greater warmth than towards the Honble. S[olomon]. W. Downs (one of your Senators). I found him firm, faithful, able and zealous in the support generally of the Compromise measures and to his exertions in no small degree was the final success of the measures owing.[2]

On such occasions as I have adverted to, the preservation of our Union has an importance so far transcending any questions of administrative policy that I have thought that those questions should be obliterated or at least suspended and he who has shown himself the faithful friend of the Union should be sustained by his Constituents.

[Asks Robb's help with the legislature to ensure the reelection of Gen. Downs to the Senate.[3] Continues:] His defeat would be a matter of exultation with the Abolitionists, the Free-Soilers and these rash men at the South whose unwise counsels would have brought upon us all the horrors of a civil war. I am aware, my Dear Sir of the very great delicacy of addressing you on this subject but I hope I shall find an excuse for it in those motives of devotion for our Country, which I am sure I share in common with you and which alone could have prompted me to take a Step which may be regarded by some as of doubtful propriety.

Copy. Printed in George E. Jordan, "Robb & Clay: Politicians & Scholars," in *The New Orleans Art Review* (Jan./Feb., 1984), 4:6. 1. James Robb (1814-81)—a wealthy banker and railroad entreprenuer—at this time lived in New Orleans. *DAB*. 2. Clay to Combs, Jan. 22, 1850. 3. Downs was not reelected. *BDAC*.

To JAMES BROWN CLAY Washington, January 3, 1851 [*sic*, 1852]

I received your two letters one dated Lexington and the other St Louis—[1]

In September last I called to see Mr. [Harvey] Miller upon the subject of the house and lot which as your agent I had sold him.[2] I stated to him that I felt very anxious that the difficulty about the title to the fraction of an Acre should be amicably adjusted, as it had been thro' my fault or rather want of recollection that it had'nt been provided for in the sale which I made him—I told him that I was desirous it should be adjusted both on his and your Account, but especially because you did not wish any difficulty to arise in the payment of his notes which you had assigned to Mr. Craig.[3] I offered him first to make him a deed with general warranty including the fraction of an Acre; hoping that you might be able to perfect the title to it hereafter—Secondly, I offered him to pay the value of the fraction of an Acre to be ascertained in any satisfactory mode and lastly, I proposed to him to rescind the contract of sale take back the property and refund to him what he had advanced—All these propositions he declined—As to the first, he said he was satisfied as to the title bond which he held—And would rather wait until February when Mr [James O.] Harrison informed him there was a prospect of your perfecting the title to a fraction of an Acre—As to the last he declined peremptorily rescinding the Contract, stating that he was delighted with the property, that the house was one of the best he ever saw in his life. And that he had been offered a thousand dollars advance upon the Amount he gave for the property—He assurred me pointedly that he would pay the note for $3000—in the hands of Mr. Craig due last October, but, intimated no purpose as to the note due next October—I told him that I was satisfied that the business might rest on that footing as before next October I trusted that the whole affair might be amicably arranged—I informed him that I had a power of Attorney from you to effect any one of the three objects above mentioned—This power I gave to Susan [Jacob Clay] with a request to take Care of it and hand it to you—

I was very glad to hear that you had got your family into your new house—[4] I hope that you did not find it too green—I do not see how you Could repel the advances made to you by the [Thomas Hart] Bentons—I never desired that my family or friends should be affected by any personal difficulties or quarrels that I might have, nor, that they should take part in them—but I tell you that unless you Consent to become a partizan of the Colonel's you will not long retain relations of friendship with him—

My health Continues feeble, my strength, my flesh, my appetite, and my sleeping are all diminishing. I am able to sit up the greater part of the day and could drive out if the horrible weather we have had did not interpose an obstacle—You think I am despondent, but if you could witness my Coughing for twenty four hours, And how much I have been reduced since we parted, you would not think so—Besides despondency implies apprehension of death; I entertain none. I am ready to go whenever it is the will of God that I should be summoned hence. And I do most sincerely desire that my present Critical Condition should be brought to a speedy issue one way or the other. All my worldly affairs are fully arranged for any event, and I could never at any former period have died with so little inconvenience to my successors as I Can at present—I would not have you Come here on my account, if you Could. I have written, indeed before I left home I stated to all my family there that I did not wish that any of them should Come to me here; Every want every wish every Attention which my situation calls for is affectionately supplied—

Give my love to Susan. Kiss all the Children for me and particularly Lucy [Jacob Clay] and dear little Harry [Clay] . . .

LS. DLC-TJC (DNA, M212, R11). 1. Not found. 2. Clay to James B. Clay, Oct. 27, 1850. 3. Probably Elijah W. or D.M. Craig. See 9:807, 792, 799, 902. 4. Clay to James B. Clay, Dec. 23, 1850.

To LUCRETIA HART CLAY Washington, January 4, 1852

I have wanted for several days past to write under my own hand to you, as I did not wish to employ anothers pen; but my faculty of writing is so impaired that [it] is only rarely that I can write at all. Sometimes I hope that my health is improving, but I am discouraged by the loss of strength, flesh, sleep and appetite. My wants are all supplied, I receive the kindest attentions, it is not necessary to sit up with me at night, and whatever may be the final issue, I am probably in no immediate danger. You will remember that I told you that one of my objects in coming to Washn. was to argue a cause before the S[upreme]. Court, in which I was to get a contingent fee of $2500.[1] I was too feeble to argue the cause and with the consent of my client I got Mr. [Joseph R.] Underwood to represent me, promising him one half of my fee. We gained the cause, and some day or other through Mr. C[harles]. S. Morehead and Mr. Underwood I shall receive $1250.

I have received remittances on account of my Illinois land,[2] and can supply you and John [Morrison Clay] with any money you may need. I will send a check shortly, or if he is hard pressed he may draw on me. Tell him that I recd. his last letter,[3] the perusal of which gave me much pleasure. I hope he and Thomas [Hart Clay] and Mary [Mentelle Clay] will continue to write fully to me, altho from my feeble condition I cannot transmit to them regular answers. How is Thomas getting along with his bank and other debts? Is he able to meet them?

Tell John that I have not heard how his horses ran at Mobile.

God bless you my dear wife and my love to all.

ALS. DLC-TJC (DNA, M212, R11). 1. The case of *Gilbert C. Russell* v. *Daniel R. Southard et al.* was argued on Clay's behalf by Underwood and Morehead for appellant Russell. A bill had been filed by Russell to redeem what he called a mortgage. The question in the case was whether it was actually a mortgage or a conditional sale. Stephen K. Williams (ed.), *Cases Argued and Decided in the Supreme Court of the United States 1850-1851* . . . (Rochester, N.Y., 1901), 53:139-57. 2. See Clay to John Hunter, Feb. 4, 1852; Memo, late June, 1852. 3. Not found.

SPEECH TO LOUIS KOSSUTH

Washington, January 9, 1852

I owe you, sir, an apology for not having acceded before to the desire you were kind enough to intimate more than once to see me; but really, my health has been so feeble that I did not dare to hazard the excitement of so interesting an interview. Besides, sir (he added, with some pleasantry), your wonderful and fascinating eloquence has mesmerized so large a portion of our people wherever you have gone, and even some of our members of Congress[1] (waving his hand toward the two or three gentlemen who were present), that I feared to come under its influence, lest you might shake my faith in some principles in regard to the foreign policy of this government, which I have long and constantly cherished.

And in regard to this matter you will allow me, I hope, to speak with that sincerity and candor which becomes the interest the subject has for you and for myself, and which is due to us both, as the votaries of freedom.

I trust you will believe me, too, when I tell you that I entertain the liveliest sympathies in every struggle for liberty in Hungary,[2] and in every country, and in this I believe I express the universal sentiment of my countrymen. But, sir, for the sake of my country, you must allow me to protest against the policy you propose to her. Waiving the grave and momentous question of the right of one nation to assume the executive power among nations for the enforcement of international law, or of the right of the United States to dictate to Russia[3] the character of her relations with the nations around her, let us come at once to the practical consideration of the matter.

You tell us yourself, with great truth and propriety, that mere sympathy, or the expression of sympathy, can not advance your purposes. You require "material aid." And indeed it is manifest that the mere declarations of sympathy of Congress, or of the President [Millard Fillmore], or of the public, would be of little avail, unless we were prepared to enforce those declarations by a resort to arms, and unless other nations could see that preparation and determination upon our part.[4]

Well, sir, suppose that war should be the issue of the course you propose to us. Could we then effect any thing for you, ourselves, or the cause of liberty? To transport men and arms across the ocean in sufficient numbers and quantities to be effective against Russia and Austria would be impossible. It is a fact which perhaps may not be generally known, that the most imperative reason with Great Britain for the close of her last war with us, was the immense cost of the transportation and maintenance of forces and munitions of war in such a distant theater, and yet she had not perhaps more than 30,000 men upon this continent at any time. Upon land, Russia is invulnerable to us, as we are to her. Upon the ocean, a war between Russia and this country would result in mutual annoyance to commerce, but probably in little else. I learn recently that her war marine is superior to that of any nation in Europe, except perhaps Great Britain. Her ports are few, her commerce limited, while we, on our part, would offer as a prey to her cruisers a rich and extensive commerce.

Thus, sir, after effecting nothing in such a war, after abandoning our ancient policy of amity and non-intervention in the affairs of other nations, and thus justifying them in abandoning the terms of forbearance and non-interference which they have hitherto preserved toward us; after the downfall, perhaps, of the friends of liberal institutions in Europe, her despots, imitating, and provoked by our fatal example, may turn upon us in the hour of our weakness and exhaustion, and, with an almost equally irresistible force of reason and of arms, they may say to us, "You have set us the example. You have quit your own to stand on foreign ground; you have abandoned the policy you professed in the day of your weakness, to interfere in the affairs of the people upon this continent, in behalf of those principles, the supremacy of which you say is necessary to your prosperity, to your existence. We, in our turn, believing that your anarchical doctrines are destructive of, and that monarchical principles are essential to the peace, security and happiness of our subjects, will obliterate the bed which has nourished such noxious weeds; we will crush you as the propagandist of doctrines so destructive of the peace and good order of the world."

The indomitable spirit of our people might and would be equal to the emergency, and we might remain unsubdued even by so tremendous a combination; but the consequences to us would be terrible enough. You must allow me, sir, to speak thus freely, as I feel deeply, though my opinion may be of but little import, as the expression of a dying man. Sir, the recent melancholy subversion of the republican government of France,[5] and that enlightened nation voluntarily placing its neck under the yoke of despotism, teach us to despair of any present success for liberal institutions in Europe. They give us an impressive warning not to rely upon others for the vindication of our principles, but to look to ourselves, and to cherish with more care than ever the security of our institutions and the preservation of our policy and principles.

By the policy to which we have adhered since the days of [George] Washington, we have prospered beyond precedent—we have done more for the cause of liberty in the world than arms could effect. We have showed to other nations the way to greatness and happiness; and, if we but continue united as one people, and persevere in the policy which our experience has so clearly and triumphantly vindicated, we may in another quarter of a century furnish an example which the reason of the world can not resist. But if we should involve ourselves in the tangled web of European politics, in a war in which we could effect nothing, and if in that struggle Hungary should go down, and we should go down with her, where, then, would be the last hope of the friends of freedom throughout the world? Far better is it for ourselves, for Hungary, and for the cause of liberty, that, adhering to our wise, pacific system, and avoiding the distant wars of Europe, we should keep our lamp burning brightly on this western shore as a light to all nations, than to hazard its utter extinction amid the ruins of fallen or falling republics in Europe.

Copy. Printed in Colton, *Clay Correspondence*, 3:221-24, with parenthetic editorial comments added by Colton. Also in John Bassett Moore, *A Digest of International Law* (Washington, 1906), 6:51-52. 1. Sens. Stephen A. Douglas, William Henry Seward, Lewis Cass, and James Shields were among Kossuth's chief supporters in the Senate. Cass was one of those who accompanied Kossuth to visit Clay. Smith, *Presidencies of Taylor & Fillmore*, 231-32; Rayback, *Millard Fillmore*, 329-31. 2. Comment in Senate, Jan. 7, 1850. 3. *Ibid.* 4. The U.S. had helped secure Kossuth's release from a Turkish prison, but President Fillmore was careful not to encourage him to believe the administration would depart from the policy of non-intervention in European affairs. Smith, *Presidencies of Taylor & Fillmore*, 231-33; Rayback, *Millard Fillmore*, 328-32. 5. In Dec., 1851 the Second French Republic had been ended and the Second Empire declared with Louis Napoleon, who had served as president of the Republic since 1848, becoming Emperor Napoleon III. Langer, *Encyclopedia of World History*, 681-83.

To THOMAS HART CLAY Washington, January 10, 1852

I received two or three letters from you[1] since I came here, and should have answered them with pleasure if my strength and health would have admitted of it. You observe now I am obliged to employ the pen of a friend. I was very thankful for the kind offer of yourself and Mary [Mentelle Clay] to come here and nurse me.[2] I should have promptly accepted, if it had been necessary, but it was not. Every want and wish that I have are kindly attended to. I am surrounded by good friends, who are ready and willing to serve me; and you and Mary yourselves could not have been more assiduous in your attentions than are my friends the [Charles B.] Calverts.

The state of my health has not very materially altered. Within the last eight or ten days there has been some improvement; not so great as my friends persuade themselves, but still some improvement. The solution of the problem of my recovery depends upon the distressing cough which I have, and I think that it is a little diminished. I am embargoed here by the severity of the winter, which has confined me to the house for the last three weeks. I hope to derive some benefit when I shall be again able to drive out in the open air. You must continue to write me without regard to my ability to reply. It is a source of great comfort to me to hear, and to hear fully, from Ashland and Mansfield. John [Morrison Clay] has been very kind in writing very frequently to me. Give my love to Mary and all the children.

Copy. Printed in Colton, *Clay Correspondence*, 4:624-25. 1. Not found. 2. See Clay to Mary M. Clay, Dec. 25, 1851.

To Samuel Austin Allibone, Philadelphia, January 11, 1852. Expresses his thanks "for your friendly offer to come hither and assist in nursing me; but I am . . . extremely well attended in that respect." Sends his "regards to your sister [Susan Allibone], and tell her, as the probability is that neither of us is long for this world, I hope that when we go hence we shall meet in one far better." LS. CSmH. Printed in Colton, *Clay Correspondence*, 4:625.

From Louis B.C. Serurier, Paris, France, January 11, 1852. After nearly "42 years since I landed on the American shore as near Envoy Extraordinary of the Emperor Napoleon," writes at length in praise of Clay's conduct during the War of 1812, a conflict that "by its origin, the rights of nations violently trampled under foot, & above all the ridiculous pretences of England, to exercise her absurd right of search, to impress your sailors under pretext of seeking her deserters is perhaps the fastest war that has been declared since the origin of political society." Intends "to write or rather to publish for it has been already written nearly 40 years, the history of this memorable war. . . . your part my dear Sir will be fine in my description—It is enough to tell you it will be true. . . . I shall limit myself to publish my correspondence with my Government." Concludes: "I learn, my dear Sir tha[t] you have just retired fro[m] the Senate. . . . I have also left great affairs to devote entirely what remains to me of life, to my family & my reminissences—But my retreat has been scarcely remarked among the acquaintances of my country, whilst yours will be for a long time, the great regret of your country." ALS. DLC-HC (DNA, M212, R6).

To LUCRETIA HART CLAY Washington, January 12, 1851 [*sic*, 1852]

If I do not write you oftener, it is owing to my feeble condition and the difficulty of writing. Since I last wrote to you, my friends think I have improved in my health, and perhaps there is a slight improvement, but not so great as they imagine, nor such as to inspire me with much confidence of regaining my health. My cough I think is somewhat diminished, but it is occasionally most tormenting. Altho' I take an opiate every night, I lay for hours and hours without any sleep. I sit up four or five hours every day, and for the rest I am on a Couch. My nursing is good and all that I want.

I have not heard from home since I last wrote to you. I am waiting to hear whether John [Morrison Clay] will draw on me, or I shall send a Check on N. York.

I hope, my dear wife, that you will take good care of my Will.[1] Its loss or destruction would produce great confusion, after I am gone, and would affect you and John most injuriously[.]

You cannot imagine what time and effort this letter has occasioned me[.]

I send you a card recd. from [Louis] Kossuth.[2]

My love to all at Ashland & Mansfield[.]

ALS. DLC-HC (DNA, M212, R6). 1. Last Will and Testament, July 10, 1851. 2. Not found.

To Garrett Davis, January 12, 1852. Thanks him for his letter [not found] and wishes "that I had the strength to respond to it, in the fullness which my heart would prompt, but I have not." Adds that "My condition is very critical," and "You have been rightly informed that I contemplate the result with composure, resignation, and submission." Concludes that "In view of my present suffering in this life, and the hopes and blessings in the next, I am ready to obey the summons of my God, whenever he may graciously please to issue it, confiding in the promises and mediation of our Saviour." Copy. Printed in the Frankfort *Tri-Weekly Commonwealth*, September 13, 1852.

From William C. Rives, Paris, France, January 15, 1852. Sends to Clay the "enclosed letter [Serurier to Clay, January 11, 1852] . . . by your old & constant friend Count [Louis B.C.] Serurier, former Minister of France to the United States." Rives also adds his "ardent wishes for the early restoration of your health, which I have heard, with deep concern, had been a good deal deranged by consequence of the untiring exertions of both mind & body you had devoted to the adjustment of the unhappy controversy which has, of late, so seriously threatened the peace & future destinies of our country [Clay to Combs, January 22, 1850]. No one, I beg leave to say, can have a profounder sense of the value of those services than I have."

Acknowledges receipt from Davies McCullough of "half a dozen canisters of his far-famed mustard." Asks Clay "to be the medium" of his thanks, adding "I have introduced his mustard to the acquaintance of some of the most competent judges here, & they all concur in pronouncing it to be decidedly superior to the boasted *Maille* of Paris, & to be in truth unrivalled in all the qualities of that popular condiment." ALS. DLC-William Cabell Rives Papers.

Samuel Davis McCullough (d. January 11, 1873, aged 71) manufactured mustard in Lexington by a process started by his relative Nathan Burrows. The mustard, which was famous for fifty years, took the premium at the World's Fair in London in 1851. Collins, *History of Kentucky*, 1:240; 2:174.

To Dr. Homer Bostwick, New York City, January 16, 1852. Thanks him for the friendly sentiments included in his letter of the 12th instant. States: "I consider my condition as highly critical.—It is a cough of some eighteen months duration, proceeding from the lower bronchial vessels; it has reduced me in strength and flesh, diminished my appetite, and lessened my sleep; it must be arrested, or it may terminate fatally." Adds that he has "felt more comfortable within the last fortnight." Copy. Printed in Frankfort *Commonwealth*, February 3, 1852.

Homer Bostwick, M.D., was located at 504 Broadway, New York City. *Wilson's Business Directory of New-York City* (New York, 1848).

From Elisha Whittlesey, Washington, January 17, 1852. Asks "whether the American Colonization Society may be favored with your presence at its next Annual meeting at the 1st Presbyterian Church" on January 20 at 7 p.m. While "No friend of this benevolent cause" would want Clay to "impair your feeble health" to attend, "all would rejoice to see you preside again over a society that you assisted to form: that has, by your sustaining influence abolished the Slave trade on the West Coast of Africa: established a Republic [Liberia]," and "carried the Bible and civilization into that benighted region." LS. DLC-Records of the American Colonization Society (DNA, M212, R20). See also McLain to Clay, February 9, 1852.

From Theodore Frelinghuysen, New Brunswick, N.J., January 19, 1852. Expresses his "great interest & anxiety of your continued feeble health—& that it had rather been more feeble, since your decided testimony, in behalf of [George] Washington's foreign policy. I was rejoiced to hear your words of soberness & truth, on the exciting question of Hungarian politics [Speech to Kossuth, January 9, 1852]." Hopes that Clay, "In this time of impaired health & sometimes trying despondency," will find it "refreshing to look away to Him" whose "blessed Gospel, that reveals the riches of God's grace in Jesus Christ, is a wonderful remedy." Prays that Clay will lean "all your hopes on the Almighty Saviour's arm . . . for life & for death, for time & eternity." ALS. DLC-HC (DNA, M212, R6). Printed in Colton, *Clay Correspondence*, 4:625-26.

To JOHN MORRISON CLAY Washington, January 20, 1852

Being able to write a little to day, I acknowledge the rect. of your letter of the 11th. inst. for which I thank you.

I send a Check of Corcoran & Riggs in N. York for $750 for the use of yourself and mother [Lucretia Hart Clay]. You will keep an a/c of what portion of it you use. I have not recd. from Bellefontaine the promised Check, altho' I wrote to Mr. [Jared] Dawson from here.[1] I think you would do well to employ a working overseer—the man you have in view. I don't see how you do without one. Why don't you employ hands to help E. Watkins abt your stable?[2]

My health continues pretty much as when I last wrote; but if there be any change perhaps it is for the better.

I wish you would let Thomas [Hart Clay] have another stack of oats.

My love to your Mama.

AL, signature removed. Josephine Simpson Collection, Lexington, Ky. 1. Not found, but see Dawson to Clay, Nov. 23, 1851; Clay to John M. Clay, Dec. 3, 1851; Dawson to Clay, Feb. 3, 1852. 2. Possibly one of the sons of Clay's half-brother John Watkins—Elijah Milton Watkins (1822-1903) or Ebenezer Watkins (1831-1906). Both Elijah and Ebenezer were born in Woodford County, died unmarried, and were buried in the Lexington Cemetery. Allen, *Henry Watkins*, 39-40.

From FRANCIS PRESTON BLAIR Silver Springs, Md., January 22, 1852

It is most gratifying to me that Mr. [Martin] Van Buren commits to my discretion the opportunity of disclosing the kind feelings and high opinion entertained for you by two of the most distinguished adversaries you have encountered in the political contests of your time. I therefore take the same liberty with Mr. Van Buren's letter[1] that he proposes with Col. [Thomas Hart] Benton's to him,[2] persuaded that nothing would more please you than the naked and unpremeditated expression of feeling contained in the very words of the private notes not meant to reach your hands.

Mr. Van Buren would not have turned over to me, I well know, an office which he would gladly have performed himself if he had not felt the delicacy of troubling you with a letter, in your present painful condition which might seem to ask reply and burden you with a matter that might cost an effort or embarrass you. My communication you can receive as you have my oral ones—take to your bosom with your benevolent thoughts without further exertion.

With the warm feelings of earlier days[.]

Copy. Printed in John C. Fitzpatrick (ed.), *The Autobiography of Martin Van Buren* in *Annual Report of the American Historical Association For The Year 1918*, 2 vols. (Washington, 1920), 2:669. 1. Van Buren had written Blair on Jan. 16, 1852, enclosing a letter he had received from Thomas Hart Benton and suggesting that Blair show the letter to Clay. Van Buren expressed the opinion that the letter revealed that Benton's "sympathies are as deeply excited as our own" by Clay's condition, and contended that "we ought" to employ "the means which have been accidently placed in our power to ameliorate the effects of past estrangements, if we cannot remove them altogether." He also sent Clay "assurances of my respect, esteem and confidence and add that no one can have derived more satisfaction from his noble bearing whilst confined to the sick bed than I have done." *Ibid.* 2. In his letter to Van Buren, Benton reported that Francis Preston Blair had told Clay what Benton had written in his autobiography concerning the election of 1825 and the corrupt bargain charge, and that Clay was very gratified by it. Benton suggested that Van Buren write Clay a letter "in which you might add, what that chapter shows, that there is a time when political animosities are to be obliterated under the great duties of historic truth." *Ibid.*, 668. The first volume of Benton's autobiography, entitled *Thirty Years' View*, was published in 1854, the second in 1856. Smith, *Magnificent Missourian*, 284-86, 299-301, 307, 310-11.

To HENRY CLAY, JR. [III] Washington, January 25, 1852

I have been sick ever since I have been here, but being now a little more comfortable, I write you. As you have been in good health, I hope, you might have written to me.

I was glad to see from the last monthly return that your marks of demerit were limited to two. If you will keep them down to that, you will be in no danger of expulsion.[1] But you did not stand as high at the Jany examination as you had done previously in your studies. How is that? What was the cause of it?

All were well at Ashland & Mansfield when I last heard from home.

Write me soon.

ALS. Henry Clay Memorial Foundation, Lexington, Ky. 1. Clay to Morehead, Dec. 14, 1848.

To JAMES O. HARRISON Washington, January 26, 1852

I received your letter,[1] respecting the Post office [a]t Lexington vacated by the death of Judge [George R.] Trotter—The Post Master General [Nathan K. Hall] called on me a few days ago to [con]fer about the appointment of his successor—I advised him to appoint Squire Bassett and he told me he would send his name into the President [Millard Fillmore]. I have no doubt therefore that he has been or will be appointed.[2]

I also received your letter transmitting interrogatories to be put to me as a witness in the case of Clay against [Harvey] Miller;[3] I will prepare my deposition in a few days and return it properly authenticated. My health continues quite feeble altho' there has been [wi]thin the last fortnight a slight improvement in it[;] if I recover at all my restoration to health must [ne]cessarily be very tedious as is always the case in chronical complaints.

Present me affectionately to your good lady [Margaretta Ross Harrison] & family . . .

LS, partially faded. DLC-HC (DNA, M212, R21). 1. Not found. 2. Trotter—lawyer, judge, and postmaster—had died on Jan. 11, 1852. Squire Bassett, a merchant and banker who had been Trotter's deputy postmaster, was nominated by President Fillmore on Jan. 28, 1852, and confirmed on Feb. 23. Walker, *History of the Lexington Post Office*, 26-28; U.S. Sen., *Executive Journal*, 8:361, 369-70. 3. Letter not found; however, the case involved a dispute about the title to part of the property sold to Miller along with James Brown Clay's house. See Clay to James B. Clay, Jan. 3, 1852.

To Eliphalet Pierson, New York City, January 26, 1852. Thanks Pierson for "suggesting a remedy for my Cough." If his "eminent physicians [Drs. Hall & Jackson]. . . . fail in their treatment of my case, I will then exercise my own judgements on the remedy you kindly propose." LS. KyU.

Pierson was a mason, located at 552 Grand in New York City. Doggett, *New-York City Directory for 1848-49.*

To A. Burnett, January 30, 1852. Acknowledges receipt of "the two Volumes,—Your work on Mexico,—which you had the goodness to send me." Assures Burnett that "they will compose a beautiful and valuable portion of my library. And I thank you also, for the compliment of the dedication, you have been pleased to make to me." Regrets he has had no opportunities to reciprocate for the "sentiments of regard and friendship, which you have long done me the honor to entertain." L. MH.

From Jared S. Dawson, Bellefontaine, Ohio, February 3, 1852. Encloses a "Draft on the Girard Bank. Philada. drawn by Mud River Vally Branch at Springfield Ohio for $350.00." Repeats the prices for which Clay's Ohio lands were sold "as I gave them in the original Statement sent," the cost per acre varying from $5.50 to $8.00. Apologizes to Clay, whose "mony should of been sent much sooner but I have not had time to go to Bank." ALS. DLC-TJC (DNA, M212, R19). See Clay to Dawson April 18, 1849; Dawson to Clay, Nov. 23, 1851.

To John Hunter, February 4, 1852. Acknowledges receipt of "the two Thousand dollars, remitted to me, thro' the Bank at Terre Haute in payment for your bond for that Amount due last Christmas," and "I take pleasure in bearing testimony to your honorable and punctual fulfillment of your engagements up to this time." Assures Hunter that "I shall be ready and take pleasure in supplying you with the two Durham Calves which I promised," but "As to the Jack, which you want, I shall not have it in my power to furnish you with one." LS. DLC-HC (DNA, M212, R21). Hunter had purchased Clay's Illinois land. See Memo, late June, 1852.

From Tilden Reynolds, Prospectville, Pa., February 7, 1852. After hearing about "your ill health I take the privelag of makeing a fue Statements to your honour Concrning a Discovery I made in medicine on the tenth of jany last." Explains that he was treating his daughter who "had a bad Cough of long Standing which was thought a Cunsumtion." Gave her "a medicine Called Fowlers Soluton five drops three times a day in distiled watter" and "sasafrc tea each night as hot as Se Could use it. this treatment Cured her of the Cough in one weeks time affectuly though not given that purpose." Adds that "Iff it Should have the astonishing and happy Cureative affect upon your honors Complaint as it had on my Daughter I Should be very hapy to See the Life of our geat Statesman and worthy citizen prolonged for the future benefit of mankind and the solace of his Relatives and friends." ALS. DLC-HC (DNA, M212, R6).

From William McLain, Washington, February 9, 1852. Sends Clay a copy of a resolution unanimously adopted at "the recent Annual Meeting of the American Colonization Society": "Resolved, That we deeply sympathise with our venerable President, the Hon. Henry Clay, in his present protracted illness, by which we are deprived of his presence and able counsels at this Annual Meeting of our Society, to which he has, from its foundation, devoted himself with signal ability and unwavering fidelity; and that we hold him in affectionate and grateful remembrance for the distinguished services he has rendered in the prosecution of the great scheme of African Colonization." ALS. DLC-HC (DNA, M212, R6). Printed in Colton, *Clay Correspondence*, 4:626.

The resolution is published in "Thirty-Fifth Annual Report of the American Colonization Society, January 20, 1852," *The African Repository* (March, 1852), 25:91.

From Daniel Ullmann *et al.*, Washington, February 9, 1852. As spokesman for a group of Clay's New York friends [Clay to Ullmann, September 26, 1851], wishes to add still another to the "many warm testimonials and enduring memorials of your great services to your country and mankind." Presents Clay with a gold medal which they hope will be "valuable as a work of art, (of an art by little practised in our country,) and as a perfect resemblance of your lineaments. We think that this effort has been successful; that no medal ever struck in this country surpasses it in beauty, and that it is the best likeness of your features ever yet attempted by any art." Hopes that "the form and expression of your countenance" is "faithfully transmitted to distant posterity," to be "fondly cherished, as are now the like images of Cicero and Brutus, not only by the antiquary and historian, but by all whom patriotism and eloquence can kindle to admiration." Notes that "All national medals hitherto struck in this country, have been commemorative of the triumphs of American arms. . . . let the first American victor of peace" also be "thus commemorated." Copy. Printed in Washington *Daily National Intelligencer*, February 10, 1852. See Speech to Citizens of New York, February 9, 1852. For a description of the medal, see Clay to Ullmann, September 26, 1851.

SPEECH TO CITIZENS OF NEW YORK

Washington,
February 9, 1852

This is among the most interesting and gratifying days of my life, although I have been confined to these rooms[1] for a long time, by a tedious and doubtful illness. You have come here, the representatives of a large and enlightened body of ardent and devoted friends of mine in the city of New-York, to present to me a beautiful and costly gold medal, intended to commemorate my public life.[2] On one face of it is engraved, all the great public measures adopted in the National Councils, in which I was supposed to have had any conspicuous agency, and on the other, a remarkable and accurate likeness of me.[3] The time, and the place of presentation, and the friends who have contributed this splendid testimonial, give to it an inestimable value. The time is, when I am about to retire forever from public life, and when I cannot expect much longer to linger here below; the place is the city of Washington, the principle theatre of those public services which have commended themselves to your approbation. Throughout my public life, I have been blessed, everywhere in the United States, with more or fewer true friends, to whom I am bound by the strongest sentiments of gratitude; but nowhere have they surpassed those in the city of New-York, in zeal, constancy and fidelity, and in distinguished and various demonstrations of their affection and attachment. Whilst one is in the ardent pursuit of public life, and is held up for its highest honors, it is not practicable always to discriminate, among his supporters, between those who bestow their suffrages from pure, patriotic and disinterested motives, and those who are actuated by selfish ends; but on this occasion no such difficulty exists. You have come, at much personal inconvenience, to the bed of a sick and afflicted friend, to present to him, in your names, and in the name of a numerous body of his personal and political friends, whom you represent, a most precious token of your esteem and affectionate regard. That friend has not now, and never will have, any public patronage to dispense. The high and honorable, and disinterested character of your motives cannot, therefore, be questioned.

Gentlemen, I request you to accept yourselves, and to communicate to my absent friends whom you represent, my cordial and heartfelt thanks, and my grateful and profound acknowledgments, for this rich tribute to the sentiments which they do me the honor to entertain towards me. I should have been most happy to have expressed my great obligations to all of them personally, if it had been in my power.

I shall soon pass from the jurisdiction of my contemporaries and of the present generation, to that of history and posterity, if the one shall deem me worthy of any record on its pages, or tradition shall transmit any recollection of me to the other.

It is not within my legitimate province to express any opinion on my own public career or public deeds. That office belongs to them, and I shall consider my future fame fortunate, if it shall be regarded by them with a small portion of the favor with which the partiality of yourselves and your associates now contemplate it.

I shall soon appear before a higher and more holy Tribunal than any earthly one, which can unerringly judge of the motives as well as the acts of man. To that Tribunal I look forward with composure and confidence, that I shall be acquitted of having ever been prompted, in the discharge of my public duties, by any mean or sordid or selfish ends, or been animated by any other purpose than to promote the honor, the prosperity, and glory of our common country.

Medals are generally struck by the authority, and paid for out of the public Treasury of Government, and most frequently are intended to reward and signalize the triumphs achieved in war. But that which you now so kindly tender to my acceptance, is the spontaneous offering of private citizens, from their private purses, for public services exclusively in the civil department. I shall fondly and gratefully cherish and preserve it whilst life endures, and transmit it to my descendants, under the hope that they will receive and carefully guard it, with emotions of lively gratitude to my New-York friends, as the proudest and richest legacy that I could leave them.

Copy. Printed in Washington *Daily National Intelligencer*, Feb. 10, 1852. 1. At the National Hotel. 2. Ullmann *et al.* to Clay, Feb. 9, 1852. 3. Clay to Ullmann, Sept. 26, 1851.

To SUSAN JACOB CLAY Washington, February 12, 1852

I recd. your letter of the 27th. Ulto, and I had recd. that of James [Brown Clay] of the 1st. I write now so uncomfortably and so slow that I take up my pen with great repugnance. I was very glad to receive both of your letters, and was delighted to contemplate the picture of your domestic happiness with your husband and children. As the world recedes from me, I feel my affections more than ever concentrated on my children, and theirs.

My health has improved a little within the last few weeks, but the cough still hangs on; and unless I can get rid of it or greatly diminish it, I cannot look for a radical cure. The winter has been excessively vigorous, and I have not been out of the house for eight weeks. You must not believe all you see in the news papers, favorable or unfavorable about my health.

I hope you and James will continue to write to me, whether you receive regular replies or not. How has the Dairy got through the winter?

My love to James & all my dear grand children[.]

ALS. DLC-HC (DNA, M212, R6). Printed in Colton, *Clay Correspondence*, 6:626-27.

From Robert P. Letcher, Mexico, February 15, 1852. Writes in behalf of "Capn Wyse, and [*sic*, an] old Sea faring man, belonging to one of the best families of Maryland." This veteran of "the naval service for many years" who "rendered distinguished services" in the Mexican War is now "very poor, very proud and high-minded" and nearly blind. Charges that "This Govt [Mexico] justly owes him about 7 or 8 thousand dollars." Noting that "There is not the slightest doubt of the justice of his claim" and that the Mexicans "promised me most positively to pay it," regrets to learn now that "they say they have no money & cant and dont expect to pay" Wyse. The captain "entreated me . . . to request, you to use your best efforts to have him paid out of the American Indemnity—He swears by all thats holy you can do '*that thing.*' " Adds: "He wishes you to see Mr. [Daniel] Webster and the President [Millard Fillmore] upon the subject." ALS. DLC-HC (DNA, M212, R6). At this time Letcher was U.S. minister to Mexico. Dougall & Chapman, *United States Chiefs of Mission*, 101.

To LUCRETIA HART CLAY Washington, February 18, 1852

A few days after I last wrote to you I got letters from John [Morrison Clay] and Mary [Mentelle Clay] which relieved me from the anxiety I felt about your health.[1] Before I received them I Telegraphed to Lexington to get information about you, but got no reply until after those letters reached me.

My own health has remained without any material change for weeks. My feebleness and the weather confine me to the House. My cough is not worse, perhaps a little better.

Tell John that I recd. his last letter, dated the 8th. He is right as to the fields which we proposed to cultivate this year. I have at last received a remittance from Bellefontaine.[2] I hope that John will not be tempted to take up Captn. Minor's banter, or any other banter for a match race. His horse Star Davis[3] is too untried. He mentioned to me that Thomas [Hart Clay] had gone or was about going to his mill, with better prospects. I wrote him advising him to sell out, but my letter must have got to Mansfield, after he left it.[4]

My love to John, Mary and her children and Mary Watkins. I hope this letter will find you perfectly well.

ALS. DLC-TJC (DNA, M212, R11). 1. Not found. 2. Dawson to Clay, Feb. 3, 1852; Clay to Dawson, Feb. 18, 1852. 3. Star Davis, a bay horse whose dam was Margaret Woods and whose sire was Glencoe, sired 1878 Kentucky Derby winner Day Star, which was bred by John M. Clay. S.D. Bruce, *The Thoroughbred Horse* (New York, 1892), 134-35. 4. Letter not found.

To Jared S. Dawson, Bellefontaine, Ohio, February 18, 1852. Acknowledges receipt of "a check for Three hundred and fifty dollars, on account of the land you sold for me." Can find "no trace of the Check for Two hundred and fifty dollars" Dawson sent earlier. Asks him "to inform me by what bank it was issued, and on what bank it was drawn." ALS. DLC-HC (DNA, M212, R21). See Clay to Dawson, April 18, 1849; Dawson to Clay, November 23, 1851; Clay to John M. Clay, December 3, 1851.

To JAMES O. HARRISON Washington, February 19, 1852

I recd. your favor to day.[1] You surprize me in stating that Mr. [Harvey] Miller denies on oath my offer to rescind the contract for the purchase of James's [Brown Clay] house.[2] Nothing can be more distinct in my memory than my recollection of having made him that offer, and his rejection of it, stating that he had been offered $1000 advance on the purchase. I gave my deposition last saturday and it was marked that afternoon for the p. office, Lexington.

I think your sale of your land a good one. It was nearly equal to $100 on the usual credits.

My health is not worse—I hope a little better; but I cannot feel entire confidence in my recovery until the cough leaves me or abates more.

My love to Margarette [Ross Harrison].

ALS. DLC-HC (DNA, M212, R21). 1. Not found. 2. Clay to James B. Clay, Oct. 27, 1850. See also Clay to Harrison, Jan. 26, 1852.

"A Correction," Washington, February 20, 1852. Clay writes to correct a story "going the rounds of the newspapers stating that the answer of Gen. LaFayette to the address [3:893-94] which, as Speaker of the House of Representatives, I made to him upon the occasion of his last visit to this country, was prepared by me, though pronounced by him." Notes that "This is a mistake. . . . It was composed by himself, as the style abundantly shows." Recalls that they breakfasted alone together the morning [December 10, 1824] of Lafayette's reception by the House, and "I stated or read to him the address which I intended to make to him on that day," and "I remarked to him that it would afford him a fine opportunity to pay us a handsome compliment, which he might do by saying . . . that he found himself surrounded by the same patriotic men, attached to liberty, devoted to free institutions, and with all the high attributes which distinguished his Revolutionary compatriots." Notes that LaFayette seemed pleased with this and incorporated it into his answer, and supposes this "trivial incident" is what gave rise to the misinformation. Copy. Printed in Washington *Daily National Intelligencer*, February 23, 1852.

To Committee for Congressional Banquet Honoring Washington's Birthday, Washington, D.C., February 21, 1852. Declines because of health an invitation to attend the banquet, but notes that it is particularly fitting "at the present time" to commemorate the day. Continues: "We have seen great principles laid down by him for the administration of this government, especially in regard to its foreign policy, drawn in question, his wisdom doubted, and serious efforts made and making to subvert those maxims of policy by the conformity to which this nation has risen to its present unparalleled greatness. We have seen serious attempts to induce the United States to depart from his great principles of peace and neutrality, of avoiding all entangling alliances with foreign Powers, and of confining ourselves to the growth, improvement, and prosperity of our new country; and, in place of them, to plunge ourselves . . . in the wars of Europe." Under such circumstances, believes it is useful "to repair to the great fountain of Washington's patriotism, and, drinking deep at it, to return refreshed and invigorated by the draught." Copy. Printed in Washington *Daily National Intelligencer*, March 5 and 20, 1852.

Clay's reference is to those who advocated U.S. intervention on behalf of the Hungarians in their revolt against Austria. See Remark in Senate, January 7, 1850; Speech to Kossuth, January 9, 1852.

To JAMES BROWN CLAY Washington, February 24, 1852

I recd. your letter of the 10th. I should have written you oftener, but I am so feeble, and write with so little comfort, that I take up the pen reluctantly. I hope that you and Susan [Jacob Clay] notwithstanding my apparent delinquency, will write me frequently, giving me full details of all your plans, improvements and business. There is nothing now that interests me so much as to receive full accounts from the members of my family frequently. Altho' you have got more in debt than I could have wished, you ought to be very happy. In dear Susan you have an excellent wife, and you have a fine parcel of promising children; and you have ample means of support.

I gave my deposition in your case with [Harvey] Miller week before the last and it was sent to Lexn.[1] It proved all that was expected of me.

My health continues very delicate. I have not been out of the house for upwards of two months. I cannot recognise any encouraging change. My cough still hangs on, altho' I some times hope that it is a little abated. If I can not get rid of it, or at least greatly diminish it, I think it must prove fatal. But I may linger for months to come. I should be glad to get home once more.

My love to Susan, and kisses for all the children. I would be glad to write more, but you cannot conceive how this little letter has exhausted me.

ALS. DLC-TJC (DNA, M212, R11). Printed in Colton, *Clay Correspondence*, 4:627. 1. Clay to Harrison, Jan. 26 and Feb. 19, 1852.

To JOHN MORRISON CLAY Washington, February 28, 1852

I received you letter of the 22d. & was highly gratified with the entire recovery of your mother [Lucretia Hart Clay] & with the general state of affairs at Ashland communicated in your letter. You & your mother naturally wish to know every thing about the state of my health my habits &c. & I wish I could satisfy you in every particular. But neither the physicians nor I know what is to be the ultimate issue of my present illness. I have less strength than when I left home, less flesh & less appetite, but still I eat quite enough to sustain life & nearly as much as when in health. I get no sleep any night, without an opiate; I sit up about seven hours in the day & the rest of the twenty four I am either in bed reclining or reclining on a couch. I have not been out of the house for nearly three months except taking two drives this week. in a close carriage. When I am sitting up I read a good deal & write a little though I write so uncomfortably that I am obliged to employ the pen of a friend occasionally, as you perceive I now do. I take two or three kinds of medicine every day, & have nearly emptied an apothecary's shop. Dr. [William W.] Hall, my physician, visits me regularly every day & I have confidence in his skill. I think my cough has abated a little, but I shall neither regain my strength flesh nor health until it is much more diminished. I do not feel any want of company, on the contrary there is a most inconvenient pressure upon me to receive the visits of strangers, & I am obliged to deny myself to the greater number of them. I am glad to hear that Zenobia & Heraldry are both foals;[1] coming so early it will require great attention to raise them. I think if you can get ninety dollars a ton for the hemp you have broken out it will be well to sell it & send it out of the way. Should you want money at any time, let me know, as I have enough in deposite with Corcoran & Riggs to supply you.

Give my love to your mama & to Cousin Mary [Watkins].

LS. Josephine Simpson Collection, Lexington, Ky. 1. For Zenobia, see Clay to John M. Clay, Jan. 13, 1851; for Heraldry, see Hampton to Clay, June 3, 1845.

To WILLIAM N. MERCER Washington, February 29, 1852

I received your letter to Mrs. [Mary Kemble] Sumner,[1] placed under cover to me, and left open, as I presumed, that I might peruse its contents, which I accordingly did. I was very glad to find that, during a part of the day, you had attained a certain degree of calmness and composure; and I could not help wishing that you would quit the scenes of Canal Street and Laurel Hill, for a time, where every object you see only serves to remind you of the great affliction which you have recently experienced.[2] I was highly gratified to find that you entertained some purpose of visiting Washington this spring. In my feeble & doubtful condition, I cannot promise to do much to assuage your grief; but I shall be most happy to see you here, and I cannot but hope that a sojourn in this City might benefit you.

I forwarded your letter to Mrs. S. and she advised me of its receipt. She wrote me about a fortnight ago that she and the General [William Sumner] were about to proceed to Havana, where I suppose they have accordingly gone.

I wish that I could say some thing encouraging about the state of my health, but I cannot. I am greatly reduced in flesh, strength and appetite, and I obtain no sleep without the aid of an opiate. For near three months I have not been out of my rooms, except to take two or three drives, on good days, in a close carriage. I am more comfortable than I was some weeks ago, but there is no such radical change as to inspire me with any confidence in my recovery. My distressing cough continues, perhaps, a little abated. To that I attribute my debilitated condition, and unless I can get rid of it, I think it must ultimately prove fatal. Still I may possibly linger on for some months.

Present my affectionate regards to Miss [Eliza] Young.

ALS. LU-Ar. 1. Not found. 2. Anna Mercer's death. See Clay to Mercer, Nov. 14, 1846.

To LUCRETIA HART CLAY Washington, March 3, 1852

I have availed myself of three or four good days to drive out in a close carriage five or six miles. There was no fatigue in the carriage, but I felt my feebleness in ascending several flights of stairs to my rooms. Whether I shall derive any benefit from this external exercise remains to be seen. I have felt none yet. I cannot say indeed that there has been any material change in my condition for many weeks. I am not worse, but I make a very slow if any advance towards a recovery.

I wrote to John [Morrison Clay] some days ago Communicating a full account of my habits, occupations and mode of passing my time.[1] I get quite worn and exhausted by my bed time which is generally eight oclock, and I rise about ten in the morning. I take less and less interest as to what is passing in the world, out side of my own family, children and personal affairs. In all these I feel the liveliest interest, however minute the details may be.

Had you not better employ a gardner for two or three months, until you get the garden laid off and planted as you wish. I do not see how you can well get along without one. Even the drunken man we had last Novr.[2] if he would come and work as well as he did then would be better than none.

John seems to be doing very well. I hope he will find nothing in the training of his horses to vex him and harass him.

I beg you to keep me informed as to your pecuniary wants, as I have ample means to supply them on deposit with Corcoran & Riggs.

My love to John [Morrison Clay] & Mary Watkins.

ALS. DLC-TJC (DNA, M212, R11). 1. Clay to John M. Clay, Feb. 28, 1852. 2. Clay to Lucretia H. Clay, Dec. 1, 1851.

To DANIEL ULLMANN Washington, March 6, 1852

I received your favor[1] transmitting an engrossed copy of the address which you did me the honor to make to me on the occasion of presenting the medal which my New York friends had offered me.[2] I thank you for this corrected copy of the address which is very beautifully engrossed.

The medal has been in the possession of the goldsmiths of this place, who desire the custody of it to gratify public curiosity.[3] You wish it returned that a more accurate impression may be made by striking another. I examined it to see if I could discern the defect in the letters to which you refer, and I confess I could not. If to strike it again will occasion any trouble or expense to my friends, I think it might well be avoided, but if you persist in your desire to have it done, I will have it sent to you by Adams' Express next week.

You rightly understood me in expressing a preference for Mr. [Millard] Fillmore as the Whig candidate for the Presidency.[4] This I did before I left home, and have frequently here in private intercourse, since my arrival at Washington. I care not how generally the fact may be known, but I should not deem it right to publish any formal avowal of that preference under my own signature in the newspapers. Such a course would subject me to the imputation of supposing that my opinions possessed more weight with the public than I apprehend they do. The foundation of my preference is, that Mr. Fillmore has administered the Executive Government with signal success and ability. He has been tried and found true, faithful, honest, and conscientious. I wish to say nothing in derogation from his eminent competitors, they have both rendered great services to their country; the one in the field, the other in the Cabinet.[5] They might, possibly administer the Government as well as Mr. Fillmore has done. But then neither of them has been tried; he has been tried in the elevated position he now holds, and I think that prudence and wisdom had better restrain us from making any change without a necessity for it, the existence of which I do not perceive.

Copy. Printed in Colton, *Clay Correspondence*, 4:628. 1. Not found. 2. Ullmann *et al.* to Clay, Feb. 9, 1852; Speech to Citizens of New York, Feb. 9, 1852. 3. Clay to Ullmann, Sept. 26, 1851. 4. Clay to Ullmann, June 14, 1851. 5. Reference is to Gen. Winfield Scott and Daniel Webster.

From Ralph Elliot, Williamsport, March 8, 1852. Expresses his admiration for Clay, and regrets "that our country did not prefer you in 1844 for President." Prays "that your health and bodily strength may be restored and that you may enjoy the sweet blessing of again meeting your dear family at Ashland." Concludes: "In 1843 my son was baptised Henry Clay. . . . would you be so kind as to send a few lines dedicated to my boy—your admo[ni]tion might be of service to him through life." ALS. DLC-TJC (DNA, M212, R11). There are towns named Williamsport in several different states; it is not known from which one Elliot was writing.

To JOHN MORRISON CLAY Washington, March 13, 1852

I recd. your letter of the 8th. inst. to day. I was sorry to hear of the misfortune of Marg[aret]. Woods[1] in losing her twins. As to our Jennies, I think you had better send the elder one to the young Jack at Mr. Wrights. By the bye he was to complete the purchase of him, by leaving his and Mr. Price's notes with you for our part of him.

As to the young Jenny, if Mr Rhodes keeps a large Jack this year you had better send her to him; if not to such other Jack as you may select.

My health does not advance. I think I took a cold by driving out, and that has thrown me back. My greatest suffering is for sleep. Altho' I take an opiate every night and lye a bed fourteen hours, I do not get two hours of refreshing sleep, and we have varied the opiates from time to time, without effect. I do not know what I shall do.

You cannot imagine how much I was gratified at hearing of your visiting at Thomas's [Hart Clay] and talking kindly together as brothers.

Your mama [Lucretia Hart Clay] has taken great trouble on herself in sending shrubbery and plants to James [Brown Clay]. He has incurred great expences, and gone more in debt than I could have wished.

I gained my other cause in the Supreme Court, which will give me a few hundred dollars.[2] But I am afraid that we shall not make much out of our case before the Brazilian Commission.[3]

My love to your Mama, and all at Ashland & Mansfield.

ALS. Courtesy of Henry Clay Simpson, Lexington, Ky. 1. Hampton to Clay, June 3, 1845. 2. The case concerning the Firemen's Insurance Company of Louisville. See Clay to Lucretia H. Clay, March 22, 1852. 3. The Ray case. See Clay to John M. Clay, Feb. 16, 1851.

To JAMES BROWN CLAY Washington, March 14, 1852

I recd. your letter of the 1st. inst. and at the same time one from Susan [Jacob Clay].[1] They both interested me, as I like to hear all the details of your business and operations. You find, as everybody finds, building and improvement more expensive than you had expected[.]

I[2] received at Xmas the $2000 I expected,[3] but some unexpected calls from John [Morrison Clay] and Thomas [Hart Clay] have been made on me, and I fear I cannot now advance the $1000 which you suppose you may want. I have taken from John $1500 from his earnings at the South, and he has needed $500 and expects he may require a similar sum before he gets through his training this Spring and the completion of his stables. And I had to advance to Thomas about $500.

I ought to receive next June $1400[4] all of which I can let you have the use of, if I get it. And I think I could negotiate the loan of $1000 for you from Corcoran and Riggs of this City, if you need it.

My health continues nearly stationary, not getting better nor worse, except in one particular, and that is sleep. Altho' I take an opiate every night and lye in bed fourteen hours, I can get no sound refreshing sleep. A man, whose flesh, strength, appetite and sleep have been greatly reduced, must be in a bad way, but that is my condition. I have taken immense quantities of drugs, but with little if any effect on my cough, the disease which threatens me. I may linger on some months, but if there be no speedy improvement, I must finally sink under it.

Had you not better send on the bond, in which I am to join you to [William B.] Astor?[5] If[6] I were to die before it is executed, you would have to negotiate about other security.

Give my love to dear Susan and all your children[.] I hope that she will continue to write to me.

ALS. DLC-TJC (DNA, M212, R11). Partially printed in Colton, *Clay Correspondence*, 4:629. 1. Not found. 2. This and the following paragraph are omitted in Colton. 3. Clay to Hunter, Feb. 4, 1852. 4. Debt due from a Mr. Blanton. See Clay to Harrison, March 15, 1852. 5. Bond of Henry Clay & James B. Clay, May 1, 1852. 6. Colton omits the remainder of this letter.

To JAMES O. HARRISON Washington, March 15, 1852

I recd. your favor of the 9th inst. I promised Mr. Blanton to give him until June to pay the balance of his debt to me,[1] and I hope that you will be able so to arrange matters as to give him the promised indulgence.

My health continues nearly stationary, neither getting better nor worse, except in the particular of sleep, of which I can get but little that is refreshing.

My love to Cousin Margaret [Margaretta Ross Harrison].

ALS. DLC-HC (DNA, M212, R21). 1. Possibly Harrison Blanton of Frankfort with whom Clay had had previous business dealings. See 8:40-41. The debt amounted to $1,400. See Clay to James B. Clay, March 14, 1852.

To DANIEL ULLMANN Washington, March 18, 1852

I received your kind letter informing me of the loss of the medal.[1] I am truly sorry for the occurrence, and the more so because I ought to have followed your direction to send it by Adams' Express.[2] But Miss Lynch[3] being in my room the evening before she started for the city of New York, and being informed that I was about to send the medal to you, she kindly offered to take charge of it, and I accordingly placed it under her care. I have no doubt she suffers as much as any of us by its loss, and I would not say one word by way of reproach to her. I should be very sorry if any trouble or expense were taken in replacing it. The fact of its presentation,[4] and even the representations upon the medal have been so widely diffused as to render the presentation of it historical. You will recollect that I jocosely remarked while you were here that some Goth, when I was laid low in the grave, might be tempted to break off my nose and use the valuable metal which it contains! I did not then, however, anticipate the possibility of such an incident occurring so quickly.[5]

Copy. Printed in Colton, *Clay Correspondence*, 4:629. 1. Not found. For the medal, see Clay to Ullmann, Sept. 26, 1851; Ullmann *et al.* to Clay, Feb. 9, 1852; Speech to Citizens of New York, Feb. 9, 1852. 2. Clay to Ullmann, March 6, 1852. 3. Charles Butler, who had accompanied Miss Lynch and her mother back to New York City, related in a letter to Ullmann, dated March 17, 1852, how his carpetbag containing the medal was stolen. Although the bag was later found, the medal was not. Butler, a lawyer who financed a railroad into Chicago, was a major contributor to educational institutions and offered to pay the approximately $2,500 worth of the medal. Bonner, *New-York, The World's Metropolis*, 475. See also New York *Herald*, March 17, 19, 1852. Miss Lynch has not been identified. 4. Ullmann *et al.* to Clay, Feb. 9, 1852; Clay to Citizens of New York, Feb. 9, 1852. 5. On May 3, 1852, Ullmann sent Clay "by Adams' Express two of the Medals executed in Bronze. . . . The head appears even better than the one struck on gold." ALS. DLC-HC (DNA, M212, R6).

To JAMES BROWN CLAY Washington, March 22, 1852

I recd. your letter of the 8th.[1] and return herewith the draught of a bond to Mr. [William B.] Astor, such I suppose as will satisfy him.[2]

I was glad to receive your letter and to peruse all the details in it.

My health continues without any material change. I am very weak, write with no comfort, sleep badly, and have very little appetite for my food[.]

You must not mind what you see in the News papers about me, such as that I was going to the Senate to make a speech &c. Not a word of truth in it.

My love to Susan [Jacob Clay] & all the children.

[P.S.] The bond can be executed and witnessed as to you in St Louis and as to me here, with our respective seals.

ALS. DLC-TJC (DNA, M212, R11). Partially printed in Colton, *Clay Correspondence*, 4:630. 1. Colton omits the remainder of this sentence and the postscript. 2. Draft not found. See Bond of Henry Clay & James B. Clay, May 1, 1852.

To LUCRETIA HART CLAY Washington, March 22, 1852

I shou'd write you oftener, if it were not very uncomfortable for me to write at all, and if I had any thing agreeable to communicate. But I am so feeble that the labor of writing soon exhausts me; and in regard to the state of my health, I have nothing encouraging to communicate. You must not believe all that you see in the news papers about it. There was not, for example, any truth in the statement that I had so much improved as to be able to attend the Senate, which I have not had the remotest thought of doing. We have had some very bad weather of late, and I have not been out of my rooms for a fortnight. The last time I went out, I caught a cold, and do not mean to venture out again until the weather gets very mild. My greatest sufferings at present is the want of sleep, and the want of appetite. My cough continues, altho' perhaps a little diminished. To day I have been spitting some blood, the first for some time. My opinion of my condition remains unchanged. I may linger on for months, but I cannot get well without the removal of the cough.

You will have heard of the loss of my Medal[1] on its return to N. York to have some slight improvement made in it. My friends intend to have another cast.[2]

I informed you through John [Morrison Clay] that I had gained the other of the two causes in the S[upreme]. Court, which formed a motive for my coming on this winter. It was for the Fire Insurance Co. of Louisville,[3] on which I have drawn for my fee, in favor of Mr. Thomas Smith, and if he receives it, I have directed him to forward it to you.

Tell them at home to continue to write to me. It is a great treat to me to get letters from there.

My love to all at Ashland and Mansfield.

ALS. DLC-TJC (DNA, M212, R11). 1. Clay to Ullmann, March 18, 1852. 2. *Ibid.* 3. The case—*Ralph S. and John Fretz* v. *John C. Bull et al., trading under the Name and Style of J.C. Bull & Co., for the use of the Firemen's Insurance Company of Louisville*—was submitted on printed argument by Clay for the appellees. Williams, *Cases Argued and Decided in the Supreme Court of the United States 1850-1851*, 464-71.

From Frances Hucknall Clay, Bretby Park, Staffordshire, England, March 25, 1852. Writes "to put in a claim of relationship." Believes that one of her grandfather's brothers "would be your Predecessor . . . if your family Tradition agrees with ours; there seems little doubt but a relationship does exist: and that we are descendants of the same family." Also claims a half-sister in America, "Adelaide Clay" of "West Fairfield Westmoreland Co. Pennsylvania."

Adds that "I have lately read an announcement in one of our newspapers that you had declined your seat in the Senate owing to declining health[.] I trust you find rest from public business a benefit." Concludes: "Your Country is greatly indebted to you for your most valuable services: I think America is destined to becom[e] a great Nation, perhaps one of the foremost in th[e] World; and your Name will descend with honour in American History to the remotest time." ALS. DLC-HC (DNA, M212, R6).

From Henry Meigs, New York City, March 25, 1852. Writes in behalf of his son-in-law Richard W. Meade, the victim of "a highly improper persecution. . . . You know Richard! I do and I proclaim him a man of religion—honour—and Naval skill—*No accident* (as it is *called*) ever troubled a boat where he had command." Asks

Clay "as the last favour to me, to persuade Secretary [of the Navy William A.] Graham to restore Richard to his place in the Navy." ALS. DNA, RG45, Misc. Letters Recd., March, 1852.

On March 30, 1852, Clay submitted Meig's letter to Graham, adding that "It is from a Most estimable gentleman with whom I formerly served in Congress. I should be extremely glad if his wishes Could be gratified." LS. *Ibid.*

For Meigs (1782-1861)—New York congressman, City alderman, and judge—see *BDAC*. Although the exact nature of the charges against Meade (1807-70) is not clear, he evidently was quickly reinstated. He was commander of the *Massachusetts* in the Pacific from 1853-55, in 1857 was dropped from active status but fought and obtained reinstatement. He attained the rank of captain in 1862. *DAB*; *NCAB*, 4:180.

To Unknown Recipient, New Orleans, March 30, 1852. Explains that "I have never distinctly understood what M[r]. [Louis] Kossuth said of me at Louisville. I certainly had given him no cause of offence. The interview between him and me [Speech to Kossuth, January 9, 1852] cannot be regarded as private, as it certainly was not a confidential one." Points out that others were present; therefore, when "What I had said . . . was variously and sometimes contradictorily represented in the newspapers," Thomas Ewing, who had been present, verified the accuracy of the statement that was published and presented a preface to it which treated Kossuth "with perfect respect." Asserts that "Over my own sentiments and language I thought I had entire control." Copy, extract. Printed in Washington *Daily National Intelligencer*, April 16, 1852.

The newspaper prefaced this letter with the statement that Kossuth had exonerated himself from the charge of disrespect to Clay but that he was "excessively 'provoked' " by the publication of the particulars of their interview. *Ibid.*

To HENRY WILLIAMS Washington, March 30, 1852

I received your letter of the 26th inst. in which you inform me that you are publishing a full length engraved portrait of Mr. [Daniel] Webster, and in which you propose to publish a Similar engraving of myself.[1] Whils't I am thankful for your Kind intentions I must frankly say, that I have no personal wish on the subject, except, that if you do engage in the undertaking it may not prove to be a loseing enterprise.

Of the full length painted portraits of me of which I have now any recollection there are four. One perhaps two in Philadelphia,[2] one in this City,[3] one in Pittsburg[h],[4] and one, in New Orleans.[5] Of these, I think that in Philadelphia by Mr. John Neagle is decidedly the best. I think he had an engraving published from it of full length tho' not as large as life. I never heard what success he had in the sale and distribution of it. Mr. Neagle first painted the bust of me, and then the full length portrait. The head upon the bust is a better likeness than that upon the portrait. Retiring, as I am about to do, from the theatre of public life I should very much fear that you would not find in the sale of the engraving an adequate indemnity for the cost and trouble in publishing it. In my present feeble and emaciated condition, I cannot promise any daguerreotype likeness of me. I should be very glad to see the engraving of Mr. Webster when it is Completed[.]

LS. MHi. 1. No engraving of Clay by Williams has been found. 2. Probably Neagle's portrait of Clay at the Union League Club of Philadelphia and John Wood Dodge's portrait at the Pennsylvania Academy of Fine Arts. See Amyx, "Portraits of Henry Clay," Special Collections, University of Kentucky Library, A:1.67 and A:1.30, respectively. 3. Probably the Chester Harding portrait at the National Portrait Gallery. See *ibid.*, A:1.45c. 4. Not found. 5. Possibly a painting by either Trevor Thomas Fowler or Theodore Sidney Moise, who had studios in New Orleans. See Amyx, A:1.36 and A:1.64.

To LUCRETIA HART CLAY Washington, April 2, 1852

I have recd no letter from home for the last ten days. If I do not write oftener it is because of my feebleness. After writing a few lines, I tire and have to stop. From the 22d. to 29h. March, I was quite unwell, as low as I have been since my arrival here. I began to think that my case was drawing to a close; but I rallied three or four days ago, and have been since better. I have had chills for the last week, but unattended by any fever. I am now taking quinine to check them and it has had good effect.

I wish most sincerely that I was at home with you; but unless I gain more strength, I doubt whether I could perform the journey. March is gone, and a very bad month it was here. and we have had two bright April days, too cold how ever for me to drive out. I still sleep badly, and have not appetite especially for dinner; but I take food enough to sustain me, if I could digest it better. I am very much troubled with constipation. Mr [Thomas] Smith writes me that he sent you the remittance I directed,[1] and I hope you received it safely. He also writes me that Mr. Jacobs [*sic*, John J. Jacob] is not expected to live, and that James [Brown Clay] had been Telegraphed to come to Louisville.[2]

Johns [Morrison Clay] last letter[3] to me was short, and he promised to write me soon a long one, but I have not got it—I want to hear every thing about home, his mares and colts, the horses in training, and the operations on the farm. I am sure that he ought to have an Overseer about this time. Why does he not get the man he wanted?

Tell Mary [Mentelle Clay] that I think she is my delinquent correspondent. I had a short letter from Thomas [Hart Clay][4] since she wrote to me.

My love to all at Ashland & Mansfield.

ALS. DLC-TJC (DNA, M212, R11). 1. Clay to Lucretia H. Clay, March 22, 1852. 2. He had died April 1. See Clay to Lucretia H. Clay, Oct. 31, 1851. 3. Not found. 4. Not found.

To Clay Festival Association of New York City, April 5, 1852. Acknowledges receipt of their note [not found] inviting him to attend a celebration on his birthday (April 12). Regrets that, because of his health, "it is utterly impracticable for me to proceed to New York." Notes that "The commemoration of my birthday . . . chiefly confined to the city of New York, I have ever regarded as being prompted by the hearts of ardent and enthusiastic friends, by their devoted attachment to me, and by their generous and unbounded confidence." Has never thought his birthday would be celebrated nationally, because "Our country has been blessed by Providence with but one man [George Washington] whose birthday ought to be, and I hope ever will be, celebrated as a great national anniversary in all times to come." Expresses his "deep obligation" for their continued regard and asks Providence to bless them. Copy. Printed in Washington *Daily National Intelligencer*, April 15, 1852.

Joseph L. White presided over the celebration on April 12. *Ibid.*

To MARY MENTELLE CLAY Washington, April 7, 1852

I received your letter of the 30th ultimo, and thank you for it. Your letters always give me satisfaction, as they go into details and tell me things which nobody else writes. The state of my health remains pretty much as it has been. But little sleep, appetite, or strength.

If I am spared, and have strength to make the journey, I think of going home in May or early in June, and in that case I wish to send for Thomas [Hart Clay] to accompany me.

I wish you would ask your mother [Lucretia Hart Clay] to pay a small note of mine held by Ike Shelby.[1] I have just heard to-day of the death of Mr. Jacobs [*sic*, John J. Jacob].[2] Poor Susan [Jacob Clay] must be overwhelmed with grief.

We have had no good weather yet.

My love to Susan and the children.

Copy. Printed in Colton, *Clay Correspondence*, 4:630. 1. Isaac Shelby, Jr. 2. Clay to Lucretia H. Clay, Oct. 31, 1851.

To JAMES BROWN CLAY Washington, April 10, 1852

I received your letters transmitting two drafts of a bond to Mr [William B.] Astor[.][1] In a day or two I will send on that which I prepared & which I think he would prefer.[2] I apprehend no difficulty in the completion of the business. When the money is received by me I will dispose of it according to your directions. I have heard of the death of Mr Jacobs [*sic*, John J. Jacob][3] & I offer to you & to Susan [Jacob Clay] assurances of my cordial condolence[.] Tell her that I hope she will bear the event with the fortitude of a Christian. My health continues very feeble, so much so that I write with no comfort or ease as you may infer from this letter being written by the pen of a friend. What will be the issue of my ilness it is impossible to predict. My own own [*sic*] opinion of the case is less favorable than that of my physicians. If my strength continues to fail me I think I cannot last a great while. I feel perfectly composed & resigned to my fate whatever it may be.

Give my love to Susan & all your children[.]

LS. DLC-TJC (DNA, M212, R11). Partially printed in Colton, *Clay Correspondence*, 4:630-31, with first four sentences omitted. 1. Not found. 2. Bond of Henry Clay & James B. Clay, May 1, 1852. 3. Clay to Lucretia H. Clay, Oct. 31, 1851.

To CLEMENT M. BUTLER[1] Washington, April 12, 1852

I thank you for your kind recollection of me, on yesterday, the day of the resurrection of our blessed Saviour, and for the sermon of the Reverend Mr. Melville, to which you called my attention, and which I perused with much edification.[2]

I should have been most happy if I had been permitted to attend your church yesterday, and to unite with my Christian brethren in the devotions and services of the occasion. I understand that your discourse was uncommonly interesting and impressive.

I cannot let this opportunity escape without expressing to you my great obligations to you for the benefit & satisfaction I have derived, under your ministration of the Gospel during the last two or three years.

May God long bless you and continue to prosper you in his service!

ALS. PHi. 1. Butler was chaplain of the Senate and pastor of various churches. *NCAB*, 10:34. 2. Not found.

To JAMES BROWN CLAY Washington, April 12, 1852

I omitted in my last[1] to advert to your fears about the title to the Orchard tract of land. Dr. John Watkins (the father of Jno under whom you claim) married Miss [Eulalie] Trudeau,[2] the daughter of Zeno [*sic*] Trudeau Govr of Upper Louisiana,[3] at St. Louis about the year 1798, 1799, or 1800, and I have no doubt that you may find the registry of their marriage in the Catholic records at St. Louis. Perhaps you may also find recorded the birth of their son, unless that happended after their arrival at N. Orleans.

I know John Watkins very well and should take him to be 48 or 50. I have conversed with him about the sale of the land, telling him how unfortunate he was to have sold it, as if he had retained it, by its rise in value, he would now be in comfortable circumstances. He said his necessities compelled him to sell it, but never stated to me that he was a Minor at the time. He is very poor.

ALS. DLC-TJC (DNA, M212, R11). 1. Clay to James B. Clay, April 10, 1852. 2. Dr. John W. Watkins (b. before 1773, d. New Orleans, 1812) was a physician and mayor of New Orleans. He first married Sarah Clay of Woodford Co., Ky., and then Eulalie Trudeau (1784-1867). Allen, *Henry Watkins*, 34. 3. For Don Zenon Trudeau, lieutenant governor of Upper Louisiana at St. Louis from 1792-99, see Conrad, *Encyclopedia of the History of Missouri*, 6:219.

To THOMAS HART CLAY Washington, April 21, 1852

I wrote to Mary [Mentelle Clay][1] stating that I should desire you to come on to this place to be with me. I have received no answer to that letter owing perhaps to the interruptions in the regular arrival of the Mail. I now wish that you would leave home about the 10th or 12th of May and join me here at the National Hotel.

My desire is to go home towards the last of May or early in June if I can command strength to take me there and if I cannot, which I fear will be the case, you can remain with me until there is a crisis in my disease[.] We have had the vilest spring I ever knew for invalids. There has not been one day when I could drive out with safety.

Hopes are entertained that when the weather gets better I may be benefited by fresh air and some exercise. There has been no material change in my condition for months except that I am getting weaker & weaker[.]

I request you to call on Mr Milton the clerk in Mr Pindle's [*sic*, Richard Pindell] office and ask him to do me the favor to go to the Clerks office and obtain a memorandum from my account as Executor of Col. [Thomas] Hart of two items, one on the last settlement of the account and the other in a previous settlement some years ago showing the amount retained by me for the heirs of Sophia Clay.[2] I wish to pay it over to Clay Taylor[3] the only heir and I cannot do it until I get the amount.

My love to Mary and all the children[.]

LS. KyU. 1. Possibly Clay to Mary M. Clay, April 7, 1852, although he does not clearly summon Thomas. 2. For Sophia Clay and the inheritance, see 1:96, 886; 3:117-18. 3. For Clay Taylor, grandson of Porter Clay and Sophia Grosch Clay, see Smith & Rogers, *The Clay Family*, 90.

To LUCRETIA HART CLAY Washington, April 25, 1852

I recd. to day a letter from Mary [Mentelle Clay] and Thomas [Hart Clay],[1] which gave me gratifying information as to affairs at Ashland and Mansfield. I wish that I had any such to communicate about myself; but I have not.

There is no improvement whatever in my health; but a constant decline in my strength, and all the essential functions of nature. I have had chills for abt. a fortnight, which I have escaped the two last days by the use of quinine and lying in bed until two oclock.

Thomas may come on and join me as soon as he pleases, altho I much fear that I shall not have strength to carry me home. He will have I suppose to resort to your purse to furnish him money for the journey.

Enocs[2] the blacksmiths bill, if it be for one year, is about fifty per cent more than any former bill I ever paid and there must be some mistake in it. Tell John [Morrison Clay] to investigate it, and if he it [*sic*], and if he is not satisfied pay him $80. and let the rest remain until I get home if I ever do.

I am afraid my dear Wife that I shall trench upon your funds. I beg John to let me know of the state of them. I have plenty of money here some $1200 dollars.

I write to nobody in my hand writing now but to you. How long I shall be able to do this is uncertain.

My love to all at Ashland and Mansfield.

ALS. DLC-TJC (DNA, M212, R11). 1. Not found. 2. Probably Enoch Clark, a coachmaker with whom Clay had done business since 1833. MacCabe, *Directory of the City of Lexington . . . 1838 & '39.*

Telegraph to James O. Harrison, Lexington, April 28, 1852. Via the New Orleans and Ohio Telegraph Company sends the following message: "Tell Thomas [Hart Clay] to come as soon as he can[.]" D. DLC-James O. Harrison Papers.

To JAMES BROWN CLAY Washington, April 28, 1852

I transmit a Check on N. York for $500, which, with the $4000 I draw on Mr. [William B.] Astor[1] for amounts to the $4500 which he authorized me to draw on him for on your a/c.

My health continues precarious & extremely critical. Unless there is a favorable change soon, I cannot hold out much longer. I have sent for Thomas [Hart Clay.][2]

My love to Susan [Jacob Clay] and the children.

ALS. DLC-TJC (DNA, M212, R11). 1. Bond of Henry Clay & James Brown Clay, May 1, 1852. 2. Telegram to James O. Harrison, April 28, 1852.

To JOHN MORRISON CLAY Washington, April 30, 1852

In addition to the slaves I have heretofore given you I send herewith a bill of sale[1] for Bill Buster whom your mother [Lucretia Hart Clay] told me you were anxious to own. I include in the same bill of sale the stud Yorkshire & as you will perceive I have relinquished to you all my interest in his earnings.

You are entitled to one half of the $1500 which Wright & Price[2] owe for my big Jack and you had better preserve this letter as evidence of your interest. I have made my dear son the most ample provision for you in what I have given you from time to time & left you by my will.[3] I hope you will take care of it & not abuse the blessings which are in your power to enjoy[.]

LS. NcD. 1. In the bill of sale, dated at Washington, April 30, 1852, Clay "in consideration of . . . love & affection" plus one dollar, conveys to John Morrison Clay "a young negro man called Bill Buster . . . also my imported stud horse Yorkshire together with all his earnings heretofore or hereafter resulting by or from serving mares." Adds that "the said Horse shall be permitted to serve the mares owned by sons Thomas [Hart Clay] & James [Brown Clay] gratis." DS. Henry Clay Memorial Foundation, Lexington, Ky. Attested to by Joseph R. Underwood. 2. Clay and Isaac Wright had concluded an agreement, dated Oct. 18, 1850, in which Clay placed two Jacks in the possession of Wright, who agreed to keep them at his own expense and prove them by making them serve mares. Wright received one-half of the elder Jack and one-fourth of the younger, and, if they were sold the proceeds were to be divided between Clay and Wright in those proportions with a sale taking place only with the concurrence of both parties. AD, in Clay's hand, signed also by Wright. DLC-TJC (DNA, M212, R19). Price has not been identified. 3. Last Will & Testament, July 10, 1851.

Bond of Henry Clay & James Brown Clay, May 1, 1852. Both men "are held and firmly bound unto William B. Astor in the sum of Twenty thousand dollars, lawful money of the U. States." Continues: "whereas the said James B. Clay has this day borrowed and received of the said W.B. Astor the sum of Ten thousand dollars, with interest at six per cent per annum," one-fourth of the principle is due on January 1, 1853, an additional one-fourth on January 1 in 1854, 1855, and 1856, and "the interest to be paid semi-annually . . . to the said Astor in the City of New York." ADS. DLC-HC (DNA, M212, R6). A record of principle and interest payments, written on the other side of the bond in an unknown hand, indicates that the debt was paid off on December 31, 1856.

From John Tappan, Boston, May 7, 1852. Sends Clay a "reprint of an English edition of the Triumph over Death." Hopes that "now when earth is receding from your view, it may convey consolation and hope, before the Nation is called to mourn the loss of one of her most illustrious Sons, & most highly gifted Statesmen." ALS. DLC-TJC (DNA, M212, R11).

For Tappan (1781-1871)—merchant, president of the American Tract Society, and older brother of Lewis and Arthur Tappan—see *NCAB*, 2:321. The book he sent Clay was probably Robert Boreman's *The Triumph of Faith Over Death*, first printed in London in 1654.

From Sir William Clay, Mayfair, England, May 8, 1852. Notes that "So many years have elapsed since the only intercourse I ever had the pleasure of holding with you—by letter and amity ceased—that I can hardly flatter myself you yet recollect its occurrence." Nevertheless, introduces his son William Dickinson Clay who "is about to make the tour of the United States." Wishes he could visit the U.S. himself but doubts his public duties will permit him to do so. Copy. Printed in Colton, *Clay Correspondence*, 4:632. See 9:6.

From Millard Fillmore, Washington, June 7, 1852. Explains that he "has a sister in town, who entertains a very high respect and veneration for Mr. Clay, and desires very much to see him." Expresses his willingness to "call with her at any day and hour that Mr. Clay shall name, but he begs Mr. Clay not to grant this indulgence if it can by any possibility injure him." L. DLC-HC (DNA, M212, R6).

Fillmore's two sisters who were living at this time were Olive Armstrong Fillmore Johnson and Julia Fillmore Harris. It is not known to which of these Fillmore referred. William A. DeGregorio, *The Complete Book of U.S. Presidents* (New York, 1984), 188.

"MEMORANDA OF H. CLAY" Washington, late June, 1852

I leave with you[1] a check on Messrs. Corcoran & Riggs for any balance standing to my credit in the books of their bank at the time you present the check. The balance now is about $1600, but it may be diminished before you have occasion to apply for it.

Mr. [Joseph R.] Underwood will draw from the secretary of the Senate[2] any balance due to me there for my services, and pay it over to you.

Out of these funds I wish you to pay Dr. [William W.] Hall's bill, the apothecary's bill, and Dr. Francis Jackson's bill of Philadelphia.[3]

Whatever may be necessary to pay those debts, and may be necessary to bear your expenses to Kentucky, had better be appropriated and reserved accordingly, and the balance to be converted in a bank check on New York, which will be safer to carry and more valuable in Kentucky.

I have settled with James G. Marshall, my servant, and at the end of this month he will have paid me all that I have advanced him, and I shall owe him two dollars. The deed for his lot in Detroit, which he assigned to me as security for being his indorser on a note in bank, is in my little trunk in your mother's [Lucretia Hart Clay] room, in the bundle marked "Notes and valuable papers." I wish the deed taken out and delivered to James as the matter is settled.

The Messrs. Hunter, who have bought my Illinois land,[4] have been very punctual in paying me the purchase money as it became due heretofore. The last payment of $2000 is due at Christmas. They have written to me that they will come over and pay it, and at the same time receive a pair of Durham calves as a present which I promised them. I wish that promise fulfilled. The heifer I bought of Mr. Hunt,[5] being a descendant of the imported cow Lucretia, I designed for one of [the] animals to be presented.

There is a note of upwards of $1000 among my papers in the pocketbook, well secured and payable in New Orleans next November. My executors[6] ought to send it down there for collection.

Copy. Printed in J.O. Harrison, "Henry Clay Reminiscences by His Executor," *Century Illustrated Monthly Magazine* (Dec., 1886), 33:176-77. Described by Harrison as "probably the last document ever signed by Mr. Clay." 1. Thomas Hart Clay. 2. Asbury Dickens of N.C. 3. Clay to Newport, *ca.* Dec. 15, 1851. 4. Clay to Hunter, Feb. 4, 1852. 5. Probably John W. Hunt. 6. James O. Harrison and Thomas A. Marshall were Clay's executors and Lucretia Hart Clay the executrix. See Last Will and Testament, July 10, 1851.

From William B. Craig, Canonsburg, Pa., June 29, 1852. "Expecting soon to stand as a watchman upon the walls of Zion," asks Clay " 'Are secret societies promotive of the Churche's interests.' " If "in the midst of sickness, disease, and pain" Clay cannot answer, "I shall nevertheless" continue to pray "that the hand which has guided and controled you through life might be your support amid all its gathering storms." ALS. DLC-HC (DNA, M212, R6).

EXECUTIVE ORDER OF MILLARD FILLMORE 12:30 P.M., Washington, June 29, 1852

The tolling bells announce the death of the Hon. Henry Clay.[1] Though this event has been long anticipated, yet the painful bereavement could never be fully realized. I am sure all hearts are too sad at this moment to attend to business, and I therefore respectfully suggest that your Department be closed for the remainder of the Day.

Copy. Printed in *MPP* (1897 edition), 6:2697. Addressed to the heads of the several Executive Departments. 1. Clay had died at 11:17 a.m. Van Deusen, *Henry Clay*, 424.

Resolution of the U.S. Senate, Washington, July 2, 1852. Resolved, "That the President [pro tempore] of the Senate [William R. King] be requested to communicate to the Executive of the State of Kentucky [Lazarus W. Powell], information of the death of the Hon. Henry Clay [Executive Order of Millard Fillmore, June 29, 1852], late a Senator from that State. DS, signed by Asbury Dickens, secretary of the Senate. Ky.

On July 2, 1852, King wrote Powell "to communicate to you, the painful intelligence of the decease of the Hon'ble Henry Clay . . . on the 29th ultimo." LS. *Ibid.*

For Gov. Lazarus W. Powell (1812-67), see Collins, *History of Kentucky*, 2:680-81.

Funeral services were held in the Senate chamber on July 1 and a committee of senators accompanied Clay's remains home. The funeral cortege passed through Baltimore, Wilmington, Philadelphia, the prinicpal places in New Jersey, New York, Albany, Ithaca, Syracuse, Rochester, Buffalo, Cleveland, Cincinnati, and Louisville on the way to Lexington. Clay was interred in the Lexington Cemetery on July 10, 1852, with approximately 30,000 persons in attendance. Van Deusen, *Henry Clay*, 424; Schurz, *Henry Clay*, 2:405-6.

CALENDAR OF UNPUBLISHED LETTERS AND OTHER DOCUMENTS

Letters deemed to have slight historical importance to an understanding of Henry Clay and his career are listed below. Copies of them are on file in the Special Collections Department, Margaret I. King Library, University of Kentucky, Lexington, and may be consulted by interested persons. The locus of the original manuscript of each letter has been included below, as has an indication of the general subject matter of each. Subject classification code numbers have been employed as follows:

1 Requests for general assistance and government assistance, information, documents, reports, correspondence, books and other printed materials.

2 Transmission of routine information and documents, including that between the Executive and Legislative branches.

3 Applications, recommendations, appointments, and resignations pertaining to government employment and political office.

4 Correspondence and transmission of information relating to the claims of private citizens against the U.S. and foreign governments:
   a. United States
   b. Great Britain
   c. France
   d. Spain
   e. Holland
   f. Other European nations
   g. Latin American nations.

5 Correspondence and transmission of information relating to land grants, pensions, and related legal actions.

6 Routine correspondence relating to:
   a. Forwarding of mail
   b. Interviews and audiences
   c. Introductions & character references
   d. Invitations, acceptances, regrets, condolences
   e. Appreciation, gratitude, social pleasantries
   f. Subject matter not clear
   g. Applications, recommendations pertaining to private employment
   h. Autograph requests.

7 Routine legal correspondence and documents relating to:
   a. Clay's law practice as counsel or executor
   b. Cases in which Clay was plaintiff, defendant, witness, or deponent

c. James Morrison Estate management
d. Eliza Jane Weir guardianship
e. James and/or Ann Hart Brown Estate management.

8 Routine correspondence and documents (including deeds, agreements, leases) relating to Clay's land purchases and sales, livestock transactions and breeding, and investments.

9 Routine bills, receipts, checks, bank drafts, promissory notes, loans, payments, rents, mortgages, tax documents.

10 Correspondence relating to routine political and professional services rendered constituents, colleagues, friends, and other politicians.

11 Remarks in Senate:
   a. Procedural matters
   b. Petitions, resolutions, memorials
   c. Asides, clarifications, brief answers
   d. Routine business with Executive department
   e. Printing of documents
   f. Salaries, appropriations, etc. relating to government employees and expenditures [*Congressional Globe* is abbreviated *CG*].

12 Miscellaneous.

JANUARY 1844
1 From Josiah Ennis, DLC-TJC, 9
1 From James Brown Clay, DLC-TJC, 9
6 To Clay Club of Montgomery, Ala., Washington *Daily National Intelligencer*, Feb. 5, 1844, 6d
6 To Francis Mahan, PHi, 6e
6 To James Dunnica, NN, 6b
23 From George Baughman, DLC-TJC, 9

FEBRUARY 1844
5 With Samuel Judah, Henry Clay, Jr., G. Schmidt, Charles J. Bayard, Fort Collins, Colo., 7a
14 *Clay* v. *Tibbatts*, Ky., 7b
15 To William H. Pollard *et al.*, Dr. Thomas W. Martin, Birmingham, Ala., 6d

MARCH 1844
16 To Montmullin & Cornwall, DLC-TJC, 9

APRIL 1844
1 From John H. Lusby, DLC-TJC, 9
1 *Clay* v. *Gilmer* DLC-TJC, 7b
8 To Edward Everett, MHi, 6c
15 To Thomas W. Duffield, Jr., *et al.*, KyLoF, 6d
19 To Rachel H. Myers, MH, 6e

MAY 1844
1 James R. Annan *et al.*, MdHi, 6d
1 To Citizens of Berkeley County, Va., F.V. Aler's *History of Martinsburg and Berkeley County, West Virginia*, 110-11, 6d
10 To Thomas L. Smith, DNA, 9
18 With Leslie Combs & Daniel Vertner, NjP, 9

JUNE 1844

ca. June To Clerk of Fayette Circuit Court, DLC-TJC, 9
8 From W.P. Browning, DLC-TJC, 9
15 To Northern Bank of Ky., DLC-TJC, 9
16 To Bank of Ky.-Lex. branch, DLC-TJC, 9
22 From John J. Dudley, DLC-TJC, 9
30 To James W. Boatner, Lincoln National Life Foundation, 6

JULY 1844

1 From Joseph Ficklin, DLC-TJC, 9
5 From Garrett Davis, DLC-TJC, 9
5 *Corder & Paul* v. *Clay*, Sc, 7b
5 From Garrett Davis, DLC-TJC, 9
8 From John J. Dudley, DLC-TJC, 9
8 To Conway D. Whittle, ViU, 7a
10 To Rufus & James Turnbull, DLC-TJC, 8
16 To Lord Ashburton, GU, 6c
17 To Northern Bank of Ky., DLC-TJC, 9
19 To Northern Bank of Ky., DLC-TJC, 9
19 To Northern Bank of Ky., DLC-TJC, 9
19 To Northern Bank of Ky., DLC-TJC, 9
19 To Northern Bank of Ky., DLC-TJC, 9
20 To Northern Bank of Ky., DLC-TJC, 9
20 To Northern Bank of Ky., DLC-TJC, 9
20 From Henry Clay Hart, DLC-TJC, 9
22 To Northern Bank of Ky., DLC-TJC, 9
22 To Northern Bank of Ky., DLC-TJC, 9
22 From James Shelby, DLC-TJC, 9
31 To Northern Bank of Ky., DLC-TJC, 9
31 To S.C. Leakin *et al.*, MdHi, 6d

AUGUST 1844

3 From Samuel Clay, DLC-TJC, 9
5 To Samuel Judah, Charles J. Bayard, Fort Collins, Colo., 7a
28 From Edmund M. Hockaday, DLC-TJC, 9
28 To Cornelius Mathews, NHi, 7a

OCTOBER 1844

7 To Northern Bank of Ky., DLC-TJC, 9
7 From Joseph Ficklin, DLC-TJC, 9
21 From Andrew McFadden, DLC-TJC, 9
31 From Kennedy, Smith & Co., DLC-TJC, 9

NOVEMBER 1844

1 From D. & J. Warner, DLC-TJC, 9
16 From Kennedy, Smith & Co., DLC-TJC, 8
30 To Henry Clay, Jr., DLC-HC, 9
30 From Henry Clay, Jr., DLC-HC, 9

DECEMBER 1844

9 From Joseph Ficklin, DLC-TJC, 9
9 From Joseph Ficklin, DLC-TJC, 9
9 From John Argabright, DLC-TJC, 8, 9
10 From Albert Florea, DLC-TJC, 9
16 To N. Guilford, ICHi, 6d
22 From R.M. Bradley, DLC-HC, 7a
26 To John J. Crittenden, DLC-Crittenden Papers, 1, 4c
27 From Edward C. Cunningham, DLC-TJC, 9
28 From James Fowler Simmons, DLC-Simmons Papers, 6c
31 From Joseph Ficklin, DLC-TJC, 9

JANUARY 1845
1845 From William Pullen, DLC-TJC, 9
ca. Jan. From D.M. Craig, DLC-TJC, 9
8 From A.M. January & Son, DLC-TJC, 9

FEBRUARY 1845
4 To Robert C. Davis, PHC, 6h
10 To Whom It May Concern, MdHi, 6c
18 From W.L. Stevenson & W.H. Henry, DLC-TJC, 9

MARCH 1845
1 From James R. Norvall, DLC-TJC, 7a
4 From Samuel Judah, DLC-TJC, 7a
8 From Kennedy, Smith & Co., DLC-TJC, 8
11 From George, Lapping, & Co., *The Dollar Farmer*, IV:10, 6e, 8
13 From John J. Dudley, DLC-TJC, 9
19 To Joseph E. Wennar, OClWHi, 6h
31 From Robert Garrett & Sons, DLC-TJC, 9

APRIL 1845
1 From John H. Lusby, DLC-TJC, 9
1 From Dudley & Carty, DLC-TJC, 9
12 To R.A. New *et al.*, PPPrHi, 6d
15 To Rufus K. Turnage, NN, 7a
25 To Unknown Recipient, Colton, *Clay Correspondence*, 3:20-21, 6e
28 To J. Phillips Phoenix, NNC, 6c
28 To Edward Everett, MHi, 6c
30 To William T. Buckner *et al.*, NhD, 6d

MAY 1845
7 From William X. Tyree, DLC-TJC, 9
14 To Edward Everett, Henry Clay Memorial Foundation, Lexington, Ky., 6c
14 To Robert Walsh, KyU, 6c
14 To Baring Brothers & Co., Henry T. Duncan, Jr., Lexington, Ky., 6c
14 To William R. King, Henry Clay Memorial Foundation, Lexington, Ky., 6c
29 To Northern Bank of Ky., DLC-TJC, 9

JULY 1845
3 From William B. Astor, DLC-HC, 9
3 To George, Lapping, & Co., *The Dollar Farmer*, IV:10, 6e
12 To Deputy Postmaster at Greencastle, Ind., InHi, 12
15 To Daniel P. King, KyU, 6e
31 To S.H. Hammond, MB, 6e

AUGUST 1845
1 To Thomas Grubbs, ViU, 9
4 To Robert Garrett & Sons, DLC-HC, 12
11 From T.W. Cridland[?], DLC-TJC, 9
12 To John Quincy Adams, KyLoF, 6c
25 From William Robertson *et al.*, Washington *Daily National Intelligencer*, Sept. 6, 1845, 6d
25 To William Robertson *et al.*, Washington *Daily National Intelligencer*, Sept. 6, 1845, 6d

SEPTEMBER 1845
4 From R.J. Atkinson, DLC-TJC, 9
12 To Bank of Ky.-Lex. branch, DLC-TJC, 9

OCTOBER 1845
4 To John Quincy Adams, MHi, 6c
7 To Bank of Ky.-Lex. branch, DLC-TJC, 9

11 To Henry Grinnell, KyU, 6c
11 To Joseph R. Ingersoll, J. Winston Coleman, Jr., Lexington, Ky., 6c

NOVEMBER 1845
1 To Samuel H. Davis, KyU, 6h

DECEMBER 1845
1 From John Argabright, DLC-TJC, 8, 9
16 To James Brown Clay, DLC-HC, 7

JANUARY 1846
1846 From John Munter, DLC-TJC, 9

FEBRUARY 1846
14 From Chouteau, Merle & Sanford, DLC-TJC, 9
17 To R.H. Chinn, Benjamin H. Branch, Jr., Arlington, Va., 6d

MARCH 1846
25 *Commonwealth* v. *Shelby*, J. Winston Coleman, Jr., Lexington, Ky., 7a

APRIL 1846
nd To Whom It May Concern, William C. Scott, New York, N.Y., 6c
17 From Charles D. Drake, DLC-TJC, 9

MAY 1846
nd To Mr. & Mrs. W. Maury, ViU, 6e
2 To Edmund Burke, DLC-Burke Papers, 6e
9 From James Fowler Simmons, DLC-Simmons Papers, 6c
12 To Henry Clay, Jr., Henry Clay Memorial Foundation, Lexington, Ky., 6c
27 To Northern Bank of Ky., DLC-TJC, 9
29 From James Shelby, DLC-TLC, 9

JUNE 1846
1 To Northern Bank of Ky., DLC-TJC, 9
1 To Northern Bank of Ky., DLC-TJC, 9
20 To Elijah W. Craig, DLC-TJC, 9

JULY 1846
nd To Andrew Jackson Donelson, DLC-HC, 6c
9 To Bank of Ky.-Lex Branch, DLC-TJC, 9
11 To Bank of Ky.-Lex Branch, DLC-TJC, 9

SEPTEMBER 1846
7 From G. Washington Anderson, DLC-TJC, 7e, 9
10 To John Wood, Jr., ViU, 6f
10 To Thomas B. Stevenson *et al.*, KyU, 6d
21 From Bush & Barley, DLC-TLC, 9

OCTOBER 1846
nd To Whom It May Concern, Mrs. Henry Jackson, Sr., Danville, Ky., 6c
12 To Thomas Helm, Jackson D. Guerrant, Danville, Ky., 6c
25 To James Brown Clay, DLC-TJC, 6
30 From William B. Astor, DLC-TJC, 9
30 *Morrison* v. *Cockerill's Heirs*, Circuit Court, Union County, Ky., 7a

NOVEMBER 1846
2 To S.H. Wiley, DLC-HC, 6h
3 To William M. Humphries, Fleming County, Ky., Deed Book 28, 7a
10 From Josiah Randall, KyLxT, 7a, 9
13 From Ambrose H. Barnett, DLC-TJC, 9

17 To Josiah Randall, KyLxT, 7a, 9
18 From Bush & Barley, DLC-TJC, 9
25 To Bank of Ky.-Lex. branch, DLC-TJC, 9

DECEMBER 1846
25 To Mr. Virtue, InU, 6h

JANUARY 1847
1847 From P. Swigert, DLC-TJC, 7a, 9
2 From William B. Astor, MH, 9
9 From J. Twinell, DLC-TJC, 9
13 From Cordeviolle & Lacroix, DLC-TJC, 9
20 From William B. Astor, DLC-TJC, 9
26 To George Eustis, DLC-HC, 6d

FEBRUARY 1847
2 To Mrs. Conrey, ICHi, 6d
22 From William B. Astor, MH, 9

MARCH 1847
3 To James Brown Clay, DLC-TJC, 9
5 From Foreman & Kennedy, DLC-TJC, 9

APRIL 1847
3 To R.W. Thompson, Lincoln National Life Foundation, 9
8 From William B. Astor, MH, 9
29 To W.G. & Eleanor Talbot, DLC-TJC, 7c, 9

MAY 1847
8 To Northern Bank of Ky., DLC-TJC, 9

JUNE 1847
3 To Harrison Gill, KyHi, 7a
3 From Thomas C. Patrick, DLC-TJC, 9
8 To Northern Bank of Ky., DLC-TJC, 9
8 From Joseph Ficklin, DLC-TJC, 9
11 From Bush & Barley, DLC-TJC, 9

JULY 1847
nd To George Bancroft, NIC, 6c
ca. 1 From Joseph Ficklin, DLC-TJC, 9
6 To Francis T. Brooke, Henry Clay Simpson, Lexington, Ky., 6h
12 To Abbott Lawrence, MH, 6c
12 To Samuel Appleton, Anna V. Parker, Ghent, Ky., 6c

AUGUST 1847
nd Testimonial for Hertz Leja, optician, Lexington *Observer & Kentucky Reporter*, July 29, 1848, 6c, 6e
nd To Mr. Butcher, PHi, 6e
16 To John H. Sherburne, KyU, 6e

SEPTEMBER 1847
8 To John A. Pool, J. Winston Coleman, Jr., Lexington, Ky., 6d
23 From Daniel Hitt, DLC-TJC, 9
24 *Clay* v. *Scott, &c., Reports of Cases at Common Law and in Equity . . . The Court of Appeals of Kentucky*, VII: 554-56, 7b

OCTOBER 1847
3 From J.R. McGowan, DLC-TJC, 9
15 From Unknown Sender, KyU, 7a
20 From William B. Astor, MH, 9

NOVEMBER 1847
1 To John H.C. Campbell, MH, 6h
2 To Northern Bank of Ky., DLC-TJC, 9
3 Bond of Alexander & Robert Carrick, KyU, 7a
3 Bond of Alexander & Robert Carrick, KyU, 7a
15 From F. Uttinger, DLC-TJC, 9
18 To Joseph Gales, Jr., CtY, 6c

DECEMBER 1847
11 From Asa Collins, DLC-TJC, 9

JANUARY 1848
8 To J.J. Speed, J. Winston Coleman, Jr., Lexington, Ky., 6d
21 To William McLain, DLC, 6e

FEBRUARY 1848
3 From A.W. Loomis *et al.*, Pittsburgh *Daily Gazette*, Feb. 17, 1848, 6d
12 To A.W. Loomis *et al.*, Pittsburgh *Daily Gazette*, Feb. 17, 1848, 6d
15 To Mrs. Jay Cooke, Ellis P. Oberholtzer, *Jay Cooke, Financier of the Civil War*, I:80, 6e
17 To George Adland, KyU, 6e, 7a
19 To William McLain, DLC, 6a, 6e
22 To Harriette McIlhany, ViU, 6e
28 To William or Carrie Richardson [?], KyLo, 6d

MARCH 1848
6 *Cordes & Paul* v. *Clay*, Sc, 7b
6 *Cordes & Paul* v. *Clay*, Sc, 7b
7 *Cordes & Paul* v. *Clay*, Sc, 7b
7 *Cordes & Paul* v. *Clay*, Sc, 7b
8 *Cordes & Paul* v. *Clay*, Sc, 7b
13 To Mrs. W. Jervis, DLC-Polk Papers, 6e
21 From Emily Bliss Souder, Henry Clay Memorial Foundation, Lexington, Ky., 12

APRIL 1848
4 Deed to James Brown Clay, DLC-TJC, 8
5 To William Maxwell, ViHi, 6e
11 To Whom It May Concern, DLC-HC, 6c
12 To William D. Bishop, CtY, 6e, 6h

MAY 1848
nd To Richard Rush, NHi, 6c
8 From William B. Astor, DLC-TJC, 9
11 To Lansing Thurber, MH, 6h
15 To William R. Lawrence, CtHT, 6h
15 To Christopher Hughes, MiU, 6c
25 To Joseph Doyle, Fleming County, Ky., Deed Book, 28, 7a
25 From John B. Tilford & Co., DLC-TJC, 9
25 To John Sloane, CtY, 6c
25 To N.B. Blunt, CtY, 6c

JULY 1848
2 From William C. Micou, DLC-TJC, 7a

AUGUST 1848
4 From Jane Tibbatts, DLC-TJC, 9
9 To R.H. Northrop, NcU, 6h
10 To Bank of Ky.-Lex. branch, DLC-TJC, 9
30 From Inskeep, Shackelford, & McKee, DLC-HC, 7a

SEPTEMBER 1848
20 From David D. Mitchell, DLC-TJC, 9

20 From St. Louis County, Mo., DLC-TJC, 9
21 To Northern Bank of Ky., DLC-TJC, 9
25 To Bank of Ky.-Lex. Branch, DLC-TJC, 9
26 To Queen's County Agricultural Society, KyU, 6d

OCTOBER 1848
3 From Thomson, Evans, & Chenault, Henry Clay Memorial Foundation, Lexington, Ky., 7a
9 To J. O'Fallon, MoSHi, 6c, 6e
20 To David D. Mitchell, MoSHi, 6c
30 From William B. Astor, DLC-HC, 9

NOVEMBER 1848
29 From Thompson heirs, DLC-TJC, 7a

DECEMBER 1848
1 To Whom It May Concern, L-M, 6c

JANUARY 1849
1 From James Jackson, DLC-TJC, 9
1 From Josiah Ennis, DLC-TJC, 9

FEBRUARY 1849
4 From Alexander Campbell, DNA, 6c
6 To Philip B. Hockaday, DNA, 3
7 From William Woodbridge, MiD, 6c
8 From James C. Jones, DNA, 6c
12 To John J. Crittenden, DNA, 6c
15 From Henry M. Shreve, DNA, 6c
15 From William Sprague, DNA, 3
17 From C.S. Hawks, DNA, 6c
ca. 17 From Daniel Henshaw, DNA, 6c
28 To John M. Clayton, DNA, 3

MARCH 1849
7 To Zebulon T. Davis, KyLoF, 3
9 To John M. Clayton, DNA, 6c
10 From William B. Preston, DNA, 3
13 To Mrs. J.W. Jervis, Washington *Daily National Intelligencer*, Jan. 7, 1850, 6e
16 To Reverdy Johnson, MdHi, 6c

APRIL 1849
6 To Whom It May Concern, OC, 6c
7 To Thomas Ewing, KyLoF, 3, 6c
9 To George Getz, DNA, 6c, 6e
11 To John M. Clayton, DNA, 3
12 To Egbert Benson, KyU, 3, 6c
16 To B.T. Kavanaugh, DNA, 3
16 To Mr. Dimmock, MB, 3
17 To John E. Lewis, DNA, 3, 6e
18 To John M. Clayton, DNA, 3
20 From James Jackson, DLC-TJC, 9

MAY 1849
nd From Capt. Angell, Henry Clay Memorial Foundation, Lexington, Ky., 12
9 From John M. Monohan, DLC-TJC, 9
12 To Northern Bank of Ky., OTU, 9
24 From William D. Henderson, DNA, 3, 6c, 6e
24 To George Bancroft, George R. Loeb, Philadelphia, Pa., 6c
28 To John M. Clayton, DNA, 3

JUNE 1849
7 From William McLain, DLC, 12
8 To William Connely, Mrs. James E. McDonald, Charleston, S.C., 3, 6e
11 To William Wickes, KyU, 3, 6e
13 To William McLain, DLC, 12
15 From William W. Hazard, DLC-TJC, 6e
16 To John M. Clayton, DNA, 3
21 To Thomas Ewing, DNA, 3
28 From S. Simpson, DLC-HC, 6e

JULY 1849
6 To Isaac N. Bernard, MoU, 6e, 6f
7 From Henry T. Duncan, DLC-TJC, 9
9 To John M. Clayton, DNA, 3
13 To John M. Clayton, DNA, 3
16 To George T. Williamson, KyU, 7a
21 From E.H. Blackburn, DLC-TJC, 9
23 To John M. Clayton, DNA, 3
23 To William Chase Barney, NRU, 3

AUGUST 1849
4 From William McLain, DLC, 12
20 To John M. Clayton, ICHi, 6c
21 To James Y. Earle, ViU, 6d
21 From Philip R. Fendall, PP, 7a
ca. 22 To Miss Smith, PPL, 6d
30 From William C. Tennant, DLC-HC, 9
31 To Susan Jacob Clay, DLC-TJC, 6e
31 To William B. Preston, KyU, 3

SEPTEMBER 1849
nd From William H. Thompson *et al.*, DNA, 3
3 From Joseph B. Weaver, DLC-TJC, 9
3 From George W. Crawford, DNA, 3
3 From William B. Preston, DNA, 3
18 To John M. Clayton, DNA, 3
19 To John M. Clayton, DNA, 3
20 To James M. Waller, MjMoHP, 3

OCTOBER 1849
15 *Clay* v. *Pindell*, Ky., 7b, 7c
15 To Henry Grinnell, Dr. Thomas D. Clark, Lexington, Ky., 6a
17 To Northern Bank of Ky., DLC-TJC, 9
22 From Frazer & Gough, DLC-TJC, 9
24 To William Crutchfield, DLC-Breckinridge Family Papers, 6e
24 To Northern Bank of Ky., DLC-TJC, 9
25 To Northern Bank of Ky., DLC-TJC, 9
25 With Thomas Hughes, DLC-TJC, 8
29 To John M. Clayton, DNA, 6c
31 From William B. Astor, DLC-TJC, 9

NOVEMBER 1849
nd To Thomas S. Redd, DLC-TJC, 7a
20 From John Sloane, MH, 6c

DECEMBER 1849
3 To John M. Clayton, DLC-Clayton Papers, 3
3 To Henry C. Wood, DLC-Wood Papers, 3
5 To John M. Clayton, DeHi, 6d
6 To Thomas Ewing, DLC-HC, 6a, 6f
8 To William H. Seward, NRU, 6a

15 Remark in Senate, *CG*, 31 Cong., 1 Sess., 36, 11d
17 To Thomas Ewing, NNPM, 3
22 To Miss L. Jewell, ViU, 6h
27 From John P. Kennedy, MdBP, 6c
27 Remark in Senate, *CG*, 31 Cong., 1 Sess., 86-87, 11b
31 From William B. Preston, DNA, 3

JANUARY 1850
1850 From E. O'Bannon, DLC-TJC, 9
1850 [?] To Alexander H.H. Stuart, ViU, 3
8 Remark in Senate, *CG*, 31 Cong., 1 Sess., Appendix, 46, 11c
9 Remark in Senate, *CG*, 31 Cong., 1 Sess., 128, 11c
10 Remark in Senate, *CG*, 31 Cong., 1 Sess., 132-33, 11b
11 From George W. Crawford, DNA, 6f
12 To John M. Clayton, DNA, 3
14 From Christopher H. Williams, DNA, 3
14 To Thomas Ewing, DNA, 3
15 Remark in Senate, *CG*, 31 Cong., 1 Sess., Appendix, 50, 11c
18 To George W. Crawford, DNA, 3
19 To Thomas Ewing, DNA, 3
21 From George W. Crawford, DNA, 3
22 Remark in Senate, *CG*, 31 Cong., 1 Sess., 212, 11c
23 Remark in Senate, *CG*, 31 Cong., 1 Sess., 220, 11b
24 From George W. Crawford, DNA, 6f, 7b
28 Remark in Senate, *CG*, 31 Cong., 1 Sess., 232, 11b
29 From William M. Meredith, DNA, 3
31 To Conway D. Whitle, ViU, 2
31 Remark in Senate, *CG*, 31 Cong., 1 Sess., 272, 11c

FEBRUARY 1850
4 Remark in Senate, *CG*, 31 Cong., 1 Sess., 283, 11c
7 To George W. Crawford, DNA, 3
7 Remark in Senate, *CG*, 31 Cong., 1 Sess., 312, 11c
8 From George W. Crawford, DNA, 3
8 Remark in Senate, *CG*, 31 Cong., 1 Sess., 323, 11c
11 Remark in Senate, *CG*, 31 Cong., 1 Sess., 334, 11a, 11c
11 From William M. Meredith, DNA, 3
ca. 12 To Joseph L. White *et al.*, Washington *Daily National Intelligencer*, Feb. 25, 1850, 6d
13 Remark in Senate, *CG*, 31 Cong., 1 Sess., 352, 11c
18 Remark in Senate, *CG*, 31 Cong., 1 Sess., 387, 11b
25 From Y. Flabionos[?], DLC-TJC, 6b, 6e

MARCH 1850
2 To A.N. Hooper, MWA, 6d
5 Remark in Senate, *CG*, 31 Cong., Called Sess., 398-99, 401-3, 11b, 11c
6 Remark in Senate, *CG*, 31 Cong., Called Sess., 469, 11a
7 Remark in Senate, *CG*, 31 Cong., Called Sess., 405, 11a
8 Remark in Senate, *CG*, 31 Cong., Called Sess., 408, 412, 11b, 11c
9 To Elizabeth Everett, NjP, 6h
11 Remark in Senate, *CG*, 31 Cong., Called Sess., 501-2, 11b, 11c
13 From J. Butterfield, DNA, 2
15 Remark in Senate, *CG*, 31 Cong., Called Sess., 542, 11b, 11c
15 To Henry Grinnell, Dr. Thomas D. Clark, Lexington, Ky., 6a
16 From J. Butterfield, DNA, 2
19 Remark in Senate, *CG*, 31 Cong., Called Sess., 555, 11b
21 To W. Ogden Niles, KyU, 6a, 6e
28 Remark in Senate, *CG*, 31 Cong., Called Sess., 616, 11b, 11c
30 To John E. Ryland, Jr., M.W. Anderson, Lexington, Ky., 6d

APRIL 1850
4 Remark in Senate, *CG*, 31 Cong., 1 Sess., 638, 11b
5 Remark in Senate, *CG*, 31 Cong., 1 Sess., 646, 11a
15 Remark in Senate, *CG*, 31 Cong., 1 Sess., 739, 11c
16 To William B. Preston, DNA, 3
16 To Thomas W. Jones, KyU, 3
16 To William C. Rives, DLC-HC, 6c
18 To George Gilman Fogg[?], NcD, 6d, 6f
22 Remark in Senate, *CG*, 31 Cong., 1 Sess., 793, 11b
23 To Abraham Faring, PHi, 6d
25 Remark in Senate, *CG*, 31 Cong., 1 Sess., 824, 11c

MAY 1850
nd To Whom It May Concern, George R. Loeb, Philadelphia, Pa., 6c
2 To William C. Rives, DLC-Rives Papers, 6c
9 Remark in Senate, *CG*, 31 Cong., 1 Sess., 967, 11a, 11c
10 From R.N. Ogden, DNA, 3, 6c
10 To Samuel Austin Allibone, CSmH, 6e
16 Remark in Senate, *CG*, 31 Cong., 1 Sess., 1016, 11b
16 To W. Elliot Woodward, KyU, 6h
20 Remark in Senate, *CG*, 31 Cong., 1 Sess., 1030, 11a
22 Remark in Senate, *CG*, 31 Cong., 1 Sess., Appendix, 638, 11c
23 Remark in Senate, *CG*, 31 Cong., 1 Sess., 1055-56, 1059, 11a
27 Remark in Senate, *CG*, 31 Cong., 1 Sess., 1074, 11a
27 Remark in Senate, *CG*, 31 Cong., 1 Sess., Appendix, 649, 11c
28 From William P. Mulchinock, DLC-HC, 6e
29 Remark in Senate, *CG*, 31 Cong., 1 Sess., 1101, 11a
30 To George R. Trotter, KyLoF, 6f
31 Remark in Senate, *CG*, 31 Cong., 1 Sess., 1107-8, 11a

JUNE 1850
3 Remark in Senate, *CG*, 31 Cong., 1 Sess., 1113, 11a, 11c
3 To Miss Dix, MH, 6e
3 From George W. Crawford, DNA, 3
4 From William B. Preston, DNA, 3
5 Remark in Senate, *CG*, 31 Cong., 1 Sess., 1129-31, 1134-36, 11a, 11b, 11c
8 Remark in Senate, *CG*, 31 Cong., 1 Sess., 1167, 11b
10 Remark in Senate, *CG*, 31 Cong., 1 Sess., 1173; *ibid*, Appendix, 678, 800, 11a
10 To Miss Dix, MH, 6e
11 Remark in Senate, *CG*, 31 Cong., 1 Sess., 1182, 11a
13 Remark in Senate, *CG*, 31 Cong., 1 Sess., 1204, 11a
14 Remark in Senate, *CG*, 31 Cong., 1 Sess., 1209-12, 11a, 11b, 11c
17 Remark in Senate, *CG*, 31 Cong., 1 Sess., 1235-36, 1238, 11a, 11b
18 Remark in Senate, *CG*, 31 Cong., 1 Sess., Appendix, 911, 11a
20 Remark in Senate, *CG*, 31 Cong., 1 Sess., 1263-64, 11a, 11c
24 Remark in Senate, *CG*, 31 Cong., 1 Sess., 1279, 11a
25 Remark in Senate, *CG*, 31 Cong., 1 Sess., 1291, 11a
26 Remark in Senate, *CG*, 31 Cong., 1 Sess., 1298, 11a
28 Remark in Senate, *CG*, 31 Cong., 1 Sess., 1314, 11a
28 Remark in Senate, *CG*, 31 Cong., 1 Sess., Appendix, 880, 11c
29 Remark in Senate, *CG*, 31 Cong., 1 Sess., 1321, 11a
29 Remark in Senate, *CG*, 31 Cong., 1 Sess., 1321, 11a
29 Remark in Senate, *CG*, 31 Cong., 1 Sess., Appendix, 881, 11c

JULY 1850
1 Remark in Senate, *CG*, 31 Cong., 1 Sess., 1326-27, 11b
3 Remark in Senate, *CG*, 31 Cong., 1 Sess., 1134, 11a, 11c
5 Remark in Senate, *CG*, 31 Cong., 1 Sess., 1342, 11c
6 Remark in Senate, *CG*, 31 Cong., 1 Sess., 1349, 11c
8 Remark in Senate, *CG*, 31 Cong., 1 Sess., 1356-57, 11a
12 To Capt. Easby, RPB, 6e

17 Remark in Senate, *CG*, 31 Cong., 1 Sess., 1398, 11a, 11c
18 Remark in Senate, *CG*, 31 Cong., 1 Sess., Appendix, 1383, 11c
19 Remark in Senate, *CG*, 31 Cong., 1 Sess., 1418, 11c
20 Remark in Senate, *CG*, 31 Cong., 1 Sess., 1424, 11a
20 From Nicholas Dean, DLC-HC, 3
22 Remark in Senate, *CG*, 31 Cong., 1 Sess., 1433, 11c
22 From Francois Bouligny, DNA, 6e
23 To Abbott Lawrence, NcD, 6c
25 Remark in Senate, *CG*, 31 Cong., 1 Sess., 1456-57, 11a
25 Remark in Senate, *CG*, 31 Cong., 1 Sess., Appendix, 1433-34, 11a
25 From M.H. Stevens, DLC-TJC, 9
26 Remark in Senate, *CG*, 31 Cong., 1 Sess., Appendix, 1444, 11a
26 Remark in Senate, *CG*, 31 Cong., 1 Sess., 1464, 11b
29 Remark in Senate, *CG*, 31 Cong., 1 Sess., Appendix, 1456, 11a
30 Remark in Senate, *CG*, 31 Cong., 1 Sess., 1481-82, 11c
30 From John W. Harris *et al.*, DNA, 3
31 Remark in Senate, *CG*, 31 Cong., 1 Sess., Appendix, 1479, 1482, 11a

AUGUST 1850
1 Remark in Senate, *CG*, 31 Cong., 1 Sess., 1502, 11c
2 Remark in Senate, *CG*, 31 Cong., 1 Sess., Appendix, 1501, 11a
5 From Thomas Corwin, DNA, 3
13 To John P. Bigelow, MH, 6d
16 To Henry Grinnell, Dr. Thomas D. Clark, Lexington, Ky., 6a
28 Remark in Senate, *CG*, 31 Cong., 1 Sess., 1687, 1690, 11b, 11c
29 From William A. Graham, DNA, 3
31 To Thomas Corwin, DNA, 3

SEPTEMBER 1850
2 Remark in Senate, *CG*, 31 Cong., 1 Sess., 1735, 11a, 11c
3 Remark in Senate, *CG*, 31 Cong., 1 Sess., 1743, 11a
3 From Thomas Corwin, DNA, 3
5 Remark in Senate, *CG*, 31 Cong., 1 Sess., 1760, 11c
5 From Charles M. Conrad, DNA, 3
6 Remark in Senate, *CG*, 31 Cong., 1 Sess., 1766, 11c
10 Remark in Senate, *CG*, 31 Cong., 1 Sess., 1794, 11a, 11c
10 Remark in Senate, *CG*, 31 Cong., 1 Sess., Appendix, 1692, 11a
12 Remark in Senate, *CG*, 31 Cong., 1 Sess., 1809-10, 11a, 11c
14 Remark in Senate, *CG*, 31 Cong., 1 Sess., 1815, 11a, 11c
16 To William A. Graham, Nc-Ar, 6f
18 To Thomas Corwin, DNA, 3
20 Remark in Senate, *CG*, 31 Cong., 1 Sess., 1897, 11b
21 Remark in Senate, *CG*, 31 Cong., 1 Sess., 1908, 1910, 11a, 11b
21 From Thomas Corwin, DNA, 3
24 Remark in Senate, *CG*, 31 Cong., 1 Sess., 1959, 11a
24 To Thomas H. Bowlus, IEN, 6h
24 To Thomas Corwin, DNA, 3
26 To Millard Fillmore, DNA, 3
27 To Thomas Corwin, DNA, 3
27 From William A. Graham, DNA, 3
27 To Thomas Corwin, DNA, 3
28 To Richard W. Thompson, Lincoln National Life Foundation, 9

NOVEMBER 1850
6 To Whom It May Concern, KyU, 8
6 Record of Stock Sales at Ashland, Josephine Simpson Collection, Lexington, Ky., 8
6 From Garrett Davis, DNA, 3
11 To Charles Lobdell, KyLoF, 6h
18 From F. Bush, Josephine Simpson Collection, Lexington, Ky., 9
30 From A. Barley, DLC-TJC, 9

DECEMBER 1850

5 From George W. Johnson, DNA, 3
7 From A.G. Hodges, DNA, 3
10 From Thomas Y. Payne, DNA, 3
17 To Editors of the *New Yorker*, ViU, 6e
20 From National Hotel, DLC-TJC, 9
21 From George S. Yerger, DNA, 3, 6c
23 Remark in Senate, *CG*, 31 Cong., 2 Sess., 114, 11b, 11c
26 Remark in Senate, *CG*, 31 Cong., 2 Sess., 124, 11a, 11c
27 To George W. Crawford, DNA, 3
27 From National Hotel, DLC-TJC, 9
27 To Millard Fillmore, NBuHi, 6c
30 Remark in Senate, *CG*, 31 Cong., 2 Sess., 138, 11a, 11c
30 To Millard Fillmore, DNA, 3
31 From Joseph Lewis, DNA, 3, 6a

JANUARY 1851

1851 From Abel Peterson, DLC-TJC, 9
nd To Millard Fillmore, DNA, 3, 6c
2 From William L. Hodge, DNA, 3
2 Remark in Senate, *CG*, 31 Cong., 2 Sess., 153, 11b
3 From National Hotel, DLC-TJC, 9
3 From Charles M. Conrad, DNA, 3
6 *Clay* v. *Blanton*, Ky., 7b
10 To Robert J. Breckinridge, DLC-Breckinridge Papers, 3, 6e
10 To Charles M. Conrad, DNA, 3
10 To Henry H. Sibley, MnHi, 6h
11 From National Hotel, DLC-TJC, 9
11 To Hezekiah G. Wells, Kalamazoo Public Museum, 6f
14 To James Linen, CSt, 6d
16 Remark in Senate, *CG*, 31 Cong., 2 Sess., 262, 11a
18 From National Hotel, DLC-TJC, 9
21 Remark in Senate, *CG*, 31 Cong., 2 Sess., 294, 11c
22 From R.A. Arnold, DNA, 3
23 To Mrs. Nathan K. Hall, NBuHi, 6d
28 Remark in Senate, *CG*, 31 Cong., 2 Sess., 357, 11b
29 Remark in Senate, *CG*, 31 Cong., 2 Sess., 369, 11b
29 To Charles M. Conrad, DNA, 3

FEBRUARY 1851

1 Remark in Senate, *CG*, 31 Cong., 2 Sess., 410, 11b
3 To Rezin D. Shepherd, NRHi, 6c
4 Remark in Senate, *CG*, 31 Cong., 2 Sess., 424-25, 11a, 11b
4 To William A. Graham, DNA, 3
5 Remark in Senate, *CG*, 31 Cong., 2 Sess., 436, 439, 11a
8 Remark in Senate, *CG*, 31 Cong., 2 Sess., 474-74, 11b
13 From D.J.A. McLaughlin, DNA, 3
14 Remark in Senate, *CG*, 31 Cong., 2 Sess., 540, 11a
17 Remark in Senate, *CG*, 31 Cong., 2 Sess., Appendix, 257, 11c
19 To F. Burrell, KyU, 6d
20 To Millard Fillmore, DNA, 3
21 Remark in Senate, *CG*, 31 Cong., 2 Sess., 659, 11b
27 Remark in Senate, *CG*, 31 Cong., 2 Sess., 736-37, 11b
27 To Millard Fillmore, NBuHi, 6c
28 Remark in Senate, *CG*, 31 Cong., 2 Sess., 805, 11c

MARCH 1851

1 Remark in Senate, *CG*, 31 Cong., 2 Sess., Appendix, 343, 11a
3 Remark in Senate, *CG*, 31 Cong., 2 Sess., 838, 11a
4 From J.C. Hall, DLC-TJC, 9

5 From William M. Gwin, DNA, 3
5 To Millard Fillmore, DNA, 3
8 Remark in Senate, *CG*, 31 Cong., 2 Sess., Appendix, 407, 11c
15 To Roswell & Jonah Baldwin, DLC-HC, 8
15 From Abel Peterson, DLC-TJC, 9

APRIL 1851
nd To William C. Rives, DLC-Rives Papers, 6c
9 From Charles Leighton, DLC-TJC, 9
11 To Thomas Butler King, Henry C. Simpson, Lexington, Ky., 6c
23 To James S. Whitney, ViU, 6e
23 To William C. Rives, DLC-Rives Papers, 6c
24 To William C. Rives, DLC-Rives Papers, 6c

MAY 1851
nd To Andrew G. Burt, Burton Milward, Lexington, Ky., 6c
nd From Henry C. Hart, DLC-TJC, 7a, 9
7 From Susan Price, DLC-TJC, 7a, 9
7 To Thomas W. Dresser, John C. White, Springfield, Ill., 6e
8 From James O. Harrison, DLC-TJC, 7a, 9
8 From Thomas H. Pindell, DLC-TJC, 7a, 9
9 To William C. Rives, DLC-Rives Papers, 6c
10 From Isaac Shelby, Jr., DLC-TJC, 7a, 9
12 From James Howard, DNA, 3, 6c
19 To Ben J. Adams, KyLoF, 6c
26 To William A. Graham, NC-Ar, 3, 6e
29 To William W. Corcoran, DLC-Corcoran Papers, 6c

JUNE 1851
8 To J. Cleves Short, DLC-Short Papers, 7a
11 To Sara A. Post, KyU, 6h
23 To Alexander H.H. Stuart, NcD, 3
23 To William C. Rives, DLC-Rives Papers, 6e

JULY 1851
nd To Whom It May Concern, Henry Clay Memorial Foundation, Lexington, Ky., 6c
16 To George Nichols, KyU, 6e
25 To Lewis P. Clover, Dr. Thomas D. Clark Lexington, Ky., 6e

AUGUST 1851
nd To Whom It May Concern, Carl Hall, Lexington, Ky., 6c

OCTOBER 1851
7 To William A. Graham, MdHi, 3
8 To James Gallaher, PPPrHi, 3
11 Record of Purchases, Josephine Simpson Collection, Lexington, Ky., 8
15 From Enoch Clark, DLC-TJC, 9

NOVEMBER 1851
6 From J.S. Halstead, DLC-TJC, 9

DECEMBER 1851
2 To Common Council of New York City, New York *Herald*, Dec. 12, 1851, 6d
2 To William A. Graham, DNA, 3
3 From William A. Graham, DNA, 3
5 From Hamilton Fish, DLC-Fish Papers, 6a
21 To Benjamin H. Brewster *et al.*, New York *Herald*, Dec. 28, 1851, 6d

JANUARY 1852
1 From E.A. Brown, DLC-TJC, 9

MARCH 1852
13 To Mr. Carroll, DNA, 7a
27 From Henry O'Rielly, NRHi, 6e
29 To Logan Hunton, KyLoF, 7a

JUNE 1852
8 To Corcoran & Riggs, Publicity bulletin, Riggs National Bank, Washington, D.C., 9

NAME & SUBJECT INDEX: VOLUME 10